# Safety Symbols

**These symbols appear in laboratory activities. They warn of possible dangers in the laboratory and remind you to work carefully.**

**Safety Goggles** Wear safety goggles to protect your eyes in any activity involving chemicals, flames or heating, or glassware.

**Lab Apron** Wear a laboratory apron to protect your skin and clothing from damage.

**Breakage** Handle breakable materials, such as glassware, with care. Do not touch broken glassware.

**Heat-Resistant Gloves** Use an oven mitt or other hand protection when handling hot materials such as hot plates or hot glassware.

**Plastic Gloves** Wear disposable plastic gloves when working with harmful chemicals and organisms. Keep your hands away from your face, and dispose of the gloves according to your teacher's instructions.

**Heating** Use a clamp or tongs to pick up hot glassware. Do not touch hot objects with your bare hands.

**Flames** Before you work with flames, tie back loose hair and clothing. Follow instructions from your teacher about lighting and extinguishing flames.

**No Flames** When using flammable materials, make sure there are no flames, sparks, or other exposed heat sources present.

**Corrosive Chemical** Avoid getting acid or other corrosive chemicals on your skin or clothing or in your eyes. Do not inhale the vapors. Wash your hands after the activity.

**Poison** Do not let any poisonous chemical come into contact with your skin, and do not inhale its vapors. Wash your hands when you are finished with the activity.

**Fumes** Work in a ventilated area when harmful vapors may be involved. Avoid inhaling vapors directly. Only test an odor when directed to do so by your teacher, and use a wafting motion to direct the vapor toward your nose.

**Sharp Object** Scissors, scalpels, knives, needles, pins, and tacks can cut your skin. Always direct a sharp edge or point away from yourself and others.

**Animal Safety** Treat live or preserved animals or animal parts with care to avoid harming the animals or yourself. Wash your hands when you are finished with the activity.

**Plant Safety** Handle plants only as directed by your teacher. If you are allergic to certain plants, tell your teacher; do not do an activity involving those plants. Avoid touching harmful plants such as poison ivy. Wash your hands when you are finished with the activity.

**Electric Shock** To avoid electric shock, never use electrical equipment around water, or when the equipment is wet or your hands are wet. Be sure cords are untangled and cannot trip anyone. Unplug equipment not in use.

**Physical Safety** When an experiment involves physical activity, avoid injuring yourself or others. Alert your teacher if there is any reason you should not participate.

**Disposal** Dispose of chemicals and other laboratory materials safely. Follow the instructions from your teacher.

**Hand Washing** Wash your hands thoroughly when finished with the activity. Use soap and warm water. Rinse well.

**General Safety Awareness** When this symbol appears, follow the instructions provided. When you are asked to develop your own procedure in a lab, have your teacher approve your plan before you go further.

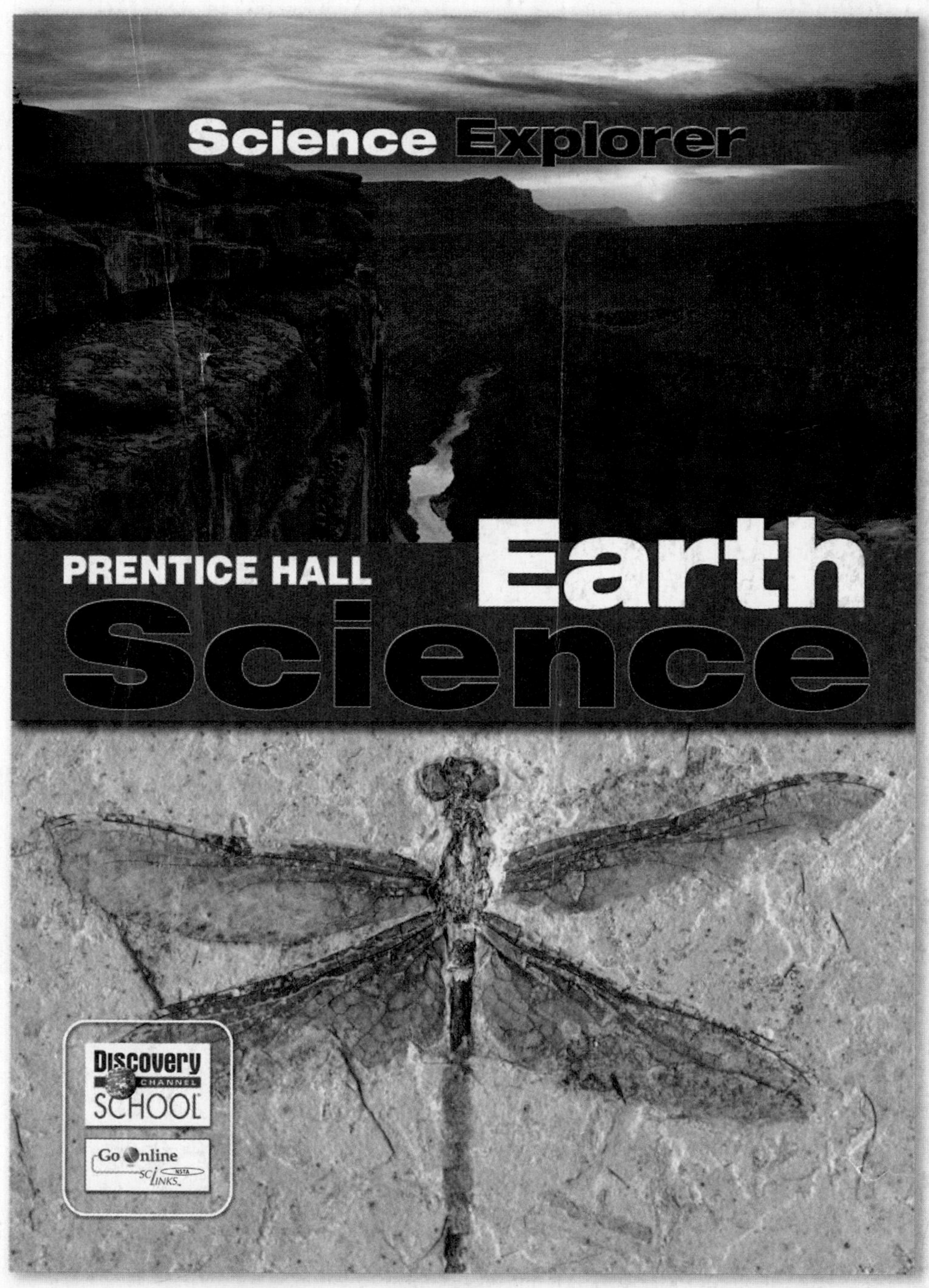


PEARSON

Boston, Massachusetts
Glenview, Illinois
Shoreview, Minnesota
Upper Saddle River, New Jersey

# Earth Science

## Program Resources
Student Edition
Student Express™ CD-ROM
Teacher's Edition
All-in-One Teaching Resources
Color Transparencies
Guided Reading and Study Workbook
Laboratory Manual
Consumable and Nonconsumable Materials Kits
Computer Microscope Lab Manual
Inquiry Skills Activity Books
Progress Monitoring Assessments
Test Preparation Workbook
Test-Taking Tips With Transparencies
Teacher's ELL Handbook
Reading Strategies for Science Content

## Program Technology Resources
TeacherExpress™ CD-ROM
Interactive Textbooks Online
PresentationExpress™ CD-ROM
Student Edition in MP3 Audio
*ExamView®* Test Generator CD-ROM
Lab zone™ Easy Planner CD-ROM
Probeware Lab Manual With CD-ROM
Computer Microscope and Lab Manual
Materials Ordering CD-ROM
Discovery Channel School® Video and DVD Library
Lab Activity Video Library—DVD and VHS
Web Site at PearsonSchool.com

## Spanish Resources for Modular Series
Spanish Student Edition
Spanish Guided Reading and Study Workbook
Spanish Teaching Guide With Tests

**Acknowledgments** appear on p. 856, which constitutes an extension of this copyright page.

**Cover**
The Colorado River eroded the Grand Canyon in Arizona over several million years (top). A fossil preserves the delicate structure of a dragonfly from the Carboniferous Period (bottom).

PEARSON

13-digit ISBN 978-0-13-366858-2
10-digit ISBN 0-13-366858-4
2 3 4 5 6 7 8 9 10 12 11 10 09 08

## Program Authors

**Michael J. Padilla, Ph.D.**
Associate Dean and Director
Eugene T. Moore School of Education
Clemson University
Clemson, South Carolina

Michael Padilla is a leader in middle school science education. He has served as an author and elected officer for the National Science Teachers Association and as a writer of the National Science Education Standards. As lead author of Science Explorer, Mike has inspired the team in developing a program that meets the needs of middle grades students, promotes science inquiry, and is aligned with the National Science Education Standards.

**Ioannis Miaoulis, Ph.D.**
President
Museum of Science
Boston, Massachusetts

Originally trained as a mechanical engineer, Ioannis Miaoulis is in the forefront of the national movement to increase technological literacy. As dean of the Tufts University School of Engineering, Dr. Miaoulis spearheaded the introduction of engineering into the Massachusetts curriculum. Currently he is working with school systems across the country to engage students in engineering activities and to foster discussions on the impact of science and technology on society.

**Martha Cyr, Ph.D.**
Director of K–12 Outreach
Worcester Polytechnic Institute
Worcester, Massachusetts

Martha Cyr is a noted expert in engineering outreach. She has over nine years of experience with programs and activities that emphasize the use of engineering principles, through hands-on projects, to excite and motivate students and teachers of mathematics and science in grades K–12. Her goal is to stimulate a continued interest in science and mathematics through engineering.

## Book Authors

**Jan Jenner, Ph.D.**
Science Writer
Talladega, Alabama

**Andrew C. Kemp, Ph.D.**
Assistant Professor of Education
University of Louisville
Louisville, Kentucky

**Jay M. Pasachoff, Ph.D.**
Professor of Astronomy
Williams College
Williamstown, Massachusetts

**Barbara Brooks Simons**
Science Writer
Boston, Massachusetts

**Thomas R. Wellnitz**
Science Instructor
The Paideia School
Atlanta, Georgia

**Michael Wysession, Ph.D.**
Associate Professor of Earth and Planetary Sciences
Washington University
St. Louis, Missouri

## Contributing Writers

**W. Russell Blake, Ph.D.**
Planetarium Director
Plymouth Community Intermediate School
Plymouth, Massachusetts

**Rose-Marie Botting**
Science Teacher
Broward County School District
Fort Lauderdale, Florida

**Jeffrey C. Callister**
Former Earth Science Instructor
Newburgh Free Academy
Newburgh, New York

**Colleen Campos**
Science Teacher
Laredo Middle School
Aurora, Colorado

**Holly Estes**
Science Teacher
Hale Middle School
Stow, Massachusetts

**Edward Evans**
Former Science Teacher
Hilton Central School
Hilton, New York

**Lauren Magruder**
Science Instructor
St. Michael's Country Day School
Newport, Rhode Island

**Beth Miaoulis**
Technology Writer
Sherborn, Massachusetts

**Naomi Pasachoff, Ph.D.**
Research Associate
Williams College
Williamstown, Massachusetts

**Emery Pineo**
Science Teacher
Barrington Middle School
Barrington, Rhode Island

**Karen Riley Sievers**
Science Teacher
Callanan Middle School
Des Moines, Iowa

**Sharon M. Stroud**
Science Teacher
Widefield High School
Colorado Springs, Colorado

## Consultants

### Reading Consultant

**Nancy Romance, Ph.D.**
Professor of Science Education
Florida Atlantic University
Fort Lauderdale, Florida

### Mathematics Consultant

**William Tate, Ph.D.**
Professor of Education and Applied Statistics and Computation
Washington University
St. Louis, Missouri

# Reviewers

## Content Reviewers

**Paul Beale, Ph.D.**
Department of Physics
University of Colorado
Boulder, Colorado

**Jeff Bodart, Ph.D.**
Chipola Junior College
Marianna, Florida

**Michael Castellani, Ph.D.**
Department of Chemistry
Marshall University
Huntington, West Virginia

**Eugene Chiang, Ph.D.**
Department of Astronomy
University of California – Berkeley
Berkeley, California

**Charles C. Curtis, Ph.D.**
Department of Physics
University of Arizona
Tucson, Arizona

**Daniel Kirk-Davidoff, Ph.D.**
Department of Meteorology
University of Maryland
College Park, Maryland

**Diane T. Doser, Ph.D.**
Department of Geological Sciences
University of Texas at El Paso
El Paso, Texas

**R. E. Duhrkopf, Ph.D.**
Department of Biology
Baylor University
Waco, Texas

**Michael Hacker**
Co-director, Center for Technological Literacy
Hofstra University
Hempstead, New York

**Michael W. Hamburger, Ph.D.**
Department of Geological Sciences
Indiana University
Bloomington, Indiana

**Alice K. Hankla, Ph.D.**
The Galloway School
Atlanta, Georgia

**Donald C. Jackson, Ph.D.**
Department of Molecular Pharmacology, Physiology, & Biotechnology
Brown University
Providence, Rhode Island

**Jeremiah N. Jarrett, Ph.D.**
Department of Biological Sciences
Central Connecticut State University
New Britain, Connecticut

**David Lederman, Ph.D.**
Department of Physics
West Virginia University
Morgantown, West Virginia

**Becky Mansfield, Ph.D.**
Department of Geography
Ohio State University
Columbus, Ohio

**Elizabeth M. Martin, M.S.**
Department of Chemistry and Biochemistry
College of Charleston
Charleston, South Carolina

**Joe McCullough, Ph.D.**
Department of Natural and Applied Sciences
Cabrillo College
Aptos, California

**Robert J. Mellors, Ph.D.**
Department of Geological Sciences
San Diego State University
San Diego, California

**Joseph M. Moran, Ph.D.**
American Meteorological Society
Washington, D.C.

**David J. Morrissey, Ph.D.**
Department of Chemistry
Michigan State University
East Lansing, Michigan

**Philip A. Reed, Ph.D.**
Department of Occupational & Technical Studies
Old Dominion University
Norfolk, Virginia

**Scott M. Rochette, Ph.D.**
Department of the Earth Sciences
State University of New York, College at Brockport
Brockport, New York

**Laurence D. Rosenhein, Ph.D.**
Department of Chemistry
Indiana State University
Terre Haute, Indiana

**Ronald Sass, Ph.D.**
Department of Biology and Chemistry
Rice University
Houston, Texas

**George Schatz, Ph.D.**
Department of Chemistry
Northwestern University
Evanston, Illinois

**Sara Seager, Ph.D.**
Carnegie Institution of Washington
Washington, D.C.

**Robert M. Thornton, Ph.D.**
Section of Plant Biology
University of California
Davis, California

**John R. Villarreal, Ph.D.**
College of Science and Engineering
The University of Texas – Pan American
Edinburg, Texas

**Kenneth Welty, Ph.D.**
School of Education
University of Wisconsin–Stout
Menomonie, Wisconsin

**Edward J. Zalisko, Ph.D.**
Department of Biology
Blackburn College
Carlinville, Illinois

## Tufts University Content Reviewers

Faculty from Tufts University in Medford, Massachusetts, developed *Science Explorer* chapter projects and reviewed the student books.

**Astier M. Almedom, Ph.D.**
Department of Biology

**Wayne Chudyk, Ph.D.**
Department of Civil and Environmental Engineering

**John L. Durant, Ph.D.**
Department of Civil and Environmental Engineering

**George S. Ellmore, Ph.D.**
Department of Biology

**David Kaplan, Ph.D.**
Department of Biomedical Engineering

**Samuel Kounaves, Ph.D.**
Department of Chemistry

**David H. Lee, Ph.D.**
Department of Chemistry

**Douglas Matson, Ph.D.**
Department of Mechanical Engineering

**Karen Panetta, Ph.D.**
Department of Electrical Engineering and Computer Science

**Jan A. Pechenik, Ph.D.**
Department of Biology

**John C. Ridge, Ph.D.**
Department of Geology

**William Waller, Ph.D.**
Department of Astronomy

## Teacher Reviewers

**David R. Blakely**
Arlington High School
Arlington, Massachusetts

**Jane E. Callery**
Two Rivers Magnet Middle School
East Hartford, Connecticut

**Melissa Lynn Cook**
Oakland Mills High School
Columbia, Maryland

**James Fattic**
Southside Middle School
Anderson, Indiana

**Dan Gabel**
Hoover Middle School
Rockville, Maryland

**Wayne Goates**
Eisenhower Middle School
Goddard, Kansas

**Katherine Bobay Graser**
Mint Hill Middle School
Charlotte, North Carolina

**Darcy Hampton**
Deal Junior High School
Washington, D.C.

**Karen Kelly**
Pierce Middle School
Waterford, Michigan

**David Kelso**
Manchester High School Central
Manchester, New Hampshire

**Benigno Lopez, Jr.**
Sleepy Hill Middle School
Lakeland, Florida

**Angie L. Matamoros, Ph.D.**
ALM Consulting, Inc.
Weston, Florida

**Tim McCollum**
Charleston Middle School
Charleston, Illinois

**Bruce A. Mellin**
Brooks School
North Andover, Massachusetts

**Ella Jay Parfitt**
Southeast Middle School
Baltimore, Maryland

**Evelyn A. Pizzarello**
Louis M. Klein Middle School
Harrison, New York

**Kathleen M. Poe**
Fletcher Middle School
Jacksonville, Florida

**Shirley Rose**
Lewis and Clark Middle School
Tulsa, Oklahoma

**Linda Sandersen**
Greenfield Middle School
Greenfield, Wisconsin

**Mary E. Solan**
Southwest Middle School
Charlotte, North Carolina

**Mary Stewart**
University of Tulsa
Tulsa, Oklahoma

**Paul Swenson**
Billings West High School
Billings, Montana

**Thomas Vaughn**
Arlington High School
Arlington, Massachusetts

**Susan C. Zibell**
Central Elementary
Simsbury, Connecticut

## Safety Reviewers

**W. H. Breazeale, Ph.D.**
Department of Chemistry
College of Charleston
Charleston, South Carolina

**Ruth Hathaway, Ph.D.**
Hathaway Consulting
Cape Girardeau, Missouri

**Douglas Mandt, M.S.**
Science Education Consultant
Edgewood, Washington

## Activity Field Testers

**Nicki Bibbo**
Witchcraft Heights School
Salem, Massachusetts

**Rose-Marie Botting**
Broward County Schools
Fort Lauderdale, Florida

**Colleen Campos**
Laredo Middle School
Aurora, Colorado

**Elizabeth Chait**
W. L. Chenery Middle School
Belmont, Massachusetts

**Holly Estes**
Hale Middle School
Stow, Massachusetts

**Laura Hapgood**
Plymouth Community Intermediate School
Plymouth, Massachusetts

**Mary F. Lavin**
Plymouth Community Intermediate School
Plymouth, Massachusetts

**James MacNeil, Ph.D.**
Cambridge, Massachusetts

**Lauren Magruder**
St. Michael's Country Day School
Newport, Rhode Island

**Jeanne Maurand**
Austin Preparatory School
Reading, Massachusetts

**Joanne Jackson-Pelletier**
Winman Junior High School
Warwick, Rhode Island

**Warren Phillips**
Plymouth Public Schools
Plymouth, Massachusetts

**Carol Pirtle**
Hale Middle School
Stow, Massachusetts

**Kathleen M. Poe**
Fletcher Middle School
Jacksonville, Florida

**Cynthia B. Pope**
Norfolk Public Schools
Norfolk, Virginia

**Anne Scammell**
Geneva Middle School
Geneva, New York

**Karen Riley Sievers**
Callanan Middle School
Des Moines, Iowa

**David M. Smith**
Eyer Middle School
Allentown, Pennsylvania

**Gene Vitale**
Parkland School
McHenry, Illinois

# Contents

# Earth Science

## Unit 1 Exploring Planet Earth

## Unit 2 Earth's Changing Surface

## Unit 3 Earth's Waters

## Unit 4 Weather and Climate

## Unit 5 Astronomy

## Reference Section

**VIDEO**

**Enhance understanding through dynamic video.**

**Preview** Get motivated with this introduction to the chapter content.

**Field Trip** Explore a real-world story related to the chapter content.

**Assessment** Review content and take an assessment.

**Get connected to exciting Web resources in every lesson.**

SciLinks NSTA Find Web links on topics relating to every section.

**Active Art** Interact with selected visuals from every chapter online.

**Planet Diary®** Explore news and natural phenomena through weekly reports.

**Science News®** Keep up to date with the latest science discoveries.

**Experience the complete text-book online and on CD-ROM.**

**Activities** Practice skills and learn content.

**Videos** Explore content and learn important lab skills.

**Audio Support** Hear key terms spoken and defined.

**Self-Assessment** Use instant feedback to help you track your progress.

# Activities

## Lab zone™ Chapter Project — Opportunities for long-term inquiry



## Lab zone Discover Activity — Exploration and inquiry before reading

## Lab zone Try This **Activity** Reinforcement of key concepts



## Lab zone Skills **Activity** Practice of specific science inquiry skills

Lab zone **Labs** In-depth practice of inquiry skills and science concepts

## Lab zone At-Home Activity — Quick, engaging activities for home and family



## • Tech & Design • Design, build, test, and communicate

## Math — Point-of-use math practice



## active art — Illustrations come alive online

SCiLINKS NSTA

Careers in **Science**

Marshall Shepherd tracks powerful thunderstorms at the Goddard Visualization Studio (left). Marshall looks at satellite images like this one of Florida (above).

# Eyes in the Sky

At the Kennedy Space Center on the east coast of Florida, a crew prepares to launch a satellite into space. The crew knows that a thunderstorm may be moving toward them. Should they launch the mission or delay it? Before deciding, the crew consults with meteorologists at the National Weather Service for the latest weather forecast.

More summer thunderstorms occur in central Florida than in any other area in the United States. Predicting when severe storms will develop and where they will move is one of the most demanding jobs for a meteorologist. One of the best people at this job is J. Marshall Shepherd.

# *Talking With* Dr. J. Marshall Shepherd

## Starting Out in Science

Marshall Shepherd is an "old hand" at predicting the weather. He's been at it since sixth grade, when his teacher suggested that he enter a science fair. He constructed a weather station for his science project. The weather station contained an anemometer to measure wind speed, a wind vane to measure wind direction, a barometer to measure air pressure, a hair hygrometer to measure humidity, and a rain gauge. "From these basic instruments, I took weather observations around my neighborhood," he explains. Marshall won prizes for his instruments and scientific work on this project at local, district, and state science fairs.

By the time he graduated from high school, he had a definite goal. "One day, I planned to be a research scientist at NASA (National Aeronautics and Space Administration)," he stated.

## Predicting Severe Storms

In graduate school, Marshall investigated the way powerful thunderstorms form and move, especially those in central Florida. The long, narrow shape of Florida is part of the reason that so many storms form there. "When you have land heating faster than water, you get something called sea-breeze circulation," he explains. "On a typical summer day, a sea-breeze forms on both the west coast and the east coast of Florida. They tend to move toward the center. When they collide, you get intense thunderstorm development."

### Career Path

**Marshall Shepherd,** the son of two school principals, grew up in the small town of Canton, Georgia. He graduated from Florida State University, where he later received his Ph.D. in meteorology. Today he works for NASA as a research meteorologist at the Goddard Space Flight Center in Maryland. Below, Marshall acts as a NASA spokesperson to TV and radio reporters.

Lightning flashes in a thunderstorm over Tucson, Arizona.

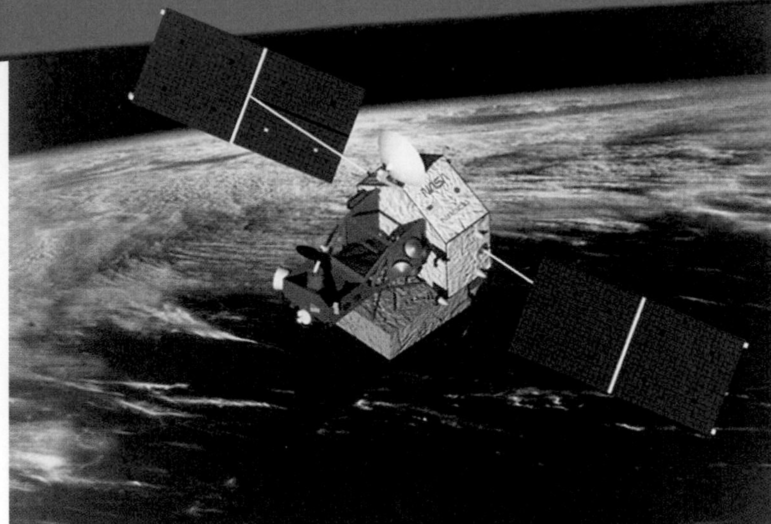

TRMM, a satellite that records weather conditions from space, contains two solar panels and instruments to collect weather data (above). TRMM orbits Earth at an altitude of about 400 kilometers. It flies over each position on Earth at a different time each day (right).

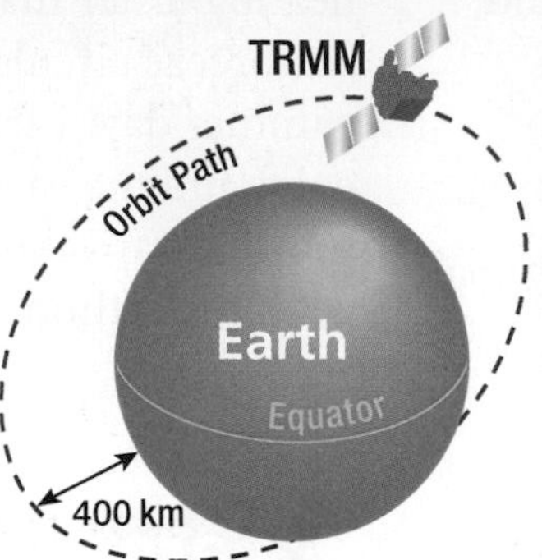


This TRMM satellite image shows an area of severe thunderstorms north of Florida.

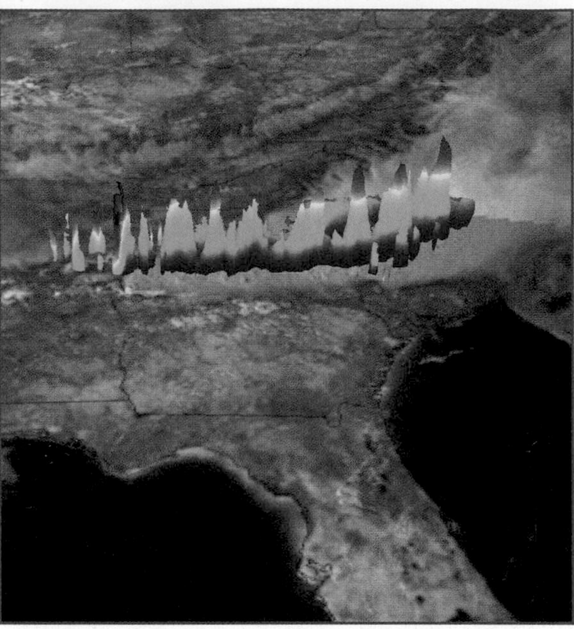

## NASA's Earth Science Enterprise

In 1993, Marshall started working at NASA. His research there contributes to NASA's Earth Science Enterprise. This long-term program uses information from satellites, aircraft, and ground stations to understand Earth as a single system. NASA scientists track changes in the atmosphere, land, ocean, and ice. They investigate how those changes affect weather and climate.

Marshall's knowledge of hurricanes and thunderstorms is especially valuable in interpreting data from the Tropical Rainfall Measuring Mission (TRMM). The TRMM is a satellite with instruments that measure tropical and subtropical rainfall. Rainfall cycles located in tropical regions affect weather throughout the world.

Marshall's work involves both observation and calculation. The instruments that Marshall uses are some of the most advanced in the world. Marshall specializes in "remote sensing"—making observations of weather conditions, such as rainfall, from a distance. After collecting data, he uses a computer to analyze it.

## Studying Global Rainfall

Recently, radar helped Marshall identify a relatively new factor in global climate—big cities. Modern cities have cars, roads, buildings, and large areas of concrete and asphalt surfaces. These surfaces hold heat, creating "urban heat islands." As a result, temperatures inside a city can be up to 5.6°C warmer than temperatures in the nearby suburbs.

But satellite pictures showed something more—"urban heat islands" may actually create local weather. Heated air rises over the city, producing clouds. As a result, summer rainfall is heavier over some cities. It is also heavier downwind, in the direction in which the wind is blowing, from the cities. Marshall and his colleagues mapped rainfall around several cities worldwide. Data showed a clear link between rainfall patterns and urban areas. This connection matters because world cities are growing quickly. As they grow, urban areas could have greater effects on the weather.

## Looking Ahead

TRMM's mission will end in a few years. Meanwhile, Marshall is already working on a new project, the Global Precipitation Measurement mission. It is scheduled to launch sometime after 2010. Its satellites will carry the next generation of space-based instruments. In planning for this next project, Marshall meets with engineers to talk about the project's scientific goals and how to design spacecraft to meet those goals.

Marshall wears other hats at NASA, too. Sometimes he acts as spokesperson to TV, radio, and magazine reporters. He also talks to government policymakers.

What is it like to fulfill his dream of working at NASA? "I am like a kid in a candy store," Dr. Shepherd says. "I got into the field by doing a science project. Now I make a living doing 'really big' science projects. . . . The biggest difference is that I no longer have to make my own instruments. I can use the satellite, aircraft, and computer model technology at NASA."

## Writing in Science

**Career Link** Marshall Shepherd credits his career success to having detailed goals. "I always write down goals, and check them off as they happen," he says. Think of a task that you would like to accomplish over the next year. In a paragraph, write the steps you will take to reach your goal. Explain how those steps help bring you closer to achieving your goal.

**For:** More on this career
**Visit:** PHSchool.com
**Web Code:** cfb-4000

**Urban Heat Islands**
**Modern cities, like Houston, Texas, help make their own weather.**

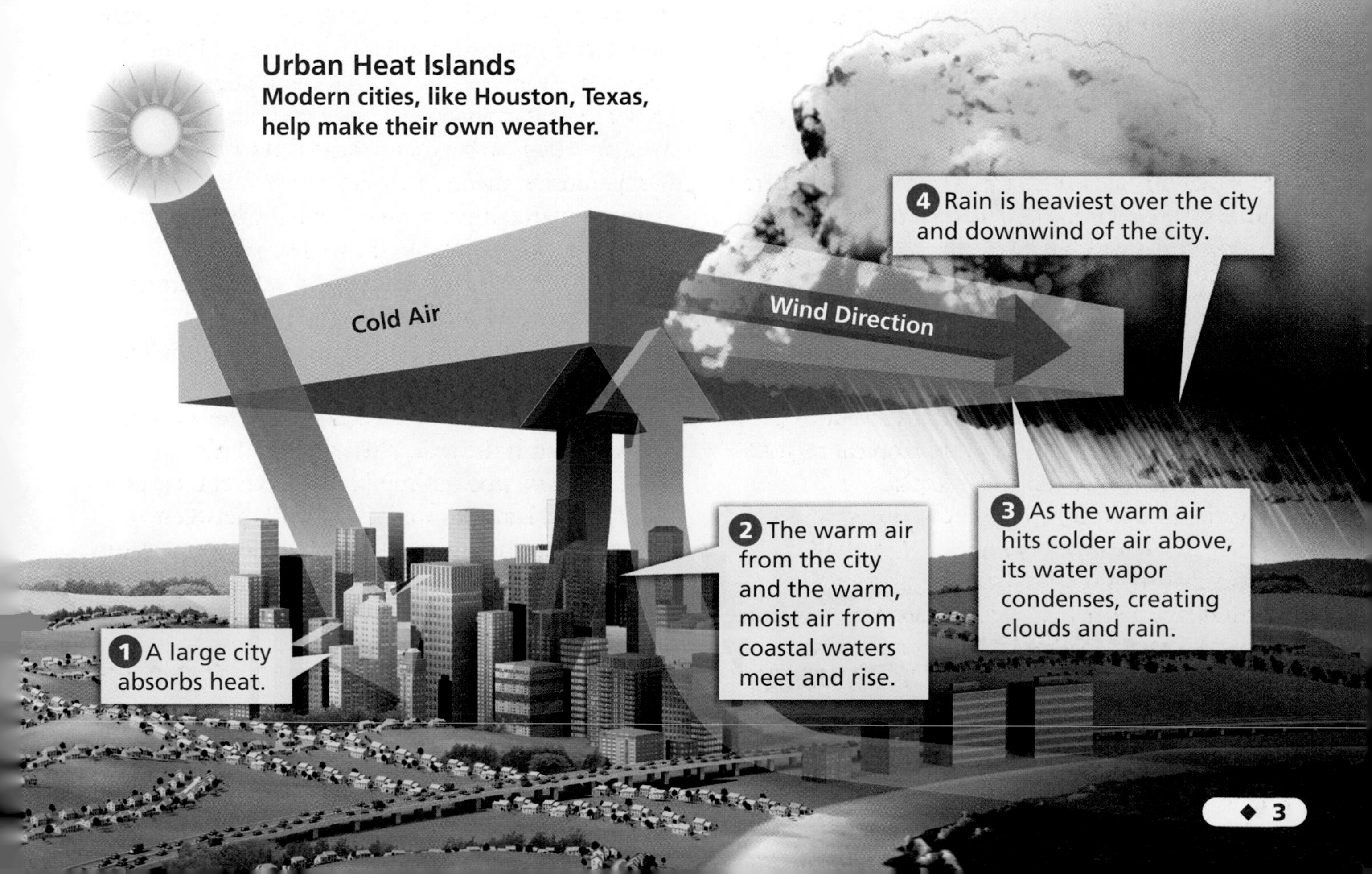

Cold Air

Wind Direction

1 A large city absorbs heat.

2 The warm air from the city and the warm, moist air from coastal waters meet and rise.

3 As the warm air hits colder air above, its water vapor condenses, creating clouds and rain.

4 Rain is heaviest over the city and downwind of the city.

Chapter 1

# Introduction to Earth Science

## The BIG Idea

Nature of Science and Inquiry

**How do scientists investigate the natural world?**

### Chapter Preview



An astronaut works on the International Space Station in orbit around Earth. ▶

*The Work of Scientists*

▶ Video Preview
Video Field Trip
Video Assessment

Lab zone™ Chapter **Project**

## Design and Build a Scale Model

How do scientists study something as large as the solar system or as tiny as an atom? One tool they use is a model. Models help scientists picture things that are difficult to see or understand. In this chapter project, you will create a three-dimensional model of a building or a room.

**Your Goal** To create a three-dimensional model that shows the size relationships among the different parts of the model

To complete this project, you must

- measure or find the actual dimensions of the structure to be modeled (To learn more about measuring, read Making Measurements in the Skills Handbook.)
- sketch your model on graph paper and calculate the size of each part you will include
- construct your three-dimensional model
- follow the safety guidelines in Appendix A

**Plan It!** Choose a familiar building or a room in your house or school to model. Think about how you could construct a smaller replica of that building or room. Preview the chapter to find out about the use of models in Earth science. Then write a brief plan detailing how you will proceed with this project. Make sure your plan includes a sketch and a list of the materials you will use. After your teacher approves your plan, start working on your model.

Section 1

# What Is Science?

## Reading Preview

### Key Concepts

- What skills and attitudes do scientists use to learn about the world?
- What is scientific inquiry?
- How do scientific theories differ from scientific laws?

### Key Terms

- science • observing
- inferring • predicting
- scientific inquiry • hypothesis
- controlled experiment
- variable
- manipulated variable
- responding variable • data
- scientific theory • scientific law

### Target Reading Skill

**Building Vocabulary** After you read this section, reread the paragraphs that contain definitions of Key Terms. Use all the information you have learned to write a definition of each Key Term in your own words.

Lab zone **Discover Activity**

### How Can Scientists Find Out What's Inside Earth?

1. Your teacher will give you a spherical object, such as a sports ball. You can think of the sphere as a model of Earth.
2. Carefully observe your sphere. What characteristics of the sphere can you observe and measure directly?
3. What characteristics of the sphere cannot be directly observed and measured?

**Think It Over**

**Posing Questions** In your notebook, list several questions that you have about Earth. Which of these questions could you answer based on direct observation? Which questions would need to be answered based on indirect evidence?

A helicopter lands near the top of an erupting volcano. With care and speed, a team of scientists get out to do their work. "I've been out there sometimes when lava is shooting out of the ground 100 meters high," says Margaret Mangan, a scientist who studies volcanoes. "The main thing you're struck with is the sound. It's like the roaring of many jet engines. Then there's the smell of sulfur, which is choking. The wind can blow particles from the lava fountain over you, little bits of congealed lava. It feels like a hot sandstorm."

Dr. Mangan has observed many volcanic eruptions of Mount Kilauea in Hawaii. She studies the characteristics of red-hot lava. She wants to know why lava sometimes erupts in huge fountains, but at other times erupts in gently flowing streams.

## Thinking Like a Scientist

Watching a volcanic eruption, you might ask yourself questions such as: "What is lava?" and "Where does lava form?" In asking these questions, you are thinking like a scientist—a person who uses science to explore problems and answer questions about the natural world. **Science** is a way of learning about the natural world. Science is also the knowledge gained through that process.

**As scientists seek to understand the natural world, they use skills such as observing, inferring, and predicting. Successful scientists also possess certain attitudes, or habits of mind.**

**Observing** Using one or more of your senses to gather information is **observing.** Your senses include sight, hearing, touch, taste, and smell. For example, Dr. Mangan not only saw lava erupting, but she heard the noise it makes, smelled volcanic gases, and felt the lava's heat.

**Inferring** When you explain or interpret the things you observe, you are **inferring,** or making an inference. Making an inference doesn't mean guessing wildly. An inference is based on reasoning from what you already know. For example, Margaret Mangan inferred that differences in the gas content of the lava result in different types of eruptions. But inferences are not always correct. There could be other factors that affect the strength of a volcanic eruption.

**Predicting** If Dr. Mangan's inferences are correct, her results may help scientists predict whether a volcanic eruption will be strong or gentle. **Predicting** means making a forecast of what will happen in the future based on past experience or evidence.

**Scientific Attitudes** As they explore scientific problems, scientists maintain a scientific attitude toward their work. Characteristics that are part of a scientific attitude include curiosity, honesty, open-mindedness, skepticism, and creativity. Curiosity is what drives a scientist to ask questions that no one has thought of before. Honesty requires that scientists report their findings truthfully. Open-mindedness helps a scientist to accept new and different ideas. At the same time, scientists are skeptical—they doubt an idea until it has been fully tested. Creativity helps scientists come up with new ways of solving problems.

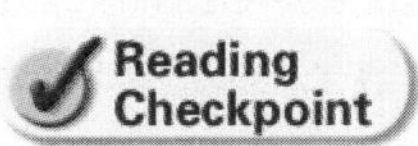

**Why is curiosity important to a scientist?**

FIGURE 1
**Observing Volcanic Eruptions**
Margaret Mangan takes samples of lava from Mount Kilauea, Hawaii. In a laboratory, she analyzes the lava to determine its gas content and other characteristics.
**Forming Operational Definitions**
*Based on what you can observe in the photograph, how would you define lava?*

## Scientific Inquiry

Thinking and asking questions about what you observe is the start of the **scientific inquiry** process. **Scientific inquiry refers to the many ways in which scientists study the natural world and propose explanations based on the evidence they gather.** Some of the methods of scientific inquiry are described below.

**Posing Questions** Scientific inquiry often begins with a problem or question about an observation. The questions may come from observations and inferences that you make, or just from curiosity. For example, you may have wondered, "What is lightning?" You could use scientific inquiry to answer this question. That's what Benjamin Franklin—the American scientist, inventor, and statesman—did in 1752.

**FIGURE 2**
**Investigating Lightning**
Franklin conducted his famous experiment near Philadelphia in 1752. As the thundercloud passed overhead, electricity was transferred between the cloud and the kite. **Inferring** *Why was Franklin's experiment extremely dangerous?*

**Developing a Hypothesis** During the mid-1700s, Franklin became interested in electricity. He thought that electricity and lightning were similar. Both electrical sparks and lightning produced a brilliant, white light. Both moved along crooked paths and made crackling noises. Could lightning be a form of electricity? In asking this question, Franklin was developing a hypothesis: Lightning consists of electricity. A **hypothesis** (plural: *hypotheses*) is a possible explanation for a set of observations or answer to a scientific question. In science, a hypothesis must be testable. This means that scientists must be able to carry out investigations and gather evidence that will either support or disprove the hypothesis.

**Designing an Experiment** Franklin designed an experiment to test his hypothesis about lightning. Franklin attached a metal wire to the frame of a kite. At the end of the kite string was a metal key. As a thunderstorm approached, Franklin launched the kite. Soon, electricity was transferred from the thunderclouds to the metal wire and down the kite string. Sparks leapt from the metal key to objects placed near it.

Franklin's experiment tested his hypothesis. But it was not a controlled experiment. A **controlled experiment** is a test of a hypothesis under conditions established by the scientist. In a controlled experiment, a scientist determines how one particular variable affects the outcome of the experiment. A **variable** is one of the factors that can change in an experiment. For example, a scientist might conduct an experiment to determine if change in temperature affects the rate at which water evaporates. In this case, change in temperature is the variable that determines the outcome of the experiment.

In an experiment, the variable that a scientist changes is called the **manipulated variable.** The variable that changes because of the manipulated variable is the **responding variable**. In the evaporation experiment, temperature is the manipulated variable. The rate of evaporation is the responding variable. In a controlled experiment, scientists control, or keep constant, all other variables. By controlling variables, scientists can eliminate the effects of the other variables as factors in their results.

**Reading Checkpoint** What is a variable?

**Lab zone Skills Activity**

### Controlling Variables

Suppose you are a scientist studying two types of crystals found on Earth's surface: salt and borax. You are designing an experiment to determine whether salt or borax dissolves more quickly in water. What is your manipulated variable? What is your responding variable? What other variables would you need to control?

**Collecting and Interpreting Data** If you wanted to investigate the weather in your area, you would need to collect data. **Data** are the facts, figures, and other evidence gathered through observations. A data table provides an organized way to collect and record observations.

After all the data have been collected, they need to be interpreted. One useful tool that can help you interpret data is a graph. Graphs like the one in the Analyzing Data feature on this page can reveal patterns or trends in data.

In Franklin's experiment, his observations were his data. He interpreted these data by comparing what he observed in the kite experiment with his earlier observations of electricity. For example, the sparks from the key tied to the kite string behaved just as electricity from other sources did.

**Drawing Conclusions** After you have gathered and interpreted your data, you can draw a conclusion about your hypothesis. A conclusion is a decision about how to interpret what you have learned from an experiment. You may decide that the data support the hypothesis. Or you may decide that the data show that the hypothesis was incorrect. Sometimes, no conclusion can be reached and more data are needed.

Franklin decided that lightning behaved exactly as electricity did in his other experiments. Therefore, he concluded that his hypothesis was correct: lightning consists of electricity.

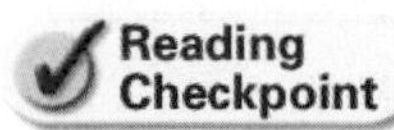

**What is a conclusion?**

## Math Analyzing Data

### Lightning Through the Year

The graph shows the average number of thunderstorms with lightning in New Mexico. Use the graph to answer the questions.

1. **Reading Graphs** What do the twelve bars on the graph represent?
2. **Reading Graphs** What does the height of each bar represent?
3. **Interpreting Data** When does lightning occur most often? Least often?
4. **Posing Questions** What are some questions that you would want to answer to help you explain the pattern in the graph?

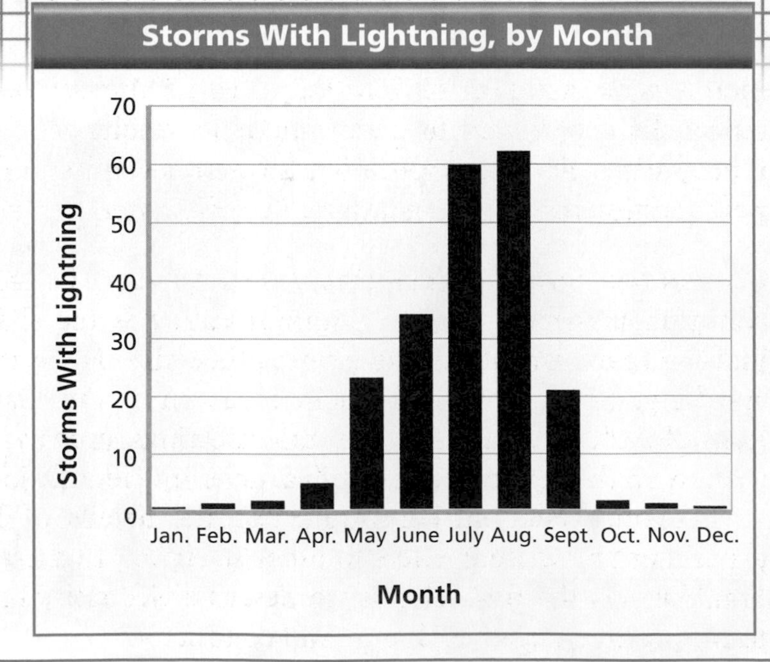

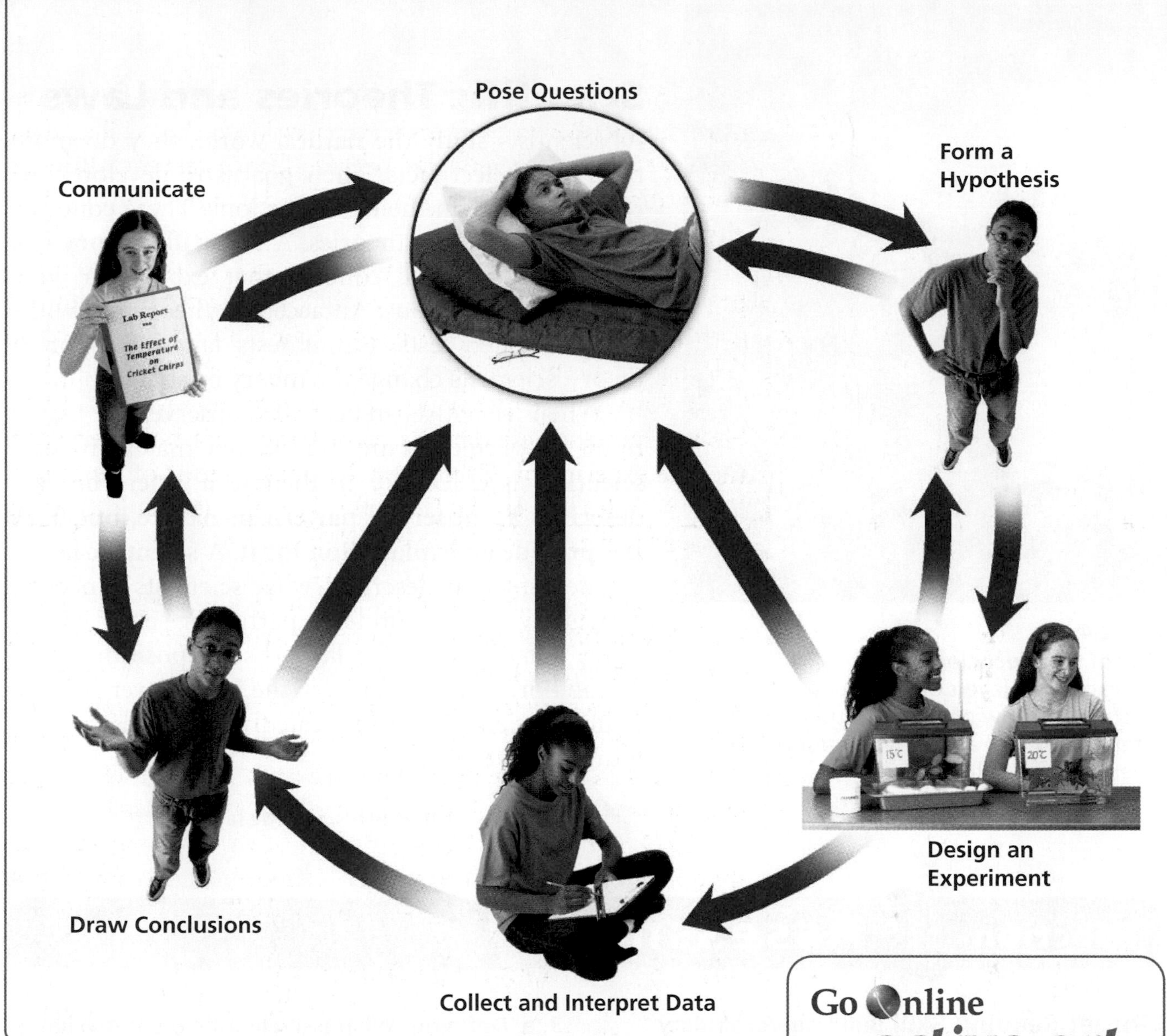


Go Online
active art
For: The Nature of Inquiry activity
Visit: PHSchool.com
Web Code: cgp-6012

FIGURE 3
**The Nature of Inquiry**
There is no set path that a scientific inquiry must follow. Observations at each stage of the process may lead you to modify your hypothesis or experiment.
**Applying Concepts** *Why is observation important as you design and conduct an experiment?*

Even after you have drawn a conclusion from one experiment, scientific inquiry usually doesn't end. Other scientists may repeat the experiment to determine if its results were correct. Often, the results of an experiment suggest new questions. These new questions can lead to new hypotheses and new experiments.

**Communicating** An important part of scientific inquiry is communicating the results. Communicating is the sharing of ideas and experimental findings with others through writing and speaking. Scientists share their ideas in many ways. For example, they give talks at scientific meetings, exchange information on the Internet, or publish articles in scientific journals.

Benjamin Franklin communicated the details of his kite experiment by writing letters to other scientists. In these letters, Franklin was the first scientist to describe electricity using the terms positive, negative, charge, and conductor.

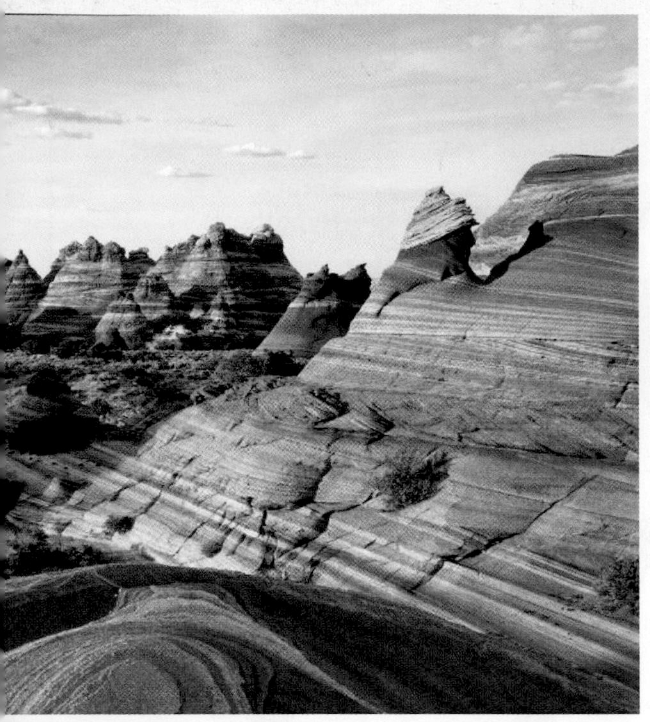

**FIGURE 4**
**Law of Superposition**
These colorful layers of sandstone in Utah illustrate the law of superposition.
**Inferring** *Where are the youngest rock layers in the photograph?*

## Scientific Theories and Laws

As scientists study the natural world, they do more than just collect facts. Their goal is to develop concepts that explain their observations. These concepts are called scientific theories. A **scientific theory** is a well-tested scientific concept that explains a wide range of observations. An accepted theory has withstood repeated tests. But if tests fail to support a theory, scientists change the theory or abandon it.

When scientists repeatedly observe the same result in specific circumstances, they may arrive at a scientific law. **Unlike a theory, a scientific law describes an observed pattern in nature, but does not provide an explanation for it.** A **scientific law** is a statement that describes what scientists expect to happen every time under a particular set of conditions. For example, the law of superposition states that in horizontal rock layers, the oldest layer is at the bottom. Scientists have repeatedly tested this law and found it to be true.

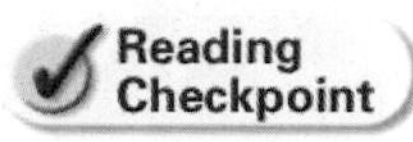
**Reading Checkpoint** What is a scientific law?

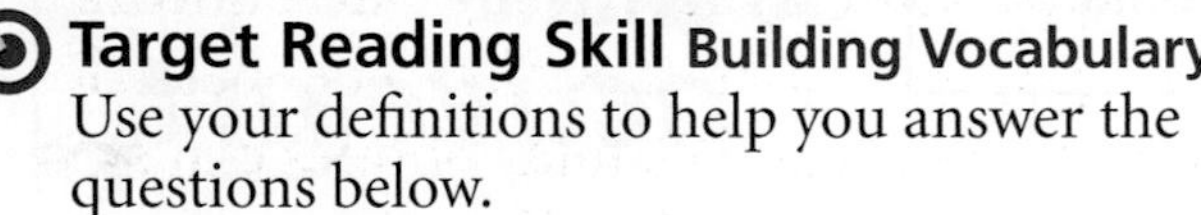

## Section 1 Assessment

**Target Reading Skill Building Vocabulary** Use your definitions to help you answer the questions below.

### Reviewing Key Concepts

1. a. **Reviewing** What is science?
   b. **Explaining** Explain three main skills that scientists use.
   c. **Applying Concepts** Can you make an inference without having made any observations? Explain your answer.
2. a. **Defining** Define the term *scientific inquiry.*
   b. **Explaining** You may have heard the saying "Red sky at morning, sailors take warning." This means that stormy weather may follow if the sky looks red around sunrise. Could you investigate this observation using scientific inquiry? Explain.
   c. **Problem Solving** To determine whether the saying in Question (b) is true, what kind of data would you need to collect?
3. a. **Defining** What is a scientific theory? What is a scientific law?
   b. **Comparing and Contrasting** How do scientific theories differ from scientific laws?

### Writing in Science

**Weather Inquiry** With a partner, think of a question about the weather in your area that you would like to answer. Write your question in your notebook. List anything you already know about the topic of your question that might help you answer it. Then state your question as a hypothesis.

Section 2

# The Study of Earth Science

## Reading Preview

### Key Concepts

- What are the big ideas of Earth science?
- What are the branches of Earth science?
- How do Earth scientists use models?

### Key Terms

- Earth science • system
- energy • constructive force
- destructive force • geologist
- oceanographer
- meteorologist • astronomer
- environmental scientist

### Target Reading Skill

**Identifying Main Ideas** As you read the Big Ideas of Earth Science section, write the main idea in a graphic organizer like the one below. Then write three supporting details that further explain the main idea.

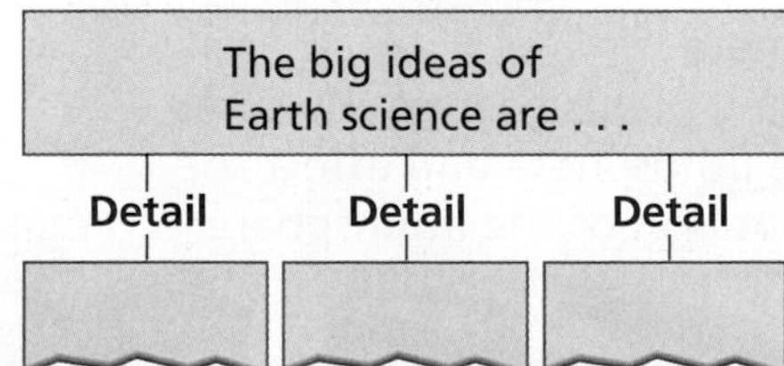


## Lab zone Discover Activity

### What Do Earth Scientists Study?

1. Preview Figure 7, which shows several different careers in Earth science.
2. Based on the figure, make a list of the different branches of Earth science.

**Think It Over**

**Predicting** What do you think a scientist in each career would study? Write your prediction beside each branch of Earth science on your list.

Leonard Strachan is an astronomer, but he doesn't study the night sky. "I'm a daytime astronomer," he says. "I study the sun." And the instruments he uses are not on a mountaintop. They are on a satellite in space between Earth and the sun. "The sun," Dr. Strachan says, "doesn't just shine as a steady yellow ball. It's always changing. Every so often the sun shoots out a huge cloud of gas particles into space. Within days the particles crash into Earth's upper atmosphere. They cause auroras: shimmering, glowing light shows in the sky. The particles interfere with radio waves. Pagers and cellular phones can stop working. Even our electrical power can be affected."

Dr. Strachan studies the sun to help scientists learn to predict this "space weather." He also collects data that can prove or disprove scientists' theories about the sun.

**FIGURE 5**
**Observing the Sun**
Dr. Strachan collects data using an instrument on this satellite, the Solar and Heliospheric Observatory, or SOHO.

## Big Ideas of Earth Science

Throughout history, people have observed the skies above them and the Earth around them. Over thousands of years, scientists have built a body of knowledge based on these observations. **Earth science** is the term for this knowledge about Earth and its place in the universe. **Earth scientists use several big ideas to guide their work: the structure of the Earth system, Earth's history, and Earth in the solar system.**

**The Structure of the Earth System** Scientists often divide Earth into four parts, or spheres: the lithosphere, hydrosphere, atmosphere, and biosphere. Earth's outermost sphere is the atmosphere (AT muh sfeer), the mixture of gases that surrounds the planet. Earth's oceans, lakes, rivers, and ice form the hydrosphere (HY druh sfeer). Earth's solid rocky outer layer is called the lithosphere (LITH uh sfeer). All living things—whether in the air, in the oceans, or on and beneath the land surface—make up the biosphere (BY uh sfeer).

These four spheres aren't separate. They make up the Earth system. A **system** is a group of parts that work together as a whole. A change in one part of the Earth system affects all the other parts. Matter and energy constantly move from one part of the Earth system to another. Matter is what makes up everything in the universe. **Energy** is the ability to do work or cause change. For example, in the water cycle, water moves from the oceans, to the atmosphere, to the land, and back to the oceans.

FIGURE 6
### Earth as a System
The atmosphere, hydrosphere, lithosphere, and biosphere together make up the Earth system. Changes in any part of the system can affect the other parts. **Interpreting Diagrams** *How does the hydrosphere affect the atmosphere?*

**Biosphere**
Growing plants change the surface of the lithosphere and affect the composition of the atmosphere.

**Lithosphere**
Volcanoes in the lithosphere release particles and gases that change the atmosphere.

The sun provides energy for the water cycle and many other processes on Earth's surface. The sun's energy is transferred to Earth as radiation, a form of energy that can move through space. The energy for other processes comes from the heat of Earth's interior. For example, deep inside Earth, some rock melts, forming the material that erupts from volcanoes.

**Earth's History** As you will learn later in this book, scientists have evidence that Earth is 4.6 billion years old! During this long span of time, Earth has not stayed the same. Instead, constructive and destructive forces have changed Earth's surface throughout its history. **Constructive forces** shape Earth's surface by building up mountains and landmasses. **Destructive forces** slowly wear away mountains and every other feature on Earth's surface.

**Earth in the Solar System** You have probably looked at the full moon and noticed the round craters in its surface. The craters formed when large objects from space struck the moon. Scientists have found similar craters on Earth. These craters are a reminder that Earth is not alone in space. It is part of the solar system.

The solar system is made up of the sun and the planets—with their moons—that move around the sun. The solar system also contains objects of different sizes, from dust-sized particles to large chunks of rock and ice. These objects are also in motion around the sun. Understanding the other planets and objects in the solar system helps scientists understand Earth and its history.

**Reading Checkpoint** How do constructive forces shape Earth?

**Lab zone Try This Activity**

### Energy for Earth

You can observe how the sun provides energy for processes on Earth's surface.

1. Pour 100 mL of tap water into a clear plastic jar and tighten the lid.
2. Place the jar in the sun for 10 minutes.
3. Move the jar to a shaded location and wait several minutes.
4. Observe the sides of the jar. What do you see?

**Predicting** If you left the jar open in the sun for a full day, what would happen to the water in the jar?

Hydrosphere
Earth's vast oceans affect the temperature of the atmosphere; flowing rivers shape the surface of the lithosphere.
Atmosphere
Storms in the atmosphere bring rains that change the surface of the lithosphere.

FIGURE 7
### Careers in Earth Science

If you worked as an Earth scientist, you might release a weather balloon into the atmosphere. You might pilot a submersible deep beneath the ocean or chip samples of rock from a mountain.

**Oceanographers ▲**
These oceanographers have donned scuba gear to observe the interactions of living things on the ocean floor.

**Geologists ▲**
The work of geologists often takes them outdoors—in this case, to a rocky mountainside.

## The Branches of Earth Science

Earth science has several different branches. **In this book, you will learn about geology, oceanography, meteorology, astronomy, and environmental science.**

**Geology** Geology is the study of the solid Earth. **Geologists** study the forces that have shaped Earth throughout its long history. Geologists study the chemical and physical characteristics of rock, the material that forms Earth's hard surface. Geologists describe the features sculpted in rock and soil by water, wind, and waves.

The science of geology began in the late 1700s. Geologists of that time studied the rocks on the surface. Those geologists concluded that Earth's land features are the work of natural forces that slowly build up and wear down the land.

**Oceanography** Oceanography is the study of Earth's oceans. **Oceanographers** study everything from the chemistry of ocean water to the shape of the ocean floor to living things in the ocean's depths. Scientists in related fields study Earth's fresh water in lakes, rivers, and glaciers and beneath the surface.

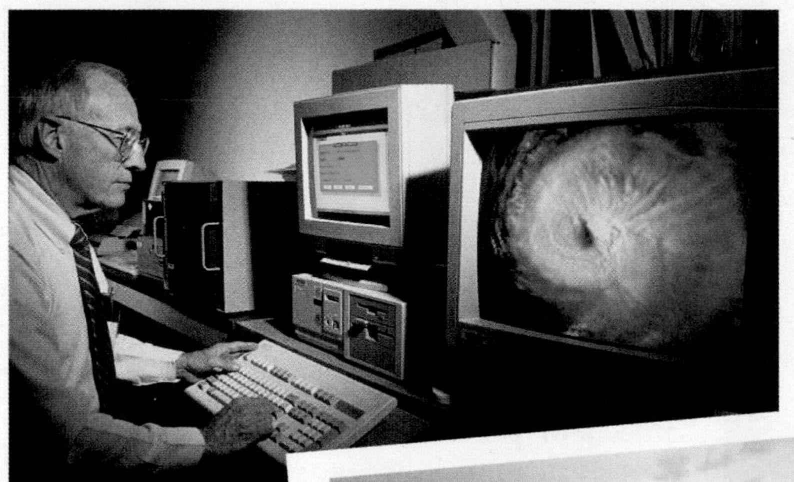

◀ **Meteorologists**
Meteorologists use data from weather satellites to monitor storms such as hurricanes. Computers process and display weather data.

**Environmental Scientists** ▶
These environmental scientists are testing water samples to find evidence of environmental change or pollution.

**Astronomers** ▲
Astronomers use telescopes to observe distant objects in space.

**Meteorology** Meteorology is the study of Earth's atmosphere. Meteorologists do much more than just forecast tomorrow's weather. **Meteorologists** are scientists who gather information about conditions in the atmosphere from around the world. Scientists in related fields study the forces that change Earth's climate.

**Astronomy** Astronomy is the study of the universe beyond Earth. Some **astronomers** focus on the solar system. Other astronomers observe stars and galaxies in an effort to understand the universe and its history.

**Environmental Science** Some Earth scientists, called **environmental scientists,** study Earth's environment and resources. Environmental scientists work together to determine the effects of human activities on Earth's land, air, water, and living things. They try to solve problems, such as pollution, that result from the use of resources.

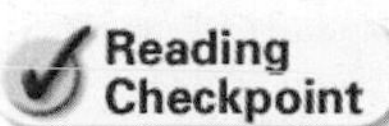

What is a meteorologist?

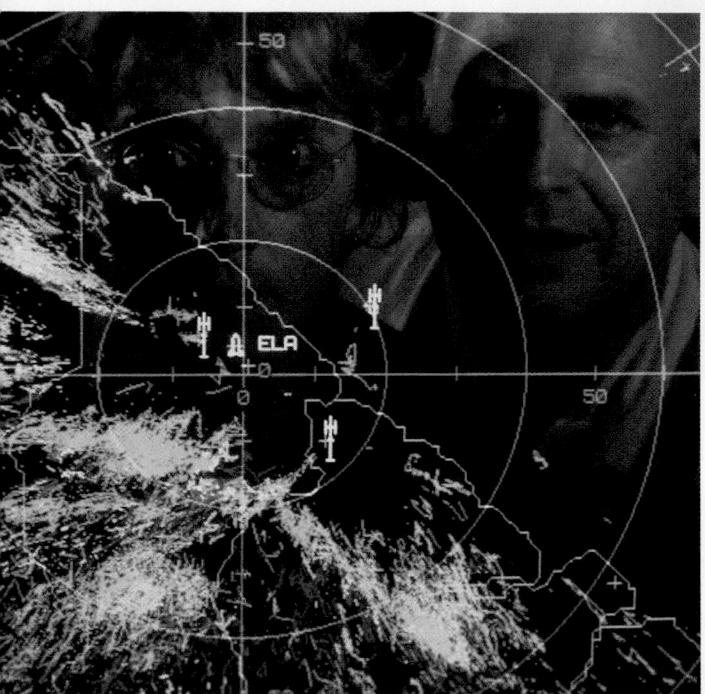


FIGURE 8
**Modeling Earth's Weather**
This weather map is a model of changing conditions in Earth's atmosphere.

## Models in Earth Science

Making models helps people study and understand things that are complex or can't be observed directly. Models are very useful in Earth science. You can't fit the whole atmosphere or lithosphere inside a laboratory! Even if you could, your experiment might need to last for millions of years. **For these reasons, Earth scientists often use models to represent complex objects or processes.** For example, meteorologists create models of how storms such as tornadoes and hurricanes form. In Figure 8 you can see one type of model used in Earth science—a weather map.

Earth scientists sometimes use models or computer simulations to test a hypothesis. A simulation is a model that imitates something in the real world. Scientists compare the results obtained from a simulation with known facts. This helps them decide whether the simulation supports the hypothesis. Because some information may be missing from a model, the model may not fully explain the process it represents.

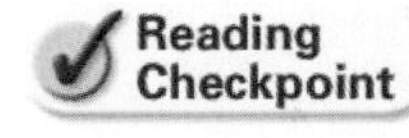

What is a simulation?

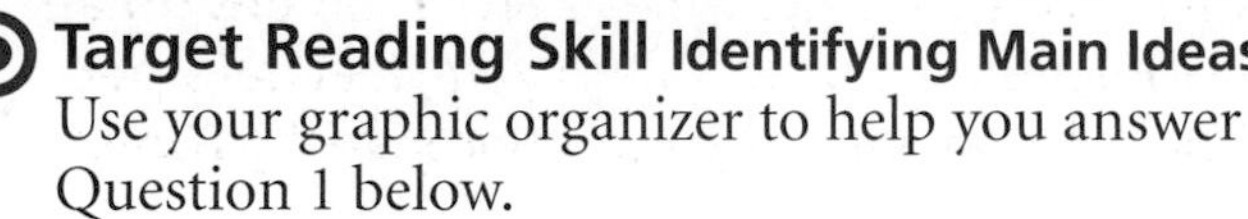


**Target Reading Skill Identifying Main Ideas** Use your graphic organizer to help you answer Question 1 below.

### Reviewing Key Concepts

1. a. **Reviewing** What are the big ideas of Earth science?
   b. **Explaining** Why do scientists view Earth as a system?
   c. **Relating Cause and Effect** Give an example of how one of the spheres of the Earth system can affect at least one of the other spheres.
2. a. **Listing** List the five branches of Earth science.
   b. **Summarizing** What do geologists do?
   c. **Classifying** What type of Earth scientist would probably study the effects of human activities on coral reefs? Explain.
3. a. **Explaining** Why are models useful in Earth science?
   b. **Applying Concepts** A geologist wants to make a model showing how a flood can change a river valley. Why would the geologist first collect data from many different floods?

### Writing in Science

**A Day in the Life** Research one of the Earth science careers in Figure 7. Based on your research, write a paragraph describing a typical workday for that type of Earth scientist. In your description, include the science inquiry skills the scientist would use on the job.

Lab zone **Skills Lab**

# Speeding Up Evaporation

## Problem

What factors increase the rate at which water evaporates?

## Skills Focus

developing hypotheses, controlling variables, drawing conclusions

## Materials

- water
- plastic dropper
- stopwatch
- 2 plastic petri dishes
- 1 petri dish cover
- 3 index cards
- paper towels
- lamp

## Procedure 

### PART 1 Effect of Heat

1. How do you think heating a water sample will affect how fast it evaporates? Record your hypothesis.
2. Place each petri dish on an index card.
3. Add a single drop of water to each of the petri dishes. Try to make the two drops the same size.
4. Position the lamp over one of the dishes as a heat source. Turn on the light. Make sure the light does not shine on the other dish. **CAUTION:** *The light bulb will become very hot. Avoid touching the bulb or getting water on it.*
5. Observe the dishes every 3 minutes to see which sample evaporates faster. Record your result.

### PART 2 Effect of Wind

6. How do you think fanning the water will affect how fast it evaporates? Record your hypothesis.
7. Dry both petri dishes and place them over the index cards. Add a drop of water to each dish as you did in Step 3.
8. Use an index card to fan one of the dishes for 5 minutes. Be careful not to fan the other dish.
9. Observe the dishes to see which sample evaporates faster. Record your result.

## Analyze and Conclude

1. **Developing Hypotheses** Did the evidence support both hypotheses? If not, which hypothesis was not supported?
2. **Controlling Variables** What was the manipulated variable in this experiment? The responding variable?
3. **Drawing Conclusions** Make a general statement about factors that increase the rate at which the water evaporates.
4. **Communicating** What everyday experiences helped you make your hypotheses at the beginning of the experiment? Explain how hypotheses differ from guesses.

## Design an Experiment

How do you think increasing the surface area of a water sample will affect how fast it evaporates? Write your hypothesis and then design an experiment to test it. *Obtain your teacher's permission before carrying out your investigation.*

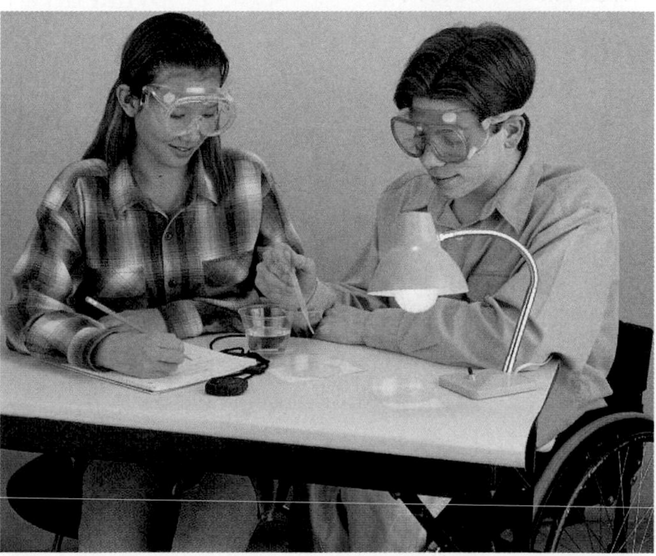

# 3 The Nature of Technology

## Reading Preview

### Key Concepts

- What is the goal of technology?
- How are science and technology related?
- How does technology affect society?

### Key Terms

- technology • engineer

### Target Reading Skill

**Using Prior Knowledge** Before you read, look at the section headings and visuals to see what this section is about. Then write what you know about technology in a graphic organizer like the one below. As you read, write what you learn.

| What You Know |
| --- |
| 1. Examples of technology include electronic devices.<br>2. |

| What You Learned |
| --- |
| 1.<br>2. |

## Lab zone Discover Activity

### What Are Some Examples of Technology?

1. Look at the objects in the photographs.
2. With a partner, discuss whether or not each object is an example of technology. Write your reasons for each decision.

**Think It Over**

**Forming Operational Definitions** On what basis did you and your partner decide whether an object was an example of technology? What is your definition of *technology*?

You have probably watched as workers constructed a school, office building, or store. But it may never have occurred to you that all of the things used in constructing these buildings—the earthmovers, crane, cement, and steel beams—are examples of technology. In fact, even the hard hats worn by the workers and the plans for the building are forms of technology. But what does *technology* mean?

## What Is Technology?

What do a pencil, a CD player, and a fork have in common? All are examples of technology—things that people have invented to suit their needs. But in addition to things that people make, technology can also refer to the knowledge and processes needed to produce those objects. In general terms, **technology** is how people change the world around them to meet their needs or to solve practical problems.

What is the purpose of technology? **The goal of technology is to improve the way people live.** Think about the many ways that technology has improved people's lives. Medicines help you recover from sickness. Eyeglasses and binoculars improve your ability to see. The Internet makes it easier for you to obtain information. The products of technology can be classified into several major areas, as shown in Figure 9.

## How Does Science Relate to Technology?

You might wonder why you are learning about technology in a science book. Are science and technology the same thing? The answer is no. In fact, people who develop technology are not called scientists, but engineers. An **engineer** is a person who is trained to use both technological and scientific knowledge to solve practical problems. Also, the goals of science and technology are different. **Science is the study of the natural world. Technology, on the other hand, changes, or modifies, the natural world to meet human needs or solve problems.**

To make the difference between science and technology clear, compare how scientists and engineers might study wind. A scientist might study how unequal heating of Earth's surface by the sun produces winds. An engineer, in contrast, might study how wind can be harnessed to produce electricity. To learn more about how engineers use technology, read the Technology Design Skills section in the Skills Handbook.

**For:** Links on Technology
**Visit:** www.SciLinks.org
**Webcode:** scn-1633

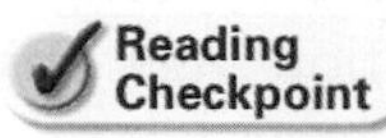


**What is an engineer?**

FIGURE 9
**Areas of Technology**
On a camping trip, you might make use of several different technologies.
**Classifying** *Besides the cellular phone, what is another example of a communication technology?*

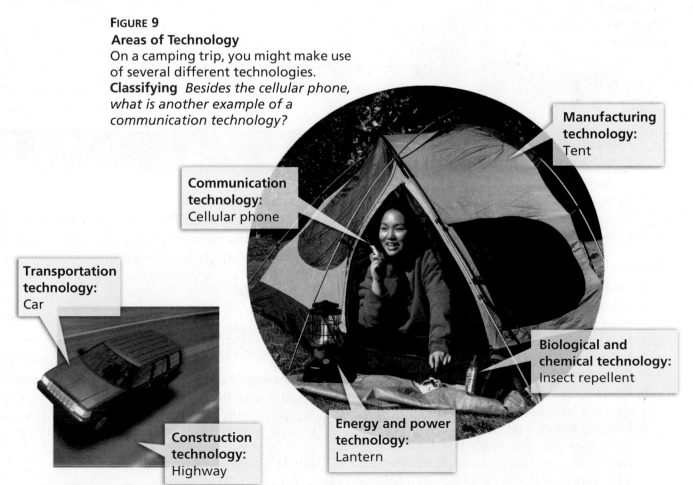

**Manufacturing technology:** Tent

**Communication technology:** Cellular phone

**Transportation technology:** Car

**Biological and chemical technology:** Insect repellent

**Construction technology:** Highway

**Energy and power technology:** Lantern

**FIGURE 10**
**Changing Technologies**
A cellular phone is smaller than an old-fashioned telephone—and it's wireless! Yet cellular phones also perform many functions that older phones did not.
**Applying Concepts** *Give an example of one way in which cellular phones have changed how people live.*

## Technology's Impact on Society

You probably know that 100 years ago, people lived very differently than they do now. Much of today's technology had not been invented. New technologies change how people live. In other words, they change society. The term *society* refers to any group of people who live together in an area, large or small, and have certain things in common. **From the Stone Age thousands of years ago to the Information Age today, technology has had a large impact on society.** During the Stone Age, for example, people used stones to make tools. Spears, axes, and spades enabled people to hunt animals and grow crops. As the food supply became more stable, people began to settle in farming communities and stay in one place.

During the Iron Age, people used iron, a strong metal, to make weapons and tools. Many machines were also invented, such as water wheels and grain mills. These inventions enabled farmers to grow more food. As food supplies increased, many people left farming behind and moved to cities.

Today, cities have grown greatly. But they are no longer isolated. The technology of the Information Age has changed societies around the world. Cellular phones, satellites, and super-fast computers allow people to share information quickly.

**What was the Iron Age?**

## Section 3 Assessment

**Target Reading Skill Using Prior Knowledge**
Review your graphic organizer and revise it based on what you just learned in the section.

### Reviewing Key Concepts

1. a. **Reviewing** What is technology?
   b. **Applying Concepts** How does a telephone meet the definition of technology?
2. a. **Identifying** Which field—science or technology—modifies the world to meet human needs?
   b. **Comparing and Contrasting** Compare and contrast science and technology.
   c. **Making Judgments** You are designing and building a dam to control floods on a large river. Is this project an example of science, technology, or both? Explain.
3. a. **Defining** What is society?
   b. **Explaining** What effect does a new technology have on society?
   c. **Predicting** Choose an example of technology that you are familiar with. Predict the impact of this technology on society.

**Lab zone At-Home Activity**

**Technology Hunt** With a family member, look around your home for ten examples of technology. In a table, list each item and the area of technology it represents. Describe how each item meets your needs and how your life might be different without it.

Section 4

# Safety in the Science Laboratory

## Reading Preview

### Key Concepts

- Why is preparation important when carrying out scientific investigations in the lab and in the field?
- What should you do if an accident occurs?

### Target Reading Skill

**Outlining** As you read, make an outline about science safety that you can use for review. Use the red headings for the main ideas and the blue headings for supporting ideas.

| Safety in the Science Laboratory |
|---|
| I. Safety in the lab<br>A. Preparing for the lab<br>B.<br>C.<br>II. Safety in the field |

## Lab zone Discover Activity

### Where Is the Safety Equipment in Your School?

1. Look around your classroom or school for any safety-related equipment.
2. Draw a floor plan of the room or building and clearly label where each item is located.

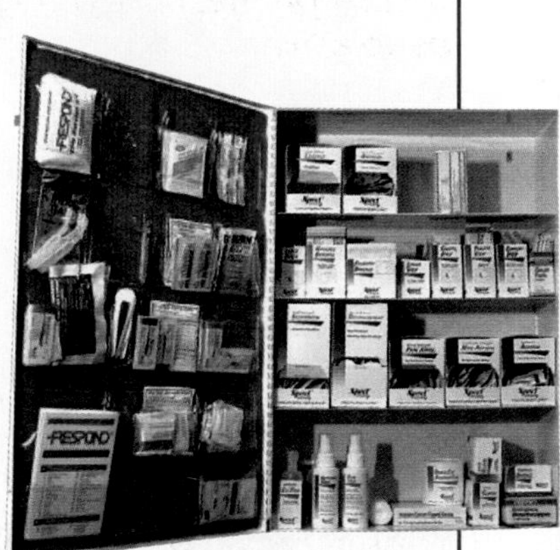

**Think It Over**

**Predicting** Why is it important to know where safety equipment is located?

You probably have a favorite summer outdoor activity. Some people enjoy watching baseball or picnicking at the beach. Others look forward to team sports or bicycling. But what if you wanted to try a new activity, such as canoeing? Before trying a new recreation, there are several things that you need to do to prepare. For example, before learning how to paddle a canoe, you would need to pass a swimming test. Then you would need to take a class to learn basic safety rules, such as always wearing a life vest.

Proper preparation is ▶ important for a canoe trip.

**Go Online** SCI LINKS NSTA

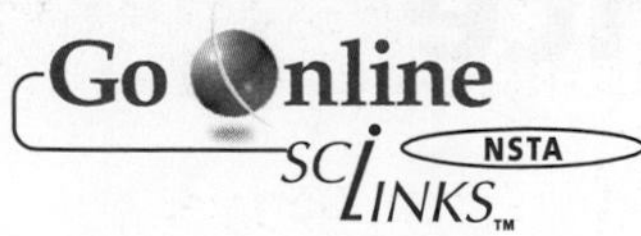

**For:** Links on laboratory safety
**Visit:** www.SciLinks.org
**Web Code:** scn-1624

## Safety in the Lab

Just as when you go canoeing, you have to be prepared before you begin any scientific investigation. **Good preparation helps you stay safe when doing science activities in the laboratory.**

Thermometers, balances, and glassware are some of the equipment you will use in science labs. Do you know how to use these items? What should you do if something goes wrong? Thinking about these questions ahead of time is an important part of being prepared.

**Preparing for the Lab** Preparing for a lab should begin the day before you will perform the lab. It is important to read through the procedure carefully and make sure you understand all the directions. Also, review the general safety guidelines in Appendix A, including those related to the specific equipment you will use. If anything is unclear, be prepared to ask your teacher about it before you begin the lab.

**Reading Checkpoint** **Why is it important to know how to use laboratory equipment?**

Wear an apron to protect yourself and your clothes from chemicals.
Wear heat-resistant gloves when handling hot objects. Wear plastic gloves to protect your skin when handling chemicals.
Make sure electric cords are untangled and out of the way.

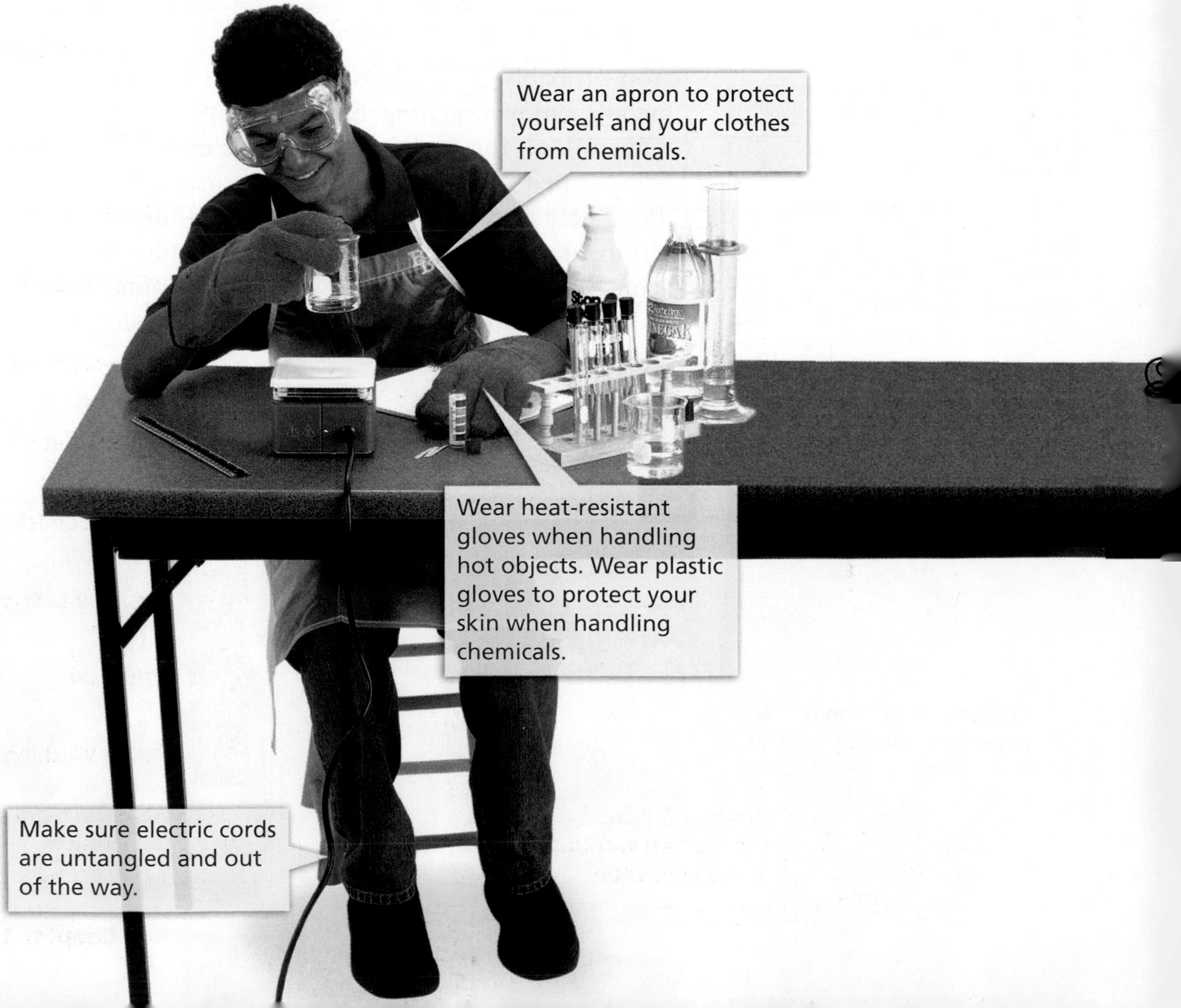

FIGURE 11
### Safety in the Lab
Good preparation for an experiment helps you stay safe in the laboratory. **Observing** *List three precautions each student is taking while performing the labs.*

**Performing the Lab** Whenever you perform a science lab, your chief concern must be the safety of yourself, your classmates, and your teacher. The most important safety rule is simple: Always follow your teacher's instructions and the textbook directions exactly. You should never try anything on your own without asking your teacher first.

Labs and activities in this textbook series include safety symbols such as those at right. These symbols alert you to possible dangers in performing the lab and remind you to work carefully. They also identify any safety equipment that you should use to protect yourself from potential hazards. The symbols are explained in detail in Appendix A. Make sure you are familiar with each safety symbol and what it means.

Other things you can do to make your lab experience safe and successful include keeping your work area clean and organized. Also, do not rush through any of the steps. Finally, always show respect and courtesy to your teacher and classmates.

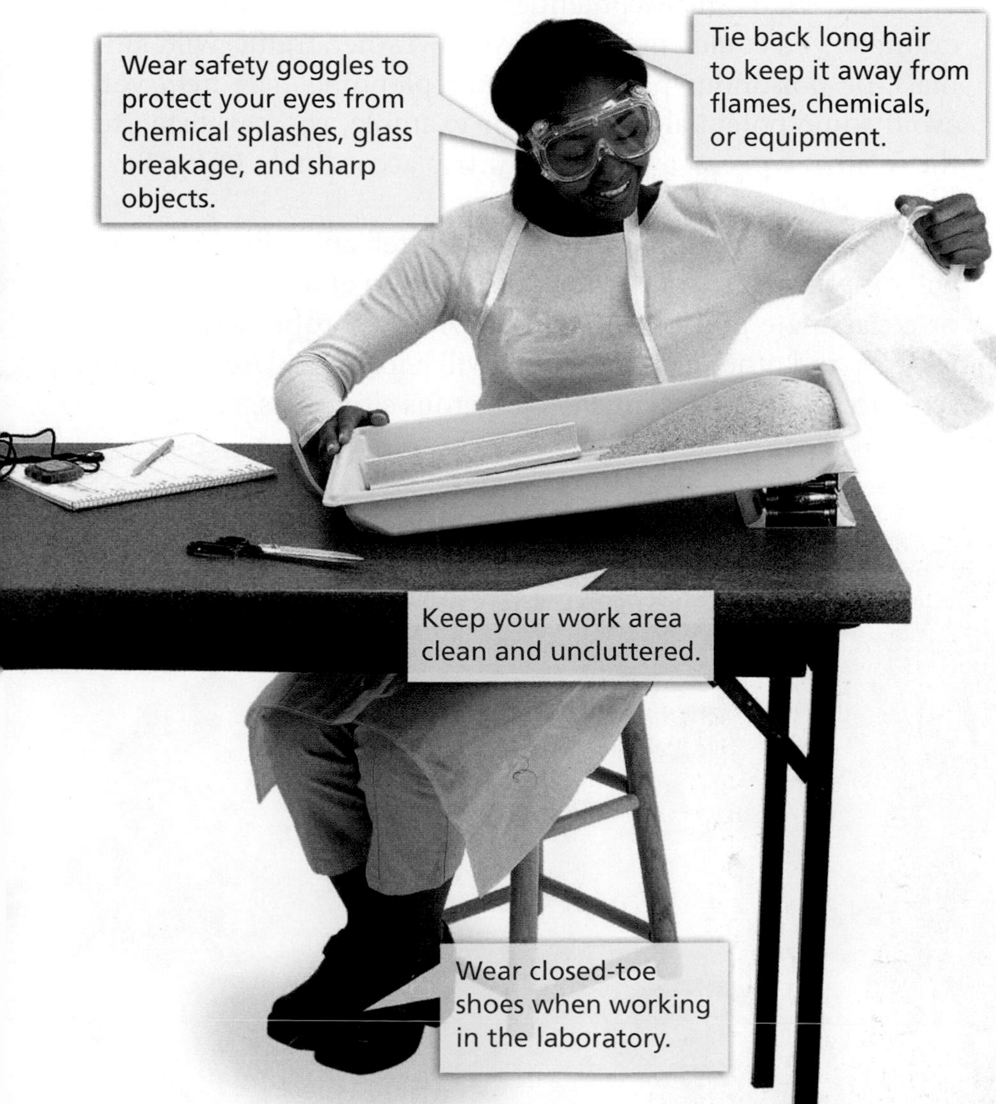
Wear safety goggles to protect your eyes from chemical splashes, glass breakage, and sharp objects.
Tie back long hair to keep it away from flames, chemicals, or equipment.
Keep your work area clean and uncluttered.
Wear closed-toe shoes when working in the laboratory.

**Safety Symbols**

 Safety Goggles

 Lab Apron

 Breakage

 Heat-Resistant Gloves

 Plastic Gloves

 Heating

 Flames

 No Flames

 Corrosive Chemical

 Poison

 Fumes

 Sharp Object

 Animal Safety

 Plant Safety

 Electric Shock

 Physical Safety

 Disposal

 Hand Washing

 General Safety Awareness

**End-of-Lab Procedures** Your lab work does not end when you reach the last step in the procedure. There are important things you need to do at the end of every lab.

When you have completed a lab, be sure to clean up your work area. Turn off and unplug any equipment and return it to its proper place. It is very important that you dispose of any waste materials properly. Some wastes should not be thrown in the trash or poured down the drain. Follow your teacher's instructions about proper disposal. Finally, be sure to wash your hands thoroughly after working in the laboratory.

FIGURE 12
### Safety in the Field
These are some of the items that might come in handy when you are out in the field.
**Applying Concepts** *What other items might be useful on a field trip to a beach?*

## Safety in the Field

The laboratory is not the only place where you will conduct scientific investigations. Some investigations will be done in the "field." The field can be any outdoor area, such as a schoolyard, a forest, a park, or a beach. **Just as in the laboratory, good preparation helps you stay safe when doing science activities in the field.**

There can be many potential safety hazards outdoors. For example, you could encounter severe weather, traffic, wild animals, or poisonous plants. Advance planning may help you avoid some potential hazards. For example, you can listen to the weather forecast and plan your trip accordingly. Other hazards may be impossible to anticipate.

Whenever you do field work, always tell an adult where you will be. Never carry out a field investigation alone. Ask an adult or a classmate to accompany you. Dress appropriately for the weather and other conditions you will encounter. Use common sense to avoid any potentially dangerous situations.

## In Case of an Accident

Good preparation and careful work habits can go a long way toward making your lab experiences safe ones. But, at some point, an accident may occur. A classmate might accidentally knock over a beaker or a chemical might spill on your sleeve. Would you know what to do?

**When any accident occurs, no matter how minor, notify your teacher immediately. Then, listen to your teacher's directions and carry them out quickly.** Make sure you know the location and proper use of all the emergency equipment in your lab room. Knowing safety and first-aid procedures beforehand will prepare you to handle accidents properly. Figure 13 lists some first-aid procedures you should know.

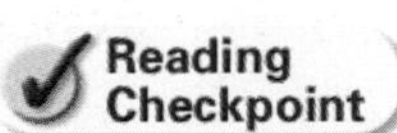

**What should you do when an accident occurs?**

**In Case of Emergency**

**ALWAYS NOTIFY YOUR TEACHER IMMEDIATELY**

| Injury | What to Do |
|---|---|
| Burns | Immerse burns in cold water. |
| Cuts | Cover cuts with a clean dressing. Apply direct pressure to the wound to stop bleeding. |
| Spills on Skin | Flush the skin with large amounts of water. |
| Foreign Object in Eye | Flush the eye with large amounts of water. Seek medical attention. |

FIGURE 13
**First-Aid Tips**
These first-aid tips can help guide your actions during emergency situations. Remember, always notify your teacher immediately if an accident occurs.

## Section 4 Assessment

**Target Reading Skill Outlining** Use the information in your outline about science safety to help you answer the questions below.

### Reviewing Key Concepts

1. a. **Listing** List two things you should do ahead of time to prepare for a lab.
   b. **Summarizing** Summarize the key steps you should take to ensure that you can perform a science lab safely.
   c. **Making Generalizations** Why is it more difficult to prepare for a lab activity in the field than for one in a laboratory?
2. a. **Reviewing** Suppose during a lab activity you get a cut and start to bleed. What is the first thing you should do?
   b. **Sequencing** Outline in order the next steps you would take to deal with your injury.
   c. **Making Judgments** Some people feel that most accidents can be prevented with proper preparation and safe behavior. Do you agree or disagree with this viewpoint? Explain your reasoning.

### Writing in Science

**Safety Poster** Make a poster of one of the safety rules in Appendix A to post in your lab. Be sure to include the safety symbol, clear directions, and additional illustrations.

Chapter 1

# Study Guide

**The BIG Idea**

**Nature of Science and Inquiry** Scientists investigate the natural world by observing, inferring, and predicting. They also pose questions, develop hypotheses, design experiments, analyze data, draw conclusions, and communicate results.

## 1 What Is Science?

**Key Concepts**

- Scientists use skills such as observing, inferring, and predicting. Successful scientists also possess certain attitudes, or habits of mind.
- Scientific inquiry refers to the many ways in which scientists study the natural world and propose explanations based on the evidence they gather.
- Unlike a theory, a scientific law describes an observed pattern in nature, but does not provide an explanation for it.

**Key Terms**

science
observing
inferring
predicting
scientific inquiry
hypothesis
controlled experiment
variable
manipulated variable
responding variable
data
scientific theory
scientific law

## 2 The Study of Earth Science

**Key Concepts**

- The big ideas of Earth science include the structure of the Earth system, Earth's history, and Earth in the solar system.
- In this book, you will learn about geology, oceanography, meteorology, astronomy, and environmental science.
- Earth scientists often use models to represent complex objects or processes.

**Key Terms**

Earth science
system
energy
constructive force
destructive force
geologist
oceanographer
meteorologist
astronomer
environmental scientist

## 3 The Nature of Technology

**Key Concepts**

- The goal of technology is to improve the way people live.
- Science is the study of the natural world. Technology, on the other hand, changes, or modifies, the natural world to meet human needs or solve problems.
- From the Stone Age thousands of years ago to the Information Age today, technology has had a large impact on society.

**Key Terms**

technology
engineer

## 4 Safety in the Science Laboratory

**Key Concepts**

- Good preparation helps you stay safe when doing science activities in the laboratory.
- Just as in the laboratory, good preparation helps you stay safe when doing science activities in the field.
- When any accident occurs, no matter how minor, notify your teacher immediately. Then, listen to your teacher's directions and carry them out quickly.

# Review and Assessment

For: Self-Assessment
Visit: PHSchool.com
Webcode: cja-1010

## Organizing Information

**Concept Mapping** Copy the concept map about the branches of Earth science onto a separate sheet of paper. Then complete it and add a title. (For more on Concept Mapping, see the Skills Handbook.)

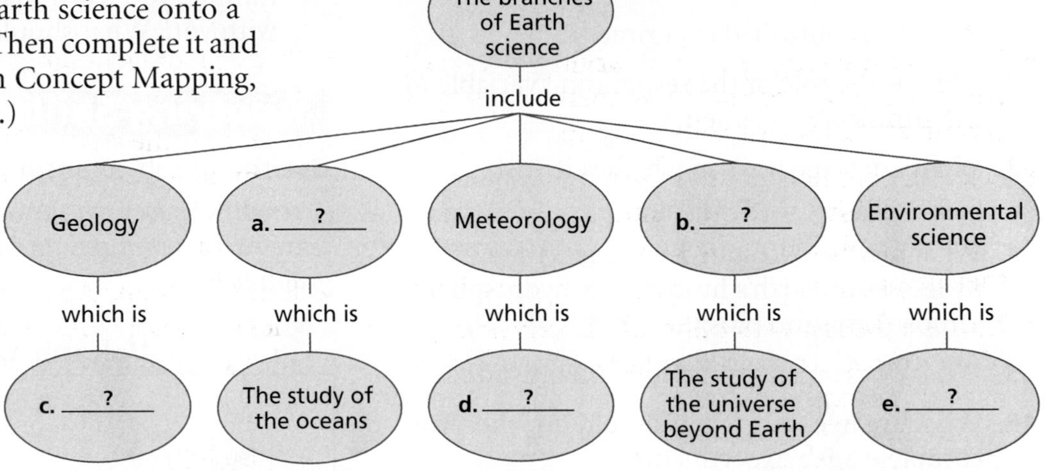


## Reviewing Key Terms

**Choose the letter of the best answer.**

1. If you explain or interpret something based on your experience, you are making a(n)
   **a.** hypothesis. **b.** prediction.
   **c.** inference. **d.** scientific law.
2. Scientific inquiry often begins with
   **a.** drawing conclusions.
   **b.** posing questions.
   **c.** making models.
   **d.** communicating results.
3. A possible explanation for a set of observations or answer to a scientific question is a
   **a.** variable. **b.** scientific theory.
   **c.** prediction. **d.** hypothesis.
4. Over time, mountains and landmasses form on Earth's surface because of
   **a.** constructive forces.
   **b.** gravity.
   **c.** destructive forces.
   **d.** energy from the sun.
5. The type of Earth scientist who studies the universe beyond Earth is a(n)
   **a.** engineer. **b.** astronomer.
   **c.** geologist. **d.** meteorologist.

**If the statement is true, write *true*. If it is false, change the underlined word or words to make the statement true.**

6. In an experiment, the variable that the scientist changes is called the <u>responding variable</u>.
7. In science, a <u>hypothesis</u> must be testable.
8. A <u>variable</u> is a group of parts that work together as a whole.
9. The <u>hydrosphere</u> is the part of the Earth made up of Earth's solid, rocky outer layer.

## Writing in Science

**Interview** You are a sports reporter interviewing an Olympic swimmer who lost the silver medal by a few hundredths of a second. Write a one-page interview in which you discuss the meaning of time and the advanced instruments used to measure time.

***The Work of Scientists***
Video Preview
Video Field Trip
▶ Video Assessment

# Review and Assessment

## Checking Concepts

**10.** In science, can a hypothesis be accepted as true after one test? Explain.

**11.** What is a controlled experiment?

**12.** What is the role of the responding variable in a controlled experiment?

**13.** What are three ways in which scientists communicate their ideas?

**14.** What are the two sources of energy for processes in Earth's lithosphere, hydrosphere, atmosphere, and biosphere?

**15.** What does an environmental scientist do?

**16.** What are five things you should do when you complete a lab experiment?

## Thinking Critically

**17. Applying Concepts** Once an experiment is complete, what must a scientist do to determine whether the data support the hypothesis?

**18. Predicting** If you could visit Earth one million years in the future, would the land surface look the same? Explain your answer.

**19. Classifying** Which type of Earth scientist studies the lithosphere? The hydrosphere? The atmosphere? Explain.

**20. Comparing and Contrasting** How are geology and astronomy similar? How are they different?

**21. Relating Cause and Effect** What are three technologies of the Information Age? How have they affected society?

**22. Interpreting Graphics** If you saw these safety icons at the beginning of an experiment's procedure, what safety steps would you need to take?

**23. Making Judgments** For an Earth science project, you and a lab partner plan to observe rocks in a park near your school. At the last minute, you learn that your partner can't go with you. What should you do? Explain.

## Applying Skills

**Use the graph to answer Questions 24–26.**

*A scientist measured the distance a lava flow traveled in 5 minutes and recorded the data in the graph below.*

**Volcanic Lava Flow**

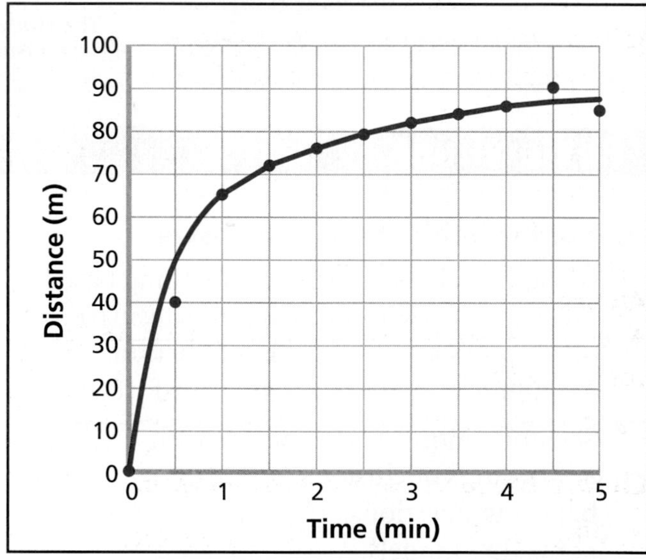


**24. Reading Graphs** What is plotted on each axis?

**25. Interpreting Data** Did the lava flow travel the same distance every minute?

**26. Predicting** Predict the movement of the lava flow between 5 and 6 minutes.

## Lab zone Chapter Project

**Performance Assessment** Display your model and explain what factors determined how you designed and built it. What was the most difficult thing about creating your model? How could you improve your model?

# Standardized Test Prep

### Test-Taking Tip

**Reading All the Answer Choices**

Always read every answer choice in a multiple-choice question before selecting the answer you think is correct. If you stop reading as soon as you find an answer that seems correct, you may not notice that another choice is more complete or accurate. Or you may not see that "all of the above" is given as one of the answer choices.

***Sample Question***

A model is a simplified representation of a complex object or process. Which of the following is an example of a model?

**A** a map showing Earth's continents and oceans
**B** a computer diagram of a new car design
**C** an architect's drawing of a new shopping mall
**D** all of the above

***Answer***

**A, B,** and **C** are all examples of models. The correct answer is **D.**

**Choose the letter of the best answer.**

**1.** What would a scientist usually do after conducting a controlled experiment?
**A** interpret the data from the experiment
**B** communicate the results of the experiment
**C** draw a conclusion and, if needed, revise the hypothesis
**D** all of the above

**2.** Which of the following are examples of technology?
**F** a laptop computer
**G** a bridge
**H** a microscope
**J** all of the above

**Use the table to answer Questions 3–4.**
*The table shows characteristics of the atmosphere, hydrosphere, and lithosphere. Density is a measure of how much mass is contained in a given volume. Density is expressed in grams per cubic centimeter ($g/cm^3$).*

**Composition of the Spheres of Earth**

| Sphere | Density ($g/cm^3$) | Type of Material | Average Thickness (km) |
|---|---|---|---|
| Atmosphere | 0.0–0.0001 | Gas | 1,000 |
| Hydrosphere | 1.0 | Liquid | 3.8 |
| Lithosphere | 2.7–3.3 | Solid | 100 |

**3.** Which answer best describes the characteristics of the lithosphere?
**A** liquid with a density of 1.0
**B** solid and less dense than the hydrosphere
**C** gas with very low density
**D** solid and more dense than the hydrosphere

**4.** What is the average thickness of the hydrosphere?
**F** 100 km
**G** 3.3 km
**H** 1,000 km
**J** 3.8 km

**5.** If an accident occurs in a science laboratory, the first thing you should do is
**A** determine the cause of the accident.
**B** notify your teacher immediately.
**C** locate the first-aid kit.
**D** put a bandage on the affected area.

### Constructed Response

**6.** Choose one of the branches of Earth science—geology, oceanography, meteorology, astronomy, or environmental science. Write a paragraph in which you define the science you picked and describe what the scientists in this branch of Earth science do.

Chapter 2

# Mapping Earth's Surface

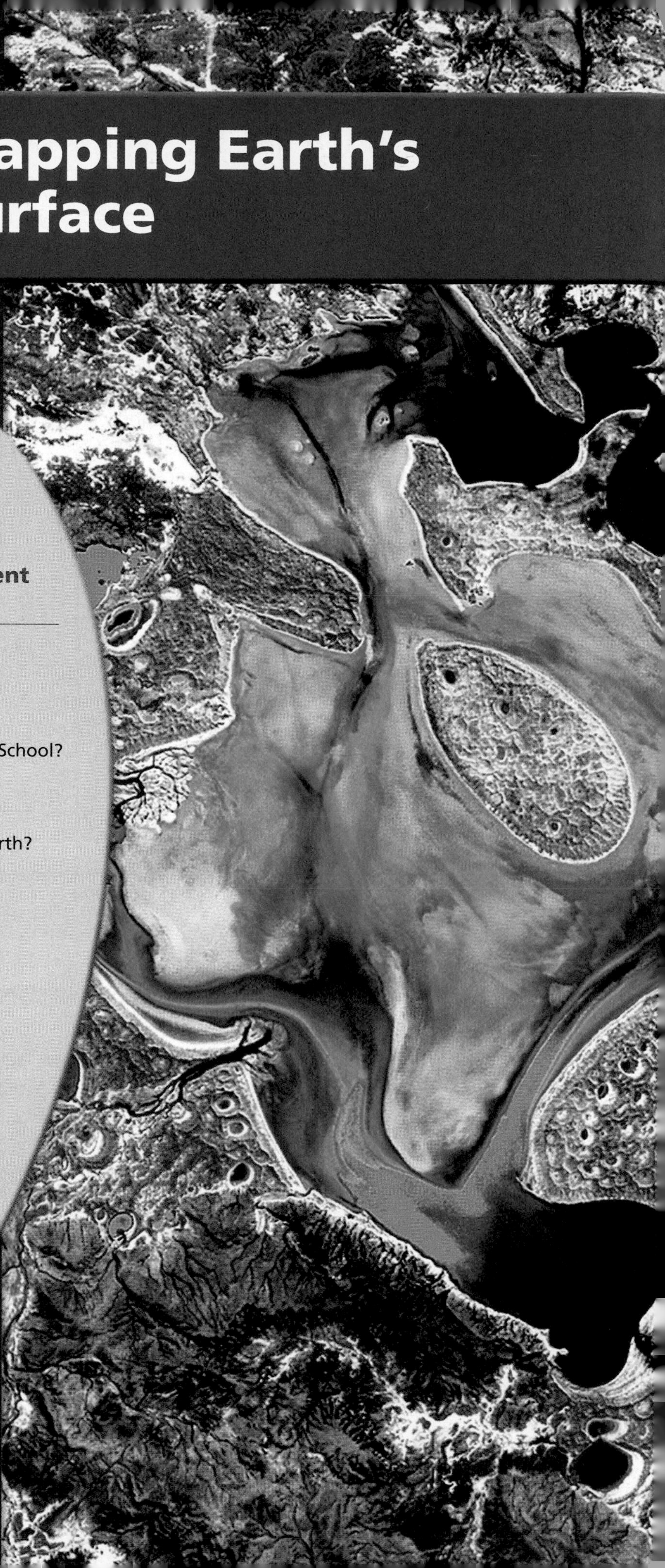

## The BIG Idea

### Modeling Earth Using Technology

**How are maps used to represent landforms and topography?**

### Chapter Preview

**❶ Exploring Earth's Surface**
- ***Discover*** What Is the Land Like Around Your School?
- ***Skills Activity*** Classifying

**❷ Models of Earth**
- ***Discover*** How Can You Flatten the Curved Earth?
- ***Math Skills*** Scale and Ratios
- ***Try This*** Where in the World?
- ***Skills Lab*** A Borderline Case

**❸ Maps and Computers**
- ***Discover*** Can You Make a Pixel Picture?
- ***At-Home Activity*** Maps in the News

**❹ Topographic Maps**
- ***Discover*** Can a Map Show Relief?
- ***Active Art*** Topographic Map
- ***Skills Activity*** Interpreting Data
- ***Analyzing Data*** Mapping Elevation Data
- ***Skills Lab*** A Map in a Pan

This satellite image shows Lake Carnegie in Western Australia. ▶

*Mapping Earth's Surface*
▶ Video Preview
Video Field Trip
Video Assessment

Lab zone™ Chapter **Project**

## Getting on the Map

For this chapter project, you will select a small piece of land and draw a map of its physical features.

**Your Goal** To create a scale map of a small area of your neighborhood

To complete this project, you must

- work with your teacher or an adult family member
- choose and measure a small square or rectangular piece of land
- use a compass to locate north
- draw a map to scale
- use symbols and a key to represent natural and human-made features of the land
- follow the safety guidelines in Appendix A

**Plan It!** Start by looking for a suitable site. Your site should be about 300 to 1,000 square meters in area. It could be part of a park, playground, or backyard. Look for an area that includes interesting natural features such as trees, a stream, and changes in elevation or slope. There may be some human-made structures on your site, such as a park bench or sidewalk. Once you have chosen a site, measure its boundaries and sketch its physical features. Then brainstorm ideas for symbols to include on your map. When you have completed your map, including a key and map scale, present it to your class.

Section 1

# Exploring Earth's Surface

## Reading Preview

### Key Concepts

- What does the topography of an area include?
- What are the main types of landforms?

### Key Terms

- topography • elevation
- relief • landform • plain
- mountain • mountain range
- plateau • landform region

### Target Reading Skill

**Comparing and Contrasting**

As you read, compare and contrast the characteristics of landforms by completing a table like the one below.

**Characteristics of Landforms**

| Landform | Elevation | Relief |
|---|---|---|
| Plain | a. ___?___ | Low |
| Mountain | b. ___?___ | c. ___?___ |
| d. ___?___ | High | e. ___?___ |

## Lab zone Discover Activity

### What Is the Land Like Around Your School?

1. On a piece of paper, draw a small square to represent your school.
2. Choose a word that describes the type of land near your school, such as flat, hilly, or rolling. Write the word next to the square.
3. Use a magnetic compass to determine the direction of north. Assume that north is at the top of your piece of paper.
4. If you travel due north 1 kilometer from your school, what type of land do you find? Choose a word to describe the land in this area. Write that word to the north of the square.
5. Repeat Step 4 for areas located 1 kilometer east, south, and west of your school.

**Think It Over**

**Forming Operational Definitions** What phrase could you use to describe the land in your area?

In 1804, an expedition set out from St. Louis to explore the land between the Mississippi River and the Pacific Ocean. The United States had just purchased a part of this vast territory, called Louisiana, from France. Before the Louisiana Purchase, the United States stretched from the Atlantic coast westward to the Mississippi River. Few United States citizens had traveled west of the Mississippi. None had ever traveled over land all the way to the Pacific.

Led by Meriwether Lewis and William Clark, the expedition first traveled up the Missouri River. Then the group crossed the Rocky Mountains and followed the Columbia River to the Pacific Ocean. They returned by a similar route. The purpose of the expedition was to map America's interior.

On the journey to the Pacific, the Lewis and Clark expedition traveled more than 5,000 kilometers. As they traveled, Lewis and Clark observed many changes in topography. **Topography** (tuh PAWG ruh fee) is the shape of the land. An area's topography may be flat, sloping, hilly, or mountainous.

◀ The compass used by Meriwether Lewis

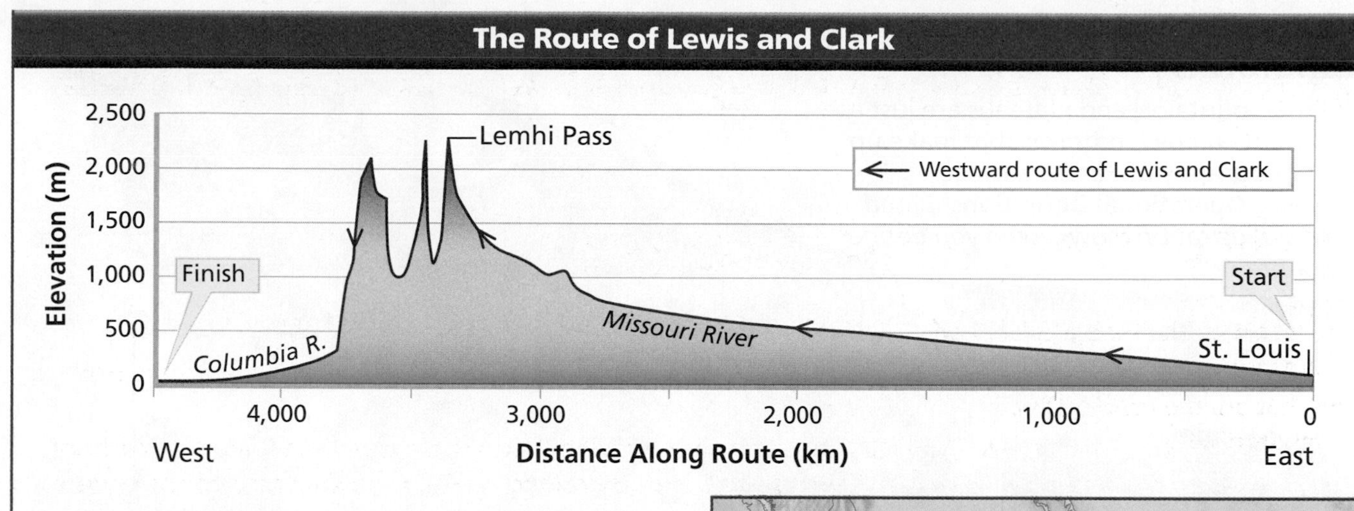


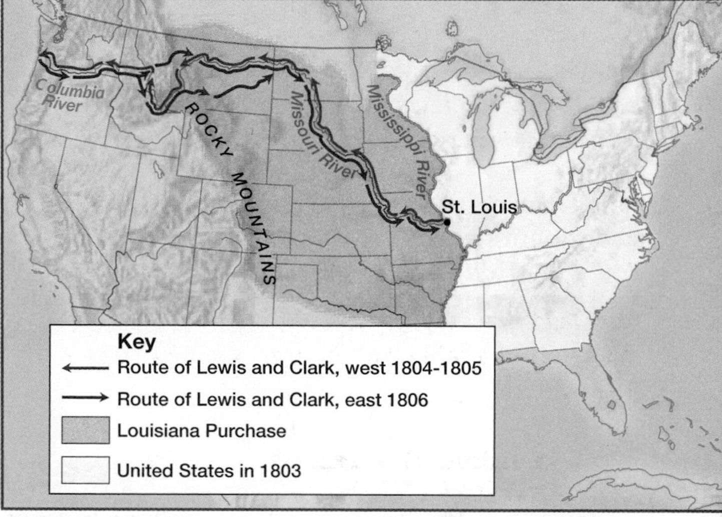


**FIGURE 1**
The route of the Lewis and Clark expedition crossed regions that differed greatly in elevation and relief. **Interpreting Graphs** *How much elevation did Lewis and Clark gain between St. Louis and Lemhi Pass?*

# Topography

**The topography of an area includes the area's elevation, relief, and landforms.** The desktop where you do homework probably has piles of books, papers, and other objects of different sizes and shapes. Your desktop has both elevation and relief!

**Elevation** The height above sea level of a point on Earth's surface is its **elevation.** When Lewis and Clark started in St. Louis, they were about 140 meters above sea level. By the time they reached Lemhi Pass in the Rocky Mountains, they were more than 2,200 meters above sea level. Look at Figure 1 to see the changes in elevation along Lewis and Clark's route.

**Relief** The difference in elevation between the highest and lowest parts of an area is its **relief.** Early in their journey, Lewis and Clark encountered flat or rolling land with low relief, or small differences in elevation. In the Rocky Mountains, they crossed huge mountains separated by deep valleys. These areas had high relief, or great differences in elevation.

**Landforms** If you followed the route of the Lewis and Clark expedition, you would see many different landforms. A **landform** is a feature of topography, such as a hill or valley, formed by the processes that shape Earth's surface. Different landforms have different combinations of elevation and relief.

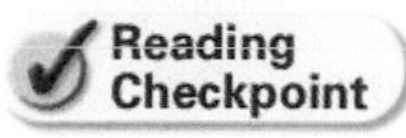

**What is the difference between elevation and relief?**

FIGURE 2
## Landforms

Plains, mountains, and plateaus are just a few of the many landforms that make up the topography of Earth's surface.
**Forming Operational Definitions** *Based on this illustration, how would you define "mountains"?*

**Plains**
Plains may occur along a continent's edges or in the interior.

# Types of Landforms

Landforms vary greatly in size and shape—from level plains extending as far as the eye can see, to low, rounded hills that you could climb on foot, to jagged mountains that would take you many days to walk around. **There are three main types of landforms: plains, mountains, and plateaus.**

**Plains** A **plain** is a landform made up of nearly flat or gently rolling land with low relief. A plain that lies along a seacoast is called a coastal plain. In North America, a coastal plain extends around the continent's eastern and southeastern shores. Coastal plains have both low elevation and low relief.

A plain that lies away from the coast is called an interior plain. Although interior plains have low relief, their elevation can vary. The broad interior plains of North America are called the Great Plains.

The Great Plains extend north from Texas into Canada. The Great Plains extend west to the Rocky Mountains from the states of North and South Dakota, Nebraska, Kansas, Oklahoma, and Texas. At the time of the Lewis and Clark expedition, the Great Plains were a vast grassland.

**For:** Links on landforms
**Visit:** www.SciLinks.org
**Web Code:** scn-0711

Mountains
A mountain's base usually covers an area of at least several square kilometers, but its peak may rise to a point. Mountains often have steeply sloping sides.
Plateaus
The top of a plateau forms a level surface.

**Mountains** A **mountain** is a landform with high elevation and high relief. Mountains usually occur as part of a mountain range. A **mountain range** is a group of mountains that are closely related in shape, structure, and age. After crossing the Great Plains, the Lewis and Clark expedition crossed a rugged mountain range in Idaho called the Bitterroot Mountains.

The different mountain ranges in a region make up a mountain system. The Bitterroot Mountains are one mountain range in the mountain system known as the Rocky Mountains.

Mountain ranges and mountain systems in a long, connected chain form a larger unit called a mountain belt. The Rocky Mountains are part of a great mountain belt that stretches down the western sides of North America and South America.

**Plateaus** A landform that has high elevation and a more or less level surface is called a **plateau.** A plateau is rarely perfectly smooth on top. Streams and rivers may cut into the plateau's surface. The Columbia Plateau in Washington State is an example. The Columbia River, which the Lewis and Clark expedition followed, slices through this plateau. The many layers of rock that make up the Columbia Plateau are stacked about 1,500 meters thick.

**Lab zone Skills Activity**

### Classifying

You take a direct flight across the United States from Walla Walla in Washington State to Washington, D.C. You have a window seat. Write a postcard to friends describing the major landforms that you see on your trip. Use Figure 3 to determine what the land is like along your route.

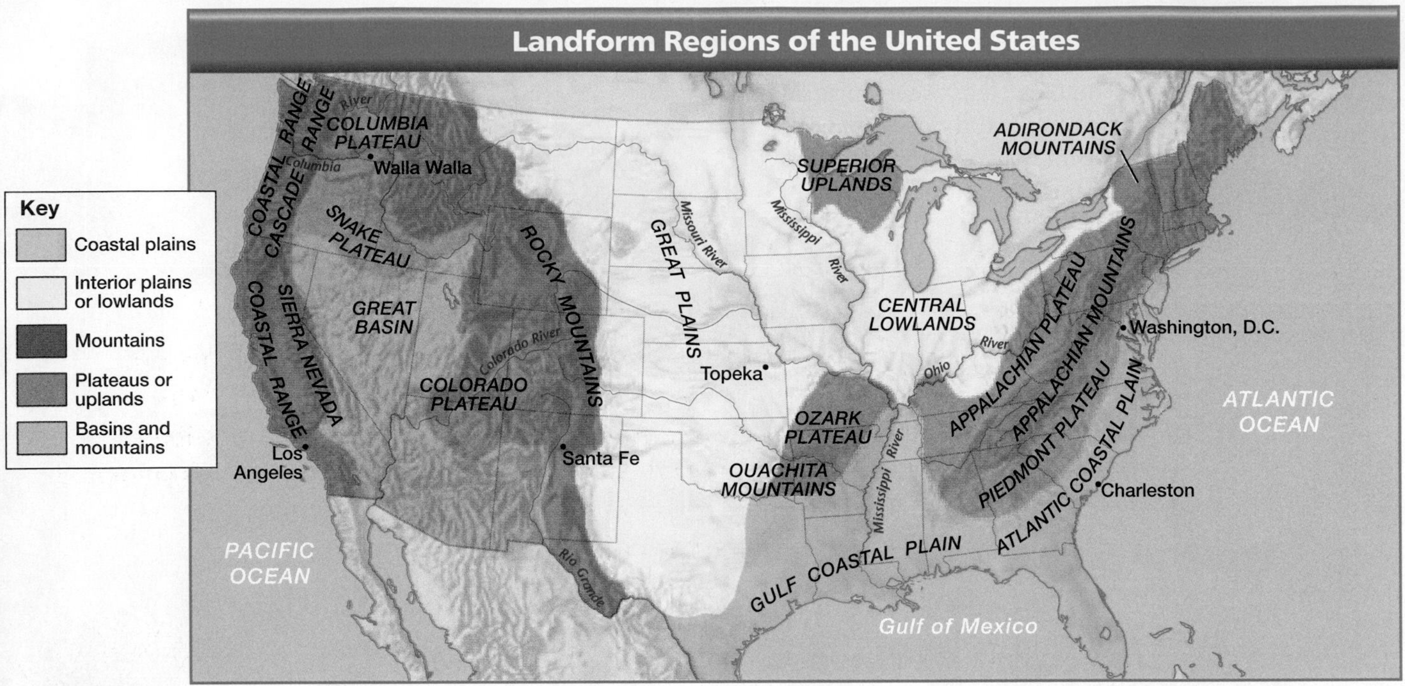


**FIGURE 3**
The United States has many different landform regions.
**Interpreting Maps** *In what regions are Charleston, Santa Fe, and Topeka?*

**Landform Regions** A large area of land where the topography is made up mainly of one type of landform is called a **landform region.** The Great Plains and Rocky Mountains are major landform regions. Other terms can be used to describe landform regions. For example, an upland is a region of hilly topography. A lowland is a region of plains with low elevation. A basin is lower than the mountains around it.

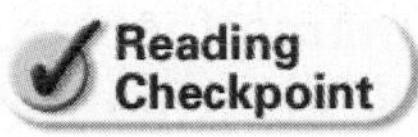


**What terms can be used to describe landform regions?**

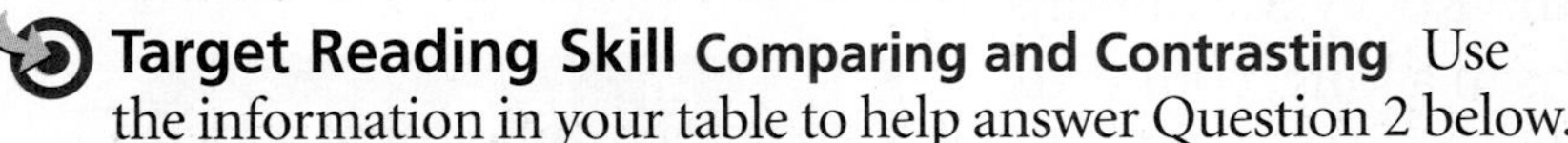

## Section 1 Assessment

**Target Reading Skill Comparing and Contrasting** Use the information in your table to help answer Question 2 below.

### Reviewing Key Concepts

1. a. **Defining** What is elevation?
   b. **Comparing and Contrasting** What is relief? How does it differ from elevation?
   c. **Calculating** What is the relief in an area where the highest point is 1,200 meters above sea level and the lowest point is 200 meters above sea level?
2. a. **Listing** What are the three main types of landforms?
   b. **Describing** What are the characteristics of a mountain?
   c. **Sequencing** Place these features in order from smallest to largest: mountain system, mountain range, mountain belt, mountain.

### Writing in Science

**Description** Look at Figure 3. Choose one of the landform regions on the map. Research the characteristics of your landform region using an encyclopedia or other reference. Write a description of the region, including characteristics such as elevation, relief, and the types of landforms found there.

Section 2

# Models of Earth

## Reading Preview

### Key Concepts

- How do maps and globes represent Earth's surface?
- What reference lines are used to locate points on Earth?
- What are three common map projections?

### Key Terms

- map • globe • scale
- symbol • key • degree
- equator • hemisphere
- prime meridian • latitude
- longitude • map projection

### Target Reading Skill

**Asking Questions** Before you read, preview the red headings. In a graphic organizer like the one below, ask a question for each heading. As you read, write the answers to your questions.

**Models of Earth**

| Question | Answer |
|---|---|
| What are maps and globes? | |
| | |

## Lab zone Discover Activity

### How Can You Flatten the Curved Earth?

1. Using a felt-tip pen, make a rough sketch of the outlines of the continents on the surface of an orange or grapefruit.
2. Using a plastic knife, carefully peel the orange. If possible, keep the peel in one large piece so that the continents remain intact.
3. Try to lay the pieces of orange peel flat on a table.

**Think It Over**

**Observing** What happens to the continents when you try to flatten the pieces? Is there any way to keep the shapes of the continents from being distorted?

Today, people know that Earth is a sphere located in space and moving around the sun. But it took hundreds of years to develop this scientific model of Earth. Around 600 B.C., one early Greek scientist, Thales of Miletus, hypothesized that Earth is a disk floating in a pool of water. Another Greek scientist, Anaximander, suggested that Earth is a cylinder floating in space. (He thought that people lived on the flat top of the cylinder!)

Around 350 B.C., the Greek scientist Aristotle used evidence from everyday observations to support the idea that Earth is a sphere. For example, Aristotle pointed out that a ship sailing away from shore appears to sink beneath the horizon because Earth's surface is curved. If Earth were flat, the ship would simply appear smaller as it moved away.

After Aristotle, other Greek scientists used the knowledge that Earth is a sphere to help them measure the size of Earth. Eratosthenes, a Greek scientist who lived in Egypt more than 2,200 years ago, calculated Earth's size. Using measurements and principles of geometry and astronomy, he arrived at a figure that was accurate to within 14 percent.

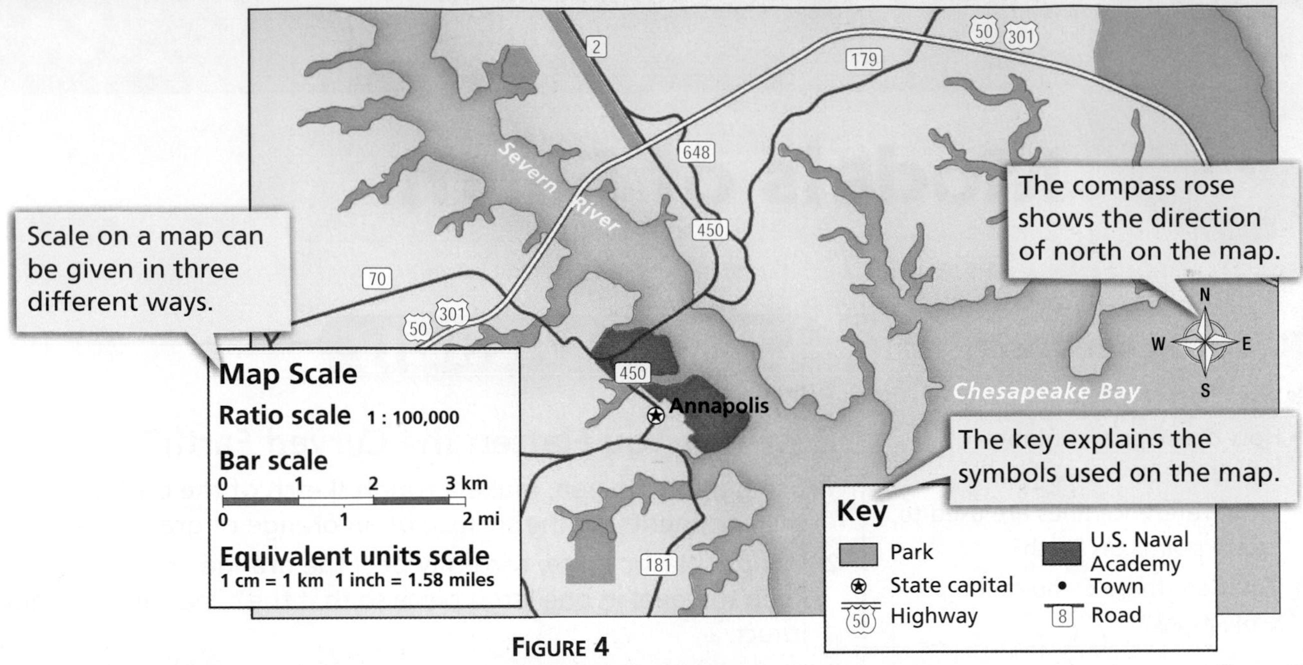


**FIGURE 4**

**What's in a Map?**

A map is drawn to scale, uses symbols explained in a map key, and usually has a compass rose to show direction. This map shows the area around Annapolis, Maryland.

**Interpreting Maps** *What is the scale of this map?*

## Math Skills

### Scale and Ratios

A ratio compares two numbers by division. For example, the scale of a map given as a ratio is 1 : 250,000. At this scale, the distance between two points on the map measures 23.5 cm. How would you find the actual distance?

1. Write the scale as a fraction.

$$\frac{1}{250,000}$$

2. Write a proportion. Let *d* represent the distance between the two points.

$$\frac{1}{250,000} = \frac{23.5 \text{ cm}}{d}$$

3. Write the cross products.

$$1 \times d = 250,000 \times 23.5 \text{ cm}$$
$$d = 5,875,000 \text{ cm}$$

(*Hint:* To convert cm to km, divide *d* by 100,000.)

**Practice Problem** A map's scale is 1 : 25,000. If two points are 4.7 cm apart on the map, how far apart are they on the ground?

## Maps and Globes

Maps and globes show the shape, size, and position of Earth's surface features. A **map** is a flat model of all or part of Earth's surface as seen from above. A **globe** is a sphere that represents Earth's entire surface. A globe correctly shows the relative size, shape, and position of landmasses and bodies of water, much as if you were viewing Earth from space.

**Maps and globes are drawn to scale and use symbols to represent topography and other features on Earth's surface.** A map's **scale** relates distance on a map to a distance on Earth's surface. Scale is often given as a ratio. For example, one unit on a map could equal 25,000 units on the ground. So one centimeter on the map would represent 0.25 kilometer. This scale, "one to twenty-five thousand," would be written "1 : 25,000." Figure 4 shows three ways of giving a map's scale.

Mapmakers use shapes and pictures called **symbols** to stand for features on Earth's surface. A symbol can represent a physical feature, such as a river, lake, mountain, or plain. A symbol also can stand for a human-made feature, such as a highway, city, or airport. A map's **key,** or legend, is a list of all the symbols used on the map with an explanation of their meaning.

Maps also include a compass rose or north arrow. The compass rose helps relate directions on the map to directions on Earth's surface. North usually is located at the top of the map.

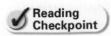

**Reading Checkpoint** **Where can you find the meaning of the symbols on a map?**

**FIGURE 5**
**A Grid System**
The checkerboard pattern made by this farmland is based on the grid lines used on maps and globes.

## An Earth Reference System

When you play checkers, the grid of squares helps you to keep track of where each piece should be. To find a point on Earth's surface, you need a reference system like the grid of squares on a checkerboard. Of course, Earth itself does not have grid lines, but most maps and globes show a grid. Because Earth is a sphere, the grid curves to cover the entire planet. **Two of the lines that make up the grid, the equator and prime meridian, are the baselines for measuring distances on Earth's surface.**

**Measuring in Degrees** To locate positions on Earth's surface, scientists use units called degrees. You probably know that degrees are used to measure the distance around a circle. As you can see in Figure 6, a **degree** (°) is $\frac{1}{360}$ of the distance around a circle. Degrees can also be used to measure distances on the surface of a sphere. On Earth's surface, each degree is a measure of an angle formed by lines drawn from the center of Earth to points on the surface. To help locate points precisely, degrees are further divided into smaller units called minutes and seconds.

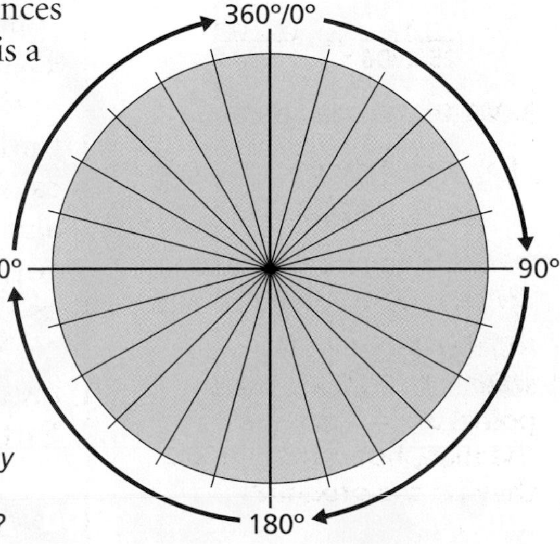


**FIGURE 6**
**Degrees Around**
Distances around a circle are measured in degrees.
**Interpreting Diagrams** *How many degrees are there in one quarter of the distance around the circle?*

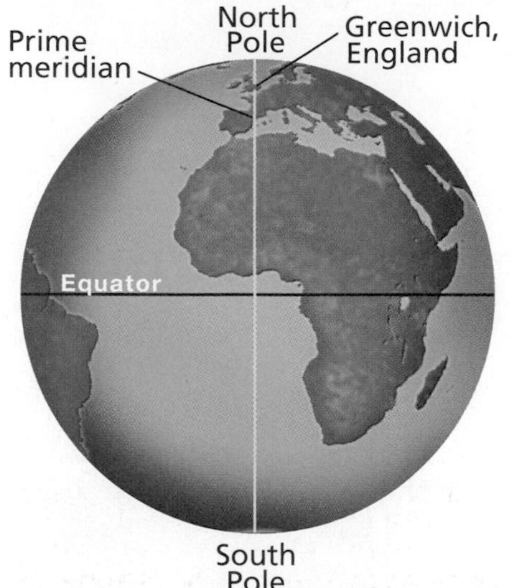


**FIGURE 7**
**Equator and Prime Meridian**
The equator and prime meridian divide Earth's surface into hemispheres.

**The Equator** Halfway between the North and South poles, the **equator** forms an imaginary line that circles Earth. The equator divides Earth into the Northern and Southern hemispheres. A **hemisphere** (HEM ih sfeer) is one half of the sphere that makes up Earth's surface. If you started at the equator and traveled to one of the poles, you would travel 90 degrees—one quarter of the distance in a full circle.

## Science and History

### Maps and Technology

Centuries ago, people invented instruments for determining compass direction, latitude, and longitude. Mapmakers developed techniques to show Earth's surface accurately.

**Around 1100**
**Magnetic Compass**
Because the needle of a magnetic compass points north, ships at sea could tell direction even when the sun and stars were not visible. Arabs and Europeans adopted this Chinese invention by the 1200s.

**1154**
**Scientific Mapmaking**
The Arab mapmaker Al-Idrisi made several world maps for King Roger of Sicily. Idrisi's maps marked a great advance over other maps of that time. They showed the Arabs' grasp of scientific mapmaking and geography. But unlike modern maps, these maps placed south at the top!

**Around 1300**
**Charts for Navigation**
Lines representing wind directions criss-crossed a type of map called a portolan chart. These charts also showed coastlines and harbors. A sea captain would use a portolan chart and a compass when sailing from one harbor to another.

1100 | 1200 | 1300 | 1400

**The Prime Meridian** Another imaginary line, called the **prime meridian,** makes a half circle from the North Pole to the South Pole. The prime meridian passes through Greenwich, England. Places east of the prime meridian are in the Eastern Hemisphere. Places west of the prime meridian are in the Western Hemisphere.

If you started at the prime meridian and traveled west along the equator, you would travel through 360 degrees before returning to your starting point. At 180 degrees east or west of the prime meridian is another half circle that lies directly opposite the prime meridian.

**What two hemispheres are separated by the equator?**

## Writing in Science

**Writing in Science** Choose one period on the timeline to learn more about. Use the library to find information about maps in that time. Who used maps? Why were they important? Share what you learn in the form of a letter written by a traveler or explorer who is using a map of that period.

**1569**
**Map Projections**
Flemish mapmaker Gerardus Mercator invented the first modern map projection, which bears his name. Mercator and his son, Rumold, also made an atlas and maps of the world such as the one shown above.

**1595**
**Determining Latitude**
To find latitude, sailors used a variety of instruments, including the backstaff. The navigator sighted along the backstaff's straight edge to measure the angle of the sun or North Star above the horizon. Later improvements led to modern instruments for navigation.

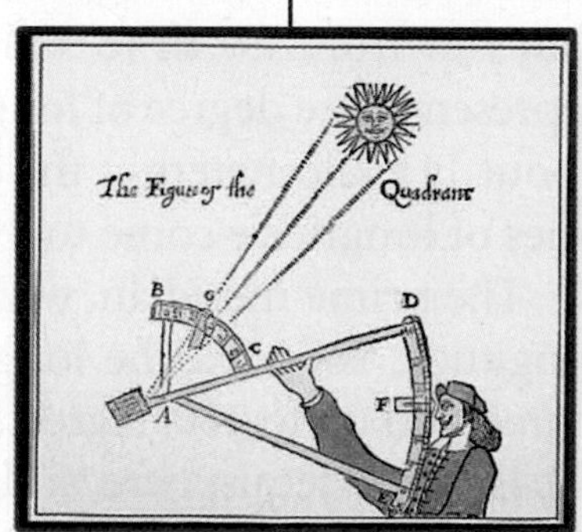


**1763**
**Determining Longitude**
John Harrison, a carpenter and mechanic, won a prize from the British navy for building a highly accurate clock called a chronometer. Harrison's invention made finding longitudes quicker and easier. With exact longitudes, mapmakers could greatly improve the accuracy of their maps.

1500 1600 1700 1800

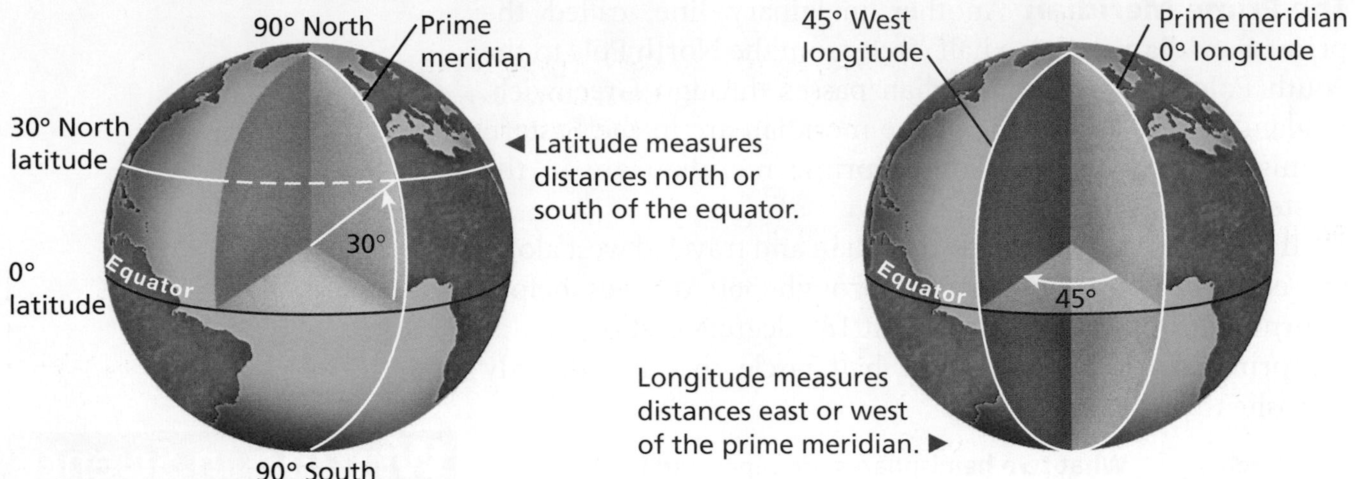


FIGURE 8
**Latitude and Longitude**
Points on Earth's surface can be located using the grid of latitude and longitude lines.

## Locating Points on Earth's Surface

Using the equator and prime meridian, mapmakers have constructed a grid made up of lines of latitude and longitude. **The lines of latitude and longitude form a grid that can be used to find locations anywhere on Earth.**

**Latitude** The equator is the starting line for measuring **latitude,** or distance in degrees north or south of the equator. The latitude of the equator is 0°. Between the equator and each pole are 90 evenly spaced, parallel lines called lines of latitude. Each degree of latitude is equal to about 111 kilometers.

A line of latitude is defined by the angle it makes with the equator and the center of Earth. Figure 8 shows how lines drawn from the center of Earth to the equator and from the center of Earth to 30° North form an angle of 30 degrees.

**Longitude** The distance in degrees east or west of the prime meridian is called **longitude.** There are 360 lines of longitude that run from north to south, meeting at the poles. Each line represents one degree of longitude. A degree of longitude equals about 111 kilometers at the equator. But at the poles, where the lines of longitude come together, the distance decreases to zero.

The prime meridian, which is the starting line for measuring longitude, is at 0°. The longitude lines in each hemisphere are numbered up to 180 degrees. Half of the lines of longitude are in the Eastern Hemisphere, and half are in the Western Hemisphere.

Each line of longitude is defined by the angle it makes with the prime meridian and the center of Earth. As you can see in Figure 8, a line drawn from the center of Earth to the prime meridian and a line drawn from the center of Earth to 45° West form an angle of 45 degrees at the equator.

**Lab zone Try This Activity**

**Where in the World?**

Using a globe, determine what city is found at each of the following points:

2° S 79° W
38° N 9° W
34° N 135° E
34° S 58° W
55° N 3° W
1° N 103° E

What word is spelled by the first letters of these cities?

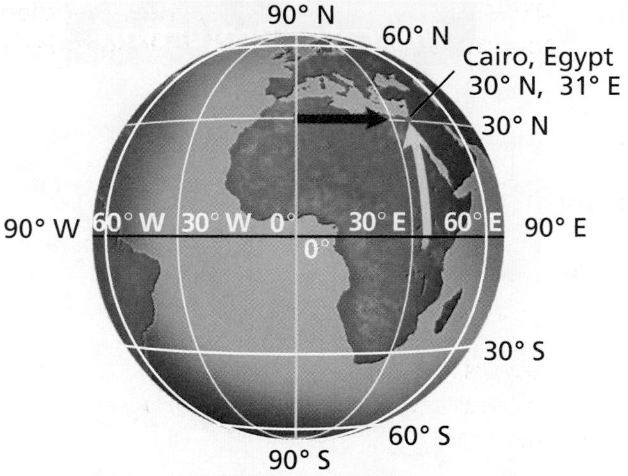


Cairo, Egypt, is located where the latitude line 30° N crosses the longitude line 31° E.

**For:** Links on latitude and longitude
**Visit:** www.SciLinks.org
**Web Code:** scn-0712

**Using Latitude and Longitude** The location of any point on Earth's surface can be expressed in terms of the latitude and longitude lines that cross at that point. For example, you can see on the map in Figure 9 that New Orleans is located where the line for 30° North latitude crosses the line for 90° West longitude. Notice that each longitude line crosses the latitude lines, including the equator, at a right angle.

How are longitude lines numbered?

FIGURE 9
Every point on Earth's surface has a particular latitude and longitude.
**Interpreting Maps** *What are the latitude and longitude of Mexico City? Of Sydney?*

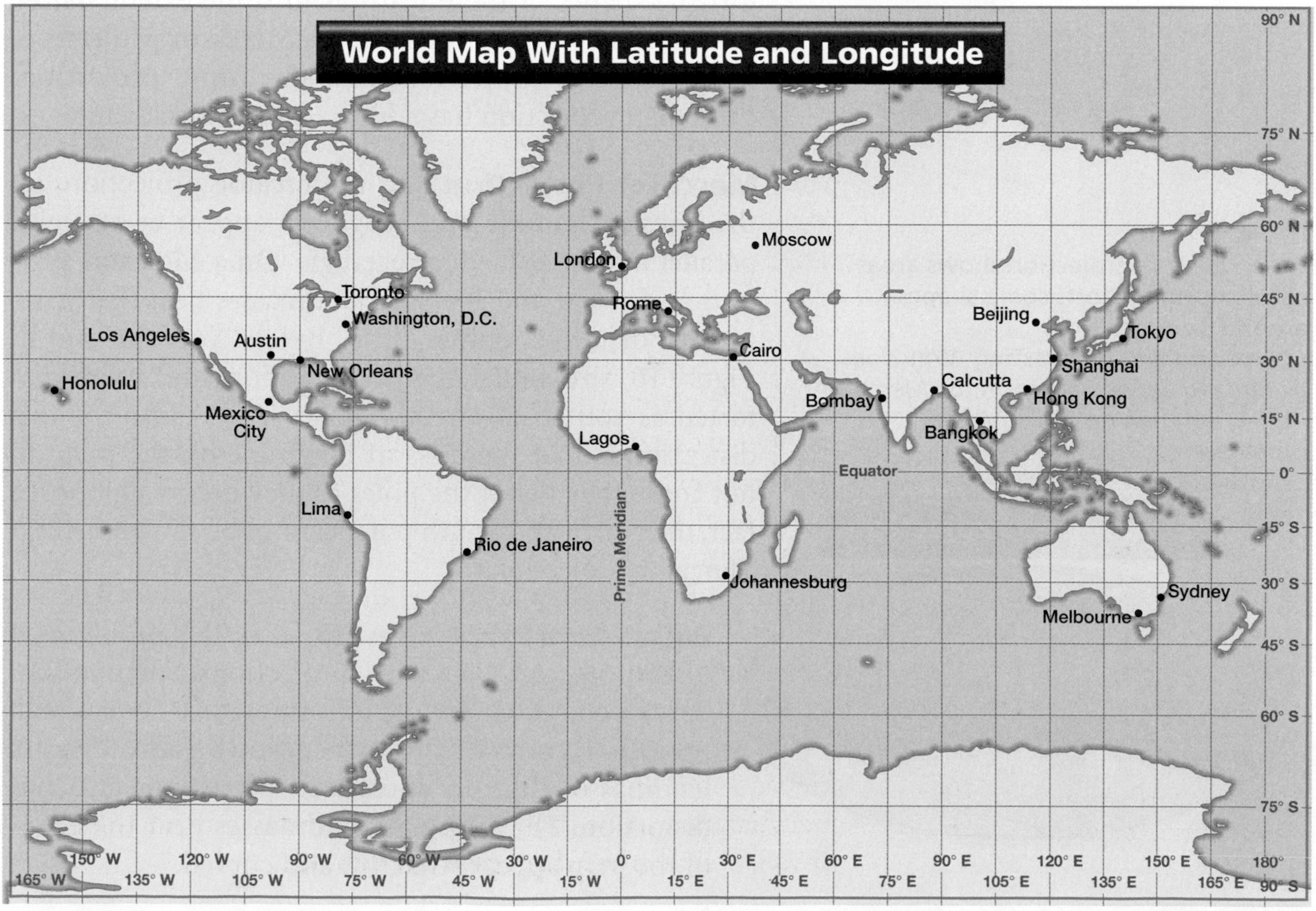

World Map With Latitude and Longitude

**FIGURE 10**
A Mercator projection is based on a cylinder with grid lines that has been flattened. On a Mercator projection, lines of longitude are parallel, so shapes near the poles are distorted.

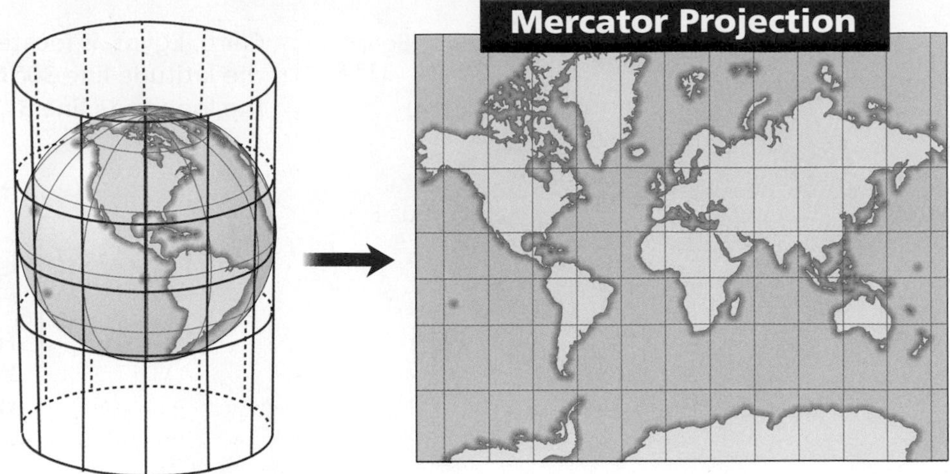


## Map Projections

To show Earth's curved surface on a flat map, mapmakers use map projections. A **map projection** is a framework of lines that helps in transferring points on Earth's three-dimensional surface onto a flat map. Features such as continents, oceans, islands, rivers, and lakes might appear to have somewhat different sizes and shapes on different map projections. All projections distort the shapes of these features to some extent. **Three common map projections are the Mercator projection, the equal-area projection, and the conic projection.** Each map projection has advantages and disadvantages.

**Mercator Projection** On a Mercator projection, all the lines of latitude and longitude appear as straight, parallel lines that form a rectangle. On a Mercator projection, the size and shape of landmasses near the equator are distorted only a little. But as you can see in Figure 10, size and shape become more and more distorted as you go toward the poles. The reason for this distortion is that the lines of longitude on the map do not come together at the poles as they do on a globe. In fact, the North and South poles cannot be shown using a Mercator projection.

**FIGURE 11**
An equal-area projection shows areas correctly, but distorts some shapes around its edges.
**Comparing and Contrasting** *Why does Greenland appear larger on the Mercator projection than on the equal-area projection?*

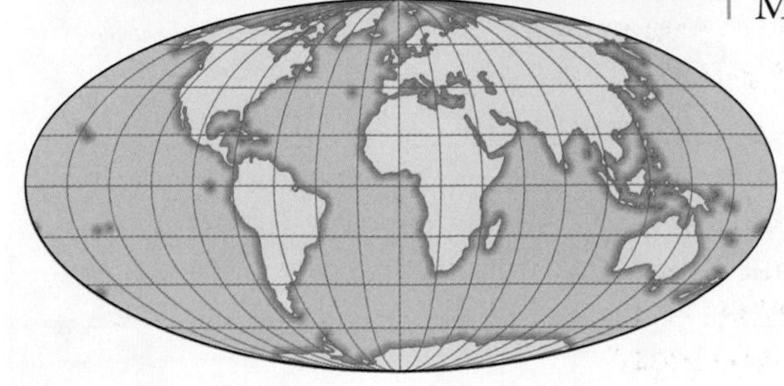


**Equal-Area Projection** To solve the problem of distortion on Mercator projections, mapmakers developed equal-area projections. An equal-area projection correctly shows the relative sizes of Earth's landmasses. But an equal-area projection also has distortion. The shapes of landmasses near the edges of the map appear stretched and curved.

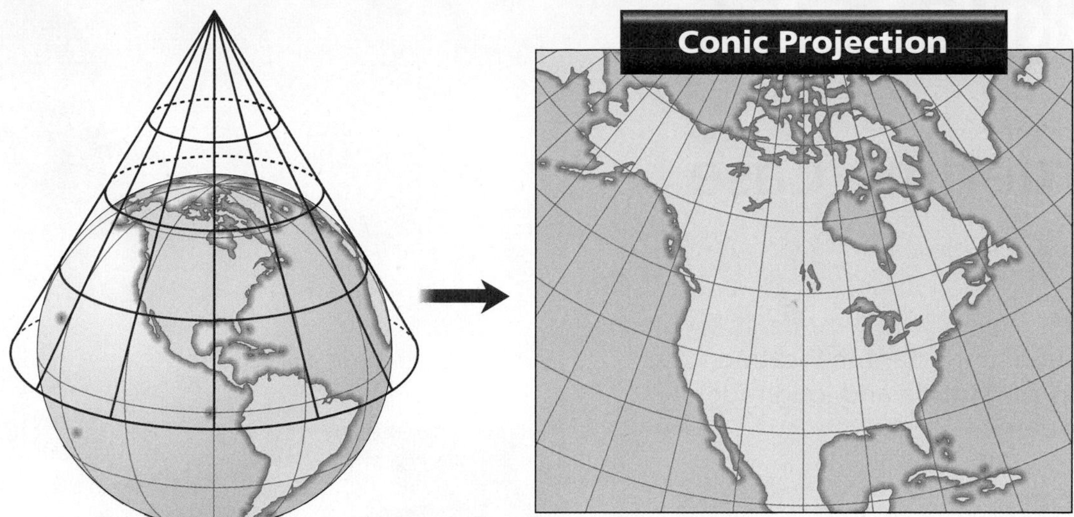


**Conic Projection** Suppose you placed a clear plastic cone over a globe, as shown in Figure 12. Then you could trace the lines of latitude and longitude onto the cone, unwrap the cone, and place it flat. The result would be a conic projection. In a conic projection, lines of longitude appear as straight lines while lines of latitude are curved. There is little distortion on maps that use this projection to show limited parts of Earth's surface. A conic projection is frequently used for maps of the continental United States.

**FIGURE 12**
A conic projection is based on a cone that covers part of Earth and is then rolled out flat. A conic projection's grid is formed from straight lines of longitude and curved lines of latitude.

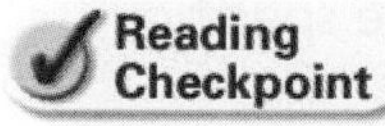


**Why is a conic projection best suited to showing only part of Earth's surface?**

## Section 2 Assessment

**Target Reading Skill Asking Questions** Work with a partner to check the answers in your graphic organizer.

### Reviewing Key Concepts

1. a. **Defining** What is a map?
   b. **Explaining** What information does a globe present?
   c. **Comparing and Contrasting** How are maps and globes similar? How are they different?
2. a. **Identifying** What two lines are baselines for measurements on Earth's surface?
   b. **Explaining** How are these baselines used to locate points on Earth's surface?
   c. **Interpreting Maps** Look at the map in Figure 9. If you fly due north from Lima, through how many degrees of latitude must you travel to reach Washington, D.C.?
3. a. **Listing** What are three common map projections?
   b. **Comparing and Contrasting** What are the advantages and disadvantages of each of the three projections?

### Math Practice

4. **Scales and Ratios** A globe has a scale of 1 : 40,000,000. Using a piece of string, you determine that the shortest distance between two cities on the globe is 7 cm. What is the actual distance between the two cities?

Lab zone **Skills Lab**

# A Borderline Case

## Problem

Which was more important in locating state borders: lines of latitude and longitude or physical features?

## Skills Focus

classifying, observing, inferring

## Materials

- United States map with latitude, longitude, and state borders
- tracing paper
- paper clips
- colored pencils
- physical map of the U.S.

## Procedure

1. Lay a sheet of tracing paper on top of a map of the United States.
2. Trace over the Pacific and Atlantic coasts of the United States with a blue pencil.
3. Using the blue pencil, trace all Great Lakes shorelines that reach nearby states.
4. Trace all state borders that go exactly north-south with a red pencil. (*Hint:* Some straight-line borders that appear to run north-south, such as the western border of Maine, do not follow lines of longitude.)
5. Use a green pencil to trace all state borders or sections of state borders that go exactly east-west. (*Hint:* Straight-line borders that are slanted, such as the southern border of Nevada, do not follow lines of latitude.)
6. Now use a blue pencil to trace the borders that follow rivers.
7. Use a brown pencil to trace any borders that are not straight lines or rivers.

## Analyze and Conclude

1. **Classifying** How many state boundaries are completely defined by longitude and latitude? How many are partially defined by longitude and latitude? How many states do not use either one to define their borders?
2. **Observing** What feature is most often used to define a state border when longitude and latitude are not used? Give specific examples.
3. **Observing** Study the physical map of the United States. What other physical features are used to define borders? Which state borders are defined by these features?
4. **Inferring** In which region of the country were lines of latitude and longitude most important in determining state borders? What do you think is the reason for this?
5. **Communicating** Pick any state and describe its borders as accurately as you can in terms of latitude, longitude, and physical features.

## More to Explore

Research the history of your state to find out when and how its borders were established. Are your state's borders based on longitude and latitude, landforms and topography, or both?

Review a map of your county or state. Are any features other than borders related to longitude and latitude? Which features seem to follow landforms and topography?

Section 3 • Tech & Design •

# Maps and Computers

## Reading Preview

### Key Concepts

- How does computer mapping differ from earlier ways of making maps?
- What sources of data are used in making computer maps?

### Key Terms

- surveying • digitizing
- satellite image • pixel
- Global Positioning System

### Target Reading Skill

**Identifying Main Ideas** As you read the Maps and Computers section, write the main idea in a graphic organizer like the one below. Then write three supporting details that further explain the main idea.

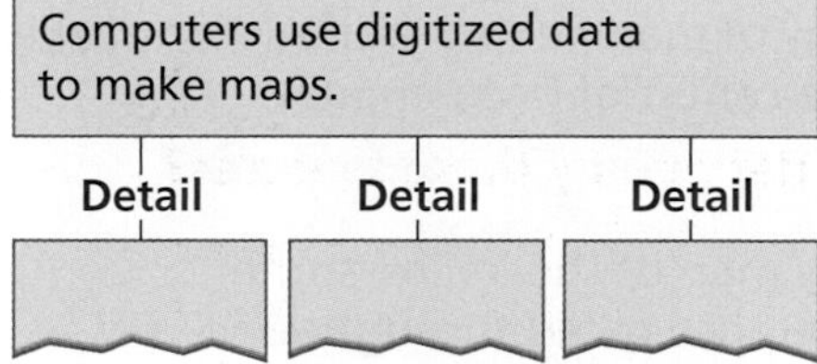


## Lab zone Discover Activity

### Can You Make a Pixel Picture?

1. With a pencil, draw a square grid of lines spaced 1 centimeter apart. The grid should have 6 squares on each side.
2. On the grid, draw the outline of a simple object, such as an apple.
3. Using a different color pencil, fill in all squares that are completely inside the object. If a square is mostly inside the object, fill it in completely. If it is mostly outside, leave it blank.
4. Each square on your grid represents one pixel, or bit of information, about your picture. Looking at your pixel picture, can you recognize the shape you started with?

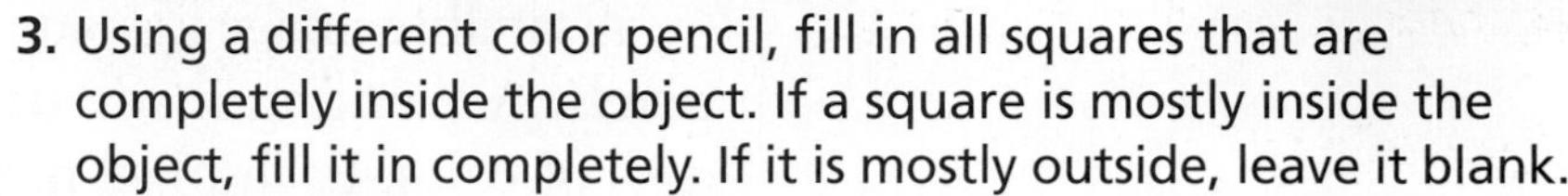

**Think It Over**

**Predicting** How would the pixel picture change if you drew the object smaller? How would the pixel picture look if you used graph paper with squares that are smaller than your grid?

For centuries, mapmakers drew maps by hand. Explorers made maps by sketching coastlines as seen from their ships. More accurate maps were made by locating points on Earth's surface in a process called surveying. In **surveying,** mapmakers determine distances and elevations using instruments and the principles of geometry. In the twentieth century, people learned to make maps using photographs taken from airplanes.

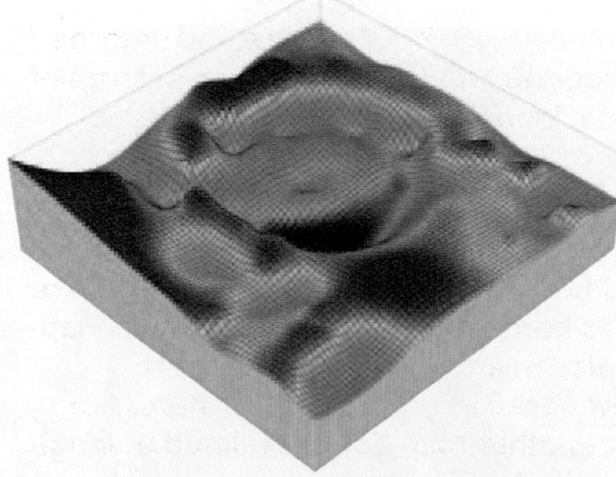

▲ A computer produced this digital model of part of Earth's surface.

## Computer Mapping

Since the 1970s, computers have revolutionized mapmaking. **With computers, mapmakers can store, process, and display map data electronically.**

All of the data used in computer mapping must be written in numbers. The process by which mapmakers convert the location of map points to numbers is called **digitizing.** These numbers are stored on a computer as a series of 0's and 1's. The digitized data can easily be displayed on a computer screen, modified, and printed in map form.

**For:** More on satellite mapping
**Visit:** PHSchool.com
**Web Code:** cfd-2013

## Sources of Map Data

Computer mapmakers use these up-to-the-minute data to produce maps quickly and easily. Computers can automatically make maps that might take a person hundreds of hours to draw by hand. **Computers produce maps using data from many sources, including satellites and the Global Positioning System.**

**Data From Satellites** Much of the data used in computer mapping is gathered by satellites in space. Mapping satellites use electronic devices to collect computer data about the land surface. Pictures of the surface based on these data are called **satellite images.**

A satellite image is made up of thousands of tiny dots called **pixels.** A painting made of pixels would have many separate dots of color. Each pixel in a satellite image contains information on the color and brightness of a small part of Earth's surface. For example, the pixels that represent a forest differ in color and brightness from the pixels that represent farmland. The data in each pixel are stored on a computer. When the satellite image is printed, the computer translates these digitized data into colors.

FIGURE 13
### Views of Yellowstone

These views of Yellowstone National Park show how computers have changed the technology of mapmaking. Yellowstone Lake is near the center of both images.

◀ This early map of the Yellowstone region was produced through surveys on the ground.

This satellite image made by the Landsat Thematic Mapper enables scientists to compare areas affected by forest fires (orange) with unburnt forest (green). ▶

Beginning in 1972, the United States launched a series of Landsat satellites designed to observe Earth's surface. Today, Landsat is just one of many different satellites used for this purpose. As a Landsat satellite orbits Earth, it collects and stores data about a strip of the surface that is 185 kilometers wide. The satellite relays the data back to a station on Earth, where computers use the data to create images. Landsat images show what covers the land surface—plants, soil, sand, rock, water, or snow and ice. Large, human-made features such as cities are also visible.

Scientists learn to identify specific features by the "signature," or combination of colors and shapes, that the feature makes on a satellite image. In a satellite image, areas covered by grass, trees, or crops are often shown as red, water as black or blue, and cities as bluish gray. Landsat images may show features such as grasslands, forests, and agricultural crops, as well as deserts, mountains, or cities.

**Data From the Global Positioning System** Today mapmakers can collect data for maps using the Global Positioning System, or GPS. The **Global Positioning System** is a method of finding latitude, longitude, and elevation of points on Earth's surface using a network of satellites. To learn more about GPS, look at the Technology and Society feature on the next pages.

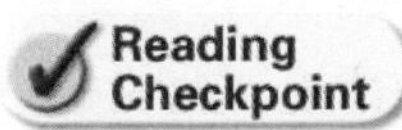

**What is a satellite image?**

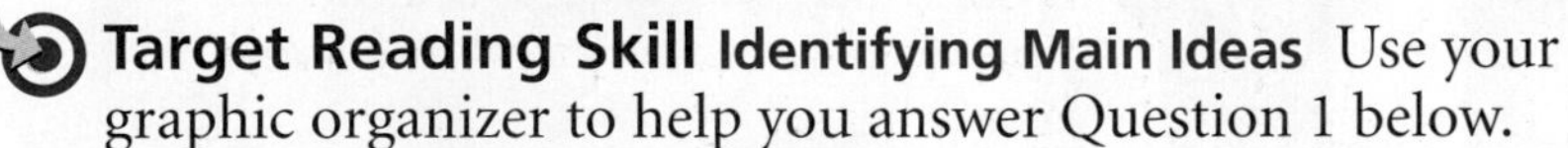


**Target Reading Skill Identifying Main Ideas** Use your graphic organizer to help you answer Question 1 below.

### Reviewing Key Concepts

1. a. **Explaining** In what form is the information for a map stored on a computer?
   b. **Defining** What is digitizing?
   c. **Applying Concepts** What are the advantages of computer mapping?
2. a. **Reviewing** How do satellites gather data for a satellite image?
   b. **Explaining** In what form are data for a satellite image stored?
   c. **Summarizing** Summarize the process by which Landsat produces a satellite image of part of Earth's surface.

### Lab zone At-Home **Activity**

**Maps in the News** Most of the maps that you see today in newspapers and magazines are made using computers. With family members, look through newspapers and news magazines. How many different types of maps can you find? Explain to your family the map's scale, symbols, and key. After you have studied the map, try to state the main point of the information shown on the map.

# Global Positioning System (GPS)

Today, being lost could be a thing of the past for many people. Why? A system of satellites orbiting nearly 20,200 km above Earth can be used to pinpoint one's location anywhere on Earth as well as in the air.

**Satellite**
Each of two dozen GPS satellites continually sends out its current location and the exact time to receivers controlled by GPS users.

## Location, Location, Location!

The Global Positioning System, or GPS, allows a user to locate his or her position anywhere on or above Earth to within a few meters or less. Hikers, drivers, boaters, and pilots use GPS to navigate. While its major use is navigation, GPS also has many scientific applications. Geologists use GPS to map some of the most rugged terrains on Earth. Points located with GPS can be entered into a computer and plotted to make maps. Archaeologists use GPS to map sites without disturbing ancient artifacts. Biologists can use the system to track threatened and endangered species.

**Navigation**
GPS systems aboard ships and boats have simplified navigation.

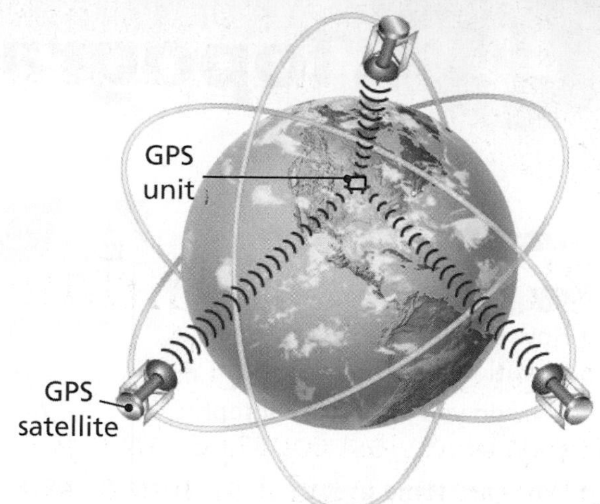


**System of Satellites**
At least three satellites must be above the horizon to pinpoint a location.

## Keeping GPS on Track

GPS has become indispensable to surveyors and mappers, many types of scientists and engineers, and many ordinary people who need to know where they are. But like all technologies, GPS has limitations. To receive signals from GPS satellites, receivers need an unobstructed view of the sky. Dense forests and tall buildings can prevent the receivers from picking up signals.

**Receiver**
GPS receivers are the size of a typical cellular phone. These devices receive and process satellite signals to determine the receiver's precise location.

## Weigh the Impact

**1. Identify the Need**
Think about activities in which knowing one's precise location is important. Make a list of at least five activities.

**2. Research**
Research the activities you listed in Question 1 to find out if GPS has been applied to them.

**3. Write**
Choose one application of GPS mentioned in this feature. Or, propose an application of this guidance system that you think might be useful. Write one or two paragraphs to explain the application or how you think GPS might be applied to an activity.

**For:** More on GPS
**Visit:** PHSchool.com
**Web Code:** cfh-2010

Section 4

# Topographic Maps

## Reading Preview

### Key Concepts

- How do mapmakers represent elevation, relief, and slope?
- How do you read a topographic map?
- What are some uses of topographic maps?

### Key Terms

- topographic map
- contour line
- contour interval
- index contour

### Target Reading Skill

**Using Prior Knowledge** Before you read, write what you know about topographic maps in a graphic organizer like the one below. As you read, write what you learn.

| What You Know |
|---|
| 1. Some maps show where mountains and plains are.<br>2. |

| What You Learned |
|---|
| 1.<br>2. |

## Lab zone Discover Activity

### Can a Map Show Relief?

1. Carefully cut the corners off 8 pieces of cardboard so that they look rounded. Each piece should be at least 1 centimeter smaller than the one before.
2. Trim the long sides of the two largest pieces so that the long sides appear wavy. Don't cut more than 0.5 centimeter into the cardboard.
3. Trace the largest cardboard piece on a sheet of paper.
4. Trace the next largest piece inside the tracing of the first. Don't let any lines cross.
5. Trace the other cardboard pieces, from largest to smallest, one inside the other, on the same paper.
6. Stack the cardboard pieces beside the paper in the same order they were traced. Compare the stack of cardboard pieces with your drawing. How are they alike? How are they different?

**Think It Over**

**Making Models** If the cardboard pieces are a model of a landform, what do the lines on the paper represent?

An orienteering meet is not an ordinary race. Participants compete to see how quickly they can find a series of locations called control points. The control points are scattered over a large park or state forest. Orienteers choose a set number of control points, and then visit the points in any order. In this sport, your ability to read a map and use a compass is often more important than how fast you can run. In a major meet, there may be several hundred orienteers on dozens of teams.

At the start of an orienteering meet, you would need to consult your map. But the maps used in orienteering are different from road maps or maps in an atlas—they're topographic maps.

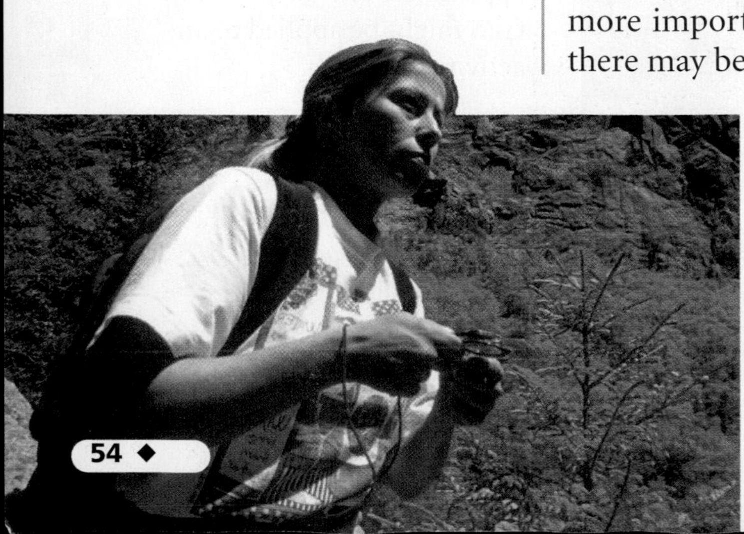

**FIGURE 14**
**Orienteering**
Orienteering helps people develop the skill of using a map and compass.

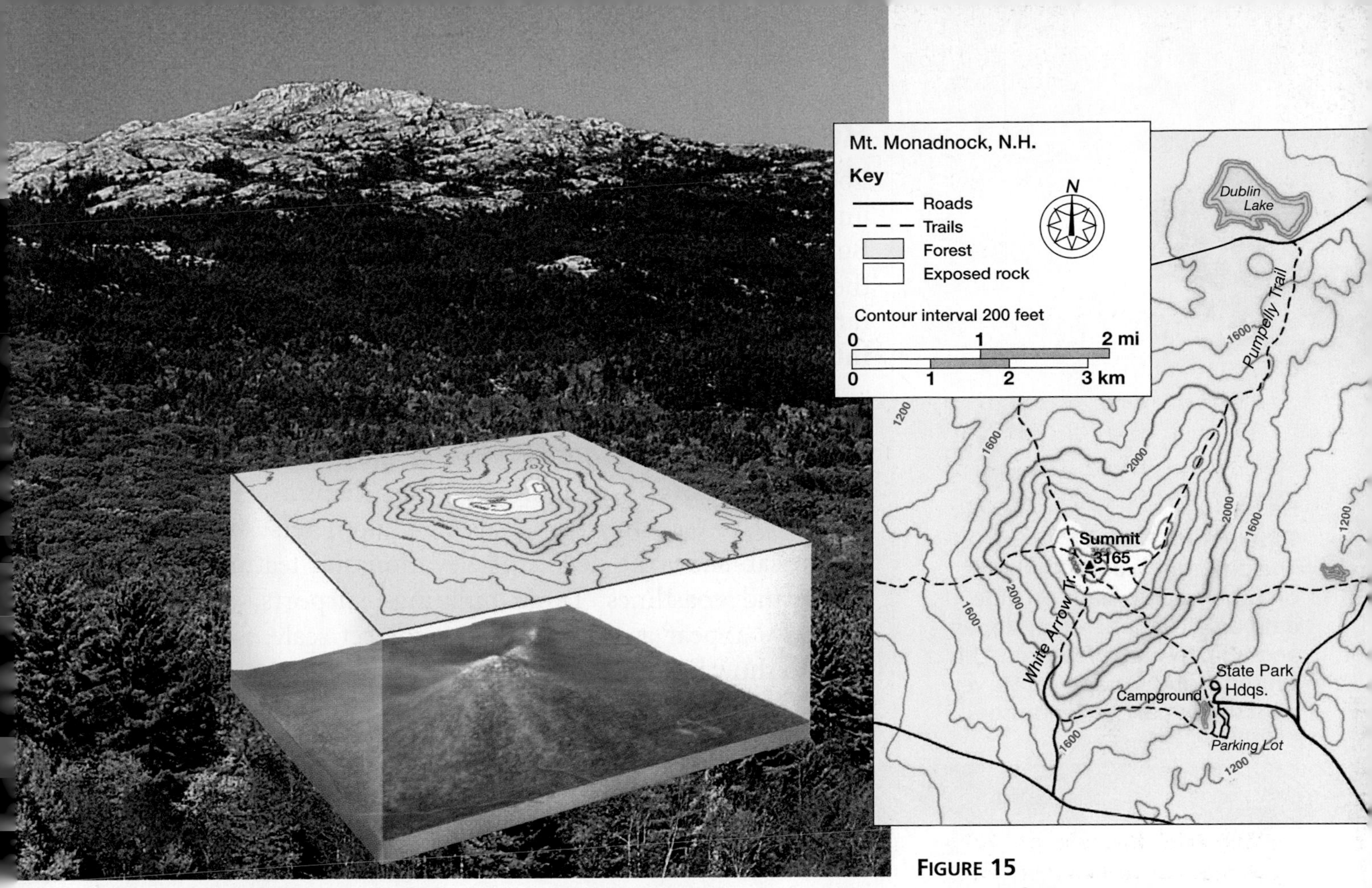

**FIGURE 15**
**Contour Lines**
The contour lines on a topographic map represent elevation and relief. **Comparing and Contrasting** *What information does the topographic map provide that the photograph does not?*

# Mapping Earth's Topography

A **topographic map** (tahp uh GRAF ik) is a map showing the surface features of an area. Topographic maps use symbols to portray the land as if you were looking down on it from above. Topographic maps provide highly accurate information on the elevation, relief, and slope of the ground surface.

**Mapmakers use contour lines to represent elevation, relief, and slope on topographic maps.** On a topographic map, a **contour line** connects points of equal elevation. In the United States, most topographic maps give contour intervals in feet rather than meters.

The change in elevation from contour line to contour line is called the **contour interval.** The contour interval for a given map is always the same. For example, the map in Figure 15 has a contour interval of 200 feet. If you start at one contour line and count up 10 contour lines, you have reached an elevation 2,000 feet above where you started. Usually, every fifth contour line, known as an index contour, is darker and heavier than the others. **Index contours** are labeled with the elevation in round units, such as 1,600 or 2,000 feet above sea level.

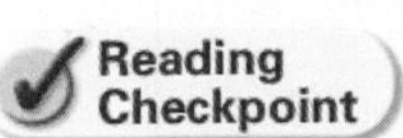

**Reading Checkpoint** **What do all the points connected by a contour line have in common?**

**Go Online**
*active art*

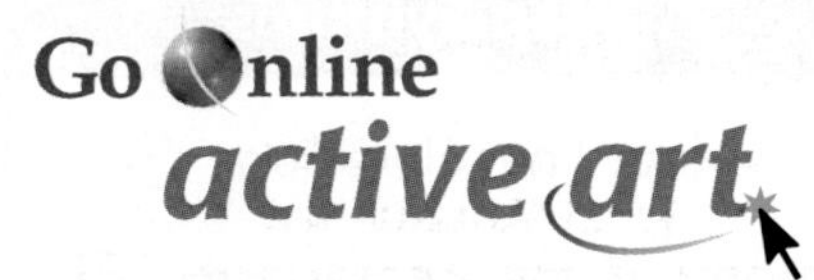

**For:** Topographic Map activity
**Visit:** PHSchool.com
**Web Code:** cfp-2014

## Reading a Topographic Map

Looking at a topographic map with many squiggly contour lines, you may feel as if you are gazing into a bowl of spaghetti. But with practice, you can learn to read a topographic map like the one in Figure 16. **To read a topographic map, you must familiarize yourself with the map's scale and symbols and interpret the map's contour lines.**

**Scale** Topographic maps are usually large-scale maps. Large-scale maps show a close-up view of part of Earth's surface. In the United States, many topographic maps are at a scale of 1 : 24,000, or 1 centimeter equals 0.24 kilometers. At this scale, a map can show the details of elevation and features such as rivers and coastlines. Large buildings, airports, and major highways appear as outlines at the correct scale. Symbols are used to show houses and other small features.

**FIGURE 16**
**Topographic Map**
The different types of symbols on topographic maps provide data on elevation, relief, slopes, and human-made features. This United States Geological Survey map shows part of Tennessee.

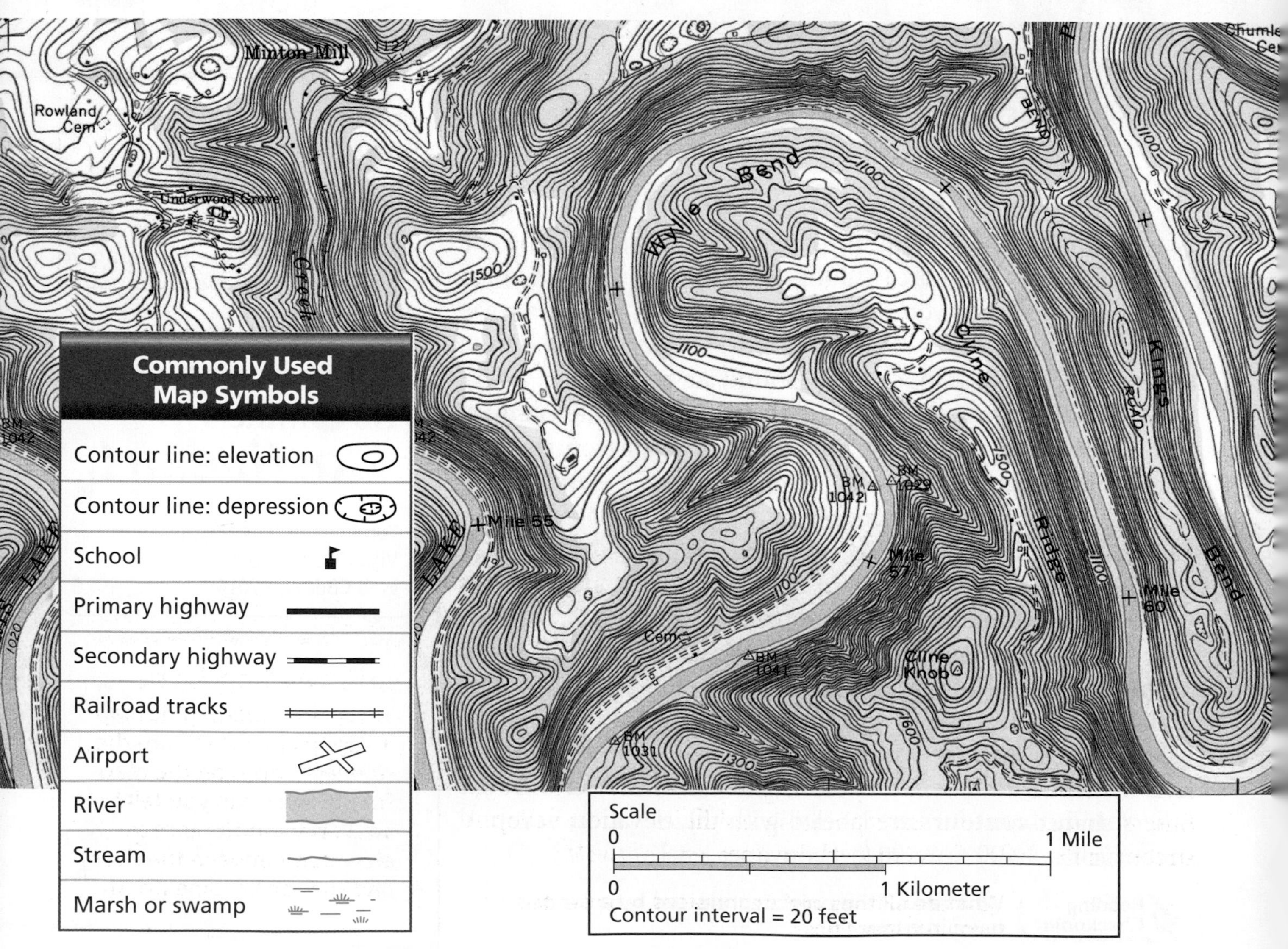

## Math Analyzing Data

### Mapping Elevation Data

The map shows the elevation data points on which the contour lines are based. Study the map and the map key, then answer the questions.

1. **Reading Maps** What is the contour interval on this map?
2. **Reading Maps** What color are the lowest points on the map? What range of elevations do these points represent?
3. **Reading Maps** What color are the highest points on the map?
4. **Applying Concepts** What is the elevation of the contour line labeled A?
5. **Inferring** Is the area between B and C a ridge or a valley? How can you tell?
6. **Interpreting Data** Describe how elevation changes along the trail from point D to point C.

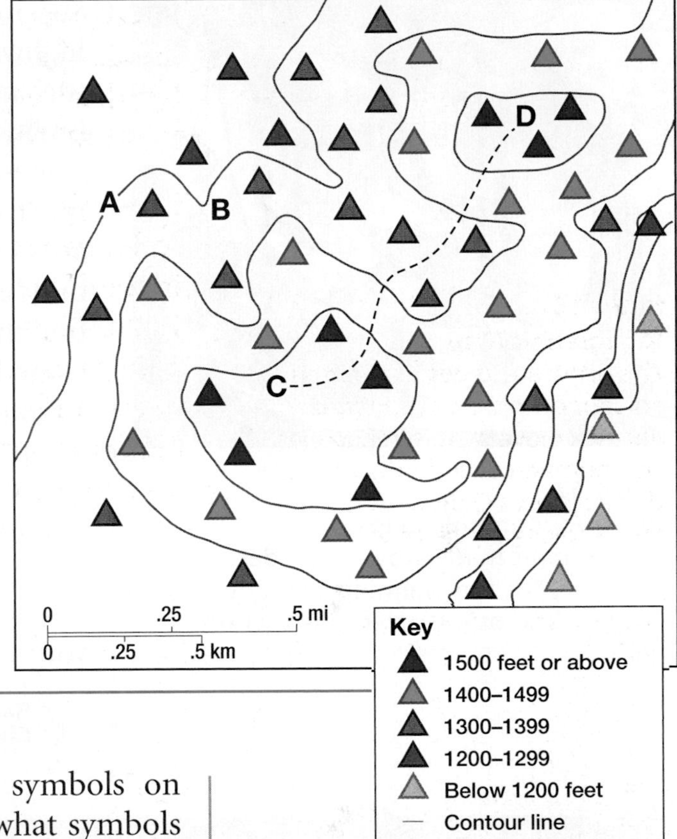


**Symbols** Mapmakers use a great variety of symbols on topographic maps. If you were drawing a map, what symbols would you use to represent a forest, a campground, an orchard, a swamp, or a school? Look at Figure 16 to see the symbols that are often used for these and other features.

**Interpreting Contour Lines** To find the elevation of a feature, begin at the labeled index contour, which is a heavier line than regular contour lines. Then, count the number of contour lines up or down to the feature.

Reading contour lines is the first step toward "seeing" an area's topography. Look at the topographic map in Figure 16. The closely spaced contour lines indicate steep slopes. The widely spaced contour lines indicate gentle slopes or relatively flat areas. A contour line that forms a closed loop with no other contour lines inside it indicates a hilltop. A closed loop with dashes inside indicates a depression, or hollow in the ground.

The shape of contour lines also help to show ridges and valleys. V-shaped contour lines pointing downhill indicate a ridge line. V-shaped contour lines pointing uphill indicate a valley. A stream in the valley flows toward the open end of the V.

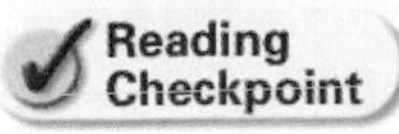


**How are hilltops and depressions represented using contour lines?**

### Lab zone Skills Activity

#### Interpreting Data

Study the topographic map in Figure 16. Where are the steepest slopes on the map found? How can you tell? What is the difference in elevation between the river and the top of Cline Knob?

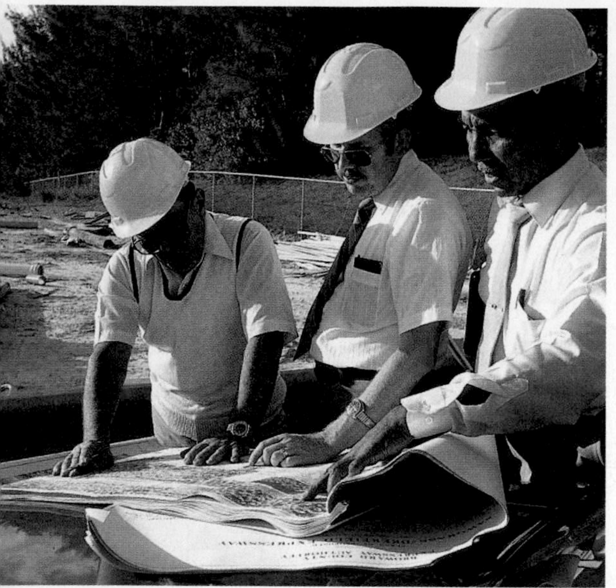

**FIGURE 17**
**Using Topographic Maps**
Topographic maps provide the data necessary for the planning of highways, bridges, and other large construction projects.

## Uses of Topographic Maps

**Topographic maps have many uses in science and engineering, business, government, and everyday life.** Suppose that you are an engineer planning a route for a highway over a mountain pass. Your design for the highway needs to solve several problems. To design a safe highway, you need a route that avoids the steepest slopes. To protect the area's water supply, the highway must stay a certain distance from rivers and lakes. You also want to find a route that avoids houses and other buildings. How would you solve these problems and find the best route for the highway? You would probably begin by studying topographic maps.

Businesses use topographic maps to help decide where to build new stores, housing, or factories. Local governments use them to decide where to build new schools and other public buildings. Topographic maps have recreational uses, too. If you were planning a bicycle trip, you could use a topographic map to see where your trip would be flat or hilly.

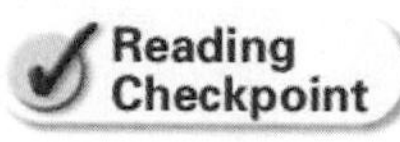

**How do businesses use topographic maps?**

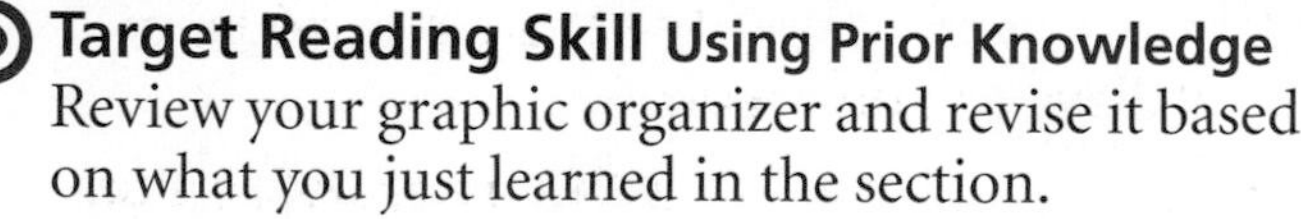


**Target Reading Skill Using Prior Knowledge** Review your graphic organizer and revise it based on what you just learned in the section.

### Reviewing Key Concepts

1. a. **Defining** What is a topographic map?
   b. **Explaining** How do topographic maps represent elevation and relief?
   c. **Calculating** If the contour interval on a topographic map is 50 meters, how much difference in elevation do 12 contour lines represent?
2. a. **Reviewing** What do you need to know about a topographic map in order to read it?
   b. **Comparing and Contrasting** Compare the way steep slopes are represented on a topographic map with the way gentle slopes are represented.
   c. **Inferring** Reading a map, you see V-shaped contour lines that point uphill. What land feature would you find in this area?
3. a. **Listing** What are four main uses of topographic maps?
   b. **Problem Solving** Suppose that your community needs a large, flat site for a new athletic field. How could you use a topographic map of your area to identify possible sites?

### Writing in Science

**Giving Directions** Write a descriptive paragraph of a simple route from one point on the map in Figure 16 to another point. Your paragraph should provide the starting point, but not the end point. Include details such as distance, compass direction, and topography along the route. Share your paragraph with classmates to see if they can follow your directions.

Lab zone **Skills Lab**

# A Map in a Pan

## Problem
How can you make a topographic map?

## Skills Focus
making models, interpreting maps

## Materials
- deep-sided pan
- water
- marking pencil
- modeling clay
- clear, hard sheet of plastic
- metric ruler
- sheet of unlined white paper
- food coloring

## Procedure
1. Place a lump of clay on the bottom of a pan. Shape the clay into a model of a hill.
2. Pour colored water into the pan to a depth of 1 centimeter to represent sea level.
3. Place a sheet of hard, clear plastic over the container.
4. Trace the outline of the pan on the plastic sheet with a marking pencil. Then, looking straight down into the pan, trace the outline the water makes around the edges of the clay model. Remove the plastic sheet from the pan.
5. Add another centimeter of water to the pan, bringing the depth of the water to 2 centimeters. Replace the plastic sheet exactly as before, then trace the water level again.
6. Repeat Step 5 several times. Stop when the next addition of water would completely cover your model.
7. Remove the plastic sheet. Trace the outlines that you drew on the plastic sheet onto a sheet of paper.

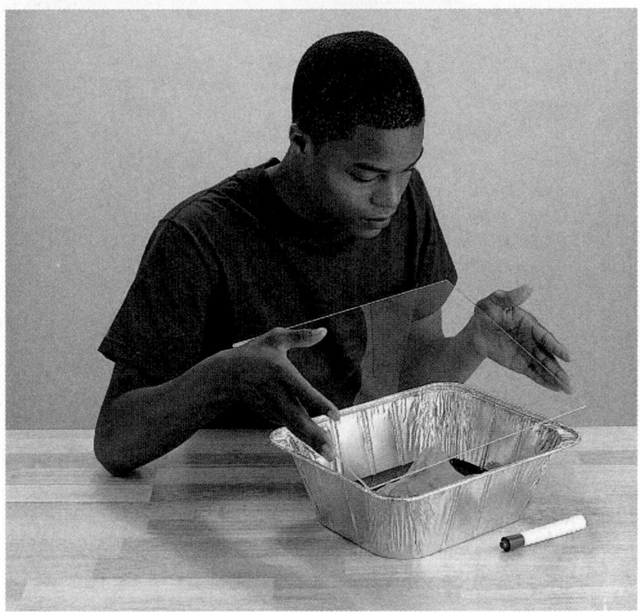

## Analyze and Conclude
1. **Interpreting Maps** Looking at your topographic map, how can you tell which parts of your model hill have a steep slope? A gentle slope?
2. **Interpreting Maps** How can you tell from the map which point on the hill is the highest?
3. **Interpreting Maps** Are there any ridges or valleys on your map?
4. **Applying Concepts** Is there any depression on your map where water would collect after it rained? What symbol should you use to identify this depression?
5. **Making Models** Compare your map with the clay landform. How are they alike? How are they different? How could you improve your map as a model of the landform?

## More to Explore
Obtain a topographic map that includes an interesting landform such as a mountain, canyon, river valley, or coastline. After studying the contour lines on the map, make a sketch of what you think the landform looks like. Then build a scale model of the landform using clay or layers of cardboard or foamboard. How does your model landform compare with your sketch?

**The BIG Idea** **Modeling Earth Using Technology** Maps are drawn to scale to represent Earth's landforms and topography. Contour lines are used to show elevation and relief.

## 1 Exploring Earth's Surface

### Key Concepts

- The topography of an area includes the area's elevation, relief, and landforms.
- There are three main types of landforms: plains, mountains, and plateaus.

### Key Terms

topography
elevation
relief
landform
plain
mountain
mountain range
plateau
landform region

## 2 Models of Earth

### Key Concepts

- Maps and globes are drawn to scale and use symbols to represent topography and other features on Earth's surface.
- Two of the lines that make up the grid, the equator and prime meridian, are the baselines for measuring distances on Earth's surface.
- The lines of latitude and longitude form a grid that can be used to find locations anywhere on Earth.
- Three common map projections are the Mercator projection, the equal-area projection, and the conic projection.

### Key Terms

map
globe
scale
symbol
key
degree
equator
hemisphere
prime meridian
latitude
longitude
map projection

## 3 Maps and Computers

### Key Concepts

- With computers, mapmakers can store, process, and display map data electronically.
- Computers produce maps using data from many sources, including satellites and the Global Positioning System.

### Key Terms

surveying
digitizing
satellite image
pixel
Global Positioning System

## 4 Topographic Maps

### Key Concepts

- Mapmakers use contour lines to represent elevation, relief, and slope on topographic maps.
- To read a topographic map, you must familiarize yourself with the map's scale and symbols and interpret the map's contour lines.
- Topographic maps have many uses in science and engineering, business, government, and everyday life.

### Key Terms

topographic map
contour line
contour interval
index contour

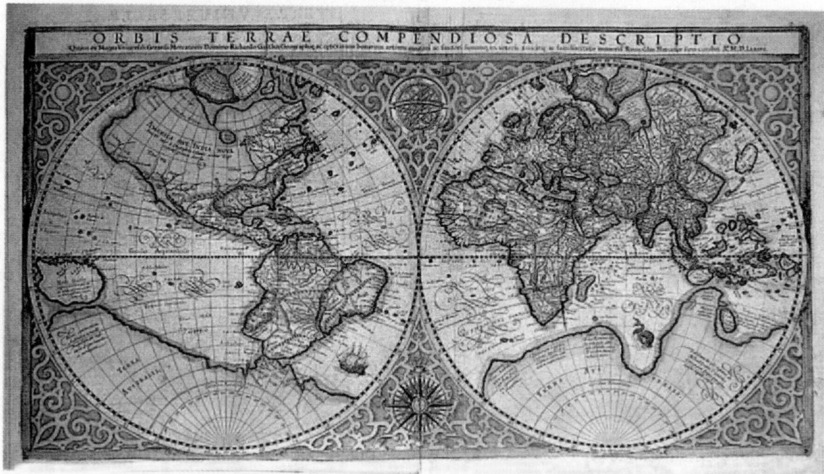

# Review and Assessment

**For:** Self-Assessment
**Visit:** PHSchool.com
**Web Code:** cfa-2010

## Organizing Information

**Concept Mapping** Copy the concept map. Then complete the map to show the characteristics of the different types of landforms. (For more about Concept Mapping, see the Skills Handbook.)

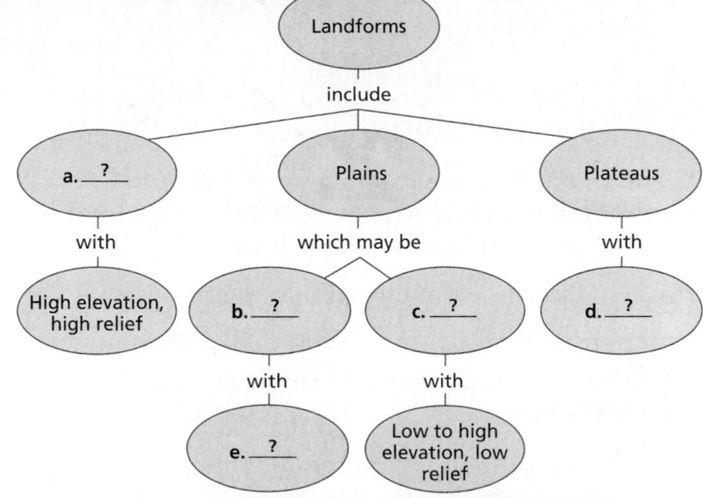


## Reviewing Key Terms

**Choose the letter of the best answer.**

1. A landform that has high elevation but a mostly flat surface is a
   **a.** plain. **b.** mountain.
   **c.** mountain range. **d.** plateau.
2. The equator divides Earth into two equal halves called
   **a.** globes. **b.** hemispheres.
   **c.** degrees. **d.** pixels.
3. Latitude is a measurement of distance north or south of the
   **a.** hemisphere. **b.** equator.
   **c.** index contour. **d.** prime meridian.
4. To show Earth's curved surface on a flat map, mapmakers choose different
   **a.** map projections. **b.** globes.
   **c.** scales. **d.** landform regions.
5. The digitized data on a computer map is made up of
   **a.** index contours. **b.** pixels.
   **c.** contour intervals. **d.** symbols.
6. On a topographic map, relief is shown using
   **a.** lines of latitude. **b.** lines of longitude.
   **c.** map projections. **d.** contour lines.

**If the statement is true, write *true.* If it is false, change the underlined word or words to make the statement true.**

7. Relief is a landform's height above sea level.
8. The equator is a half circle that extends from the North Pole to the South Pole.
9. If an airplane flew around Earth in a straight line from east to west, the airplane would cross lines of longitude.
10. An index contour is labeled to indicate the elevation along a contour line.

## Writing in Science

**Advertisement** Suppose that you are a manufacturer of GPS tracking and mapping devices. Write an advertisement that describes as many uses for your device as you can think of.

***Mapping Earth's Surface***
Video Preview
Video Field Trip
▶ Video Assessment

# Review and Assessment

## Checking Concepts

11. Compare the elevation of a coastal plain to that of an interior plain.
12. What is a mountain range?
13. What do geologists call an area where there is mostly one kind of topography?
14. The South Island of New Zealand lies at about 170° E. What hemisphere is it in?
15. What is one advantage of a Mercator projection? What is one disadvantage?
16. What information does a map's contour interval provide?
17. How do the contour lines on a topographic map indicate the slope of the land?

## Math Practice

18. **Scale and Ratios** Earth's diameter is about 13,000 kilometers. If a globe has a diameter of 0.5 meter, write the globe's scale as a ratio. What distance on Earth would 1 centimeter on the globe represent?

## Thinking Critically

19. **Applying Concepts** Which would be more likely to show a shallow, 1.5-meter-deep depression in the ground: a 1-meter contour interval or a 5-meter contour interval?
20. **Interpreting Maps** Use the map below to answer the question. What is the latitude and longitude of Point A? In which two hemispheres is Point A located?

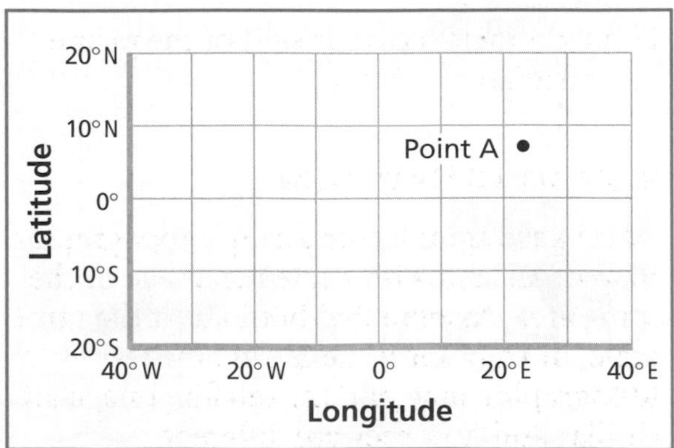


21. **Comparing and Contrasting** How would the colors in a satellite image of an area compare with a color photograph of the same area?
22. **Problem Solving** Describe one way in which you could use a topographic map of your community.

## Applying Skills

**Use the map below to answer Questions 23–25.**

*This map shows part of Acadia National Park in Maine. The contour interval is 20 feet.*

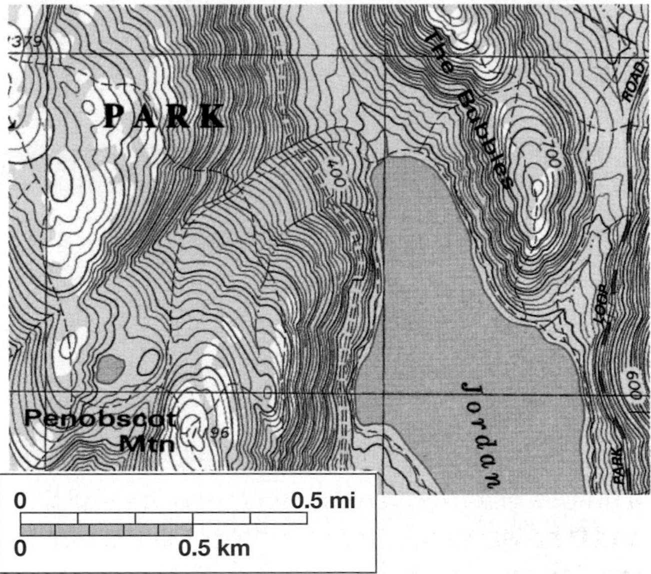


23. **Interpreting Maps** What is the elevation of the large lake? Which of the two Bubbles is higher?
24. **Calculating** Use the map scale to calculate the distance from the top of Penobscot Mountain to the large lake.
25. **Inferring** How can you tell whether the streams flow into or out of the large lake?

## Lab zone Chapter Project

**Performance Assessment** Present your map to the class. What symbols did you use to represent the natural and physical features of your site? How did you measure and locate them on your map? How accurate is your map? Does your map give others a clear idea of what the land looks like?

# Standardized Test Prep

## Test-Taking Tip

**Selecting the Right Unit of Measurement**

In some multiple-choice questions, selecting the right units of measurement may help you find the correct answer or eliminate one or more answers. For example, if the question asks for the length of something, you can eliminate any answers that are expressed in units of volume or mass. You can also eliminate answers of the measurements are much too large or small. The distance that hikers travel in a day, for example, will usually be expressed in kilometers rather than centimeters.

***Sample Question***

The 90 degrees of latitude from the equator to the North Pole equals approximately 10,000 kilometers. What is the approximate length of one degree of latitude?

**A** 111 grams
**B** 111 kilometers
**C** 11 meters
**D** 111 centimeters

***Answer***

The answer is **B.** You can eliminate **A** because it is a unit of mass, not length. You can eliminate **C** and **D** because the meters and centimeters are too small to measure half of the Earth.

**Choose the letter of the best answer.**

**1.** On a map, what is the height above sea level of a point on Earth's surface?
**A** topography **B** relief
**C** elevation **D** latitude

**2.** You are an engineer preparing to build a new highway exit. You will need to look at details of the area where the new exit will be located. Which map scale would it be best to use, in order to see the needed topographic details?
**F** 1 centimeter = 0.25 kilometers
**G** 1 centimeter = 10.0 kilometers
**H** 1 centimeter = 5.0 kilometers
**J** 1 centimeter = 2.5 kilometers

*Use the map below and your knowledge of science to answer Questions 3–4.*

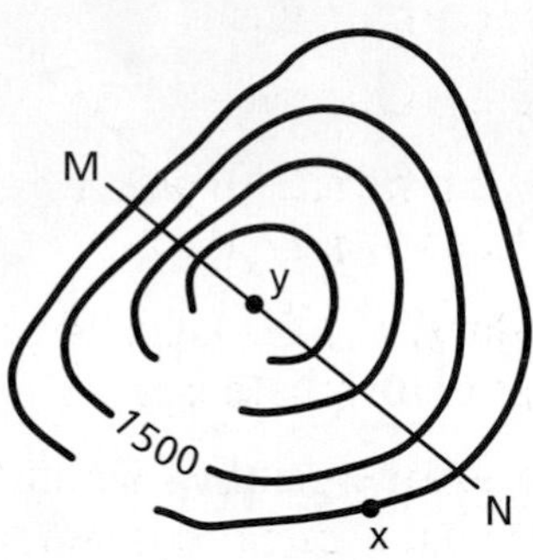


Contour interval = 15 meters

**3.** A topographic profile shows the shape or relief of the land along a given line. Along line M-N on the map, which of the following would the profile most closely resemble?

**A** 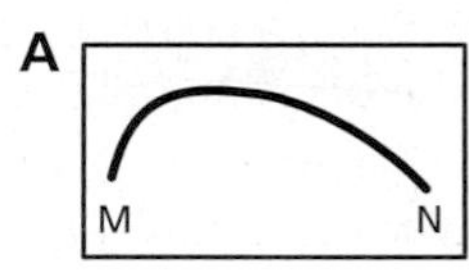


**B** 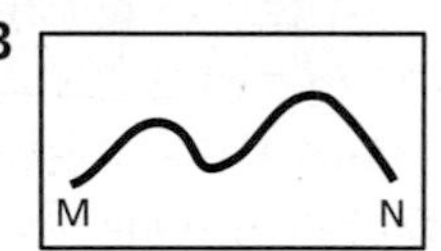


**C** 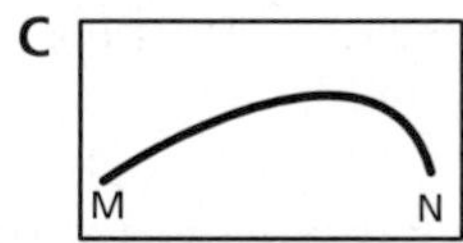


**D** 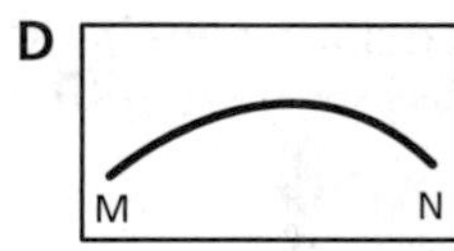


**4.** What is the elevation of the point marked *x* on the map?
**F** 1400 meters **G** 1500 meters
**H** 1485 meters **J** 1515 meters

**5.** How is longitude measured?
**A** in degrees east or west of the prime meridian
**B** in degrees east or west of the equator
**C** in degrees north or south of the prime meridian
**D** in kilometers east or west of the prime meridian

## Constructed Response

**6.** Write a paragraph comparing a topographic map of an area with a satellite image of the same area. Assume that both are at the same scale. In your answer, explain how the topographic map and the satellite image are similar and how they are different.

Chapter 3

# Minerals

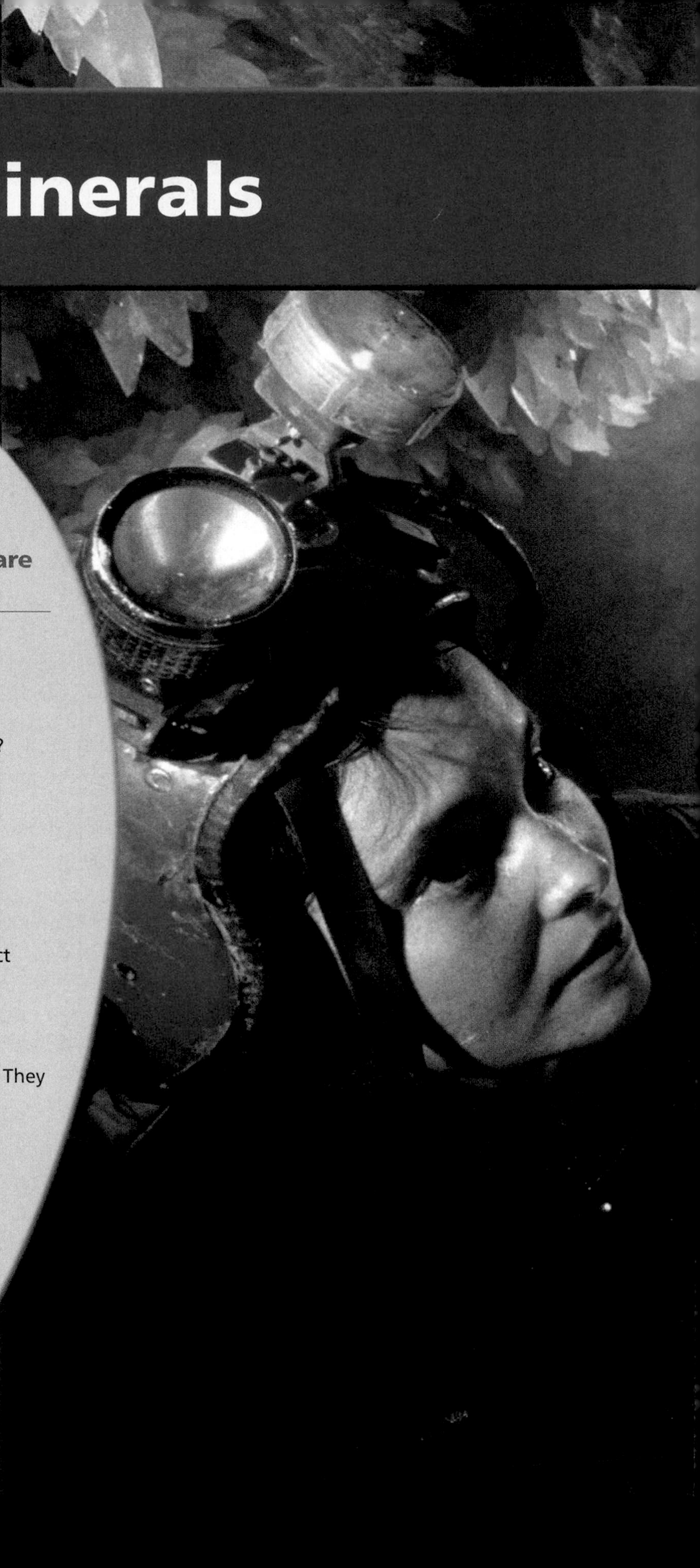

## The BIG Idea

Properties of Matter

**What are minerals and how are they used?**

### Chapter Preview

❶ **Properties of Minerals**

***Discover*** What Is the True Color of a Mineral?

***Math Skills*** Calculating Density

***Analyzing Data*** Mineral Density

***Skills Activity*** Classifying

***Active Art*** Crystal Systems

***Skills Lab*** Finding the Density of Minerals

❷ **How Minerals Form**

***Discover*** How Does the Rate of Cooling Affect Crystals?

***Try This*** Crystal Hands

❸ **Using Mineral Resources**

***Discover*** How Are Minerals Processed Before They Are Used?

***At-Home Activity*** Rust Protection

***Consumer Lab*** A Mouthful of Minerals

*Minerals*

▶ Video Preview
Video Field Trip
Video Assessment

Lab zone™ Chapter **Project**

## Growing a Crystal Garden

Minerals occur in an amazing variety of colors and shapes—from clear, tiny cubes of halite (table salt), to the masses of calcite crystals in the photograph, to precious rubies and sapphires. In this project, you will grow crystals to see how different types of chemicals form different crystal shapes.

**Your Goal** To design and grow a crystal garden

To complete this project successfully, you must

- create a three-dimensional garden scene as a base on which to grow crystals
- prepare at least two different crystal-growth solutions
- observe and record the shapes and growth rates of your crystals
- follow the safety guidelines in Appendix A

**Plan It!** Begin by deciding what materials you will use to create your garden scene. Your teacher will suggest a variety of materials and also describe the types of crystal-growth solutions that you can use. Then, design and build a setting for your crystal garden and add the solutions. Observe and record the growth of the crystals. Finally, display your finished crystal garden to your class. Be prepared to describe your procedure, observations, and conclusions.

Section 1

# Properties of Minerals

## Reading Focus

### Key Concepts

- What is a mineral?
- How are minerals identified?

### Key Terms

- mineral • inorganic
- crystal • streak • luster
- Mohs hardness scale
- cleavage • fracture

### Target Reading Skill

**Outlining** An outline shows the relationship between major ideas and supporting ideas. As you read, make an outline about the properties of minerals. Use the red headings for the main topics and the blue headings for the subtopics.

**Properties of Minerals**

I. What is a mineral?
  A. Naturally occurring
  B. Inorganic
  C.
  D.
  E.
II. Identifying minerals

## Lab zone Discover Activity

### What Is the True Color of a Mineral?

1. Examine samples of magnetite and black hematite. Both minerals contain iron. Describe the color and appearance of the two minerals. Are they similar or different?
2. Rub the black hematite across the back of a porcelain or ceramic tile. Observe the color of the streak on the tile.
3. Wipe the tile clean before you test the next sample.
4. Rub the magnetite across the back of the tile. Observe the color of the streak.

**Think It Over**

**Observing** Does the color of each mineral match the color of its streak? How could this streak test be helpful in identifying them as two different minerals?

Look at the two different substances in Figure 1. On the left are beautiful quartz crystals. On the right is a handful of coal. Both are solid materials that form beneath Earth's surface. But only one is a mineral. To determine which of the two is a mineral, you need to become familiar with the characteristics of minerals. Then you can decide what's a mineral and what's not!

## What Is a Mineral?

**A mineral is a naturally occurring, inorganic solid that has a crystal structure and a definite chemical composition.** For a substance to be a **mineral,** it must have all five of these characteristics.

**Naturally Occurring** To be classified as a mineral, a substance must be formed by processes in the natural world. The mineral quartz forms naturally as molten material cools and hardens deep beneath Earth's surface. Materials made by people, such as plastic, brick, glass, and steel, are not minerals.

**Inorganic** A mineral must also be **inorganic.** This means that the mineral cannot form from materials that were once part of a living thing. For example, coal forms naturally in the crust. But geologists do not classify coal as a mineral because it comes from the remains of plants that lived millions of years ago.

**Solid** A mineral is always a solid, with a definite volume and shape. The particles that make up a solid are packed together very tightly, so they cannot move like the particles that make up a liquid.

**Crystal Structure** The particles of a mineral line up in a pattern that repeats over and over again. The repeating pattern of a mineral's particles forms a solid called a **crystal.** A crystal has flat sides, called faces, that meet at sharp edges and corners. The quartz in Figure 1 has a crystal structure. In contrast, most coal lacks a crystal structure.

**Definite Chemical Composition** A mineral has a definite chemical composition or range of compositions. This means that a mineral always contains certain elements in definite proportions.

Almost all minerals are compounds. For example, a crystal of the mineral quartz has one atom of silicon for every two atoms of oxygen. Each compound has its own properties, or characteristics, which usually differ greatly from the properties of the elements that form it.

Some elements occur in nature in a pure form, and not as part of a compound with other elements. Elements such as copper, silver, and gold are also minerals. Almost all pure, solid elements are metals.

FIGURE 1
**Quartz and Coal**
Quartz (below) has all the characteristics of a mineral. But coal (above) is formed from the remains of plants, lacks a crystal structure, and has no definite chemical composition.

**Reading Checkpoint** What does the phrase "definite chemical composition" mean?

Mineral Characteristics
Quartz
Coal
Naturally occurring
Inorganic
Solid
Crystal structure
Definite chemical composition
✓
✓
No
✓
✓
✓
No
✓
No

## Identifying Minerals

Geologists have identified about 3,800 minerals. Because there are so many different kinds of minerals, telling them apart can often be a challenge. **Each mineral has characteristic properties that can be used to identify it.** When you have learned to recognize the properties of minerals, you will be able to identify many common minerals around you.

You can see some of the properties of a mineral just by looking at a sample. To observe other properties, however, you need to conduct tests on that sample. As you read about the properties of minerals, think about how you could use them to identify a mineral.

**Color** The color of a mineral is an easily observed physical property. But the color of a mineral alone often provides too little information to make an identification. All three minerals in Figure 2 are the color gold, yet only one is the real thing. Color can be used to identify only those few minerals that always have their own characteristic color. The mineral malachite is always green. The mineral azurite is always blue. No other minerals look quite the same as these.

**FIGURE 2**
**Color of Minerals**
These women in India are searching for bits of gold in river sand. Just because a mineral is gold in color doesn't mean it really is gold. Chalcopyrite and pyrite, also known as "fool's gold," are similar in color to real gold.

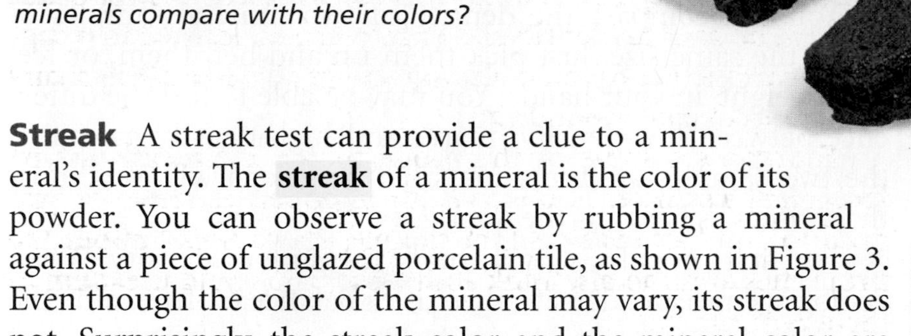

**FIGURE 3**
**Streak**
A mineral's streak can be the same as or quite different from its color.
**Observing** *How do the streaks of these minerals compare with their colors?*

**Streak** A streak test can provide a clue to a mineral's identity. The **streak** of a mineral is the color of its powder. You can observe a streak by rubbing a mineral against a piece of unglazed porcelain tile, as shown in Figure 3. Even though the color of the mineral may vary, its streak does not. Surprisingly, the streak color and the mineral color are often different. For example, although pyrite has a gold color, it always produces a greenish black streak. Real gold, on the other hand, produces a golden yellow streak.

**Luster** Another simple test to identify a mineral is to check its luster. **Luster** is the term used to describe how light is reflected from a mineral's surface. Minerals containing metals are often shiny. For example, galena is an ore of lead that has a bright, metallic luster. Quartz has a glassy luster. Some of the other terms used to describe luster include earthy, waxy, and pearly. Figure 4 shows the luster of several minerals.

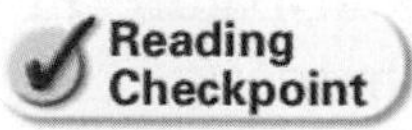

**What characteristic of minerals does the term *luster* describe?**

**FIGURE 4**
Geologists use many different terms to describe the luster of minerals.
**Interpreting Tables** *Which mineral has an earthy luster?*

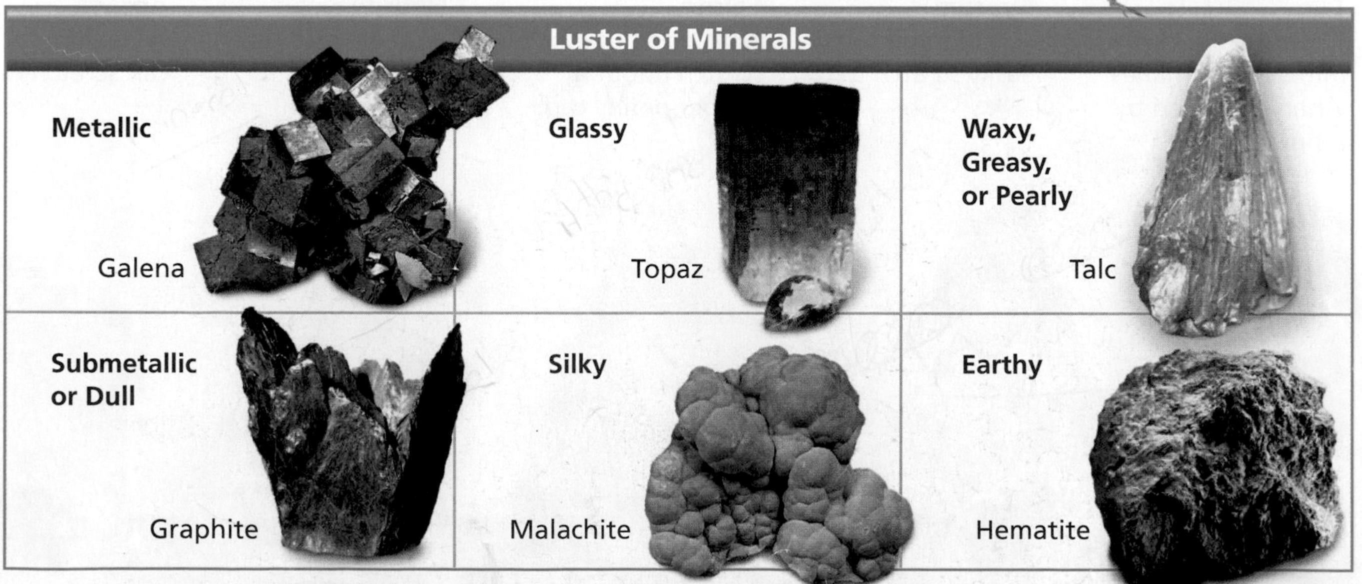

Luster of Minerals
Metallic
Galena
Glassy
Topaz
Waxy, Greasy, or Pearly
Talc
Submetallic or Dull
Graphite
Silky
Malachite
Earthy
Hematite

## Math Skills

### Calculating Density

To calculate the density of a mineral, divide the mass of the mineral sample by its volume.

$$\text{Density} = \frac{\text{Mass}}{\text{Volume}}$$

For example, if a sample of olivine has a mass of 237 g and a volume of 72 cm$^3$, then the density is

$$\frac{237\text{ g}}{72\text{ cm}^3} = 3.3\text{ g/cm}^3$$

**Practice Problem** A sample of calcite has a mass of 324 g and a volume of 120 cm$^3$. What is its density?

**Density** Each mineral has a characteristic density. Recall that density is the mass in a given space, or mass per unit volume. No matter what the size of a mineral sample, the density of that mineral always remains the same.

You can compare the density of two mineral samples of about the same size. Just pick them up and heft them, or feel their weight, in your hands. You may be able to feel the difference between low-density quartz and high-density galena. If the two samples are the same size, the galena will be almost three times as heavy as the quartz.

But heft provides only a rough measure of density. When geologists measure density, they use a balance to determine the precise mass of a mineral sample. Then they place the mineral in water to determine how much water the sample displaces. The volume of the displaced water equals the volume of the sample. Dividing the sample's mass by its volume gives the density of the mineral:

$$\text{Density} = \frac{\text{Mass}}{\text{Volume}}$$

**Hardness** When you identify a mineral, one of the best clues you can use is the mineral's hardness. In 1812, Friedrich Mohs, an Austrian mineral expert, invented a test to describe the hardness of minerals. Called the **Mohs hardness scale,** this scale ranks ten minerals from softest to hardest. Look at Figure 5 to see which mineral is the softest and which is the hardest.

FIGURE 5
### Mohs Hardness Scale

Geologists determine a mineral's hardness by comparing it to the hardness of the minerals on the Mohs scale.

Talc
The softest known mineral, talc flakes when scratched by a fingernail.
Gypsum
A fingernail can easily scratch it.
Calcite
A fingernail cannot scratch it, but a copper penny can.
Fluorite
A steel knife can easily scratch it.
Apatite
A steel knife can scratch it.
1
2
3
4
5

## Math Analyzing Data

### Mineral Density

Use the line graph of the mass and volume of pyrite samples to answer the questions.

1. **Reading Graphs** What is the mass of Sample B? What is the volume of Sample B?
2. **Calculating** What is the density of Sample B?
3. **Reading Graphs** What is the mass of Sample C? What is the volume of Sample C?
4. **Calculating** What is the density of Sample C?
5. **Comparing and Contrasting** Compare the density of Sample B to that of Sample C.
6. **Predicting** A piece of pyrite has a volume of 40 $cm^3$. What is its mass?

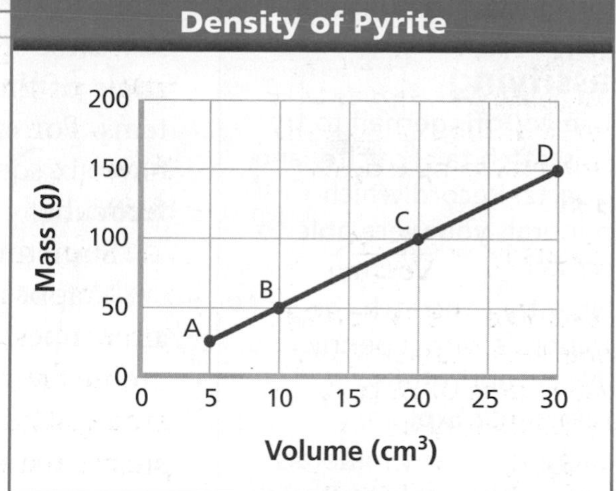


7. **Drawing Conclusions** Does the density of a mineral depend on the size of the mineral sample? Explain.

Hardness can be determined by a scratch test. A mineral can scratch any mineral softer than itself, but can be scratched by any mineral that is harder. To determine the hardness of azurite, a mineral not on the Mohs scale, you could try to scratch it with talc, gypsum, or calcite. But none of these minerals scratch azurite. Apatite, rated 5 on the scale, does scratch azurite. Therefore, azurite's hardness is about 4.

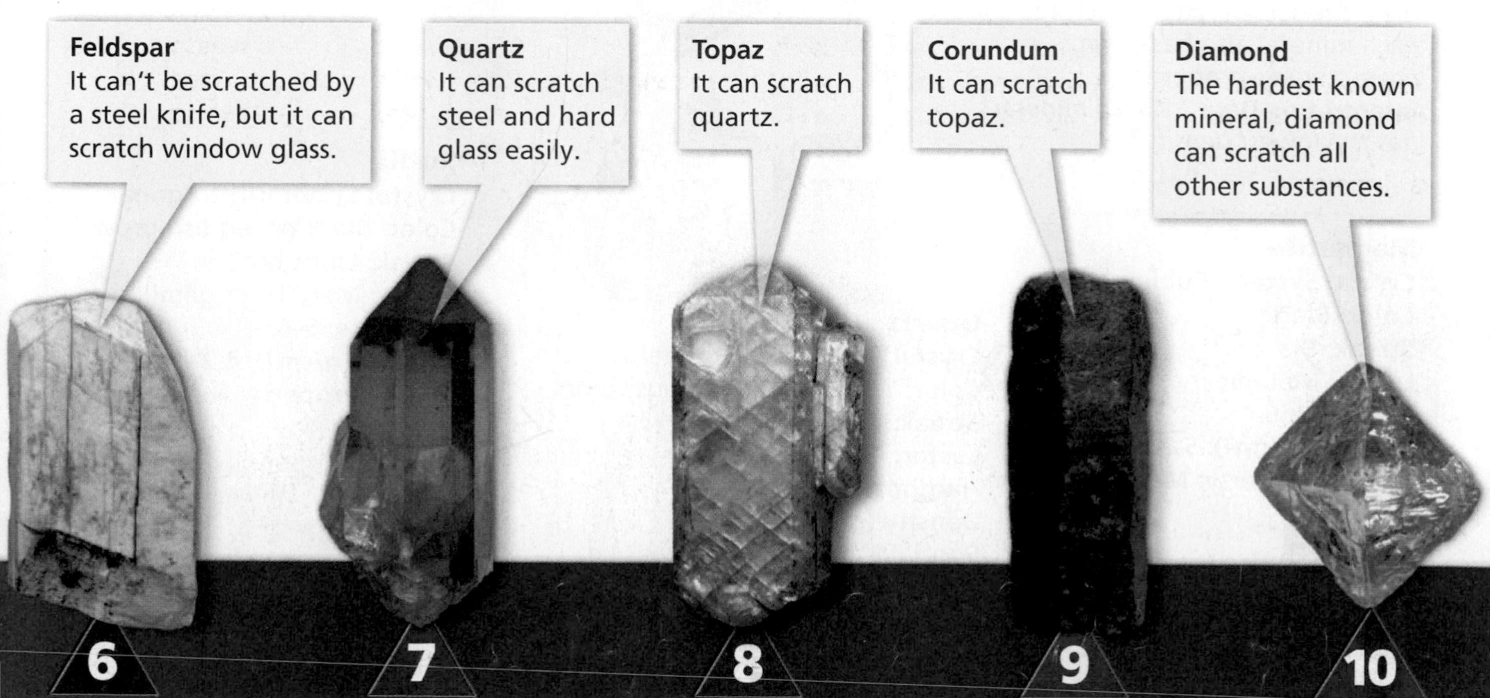

Feldspar
It can't be scratched by a steel knife, but it can scratch window glass.
Quartz
It can scratch steel and hard glass easily.
Topaz
It can scratch quartz.
Corundum
It can scratch topaz.
Diamond
The hardest known mineral, diamond can scratch all other substances.
6
7
8
9
10

## Lab zone Skills Activity

### Classifying

1. Use your fingernail to try to scratch talc, calcite, and quartz. Record which minerals you were able to scratch.
2. Now try to scratch the minerals with a penny. Were your results different? Explain.
3. Were there any minerals you were unable to scratch with either your fingernail or the penny?
4. In order of increasing hardness, how would you classify the three minerals?

**Crystal Systems** The crystals of each mineral grow atom by atom to form that mineral's crystal structure. Geologists classify these structures into six groups based on the number and angle of the crystal faces. These groups are called crystal systems. For example, all halite crystals are cubic. Halite crystals have six square faces that meet at right angles, forming a perfect cube.

Sometimes, the crystal structure is obvious from the mineral's appearance. Crystals that grow in an open space can be almost perfectly formed. But crystals that grow in a tight space are often incompletely formed. In other minerals, the crystal structure is visible only under a microscope. A few minerals, such as opal, are considered minerals even though their particles are not arranged in a crystal structure. Figure 6 shows minerals that belong to each of the six crystal systems.

**Cleavage and Fracture** The way a mineral breaks apart can help to identify it. A mineral that splits easily along flat surfaces has the property called **cleavage.** Whether a mineral has cleavage depends on how the atoms in its crystals are arranged. The arrangement of atoms in the mineral causes it to break apart more easily in one direction than another. Look at the photo of mica in Figure 7. Mica separates easily in only one direction, forming flat sheets. Therefore, mica has cleavage. Feldspar is another common mineral that has cleavage.

FIGURE 6
**Properties of Minerals**
All crystals of the same mineral have the same crystal structure. Each mineral also has other characteristic properties.
**Interpreting Data** *Which mineral has the lowest density?*

**Quartz**
**Crystal System:** Hexagonal
**Color:** Transparent, various colors
**Streak:** Colorless
**Luster:** Glassy
**Hardness:** 7
**Density (g/cm³):** 2.6
**Special Property:** Fractures like broken glass

**Magnetite**
**Crystal System:** Cubic
**Color:** Black
**Streak:** Black
**Luster:** Metallic
**Hardness:** 6
**Density (g/cm³):** 5.2
**Special Property:** Magnetic

**Rutile**
**Crystal System:** Tetragonal
**Color:** Black or reddish brown
**Streak:** Light brown
**Luster:** Metallic or gemlike
**Hardness:** 6–6.5
**Density (g/cm³):** 4.2–4.3
**Special Property:** Not easily melted

**Cleavage**
Mica cleaves into thin, flat sheets that are almost transparent.

**Fracture**
When quartz fractures, the break looks like the surface of a seashell.

**FIGURE 7**
**Cleavage and Fracture**
How a mineral breaks apart can help to identify it.
**Applying Concepts** *How would you test a mineral to determine whether it has cleavage or fracture?*

Most minerals do not split apart evenly. Instead, they have a characteristic type of fracture. **Fracture** describes how a mineral looks when it breaks apart in an irregular way. Geologists use a variety of terms to describe fracture. For example, quartz has a shell-shaped fracture. When quartz breaks, it produces curved, shell-like surfaces that look like chipped glass. Pure metals, like copper and iron, have a hackly fracture—they form jagged points. Some soft minerals that crumble easily like clay have an earthy fracture. Minerals that form rough, irregular surfaces when broken have an uneven fracture.

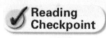

**Reading Checkpoint** **Compare the fracture of quartz to the fracture of a pure metal, such as iron.**

Go Online
*active art*

**For:** Crystal Systems activity
**Visit:** PHSchool.com
**Web Code:** cfp-1041

**Sulfur**
**Crystal System:** Orthorhombic
**Color:** Lemon yellow to yellowish brown
**Streak:** White
**Luster:** Greasy
**Hardness:** 2
**Density (g/cm³):** 2.0–2.1
**Special Property:** Melts easily

**Azurite**
**Crystal System:** Monoclinic
**Color:** Blue
**Streak:** Pale blue
**Luster:** Glassy to dull or earthy
**Hardness:** 3.5–4
**Density (g/cm³):** 3.8
**Special Property:** Reacts to acid

**Microcline Feldspar**
**Crystal System:** Triclinic
**Color:** Pink, white, red-brown, or green
**Streak:** Colorless
**Luster:** Glassy
**Hardness:** 6
**Density (g/cm³):** 2.6
**Special Property:** Cleaves well in two directions

**FIGURE 8**
**Special Properties**
The special properties of minerals include fluorescence, magnetism, radioactivity, and reaction to acids. Other minerals have useful optical or electrical properties.

**Special Properties** Some minerals can be identified by special physical properties. For example, magnetism occurs naturally in a few minerals. Minerals that glow under ultraviolet light have a property known as fluorescence (floo RES uns). The mineral scheelite is fluorescent. Figure 8 shows several minerals with special properties.

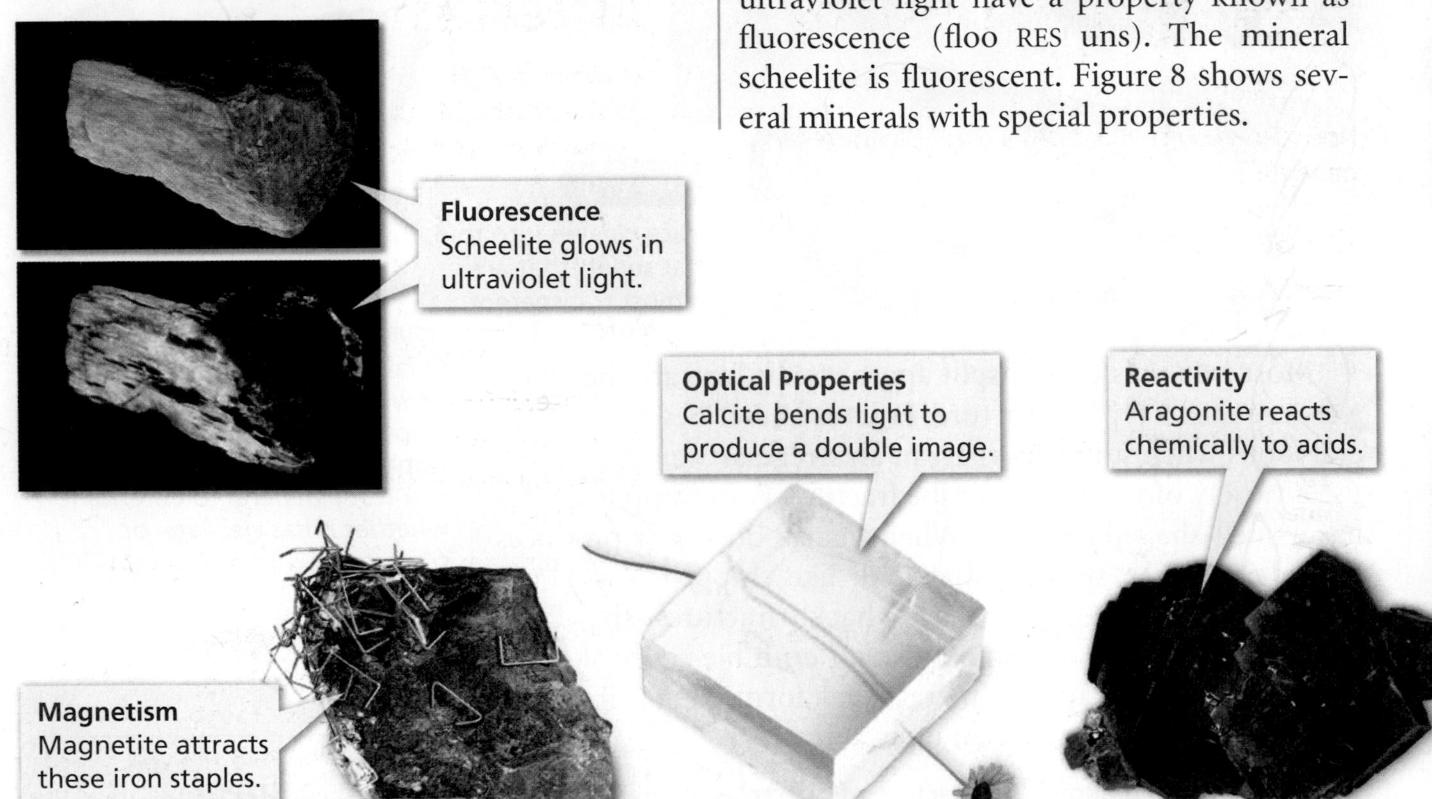
**Fluorescence**
Scheelite glows in ultraviolet light.
**Optical Properties**
Calcite bends light to produce a double image.
**Reactivity**
Aragonite reacts chemically to acids.
**Magnetism**
Magnetite attracts these iron staples.

## Section 1 Assessment

**Target Reading Skill Outlining** Use the information in your outline about the properties of minerals to help you answer the questions.

### Reviewing Key Concepts

1. a. **Defining** Write a definition of "mineral" in your own words.
   b. **Explaining** What does it mean to say that a mineral is inorganic?
   c. **Classifying** Amber is a precious material used in jewelry. It forms when the resin of pine trees hardens into stone. Is amber a mineral? Explain.
2. a. **Listing** Name eight properties that can be used to identify minerals.
   b. **Comparing and Contrasting** What is the difference between fracture and cleavage?
   c. **Predicting** Graphite is a mineral made up of carbon atoms that form thin sheets. But the sheets are only weakly held together. Predict whether graphite will break apart with fracture or cleavage. Explain.

### Math Practice

3. **Calculating Density** The mineral platinum is an element that often occurs as a pure metal. If a sample of platinum has a mass of 430 g and a volume of 20 $cm^3$, what is its density?

For: Data sharing
Visit: PHSchool.com
Web Code: cfd-1041

# Finding the Density of Minerals

## Problem

How can you compare the density of different minerals?

## Skills Focus

measuring

## Materials (per student)

- graduated cylinder, 100-mL
- 3 mineral samples: pyrite, quartz, and galena
- water
- balance

## Procedure 

1. Check to make sure the mineral samples are small enough to fit in the graduated cylinder.
2. Copy the data table into your notebook. Place the pyrite on the balance and record its mass in the data table.
3. Fill the cylinder with water to the 50-mL mark.
4. Carefully place the pyrite in the cylinder of water. Try not to spill any of the water.
5. Read the level of the water on the scale of the graduated cylinder. Record the level of the water with the pyrite in it.

| Data Table | | | |
|---|---|---|---|
| | Pyrite | Quartz | Galena |
| Mass of Mineral (g) | | | |
| Volume of Water Without Mineral (mL) | 50 | 50 | 50 |
| Volume of Water With Mineral (mL) | | | |
| Volume of Water Displaced (mL) | | | |
| Volume of Water Displaced (cm³) | | | |
| Density (g/cm³) | | | |

6. Calculate the volume of water displaced by the pyrite. To do this, subtract the volume of water without the pyrite from the volume of water with the pyrite. Record your answer.
7. Calculate the density of the pyrite by using this formula.

$$\textbf{Density} = \frac{\textbf{Mass of mineral}}{\textbf{Volume of water displaced by mineral}}$$

(Note: Density is expressed as g/cm$^3$. One mL of water has a volume of 1 cm$^3$.)

8. Remove the water and mineral from the cylinder.
9. Repeat Steps 2–8 for quartz and galena.

## Analyze and Conclude

1. **Interpreting Data** Which mineral had the highest density? The lowest density?
2. **Measuring** How does finding the volume of the water that was displaced help you find the volume of the mineral itself?
3. **Drawing Conclusions** Does the shape of a mineral sample affect its density? Explain.
4. **Predicting** Would the procedure you used in this lab work for a substance that floats or one that dissolves in water?

## Designing Experiments

Pyrite is sometimes called "fool's gold" because its color and appearance are similar to real gold. Design an experiment to determine if a sample that looks like gold is in fact real gold.

Section 2

# How Minerals Form

## Reading Focus

### Key Concepts

- How do minerals form from magma and lava?
- How do minerals form from water solutions?

### Key Terms

- geode
- crystallization
- magma
- lava
- solution
- vein

### Target Reading Skill

**Asking Questions** Before you read, preview the red headings. In a graphic organizer like the one below, ask a *how* or *what* question for each heading. As you read, write answers to your questions.

**Formation of Minerals**

| Question | Answer |
|---|---|
| How do minerals form from magma? | |
| | |

Lab zone **Discover Activity**

### How Does the Rate of Cooling Affect Crystals?

1. Put on your goggles. Use a plastic spoon to place a small amount of salol near one end of each of two microscope slides. You need just enough to form a spot 0.5 to 1.0 cm in diameter.
2. Carefully hold one slide with tongs. Warm it gently over a lit candle until the salol is almost completely melted. **CAUTION:** *Move the slide in and out of the flame to avoid cracking the glass.*
3. Set the slide aside to cool slowly. While the first slide is cooling, hold the second slide with tongs and heat it as in Step 2.
4. Cool the second slide quickly by placing it on an ice cube. Carefully blow out the candle.
5. Observe the slides under a hand lens. Compare the appearance of the crystals that form on the two slides.
6. Wash your hands when you are finished.

**Think It Over**

**Developing Hypotheses** Which sample had larger crystals? If a mineral forms by rapid cooling, would you expect the crystals to be large or small?

On a rock-collecting field trip, you spot an egg-shaped rock about the size of a football. No, it's not a dinosaur egg—but what is it? You collect the rock and bring it to a geologic laboratory. There, you carefully split the rock open. The rock is hollow! Its inside surface sparkles with large, colorful amethyst crystals.

You have found a geode (JEE ohd). A **geode** is a rounded, hollow rock that is often lined with mineral crystals. Crystals form inside a geode when water containing dissolved minerals seeps into a crack or hollow in a rock. Slowly, crystallization occurs, lining the inside with large crystals that are often perfectly formed. **Crystallization** is the process by which atoms are arranged to form a material with a crystal structure. In general, minerals can form in two ways: by crystallization of molten material or by crystallization of materials dissolved in water.

Amethyst geode ▼

## Minerals From Magma and Lava

Many minerals form from magma and lava. **Magma** is molten material from inside Earth that hardens to form rock. **Lava** is magma that reaches the surface. Lava also forms rock when it cools and hardens. **Minerals form as hot magma cools inside Earth, or as lava hardens on the surface. When these liquids cool to a solid state, they form crystals.** The size of the crystals depends on the rate at which the magma cools.

When magma remains deep below the surface, it cools slowly over many thousands of years. Slow cooling leads to the formation of large crystals, like the amethyst crystals in a geode. If the crystals remain undisturbed while cooling, they grow by adding atoms according to a regular pattern.

Magma closer to the surface cools much faster than magma that hardens deep below ground. With more rapid cooling, there is no time for magma to form large crystals. Instead, small crystals form. If magma erupts to the surface and becomes lava, the lava will also cool quickly and form minerals with small crystals.

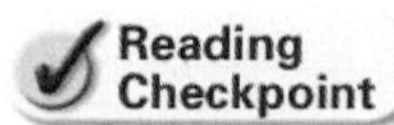


**What size crystals form when magma cools rapidly?**

## Minerals From Solutions

Sometimes the elements and compounds that form minerals can be dissolved in water to form solutions. A **solution** is a mixture in which one substance is dissolved in another. **When elements and compounds that are dissolved in water leave a solution, crystallization occurs.** Minerals can form in this way underground and in bodies of water on Earth's surface.

**Lab zone Try This Activity**

### Crystal Hands

1. Put on your goggles.
2. Pour a solution of table salt into one shallow pan and a solution of Epsom salts into another shallow pan.
3. Put a large piece of black construction paper on a flat surface.

   Dip one hand in the table salt solution. Shake off the excess liquid and make a palm print on the paper. Repeat with the other hand and the Epsom salt solution, placing your new print next to the first one. Wash your hands after making your hand prints. **CAUTION:** *Do not do this activity if you have a cut on your hand.*
4. Let the prints dry overnight.

**Observing** Use a hand lens to compare the shape of the crystals. Which hand print has more crystals?

FIGURE 9
**Selenite Crystals**
These huge selenite crystals in a cave in Mexico formed from the crystallization of minerals in a solution.

A gypsum "rose" forms by evaporation of a mineral solution.

Minerals formed by evaporation

Water containing dissolved minerals

**Minerals Formed by Evaporation** Some minerals form when solutions evaporate. If you stir salt crystals into a beaker of water, the salt dissolves, forming a solution. But if you allow the water in the solution to evaporate, it will leave salt crystals on the bottom of the beaker. In a similar way, deposits of the mineral halite formed over millions of years when ancient seas slowly evaporated. In the United States, such halite deposits are found in the Midwest, the Southwest, and along the Gulf Coast. Other useful minerals that can form by evaporation include gypsum and calcite.

**Minerals From Hot Water Solutions** Deep underground, magma can heat water to a high temperature. Sometimes, the elements and compounds that form a mineral dissolve in this hot water. When the water solution begins to cool, the elements and compounds leave the solution and crystallize as minerals. The silver in Figure 10 was deposited from a hot water solution.

Pure metals that crystallize from hot water solutions underground often form veins. A **vein** is a narrow channel or slab of a mineral that is different from the surrounding rock. Solutions of hot water and metals often flow through cracks within the rock. Then the metals crystallize into veins that resemble the streaks of fudge in vanilla fudge ice cream.

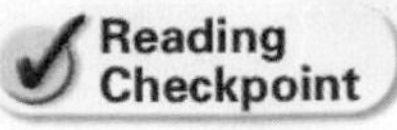

What is a vein?

**For:** More on mineral formation
**Visit:** PHSchool.com
**Web Code:** cfd-1042

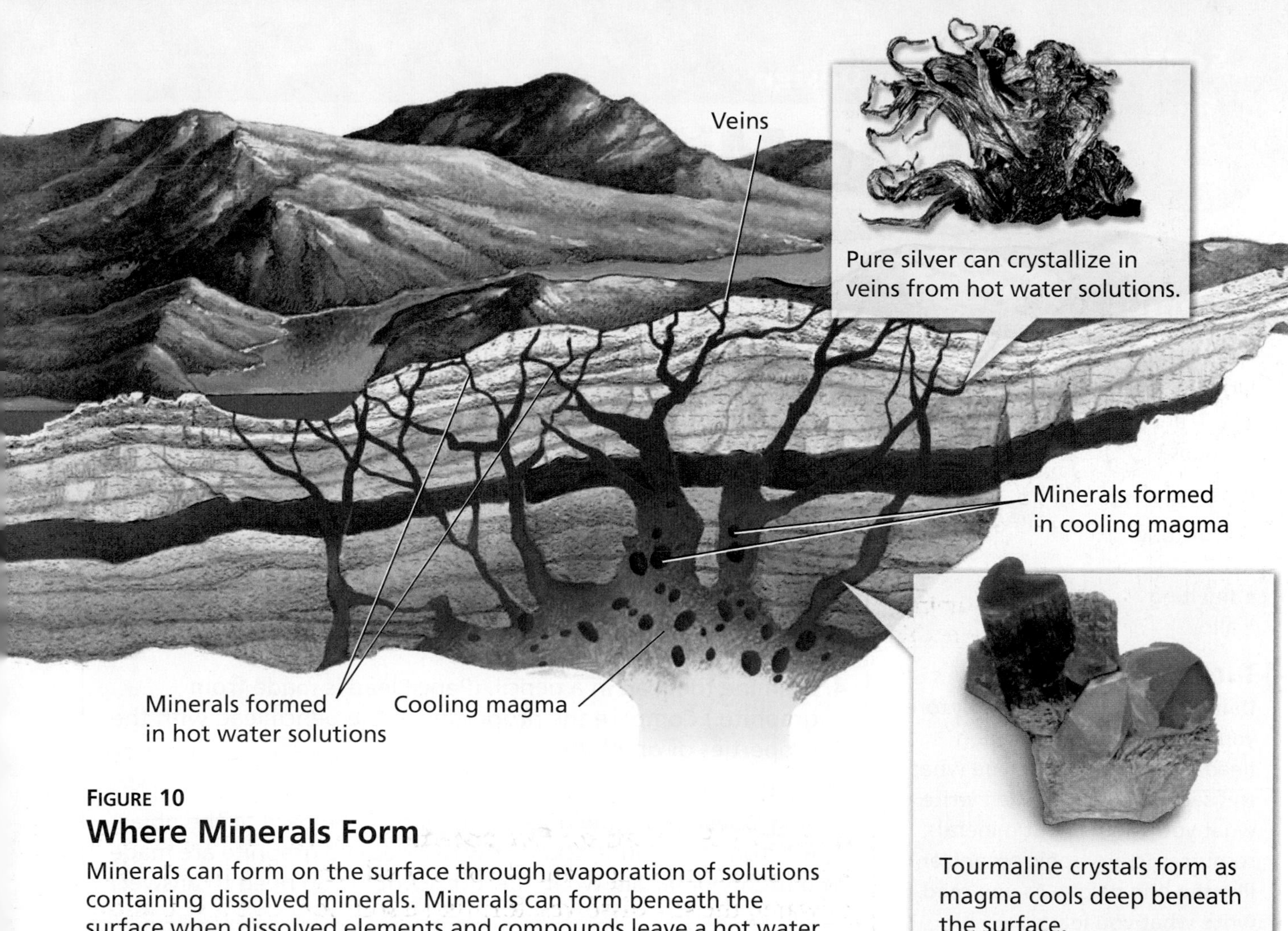


Tourmaline crystals form as magma cools deep beneath the surface.

FIGURE 10
**Where Minerals Form**
Minerals can form on the surface through evaporation of solutions containing dissolved minerals. Minerals can form beneath the surface when dissolved elements and compounds leave a hot water solution or when magma cools and hardens.
**Interpreting Diagrams** *What process can form veins of underground minerals?*

## Section 2 Assessment

**Target Reading Skill Asking Questions** Use your chart to explain two ways in which minerals can form on Earth's surface.

### Reviewing Key Concepts

1. a. **Defining** What is crystallization?
   b. **Relating Cause and Effect** What factor affects the size of the crystals that form as magma cools?
   c. **Predicting** Under what conditions will cooling magma produce minerals with large crystals?
2. a. **Defining** What is a solution?
   b. **Explaining** What are two ways in which minerals can form from a solution?
   c. **Relating Cause and Effect** Describe the process by which a deposit of rock salt, or halite, could form from a solution.

### Writing in Science

**Dialogue** Suppose that you are a scientist exploring a cave. The light on your helmet suddenly reveals a wall covered with large crystals. Scientists on the surface ask you about your observations. Write a dialogue made up of their questions and your replies. Include the different ways in which the minerals you see might have formed.

Section 3 • Tech & Design •

# Using Mineral Resources

## Reading Focus

### Key Concepts

- How are minerals used?
- How are ores processed to obtain metals?

### Key Terms

- gemstone
- ore
- smelting
- alloy

### Target Reading Skill

**Using Prior Knowledge** Before you read, look at the section headings and visuals to see what this section is about. Then write what you know about mineral resources in a graphic organizer like the one below. As you read, write what you learn.

| What You Know |
|---|
| 1. The gems used in jewelry are minerals.<br>2. |

| What You Learned |
|---|
| 1.<br>2. |

## Lab zone Discover Activity

### How Are Minerals Processed Before They Are Used?

1. Examine a piece of the mineral bauxite carefully. Use your knowledge of the properties of minerals to describe it.
2. Examine an aluminum can. (The metal aluminum comes from bauxite.) Compare the properties of the aluminum can with the properties of bauxite.
3. Examine a piece of the mineral graphite and describe its properties.
4. Examine the lead in a pencil. (Pencil lead is made from graphite.) Compare the properties of the pencil lead with the properties of graphite.

**Think It Over**

**Posing Questions** How does each mineral compare to the object made from it? To understand how bauxite and graphite are made into useful materials, what questions would you need to answer?

More than a thousand years ago, the Hopewell people lived in the Ohio River valley. These ancient Native Americans are famous for the mysterious earthen mounds they built near the river. There these people left beautiful objects made from minerals. Some of these objects are tools chipped from flint (a variety of quartz). Others are animals made from thin sheets of copper, like the fish in Figure 11.

To obtain these minerals, the Hopewell people traded with peoples across North America. The copper, for example, came from near Lake Superior. There, copper could be found as a pure metal. Because pure copper is soft, it was easy to shape into ornaments or weapons.

**FIGURE 11**
**Hopewell Fish**
The ancient Hopewell people used a thin sheet of copper to make this fish.

## The Uses of Minerals

Like the Hopewell people, modern civilizations use many minerals. You are surrounded by materials that come from minerals, such as the metal body and window glass of a car. **Minerals are the source of gemstones, metals, and a variety of materials used to make many products.** How many products that are made from minerals can you name? You might be surprised at how important minerals are in everyday life.

FIGURE 12
**Gems**
Precious gems like the diamonds and large blue sapphires on this necklace are among the most valuable minerals.
**Observing** *How would you describe the luster of these gems?*

**Gemstones** Beautiful gemstones such as rubies and sapphires have captured the imagination of people throughout the ages. Usually, a **gemstone** is a hard, colorful mineral that has a brilliant or glassy luster. People value gemstones for their color, luster, and durability, and for the fact that they are rare. Once a gemstone is cut and polished, it is called a gem. Gems are used mainly for jewelry and decoration. They are also used for mechanical parts and for grinding and polishing.

**Metals** Some minerals are the sources of metals such as aluminum, iron, copper, or silver. Metals are generally not as hard as gemstones. But metals are useful because they can be stretched into wire, flattened into sheets, and hammered or molded without breaking. Metal tools and machinery, the metal filament in a light bulb, aluminum foil, and the steel beams used to frame office buildings all began as minerals inside Earth's crust.

**Other Useful Minerals** There are many other useful minerals besides metals and gems. People use materials from these minerals in foods, medicines, fertilizers, and building materials. The very soft mineral talc is ground up to make talcum powder. Clear crystals of the mineral calcite are used in optical instruments such as microscopes. Quartz, a mineral found in sand, is used in making glass as well as in electronic equipment and watches. Gypsum, a soft, white mineral, is used to make wallboard, cement, and stucco.

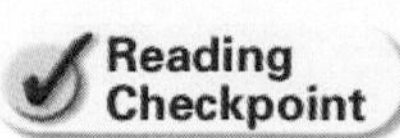


How do people use talc and calcite?

Discovery
CHANNEL
SCHOOL
Minerals
Video Preview
▶ Video Field Trip
Video Assessment

## Producing Metals From Minerals

How is a mineral containing metal made into a finished product? **To produce metal from a mineral, a rock containing the mineral must be located through prospecting and mined, or removed from the ground. Then the rock must be processed to extract the metal.** Look at the Tech & Design in History timeline to see how the technology of producing metals has developed through the ages.

A rock that contains a metal or other useful mineral that can be mined and sold at a profit is called an **ore.** Unlike the copper used by the Hopewell people, most metals do not occur in a pure form. A metal usually occurs as a mineral that is a combination of that metal and other elements. Much of the world's copper, for example, comes from ores containing the mineral chalcopyrite (kal koh PY ryt). In addition to copper, chalcopyrite contains iron and sulfur.

### • Tech & Design in History •

#### Advances in Metal Technology

For thousands of years, people have been inventing and improving methods for smelting metals and making alloys.

**4000 B.C. Copper**
The island of Cyprus was one of the first places where copper was mined and smelted. In fact, the name of the island provided the name of the metal. In Latin, *aes cyprium* meant "metal of Cyprus." It was later shortened to *cuprum*, meaning "copper." The sculpted figure is carrying a large piece of smelted copper.

**3500 B.C. Bronze**
Metalworkers in Sumer, a city between the Tigris and Euphrates rivers, made an alloy of tin and copper to produce a harder metal—bronze. Bronze was poured into molds to form statues, weapons, or vessels for food and drink.

**1500 B.C. Iron**
The Hittites learned to mine and smelt iron ore. Because iron is stronger than copper or bronze, its use spread rapidly. Tools and weapons could be made of iron. This iron dagger was made in Austria several hundred years after the Hittites' discovery.

4000 B.C. | 2500 B.C. | 1000 B.C.

**Prospecting** A prospector is anyone who searches, or prospects, for an ore deposit. Geologists prospect for ores by observing rocks on the land surface and by studying maps of rocks beneath the surface. Geologists can often map the size and shape of an ore deposit by making careful measurements of Earth's magnetic field over the deposit. This works well for minerals that contain magnetic elements such as iron and nickel.

**Mining** The geologist's map of an ore deposit helps miners decide how to remove the ore from the ground. There are three types of mines: strip mines, open pit mines, and shaft mines. In strip mining, earthmoving equipment scrapes away soil to expose ore. In open pit mining, miners use giant earthmoving equipment to dig a tremendous pit and remove ore deposits. For ore deposits that occur in veins, miners dig shaft mines. Shaft mines often have a network of tunnels that extend deep into the ground, following the veins of ore.

## Writing in Science

**Diary Entry** When people discover how to use metals in a new way, the discovery often produces big changes in the way those people live. Choose a development in the history of metals to research. Write a diary entry telling how the discovery happened and how it changed people's lives.

**A.D. 500**
**Early Steel-Making**
Sri Lankans made steel in outdoor furnaces. Steady winds blowing over the top of the furnace's front wall created the high temperatures needed to make steel. Because their steel was so much harder than iron, the Sri Lankans were able to trade it throughout the Indian Ocean region.

**A.D. 1860s**
**Modern Steel-Making**
Steel-making techniques invented by Henry Bessemer and William Siemens made it possible to produce steel cheaply on a large scale. Siemens' invention, the open-hearth furnace, is still widely used, although more modern methods account for most steel production today.

**A.D. 1960s Space-Age Alloys**
Scientists working on the space program have developed light and strong alloys for use in products ranging from bicycles to soda cans. For example, a new alloy of nickel and titanium can "remember" its shape. It is used for eyeglasses that return to their original shape after being bent.

A.D. 500 — A.D. 2000

**For:** Links on mining minerals
**Visit:** www.SciLinks.org
**Web Code:** scn-1043

**Smelting** Ores must be processed before the metals they contain can be used. In the process of **smelting,** an ore is mixed with other substances and then melted to separate the useful metal from other elements the ore contains. Look at Figure 13 to see how smelting separates iron metal from hematite, a common form of iron ore.

1. Iron ore is crushed and mixed with crushed limestone and coke (baked coal), which is rich in carbon.
2. The mixture is placed in a blast furnace, where extremely hot air is blown through, making the coke burn easily.
3. As the coke burns, chemical changes in the mixture produce carbon dioxide gas and molten iron.
4. The dense, molten iron sinks to the bottom of the furnace. Impurities left in the ore combine with the limestone to create slag.
5. The slag and molten iron are poured off through taps.

**FIGURE 13**
**Smelting Iron Ore**
Iron ores must be smelted to separate the iron from the oxygen and other substances in the ores. Then the iron is refined and processed into steel.
**Inferring** *Why does the molten iron sink to the bottom of the blast furnace?*

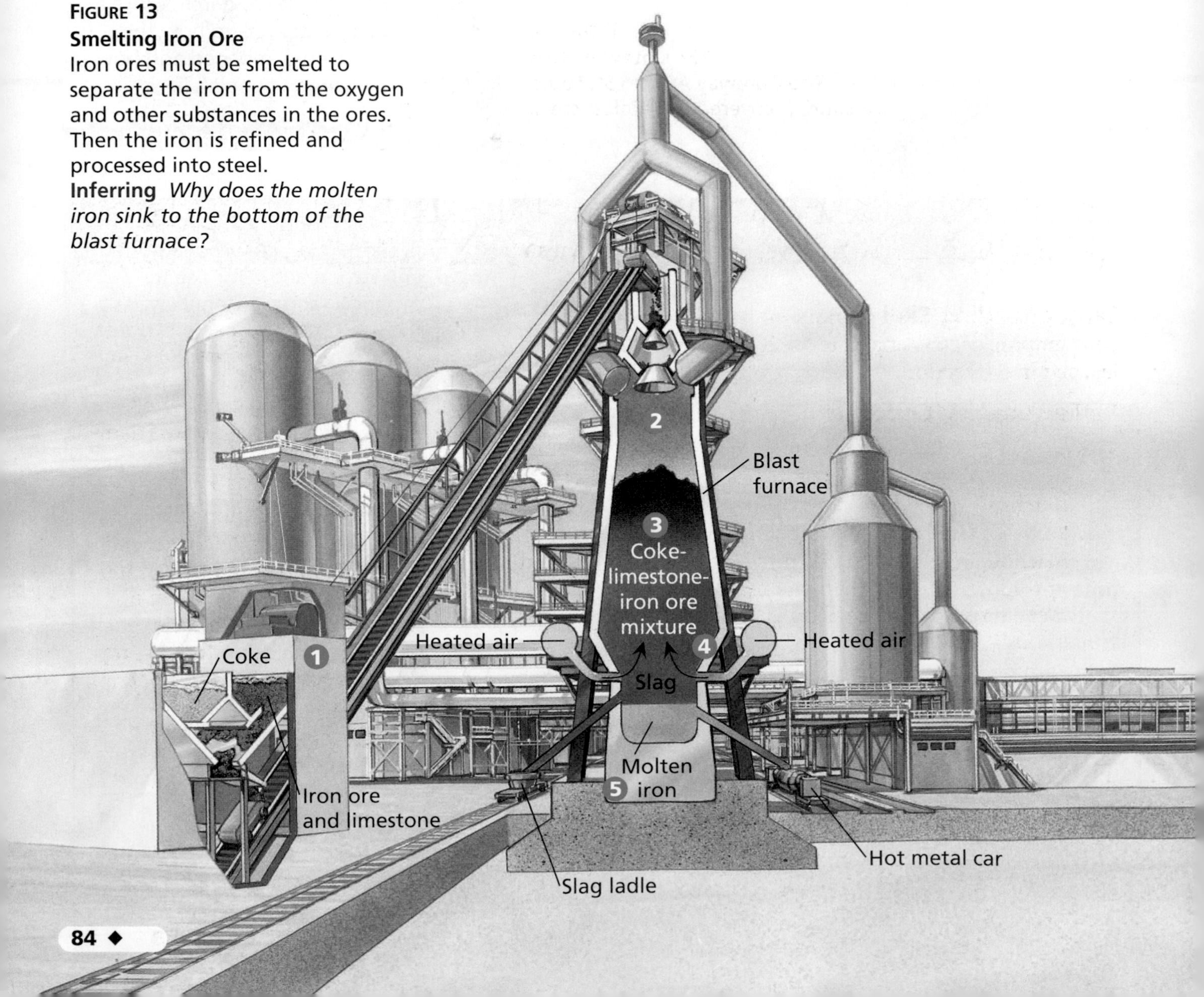

2
Blast furnace
3 Coke-limestone-iron ore mixture
Heated air
Heated air
4
Coke
1
Slag
Molten iron
5
Iron ore and limestone
Hot metal car
Slag ladle

**Further Processing** After smelting, additional processing is needed to remove impurities from the metal. After the iron is purified, a small amount of carbon may be added to it. The result is steel, which is harder and stronger than iron. Steel is an **alloy,** a solid mixture of two or more elements, at least one of which is a metal. To be considered an alloy, the mixture must have the characteristic properties of a metal.

After adding carbon to iron, steelmakers may add other elements to create alloys with specific properties. For stronger steel, the metal manganese is added. For rust-resistant steel, the metals chromium and nickel are added. Figure 14 shows how rust-resistant stainless steel was used in the construction of one of America's most famous monuments.

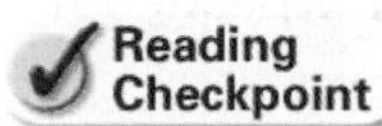

**What is an alloy?**

FIGURE 14
**The Gateway Arch**
The Gateway Arch in St. Louis, Missouri, is covered in stainless steel.

## Section 3 Assessment

**Target Reading Skill Using Prior Knowledge** Review your graphic organizer and revise it based on what you just learned in the section.

### Reviewing Key Concepts

1. **a. Defining** What are gemstones? Why are they valuable?
   **b. Listing** What properties of metals make them useful to humans?
   **c. Problem Solving** Suppose that you are designing a machine with many small, moving parts that will need to run constantly. Would you make the parts from metal or gemstone? Explain your answer.
2. **a. Identifying** What is an ore?
   **b. Summarizing** Explain the steps that must take place before an ore can be made into a useful product.
   **c. Inferring** Which material formed during smelting is denser—molten metal or slag? How can you tell?

### Lab zone At-Home Activity

**Rust Protection** You can demonstrate to your family how rust damages objects that contain iron. Obtain three iron nails. Coat one of the nails with petroleum jelly and coat the second nail with clear nail polish. Do not put anything on the third nail. Place all the nails in a glass of water with a little vinegar. (The vinegar speeds up the rusting process.) Allow the nails to stand in the glass overnight. Which nails show signs of rusting? Explain these results to your family.

Lab zone **Consumer Lab**

# A Mouthful Of Minerals

## Problem
What effect do the minerals in toothpaste have on the toothpaste's ability to clean?

## Skills Focus
observing, controlling variables, drawing conclusions

## Materials
- samples of 3 different types of toothpaste
- worn-out toothbrushes
- tap water
- a ceramic tile stained on the unglazed side with a felt-tip marker or pen

## Procedure   

1. Copy the data table into your notebook.
2. Your teacher will give you samples of toothpaste, a list of the mineral or minerals in each type of toothpaste, a toothbrush, and a ceramic tile.
3. In your data table, record the substances found in each toothpaste sample. Common minerals in toothpaste include mica, calcite, and quartz (silica). Toothpaste also may include compounds such as sodium bicarbonate (baking soda), sodium fluoride, aluminum or calcium phosphates, and titanium dioxide.
4. For each toothpaste sample, predict how effective you think it will be in removing the stain from the tile. Record your predictions in the data table.
5. Put a pea-sized amount of the first toothpaste onto a toothbrush. **CAUTION:** *Do not ingest any of the toothpaste.*
6. Brush one of the stain marks on the tile 50 times. As you brush, try to use the same amount of force for each stroke.
7. Using tap water, rinse the tile to remove all of the paste. Then rinse the toothpaste out of the toothbrush.
8. Repeat Steps 5–7 for the other toothpaste samples, using a different stain mark for each test. Be sure to brush with the same amount of force and for the same number of times.
9. Compare how well the different toothpastes cleaned the stains. Record your observations in the data table.

## Analyze and Conclude

1. **Classifying** Which mineral or minerals were found in all of the toothpastes tested? Did any toothpaste contain minerals not found in the other toothpastes?
2. **Observing** Which toothpaste was most effective in removing stains from the tile?
3. **Interpreting Data** Were your predictions about which toothpaste would be most effective correct?
4. **Interpreting Data** Does the toothpaste that was most effective in cleaning the tile differ in mineral content from the other toothpastes that were tested?

Data Table

| Toothpaste | Minerals Present | Predictions | Observations |
|---|---|---|---|
| 1 | | | |
| 2 | | | |
| 3 | | | |

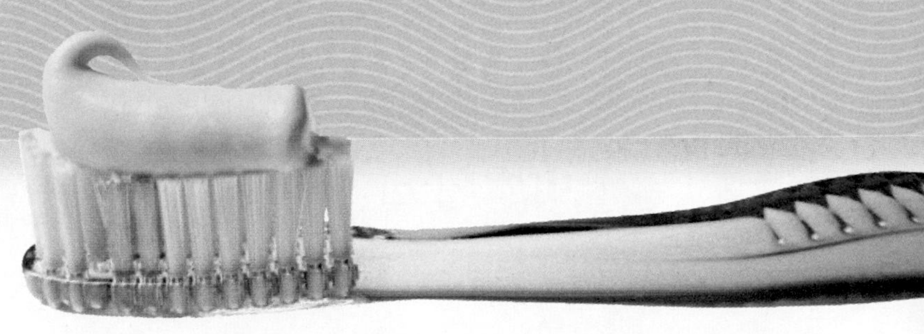

5. **Controlling Variables** What was the independent variable in this experiment? What was the dependent variable? Why did you use the same amount of toothpaste, force, and number of brushstrokes in each trial?
6. **Drawing Conclusions** How do the minerals in toothpaste affect the toothpaste's cleaning ability? Explain.
7. **Developing Hypotheses** Your teeth have the same composition as apatite, which has a hardness of 5 on the Mohs scale. What would be the advantages and disadvantages of using a toothpaste containing a mineral that is harder than apatite? Softer than apatite? Explain.
8. **Communicating** Write a lab report for this experiment. In your report, describe your predictions, your procedure, how you controlled variables, and whether or not your results supported your predictions.

## Design Your Own Experiment

Some brands of toothpaste claim that they whiten teeth. Design an experiment to test the effectiveness of different kinds of whitening toothpaste. Make a data table to organize your findings. *Obtain your teacher's permission before carrying out your investigation.*

# Chapter 3 Study Guide

**The BIG Idea**

**Properties of Matter** Minerals are naturally occurring, inorganic solids with a crystal structure and a definite chemical composition. Minerals are used as gemstones, metals, and raw materials for many products.

## 1 Properties of Minerals

**Key Concepts**

- A mineral is a naturally occurring, inorganic solid that has a crystal structure and a definite chemical composition.
- Each mineral has characteristic properties that can be used to identify it.
- Density can be determined with the following formula:

$$\text{Density} = \frac{\text{Mass}}{\text{Volume}}$$

**Key Terms**

mineral
inorganic
crystal
streak
luster
Mohs hardness scale
cleavage
fracture

## 2 How Minerals Form

**Key Concepts**

- Minerals form as hot magma cools inside Earth, or as lava hardens on the surface. When these liquids cool to a solid state, they form crystals.
- When elements and compounds that are dissolved in water leave a solution, crystallization of minerals occurs.

**Key Terms**

geode
crystallization
magma
lava
solution
vein

## 3 Mineral Resources

**Key Concepts**

- Minerals are the source of gemstones, metals, and a variety of materials used to make many products.
- To produce metal from a mineral, a rock containing the mineral must be located through prospecting and mined, or removed from the ground. Then the rock must be processed to extract the metal.

**Key Terms**

gemstone
ore
smelting
alloy

# Review and Assessment

For: Self-assessment
Visit: PHSchool.com
Web Code: cja-1030

## Organizing Information

**Comparing and Contrasting** Fill in the Venn diagram to compare the characteristics of a mineral and a material that is not a mineral.

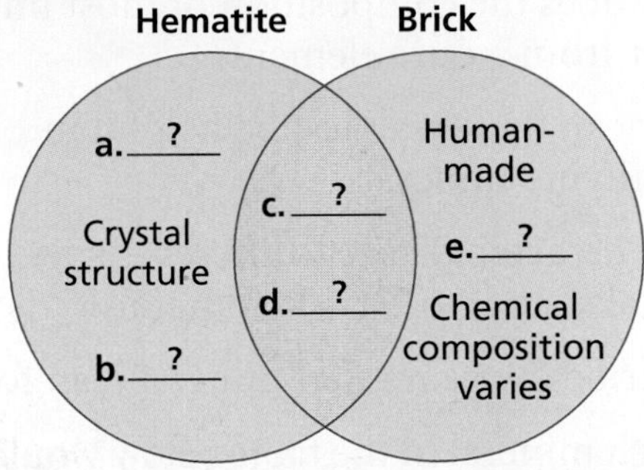


## Reviewing Key Terms

**Choose the letter of the best answer.**

1. Because minerals do not come from once-living material, they are said to be
   a. crystalline.
   b. solid.
   c. colorful.
   d. inorganic.
2. In a mineral, the particles line up in a repeating pattern to form a(n)
   a. element.
   b. crystal.
   c. mixture.
   d. compound.
3. Which characteristic is used to determine the color of a mineral's powder?
   a. luster
   b. fracture
   c. cleavage
   d. streak
4. Halite is a mineral formed through the evaporation of
   a. magma.
   b. a vein.
   c. a solution.
   d. lava.
5. Minerals from which metals can be removed in usable amounts are called
   a. gemstones. b. crystals.
   c. alloys. d. ores.

**If the statement is true, write *true*. If it is false, change the underlined word or words to make the statement true.**

6. A hollow rock lined with crystals is a <u>geode</u>.
7. <u>Fracture</u> is the term that describes how a mineral reflects light from its surface.
8. Mineral deposits beneath Earth's surface that are different from the surrounding rocks are called <u>veins</u>.
9. Hard, shiny crystals used in jewelry are called <u>ores</u>.
10. Steel is an example of a(n) <u>alloy</u>.

## Writing in Science

**Descriptive Paragraph** Choose a mineral such as gold or jade. Write a paragraph about the properties of this mineral. Explain why it is valuable and how it is useful to society.

*Minerals*

Video Preview
Video Field Trip
▶ Video Assessment

# Review and Assessment

## Checking Concepts

**11.** How does the composition of most minerals differ from a pure element?

**12.** How can the streak test be helpful in identifying minerals?

**13.** How do geologists use different types of crystal shapes to classify minerals?

**14.** Describe two ways that minerals can form.

**15.** Which mineral in the table below would make the best gemstone? Explain your answer.

**Properties of Minerals**

| Mineral | Hardness | Density ($g/cm^3$) | Luster |
|---|---|---|---|
| Galena | 2.5 | 7.5 | metallic |
| Fluorite | 4.0 | 3.3 | glassy |
| Corundum | 9.0 | 4.0 | glassy |
| Talc | 1.0 | 2.8 | pearly |

**16.** Describe what happens to a mineral during smelting.

## Thinking Critically

**17. Classifying** Obsidian is a solid that occurs in volcanic areas. Obsidian forms when magma cools very quickly, creating a type of glass. In glass, the particles are not arranged in an orderly pattern as in a crystal. Should obsidian be classified as a mineral? Explain why or why not.

**18. Comparing and Contrasting** Color and luster are both properties of minerals. How are they similar? How are they different? How can each be used to help identify a mineral?

**19. Relating Cause and Effect** Describe how a vein of ore forms underground. What is the energy source for this process?

**20. Predicting** What would happen if steel-makers forgot to add enough chromium and nickel to a batch of stainless steel?

## Math Practice

**21. Calculating** A platinum ring has a volume of 0.8 $cm^3$ and a mass of 15.2 g. What is its density?

**22. Calculating** A diamond has a mass of 10.56 g and a volume of 3 $cm^3$. Calculate the density of the diamond.

## Applying Skills

**Use the photograph below to answer Questions 23–25.**

*You have found a sample of the mineral wulfenite. The wulfenite has a hardness of about 3 on the Mohs hardness scale and a density of 6.8 $g/cm^3$. The mineral contains oxygen as well as the metals lead and molybdenum.*

**23. Observing** Describe wulfenite's color and luster and the shape of its crystals.

**24. Inferring** Did the wulfenite form slowly or quickly? Explain your answer.

**25. Drawing Conclusions** Is wulfenite hard enough for use as a gem? What would you use these crystals for? Explain.

## Lab zone Chapter Project

**Performance Assessment** Share your crystal garden with a classmate. Can your classmate identify which solution created which crystals? Do your data show differences in crystal growth rates? Which materials worked best for crystals to grow on? Share the answers to these questions when you present your project.

# Standardized Test Prep

### Test-Taking Tip

**Choosing Among Similar Answers**

Sometimes two or more answers to a question are almost identical. If you do not read each answer carefully, you may select an incorrect answer.

*Sample Question*

Which of the following is the best definition of a mineral?

**A** a naturally occurring, inorganic solid that has a crystal shape and a definite chemical composition
**B** a naturally occurring, inorganic solid that forms through crystallization of melted materials
**C** a naturally occurring, inorganic solid that forms through crystallization of materials dissolved in water
**D** a naturally occurring, organic solid that has a crystal shape and a definite chemical composition

*Answer*

Choices **A** and **D** are similar, but the correct answer is **A. D** is incorrect because minerals do not contain organic material. Although correct, **B** and **C** are not the most complete definition of a mineral.

### Choose the letter of the best answer.

**1.** Which of the following is a mineral?
**A** salt
**B** pearl
**C** coal
**D** cement

**2.** You could distinguish gold from pyrite (fool's gold) by
**F** comparing their hardness.
**G** testing their chemical composition.
**H** comparing their density.
**J** all of the above

**3.** Veins of silver can be found in rock. These veins formed when
**A** hot water solutions escaped from cracks in the rock.
**B** hot water solutions crystallized in cracks in the rock.
**C** magma crystallized in cracks in the rock.
**D** hot water solutions evaporated in cracks in the rock.

**4.** An ore is a mineral that
**F** is beautiful and rare.
**G** can be mined at a profit.
**H** is dense and metallic.
**J** is light and durable.

**5.** The following diagrams show four different mineral samples. Based on these diagrams, what property is the same for all four minerals?

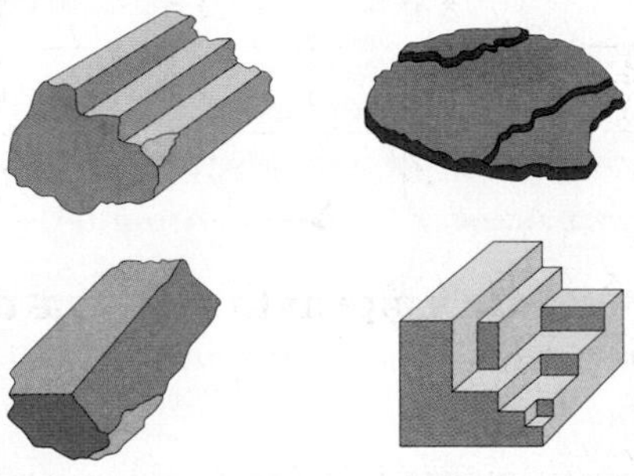

**A** crystal structure
**B** cleavage
**C** hardness
**D** color

### Constructed Response

**6.** A geologist finds an unknown mineral while working in a national park. The geologist is carrying a kit that contains a geologic hammer, a jackknife, a hand lens, a piece of tile, and a penny. In a paragraph, describe how the geologist could use these items to determine some of the mineral's properties.

# Chapter 4 Rocks

## The BIG Idea

Cycles of Matter and Energy

**What are the three main types of rocks and how do they form?**

### Chapter Preview



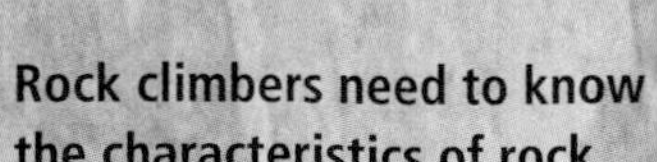

Rock climbers need to know the characteristics of rock.

Rocks

▶ Video Preview
Video Field Trip
Video Assessment

Lab zone™ Chapter **Project**

## Collecting Rocks

Each rock, whether a small pebble or a mountain peak, tells a story. The rocks in your own community tell part of the story of Earth's crust.

In this chapter, you will learn how three different types of rocks form. You can apply what you learn about rocks to create your own rock collection and explore the properties of your rocks.

**Your Goal** To make a collection of the rocks in your area

To complete this project, you must

- collect samples of rocks, keeping a record of where you found each sample
- describe the characteristics of your rocks, including their color, texture, and density
- classify each rock as igneous, sedimentary, or metamorphic
- create a display for your rock collection
- follow the safety guidelines in Appendix A

**Plan It!** With your classmates and teacher, brainstorm locations in your community where rocks are likely to be found. Are there road cuts, outcroppings of bedrock, riverbanks, or beaches where you could safely and legally collect your rocks? Plan your rock-hunting expeditions. Collect your rocks, and then describe, test, and classify your rock collection.

Section 1

# Classifying Rocks

## Reading Focus

### Key Concepts

- What characteristics do geologists use to identify rocks?
- What are the three main groups of rocks?

### Key Terms

- rock-forming mineral
- granite
- basalt
- grains
- texture
- igneous rock
- sedimentary rock
- metamorphic rock

### Target Reading Skill

**Asking Questions** Before you read, preview the red headings. In a graphic organizer like the one below, ask a *what* or *how* question for each heading. As you read, write answers to your questions.

| Question | Answer |
|---|---|
| What does a rock's color tell about the rock? | |
| | |

## Lab zone Discover Activity

### How Do Rocks Compare?

1. Look at samples of conglomerate and marble with a hand lens.
2. Describe the two rocks. What is the color and texture of each?
3. Try scratching the surface of each rock with the edge of a penny. Which rock seems harder?
4. Hold each rock in your hand. Allowing for the fact that the samples aren't exactly the same size, which rock seems denser?

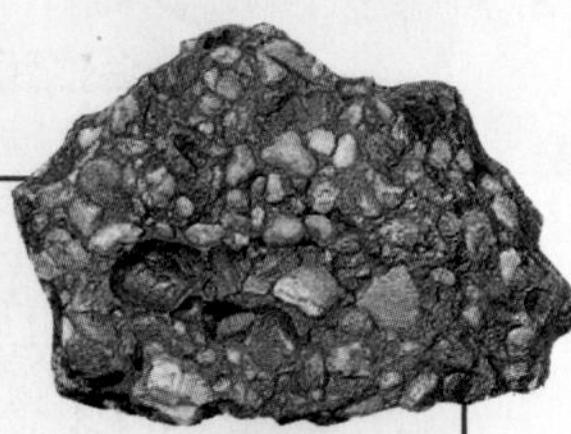

Conglomerate

Marble

**Think It Over**

**Observing** Based on your observations, how would you compare the physical properties of marble and conglomerate?

If you were a geologist, how would you examine a rock for the first time? You might use a camera or notebook to record information about the setting where the rock was found. Then, you would use a chisel or the sharp end of a rock hammer to remove samples of the rock. Finally, you would break open the samples with a hammer to examine their inside surfaces. You must look at the inside of a rock because the effects of ice, liquid water, and weather can change the outer surface of a rock.

You can find interesting rocks almost anywhere. The rock of Earth's crust forms mountains, hills, valleys, beaches, even the ocean floor. **When studying a rock sample, geologists observe the rock's mineral composition, color, and texture.**

FIGURE 1
**Inspecting a Rock**
This geologist is using a hand lens to observe a piece of shale.

## Mineral Composition and Color

Rocks are made of mixtures of minerals and other materials. Some rocks contain only a single mineral. Others contain several minerals. For example, the granite in Figure 2 is made up of the minerals quartz, feldspar, hornblende, and mica. About 20 minerals make up most of the rocks of Earth's crust. These minerals are known as **rock-forming minerals.** Appendix B at the back of this book lists some of the most common rock-forming minerals.

A rock's color provides clues to the rock's mineral composition. For example, **granite** is generally a light-colored rock that has high silica content. **Basalt,** shown in Figure 3, is a dark-colored rock that is low in silica. But as with minerals, color alone does not provide enough information to identify a rock.

Geologists observe the shape and color of crystals in a rock to identify the minerals that the rock contains. In identifying rocks, geologists also use some of the tests that are used to identify minerals. For example, testing the surface of a rock with acid determines whether the rock includes minerals made of compounds called carbonates.

FIGURE 2
**Minerals in Granite**
Granite is made up of quartz, feldspar, hornblende, and mica. It may also contain other minerals.
**Observing** *Which mineral seems most abundant in the sample of granite shown?*

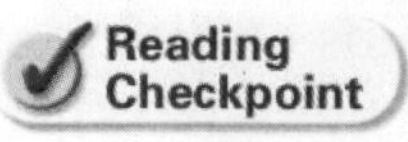

**How would you define "rock-forming mineral"?**

FIGURE 3
**Basalt**
Basalt is a dark-colored rock that has low silica content. Unlike granite, basalt has mineral crystals that are too small to be seen without a hand lens.

## Texture

As with minerals, color alone does not provide enough information to identify a rock. But a rock's texture is very useful in identifying a rock. Most rocks are made up of particles of minerals or other rocks, which geologists call **grains.** Grains give the rock its texture. To a geologist, a rock's **texture** is the look and feel of the rock's surface. Some rocks are smooth and glassy. Others are rough or chalky. To describe a rock's texture, geologists use terms based on the size, shape, and pattern of the grains.

**FIGURE 4**
**Rock Textures**
Texture helps classify rocks.
**Comparing and Contrasting** *How would you compare the texture of diorite with the texture of gneiss?*

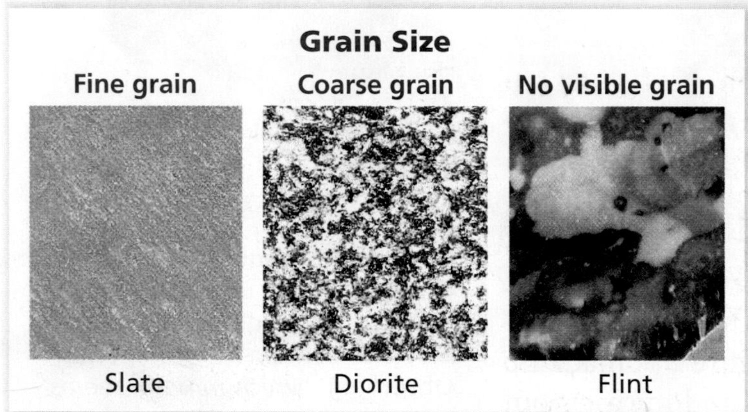


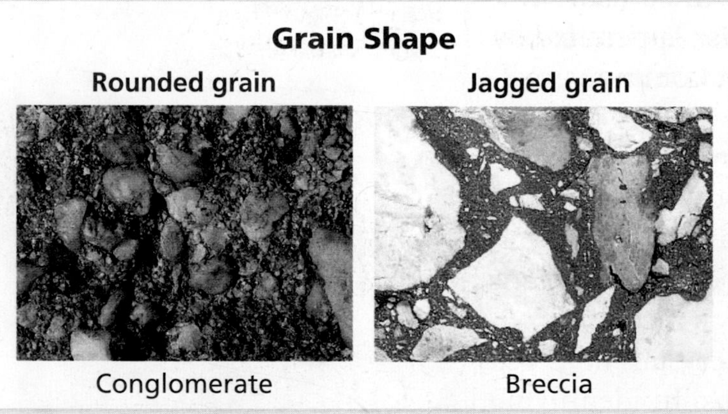


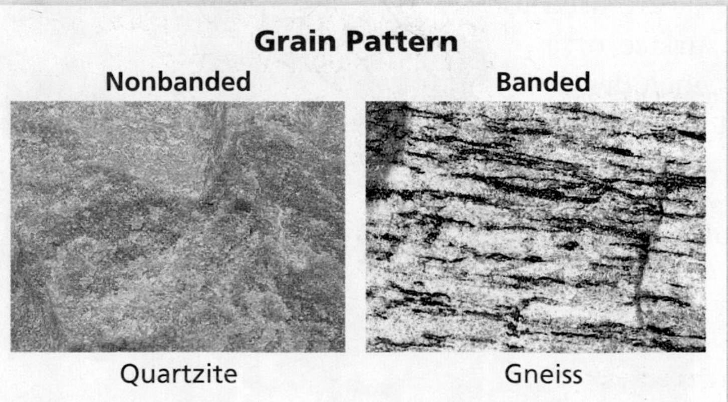


**Grain Size** Often, the grains in a rock are large and easy to see. Such rocks are said to be coarse-grained. In other rocks, the grains are so small that they can only be seen with a microscope. These rocks are said to be fine-grained. Notice the difference in texture between the fine-grained slate and the coarse-grained diorite in Figure 4 at left. Some rocks have no visible grain even when they are examined under a microscope.

**Grain Shape** The grains in a rock vary widely in shape. Some grains look like tiny particles of sand. Others look like small seeds or exploding stars. In some rocks, such as granite, the grain results from the shapes of the crystals that form the rock. In other rocks, the grain shape results from fragments of several rocks. These fragments can be smooth and rounded or they can be jagged.

**Grain Pattern** The grains in a rock often form patterns. Some grains lie in flat layers that look like a stack of pancakes. Other grains form swirling patterns. Some rocks have grains of different colors in bands, like the gneiss (NYS) in Figure 4. In other rocks, the grains occur randomly throughout.

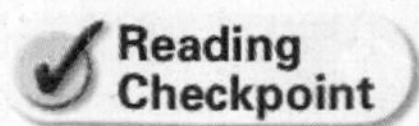


**What does it mean to say that a rock is coarse-grained?**

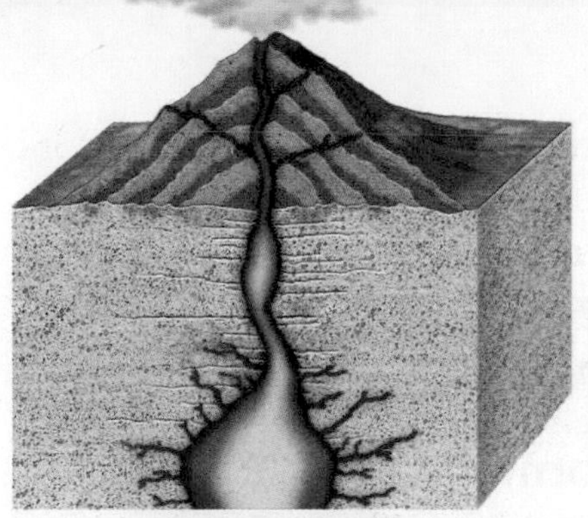

**Igneous Rock** forms when magma or lava cools and hardens.

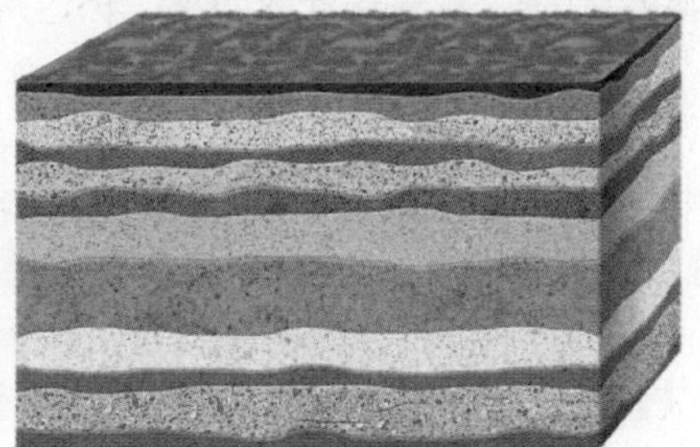

**Sedimentary Rock** forms when pieces of rock are pressed and cemented together.

**Metamorphic Rock** forms from other rocks that are changed by heat and pressure.

## How Rocks Form

Using color, texture, and mineral composition, geologists can classify a rock according to its origin. A rock's origin is how the rock formed. **Geologists classify rocks into three major groups: igneous rock, sedimentary rock, and metamorphic rock.**

Each of these groups of rocks forms in a different way. **Igneous rock** (IG nee us) forms from the cooling of magma or lava. Most **sedimentary rock** (seduh MEN turee) forms when particles of other rocks or the remains of plants and animals are pressed and cemented together. Sedimentary rock forms in layers that are buried below the surface. **Metamorphic rock** (metuh MAWR fik) forms when an existing rock is changed by heat, pressure, or chemical reactions. Most metamorphic rock forms deep underground.

FIGURE 5
**Kinds of Rocks**
Rocks can be igneous, sedimentary, or metamorphic, depending on how the rock formed.

**For:** More on rock identification
**Visit:** PHSchool.com
**Web Code:** cfd-1051

## Section 1 Assessment

**Target Reading Skill Asking Questions** Work with a partner to check the answers in your graphic organizer about the section headings.

### Reviewing Key Concepts

1. a. **Naming** What three characteristics do geologists use to identify rocks?
   b. **Defining** What are the grains of a rock?
   c. **Comparing and Contrasting** In your own words, compare the grain size, shape, and pattern of the conglomerate and breccia in Figure 4.
2. a. **Reviewing** What are the three main groups of rocks?
   b. **Explaining** How do igneous rocks form?
   c. **Classifying** Gneiss is a kind of rock that forms when heat and pressure inside Earth change granite. To what group of rocks does gneiss belong?

### Writing in Science

**Wanted Poster** Write a paragraph for a wanted poster in which you describe the characteristics of granite. In your wanted poster, be sure to describe granite's mineral composition, color, and texture. Also mention the group of rocks to which granite belongs.

Section 2

# Igneous Rocks

## Reading Focus

### Key Concepts

- What characteristics are used to classify igneous rocks?
- How are igneous rocks used?

### Key Terms

- extrusive rock
- intrusive rock
- silica

### Target Reading Skill

**Identifying Main Ideas** As you read Classifying Igneous Rocks, write the main idea in a graphic organizer like the one below. Then write three supporting details that further explain the main idea.

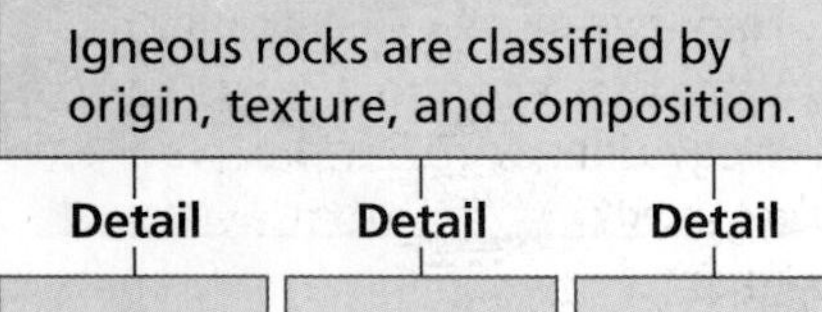

For: Links on igneous rocks
Visit: www.SciLinks.org
Web Code: scn-1052

### Lab zone Discover Activity

#### How Do Igneous Rocks Form?

1. Use a hand lens to examine samples of granite and obsidian.
2. Describe the texture of both rocks using the terms coarse, fine, or glassy.
3. Which rock has coarse-grained crystals? Which rock has no crystals or grains?

**Think It Over**

**Inferring** Granite and obsidian are igneous rocks. From your observations, what can you infer about how each type of rock formed?

Obsidian

Granite

The time is 4.6 billion years ago. You are in a spacecraft orbiting Earth. Do you see the blue and green globe of Earth that astronauts today see from space? No—instead, Earth looks like a charred and bubbling marshmallow heated over hot coals.

Soon after Earth formed, the planet's interior became so hot that magma formed. Lava repeatedly flowed over the surface. The lava quickly hardened, forming a rocky crust. Because this early crust was denser than the material beneath it, chunks of crust sank into Earth's interior. This allowed more lava to erupt over the surface and harden to form rock.

## Classifying Igneous Rocks

The first rocks to form on Earth probably looked like the igneous rocks that can be seen today. Igneous rock is any rock that forms from magma or lava. The name *igneous* comes from the Latin word *ignis*, meaning "fire." **Igneous rocks are classified according to their origin, texture, and mineral composition.**

**Origin** Igneous rock may form on or beneath Earth's surface. **Extrusive rock** is igneous rock formed from lava that erupted onto Earth's surface. Basalt is the most common extrusive rock. Basalt is one of the most common rocks on Earth. A layer of basalt forms much of Earth's ocean floors.

Igneous rock that formed when magma hardened beneath Earth's surface is called **intrusive rock.** The most abundant intrusive rock on Earth's continents is granite. Granite forms the core of many mountain ranges.

**Texture** The texture of an igneous rock depends on the size and shape of its mineral crystals. The only exceptions to this rule are certain types of rock that have a texture like glass. These igneous rocks lack a crystal structure.

Igneous rocks may be similar in mineral composition and yet have very different textures. Rapidly cooling lava forms fine-grained igneous rocks with small crystals. Slowly cooling magma forms coarse-grained rocks with large crystals. Therefore, intrusive and extrusive rocks usually have different textures.

Intrusive rocks have larger crystals than extrusive rocks. If you examine a coarse-grained rock such as granite, you can easily see that the crystals vary in size and color. Some intrusive rocks, like the porphyry in Figure 6, have a texture that looks like a gelatin dessert with chopped-up fruit mixed in.

Extrusive rocks have a fine-grained or glassy texture. Basalt is a fine-grained extrusive rock. It consists of crystals too small to be seen without a microscope. Obsidian is an extrusive rock that cooled very rapidly without forming crystals. As a result, obsidian has the smooth, shiny texture of a thick piece of glass.

**Figure 6**
**Igneous Rock Textures**
Igneous rocks such as rhyolite, pegmatite, and porphyry can vary greatly in texture depending on whether they are intrusive or extrusive.
**Relating Cause and Effect** *What conditions caused rhyolite to have a fine-grained texture?*

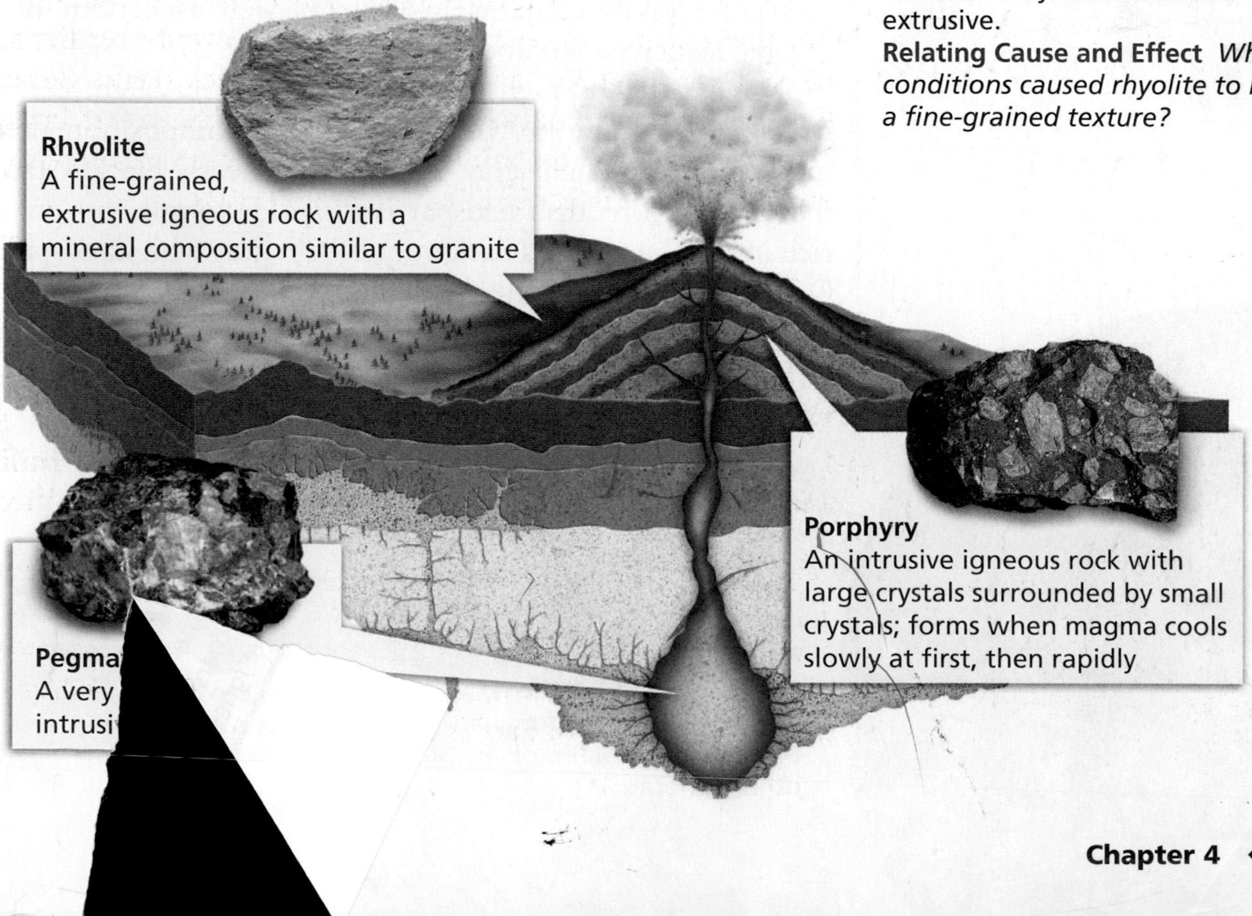

**Rhyolite**
A fine-grained, extrusive igneous rock with a mineral composition similar to granite

**Porphyry**
An intrusive igneous rock with large crystals surrounded by small crystals; forms when magma cools slowly at first, then rapidly

**Pegma**
A very
intrusi

## Math Analyzing Data

### Mineral Mixture

Granite is a mixture of light-colored minerals such as feldspar and quartz and dark-colored minerals including hornblende and mica. But, granite can vary in mineral composition, affecting its color and texture.

Study the circle graph and then answer the questions.

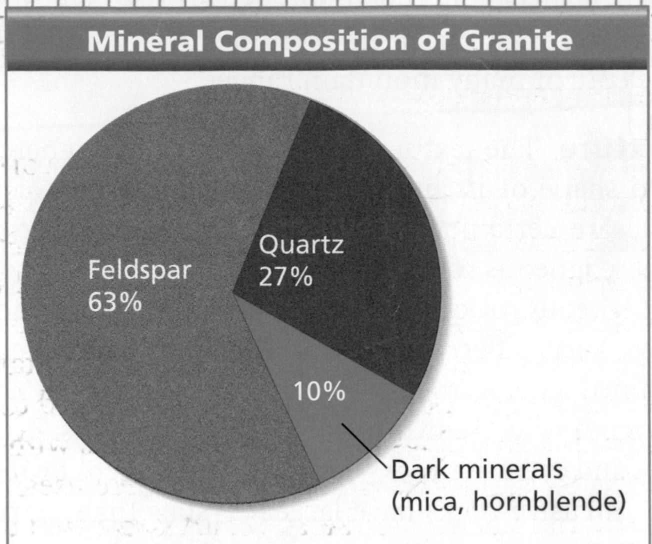


1. **Reading Graphs** What mineral is most abundant in granite?
2. **Reading Graphs** About what percentage of granite is made up of dark minerals?
3. **Calculating** If the amount of quartz increases to 35 percent and the amount of dark-colored minerals stays the same, what percentage of the granite will be made up of feldspar?
4. **Predicting** How would the color of the granite change if it contained less feldspar and more mica and hornblende?

**Mineral Composition** Most of Earth's minerals contain **silica,** a material formed from oxygen and silicon. The silica content of magma and lava affects the types of rock they form. Lava that is low in silica usually forms dark-colored rocks such as basalt. Basalt contains feldspar as well as certain dark-colored minerals, but does not contain quartz.

Magma that is high in silica usually forms light-colored rocks, such as granite. Granite's mineral composition determines its color—light gray, red, pink, or nearly black. Granite that is rich in reddish feldspar is a speckled pink. But granite rich in hornblende and dark mica is light gray with dark specks. Quartz crystals in granite add light gray or smoky specks.

Geologists can make thin slices of a rock, such as the gabbro in Figure 7. They study the rock's crystals under a microscope to determine the rock's mineral composition.

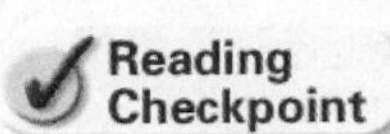


**What is silica?**

FIGURE 7
**Thin Section of a Rock**
This thin slice of gabbro, viewed under a microscope, contains olivine, feldspar, and other minerals.

## Uses of Igneous Rocks

Many igneous rocks are hard, dense, and durable. **People throughout history have used igneous rock for tools and building materials.**

**Building Materials** Granite has a long history as a building material. More than 3,500 years ago, the ancient Egyptians used granite for statues like the one shown in Figure 8. About 600 years ago, the Incas of Peru carefully fitted together great blocks of granite and other igneous rocks to build a fortress near Cuzco, their capital city. In the United States during the 1800s and early 1900s, granite was widely used to build bridges and public buildings and for paving streets with cobblestones. Today, thin, polished sheets of granite are used in curbstones, floors, and kitchen counters. Basalt is crushed to make gravel that is used in construction.

**Other Uses** Igneous rocks such as pumice and obsidian also have important uses. The rough surface of pumice makes it a good abrasive for cleaning and polishing. Ancient native Americans used obsidian to make sharp tools for cutting and scraping. Perlite, formed from the heating of obsidian, is often mixed with soil for starting vegetable seeds.

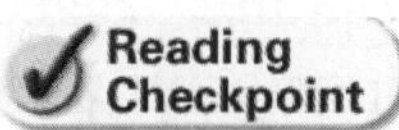

**What igneous rock is most often used as a building material?**

**FIGURE 8**
**Durable Granite**
The ancient Egyptians valued granite for its durability. These statues from a temple in Luxor, Egypt, were carved in granite.

## Section 2 Assessment

**Target Reading Skill Identifying Main Ideas** Use your graphic organizer about the characteristics of igneous rock to help you answer Question 1 below.

### Reviewing Key Concepts

1. a. **Explaining** How are igneous rocks classified?
   b. **Defining** What are extrusive rocks and intrusive rocks?
   c. **Comparing and Contrasting** Compare granite and basalt in terms of their origin and texture. Which is extrusive? Which is intrusive?
2. a. **Summarizing** What are two common uses of igneous rocks?
   b. **Reviewing** What characteristics make igneous rocks useful?
   c. **Making Judgments** Would pumice be a good material to use to make a floor? Explain.

### Lab zone At-Home Activity

**The Rocks Around Us** Many common household products contain minerals found in igneous rock. For example, glass contains quartz, which is found in granite. Research one of the following materials and the products in which it is used: garnet, granite, perlite, pumice, or vermiculite. Explain to family members how the rock or mineral formed and how it is used.

Section 3

# Sedimentary Rocks

## Reading Focus

### Key Concepts

- How do sedimentary rocks form?
- What are the three major types of sedimentary rocks?
- How are sedimentary rocks used?

### Key Terms

- sediment
- erosion
- deposition
- compaction
- cementation
- clastic rock
- organic rock
- chemical rock

### Target Reading Skill

**Outlining** As you read, make an outline about sedimentary rocks. Use the red section headings for the main topics and the blue headings for the subtopics.

**Sedimentary Rocks**

I. From sediment to rock
   A. Erosion
   B.
II.
   A.

## Lab zone Discover Activity

### How Does Pressure Affect Particles of Rock?

1. Place a sheet of paper over a slice of soft bread.
2. Put a stack of several heavy books on top of the paper. After 10 minutes, remove the books. Observe what happened to the bread.
3. Slice the bread so you can observe its cross section.
4. Carefully slice a piece of fresh bread and compare its cross section to that of the pressed bread.

**Think It Over**

**Observing** How did the bread change after you removed the books? Describe the texture of the bread. How does the bread feel? What can you predict about how pressure affects the particles that make up sedimentary rocks?

Visitors to Badlands National Park in South Dakota see some of the strangest scenery on Earth. The park contains jagged peaks, steep cliffs, and deep canyons sculpted in colorful rock that is layered like a birthday cake. The layers of this cake are red, orange, pink, yellow, or tan. These rocks formed over millions of years as particles of mud, sand, and volcanic ash were deposited in thick layers. The mud and sand slowly changed to sedimentary rock. Then, uplift of the land exposed the rocks to the forces that wear away Earth's surface.

Badlands National Park ▲

## From Sediment to Rock

If you have ever walked along a stream or beach you may have noticed tiny sand grains, mud, and pebbles. These are particles of sediment. **Sediment** is small, solid pieces of material that come from rocks or living things. In addition to particles of rock, sediment may include shells, bones, leaves, stems, and other remains of living things. Sedimentary rocks form when sediment is deposited by water and wind. **Most sedimentary rocks are formed through a series of processes: erosion, deposition, compaction, and cementation.** Figure 9 shows how sedimentary rocks form.

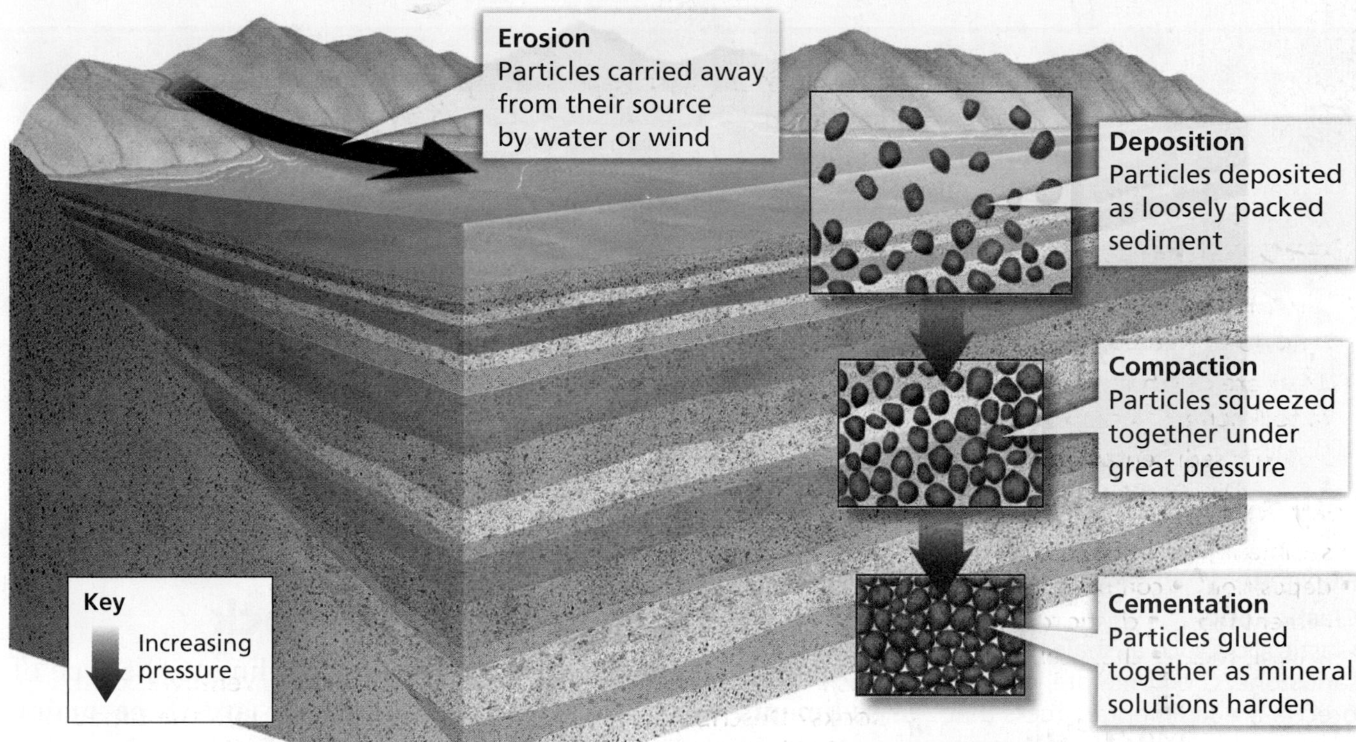
Erosion
Particles carried away from their source by water or wind
Deposition
Particles deposited as loosely packed sediment
Compaction
Particles squeezed together under great pressure
Cementation
Particles glued together as mineral solutions harden
Key
Increasing pressure

FIGURE 9
**How Sedimentary Rocks Form**
Sedimentary rocks form through the deposition, compaction, and cementation of sediments over millions of years.
**Relating Cause and Effect** *What conditions are necessary for sedimentary rocks to form?*

**Erosion** Destructive forces are constantly breaking up and wearing away all the rocks on Earth's surface. These forces include heat and cold, rain, waves, and grinding ice. The forces of erosion form sediment. In **erosion,** running water, wind, or ice loosen and carry away fragments of rock.

**Deposition** Eventually, the moving water, wind, or ice slows and deposits the sediment in layers. If water is carrying the sediment, rock fragments and other materials sink to the bottom of a lake or ocean. **Deposition** is the process by which sediment settles out of the water or wind carrying it.

**Compaction** The process that presses sediments together is **compaction.** Thick layers of sediment build up gradually over millions of years. These heavy layers press down on the layers beneath them. The weight of new layers further compacts the sediments, squeezing them tightly together. The layers often remain visible in sedimentary rock.

**Cementation** While compaction is taking place, the minerals in the rock slowly dissolve in the water. **Cementation** is the process in which dissolved minerals crystallize and glue particles of sediment together. In cementation, dissolved minerals seep into the spaces between particles and then harden.

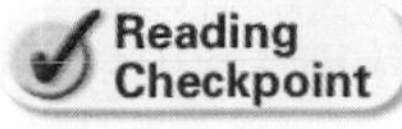
Reading Checkpoint
**What is deposition?**

Go Online
SCI LINKS
NSTA
**For:** Links on sedimentary rocks
**Visit:** www.SciLinks.org
**Web Code:** scn-1053

Clastic

**Shale**
Fossils are often found in shale, which splits easily into flat pieces.

**Sandstone**
Many small holes between sand grains allow sandstone to absorb water.

**Conglomerate**
Rock fragments with rounded edges make up conglomerate.

FIGURE 10
**Clastic Rocks**
Clastic rocks such as shale, sandstone, conglomerate, and breccia are sedimentary rocks that form from particles of other rocks.

# Types of Sedimentary Rock

Geologists classify sedimentary rocks according to the type of sediments that make up the rock. **There are three major groups of sedimentary rocks: clastic rocks, organic rocks, and chemical rocks.** Different processes form each of these types of sedimentary rocks.

**Clastic Rocks** Most sedimentary rocks are made up of broken pieces of other rocks. A **clastic rock** is a sedimentary rock that forms when rock fragments are squeezed together. These fragments can range in size from clay particles that are too small to be seen without a microscope to large boulders that are too heavy for you to lift. Clastic rocks are grouped by the size of the rock fragments, or particles, of which they are made. Common clastic rocks include shale, sandstone, conglomerate, and breccia (BRECH ee uh), shown in Figure 10.

Shale forms from tiny particles of clay. Water must deposit the clay particles in thin, flat layers. Sandstone forms from the sand on beaches, the ocean floor, riverbeds, and sand dunes. Most sand particles consist of quartz.

Some sedimentary rocks contain a mixture of rock fragments of different sizes. If the fragments have rounded edges, they form a clastic rock called conglomerate. A rock made up of large fragments with sharp edges is called breccia.

**Organic Rocks** Not all sedimentary rocks are made from particles of other rocks. **Organic rock** forms where the remains of plants and animals are deposited in thick layers. The term "organic" refers to substances that once were part of living things or were made by living things. Two important organic sedimentary rocks are coal and limestone, shown in Figure 11.

**Lab zone Try This Activity**

### Rock Absorber

Here's how to find out if water can soak into rock.

1. Using a hand lens, compare samples of sandstone and shale.
2. Use a balance to measure the mass of each rock.
3. Place the rocks in a pan of water and watch closely. Which sample has bubbles escaping? Predict which sample will gain mass.
4. Leave the rocks submerged in the pan overnight.
5. The next day, remove the rocks from the pan and find the mass of each rock.

**Drawing Conclusions** How did the masses of the two rocks change after soaking? What can you conclude about each rock?

## Organic

Breccia
Rock fragments with sharp edges form breccia.

Coal
Swamp plants that formed millions of years ago slowly changed to form coal.

Limestone
Coquina is a form of limestone in which the shells that makeup the rock are easy to see.


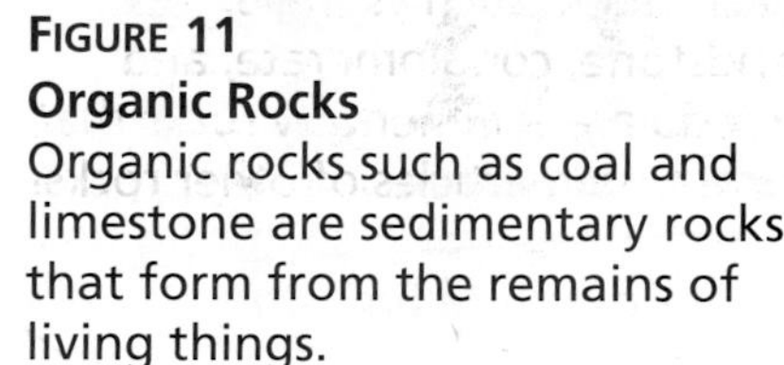

FIGURE 11
**Organic Rocks**
Organic rocks such as coal and limestone are sedimentary rocks that form from the remains of living things.

Coal forms from the remains of swamp plants buried in water. As layer upon layer of plant remains build up, the weight of the layers squeezes the decaying plants. Over millions of years, they slowly change into coal.

Limestone forms in the ocean, where many living things, such as coral, clams, and oysters, have hard shells or skeletons made of calcite. When these animals die, their shells pile up on the ocean floor. Over millions of years, these layers of sediment can grow to a depth of hundreds of meters. Slowly, compaction and cementation change the sediment to limestone.

**Chemical Rocks** When minerals that are dissolved in a solution crystallize, **chemical rock** forms. For example, limestone can form when calcite that is dissolved in lakes, seas, or underground water comes out of solution and forms crystals. This kind of limestone is considered a chemical rock. Chemical rocks can also form from mineral deposits left when seas or lakes evaporate. For example, rock salt is made of the mineral halite, which forms by evaporation.

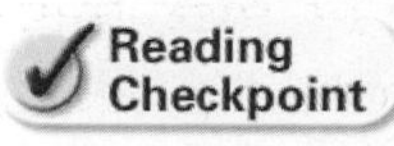


**How does coal form?**

FIGURE 12
**Chemical Rocks**
These rock "towers" in Mono Lake California, are made of tufa, a form of limestone. Tufa is a chemical rock that forms from solutions containing dissolved materials. **Classifying** *What type of sedimentary rock is tufa?*

**FIGURE 13**
**Carving Limestone**
This stone carver is sculpting designs on a sphere of white limestone.

## Uses of Sedimentary Rocks

**People have used sedimentary rocks throughout history for many different purposes, including building materials and tools.** For example, people made arrowheads out of flint for thousands of years. Flint is a hard rock, yet it can be shaped to a point. Flint is formed when small particles of silica settle out of water.

Sedimentary rocks such as sandstone and limestone have been used as building materials for thousands of years. Both types of stone are soft enough to be cut easily into blocks or slabs. You may be surprised to learn that the White House in Washington, D.C., is built of sandstone. Builders today use sandstone and limestone on the outside walls of buildings. Limestone also has many industrial uses. For example, limestone is used in making cement and steel.

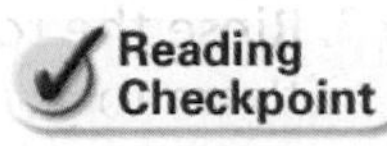

**Why are sandstone and limestone useful as building materials?**

## Section 3 Assessment

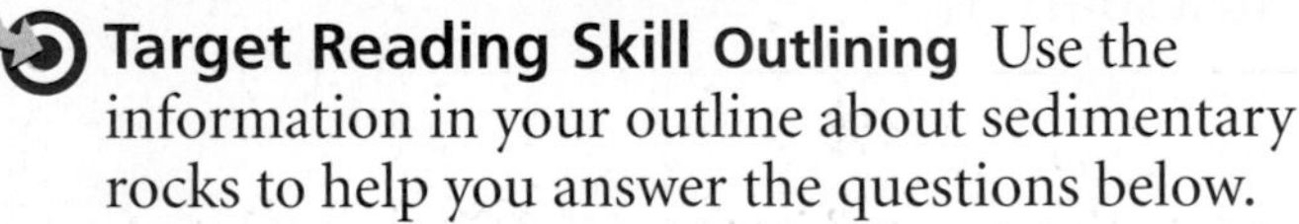

**Target Reading Skill Outlining** Use the information in your outline about sedimentary rocks to help you answer the questions below.

### Reviewing Key Concepts

1. a. **Defining** What is sediment?
   b. **Sequencing** Place these steps in the formation of sedimentary rock in the proper sequence: compaction, erosion, cementation, deposition.
   c. **Inferring** In layers of sedimentary rock, where would you expect to find the oldest sediment? Explain your answer.
2. a. **Listing** What are the three main types of sedimentary rock?
   b. **Explaining** Which type of sedimentary rock forms from the remains of living things? Explain how this sedimentary rock forms.
   c. **Relating Cause and Effect** What process causes deposits of rock salt to form? What type of sedimentary rock is rock salt?
3. a. **Listing** What are some uses of sedimentary rocks?
   b. **Predicting** The particles of sediment that make up shale are not usually well cemented. Would shale be a good choice of building material in a wet climate?

### Writing in Science

**Explaining a Process** Suppose that a large mass of granite lies exposed on Earth's surface. Explain the steps in the process by which the granite could become sedimentary rock. Your answer should also state which of the main types of sedimentary rock will result from this process.

Section 4

Integrating Life Science

# Rocks From Reefs

## Reading Focus

### Key Concepts

- How do coral reefs form?
- What evidence do limestone deposits from coral reefs provide about Earth's history?

### Key Term

- coral reef

### Target Reading Skill

**Using Prior Knowledge**

Before you read, look at the section headings to see what this section is about. Then write what you know about coral reefs in a graphic organizer like the one below. As you read, write what you learn.

| What You Know |
|---|
| 1. Coral reefs grow in the oceans.<br>2. |

| What You Learned |
|---|
| 1.<br>2. |

## Lab zone Discover Activity

### How Does a Rock React to Acid?

1. Using a hand lens, observe the color and texture of limestone and coquina.
2. Put on your goggles and apron.
3. Obtain a small amount of dilute hydrochloric acid from your teacher. Hydrochloric acid is used to test rocks for the presence of the mineral calcite. Using a plastic dropper, place a few drops of dilute hydrochloric acid on the limestone. **CAUTION:** *Hydrochloric acid can cause burns.*
4. Record your observations.
5. Repeat Steps 2 through 4 with the sample of coquina and observe the results.
6. Rinse the rock samples with lots of water before returning them to your teacher. Wash your hands.

**Think It Over**

**Drawing Conclusions** How did the two rocks react to the test? A piece of coral reacts to hydrochloric acid the same way as limestone and coquina. What could you conclude about the mineral composition of coral?

Off the coast of Florida lies a "city" in the sea. It is a coral reef providing both food and shelter for many sea animals. The reef shimmers with life—clams, sponges, sea urchins, starfish, marine worms and, of course, fish. Schools of brilliantly colored fish dart in and out of forests of equally colorful corals. Octopuses lurk in underwater caves, scooping up crabs that pass too close. A reef forms a sturdy wall that protects the shoreline from battering waves. This city was built by billions of tiny, soft-bodied animals that have skeletons made of calcite.

**FIGURE 14**
**A City in the Sea**
A coral reef provides food and shelter for many different kinds of living things.

For: More on coral landforms
Visit: PHSchool.com
Web Code: cfd-1054

## Coral Reefs

Coral animals are tiny relatives of jellyfish that live together in vast numbers. They produce skeletons that grow together to form a structure called a **coral reef.**

**How Coral Animals Live** Most coral animals are smaller than your fingernail. Each one looks like a small sack with a mouth surrounded by tentacles. These animals use their tentacles to capture and eat microscopic creatures that float by.

Tiny algae grow within the body of each coral animal. The algae provide substances that the coral animals need to live. In turn, the coral animals provide a framework for the algae to grow on. Like plants, algae need sunlight. Below 40 meters, there is not enough light for the algae to grow. For this reason, almost all coral growth occurs within 40 meters of the water's surface.

**How a Coral Reef Forms** To form their skeletons, coral animals absorb the element calcium from the ocean water. The calcium is then combined with carbon and oxygen to form calcite. Recall that calcite is a mineral. **When coral animals die, their skeletons remain. More corals build on top of them, gradually forming a coral reef.**

Coral animals cannot grow in cold water. As a result, coral reefs form only in the warm, shallow water of tropical oceans. Reefs are most abundant around islands and along the eastern coasts of continents. In the United States, only the coasts of southern Florida and Hawaii have coral reefs.

Over thousands of years, reefs may grow to be hundreds of kilometers long and hundreds of meters thick. Reefs usually grow outward toward the open ocean. If the sea level rises or if the sea floor sinks, the reef will grow upward, too.

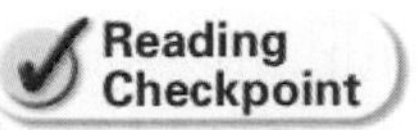


**What conditions of light and temperature do coral animals require?**

FIGURE 15
**Coral Animals and Reefs**
The coral animals in the close-up feed on tiny organisms carried their way by the movement of ocean water. (The view has been magnified to show detail.) The aerial photograph shows an island in the South Pacific Ocean that is ringed by a coral reef (light blue areas). **Inferring** *Why are there no coral reefs in the dark blue areas of ocean water?*

## Limestone From Coral Reefs

A coral reef is really organic limestone. **Limestone deposits that began as coral reefs provide evidence of how Earth's surface has changed. These deposits also provide evidence of past environments.**

Limestone from coral reefs has been forming in Earth's oceans for more than 400 million years. The limestone formed when shallow seas covered the low-lying parts of the continents. The limestone was exposed when the seas retreated. In the United States, reefs that formed millions of years ago are exposed in Wisconsin, Illinois, Indiana, Texas, New Mexico, and many other places.

Deposits of organic limestone help geologists understand past environments. Where geologists find fossils of an ancient coral reef, they know that the reef formed in an area with a warm climate and shallow ocean water. In North America, these conditions existed for millions of years when much of the continent lay closer to the equator than it does today. Shallow seas covered the central part of North America, allowing large coral reefs to form. Today, the reefs are thick deposits of sedimentary rock.

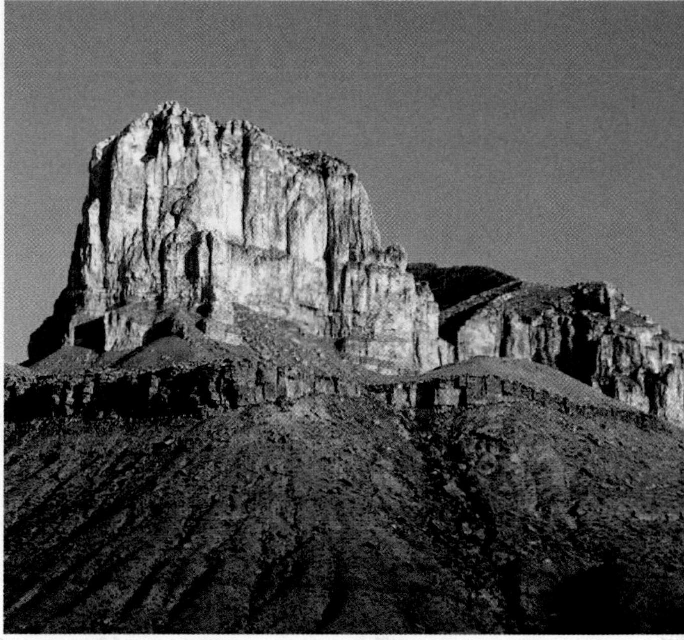

**FIGURE 16**
**Limestone From Coral**
A band of light-colored limestone marks an ancient reef that forms part of Guadalupe Peak in Texas. This reef is now 2,600 meters above sea level!

## Section 4 Assessment

**Target Reading Skill Using Prior Knowledge** Review your graphic organizer about coral reefs and revise it based on what you just learned.

### Reviewing Key Concepts

1. a. **Describing** What is a coral animal?
   b. **Summarizing** How do coral animals build a coral reef?
   c. **Predicting** If sea level rises above a coral reef, what may happen to the reef?
2. a. **Identifying** What type of rock is made up of ancient coral?
   b. **Inferring** A geologist finds an area where the rocks were formed from an ancient coral reef. What can the geologist infer about the ancient environment where the rocks formed?

### Lab zone At-Home Activity

**Earth's Coral Reefs** Obtain a globe or world map. Find the lines that represent the tropic of Cancer and the tropic of Capricorn. The area that lies between these two lines, called the Tropics, is where most coral reefs form in warm ocean water. Locate the northeast coast of Australia, the Red Sea, and groups of tropical islands in the Caribbean Sea, Indian Ocean, and Pacific Ocean. Point out these features to family members and explain that these are areas where coral reefs occur today.

Section 5

# Metamorphic Rocks

## Reading Preview

### Key Concepts

- Under what conditions do metamorphic rocks form?
- How do geologists classify metamorphic rocks?
- How are metamorphic rocks used?

### Key Term

- foliated

### Target Reading Skill

**Previewing Visuals** Before you read, preview Figure 17. Then write two questions that you have about metamorphic rocks in a graphic organizer like the one below. As you read, answer your questions.

**Metamorphic Rocks**

| |
|---|
| **Q.** Why do the crystals in gneiss line up in bands? |
| **A.** |
| **Q.** |

**For:** Links on metamorphic rocks
**Visit:** www.SciLinks.org
**Web Code:** scn-1055

## Lab zone Discover Activity

### How Do Grain Patterns Compare?

1. Using a hand lens, observe samples of gneiss and granite. Look carefully at the grains or crystals in both rocks.
2. Observe how the grains or crystals are arranged in both rocks. Draw a sketch of both rocks and describe their textures.

**Think It Over**

**Inferring** Within the crust, some granite becomes gneiss. What do you think must happen to cause this change?

Every metamorphic rock is a rock that has changed its form. In fact, the word *metamorphic* comes from the Greek words *meta*, meaning "change," and *morphosis*, meaning "form." But what causes a rock to change into metamorphic rock? The answer lies inside Earth.

**Heat and pressure deep beneath Earth's surface can change any rock into metamorphic rock.** When rock changes into metamorphic rock, its appearance, texture, crystal structure, and mineral content change. Metamorphic rock can form out of igneous, sedimentary, or other metamorphic rock.

Sometimes, forces inside Earth can push the rock down toward the heat of the mantle. Pockets of magma rising through the crust also provide heat that can produce metamorphic rocks. The deeper a rock is buried, the greater the pressure on that rock. Under high temperature and pressure many times greater than at Earth's surface, the minerals in a rock can be changed into other minerals. The rock has become a metamorphic rock.

## Types of Metamorphic Rocks

While metamorphic rocks are forming, high temperatures change the size and shape of the grains, or mineral crystals, in the rock. Extreme pressure squeezes rock so tightly that the mineral grains may line up in flat, parallel layers. **Geologists classify metamorphic rocks according to the arrangement of the grains that make up the rocks.**

**Foliated Rocks** Metamorphic rocks that have their grains arranged in parallel layers or bands are said to be **foliated.** The term *foliated* comes from the Latin word for "leaf." It describes the thin, flat layering found in most metamorphic rocks. Foliated rocks—including slate, schist, and gneiss—may split apart along these bands. In Figure 17, notice how the crystals in granite have been flattened to create the foliated texture of gneiss.

One common foliated rock is slate. Heat and pressure change the sedimentary rock shale into slate. Slate is basically a denser, more compact version of shale. During the change, new minerals such as mica form in the slate.

**Nonfoliated Rocks** Some metamorphic rocks are nonfoliated. The mineral grains in these rocks are arranged randomly. Metamorphic rocks that are nonfoliated do not split into layers. Marble and quartzite are two metamorphic rocks that have a nonfoliated texture. Quartzite forms out of sandstone. The weakly cemented quartz particles in the sandstone recrystallize to form quartzite, which is extremely hard. Notice in Figure 17 how much smoother quartzite looks than sandstone.

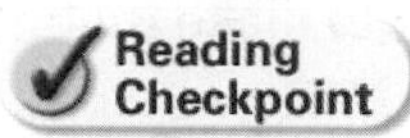

**What is a foliated rock?**

## Lab zone Try This **Activity**

### A Sequined Rock

1. Make three balls of clay about 3 cm in diameter. Gently mix about 25 sequins into one ball.
2. Use a 30-cm piece of string to cut the ball in half. How are the sequins arranged?
3. Roll the clay with the sequins back into a ball. Stack the three balls with the sequin ball in the middle. Set these on a block of wood. With another block of wood, press slowly down until the stack is about 3 cm high.
4. Use the string to cut the stack in half. How are the sequins arranged?

**Making Models** What do the sequins in your model rock represent? Is this rock foliated or nonfoliated?

FIGURE 17
**Forming Metamorphic Rocks**
Great heat and pressure can change one type of rock into another. **Observing** *How does slate differ from shale?*

**Granite**
igneous

Heat and pressure

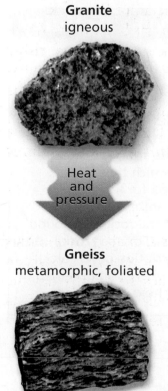

**Gneiss**
metamorphic, foliated

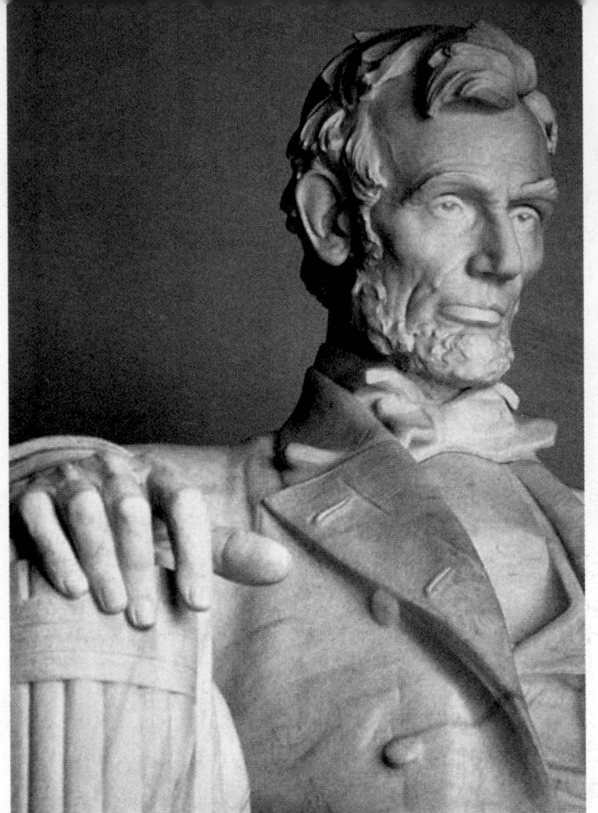

**FIGURE 18**
**The Lincoln Memorial**
The statue of Abraham Lincoln in the Lincoln Memorial in Washington, D.C., is made of gleaming white marble.

## Uses of Metamorphic Rock

**Certain metamorphic rocks are important materials for building and sculpture.** Marble and slate are two of the most useful metamorphic rocks. Marble usually forms when limestone is subjected to heat and pressure deep beneath the surface. Because marble has a fine, even grain, it can be cut into thin slabs or carved into many shapes. And marble is easy to polish. These qualities have led architects and sculptors to use marble for many buildings and statues. For example, one of America's most famous sculptures is in the Lincoln Memorial in Washington, D.C. Sculptor Daniel Chester French carved this portrait of Abraham Lincoln in gleaming white marble.

Like marble, slate comes in a variety of colors, including gray, black, red, and purple. Because it is foliated, slate splits easily into flat pieces. These pieces can be used for flooring, roofing, outdoor walkways, chalkboards, and as trim for stone buildings.

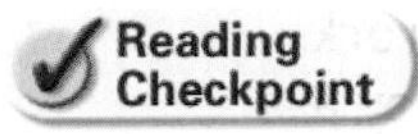

**What characteristics of slate make it useful?**

## Section 5 Assessment

**Target Reading Skill Previewing Visuals** Compare your questions and answers about Figure 17 with those of a partner.

### Reviewing Key Concepts

1. a. **Explaining** What does *metamorphic* mean?
   b. **Relating Cause and Effect** Where and under what conditions are metamorphic rocks formed?
2. a. **Identifying** What characteristic of metamorphic rocks do geologists use to classify them?
   b. **Explaining** How does a foliated metamorphic rock form?
   c. **Classifying** Which of the rocks in Figure 17 is foliated? How can you tell?
3. a. **Identifying** What is the main use of metamorphic rocks?
   b. **Making Judgments** Which might be more useful for carving chess pieces—marble or slate? Explain your answer.

### Lab zone At-Home Activity

**Rocks Around the Block** How are rocks used in your neighborhood? Take a walk with your family to see how many uses you can observe. Identify statues, walls, and buildings made from rocks. Can you identify which type of rock was used? Look for limestone, sandstone, granite, and marble. Share a list of the rocks you found with your class. For each rock, include a description of its color and texture, where you observed the rock, and how it was used.

Lab zone **Skills Lab**

# Mystery Rocks

## Problem

What properties can be used to classify rocks?

## Skills Focus

inferring, classifying

## Materials

- 1 "mystery rock"
- 2 unknown igneous rocks
- 2 unknown sedimentary rocks
- 2 unknown metamorphic rocks
- hand lens

## Procedure 

1. For this activity, you will be given six rocks and one sample that is not a rock. They are labeled A through G.
2. Copy the data table into your notebook.
3. Using the hand lens, examine each rock for clues that show the rock formed from molten material. Record the rock's color and texture. Observe if there are any crystals or grains in the rock.
4. Use the hand lens to look for clues that show the rock formed from particles of other rocks. Observe the texture of the rock to see if it has any tiny, well-rounded grains.
5. Use the hand lens to look for clues that show the rock formed under heat and pressure. Observe if the rock has a flat layer of crystals or shows colored bands.
6. Record your observations in the data table.

| Data Table | | | | |
|---|---|---|---|---|
| Sample | Color | Texture (fine, medium, or coarse-grained) | Foliated or Banded | Rock Group (igneous, metamorphic, sedimentary) |
| A | | | | |
| B | | | | |
| | | | | |

## Analyze and Conclude

1. **Inferring** Infer from your observations the group in which each rock belongs.
2. **Classifying** Which of the samples could be classified as igneous rocks? What physical properties do these rocks share with the other samples? How are they different?
3. **Classifying** Which of the samples could be classified as sedimentary rocks? How do you think these rocks formed? What are the physical properties of these rocks?
4. **Classifying** Which of the samples could be classified as metamorphic rocks? What are their physical properties?
5. **Drawing Conclusions** Decide which sample is not a rock. How did you determine that the sample you chose is not a rock? What do you think the "mystery rock" is? Explain.
6. **Communicating** What physical property was most useful in classifying rocks? Which physical property was least useful? Explain your answer.

## More to Explore

Can you name each rock? Use a field guide to rocks and minerals to find the specific name of each rock sample.

Section 6

# The Rock Cycle

## Reading Preview

### Key Concepts

- What is the rock cycle?

### Key Term

- rock cycle

### Target Reading Skill

**Sequencing** As you read, make a cycle diagram that shows the stages in the rock cycle. Write each stage of the rock cycle in a separate circle in your diagram.

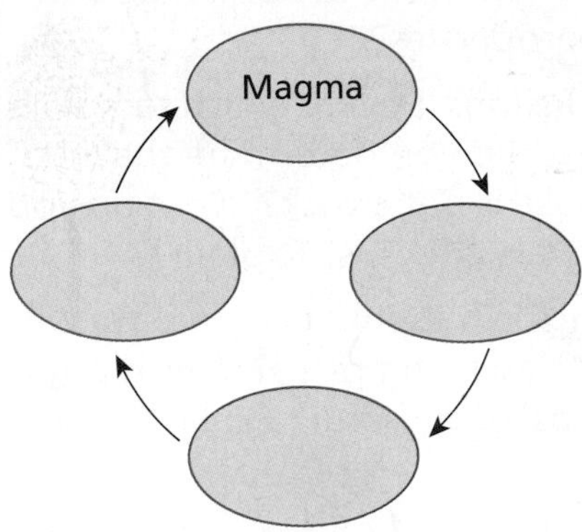


## Lab zone Discover Activity

### Which Rock Came First?

1. Referring to the photos below, make sketches of quartzite, granite, and sandstone on three index cards.
2. Observe the color and texture of each rock. Look for similarities and differences.
3. To which major group does each rock belong?

**Think It Over**

**Developing Hypotheses** How are quartzite, granite, and sandstone related? Arrange your cards in the order in which these three rocks formed. Given enough time in Earth's crust, what might happen to the third rock in your series?

**Sandstone** **Quartzite** **Granite**

Earth's rocks are not as unchanging as they seem. **Forces deep inside Earth and at the surface produce a slow cycle that builds, destroys, and changes the rocks in the crust.** The **rock cycle** is a series of processes on Earth's surface and in the crust and mantle that slowly change rocks from one kind to another.

## A Cycle of Many Pathways

As shown in Figure 19, the rock cycle can follow many different pathways. To take one pathway as an example, you can follow the rock of Stone Mountain, Georgia, through the rock cycle.

**Beginning the Rock Cycle** In the case of Stone Mountain, the rock cycle began millions of years ago. First, a huge mass of granite formed deep beneath Earth's surface. Then the forces of mountain building slowly pushed the granite upward. Over millions of years, water and weather began to wear away the granite of Stone Mountain, forming sediment. Today, particles of granite sediment still break off the mountain and become sand. Streams carry the sand to the ocean.

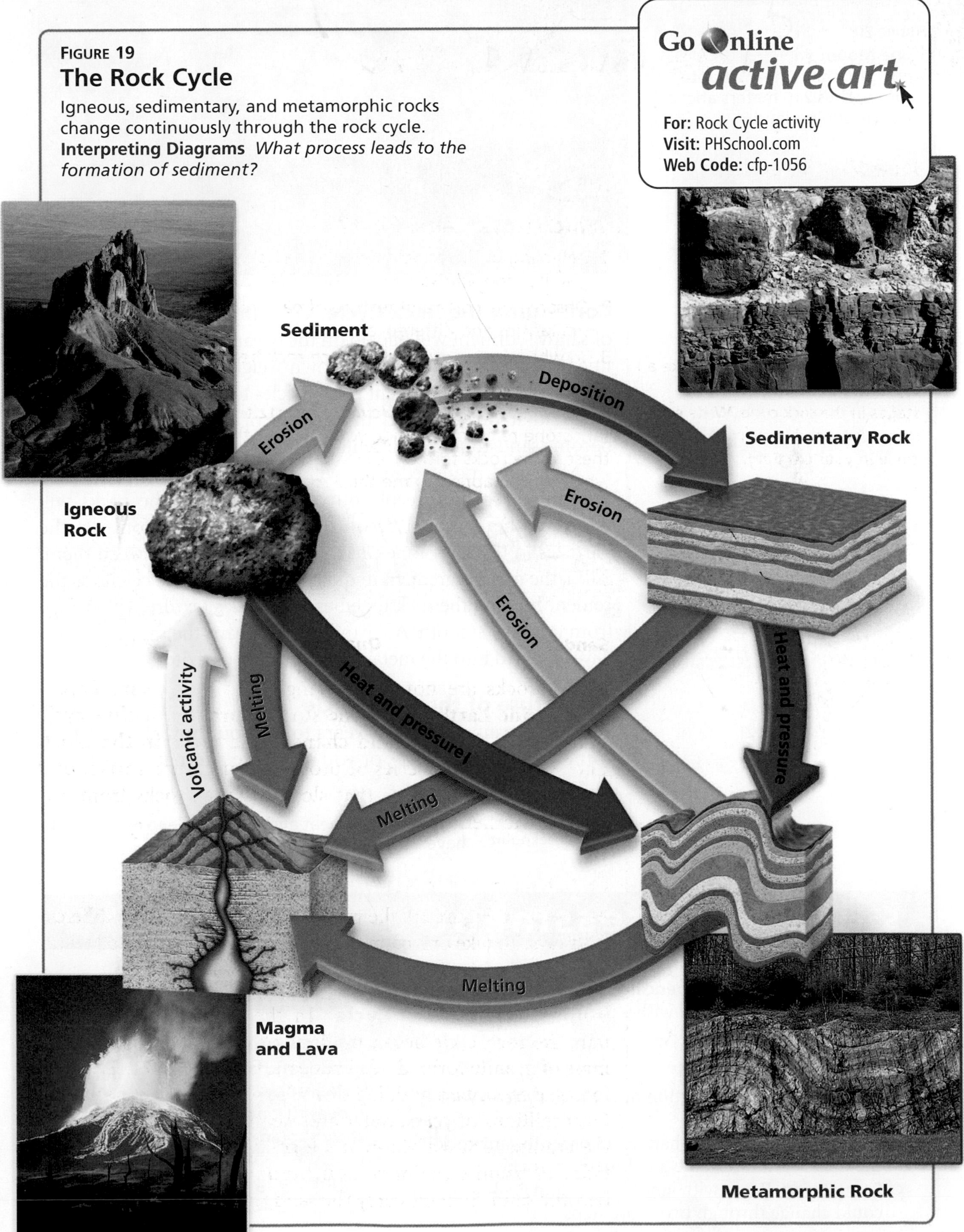


FIGURE 19
## The Rock Cycle
Igneous, sedimentary, and metamorphic rocks change continuously through the rock cycle. **Interpreting Diagrams** *What process leads to the formation of sediment?*

**FIGURE 20**
**Stone Mountain**
Stone Mountain, near Atlanta, Georgia, rises 210 meters above the surrounding land.

**Continuing the Rock Cycle** Over millions of years, layers of sandy sediment will pile up on the ocean floor. Slowly, the sediment will be compacted by its own weight. Dissolved calcite in the ocean water will cement the particles together. Eventually, the quartz that once formed the granite of Stone Mountain will become sandstone, a sedimentary rock.

More and more sediment will pile up on the sandstone. As sandstone becomes deeply buried, pressure on the rocks will increase. The rock will become hot. Pressure will compact the particles in the sandstone until no spaces are left between them. Silica, the main ingredient in quartz, will replace the calcite as the cement holding the rock together. The rock's texture will change from gritty to smooth. After millions of years, the sandstone will have changed into the metamorphic rock quartzite.

**The Future of the Rock Cycle** What will happen next? You could wait millions of years to find out how the quartzite completes the rock cycle, or you can trace alternative pathways in Figure 19.

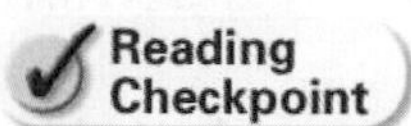


**What effect do heat and pressure deep inside Earth have on sandstone?**

## Section 6 Assessment

**Target Reading Skill Sequencing** Review your cycle diagram about the rock cycle with a partner. Add any necessary information.

### Reviewing Key Concepts

1. a. **Defining** Write a definition of the rock cycle in your own words.
   b. **Explaining** What must happen in order for any rock in the rock cycle to become a sedimentary rock?
   c. **Sequencing** Begin with igneous rock and explain how it could change through two more steps in the rock cycle.

### Writing in Science

**Rock Legend** Pick one type of rock and write a possible "biography" of the rock as it moves through the rock cycle. Your story should state the type of rock, how the rock formed, and how it might change.

Lab zone **Design Your Own Lab**

# Testing Rock Flooring

## Problem

What kind of building stone makes the best flooring?

## Skills Focus

designing experiments, controlling variables, drawing conclusions

## Suggested Materials

- steel nail • wire brush • water
- plastic dropper • hand lens
- samples of igneous, sedimentary, and metamorphic rocks with flat surfaces
- greasy materials such as butter and crayons
- materials that form stains, such as ink and paints

## Procedure 

1. Brainstorm with your partner the qualities of good flooring. For example, good flooring should resist stains, scratches, and grease marks, and be safe to walk on when wet.
2. Predict what you think is the best building stone for a kitchen floor. Why is it the best?
3. Write the steps you plan to follow in answering the problem question. As you design your plan, consider the following factors:
   - What igneous, sedimentary, and metamorphic rocks will you test? (Pick at least one rock from each group.)
   - What materials or equipment will you need to acquire, and in what amounts?
   - What tests will you perform on the samples?
   - How will you control the variables in each test?
   - How will you measure each sample's resistance to staining, grease, and scratches?
   - How will you measure slipperiness?
4. Review your plan. Will it lead to an answer to the problem question?
5. Check your procedure and safety plan with your teacher.
6. Create a data table that includes a column in which you predict how each material will perform in each test.

## Analyze and Conclude

1. **Interpreting Data** Which material performed the best on each test? Which performed the worst on each test?
2. **Drawing Conclusions** Which material is best for the kitchen flooring? Which material would you least want to use?
3. **Drawing Conclusions** Do your answers support your initial prediction? Why or why not?
4. **Applying Concepts** The person installing the floor might want stone that is easy to cut to the correct size or shape. What other qualities would matter to the flooring installer?
5. **Communicating** Based on your results, write an advertisement for the building stone that performed best as a flooring material.

## Design an Experiment

Suppose you are trying to select flooring material for a laboratory where heavy equipment is frequently moved across the floor. Make a hypothesis predicting which type of stone flooring will be strongest. Then design an experiment to compare how well each type resists breakage.

Chapter 4

# Study Guide

**The BIG Idea**

**Cycles of Matter and Energy** Earth's crust is made up of igneous, sedimentary, and metamorphic rocks. Rocks are formed through the rock cycle, a series of processes on and beneath Earth's surface.

## 1 Classifying Rocks

### Key Concepts

- When studying a rock sample, geologists observe the rock's mineral composition, color, and texture.
- Geologists classify rocks into three major groups: igneous rock, sedimentary rock, and metamorphic rock.

### Key Terms

rock-forming mineral
granite
basalt
grains
texture
igneous rock
sedimentary rock
metamorphic rock

## 2 Igneous Rocks

### Key Concepts

- Igneous rocks are classified according to their origin, texture, and mineral composition.
- People throughout history have used igneous rock for tools and building materials.

### Key Terms

• extrusive rock • intrusive rock • silica

## 3 Sedimentary Rocks

### Key Concepts

- Most sedimentary rocks are formed through a series of processes: erosion, deposition, compaction, and cementation.
- There are three major groups of sedimentary rocks: clastic rocks, organic rocks, and chemical rocks.
- People have used sedimentary rocks throughout history for many different purposes, including building materials and tools.

### Key Terms

sediment
erosion
deposition
compaction
cementation
clastic rock
organic rock
chemical rock

## 4 Rocks From Reefs

### Key Concepts

- When coral animals die, their skeletons remain. More corals build on top of them, gradually forming a reef.
- Limestone deposits that began as coral reefs provide evidence of how Earth's surface has changed. These deposits also provide evidence of past environments.

### Key Term

coral reef

## 5 Metamorphic Rocks

### Key Concepts

- Heat and pressure deep beneath Earth's surface can change any rock into metamorphic rock.
- Geologists classify metamorphic rocks according to the arrangement of the grains that make up the rocks.
- Certain metamorphic rocks are important materials for building and sculpture.

### Key Term

foliated

## 6 The Rock Cycle

### Key Concepts

- Forces deep inside Earth and at the surface produce a slow cycle that builds, destroys, and changes the rocks in the crust.

### Key Term

rock cycle

# Review and Assessment

For: Self-Assessment
Visit: PHSchool.com
Web Code: cja-1040

## Organizing Information

**Concept Mapping** Copy the concept map about classifying rocks onto a separate sheet of paper. Then complete it and give it a title. (For more on concept maps, see the Skills Handbook.)

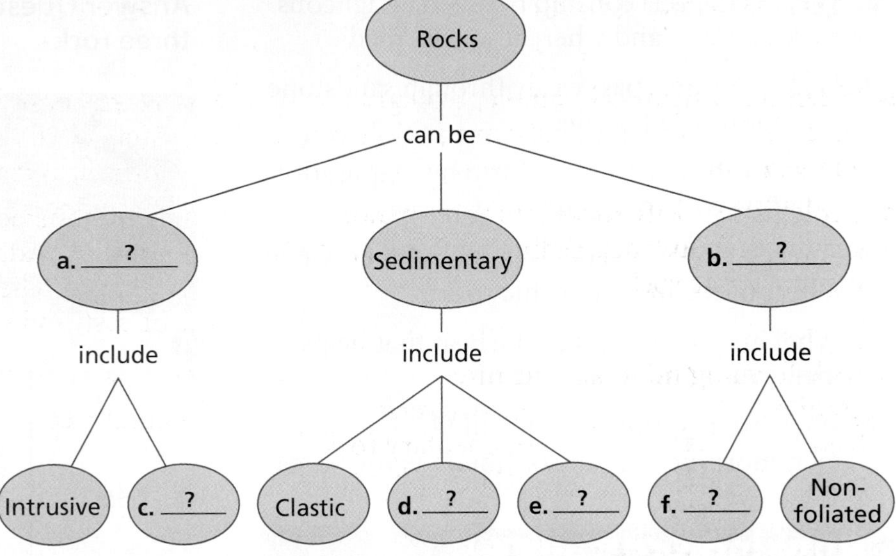


## Reviewing Key Terms

**Choose the letter of the best answer.**

1. A rock formed from fragments of other rocks is a(n)
   **a.** metamorphic rock. **b.** extrusive rock.
   **c.** sedimentary rock. **d.** igneous rock.

2. An igneous rock containing large crystals is most likely a(n)
   **a.** chemical rock. **b.** extrusive rock.
   **c.** foliated rock. **d.** intrusive rock.

3. A sedimentary rock formed from pieces of other rocks is called a(n)
   **a.** organic rock. **b.** chemical rock.
   **c.** clastic rock. **d.** compacted rock.

4. A deposit of organic limestone on land probably formed millions of years ago as a(n)
   **a.** extrusive rock. **b.** coral reef.
   **c.** chemical rock. **d.** metamorphic rock.

5. A metamorphic rock in which the grains line up in parallel bands is a
   **a.** clastic rock. **b.** nonclastic rock.
   **c.** nonfoliated rock. **d.** foliated rock.

6. In the rock cycle, the process by which an igneous rock changes to a sedimentary rock must begin with
   **a.** cementation.
   **b.** deposition.
   **c.** erosion.
   **d.** compaction.

## Writing in Science

**Field Guide** Research and write a field guide for geologists and visitors to an area such as the Grand Canyon. Describe the types of rocks you might find there, what the rocks look like, and what their properties are. Briefly explain the kinds of forces that shaped the rocks in the area you chose.

*Rocks*
Video Preview
Video Field Trip
▶ Video Assessment

# Review and Assessment

## Checking Concepts

7. What is the relationship between an igneous rock's texture and where it was formed?
8. Why can water pass easily through sandstone but not through shale?
9. Describe how a rock can form by evaporation. What type of rock is it?
10. How do the properties of a rock change when it becomes a metamorphic rock?
11. What are the sources of the heat that helps metamorphic rocks to form?
12. What are two things that could happen to a metamorphic rock to continue the rock cycle?

## Thinking Critically

13. **Developing Hypotheses** The sedimentary rocks limestone and sandstone are used as building materials. However, they wear away more rapidly than marble and quartzite, the metamorphic rocks that are formed from them. Why do you think this is so?
14. **Inferring** A geologist finds an area where the rocks are layers of coal and shale as shown in the diagram below. What kind of environment probably existed in this area millions of years ago when these rocks formed?

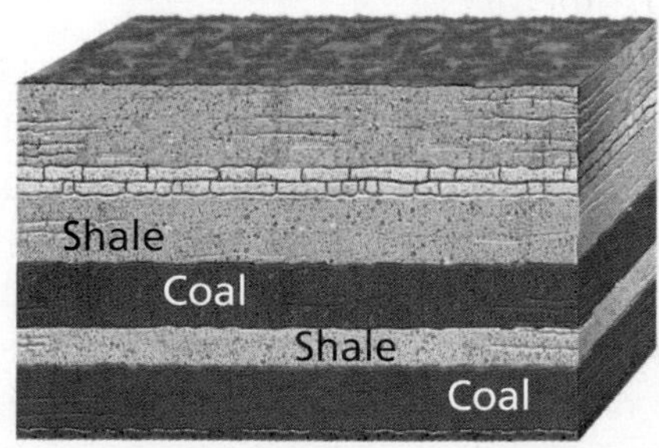


15. **Comparing and Contrasting** How are clastic rocks and organic rocks similar? How are they different?
16. **Predicting** Would you be less likely to find fossils in metamorphic rocks than in sedimentary rocks? Explain your answer.

## Applying Skills

**Answer Questions 17–20 using the photos of three rocks.**

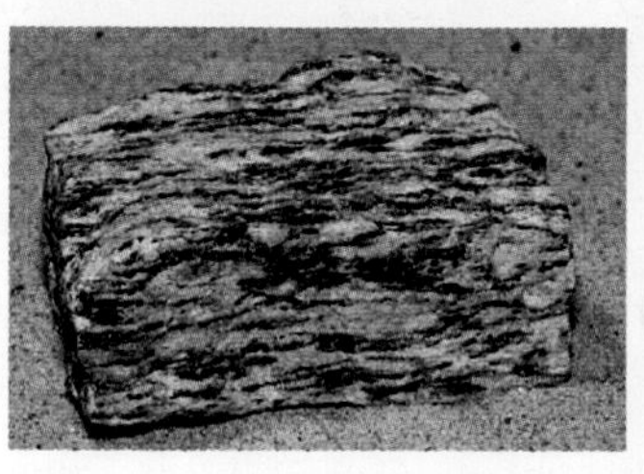

A

B

C

17. **Observing** How would you describe the texture of each rock?
18. **Classifying** Which of the three rocks would you classify as a metamorphic rock? Why?
19. **Inferring** A rock's texture gives clues about how the rock formed. What can you infer about the process by which Rock B formed?
20. **Relating Cause and Effect** What conditions led to the formation of the large crystals in Rock C? Explain your answer.

## Lab zone Chapter Project

**Performance Assessment** Construct a simple display for your rocks. It should show your classification for each rock sample. In your presentation, describe where you hunted and what kinds of rocks you found. Were any rocks hard to classify? Did you find rocks from each of the three major groups? Can you think of any reason why certain types of rocks would not be found in your area?

# Standardized Test Prep

**Test-Taking Tip**

**Watching for Qualifiers**

Many multiple-choice questions use qualifying words such as *most, least, best,* or *always.* For example, you might be asked what is the best conclusion you can draw from experimental data. When you answer that kind of question, read the choices very carefully. Some answers may be partially correct. Look for the best and most complete answer.

***Sample Question***

Which statement best describes how an intrusive igneous rock forms?

**A** Slowly cooling magma forms rock with large crystals.
**B** Slowly cooling magma forms veins of ore.
**C** Slowly cooling magma forms rock with small crystals.
**D** Fast-cooling magma forms rock with foliated crystals.

***Answer***

**A** is correct. An intrusive igneous rock forms when magma cools slowly, allowing large crystals to form. **B** and **C** are only partly correct. **D** incorrectly identifies the type of magma involved and the type of crystals that form.

**Choose the letter of the best answer.**

**1.** You find a rock in which the grains are arranged in parallel bands of white and black crystals. The rock is probably a(n)
**A** igneous rock.
**B** sedimentary rock.
**C** metamorphic rock.
**D** reef rock.

**2.** Many sedimentary rocks have visible layers because of the process of
**F** eruption.
**G** deposition.
**H** intrusion.
**J** crystallization.

**3.** Rock salt, made of the mineral halite, is an organic sedimentary rock. A deposit of rock salt is most likely to be formed when
**A** magma cools and hardens inside Earth.
**B** hot water solutions form veins of rock salt.
**C** the minerals form a solution in magma.
**D** a solution of halite and water evaporates.

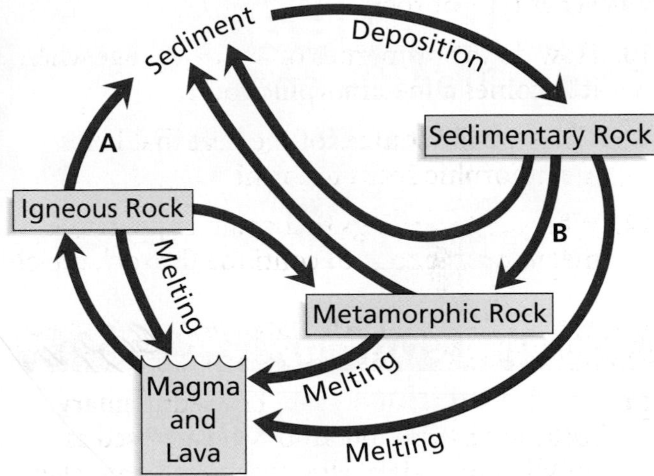


*Use the diagram above to answer Questions 4 and 5.*

**4.** If the heat and pressure inside Earth cause a rock to melt, the material that formed would be
**F** metamorphic rock.
**G** magma.
**H** sedimentary rock.
**J** igneous rock.

**5.** How can a metamorphic rock change into a sedimentary rock?
**A** erosion and deposition
**B** melting and crystallization
**C** heat and pressure
**D** all of the above

## Constructed Response

**6.** You are studying some moon rocks. Some of the moon rocks are made up of jagged pieces of other rocks. The pieces are cemented together by fine, dust-sized particles called rock powder. How would you classify this type of moon rock? Explain how you used the rock's characteristics to classify it.

Chapter 5

# Plate Tectonics

## The BIG Idea

Energy Transfer and Earth's Structure

**How does the transfer of energy inside Earth affect its surface?**

### Chapter Preview

**1 Earth's Interior**

*Discover* How Do Scientists Find Out What's Inside Earth?

*Skills Activity* Creating Data Tables

*Analyzing Data* Temperature Inside Earth

**2 Convection and the Mantle**

*Discover* How Can Heat Cause Motion in a Liquid?

**3 Drifting Continents**

*Discover* How Are Earth's Continents Linked Together?

**4 Sea-Floor Spreading**

*Discover* What Is the Effect of a Change in Density?

*Try This* Reversing Poles

*Skills Lab* Modeling Sea-Floor Spreading

**5 The Theory of Plate Tectonics**

*Discover* How Well Do the Continents Fit Together?

*Skills Activity* Predicting

*Math Skills* Calculating a Rate

*Active Art* Continental Drift

*Skills Lab* Modeling Mantle Convection Currents

The huge gash in the ground is a rift valley formed where the mid-Atlantic ridge cuts through Iceland.

Lab zone™ Chapter **Project**

## Make a Model of Earth

In this chapter, you will learn how movements deep within Earth help to create mountains and other surface features. As you read this chapter, you will build a model that shows Earth's interior.

**Your Goal** To build a three-dimensional model that shows Earth's surface features, as well as a cutaway view of Earth's interior

Your model must

- be built to scale to show the layers of Earth's interior
- include at least three of the plates that form Earth's surface, as well as two landmasses or continents
- show how the plates push together, pull apart, or slide past each other and indicate their direction of movement
- follow the safety guidelines in Appendix A

**Plan It!** Think about the materials you could use to make a three-dimensional model. How will you show what happens beneath the crust? As you learn about sea-floor spreading and plate tectonics, add the appropriate features to your model.

## Section 1

# Earth's Interior

## Reading Preview

### Key Concepts

- How have geologists learned about Earth's inner structure?
- What are the characteristics of Earth's crust, mantle, and core?

### Key Terms

- seismic waves • pressure
- crust • basalt • granite
- mantle • lithosphere
- asthenosphere • outer core
- inner core

### Target Reading Skill

**Using Prior Knowledge** Before you read, look at the section headings and visuals to see what this section is about. Then write what you know about Earth's interior in a graphic organizer like the one below. As you read, write what you learn.

| What You Know |
|---|
| 1. Earth's crust is made of rock.<br>2. |

| What You Learned |
|---|
| 1.<br>2. |

## Lab zone Discover Activity

### How Do Scientists Find Out What's Inside Earth?

1. Your teacher will provide you with three closed film canisters. Each canister contains a different material. Your goal is to determine what is inside each canister—even though you can't directly observe what it contains.
2. Tape a paper label on each canister.
3. To gather evidence about what is in the canisters, you may tap, roll, shake, or weigh them. Record your observations.
4. What differences do you notice between the canisters? Apart from their appearance on the outside, are the canisters similar in any way? How did you obtain this evidence?

**Think It Over**

**Inferring** From your observations, what can you infer about the contents of the canisters? How is a canister like Earth?

Imagine watching an island grow! That's exactly what you can do on the island of Hawaii. On the south side of the island, molten material pours out of cracks in Mount Kilauea (kee loo AY uh) and flows into the ocean. As this lava flows over the land, it cools and hardens into rock.

The most recent eruptions of Mount Kilauea began in 1983. An area of cracks 7 kilometers long opened in Earth's surface. Through the cracks spurted "curtains of fire"—fountains of hot liquid rock from deep inside Earth. Since that time, the lava has covered more than 100 square kilometers of land with a layer of rock. When the lava reaches the sea, it extends the borders of the island into the Pacific Ocean.

FIGURE 1
**Lava Flows in Hawaii**
These people are watching lava from vents in Kilauea flow into the Pacific Ocean.

**FIGURE 2**
**Getting Beneath the Surface**
Geologists (left) examine rocks for clues about what's inside Earth. Even though caves like this one in Georgia (below) may seem deep, they reach only a relatively short distance beneath the surface.

## Exploring Inside Earth

Earth's surface is constantly changing. Throughout our planet's long history, its surface has been lifted up, pushed down, bent, and broken. Thus Earth looks different today from the way it did millions of years ago.

Volcanic eruptions like those at Mount Kilauea make people wonder, What's inside Earth? Yet this question is very difficult to answer. Much as geologists would like to, they cannot dig a hole to the center of Earth. The extreme conditions in Earth's interior prevent exploration far below the surface.

The deepest mine in the world, a gold mine in South Africa, reaches a depth of 3.8 kilometers. But that mine only scratches the surface. You would have to travel more than 1,600 times that distance—over 6,000 kilometers—to reach Earth's center. **Geologists have used two main types of evidence to learn about Earth's interior: direct evidence from rock samples and indirect evidence from seismic waves.** The geologists in Figure 2 are observing rock on Earth's surface.

**For:** Links on the structure of Earth
**Visit:** www.SciLinks.org
**Web Code:** scn-1011

**Evidence From Rock Samples** Rocks from inside Earth give geologists clues about Earth's structure. Geologists have drilled holes as much as 12 kilometers into Earth. The drills bring up samples of rock. From these samples, geologists can make inferences about conditions deep inside Earth, where these rocks formed. In addition, forces inside Earth sometimes blast rock to the surface from depths of more than 100 kilometers. These rocks provide more information about the interior.

**Evidence From Seismic Waves** Geologists cannot look inside Earth. Instead, they must rely on indirect methods of observation. Have you ever hung a heavy picture on a wall? If you have, you know that you can knock on the wall to locate the wooden beam underneath the plaster that will support the picture. When you knock on the wall, you listen carefully for a change in the sound.

To study Earth's interior, geologists also use an indirect method. But instead of knocking on walls, they use seismic waves. When earthquakes occur, they produce **seismic waves** (SYZ mik). Geologists record the seismic waves and study how they travel through Earth. The speed of seismic waves and the paths they take reveal the structure of the planet.

Using data from seismic waves, geologists have learned that Earth's interior is made up of several layers. Each layer surrounds the layers beneath it, much like the layers of an onion. In Figure 3, you can see how seismic waves travel through the layers that make up Earth.

**What causes seismic waves?**

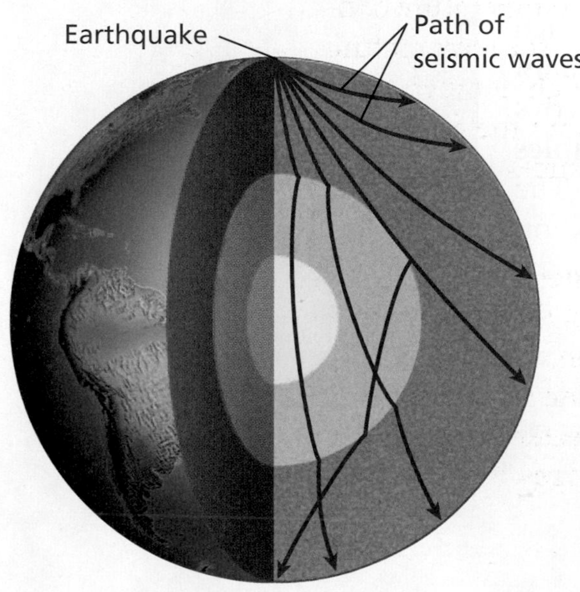


**FIGURE 3**
**Seismic Waves**
Scientists infer Earth's inner structure by recording and studying how seismic waves travel through Earth.

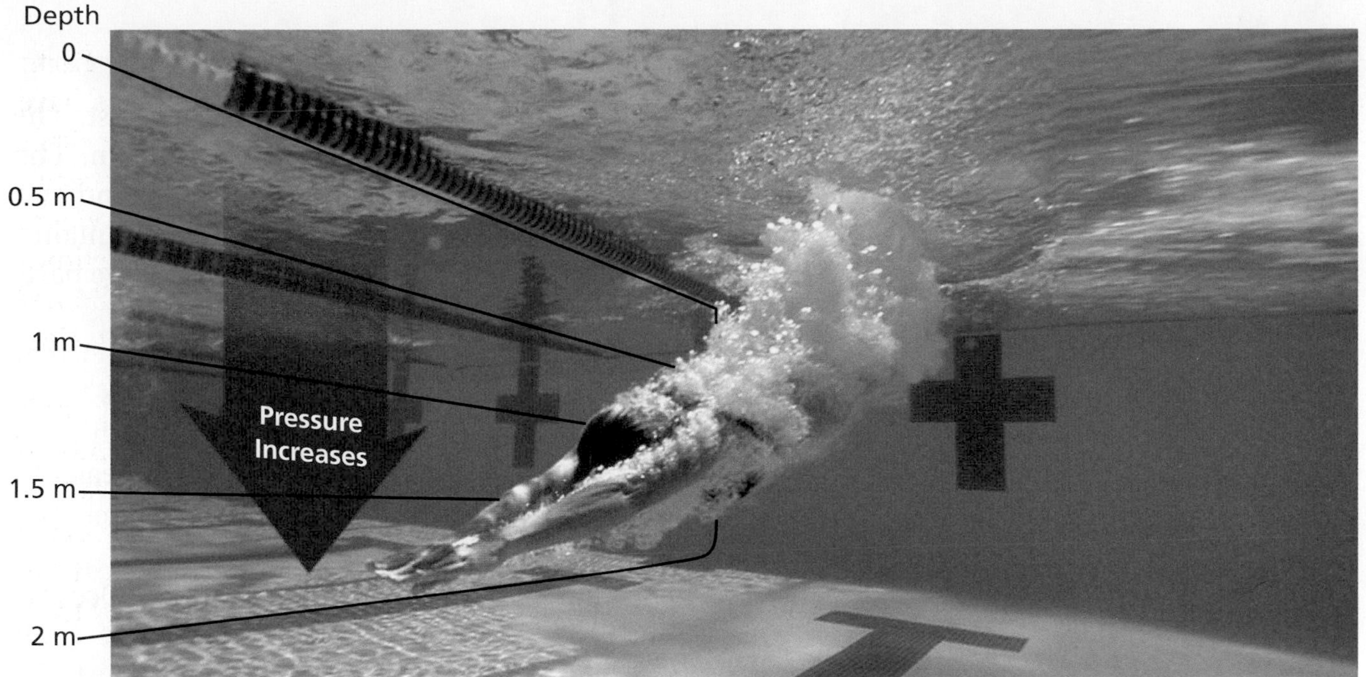


## A Journey to the Center of Earth

**The three main layers of Earth are the crust, the mantle, and the core. These layers vary greatly in size, composition, temperature, and pressure.** If you could travel through these layers to the center of Earth, what would your trip be like? To begin, you will need a vehicle that can travel through solid rock. The vehicle will carry scientific instruments to record changes in temperature and pressure as you descend.

**Temperature** As you start to tunnel beneath the surface, the surrounding rock is cool. Then at about 20 meters down, your instruments report that the rock is getting warmer. For every 40 meters that you descend from that point, the temperature rises 1 Celsius degree. This rapid rise in temperature continues for several tens of kilometers. After that, the temperature increases more slowly, but steadily. The high temperatures inside Earth are the result of heat left over from the formation of the planet. In addition, radioactive substances inside Earth release energy. This further heats the interior.

**Pressure** During your journey to the center of Earth, your instruments record an increase in pressure in the surrounding rock. **Pressure** results from a force pressing on an area. Because of the weight of the rock above, pressure inside Earth increases as you go deeper. The deeper you go, the greater the pressure. Pressure inside Earth increases much as it does in the swimming pool in Figure 4.

**FIGURE 4**
**Pressure and Depth**
The deeper this swimmer goes, the greater the pressure from the surrounding water.
**Comparing and Contrasting** *How is the water in the swimming pool similar to Earth's interior? How is it different?*

## The Crust

Your journey to the center of Earth begins in the crust. The **crust** is the layer of rock that forms Earth's outer skin. **The crust is a layer of solid rock that includes both dry land and the ocean floor.** On the crust you find rocks and mountains. The crust also includes the soil and water that cover large parts of Earth's surface.

This outer rind of rock is much thinner than the layer that lies beneath it. In fact, you can think of Earth's crust as being similar to the paper-thin skin of an onion. The crust is thickest under high mountains and thinnest beneath the ocean. In most places, the crust is between 5 and 40 kilometers thick. But it can be up to 70 kilometers thick beneath mountains.

The crust beneath the ocean is called oceanic crust. Oceanic crust consists mostly of rocks such as basalt. **Basalt** (buh SAWLT) is dark rock with a fine texture. Continental crust, the crust that forms the continents, consists mainly of rocks such as granite. **Granite** is a rock that usually is a light color and has a coarse texture.

**Reading Checkpoint** **What is the main type of rock in oceanic crust?**

**FIGURE 5**
**Earth's Interior**
Earth's interior is divided into layers: the crust, mantle, outer core, and inner core.
**Interpreting Diagrams** *Which of Earth's layers is the thickest?*

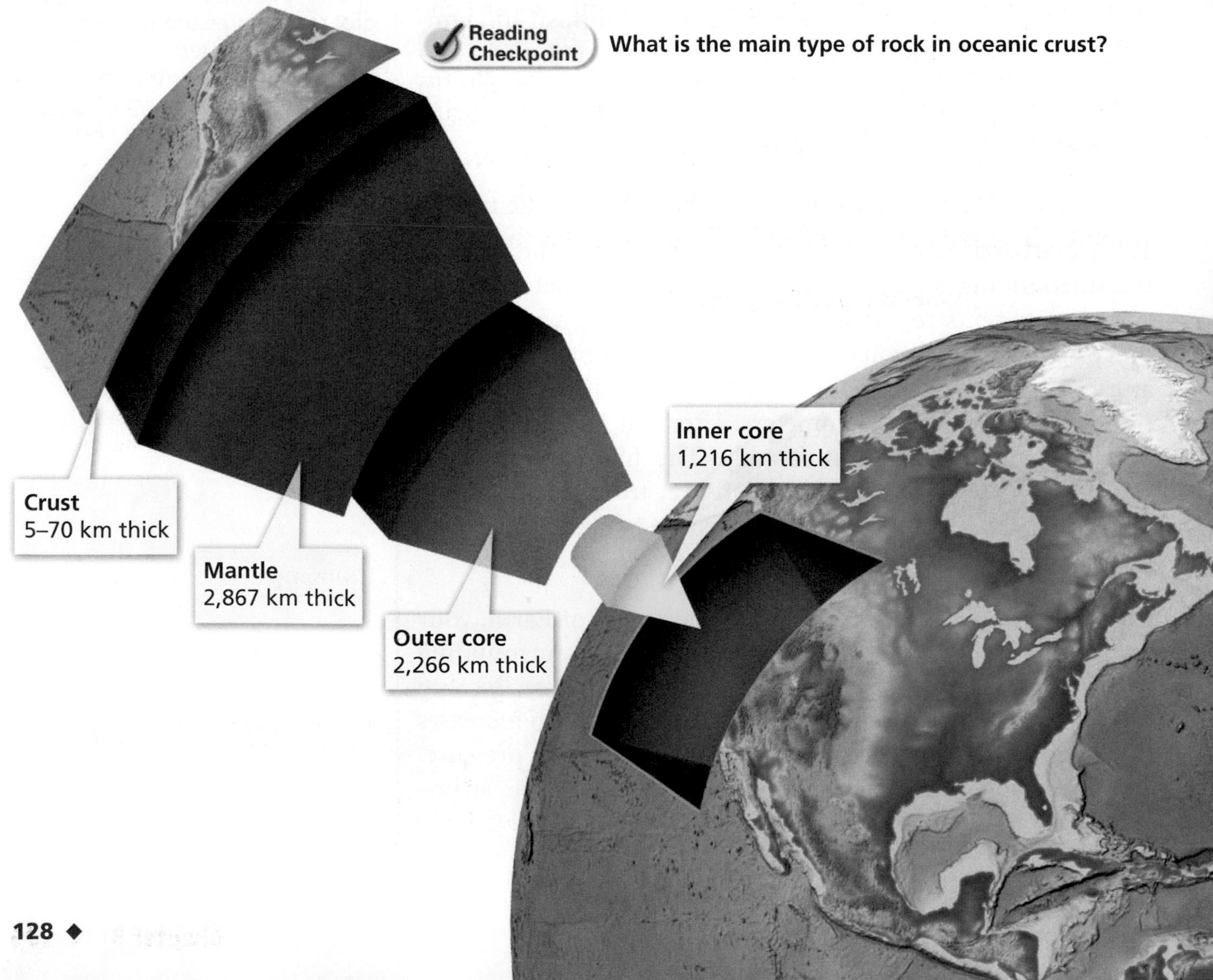

## The Mantle

Your journey downward continues. About 40 kilometers beneath the surface, you cross a boundary. Below the boundary is the solid material of the **mantle,** a layer of hot rock. **Earth's mantle is made up of rock that is very hot, but solid. Scientists divide the mantle into layers based on the physical characteristics of those layers. Overall, the mantle is nearly 3,000 kilometers thick.**

**The Lithosphere** The uppermost part of the mantle is very similar to the crust. The uppermost part of the mantle and the crust together form a rigid layer called the **lithosphere** (lith UH sphere). In Greek, *lithos* means "stone." As you can see in Figure 6, the lithosphere averages about 100 kilometers thick.

**The Asthenosphere** Below the lithosphere, your vehicle encounters material that is hotter and under increasing pressure. As a result, the part of the mantle just beneath the lithosphere is less rigid than the rock above. Like road tar softened by the heat of the sun, this part of the mantle is somewhat soft—it can bend like plastic. This soft layer is called the **asthenosphere** (as THEN uh sfeer). In Greek, *asthenes* means "weak." Although the asthenosphere is softer than the rest of the mantle, it's still solid. If you kicked it, you would stub your toe.

**The Lower Mantle** Beneath the asthenosphere, the mantle is solid. This solid material extends all the way to Earth's core.

**Reading Checkpoint** What is the asthenosphere?

**Lab zone Skills Activity**

### Creating Data Tables

Imagine that you are in a super-strong vehicle that is tunneling deep into Earth's interior. You stop several times on your trip to collect data. Copy the data table. For each depth, identify the layer and what that layer is made of. Then complete the table.

Data Table

| Depth | Name of Layer | What Layer Is Made Of |
|---|---|---|
| 20 km | | |
| 150 km | | |
| 2,000 km | | |
| 4,000 km | | |
| 6,000 km | | |

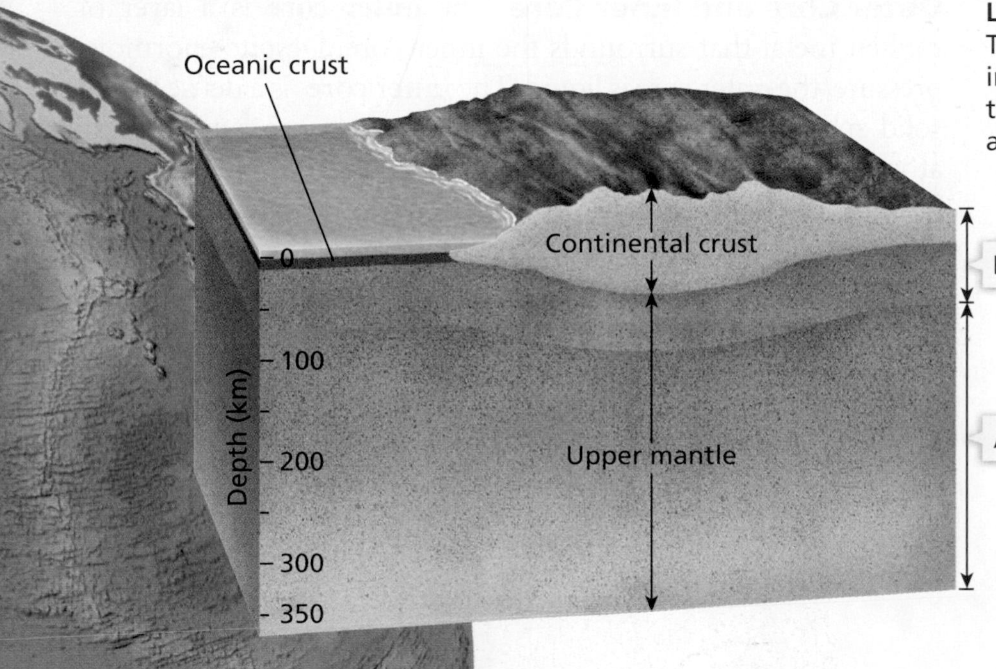


FIGURE 6
**Lithosphere and Asthenosphere**
The rigid lithosphere, which includes the crust, rests on the softer material of the asthenosphere.

**Math** Analyzing Data

## Temperature Inside Earth

The graph shows how temperatures change between Earth's surface and the bottom of the mantle. On this graph, the temperature at Earth's surface is 0°C. Study the graph carefully and then answer the questions.

1. **Reading Graphs** As you move from left to right on the *x*-axis, how does depth inside Earth change?
2. **Estimating** What is the temperature at the boundary between the lithosphere and the asthenosphere?
3. **Estimating** What is the temperature at the boundary between the lower mantle and the core?
4. **Interpreting Data** How does temperature change with depth in Earth's interior?

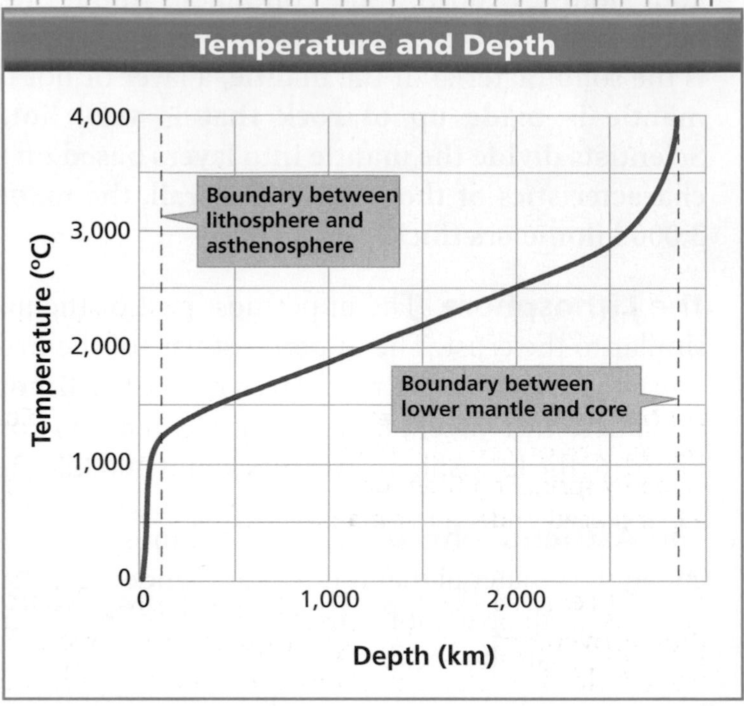


# The Core

After traveling through the mantle, you reach Earth's core. **The core is made mostly of the metals iron and nickel. It consists of two parts—a liquid outer core and a solid inner core.** Together, the inner and outer core are 3,486 kilometers thick.

**Outer Core and Inner Core** The **outer core** is a layer of molten metal that surrounds the inner core. Despite enormous pressure, the outer core is liquid. The **inner core** is a dense ball of solid metal. In the inner core, extreme pressure squeezes the atoms of iron and nickel so much that they cannot spread out and become liquid.

Most of the current evidence suggests that both parts of the core are made of iron and nickel. But scientists have found data suggesting that the core also contains substances such as oxygen, sulfur, and silicon. Scientists must seek more data before they decide which of these other substances is most important.

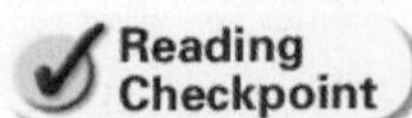


**What is the main difference between the outer core and the inner core?**

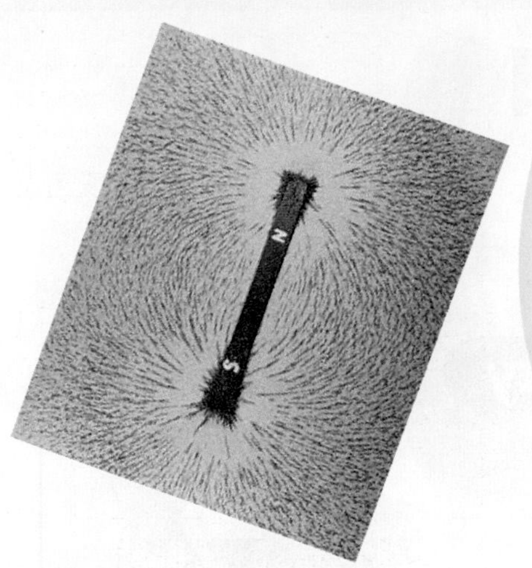

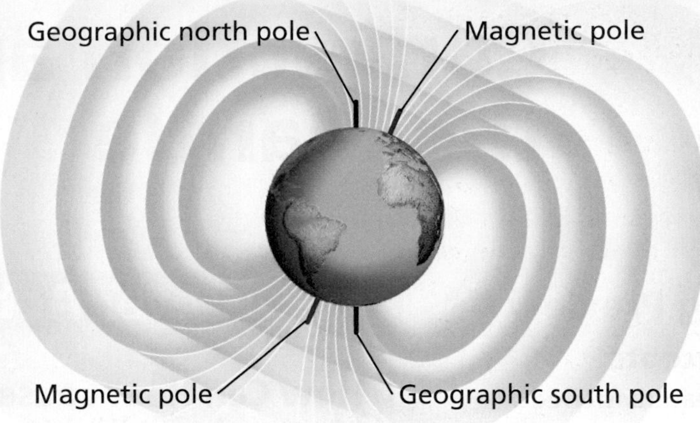


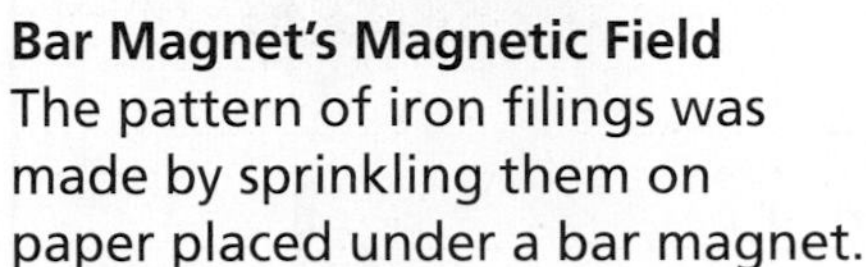

**Bar Magnet's Magnetic Field**
The pattern of iron filings was made by sprinkling them on paper placed under a bar magnet.

**Earth's Magnetic Field**
Like a magnet, Earth's magnetic field has north and south poles.

**FIGURE 7**
**Earth's Magnetic Field**
Just as a bar magnet is surrounded by its own magnetic field, Earth's magnetic field surrounds the planet.
**Relating Cause and Effect** *If you shifted the magnet beneath the paper, what would happen to the iron filings?*

**The Core and Earth's Magnetic Field** Scientists think that movements in the liquid outer core create Earth's magnetic field. Because Earth has a magnetic field, the planet acts like a giant bar magnet. As you can see in Figure 7, the magnetic field affects the whole Earth.

Consider an ordinary bar magnet. If you place it on a piece of paper and sprinkle iron filings on the paper, the iron filings line up with the bar's magnetic field. If you could cover the entire planet with iron filings, they would form a similar pattern. When you use a compass, the compass needle aligns with the lines of force in Earth's magnetic field.

## Section 1 Assessment

**Target Reading Skill Using Prior Knowledge** Review your graphic organizer and revise it based on what you just learned in the section.

### Reviewing Key Concepts

1. a. **Explaining** Why is it difficult to determine Earth's inner structure?
   b. **Inferring** How are seismic waves used to provide evidence about Earth's interior?
2. a. **Listing** List Earth's three main layers.
   b. **Comparing and Contrasting** What is the difference between the lithosphere and the asthenosphere? In which layer is each located?
   c. **Classifying** Classify each of the following layers as liquid, solid, or solid but able to flow slowly: lithosphere, asthenosphere, lower mantle, outer core, inner core.

### Writing in Science

**Narrative** Write a narrative of your own imaginary journey to the center of Earth. Your narrative should describe the layers of Earth through which you travel and how temperature and pressure change beneath the surface.

Section 2

Integrating Physics

# Convection and the Mantle

## Reading Preview

### Key Concepts

- How is heat transferred?
- What causes convection currents?
- What causes convection currents in Earth's mantle?

### Key Terms

- radiation
- conduction
- convection
- density
- convection current

### Target Reading Skill

**Outlining** An outline shows the relationship between major ideas and supporting ideas. As you read, make an outline about heat transfer. Use the red headings for the main topics and the blue headings for the subtopics.

**Convection and the Mantle**

I. Types of Heat Transfer
  A. Radiation
  B.
  C.
II. Convection Currents

## Lab zone Discover **Activity**

### How Can Heat Cause Motion in a Liquid?

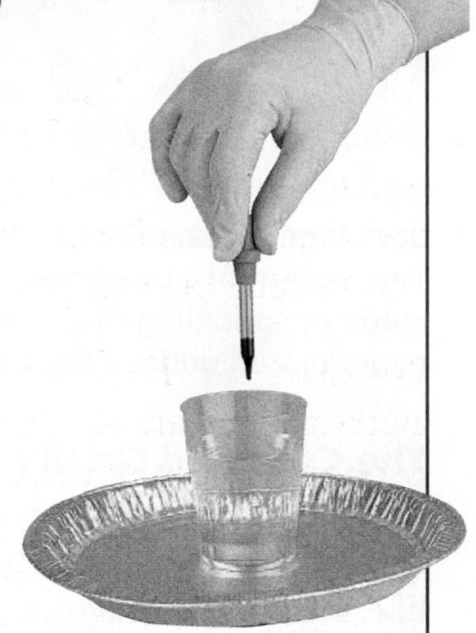

1. Carefully pour some hot water into a small, shallow pan. Fill a clear, plastic cup about half full with cold water. Place the cup in the pan.
2. Allow the water to stand for two minutes until all motion stops.
3. Fill a plastic dropper with some food coloring. Then, holding the dropper under the water's surface and slightly away from the edge of the cup, gently squeeze a small droplet of the food coloring into the water.
4. Observe the water for one minute.
5. Add another droplet at the water's surface in the middle of the cup and observe again.

**Think It Over**

**Inferring** How do you explain what happened to the droplets of food coloring? Why do you think the second droplet moved in a way that was different from the way the first droplet moved?

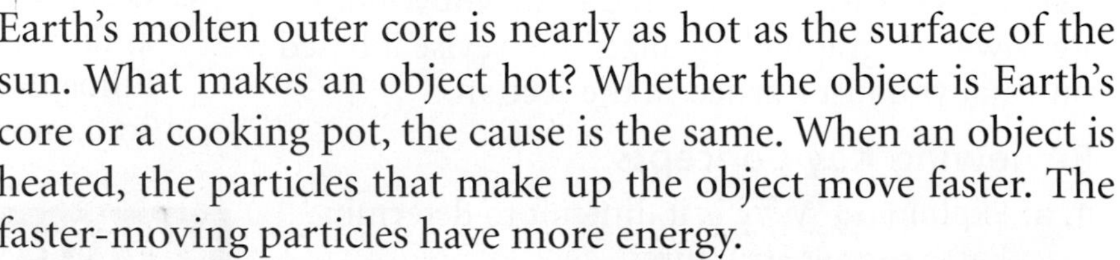

Earth's molten outer core is nearly as hot as the surface of the sun. What makes an object hot? Whether the object is Earth's core or a cooking pot, the cause is the same. When an object is heated, the particles that make up the object move faster. The faster-moving particles have more energy.

If you have ever touched a hot pot accidentally, you have discovered for yourself (in a painful way) that heat moves. In this case, it moved from the hot pot to your hand. The movement of energy from a warmer object to a cooler object is called heat transfer. To explain how heat moves from Earth's core through the mantle, you need to know how heat is transferred.

## Types of Heat Transfer

Heat always moves from a warmer substance to a cooler substance. For example, holding an ice cube will make your hand begin to feel cold in a few seconds. But is the coldness in the ice cube moving to your hand? No! Since cold is the absence of heat, it's the heat in your hand that moves to the ice cube. This is one of the ways that heat is transferred. **There are three types of heat transfer: radiation, conduction, and convection.**

**Radiation** The transfer of energy through space is called **radiation.** Heat transfer by radiation takes place with no direct contact between a heat source and an object. Sunlight is radiation that warms Earth's surface. Other familiar forms of radiation include the heat you feel around a flame or open fire.

**Conduction** Heat transfer within a material or between materials that are touching is called **conduction.** For example, a spoon in a pot of soup heats up by conduction, as shown in Figure 8. Heat moves from the hot soup and the pot to the particles that make up the spoon. The particles near the bottom of the spoon vibrate faster as they are heated, so they bump into other particles and heat them, too. Gradually the entire spoon heats up. When your hand touches the spoon, conduction transfers heat from the spoon directly to your skin. Then you feel the heat. Conduction is responsible for some of the heat transfer inside Earth.

**Reading Checkpoint** **What is conduction?**

FIGURE 8
**Conduction**
In conduction, the heated particles of a substance transfer heat through contact with other particles in the substance. Conduction heats the spoon and the pot itself. That's why you need a mitt to protect your hand from the hot handle.

For: More on convection currents in the mantle
Visit: PHSchool.com
Web Code: cfd-1012

**Convection** Heat can also be transferred by the movement of fluids—liquids and gases. **Convection** is heat transfer by the movement of currents within a fluid. During convection, heated particles of fluid begin to flow. This flow transfers heat from one part of the fluid to another.

Heat transfer by convection is caused by differences of temperature and density within a fluid. **Density** is a measure of how much mass there is in a volume of a substance. For example, rock is more dense than water because a given volume of rock has more mass than the same volume of water.

When a liquid or gas is heated, the particles move faster and spread apart. As a result, the particles of the heated fluid occupy more space. The fluid's density decreases. But when a fluid cools, its particles move more slowly and settle together more closely. As the fluid becomes cooler, its density increases.

## Convection Currents

When you heat soup on a stove, convection occurs in the soup, as shown in Figure 9. As the soup at the bottom of the pot gets hot, it expands and therefore becomes less dense. The warm, less dense soup moves upward and floats over the cooler, denser soup. At the surface, the warm soup cools, becoming denser. Then gravity pulls this cooler, denser soup back down to the bottom of the pot, where it is heated again.

A constant flow begins as the cooler, denser soup sinks to the bottom of the pot and the warmer, less dense soup rises. A **convection current** is the flow that transfers heat within a fluid. **Heating and cooling of the fluid, changes in the fluid's density, and the force of gravity combine to set convection currents in motion.** Convection currents continue as long as heat is added. Without heat, convection currents eventually stop.

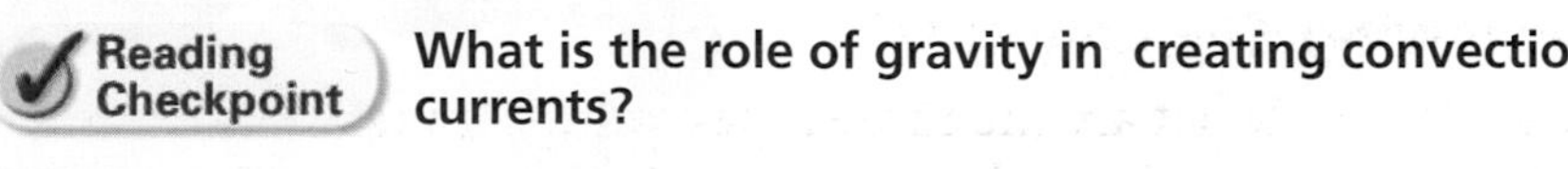

**Reading Checkpoint** What is the role of gravity in creating convection currents?

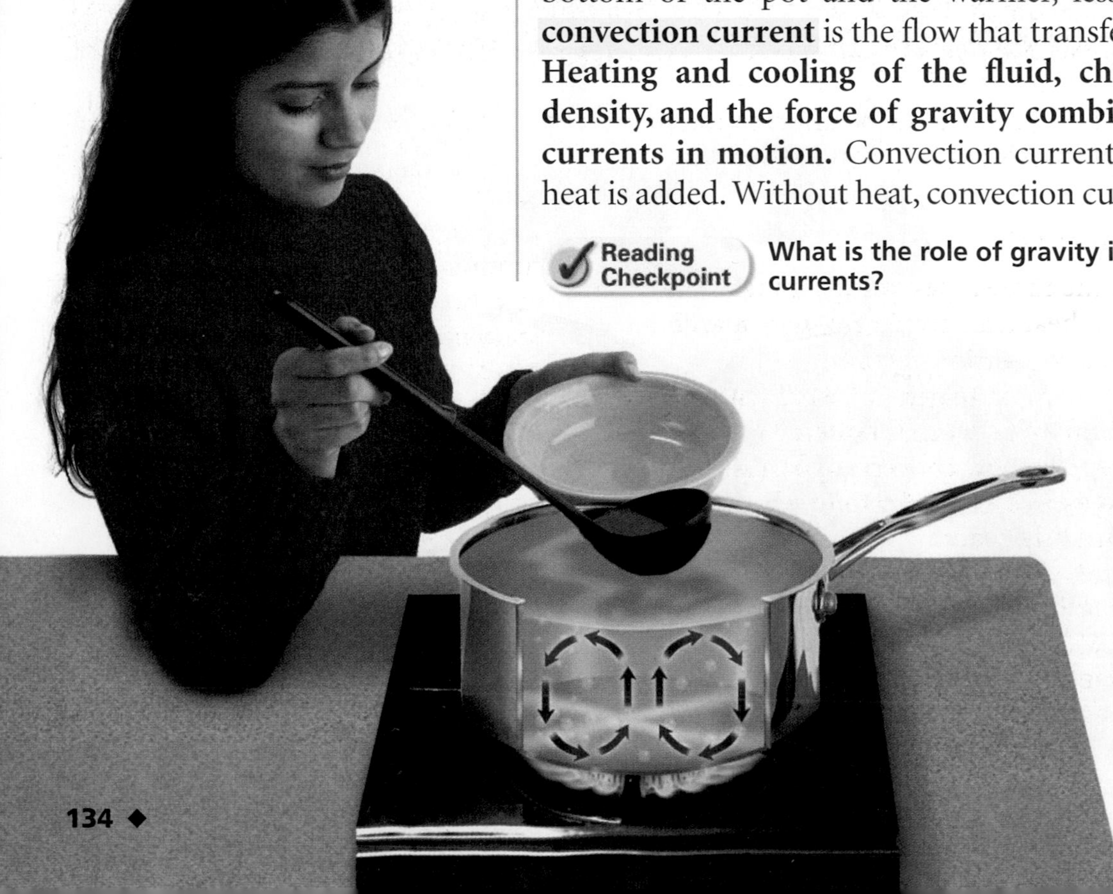

**FIGURE 9**
**Convection Currents**
Differences in temperature and density cause convection currents. In the pot, convection currents arise because the soup close to the heat source is hotter and less dense than the soup near the surface.

## Convection Currents in Earth

In Earth's mantle, large amounts of heat are transferred by convection currents, as shown in Figure 10. **Heat from the core and the mantle itself causes convection currents in the mantle.**

How is it possible for mantle rock to flow? Over millions of years, the great heat and pressure in the mantle cause solid mantle rock to flow very slowly. Many geologists think that plumes of mantle rock rise slowly from the bottom of the mantle toward the top. The hot rock eventually cools and sinks back through the mantle. Over and over, the cycle of rising and sinking takes place. Convection currents like these have been moving inside Earth for more than four billion years!

There are also convection currents in the outer core. These convection currents cause Earth's magnetic field.

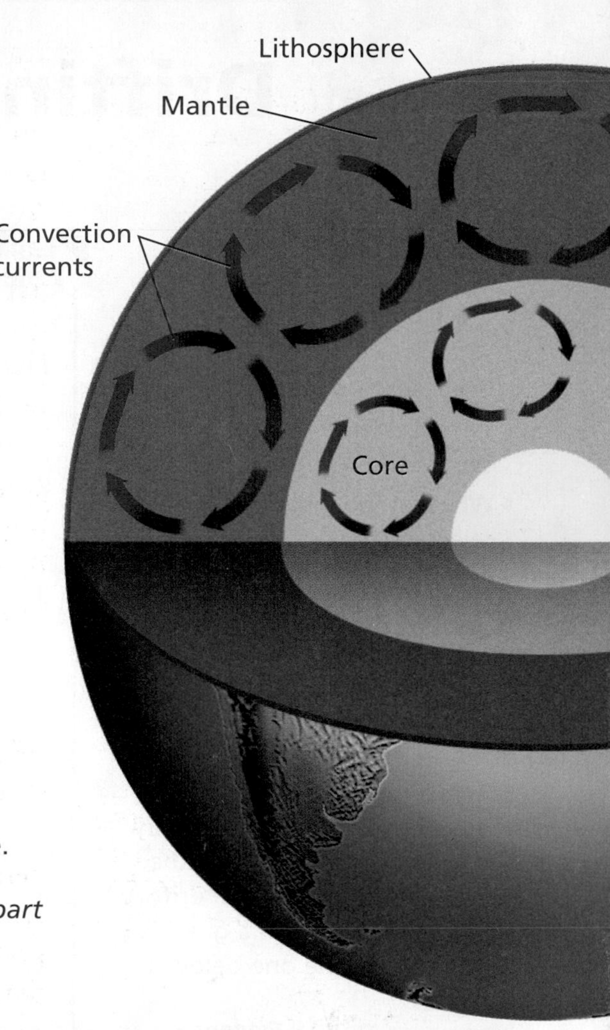


**FIGURE 10**
**Mantle Convection**
Most geologists think that convection currents rise and sink through the mantle.
**Applying Concepts** *What part of Earth's interior is like the soup in the pot? What part is like the burner on the stove?*

## Section 2 Assessment

**Target Reading Skill Outlining** Use the information in your outline about heat transfer to help you answer the questions below.

### Reviewing Key Concepts

1. a. **Listing** What are the three types of heat transfer?
   b. **Explaining** How is heat transferred through space?
2. a. **Defining** What is a convection current?
   b. **Relating Cause and Effect** In general, what happens to the density of a fluid as it becomes hotter?
   c. **Summarizing** Describe how convection currents form.
3. a. **Identifying** Name two layers of Earth in which convection currents take place.
   b. **Relating Cause and Effect** What causes convection currents in the mantle?
   c. **Predicting** What will happen to the convection currents in the mantle if Earth's interior eventually cools down? Explain.

### Lab zone At-Home Activity

**Tracing Heat Flow** Convection currents may keep the air inside your home at a comfortable temperature. Air is made up of gases, so it is a fluid. Regardless of the type of home heating system, heated air circulates through a room by convection. You may have tried to adjust the flow of air in a stuffy room by opening a window. When you did so, you were making use of convection currents. With an adult family member, study how your home is heated. Look for evidence of convection currents.

# Section 3 Drifting Continents

## Reading Preview

### Key Concepts

- What was Alfred Wegener's hypothesis about the continents?
- What evidence supported Wegener's hypothesis?
- Why was Wegener's hypothesis rejected by most scientists of his day?

### Key Terms

- continental drift
- Pangaea
- fossil

### Target Reading Skill

**Identifying Supporting Evidence** As you read, identify the evidence that supports the hypothesis of continental drift. Write the evidence in a graphic organizer like the one below.

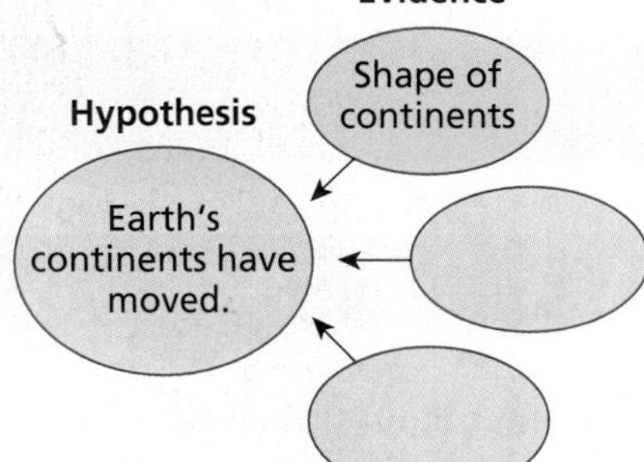


## Lab zone Discover Activity

### How Are Earth's Continents Linked Together?

1. Find the oceans and the seven continents on a globe showing Earth's physical features.
2. How much of the globe is occupied by the Pacific Ocean? Does most of Earth's dry land lie in the Northern or Southern Hemisphere?
3. Find the points or areas where most of the continents are connected. Find the points at which several of the continents almost touch, but are not connected.
4. Examine the globe more closely. Find the great belt of mountains running from north to south along the western side of North and South America. Can you find another great belt of mountains on the globe?

**Think It Over**

**Posing Questions** What questions can you pose about how oceans, continents, and mountains are distributed on Earth's surface?

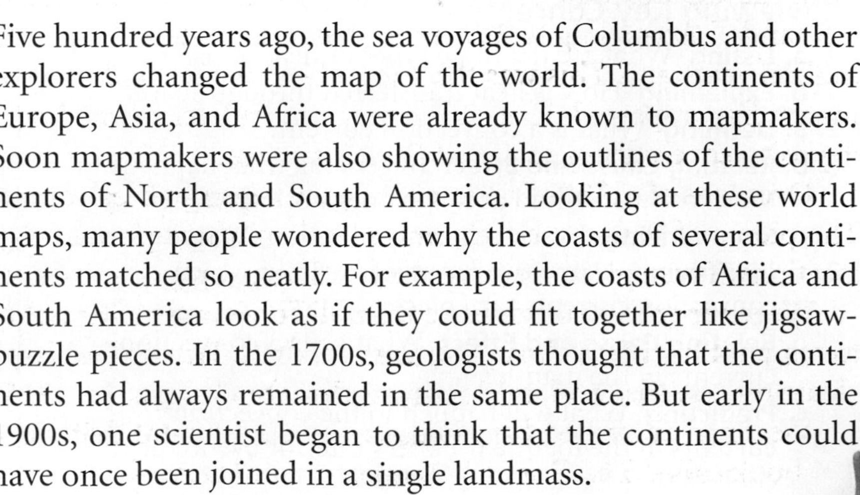

Five hundred years ago, the sea voyages of Columbus and other explorers changed the map of the world. The continents of Europe, Asia, and Africa were already known to mapmakers. Soon mapmakers were also showing the outlines of the continents of North and South America. Looking at these world maps, many people wondered why the coasts of several continents matched so neatly. For example, the coasts of Africa and South America look as if they could fit together like jigsaw-puzzle pieces. In the 1700s, geologists thought that the continents had always remained in the same place. But early in the 1900s, one scientist began to think that the continents could have once been joined in a single landmass.

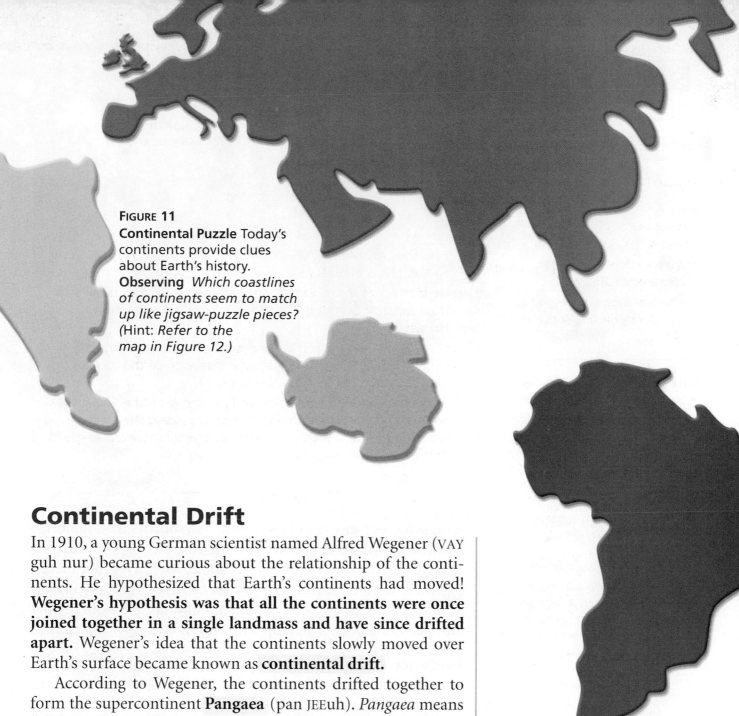

**FIGURE 11**
**Continental Puzzle** Today's continents provide clues about Earth's history.
**Observing** *Which coastlines of continents seem to match up like jigsaw-puzzle pieces?* (Hint: *Refer to the map in Figure 12.)*

## Continental Drift

In 1910, a young German scientist named Alfred Wegener (VAY guh nur) became curious about the relationship of the continents. He hypothesized that Earth's continents had moved! **Wegener's hypothesis was that all the continents were once joined together in a single landmass and have since drifted apart.** Wegener's idea that the continents slowly moved over Earth's surface became known as **continental drift.**

According to Wegener, the continents drifted together to form the supercontinent **Pangaea** (pan JEEuh). *Pangaea* means "all lands." According to Wegener, Pangaea existed about 300 million years ago. This was the time when reptiles and winged insects first appeared. Tropical forests, which later formed coal deposits, covered large parts of Earth's surface.

Over tens of millions of years, Pangaea began to break apart. The pieces of Pangaea slowly moved toward their present-day locations. These pieces became the continents as they are today.

**Wegener gathered evidence from different scientific fields to support his ideas about continental drift. He studied land features, fossils, and evidence of climate change.** In 1915, Wegener published his evidence for continental drift in a book called *The Origin of Continents and Oceans.*

**For:** Links on continental drift
**Visit:** www.SciLinks.org
**Web Code:** scn-1013

## Evidence for Continental Drift

**Pangaea**

NORTH AMERICA
EURASIA
Equator
Tethys Sea
AFRICA
SOUTH AMERICA
INDIA
AUSTRALIA
ANTARCTICA

NORTH AMERICA
Atlantic Ocean
Equator
SOUTH AMERICA
Pacific Ocean

**Key**

| | |
|---|---|
| Folded mountains | Glossopteris fossils |
| Coal beds | Lystrosaurus fossils |
| Glacial deposits | Mesosaurus fossils |

**FIGURE 12**
Fossils and rocks found on different continents provide evidence that Earth's landmasses once were joined together in the supercontinent Pangaea.
**Inferring** *What do the matching mountain ranges in Africa and South America show, according to Wegener's hypothesis?*

**Evidence From Land Features** As shown in Figure 12, mountains and other features on the continents provided evidence for continental drift. For example, when Wegener pieced together maps of Africa and South America, he noticed that mountain ranges on both continents line up. He noticed that European coal fields match up with coal fields in North America.

**Evidence From Fossils** Wegener also used fossils to support his argument for continental drift. A **fossil** is any trace of an ancient organism that has been preserved in rock. For example, *Glossopteris* (glaw SAHP tuh ris), was a fernlike plant that lived 250 million years ago. *Glossopteris* fossils have been found in rocks in Africa, South America, Australia, India, and Antarctica. The occurrence of *Glossopteris* on these widely separated landmasses convinced Wegener that Pangaea had existed.

Other examples include fossils of the freshwater reptiles *Mesosaurus* and *Lystrosaurus.* These fossils have also been found in places now separated by oceans. Neither reptile could have swum great distances across salt water. Wegener inferred that these reptiles lived on a single landmass that has since split apart.

**Lystrosaurus**

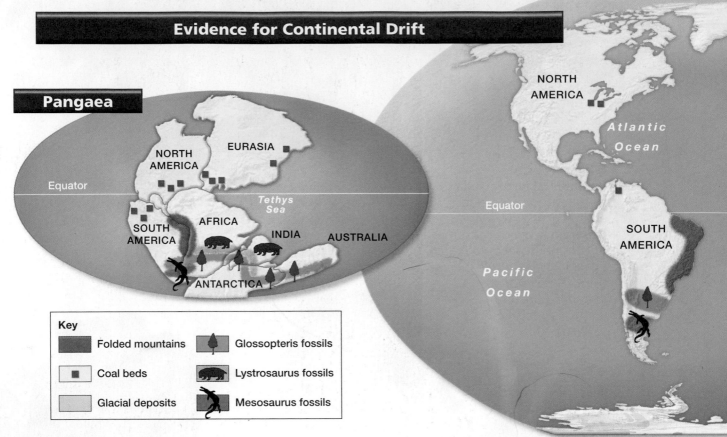

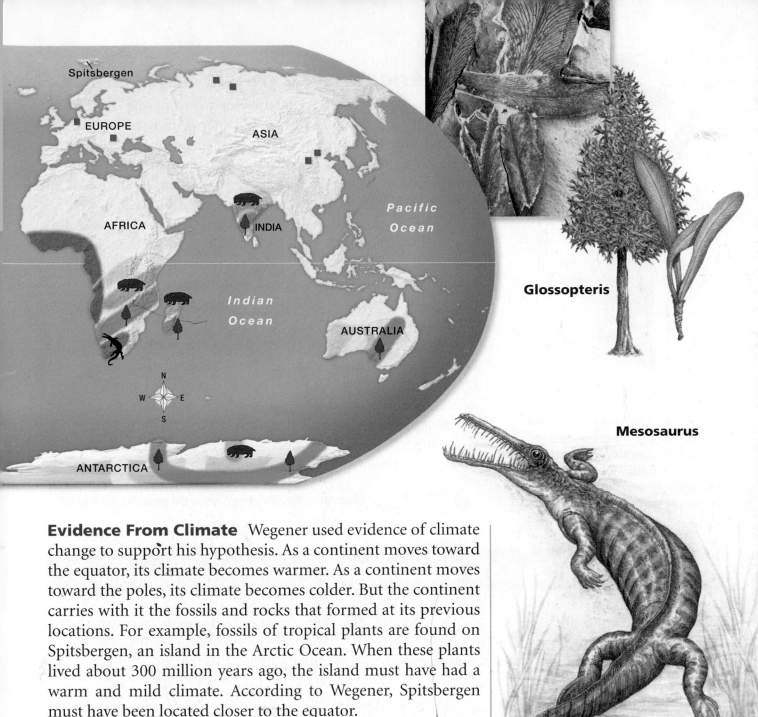

Spitsbergen
EUROPE
ASIA
AFRICA
INDIA
Pacific Ocean
Indian Ocean
AUSTRALIA
ANTARCTICA
N
W
E
S

Glossopteris

Mesosaurus

**Evidence From Climate** Wegener used evidence of climate change to support his hypothesis. As a continent moves toward the equator, its climate becomes warmer. As a continent moves toward the poles, its climate becomes colder. But the continent carries with it the fossils and rocks that formed at its previous locations. For example, fossils of tropical plants are found on Spitsbergen, an island in the Arctic Ocean. When these plants lived about 300 million years ago, the island must have had a warm and mild climate. According to Wegener, Spitsbergen must have been located closer to the equator.

Geologists found evidence that when it was warm in Spitsbergen, the climate was much colder in South Africa. Deep scratches in rocks showed that continental glaciers once covered South Africa. Continental glaciers are thick layers of ice that cover hundreds of thousands of square kilometers. But the climate of South Africa is too mild today for continental glaciers to form. Wegener concluded that when Pangaea existed, South Africa was much closer to the South Pole. According to Wegener, the climates of Spitsbergen and South Africa changed because these landmasses had moved.

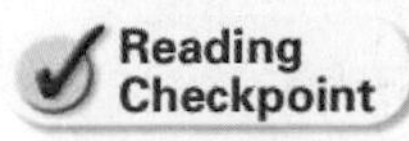


**How would continental drift affect a continent's climate?**

**FIGURE 13**
**Alfred Wegener**
Although scientists rejected his theory, Wegener continued to collect evidence on continental drift and to update his book. He died in 1930 on an expedition to explore Greenland's continental glacier.

## Wegener's Hypothesis Rejected

Wegener attempted to explain how continental drift took place. He suggested that the continents plowed across the ocean floors. **Unfortunately, Wegener could not provide a satisfactory explanation for the force that pushes or pulls the continents.** Because Wegener could not identify the cause of continental drift, most geologists rejected his idea.

For geologists to accept continental drift, they would also have had to change their ideas about how mountains form. In the early 1900s, many geologists thought that mountains formed because Earth was slowly cooling and shrinking. According to this hypothesis, mountains formed when the crust wrinkled like the skin of a dried-up apple.

Wegener said that if these geologists were correct, then mountains should be found all over Earth's surface. But mountains usually occur in narrow bands along the edges of continents. Wegener developed a hypothesis that better explained where mountains occur and how they form. Wegener proposed that when continents collide, their edges crumple and fold. The folding continents push up huge mountains.

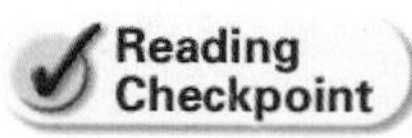


**According to Wegener, how do mountains form?**

## Section 3 Assessment

### Target Reading Skill

**Identifying Supporting Evidence** Refer to your graphic organizer about continental drift as you answer Question 2 below.

### Reviewing Key Concepts

1. a. **Identifying** Who proposed the concept of continental drift?
   b. **Summarizing** According to the hypothesis of continental drift, how would a world map have changed over the last 250 million years?
2. a. **Reviewing** What evidence supported the hypothesis of continental drift?
   b. **Explaining** How did fossils provide evidence for continental drift?
   c. **Forming Hypotheses** Deposits of coal have been found beneath the ice of Antarctica. But coal only forms in warm swamps. Use Wegener's hypothesis to explain how coal could be found so near to the South Pole.
3. a. **Explaining** Why did most scientists reject Wegener's hypothesis of continental drift?
   b. **Making Judgments** Do you think the scientists of Wegener's time should have accepted his hypothesis? Why or why not?

### Lab zone At-Home Activity

**Moving the Continents** Using a world map and tracing paper, trace the outlines of the continents that border the Atlantic Ocean. Label the continents. Then use scissors to carefully cut your map along the edges of the continents. Throw away the Atlantic Ocean. Place the two remaining pieces on a dark surface and ask family members to try to fit the two halves together. Explain to them about continental drift and Pangaea.

Section 4

# Sea-Floor Spreading

## Reading Preview

### Key Concepts

- What is the process of sea-floor spreading?
- What is the evidence for sea-floor spreading?
- What happens at deep-ocean trenches?

### Key Terms

- mid-ocean ridge
- sonar
- sea-floor spreading
- deep-ocean trench
- subduction

### Target Reading Skill

**Sequencing** Make a flowchart to show the process of sea-floor spreading.

Magma erupts along mid-ocean ridge
↓
[ ]
↓
[ ]

## Lab zone Discover Activity

### What Is the Effect of a Change in Density?

1. Partially fill a sink or dishpan with water.
2. Open up a dry washcloth in your hand. Does the washcloth feel light or heavy?
3. Moisten one edge of the washcloth in the water. Then gently place the washcloth so that it floats on the water's surface. Observe the washcloth carefully (especially at its edges) as it starts to sink.
4. Remove the washcloth from the water and open it up in your hand. Is the mass of the washcloth the same as, less than, or greater than when it was dry?

**Think It Over**

**Observing** How did the washcloth's density change? What effect did this change in density have on the washcloth?

Deep in the ocean, the temperature is near freezing. There is no light, and living things are generally scarce. Yet some areas of the deep-ocean floor are teeming with life. One of these areas is the East Pacific Rise. This area forms part of the Pacific Ocean floor off the coasts of Mexico and South America. Here, ocean water sinks through cracks, or vents, in the crust. The water is heated by contact with hot material from the mantle. The hot water then spurts back into the ocean.

Around these hot-water vents live some of the most bizarre creatures ever discovered. Giant, red-tipped tube worms sway in the water. Nearby sit giant clams nearly a meter across. Strange spider-like crabs scuttle by. Surprisingly, the geological features of this strange environment provided some of the best evidence for Wegener's hypothesis of continental drift.

**FIGURE 14**
**The Deep-Ocean Floor**
Shrimp, crabs, and other organisms cluster near hot water vents in the ocean floor.

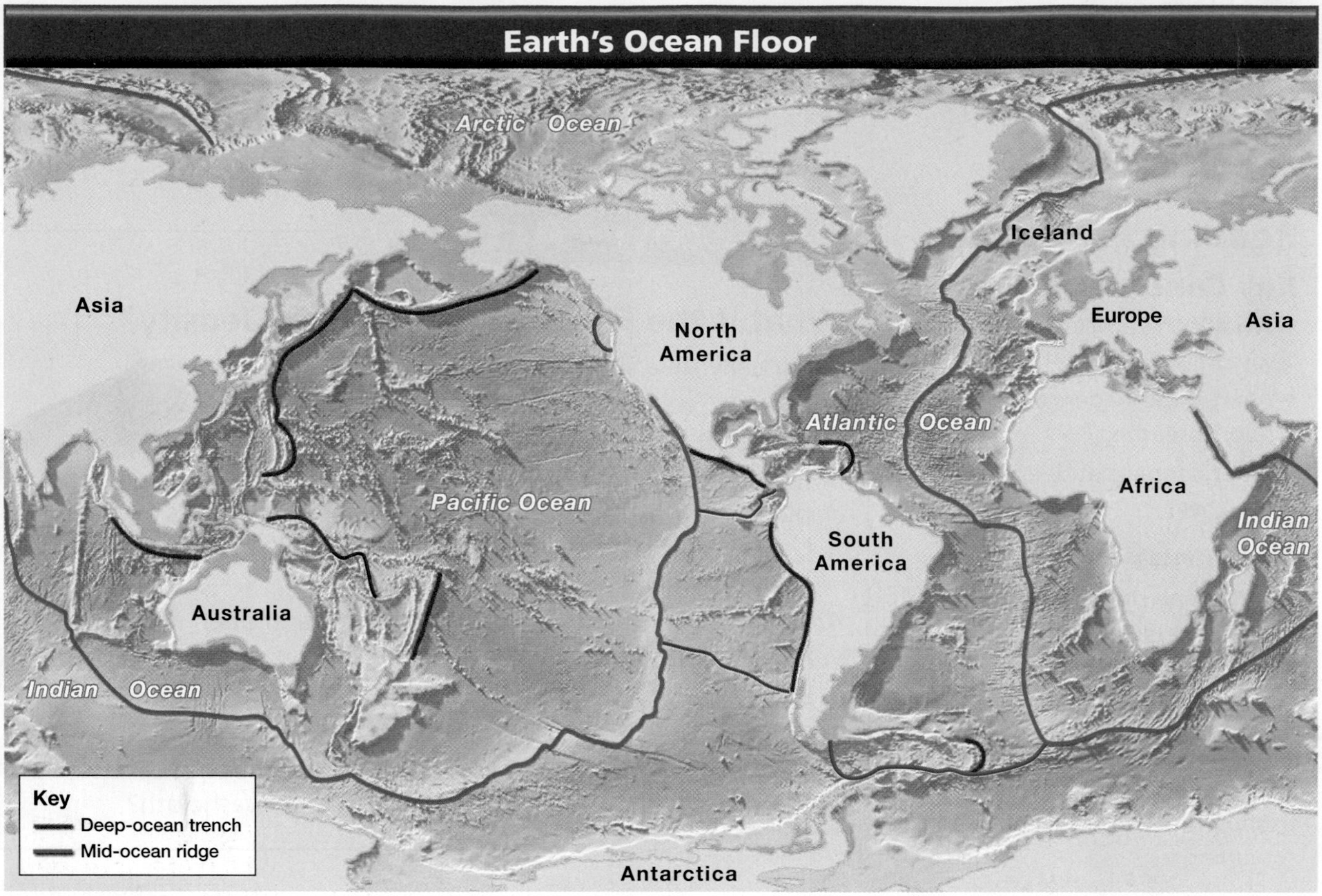

**Earth's Ocean Floor**

Key
Deep-ocean trench
Mid-ocean ridge

**FIGURE 15**
The mid-ocean ridge system is more than 50,000 kilometers long.
**Interpreting Maps** *What is unusual about Iceland?*

## Mid-Ocean Ridges

The East Pacific Rise is just one of many **mid-ocean ridges** that wind beneath Earth's oceans. In the mid-1900s, scientists mapped the mid-ocean ridges using sonar. **Sonar** is a device that bounces sound waves off underwater objects and then records the echoes of these sound waves. The time it takes for the echo to arrive indicates the distance to the object.

Mid-ocean ridges curve like the seam of a baseball along the sea floor. They extend into all of Earth's oceans. Figure 15 shows the location of these ridges. Most of the mountains in the mid-ocean ridge system lie hidden under hundreds of meters of water. But in a few places the ridge pokes above the surface. For example, the island of Iceland is a part of the mid-ocean ridge that rises above the surface in the North Atlantic Ocean. A steep-sided valley splits the top of some mid-ocean ridges.

The mapping of mid-ocean ridges made scientists curious to know more about them. What are the ridges? How do they form?

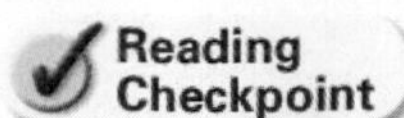

**What device is used to map the ocean floor?**

## What Is Sea-Floor Spreading?

Harry Hess, an American geologist, was one of the scientists who studied mid-ocean ridges. Hess carefully examined maps of the mid-ocean ridge system. Then he began to think about the ocean floor in relation to the problem of continental drift. Finally, he reached a startling conclusion: Maybe Wegener was right! Perhaps the continents do move.

In 1960, Hess proposed a radical idea. He suggested that a process he called **sea-floor spreading** continually adds new material to the ocean floor. **In sea-floor spreading, the sea floor spreads apart along both sides of a mid-ocean ridge as new crust is added. As a result, the ocean floors move like conveyor belts, carrying the continents along with them.** Look at Figure 16 to see the process of sea-floor spreading.

Sea-floor spreading begins at a mid-ocean ridge, which forms along a crack in the oceanic crust. Along the ridge, molten material that forms several kilometers beneath the surface rises and erupts. At the same time, older rock moves outward on both sides of the ridge. As the molten material cools, it forms a strip of solid rock in the center of the ridge. When more molten material flows into the crack, it forms a new strip of rock.

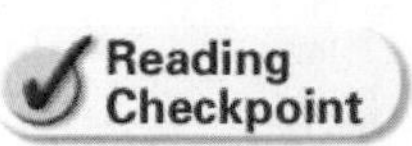


**How does new oceanic crust form?**

**Go Online** PHSchool.com
**For:** More on sea-floor spreading
**Visit:** PHSchool.com
**Web Code:** cfd-1014

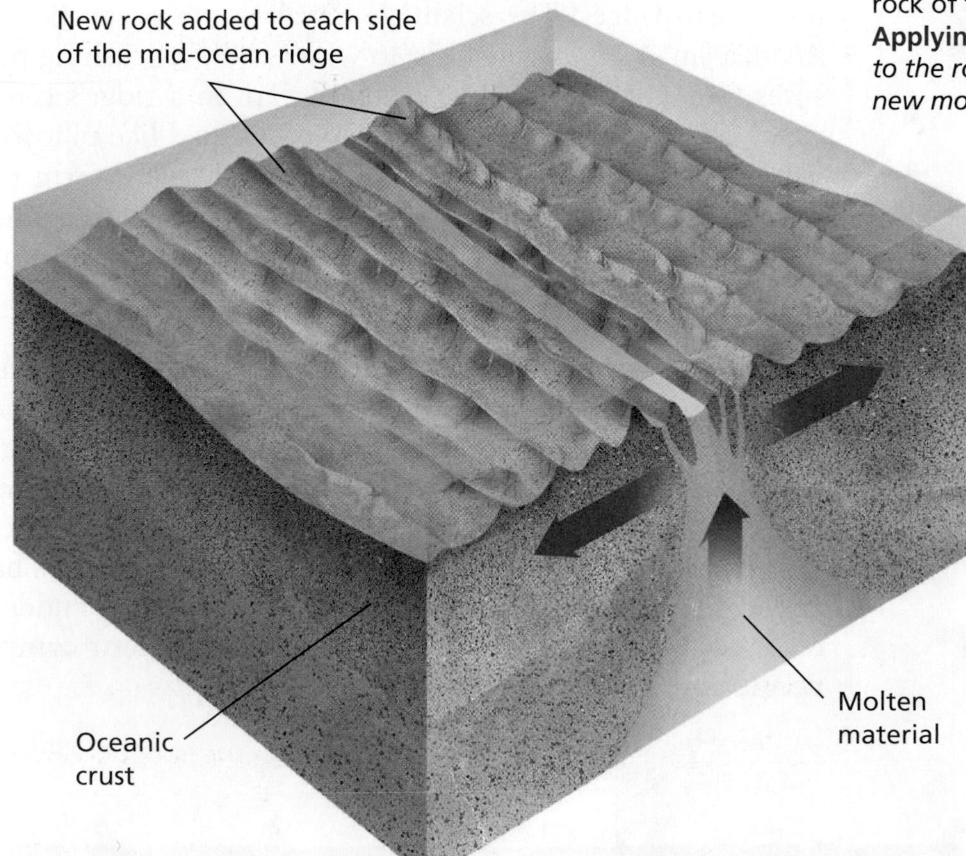


FIGURE 16
**Sea-Floor Spreading**
Molten material erupts through the valley that runs along the center of some mid-ocean ridges. This material hardens to form the rock of the ocean floor.
**Applying Concepts** *What happens to the rock along the ridge when new molten material erupts?*

Rock formed when Earth's magnetic field was normal

Rock formed when Earth's magnetic field was reversed

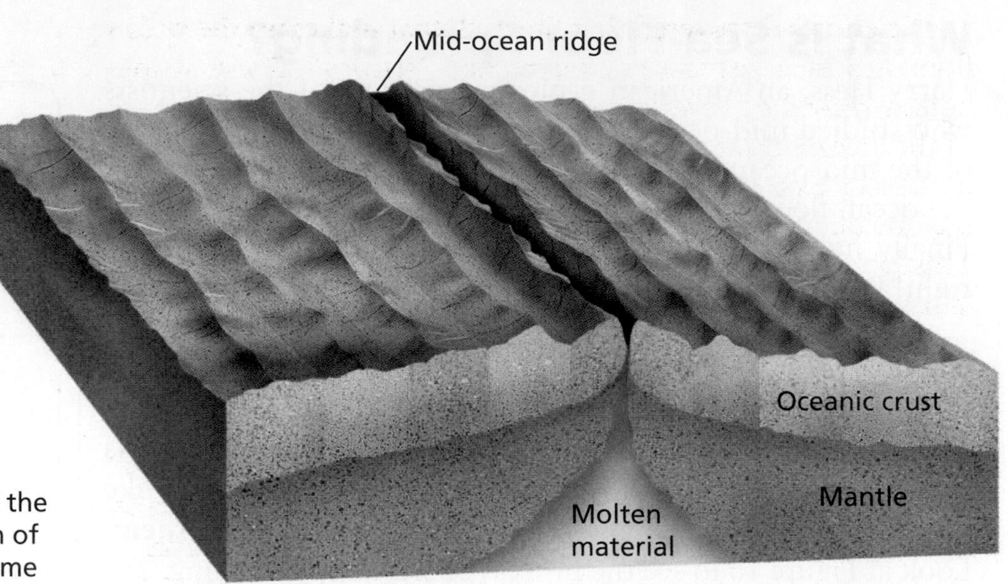


**FIGURE 17**
**Magnetic Stripes**
Magnetic stripes in the rock of the ocean floor show the direction of Earth's magnetic field at the time the rock hardened.
**Interpreting Diagrams** *How are these matching stripes evidence of sea-floor spreading?*

# Evidence for Sea-Floor Spreading

**Several types of evidence supported Hess's theory of sea-floor spreading: eruptions of molten material, magnetic stripes in the rock of the ocean floor, and the ages of the rocks themselves.** This evidence led scientists to look again at Wegener's hypothesis of continental drift.

**Evidence From Molten Material** In the 1960s, scientists found evidence that new material is indeed erupting along mid-ocean ridges. The scientists dived to the ocean floor in *Alvin*, a small submarine built to withstand the crushing pressures four kilometers down in the ocean. In a ridge's central valley, *Alvin's* crew found strange rocks shaped like pillows or like toothpaste squeezed from a tube. Such rocks form only when molten material hardens quickly after erupting under water. These rocks showed that molten material has erupted again and again along the mid-ocean ridge.

**Evidence From Magnetic Stripes** When scientists studied patterns in the rocks of the ocean floor, they found more support for sea-floor spreading. You read earlier that Earth behaves like a giant magnet, with a north pole and a south pole. Surprisingly, Earth's magnetic poles have reversed themselves many times during Earth's history. The last reversal happened 780,000 years ago. If the magnetic poles suddenly reversed themselves today, you would find that your compass needle points south.

Scientists discovered that the rock that makes up the ocean floor lies in a pattern of magnetized "stripes." These stripes hold a record of reversals in Earth's magnetic field. The rock of the ocean floor contains iron. The rock began as molten material that cooled and hardened. As the rock cooled, the iron bits inside lined up in the direction of Earth's magnetic poles. This locked the iron bits in place, giving the rocks a permanent "magnetic memory."

Using sensitive instruments, scientists recorded the magnetic memory of rocks on both sides of a mid-ocean ridge. They found that stripes of rock that formed when Earth's magnetic field pointed north alternate with stripes of rock that formed when the magnetic field pointed south. As shown in Figure 17, the pattern is the same on both sides of the ridge.

**Evidence From Drilling Samples** The final proof of sea-floor spreading came from rock samples obtained by drilling into the ocean floor. The *Glomar Challenger,* a drilling ship built in 1968, gathered the samples. The *Glomar Challenger* sent drilling pipes through water six kilometers deep to drill holes in the ocean floor. This feat has been compared to using a sharp-ended wire to dig a hole into a sidewalk from the top of the Empire State Building.

Samples from the sea floor were brought up through the pipes. Then the scientists determined the age of the rocks in the samples. They found that the farther away from a ridge the samples were taken, the older the rocks were. The youngest rocks were always in the center of the ridges. This showed that sea-floor spreading really has taken place.

**Why does the rock of the ocean floor have a pattern of magnetic stripes?**

**Lab zone Try This Activity**

### Reversing Poles

1. Cut six short pieces, each about 2.5 cm long, from a length of audiotape.
2. Tape one end of each piece of audiotape to a flat surface. The pieces should be spaced 1 cm apart and lined up lengthwise in a single row.
3. Touch a bar magnet's north pole to the first piece of audiotape. Then reverse the magnet and touch its south pole to the next piece.
4. Repeat Step 3 until you have applied the magnet to each piece of audiotape.
5. Sweep one end of the magnet about 1 cm above the line of audiotape pieces. Observe what happens.

**Making Models** What characteristic of the ocean floor did you observe as you swept the magnet along the line of audiotape pieces?

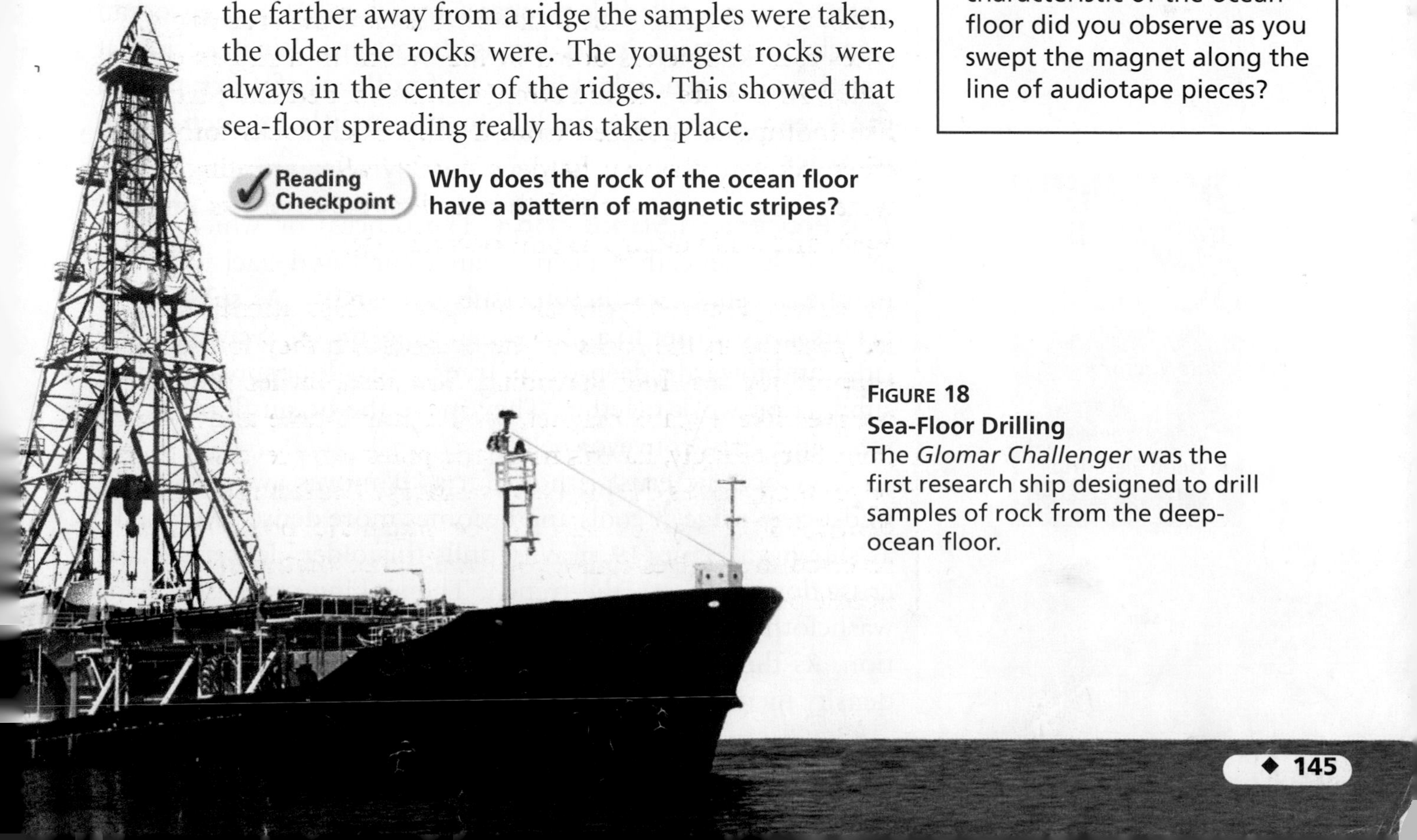

FIGURE 18
**Sea-Floor Drilling**
The *Glomar Challenger* was the first research ship designed to drill samples of rock from the deep-ocean floor.

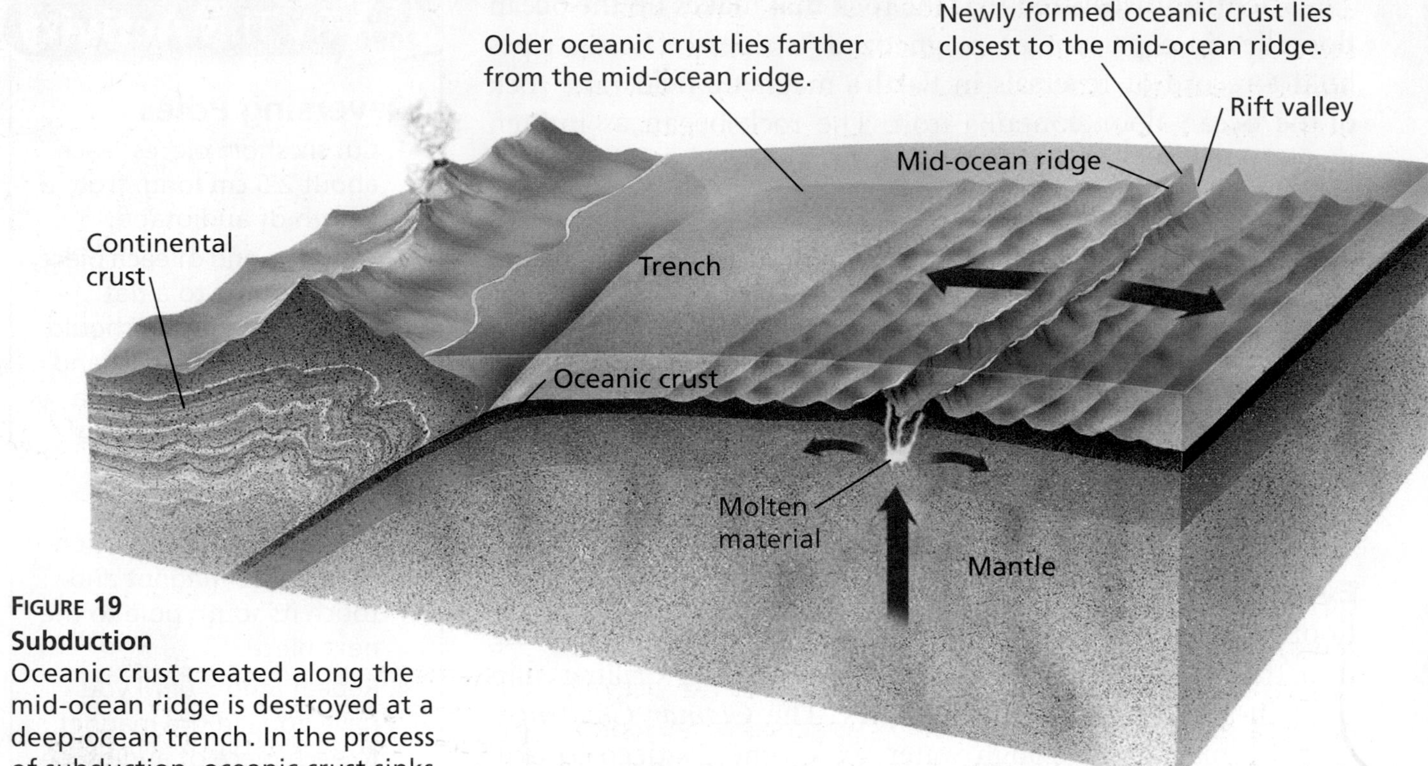


**FIGURE 19**
**Subduction**
Oceanic crust created along the mid-ocean ridge is destroyed at a deep-ocean trench. In the process of subduction, oceanic crust sinks down beneath the trench into the mantle.
**Drawing Conclusions** *Where would the densest oceanic crust be found?*

## Subduction at Trenches

How can the ocean floor keep getting wider and wider? The answer is that the ocean floor generally does not just keep spreading. Instead, the ocean floor plunges into deep underwater canyons called **deep-ocean trenches.** At a deep-ocean trench, the oceanic crust bends downward. What occurs at trenches? **In a process taking tens of millions of years, part of the ocean floor sinks back into the mantle at deep-ocean trenches.**

**The Process of Subduction** The process by which ocean floor sinks beneath a deep-ocean trench and back into the mantle is called **subduction** (sub DUC shun). As subduction occurs, crust closer to a mid-ocean ridge moves away from the ridge and toward a deep-ocean trench. Sea-floor spreading and subduction work together. They move the ocean floor as if it were on a giant conveyor belt.

New oceanic crust is hot. But as it moves away from the mid-ocean ridge, it cools and becomes more dense. Eventually, as shown in Figure 19, gravity pulls this older, denser oceanic crust down beneath the trench. The sinking crust is like the washcloth in the Discover activity at the beginning of this section. As the dry washcloth floating on the water gets wet, its density increases and it begins to sink.

**Subduction and Earth's Oceans** The processes of subduction and sea-floor spreading can change the size and shape of the oceans. Because of these processes, the ocean floor is renewed about every 200 million years. That is the time it takes for new rock to form at the mid-ocean ridge, move across the ocean, and sink into a trench.

The vast Pacific Ocean covers almost one third of the planet. And yet it is shrinking. How can that be? Sometimes a deep ocean trench swallows more oceanic crust than a mid-ocean ridge can produce. Then, if the ridge does not add new crust fast enough, the width of the ocean will shrink. In the Pacific Ocean, subduction through the many trenches that ring the ocean is occurring faster than new crust can be added.

On the other hand, the Atlantic Ocean is expanding. Unlike the Pacific Ocean, the Atlantic Ocean has only a few short trenches. As a result, the spreading ocean floor has virtually nowhere to go. In most places, the oceanic crust of the Atlantic Ocean floor is attached to the continental crust of the continents around the ocean. So as the Atlantic's ocean floor spreads, the continents along its edges also move. Over time, the whole ocean gets wider.

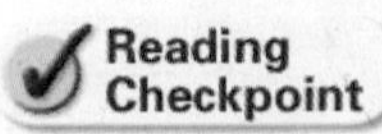

**Why is the Pacific Ocean shrinking?**

**FIGURE 20**
**Growing an Ocean**
Because of sea-floor spreading, the distance between Europe and North America is increasing by a few centimeters per year.

## Section 4 Assessment

**Target Reading Skill** **Sequencing** Refer to your flowchart on sea-floor spreading as you answer the questions below.

### Reviewing Key Concepts

1. a. **Naming** What scientist helped to discover the process of sea-floor spreading?
   b. **Identifying** Along what feature of the ocean floor does sea-floor spreading begin?
   c. **Sequencing** What are the steps in the process of sea-floor spreading?
2. a. **Reviewing** What three types of evidence provided support for the theory of sea-floor spreading?
   b. **Applying Concepts** How do rocks along the central valley of the mid-ocean ridge provide evidence of sea-floor spreading?
   c. **Predicting** Where would you expect to find the oldest rock on the ocean floor?
3. a. **Defining** What is a deep-ocean trench?
   b. **Relating Cause and Effect** What happens to oceanic crust at a deep-ocean trench?

### Writing in Science

**Description** Write a description of what you might see if you could explore a mid-ocean ridge in a vessel like the *Alvin.* In your description, be sure to include the main features of the ocean floor along and near the ridge.

# Modeling Sea-Floor Spreading

## Problem

How does sea-floor spreading add material to the ocean floor?

## Skills Focus

making models

## Materials

- scissors
- colored marker
- metric ruler
- 2 sheets of unlined paper

## Procedure  

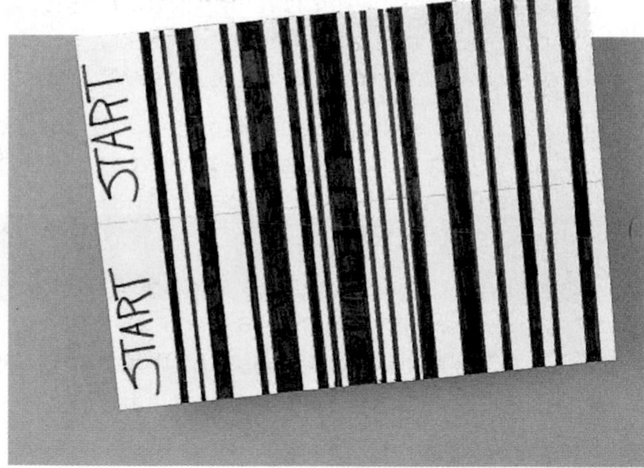


1. Draw stripes across one sheet of paper, parallel to the short sides of the paper. The stripes should vary in spacing and thickness.
2. Fold the paper in half lengthwise and write the word "Start" at the top of both halves of the paper. Using the scissors, carefully cut the paper in half along the fold line to form two strips.

3. Lightly fold the second sheet of paper into eighths. Then unfold it, leaving creases in the paper. Fold this sheet in half lengthwise.
4. Starting at the fold, draw lines 5.5 cm long on the middle crease and the two creases closest to the ends of the paper.

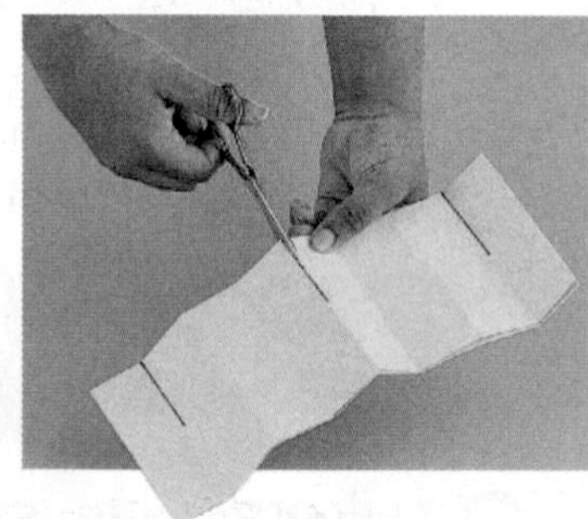

5. Now carefully cut along the lines you drew. Unfold the paper. There should be three slits in the center of the paper.
6. Put the two striped strips of paper together so their Start labels touch one another. Insert the Start ends of the strips up through the center slit and then pull them toward the side slits.

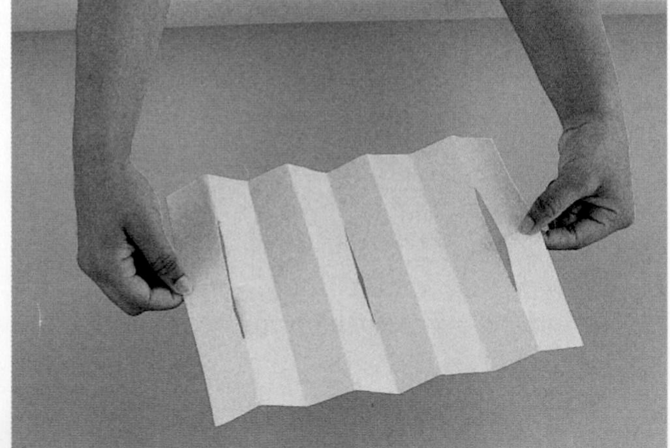

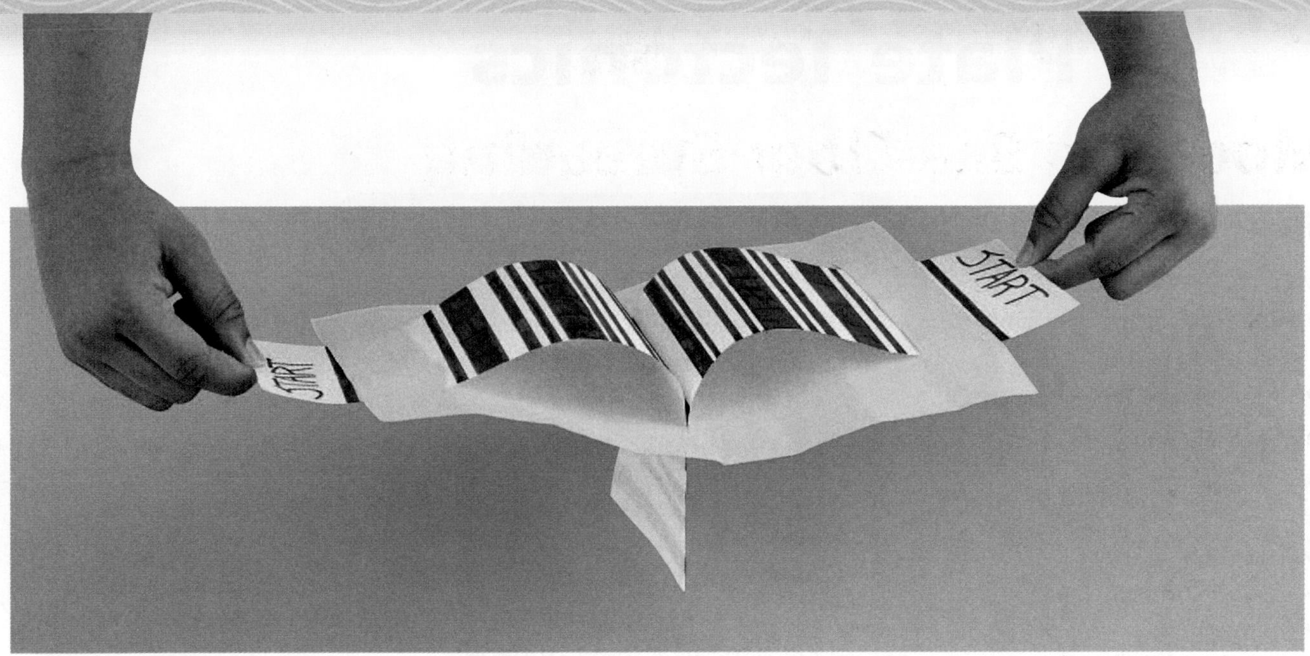


7. Insert the ends of the strips into the side slits. Pull the ends of the strips and watch what happens at the center slit.
8. Practice pulling the strips until you can make the two strips come up through the center and go down through the sides at the same time.

## Analyze and Conclude

1. **Making Models** What feature of the ocean floor does the center slit stand for? What prominent feature of the ocean floor is missing from the model at this point?
2. **Making Models** What do the side slits stand for? What does the space under the paper stand for?
3. **Comparing and Contrasting** As shown by your model, how does the ocean floor close to the center slit differ from the ocean floor near a side slit? How does this difference affect the depth of the ocean?
4. **Making Models** What do the stripes on the strips stand for? Why is it important that your model have an identical pattern of stripes on both sides of the center slit?
5. **Applying Concepts** Explain how differences in density and temperature provide some of the force needed to cause sea-floor spreading and subduction.
6. **Communicating** Use your own words to describe the process of sea-floor spreading. What parts of the process were not shown by your model?

## More to Explore

How could you modify your model to show an island that formed where a large amount of molten rock erupted from the mid-ocean ridge? How could you show what would happen to the island over a long period of time?

Section 5

# The Theory of Plate Tectonics

## Reading Preview

### Key Concepts

- What is the theory of plate tectonics?
- What are the three types of plate boundaries?

### Key Terms

- plate
- scientific theory
- plate tectonics
- fault
- divergent boundary
- rift valley
- convergent boundary
- transform boundary

### Target Reading Skill

**Building Vocabulary** A definition states the meaning of a word or phrase by telling about its most important feature or function. After you read the section, reread the paragraphs that contain definitions of Key Terms. Use all the information you have learned to write a definition of each Key Term in your own words.

## Lab zone Discover Activity

### How Well Do the Continents Fit Together?

1. Using a world map in an atlas, trace the shape of each continent and Madagascar on a sheet of paper. Also trace the shape of India and the Arabian Peninsula.
2. Carefully cut apart the landmasses, leaving Asia and Europe as one piece. Separate India and the Arabian Peninsula from Asia.
3. Piece together the continents as they may have looked before the breakup of Pangaea. Then attach your reconstruction of Pangaea to a sheet of paper.

**Think It Over**

**Drawing Conclusions** How well did the pieces of your continents fit together? Do your observations support the idea that today's landmasses were once joined together? Explain.

Have you ever dropped a hard-boiled egg? If so, you may have noticed that the eggshell cracked in an irregular pattern of pieces. Earth's lithosphere, its solid outer shell, is not one unbroken layer. It is more like that cracked eggshell. It's broken into pieces separated by jagged cracks.

A Canadian scientist, J. Tuzo Wilson, observed that there are cracks in the continents similar to those on the ocean floor. In 1965, Wilson proposed a new way of looking at these cracks. According to Wilson, the lithosphere is broken into separate sections called **plates.** The plates fit together along cracks in the lithosphere. As shown in Figure 22, the plates carry the continents or parts of the ocean floor, or both. Wilson combined what geologists knew about sea-floor spreading, Earth's plates, and continental drift into a single theory. A **scientific theory** is a well-tested concept that explains a wide range of observations.

**FIGURE 21**
**A Cracked Eggshell**
Earth's lithosphere is broken into plates like the cracked shell of a hard-boiled egg.

## How Plates Move

The theory of **plate tectonics** (tek TAHN iks) states that pieces of Earth's lithosphere are in slow, constant motion, driven by convection currents in the mantle. **The theory of plate tectonics explains the formation, movement, and subduction of Earth's plates.**

How can Earth's plates move? What force is great enough to move the heavy continents? Geologists think that movement of convection currents in the mantle is the major force that causes plate motion. During subduction, gravity pulls one edge of a plate down into the mantle. The rest of the plate also moves. This slow movement is similar to what happens in a pot of soup when gravity causes the cooler, denser soup near the surface to sink.

As the plates move, they collide, pull apart, or grind past each other, producing spectacular changes in Earth's surface. These changes include volcanoes, mountain ranges, and deep-ocean trenches.

**Lab zone Skills Activity**

### Predicting

Study the map of Earth's plates in Figure 22. Notice the arrows that show the direction of plate movement. Now find the Nazca plate on the map. Which direction is it moving? Find the South American plate and describe its movement. What do you think will happen as these plates continue to move?

**FIGURE 22**
Plate boundaries divide the lithosphere into large plates.
**Interpreting Maps** *Which plates include only ocean floor? Which plates include both continents and ocean floor?*

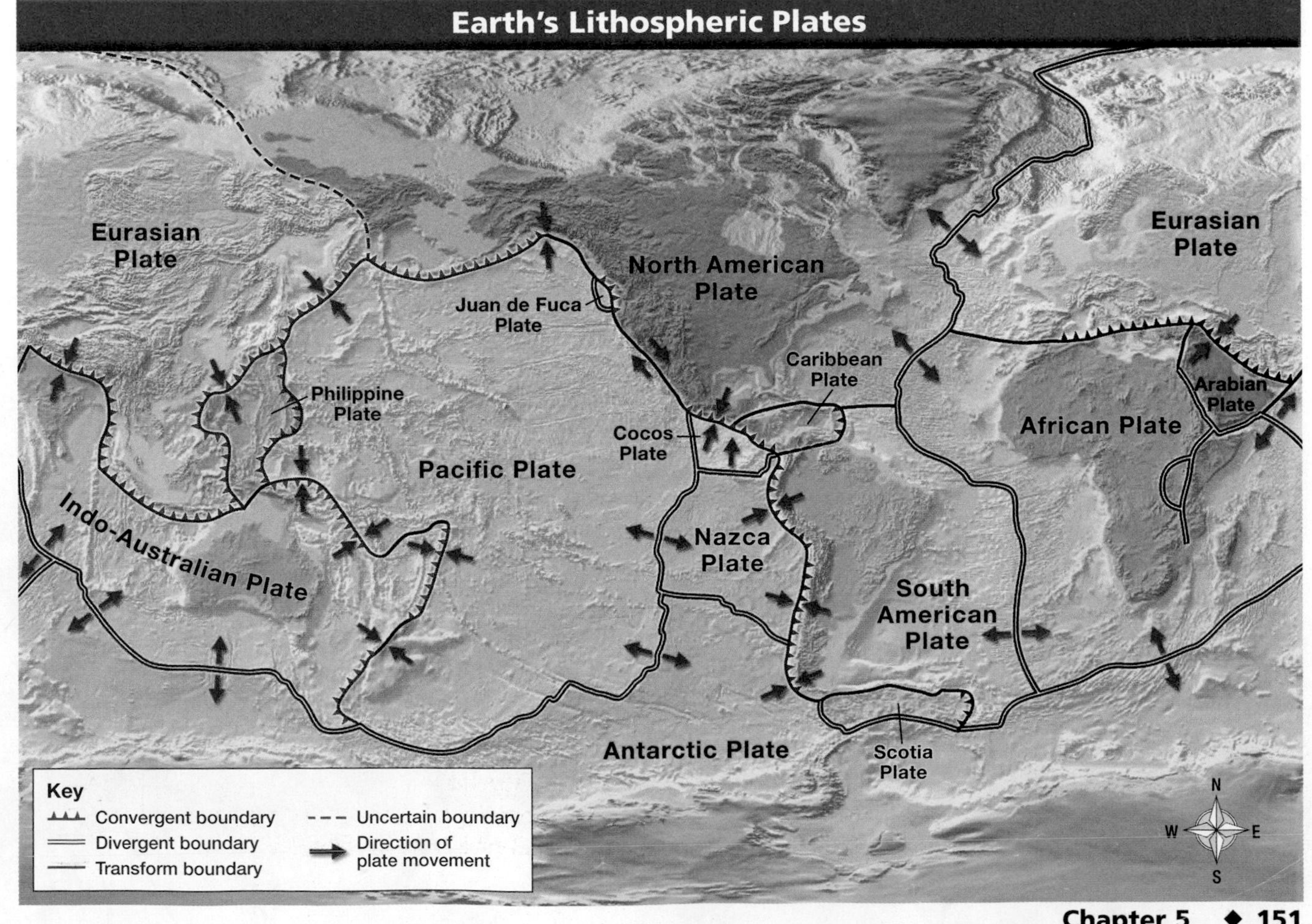

## Plate Boundaries

The edges of Earth's plates meet at plate boundaries. Plate boundaries extend deep into the lithosphere. **Faults** —breaks in Earth's crust where rocks have slipped past each other—form along these boundaries. **As shown in Figure 23, there are three kinds of plate boundaries: divergent boundaries, convergent boundaries, and transform boundaries. A different type of plate movement occurs along each type of boundary.**

Scientists have used instruments on satellites to measure plate motion very precisely. The plates move at amazingly slow rates: from about 1 to 24 centimeters per year. The North American and Eurasian plates are moving apart at a rate of 2.5 centimeters per year. That's about as fast as your fingernails grow. This may not seem like much, but these plates have been moving apart for tens of millions of years.

**Divergent Boundaries** The place where two plates move apart, or diverge, is called a **divergent boundary** (dy VUR junt). Most divergent boundaries occur along the mid-ocean ridges where sea-floor spreading occurs.

Divergent boundaries also occur on land. When a divergent boundary develops on land, two of Earth's plates slide apart. A deep valley called a **rift valley** forms along the divergent boundary. For example, the Great Rift Valley in East Africa marks a deep crack in the African continent.

FIGURE 23
### Plate Tectonics
Plate movements have built many of the features of Earth's land surfaces and ocean floors.
**Predicting** *What will eventually happen if a rift valley continues to pull apart?*

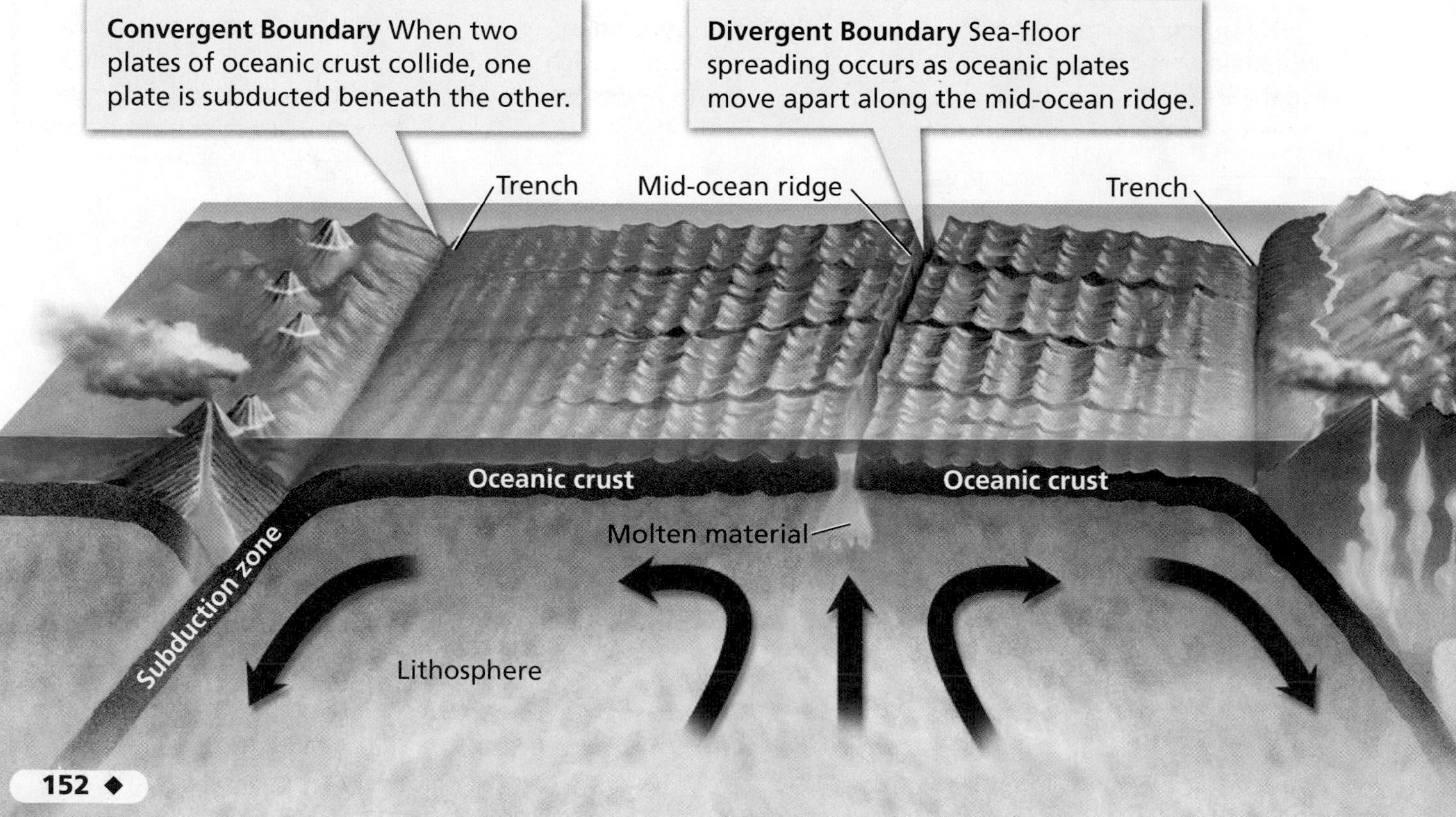
**Convergent Boundary** When two plates of oceanic crust collide, one plate is subducted beneath the other.
**Divergent Boundary** Sea-floor spreading occurs as oceanic plates move apart along the mid-ocean ridge.
Trench
Mid-ocean ridge
Trench
Oceanic crust
Oceanic crust
Molten material
Subduction zone
Lithosphere

**Convergent Boundaries** The place where two plates come together, or converge, is called a **convergent boundary** (kun VUR junt). When two plates converge, the result is called a collision. When two plates collide, the density of the plates determines which one comes out on top.

Oceanic crust becomes cooler and denser as it spreads away from the mid-ocean ridge. Where two plates carrying oceanic crust meet at a trench, the plate that is more dense sinks under the other plate.

Sometimes a plate carrying oceanic crust collides with a plate carrying continental crust. Oceanic crust is more dense than continental crust. The less dense continental crust can't sink under the more dense oceanic crust. Instead, subduction occurs as the oceanic plate sinks beneath the continental plate.

When two plates carrying continental crust collide, subduction does not take place. Neither piece of crust is dense enough to sink very far into the mantle. Instead, the collision squeezes the crust into mighty mountain ranges.

**Transform Boundaries** A **transform boundary** is a place where two plates slip past each other, moving in opposite directions. Earthquakes often occur along transform boundaries, but crust is neither created nor destroyed.

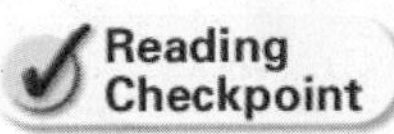


**What features form where two continental plates come together?**

### Calculating a Rate

To calculate the rate of plate motion, divide the distance the plate moves by the time it takes to move that distance.

$$\text{Rate} = \frac{\text{Distance}}{\text{Time}}$$

For example, a plate takes 2 million years to move 156 km. Calculate its rate of motion.

$$\frac{156 \text{ km}}{2{,}000{,}000 \text{ years}} = 7.8 \text{ cm per year}$$

**Practice Problem** The Pacific plate is sliding past the North American plate. It has taken 10 million years for the plate to move 600 km. What is the Pacific plate's rate of motion?

**Divergent Boundary** A rift valley forms when two pieces of continental crust pull apart.

**Transform Boundary** Two plates slide past each other.

**Convergent Boundary** Two continental plates collide, forming a mountain range.

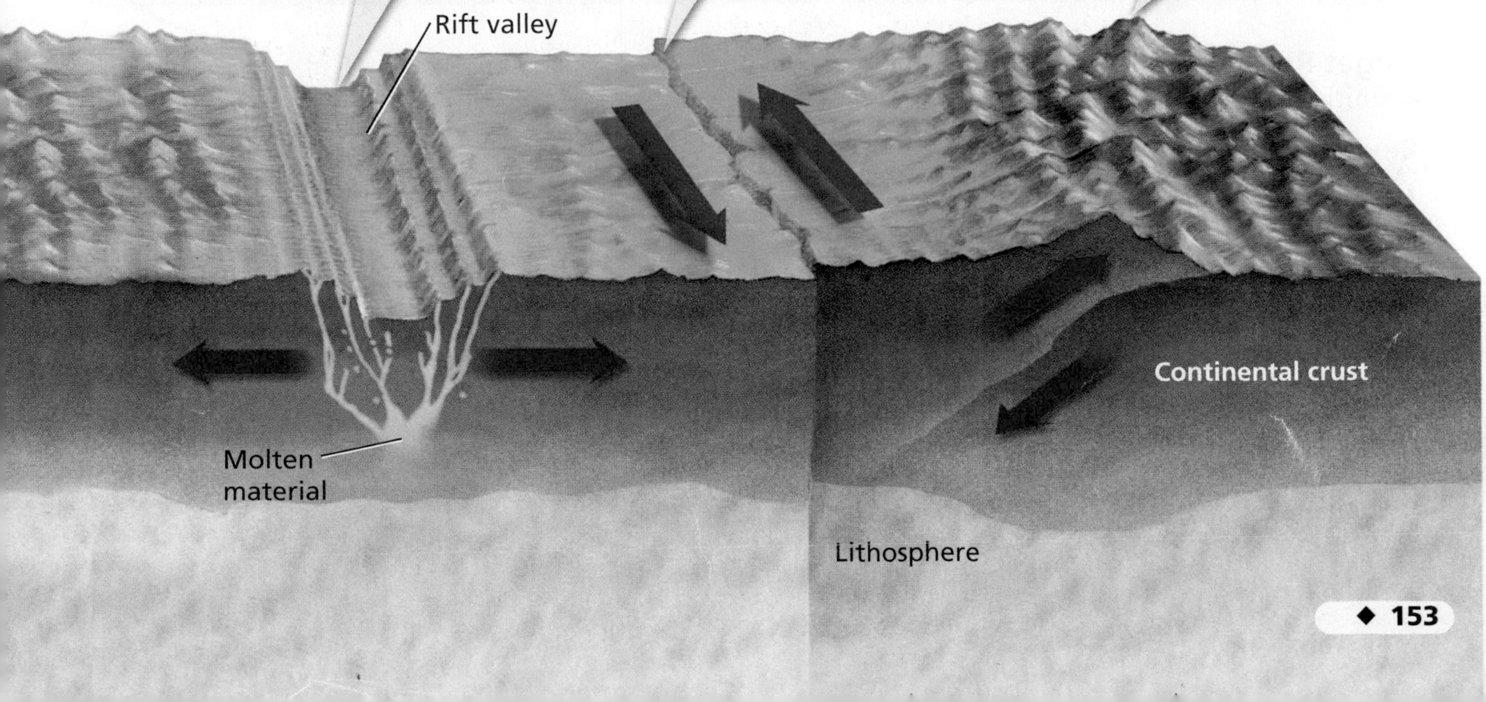

Rift valley

Molten material

Continental crust

Lithosphere

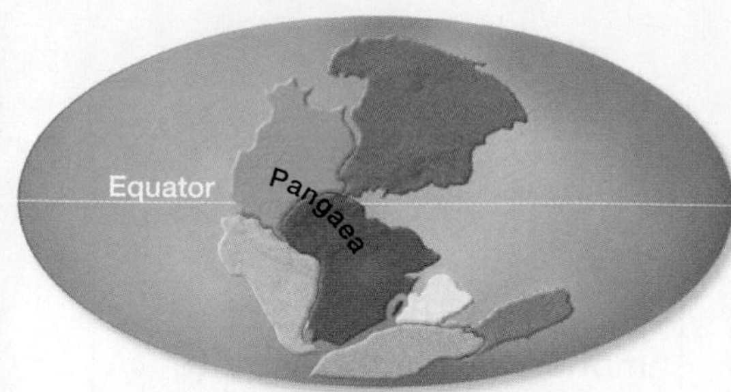


225 Million Years Ago

**Plate Motions Over Time** The movement of Earth's plates has greatly changed Earth's surface. Geologists have evidence that, before Pangaea existed, other supercontinents formed and split apart over billions of years. Pangaea itself formed when Earth's landmasses drifted together about 260 million years ago. Then, about 225 million years ago, Pangaea began to break apart. Figure 24 shows how major landmasses have moved since the breakup of Pangaea.

Laurasia
Equator
Gondwanaland

180–200 Million Years Ago

FIGURE 24
**Continental Drift**
It has taken the continents about 225 million years since the breakup of Pangaea to move to their present locations. **Posing Questions** *What questions would you need to answer in order to predict where the continents will be in 50 million years?*

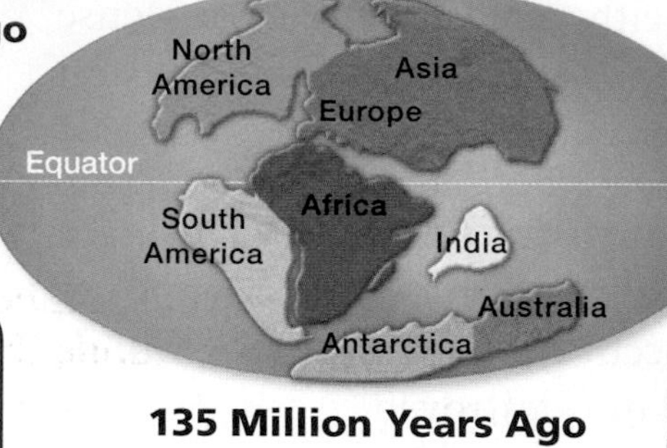

135 Million Years Ago

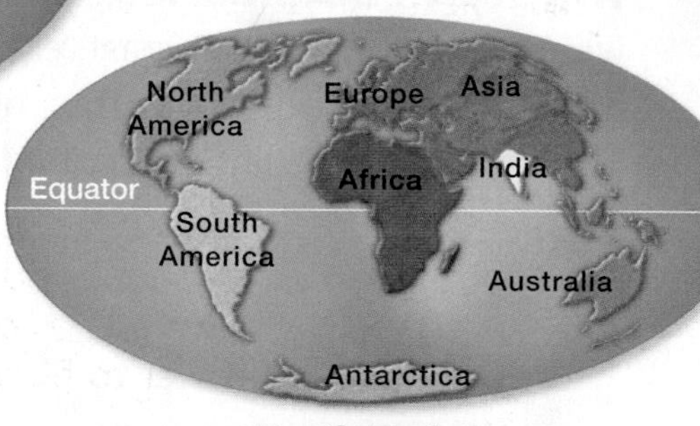


Earth Today

**Go Online**
*active art*
**For:** Continental Drift activity
**Visit:** PHSchool.com
**Web Code:** cfp-1015

## Section 5 Assessment

**Target Reading Skill Building Vocabulary** Use your definitions to help answer the questions.

### Reviewing Key Concepts

1. a. **Defining** What are plates?
   b. **Summarizing** In your own words, what is the theory of plate tectonics?
   c. **Relating Cause and Effect** What do scientists think causes the movement of Earth's plates?
2. a. **Listing** What are the three types of plate boundaries?
   b. **Describing** Describe the type of movement that occurs at each type of plate boundary.
   c. **Predicting** What is likely to occur at a plate boundary where oceanic crust collides with continental crust?

**Math Practice**

3. **Calculating a Rate** There are two islands on opposite sides of a mid-ocean ridge in the Atlantic Ocean. During the last 8 million years, the distance between the islands has increased by 200 kilometers. Calculate the rate at which the two plates are diverging.

Lab zone **Skills Lab**

# Modeling Mantle Convection Currents

## Problem

How might convection in Earth's mantle affect tectonic plates?

## Skills Focus

making models, observing

## Materials

- large plastic bottle
- food coloring
- small glass jar
- aluminum foil or plastic wrap
- rubber band
- several paper hole punches or small pieces of paper
- tap water

## Procedure

1. Fill the large bottle about half full with cold tap water.
2. Partly fill the small jar with hot tap water and stir in 6 drops of food coloring. Carefully add enough hot water to fill the jar to the brim.
3. Cover the top of the jar with aluminum foil or plastic wrap and secure with a rubber band.
4. Carefully lower the jar into the bottle of tap water.
5. Place the pieces of paper on the surface of the water.
6. Without disturbing the water, use the tip of the pencil to make two small holes about 2–4 mm in diameter in the material covering the jar.
7. Predict what will happen to the colored water and to the pieces of paper floating on the surface.
8. Observe the contents of the jar, as well as the paper pieces on the surface of the water.

## Analyze and Conclude

1. **Observing** Describe what happened to the colored water and to the pieces of paper after the holes were punched in the material covering the jar.
2. **Drawing Conclusions** How did your prediction compare with what actually happened to the colored water and pieces of paper?
3. **Inferring** What type of heat transfer took place in the bottle? Describe how the transfer occurred.
4. **Making Models** Which part of your model represents a tectonic plate? Which part represents Earth's mantle?
5. **Communicating** How well do you think this lab modeled the movement of Earth's plates? What similarities exist between this model and actual plate movement? What factors weren't you able to model in this lab?

## Designing Experiments

Repeat this activity, but develop a plan to measure the temperature of the water inside the large bottle. Is there a difference in temperature between the water's surface and the water near the top of the small jar? Do you observe any change in the convection currents as the water temperature changes? With your teacher's approval, carry out your plan.

**The BIG Idea** **Energy Transfer and Earth's Structure** Mantle convection causes the movement of pieces of the lithosphere called plates. Plate motions produce faults, mountain ranges, earthquakes, and volcanoes.

## 1 Earth's Interior

### Key Concepts

- Geologists have used two main types of evidence to learn about Earth's interior: direct evidence from rock samples and indirect evidence from seismic waves.
- The three main layers of Earth are the crust, the mantle, and the core. These layers vary in size, composition, temperature, and pressure.
- The crust is a layer of solid rock that includes both dry land and the ocean floor.
- Earth's mantle is made up of rock that is very hot, but solid. Scientists divide the mantle into layers based on physical characteristics.
- The core is made mostly of the metals iron and nickel. It consists of two parts—a liquid outer core and a solid inner core.

### Key Terms

• seismic waves • pressure • crust • basalt
• granite • mantle • lithosphere
• asthenosphere • outer core • inner core

## 2 Convection and the Mantle

### Key Concepts

- There are three types of heat transfer: radiation, conduction, and convection.
- Heating and cooling of the fluid, changes in the fluid's density, and the force of gravity combine to set convection currents in motion.
- Heat from the core and the mantle itself causes convection currents in the mantle.

### Key Terms

• radiation • conduction • convection
• density • convection current

## 3 Drifting Continents

### Key Concepts

- Wegener's hypothesis was that all the continents had once been joined together in a single landmass and have since drifted apart.
- Wegener gathered evidence from different scientific fields to support his ideas about continental drift. He studied land features, fossils, and evidence of climate change.
- Wegener could not provide a satisfactory explanation for the force that pushes or pulls the continents.

### Key Terms

• continental drift • Pangaea • fossil

## 4 Sea-Floor Spreading

### Key Concepts

- In sea-floor spreading, the sea floor spreads apart along both sides of a mid-ocean ridge as new crust is added. As a result, the ocean floors move like conveyor belts, carrying the continents along with them.
- Several types of evidence supported Hess's theory of sea-floor spreading: eruptions of molten material, magnetic stripes in the rock of the ocean floor, and the ages of the rocks.
- In a process taking tens of millions of years, part of the ocean floor sinks back into the mantle at deep-ocean trenches.

### Key Terms

• mid-ocean ridge • sonar • sea-floor spreading
• deep-ocean trench • subduction

## 5 The Theory of Plate Tectonics

### Key Concepts

- The theory of plate tectonics explains the formation, movement, and subduction of Earth's plates.
- There are three kinds of plate boundaries: divergent boundaries, convergent boundaries, and transform boundaries. A different type of plate movement occurs along each.

### Key Terms

• plate • scientific theory • plate tectonics
• fault • divergent boundary • rift valley
• convergent boundary • transform boundary

# Review and Assessment

For: Self-Assessment
Visit: PHSchool.com
Web Code: cfa-1010

## Organizing Information

**Comparing and Contrasting** Fill in the compare-and-contrast table to compare the characteristics of the different types of plate boundaries.

| Type of Plate Boundary | Type of Motion | Effect on Crust | Feature(s) Formed |
|---|---|---|---|
| a. ___?___ boundary | Plates slide past each other. | b. ___?___ | c. ___?___ |
| d. ___?___ boundary | e. ___?___ | Subduction or mountain building | f. ___?___ |
| g. ___?___ boundary | h. ___?___ | i. ___?___ | Mid-ocean ridge, ocean floor |

## Reviewing Key Terms

**Choose the letter of the best answer.**

1. The relatively soft layer of the upper mantle is the
   a. asthenosphere.
   b. lithosphere.
   c. inner core.
   d. continental crust.
2. The transfer of heat by the direct contact of particles of matter is
   a. pressure.
   b. radiation.
   c. conduction.
   d. convection.
3. Subduction of the ocean floor takes place at
   a. the lower mantle.
   b. mid-ocean ridges.
   c. rift valleys.
   d. trenches.
4. The process that powers plate tectonics is
   a. radiation.
   b. convection.
   c. conduction.
   d. subduction.
5. Two plates collide with each other at
   a. a divergent boundary.
   b. a convergent boundary.
   c. the boundary between the mantle and the crust.
   d. a transform boundary.

**If the statement is true, write *true*. If it is false, change the underlined word or words to make the statement true.**

6. Continental <u>crust</u> is made of rocks such as granite.
7. Slow movements of mantle rock called <u>radiation</u> transfer heat in the mantle.
8. The single landmass that broke apart 250 million years ago was <u>Pangaea</u>.
9. <u>Mid-ocean ridges</u> are places where oceanic crust sinks back to the mantle.
10. When two continental plates diverge, a <u>transform boundary</u> forms.

## Writing in Science

**Prediction** Now that you have learned about the theory of plate tectonics, write a paragraph predicting what the shape and positions of Earth's continents will be 50 million years in the future. Include what would happen to the oceans if continental landmasses became connected in new ways or drifted from their present locations.

*Plate Tectonics*
Video Preview
Video Field Trip
▶ Video Assessment

# Review and Assessment

## Checking Concepts

**11.** What kinds of indirect evidence do geologists use to study the structure of Earth?

**12.** How do temperature and pressure change as you go deeper into Earth?

**13.** What happens in Earth's interior to produce Earth's magnetic field? Describe the layer where the magnetic field is produced.

**14.** Why are there convection currents in the mantle?

**15.** Why are the oldest parts of the ocean floor no older than about 200 million years old?

**16.** How do magnetic stripes form on the ocean floor? Why are these stripes significant?

## Thinking Critically

**17. Comparing and Contrasting** How are oceanic and continental crust alike? How do they differ?

**18. Sequencing** Place these terms in correct order so they begin at Earth's surface and move toward the center: inner core, asthenosphere, lower mantle, lithosphere, outer core.

**19. Predicting** In the diagram below, a plate of oceanic crust is colliding with a plate of continental crust. What will happen? Why?

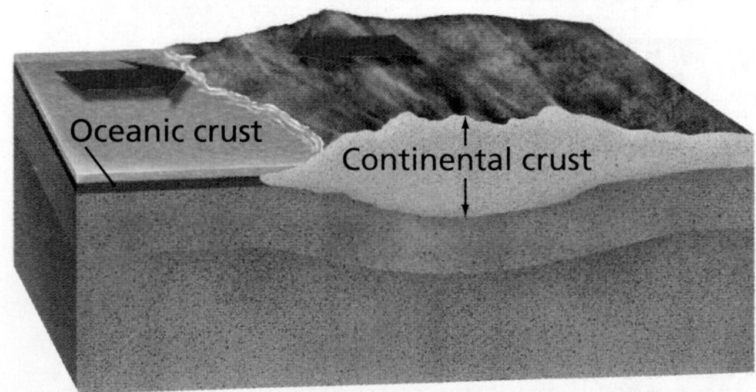


**20. Relating Cause and Effect** What do many geologists think is the driving force of plate tectonics? Explain.

**21. Making Judgments** Scientists refer to plate tectonics as a *theory*. What is a theory? How is plate tectonics a theory? Why isn't continental drift considered a theory? (*Hint*: Refer to the Skills Handbook for more on theories.)

## Math Practice

**22. Calculating a Rate** It takes 100,000 years for a plate to move about 14 kilometers. Calculate the rate of plate motion.

## Applying Skills

**Use the map to answer Questions 23–25.**

*Geologists think that a new plate boundary is forming in the Indian Ocean. The part of the plate carrying Australia is twisting away from the part of the plate carrying India.*

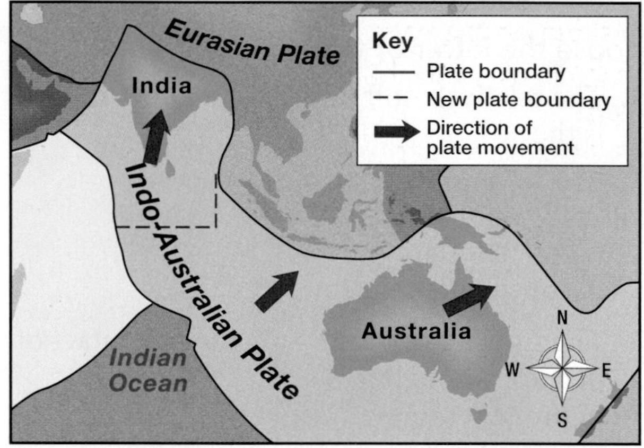


**23. Interpreting Maps** In what direction is the part of the plate carrying Australia moving? In what direction is the part carrying India moving?

**24. Predicting** As India and Australia move in different directions, what type of plate boundary will form between them?

**25. Inferring** What features could occur where the northern part of the Indo-Australian plate is colliding with the Eurasian plate?

## Lab zone Chapter Project

**Performance Assessment** Present your model to the class. Point out the types of plate boundaries on your model. Discuss the plate motions and landforms that result in these areas.

# Standardized Test Prep

**Test-Taking Tip**

**Using Formulas**

Some test questions require you to use a formula to answer a question. For example, in the question below you should recall that speed can be found using the following formula.

$$\text{Speed} = \frac{\text{Distance}}{\text{Time}}$$

To solve for a quantity in a formula, substitute known values, including units, for the variables. Be sure to include units in your final answer.

***Sample Question***

An island on the Pacific plate moves a distance of 550 cm in 50 years. What is the plate's rate of speed?

**A** 44 cm per year
**B** 110 cm per year
**C** 2,750 cm per year
**D** 11 cm per year

***Answer***

The answer is **D**.

$$\frac{550 \text{ cm}}{50 \text{ years}} = 11 \text{ cm per year}$$

**Choose the letter that best answers the question or completes the statement.**

**1.** Which of the following is evidence for sea-floor spreading?
**A** matching patterns of magnetic stripes in the ocean floor
**B** volcanic eruptions along mid-ocean ridges
**C** older rock found farther from mid-ocean ridges
**D** all of the above

**2.** Wegener thought the continents moved because fossils of the same organisms are found on widely separated continents. Wegener's use of fossil evidence is an example of a(n)
**F** prediction.
**G** observation.
**H** inference.
**J** controlled experiment.

**3.** The table below shows the movement of rock away from a mid-ocean ridge, and the time in years it takes sea-floor spreading to move the rock that distance.

| Distance (meters) | Time (years) |
|---|---|
| 50 | 4,000 |
| 100 | 8,000 |
| 150 | 12,000 |

What is the speed of the rock?
**A** 0.0125 m per year
**B** 12.5 m per year
**C** 80 m per year
**D** 200,000 m per year

**4.** Which of the following best describes the process in the diagram below?
**F** Converging plates form a transform boundary.
**G** Converging plates form volcanoes.
**H** Diverging plates form a mid-ocean ridge.
**J** Diverging plates form a rift valley.

### Constructed Response

**5.** Today, the Mediterranean Sea lies between Europe and Africa. But the African plate is moving toward the Eurasian plate at a rate of a few centimeters per year. Predict how this area will change in 100 million years. In your answer, first explain how the Mediterranean Sea will change. Then explain what will happen on land.

Chapter 6

# Earthquakes

## The BIG Idea

Energy Transfer and Earth's Structure

**What force deforms Earth's crust and causes earthquakes?**

### Chapter Preview



An earthquake destroyed this freeway in Oakland, California, in 1989. ▶

*Earthquakes*

▶ Video Preview
Video Field Trip
Video Assessment

Lab zone™ Chapter **Project**

## Design and Build an Earthquake-Safe House

Earthquakes like the ones that caused the damage in this picture are proof that our planet is subject to great forces from within. Earthquakes remind us that we live on the moving pieces of Earth's crust. In this Chapter Project you will design a structure that can withstand earthquakes.

**Your Goal** To design, build, and test a model structure that is earthquake resistant

Your structure must

- be made of materials that have been approved by your teacher
- be built to specifications agreed on by your class
- be able to withstand several "earthquakes" of increasing intensity
- be built following the safety guidelines in Appendix A

**Plan It!** Before you design your model, find out how earthquakes damage structures such as homes, office buildings, and highways. Preview the chapter to find out how engineers design structures to withstand earthquakes. Then choose materials for your structure and sketch your design. When your teacher has approved your design, build and test your structure.

Section 1

# Forces in Earth's Crust

## Reading Preview

### Key Concepts

- How does stress in the crust change Earth's surface?
- Where are faults usually found, and why do they form?
- What land features result from the forces of plate movement?

### Key Terms

- stress • tension
- compression • shearing
- normal fault • hanging wall
- footwall • reverse fault
- strike-slip fault • anticline
- syncline • plateau

### Target Reading Skill

**Building Vocabulary**
A definition states the meaning of a word or phrase. As you read, write a definition of each Key Term in your own words.

## Lab zone Discover Activity

### How Does Stress Affect Earth's Crust?

1. Put on your goggles.
2. Holding a popsicle stick at both ends, slowly bend it into an arch.
3. Release the pressure on the popsicle stick and observe what happens.
4. Repeat Steps 1 and 2. This time, however, keep bending the ends of the popsicle stick toward each other. What happens to the wood?

**Think It Over**
**Predicting** Think of the popsicle stick as a model for part of Earth's crust. What do you think might eventually happen as the forces of plate movement bend the crust?

The movement of Earth's plates creates enormous forces that squeeze or pull the rock in the crust as if it were a candy bar. These forces are examples of **stress,** a force that acts on rock to change its shape or volume. (A rock's volume is the amount of space the rock takes up.) Because stress is a force, it adds energy to the rock. The energy is stored in the rock until the rock changes shape or breaks.

If you try to break a caramel candy bar in two, it may only bend and stretch at first. Like a candy bar, many types of rock can bend or fold. But beyond a certain limit, even these rocks will break.

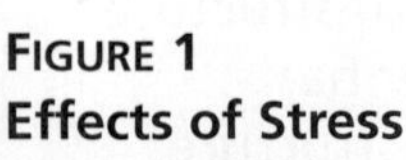

**FIGURE 1**
**Effects of Stress**
Powerful forces in Earth's crust caused the ground beneath this athletic field in Taiwan to change its shape.

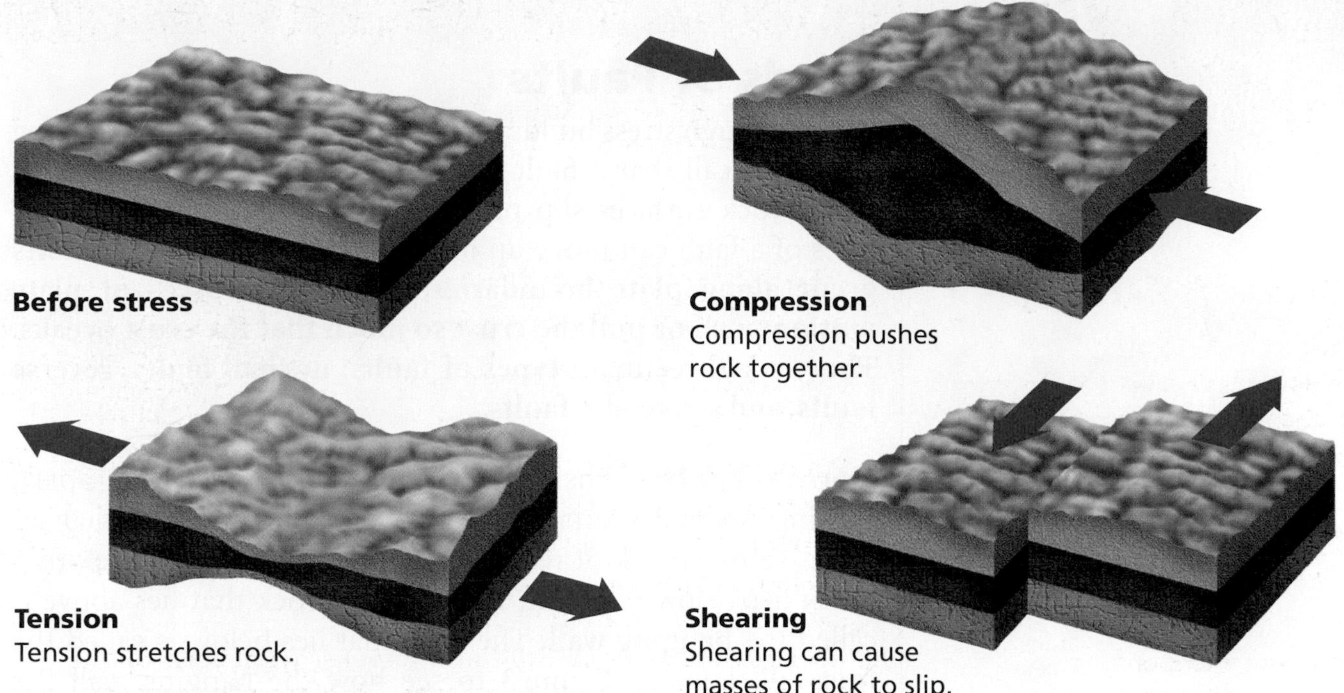


Before stress

Compression pushes rock together.

Shearing can cause masses of rock to slip.

## Types of Stress

Three different kinds of stress can occur in the crust—tension, compression, and shearing. **Tension, compression, and shearing work over millions of years to change the shape and volume of rock.** These forces cause some rocks to become brittle and snap. Other rocks bend slowly, like road tar softened by the sun. Figure 2 shows how stress affects the crust.

Most changes in the crust occur so slowly that they cannot be observed directly. But if you could speed up time so a billion years passed by in minutes, you could see the crust bend, stretch, break, tilt, fold, and slide. The slow shift of Earth's plates causes these changes.

**Tension** The stress force called **tension** pulls on the crust, stretching rock so that it becomes thinner in the middle. The effect of tension on rock is somewhat like pulling apart a piece of warm bubble gum. Tension occurs where two plates are moving apart.

**Compression** The stress force called **compression** squeezes rock until it folds or breaks. One plate pushing against another can compress rock like a giant trash compactor.

**Shearing** Stress that pushes a mass of rock in two opposite directions is called **shearing.** Shearing can cause rock to break and slip apart or to change its shape.

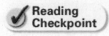

**Reading Checkpoint** **How does shearing affect rock in Earth's crust?**

Tension stretches rock.

FIGURE 2
**Stress in Earth's Crust**
Stress forces push, pull, or twist the rocks in Earth's crust.
**Relating Cause and Effect** *Which type of stress tends to shorten part of the crust?*

## Kinds of Faults

When enough stress builds up in rock, the rock breaks, creating a fault. Recall that a fault is a break in the rock of the crust where rock surfaces slip past each other. The rocks on both sides of a fault can move up or down or sideways. **Most faults occur along plate boundaries, where the forces of plate motion push or pull the crust so much that the crust breaks. There are three main types of faults: normal faults, reverse faults, and strike-slip faults.**

**Normal Faults** Tension in Earth's crust pulls rock apart, causing **normal faults.** In a normal fault, the fault is at an angle, so one block of rock lies above the fault while the other block lies below the fault. The block of rock that lies above is called the **hanging wall.** The rock that lies below is called the **footwall.** Look at Figure 3 to see how the hanging wall lies above the footwall. When movement occurs along a normal fault, the hanging wall slips downward. Normal faults occur where plates diverge, or pull apart. For example, normal faults are found along the Rio Grande rift valley in New Mexico, where two pieces of Earth's crust are under tension.

FIGURE 3
**Kinds of Faults**
There are three main kinds of faults: normal faults, reverse faults, and strike-slip faults.
**Inferring** *Which half of a normal fault would you expect to form the floor of a valley? Why?*

**Normal fault**
In a normal fault, the hanging wall slips down relative to the footwall.

**Reverse Faults** In places where the rock of the crust is pushed together, compression causes reverse faults to form. A **reverse fault** has the same structure as a normal fault, but the blocks move in the opposite direction. Look at Figure 3 to see how the rocks along a reverse fault move. As in a normal fault, one side of a reverse fault lies at an angle above the other side. The rock forming the hanging wall of a reverse fault slides up and over the footwall. Movement along reverse faults produced part of the northern Rocky Mountains in the western United States and Canada.

For: Links on faults
Visit: www.SciLinks.org
Web Code: scn-1021

**Strike-Slip Faults** In places where plates move past each other, shearing creates strike-slip faults. In a **strike-slip fault,** the rocks on either side of the fault slip past each other sideways, with little up or down motion. A strike-slip fault that forms the boundary between two plates is called a transform boundary. The San Andreas fault in California is an example of a strike-slip fault that is a transform boundary.

**What is the difference between a hanging wall and a footwall?**

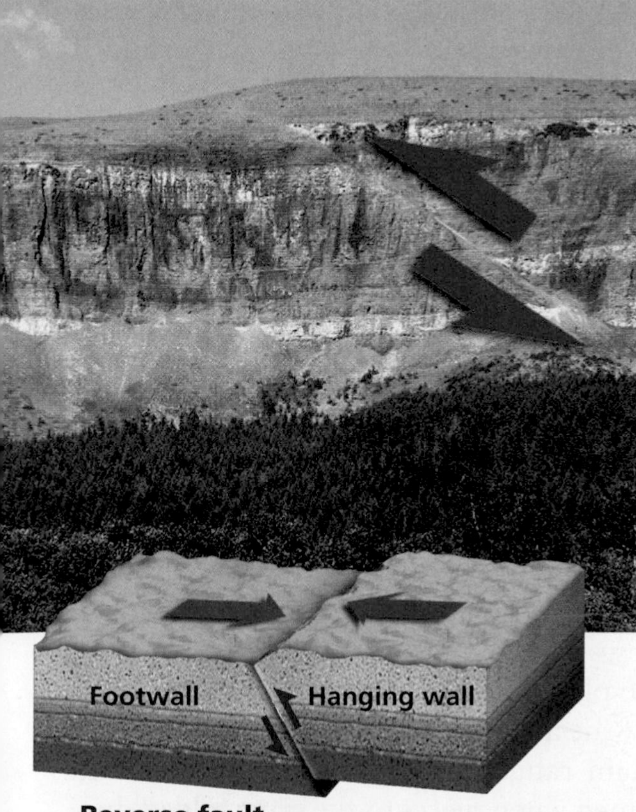


**Reverse fault**
In a reverse fault, the hanging wall moves up relative to the footwall.

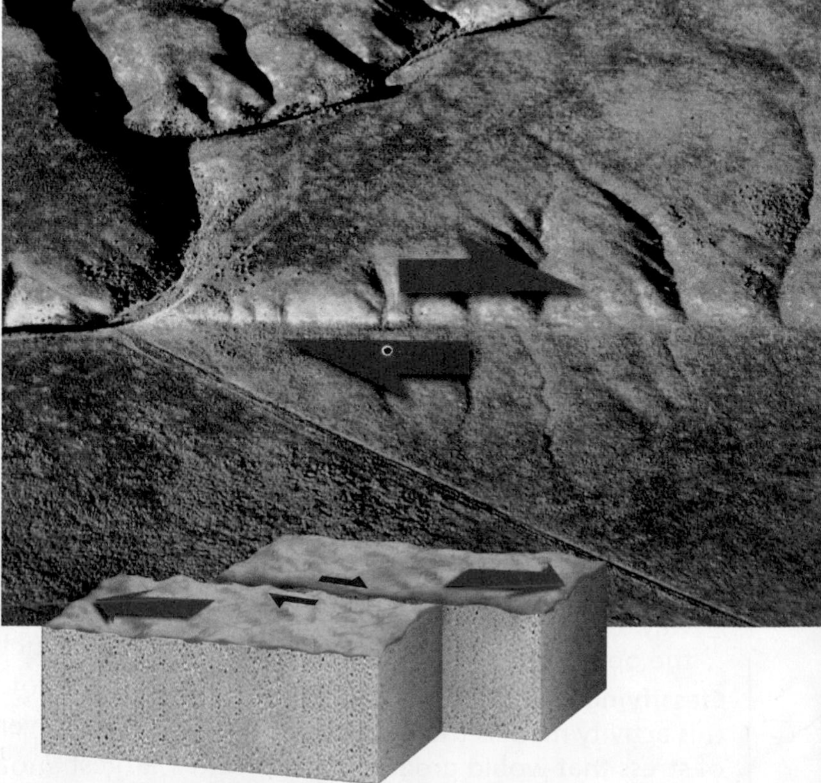

**Strike-slip fault**
Rocks on either side of a strike-slip fault slip past each other.

**FIGURE 4**
**Effects of Folding**
Compression and folding of the crust produce anticlines, which arch upward, and synclines, which dip downward. Over millions of years, folding can push up high mountain ranges.
**Predicting** *If the folding in the diagram continued, what kind of fault might form?*

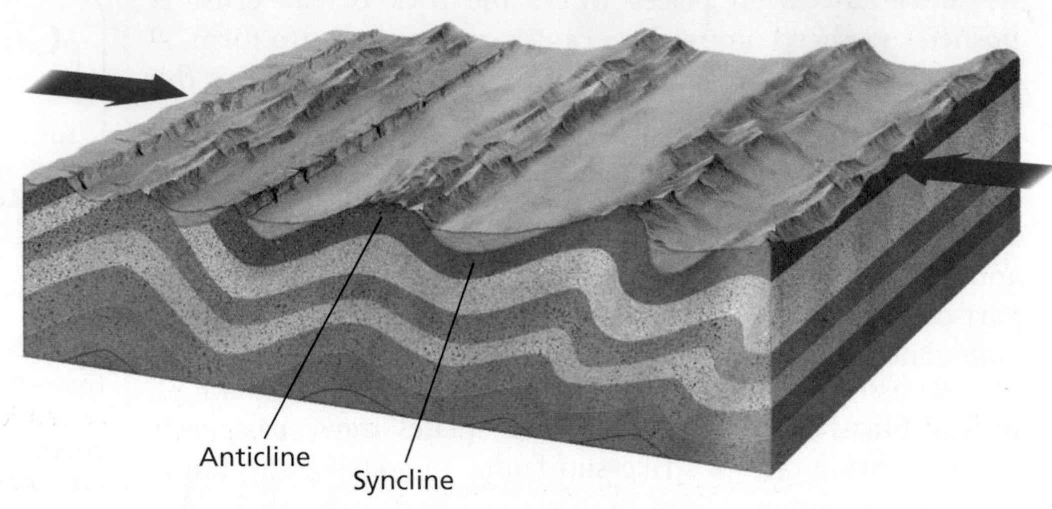


## Changing Earth's Surface

The forces produced by the movement of Earth's plates can fold, stretch, and uplift the crust. **Over millions of years, the forces of plate movement can change a flat plain into landforms such as anticlines and synclines, folded mountains, fault-block mountains, and plateaus.**

**Folding Earth's Crust** Sometimes plate movement causes the crust to fold. Have you ever skidded on a rug that wrinkled up as your feet pushed it across the floor? Much as the rug wrinkles, rock stressed by compression may bend without breaking. Folds are bends in rock that form when compression shortens and thickens part of Earth's crust. A fold can be only a few centimeters across or hundreds of kilometers wide. You can often see small folds in the rock exposed where a highway has been cut through a hillside.

Geologists use the terms anticline and syncline to describe upward and downward folds in rock. A fold in rock that bends upward into an arch is an **anticline,** shown in Figure 4. A fold in rock that bends downward to form a valley is a **syncline.** Anticlines and synclines are found in many places where compression forces have folded the crust. The central Appalachian Mountains in Pennsylvania are folded mountains made up of anticlines and synclines.

The collision of two plates can cause compression and folding of the crust over a wide area. Folding produced some of the world's largest mountain ranges. The Himalayas in Asia and the Alps in Europe formed when pieces of the crust folded during the collision of two plates.

**Lab zone** **Try This Activity**

### Modeling Stress

You can model the stresses that create faults.

1. Knead a piece of plastic putty until it is soft.
2. Push the ends of the putty toward the middle.
3. Pull the ends apart.
4. Push half of the putty one way and the other half in the opposite direction.

**Classifying** Which step in this activity models the type of stress that would produce anticlines and synclines?

**Stretching Earth's Crust** When two normal faults cut through a block of rock, a fault-block mountain forms. You can see a diagram of this process in Figure 5. How does this process begin? Where two plates move away from each other, tension forces create many normal faults. When two of these normal faults form parallel to each other, a block of rock is left lying between them. As the hanging wall of each normal fault slips downward, the block in between moves upward, forming a fault-block mountain.

If you traveled by car from Salt Lake City to Los Angeles, you would cross the Great Basin. This region contains many ranges of fault-block mountains separated by broad valleys, or basins.

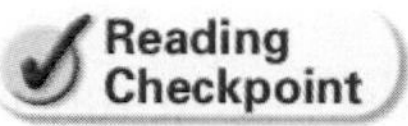

**What type of plate movement causes fault-block mountains to form?**

**FIGURE 5**
**Fault-Block Mountains**
As tension forces pull the crust apart, two parallel normal faults can form a range of fault-block mountains, like this mountain range in Idaho.

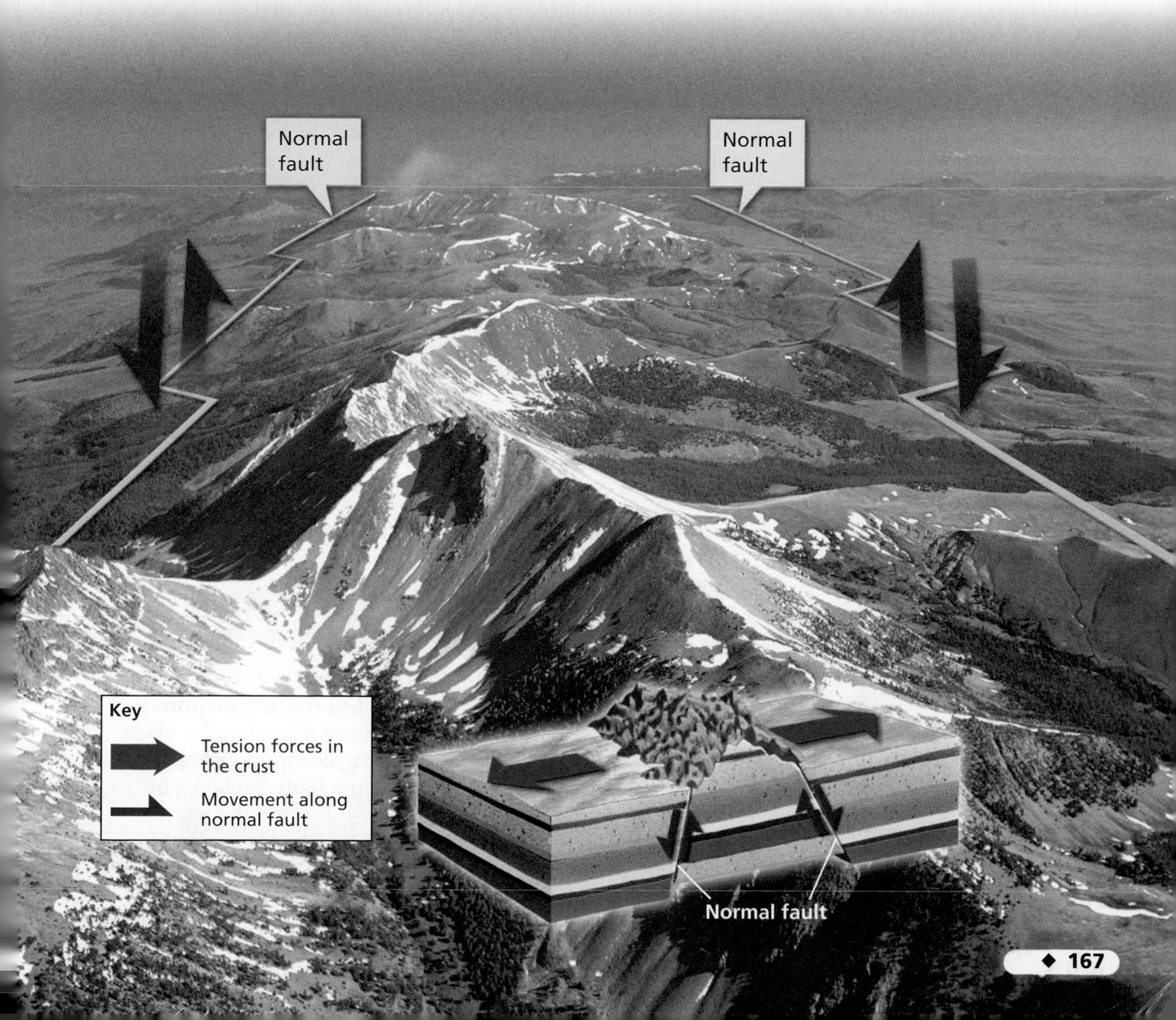

**FIGURE 6**
**The Kaibab Plateau**
The flat land on the horizon is the Kaibab Plateau, which forms the North Rim of the Grand Canyon in Arizona. The Kaibab Plateau is part of the Colorado Plateau.

**Uplifting Earth's Crust** The forces that raise mountains can also uplift, or raise, plateaus. A **plateau** is a large area of flat land elevated high above sea level. Some plateaus form when forces in Earth's crust push up a large, flat block of rock. Like a fancy sandwich, a plateau consists of many different flat layers, and is wider than it is tall.

Forces deforming the crust uplifted the Colorado Plateau in the "Four Corners" region of Arizona, Utah, Colorado, and New Mexico. Much of the Colorado Plateau lies more than 1,500 meters above sea level. Figure 6 shows one part of that plateau in northern Arizona.

## Section 1 Assessment

**Target Reading Skill** **Building Vocabulary** Refer to your definitions of the Key Terms to help you answer the following questions.

### Reviewing Key Concepts

1. a. **Reviewing** What are the three main types of stress in rock?
   b. **Relating Cause and Effect** How does tension change the shape of Earth's crust?
   c. **Comparing and Contrasting** Compare the way that compression affects the crust to the way that tension affects the crust.
2. a. **Describing** What is a fault?
   b. **Explaining** Why do faults often occur along plate boundaries?
   c. **Relating Cause and Effect** What type of fault is formed when plates diverge, or pull apart? What type of fault is formed when plates are pushed together?
3. a. **Listing** Name five kinds of landforms caused by plate movement.
   b. **Relating Cause and Effect** What are three landforms produced by compression in the crust? What landform is produced by tension?

### Lab zone At-Home Activity

**Modeling Faults** To model Earth's crust, roll modeling clay into layers and then press the layers together to form a rectangular block. Use a plastic knife to slice through the block at an angle, forming a fault. Explain which parts of your model represent the land surface, the hanging wall, and the footwall. Then show the three ways in which the sides of the fault can move.

Section 2

# Earthquakes and Seismic Waves

## Reading Preview

### Key Concepts

- How does the energy of an earthquake travel through Earth?
- What are the scales used to measure the strength of an earthquake?
- How do scientists locate the epicenter of an earthquake?

### Key Terms

- earthquake
- focus
- epicenter
- P wave
- S wave
- surface wave
- Mercalli scale
- magnitude
- Richter scale
- seismograph
- moment magnitude scale

### Target Reading Skill

**Identifying Main Ideas** As you read Types of Seismic Waves, write the main idea in a graphic organizer like the one below. Then write three supporting details. The supporting details further explain the main idea.

Main Idea

Seismic waves carry the energy of an earthquake.

Detail | Detail | Detail

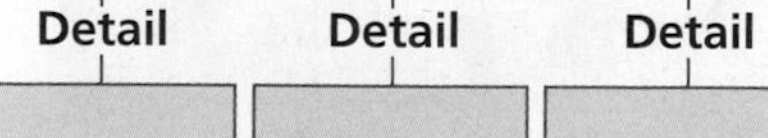

## Lab zone Discover Activity

### How Do Seismic Waves Travel Through Earth?

1. Stretch a spring toy across the floor while a classmate holds the other end. Do not overstretch the toy.
2. Gather together about four coils of the spring toy and release them. In what direction do the coils move?
3. Once the spring toy has stopped moving, jerk one end of the toy from side to side once. Be certain your classmate has a secure grip on the other end. In what direction do the coils move?

**Think It Over**

**Observing** Describe the two types of wave motion that you observed in the spring toy.

Earth is never still. Every day, worldwide, there are several thousand earthquakes. An **earthquake** is the shaking and trembling that results from the movement of rock beneath Earth's surface. Most earthquakes are too small to notice. But a large earthquake can produce dramatic changes in Earth's surface and cause great damage.

The forces of plate movement cause earthquakes. Plate movements produce stress in Earth's crust, adding energy to rock and forming faults. Stress increases along a fault until the rock breaks. An earthquake begins. In seconds, the earthquake releases an enormous amount of stored energy.

Most earthquakes begin in the lithosphere within about 100 kilometers of Earth's surface. The **focus** (FOH kus) is the area beneath Earth's surface where rock that is under stress breaks, triggering an earthquake. The point on the surface directly above the focus is called the **epicenter** (EP uh sen tur).

## Types of Seismic Waves

Like a pebble thrown into a pond, an earthquake produces vibrations called waves. These waves carry energy as they travel outward. During an earthquake, seismic waves race out from the focus in all directions. Seismic waves are vibrations that travel through Earth carrying the energy released during an earthquake. The seismic waves move like ripples in a pond. **Seismic waves carry energy from an earthquake away from the focus, through Earth's interior, and across the surface.** That's what happened in 2002, when a powerful earthquake ruptured the Denali fault in Alaska, shown in Figure 7.

There are three main categories of seismic waves: P waves, S waves, and surface waves. An earthquake sends out two types of waves from its focus: P waves and S waves. When these waves reach Earth's surface at the epicenter, surface waves develop.

FIGURE 7
### Seismic Waves
This diagram shows an earthquake along the Denali fault. An earthquake occurs when rocks fracture deep in the crust. The seismic waves move out in all directions from the focus.
**Interpreting Diagrams** *At what point do seismic waves first reach the surface?*

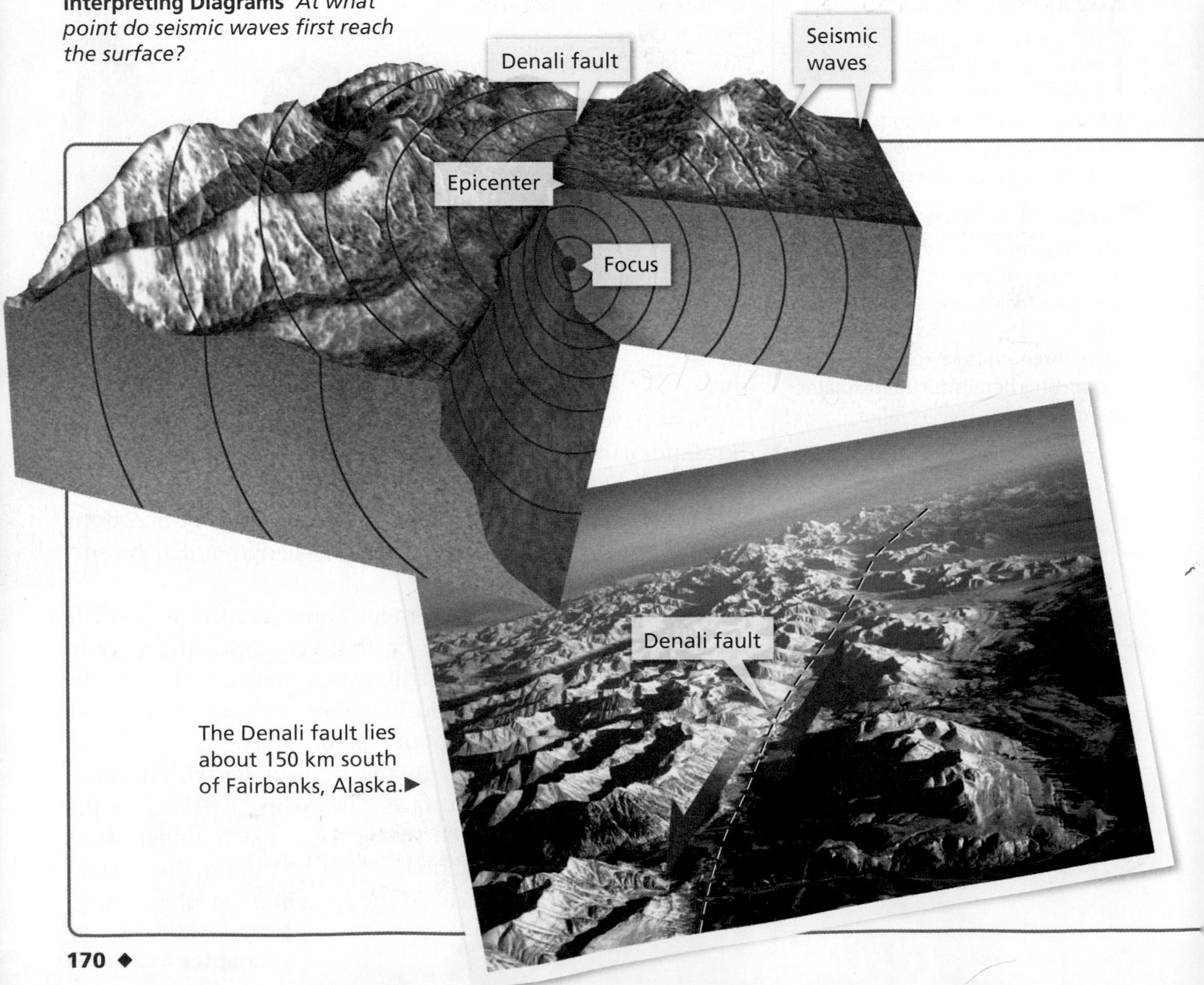


The Denali fault lies about 150 km south of Fairbanks, Alaska.▶

**P Waves** The first waves to arrive are primary waves, or P waves. **P waves** are seismic waves that compress and expand the ground like an accordion. Like the other types of seismic waves, P waves can damage buildings. Look at Figure 7 to see how P waves move.

**S Waves** After P waves come secondary waves, or S waves. **S waves** are seismic waves that vibrate from side to side as well as up and down. They shake the ground back and forth. When S waves reach the surface, they shake structures violently. Unlike P waves, which travel through both solids and liquids, S waves cannot move through liquids.

**Surface Waves** When P waves and S waves reach the surface, some of them become surface waves. **Surface waves** move more slowly than P waves and S waves, but they can produce severe ground movements. Some surface waves make the ground roll like ocean waves. Other surface waves shake buildings from side to side.

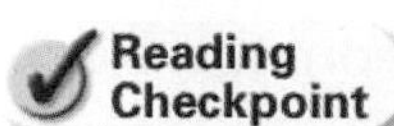


**Which type of seismic wave causes the ground to roll like ocean waves?**

**For:** Seismic Waves activity
**Visit:** PHSchool.com
**Web Code:** cfp-1022

**P waves ▼**
The crust vibrates forward and back along the path of the wave.

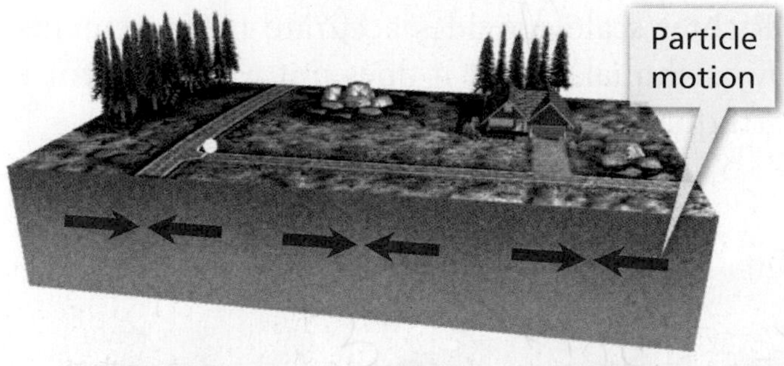


**S waves ▼**
The crust vibrates from side to side and up and down.

**◀ Surface waves**
The ground surface rolls with a wavelike motion.

## Measuring Earthquakes

When an earthquake occurs, people want to know "How big was the quake?" and "Where was it centered?" When geologists want to know the size of an earthquake, they must consider many factors. As a result, there are at least 20 different measures for rating earthquakes, each with its strengths and shortcomings. **Three commonly used methods of measuring earthquakes are the Mercalli scale, the Richter scale, and the moment magnitude scale.**

**The Mercalli Scale** The **Mercalli scale** was developed to rate earthquakes according to the level of damage at a given place. The 12 steps of the Mercalli scale, shown in Figure 9, describe an earthquake's effects. The same earthquake can have different Mercalli ratings because it causes different amounts of ground motion at different locations.

**The Richter Scale** An earthquake's **magnitude** is a number that geologists assign to an earthquake based on the earthquake's size. Geologists determine magnitude by measuring the seismic waves and fault movement that occur during an earthquake. The **Richter scale** is a rating of an earthquake's magnitude based on the size of the earthquake's seismic waves. The seismic waves are measured by a **seismograph.** A seismograph is an instrument that records and measures seismic waves. The Richter scale provides accurate measurements for small, nearby earthquakes. But it does not work well for large or distant earthquakes.

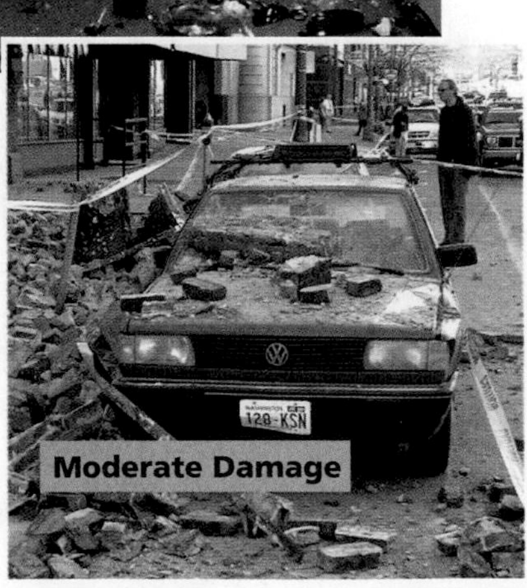


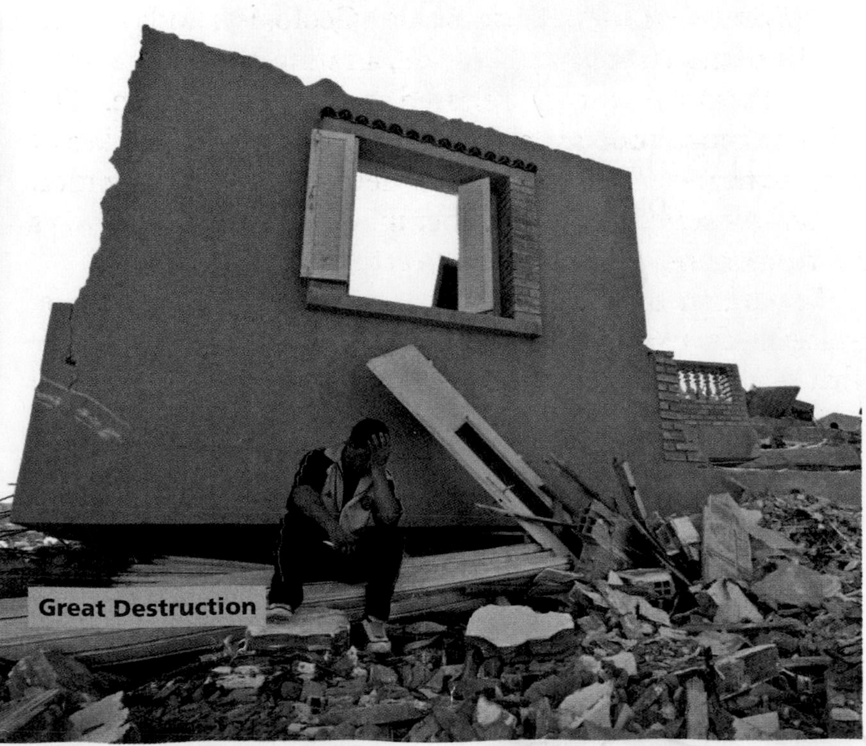


**FIGURE 8**
**Levels of Earthquake Damage**
The level of damage caused by an earthquake varies depending on the magnitude of the earthquake and the distance from the epicenter.

FIGURE 9
**The Mercalli Scale**
The Mercalli scale uses Roman numerals to rank earthquakes by how much damage they cause.
**Applying Concepts** *How would you rate the three examples of earthquake damage in Figure 8?*

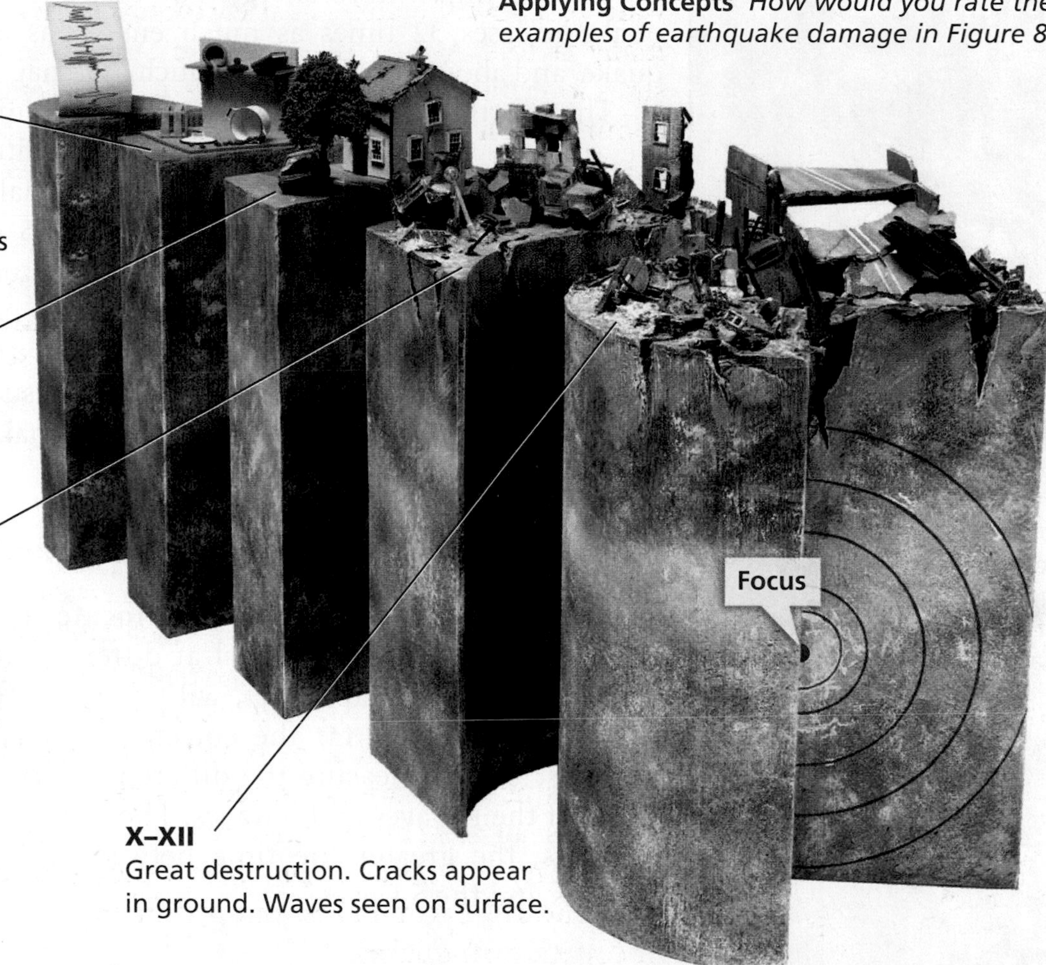
I–III
People notice vibrations like those from a passing truck. Unstable objects disturbed.
IV–VI
Slight damage. People run outdoors.
VII–IX
Moderate to heavy damage. Buildings jolted off foundations or destroyed.
X–XII
Great destruction. Cracks appear in ground. Waves seen on surface.
Focus

**The Moment Magnitude Scale** Geologists today often use the **moment magnitude scale,** a rating system that estimates the total energy released by an earthquake. The moment magnitude scale can be used to rate earthquakes of all sizes, near or far. You may hear news reports that mention the Richter scale. But the number they quote is almost always the moment magnitude for that earthquake.

To rate an earthquake on the moment magnitude scale, geologists first study data from seismographs. The data show what kinds of seismic waves the earthquake produced and how strong they were. The data also help geologists infer how much movement occurred along the fault and the strength of the rocks that broke when the fault slipped. Geologists use all this information to rate the quake on the moment magnitude scale.

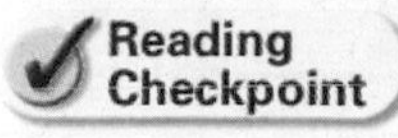
Reading Checkpoint

**What evidence do geologists use to rate an earthquake on the moment magnitude scale?**

**Lab zone Skills Activity**

## Classifying

Classify the earthquake damage at these locations using the Mercalli scale.

1. Many buildings are destroyed; cracks form in the ground.
2. Several old brick buildings and a bridge collapse.
3. Canned goods fall off shelves; walls crack; people go outside to see what's happening.

**FIGURE 10**
**Collecting Seismic Data**
This geologist is checking data collected after an earthquake. These data can be used to pinpoint the epicenter of an earthquake.

**Comparing Magnitudes** An earthquake's magnitude tells geologists how much energy was released by the earthquake. Each one-point increase in magnitude represents the release of roughly 32 times more energy. For example, a magnitude 6 quake releases 32 times as much energy as a magnitude 5 quake, and about 1,000 times as much as a magnitude 4 quake.

The effects of an earthquake increase with magnitude. People scarcely notice earthquakes with magnitudes below 3. Earthquakes with a magnitude below 5 are small and cause little damage. Those with a magnitude between 5 and 6 can cause moderate damage. Earthquakes with a magnitude above 6 can cause great damage. Fortunately, the most powerful earthquakes, with a magnitude of 8 or above, are rare. During the twentieth century, only two earthquakes measured above 9 on the moment magnitude scale. These earthquakes occurred in Chile in 1960 and in Alaska in 1964.

## Locating the Epicenter

**Geologists use seismic waves to locate an earthquake's epicenter.** Seismic waves travel at different speeds. P waves arrive at a seismograph first, with S waves following close behind. To tell how far the epicenter is from the seismograph, scientists measure the difference between the arrival times of the P waves and S waves. The farther away an earthquake is, the greater the time between the arrival of the P waves and the S waves.

## Math Analyzing Data

### Seismic Wave Speeds

Seismographs at five observation stations recorded the arrival times of the P and S waves produced by an earthquake. These data are shown in the graph.

1. **Reading Graphs** What variable is shown on the *x*-axis of the graph? The *y*-axis?
2. **Reading Graphs** How long did it take the S waves to travel 2,000 km?
3. **Estimating** How long did it take the P waves to travel 2,000 km?
4. **Calculating** What is the difference in the arrival times of the P waves and the S waves at 2,000 km? At 4,000 km?

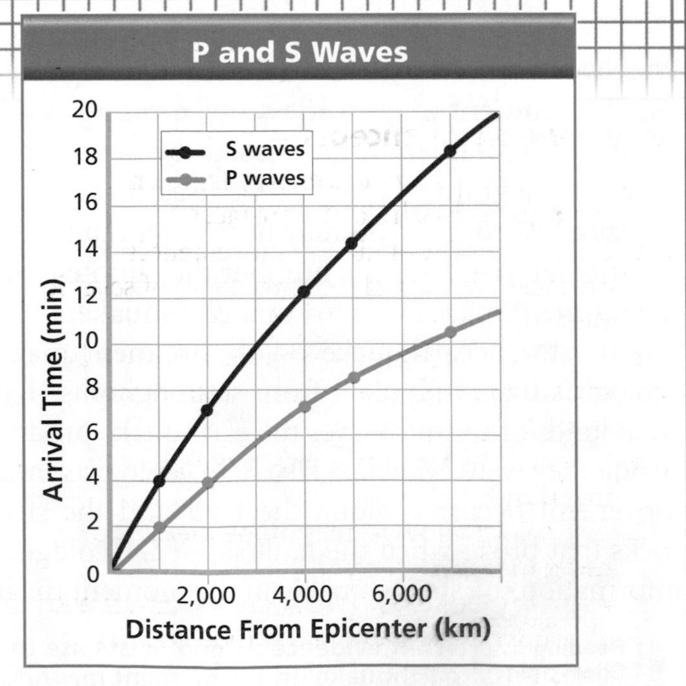

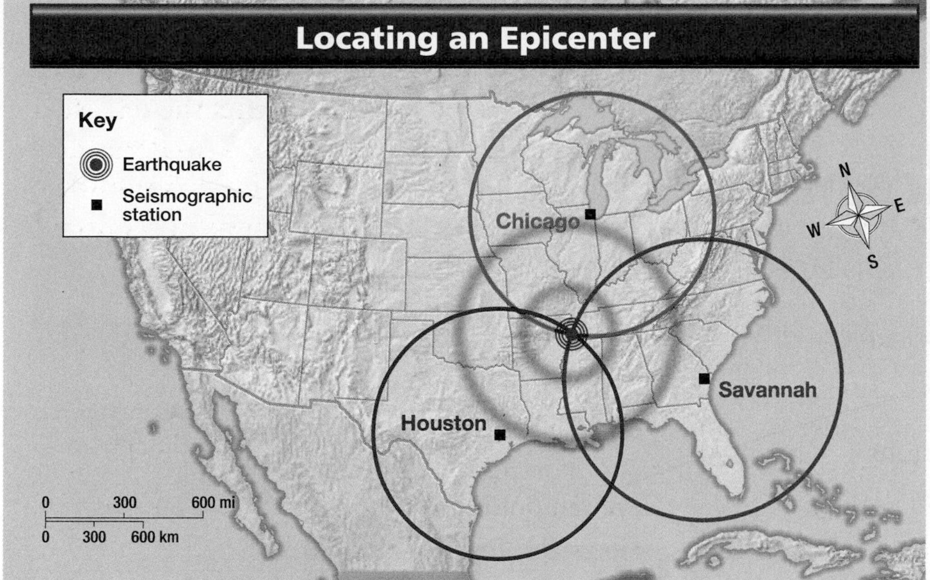


**FIGURE 11**
The map shows how to find the epicenter of an earthquake using data from three seismographic stations. **Measuring** *Use the map scale to determine the distances from Savannah and Houston to the epicenter. Which is closer?*

Geologists then draw at least three circles using data from different seismographs set up at stations all over the world. The center of each circle is a particular seismograph's location. The radius of each circle is the distance from that seismograph to the epicenter. As you can see in Figure 11, the point where the three circles intersect is the location of the epicenter.

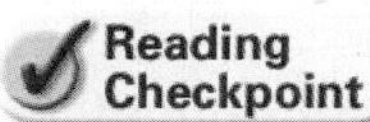


**What do geologists measure to determine the distance from a seismograph to an epicenter?**

## Section 2 Assessment

### Target Reading Skill

**Identifying Main Ideas** Use your graphic organizer to help you answer Question 1 below.

### Reviewing Key Concepts

1. a. **Reviewing** How does energy from an earthquake reach Earth's surface?
   b. **Describing** What kind of movement is produced by each of the three types of seismic waves?
   c. **Sequencing** When do P waves arrive at the surface in relation to S waves and surface waves?
2. a. **Defining** What is an earthquake's magnitude?
   b. **Describing** How is magnitude measured using the Richter scale?
   c. **Applying Concepts** What are the advantages of using the moment magnitude scale to measure an earthquake?
3. a. **Explaining** What type of data do geologists use to locate an earthquake's epicenter?
   b. **Interpreting Maps** Study the map in Figure 11 above. Then describe the method that scientists use to determine the epicenter of an earthquake.

### Writing in Science

**News Report** As a television news reporter, you are covering an earthquake rated between IV and V on the Mercalli scale. Write a short news story describing the earthquake's effects. Your lead paragraph should tell *who, what, where, when,* and *how*. (*Hint:* Refer to Figure 9 for examples of earthquake damage.)

Lab zone **Skills Lab**

# Finding the Epicenter

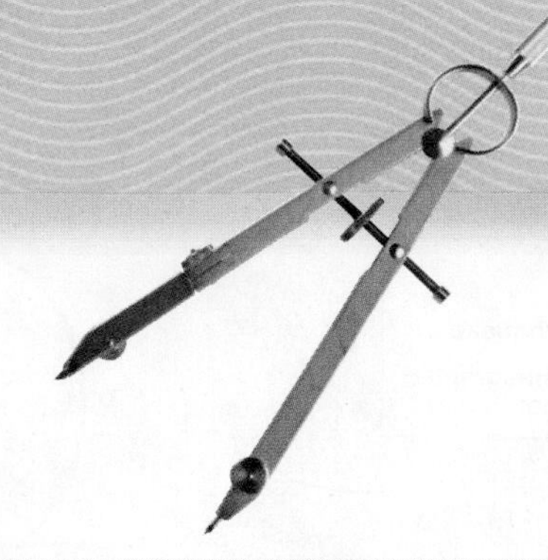

## Problem

How can you locate an earthquake's epicenter?

## Skills Focus

interpreting data, drawing conclusions

## Materials

- drawing compass with pencil
- outline map of the United States

| Data Table | | |
|---|---|---|
| City | Difference in P and S Wave Arrival Times | Distance to Epicenter |
| Denver, Colorado | 2 min 40 s | |
| Houston, Texas | 1 min 50 s | |
| Chicago, Illinois | 1 min 10 s | |

## Procedure

1. Make a copy of the data table showing differences in earthquake arrival times.
2. The graph shows how the difference in arrival time between P waves and S waves depends on the distance from the epicenter of the earthquake. Find the difference in arrival time for Denver on the *y*-axis of the graph. Follow this line across to the point at which it crosses the curve. To find the distance to the epicenter, read down from this point to the *x*-axis of the graph. Enter this distance in the data table.
3. Repeat Step 2 for Houston and Chicago.
4. Set your compass at a radius equal to the distance from Denver to the earthquake epicenter that you previously recorded in your data table.
5. Draw a circle with the radius determined in Step 4, using Denver as the center. Draw the circle on your copy of the map. (*Hint:* Draw your circles carefully. You may need to draw some parts of the circles off the map.)
6. Repeat Steps 4 and 5 for Houston and Chicago.

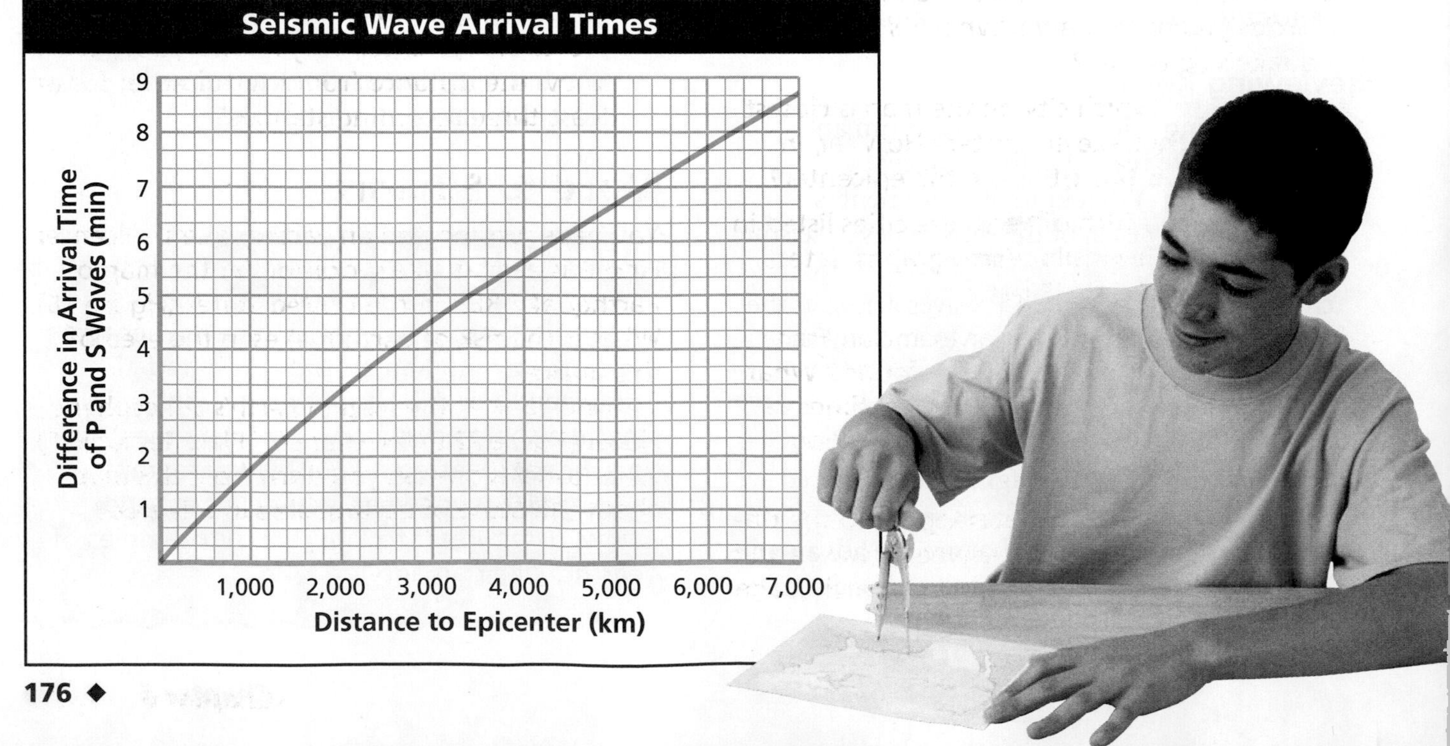

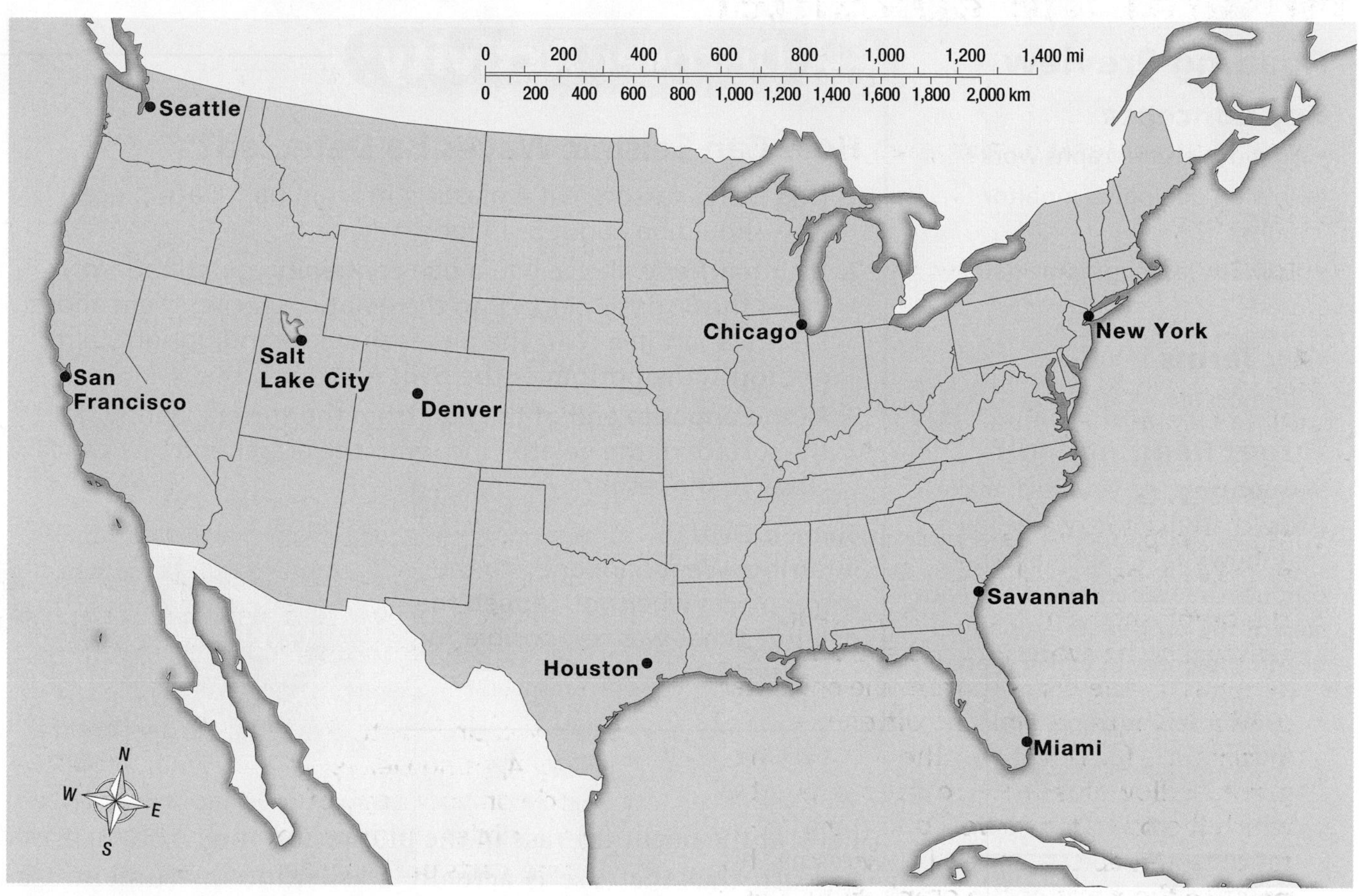


## Analyze and Conclude

1. **Drawing Conclusions** Observe the three circles you have drawn. Where is the earthquake's epicenter?
2. **Measuring** Which city on the map is closest to the earthquake epicenter? How far, in kilometers, is this city from the epicenter?
3. **Inferring** In which of the three cities listed in the data table would seismographs detect the earthquake first? Last?
4. **Estimating** About how far from San Francisco is the epicenter that you found? What would be the difference in arrival times of the P waves and S waves for a recording station in San Francisco?
5. **Interpreting Data** What happens to the difference in arrival times between P waves and S waves as the distance from the earthquake increases?
6. **Communicating** Review the procedure you followed in this lab and then answer the following question. When you are trying to locate an epicenter, why is it necessary to know the distance from the epicenter for at least three recording stations?

## More to Explore

You have just located an earthquake's epicenter. Find this earthquake's location on the map of Earthquake Risk in the United States (Figure 18). What is the risk of earthquakes in the area of this quake?

Now look at the map of Earth's Lithospheric Plates (Figure 22 in the chapter "Plate Tectonics"). What conclusions can you draw from this map about the cause of earthquakes in this area?

Section 3 • Tech & Design •

# Monitoring Earthquakes

## Reading Preview

### Key Concepts

- How do seismographs work?
- How do geologists monitor faults?
- How are seismographic data used?

### Key Terms

- seismogram
- friction

### Target Reading Skill

**Sequencing** As you read, make a flowchart like the one below that shows how a seismograph produces a seismogram. Write each step of the process in a separate box in the order in which it occurs.

**How a Seismograph Works**

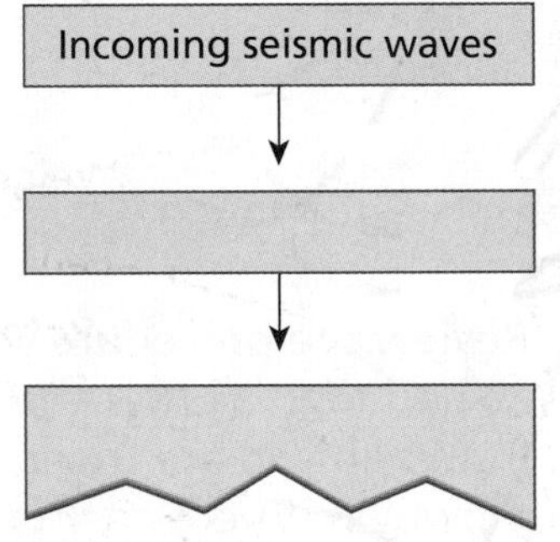


## Lab zone Discover Activity

### How Can Seismic Waves Be Detected?

1. Using scissors, cut 4 plastic stirrers in half. Each piece should be about 5 cm long.
2. Your teacher will give you a pan containing gelatin. Gently insert the 8 stirrer pieces into the gelatin, spacing them about 2–3 cm apart in a row. The pieces should stand upright, but not touch the bottom of the pan.
3. At the opposite end of the pan from the stirrers, gently tap the surface of the gelatin once with the eraser end of a pencil. Observe the results.

**Think It Over**

**Inferring** What happened to the stirrer pieces when you tapped the gelatin? What was responsible for this effect?

Look at the beautiful vase in the photo. You might be surprised to learn that the vase is actually a scientific instrument. Can you guess what it was designed to do? Zhang Heng, an astronomer, designed and built this earthquake detection device in China nearly 2,000 years ago. It is said to have detected an earthquake centered several hundred kilometers away.

Earthquakes are dangerous, so people want to monitor them. To *monitor* means to "watch closely." Like the ancient Chinese, many societies have used technology to determine when and where earthquakes have occurred. During the late 1800s, scientists developed seismographs that were much more sensitive and accurate than any earlier devices.

FIGURE 12
**Earthquake Detector**
Nearly 2,000 years ago, a Chinese scientist invented this instrument to detect earthquakes.

## The Seismograph

A simple seismograph can consist of a heavy weight attached to a frame by a spring or wire. A pen connected to the weight rests its point on a drum that can rotate. As the drum rotates slowly, the pen draws a straight line on paper wrapped tightly around the drum. **Seismic waves cause the seismograph's drum to vibrate. But the suspended weight with the pen attached moves very little. Therefore, the pen stays in place and records the drum's vibrations.**

**Measuring Seismic Waves** When you write a sentence, the paper stays in one place while your hand moves the pen. But in a seismograph, it's the pen that remains stationary while the paper moves. Why is this? All seismographs make use of a basic principle of physics: Whether it is moving or at rest, every object resists any change to its motion. A seismograph's heavy weight resists motion during a quake. But the rest of the seismograph is anchored to the ground and vibrates when seismic waves arrive.

**Reading a Seismogram** You have probably seen a zigzag pattern of lines used to represent an earthquake. The pattern of lines, called a **seismogram,** is the record of an earthquake's seismic waves produced by a seismograph. Study the seismogram in Figure 13 and notice when the P waves, S waves, and surface waves arrive. The height of the jagged lines drawn on the seismograph's drum is greater for a more severe earthquake or for an earthquake close to the seismograph.

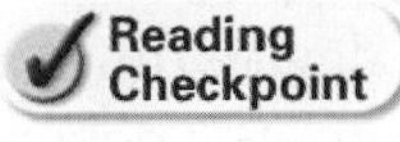

What is a seismogram?

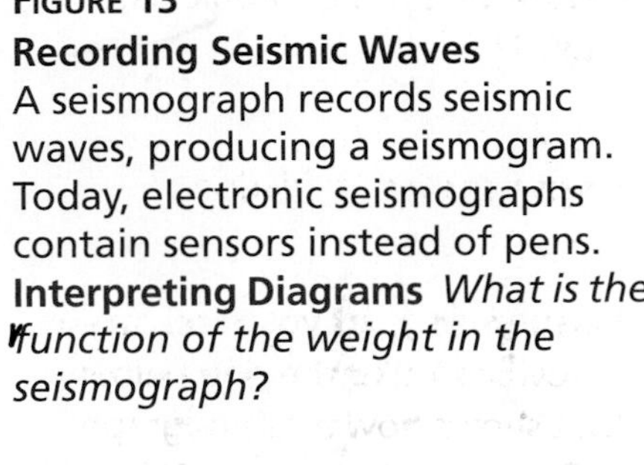

FIGURE 13
**Recording Seismic Waves**
A seismograph records seismic waves, producing a seismogram. Today, electronic seismographs contain sensors instead of pens.
**Interpreting Diagrams** *What is the function of the weight in the seismograph?*

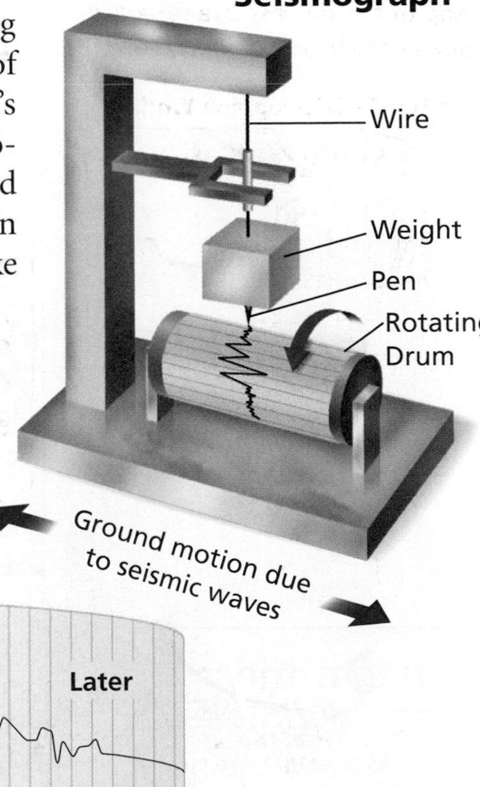


**Seismogram**

Earlier

Later

**P waves** travel fastest and arrive first.

**S waves** arrive shortly after P waves.

**Surface waves** produce the largest disturbance on the seismogram.

## Instruments That Monitor Faults

Along a fault, scientists may detect a slight rise or fall in the elevation and tilt of the land. Geologists hypothesize that such changes signal a buildup of stress in rock. Increasing stress could eventually lead to an earthquake. **To monitor faults, geologists have developed instruments to measure changes in elevation, tilting of the land surface, and ground movements along faults.** Some of the instruments that geologists use to monitor these movements include tiltmeters, creep meters, laser-ranging devices, and satellites.

**Tiltmeters** A tiltmeter measures tilting or raising of the ground. If you have ever used a carpenter's level, you have used a type of tiltmeter. The tiltmeters used by geologists consist of two bulbs that are filled with a liquid and connected by a hollow stem. Notice that if the land rises or falls slightly, the liquid will flow from one bulb to the other. Each bulb contains a measuring scale to measure the depth of the liquid in that bulb. Geologists read the scales to measure the amount of tilt occurring along the fault.

**Creep Meters** A creep meter uses a wire stretched across a fault to measure horizontal movement of the ground. On one side of the fault, the wire is anchored to a post. On the other side, the wire is attached to a weight that can slide if the fault moves. Geologists determine how much the fault has moved by measuring how much the weight has moved against a scale.

**Laser-Ranging Devices** A laser-ranging device uses a laser beam to detect horizontal fault movements. The device times a laser beam as it travels to a reflector and back. Thus, the device can detect any change in distance to the reflector.

**GPS Satellites** Scientists can monitor changes in elevation as well as horizontal movement along faults using a network of Earth-orbiting satellites called GPS. GPS, the Global Positioning System, was developed to help ships and planes find their routes. As shown in Figure 14, GPS can also be used to locate points on Earth's surface with great precision. Using GPS, scientists measure tiny movements of markers set up on the opposite sides of a fault.

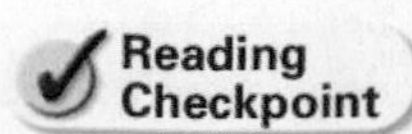

How does a creep meter work?

**For:** Links on earthquake measurement
**Visit:** www.SciLinks.org
**Web Code:** scn-1023

FIGURE 14
## Motion Detectors

To detect slight motions along faults, geologists use several types of devices.

**Comparing and Contrasting** *Which of these devices measure horizontal movement? Which ones measure vertical movement?*

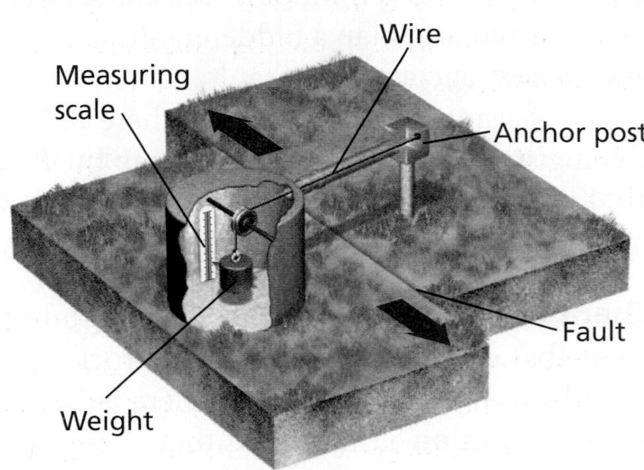


**Creep Meter**
A creep meter measures horizontal movement.

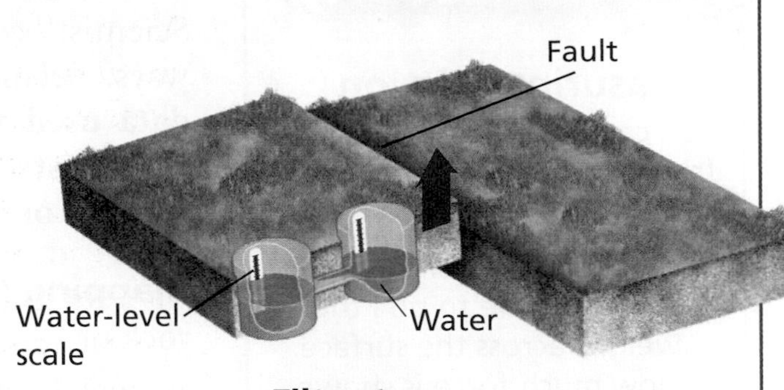


**Tiltmeter**
A tiltmeter measures vertical movement.

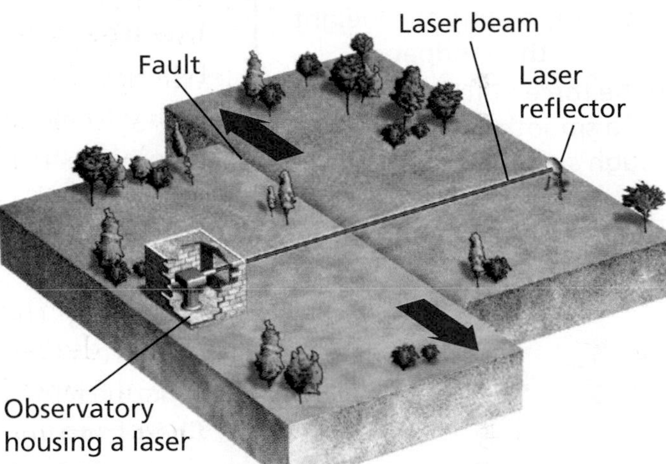


**Laser-Ranging Device**
A laser-ranging device measures horizontal movement.

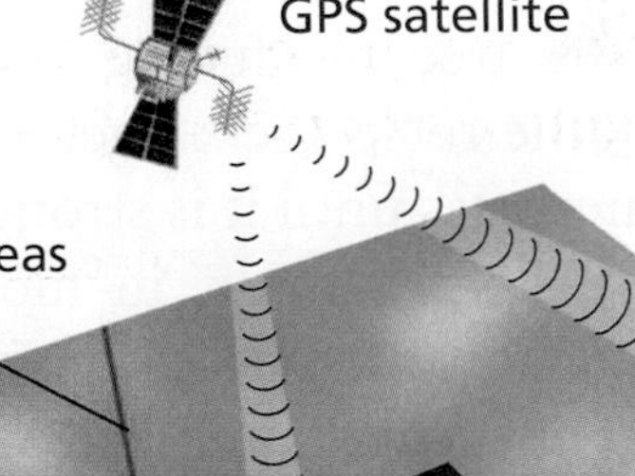

**GPS Satellites**
Ground-based receivers use the GPS satellite system to measure changes in elevation and tilt of the land as well as horizontal movement along a fault.

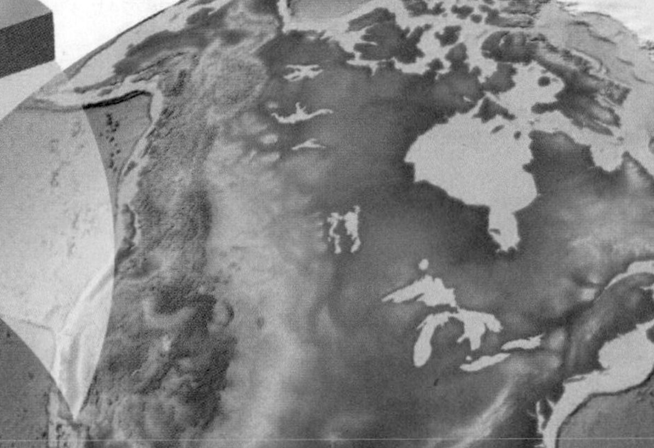

## Lab zone Skills Activity

### Measuring Friction

You can measure the force of friction.

1. Place a small weight on a smooth, flat tabletop. Use a spring scale to pull the weight across the surface. How much force is shown on the spring scale? (*Hint:* The unit of force is newtons.)
2. Tape a piece of sandpaper to the tabletop. Repeat Step 1, pulling the weight across the sandpaper.

Is the force of friction greater for a smooth surface or for a rough surface?

# Using Seismographic Data

Scientists collect and use seismographic data in a variety of ways. **Seismographs and fault-monitoring devices provide data used to map faults and detect changes along faults. Geologists are also trying to use these data to develop a method of predicting earthquakes.**

**Mapping Faults** Faults are often hidden by a thick layer of rock or soil. How can geologists map a hidden fault?

When seismic waves encounter a fault, the waves are reflected off the fault. Seismographs can detect these reflected seismic waves. Geologists then use these data to map the fault's length and depth. Knowing the location of hidden faults helps scientists determine the earthquake risk for the area.

**Monitoring Changes Along Faults** Geologists study the types of movement that occur along faults. How rocks move along a fault depends on how much friction there is between the sides of the fault. **Friction** is the force that opposes the motion of one surface as it moves across another surface. Friction exists because surfaces are not perfectly smooth.

Where friction along a fault is low, the rocks on both sides of the fault slide by each other without much sticking. Therefore stress does not build up, and big earthquakes are unlikely. Where friction is moderate, the sides of the fault jam together. Then from time to time they jerk free, producing small earthquakes. Where friction is high, the rocks lock together and do not move. In this case, stress increases until it is strong enough to overcome the friction force. For example, in most places along the San Andreas fault in California, friction is high and the plates lock. Stress builds up until an earthquake occurs.

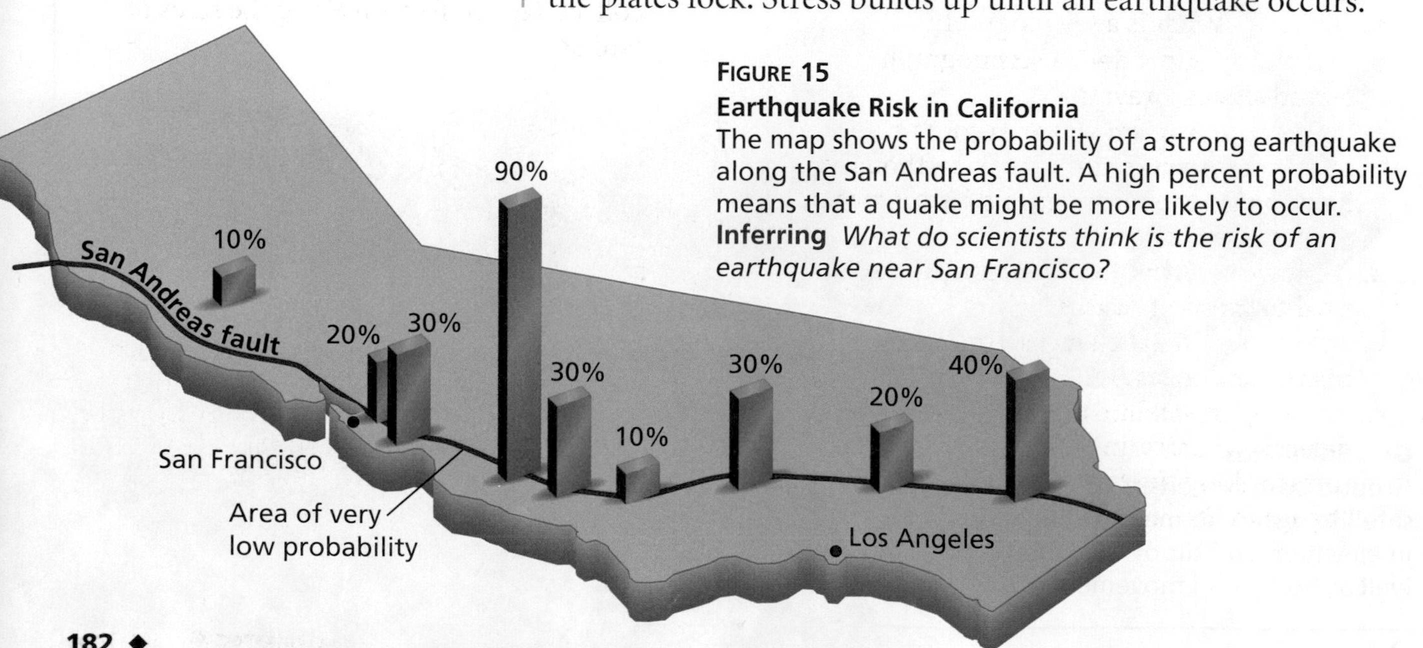


**FIGURE 15**
**Earthquake Risk in California**
The map shows the probability of a strong earthquake along the San Andreas fault. A high percent probability means that a quake might be more likely to occur.
**Inferring** *What do scientists think is the risk of an earthquake near San Francisco?*

Figure 15 shows how geologists in California have used data about how the San Andreas fault moves. They have tried to estimate the earthquake risk along different parts of the fault. Unfortunately, this attempt at forecasting earthquakes has not worked yet.

**Trying to Predict Earthquakes** Even with data from many sources, geologists can't predict when and where a quake will strike. Usually, stress along a fault increases until an earthquake occurs. Yet sometimes stress builds up along a fault, but an earthquake fails to occur. Or, one or more earthquakes may relieve stress along another part of the fault. Exactly what will happen remains uncertain.

The problem of predicting earthquakes is one of many scientific questions that remain unsolved. If you become a scientist, you can work to find answers to these questions. Much remains to be discovered!

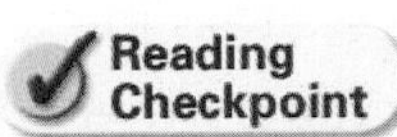


**Why is it difficult to predict earthquakes?**

**FIGURE 16**
**Seismographic Data**
A geologist interprets a seismogram. Understanding changes that precede earthquakes may help in efforts to predict them.

## Section 3 Assessment

**Target Reading Skill Sequencing** Refer to your flowchart about seismographs as you answer Question 1.

### Reviewing Key Concepts

1. a. **Defining** What is a seismograph?
   b. **Explaining** How does a seismograph record seismic waves?
   c. **Predicting** A seismograph records a strong earthquake and a weak earthquake. How would the seismograms for the two earthquakes compare?
2. a. **Reviewing** What four instruments are used to monitor faults?
   b. **Describing** What changes does each instrument measure?
   c. **Inferring** A satellite that monitors a fault detects an increasing tilt in the land surface along the fault. What could this change in the land surface indicate?
3. a. **Listing** What are three ways in which geologists use seismographic data?
   b. **Explaining** How do geologists use seismographic data to make maps of faults?
   c. **Making Generalizations** Why do geologists collect data on friction along the sides of faults?

### Writing in Science

**Patent Application** You are an inventor who has created a simple device that can detect an earthquake. To protect your rights to the invention, you apply for a patent. In your patent application, describe your device and how it will indicate the direction and strength of an earthquake. You may include a sketch.

Lab zone **Technology Lab**

# Design a Seismograph

## Problem

Can you design and build a seismograph that can record the movements of simulated earthquakes?

## Skills Focus

designing, evaluating, troubleshooting

## Materials

- large book
- pencil
- pen
- 2 strips of paper
- optional materials provided by your teacher

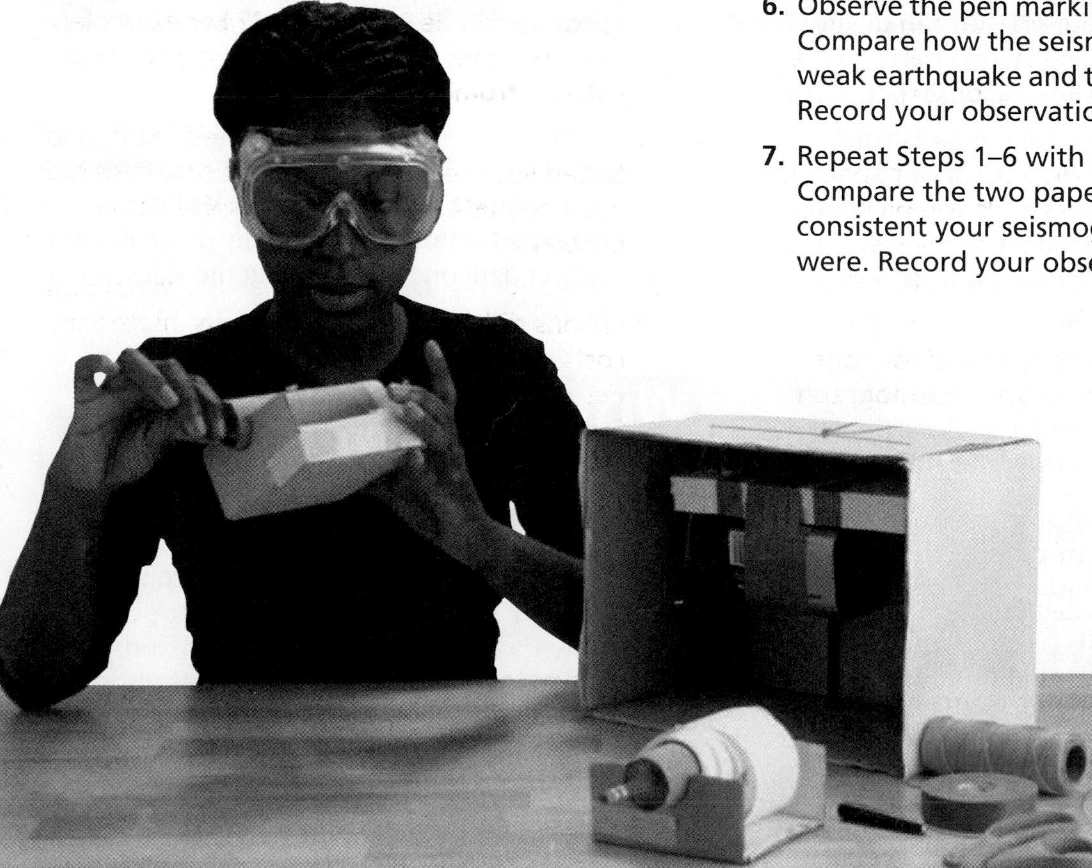

## Procedure 

### PART 1 Research and Investigate

1. With two lab partners, create a model of a seismograph. Begin by placing a large book on a table.
2. Wind a strip of paper about one meter long around a pencil.
3. Hold the pencil with the paper wound around it in one hand. In your other hand, hold a pen against the paper.
4. As you hold the pen steady, have one lab partner slowly pull on the paper so that it slides across the book.
5. After a few seconds, the other lab partner should jiggle the book gently for 10 seconds to model a weak earthquake, and then for 10 seconds to model a strong earthquake.
6. Observe the pen markings on the paper strip. Compare how the seismograph recorded the weak earthquake and the strong earthquake. Record your observations in your notebook.
7. Repeat Steps 1–6 with a new paper strip. Compare the two paper strips to see how consistent your seismograph recordings were. Record your observations.

## PART 2 Design and Build

8. Using what you learned from the seismograph model in Part 1, develop your own design for a seismograph. Your seismograph should be able to
   - record vibrations continuously for 30 seconds
   - produce a seismogram that can distinguish between gentle and strong earthquakes
   - record seismic readings consistently from trial to trial
9. Sketch your design on a sheet of paper. Then make a list of the materials you will need. Materials might include a heavy weight, a roll of paper, a pen, wood blocks, wood dowels, and duct tape.
10. Obtain your teacher's approval for your design. Then construct your seismograph.

## PART 3 Evaluate and Redesign

11. Test your seismograph in a series of simulated earthquakes of different strengths. Evaluate how well your seismograph functions. Does it meet the criteria outlined in Step 8? Make note of any problems.
12. Based on your tests, decide how you could improve the design of your seismograph. Then make any necessary changes to your seismograph and test how it functions.

## Analyze and Conclude

1. **Evaluating** What problems or shortcomings did you encounter with the seismograph you tested in Part 1? Why do you think these problems occurred?
2. **Designing a Solution** How did you incorporate what you learned in Part 1 into your seismograph design in Part 2? For example, what changes did you make to improve consistency from trial to trial?
3. **Troubleshooting** As you designed, built, and tested your seismograph, what problems did you encounter? How did you solve these problems?
4. **Working With Design Constraints** What limitations did factors such as gravity, materials, costs, time, or other factors place on the design and function of your seismograph? Describe how you adapted your design to work within these limitations.
5. **Evaluating the Impact on Society** Why is it important for scientists around the world to have access to accurate and durable seismographs?

## Communicate

Write an advertisement trying to "sell" your seismograph. In your ad, explain how your design and evaluation process helped you improve your seismograph. Include a labeled sketch of your design.

Section 4

# Earthquake Safety

## Reading Preview

### Key Concepts

- How do geologists determine earthquake risk?
- What kinds of damage does an earthquake cause?
- What can be done to increase earthquake safety and reduce earthquake damage?

### Key Terms

- liquefaction
- aftershock
- tsunami
- base-isolated building

### Target Reading Skill

**Asking Questions** Before you read, preview the red headings and ask a *what, how,* or *where* question for each. As you read, write answers to your questions.

**Earthquake Safety**

| Question | Answer |
|---|---|
| Where is quake risk highest? | Earthquake risk is highest . . . |
| | |

## Lab zone Discover Activity

### Can Bracing Prevent Building Collapse?

1. Tape four straws together to make a square frame. Hold the frame upright on a flat surface.
2. Hold the bottom straw down with one hand while you push the top straw to the left with the other. Push it as far as it will go without breaking the frame.
3. Tape a fifth straw horizontally across the middle of the frame. Repeat Step 2.

**Think It Over**

**Predicting** What effect did the fifth straw have? What effect would a piece of cardboard taped to the frame have? Based on your observations, how would an earthquake affect the frame of a house?

Imagine being sound asleep in your bed in the middle of the night. Suddenly, you are jolted wide awake as your home begins to rattle and shake. As objects fall off shelves and walls crack, you crouch under a desk for protection. Around the city, large buildings collapse and fires break out. The quake lasts less than a minute, but leaves behind great devastation. That's what happened in September 1999 when a magnitude 7.6 earthquake hit Taipei, Taiwan. The quake killed more than 2,000 people, and injured thousands more.

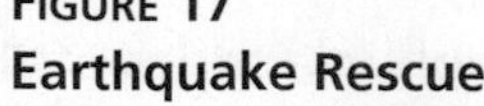

**FIGURE 17**
**Earthquake Rescue**
After an earthquake in Taipei, emergency crews worked to put out fires and rescue victims in collapsed buildings.

## Earthquake Risk in the United States

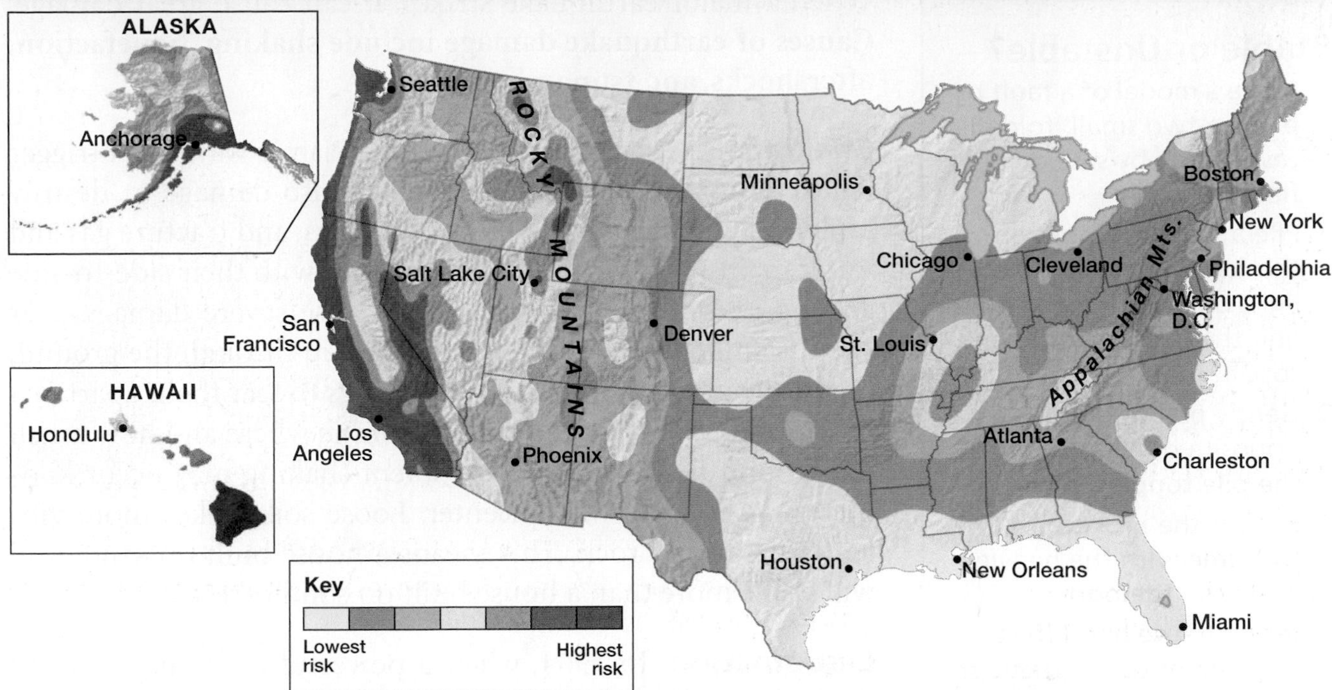


**FIGURE 18**
The map shows areas where serious earthquakes are likely to occur, based on the locations of previous earthquakes.
**Interpreting Maps** *Where are damaging earthquakes least likely to occur? Most likely to occur?*

# Earthquake Risk

Geologists know that earthquakes are likely wherever plate movement stores energy in the rock along faults. **Geologists can determine earthquake risk by locating where faults are active and where past earthquakes have occurred.**

Look at Figure 18. In the United States, the risk is highest along the Pacific coast in California, Washington, and Alaska. Plates meet along the Pacific coast, causing many active faults. In California, the Pacific plate and North American plate meet along the San Andreas fault. In Washington, earthquakes result from the subduction of the Juan de Fuca plate beneath the North American plate. In Alaska, subduction of the Pacific plate causes many earthquakes.

The eastern United States generally has a low risk of earthquakes because this region lies far from plate boundaries. But, the East has experienced some of the most powerful quakes in the nation's history. Scientists hypothesize that the continental plate forming most of North America is under stress. This stress could disturb faults that lie hidden beneath thick layers of soil and rock.

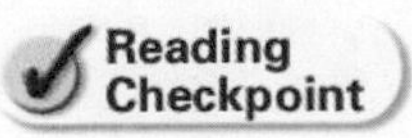


**What area of the United States has the highest earthquake risk?**

**Lab zone** **Try This Activity**

### Stable or Unstable?

1. Make a model of a fault by placing two small, folded towels side by side on a flat surface.
2. Pile a stack of books on the fault by placing the light books on the bottom and the heaviest ones on top.
3. Gently pull the towels in opposite directions until the pile topples.
4. Repeat the process, but this time with the heavier books on the bottom.

**Relating Cause and Effect** Which one of your structures was more stable than the other? Why?

## How Earthquakes Cause Damage

When a major earthquake strikes, it can cause great damage. **Causes of earthquake damage include shaking, liquefaction, aftershocks, and tsunamis.**

**Shaking** The shaking produced by seismic waves can trigger landslides or avalanches. Shaking can also damage or destroy buildings and bridges, topple utility poles, and fracture gas and water mains. S waves and surface waves, with their side-to-side and up-and-down movement, can cause severe damage near the epicenter. As the seismic waves sweep through the ground, they can put enough stress on buildings to tear them apart.

The types of rock and soil determine where and how much the ground shakes. The most violent shaking may occur kilometers away from the epicenter. Loose soil shakes more violently than solid rock. This means a house built on sandy soil will shake more than a house built on solid rock.

**Liquefaction** In 1964, when a powerful earthquake roared through Anchorage, Alaska, cracks opened in the ground. Some of the cracks were 9 meters wide. The cracks were created by liquefaction. **Liquefaction** (lik wih FAK shun) occurs when an earthquake's violent shaking suddenly turns loose, soft soil into liquid mud. Liquefaction is likely where the soil is full of moisture. As the ground gives way, buildings sink and pull apart.

**Aftershocks** Sometimes, buildings weakened by an earthquake collapse during an aftershock. An **aftershock** is an earthquake that occurs after a larger earthquake in the same area. Aftershocks may strike hours, days, or even months later.

FIGURE 19
**Liquefaction Damage**
An earthquake caused the soil beneath this building to liquefy. Liquefaction can change soil to liquid mud.
**Posing Questions** *What are some questions people might ask before building in a quake-prone area?*

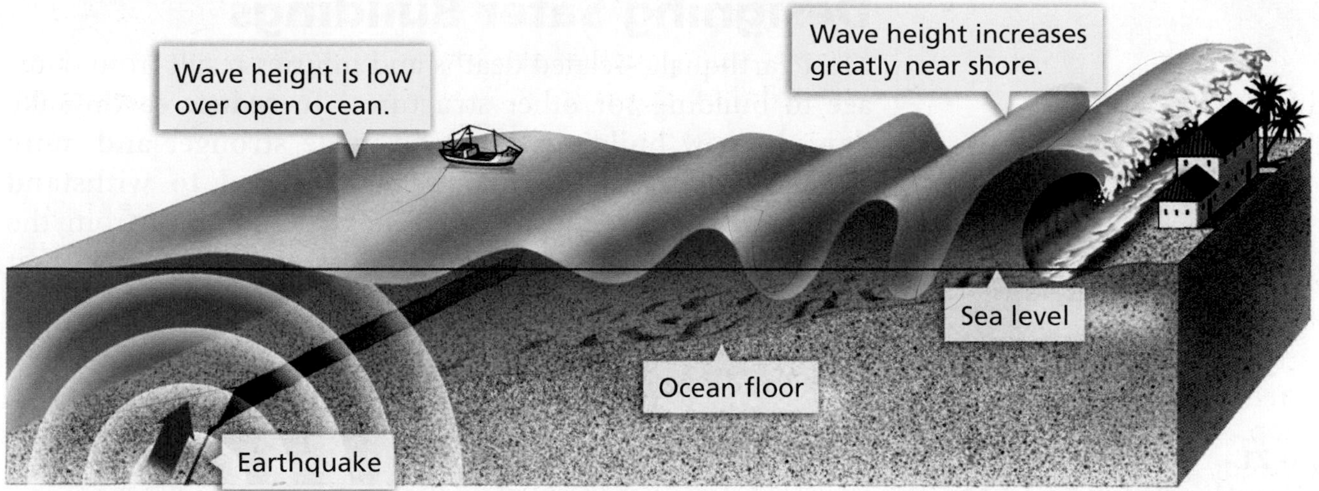


**FIGURE 20**
**How a Tsunami Forms**
A tsunami begins as a low wave, but turns into a huge wave as it nears the shore. In 2004, a powerful earthquake in the Indian Ocean triggered several tsunamis. The tsunamis caused great loss of life and destruction to coastal areas around the Indian Ocean.

**Tsunamis** When an earthquake jolts the ocean floor, plate movement causes the ocean floor to rise slightly and push water out of its way. The water displaced by the earthquake may form a large wave called a **tsunami** (tsoo NAH mee), shown in Figure 20. A tsunami spreads out from an earthquake's epicenter and speeds across the ocean. In the open ocean, the height of the wave is low. As a tsunami approaches shallow water, the wave grows into a mountain of water.

## Steps to Earthquake Safety

What should you do if an earthquake strikes? The main danger is from falling objects and flying glass. **The best way to protect yourself is to drop, cover, and hold.**

If you are indoors when a quake strikes, crouch beneath a sturdy table or desk and hold on to it. If no desk or table is available, crouch against an inner wall, away from the outside of a building, and cover your head and neck with your arms. Avoid windows, mirrors, wall hangings, and furniture that might topple.

If you are outdoors, move to an open area such as a playground. Avoid vehicles, power lines, trees, and buildings. Sit down to avoid being thrown down.

After a quake, water and power supplies may fail, food stores may be closed, and travel may be difficult. People may have to wait days for these services to be restored. To prepare, an earthquake kit containing canned food, water, and first aid supplies should be stored where it is easy to reach.

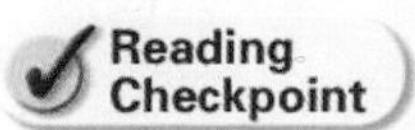


**How can furniture be dangerous during a quake? How can it protect you?**

## Designing Safer Buildings

Most earthquake-related deaths and injuries result from damage to buildings or other structures. **To reduce earthquake damage, new buildings must be made stronger and more flexible. Older buildings may be modified to withstand stronger quakes.** People can protect their homes from the dangers of earthquakes. Figure 21 shows some of the steps that can make houses earthquake-safe. Some steps strengthen the house itself. Others may help to keep objects from tipping or falling and causing injury.

**FIGURE 21**

### An Earthquake-Safe House

People can take a variety of steps to make their homes safer in an earthquake.
**Predicting** *During a quake, what might happen to a house that was not bolted to its foundation?*

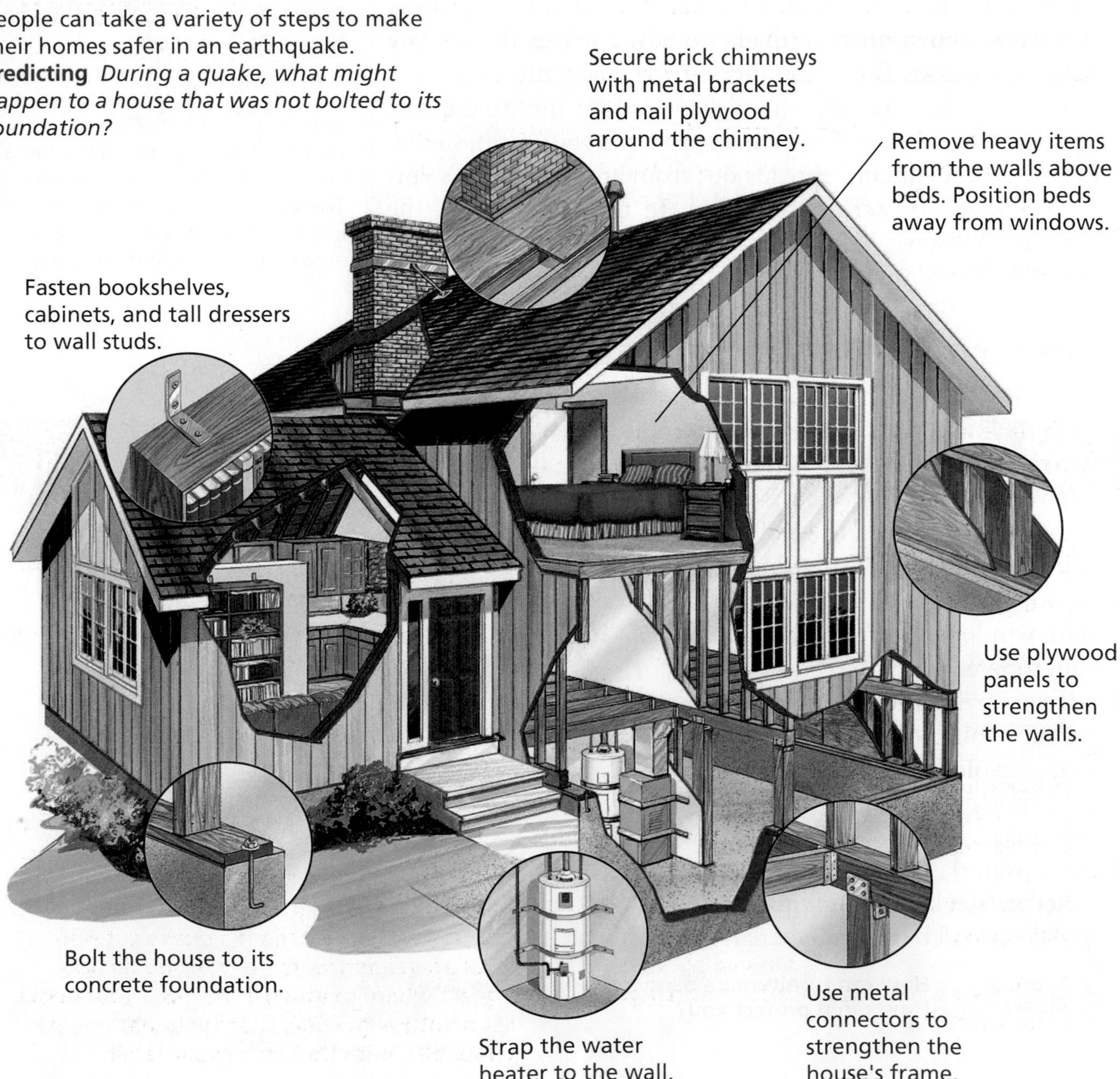

Secure brick chimneys with metal brackets and nail plywood around the chimney.
Remove heavy items from the walls above beds. Position beds away from windows.
Fasten bookshelves, cabinets, and tall dressers to wall studs.
Use plywood panels to strengthen the walls.
Bolt the house to its concrete foundation.
Strap the water heater to the wall.
Use metal connectors to strengthen the house's frame.

**Protecting Structures** The way in which a building is constructed determines whether it can withstand an earthquake. During an earthquake, brick buildings and some wood-frame buildings may collapse if their walls have not been reinforced, or strengthened. To combat damage caused by liquefaction, new homes built on soft ground should be anchored to solid rock below the soil. Bridges and highway overpasses can be built on supports that go through soft soil to firmer ground. To find out more about how buildings can withstand earthquakes, look at *Seismic-Safe Buildings* on the following pages.

A **base-isolated building** is designed to reduce the amount of energy that reaches the building during an earthquake. A base-isolated building rests on shock-absorbing rubber pads or springs. Like the suspension of a car, the pads and springs smooth out a bumpy ride. During a quake, the building moves gently back and forth without any violent shaking.

**Making Utilities Safer** Earthquakes can cause fire and flooding when gas pipes and water mains break. Flexible joints can be installed in gas and water lines to keep them from breaking. Automatic shut-off valves also can be installed on these lines to cut off gas and water flow.

For: More on earthquake risk
Visit: PHSchool.com
Web Code: cfd-1024

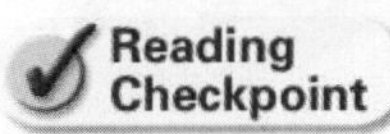


**How can utilities be protected from earthquake damage?**

## Section 4 Assessment

**Target Reading Skill** **Asking Questions** Work with a partner to check the answers in your graphic organizer.

### Reviewing Key Concepts

1. a. **Identifying** What factors help geologists determine earthquake risk for a region?
   b. **Comparing and Contrasting** Why does the risk of quakes vary across the United States?
2. a. **Listing** What are four ways that earthquakes cause damage?
   b. **Relating Cause and Effect** How does liquefaction cause damage during an earthquake?
   c. **Developing Hypotheses** How might heavy rain before an earthquake affect the danger of liquefaction?
3. a. **Reviewing** How can you protect yourself during an earthquake?
   b. **Describing** What will happen to a base-isolated building when seismic waves strike the building during an earthquake?

### Lab zone At-Home Activity

**Quake Safety Plan** Work with an adult family member to develop an earthquake safety plan. The plan should tell family members what to do during an earthquake. It should list items your family would need if a quake cut electrical power and water lines. It should also explain where to shut off the gas if your home has a natural gas line. Share your earthquake safety plan with the rest of your family.

# Technology and Society • Tech & Design •

## Seismic-Safe Buildings

Breaking one thin twig doesn't require much force. Breaking a bundle of thin twigs does. Like one thin twig, the walls, beams, and other supporting parts of a building can snap as seismic energy travels through the structure. Reinforcing a building's parts makes them more like the bundle of twigs—stronger and less likely to snap when a quake occurs.

### What Are Seismic-Safe Buildings?

Seismic-safe buildings have features that reduce earthquake damage. Some of these features strengthen a building. Others allow the building to move, or shield the building from the energy of seismic waves. In earthquake-prone areas, most tall, steel-frame buildings may have one or more of the seismic-safe features shown here.

**Shear Walls** A shear wall transfers some of a quake's energy from roofs and floors to the building's foundation.

**Tension Ties** These devices firmly "tie" the floors and ceilings of a building to the walls. Tension ties absorb and scatter earthquake energy and thus reduce damage.

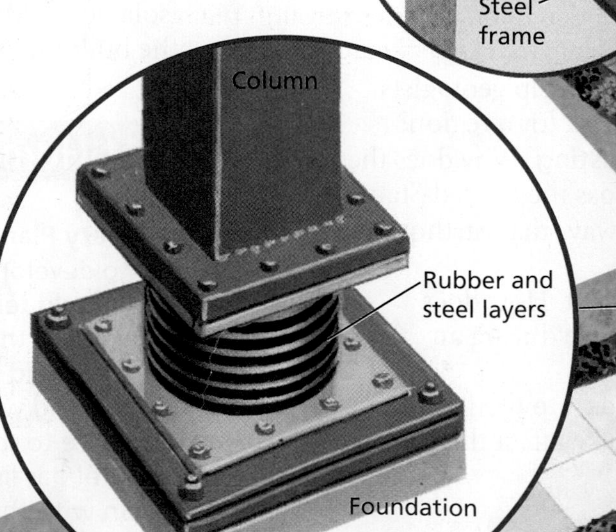


**Base Isolators** These pads separate, or isolate, a building from its foundation and prevent some of an earthquake's energy from entering the building.

## Seismic-Safe, But at What Cost?

Seismic-safe buildings save lives and reduce damage. Despite these benefits, the technologies have drawbacks. Seismic-safe features, such as cross braces, may reduce the amount of usable space in a building. It is also expensive to add seismic-safe features to an existing building. Communities must make trade-offs between the benefits and the costs of seismic-safe buildings.

Even steel-frame buildings need seismic-safe design features.

**Cross Braces** Steel cross braces are placed between stories to stiffen a building's frame and absorb energy during an earthquake.

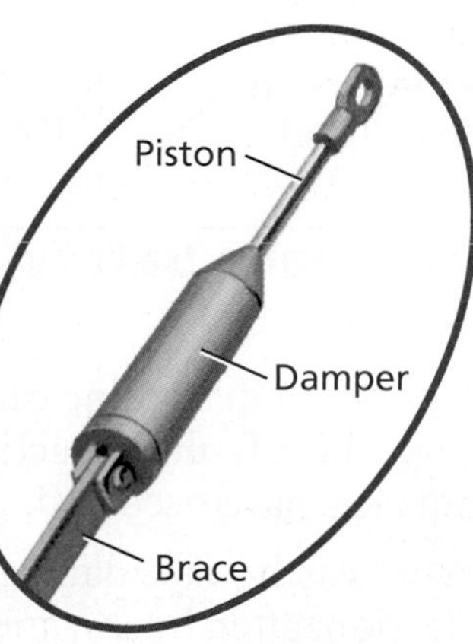


**Dampers**
Dampers work like the shock absorbers in a car to absorb some of the energy of seismic waves.

**Flexible Pipes** Water and gas pipes have flexible joints. Flexible pipes bend as energy passes through them, greatly reducing damage.

## Weigh the Impact

### 1. Identify the Need

Your city has hired you to decide which buildings or other structures most need to be able to withstand an earthquake. List three types of structures that you think need to be seismic-safe.

### 2. Research

Research how the structures on your list can be made safe. Choose one structure from your list and make notes on how it can be made safe.

### 3. Write

Using your notes, write a report that explains how your structure can be designed or modified to withstand earthquakes.

**For:** More on seismic-safe buildings
**Visit:** PHSchool.com
**Web Code:** cfh-1020

# Chapter 6 Study Guide

**The BIG Idea** **Energy Transfer and Earth's Structure** The forces of plate movement deform Earth's crust, forming faults, folds, and mountains. Plate movements also cause earthquakes.

## 1 Forces in Earth's Crust

### Key Concepts

- Tension, compression, and shearing work over millions of years to change the shape and volume of rock.
- Faults usually occur along plate boundaries, where the forces of plate motion push or pull the crust so much that the crust breaks. There are three main types of faults: normal faults, reverse faults, and strike-slip faults.
- Over millions of years, the forces of plate movement can change a flat plain into landforms such as anticlines and synclines, folded mountains, fault-block mountains, and plateaus.

### Key Terms

stress
tension
compression
shearing
normal fault
hanging wall
footwall
reverse fault
strike-slip fault
anticline
syncline
plateau

## 2 Earthquakes and Seismic Waves

### Key Concepts

- Seismic waves carry energy from an earthquake away from the focus, through Earth's interior, and across the surface.
- Three commonly used ways of measuring earthquakes are the Mercalli scale, the Richter scale, and the moment magnitude scale.
- Geologists use seismic waves to locate an earthquake's epicenter.

### Key Terms

earthquake
focus
epicenter
P wave
S wave
surface wave
Mercalli scale
magnitude
Richter scale
seismograph
moment magnitude scale

## 3 Monitoring Earthquakes

### Key Concepts

- During an earthquake, seismic waves cause the seismograph's drum to vibrate. But the suspended weight with the pen attached moves very little. Therefore, the pen stays in place and records the drum's vibrations.
- To monitor faults, geologists have developed instruments to measure changes in elevation, tilting of the land surface, and ground movements along faults.
- Seismographs and fault-monitoring devices provide data used to map faults and detect changes along faults.

### Key Terms

seismogram
friction

## 4 Earthquake Safety

### Key Concepts

- Geologists can determine earthquake risk by locating where faults are active and where past earthquakes have occurred.
- Causes of earthquake damage include shaking, liquefaction, aftershocks, and tsunamis.
- The best way to protect yourself is to drop, cover, and hold.
- To reduce earthquake damage, new buildings must be made stronger and more flexible. Older buildings may be modified to withstand stronger quakes.

### Key Terms

liquefaction
aftershock
tsunami
base-isolated building

# Review and Assessment

**For:** Self-assessment
**Visit:** PHSchool.com
**Web Code:** cfa-1020

## Organizing Information

**Relating Cause and Effect** Fill in the cause-and-effect graphic organizer to show how different stress forces produce different kinds of faults.

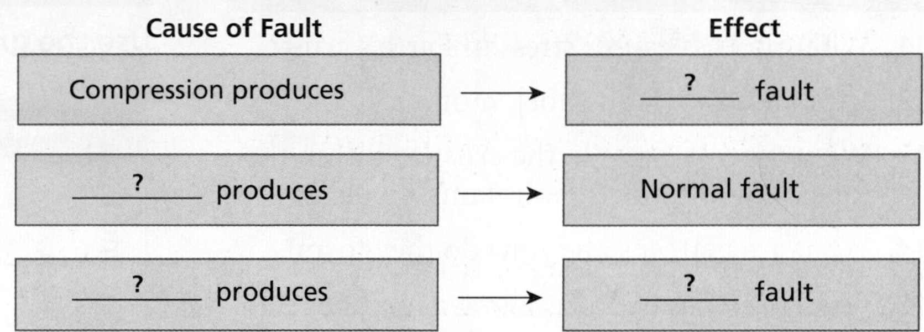


## Reviewing Key Terms

**Choose the letter of the best answer.**

1. The force that causes part of the crust to become shorter and thicker is
   **a.** tension.
   **b.** compression.
   **c.** shearing.
   **d.** normal force.
2. When the hanging wall of a fault slips down with respect to the footwall, the result is a
   **a.** reverse fault.
   **b.** syncline.
   **c.** normal fault.
   **d.** strike-slip fault.
3. Which of the following is a rating of earthquake damage at a particular location?
   **a.** moment magnitude scale
   **b.** focus scale
   **c.** Mercalli scale
   **d.** Richter scale
4. The largest waves on a seismogram are
   **a.** P waves.
   **b.** S waves.
   **c.** surface waves.
   **d.** tsunamis.
5. In the hours after an earthquake, people should not go inside a building, even if it appears undamaged, because of
   **a.** aftershocks.
   **b.** liquefaction.
   **c.** tsunamis.
   **d.** deformation.

**If the statement is true, write *true.* If it is false, change the underlined word or words to make the statement true.**

6. Liquefaction forces squeeze or pull the rock in Earth's crust.
7. Rock uplifted by normal faults creates fault-block mountains.
8. An earthquake's epicenter is located deep underground.
9. As S waves move through the ground, they cause it to compress and then expand.
10. Tsunamis are triggered by earthquakes originating beneath the ocean floor.

## Writing in Science

**Cause-and-Effect Paragraph** Now that you have learned about the awesome power of earthquakes, write a paragraph about how earthquakes cause damage. Discuss both the natural and human-made factors that contribute to an earthquake's destructive power.

*Earthquakes*
Video Preview
Video Field Trip
▶ Video Assessment

# Review and Assessment

## Checking Concepts

11. What process causes stress in Earth's crust?
12. Explain how a fault-block mountain forms.
13. What type of stress in the crust results in the formation of folded mountains? Explain.
14. What are plateaus and how do they form?
15. Describe what happens along a fault beneath Earth's surface when an earthquake occurs.
16. How is the amount of energy released by an earthquake related to its magnitude?
17. What does the height of the jagged lines on a seismogram indicate?
18. How can homes and other structures be protected from liquefaction?

## Thinking Critically

19. **Classifying** Look at the diagram of a fault below. Describe how the hanging wall moves in relation to the footwall. What kind of fault is this?

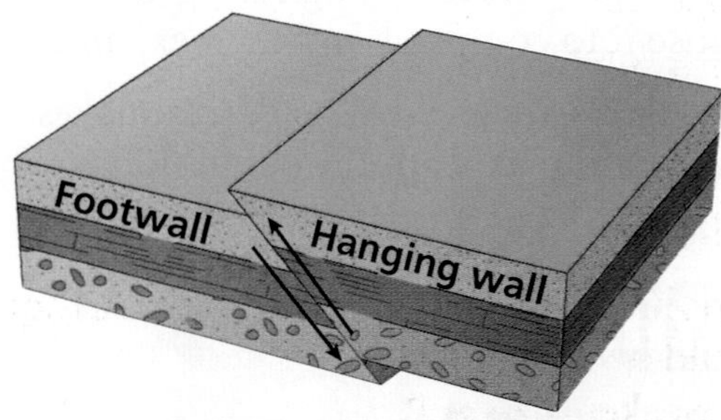


20. **Analyzing Data** A geologist has data about an earthquake from two seismographic stations. Is this enough information to determine the location of the epicenter? Why or why not?
21. **Predicting** A community has just built a street across a strike-slip fault that has frequent earthquakes. How will movement along the fault affect the street?
22. **Making Generalizations** How can filled land and loose, soft soil affect the amount of damage caused by an earthquake? Explain.

## Applying Skills

**Use the graph to answer Questions 23–26.**

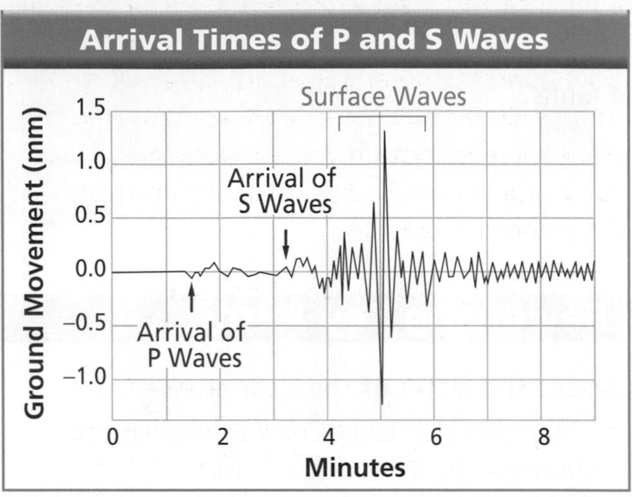


23. **Interpreting Diagrams** In what order did the seismic waves arrive at the seismograph station?
24. **Interpreting Diagrams** Which type of seismic wave produced the largest ground movement?
25. **Analyzing Data** What was the difference in arrival times for the P waves and S waves?
26. **Predicting** What would the seismogram look like several hours after this earthquake? How would it change if an aftershock occurred?

## Lab zone Chapter Project

**Performance Assessment** Before testing how your model withstands an earthquake, explain to your classmates how and why you changed your model. When your model is tested, observe how it withstands the earthquake. How would a real earthquake compare with the method used to test your model? If it were a real building, could your structure withstand an earthquake? How could you improve your model?

# Standardized Test Prep

### Test-Taking Tip

When answering questions about diagrams, read all parts of the diagram carefully, including title, captions, and labels. Make sure that you understand the meaning of arrows and other symbols. Determine exactly what the question asks. Then eliminate those answer choices that are not supported by the diagram. Practice answering this question.

**Stress in the Crust**

***Sample Question***

The diagram shows how stress affects a mass of rock in a process called

**A** compression.
**B** tension.
**C** squeezing.
**D** shearing.

***Answer***

The correct answer is **D** because the arrows show forces pulling the rock in opposite directions.

**Choose the letter that best answers the question or completes the statement.**

**1.** Stress will build until an earthquake occurs if friction along a fault is
**A** decreasing.
**B** high.
**C** low.
**D** changed to heat.

**2.** To estimate the total energy released by an earthquake, a geologist should use the
**F** Mercalli scale.
**G** Richter scale.
**H** epicenter scale.
**J** moment magnitude scale.

*Use the information below and your knowledge of science to answer Questions 3 through 5.*

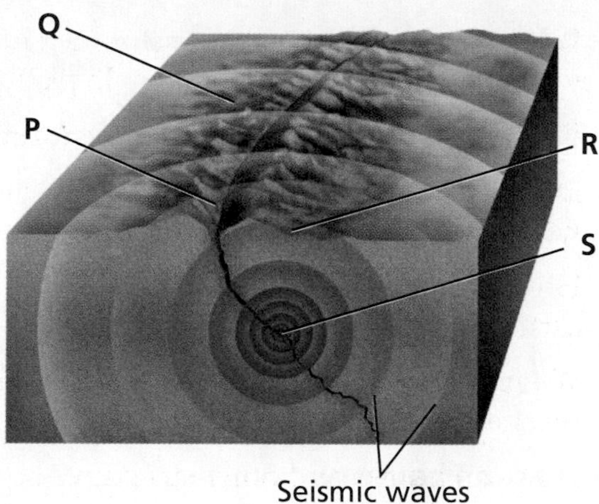


**3.** In the diagram, the epicenter is located at point
**A** Q.
**B** P.
**C** R.
**D** S.

**4.** When an earthquake occurs, seismic waves travel
**F** from P in all directions.
**G** from R to S.
**H** from S in all directions.
**J** from Q to P.

**5.** At point R, seismic waves from an earthquake would be
**A** weaker than at P.
**B** likely to cause little damage.
**C** weaker than at Q.
**D** likely to cause the most damage.

## Constructed Response

**6.** Explain the process that forms a strike-slip fault and leads to an earthquake along the fault. In your answer, discuss the force that causes stress in Earth's crust, the type of stress that produces a strike-slip fault, the characteristics of a strike-slip fault, and what happens before and during the earthquake.

# Chapter 7 Volcanoes

## The BIG Idea

### Forces Inside Earth

**What causes volcanoes and how do they affect Earth's surface?**

### Chapter Preview

**1 Volcanoes and Plate Tectonics**

*Discover* Where Are Volcanoes Found on Earth's Surface?

*Try This* Hot Spot in a Box

*Skills Lab* Mapping Earthquakes and Volcanoes

**2 Properties of Magma**

*Discover* How Fast Do Liquids Flow?

*Analyzing Data* Magma Composition

*At-Home Activity* Cooling Lava

**3 Volcanic Eruptions**

*Discover* What Are Volcanic Rocks Like?

*Active Art* Composite Volcano Eruption

*Try This* Gases in Magma

**4 Volcanic Landforms**

*Discover* How Can Volcanic Activity Change Earth's Surface?

*Skills Lab* Gelatin Volcanoes

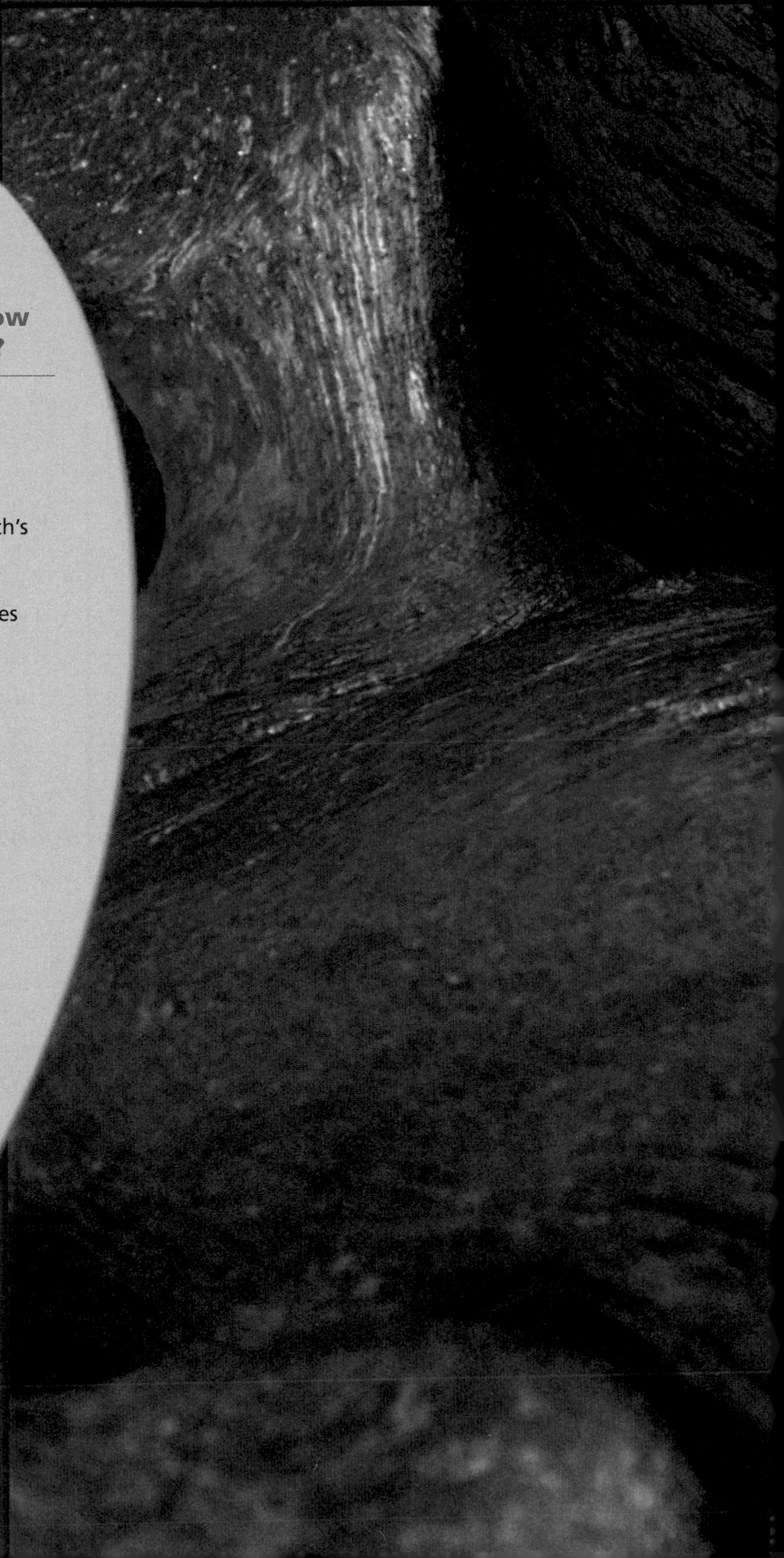

Red-hot lava from Mount Kilauea, a volcano in Hawaii, cools to form solid rock. ▶

*Volcanoes*

▶ Video Preview
Video Field Trip
Video Assessment

Lab zone™ Chapter **Project**

## Volcanoes and People

The eruptions of a volcano can be dangerous. Yet volcanoes and people have been closely connected throughout history. People often live near volcanoes because of the benefits they offer, from rich soil, to minerals, to hot springs. In this chapter project, you will investigate how volcanoes have affected the people living in a volcanic region.

**Your Goal** To make a documentary about life in a volcanic region

Your documentary must

- describe the type of volcano you chose and give its history
- focus on one topic, such as how people have benefited from living near the volcano or how people show the volcano in their art and stories
- use a variety of media

**Plan It!** Brainstorm with a group of other students which geographic area you would like to learn about. Your teacher may suggest some volcanic regions for you to check out. Decide what research resources you will need and what media you want to use. For media, you might consider video, computer art, overhead transparencies, a skit, or a mural. Be creative! When your documentary is finished, rehearse your presentation. Then present your documentary to your class.

Section 1

# Volcanoes and Plate Tectonics

## Reading Preview

### Key Concepts

- Where are most of Earth's volcanoes found?
- How do hot spot volcanoes form?

### Key Terms

- volcano
- magma
- lava
- Ring of Fire
- island arc
- hot spot

### Target Reading Skill

**Asking Questions** Before you read, preview the red headings. In a graphic organizer like the one below, ask a *where, what,* or *how* question for each heading. As you read, write the answers to your questions.

**Volcanoes and Plate Tectonics**

| Question | Answer |
|---|---|
| Where are volcanoes found? | Most volcanoes are found along plate boundaries. |
| | |

## Lab zone Discover Activity

### Where Are Volcanoes Found on Earth's Surface?

1. Look at the map of Earth's Active Volcanoes in Figure 2. What symbols are used to represent volcanoes? What other symbols are shown on the map?
2. Do the locations of the volcanoes form a pattern? Do the volcanoes seem related to any other features on Earth's surface?

**Think About It**

**Developing Hypotheses** Develop a hypothesis to explain where Earth's volcanoes are located.

In 2002, Mount Etna erupted in glowing fountains and rivers of molten rock. Located on the island of Sicily in the Mediterranean Sea, Mount Etna is Europe's largest volcano. Over the last 2,500 years, it has erupted often. The ancient Greeks believed that Mount Etna was one home of Hephaestus, the Greek god of fire. Beneath the volcano was the forge where Hephaestus made beautiful metal objects for the other Greek gods.

The eruption of a volcano is among the most awe-inspiring events on Earth. A **volcano** is a weak spot in the crust where molten material, or magma, comes to the surface. **Magma** is a molten mixture of rock-forming substances, gases, and water from the mantle. When magma reaches the surface, it is called **lava.** After lava has cooled, it forms solid rock. Lava released during volcanic activity builds up Earth's surface.

FIGURE 1
**Lava Flow on Mount Etna**
A lava flow from Mount Etna in Sicily almost buried this small building.

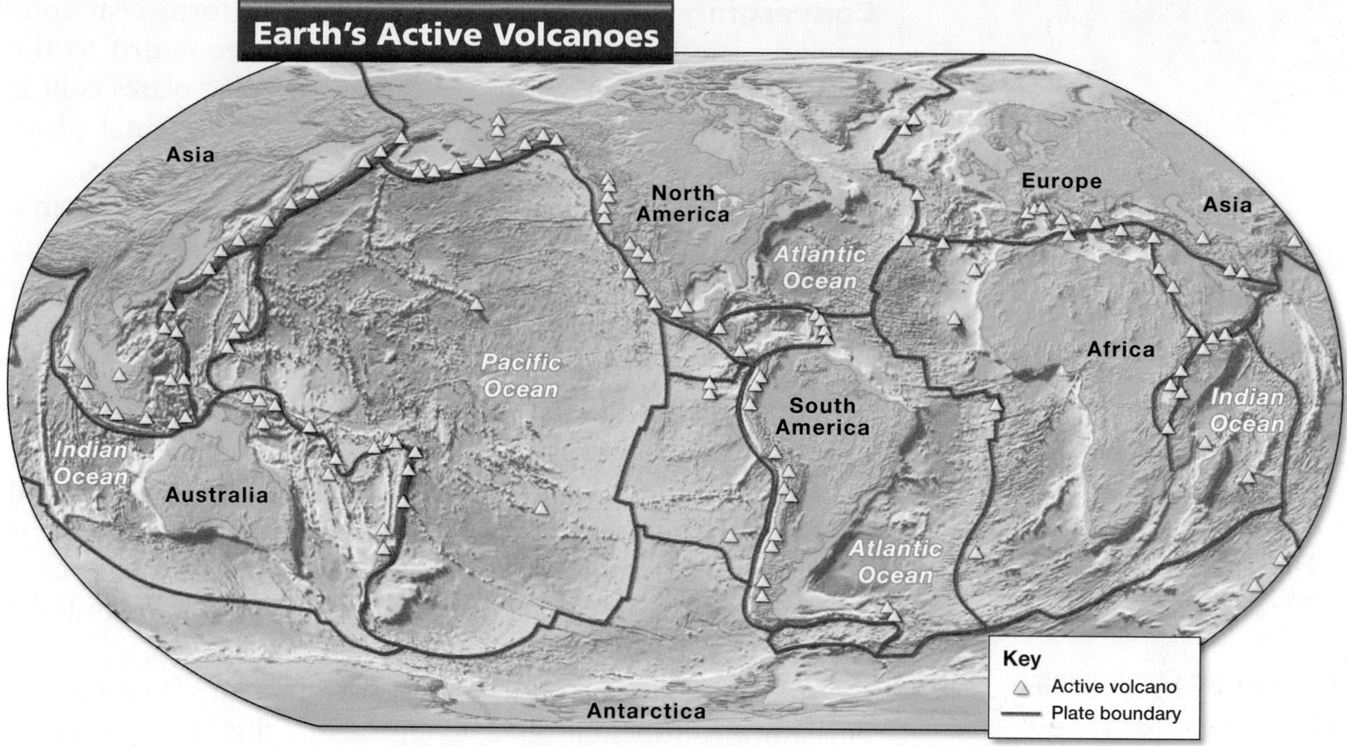


**FIGURE 2**
Many of Earth's volcanoes are located along the boundaries of tectonic plates. The Ring of Fire is a belt of volcanoes that circles the Pacific Ocean. **Observing** *What other regions have a large number of volcanoes?*

## Volcanoes and Plate Boundaries

There are about 600 active volcanoes on land. Many more lie beneath the sea, where it is difficult for scientists to observe and map them. Figure 2 shows the location of some of Earth's major volcanoes. Notice how volcanoes occur in belts that extend across continents and oceans. One major volcanic belt is the **Ring of Fire,** formed by the many volcanoes that rim the Pacific Ocean.

**Volcanic belts form along the boundaries of Earth's plates.** At plate boundaries, huge pieces of the crust diverge (pull apart) or converge (push together). As a result, the crust often fractures, allowing magma to reach the surface. Most volcanoes form along diverging plate boundaries such as mid-ocean ridges and along converging plate boundaries where subduction takes place. For example, Mount Etna formed near the boundary of the Eurasian and African plates.

**Diverging Boundaries** Volcanoes form along the mid-ocean ridges, which mark diverging plate boundaries. Recall that ridges are long, underwater mountain ranges that sometimes have a rift valley down their center. Along the rift valley, lava pours out of cracks in the ocean floor, gradually building new mountains. Volcanoes also form along diverging plate boundaries on land. For example, there are several large volcanoes along the Great Rift Valley in East Africa.

**For:** More on volcanoes
**Visit:** PHSchool.com
**Web Code:** cfd-1031

**Converging Boundaries** Many volcanoes form near converging plate boundaries where oceanic plates return to the mantle. Volcanoes may form where two oceanic plates collide or where an oceanic plate collides with a continental plate. Figure 3 shows how converging plates produce volcanoes.

Many volcanoes occur near boundaries where two oceanic plates collide. Through subduction, the older, denser plate sinks beneath a deep-ocean trench into the mantle. Some of the rock above the subducting plate melts and forms magma. Because the magma is less dense than the surrounding rock, it rises toward the surface. Eventually, the magma breaks through the ocean floor, creating volcanoes.

The resulting volcanoes create a string of islands called an **island arc.** The curve of an island arc echoes the curve of its deep-ocean trench. Major island arcs include Japan, New Zealand, Indonesia, the Philippines, the Aleutians, and the Caribbean islands.

Volcanoes also occur where an oceanic plate is subducted beneath a continental plate. Collisions of this type produced the volcanoes of the Andes Mountains in South America and the volcanoes of the Pacific Northwest in the United States.

**How did the volcanoes in the Andes Mountains form?**

FIGURE 3
**Volcanoes at Converging Boundaries**
Volcanoes often form where two oceanic plates collide or where an oceanic plate collides with a continental plate. In both situations, an oceanic plate sinks beneath a trench. Rock above the plate melts to form magma, which then erupts to the surface as lava.

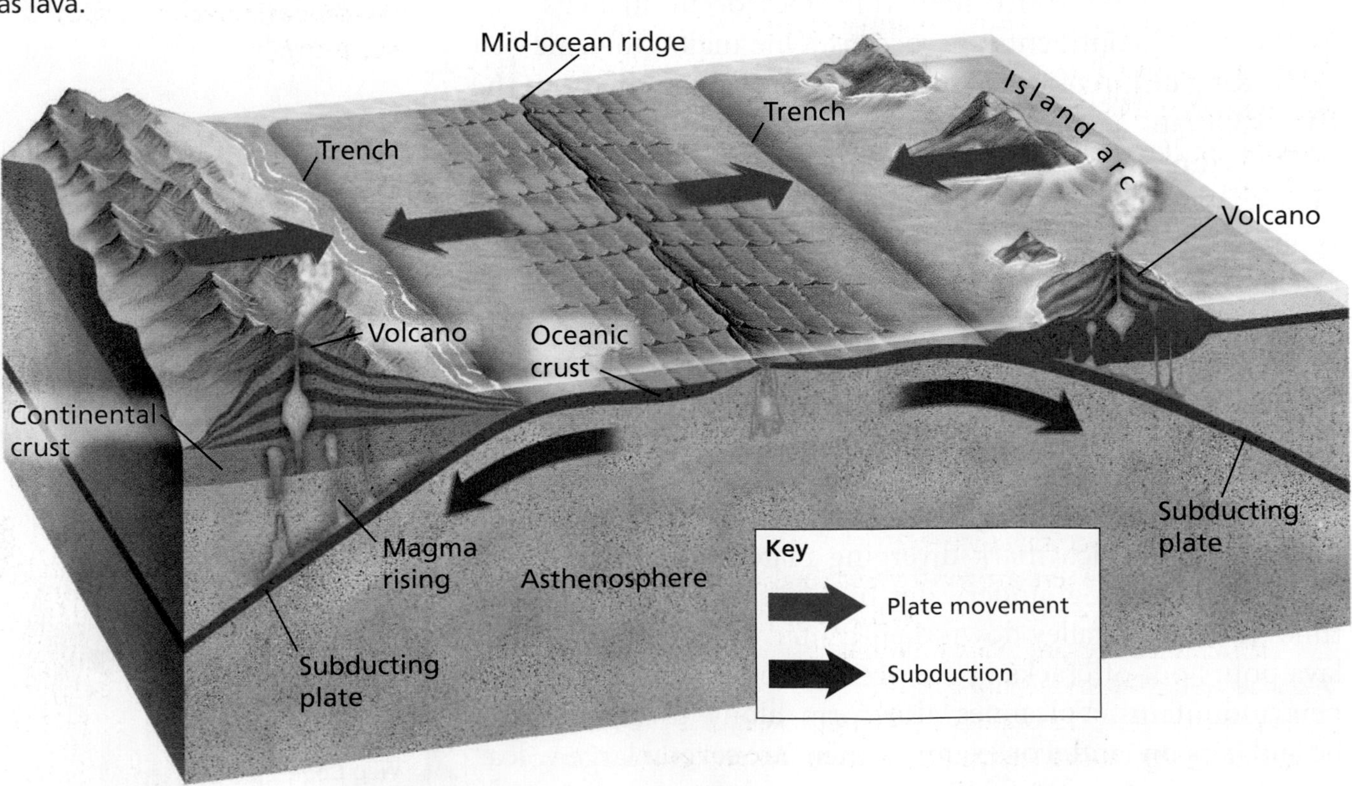

**FIGURE 4**
**Hot Spot Volcanoes**
Eventually, the Pacific plate's movement will carry the island of Hawaii away from the hot spot.
**Inferring** *Which island on the map formed first?*

## Hot Spot Volcanoes

Some volcanoes result from "hot spots" in Earth's mantle. A **hot spot** is an area where material from deep within the mantle rises and then melts, forming magma. **A volcano forms above a hot spot when magma erupts through the crust and reaches the surface.** Some hot spot volcanoes lie in the middle of plates far from any plate boundaries. Other hot spots occur on or near plate boundaries.

A hot spot in the ocean floor can gradually form a series of volcanic mountains. For example, the Hawaiian Islands formed one by one over millions of years as the Pacific plate drifted over a hot spot. Hot spots can also form under the continents. Yellowstone National Park in Wyoming marks a hot spot under the North American plate.

**Lab zone Try This Activity**

### Hot Spot in a Box

1. Fill a plastic box half full of cold water. This represents the mantle.
2. Mix red food coloring with hot water in a small, narrow-necked bottle to represent magma.
3. Hold your finger over the mouth of the bottle as you place the bottle in the center of the box. The mouth of the bottle must be under water.
4. Float a flat piece of plastic foam on the water above the bottle to model a tectonic plate.
5. Take your finger off the bottle and observe what happens to the "magma."

**Making Models** Move the plastic foam slowly along. Where does the magma touch the "plate"? How does this model a hot spot volcano?

## Section 1 Assessment

**Target Reading Skill** **Asking Questions** Work with a partner to check the answers in your graphic organizer.

### Reviewing Key Concepts

1. a. **Defining** What is a volcano?
   b. **Reviewing** Where are most volcanoes located?
   c. **Relating Cause and Effect** What causes volcanoes to form at a diverging plate boundary?
2. a. **Defining** What is a hot spot?
   b. **Summarizing** How does a hot spot volcano form?
   c. **Predicting** What features form as an oceanic plate moves across a hot spot?

### Writing in Science

**Travel Brochure** As a travel agent, you are planning a Pacific Ocean cruise that will visit volcanoes in the Ring of Fire and Hawaii. Write a travel brochure describing the types of volcanoes the group will see and explaining why the volcanoes formed where they did.

Lab zone **Skills Lab**

# Mapping Earthquakes and Volcanoes

## Problem

Is there a pattern in the locations of earthquakes and volcanoes?

## Skills Focus

interpreting data

## Materials

- outline world map showing longitude and latitude
- 4 pencils of different colors

## Procedure 

1. Use the information in the table to mark the location of each earthquake on the world map. Use a colored pencil to draw a letter E inside a circle at each earthquake location.
2. Use a pencil of a second color to mark the volcanoes on the world map. Indicate each volcano with the letter V inside a circle.
3. Use a third pencil to lightly shade the areas in which earthquakes are found.
4. Use a fourth colored pencil to lightly shade the areas in which volcanoes are found.

## Analyze and Conclude

1. **Interpreting Data** How are earthquakes distributed on the map? Are they scattered evenly or concentrated in zones?
2. **Interpreting Data** How are volcanoes distributed? Are they scattered evenly or concentrated in zones?
3. **Inferring** From your data, what can you infer about the relationship between earthquakes and volcanoes?
4. **Communicating** Suppose you added the locations of additional earthquakes and volcanoes to your map. Would the overall pattern of earthquakes and volcanoes change? Explain in writing why you think the pattern would or would not change.

**Earthquakes and Volcanoes**

| Earthquakes | | Volcanoes | |
|---|---|---|---|
| Longitude | Latitude | Longitude | Latitude |
| 120° W | 40° N | 150° W | 60° N |
| 110° E | 5° S | 70° W | 35° S |
| 77° W | 4° S | 120° W | 45° N |
| 88° E | 23° N | 61° W | 15° N |
| 121° E | 14° S | 105° W | 20° N |
| 34° E | 7° N | 75° W | 0° |
| 74° W | 44° N | 122° W | 40° N |
| 70° W | 30° S | 30° E | 40° N |
| 10° E | 45° N | 60° E | 30° N |
| 85° W | 13° N | 160° E | 55° N |
| 125° E | 23° N | 37° E | 3° S |
| 30° E | 35° N | 145° E | 40° N |
| 140° E | 35° N | 120° E | 10° S |
| 12° E | 46° N | 14° E | 41° N |
| 75° E | 28° N | 105° E | 5° S |
| 150° W | 61° N | 35° E | 15° N |
| 68° W | 47° S | 70° W | 30° S |
| 175° E | 41° S | 175° E | 39° S |
| 121° E | 17° N | 123° E | 38° N |

## More to Explore

On a map of the United States, locate active volcanoes and areas of earthquake activity. Determine the distance from your home to the nearest active volcano.

Section 2

Integrating Chemistry

# Properties of Magma

## Reading Preview

### Key Concepts

- Why is it helpful to know the physical and chemical properties of a substance?
- What causes some liquids to flow more easily than others?
- What factors determine the viscosity of magma?

### Key Terms

- element
- compound
- physical property
- chemical property
- viscosity
- silica
- pahoehoe
- aa

### Target Reading Skill

**Identifying Main Ideas**

As you read Viscosity of Magma, write the main idea in a graphic organizer like the one below. Then write three supporting details that further explain the main idea.

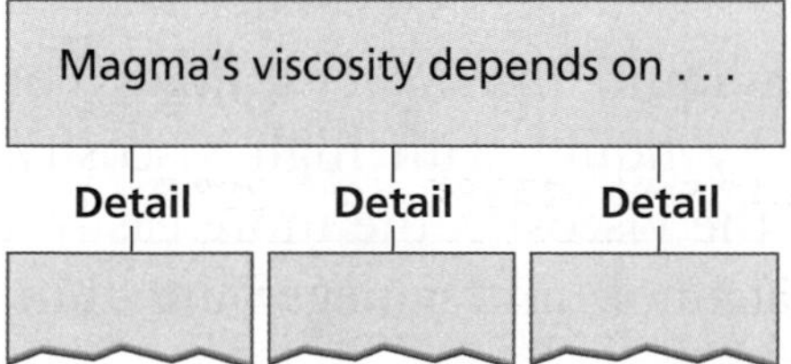


## Lab zone Discover Activity

### How Fast Do Liquids Flow?

1. Fill one third of a small plastic cup with honey. Fill one third of another cup with cooking oil.
2. Hold the cup containing honey over a third cup and tip it until the liquid begins to flow out of the cup. Time how long it takes from the time the cup was tipped until all the liquid drains out of the cup. Record the time.
3. Repeat Step 2 with the cup filled with oil.

**Think About It**

**Forming Operational Definitions** The tendency of a fluid to resist flowing is called viscosity. How did you measure the viscosity of honey and cooking oil? Which had a greater viscosity?

Measured from the bottom of the Pacific Ocean, the Big Island of Hawaii is the largest mountain on Earth. The island is made up of massive volcanoes. One of these volcanoes, Mount Kilauea (kee loo AY uh) erupts frequently and produces huge amounts of lava.

At a temperature of around 1,000°C, lava from Mount Kilauea is very dangerous. Yet most of the time, the lava moves slower than a person can walk—about 1 kilometer per hour. Some types of lava move much more slowly—less than the length of a football field in an entire day. How fast lava flows depends on the properties of the magma from which it formed.

## Physical and Chemical Properties

Like all substances, magma and lava are made up of elements and compounds. An **element** is a substance that cannot be broken down into other substances. Carbon, hydrogen, and oxygen are examples of elements. A **compound** is a substance made of two or more elements that have been chemically combined. Water, carbon dioxide, and table salt are familiar compounds. **Each substance has a particular set of physical and chemical properties. These properties can be used to identify a substance or to predict how it will behave.**

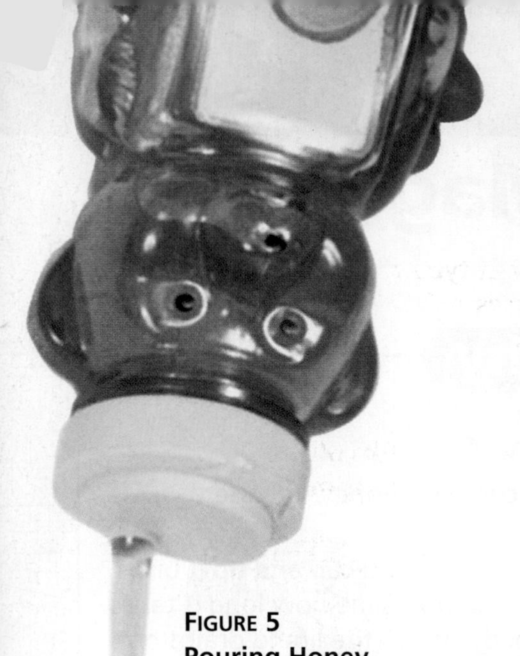

FIGURE 5
**Pouring Honey**
A liquid with high viscosity, such as honey, pours slowly from its container.
**Predicting** *If you poured water out of a similar container, how would its behavior differ from the honey? Explain your answer.*

**Physical Properties** A **physical property** is any characteristic of a substance that can be observed or measured without changing the composition of the substance. Examples of physical properties include density, hardness, melting point, boiling point, and whether a substance is magnetic. A substance always has the same physical properties under particular conditions. Under normal conditions at sea level, for example, water's freezing point is 0°C and its boiling point is 100°C. Between its freezing and boiling points, water is a liquid.

**Chemical Properties** A **chemical property** is any property that produces a change in the composition of matter. Examples of chemical properties include a substance's ability to burn and its ability to combine, or react, with other substances. You can often tell that one substance has reacted with another if it changes color, produces a gas, or forms a new, solid substance. For example, a piece of silver jewelry darkens when exposed to air. This change indicates that silver has reacted with oxygen to form tarnish. The ability to react with oxygen is a chemical property of silver.

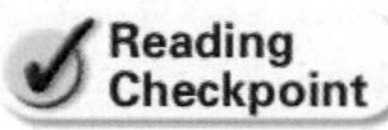
**Is the boiling point of a substance a physical property or a chemical property?**

## What Is Viscosity?

When you pour yourself a glass of milk, you are making use of a familiar physical property of liquids. Because particles in a liquid are free to move around one another, a liquid can flow from place to place. The physical property of liquids called **viscosity** (vis KAHS uh tee) is the resistance of a liquid to flowing. **Because liquids differ in viscosity, some liquids flow more easily than others.**

The greater the viscosity of a liquid, the slower it flows. For example, honey is a thick, sticky liquid with high viscosity. Honey flows slowly. The lower the viscosity, the more easily a liquid flows. Water, rubbing alcohol, and vinegar are thin, runny liquids with low viscosities.

Why do different liquids have different viscosities? The answer lies in the movement of the particles that make up each type of liquid. In some liquids, there is a greater degree of friction among the liquid's particles. These liquids have higher viscosity.

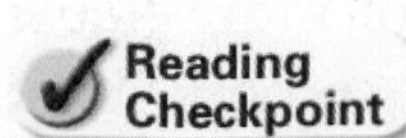
**Why do liquids differ in viscosity?**

**For:** Links on volcanic eruptions
**Visit:** www.SciLinks.org
**Web Code:** scn-1032

## Math Analyzing Data

### Magma Composition

Magma varies in composition and is classified according to the amount of silica it contains. The graphs show the average composition of two types of magma. Use the graphs to answer the questions.

1. **Reading Graphs** Study both graphs. What materials make up both types of magma?
2. **Reading Graphs** Which type of magma has more silica? About how much silica does this type of magma contain?
3. **Estimating** A third type of magma has a silica content that is halfway between that of the other two types. About how much silica does this magma contain?
4. **Predicting** What type of magma would have a higher viscosity? Explain.

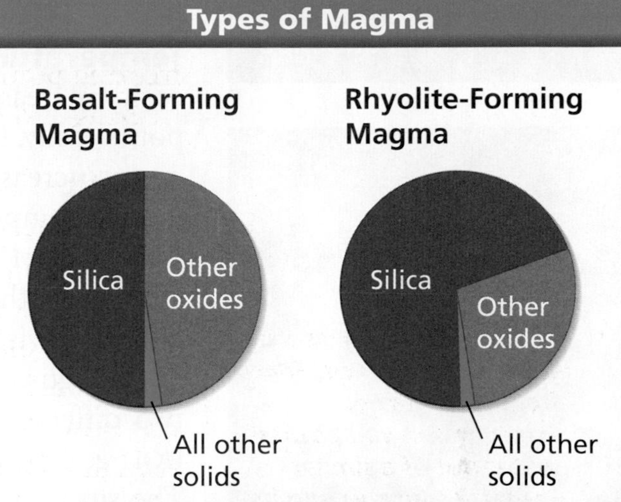


## Viscosity of Magma

At the extremely high temperatures and pressures inside Earth, mantle rock sometimes melts to form magma. Surprisingly, the properties of magma can vary. For example, not all types of magma have the same viscosity. **The viscosity of magma depends upon its silica content and temperature.**

**Silica Content** Magma is a complex mixture, but its major ingredient is silica. The compound **silica** is made up of particles of the elements oxygen and silicon. Silica is one of the most abundant materials in Earth's crust. The silica content of magma ranges from about 50 percent to 70 percent.

The amount of silica in magma helps to determine its viscosity. The more silica magma contains, the higher its viscosity. Magma that is high in silica produces light-colored lava that is too sticky to flow very far. When this type of lava cools, it forms the rock rhyolite, which has the same composition as granite.

The less silica magma contains, the lower its viscosity. Low-silica magma flows readily and produces dark-colored lava. When this kind of lava cools, it forms rocks like basalt.

FIGURE 6
**Sampling Magma**
A geologist samples magma from a lava flow in Hawaii.

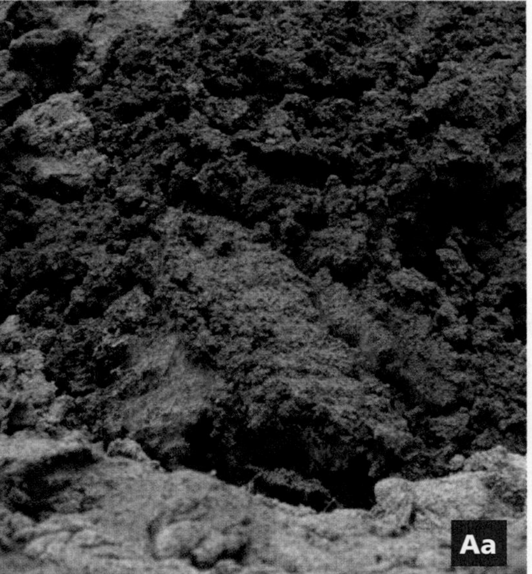


**FIGURE 7**
**Pahoehoe and Aa**
Both pahoehoe and aa can come from the same volcano. Pahoehoe flows easily and hardens into a rippled surface. Aa hardens into rough chunks. **Inferring** *Which type of lava has lower viscosity?*

**Temperature** How does temperature affect viscosity? Viscosity increases as temperature decreases. On a hot day, honey pours easily. But if you put the honey in the refrigerator, its viscosity increases. The cold honey flows very slowly.

The temperature of magma and lava can range from about 750°C to 1,175°C. The hotter the magma is, the lower its viscosity and the more rapidly it flows. Cooler types of magma have high viscosity and flow very slowly.

In Figure 7, you can see how temperature differences produce two different types of lava: pahoehoe and aa. **Pahoehoe** (pah HOH ee hoh ee) is fast-moving, hot lava that has low viscosity. The surface of a lava flow formed from pahoehoe looks like a solid mass of wrinkles, billows, and ropelike coils. Lava that is cooler and slower-moving is called **aa** (AH ah). Aa has higher viscosity than pahoehoe. When aa hardens, it forms a rough surface consisting of jagged lava chunks.

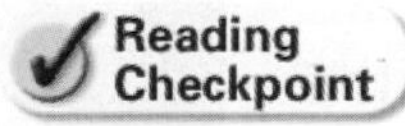


**How hot are magma and lava?**

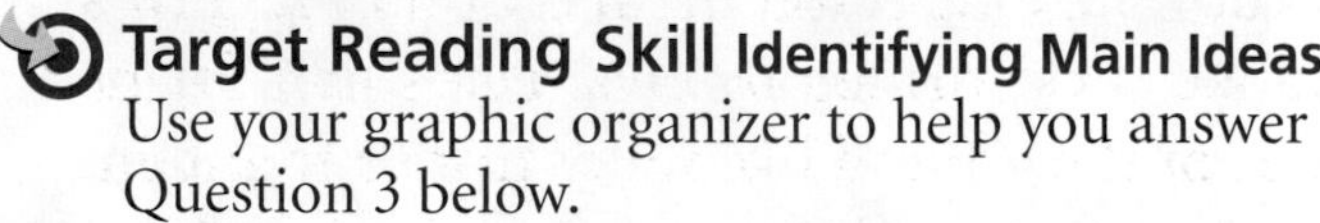


**Target Reading Skill Identifying Main Ideas** Use your graphic organizer to help you answer Question 3 below.

### Reviewing Key Concepts

1. a. **Defining** What is a physical property?
   b. **Defining** What is a chemical property?
   c. **Classifying** Magma is a hot, liquid mixture that changes to solid rock when it cools and hardens. Which of these characteristics are physical properties?
2. a. **Identifying** What is viscosity?
   b. **Applying Concepts** Which has a higher viscosity, a fast-flowing liquid or a slow-flowing liquid?
   c. **Inferring** What can you infer about the amount of friction among the particles of a liquid that has low viscosity?
3. a. **Reviewing** What two main factors affect magma's viscosity?
   b. **Predicting** A lava flow cools as it moves away from the vent. How would this affect the surface appearance of the lava flow?

### Lab zone At-Home Activity

**Cooling Lava** Place cold water in one cup and hot tap water in another. Ask members of your family to predict what will happen when melted candle wax drops into each cup of water. Have an adult family member drip melted wax from a candle into each cup. **CAUTION:** *Handle the lit candle carefully.* Explain how this models what happens when lava cools quickly or slowly.

Section 3

# Volcanic Eruptions

## Reading Preview

### Key Concepts

- What happens when a volcano erupts?
- What are the two types of volcanic eruptions?
- What are a volcano's stages of activity?

### Key Terms

- magma chamber
- pipe
- vent
- lava flow
- crater
- pyroclastic flow
- dormant
- extinct

### Target Reading Skill

**Using Prior Knowledge** Before you read, look at the section headings to see what the section is about. Then write what you know about how a volcano erupts in a graphic organizer like the one below. As you read, write what you learn.

| What You Know |
|---|
| 1. Lava flows out of a volcano.<br>2. |

| What You Learned |
|---|
| 1.<br>2. |

## Lab zone Discover Activity

### What Are Volcanic Rocks Like?

Volcanoes produce lava, which hardens into rock. Two of these rocks are pumice and obsidian.

Pumice

Obsidian

1. Observe samples of pumice and obsidian with a hand lens.
2. How would you describe the texture of the pumice? What could have caused this texture?
3. Observe the surface of the obsidian. How does the surface of the obsidian differ from pumice?

**Think It Over**

**Developing Hypotheses** What could have produced the difference in texture between the two rocks? Explain your answer.

In Hawaii, there are many myths about Pele (PAY lay), the fire goddess of volcanoes. Pele lives in the depths of Hawaii's erupting volcanoes. According to legend, when Pele is angry, she causes a volcanic eruption. One result of an eruption is "Pele's hair," a fine, threadlike rock formed by lava. Pele's hair forms when lava sprays out of the ground like water from a fountain. As it cools, the lava stretches and hardens into thin strands, as shown in Figure 8.

Where does this lava come from? Lava begins as magma, which usually forms in the asthenosphere. The materials of the asthenosphere are under great pressure. Liquid magma is less dense than the solid material around it. Therefore, magma flows upward into any cracks in the rock above. As magma rises, it sometimes becomes trapped beneath layers of rock. But if an opening in weak rock allows the magma to reach the surface, a volcano forms.

**FIGURE 8**
**Pele's Hair**
Pele's hair is a type of rock formed from lava. Each strand is as fine as spun glass.

## Magma Reaches Earth's Surface

A volcano is more than a large, cone-shaped mountain. Inside a volcano is a system of passageways through which magma moves.

**Inside a Volcano** All volcanoes have a pocket of magma beneath the surface and one or more cracks through which the magma forces its way. Beneath a volcano, magma collects in a pocket called a **magma chamber.** The magma moves upward through a **pipe,** a long tube in the ground that connects the magma chamber to Earth's surface. You can see these features in Figure 10.

Molten rock and gas leave the volcano through an opening called a **vent.** Often, there is one central vent at the top of a volcano. However, many volcanoes also have other vents that open on the volcano's sides. A **lava flow** is the area covered by lava as it pours out of a vent. A **crater** is a bowl-shaped area that may form at the top of a volcano around the central vent.

**A Volcanic Eruption** What pushes magma to the surface? The explosion of a volcano is similar to the soda water bubbling out of a warm bottle of soda pop. You cannot see the carbon dioxide gas in a bottle of soda pop because it is dissolved in the liquid. But when you open the bottle, the pressure is released. The carbon dioxide expands and forms bubbles, which rush to the surface. Like the carbon dioxide in soda pop, dissolved gases are trapped in magma. These dissolved gases are under tremendous pressure.

FIGURE 9
**Lava Burp**
During an eruption on Mount Kilauea, the force of a bursting gas bubble pushes up a sheet of red-hot lava.

**Go Online** *active art*

**For:** Composite Volcano Eruption activity
**Visit:** PHSchool.com
**Web Code:** cfp-1033

FIGURE 10
**A Volcano Erupts**
A volcano forms where magma breaks through Earth's crust and lava flows over the surface.
**Interpreting Diagrams** *What part of a volcano connects the vent with the magma chamber?*

As magma rises toward the surface, the pressure of the surrounding rock on the magma decreases. The dissolved gases begin to expand, forming bubbles. As pressure falls within the magma, the size of the gas bubbles increases greatly. These expanding gases exert an enormous force. **When a volcano erupts, the force of the expanding gases pushes magma from the magma chamber through the pipe until it flows or explodes out of the vent.** Once magma escapes from the volcano and becomes lava, the remaining gases bubble out.

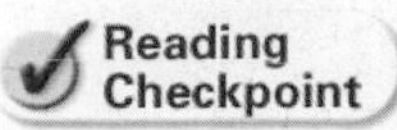


**What happens to the pressure in magma as the magma rises toward the surface?**

Lab zone **Try This Activity**

### Gases in Magma

This activity models the gas bubbles in a volcanic eruption.

1. In a 1- or 2-liter plastic bottle, mix 10 g of baking soda into 65 mL of water.
2. Put about six raisins in the water.
3. While swirling the water and raisins, add 65 mL of vinegar and stir vigorously.
4. Once the liquid stops moving, observe the raisins.

**Making Models** What happens after you add the vinegar? What do the raisins and bubbles represent? How is this model similar to the way magma behaves in a volcano?

## Kinds of Volcanic Eruptions

Some volcanic eruptions occur gradually. Others are dramatic explosions. **Geologists classify volcanic eruptions as quiet or explosive.** The physical properties of its magma determine how a volcano erupts. Whether an eruption is quiet or explosive depends on the magma's silica content and viscosity.

**Quiet Eruptions** A volcano erupts quietly if its magma is low in silica. Low-silica magma has low viscosity and flows easily. The gases in the magma bubble out gently. Lava with low viscosity oozes quietly from the vent and can flow for many kilometers. Quiet eruptions can produce both pahoehoe and aa.

The Hawaiian Islands were formed from quiet eruptions. On the Big Island of Hawaii, lava pours out of the crater near the top of Mount Kilauea. But lava also flows out of long cracks on the volcano's sides. Quiet eruptions have built up the Big Island over hundreds of thousands of years.

**Explosive Eruptions** A volcano erupts explosively if its magma is high in silica. High-silica magma has high viscosity, making it thick and sticky. The high-viscosity magma does not always flow out of the crater. Instead, it builds up in the volcano's pipe, plugging it like a cork in a bottle. Dissolved gases, including water vapor, cannot escape from the thick magma. The trapped gases build up pressure until they explode. The erupting gases and steam push the magma out of the volcano with incredible force. That's what happened during the eruption of Mount St. Helens, shown in Figure 11.

An explosive eruption breaks lava into fragments that quickly cool and harden into pieces of different sizes. The smallest pieces are volcanic ash—fine, rocky particles as small as a speck of dust. Pebble-sized particles are called cinders. Larger pieces, called bombs, may range from the size of a baseball to the size of a car. A **pyroclastic flow** (py roh KLAS tik) occurs when an explosive eruption hurls out a mixture of hot gases, ash, cinders, and bombs.

Pumice and obsidian, which you observed if you did the Discover Activity, form from high-silica lava. Obsidian forms when lava cools very quickly, giving it a smooth, glossy surface like glass. Pumice forms when gas bubbles are trapped in fast-cooling lava, leaving spaces in the rock.

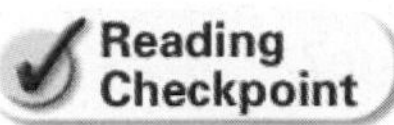


**What is a pyroclastic flow?**

**FIGURE 11**
**An Explosive Eruption**
Mount St. Helens in Washington State erupted at 8:30 A.M. on May 18, 1980. The explosion blew off the top of the mountain, leaving a huge crater and causing great destruction.

**After Eruption**

**Volcano Hazards** Although quiet eruptions and explosive eruptions produce different hazards, both types of eruption can cause damage far from the crater's rim.

During a quiet eruption, lava flows from vents, setting fire to, and then burying, everything in its path. A quiet eruption can cover large areas with a thick layer of lava.

During an explosive eruption, a volcano can belch out hot clouds of deadly gases as well as ash, cinders, and bombs. Volcanic ash can bury entire towns. If it becomes wet, the heavy ash can cause roofs to collapse. If a jet plane sucks ash into its engine, the engine may stall. Eruptions can cause landslides and avalanches of mud, melted snow, and rock. The Science and History timeline shows the effects of several explosive eruptions.

**How does volcanic ash cause damage?**

## Science and **History**

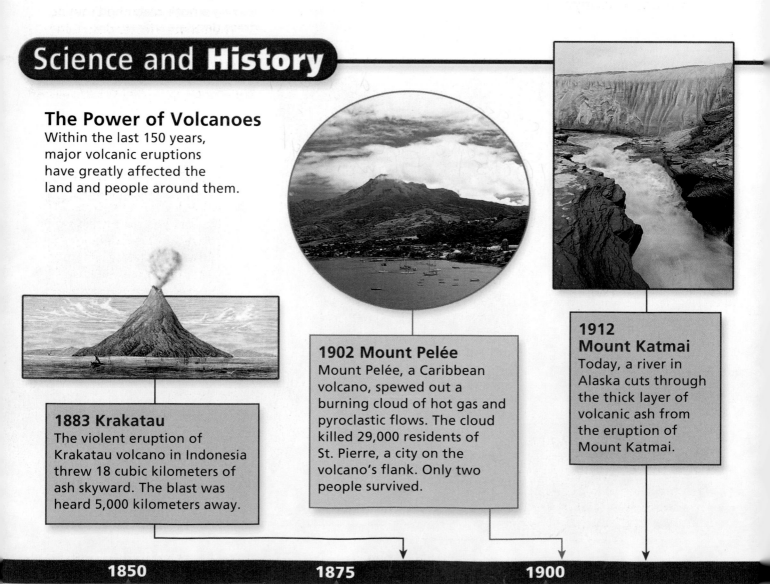

### The Power of Volcanoes

Within the last 150 years, major volcanic eruptions have greatly affected the land and people around them.

**1883 Krakatau**
The violent eruption of Krakatau volcano in Indonesia threw 18 cubic kilometers of ash skyward. The blast was heard 5,000 kilometers away.

**1902 Mount Pelée**
Mount Pelée, a Caribbean volcano, spewed out a burning cloud of hot gas and pyroclastic flows. The cloud killed 29,000 residents of St. Pierre, a city on the volcano's flank. Only two people survived.

**1912 Mount Katmai**
Today, a river in Alaska cuts through the thick layer of volcanic ash from the eruption of Mount Katmai.

1850 1875 1900

## Stages of Volcanic Activity

The activity of a volcano may last from less than a decade to more than 10 million years. Most long-lived volcanoes, however, do not erupt continuously. Geologists try to determine a volcano's past and whether the volcano will erupt again.

**Life Cycle of a Volcano** **Geologists often use the terms *active, dormant,* or *extinct* to describe a volcano's stage of activity.** An active, or live, volcano is one that is erupting or has shown signs that it may erupt in the near future. A dormant, or sleeping, volcano is like a sleeping bear. Scientists expect a **dormant** volcano to awaken in the future and become active. An **extinct,** or dead, volcano is unlikely to erupt again.

The time between volcanic eruptions may span hundreds to many thousands of years. People living near a dormant volcano may be unaware of the danger. But a dormant volcano can become active at any time.

### Writing in Science

**Research and Write** People have written eyewitness accounts of famous volcanic eruptions. Research one of the eruptions in the timeline. Then write a letter describing what someone observing the eruption might have seen.

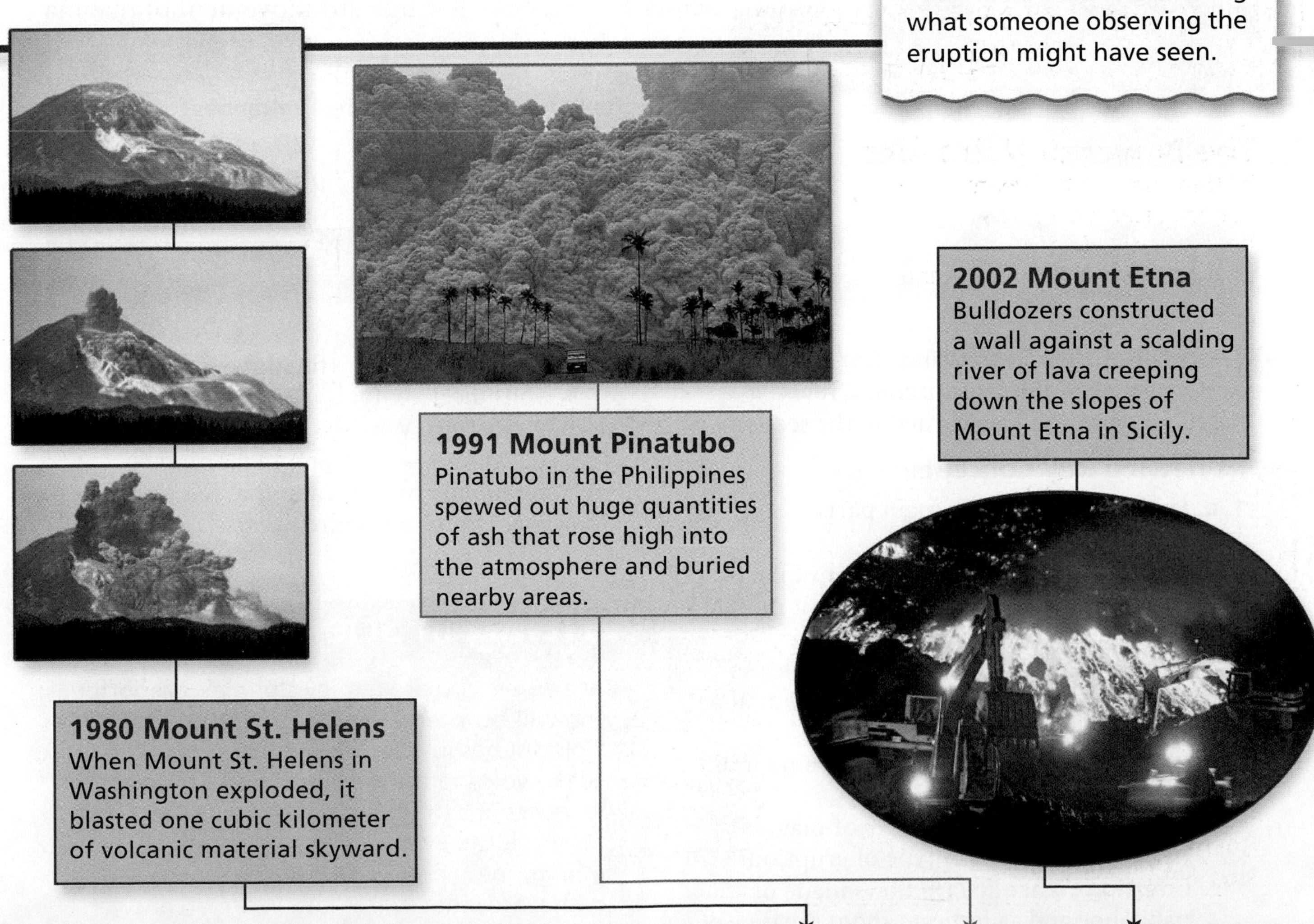


**1980 Mount St. Helens** When Mount St. Helens in Washington exploded, it blasted one cubic kilometer of volcanic material skyward.

**1991 Mount Pinatubo** Pinatubo in the Philippines spewed out huge quantities of ash that rose high into the atmosphere and buried nearby areas.

**2002 Mount Etna** Bulldozers constructed a wall against a scalding river of lava creeping down the slopes of Mount Etna in Sicily.

**FIGURE 12**
**Volcano Watch**
Near Mount Kilauea in Hawaii, these geologists are testing instruments to monitor temperatures in and around a crater.

**Monitoring Volcanoes** Geologists have been more successful in predicting volcanic eruptions than in predicting earthquakes. Geologists use instruments to detect changes in and around a volcano. These changes may give warning a short time before a volcano erupts. But geologists cannot be certain about the type of eruption or how powerful it will be.

Geologists use tiltmeters and other instruments to detect slight surface changes in elevation and tilt caused by magma moving underground. They monitor any gases escaping from the volcano. A temperature increase in underground water may be a sign that magma is nearing the surface. Geologists also monitor the many small earthquakes that occur around a volcano before an eruption. The upward movement of magma triggers these quakes.

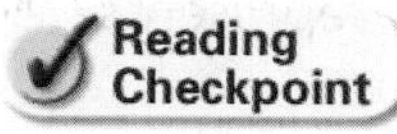

**How do geologists monitor volcanoes?**

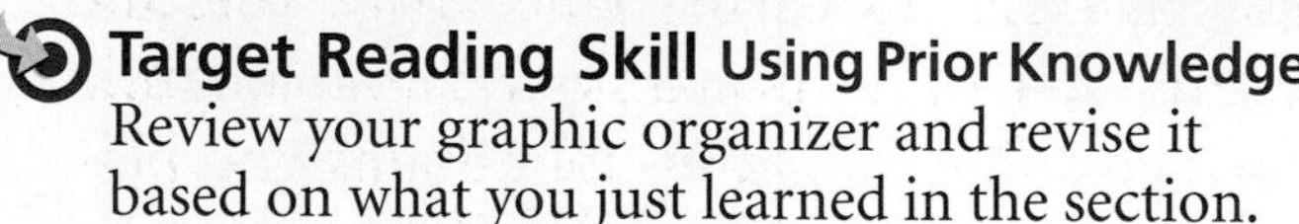


## Section 3 Assessment

**Target Reading Skill Using Prior Knowledge** Review your graphic organizer and revise it based on what you just learned in the section.

### Reviewing Key Concepts

1. a. **Listing** What are the main parts of a volcano?
   b. **Sequencing** Describe the order of parts through which magma travels as it moves to the surface.
   c. **Relating Cause and Effect** As a volcano erupts, what force pushes magma out of a volcano onto the surface?
2. a. **Identifying** What are the two main kinds of volcanic eruptions?
   b. **Explaining** What properties of magma help to determine the type of eruption?
   c. **Inferring** What do lava flows made of pahoehoe and aa indicate about the type of volcanic eruption that occurred?
3. a. **Naming** What are the three stages of volcanic activity?
   b. **Predicting** Which is more likely to be dangerous—a volcano that erupts frequently or a volcano that has been inactive for a hundred years? Why?

### Writing in Science

**Interview** You are a television news reporter who will be interviewing a geologist. The geologist has just returned from studying a nearby volcano that may soon erupt. Write the questions that you would ask. Be sure to ask about the evidence that an eruption is coming, the type of eruption expected, and any hazards that will result. Write an answer for each question.

Section 4

# Volcanic Landforms

## Reading Preview

### Key Concepts

- What landforms do lava and ash create?
- How does magma that hardens beneath the surface create landforms?
- What other distinctive features occur in volcanic areas?

### Key Terms

- shield volcano • cinder cone
- composite volcano • caldera
- volcanic neck • dike
- sill • batholith
- geothermal activity • geyser

### Target Reading Skill

**Outlining** As you read, make an outline about volcanic landforms that you can use for review. Use the red headings for main topics and the blue headings for subtopics.

**Volcanic Landforms**

I. Landforms From Lava and Ash
  A. Shield Volcanoes
  B.
  C.
  D.
  E.
II. Landforms From Magma

## Lab zone Discover Activity

### How Can Volcanic Activity Change Earth's Surface?

1. Use tape to secure the neck of a balloon over one end of a straw.
2. Place the balloon in the center of a box with the straw protruding.
3. Partially inflate the balloon.
4. Put damp sand on top of the balloon until it is covered.
5. Slowly inflate the balloon more. Observe what happens to the surface of the sand.

**Think It Over**

**Making Models** This activity models one of the ways in which volcanic activity can cause a mountain to form. What do you think the sand represents? What does the balloon represent?

Volcanoes have created some of Earth's most spectacular landforms. The perfect cone of Mount Fuji in Japan, shown in Figure 13, is famous around the world.

For much of Earth's history, volcanic activity on and beneath the surface has built up Earth's land areas. Volcanic activity also formed the rock of the ocean floor. Some volcanic landforms arise when lava flows build up mountains and plateaus on Earth's surface. Other volcanic landforms are the result of the buildup of magma beneath the surface.

**FIGURE 13**
**Mount Fuji**
The almost perfect volcanic cone of Mount Fuji in Japan has long been a favorite subject for artists.

## Landforms From Lava and Ash

**Volcanic eruptions create landforms made of lava, ash, and other materials. These landforms include shield volcanoes, cinder cone volcanoes, composite volcanoes, and lava plateaus.** Look at Figure 14 to see these features. Another landform results from the collapse of a volcanic mountain.

**Shield Volcanoes** At some places on Earth's surface, thin layers of lava pour out of a vent and harden on top of previous layers. Such lava flows gradually build a wide, gently sloping mountain called a **shield volcano.** Shield volcanoes rising from a hot spot on the ocean floor created the Hawaiian Islands.

**Cinder Cone Volcanoes** If a volcano's lava has high viscosity, it may produce ash, cinders, and bombs. These materials build up around the vent in a steep, cone-shaped hill or small mountain called a **cinder cone.** For example, Paricutín in Mexico erupted in 1943 in a farmer's cornfield. The volcano built up a cinder cone about 400 meters high.

FIGURE 14

### Volcanic Mountains

Volcanic activity is responsible for building up much of Earth's surface. Lava from volcanoes cools and hardens into three types of mountains. It can also form lava plateaus. **Classifying** *What type of volcano is formed from thin, low-silica lava?*

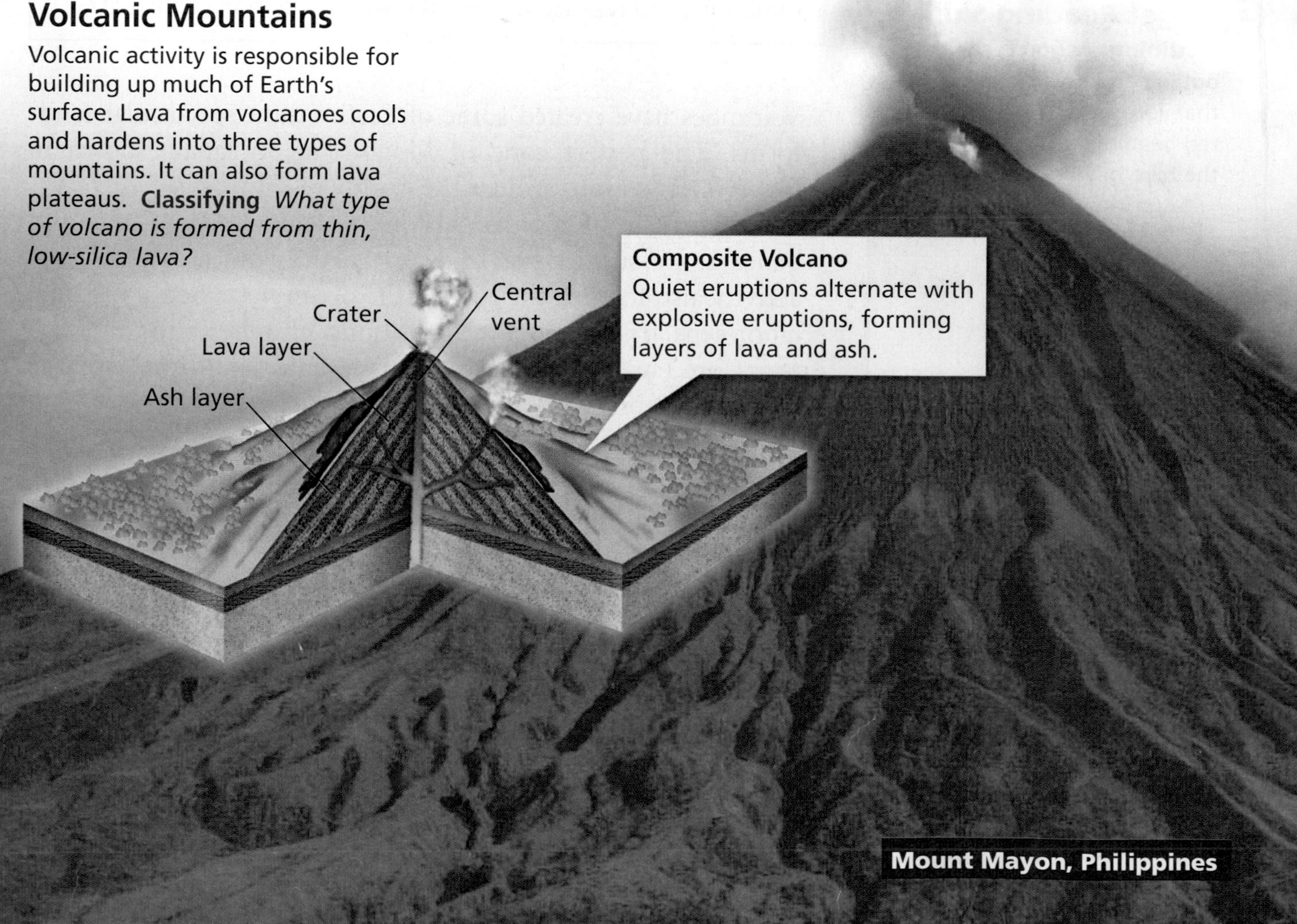

**Composite Volcanoes** Sometimes, lava flows alternate with explosive eruptions of ash, cinder, and bombs. The result is a composite volcano. **Composite volcanoes** are tall, cone-shaped mountains in which layers of lava alternate with layers of ash. Examples of composite volcanoes include Mount Fuji in Japan and Mount St. Helens in Washington State.

**Lava Plateaus** Instead of forming mountains, some eruptions of lava form high, level areas called lava plateaus. First, lava flows out of several long cracks in an area. The thin, runny lava travels far before cooling and solidifying. Again and again, floods of lava flow on top of earlier floods. After millions of years, these layers of lava can form high plateaus. One example is the Columbia Plateau, which covers parts of the states of Washington, Oregon, and Idaho.

Discovery Channel School

*Volcanoes*

Video Preview
▶ Video Field Trip
Video Assessment

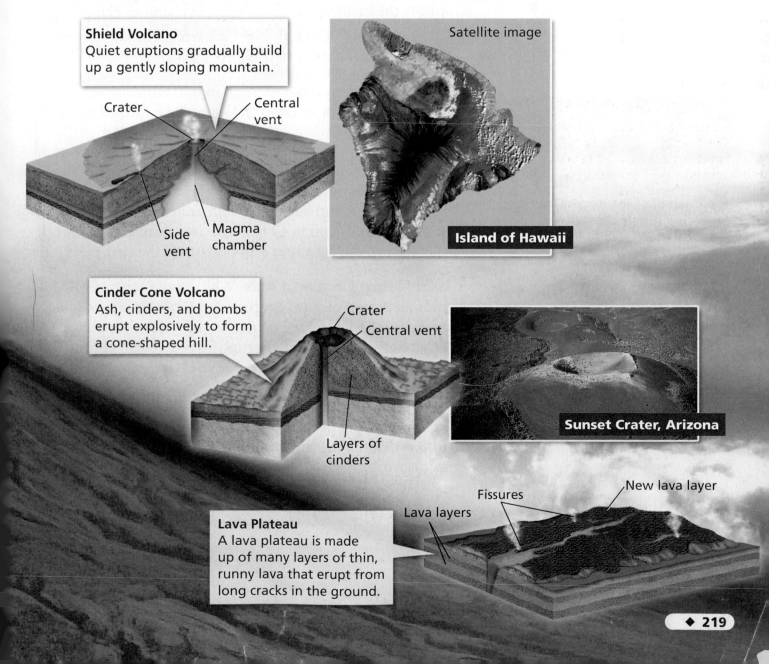

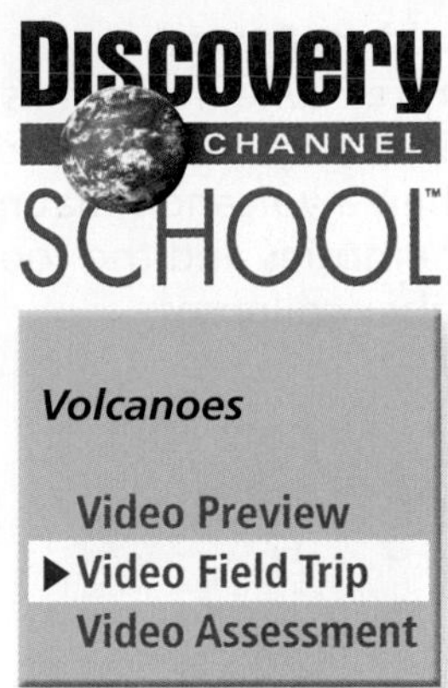

**Shield Volcano**
Quiet eruptions gradually build up a gently sloping mountain.

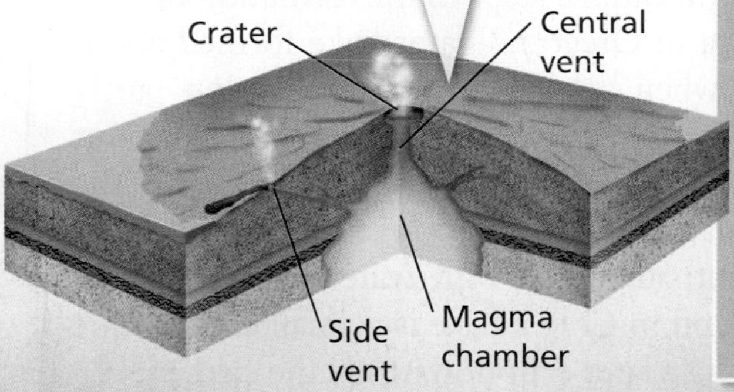

Crater
Central vent
Side vent
Magma chamber

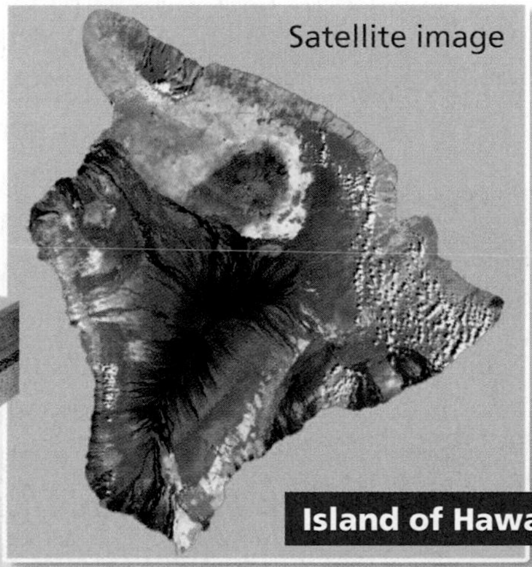

Satellite image

**Island of Hawaii**

**Cinder Cone Volcano**
Ash, cinders, and bombs erupt explosively to form a cone-shaped hill.

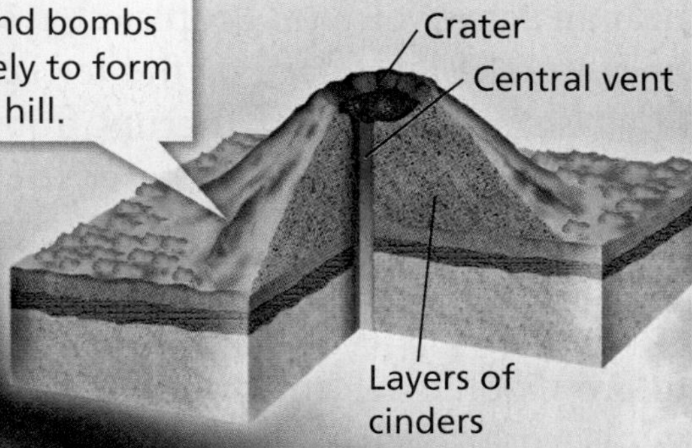

Crater
Central vent
Layers of cinders

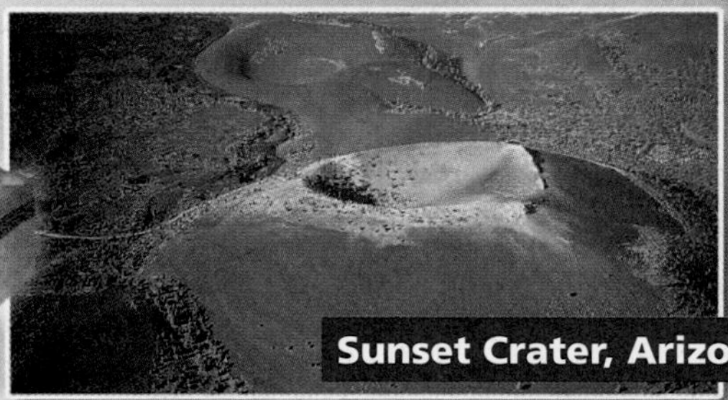

**Sunset Crater, Arizona**

**Lava Plateau**
A lava plateau is made up of many layers of thin, runny lava that erupt from long cracks in the ground.

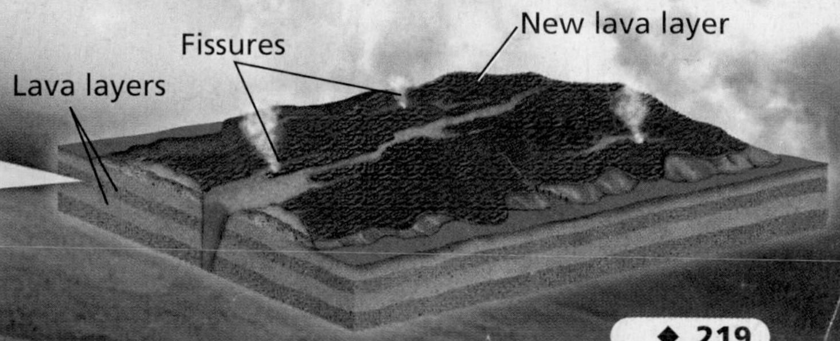

Fissures
New lava layer
Lava layers

**FIGURE 15**
**How a Caldera Forms**
Today, Crater Lake (right) fills an almost circular caldera. A caldera forms when a volcano's magma chamber empties and the roof of the chamber collapses.

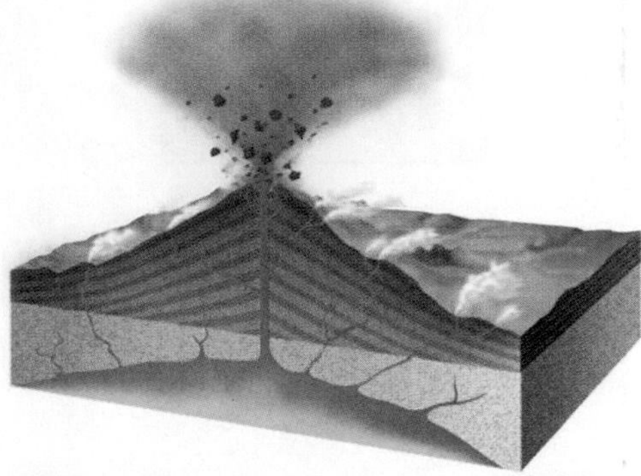

1 The top of a composite volcano explodes. Lava flows partially empty the magma chamber.

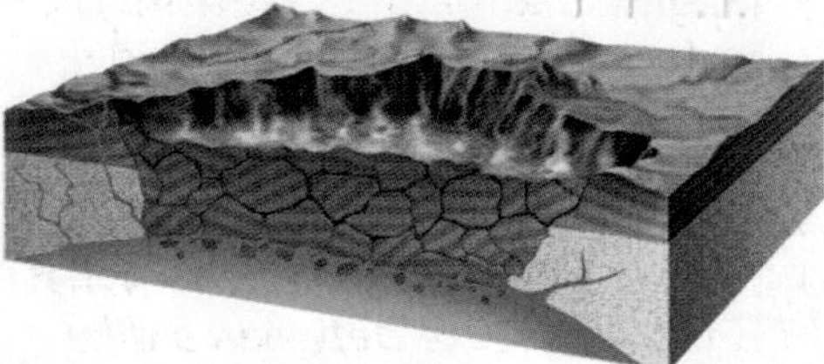

2 The roof of the magma chamber collapses, forming a caldera.

3 Later, a small cinder cone forms in the caldera, which partly fills with water.

**Calderas** The huge hole left by the collapse of a volcanic mountain is called a **caldera** (kal DAIR uh). The hole is filled with the pieces of the volcano that have fallen inward, as well as some lava and ash.

How does a caldera form? Enormous eruptions may empty the main vent and the magma chamber beneath a volcano. The mountain becomes a hollow shell. With nothing to support it, the top of the mountain collapses inward, forming a caldera.

In Figure 15 you can see steps in the formation of Crater Lake, a caldera in Oregon. Crater Lake formed about 7,700 years ago when a huge explosive eruption partly emptied the magma chamber of a volcano called Mount Mazama. When the volcano exploded, the top of the mountain was blasted into the atmosphere. The caldera that formed eventually filled with water from rain and snow. Wizard Island in Crater Lake is a small cinder cone that formed during a later eruption inside the caldera.

**Soils From Lava and Ash** Why would anyone live near an active volcano? People often settle close to volcanoes to take advantage of the fertile volcanic soil. The lava, ash, and cinders that erupt from a volcano are initially barren. Over time, however, the hard surface of the lava breaks down to form soil. When volcanic ash breaks down, it releases potassium, phosphorus, and other substances that plants need. As soil develops, plants are able to grow. Some volcanic soils are among the richest soils in the world. Saying that soil is rich means that it's fertile, or able to support plant growth.

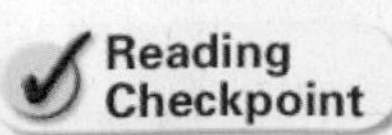

**How are volcanic soils important?**

## Landforms From Magma

Sometimes magma forces its way through cracks in the upper crust, but fails to reach the surface. There the magma cools and hardens into rock. Over time, the forces that wear away Earth's surface—such as flowing water, ice, or wind—may strip away the layers above the hardened magma and finally expose it. **Features formed by magma include volcanic necks, dikes, and sills, as well as batholiths and dome mountains.**

**Volcanic Necks** A volcanic neck looks like a giant tooth stuck in the ground. A **volcanic neck** forms when magma hardens in a volcano's pipe. The softer rock around the pipe wears away, exposing the hard rock of the volcanic neck. Ship Rock in New Mexico, shown in Figure 16, is a volcanic neck formed from a volcano that erupted about 30 million years ago.

**Dikes and Sills** Magma that forces itself across rock layers hardens into a **dike.** Sometimes, a dike can be seen slanting through bedrock along a highway cut.

When magma squeezes between horizontal layers of rock, it forms a **sill.** One famous example of a sill is the Palisades in New York State and New Jersey. The Palisades form a series of long, dark cliffs. These cliffs stretch for about 30 kilometers along the west bank of the Hudson River.

For: Links on volcanic effects
Visit: www.SciLinks.org
Web Code: scn-1034

**FIGURE 16**
**Volcanic Necks, Dikes, and Sills**
Magma that hardens beneath the surface may form volcanic necks, dikes, and sills. A dike extends outward from Ship Rock, a volcanic neck in New Mexico.
**Comparing and Contrasting** *What is the difference between a dike and a sill?*

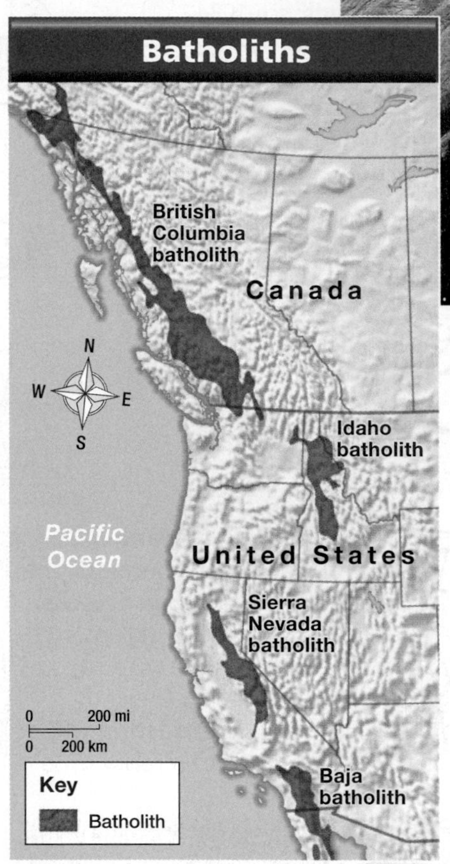


**FIGURE 17**
**Batholiths**
Several large batholiths form the core of mountain ranges in western North America. Half Dome in Yosemite National Park, California is part of the Sierra Nevada batholith.

**Batholiths** Large rock masses called batholiths form the core of many mountain ranges. A **batholith** (BATH UH lith) is a mass of rock formed when a large body of magma cools inside the crust. The map in Figure 17 shows just how big batholiths really are. The photograph shows how a batholith looks when the layers of rock above it have worn away.

**Dome Mountains** Other, smaller bodies of hardened magma can create dome mountains. A dome mountain forms when uplift pushes a batholith or smaller body of hardened magma toward the surface. The hardened magma forces the layers of rock to bend upward into a dome shape. Eventually, the rock above the dome mountain wears away, leaving it exposed. This process formed the Black Hills in South Dakota.

## Geothermal Activity

The word *geothermal* comes from the Greek *geo* meaning "Earth" and *therme* meaning "heat." In **geothermal activity,** magma a few kilometers beneath Earth's surface heats underground water. A variety of geothermal features occur in volcanic areas. **Hot springs and geysers are types of geothermal activity that are often found in areas of present or past volcanic activity.**

**Hot Springs** A hot spring forms when groundwater is heated by a nearby body of magma or by hot rock deep underground. The hot water rises to the surface and collects in a natural pool. (Groundwater is water that has seeped into the spaces among rocks deep beneath Earth's surface.) Water from hot springs may contain dissolved gases and other substances from deep within Earth.

**Geysers** Sometimes, rising hot water and steam become trapped underground in a narrow crack. Pressure builds until the mixture suddenly sprays above the surface as a geyser. A **geyser** (GY zur) is a fountain of water and steam that erupts from the ground. Figure 18 shows one of Earth's most famous geysers.

**Geothermal Energy** In some volcanic areas, water heated by magma can provide an energy source called geothermal energy. The people of Reykjavik, Iceland, pipe this hot water into homes for warmth. Geothermal energy can also be used as a source of electricity. Steam from underground is piped into turbines. Inside a turbine, the steam spins a wheel in the same way that blowing on a pinwheel makes the pinwheel turn. The moving wheel in the turbine turns a generator that changes the energy of motion into electrical energy. Geothermal energy provides some electrical power in California and New Zealand.

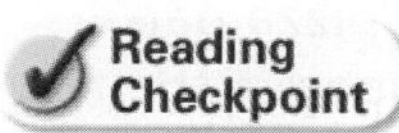


**How can geothermal energy be used to generate electricity?**

FIGURE 18
**A Geyser Erupts**
Old Faithful, a geyser in Yellowstone National Park, erupts about every 33 to 93 minutes. That's how long it takes for the pressure to build up again after each eruption.

## Section 4 Assessment

**Target Reading Skill Outlining** Use the information in your outline about volcanic landforms to help you answer the questions below.

### Reviewing Key Concepts

1. a. **Identifying** What are the three main types of volcanoes?
   b. **Comparing and Contrasting** Compare the three types of volcanic mountains in terms of shape, type of eruption, and the materials that make up the volcano.
2. a. **Listing** What features form as a result of magma hardening beneath Earth's surface?
   b. **Explaining** What are two ways in which mountains can form as a result of magma hardening beneath Earth's surface?
   c. **Predicting** After millions of years, what landform forms from hardened magma in the pipe of an extinct volcano?
3. a. **Listing** What are some features found in areas of geothermal activity?
   b. **Relating Cause and Effect** What causes a geyser to erupt?

### Writing in Science

**Explaining a Process** Write an explanation of the process that formed Crater Lake. In your answer, include the type of volcanic mountain and eruption involved, as well as the steps in the process. (*Hint:* Look at the diagram in Figure 15 before you write.)

Lab zone **Skills Lab**

# Gelatin Volcanoes

## Problem
How does magma move inside a volcano?

## Skills Focus
developing hypotheses, making models, observing

## Materials
- plastic cup
- tray or shallow pan
- aluminum pizza pan with holes punched at 2.5-cm intervals
- plastic knife
- unflavored gelatin mold in bowl
- red food coloring and water
- plastic syringe, 10 cc
- rubber gloves
- unlined paper
- 3 small cardboard oatmeal boxes

## Procedure 

1. Before magma erupts as lava, how does it travel up from underground magma chambers? Record your hypothesis.
2. Remove the gelatin from the refrigerator. Loosen the gelatin from its container by briefly placing the container of gelatin in a larger bowl of hot water.
3. Place the pizza pan over the gelatin so the mold is near the center of the pizza pan. While holding the pizza pan against the top of the mold, carefully turn the mold and the pizza pan upside down.
4. Carefully lift the bowl off the gelatin mold to create a gelatin volcano.
5. Place the pizza pan with the gelatin mold on top of the oatmeal boxes as shown below.
6. Mix the red food coloring and water in the plastic cup. Then fill the syringe with "magma" (the red water). Remove air bubbles from the syringe by holding it upright and squirting out a small amount of water.
7. Insert the tip of the syringe through a hole in the pizza pan near the center of the gelatin volcano. Inject the magma into the gelatin very slowly. Observe what happens to the magma.
8. Repeat steps 6 and 7 as many times as possible. Observe the movement of the magma each time. Note any differences in the direction the magma takes when the syringe is inserted into different parts of the gelatin volcano. Record your observations.

| Data Table | | | |
|---|---|---|---|
| Test | Initial Location of Magma | Position and Shape of Magma Bodies | Other Observations |
| 1. | | | |
| 2. | | | |
| 3. | | | |
| 4. | | | |
| | | | |

9. Look down on your gelatin volcano from above. Make a sketch of the positions and shapes of the magma bodies. Label your drawing "Top View."
10. Carefully use a knife to cut your volcano in half. Separate the pieces and examine the cut surfaces for traces of the magma bodies.
11. Sketch the positions and shapes of the magma bodies on one of the cut faces. Label your drawing "Cross Section."

## Analyze and Conclude

1. **Observing** Describe how the magma moved through your model. Did the magma move straight up through the center of your model volcano or did it branch off in places? Explain why you think the magma moved in this way.
2. **Developing Hypotheses** What knowledge or experience did you use to develop your hypothesis? How did the actual movement compare with your hypothesis?
3. **Inferring** How would you explain any differences in the direction the magma flowed when the syringe was inserted in different parts of the gelatin volcano?
4. **Making Models** How does what you observed in your model compare to the way magma moves through real volcanoes? How could you change your model to be more like a real volcano?
5. **Communicating** Prepare your model as a display to teach other students about volcanoes. Make a list of the volcanic features in your model. For each feature, write a description of how the feature would form in a real volcano.

## More to Explore

Plan to repeat the investigation using a mold made of two layers of gelatin. Before injecting the magma, predict what effect the layering will have on the movement of magma. Record your observations to determine if your hypothesis was correct. What volcanic feature is produced by this version of the model? Can you think of other volcanic features that you could model using gelatin layers? *Obtain your teacher's permission before carrying out your investigation.*

An eruption of Mount Kilauea, Hawaii

# Chapter 7 Study Guide

**The BIG Idea** **Forces Inside Earth** Most volcanoes form where Earth's plates collide or move apart, allowing magma to reach the surface. Lava forms landforms such as volcanic mountains or lava plateaus.

## 1 Volcanoes and Plate Tectonics

**Key Concepts**

- Volcanic belts form along the boundaries of Earth's plates.
- A volcano forms above a hot spot when magma erupts through the crust and reaches the surface.

**Key Terms**

• volcano • magma • lava • Ring of Fire
• island arc • hot spot

## 2 Properties of Magma

**Key Concepts**

- Each substance has a particular set of physical and chemical properties. These properties can be used to identify a substance or to predict how it will behave.
- Because liquids differ in viscosity, some liquids flow more easily than others.
- The viscosity of magma depends upon its silica content and temperature.

**Key Terms**

element
compound
physical property
chemical property
viscosity
silica
pahoehoe
aa

## 3 Volcanic Eruptions

**Key Concepts**

- When a volcano erupts, the force of the expanding gases pushes magma from the magma chamber through the pipe until it flows or explodes out of the vent.
- Geologists classify volcanic eruptions as quiet or explosive.
- Geologists often use the terms *active, dormant,* or *extinct* to describe a volcano's stage of activity.

**Key Terms**

• magma chamber • pipe • vent • lava flow
• crater • pyroclastic flow • dormant
• extinct

## 4 Volcanic Landforms

**Key Concepts**

- Volcanic eruptions create landforms made of lava, ash, and other materials. These landforms include shield volcanoes, cinder cone volcanoes, composite volcanoes, and lava plateaus.
- Features formed by magma include volcanic necks, dikes, and sills, as well as batholiths and dome mountains.
- Hot springs and geysers are types of geothermal activity that are often found in areas of present or past volcanic activity.

**Key Terms**

shield volcano
cinder cone
composite volcano
caldera
volcanic neck
dike
sill
batholith
geothermal activity
geyser

# Review and Assessment

For: Self-assessment
Visit: PHSchool.com
Web Code: cfa-1030

## Organizing Information

**Concept Mapping** Fill in the concept map to show the characteristics of the different types of volcanic mountains.

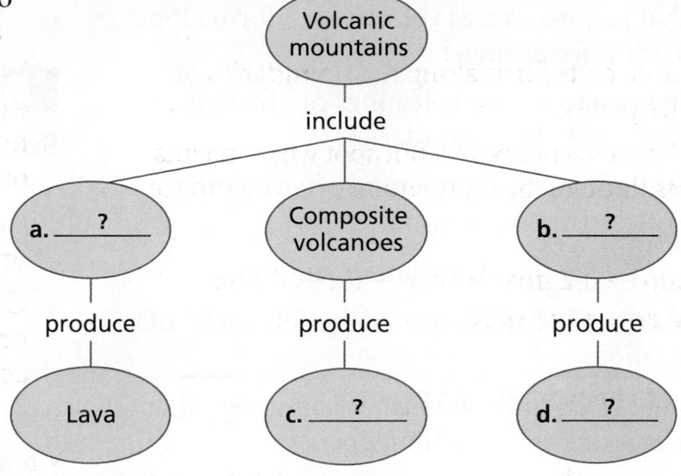


## Reviewing Key Terms

**Choose the letter of the best answer.**

1. Volcanoes found where two oceanic plates collide form a(n)
   a. cinder cone. b. island arc.
   c. hot spot. d. Ring of Fire.
2. Magma becomes lava when it reaches a volcano's
   a. geyser. b. magma chamber.
   c. pipe. d. vent.
3. Lava that forms smooth, ropelike coils when it hardens is called
   a. aa. b. silica.
   c. pahoehoe. d. pyroclastic flow.
4. A volcanic mountain made up of volcanic ash, cinders, and bombs is called a
   a. shield volcano.
   b. cinder cone.
   c. composite volcano.
   d. caldera.
5. The collapse of a volcano's magma chamber may produce a(n)
   a. crater.
   b. island arc.
   c. caldera.
   d. batholith.
6. Lava that cuts across rock layers hardens to form a feature called a
   a. dike. b. caldera.
   c. volcanic neck. d. sill.
7. When magma heats underground water, the result may be a
   a. lava flow.
   b. vent.
   c. hot spot.
   d. hot spring.

## Writing in Science

**Comparison** Write a comparison of the three different kinds of volcanoes. Discuss the ways in which all three are similar and the ways in which they are different. Use the correct terms to describe each type of volcano.

*Volcanoes*
Video Preview
Video Field Trip
▶ Video Assessment

# Review and Assessment

## Checking Concepts

8. What is the Ring of Fire?
9. What process causes volcanoes to form along the mid-ocean ridge?
10. What are two ways volcanoes can form near converging plate boundaries?
11. What effect does temperature have on the characteristics of magma?
12. How does a shield volcano form?
13. Describe the three stages in the "life cycle" of a volcano.
14. Why can earthquakes be a warning sign that an eruption is about to happen?
15. How do hot springs form?

## Thinking Critically

16. **Predicting** Is a volcanic eruption likely to occur on the East Coast of the United States? Explain your answer.
17. **Comparing and Contrasting** Compare the way in which an island arc forms with the way in which a hot spot volcano forms.
18. **Making Generalizations** How might a volcanic eruption affect the area around a volcano, including its plant and animal life?
19. **Relating Cause and Effect** Look at the diagram of a lava plateau below. Why doesn't the type of eruption that produces a lava plateau produce a volcanic mountain instead?

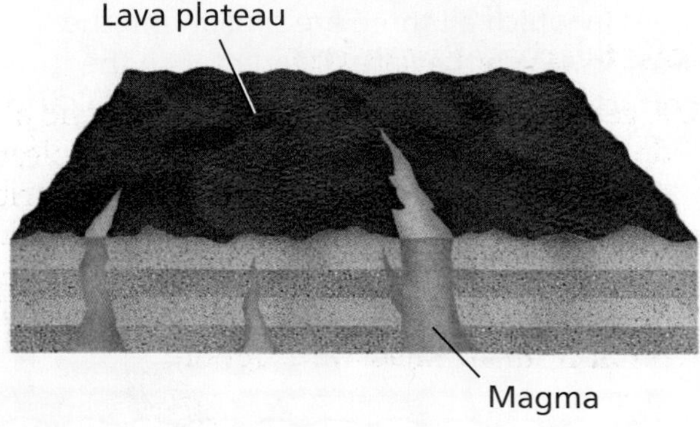


20. **Predicting** In a particular volcanic region, many small faults fracture the rocks of the crust. What features are likely to form beneath the surface? Explain your answer.

## Applying Skills

**Refer to the diagram to answer Questions 21–24.**

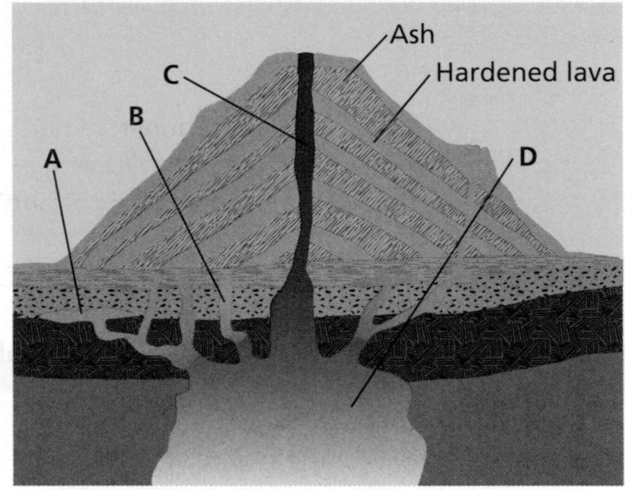


21. **Classifying** What is this volcano made of? How do geologists classify a volcano made of these materials?
22. **Developing Hypotheses** What is the feature labeled A in the diagram? What is the feature labeled B? How do these features form?
23. **Predicting** What is the feature labeled C in the diagram? If this feature becomes plugged with hardened magma, what could happen to the volcano? Explain.
24. **Inferring** What is the feature labeled D in the diagram? What can you infer about this feature if the volcano becomes dormant?

## Lab zone Chapter Project

**Performance Assessment** Present your documentary about a volcanic region to your class. Evaluate how well your documentary presented the information you collected. As you watched the other documentaries, did you see any similarities between how people in different regions live with volcanoes?

# Standardized Test Prep

## Test-Taking Tip

**Sequencing Events**

Some test questions require you to arrange a series of events in order. For example, you might be asked which event comes first or last. Before looking at the answer choices, first try to determine the correct sequence in which the events occur.

***Sample Question***

Composite volcanoes form on a continental plate in a sequence of steps. Which of the following is the first step toward forming this type of volcano?

**A** Subduction occurs.
**B** Crust above the subducting plate melts and forms magma.
**C** An oceanic plate collides with a continental plate.
**D** A deep-ocean trench forms.

***Answer***

**C** is correct. **A** cannot be correct because subduction can only occur if a trench has formed. You can eliminate **B** because the formation of magma occurs near the end of the process. **D** cannot be correct because two plates must collide before a trench can form.

**Choose the letter that best answers the question or completes the statement.**

**1.** A composite volcano is most likely to form
**A** above a hot spot.
**B** where an oceanic plate collides with a continental plate.
**C** along the mid-ocean ridge.
**D** along a rift valley.

**2.** As the temperature of magma increases, its viscosity
**F** affects the magma's silica content.
**G** increases.
**H** stays the same.
**J** decreases.

**3.** Which step in a volcanic eruption occurs just before the volcano erupts?
**A** Magma collects in the magma chamber.
**B** Lava hardens to form volcanic rock.
**C** Expanding gases push magma through the pipe.
**D** The roof of the empty magma chamber collapses.

**4.** Magma that hardens between layers of rock forms a
**F** volcanic neck.
**G** dike.
**H** batholith.
**J** sill.

**5.** The diagram below shows the formation of what volcanic feature?
**A** caldera
**B** island arc volcano
**C** hot spot
**D** mid-ocean ridge

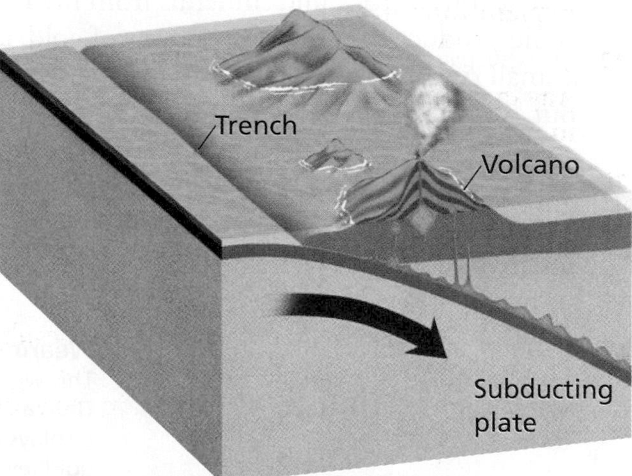


## Constructed Response

**6.** A geologist was observing the area around a dormant volcano. She decided that this volcano must have had an explosive eruption. Describe the evidence geologists would use to make this decision. In your answer, discuss the properties of the magma and the types of rock that would result from an explosive eruption.

# Interdisciplinary **Exploration**

◀ A gold crown is a symbol of royalty.

# Gold—The Noble Metal

## You can find it —

## on people's wrists, in your computer, on dinner plates, satellites, and in spacesuits

Because gold is both rare and beautiful, people have prized it since ancient times. Gold was so valuable that it was used to make crowns for rulers and coins for trade. In some cultures, people wear gold bracelets and necklaces to show their wealth.

In spite of its many uses, gold is scarce. For every 23,000 metric tons of rock and minerals from the Earth's crust, you could produce only about 14 grams of gold, enough to make a small ring. Today, gold is found in many parts of the world. But even rich gold fields produce only small amounts of gold. In fact, if all the gold mined over the years were gathered and melted down, you would have a cube only about 15 meters on a side—about the size of a four-story square building.

**Wearing Gold**
This woman from Ghana in Africa displays her wealth in gold jewelry.

**Gold Nugget**
A nugget is gold in one of its natural forms.

# Properties of Gold

Why is gold used for everything from bracelets to space helmets to medicine? You'll find the answers in this precious metal's unusual chemical and physical properties. Gold is deep yellow in color and so shiny, or lustrous, that its Latin name, *aurum,* means "glowing dawn." Gold's chemical symbol—Au—comes from that Latin word. Gold is very heavy—one of the densest metals.

Gold is very soft and malleable. That is, it's easy to bend or hammer into shapes without breaking. It can be pounded into very thin sheets called gold leaf. Gold is also the most ductile metal. You can draw out 30 grams of gold into a fine thread as long as 8 kilometers without breaking it.

Gold is very stable. Unlike iron, gold doesn't rust. It also doesn't tarnish in air as silver does. Ancient chemists thought that gold was superior to other metals. They classified it as one of the "noble" metals.

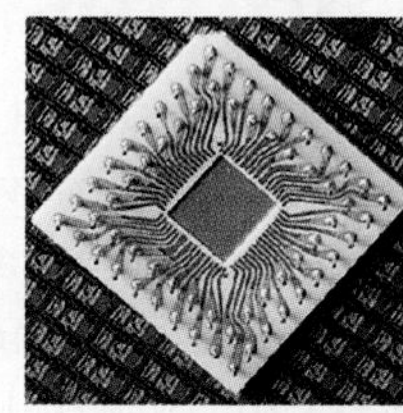

**Ductile**
Because gold is so ductile, it can be made into fine wires like the ones in this computer chip.

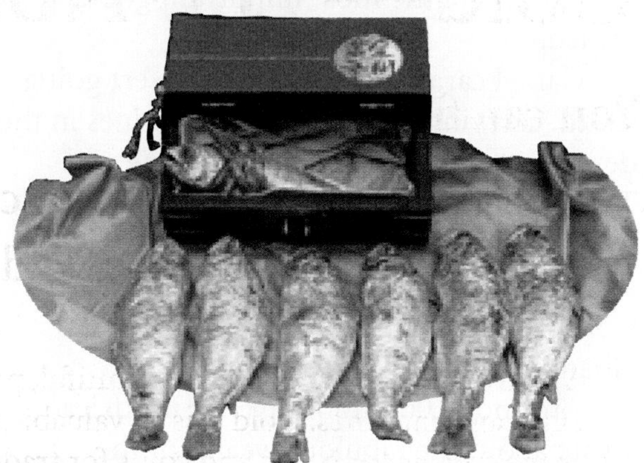

**Malleable**
A Korean delicacy is dried fish coated with gold leaf.

**Stable and Lustrous**
Hundreds of years ago, traders used these gold doubloons as money.

## Science Activity

The gold hunters who flocked to California during the Gold Rush of 1849 were searching for gold in streams and rivers. Although they had very simple equipment, their technique worked because gold is so dense. Using pans, miners washed gold-bearing gravel in running water. Try your own gold panning.

Set up your own model of gold panning, using a large pan, a gravel mixture, and a very dense material as a substitute for gold. Use a sink trap. Under running water, shake and swirl the pan until the lighter materials wash away. What's left is your "gold."

- Why is "gold" left in the pan while other materials are washed away?

## Golden Trade Routes

In West Africa nearly 1,000 years ago, salt was said to be worth its weight in gold. It may be hard to imagine how valuable this mineral was to people. But if you lived in a very hot, dry climate, you would need salt. It would be as valuable to you as gold. In West Africa, salt and gold were the most important goods traded.

Camel caravans crossed the desert going south, carrying slabs of salt from mines in the desert to trade centers, such as Jenne and Timbuktu. But several hundred kilometers south in the Kingdom of Ghana, salt was scarce and gold was plentiful. Salt traders from the north traveled into the forests of Ghana to trade salt for gold.

Around 1100, Arab travelers in Africa wrote about the fabulous wealth of the Kingdom of Ghana. The most popular tale was that the salt traders and gold miners never met, as a way of keeping secret the location of gold mines. Traders from the north left slabs of salt in an agreed-upon trading place, pounded their drums to indicate a trade, and then withdrew. Miners from the south arrived, left an amount of gold that seemed fair, and withdrew. The salt traders returned. If they thought the trade was fair, they took the gold and left. If they were not satisfied, the silent trade continued.

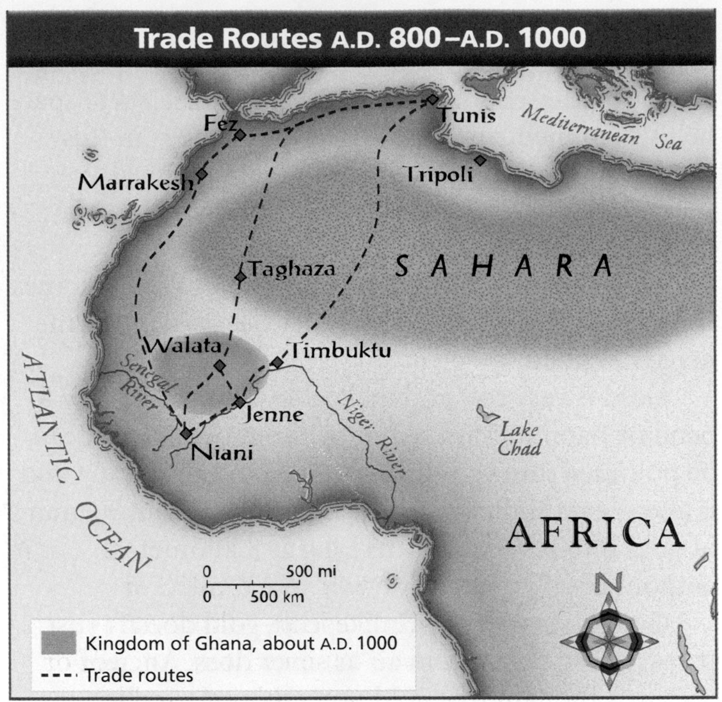


**Gold Trade Routes**
The map shows the busy north-south trade routes in West Africa about 1,000 years ago.

### Social Studies Activity

How would you succeed as a gold or salt trader? Find out by carrying out your own silent trade. Work in teams of Salt Traders and Gold Miners. Before trading, each team should decide how much a bag of gold or a block of salt is worth. Then, for each silent trade, make up a situation that would change the value of gold or salt, such as, "Demand for gold in Europe increases."

- Suppose you are selling a product today. How would the supply of the product affect the value or sale price of the product?

**Salt Caravan**
Camels carrying salt slabs travel to Timbuktu.

## Go for the Gold

What do these sayings have in common?

"It's worth its weight in gold."

"Speech is silver, silence is golden."

"All that glitters is not gold."

"Go for the gold!"

All of these sayings use gold as a symbol of excellence, richness, and perfection—things that people want and search for. When writers use *gold* or *golden,* they are referring to something desirable, of value or worth. These words may also represent the beauty of gold.

In literature, writers and poets often use *gold* to make a comparison in a simile or metaphor. Similes and metaphors are figures of speech.

- A simile makes a comparison between two things, using *like* or *as* in the comparison. Here's an example: "An honest person's promise is as good as gold."
- A metaphor is a comparison without the use of like or as, such as, "When you're in trouble, true friends are golden."

Look for similes and metaphors in the poem by Florence Converse. What similes or metaphors has Converse made? What would this poem be like without the comparisons?

### Rune of Riches*

I have a golden ball,
A big, bright, shining one,
Pure gold; and it is all
Mine—It is the sun.

I have a silver ball
A white and glistening stone
That other people call
The moon;—my very own!

The jewel things that prick
My cushion's soft blue cover
Are mine,—my stars, thick, thick,
Scattered the sky all over.

And everything that's mine
Is yours, and yours, and yours,—
The shimmer and the shine!—
Let's lock our wealth out-doors!

—Florence Converse

*A rune is a song or poem.

### Language Arts Activity

What does gold symbolize for you? Think of some comparisons of your own in which you use gold in a simile or metaphor. After jotting down all of your ideas, choose one (or more) and decide what comparison you will make. Write a short saying, a proverb, or a short poem that includes your own simile or metaphor.

- How does your comparison make your saying or poem more interesting?

## Measuring Gold

People often say that something is "worth its weight in gold." But modern-day jewelry is seldom made of pure gold. Because gold is so soft, it is usually mixed with another metal to form an alloy—a mixture of two or more metals. Most commonly the other metal in a gold alloy is copper, although alloys of gold can also contain silver, zinc, or other metals.

Suppose you are shopping for a gold chain. You see two chains that look the same and are exactly the same size. How do you decide which one to buy? If you look closely at the gold jewelry, you'll probably see in small print the numbers "20K," "18K," "14K," or "12K." The "K" is the abbreviation for karat, which is the measure of how pure an alloy of gold is. Pure gold is 24 karat. Gold that is 50 percent pure is $\frac{12}{24}$ gold, or 12 karat. The greater the amount of gold in a piece of jewelry, the higher the value.

You look again at the two gold chains and decide that your favorite is the 18-karat gold chain. It has copper in it. What percent of the 18 K gold chain is gold? What percent is copper?

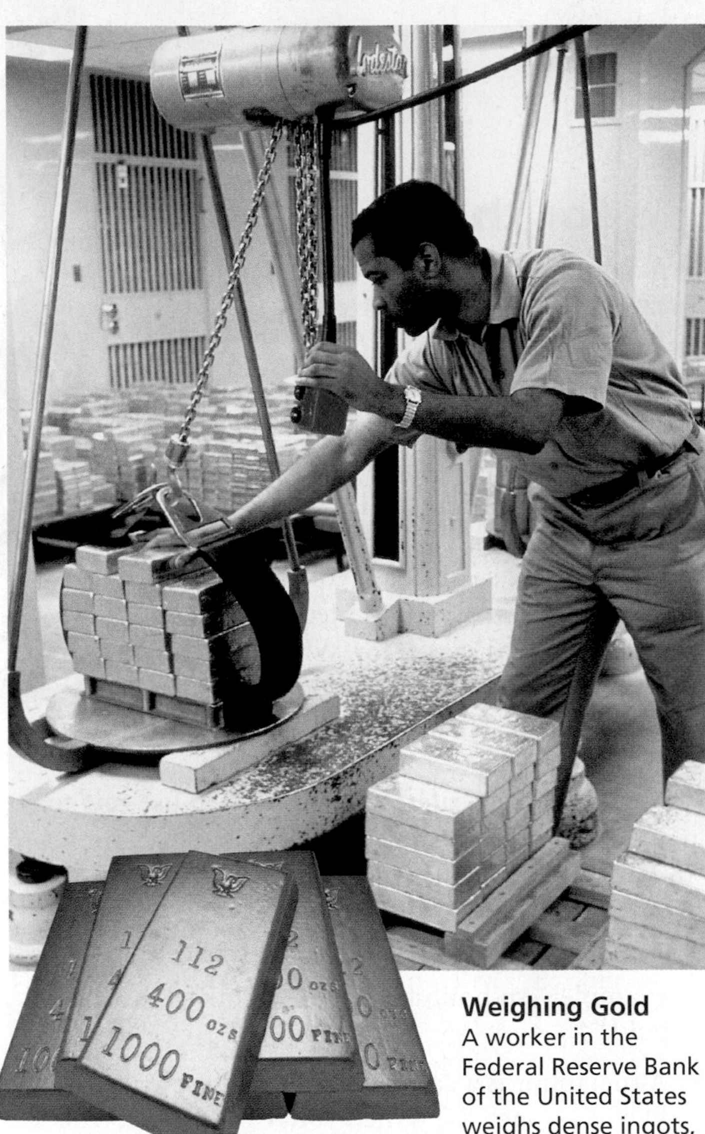


**Weighing Gold**
A worker in the Federal Reserve Bank of the United States weighs dense ingots, or bars, of pure gold.

### 1 Read and Understand

You know that pure gold is $\frac{24}{24}$ gold,

and an 18 karat chain is $\frac{18}{24}$ gold.

### 2 Plan and Solve

In order to find out what percent of an 18 K chain is gold, you need to write a proportion.

$$\frac{\text{Number of gold parts}}{\text{Number of parts in the whole}} \begin{matrix} \rightarrow \\ \rightarrow \end{matrix} \frac{18}{24}$$

Then simplify the fraction and convert it to a percentage.

$$\frac{18}{24} = \frac{3}{4} = 75\%$$

### 3 Look Back and Check

If 75% of the chain is gold, then 25% of the chain must be copper.

## Math Activity

How would you choose a gold ring? To decide, you might determine what percent of each ring is gold.

- What percent of a 14 K gold ring is gold? What percent is another metal? Round decimals to the nearest hundredth.
- What percent of a 12 K ring is gold? What percent of the 20 K ring is gold?
- Which ring would you like to own—the 12 K or the 20 K? Why?

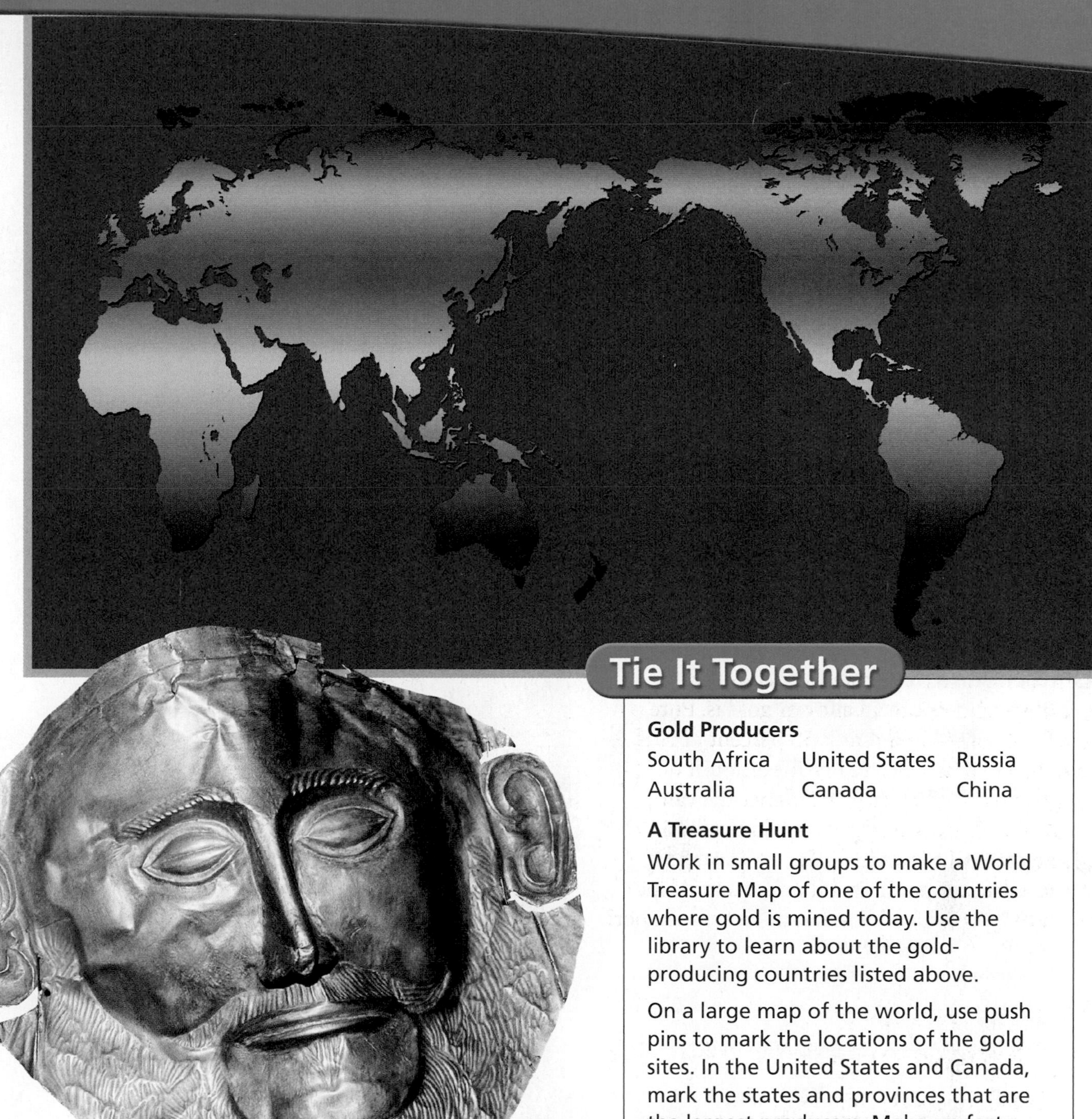

Gold Mask
This gold mask was found in the tomb of a ruler of Mycenae, a city in ancient Greece. The mask is about 3,500 years old.

## Tie It Together

**Gold Producers**

| | | |
|---|---|---|
| South Africa | United States | Russia |
| Australia | Canada | China |

**A Treasure Hunt**

Work in small groups to make a World Treasure Map of one of the countries where gold is mined today. Use the library to learn about the gold-producing countries listed above.

On a large map of the world, use push pins to mark the locations of the gold sites. In the United States and Canada, mark the states and provinces that are the largest producers. Make up fact sheets to answer questions such as:

- Where are gold sites located in each country?
- When was gold first discovered there?
- Did a gold rush influence the history of that area?

If possible, collect photographs to illustrate gold products in each country. Post your pictures and fact sheets at the side of the World Treasure Map.

Chapter 8

# Weathering and Soil Formation

## The BIG Idea

Processes on Earth's Surface

What are the processes of weathering and soil formation?

### Chapter Preview

1. **Rocks and Weathering**
   - ***Discover*** How Fast Can It Fizz?
   - ***Try This*** Rusting Away
   - ***Analyzing Data*** Which Weathered Faster?
   - ***At-Home Activity*** Ice in a Straw
   - ***Skills Lab*** Rock Shake
2. **How Soil Forms**
   - ***Discover*** What Is Soil?
   - ***Active Art*** Soil Layers
   - ***Try This*** A Square Meter of Soil
   - ***Consumer Lab*** Comparing Soils
3. **Soil Conservation**
   - ***Discover*** How Can You Keep Soil From Washing Away?

The rich soil on this farm is a valuable natural resource. ▶

Weathering and Soil Formation

▶ Video Preview
Video Field Trip
Video Assessment

Lab zone™ Chapter **Project**

## Soils for Seeds

The process of weathering affects all rocks exposed on Earth's surface. Weathering breaks rock into smaller and smaller particles. When the rock particles mix with other ingredients, such as leaves, the mixture is called soil. In this project you will test how soil and other growing materials affect the growth of plants.

**Your Goal** To determine how soil composition affects the growth of bean seeds

To complete this project, you must

- compare the particle size, shape, and composition of different growing materials
- compare how bean seeds grow in several different growing materials
- determine what type of soil or growing material is best for young bean plants
- follow the safety guidelines in Appendix A

**Plan It!** In a group, brainstorm what types of soil and other growing materials you will use in your experiment. What are the different variables that affect the growth of plants? How will you measure the growth of your bean plants? Plan your experiment and obtain your teacher's approval. As you carry out your experiment, observe and record the growth of your plants. Then present your results to your class.

Section 1

# Rocks and Weathering

## Reading Preview

### Key Concepts

- How do weathering and erosion affect Earth's surface?
- What are the causes of mechanical weathering and chemical weathering?
- What determines how fast weathering occurs?

### Key Terms

- weathering
- erosion
- uniformitarianism
- mechanical weathering
- abrasion
- ice wedging
- chemical weathering
- oxidation
- permeable

### Target Reading Skill

**Relating Cause and Effect** A cause makes something happen. An effect is what happens. As you read, identify the causes of chemical weathering. Write them in a graphic organizer like the one below.

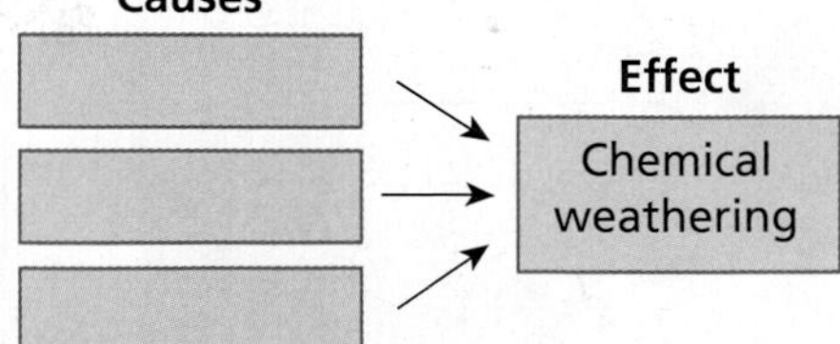


## Lab zone Discover Activity

### How Fast Can It Fizz?

1. Place a fizzing antacid tablet in a small beaker. Then grind up a second tablet and place it in another beaker. The whole tablet is a model of solid rock. The ground-up tablet is a model of rock fragments.
2. Add 100 mL of warm water to the beaker containing the whole tablet. Then stir with a stirring rod until the tablet dissolves completely. Use a stopwatch to time how long it takes.
3. Add 100 mL of warm water to the beaker containing the ground-up tablet. Then stir until all of the ground-up tablet dissolves. Time how long it takes.

**Think It Over**

**Drawing Conclusions** Which dissolved faster, the whole antacid tablet or the ground-up tablet? What variable affected how long it took each of them to dissolve?

Imagine a hike that lasts for months and covers hundreds of kilometers. Each year, many hikers go on such treks. They hike trails that run the length of America's great mountain ranges. For example, the John Muir Trail follows the Sierra Nevada mountains. The Sierras extend about 640 kilometers along the eastern side of California. In the east, the Appalachian Trail follows the Appalachian Mountains. The Appalachians stretch more than 3,000 kilometers from Alabama to Canada.

The two trails cross very different landscapes. The Sierras are rocky and steep, with many peaks rising 3,000 meters above sea level. The Appalachians are more rounded and gently sloping, and are covered with soil and plants. The highest peaks in the Appalachians are less than half the elevation of the highest peaks in the Sierras. Which mountain range do you think is older? The Appalachians formed more than 250 million years ago. The Sierras formed only within the last 10 million years. The forces that wear down rock on Earth's surface have had much longer to grind down the Appalachians.

## Weathering and Erosion

The process of mountain building thrusts rock up to the surface of Earth. There, the rock is exposed to weathering. **Weathering** is the process that breaks down rock and other substances at Earth's surface. Heat, cold, water, and ice all contribute to weathering. So do the oxygen and carbon dioxide in the atmosphere. Repeated freezing and thawing, for example, can crack rock apart into smaller pieces. Rainwater can dissolve minerals that bind rock together. You don't need to go to the mountains to see examples of weathering. The forces that wear down mountains also cause bicycles to rust, paint to peel, sidewalks to crack, and potholes to form.

The forces of weathering break rocks into smaller and smaller pieces. Then the forces of erosion carry the pieces away. **Erosion** (ee ROH zhun) is the removal of rock particles by wind, water, ice, or gravity. **Weathering and erosion work together continuously to wear down and carry away the rocks at Earth's surface.** The weathering and erosion that geologists observe today also shaped Earth's surface millions of years ago. How do geologists know this? Geologists make inferences based on the principle of **uniformitarianism** (yoon uh fawrm uh TAYR ee un iz um). This principle states that the same processes that operate today operated in the past.

There are two kinds of weathering: mechanical weathering and chemical weathering. Both types of weathering act slowly, but over time they break down even the biggest, hardest rocks.

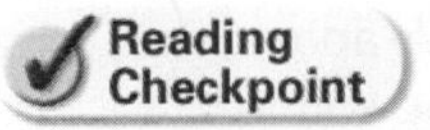


**What is the difference between weathering and erosion?**

FIGURE 1
**Effects of Weathering**
The jagged peaks of the Sierra Nevadas (bottom) formed within the last 10 million years. The more gently sloping Appalachians (top) have been exposed to weathering for 250 million years.
**Inferring** *How can you tell that the Sierra Nevadas formed much more recently than the Appalachians?*

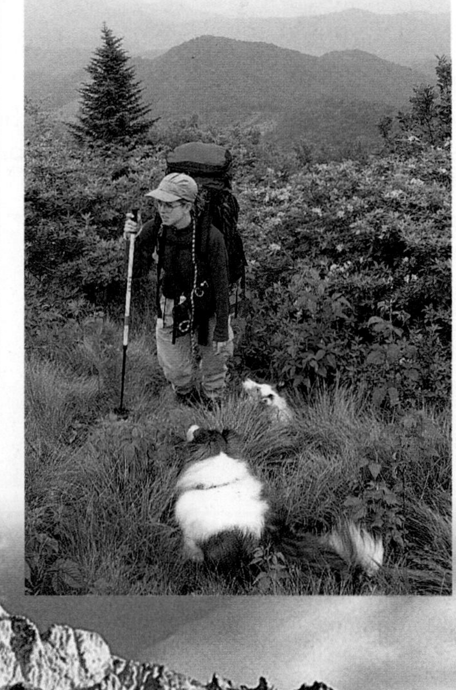

FIGURE 2
**Forces of Mechanical Weathering**

Mechanical weathering affects all the rock on Earth's surface.
**Forming Operational Definitions** *Study the examples of mechanical weathering, and then write a definition of each term in your own words.*

**Freezing and Thawing**
When water freezes in a crack in a rock, it expands and makes the crack bigger. The process of ice wedging also widens cracks in sidewalks and causes potholes in streets.

**Release of Pressure**
As erosion removes material from the surface of a mass of rock, pressure on the rock is reduced. This release of pressure causes the outside of the rock to crack and flake off like the layers of an onion.

**Animal Actions**
Animals that burrow in the ground—including moles, gophers, prairie dogs, and some insects—loosen and break apart rocks in the soil.

## Mechanical Weathering

If you hit a rock with a hammer, the rock may break into pieces. Like a hammer, some forces of weathering break rock into pieces. The type of weathering in which rock is physically broken into smaller pieces is called **mechanical weathering.** These smaller pieces of rock have the same composition as the rock they came from. If you have seen rocks that are cracked or split in layers, then you have seen rocks that are undergoing mechanical weathering. Mechanical weathering works slowly. But over very long periods of time, it does more than wear down rocks. Mechanical weathering eventually wears away whole mountains.

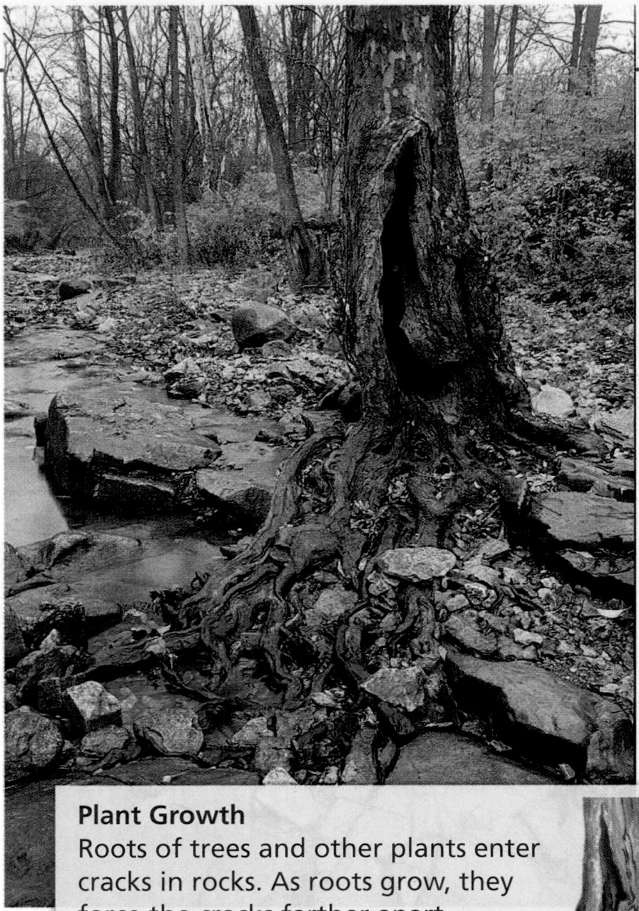

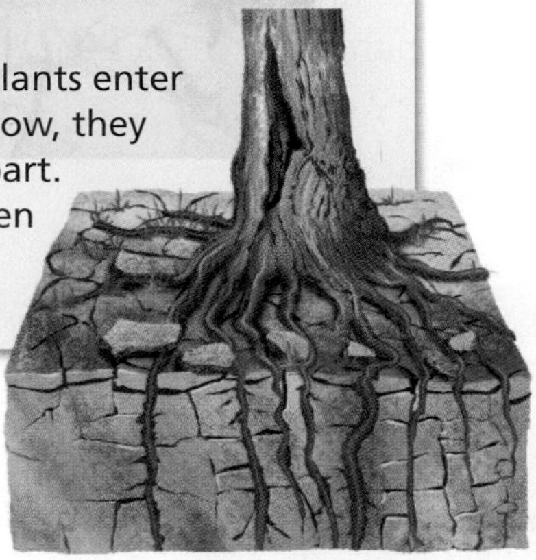

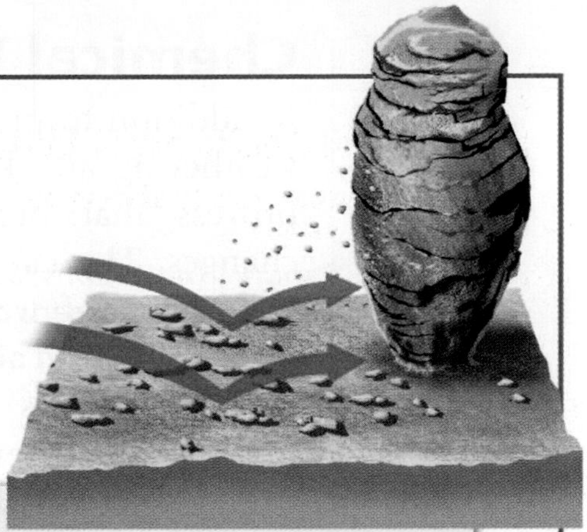

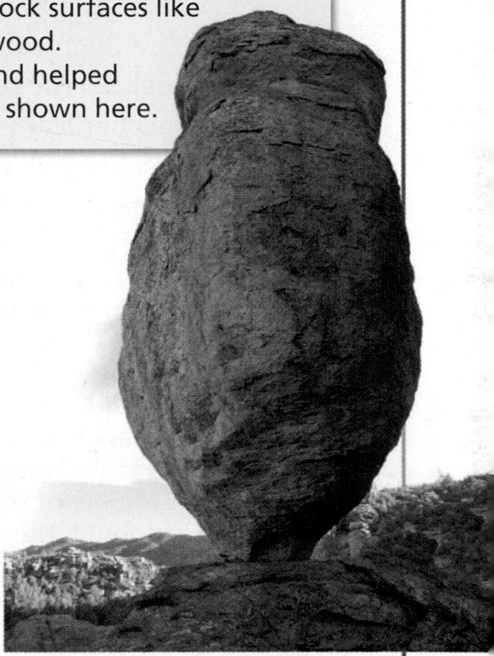

**Plant Growth**
Roots of trees and other plants enter cracks in rocks. As roots grow, they force the cracks farther apart. Over time, the roots of even small plants can pry apart cracked rocks.

**Abrasion**
Sand and other rock particles that are carried by wind, water, or ice can wear away exposed rock surfaces like sandpaper on wood. Wind-driven sand helped shape the rocks shown here.

**The causes of mechanical weathering include freezing and thawing, release of pressure, plant growth, actions of animals, and abrasion.** The term **abrasion** (uh BRAY zhun) refers to the grinding away of rock by rock particles carried by water, ice, wind, or gravity.

In cool climates, the most important force of mechanical weathering is the freezing and thawing of water. Water seeps into cracks in rocks and then freezes when the temperature drops. Water expands when it freezes. Ice therefore acts like a wedge that forces things apart. Wedges of ice in rocks widen and deepen cracks. This process is called **ice wedging.** When the ice melts, the water seeps deeper into the cracks. With repeated freezing and thawing, the cracks slowly expand until pieces of rock break off.

**Reading Checkpoint** How does ice wedging weather rock?

Go Online
PHSchool.com

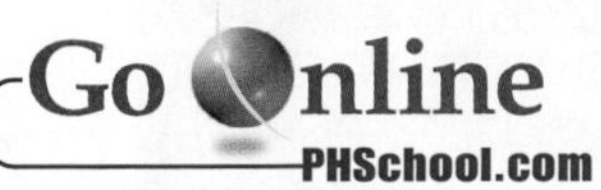

**For:** More on weathering
**Visit:** PHSchool.com
**Web Code:** cfd-2021

## Chemical Weathering

In addition to mechanical weathering, another type of weathering attacks rock. **Chemical weathering** is the process that breaks down rock through chemical changes. **The causes of chemical weathering include the action of water, oxygen, carbon dioxide, living organisms, and acid rain.**

Each rock is made up of one or more minerals. Chemical weathering can produce new minerals as it breaks down rock. For example, granite is made up of several minerals, including feldspar, quartz, and mica. As a result of chemical weathering, granite eventually changes the feldspar minerals to clay minerals.

Chemical weathering creates holes or soft spots in rock, so the rock breaks apart more easily. Chemical and mechanical weathering often work together. As mechanical weathering breaks rock into pieces, more surface area becomes exposed to chemical weathering. The Discover activity at the beginning of this section shows how increasing the surface area increases the rate of a chemical reaction.

**FIGURE 3**
**Weathering and Surface Area**
As weathering breaks apart rock, the surface area exposed to weathering increases. The total volume of the rock stays the same even though the rock is broken into smaller and smaller pieces.
**Predicting** *What will happen to the surface area if each cube is again divided into eight cubes?*

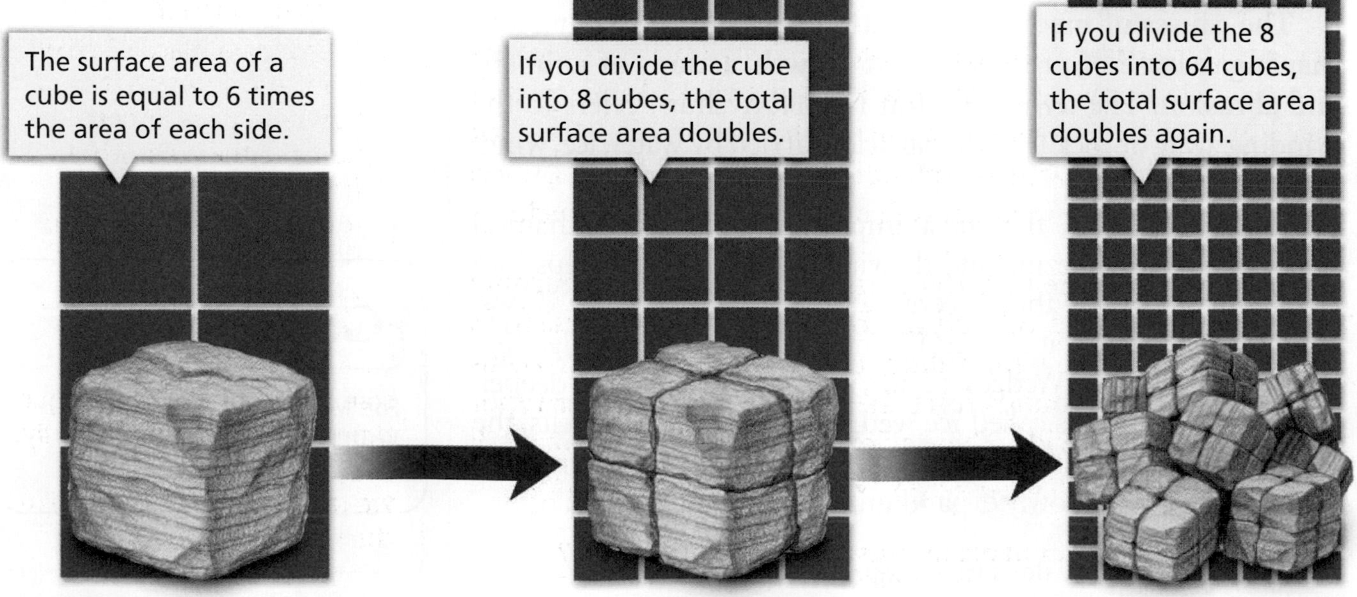

The surface area of a cube is equal to 6 times the area of each side.

If you divide the cube into 8 cubes, the total surface area doubles.

If you divide the 8 cubes into 64 cubes, the total surface area doubles again.

**FIGURE 4**
**Effects of Chemical Weathering**
Acid rain chemically weathered these stone gargoyles on the cathedral of Notre Dame in Paris, France.

**Water** Water is the most important cause of chemical weathering. Water weathers rock by dissolving it. When a rock or other substance dissolves in water, it mixes uniformly throughout the water to make a solution. Over time, many rocks will dissolve in water.

**Oxygen** The oxygen gas in air is an important cause of chemical weathering. If you have ever left a bicycle or metal tool outside in the rain, then you have seen how oxygen can weather iron. Iron combines with oxygen in the presence of water in a process called **oxidation.** The product of oxidation is rust. Rock that contains iron also oxidizes, or rusts. Rust makes rock soft and crumbly and gives it a red or brown color.

**Carbon Dioxide** Another gas found in air, carbon dioxide, also causes chemical weathering. Carbon dioxide dissolves in rainwater and in water that sinks through air pockets in the soil. The result is a weak acid called carbonic acid. Carbonic acid easily weathers rocks such as marble and limestone.

**Living Organisms** Imagine a seed landing on a rock face. As it sprouts, its roots push into cracks in the rock. As the plant's roots grow, they produce weak acids that slowly dissolve rock around the roots. Lichens—plantlike organisms that grow on rocks—also produce weak acids that chemically weather rock.

**Acid Rain** Over the past 150 years, people have been burning large amounts of coal, oil, and gas for energy. Burning these fuels can pollute the air with sulfur, carbon, and nitrogen compounds. Such compounds react chemically with the water vapor in clouds, forming acids. These acids mix with raindrops and fall as acid rain. Acid rain causes very rapid chemical weathering.

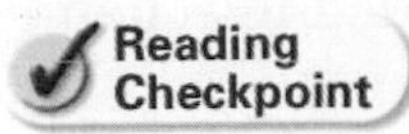

**How can plants cause chemical weathering?**

**Lab zone Try This Activity**

### Rusting Away

Here's how you can observe weathering.

1. Moisten some steel wool and place it in a closed container so it will not dry out.
2. Observe the steel wool after a few days. What has happened to it?
3. Take a new piece of steel wool and squeeze it between your fingers. Remove the steel wool from the container and squeeze it between your fingers. What happens? Wash your hands when you have finished.

**Predicting** If you kept the steel wool moist for a longer time, what would eventually happen to it? How is the weathering of steel wool like the weathering of a rock?

## Math Analyzing Data

### Which Weathered Faster?

The graph shows the rate of weathering for two identical pieces of limestone that weathered in different locations.

1. **Reading Graphs** What does the *x*-axis of the graph represent?
2. **Reading Graphs** What does the *y*-axis of the graph represent?
3. **Reading Graphs** How much thickness did Stone A lose in 1,000 years? How much thickness did Stone B lose in the same period?
4. **Drawing Conclusions** Which stone weathered at a faster rate?
5. **Inferring** Since the two identical pieces of limestone weathered at different rates, what can you infer caused the difference in their rates of weathering?

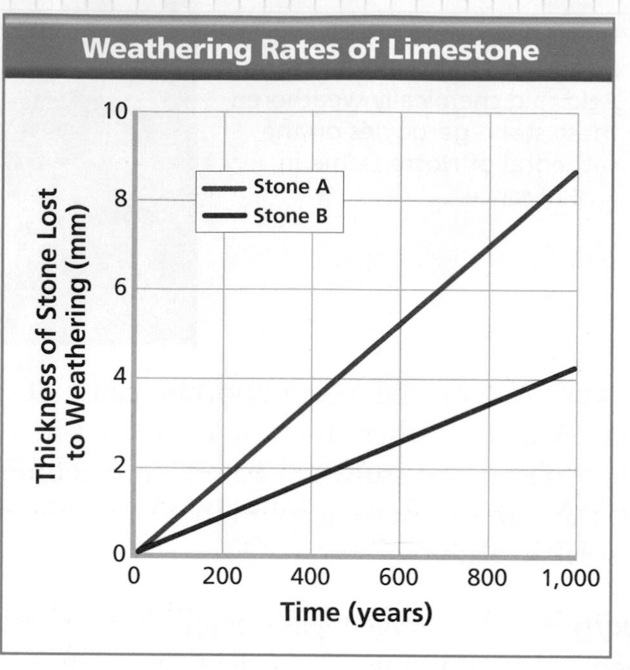


# Rate of Weathering

Visitors to New England's historic cemeteries may notice a surprising fact. Slate tombstones carved in the 1700s are less weathered and easier to read than marble gravestones from the 1800s. Why is this so? Some kinds of rocks weather more rapidly than others. **The most important factors that determine the rate at which weathering occurs are the type of rock and the climate.**

**Type of Rock** The minerals that make up the rock determine how fast it weathers. Rock made of minerals that do not dissolve easily in water weathers slowly. Rock made of minerals that dissolve easily in water weathers faster.

Some rock weathers more easily because it is permeable. **Permeable** (PUR mee uh bul) means that a material is full of tiny, connected air spaces that allow water to seep through it. Permeable rock weathers chemically at a fast rate. Why? As water seeps through the spaces in the rock, it dissolves and removes material broken down by weathering.

**Climate** Climate refers to the average weather conditions in an area. Both chemical and mechanical weathering occur faster in wet climates. Rainfall provides the water needed for chemical changes as well as for freezing and thawing.

Chemical reactions occur faster at higher temperatures. That is why chemical weathering occurs more quickly where the climate is both hot and wet.

**Human Activities** Human activities, such as those that produce acid rain, can increase the rate of weathering. Sulfur compounds in acid rain caused the weathering of the marble in Figure 5.

**FIGURE 5**
**Which Rock Weathers Faster?**
These two tombstones are about the same age, yet one has weathered much less than the other. **Observing** *Which type of stone weathered faster, granite or marble?*

**Reading Checkpoint** **How does rainfall affect the rate of weathering?**

## Section 1 Assessment

**Target Reading Skill** **Relating Cause and Effect** Refer to your graphic organizer about the causes of chemical weathering to help you answer Question 2 below.

### Reviewing Key Concepts

1. a. **Defining** What is weathering?
   b. **Defining** What is erosion?
   c. **Predicting** Over millions of years, how do weathering and erosion change a mountain made of solid rock?
2. a. **Defining** What is chemical weathering?
   b. **Comparing and Contrasting** Compare and contrast mechanical weathering and chemical weathering.
   c. **Classifying** Classify each as chemical or mechanical weathering: freezing or thawing, oxidation, water dissolving chemicals in rock, abrasion, acid rain.
3. a. **Identifying** What are two factors that affect the rate of weathering?
   b. **Relating Cause and Effect** A granite monument is placed outside for 200 years in a region with a cool, dry climate. What would its rate of weathering be? Explain.

### Lab zone At-Home **Activity**

**Ice in a Straw** Demonstrate one type of weathering for your family. Plug one end of a drinking straw with a small piece of clay. Fill the straw with water. Now plug the top of the straw with clay. Make sure that the clay plugs do not leak. Lay the straw flat in the freezer overnight. Remove the straw the next day. What happened to the clay plugs? What process produced this result? Be sure to dispose of the straw so that no one will use it for drinking.

Lab zone **Skills Lab**

# Rock Shake

## Problem

How will shaking and acid conditions affect the rate at which limestone weathers?

## Skills Focus

interpreting data, calculating, drawing conclusions

## Materials

- 300 mL of water
- balance
- paper towels
- masking tape
- 2 pieces of thin cloth
- marking pen or pencil
- 300 mL of vinegar, an acid
- plastic graduated cylinder, 250 mL
- 80 small pieces of water-soaked limestone
- 4 watertight plastic containers with screw-on caps, 500 mL

## Procedure 

**PART 1** Day 1

1. Using masking tape, label the four 500-mL containers A, B, C, and D.
2. Separate the 80 pieces of limestone into four sets of 20.
3. Copy the data table in your notebook. Then place the first 20 pieces of limestone on the balance and record their mass in the data table. Place the rocks in container A.
4. Repeat Step 3 for the other sets of rocks and place them in containers B, C, and D.
5. Pour 150 mL of water into container A and container B. Put caps on both containers.
6. Pour 150 mL of vinegar into container C and container D. Put caps on both containers.
7. Predict the effect of weathering on the mass of the limestone pieces. Which will weather more: the limestone in water or the limestone in vinegar? (*Hint:* Vinegar is an acid.) Also predict the effect of shaking on the limestone in containers B and D. Record your predictions in your notebook.
8. Allow the pieces to soak overnight.

Data Table

| Container | Total Mass at Start | Total Mass Next Day | Change in Mass | Percent Change in Mass |
|---|---|---|---|---|
| A (water, no shaking) | | | | |
| B (water, shaking) | | | | |
| C (vinegar, no shaking) | | | | |
| D (vinegar, shaking) | | | | |
| | | | | |

## PART 2 Day 2

9. Screw the caps tightly on containers B and D. Shake both containers for 10 to 15 minutes. Make sure that each container is shaken for exactly the same amount of time and at the same intensity. After shaking, set the containers aside. Do not shake containers A and C.
10. Open the top of container A. Place one piece of thin cloth over the opening of the container. Carefully pour all of the water out through the cloth into a waste container. Be careful not to let any of the pieces flow out with the water. Dry these pieces carefully and record their mass in your data table.
11. Next, determine how much limestone was lost through weathering in container A. (*Hint*: Subtract the mass of the limestone pieces remaining on Day 2 from the mass of the pieces on Day 1.)
12. Repeat Steps 10 and 11 for containers B, C, and D.

## Analyze and Conclude

1. **Calculating** Calculate the percent change in mass of the 20 pieces for each container.

$$\% \text{ change} = \frac{\text{Change in mass} \times 100}{\text{Total mass at start}}$$

Record the results in the data table.

2. **Interpreting Data** Do your data show a change in mass of the 20 pieces in each of the four containers?
3. **Interpreting Data** Is there a greater change in total mass for the pieces in one container than for the pieces in another? Explain.
4. **Drawing Conclusions** How correct were your predictions of how shaking and acid would affect the weathering of limestone? Explain.
5. **Developing Hypotheses** If your data showed a greater change in the mass of the pieces in one of the containers, how might this change be explained?
6. **Drawing Conclusions** Based on your data, which variable do you think was more responsible for breaking down the limestone: the vinegar or the shaking? Explain.
7. **Communicating** Write a paragraph that explains why you allowed two of the containers to stand without shaking, and why you were careful to shake the other two containers for the same amount of time.

## Design an Experiment

Would your results for this experiment change if you changed the variables? For example, you could soak or shake the pieces for a longer time, or test rocks other than limestone. You could also test whether adding more limestone pieces (30 rather than 20 in each set) would make a difference in the outcome. Design an experiment on the rate of weathering to test the effects of changing one of these variables. *Have your teacher approve your plan before you begin.*

Section 2

# How Soil Forms

## Reading Preview

### Key Concepts

- What is soil made of and how does it form?
- How do scientists classify soils?
- What is the role of plants and animals in soil formation?

### Key Terms

- soil
- bedrock
- humus
- fertility
- loam
- soil horizon
- topsoil
- subsoil
- litter
- decomposer

### Target Reading Skill

**Building Vocabulary** A definition states the meaning of a word or phrase by telling about its most important feature or function. Carefully read the definition of each Key Term and also read the neighboring sentences. Then write a definition of each Key Term in your own words.

## Lab zone Discover Activity

### What Is Soil?

1. Use a toothpick to separate a sample of soil into individual particles. With a hand lens, try to identify the different types of particles in the sample. Wash your hands when you are finished.
2. Write a "recipe" for the sample of soil, naming each of the "ingredients" that you think the soil contains. Include what percentage of each ingredient would be needed to make up the soil.
3. Compare your recipe with those of your classmates.

**Think It Over**
**Forming Operational Definitions** Based on your observations, how would you define *soil*?

A bare rock surface does not look like a spot where a plant could grow. But look more closely. In that hard surface is a small crack. Over many years, mechanical and chemical weathering will slowly enlarge the crack. Rain and wind will bring bits of weathered rock, dust, and dry leaves. The wind also may carry tiny seeds. With enough moisture, a seed will sprout and take root. Then, a few months later, the plant blossoms.

## What Is Soil?

The crack in the rock seems to have little in common with a flower garden containing thick, rich soil. But soil is what the weathered rock and other materials in the crack have started to become. **Soil** is the loose, weathered material on Earth's surface in which plants can grow.

One of the main ingredients of soil comes from bedrock. **Bedrock** is the solid layer of rock beneath the soil. Once exposed at the surface, bedrock gradually weathers into smaller and smaller particles that are the basic material of soil.

**Soil Composition** Soil is more than just particles of weathered bedrock. **Soil is a mixture of rock particles, minerals, decayed organic material, water, and air.** Together, sand, silt, and clay make up the portion of soil that comes from weathered rock.

The decayed organic material in soil is called humus. **Humus** (HYOO mus) is a dark-colored substance that forms as plant and animal remains decay. Humus helps create spaces in soil for the air and water that plants must have. Humus also contains substances called nutrients, including nitrogen, sulfur, phosphorus, and potassium. Plants need nutrients in order to grow. As plants grow, they absorb nutrients from the soil.

Fertile soil is rich in the nutrients that plants need to grow. The **fertility** of soil is a measure of how well the soil supports plant growth. Soil that is rich in humus has high fertility. Sandy soil containing little humus has low fertility.

**Soil Texture** Sand feels coarse and grainy, but clay feels smooth and silky. These differences are differences in texture. Soil texture depends on the size of individual soil particles.

The particles of rock in soil are classified by size. As you can see in Figure 7, the largest soil particles are gravel. The smallest soil particles are clay. Clay particles are smaller than the period at the end of this sentence.

Soil texture is important for plant growth. Soil that is mostly clay has a dense, heavy texture. Some clay soils hold a lot of water, so plants grown in them may "drown" for lack of air. In contrast, sandy soil has a coarse texture. Water quickly drains through it, so plants may die for lack of water.

Soil that is made up of about equal parts of clay, sand, and silt is called **loam.** It has a crumbly texture that holds both air and water. Loam is best for growing most types of plants.

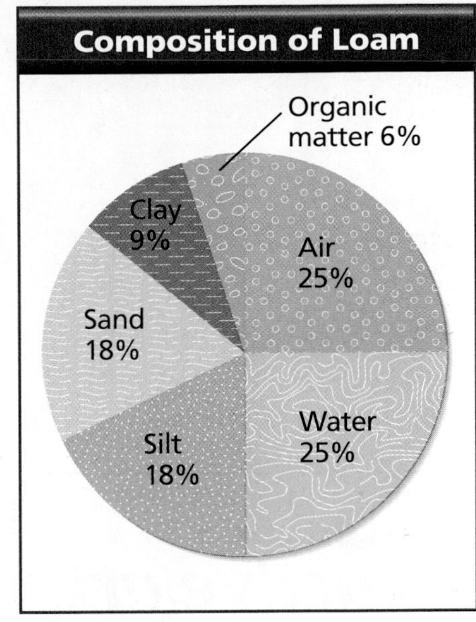


**FIGURE 6**
Loam, a type of soil, is made up of air, water, and organic matter as well as materials from weathered rock. **Interpreting Graphs** *What two materials make up the major portion of this soil?*

**FIGURE 7**
Soil particles range in size from gravel to clay particles too small to be seen by the unaided eye. The sand, silt, and clay shown here have been enlarged.

**Soil Particle Size**

| Clay | Silt | Sand | Gravel |
|---|---|---|---|
| Less than $\frac{1}{256}$ mm | Less than $\frac{1}{16}$ mm | Less than 2 mm | 2 mm and larger |

## The Process of Soil Formation

**Soil forms as rock is broken down by weathering and mixes with other materials on the surface. Soil is constantly being formed wherever bedrock is exposed.** Soil formation continues over a long period of time.

Gradually, soil develops layers called horizons. A **soil horizon** is a layer of soil that differs in color and texture from the layers above or below it.

If you dug a hole in the ground about half a meter deep, you would see the different soil horizons. Figure 8 shows how soil scientists classify the soil into three horizons. The A horizon is made up of **topsoil,** a crumbly, dark brown soil that is a mixture of humus, clay, and other minerals. The B horizon, often called **subsoil,** usually consists of clay and other particles washed down from the A horizon, but little humus. The C horizon contains only partly weathered rock.

The rate at which soil forms depends on the climate and type of rock. Remember that weathering occurs most rapidly in areas with a warm, rainy climate. As a result, soil develops more quickly in these areas. In contrast, weathering and soil formation take place slowly in areas where the climate is cold and dry.

Some types of rock weather and form soil faster than others. For example, limestone, a type of rock formed from the shells and skeletons of once-living things, weathers faster than granite. Thus, soil forms more quickly from limestone than from granite.

Go Online
*active art*

**For:** Soil Layers activity
**Visit:** PHSchool.com
**Web Code:** cfp-2022

**FIGURE 8**
**Soil Layers**
Soil horizons form in three steps.
**Inferring** *Which soil horizon is responsible for soil's fertility? Explain.*

1 The C horizon forms as bedrock weathers and rock breaks up into soil particles.

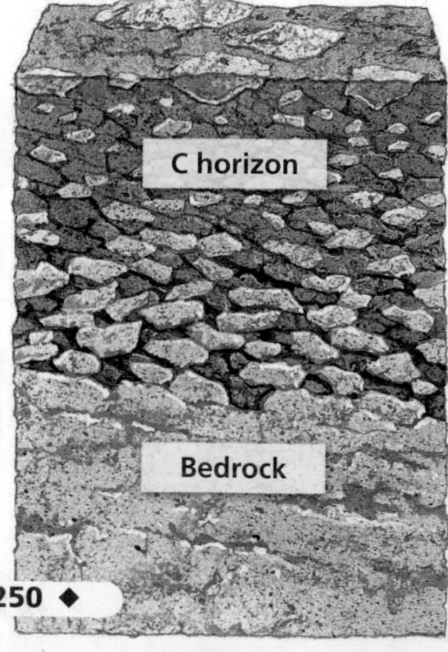


2 The A horizon develops as plants add organic material to the soil and plant roots weather pieces of rock.

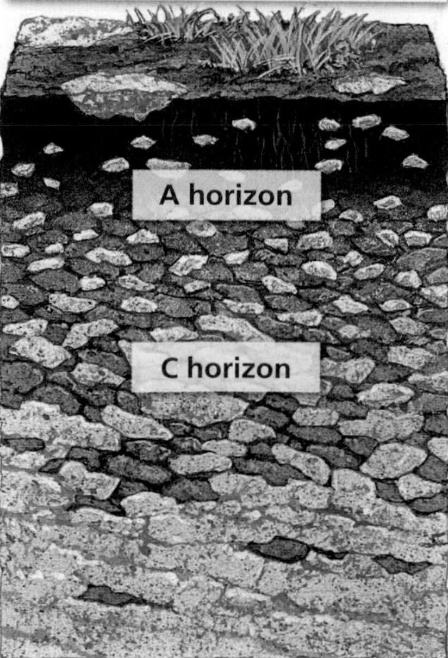


3 The B horizon develops as rainwater washes clay and minerals from the A horizon to the B horizon.

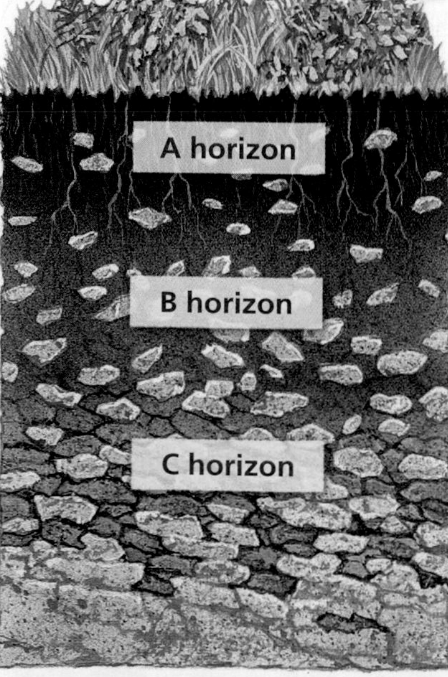

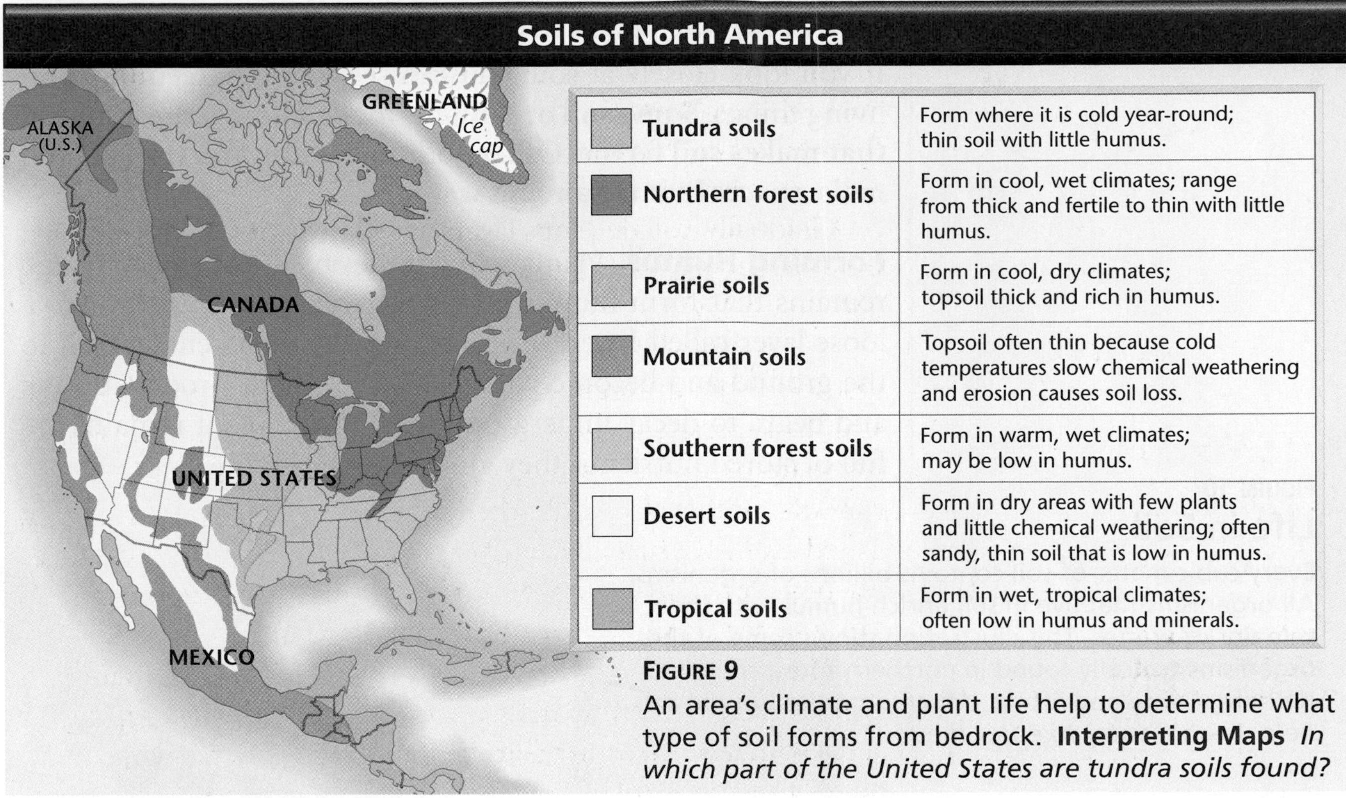


| | |
|---|---|
| **Tundra soils** | Form where it is cold year-round; thin soil with little humus. |
| **Northern forest soils** | Form in cool, wet climates; range from thick and fertile to thin with little humus. |
| **Prairie soils** | Form in cool, dry climates; topsoil thick and rich in humus. |
| **Mountain soils** | Topsoil often thin because cold temperatures slow chemical weathering and erosion causes soil loss. |
| **Southern forest soils** | Form in warm, wet climates; may be low in humus. |
| **Desert soils** | Form in dry areas with few plants and little chemical weathering; often sandy, thin soil that is low in humus. |
| **Tropical soils** | Form in wet, tropical climates; often low in humus and minerals. |

**FIGURE 9**
An area's climate and plant life help to determine what type of soil forms from bedrock. **Interpreting Maps** *In which part of the United States are tundra soils found?*

## Soil Types

If you were traveling across the hills of north-central Georgia, you would see soils that seem to be made of red clay. In other parts of the country, soils can be black, brown, yellow, or gray. In the United States alone, there are thousands of different types of soil.

**Scientists classify the different types of soil into major groups based on climate, plants, and soil composition.** Fertile soil can form in regions with hot, wet climates, but rain may wash humus and minerals out of the A horizon. In mountains and polar regions with cold, dry climates, the soil is often very thin. The thickest, most fertile soil forms in climate regions with moderate temperatures and rainfall.

The most common plants found in a region are also used to help classify the soil. For example, grassland soils are very different from forest soils. In addition, scientists classify soil by its composition—whether it is rocky, sandy, or rich in clay. Other factors in the classification of soil include the type of bedrock and the amount of time the soil has been developing.

Major soil types found in North America include forest, prairie, desert, mountain, tundra, and tropical soils. Look at Figure 9 to see where each of the major soil types is found.

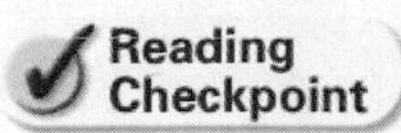

**What major soil types are found in North America?**

**Lab zone Try This Activity**

### A Square Meter of Soil

1. Outdoors, measure an area of one square meter. Mark your square with string.
2. Observe the color and texture of the soil at the surface and a few centimeters below the surface. Is it dry or moist? Does it contain sand, clay, or gravel? Are there plants, animals, or humus?
3. When you finish, leave the soil as you found it. Wash your hands.

**Drawing Conclusions** What can you conclude about the soil's fertility? Explain.

## Living Organisms in Soil

If you look closely at soil, you can see that it is teeming with living things. **Some soil organisms make humus, the material that makes soil fertile. Other soil organisms mix the soil and make spaces in it for air and water.**

**Forming Humus** Plants contribute most of the organic remains that form humus. As plants shed leaves, they form a loose layer called **litter.** When plants die, their remains fall to the ground and become part of the litter. Plant roots also die and begin to decay underground. Although plant remains are full of stored nutrients, they are not yet humus.

FIGURE 10
### Life in Soil

Every cubic meter of soil contains billions of organisms. All organisms that live in soil enrich humus with their remains or wastes. This illustration shows some of the organisms typically found in northern forest soil.
**Relating Cause and Effect** *Which organisms in the art help air and water to enter the soil?*

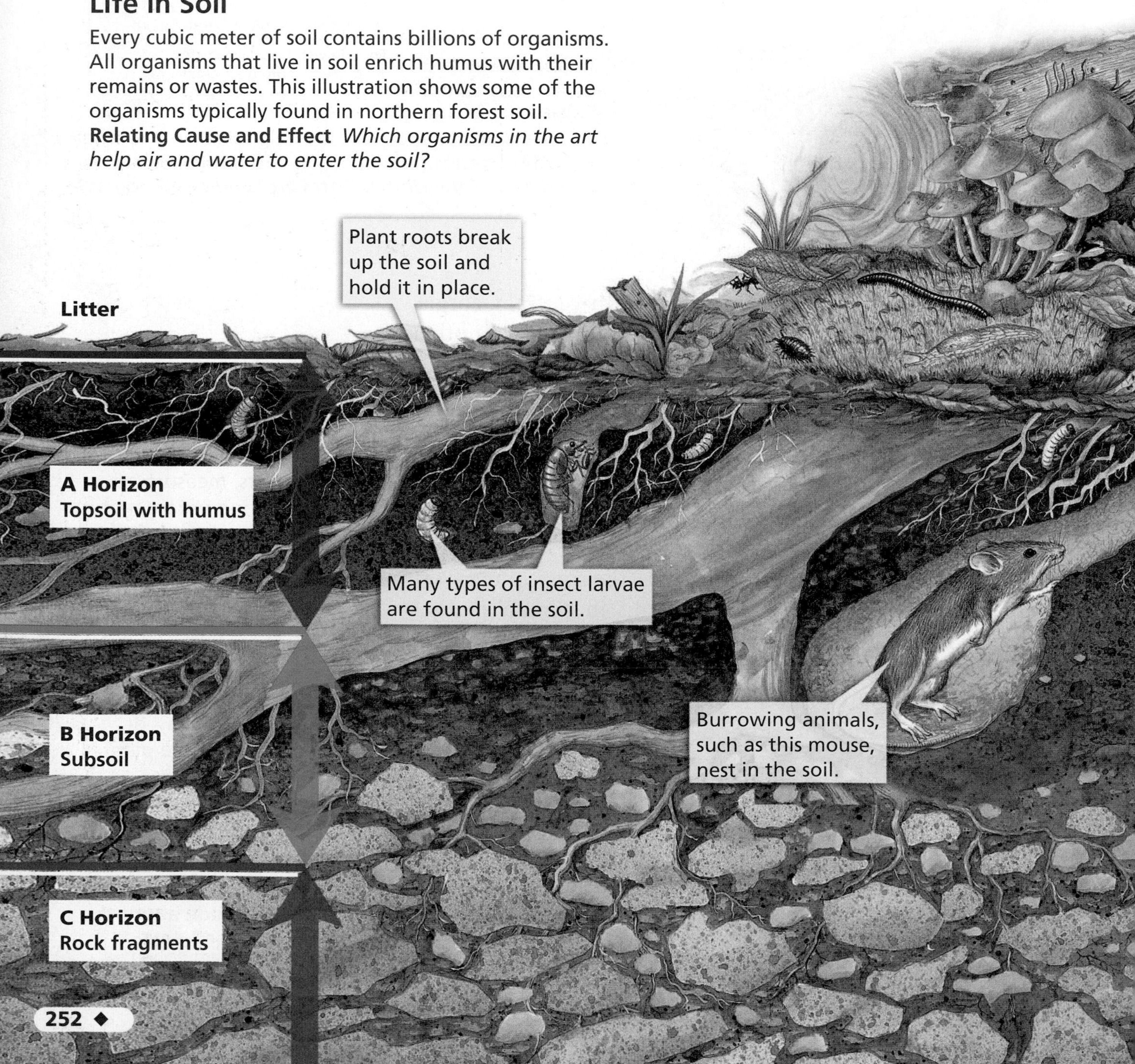

Plant roots break up the soil and hold it in place.
Litter
A Horizon
Topsoil with humus
Many types of insect larvae are found in the soil.
B Horizon
Subsoil
Burrowing animals, such as this mouse, nest in the soil.
C Horizon
Rock fragments

Humus forms in a process called decomposition. During decomposition, organisms that live in soil turn dead organic material into humus. These organisms are called decomposers. **Decomposers** are the organisms that break the remains of dead organisms into smaller pieces and digest them with chemicals.

Soil decomposers include fungi, bacteria, worms, and other organisms. Fungi are organisms such as molds and mushrooms. Fungi grow on, and digest, plant remains. Bacteria are microscopic decomposers that cause decay. Bacteria attack dead organisms and their wastes in soil. Very small animals, such as mites and worms, also decompose dead organic material and mix it with the soil.

Organisms such as snails and beetles feed on decaying organic material.
Chipmunks live in dens in the soil and search the litter for seeds and nuts.
The leaves, roots, and stems of plants are a major source of humus.
Ants are insects that live together in colonies in the soil.
Earthworms break up hard, compacted soil, making it easier for plant roots to spread and for air and water to enter the soil.
Bacteria are decomposers that break down animal and plant remains and wastes.
Fungi are decomposers that send out long, rootlike threads. From these threads, fungi release chemicals that digest plant remains.

FIGURE 11
**Soil Mixers**
Earthworms break up the soil, allowing in air and water. An earthworm eats its own weight in soil every day. **Predicting** *How fertile is soil that contains many earthworms likely to be? Explain.*

**Mixing the Soil** Earthworms do most of the work of mixing humus with other materials in soil. As earthworms eat their way through the soil, they carry humus down to the subsoil and subsoil up to the surface. Earthworms also pass out the soil they eat as waste. The waste soil is enriched with substances that plants need to grow, such as nitrogen.

Many burrowing mammals such as mice, moles, prairie dogs, and gophers break up hard, compacted soil and mix humus through it. These animals also add nitrogen to the soil when they produce waste. They add organic material when they die and decay.

Earthworms and burrowing animals also help to aerate, or mix air into, the soil. Plant roots need the oxygen that this process adds to the soil.

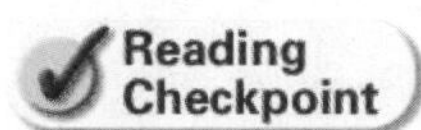


**Which animals are most important in mixing humus into the soil?**

## Section 2 Assessment

### Target Reading Skill

**Building Vocabulary** Use your definitions to help you answer the questions below.

### Reviewing Key Concepts

1. a. **Describing** What five materials make up soil?
   b. **Explaining** How do soil horizons form?
   c. **Sequencing** Place these terms in the correct order starting from the surface: C horizon, subsoil, bedrock, topsoil.
2. a. **Reviewing** What are three main factors used to classify soils?
   b. **Interpreting Maps** Soil forms more rapidly in warm, wet areas than in cold, dry areas. Study the map in Figure 9. Which soil type on the map would you expect to form most slowly? Explain.
3. a. **Identifying** What are two main ways in which soil organisms contribute to soil formation?
   b. **Describing** Give examples of three types of decomposers and describe their effects on soil.
   c. **Predicting** What would happen to the fertility of a soil if all decomposers were removed? Explain.

### Writing in Science

**Product Label** Write a product label for a bag of topsoil. Your label should give the soil a name that will make consumers want to buy it, state how and where the soil formed, give its composition, and suggest how it can be used.

Lab zone **Consumer Lab**

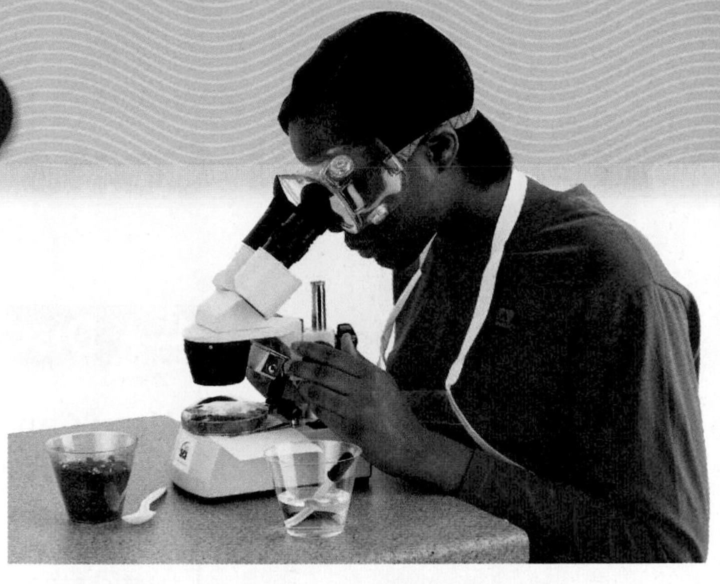

# Comparing Soils

## Problem

What are the characteristics of two samples of soil?

## Skills Focus

observing, inferring, developing hypotheses

## Materials

- 20–30 grams of local soil
- 20–30 grams of bagged topsoil
- plastic spoon • plastic dropper • toothpick
- water • stereomicroscope
- plastic petri dish or jar lid
- graph paper ruled with 1- or 2-mm spacing

## Procedure  

1. Obtain a sample of local soil. As you observe the sample, record your observations in your lab notebook.
2. Spread half of the sample on the graph paper. Spread the soil thinly so that you can see the lines on the paper through the soil. Using the graph paper as a background, estimate the sizes of the particles that make up the soil.
3. Place the rest of the sample in the palm of your hand, rub it between your fingers, and squeeze it. Is it soft or gritty? Does it clump together or crumble when you squeeze it?
4. Place about half the sample in a plastic petri dish. Using the dropper, add water one drop at a time. Watch how the sample changes. Does any material in the sample float? As the sample gets wet, do you notice any odor? (*Hint:* If the wet soil has an odor or contains material that floats, it is likely to contain organic material.)
5. Look at some of the soil under the stereomicroscope. (*Hint:* Use the toothpick to separate the particles in the soil.) Sketch what you see. Label the particles, such as gravel, organic matter, or strangely shaped grains.
6. Repeat Steps 1–5 with the topsoil. Be sure to record your observations.
7. Clean up and dispose of your samples as directed by your teacher. **CAUTION:** *Wash your hands when you finish handling soil.*

## Analyze and Conclude

1. **Observing** Did you observe any similarities between the local soil sample and the topsoil? Any differences?
2. **Inferring** What can you infer about the composition of both types of soil from the different sizes of their particles? From your observations of texture? From how the samples changed when water was added?
3. **Inferring** Do you think that both types of soil were formed in the same way? Explain.
4. **Developing Hypotheses** Based on your observations and study of the chapter, develop a hypothesis about which soil would be better for growing flowers and vegetables.
5. **Communicating** Write a report for consumers that summarizes your analysis of the two soil samples. Be sure to describe what factors you analyzed and give a suggestion for which soil consumers should use for growing flowers and vegetables.

## Design an Experiment

In Question 4 you developed a hypothesis about which soil would be better for growing flowers and vegetables. Design an experiment that would test this hypothesis. Be sure to indicate how you would control variables. *After you receive your teacher's approval, carry out your experiment.*

# 3 Soil Conservation

## Reading Preview

### Key Concepts

- Why is soil a valuable resource?
- How can soil lose its value?
- What are some ways that soil can be conserved?

### Key Terms

- sod • natural resource
- Dust Bowl • soil conservation
- contour plowing
- conservation plowing
- crop rotation

### Target Reading Skill

**Previewing Visuals** Before you read, preview Figure 13, The Dust Bowl. Then write two questions that you have about the photo and map in a graphic organizer like the one below. As you read, answer your questions.

**The Dust Bowl**

| Q. Where was the Dust Bowl? |
|---|
| A. |
| Q. |

## Lab zone Discover Activity

### How Can You Keep Soil From Washing Away?

1. Pour about 500 mL of soil into a pie plate, forming a pile.
2. Devise a way to keep the soil from washing away when water is poured over it. To protect the pile of soil, you may use craft sticks, paper clips, pebbles, modeling clay, strips of paper, or other materials approved by your teacher.
3. After arranging your materials to protect the soil, hold a container filled with 200 mL of water about 20 cm above the center of the soil. Slowly pour the water in a stream onto the pile of soil.
4. Compare your pan of soil with those of your classmates.

**Think It Over**

**Observing** Based on your observations, what do you think is the best way to prevent soil on a slope from washing away?

Suppose you were a settler traveling west in the mid 1800s. Much of your journey would have been through vast, open grasslands called prairies. After the forests and mountains of the East, the prairies were an amazing sight. Grass taller than a person rippled and flowed in the wind like a sea of green.

The prairie soil was very fertile. It was rich with humus because of the tall grass. The **sod**—the thick mass of tough roots at the surface of the soil—kept the soil in place and held onto moisture.

The prairies covered a vast area. They included Iowa and Illinois, as well as the eastern parts of Kansas, Nebraska, and North and South Dakota. Today, farms growing crops such as corn, soybeans, and wheat have replaced the prairies. But prairie soils are still among the most fertile in the world.

Prairie grasses and wildflowers ▼

## The Value of Soil

A **natural resource** is anything in the environment that humans use. **Soil is one of Earth's most valuable natural resources because everything that lives on land, including humans, depends directly or indirectly on soil.** Plants depend directly on the soil to live and grow. Humans and animals depend on plants—or on other animals that depend on plants—for food.

Fertile soil is valuable because there is a limited supply. Less than one eighth of the land on Earth has soils that are well suited for farming. Soil is also in limited supply because it takes a long time to form. It can take hundreds of years for just a few centimeters of soil to form. The thick, fertile soil of the prairies took many thousands of years to develop.

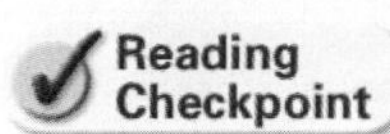


**Why is fertile soil valuable?**

## Soil Damage and Loss

Human activities and changes in the environment can affect the soil. **The value of soil is reduced when soil loses its fertility and when topsoil is lost due to erosion.**

**Loss of Fertility** Soil can be damaged when it loses its fertility. Soil that has lost its fertility is said to be exhausted. This type of soil loss occurred in large parts of the South in the late 1800s. Soils in which only cotton had been grown were exhausted. Many farmers abandoned their farms. Early in the 1900s in Alabama, a scientist named George Washington Carver developed new crops and farming methods that helped to restore soil fertility in the South. Peanuts were one crop that helped make the soil fertile again. Peanut plants are legumes. Legumes have small lumps on their roots that contain nitrogen-fixing bacteria. These bacteria make nitrogen, an important nutrient, available in a form that plants can use.

FIGURE 12
**Restoring Soil Fertility**
George Washington Carver (1864–1943) taught new methods of soil conservation. He also encouraged farmers to plant peanuts, which helped restore soil fertility.
**Applying Concepts** *What nutrient do peanut plants add to the soil?*

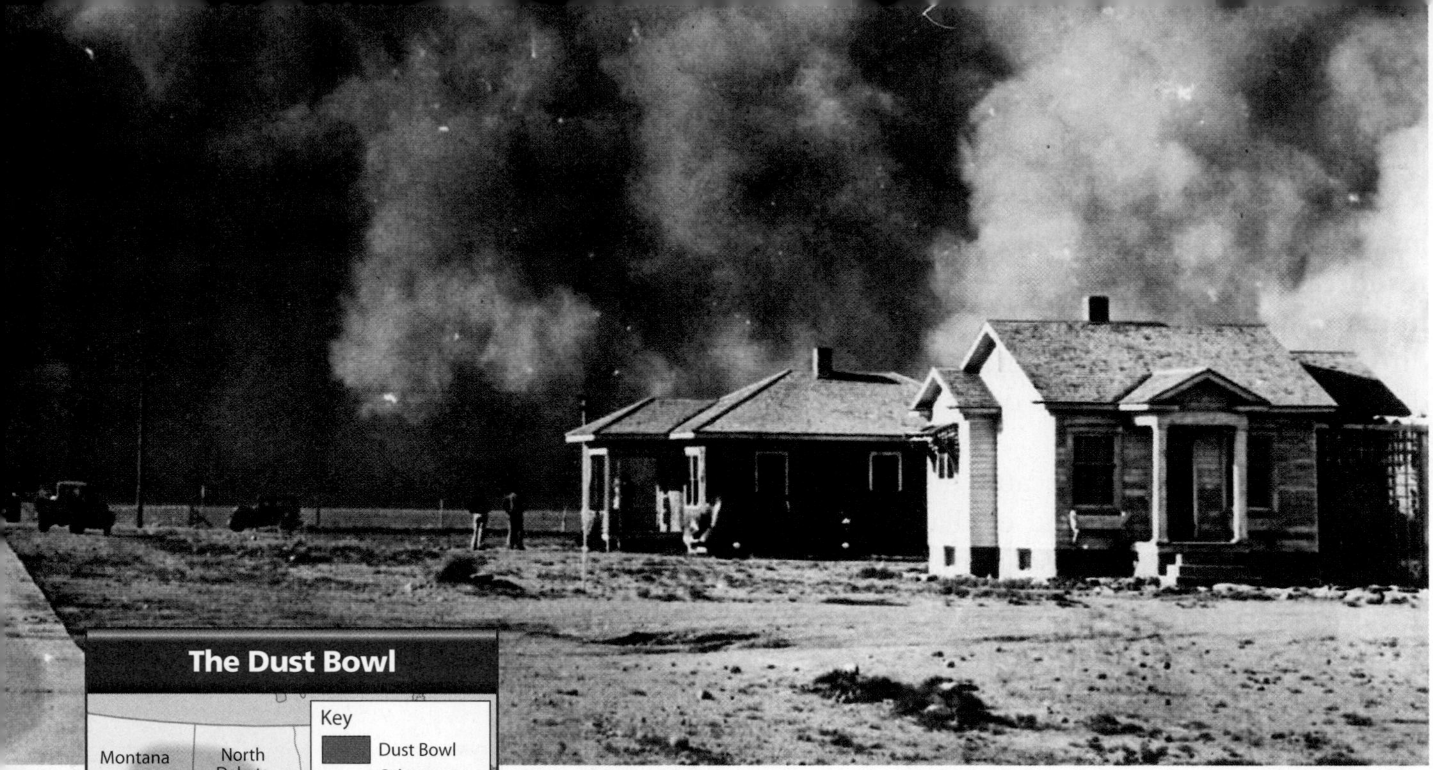

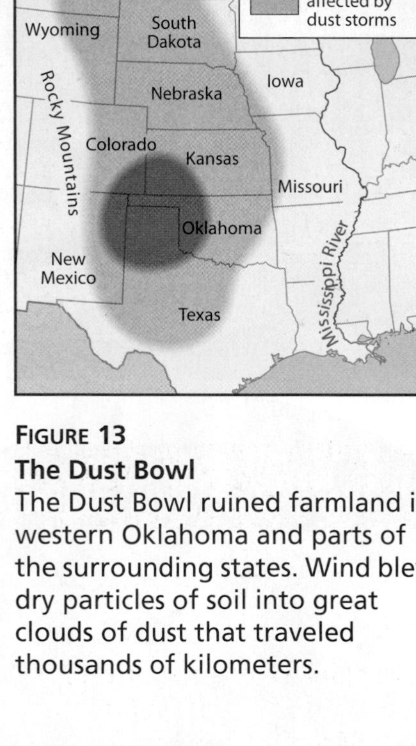


**FIGURE 13**
**The Dust Bowl**
The Dust Bowl ruined farmland in western Oklahoma and parts of the surrounding states. Wind blew dry particles of soil into great clouds of dust that traveled thousands of kilometers.

**Loss of Topsoil** Whenever soil is exposed, water and wind can quickly erode it. Plant cover can protect soil from erosion. Plants break the force of falling rain, and plant roots hold the soil together. Wind is another cause of soil loss. Wind erosion is most likely in areas where farming methods are not suited to dry conditions. For example, wind erosion contributed to the Dust Bowl on the Great Plains.

**Soil Loss in the Dust Bowl** Toward the end of the 1800s, farmers settled the Great Plains. The soil of the Great Plains is fertile. But rainfall decreases steadily from east to west across the Great Plains. The region also has droughts—years when rainfall is scarce. Plowing removed the grass from the Great Plains and exposed the soil. In times of drought, the topsoil quickly dried out, turned to dust, and blew away.

By 1930, almost all of the Great Plains had been turned into farms or ranches. Then, a long drought turned the soil on parts of the Great Plains to dust. The wind blew the soil east in great, black clouds that reached Chicago and New York City. The erosion was most serious in the southern Plains states. This area, shown in Figure 13, was called the **Dust Bowl.** The Dust Bowl helped people appreciate the value of soil. With government support, farmers in the Great Plains and throughout the country began to take better care of their land. They adopted methods of farming that helped save the soil. Some methods were new. Others had been practiced for hundreds of years.

**What caused the Dust Bowl?**

**For:** Links on soil conservation
**Visit:** www.SciLinks.org
**Web Code:** scn-0723

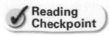

## Soil Conservation

Since the Dust Bowl, farmers have adopted modern methods of soil conservation. **Soil conservation** is the management of soil to prevent its destruction. **Soil can be conserved through contour plowing, conservation plowing, and crop rotation.**

In **contour plowing,** farmers plow their fields along the curves of a slope. This helps slow the runoff of excess rainfall and prevents it from washing the soil away.

In **conservation plowing,** farmers disturb the soil and its plant cover as little as possible. Dead weeds and stalks of the previous year's crop are left in the ground to help return soil nutrients, retain moisture, and hold soil in place. This method is also called low-till or no-till plowing.

In **crop rotation,** a farmer plants different crops in a field each year. Different types of plants absorb different amounts of nutrients from the soil. Some crops, such as corn and cotton, absorb large amounts of nutrients. The year after planting these crops, the farmer plants crops that use fewer soil nutrients, such as oats, barley, or rye. The year after that the farmer sows legumes such as alfalfa or beans to restore the nutrient supply.

**Reading Checkpoint** **How does conservation plowing help conserve soil?**

**FIGURE 14**
**Soil Conservation Methods**
This farm's fields show evidence of contour plowing and crop rotation. **Predicting** *How might contour plowing affect the amount of topsoil?*

## Section 3 Assessment

**Target Reading Skill** **Previewing Visuals** Compare your questions and answers about Figure 13 with those of a partner.

### Reviewing Key Concepts

1. a. **Defining** What is a natural resource?
   b. **Explaining** Why is soil valuable as a natural resource?
2. a. **Listing** What are two ways in which the value of soil can be reduced?
   b. **Explaining** Explain how topsoil can be lost.
   c. **Relating Cause and Effect** What caused the Dust Bowl?
3. a. **Defining** What is soil conservation?
   b. **Listing** What are three methods by which farmers can conserve soil?
   c. **Problem Solving** A farmer growing corn wants to maintain soil fertility and reduce erosion. What conservation methods could the farmer try? Explain.

### Writing in Science

**Public Service Announcement**
A severe drought in a farming region threatens to produce another Dust Bowl. Write a paragraph about soil conservation to be read as a public service announcement on radio stations. The announcement should identify the danger of soil loss due to erosion. It should also describe the steps farmers can take to conserve the soil.

# Chapter 8 Study Guide

**The BIG Idea**

**Processes on Earth's Surface** Weathering breaks down rock physically or chemically. Soil forms as weathered rock particles mix with decayed organic material, water, and air.

## 1 Rocks and Weathering

### Key Concepts

- Weathering and erosion continuously wear down and carry away rock at Earth's surface.
- The causes of mechanical weathering include freezing and thawing, release of pressure, plant growth, actions of animals, and abrasion.
- The causes of chemical weathering include the action of water, oxygen, carbon dioxide, living organisms, and acid rain.
- The most important factors that determine the rate at which weathering occurs are the type of rock and the climate.

### Key Terms

weathering
erosion
uniformitarianism
mechanical weathering
abrasion
ice wedging
chemical weathering
oxidation
permeable

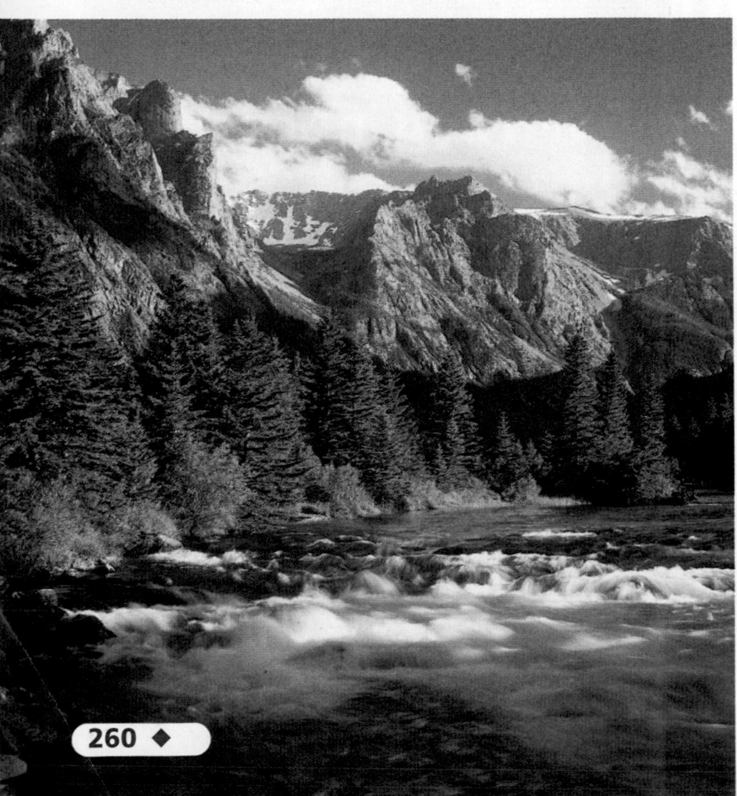

## 2 How Soil Forms

### Key Concepts

- Soil is a mixture of rock particles, minerals, decayed organic material, water, and air.
- Soil forms as rock is broken down by weathering and mixes with other materials on the surface. Soil is constantly being formed wherever bedrock is exposed.
- Scientists classify soils into major groups based on climate, plants, and soil composition.
- Some soil organisms make humus, the material that makes soil fertile. Other soil organisms mix the soil and make spaces in it for air and water.

### Key Terms

soil
bedrock
humus
fertility
loam
soil horizon
topsoil
subsoil
litter
decomposer

## 3 Soil Conservation

### Key Concepts

- Soil is one of Earth's most valuable natural resources because everything that lives on land, including humans, depends directly or indirectly on soil.
- The value of soil is reduced when soil loses its fertility and when topsoil is lost due to erosion.
- Soil can be conserved through contour plowing, conservation plowing, and crop rotation.

### Key Terms

sod
natural resource
Dust Bowl
soil conservation
contour plowing
conservation plowing
crop rotation

# Review and Assessment

**Go Online** PHSchool.com
**For:** Self-Assessment
**Visit:** PHSchool.com
**Web Code:** cfa-2020

## Organizing Information

**Sequencing** Fill in the flowchart to show how soil horizons form. (For more information on flowcharts, see the Skills Handbook.)

**Soil Horizons**

Bedrock begins to weather.
↓
a. ___?___
↓
b. ___?___
↓
c. ___?___

## Reviewing Key Terms

**Choose the letter of the best answer.**

1. The process that splits rock through freezing and thawing is called
   a. erosion.
   b. chemical weathering.
   c. ice wedging.
   d. abrasion.
2. Acid rain results in
   a. chemical weathering.
   b. abrasion.
   c. oxidation.
   d. mechanical weathering.
3. Soil that is made up of roughly equal parts of clay, sand, and silt is called
   a. sod.
   b. loam.
   c. tropical soil.
   d. subsoil.
4. The B horizon consists of
   a. subsoil.
   b. topsoil.
   c. litter.
   d. bedrock.
5. The humus in soil is produced by
   a. mechanical weathering.
   b. bedrock.
   c. chemical weathering.
   d. decomposers.

**If the statement is true, write *true.* If it is false, change the underlined word or words to make the statement true.**

6. <u>Mechanical weathering</u> is the removal of rock particles by gravity, wind, water, or ice.
7. Rock that is <u>permeable</u> weathers easily because it is full of tiny air spaces.
8. The decayed organic material in soil is called <u>loam</u>.
9. The layer of plant remains at the surface of the soil is called <u>litter</u>.
10. In <u>contour plowing</u>, farmers conserve soil fertility by leaving dead stalks and weeds in the ground.

## Writing in Science

**Journal Entry** You are a farmer on the tall grass prairie in the midwestern United States. Write a journal entry describing prairie soil. Include the soil's composition, how it formed, and how animals helped it develop.

*Weathering and Soil Formation*
Video Preview
Video Field Trip
▶ Video Assessment

# Review and Assessment

## Checking Concepts

**11.** What is the principle of uniformitarianism?

**12.** Explain how plants can act as agents of both mechanical and chemical weathering.

**13.** What is the role of gases such as oxygen and carbon dioxide in chemical weathering?

**14.** Briefly describe how soil is formed.

**15.** Which contains more humus, topsoil or subsoil? Which has higher fertility? Explain.

**16.** What organism does most of the work in mixing humus into soil?

**17.** What role did grass play in conserving the soil of the prairies?

**18.** How do conservation plowing and crop rotation contribute to soil conservation?

## Thinking Critically

**19. Predicting** If mechanical weathering breaks a rock into pieces, how would this affect the rate at which the rock weathers chemically?

**20. Comparing and Contrasting** Compare the layers in the diagram below in terms of their composition and humus content.

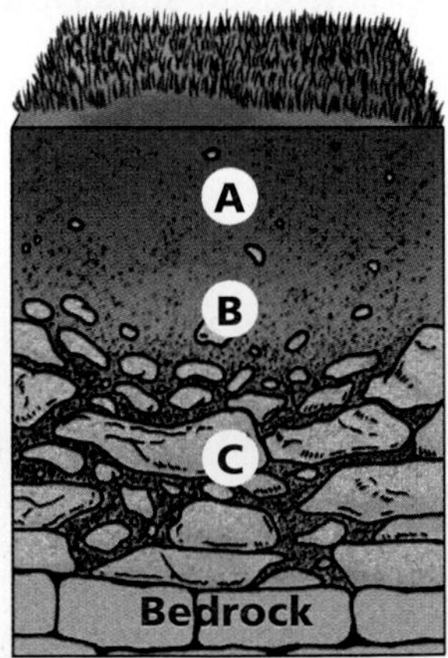


**21. Classifying** Classify as mechanical or chemical weathering: cracks in a sidewalk next to a tree; limestone with holes like Swiss cheese; a rock that slowly turns reddish brown.

## Applying Skills

**Use the following information to answer Questions 22–24.**

*You have two samples of soil. One is mostly sand and one is mostly clay.*

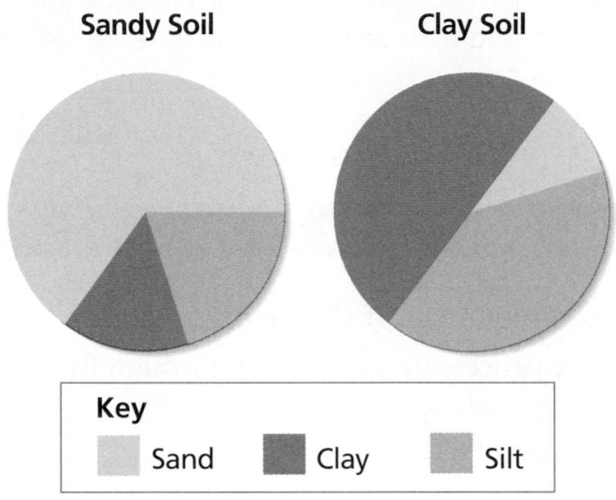


**22. Developing Hypotheses** Which soil sample would lose water more quickly? Why?

**23. Designing Experiments** Design an experiment to test how quickly water passes through each soil sample.

**24. Posing Questions** You are a farmer who wants to grow soybeans in one of these two soils. What questions would you need to answer before choosing where to plant your soybeans?

## Lab zone Chapter Project

**Performance Assessment** You are ready to present your data and conclusions about what type of material is best for growing bean plants. How did your group's results compare with those of the other groups in your class?

In your journal, describe how well the results of your experiment matched your predictions. What have you learned from this project about soil characteristics that help plants to grow? How could you improve your experiment?

# Standardized Test Prep

## Test-Taking Tip

**Reading All the Answer Choices**

Always read *every* answer choice in a multiple-choice question before selecting the answer you think is correct. There may be more than one correct response, but one choice will be more complete and precise than the others. Or "all of the above" may be a possible answer. If you stop reading as soon as you find an answer that seems correct, you won't notice that "all of the above" is an option.

***Sample Question***

What is the term for the process that breaks down rock through chemical changes?

**A** acid rain
**B** ice wedging
**C** chemical weathering
**D** all of the above

***Answer***

The correct answer is **C**. **A** is an agent of chemical weathering, but it is not the term for the process. **B** is a type of mechanical weathering.

**Choose the letter of the best answer.**

**1.** Which of the following is a type of mechanical weathering?
**A** abrasion
**B** freezing and thawing
**C** plant growth
**D** all of the above

**2.** You are designing an experiment to test the resistance to weathering of various types of materials. What weathering process could be modeled using sandpaper?
**F** acid rain
**G** freezing and thawing
**H** abrasion
**J** all of the above

**3.** In what type of climate would soil form fastest from limestone bedrock?
**A** a cold, dry climate **B** a cold, wet climate
**C** a hot, dry climate **D** a hot, wet climate

*Use the data table below and your knowledge of science to answer Questions 4–5.*

**Soil Erosion by State**

| State | Tons per Acre per Year | | |
|---|---|---|---|
| | Water Erosion | Wind Erosion | Total Erosion |
| Montana | 1.08 | 3.8 | 4.9 |
| Wyoming | 1.57 | 2.4 | 3.97 |
| Texas | 3.47 | 14.9 | 18.4 |
| New Mexico | 2.00 | 11.5 | 13.5 |
| Colorado | 2.5 | 8.9 | 11.4 |
| Tennessee | 14.12 | 0.0 | 14.12 |
| Hawaii | 13.71 | 0.0 | 13.71 |

**4.** Of the states listed in the table, which two have the greatest amount of erosion by water?
**F** Texas and Tennessee
**G** Texas and Hawaii
**H** New Mexico and Colorado
**J** Tennessee and Hawaii

**5.** What state in the table has the greatest soil erosion?
**A** Texas
**B** Hawaii
**C** Tennessee
**D** New Mexico

## Constructed Response

**6.** Two rocks, each in a different location, have been weathering for the same amount of time. Mature soil has formed from one rock, but only immature soil has formed from the other. What factors might have caused this difference in rate of soil formation? In your answer, include examples of both mechanical and chemical weathering.

Chapter 9

# Erosion and Deposition

## The BIG Idea

Processes on Earth's Surface

**How do erosion and deposition change Earth's surface?**

### Chapter Preview

**1 Changing Earth's Surface**

***Discover*** How Does Gravity Affect Materials on a Slope?

***Skills Activity*** Making Models

***Active Art*** Mass Movement

***Skills Lab*** Sand Hills

**2 Water Erosion**

***Discover*** How Does Moving Water Wear Away Rocks?

***Try This*** Raindrops Falling

***Skills Lab*** Streams in Action

**3 The Force of Moving Water**

***Discover*** How Are Sediments Deposited?

***Skills Activity*** Developing Hypotheses

***Analyzing Data*** Sediment on the Move

**4 Glaciers**

***Discover*** How Do Glaciers Change the Land?

**5 Waves**

***Discover*** What Is Sand Made of?

***Skills Activity*** Calculating

**6 Wind**

***Discover*** How Does Moving Air Affect Sediment?

***At-Home Activity*** Desert Pavement

**Water erosion formed the Grand Canyon, viewed here from Toroweap Point.** ▶

*Erosion and Deposition*

▶ Video Preview
Video Field Trip
Video Assessment

Lab zone™ Chapter **Project**

## Design and Build a Dam

Dams on major rivers are among the most spectacular works of engineering. These structures serve many purposes. Dams help to control flooding, generate power, and store water for drinking and watering crops. Dams can be constructed out of a variety of materials—wood, concrete, and even soil.

**Your Goal** To build a dam using various types of soil. To complete this project, you must

- conduct an experiment to determine the permeability of different soils
- investigate how readily the different soils erode when water passes over them
- design and build a dam
- test the dam and redesign if time allows
- follow the safety guidelines in Appendix A

**Plan It!** You will use a combination of three different soils to build the dam. First, you will need to test the permeability of each type of soil. Then develop an experiment to test how easily water erodes the soil. The results of the two experiments will provide you with information about the soils you tested. As you design your dam, think about what layers or combinations of materials will make the most effective dam. When you have tested your dam, present your conclusions to your class.

# Changing Earth's Surface

## Reading Preview

### Key Concepts

- What processes wear down and build up Earth's surface?
- What causes the different types of mass movement?

### Key Terms

- erosion
- sediment
- deposition
- gravity
- mass movement

### Target Reading Skill

**Comparing and Contrasting** As you read, compare and contrast the different types of mass movement by completing a table like the one below.

**Mass Movement**

| Type of Mass Movement | Speed | Slope |
|---|---|---|
| Landslide | | |
| | | |

## Lab zone Discover **Activity**

### How Does Gravity Affect Materials on a Slope?

1. Place a small board flat on your desk. Place a marble on the board and slowly tip one end of the board up slightly. Observe what happens.
2. Place a block of wood on the board. Slowly lift one end of the board and observe the result.
3. Next, cover the board and the wood block with sandpaper and repeat Step 2.

**Think It Over**

**Developing Hypotheses** How do the results of each step compare? Develop a hypothesis to explain the differences in your observations.

The ground you stand on is solid. But under certain conditions, solid earth can quickly change to thick, soupy mud. For example, high rains soaked into the soil and triggered the devastating mudflow in Figure 1. A river of mud raced down the mountainside, burying homes and cars. Several lives were lost. In moments, the mudflow moved a huge volume of soil mixed with water and rock downhill.

## Wearing Down and Building Up

A mudflow is a spectacular example of erosion. **Erosion** is the process by which natural forces move weathered rock and soil from one place to another. You may have seen water carrying soil and gravel down a driveway after it rains. That's an example of erosion. A mudflow is a very rapid type of erosion. Other types of erosion move soil and rock more slowly. Gravity, running water, glaciers, waves, and wind are all causes, or agents, of erosion. In geology, an agent is a force or material that causes a change in Earth's surface.

**FIGURE 1**
**Mudflow**
A mudflow caused by heavy rains in San Bernardino, California, brought this ambulance to a stop.

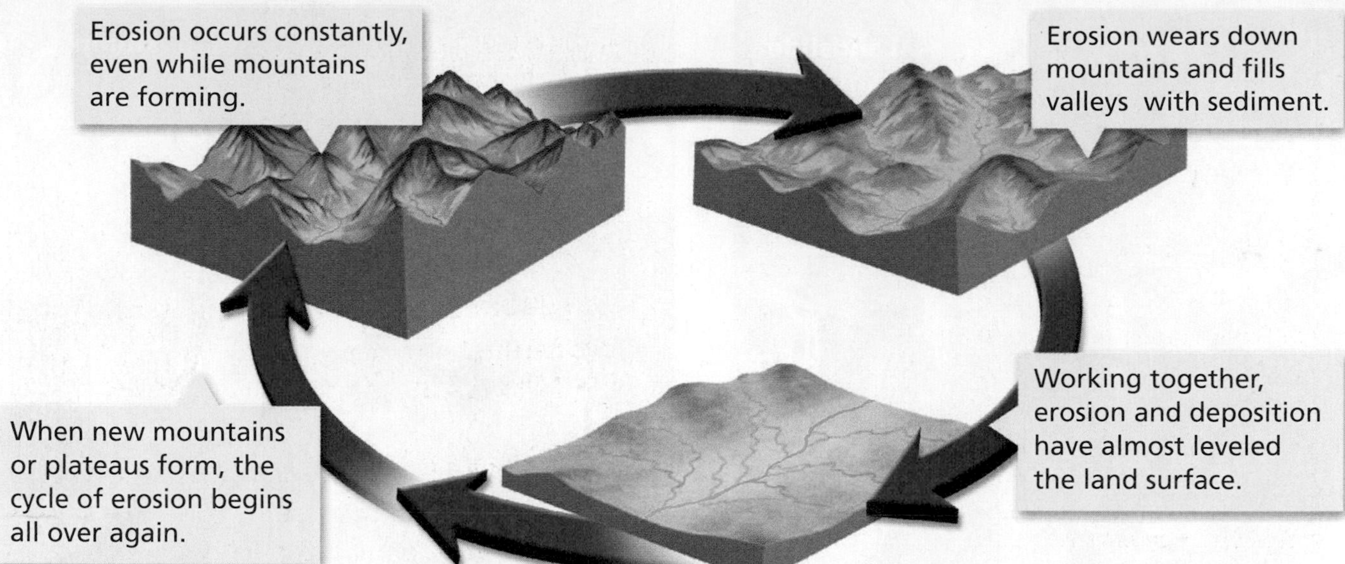

Erosion occurs constantly, even while mountains are forming.
Erosion wears down mountains and fills valleys with sediment.
Working together, erosion and deposition have almost leveled the land surface.
When new mountains or plateaus form, the cycle of erosion begins all over again.

**FIGURE 2**
**Cycle of Erosion and Deposition**
Over millions of years, erosion gradually wears away mountains while deposition fills in valleys with sediment.
**Predicting** *What would happen to the surface of the land if uplift did not occur?*

The material moved by erosion is **sediment.** Sediment may consist of pieces of rock or soil or the remains of plants and animals. Both weathering and erosion produce sediment. **Deposition** occurs where the agents of erosion, deposit, or lay down, sediment. Deposition changes the shape of the land. You may have watched a playing child who picked up several toys, carried them across a room, and then put them down. This child was acting something like an agent of erosion and deposition.

**Weathering, erosion, and deposition act together in a cycle that wears down and builds up Earth's surface.** Erosion and deposition are at work everywhere on Earth. As a mountain wears down in one place, new landforms build up in other places. The cycle of erosion and deposition is never-ending.

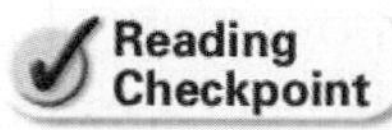 **Reading Checkpoint** What is sediment?

## Mass Movement

Imagine that you are sitting on a bicycle at the top of a hill. With only a slight push, you can coast down the hill. If the slope of the hill is very steep, you will reach a high speed before reaching the bottom. The force that pulls you and your bicycle downward is gravity. Gravity pulls everything toward the center of Earth.

**Gravity** is the force that moves rock and other materials downhill. Gravity causes **mass movement,** any one of several processes that move sediment downhill. **The different types of mass movement include landslides, mudflows, slump, and creep.** Mass movement can be rapid or slow.

**Lab zone Skills Activity**

### Making Models

You can make a model of mass movement. Design a plan to model one of the types of mass movement using sand, pebbles, and water. With your teacher's approval, make and test your model.

How well did your model represent the type of mass movement you chose? How could you improve your model?

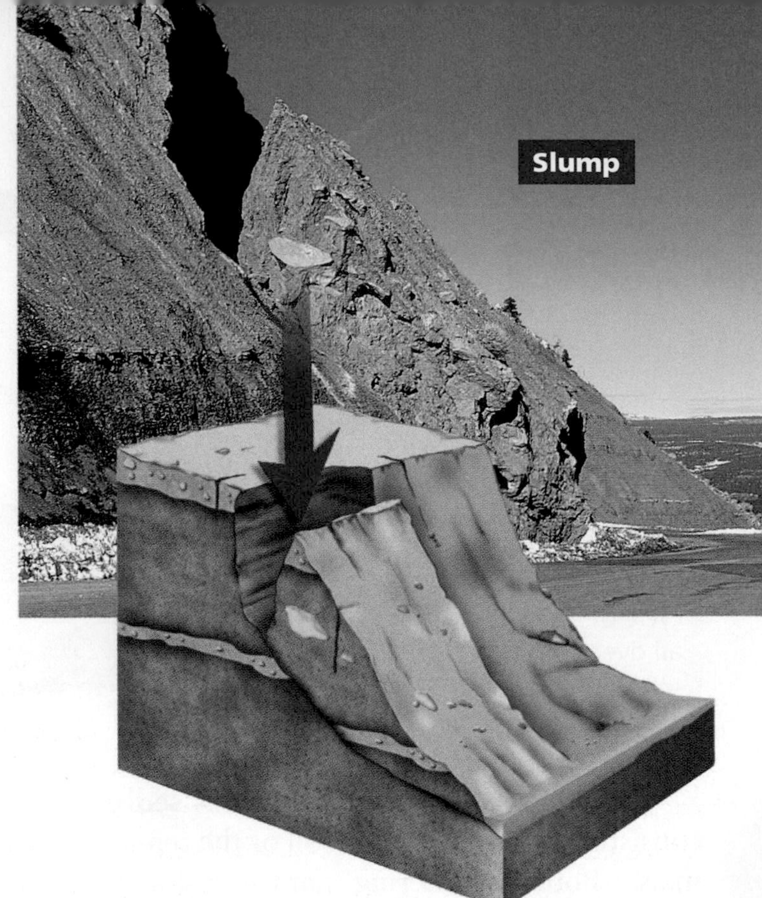


**FIGURE 3**
**Mass Movement**
In addition to mudflows, types of mass movement include landslides, slump, and creep.
**Making Judgments** *Which form of mass movement produces the most drastic change in the surface?*

**Landslides** The most destructive kind of mass movement is a landslide, which occurs when rock and soil slide quickly down a steep slope. Some landslides contain huge masses of rock. But many landslides contain only a small amount of rock and soil. Some landslides occur where road builders have cut highways through hills or mountains. Figure 3 shows an example of a landslide.

**Mudflows** A mudflow is the rapid downhill movement of a mixture of water, rock, and soil. The amount of water in a mudflow can be as high as 60 percent. Mudflows often occur after heavy rains in a normally dry area. In clay soils with a high water content, mudflows may occur even on very gentle slopes. Under certain conditions, clay soils suddenly turn to liquid and begin to flow. An earthquake can trigger both mudflows and landslides. Mudflows can be very dangerous.

**Slump** If you slump your shoulders, the entire upper part of your body drops down. In the type of mass movement known as slump, a mass of rock and soil suddenly slips down a slope. Unlike a landslide, the material in a slump moves down in one large mass. It looks as if someone pulled the bottom out from under part of the slope. A slump often occurs when water soaks the bottom of soil that is rich in clay.

**Go Online** *active art*

**For:** Mass Movement activity
**Visit:** PHSchool.com
**Web Code:** cfp-2031

**Creep** Creep is the very slow downhill movement of rock and soil. It can even occur on gentle slopes. Creep often results from the freezing and thawing of water in cracked layers of rock beneath the soil. Like the movement of an hour hand on a clock, creep is so slow you can barely notice it. But you can see the effects of creep in objects such as telephone poles, gravestones, and fenceposts. Creep may tilt these objects at spooky angles. Landscapes affected by creep may have the eerie, out-of-kilter look of a funhouse in an amusement park.

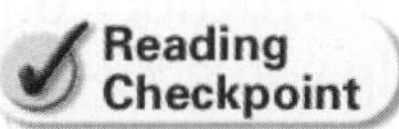

**What is the main difference between a slump and a landslide?**

## Section 1 Assessment

**Target Reading Skill Comparing and Contrasting** Use the information in your table to help you answer Question 2 below.

### Reviewing Key Concepts

1. a. **Listing** What are five agents of erosion?
   b. **Defining** In your own words, write a definition of *deposition.*
   c. **Predicting** Over time, how will erosion and deposition affect a mountain range? Explain.
2. a. **Listing** What are the four types of mass movement?
   b. **Relating Cause and Effect** What force causes all types of mass movement?
   c. **Inferring** A fence runs across a steep hillside. The fence is tilted downhill and forms a curve rather than a straight line. What can you infer happened to the fence? Explain.

### Lab zone At-Home Activity

**Evidence of Erosion** After a rainstorm, take a walk with an adult family member around your neighborhood. Look for evidence of erosion. Try to find areas where there is loose soil, sand, gravel, or rock. **CAUTION:** *Stay away from any large pile of loose sand or soil—it may slide without warning.* Which areas have the most erosion? The least erosion? How does the slope of the ground affect the amount of erosion? Sketch or take photographs of the areas showing evidence of erosion.

Lab zone **Skills Lab**

# Sand Hills

## Problem

What is the relationship between the height and width of a sand hill?

## Skills

developing hypotheses, interpreting data, predicting

## Materials

- dry sand, 500 mL • cardboard tube
- tray (about 15 cm × 45 cm × 60 cm)
- wooden barbecue skewer • masking tape
- spoon • ruler • pencil or crayon
- several sheets of white paper

## Procedure

1. Begin by observing how gravity causes mass movement. To start, place the cardboard tube vertically in the center of the tray.
2. Using the spoon, fill the cardboard tube with the dry sand. Take care not to spill the sand around the outside of the tube.
3. Carefully lift the sand-filled tube straight up so that all the sand flows out. As you lift the tube, observe the sand's movement.
4. Develop a hypothesis explaining how you think the width of the sand pile is related to its height for different amounts of sand.
5. Empty the sand in the tray back into a container. Then set up your system for measuring the sand hill.
6. Copy the data table into your lab notebook.
7. Following Steps 1 through 3, make a new sand hill.

**Data Table**

| Test | 1 | 2 | 3 | 4 | 5 |
|---|---|---|---|---|---|
| Width | | | | | |
| Height | | | | | |

8. Measure and record the sand hill's height and width for Test 1. (See the instructions on the bottom of the page to help you accurately measure the height and width.)

### How to Measure a Sand Hill

1. Cover the bottom of the tray with unlined white paper and tape it firmly in place.
2. Mark off points 0.5 cm apart along one side of the paper in the tray.
3. Carefully draw the sand hill's outline on the paper. The line should go completely around the base of the hill.
4. Now measure the width of the hill against the marks you made along the edge of the paper.
5. Measure the sand hill's height by inserting a barbecue skewer through its center. Make a mark on the skewer at the top of the hill.
6. Remove the skewer and use the ruler to measure how much of the skewer was buried in the hill. Try not to disturb the sand.

For: Data sharing
Visit: PHSchool.com
Web Code: cfd-2031

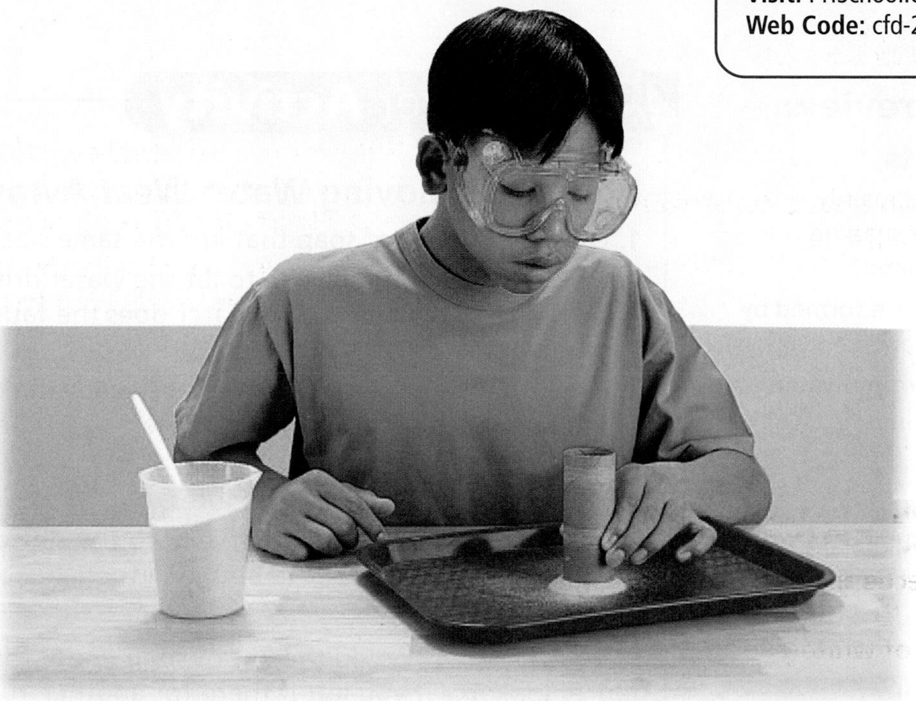

9. Now test what happens when you add more sand to the sand hill. Place your cardboard tube vertically at the center of the sand hill. Be careful not to push the tube down into the sand hill! Using the spoon, fill the tube with sand as before.
10. Carefully raise the tube and observe the sand's movement.
11. Measure and record the sand hill's height and width for Test 2.
12. Repeat Steps 9 through 11 at least three more times. After each test, record your results. Be sure to number each test.

## Analyze and Conclude

1. **Graphing** Make a graph showing how the sand hill's height and width changed with each test. (Hint: Use the *x*-axis of the graph for height. Use the *y*-axis of the graph for width.)
2. **Interpreting Data** What does your graph show about the relationship between the sand hill's height and width?
3. **Drawing Conclusions** Does your graph support your hypothesis about the sand hill's height and width? Why or why not?
4. **Developing Hypotheses** How would you revise your original hypothesis after examining your data? Give reasons for your answer.
5. **Predicting** Predict what would happen if you continued the experiment for five more tests. Extend your graph with a dashed line to show your prediction. How could you test your prediction?
6. **Communicating** Write a paragraph in which you discuss how you measured your sand hill. Did any problems you had in making your measurements affect your results? How did you adjust your measurement technique to solve these problems?

## Design an Experiment

Do you think the use of different materials, such as wet sand or gravel, would produce different results from those using dry sand? Make a new hypothesis about the relationship between slope and width in hills made of materials other than dry sand. Design an experiment in which you test how these different materials form hills. *Obtain your teacher's approval before you try the experiment.*

Section 2

# Water Erosion

## Reading Preview

### Key Concepts

- What process is mainly responsible for shaping the surface of the land?
- What features are formed by water erosion and deposition?
- What causes groundwater erosion?

### Key Terms

- runoff • rill • gully • stream
- tributary • flood plain
- meander • oxbow lake
- alluvial fan • delta
- groundwater • stalactite
- stalagmite • karst topography

### Target Reading Skill

**Previewing Visuals** Before you read, preview Figure 10. Then write two questions that you have about the illustration in a graphic organizer like the one below. As you read, answer your questions.

**The Course of a River**

| | |
|---|---|
| Q. | What features does a river produce by erosion? |
| A. | |
| Q. | |

## Lab zone Discover Activity

### How Does Moving Water Wear Away Rocks?

1. Obtain two bars of soap that are the same size and brand.
2. Open a faucet just enough to let the water drip out very slowly. How many drops of water does the faucet release per minute?
3. Place one bar of soap in a dry place. Place the other bar of soap under the faucet. Predict the effect of the dripping water droplets on the soap.
4. Let the faucet drip for 10 minutes.
5. Turn off the faucet and observe both bars of soap. What difference do you observe between them?

**Think It Over**

**Predicting** What would the bar of soap under the dripping faucet look like if you left it there for another 10 minutes? For an hour? How could you speed up the process? Slow it down?

Walking in the woods in summer, you can hear the racing water of a stream before you see the stream itself. The water roars as it foams over rock ledges and boulders. When you reach the stream, you see water rushing by. Sand and pebbles tumble along the bottom of the stream. As it swirls downstream, the water also carries twigs, leaves, and bits of soil. In sheltered pools, insects such as water striders skim the water's calm surface. Beneath the surface, a rainbow trout swims in the clear water.

In winter, the stream freezes. Chunks of ice scrape and grind away at the stream's bed and banks. In spring, the stream floods. Then the flow of water may be strong enough to move large rocks. But throughout the year, the stream continues to erode its small part of Earth's surface.

▼ A stream in summer

## Runoff and Erosion

**Moving water is the major agent of the erosion that has shaped Earth's land surface.** Erosion by water begins with the splash of rain. Some rainfall sinks into the ground. Some evaporates or is taken up by plants. The force of a falling raindrop can loosen and pick up soil particles. As water moves over the land, it carries these particles with it. This moving water is called runoff. **Runoff** is water that moves over Earth's surface. When runoff flows in a thin layer over the land, it may cause a type of erosion called sheet erosion.

**Amount of Runoff** The amount of runoff in an area depends on five main factors. The first factor is the amount of rain an area receives. A second factor is vegetation. Grasses, shrubs, and trees reduce runoff by absorbing water and holding soil in place. A third factor is the type of soil. Some types of soils absorb more water than others. A fourth factor is the shape of the land. Land that is steeply sloped has more runoff than flatter land. Finally, a fifth factor is how people use the land. For instance, a paved parking lot absorbs no water, so all the rain that falls on it becomes runoff. Runoff also increases when a farmer cuts down crops, since this removes vegetation from the land.

Generally, more runoff means more erosion. In contrast, factors that reduce runoff will reduce erosion. Even though deserts have little rainfall, they often have high runoff and erosion because they have few plants. In wet areas, runoff and erosion may be low because there are more plants to protect the soil.

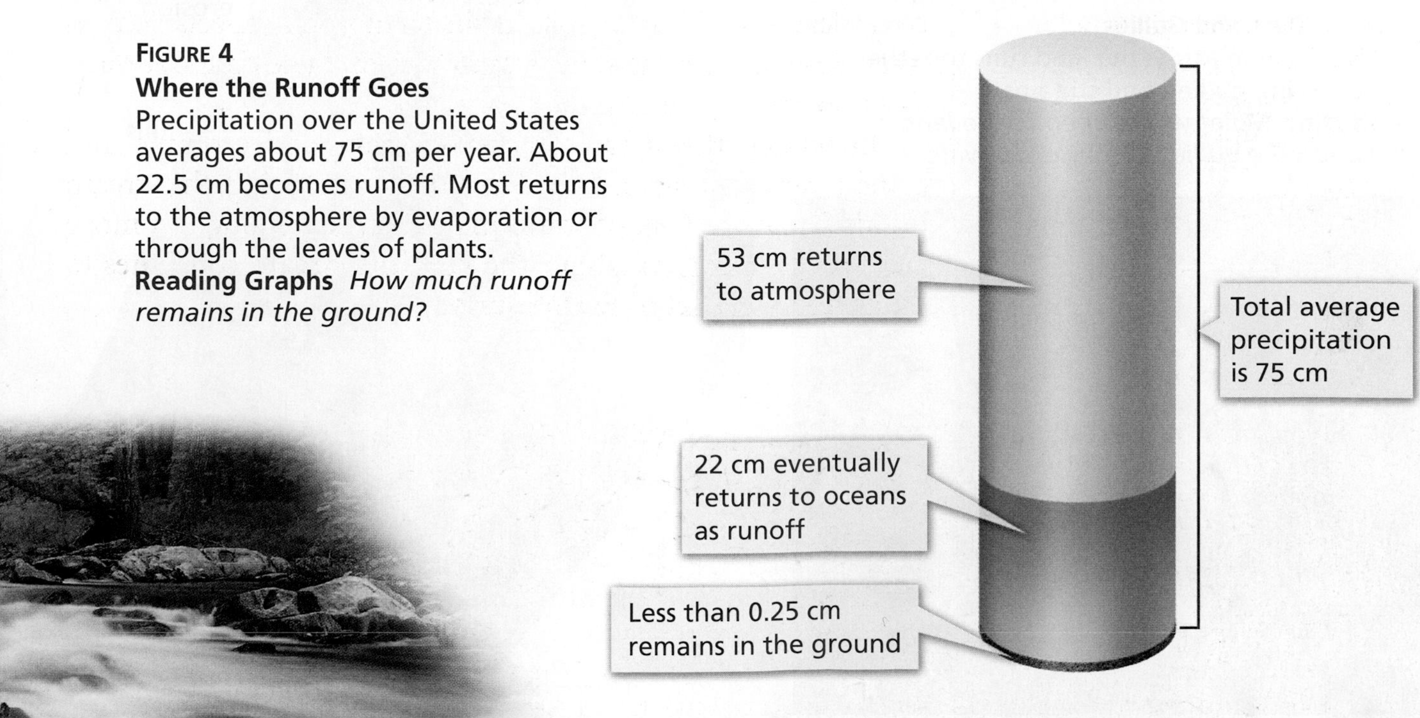

53 cm returns to atmosphere
Total average precipitation is 75 cm
22 cm eventually returns to oceans as runoff
Less than 0.25 cm remains in the ground

**FIGURE 4**
**Where the Runoff Goes**
Precipitation over the United States averages about 75 cm per year. About 22.5 cm becomes runoff. Most returns to the atmosphere by evaporation or through the leaves of plants.
**Reading Graphs** *How much runoff remains in the ground?*

**Lab zone** Try This **Activity**

### Raindrops Falling

Find out how the force of falling raindrops affects soil.

1. Fill a petri dish with fine-textured soil to a depth of about 1 cm. Make sure the soil has a smooth flat surface, but do not pack it firmly in the dish.
2. Place the dish in the center of a newspaper.
3. Fill a dropper with water. Squeeze a large water drop from a height of 1 m onto the surface of the soil. Repeat 4 times.
4. Use a meter stick to measure the distance the soil splashed from the dish. Record your observations.
5. Repeat Steps 1 through 4, this time from a height of 2 m.

**Drawing Conclusions** Which test produced the greater amount of erosion? Why?

**Rills and Gullies** Because of gravity, runoff and the material it contains move downhill. As runoff travels, it forms tiny grooves in the soil called **rills.** As many rills flow into one another, they grow larger, forming gullies. A **gully** is a large groove, or channel, in the soil that carries runoff after a rainstorm. As water flows through gullies, it moves soil and rocks with it, thus enlarging the gullies through erosion. Gullies contain water only after it rains.

**Streams and Rivers** Gullies join together to form a larger channel called a stream. A **stream** is a channel along which water is continually flowing down a slope. Unlike gullies, streams rarely dry up. Small streams are also called creeks or brooks. As streams flow together, they form larger and larger bodies of flowing water. A large stream is often called a river.

**Tributaries** A stream grows into a larger stream or river by receiving water from tributaries. A **tributary** is a stream or river that flows into a larger river. For example, the Missouri and Ohio rivers are tributaries of the Mississippi River. A drainage basin, or watershed, is the area from which a river and its tributaries collect their water.

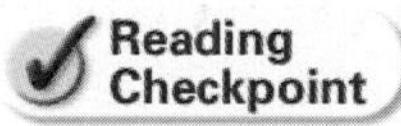


**What is a tributary?**

FIGURE 5
**Runoff, Rills, and Gullies**
Water flowing across the land runs together to form rills, gullies, and streams.
**Predicting** *What will happen to the land between the gullies as they grow wider?*

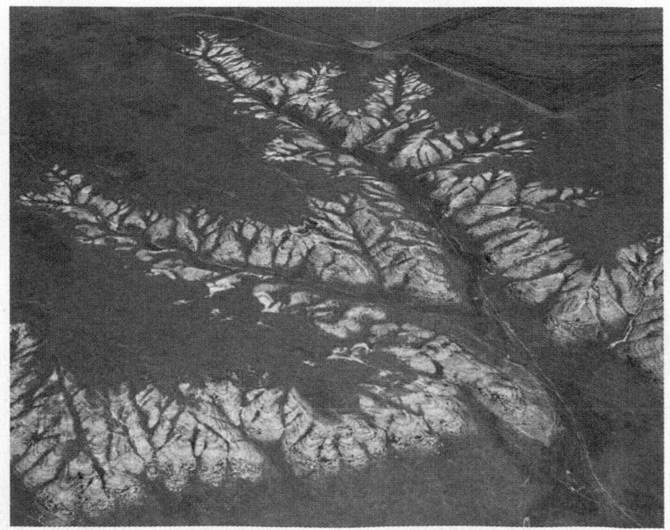

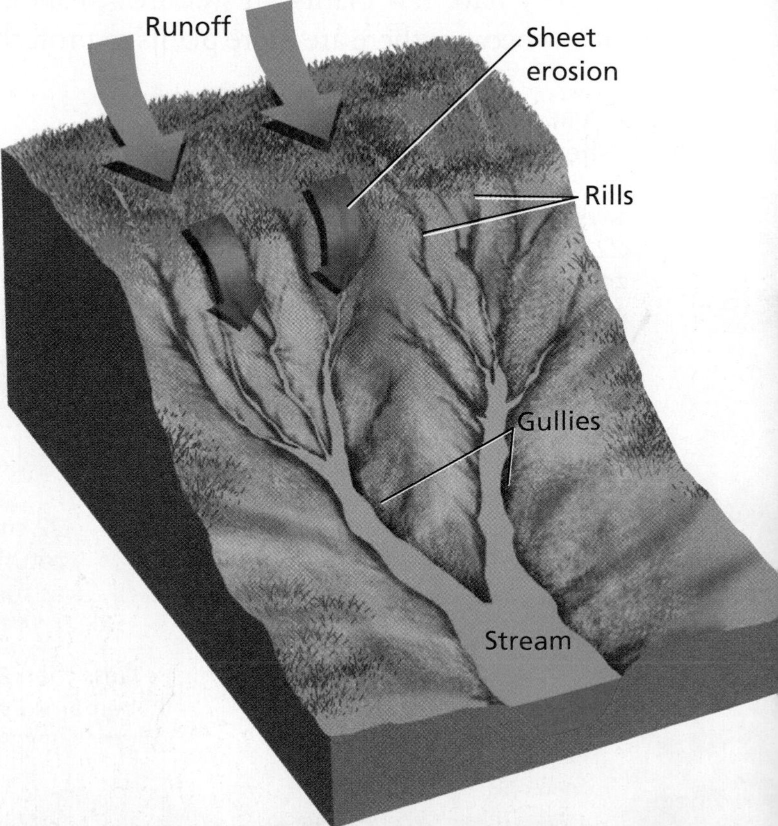

## Erosion by Rivers

As a river flows from the mountains to the sea, the river forms a variety of features. **Through erosion, a river creates valleys, waterfalls, flood plains, meanders, and oxbow lakes.**

Rivers often form on steep mountain slopes. Near its source, a river is often fast flowing and generally follows a straight, narrow course. The steep slopes along the river erode rapidly. The result is a deep, V-shaped valley.

**Waterfalls** Waterfalls may occur where a river meets an area of rock that is very hard and erodes slowly. The river flows over this rock and then flows over softer rock downstream. As you can see in Figure 6, the softer rock wears away faster than the harder rock. Eventually a waterfall develops where the softer rock was removed. Areas of rough water called rapids also occur where a river tumbles over hard rock.

**Flood Plain** Lower down on its course, a river usually flows over more gently sloping land. The river spreads out and erodes the land, forming a wide river valley. The flat, wide area of land along a river is a **flood plain.** A river often covers its flood plain when it overflows its banks during floods. On a wide flood plain, the valley walls may be kilometers away from the river itself.

Go Online
PLANET DIARY

For: More on floods
Visit: PHSchool.com
Web Code: cfd-2032

Harder rock layers eventually break off.
Softer rock layers erode first.
Rapids are areas of turbulence below the falls where water rushes over rocks.

**FIGURE 6**
**How a Waterfall Forms**
A waterfall forms where a flat layer of tough rock lies over a layer of softer rock that erodes easily. When the softer rock erodes, pieces of the harder rock above break off, creating the waterfall's sharp drop.

**FIGURE 7**
**Meanders and Oxbow Lakes**
Erosion often forms meanders and oxbow lakes where a river winds across its floodplain.

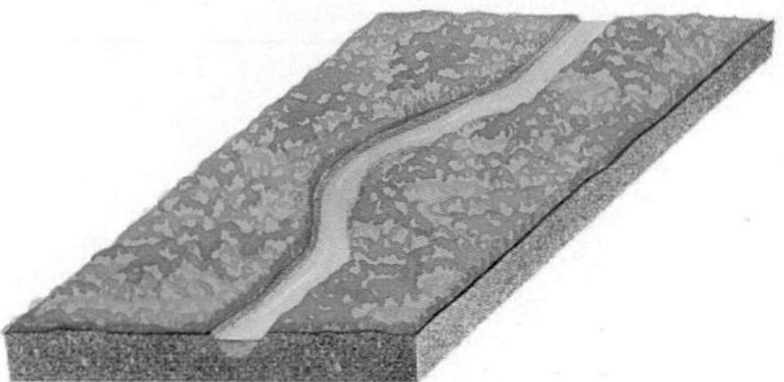

1 A small obstacle creates a slight bend in the river.

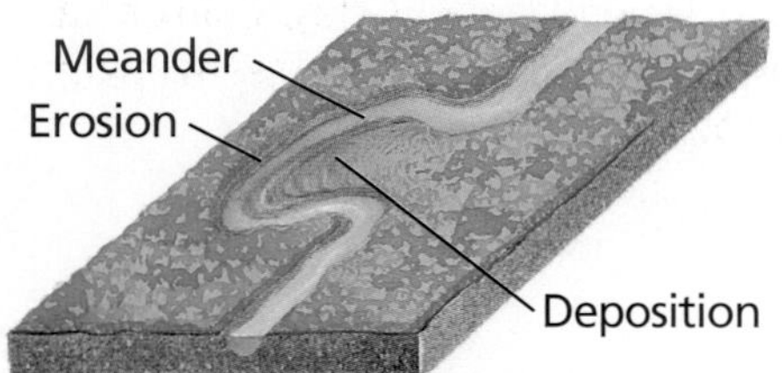


2 As water erodes the outer edge of a meander, the bend becomes bigger. Deposition occurs along the inner edge.

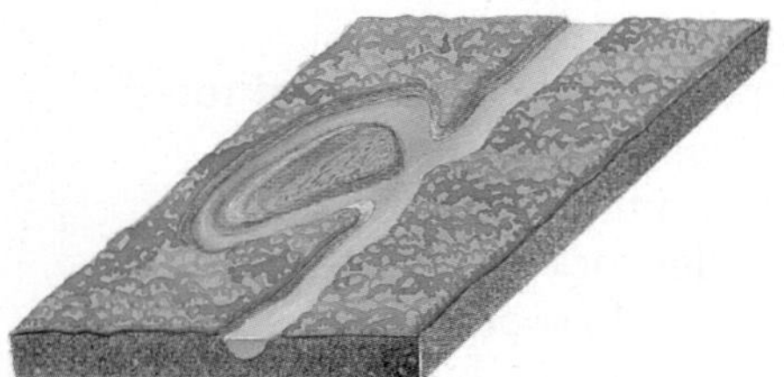

3 Gradually, the meander becomes more curved. The river breaks through and takes a new course.

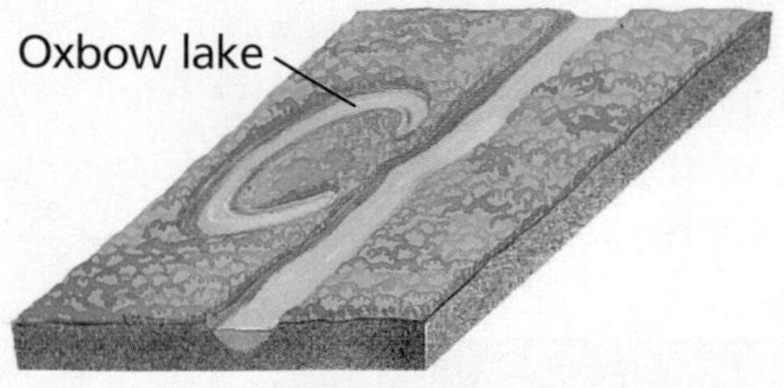


4 An oxbow lake remains.

**Meanders** A river often develops meanders where it flows through easily eroded rock or sediment. A **meander** is a loop-like bend in the course of a river. As the river winds from side to side, it tends to erode the outer bank and deposit sediment on the inner bank of a bend. Over time, the meander becomes more and more curved.

Because of the sediment a river carries, it can erode a very wide flood plain. Along this part of a river's course, its channel is deep and wide. Meanders are common. The southern stretch of the Mississippi River is one example of a river that meanders on a wide, gently sloping flood plain.

**Oxbow Lakes** Sometimes a meandering river forms a feature called an oxbow lake. As Figure 7 shows, an **oxbow lake** is a meander that has been cut off from the river. An oxbow lake may form when a river floods. During the flood, high water finds a straighter route downstream. As the flood waters fall, sediments dam up the ends of a meander. The meander has become an oxbow lake.

Reading Checkpoint **How does an oxbow lake form?**

## Deposits by Rivers

As water moves, it carries sediments with it. Any time moving water slows down, it drops, or deposits, some of the sediment. As the water slows down, fine particles fall to the river's bed. Larger stones quit rolling and sliding. **Deposition creates landforms such as alluvial fans and deltas. It can also add soil to a river's flood plain.** In Figure 10, you can see these and other features shaped by rivers and streams.

**Alluvial Fans** Where a stream flows out of a steep, narrow mountain valley, the stream suddenly becomes wider and shallower. The water slows down. Here sediments are deposited in an alluvial fan. An **alluvial fan** is a wide, sloping deposit of sediment formed where a stream leaves a mountain range. As its name suggests, this deposit is shaped like a fan. You can see an alluvial fan in Figure 8.

**FIGURE 8**
**Alluvial Fan**
This alluvial fan in Death Valley, California, was formed from deposits by streams from the mountains.

**Deltas** A river ends its journey when it flows into a still body of water, such as an ocean or a lake. Because the river water is no longer flowing downhill, the water slows down. At this point, the sediment in the water drops to the bottom. Sediment deposited where a river flows into an ocean or lake builds up a landform called a **delta.** Deltas can be a variety of shapes. Some are arc shaped, others are triangle shaped. The delta of the Mississippi River, shown in Figure 9, is an example of a type of delta called a "bird's foot" delta.

**Soil on Flood Plains** Deposition can also occur during floods. Then heavy rains or melting snow cause a river to rise above its banks and spread out over its flood plain. When the flood water finally retreats, it deposits sediment as new soil. Deposition of new soil over a flood plain is what makes a river valley fertile. Dense forests can grow in the rich soil of a flood plain. The soil is also perfect for growing crops.

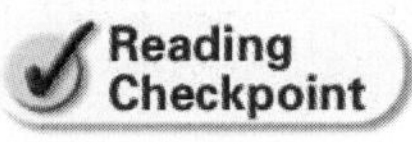

**How can a flood be beneficial?**

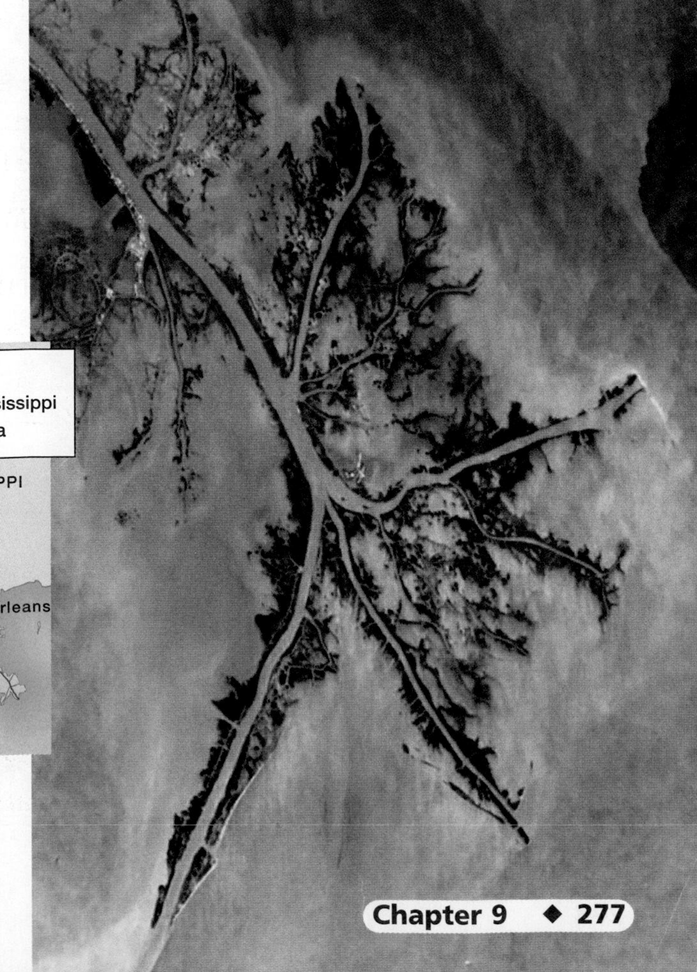


**FIGURE 9**
**Mississippi Delta**
This satellite image shows part of the Mississippi River delta after erosion caused by Hurricane Katrina in 2004.
**Observing** *What happens to the Mississippi River as it flows through its delta? Can you find the river's main channel?*

Waterfalls and Rapids
Waterfalls and rapids are common where the river passes over harder rock.
V-Shaped Valley
Near its source, the river flows through a deep, V-shaped valley. As the river flows, it cuts the valley deeper.
Flood Plain
A flood plain forms where the river's power of erosion widens its valley rather than deepening it.
Meanders
Where the river flows across easily eroded sediment, its channel bends from side to side in a series of meanders.
Beaches
Sand carried downstream by the river spreads along the coast to form beaches.

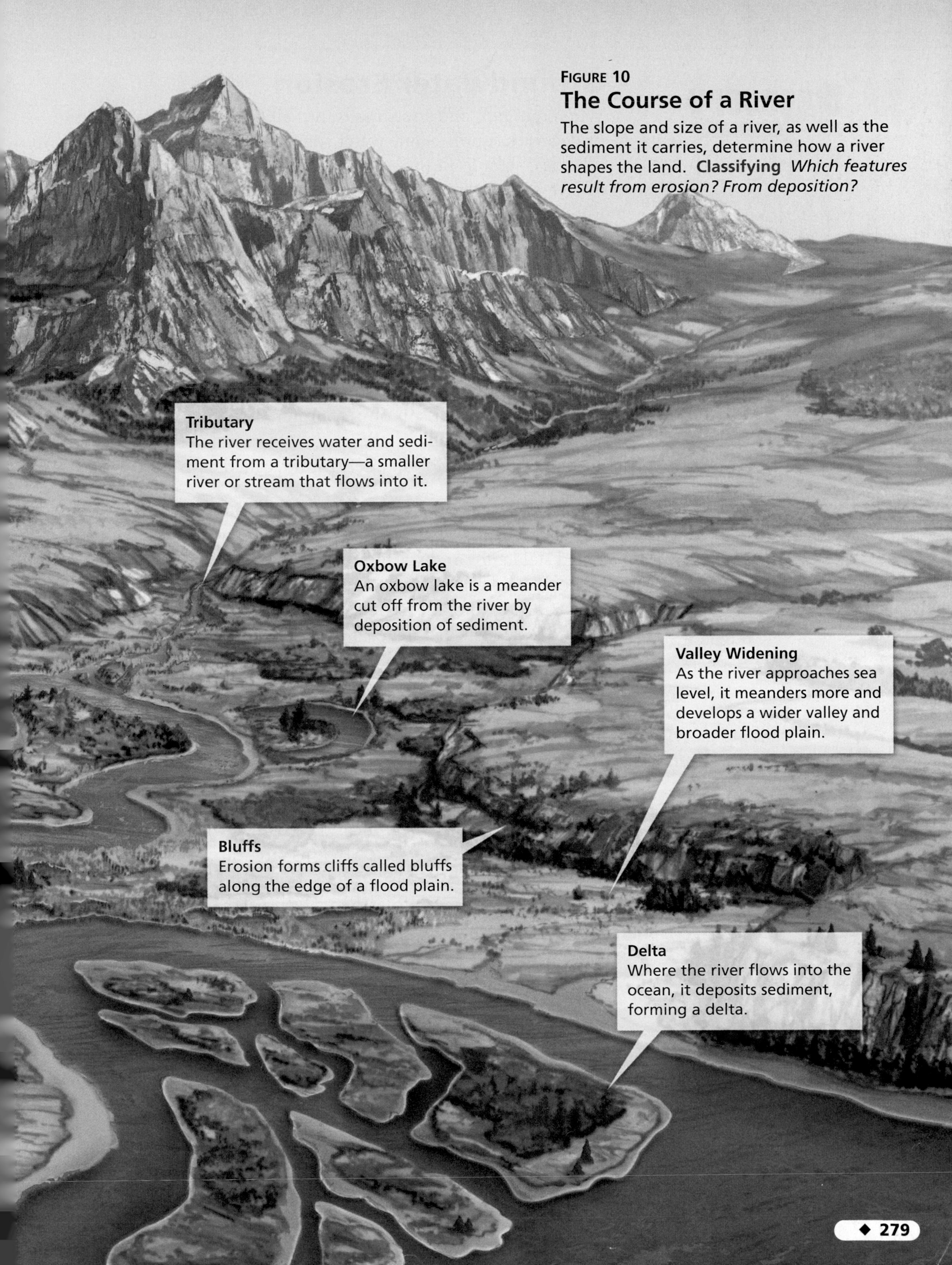

Tributary
The river receives water and sediment from a tributary—a smaller river or stream that flows into it.
Oxbow Lake
An oxbow lake is a meander cut off from the river by deposition of sediment.
Valley Widening
As the river approaches sea level, it meanders more and develops a wider valley and broader flood plain.
Bluffs
Erosion forms cliffs called bluffs along the edge of a flood plain.
Delta
Where the river flows into the ocean, it deposits sediment, forming a delta.

FIGURE 10
**The Course of a River**
The slope and size of a river, as well as the sediment it carries, determine how a river shapes the land. **Classifying** *Which features result from erosion? From deposition?*

## Groundwater Erosion

When rain falls and snow melts, not all of the water evaporates or becomes runoff. Some water soaks into the ground. There it fills the openings in the soil and trickles into cracks and spaces in layers of rock. **Groundwater** is the term geologists use for this underground water. Like running water on the surface, groundwater affects the shape of the land.

**Groundwater can cause erosion through a process of chemical weathering.** When water sinks into the ground, it combines with carbon dioxide to form a weak acid, called carbonic acid. Carbonic acid can break down limestone. Groundwater containing carbonic acid flows into any cracks in the limestone. Then some of the limestone changes chemically and is carried away in a solution of water. This process gradually hollows out pockets in the rock. Over time, these pockets develop into large holes underground, called caves or caverns.

**Cave Formations** The action of carbonic acid on limestone can also result in deposition. Inside limestone caves, deposits called stalactites and stalagmites often form. Water containing carbonic acid and calcium from limestone drips from a cave's roof. Carbon dioxide is released from the solution, leaving behind a deposit of calcite. A deposit that hangs like an icicle from the roof of a cave is known as a **stalactite** (stuh LAK tyt). Slow dripping builds up a cone-shaped **stalagmite** (stuh LAG myt) from the cave floor.

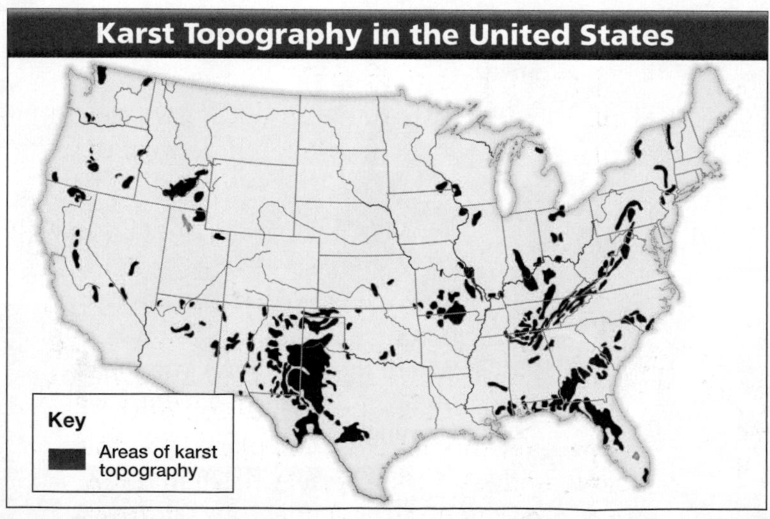


FIGURE 11
Karst topography is found in many parts of the United States where the bedrock is made up of thick layers of limestone.

**Karst Topography** In rainy regions where there is a layer of limestone near the surface, groundwater erosion can significantly change the shape of the land. Streams are rare, because water easily sinks down into the weathered limestone. Deep valleys and caverns are common. If the roof of a cave collapses because of the erosion of the underlying limestone, the result is a depression called a sinkhole. This type of landscape is called **karst topography** after a region in Eastern Europe. In the United States, regions of karst topography are found in Florida, Texas, and many other states.

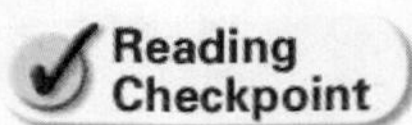


**How does deposition occur in a limestone cave?**

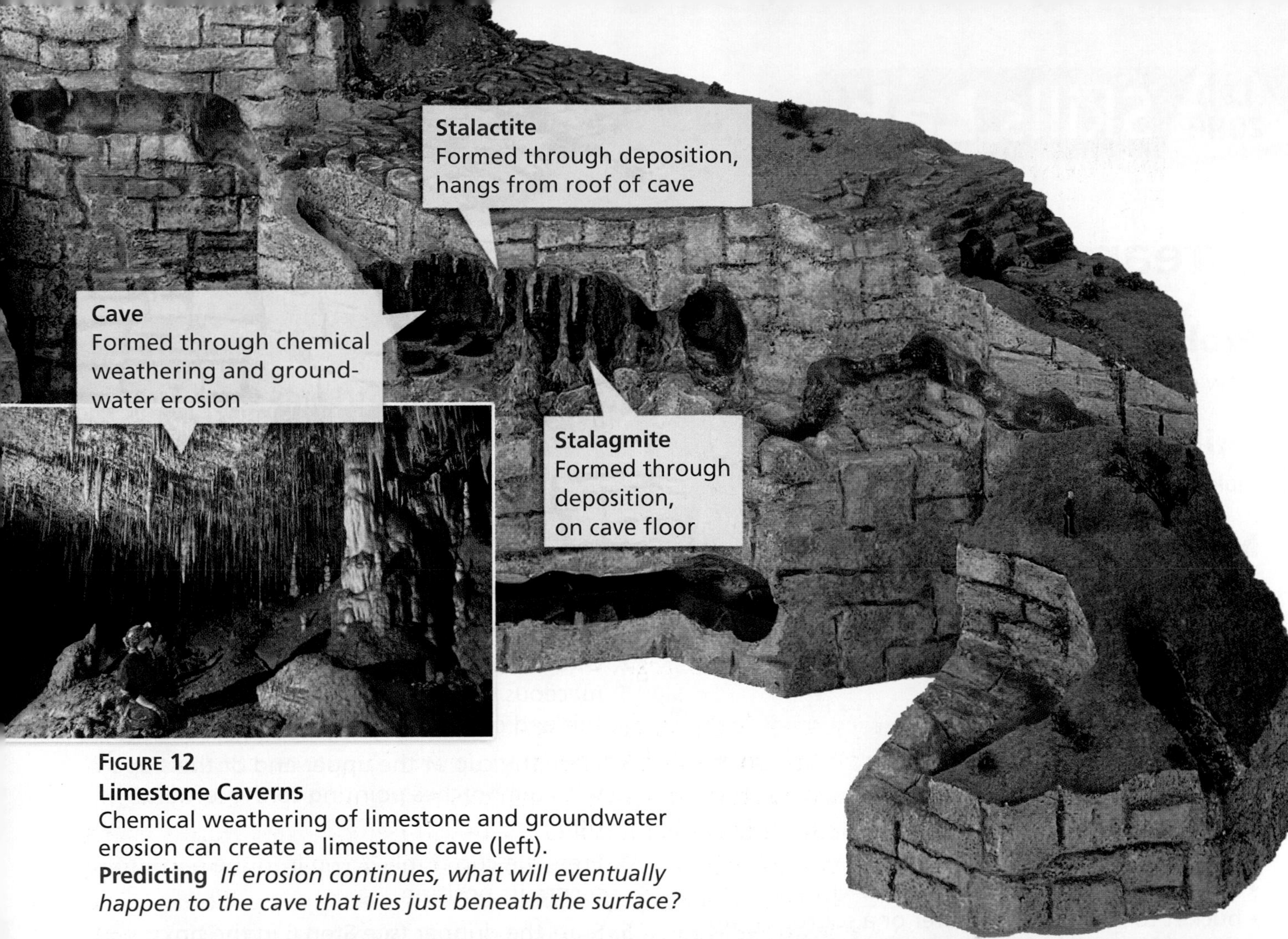


**FIGURE 12**
**Limestone Caverns**
Chemical weathering of limestone and groundwater erosion can create a limestone cave (left).
**Predicting** *If erosion continues, what will eventually happen to the cave that lies just beneath the surface?*

## Section 2 Assessment

**Target Reading Skill Previewing Visuals** Refer to your questions and answers about Figure 10 to help you answer Question 2 below.

### Reviewing Key Concepts

1. a. **Reviewing** What is the major agent of erosion on Earth's surface?
   b. **Sequencing** List these in order of size: tributary, stream, rill, gully, runoff, river.
   c. **Predicting** Where would gullies be more likely to form: a field with plowed soil and no plants, or a field covered with thick grass? Explain.
2. a. **Listing** What are five features that erosion forms along a river?
   b. **Listing** What are three features that result from deposition along a river?
   c. **Relating Cause and Effect** Why does a delta often form where a river empties into the ocean?
3. a. **Identifying** What process is the cause of groundwater erosion?
   b. **Explaining** How do groundwater erosion and deposition produce a limestone cave?

### Lab zone At-Home Activity

**Erosion Cube** In a small dish, build a cube out of 27 small sugar cubes. Your cube should be three sugar cubes on a side. Fold a square piece of paper towel to fit the top of the cube. Wet the paper towel, place it on the cube, and let it stand for 15 or 20 minutes. Every few minutes, sprinkle a few drops of water on the paper towel to keep it wet. Then remove the paper towel. What happened to your cube? How is the effect of water on a sugar cube similar to groundwater eroding limestone? How is it different?

Lab zone **Skills Lab**

# Streams in Action

## Problem

How do rivers and streams erode the land?

## Skills Focus

making models, observing

## Materials   

- diatomaceous earth
- plastic measuring cup
- spray bottle
- hand lens
- watch or clock
- water
- 1 metal spoon
- plastic foam cup
- blue food coloring
- liquid detergent
- scissors
- 2 wood blocks about 2.5 cm thick
- bucket to hold 2–3 L of water or a source of tap water
- plastic stirrers, 10–12 cm long, with two small holes each
- wire, 13–15 cm long, 20 gauge

## Procedure

### PART 1 Creating Streams Over Time

1. Your teacher will give you a plastic tub containing diatomaceous earth that has been soaked with water. Place the tub on a level surface. **CAUTION:** *Dry diatomaceous earth produces dust that may be irritating if inhaled.* To keep the diatomaceous earth from drying out, spray it lightly with water.
2. One end of the tub will contain more diatomaceous earth. Use a block of wood to raise this end of the tub 2.5 cm.
3. Place the cup at the upper end of the slope with the notches pointing to the left and right.
4. Press the cup firmly down into the earth to secure its position.
5. Start the dripper (see Step 6 in the box below). Allow the water to drip to the right onto the diatomaceous earth.
6. Allow the dripper to drip for 5 minutes. (*Hint:* When you need to add more water, be careful not to disturb the dripper.)

## Making the Dripper

1. Insert the wire into one of the two holes in a plastic stirrer. The ends of the wire should protrude from the stirrer.
2. Gently bend the stirrer into a **U** shape. Be careful not to make any sharp bends. This is the dripper.
3. With scissors, carefully cut two small notches on opposite sides of the top of the foam cup.
4. Fill the cup to just below the notches with water colored with two drops of blue food coloring. Add more food coloring later as you add more water to the cup.

5. Add one drop of detergent to keep air bubbles out of the dripper and increase flow.
6. To start the dripper, fill it with water. Then quickly tip it and place it in one of the notches in the cup, as shown at left.
7. Adjust the flow rate of the dripper to about 2 drips per 1 second. (*Hint:* Bend the dripper into more of a **U** shape to increase flow. Lessen the curve to reduce flow.)

7. Observe the flow of water and the changes it makes. Use the hand lens to look closely at the stream bed.
8. After 5 minutes, remove the dripper.
9. In your lab notebook, draw a picture of the resulting stream and label it "5 minutes."
10. Now switch the dripper to the left side of the cup. Restart the dripper and allow it to drip for 10 minutes. Then remove the dripper.
11. Draw a picture and label it "10 minutes."

### PART 2 Changing the Angle of Slope

1. Remove the cup from the stream table.
2. Save the stream bed on the right side of the tub. Using the bowl of the spoon, smooth out the diatomaceous earth on the left side.
3. To increase the angle of slope of your stream table, raise the end of the tub another 2.5 cm.
4. In your lab notebook, predict the effects of increasing the angle of slope.
5. Replace the cup and restart the dripper, placing it in the notch on the left side of the cup. Allow the dripper to drip for 5 minutes. Notice any changes in the new stream bed.
6. At the end of 5 minutes, remove the dripper.
7. Draw the new stream bed in your lab notebook. Label it "Increased Angle."
8. Follow your teacher's instructions for cleanup after this activity. Wash your hands when you have finished.

## Analyze and Conclude

1. **Observing** Compare the 5-minute stream with the 10-minute stream. How did the length of time that the water flowed affect erosion along the stream bed?
2. **Drawing Conclusions** Were your predictions about the effects of increasing the angle of slope correct? Explain your answer.
3. **Observing** What happened to the eroded material that was carried downstream?
4. **Making Models** What features of streams were you able to observe using your model? How could you modify the model to observe additional features?
5. **Controlling Variables** What other variables besides time and angle of slope might affect the way rivers and streams erode the land?
6. **Communicating** Describe an example of water erosion that you have seen, such as water flowing down a hillside or street after a heavy rain. Include in your answer details such as the slope of the land, the color of the water, and the effects of the erosion.

## Design an Experiment

Design an experiment in which you use your model to measure how the amount of sediment carried by a river changes as the volume of flow of the river increases. *Obtain your teacher's approval before you try the experiment.*

# Science and Society

# Protecting Homes in Flood Plains

**Evacuation**
In 2005, floodwaters from Hurricane Katrina rose to the rooftops of many New Orleans houses. Thousands of people were stranded and had to be evacuated by boat.

In 2005, water from Hurricane Katrina flooded New Orleans, Louisiana. The city lies on the Mississippi River's flood plain. High levees were supposed to protect the city. But several levees failed, and flood waters poured in. At least ten million American households are located on flood plains. The cost of flood damage has been growing. How can communities along rivers limit the cost of flooding and protect people and buildings?

## The Issues

### Should the Government Insure People Against Flood Damage?

The United States government offers insurance to households in flood plains. The insurance pays part of the cost of repairs after a flood. However, government flood insurance is available only to towns and cities that take steps to reduce flood damage. Cities must allow new building only on high ground. In addition, the insurance will not pay to rebuild homes that are badly damaged by flood water. Instead, these people must use the money to find a home somewhere else.

Critics say that government insurance just encourages development in areas that flood. Another problem with the insurance is cost. It is very expensive, so most people who live in flood plains don't buy the government insurance. Supporters say government insurance rewards towns and cities that make rules to control building on flood plains. Over time, this approach would mean fewer homes and other buildings on flood plains—and less damage from flooding.

**Floodwater Rising** Floodwaters engulfed much of New Orleans after the historic city's levees were breached by Hurricane Katrina.

## How Much of the Flood Plain Should Be Protected?

Government flood insurance is available only in areas where scientists expect flooding at least once in 100 years. But such figures are just estimates. Three floods occurred in only 12 years in a government flood insurance area near Sacramento, California.

## Should the Government Tell People Where They Can Live?

The frequency and severity of flooding is an important factor in land-use decisions. Sometimes, no construction on a flood plain is advisable. Some programs of flood control forbid all new building.

Other programs may also encourage people to move to safer areas. The 1997 flood on the Red River in Grand Forks, North Dakota, is one example. After the flood, the city of Grand Forks offered to buy all the damaged buildings near the river. The city wants to build high walls of earth to protect the rest of the town.

The Grand Forks plan might prevent future damage, but is it fair? Supporters say that since the government has to pay for flood damage, it has the right to make people leave flood plains. Critics of such plans say that people should be free to live where they want, even in risky areas.

Who should decide that no new houses can be built in a certain area—the local, state, or federal government? Some believe scientists should make the decision.

## You Decide

**1. Identify the Problem**
In your own words, describe the controversy surrounding flood plains and housing.

**2. Analyze the Options**
List several steps that could be taken to reduce the damage done to buildings in flood plains. For each step, include who would benefit from the step and who would pay the costs.

**3. Find a Solution**
Your town has to decide what to do about a neighborhood damaged by the worst flood in 50 years. Write a speech that argues for your solution.

**For:** More on protecting homes in flood plains
**Visit:** PHSchool.com
**Web Code:** cfh-2030

# The Force of Moving Water

## Reading Preview

### Key Concepts

- What enables water to do work?
- How does sediment enter rivers and streams?
- What factors affect a river's ability to erode and carry sediment?

### Key Terms

- energy • potential energy
- kinetic energy • abrasion
- load • friction • turbulence

### Target Reading Skill

**Building Vocabulary** A definition states the meaning of a word or phrase by telling about its most important feature or function. Carefully read the definition of each Key Term and also read the neighboring sentences. Then write a definition of each Key Term in your own words.

## Lab zone Discover Activity

### How Are Sediments Deposited?

1. Put on your goggles.
2. Obtain a clear plastic jar or bottle with a top. Fill the jar about two-thirds full with water.
3. Fill a plastic beaker with 200 mL of fine and coarse sand, soil, clay, and small pebbles.
4. Pour the mixture into the jar of water. Screw on the top tightly and shake for two minutes. Be sure to hold onto the jar firmly.
5. Set the jar down and observe it for 10 to 15 minutes.

**Think It Over**

**Inferring** In what order are the sediments in the jar deposited? What do you think causes this pattern?

The Merrimack River in New Hampshire and Massachusetts is only 180 kilometers long. But the Merrimack does a great deal of work as it runs from the mountains to the sea. The river's waters fall 82 meters through many rapids and waterfalls. During the 1800s, people harnessed this falling water to run machines that could spin thread and weave cloth.

## Work and Energy

A river's water has energy. **Energy** is the ability to do work or cause change. There are two kinds of energy. **Potential energy** is energy that is stored and waiting to be used later. The Merrimack's waters begin with potential energy due to their position above sea level. **Kinetic energy** is the energy an object has due to its motion. **As gravity pulls water down a slope, the water's potential energy changes to kinetic energy that can do work.**

When energy does work, the energy is transferred from one object to another. Along the Merrimack River, the kinetic energy of the moving water was transferred to the spinning machines. It became mechanical energy harnessed for making cloth. But all along a river, moving water has other effects. A river is always moving sediment from the mountains to the sea. At the same time, a river is also eroding its banks and valley.

**FIGURE 13**
**Water Power**
Dams like this one on the Merrimack River in Lowell, Massachusetts, help to harness the power of flowing water.

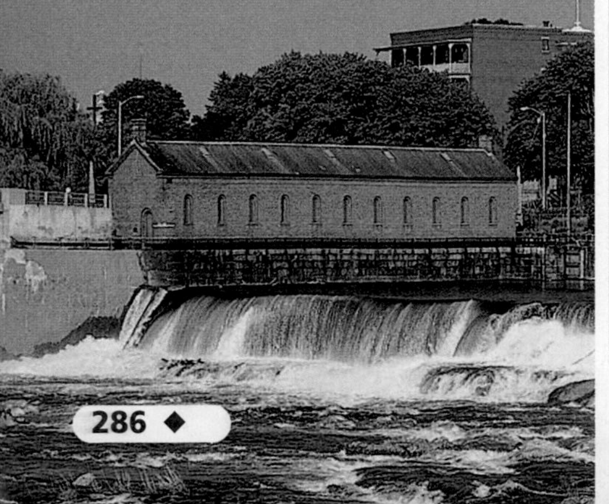

## How Water Erodes

Gravity causes the movement of water across Earth's land surface. But how does water cause erosion? In the process of water erosion, water picks up and moves sediment. Sediment includes soil, rock, clay, and sand. Sediment can enter rivers and streams in a number of ways. **Most sediment washes or falls into a river as a result of mass movement and runoff. Other sediment erodes from the bottom or sides of the river.** Wind may also drop sediment into the water.

Abrasion is another process by which a river obtains sediment. **Abrasion** is the wearing away of rock by a grinding action. Abrasion occurs when particles of sediment in flowing water bump into the streambed again and again. Abrasion grinds down sediment particles. For example, boulders become smaller as they are moved down a streambed. Sediments also grind and chip away at the rock of the streambed, deepening and widening the stream's channel.

The amount of sediment that a river carries is its **load.** Gravity and the force of the moving water cause the sediment load to move downstream. Most large sediment falls to the bottom and moves by rolling and sliding. Fast-moving water actually lifts sand and other, smaller sediment and carries it downstream. Water dissolves some sediment completely. The river carries these dissolved sediments in solution. Figure 14 shows other ways in which water can carry sediment. For example, grains of sand or small stones can move by bouncing.

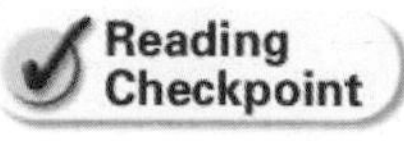


**What causes the sediment in a river to move downstream?**

### Lab zone Skills Activity

**Developing Hypotheses**

A geologist is comparing alluvial fans. One alluvial fan is composed of gravel and small boulders. The other fan is composed of sand and silt. Propose a hypothesis to explain the difference in the size of the particles in the two fans. (*Hint:* Think of the characteristics of the streams that formed each alluvial fan.)

FIGURE 14
**Movement of Sediment**
Rivers and streams carry sediment in several ways.The salmon at right are swimming upstream through water that looks clear, but contains dissolved sediment. **Predicting** *How would a boulder in a stream be likely to move?*

Direction of flow

Dissolved sediment

Larger particles pushed or rolled along streambed

Smaller particles move by bouncing

Suspended sediment

For: More on river erosion
Visit: PHSchool.com
Web Code: cfd-2033

# Erosion and Sediment Load

The power of a river to cause erosion and carry sediment depends on several factors. **A river's slope, volume of flow, and the shape of its streambed all affect how fast the river flows and how much sediment it can erode.**

A fast-flowing river carries more and larger particles of sediment. When a river slows down, it drops its sediment load. The larger particles of sediment are deposited first.

**Slope** Generally, if a river's slope increases, the water's speed also increases. A river's slope is the amount the river drops toward sea level over a given distance. If a river's speed increases, its sediment load and power to erode may increase. But other factors are also important in determining how much sediment the river erodes and carries.

**Volume of Flow** A river's flow is the volume of water that moves past a point on the river in a given time. As more water flows through a river, its speed increases. During a flood, the increased volume of water helps the river to cut more deeply into its banks and bed. When a river floods, its power to erode may increase by a hundredfold. A flooding river can carry huge amounts of sand, soil, and other sediments. It may move giant boulders as if they were pebbles.

**How does a river's slope affect its speed?**

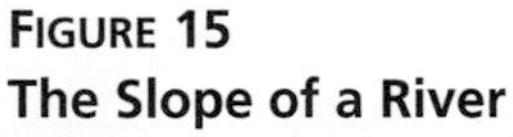

FIGURE 15
**The Slope of a River**
A river's slope is usually greatest near the river's source. As a river approaches its mouth, its slope lessens. **Inferring** *Where would you expect the water in this river to have the greatest amount of potential energy?*

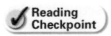

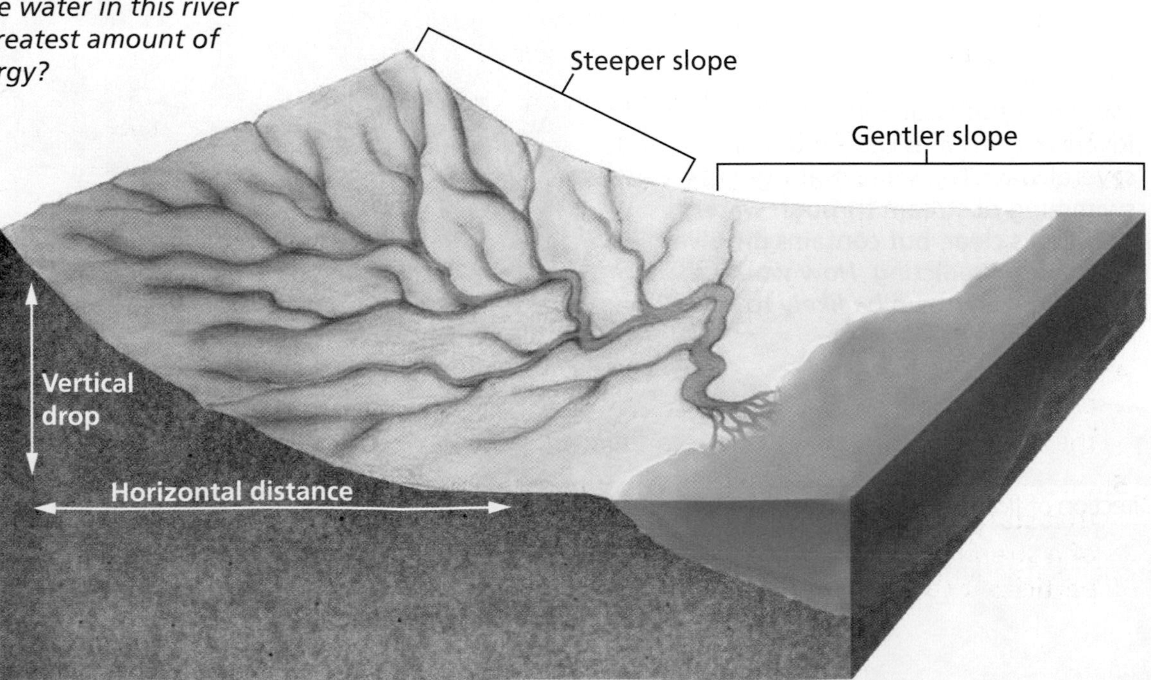

**Streambed Shape** A streambed's shape affects the amount of friction between the water and the streambed. **Friction** is the force that opposes the motion of one surface as it moves across another surface. Friction, in turn, affects a river's speed. Where a river is deep, less water comes in contact with the streambed. The reduced friction allows the river to flow faster. In a shallow river, much of the water comes in contact with the streambed. Therefore friction increases, reducing the river's speed.

A streambed is often full of boulders and other obstacles. This roughness prevents the water from flowing smoothly. Roughness thus increases friction and reduces the river's speed. Instead of moving downstream, the water moves every which way in a type of movement called **turbulence.** For example, a stream on a steep slope may flow at a slower speed than a large river on a gentle slope. Friction and turbulence slow the stream's flow. But a turbulent stream or river may have great power to erode.

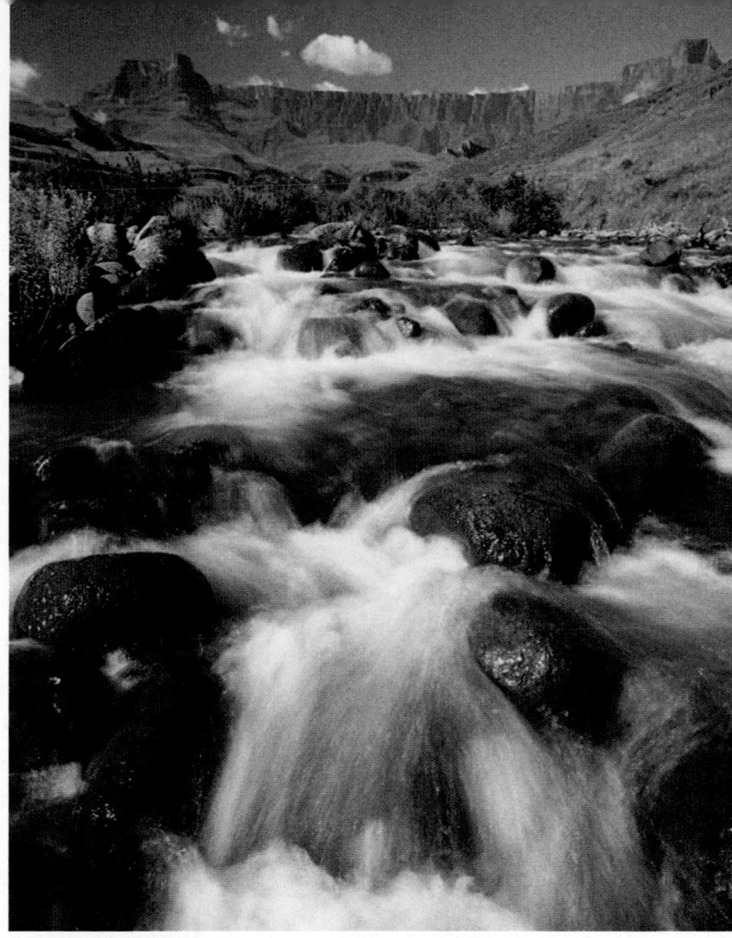

**FIGURE 16**
**Turbulence**
The turbulent flow of this stream increases the stream's power to cause erosion.

## Math Analyzing Data

### Sediment on the Move

The speed, or velocity, of a stream affects the size of the sediment particles the stream can carry. Study the graph, then answer the questions below.

1. **Reading Graphs** What variable is shown on the *x*-axis of the graph?
2. **Reading Graphs** What variable is shown on the *y*-axis of the graph?
3. **Interpreting Data** What is the speed at which a stream can move coarse sand? Small pebbles? Large boulders?
4. **Predicting** A stream's speed increases to about 600 cm per second during a flood. What are the largest particles the stream can move?
5. **Developing Hypotheses** Write a hypothesis that states the relationship between the speed of a stream and the size of the sediment particles it can move.

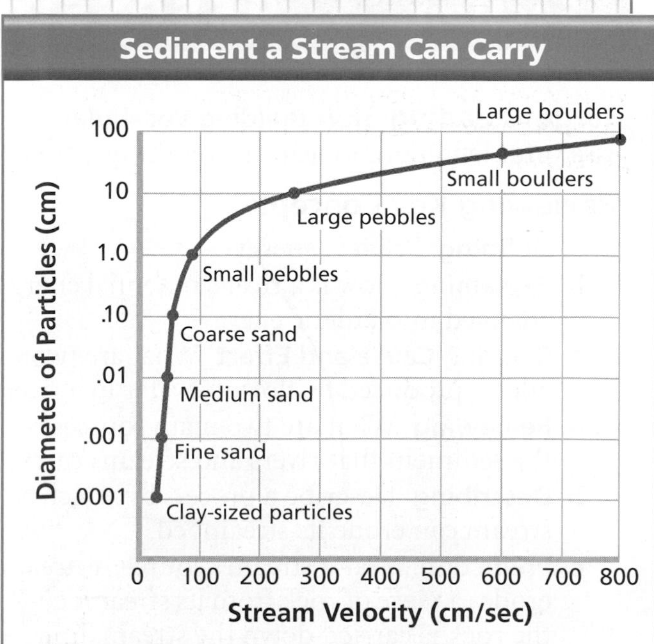

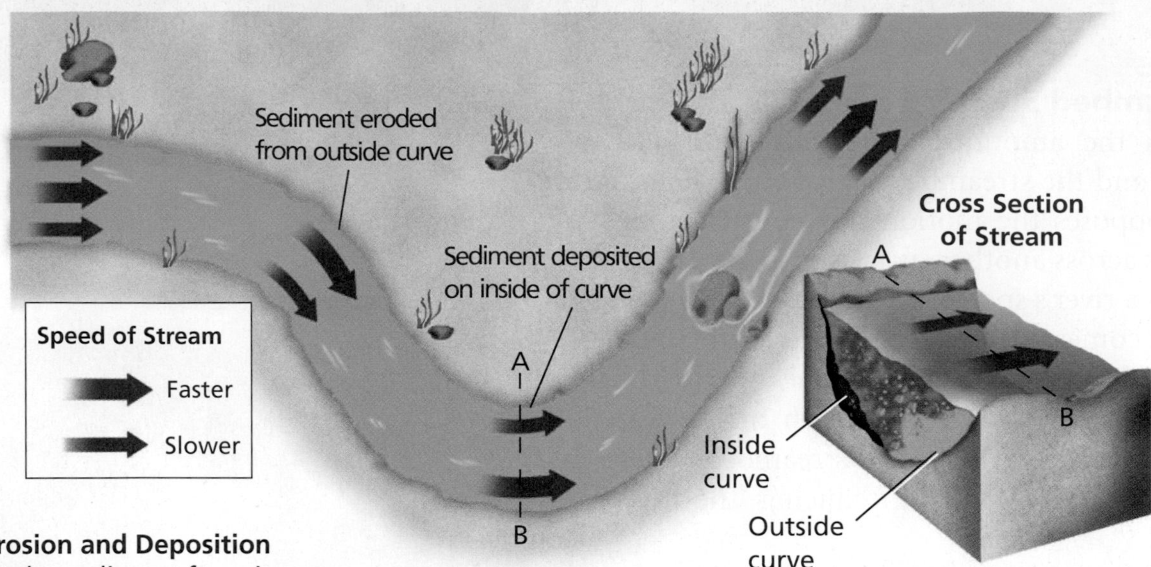


**FIGURE 17**
**Stream Erosion and Deposition**
A river erodes sediment from its banks on the outside curve and deposits sediment on the inside curve.
**Relating Cause and Effect** *Why does a river deposit sediment on the inside of a curve?*

**Factors Affecting Erosion and Deposition** Whether a river flows in a straight line or a curved line affects the way it erodes and deposits sediment. Where a river flows in a straight line, the water flows faster near the center of the river than along its sides. Deposition occurs along the sides of the river, where the water moves more slowly.

If a river curves, the water moves fastest along the outside of the curve. There, the river tends to cut into its bank, causing erosion. Sediment is deposited on the inside curve, where the water speed is slowest. You can see this process in Figure 17.

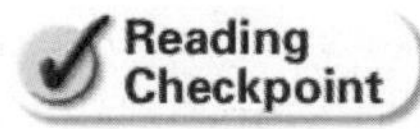

**Where a stream curves, in what part of the stream does the water flow fastest?**

## Section 3 Assessment

**Target Reading Skill Building Vocabulary**
Use your definitions to help answer the questions.

### Reviewing Key Concepts

1. a. **Defining** What is energy?
   b. **Explaining** How is a river's potential energy changed into kinetic energy?
   c. **Relating Cause and Effect** What are two effects produced by flowing water in a river?
2. a. **Reviewing** What are two main sources of the sediment that rivers and streams carry?
   b. **Describing** Describe a process by which a stream can erode its streambed.
   c. **Predicting** Near a stream's source, a stream erodes a piece of rock from its streambed. As the rock is carried down the stream, how will its size and shape change? Explain.
3. a. **Identifying** What three factors affect how fast a river flows?
   b. **Interpreting Diagrams** Study Figure 17 above. Over time, what will happen to the river's bank at B? Why?

### Writing in Science

**Comparison Paragraph** A river transports different types of sediment particles from its source to its mouth: tiny clay particles, grains of sand, pebbles, and boulders. Write a paragraph that compares clay particles and pebbles in terms of how they move, how fast they travel, and how their potential energy changes during the journey.

Section 4

# Glaciers

## Reading Preview

### Key Concepts

- What are the two kinds of glaciers?
- How does a valley glacier form and move?
- How do glaciers cause erosion and deposition?

### Key Terms

- glacier • continental glacier
- ice age • valley glacier
- plucking • till • moraine • kettle

### Target Reading Skill

**Asking Questions** Before you read, preview the red headings. In a graphic organizer like the one below, ask a *what, how,* or *where* question for each heading. As you read, answer your questions.

**Glaciers**

| Question | Answer |
|---|---|
| What kinds of glaciers are there? | Valley glaciers and . . . |
| | |

## Lab zone Discover Activity

### How Do Glaciers Change the Land?

1. Put some sand in a small plastic container.
2. Fill the container with water and place the container in a freezer until the water turns to ice.
3. Remove the block of ice from the container. Hold the ice with a paper towel.

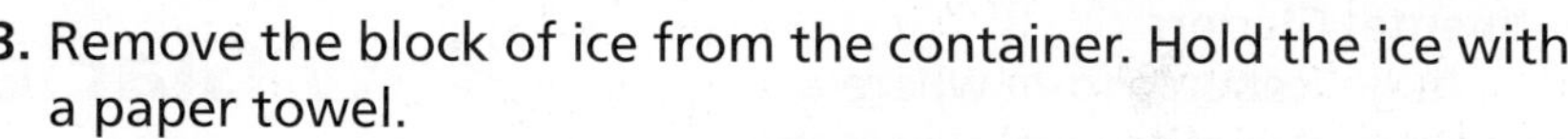

4. Rub the ice, sand side down, over a bar of soap. Observe what happens to the surface of the soap.

**Think It Over**

**Inferring** Based on your observations, how do you think moving ice could change the surface of the land?

You are on a boat trip near the coast of Alaska. You sail by vast evergreen forests and snow-capped mountains. Then, as your boat rounds a point of land, you see an amazing sight. A great mass of ice winds like a river between rows of mountains. Suddenly you hear a noise like thunder. Where the ice meets the sea, a giant chunk of ice breaks off and plunges into the water. Carefully, the pilot steers your boat around the iceberg and toward the mass of ice. It towers over your boat. You see that it is made up of solid ice that is deep blue and green as well as white. What is this river of ice?

▼ The Hubbard Glacier in Alaska

Huge icebergs form where Antarctica's continental glacier meets the ocean.


**FIGURE 18**
**Continental Glaciers**
Today, huge icebergs form where a continental glacier (above) meets the ocean. During the last ice age (below), a continental glacier covered most of northern North America.

**The Ice Age in North America**

Key
Area covered by continental glacier

## How Glaciers Form and Move

Geologists define a **glacier** as any large mass of ice that moves slowly over land. **There are two kinds of glaciers—continental glaciers and valley glaciers.**

**Continental Glaciers** A **continental glacier** is a glacier that covers much of a continent or large island. They can spread out over millions of square kilometers. Today, continental glaciers cover about 10 percent of Earth's land. They cover Antarctica and most of Greenland. In places, the glacier covering Antarctica is over 3 kilometers thick. Continental glaciers can flow in all directions as they move. Continental glaciers spread out much as pancake batter spreads out in a frying pan.

Many times in the past, continental glaciers have covered larger parts of Earth's surface. These times are known as **ice ages.** For example, beginning about 2.5 million years ago, continental glaciers covered about one third of Earth's land. The glaciers advanced and retreated, or melted back, several times. They finally retreated about 10,000 years ago.

**Valley Glaciers** A **valley glacier** is a long, narrow glacier that forms when snow and ice build up high in a mountain valley. The sides of mountains keep these glaciers from spreading out in all directions. Instead, they usually move down valleys that have already been cut by rivers. Valley glaciers are found on many high mountains. Although they are much smaller than continental glaciers, valley glaciers can be tens of kilometers long.

High in mountain valleys, temperatures seldom rise above freezing. Snow builds up year after year. The weight of more and more snow compacts the snow at the bottom into ice. **Glaciers can form only in an area where more snow falls than melts. Once the depth of snow and ice reaches more than 30 to 40 meters, gravity begins to pull the glacier downhill.**

Valley glaciers flow at a rate of a few centimeters to a few meters per day. But sometimes a valley glacier slides down more quickly in what is called a surge. A surging glacier can flow as much as 6 kilometers a year.

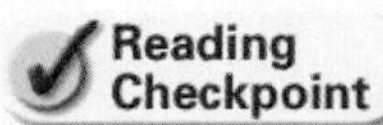


**On what type of landform are valley glaciers found?**

**FIGURE 19**
**Glacial Erosion**
As a glacier moves (above), plucking breaks pieces of bedrock from the ground. Erosion by glaciers (below) can carve a mountain peak into a sharp horn and grind out a **V**-shaped valley to form a **U**-shaped valley.
**Observing** *What other changes did the glacier produce in this landscape?*

## How Glaciers Shape the Land

The movement of a glacier changes the land beneath it. Although glaciers work slowly, they are a major force of erosion. **The two processes by which glaciers erode the land are plucking and abrasion.**

**Glacial Erosion** As a glacier flows over the land, it picks up rocks in a process called **plucking.** Beneath a glacier, the weight of the ice can break rocks apart. These rock fragments freeze to the bottom of the glacier. When the glacier moves, it carries the rocks with it. Figure 19 shows plucking by a glacier. Plucking can move even huge boulders.

Many rocks remain on the bottom of the glacier, and the glacier drags them across the land. This process, called abrasion, gouges and scratches the bedrock. You can see the results of erosion by glaciers in Figure 19.

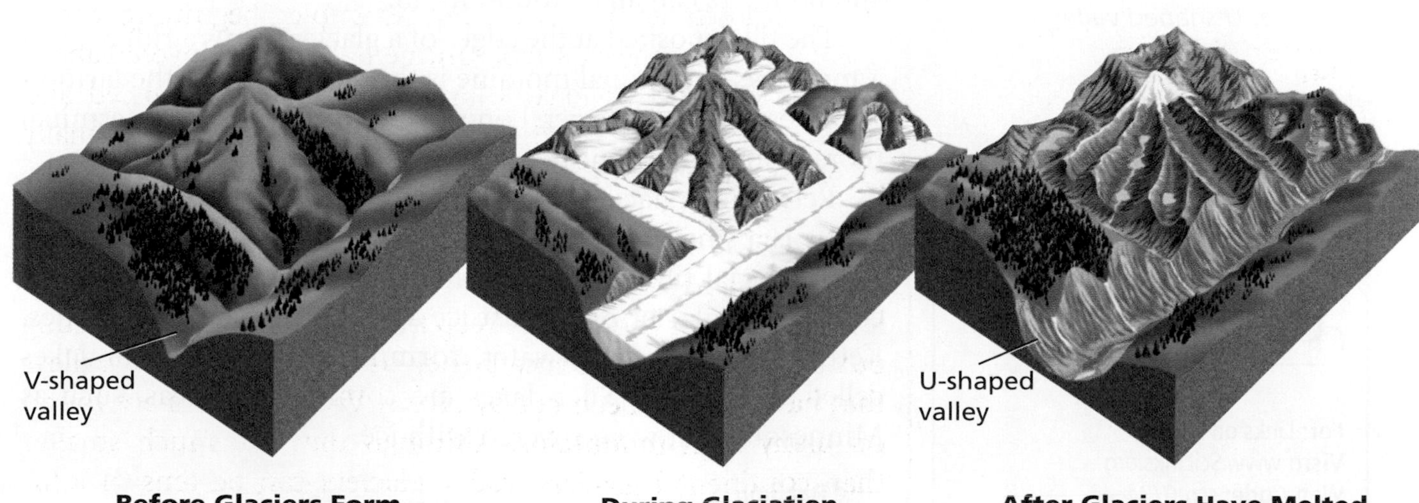

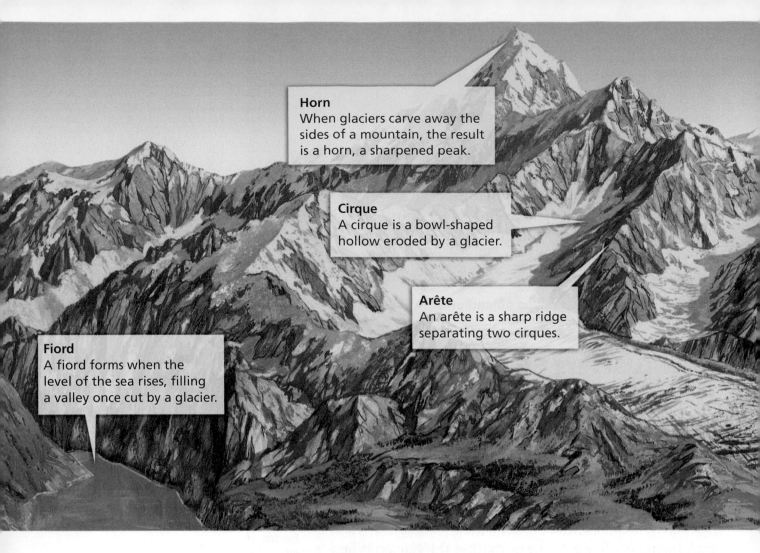

**Horn**
When glaciers carve away the sides of a mountain, the result is a horn, a sharpened peak.

**Cirque**
A cirque is a bowl-shaped hollow eroded by a glacier.

**Arête**
An arête is a sharp ridge separating two cirques.

**Fiord**
A fiord forms when the level of the sea rises, filling a valley once cut by a glacier.

FIGURE 20
**Glacial Landforms**
As glaciers advance and retreat, they sculpt the landscape by erosion and deposition.
**Classifying** *Classify these glacial features according to whether they result from erosion or deposition: drumlin, horn, cirque, moraine, U-shaped valley.*

**Glacial Deposition** A glacier gathers a huge amount of rock and soil as it erodes the land in its path. **When a glacier melts, it deposits the sediment it eroded from the land, creating various landforms.** These landforms remain for thousands of years after the glacier has melted. The mixture of sediments that a glacier deposits directly on the surface is called **till.** Till is made up of particles of many different sizes. Clay, silt, sand, gravel, and boulders can all be found in till.

The till deposited at the edges of a glacier forms a ridge called a **moraine.** A terminal moraine is the ridge of till at the farthest point reached by a glacier. Long Island in New York is a terminal moraine from the continental glaciers of the last ice age.

Retreating glaciers also create features called kettles. A **kettle** is a small depression that forms when a chunk of ice is left in glacial till. When the ice melts, the kettle remains. The continental glacier of the last ice age left behind many kettles. Kettles often fill with water, forming small ponds or lakes called kettle lakes. Such lakes are common in areas, such as Minnesota, that were covered with ice.

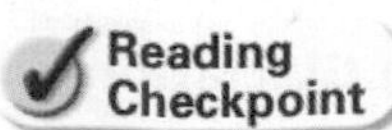

**What is a terminal moraine?**

**For:** Links on glaciers
**Visit:** www.SciLinks.org
**Web Code:** scn-0734

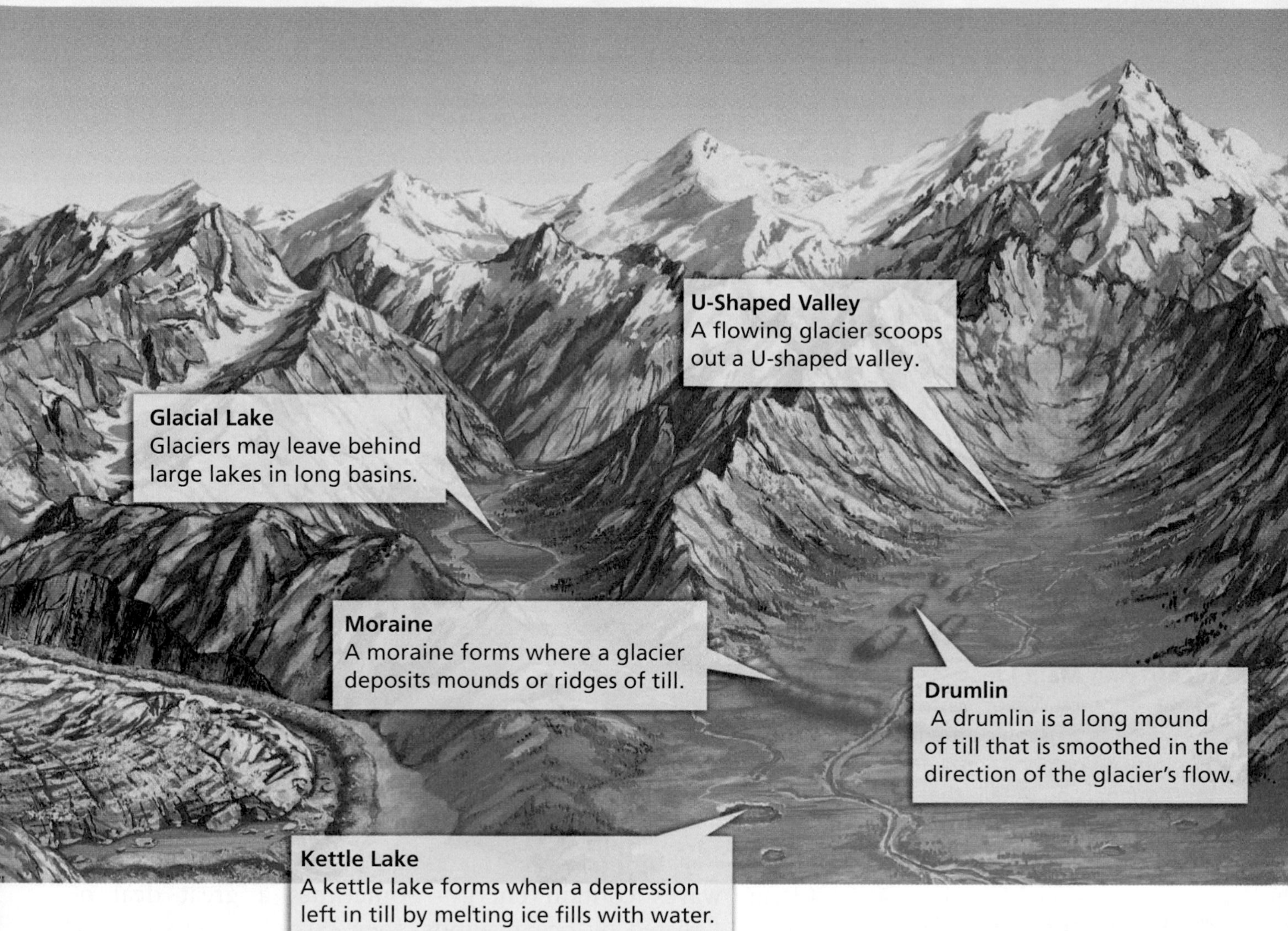

U-Shaped Valley
A flowing glacier scoops out a U-shaped valley.
Glacial Lake
Glaciers may leave behind large lakes in long basins.
Moraine
A moraine forms where a glacier deposits mounds or ridges of till.
Drumlin
A drumlin is a long mound of till that is smoothed in the direction of the glacier's flow.
Kettle Lake
A kettle lake forms when a depression left in till by melting ice fills with water.

## Section 4 Assessment

**Target Reading Skill** **Asking Questions** Use the answers to the questions you wrote about the headings to help you answer the questions below.

### Reviewing Key Concepts

1. a. **Defining** What is a continental glacier?
   b **Defining** What is a valley glacier?
   c. **Comparing and Contrasting** How are the two types of glaciers similar? How are they different?
2. a. **Reviewing** What condition is necessary for a glacier to form?
   b. **Explaining** How does a glacier move?
   c. **Relating Cause and Effect** Why does the snow that forms a glacier change to ice?
3. a. **Identifying** What are two ways in which glaciers erode Earth's surface?
   b. **Describing** How does glacial deposition occur?

### Writing in Science

**Travel Brochure** A travel agency wants people to go on a tour of a mountain region with many glaciers. Write a paragraph for a travel brochure describing what people will see on the tour. In your answer, include features formed by glacial erosion and deposition.

# 5 Waves

## Reading Preview

### Key Concepts

- What gives waves their energy?
- How do waves erode a coast?
- What features result from deposition by waves?

### Key Terms

- headland
- beach
- longshore drift
- spit

### Target Reading Skill

**Identifying Main Ideas** As you read Erosion by Waves, write the main idea in a graphic organizer like the one below. Then write three supporting details that further explain the main idea.

**Main Idea**

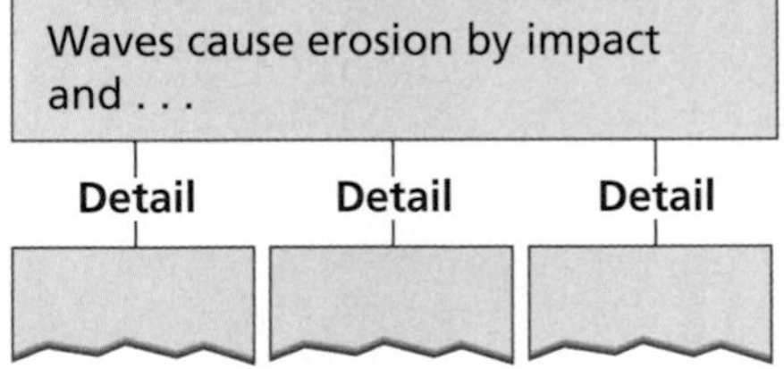


▼ **Waves on the Oregon coast**

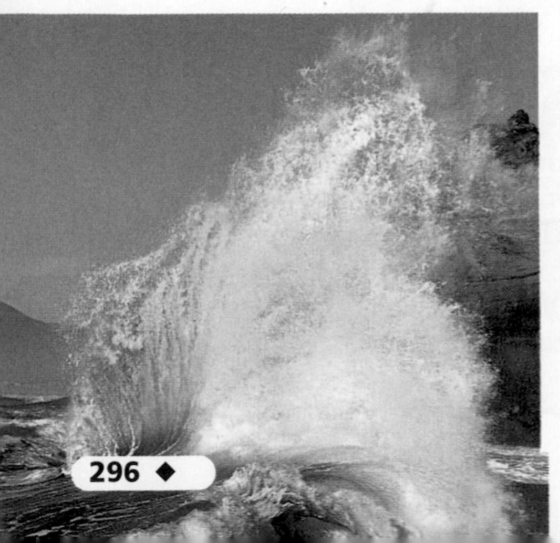

## Lab zone Discover **Activity**

### What Is Sand Made Of?

1. Collect a spoonful of sand from each of two different beaches.
2. Examine the first sample of beach sand with a hand lens.
3. Record the properties of the sand grains, for example, color and shape. Are the grains smooth and rounded or angular and rough?
4. Examine the second sample and repeat Step 3. How do the two samples compare?

**Think It Over**

**Posing Questions** What questions do you need to answer to understand beach sand? Use what you know about erosion and deposition to help you think of questions.

Ocean waves contain energy—sometimes a great deal of energy. Created by ocean winds, they carry energy vast distances across the Pacific Ocean. Acting like drills or buzz saws, the waves erode the solid rock of the coast into cliffs and caves. Waves also carry sediment that forms features such as beaches.

## How Waves Form

**The energy in waves comes from wind that blows across the water's surface.** As the wind makes contact with the water, some of its energy transfers to the water. Large ocean waves are the result of powerful storms far out at sea. But ordinary breezes can produce waves in lakes or small ponds.

The energy that water picks up from the wind causes water particles to move up and down as the wave goes by. But the water particles themselves don't move forward.

A wave changes as it approaches land. In deep water, a wave only affects the water near the surface. But as it approaches shallow water, the wave begins to drag on the bottom. The friction between the wave and the bottom causes the wave to slow down. Now the water actually does move forward with the wave. This forward-moving water provides the force that shapes the land along the shoreline.

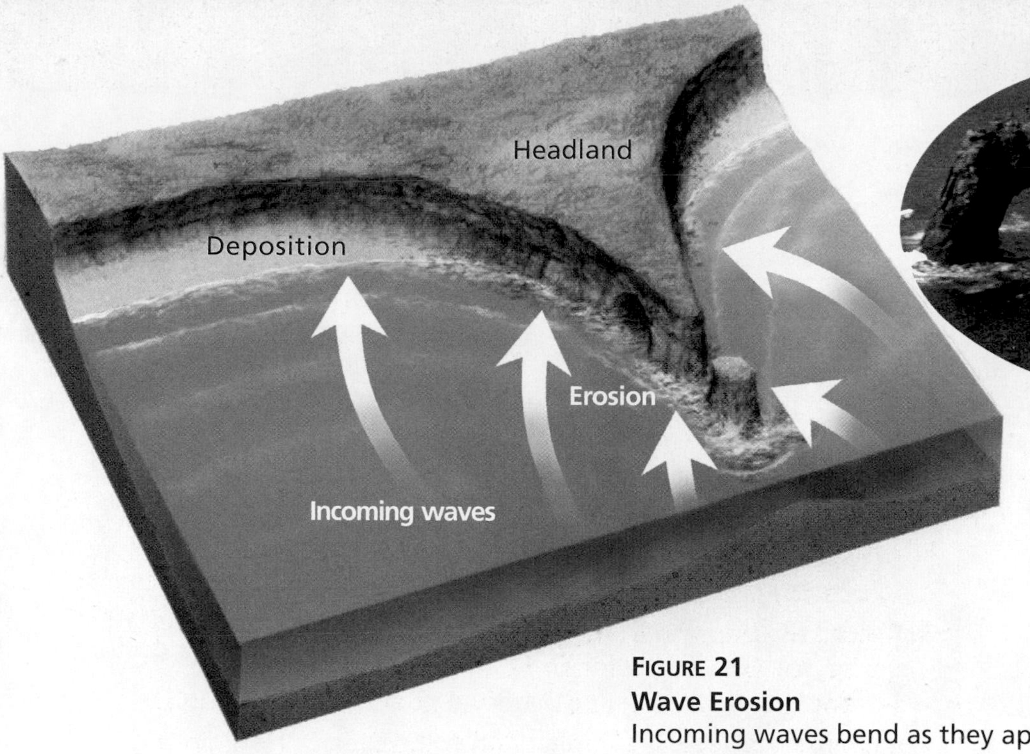

Headland

Deposition

Erosion

Incoming waves

▲ Sea arch

FIGURE 21
**Wave Erosion**
Incoming waves bend as they approach the shore, concentrating their energy on headlands. Waves have shaped these spectacular cliffs (right) along the coast of Cornwall in England.
**Relating Cause and Effect** *What will eventually happen to the headlands?*

# Erosion by Waves

Waves are the major force of erosion along coasts. **Waves shape the coast through erosion by breaking down rock and transporting sand and other sediment.**

**How Waves Erode** One way waves erode the land is by impact. Large waves can hit rocks along the shore with great force. This energy in waves can break apart rocks. Over time, waves can make small cracks larger. Eventually, the waves cause pieces of rock to break off.

Waves also erode by abrasion. As a wave approaches shallow water, it picks up sediment, including sand and gravel. This sediment is carried forward by the wave. When the wave hits land, the sediment wears away rock like sandpaper wearing away wood.

Waves coming to shore gradually change direction. The change in direction occurs as different parts of a wave begin to drag on the bottom. Notice how the waves in Figure 21 change direction as they approach the shore. The energy of these waves is concentrated on headlands. A **headland** is a part of the shore that sticks out into the ocean. Headlands stand out from the coast because they are made of harder rock that resists erosion by the waves. But, over time, waves erode the headlands and even out the shoreline.

**For:** Links on waves
**Visit:** www.SciLinks.org
**Web Code:** scn-0735

FIGURE 22
**The Changing Coast**
Erosion and deposition create a variety of features along a coast.
**Predicting** *What will eventually happen to the sea arch?*

**Landforms Created by Wave Erosion** When waves hit a steep, rocky coast, they strike the area again and again. Think of an ax striking the trunk of a tree. The cut gets bigger and deeper with each strike of the blade. Finally the tree falls. In a similar way, ocean waves erode the base of the land along a steep coast. Where the rock is softer, the waves erode the land faster. Over time the waves may erode a hollow area in the rock called a sea cave.

Eventually, waves may erode the base of a cliff so much that the rock above collapses. The result is a wave-cut cliff. You can see an example of such a cliff in Figure 22.

Another feature created by wave erosion is a sea arch. A sea arch forms when waves erode a layer of softer rock that underlies a layer of harder rock. If an arch collapses, the result might be a sea stack, a pillar of rock rising above the water.

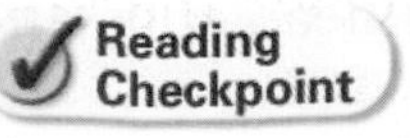

**Over a long period of time, what effect do waves have on a steep, rocky coast?**

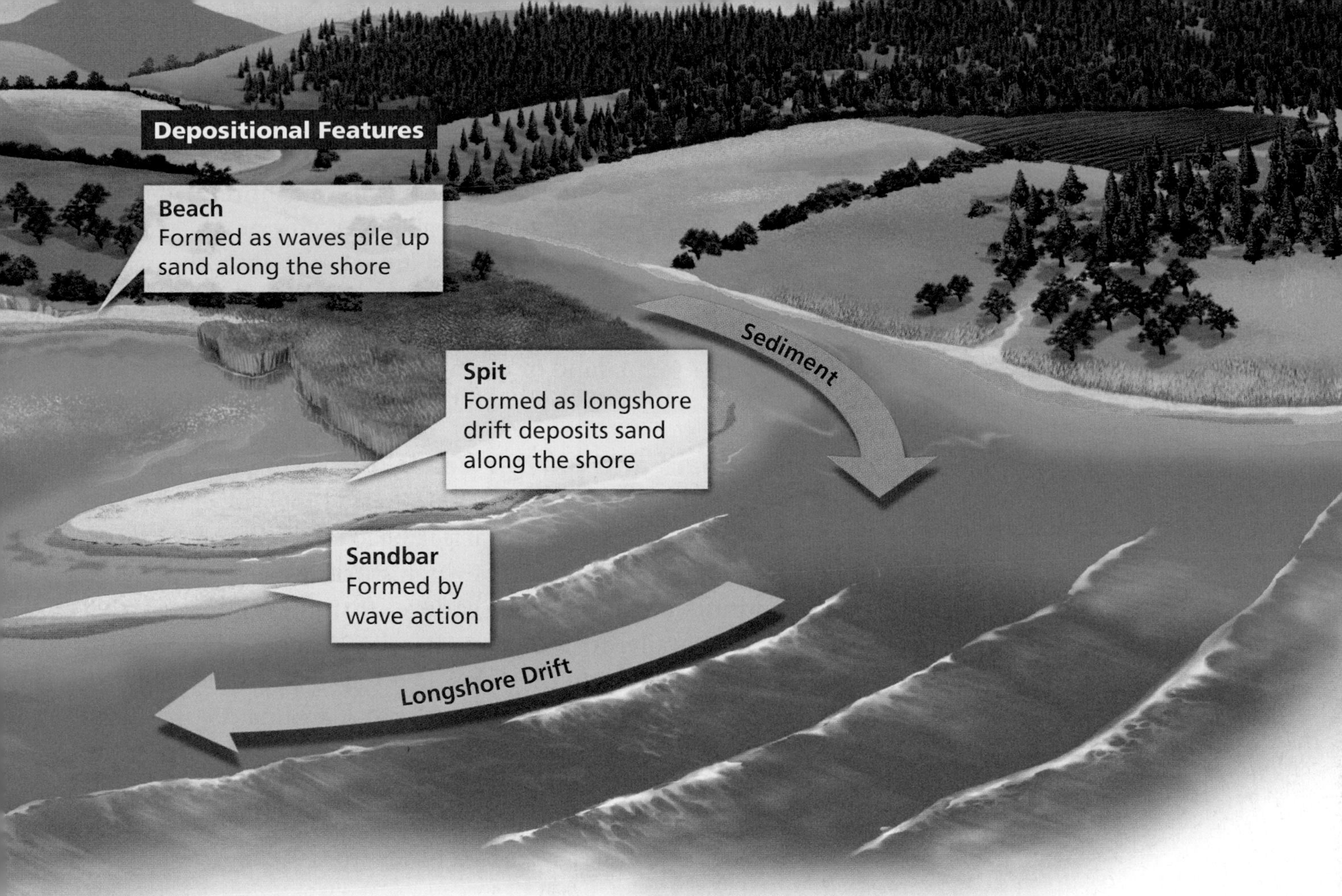


## Deposits by Waves

**Waves shape a coast when they deposit sediment, forming coastal features such as beaches, spits, and barrier beaches.** Deposition occurs when waves slow down, causing the water to drop its sediment. This process is similar to the deposition that occurs on a river delta when the river slows down and drops its sediment load.

**Beaches** As waves reach the shore, they drop the sediment they carry, forming a beach. A **beach** is an area of wave-washed sediment along a coast. The sediment deposited on beaches is usually sand. Most sand comes from rivers that carry eroded particles of rock into the ocean. But not all beaches are made of sand. Some beaches are made of small fragments of coral or sea shells piled up by wave action. Florida has many such beaches.

The sediment on a beach usually moves down the beach after it has been deposited. Waves usually hit the beach at an angle instead of straight on. These angled waves create a current that runs parallel to the coastline. As waves repeatedly hit the beach, some of the beach sediment moves down the beach with the current, in a process called **longshore drift.**

**Lab zone Skills Activity**

**Calculating** A sandy coast erodes at a rate of 1.25 m per year. But a severe storm can erode an additional 3.75 m from the shore. If 12 severe storms occur during a 50-year period, how much will the coast erode? If you wish, you may use an electronic calculator to find the answer.

**Spits** One result of longshore drift is the formation of a spit. A **spit** is a beach that projects like a finger out into the water. Spits form as a result of deposition by longshore drift. Spits occur where a headland or other obstacle interrupts longshore drift, or where the coast turns abruptly.

FIGURE 23
**Spits**
This aerial photograph shows how longshore drift can carry sand and deposit it to form a spit.
**Observing** *How many spits can you find in this image?*

**Sandbars and Barrier Beaches** Incoming waves carrying sand may build up sandbars, long ridges of sand parallel to the shore. A barrier beach is similar to a sandbar. A barrier beach forms when storm waves pile up large amounts of sand above sea level forming a long, narrow island parallel to the coast. Barrier beaches are found in many places along the Atlantic coast of the United States, such as the Outer Banks of North Carolina. People have built homes on many of these barrier beaches. But the storm waves that build up the beaches can also wash them away. Barrier beach communities must be prepared for the damage that hurricanes and other storms can bring.

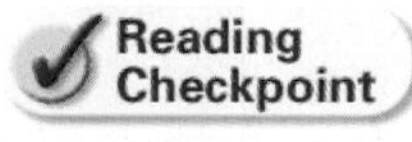

**How does a barrier beach form?**

## Section 5 Assessment

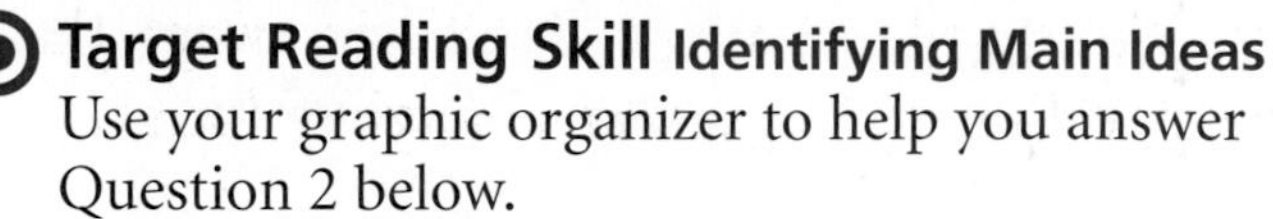

**Target Reading Skill Identifying Main Ideas** Use your graphic organizer to help you answer Question 2 below.

### Reviewing Key Concepts

1. a. **Explaining** What is the source of the energy in ocean waves?
   b. **Describing** How does an ocean wave change when it reaches shallow water?
   c. **Inferring** Does an ocean wave possess potential energy or kinetic energy? Explain.
2. a. **Identifying** What are two results of wave erosion along a coast?
   b. **Describing** What are two ways in which waves erode rock?
   c. **Sequencing** Place these features in the order in which they would probably form: sea stack, sea cave, headland, cliff, sea arch.
3. a. **Listing** What are three features formed by wave deposition?
   b. **Relating Cause and Effect** Beginning with the source of sand, explain the process by which a spit forms.

### Writing in Science

**Explaining a Process** Suppose that you live in a coastal area that has a barrier beach. Write a paragraph in which you explain the processes that formed the barrier beach. Also describe how the forces might change it over time.

Section 6

# Wind

## Reading Preview

### Key Concepts

- How does wind cause erosion?
- What features result from deposition by wind?

### Key Terms

- sand dune
- deflation
- loess

### Target Reading Skill

**Sequencing** As you read, make a flowchart like the one below that shows the process of wind erosion and deposition. Write each step of the process in a separate box in the flowchart in the order in which it occurs.

**Wind Erosion**

Wind picks up smallest particles of sediment.

↓

↓

## Lab zone Discover Activity

### How Does Moving Air Affect Sediment?

1. Cover the bottom of a pan with a flat layer of cornmeal 1–2 cm deep.
2. Gently blow over the layer of cornmeal using a straw to direct your breath. Observe what happens. **CAUTION:** *Do not blow the cornmeal in the direction of another student.*

**Think It Over**

**Observing** What changes did the wind you created make in the flat layer of cornmeal?

Imagine a landscape made almost entirely of sand. One such place is the Namib Desert. The desert stretches 1,900 kilometers along the coast of Namibia in Africa. In the southern half of the Namib are rows of giant sand dunes. A **sand dune** is a deposit of wind-blown sand. Some sand dunes in the Namib are more than 200 meters high and 15 kilometers long. Much of the sand in the dunes originally came from the nearby Orange River. Over thousands of years, wind has swept the sand across the desert, piling up huge, ever-changing dunes.

## How Wind Causes Erosion

Wind by itself is the weakest agent of erosion. Water, waves, moving ice, and even mass movement have more effect on the land. Yet wind can be a powerful force in shaping the land in areas where there are few plants to hold the soil in place. For example, few plants grow in deserts, so wind can easily move the grains of dry sand. **Wind causes erosion by deflation and abrasion.**

**Wind erosion constantly shapes the giant sand dunes in the Namib Desert of southwestern Africa. ▼**

**FIGURE 24**
**Wind Erosion**
Wind erosion moves sediment particles of different sizes in the three ways shown at right.
**Comparing and Contrasting**
*Compare the movement of sediment by wind with the movement of sediment by water in Figure 14 earlier in the chapter. How are the processes similar? How are they different?*

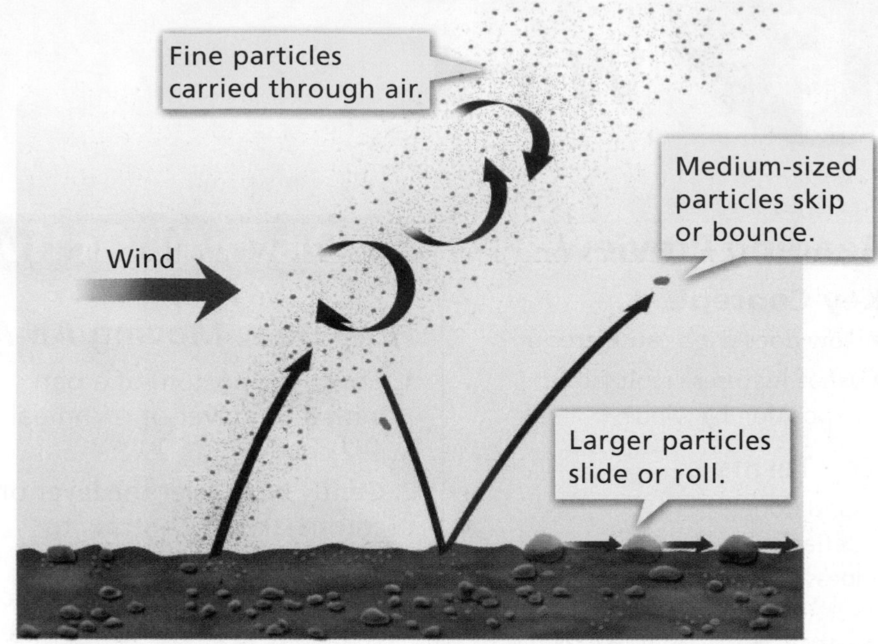
Fine particles carried through air.
Medium-sized particles skip or bounce.
Wind
Larger particles slide or roll.

**Deflation** The main way that wind causes erosion is by deflation. Geologists define **deflation** as the process by which wind removes surface materials. When wind blows over the land, it picks up the smallest particles of sediment. This sediment is made of bits of clay and silt. The stronger the wind, the larger the particles that it can pick up. Slightly heavier particles, such as sand, might skip or bounce for a short distance. But sand soon falls back to the ground. Strong winds can even roll heavier sediment particles over the ground. Figure 24 shows how wind erodes by deflation.

Deflation does not usually have a great effect on land. However, in parts of the Great Plains in the 1930s, deflation caused the loss of about 1 meter of topsoil in just a few years. In deserts, deflation can sometimes create an area of rock fragments called desert pavement. You can see an area of desert pavement in Figure 25. There, wind has blown away the smaller sediment. All that remains are rocky materials that are too heavy to be moved. Where there is already a slight depression in the ground, deflation can produce a bowl-shaped hollow called a blowout.

**FIGURE 25**
**Desert Pavement**
Wind erosion formed this desert pavement in the Arizona desert. Wind-driven sand may polish and shape individual stones.

**Abrasion** Abrasion by wind-carried sand can polish rock, but it causes little erosion. At one time, geologists thought that the sediment carried by wind cut the stone shapes seen in deserts. But now evidence shows that most desert landforms are the result of weathering and water erosion.

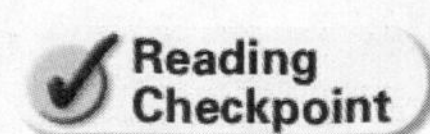
Reading Checkpoint
**Where would you be most likely to see evidence of wind erosion?**

## Wind Deposition

All the sediment picked up by wind eventually falls to the ground. This happens when the wind slows down or some obstacle, such as a boulder or a clump of grass, traps the windblown sand sediment. **Wind erosion and deposition may form sand dunes and loess deposits.** When the wind strikes an obstacle, the result is usually a sand dune. Sand dunes can be seen on beaches and in deserts where wind-blown sediment has built up.

**Sand Dunes** Sand dunes come in many shapes and sizes. Some are long, with parallel ridges, while others are U-shaped. They can also be very small or very large—some sand dunes in China have grown to heights of 500 meters. Sand dunes move over time. Little by little, the sand shifts with the wind from one side of the dune to the other. This process is shown in Figure 26. Sometimes plants begin growing on a dune. Plant roots can help to anchor the dune in one place.

**Loess Deposits** Sediment that is finer than sand, such as particles of clay and silt, is sometimes deposited in layers far from its source. This fine, wind-deposited sediment is **loess** (LES). Large loess deposits are found in central China and in such states as Nebraska, South Dakota, Iowa, Missouri, and Illinois. Loess helps to form fertile soil. Many areas with thick loess deposits are valuable farmlands.

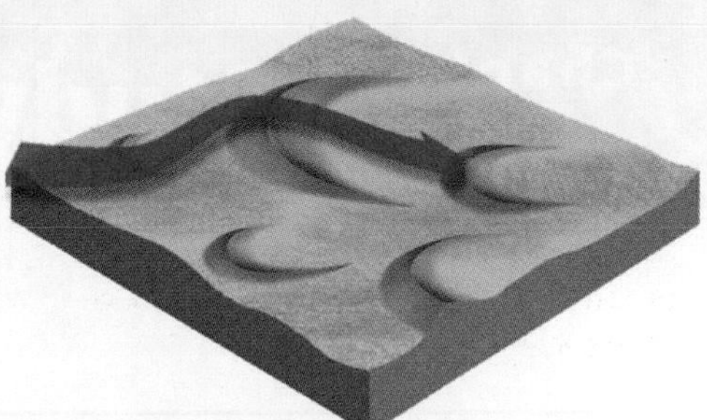

Crescent-shaped dunes form where the wind usually blows in the same direction.

Star-shaped dunes form where the wind direction changes frequently.

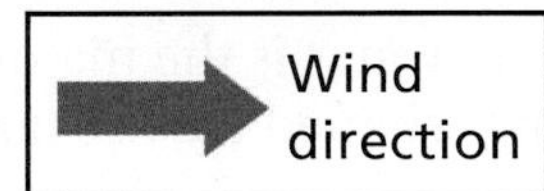


**FIGURE 26**
**Movement of Sand Dunes**
Wind direction is one factor that helps determine the shape and size of sand dunes.

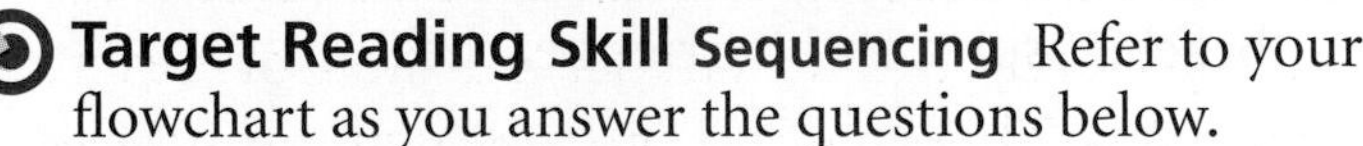

## Section 6 Assessment

**Target Reading Skill Sequencing** Refer to your flowchart as you answer the questions below.

### Reviewing Key Concepts

1. a. **Reviewing** What are two kinds of wind erosion?
   b. **Explaining** Explain how sediment particles of different sizes move during wind erosion.
   c. **Predicting** In a desert, soil containing a mixture of sand and small rocks is exposed to wind erosion. Over time, how would the land surface change? Explain.
2. a. **Relating Cause and Effect** What causes wind to deposit sand or other sediment?
   b. **Identifying** What are two types of features that result from wind deposition?
   c. **Problem Solving** How could sand dunes be held in place to keep them from drifting onto a parking lot?

### Lab zone At-Home Activity

**Desert Pavement** To model desert pavement, put a few coins in a shallow pan. Sprinkle enough flour over the coins to cover them. Then blow air gently through a straw across the surface of the flour. Be careful not to draw in any flour through the straw. Be certain the blown flour will not get in your or anyone else's eyes. Ask your family to predict what would happen if the "wind" blew for a long time.

**The BIG Idea** **Processes on Earth's Surface** Erosion and deposition by mass movements, flowing water, ice, waves, and wind wear down and build up the land.

## 1 Changing Earth's Surface

### Key Concepts

- Weathering, erosion, and deposition act together in a cycle that wears down and builds up Earth's surface.
- Gravity causes mass movement, including landslides, mudflows, slump, and creep.

### Key Terms

• erosion • sediment • deposition • gravity • mass movement

## 2 Water Erosion

### Key Concepts

- Moving water is the major agent of the erosion that has shaped Earth's land surface.
- Through erosion, a river creates valleys, waterfalls, flood plains, meanders, and oxbow lakes.
- Deposition creates alluvial fans and deltas. It can also add soil to a river's flood plain.
- Groundwater can cause erosion through a process of chemical weathering.

### Key Terms

• runoff • rill • gully • stream • tributary • flood plain • meander • oxbow lake • alluvial fan • delta • groundwater • stalactite • stalagmite • karst topography

## 3 The Force of Moving Water

### Key Concepts

- As gravity pulls water down a slope, the water's potential energy changes to kinetic energy.
- Most sediment washes or falls into a river as a result of mass movement and runoff.
- A river's slope, volume of flow, and the shape of its streambed all affect how fast the river flows and how much sediment it can erode.

### Key Terms

• energy • potential energy • kinetic energy • abrasion • load • friction • turbulence

## 4 Glaciers

### Key Concepts

- There are two kinds of glaciers—continental glaciers and valley glaciers.
- Glaciers can form only in an area where more snow falls than melts. Once the depth of snow and ice reaches more than 30 to 40 meters, gravity begins to pull the glacier downhill.
- The two processes by which glaciers erode the land are plucking and abrasion.
- When a glacier melts, it deposits the sediment it eroded from the land, creating various landforms.

### Key Terms

• glacier • continental glacier • ice age • valley glacier • plucking • till • moraine • kettle

## 5 Waves

### Key Concepts

- The energy in waves comes from wind that blows across the water's surface.
- Waves shape the coast through erosion by breaking down rock and transporting sand and other sediment.
- Waves shape a coast when they deposit sediment, forming coastal features such as beaches, spits, and barrier beaches.

### Key Terms

• headland • beach • longshore drift • spit

## 6 Wind

### Key Concepts

- Wind causes erosion by deflation and abrasion.
- Wind erosion and deposition may form sand dunes and loess deposits.

### Key Terms

• sand dune • deflation • loess

# Review and Assessment

For: Self-Assessment
Visit: PHSchool.com
Web Code: cfa-2030

## Organizing Information

**Flowcharts** Copy the flowchart about stream formation onto a separate sheet of paper. Then complete it and add a title. (For more on flowcharts, see the Skills Handbook).

**Stream Formation**

Raindrops strike ground.
↓
Runoff forms.
↓
a. ___?___
↓
b. ___?___
↓
c. ___?___
↓
d. ___?___

## Reviewing Key Terms

**Choose the letter of the best answer.**

1. The eroded materials carried by water or wind are called
   a. stalactites.
   b. desert pavement.
   c. sediment.
   d. moraines.
2. The downhill movement of eroded materials is known as
   a. mass movement.
   b. abrasion.
   c. deposition.
   d. deflation.
3. Where a streambed is rough, the stream flows more slowly because of
   a. sediment.
   b. friction.
   c. deposition.
   d. potential energy.
4. A mass of rock and soil deposited directly by a glacier is called
   a. load. b. till.
   c. loess. d. erosion.
5. The erosion of sediment by wind is
   a. deposition. b. deflation.
   c. plucking. d. glaciation.

**If the statement is true, write *true*. If it is false, change the underlined word or words to make the statement true.**

6. The process by which sediment in water settles in new locations is <u>mass movement</u>.
7. <u>Groundwater</u> that flows in a thin layer over the land causes sheet erosion.
8. Because it is moving, flowing water has a type of energy called <u>kinetic energy</u>.
9. A looplike bend in the river is a <u>meander</u>.
10. The sediment deposited at the edge of a glacier forms a ridge called a <u>kettle</u>.

## Writing in Science

**Article** Suppose that you have just returned from a visit to a limestone cave, such as Mammoth Cave in Kentucky. Write an article describing your visit to the cave. Include how the cave formed, what you saw during your visit, and how features inside the cave developed.

*Erosion and Deposition*
Video Preview
Video Field Trip
▶ Video Assessment

# Review and Assessment

## Checking Concepts

11. What agents of erosion are assisted by the force of gravity?
12. How do a river's slope and volume of flow affect the river's sediment load?
13. What is turbulence? How does it affect the speed of a river and the river's power to cause erosion?
14. Where is the speed of the flowing water in a river the slowest? Explain.
15. What are ice ages?
16. How does a kettle lake form?
17. How does a loess deposit form?

## Thinking Critically

18. **Comparing and Contrasting** Compare and contrast landslides and mudflows.
19. **Applying Concepts** Under what conditions would you expect abrasion to cause the most erosion of a riverbed?
20. **Making Judgments** A salesperson offers to sell your family a new house right on a riverbank for very little money. Why might your family hesitate to buy this house?
21. **Relating Cause and Effect** What caused the features labeled A, B, and C in the diagram below to form? Explain.

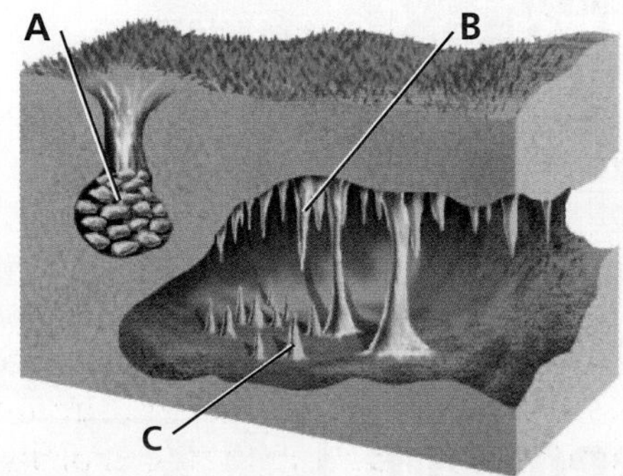


22. **Problem Solving** Suppose you are a geologist studying a valley glacier. What method could you use to tell if it is advancing or retreating?
23. **Inferring** You see a sandy beach along a coastline. Where did the sand come from?

## Applying Skills

**Use the table below to answer Questions 24–26.**

*The table shows how a river's volume of flow and sediment load change over six months.*

| Month | Volume of Flow (cubic meters/ second) | Sediment Load (metric tons/day) |
|---|---|---|
| January | 1.5 | 200 |
| February | 1.7 | 320 |
| March | 2.6 | 725 |
| April | 4.0 | 1,600 |
| May | 3.2 | 1,100 |
| June | 2.8 | 900 |

24. **Graphing** Make one graph with the month on the *x*-axis and the volume of flow on the *y*-axis. Make a second graph with the sediment load on the *y*-axis. Compare your two graphs. When were the river's volume of flow and load the greatest? The lowest?
25. **Developing Hypotheses** Use your graphs to develop a hypothesis about the relationship between volume of flow and sediment load.
26. **Relating Cause and Effect** What may have occurred in the river's drainage basin in April to cause the changes in volume of flow and sediment load? Explain.

## Lab zone Chapter Project

**Performance Assessment** Now you are ready to present to your class. Explain which types of soil you chose and why you chose them. Discuss the design of your dam, the tests you conducted, and the results. In your journal, write about the easiest and hardest parts of this project. How would you design your dam differently if you did the project again?

# Standardized Test Prep

### Test-Taking Tip

**Eliminating Incorrect Answers**

When answering a multiple-choice question, you can often eliminate some answer choices immediately because they are clearly incorrect. By doing this, you increase your odds of choosing the correct answer.

***Sample Question***

What is the slow, downhill mass movement of rock and soil, caused by gravity?

**A** a landslide
**B** creep
**C** runoff
**D** a glacier

***Answer***

You can eliminate **C** and **D,** because neither are examples of mass movement due to gravity. Runoff is water moving over the land, and a glacier is a moving mass of ice. **A** is incorrect because a landslide is a rapid type of mass movement. The correct answer is **B.**

**Choose the letter of the best answer.**

**1.** As a stream flows from a mountainous area to a flatter area, what happens to the size of the sediment the stream normally carries?
**A** The sediment size does not change.
**B** The sediment size carried by the stream increases.
**C** The sediment size carried by the stream decreases.
**D** The stream drops all the sediment it was carrying.

**2.** How does wind carry sediment particles?
**F** as fine particles carried through the air
**G** as particles that bounce along the ground
**H** as larger particles that slide or roll along the ground
**J** all of the above

*Use the diagram below and your knowledge of science to answer Questions 3–4.*

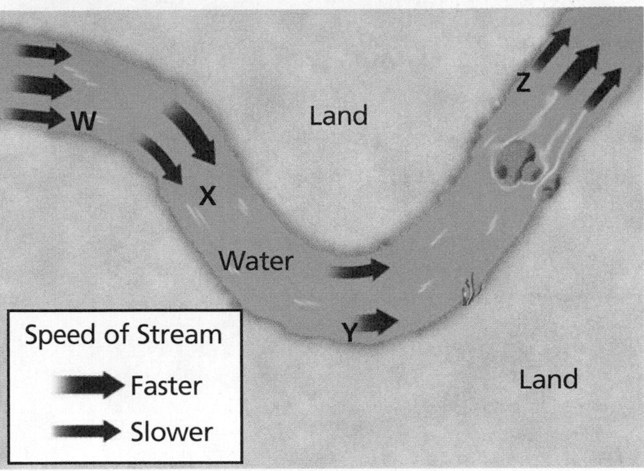


**3.** What is the erosional feature in the diagram?
**A** a meander
**B** a delta
**C** a flood plain
**D** karst topography

**4.** In the diagram, where is the speed of the stream the greatest?
**F** at Y
**G** at X
**H** at W
**J** at Z

**5.** What is the process by which weathered rock, sediment, and soil is moved from place to place?
**A** erosion
**B** delta formation
**C** running water
**D** runoff

### Constructed Response

**6.** Describe how gravity is involved in the erosion of Earth's surface by mass movement, running water, and glaciers. Be sure to first explain what erosion is.

# Chapter 10 A Trip Through Geologic Time

## The BIG Idea
Earth's History

**What have geologists learned from the study of Earth's past?**

### Chapter Preview

1. **Fossils**
   *Discover* What's in a Rock?
   *Try This* Sweet Fossils
2. **The Relative Age of Rocks**
   *Discover* Which Layer Is the Oldest?
   *Try This* Sampling a Sandwich
   *Active Art* Index Fossils
   *Skills Lab* Finding Clues to Rock Layers
3. **Radioactive Dating**
   *Discover* How Long Till It's Gone?
   *Math Skills* Percentage
4. **The Geologic Time Scale**
   *Discover* This Is Your Life!
5. **Early Earth**
   *Discover* How Could Planet Earth Form in Space?
   *Skills Activity* Calculating
6. **Eras of Earth's History**
   *Discover* What Do Fossils Reveal About Earth's History?
   *Analyzing Data* Mass Extinctions
   *Try This* Life and Times
   *Skills Lab* As Time Goes By

A paleontologist examines a fossilized dinosaur skeleton in the Denver Museum of Nature and Science.

*A Trip Through Geologic Time*

▶ Video Preview
Video Field Trip
Video Assessment

Lab zone™ Chapter **Project**

## A Journey Back in Time

This chapter will take you on a journey through geologic time. You will learn how fossils reveal the history of life on Earth. To guide you on your journey, you and your classmates will make a timeline showing the many periods of geologic time.

**Your Goal** To become an expert on one geologic time period and assist in constructing a timeline

To complete this project, you must

- research a geologic time period of your choice
- create a travel brochure that shows what life was like in this time period
- illustrate your time period for the timeline
- follow the safety guidelines in Appendix A

**Plan It!** Begin by selecting a time period you would like to investigate. Check with your teacher to be sure that all the time periods will be covered by members of your class. Then, collect information on your time period's animals, plants, and environment. Use this information to write a travel brochure about your time period. Create illustrations that depict your time period and place them on the timeline. Use the travel brochure to present your geologic time period to your classmates.

Section 1

# Fossils

## Reading Preview

### Key Concepts

- How do fossils form?
- What are the different kinds of fossils?
- What does the fossil record tell about organisms and environments of the past?

### Key Terms

- fossil
- sedimentary rock
- mold
- cast
- petrified fossil
- carbon film
- trace fossil
- paleontologist
- scientific theory
- evolution
- extinct

### Target Reading Skill

**Using Prior Knowledge** Before you read, look at the section headings and visuals to see what this section is about. Then write what you know about fossils in a graphic organizer like the one below. As you read, write what you learn.

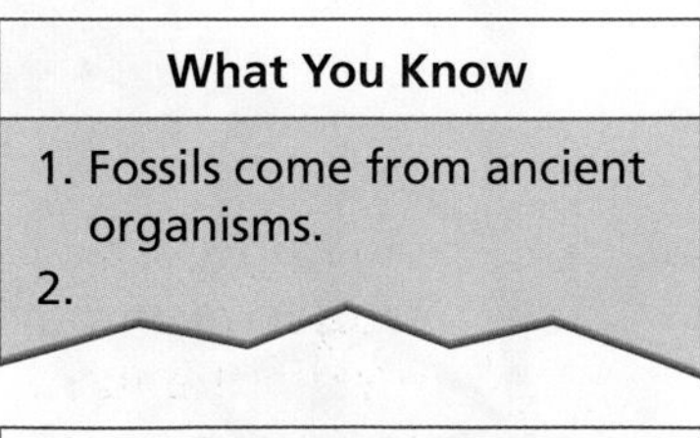

## Lab zone Discover Activity

### What's in a Rock?

1. Use a hand lens to carefully observe the rock sample provided by your teacher. You may also study the photograph of limestone below.
2. Make a drawing of any shapes you see in the rock. Include as many details as you can. Beneath your drawing, write a description of what you see.

**Think It Over**

**Inferring** What do you think the rock contains? How do you think the shapes you observed in the rock got there?

Millions of years ago, a fish died and sank to the bottom of a lake. Before the fish could decay completely, layers of sediment covered it. Minerals in the sediment seeped into the fish's bones. Slowly, pressure changed the sediment into solid rock. Inside the rock, the fish became a fossil.

**Fossils** are the preserved remains or traces of living things. Fossils like the ancient fish in Figure 1 provide evidence of how life has changed over time. Fossils can also help scientists infer how Earth's surface has changed. Fossils are clues to what past environments were like.

## How a Fossil Forms

**Most fossils form when living things die and are buried by sediments. The sediments slowly harden into rock and preserve the shapes of the organisms.** Fossils are usually found in sedimentary rock. **Sedimentary rock** is the type of rock that is made of hardened sediment. Recall that sediment is the material removed by erosion. Sediment is made up of rock particles or the remains of living things. Sandstone, limestone, and coal are examples of sedimentary rocks. Most fossils form from animals or plants that once lived in or near quiet water such as swamps, lakes, or shallow seas where sediments build up. In Figure 1, you can see how a fossil might form.

**FIGURE 1**
**How a Fossil Forms**
A fossil may form when sediment quickly covers an animal's body. **Classifying** *In what type of rock would this fossil be found?*

An animal dies and sinks into shallow water.
1

Sediment covers the animal.
2

The sediment becomes rock, preserving parts of the animal.
3

Weathering and erosion eventually expose the fossil at the surface.
4

When an organism dies, its soft parts often decay quickly or are eaten by animals. That is why only hard parts of an organism generally leave fossils. These hard parts include bones, shells, teeth, seeds, and woody stems. It is rare for the soft parts of an organism to become a fossil.

For a fossil to form, the remains or traces of an organism must be protected from decay. Then several processes may cause a fossil to form. **Fossils found in rock include molds and casts, petrified fossils, carbon films, and trace fossils. Other fossils form when the remains of organisms are preserved in substances such as tar, amber, or ice.**

**Molds and Casts** The most common fossils are molds and casts. Both copy the shape of ancient organisms. A **mold** is a hollow area in sediment in the shape of an organism or part of an organism. A mold forms when the hard part of the organism, such as a shell, is buried in sediment.

Later, water carrying dissolved minerals and sediment may seep into the empty space of a mold. If the water deposits the minerals and sediment there, the result is a cast. A **cast** is a solid copy of the shape of an organism. A cast is the opposite of its mold. Both the mold and cast preserve details of the animal's structure. Figure 1 shows a process that could form a mold and cast fossil.

For: Links on fossils
Visit: www.SciLinks.org
Web Code: scn-0741

**Petrified Fossils** A fossil may form when the remains of an organism become petrified. The term *petrified* means "turned into stone." **Petrified fossils** are fossils in which minerals replace all or part of an organism. The fossil tree trunks shown in Figure 2 are examples of petrified wood. These fossils formed after sediment covered the wood. Then water rich in dissolved minerals seeped into spaces in the plant's cells. Over time, the minerals come out of solution and harden, filling in all of the spaces. Some of the original wood remains, but the minerals have hardened and preserved it.

**Carbon Films** Another type of fossil is a **carbon film,** an extremely thin coating of carbon on rock. How does a carbon film form? Remember that all living things contain carbon. When sediment buries an organism, some of the materials that make up the organism evaporate, or become gases. These gases escape from the sediment, leaving carbon behind. Eventually, only a thin film of carbon remains. This process can preserve the delicate parts of plant leaves and insects.

**Trace Fossils** Most types of fossils preserve the shapes of ancient animals and plants. In contrast, **trace fossils** provide evidence of the activities of ancient organisms. A fossilized footprint is one example of a trace fossil. A dinosaur made the fossil footprint shown in Figure 2. The mud or sand that the animal stepped in was buried by layers of sediment. Slowly the sediment became solid rock, preserving the footprint for millions of years.

FIGURE 2

## Kinds of Fossils

In addition to petrified fossils, fossils may be molds and casts, carbon films, trace fossils, or preserved remains.
**Classifying** *You split apart a rock and find the imprint of a seashell on one half of the rock. What type of fossil have you found?*

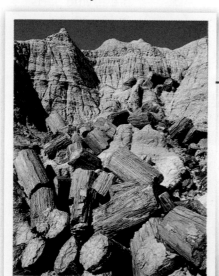

▲ **Petrified Fossils**
These petrified tree trunks in Arizona were formed 200 million years ago, yet look as if they were just cut down.

**Molds and Casts ▼**
The fossil mold (left) clearly shows the shape of the animal called *Cryptolithus*. So does the fossil cast (right). *Cryptolithus* lived in the oceans about 450 million years ago.

▲ **Carbon Films**
This carbon film fossil of insects is between 5 million and 23 million years old.

From fossil footprints, scientists can find answers to questions about an animal's size and behavior. Did the animal walk on two or four legs? Did it live alone or as part of a group?

Other types of trace fossils also provide clues about ancient organisms. A trail or burrow can give clues about the size and shape of an organism, where it lived, and how it obtained food.

**Preserved Remains** Some processes preserve the remains of organisms with little or no change. For example, some remains are preserved when organisms become trapped in tar. Tar is sticky oil that seeps from Earth's surface. Many fossils preserved in tar have been found at the Rancho La Brea tar pits in Los Angeles, California. Thousands of years ago, animals came to drink the water that covered these pits. Somehow, they became stuck in the tar and then died. The tar soaked into their bones, preserving the bones from decay.

Ancient organisms also have been preserved in amber. Amber is the hardened resin, or sap, of evergreen trees. First, an insect is trapped on sticky resin. After the insect dies, more resin covers it, sealing it from air and protecting its body from decay.

Freezing can also preserve remains. The frozen remains of woolly mammoths, huge ancient relatives of elephants, have been found in very cold regions of Siberia and Alaska. Freezing has preserved even the mammoths' hair and skin.

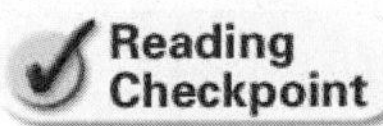


**What are three ways in which the remains of an organism can be preserved with little change?**

**Lab zone Try This Activity**

### Sweet Fossils

1. Wrap a piece of clay around one sugar cube so that half of it is covered with clay.
2. Wrap clay entirely around a second sugar cube and seal it tightly.
3. Drop both cubes into a bowl of water, along with an uncovered sugar cube.
4. Stir until the uncovered sugar cube dissolves completely.
5. Remove the other cubes from the water and examine the remains.

**Observing** Describe the appearance of the two sugar cubes. Did the clay preserve the sugar cubes? How does this activity model the way fossils form?

▲ **Dinosaur Footprint**

◀ **Trace Fossils**
These students are measuring a dinosaur footprint in Zilker Park in Austin, Texas.

**Amber**
A fossil preserved in amber provides a window into the history of past life on Earth. Body parts, including the hairlike bristles on an insect's legs, its antennae, and its delicate wings, are often perfectly preserved. ▼

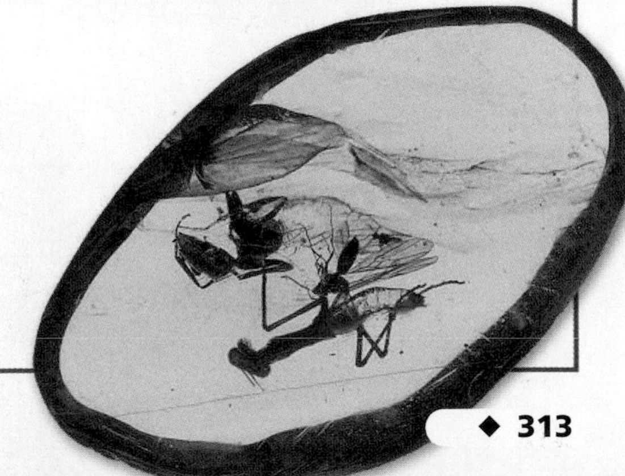

FIGURE 3
### Fossil Clues to Past Environments
Fossils of many different kinds of organisms were formed in this ancient lakeshore environment. **Inferring** *How do you think the fossil of the bat was preserved?*

## Change Over Time

Scientists who study fossils are called **paleontologists** (pay lee un TAHL uh jists). Paleontologists collect fossils from sedimentary rocks all over the world. They use this information to determine what past life forms were like. They want to learn what these organisms ate, what ate them, and in what kind of environment they lived.

Paleontologists also classify organisms. They group similar organisms together. They arrange organisms in the order in which they lived, from earliest to latest. Together, all the information that paleontologists have gathered about past life is called the fossil record. **The fossil record provides evidence about the history of life and past environments on Earth. The fossil record also shows that different groups of organisms have changed over time.**

**Fossils and Past Environments** Paleontologists use fossils to build up a picture of Earth's past environments. The fossils found in an area tell whether the area was a shallow bay, an ocean bottom, or a freshwater swamp.

Fossils also provide evidence about the past climate of a region. For example, coal has been found in Antarctica. But coal only forms from the remains of plants that grow in warm, swampy regions. As you probably know, thick layers of ice and snow now cover Antarctica. The presence of coal shows that the climate of Antarctica was once much warmer than it is today.

Scientists can use fossils to learn about changes in Earth's surface. For example, the fossils in Figure 3 are about 50 million years old. They were found in a region of dry plains and plateaus in the state of Wyoming. From these fossils, scientists have inferred that back then the region had many shallow lakes and swamps. Lush forests with many different kinds of plants and animals flourished in a warm, subtropical climate.

**FIGURE 4**
**Ancestry of the Elephant**
From fossils, scientists have reconstructed the paleomastodon (left). This animal had a short trunk and short tusks on both upper and lower jaws. The paleomastodon is an ancestor of the modern elephant (right).
**Inferring** *Why is the paleomastodon only known from its fossils?*

**Change and the Fossil Record** The fossil record reveals a surprising fact: Fossils occur in a particular order. Older rocks contain fossils of simpler organisms. Younger rocks contain fossils of more complex organisms. In other words, the fossil record shows that life on Earth has evolved, or changed over time. Simple, one-celled organisms have given rise to complex plants and animals.

The fossil record provides evidence to support the theory of evolution. A **scientific theory** is a well-tested concept that explains a wide range of observations. **Evolution** is the gradual change in living things over long periods of time.

The fossil record shows that millions of types of organisms have evolved. But many others have become extinct. A type of organism is **extinct** if it no longer exists and will never again live on Earth.

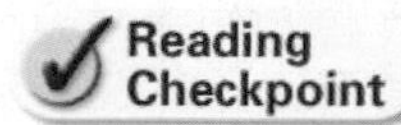

**What is a scientific theory?**

## Section 1 Assessment

**Target Reading Skill Using Prior Knowledge** Review your graphic organizer and revise it based on what you just learned in the section.

### Reviewing Key Concepts

1. a. **Defining** What is a fossil?
   b. **Summarizing** In general, how does a fossil form?
   c. **Relating Cause and Effect** Which parts of an organism are most likely to be preserved as fossils? Why?
2. a. **Listing** What are the five different kinds of fossils?
   b. **Explaining** How does a carbon film fossil form?
   c. **Comparing and Contrasting** How are petrified fossils similar to preserved remains? How are they different?
3. a. **Reviewing** What are two things that scientists can learn from the fossil record?
   b. **Making Generalizations** What does the fossil record show about how life has changed over time?

### Lab zone At-Home **Activity**

**Family Fossils** A fossil is something old that has been preserved. With your parents' permission, look around your house for the oldest object you can find. Interview family members to determine how old the object is, why it has been preserved, and how it may have changed since it was new. Make a drawing of the object and bring it to class. Tell your class the story of this "fossil."

Section 2

# The Relative Age of Rocks

## Reading Preview

### Key Concepts

- What is the law of superposition?
- How do geologists determine the relative age of rocks?
- How are index fossils useful to geologists?

### Key Terms

- relative age
- absolute age
- law of superposition
- extrusion
- intrusion
- fault
- unconformity
- index fossil

### Target Reading Skill

**Asking Questions** Before you read, preview the red headings. In a graphic organizer like the one below, ask a *what* or *how* question for each heading. As you read, write answers to your questions.

**Relative Age**

| Question | Answer |
|---|---|
| What does the position of rock layers reveal? | The position of rock layers shows . . . |
| | |

## Lab zone Discover Activity

### Which Layer Is the Oldest?

1. Make a stack of different-colored layers of clay. Each layer should be about the size and thickness of a pancake. If these flat layers are sediments, which layer of sediment was deposited first? (*Hint:* This is the oldest layer.)
2. Now form the stack into a dome by pressing it over a small rounded object, such as a small bowl. With a cheese-slicer or plastic knife, carefully cut off the top of the dome. Look at the layers that you have exposed. Which layer is the oldest?

**Think It Over**

**Inferring** If you press the stack into a small bowl and trim away the clay that sticks above the edge, where will you find the oldest layer?

As sedimentary rock forms, the remains of organisms in the sediment may become fossils. Millions of years later, if you split open the rock, you might see the petrified bones of an extinct reptile or insect.

Your first question about a new fossil might be, "What is it?" Your next question would probably be, "How old is it?" Geologists have two ways to express the age of a rock and any fossil it contains. The **relative age** of a rock is its age compared to the ages of other rocks. You have probably used the idea of relative age when comparing your age with someone else's age. For example, if you say that you are older than your brother but younger than your sister, you are describing your relative age.

The relative age of a rock does not provide its absolute age. The **absolute age** of a rock is the number of years since the rock formed. It may be impossible to know a rock's absolute age exactly. But sometimes geologists can determine a rock's absolute age to within a certain number of years.

◄ The age of each family member could be given as relative age or absolute age.

## The Position of Rock Layers

Have you ever seen rock layers of different colors on a cliff beside a road? What are these layers, and how did they form? The sediment that forms sedimentary rocks is deposited in flat layers one on top of the other. Over time, the sediment hardens and changes into sedimentary rock. These rock layers provide a record of Earth's geologic history.

It can be difficult to determine the absolute age of a rock. So geologists use a method to find a rock's relative age. Geologists use the **law of superposition** to determine the relative ages of sedimentary rock layers. **According to the law of superposition, in horizontal sedimentary rock layers the oldest layer is at the bottom. Each higher layer is younger than the layers below it.**

The walls of the Grand Canyon in Arizona illustrate the law of superposition. You can see some of the rock layers found in the Grand Canyon in Figure 5. The deeper down you go in the Grand Canyon, the older the rocks.

**Reading Checkpoint** Why do sedimentary rocks have layers?

FIGURE 5
**The Grand Canyon**
More than a dozen rock layers make up the walls of the Grand Canyon. You can see five layers clearly in the photograph. **Applying Concepts** *In which labeled layers would you find the oldest fossils? Explain.*

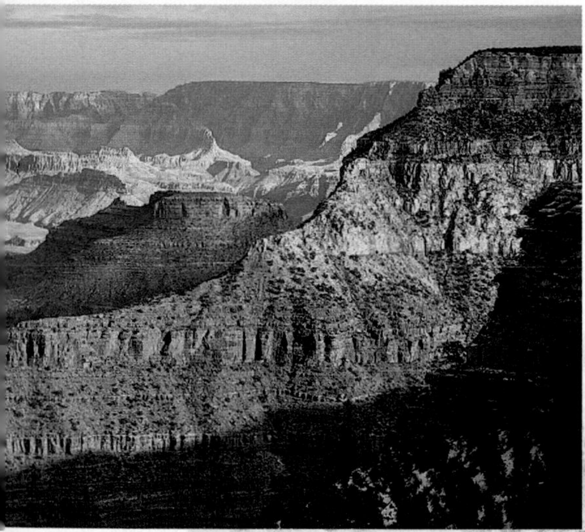

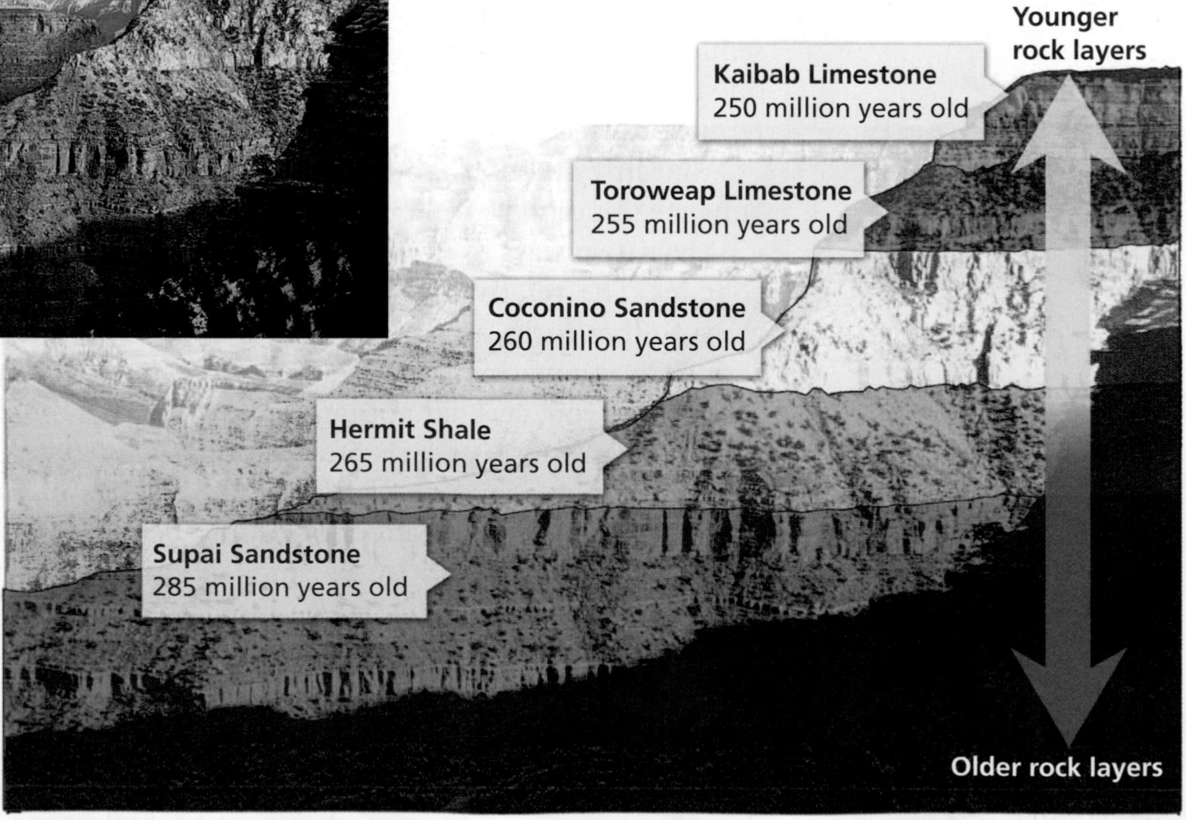

Younger rock layers
Kaibab Limestone 250 million years old
Toroweap Limestone 255 million years old
Coconino Sandstone 260 million years old
Hermit Shale 265 million years old
Supai Sandstone 285 million years old
Older rock layers

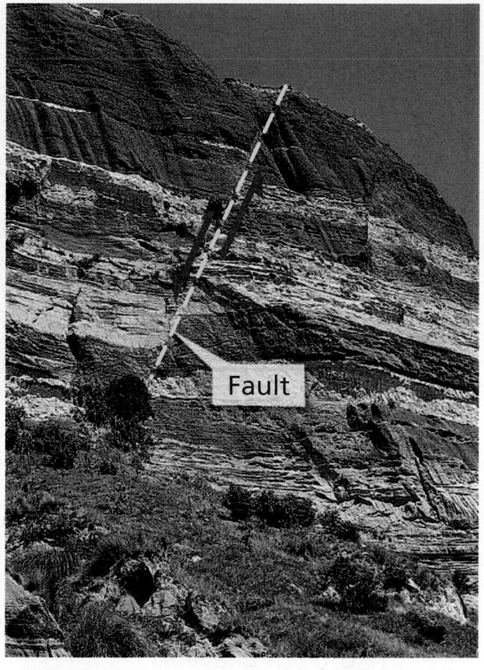

**FIGURE 6**
**Intrusions and Faults**
Intrusions and faults give clues to the relative ages of rocks. An intrusion (left) cuts through rock layers. Rock layers are broken and shifted along a fault (right).

## Determining Relative Age

There are other clues besides the position of rock layers to the relative ages of rocks. **To determine relative age, geologists also study extrusions and intrusions of igneous rock, faults, and gaps in the geologic record.**

**Clues From Igneous Rock** Igneous rock forms when magma or lava hardens. Magma is molten material beneath Earth's surface. Magma that flows onto the surface is called lava.

Lava that hardens on the surface is called an **extrusion.** An extrusion is always younger than the rocks below it.

Beneath the surface, magma may push into bodies of rock. There, the magma cools and hardens into a mass of igneous rock called an **intrusion.** An intrusion is always younger than the rock layers around and beneath it. Figure 6 shows an intrusion. Geologists study where intrusions and extrusions formed in relation to other rock layers. This helps geologists understand the relative ages of the different types of rock.

**Clues From Faults** More clues come from the study of faults. A **fault** is a break in Earth's crust. Forces inside Earth cause movement of the rock on opposite sides of a fault.

A fault is always younger than the rock it cuts through. To determine the relative age of a fault, geologists find the relative age of the youngest layer cut by the fault.

Movements along faults can make it harder for geologists to determine the relative ages of rock layers. You can see in Figure 6 how the rock layers no longer line up because of movement along the fault.

**Lab zone** Try This **Activity**

### Sampling a Sandwich

Your teacher will give you a sandwich that represents rock layers in Earth's crust.

1. Use a round, hollow, uncooked noodle as a coring tool. Push the noodle through the layers of the sandwich.
2. Pull the noodle out of the sandwich. Break the noodle gently to remove your core sample.
3. Draw a picture of what you see in each layer of the core.

**Making Models** Which layer of your sandwich is the "oldest"? The "youngest"? Why do you think scientists study core samples?

FIGURE 7
**Unconformity**
An unconformity occurs where erosion wears away layers of sedimentary rock. Other rock layers then form on top.
**Sequencing** *What two processes must take place before an unconformity can form?*

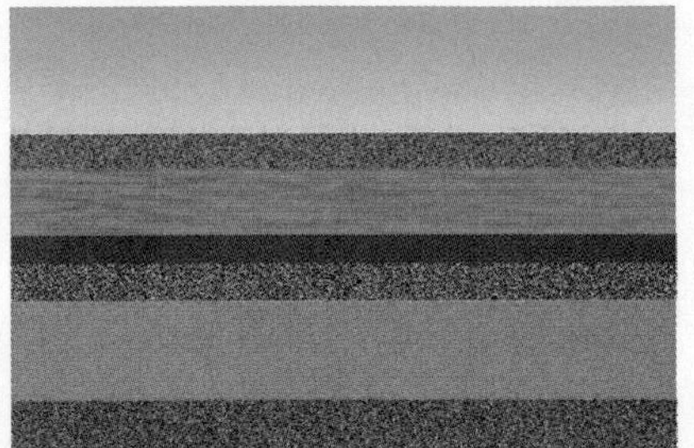

1 Sedimentary rocks form in horizontal layers.

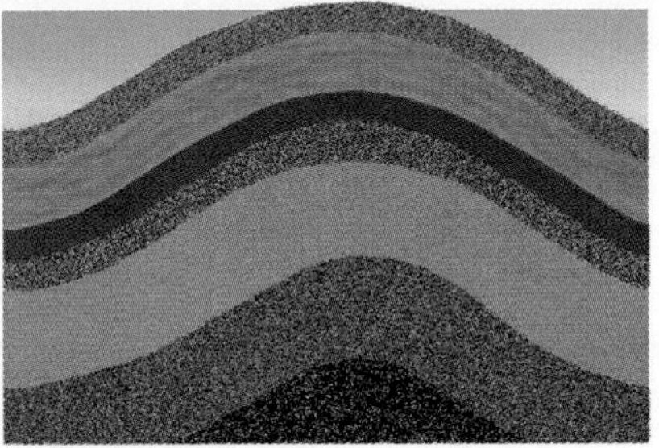

2 Folding tilts the rock layers.

3 The surface is eroded.

4 New sediment is deposited, forming rock layers above the unconformity.

**Gaps in the Geologic Record** The geologic record of sedimentary rock layers is not always complete. Deposition slowly builds layer upon layer of sedimentary rock. But some of these layers may erode away, exposing an older rock surface. Then deposition begins again, building new rock layers.

The surface where new rock layers meet a much older rock surface beneath them is called an **unconformity**. An unconformity is a gap in the geologic record. An unconformity shows where some rock layers have been lost because of erosion. Figure 7 shows how an unconformity forms.

**What is an unconformity?**

## Using Fossils to Date Rocks

To date rock layers, geologists first give a relative age to a layer of rock at one location. Then they can give the same age to matching layers of rock at other locations.

Certain fossils, called index fossils, help geologists match rock layers. To be useful as an **index fossil,** a fossil must be widely distributed and represent a type of organism that existed only briefly. A fossil is considered widely distributed if it occurs in many different areas. Geologists look for index fossils in layers of rock. **Index fossils are useful because they tell the relative ages of the rock layers in which they occur.**

Geologists use particular types of organisms as index fossils—for example, certain types of ammonites. Ammonites (AM uh nyts) were a group of hard-shelled animals. Ammonites evolved in shallow seas more than 500 million years ago and became extinct about 65 million years ago.

Ammonite fossils make good index fossils for two reasons. First, they are widely distributed. Second, many different types of ammonites evolved and then became extinct after a few million years.

Geologists can identify the different types of ammonites through differences in the structure of their shells. Based on these differences, geologists can identify the rock layers in which a particular type of ammonite fossil occurs.

You can use index fossils to match rock layers. Look at Figure 8, which shows rock layers from four different locations. Notice that two of the fossils are found in only one of these rock layers. These are the index fossils.

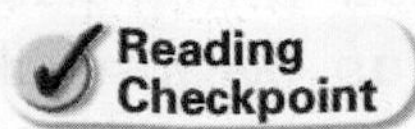

**What characteristics must a fossil have to be useful as an index fossil?**

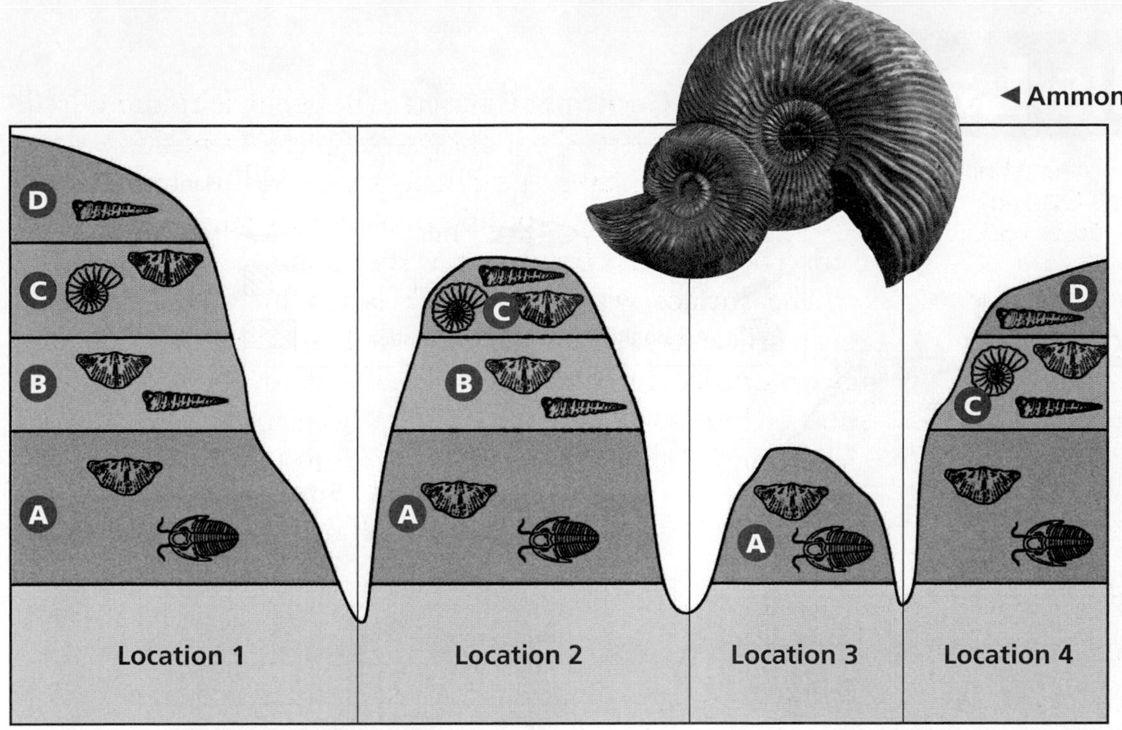


**FIGURE 8**
**Using Index Fossils**
Scientists use index fossils to match up rock layers at locations that may be far apart. The ammonites in layer C are index fossils. **Interpreting Diagrams** *Can you find another index fossil in the diagram? (Hint: Look for a fossil that occurs in only one time period, but in several different locations.)*

**For:** Index Fossils activities
**Visit:** PHSchool.com
**Web Code:** cfp-2042

## Section 2 Assessment

**Target Reading Skill Asking Questions** Use the answers to the questions you wrote about the headings to help you answer the questions below.

### Reviewing Key Concepts

1. a. **Defining** In your own words, define the terms *relative age* and *absolute age*.
   b. **Explaining** What is the law of superposition?
   c. **Inferring** A geologist finds a cliff where the edges of several different rock layers can be seen. Which layer is the oldest? Explain.
2. a. **Reviewing** Besides the law of superposition, what are three types of clues to the relative age of rock layers?
   b. **Comparing and Contrasting** Compare and contrast extrusions and intrusions.
   c. **Sequencing** An intrusion crosses an extrusion. Which layer is the older? Explain.
3. a. **Defining** What is an index fossil?
   b. **Applying Concepts** The fossil record shows that horseshoe crabs have existed with very little change for about 200 million years. Would horseshoe crabs be useful as an index fossil? Explain why or why not.

### Lab zone At-Home Activity

**Drawer to the Past** Collect ten items out of a drawer full of odds and ends such as keys, coins, receipts, photographs, and souvenirs. Have your family members put them in order from oldest to newest. What clues will you use to determine their relative ages? How can you determine the oldest object of all? List the ten items in order of their relative age. Do you know the absolute age of any of the items?

Lab zone **Skills Lab**

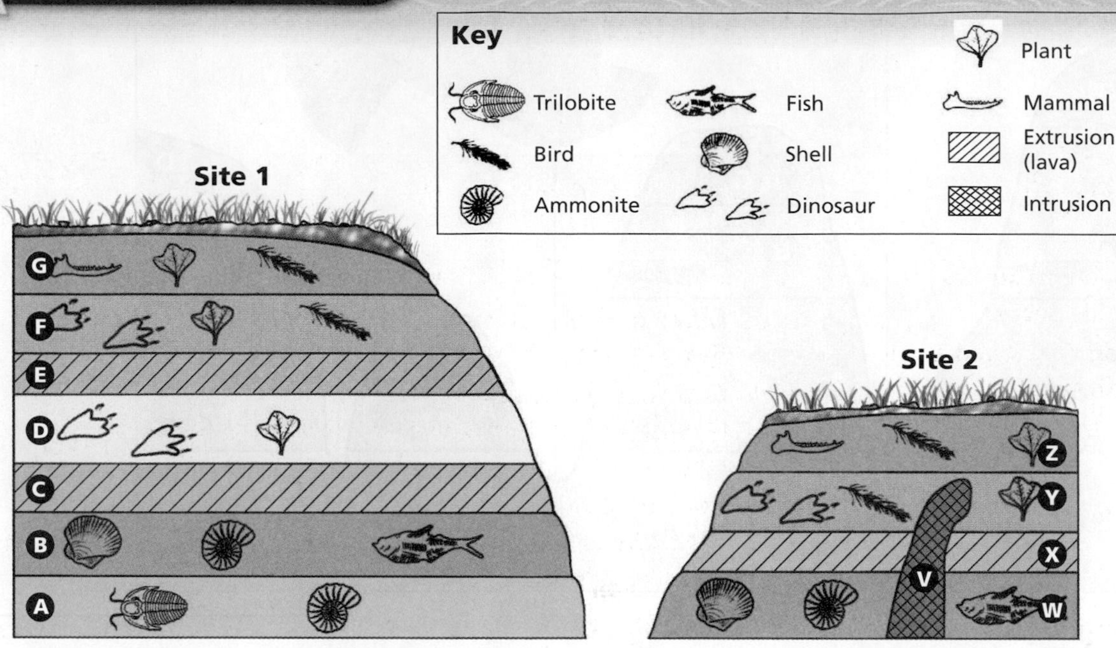


# Finding Clues to Rock Layers

## Problem

How can you use fossils and geologic features to interpret the relative ages of rock layers?

## Skills Focus

interpreting data, drawing conclusions

## Procedure

1. Study the rock layers at Sites 1 and 2. Write down the similarities and differences between the layers at the two sites.
2. List the kinds of fossils that are found in each rock layer of Sites 1 and 2.

## Analyze and Conclude

### Site 1

1. **Interpreting Data** What "fossil clues" in layers A and B indicate the kind of environment that existed when these rock layers were formed? How did the environment change in layer D?
2. **Drawing Conclusions** Which layer is the oldest? How do you know?
3. **Drawing Conclusions** Which of the layers formed most recently? How do you know?
4. **Inferring** Why are there no fossils in layers C and E?
5. **Observing** What kind of fossils are found in layer F?

### Site 2

6. **Inferring** Which layer at Site 1 might have formed at the same time as layer W at Site 2?
7. **Interpreting Data** What clues show an unconformity or gap in the horizontal rock layers? Which rock layers are missing? What might have happened to these rock layers?
8. **Drawing Conclusions** Which is older, intrusion V or layer Y? How do you know?
9. **Communicating** Write a journal entry describing how the environment at Site 2 changed over time. Starting with the earliest layer, describe the types of organisms, their environment, and how the environment changed.

## More to Explore

Draw a sketch similar to Site 2 and include a fault that cuts across the intrusion. Have a partner then identify the relative age of the fault, the intrusion, and the layers cut by the fault.

# Radioactive Dating

## Reading Preview

### Key Concepts

- What happens during radioactive decay?
- What can be learned from radioactive dating?

### Key Terms

- atom
- element
- radioactive decay
- half-life

### Target Reading Skill

**Identifying Main Ideas** As you read the Determining Absolute Ages section, write the main idea in a graphic organizer like the one below. Then write three supporting details that give examples of the main idea.

**Main Idea**

Using radioactive dating, scientists can determine . . .

**Detail** | **Detail** | **Detail**

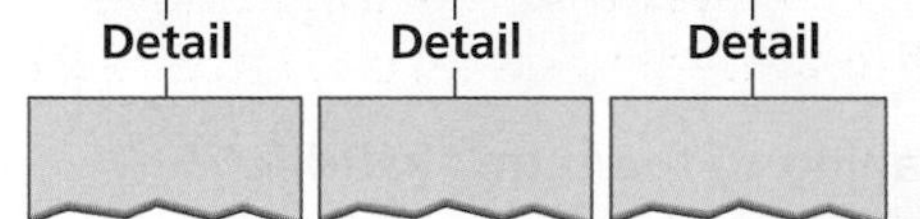

## Lab zone Discover Activity

### How Long Till It's Gone?

1. Make a small cube—about 5 cm × 5 cm × 5 cm —from modeling clay.
2. Carefully use a knife to cut the clay in half. Put one half of the clay aside.
3. Cut the clay in half two more times. Each time you cut the clay, put one half of it aside.

**Think It Over**

**Predicting** How big will the remaining piece of clay be if you repeat the process several more times?

In Australia, scientists have found sedimentary rocks that contain some of the world's oldest fossils. These are fossils of stromatolites (stroh MAT uh lyts). Stromatolites are the remains of reefs built by organisms similar to present-day bacteria. Sediment eventually covered these reefs. As the sediment changed to rock, so did the reefs. Using absolute dating, scientists have determined that some stromatolites are more than 3 billion years old. To understand absolute dating, you need to learn more about the chemistry of rocks.

**FIGURE 9**
**Stromatolites**
Scientists think that ancient stromatolites were formed by organisms similar to blue-green bacteria (above). Modern stromatolites (right) still form reefs along the western coast of Australia.

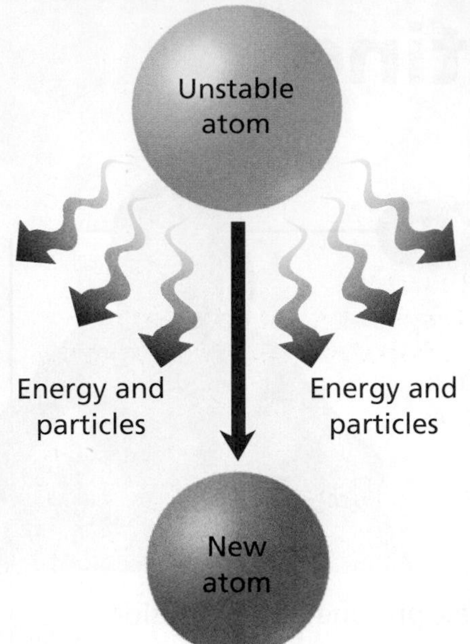


**FIGURE 10**
**Radioactive Decay**
In the process of radioactive decay, an atom releases energy and particles as it changes to a new kind of atom.

## Radioactive Decay

Rocks are a form of matter. All the matter you see, including rocks, is made of tiny particles called **atoms.** When all the atoms in a particular type of matter are the same, the matter is an **element.** Carbon, oxygen, iron, lead, and potassium are just some of the more than 110 currently known elements.

Most elements are stable. They do not change under normal conditions. But some elements exist in forms that are unstable. Over time, these elements break down, or decay, by releasing particles and energy in a process called **radioactive decay.** These unstable elements are said to be radioactive. **During radioactive decay, the atoms of one element break down to form atoms of another element.**

Radioactive elements occur naturally in igneous rocks. Scientists use the rate at which these elements decay to calculate the rock's age. You calculate your age based on a specific day—your birthday. What's the "birthday" of a rock? For an igneous rock, that "birthday" is when it first hardens to become rock. As a radioactive element within the igneous rock decays, it changes into another element. So the composition of the rock changes slowly over time. The amount of the radioactive element goes down. But the amount of the new element goes up.

The rate of decay of each radioactive element is constant—it never changes. This rate of decay is the element's half-life. The **half-life** of a radioactive element is the time it takes for half of the radioactive atoms to decay. You can see in Figure 11 how a radioactive element decays over time.

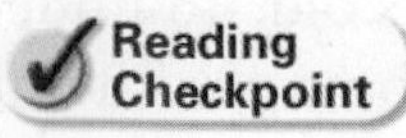


**What is the meaning of the term "half-life"?**

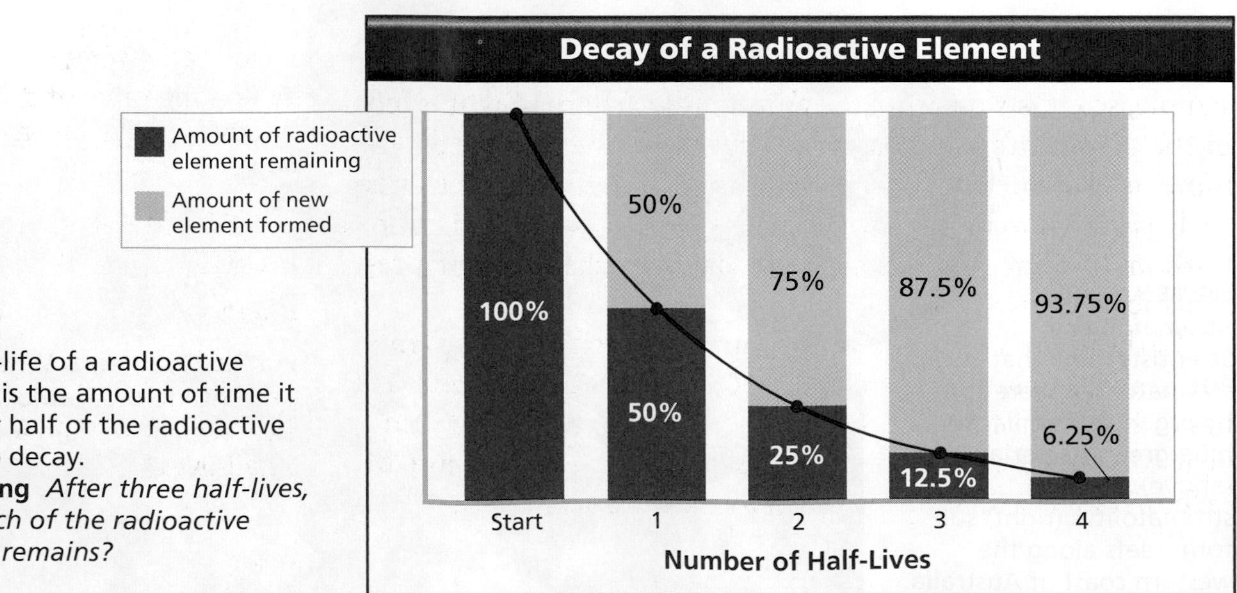


**FIGURE 11**
The half-life of a radioactive element is the amount of time it takes for half of the radioactive atoms to decay.
**Calculating** *After three half-lives, how much of the radioactive element remains?*

| Elements Used in Radioactive Dating | | |
|---|---|---|
| **Radioactive Element** | **Half-life (years)** | **Dating Range (years)** |
| Carbon-14 | 5,730 | 500–50,000 |
| Potassium-40 | 1.3 billion | 50,000–4.6 billion |
| Rubidium-87 | 48.8 billion | 10 million–4.6 billion |
| Thorium-232 | 14 billion | 10 million–4.6 billion |
| Uranium-235 | 713 million | 10 million–4.6 billion |
| Uranium-238 | 4.5 billion | 10 million–4.6 billion |

**FIGURE 12**
The half-lives of different radioactive elements vary greatly.

## Determining Absolute Ages

**Geologists use radioactive dating to determine the absolute ages of rocks.** In radioactive dating, scientists first determine the amount of a radioactive element in a rock. Then they compare that amount with the amount of the stable element into which the radioactive element decays. Figure 12 lists several common radioactive elements and their half-lives.

**Potassium–Argon Dating** Scientists often date rocks using potassium-40. This form of potassium decays to stable argon-40 and has a half-life of 1.3 billion years. Potassium-40 is useful in dating the most ancient rocks because of its long half-life.

**Carbon-14 Dating** A radioactive form of carbon is carbon-14. All plants and animals contain carbon, including some carbon-14. As plants and animals grow, carbon atoms are added to their tissues. After an organism dies, no more carbon is added. But the carbon-14 in the organism's body decays. It changes to stable nitrogen-14. To determine the age of a sample, scientists measure the amount of carbon-14 that is left in the organism's remains. From this amount, they can determine its absolute age. Carbon-14 has been used to date fossils such as frozen mammoths, as well as pieces of wood and bone. Carbon-14 even has been used to date the skeletons of prehistoric humans.

Carbon-14 is very useful in dating materials from plants and animals that lived up to about 50,000 years ago. Carbon-14 has a half-life of only 5,730 years. For this reason, it can't be used to date very ancient fossils or rocks. The amount of carbon-14 left would be too small to measure accurately.

### Math Skills

**Percentage** What percentage of a radioactive element will be left after 3 half-lives? First, multiply $\frac{1}{2}$ three times to determine what fraction of the element will remain.

$$\frac{1}{2} \times \frac{1}{2} \times \frac{1}{2} = \frac{1}{8}$$

You can convert this fraction to a percentage by setting up a proportion:

$$\frac{1}{8} = \frac{d\%}{100\%}$$

To find the value of $d$, begin by cross multiplying, as for any proportion:

$1 \times 100 = 8 \times d$

$d = \frac{100}{8}$

$d = 12.5\%$

**Practice Problems** What percentage of a radioactive element will remain after 5 half-lives?

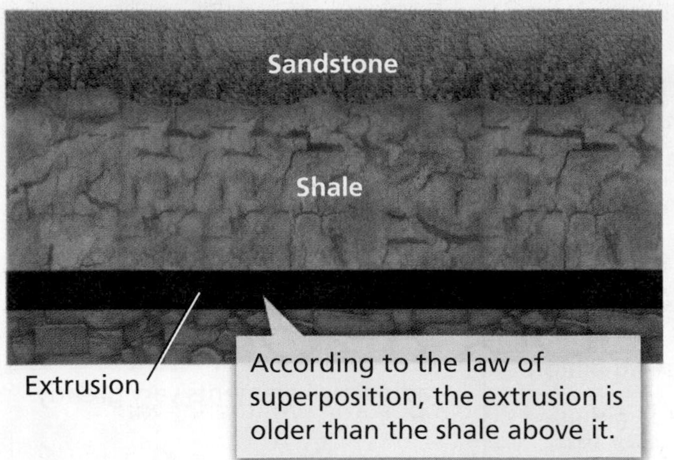

Sandstone
Shale
Extrusion
According to the law of superposition, the extrusion is older than the shale above it.

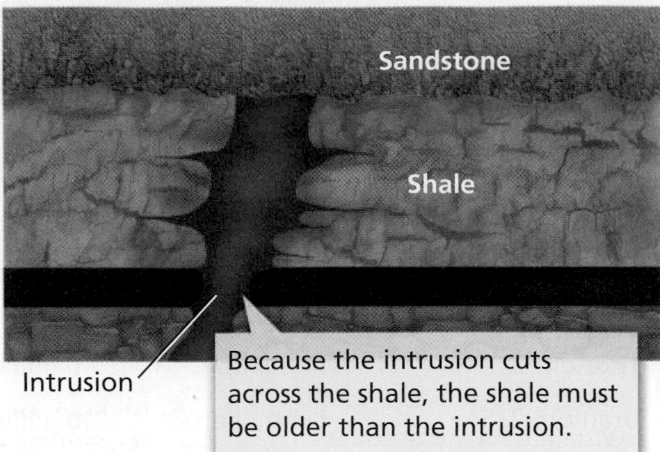

Sandstone
Shale
Intrusion
Because the intrusion cuts across the shale, the shale must be older than the intrusion.

**FIGURE 13**
**Inferring the Age of Rocks**
A layer of shale forms above an extrusion (left). Later (right), an intrusion crosses the shale.
**Inferring** *What can you infer about the age of the shale?*

**Radioactive Dating of Rock Layers** Radioactive dating works well for igneous rocks, but not for sedimentary rocks. The rock particles in sedimentary rocks are from other rocks, all of different ages. Radioactive dating would provide the age of the particles. It would not provide the age of the sedimentary rock.

How, then, do scientists date sedimentary rock layers? They date the igneous intrusions and extrusions near the sedimentary rock layers. Look at Figure 13. As you can see, sedimentary rock (sandstone) above an igneous intrusion must be younger than that intrusion.

**For:** More on radioactive dating
**Visit:** PHSchool.com
**Web Code:** cfd-2043

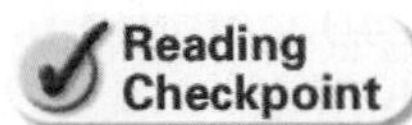


**What are two types of radioactive dating?**

## Section 3 Assessment

**Target Reading Skill Identifying Main Ideas** Use your graphic organizer to help you answer Question 2 below.

### Reviewing Key Concepts

1. a. **Defining** In your own words, define the term *radioactive decay.*
   b. **Describing** How does the composition of a rock containing a radioactive element change over time?
   c. **Applying Concepts** How is a radioactive element's rate of decay like the ticking of a clock? Explain.
2. a. **Identifying** What method do geologists use to determine the absolute age of a rock?
   b. **Explaining** Why is it difficult to determine the absolute age of a sedimentary rock?
   c. **Problem Solving** A geologist finds a fossil in a layer of sedimentary rock that lies in between two igneous extrusions. How could the geologist determine the age of the fossil?

**Math Practice**

3. **Percentage** What percentage of a radioactive element will remain after 7 half-lives?

# 4 The Geologic Time Scale

## Reading Preview

### Key Concepts

- Why is the geologic time scale used to show Earth's history?
- What are the different units of the geologic time scale?

### Key Terms

- geologic time scale
- era
- period

### Target Reading Skill

**Sequencing** As you read, make a flowchart like the one below that shows the eras and periods of geologic time. Write the name of each era and period in the flowchart in the order in which it occurs.

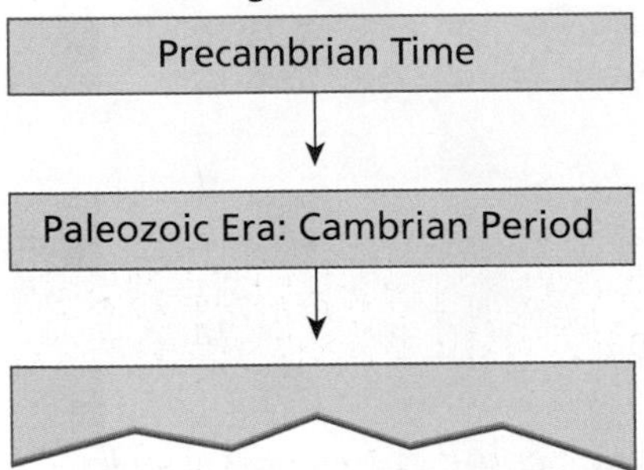


## Lab zone Discover Activity

### This Is Your Life!

1. Make a list of about 10 to 15 important events that you remember in your life.
2. On a sheet of paper, draw a timeline to represent your life. Use a scale of 3.0 cm to 1 year.
3. Write each event in the correct year along the timeline.
4. Now divide the timeline into parts that describe major periods in your life, such as preschool years, elementary school years, and middle school years.

**Think It Over**

**Making Models** Along which part of your timeline are most of the events located? Which period of your life does this part of the timeline represent? Why do you think this is so?

Imagine squeezing Earth's 4.6-billion-year history into a 24-hour day. Earth forms at midnight. About seven hours later, the earliest one-celled organisms appear. Over the next 14 hours, simple, soft-bodied organisms such as jellyfish and worms develop. A little after 9:00 P.M.—21 hours later—larger, more complex organisms evolve in the oceans. Reptiles and insects first appear about an hour after that. Dinosaurs arrive just before 11:00 P.M., but are extinct by 11:30 P.M. Modern humans don't appear until less than a second before midnight!

## The Geologic Time Scale

Months, years, or even centuries aren't very helpful for thinking about Earth's long history. **Because the time span of Earth's past is so great, geologists use the geologic time scale to show Earth's history.** The **geologic time scale** is a record of the life forms and geologic events in Earth's history. You can see this time scale in Figure 14.

Scientists first developed the geologic time scale by studying rock layers and index fossils worldwide. With this information, scientists placed Earth's rocks in order by relative age. Later, radioactive dating helped determine the absolute age of the divisions in the geologic time scale.

FIGURE 14

## The Geologic Time Scale

The eras and periods of the geologic time scale are used to date the events in Earth's long history.
**Interpreting Diagrams** *How long ago did the Paleozoic Era end?*

**Cenozoic Era**
The Cenozoic (sen uh ZOH ik) began about 66 million years ago and continues to the present. The word part *ceno-* means "recent," and *-zoic* means "life." Mammals became common during this time.

**Mesozoic Era**
People often call the Mesozoic (mez uh ZOH ik) the Age of Reptiles. The Mesozoic began about 245 million years ago and lasted about 180 million years. The word part *meso-* means "middle."

**Paleozoic Era**
The Paleozoic (pay lee uh ZOH ik) began about 544 million years ago and lasted for 300 million years. The word part *paleo-* means "ancient or early."

**Geologic Time Scale**

| Era | Period | Millions of Years Ago | Duration (millions of years) |
|---|---|---|---|
| Cenozoic | *Quaternary* | | 1.8 to present |
| | | 1.8 | |
| | *Tertiary* | | 65 |
| | | 66.4 | |
| Mesozoic | *Cretaceous* | | 78 |
| | | 144 | |
| | *Jurassic* | | 64 |
| | | 208 | |
| | *Triassic* | | 37 |
| | | 245 | |
| Paleozoic | *Permian* | | 41 |
| | | 286 | |
| | *Carboniferous* | | 74 |
| | | 360 | |
| | *Devonian* | | 48 |
| | | 408 | |
| | *Silurian* | | 30 |
| | | 438 | |
| | *Ordovician* | | 67 |
| | | 505 | |
| | *Cambrian* | | 39 |
| | | 544 | |
| Precambrian | | | *544 million years ago–4.6 billion years ago* |

## Divisions of Geologic Time

As geologists studied the fossil record, they found major changes in life forms at certain times. They used these changes to mark where one unit of geologic time ends and the next begins. Therefore the divisions of the geologic time scale depend on events in the history of life on Earth.

When speaking of the past, what names do you use for different spans of time? You probably use names such as century, decade, year, month, week, and day. Scientists use similar divisions for the geologic time scale.

Geologic time begins with a long span of time called Precambrian Time (pree KAM bree un). Precambrian Time, which covers about 88 percent of Earth's history, ended 544 million years ago. **After Precambrian Time, the basic units of the geologic time scale are eras and periods.** Geologists divide the time between Precambrian Time and the present into three long units of time called **eras.** They are the Paleozoic Era, the Mesozoic Era, and the Cenozoic Era.

Eras are subdivided into units of geologic time called **periods.** You can see in Figure 14 that the Mesozoic Era includes three periods: the Triassic Period, the Jurassic Period, and the Cretaceous Period.

The names of many of the geologic periods come from places around the world where geologists first described the rocks and fossils of that period. For example, the name Cambrian refers to Cambria, the old Roman name for Wales.

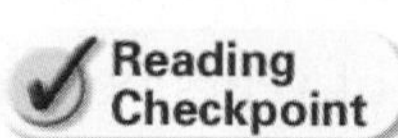


**To what era does the Jurassic Period belong?**

FIGURE 15
**Fossil of the Quaternary Period**
This saber-toothed cat lived during the Quaternary Period.

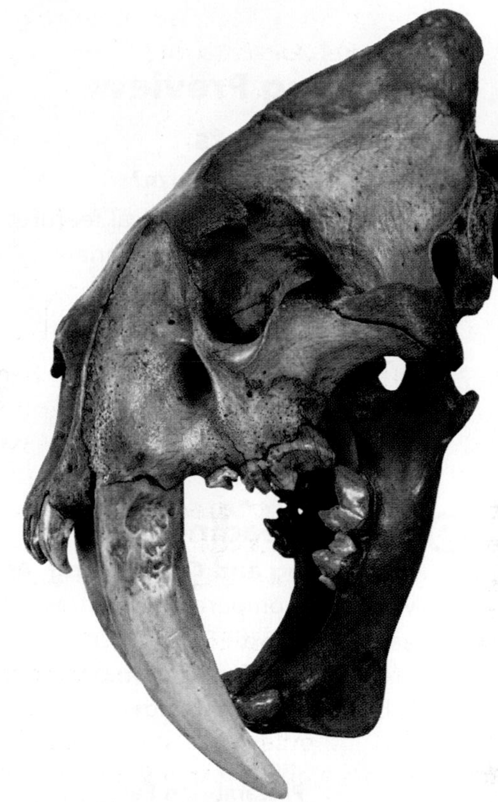

**For:** More on the geologic time scale
**Visit:** PHSchool.com
**Web Code:** cfd-2044

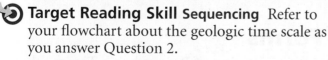

## Section 4 Assessment

**Target Reading Skill Sequencing** Refer to your flowchart about the geologic time scale as you answer Question 2.

### Reviewing Key Concepts

1. a. **Defining** What is the geologic time scale?
   b. **Explaining** What information did geologists use in developing the geologic time scale?
2. a. **Listing** What are the basic units into which the geologic time scale is divided?
   b. **Interpreting Diagrams** Study Figure 14. Which major division of geologic time was the longest? When did it begin? When did it end?
   c. **Sequencing** Place the following in the correct order from earliest to latest: Tertiary, Jurassic, Quaternary, Triassic, Cretaceous.

### Writing in Science

**An Address in Time** Pick one of the periods in the geologic time scale. Write a paragraph that describes, as completely as you can, that period's place in geologic time relative to the other periods and eras.

# Early Earth

## Reading Preview

### Key Concepts

- When did Earth form?
- How did Earth's physical features develop during Precambrian Time?
- What were early Precambrian organisms like?

### Key Terms

- comet
- continental drift

### Target Reading Skill

**Comparing and Contrasting** As you read, compare and contrast early Earth with Earth later in Precambrian Time by completing a table like the one below.

**Precambrian Earth**

| Feature | Early Earth | Later Precambrian Earth |
|---|---|---|
| Atmosphere | | |
| Oceans | | |
| Continents | | |

## Lab zone Discover Activity

### How Could Planet Earth Form in Space?

1. Place a sheet of paper on top of a small magnet. The paper represents outer space and the magnet models gravity.
2. Sprinkle a half teaspoon of iron filings along one end of the paper to model the materials that formed Earth.
3. Gently blow through a straw for about 10 seconds from the end of the paper with the iron filings toward the magnet. **CAUTION:** *Be sure the straw is pointed away from other students.*
4. Observe what happens to the iron filings.

**Think It Over**

**Making Models** If you repeated Steps 2 and 3, what would happen to the size of your "planet"? How is this model like the early Earth? How is it different?

Your science class is going on a field trip, but this trip is a little out of the ordinary. You're going to travel back billions of years to the earliest days on Earth. Then you will move forward through time to the present. Enter the time machine and strap yourself in. Take a deep breath—you're off!

A dial on the dashboard shows the number of years before the present. You stare at the dial—it reads 4.6 billion years. You peer out the window as the time machine flies above the planet. Earth looks a little strange. Where are the oceans? Where are the continents? How will Earth change over the next billions of years? You'll answer these and other questions about Earth's history as you take this extraordinary trip.

## The Planet Forms

Your journey starts at the beginning of Precambrian Time with the formation of planet Earth. **Scientists hypothesize that Earth formed at the same time as the other planets and the sun, roughly 4.6 billion years ago.**

**The Age of Earth** How do scientists know the age of Earth? Using radioactive dating, scientists have determined that the oldest rocks ever found on Earth are about 4 billion years old. But scientists think Earth formed even earlier than that.

According to this hypothesis, Earth and the moon are about the same age. When Earth was very young, it collided with a large object. The collision threw a large amount of material from both bodies into orbit around Earth. This material combined to form the moon. Scientists have dated moon rocks that were brought to Earth by astronauts during the 1970s. Radioactive dating shows that the oldest moon rocks are about 4.6 billion years old. Scientists infer that Earth is also roughly 4.6 billion years old—only a little older than those moon rocks.

**Earth Takes Shape** Scientists think that Earth began as a ball of dust, rock, and ice in space. Gravity pulled this mass together. As Earth grew larger, its gravity increased, pulling in dust, rock, and ice nearby. As objects made of these materials struck Earth at high speed, their kinetic energy was changed into thermal energy.

The energy from these collisions caused Earth's temperature to rise until the planet was very hot. Scientists think that Earth may have become so hot that it melted. Denser materials sank toward the center, forming Earth's dense, iron core. At the same time, Earth continuously lost heat to the cold of space. Less dense, molten material hardened to form Earth's outer layers—the solid crust and mantle.

As the growing Earth traveled around the sun, its gravity also captured gases such as hydrogen and helium. But this first atmosphere was lost when the sun released a strong burst of particles. These particles blew away Earth's first atmosphere.

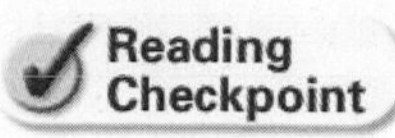


**What force caused the materials that formed Earth to come together?**

**FIGURE 16**
**Early Earth**
This artist's illustration shows Earth shortly after the moon formed. Notice the rocky objects from space striking Earth, and the molten rock flowing over the surface.

**For:** Links on Precambrian Earth
**Visit:** www.SciLinks.org
**Web Code:** scn-0745

FIGURE 17
**Development of the Atmosphere**
Earth soon lost its first atmosphere (left) of hydrogen and helium. Earth's second atmosphere (right) slowly developed the mixture of gases—nitrogen, oxygen, carbon dioxide, water vapor, and argon—of the atmosphere today. As oxygen levels increased, the ozone layer also developed.
**Comparing and Contrasting** *Compare and contrast Earth's first and second atmospheres.*

## Earth's Surface Forms

Watching early Earth from your time machine, you can see the planet change as the years speed by. **During the first several hundred million years of Precambrian Time, an atmosphere, oceans, and continents began to form.**

**The Atmosphere** After Earth lost its first atmosphere, a second atmosphere formed. This new atmosphere was made up mostly of carbon dioxide, water vapor, and nitrogen. Volcanic eruptions released carbon dioxide, water vapor, and other gases from Earth's interior. Collisions with comets added other gases to the atmosphere. A **comet** is a ball of dust and ice that orbits the sun. The ice in a comet consists of water and frozen gases, including carbon dioxide.

**The Oceans** At first, Earth's surface was too hot for water to remain as a liquid. All water evaporated into water vapor. However, as Earth's surface cooled, the water vapor began to condense to form rain. Gradually, rainwater began to accumulate to form an ocean. Rain also began to erode Earth's rocky surface. Over time, the oceans affected the composition of the atmosphere by absorbing much of the carbon dioxide.

**The Continents** During early Precambrian Time, more and more of Earth's rock cooled and hardened. Less than 500 million years after Earth's formation, the less dense rock at the surface formed large landmasses called continents.

Scientists have found that the continents move very slowly over Earth's surface because of forces inside Earth. This process is called **continental drift.** The movement is very slow—only a few centimeters per year. Over billions of years, Earth's landmasses have repeatedly formed, broken apart, and then crashed together again, forming new continents.

What is continental drift?

**Lab zone Skills Activity**

### Calculating

Precambrian Time lasted about 4 billion years. What percentage is this of Earth's entire history of 4.6 billion years? If the first continents formed about 500 million years after Earth itself formed, what percentage of Precambrian Time had elapsed? (*Hint:* To review percentages, see the Math Review section in the Skills Handbook.)

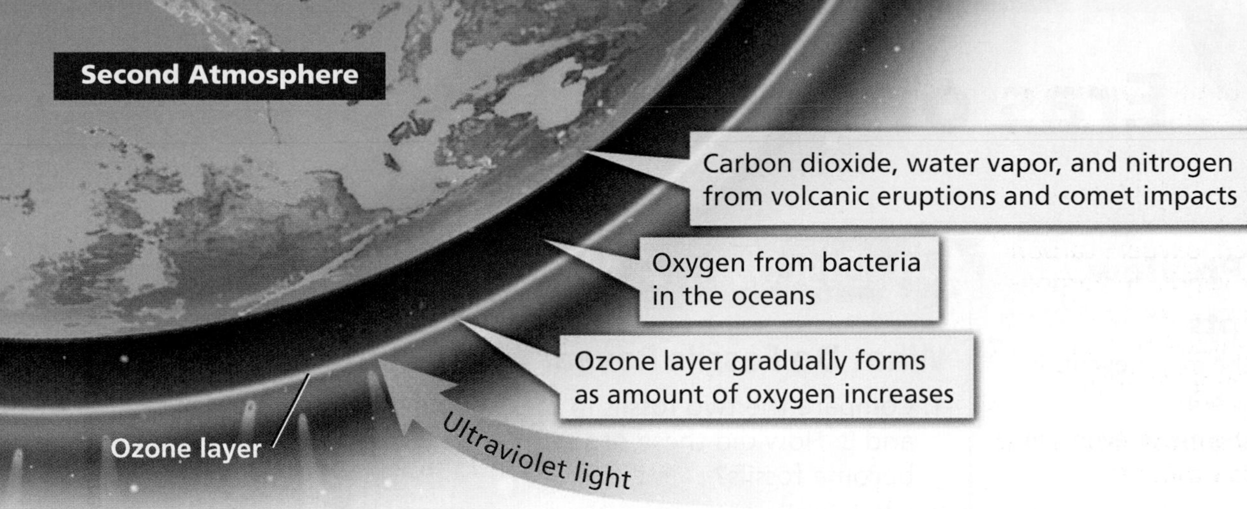
Second Atmosphere
Carbon dioxide, water vapor, and nitrogen from volcanic eruptions and comet impacts
Oxygen from bacteria in the oceans
Ozone layer gradually forms as amount of oxygen increases
Ozone layer
Ultraviolet light

## Life Develops

Scientists cannot pinpoint when or where life began on Earth. **But scientists have found fossils of single-celled organisms in rocks that formed about 3.5 billion years ago. These earliest life forms were probably similar to present-day bacteria.** Scientists hypothesize that all other forms of life on Earth arose from these simple organisms.

About 2.5 billion years ago, many organisms began using energy from the sun to make their own food. This process is called photosynthesis. One waste product of photosynthesis is oxygen. As organisms released oxygen into the air, the amount of oxygen in the atmosphere slowly increased. Processes in the atmosphere changed some of this oxygen into a form called ozone. The atmosphere developed a layer rich in ozone that blocked out the deadly ultraviolet rays of the sun. Shielded from the sun's ultraviolet rays, organisms could live on land.

## Section 5 Assessment

**Target Reading Skill Comparing and Contrasting** Use the information in your table about early Earth to answer the questions below.

### Reviewing Key Concepts

1. a. **Reviewing** How long ago did Earth form?
   b. **Summarizing** Summarize the process by which scientists determined the age of Earth.
2. a. **Listing** What physical features formed during Earth's first several hundred million years?
   b. **Explaining** How did volcanic eruptions and comets change early Earth?
   c. **Relating Cause and Effect** What caused water erosion to begin on Earth's surface?
3. a. **Identifying** What do scientists think were the first organisms to evolve on Earth?
   b. **Predicting** How would Earth's atmosphere be different if organisms capable of photosynthesis had not evolved? Explain.

### Writing in Science

**Web Site** Plan a Web site for early Earth. To plan your Web site, make a list of the topics you will include. Make sketches of the screens that visitors to the Web site will see. Then write short descriptions for each topic.

Section 6

# Eras of Earth's History

## Reading Preview

### Key Concepts

- What were the major events in the Paleozoic Era?
- What were the major events in the Mesozoic Era?
- What were the major events in the Cenozoic Era?

### Key Terms

- invertebrate
- vertebrate
- amphibian
- reptile
- mass extinction
- mammal

### Target Reading Skill

**Previewing Visuals** Before you read, preview Figure 22. Then write three questions that you have about Earth's history in a graphic organizer like the one below. As you read, answer your questions.

**Earth's History**

| |
|---|
| **Q.** What geologic events happened during Precambrian Time? |
| **A.** |
| **Q.** |

## Lab zone Discover Activity

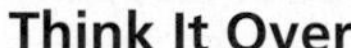

### What Do Fossils Reveal About Earth's History?

1. Compare the two fossils in photos A and B. How did these organisms become fossils?
2. Work with one or two other students to study the organisms in the two photos. Think about how these organisms may have lived. Then make sketches showing what each of these organisms may have looked like.

**Think It Over**

**Posing Questions** If you were a paleontologist, what questions would you want to ask about these organisms?

As your time machine nears the end of Precambrian Time, you notice that Earth's organisms have begun to change. Along with organisms made up of single cells, living things resembling jellyfish now float in Earth's oceans. You also notice the fronds of feathery, plantlike organisms anchored to the seafloor. Scientists have found fossils of such organisms in Australia, Russia, China, and southern Africa. Fossils like the ones in Figure 18 are more than 600 million years old! But a much greater variety of living things evolved during the next phase of geologic time—the Paleozoic Era.

**FIGURE 18**
**Paleontologist at Work**
This paleontologist in Australia is uncovering fossil animals from late Precambrian Time.

**FIGURE 19**
**The Cambrian Explosion**
During the early Cambrian period, Earth's oceans were home to many strange organisms unlike any animals that are alive today.

## The Paleozoic Era

Your time machine slows. You observe the "explosion" of life that began the Paleozoic Era.

**The Cambrian Explosion** During the Cambrian Period life took a big leap forward. **At the beginning of the Paleozoic Era, a great number of different kinds of organisms evolved.** Paleontologists call this event the Cambrian Explosion because so many new life forms appeared within a relatively short time. For the first time, many organisms had hard parts, including shells and outer skeletons.

At this time, all animals lived in the sea. Many were animals without backbones, or **invertebrates.** Invertebrates such as jellyfish, worms, and sponges drifted through the water, crawled along the sandy bottom, or attached themselves to the ocean floors.

Brachiopods and trilobites were common in the Cambrian seas. Brachiopods were small ocean animals with two shells. They resembled modern clams, but are only distantly related.

**Vertebrates Arise** During the Ordovician (awr duh VISH ee un) and Silurian (sih LOOR ee un) periods, the ancestors of the modern octopus and squid appeared. But these invertebrates soon shared the seas with a new type of organism. **During this time, jawless fishes evolved. Jawless fishes were the first vertebrates.** A **vertebrate** is an animal with a backbone. These fishes had suckerlike mouths, and they soon became common.

**FIGURE 20**
**Devonian Armored Fish**
Paleontologists have found fossils of huge armored fish, like this *Dunkleosteus,* that lived during the Devonian Period.

**Life Reaches Land** Until the Silurian Period, only one-celled organisms lived on the land. But during the Silurian Period, plants became abundant. These first, simple plants grew low to the ground in damp areas. By the Devonian Period (dih VOH nee un), plants that could grow in drier areas had evolved. Among these plants were the earliest ferns. The first insects also appeared during the Silurian Period.

Both invertebrates and vertebrates lived in the Devonian seas. Even though the invertebrates were more numerous, the Devonian Period is often called the Age of Fishes. Every main group of fishes was present in the oceans at this time. Most fishes now had jaws, bony skeletons, and scales on their bodies. Some fishes, like the one in Figure 20, were huge. Sharks appeared in the late Devonian Period.

**During the Devonian Period, animals began to invade the land.** The first vertebrates to crawl onto land were lungfish with strong, muscular fins. The first amphibians evolved from these lung fish. An **amphibian** (am FIB ee un) is an animal that lives part of its life on land and part of its life in water.

**The Carboniferous Period** Throughout the rest of the Paleozoic, life expanded over Earth's continents. Other vertebrates evolved from the amphibians. For example, small reptiles developed during the Carboniferous Period. **Reptiles** have scaly skin and lay eggs with tough, leathery shells. Some types of reptiles became very large during the later Paleozoic.

**FIGURE 21**
**The Coal Forest**
Forests of the Carboniferous Period later formed coal deposits. **Predicting** *What types of fossils would you expect to find from the Carboniferous Period?*

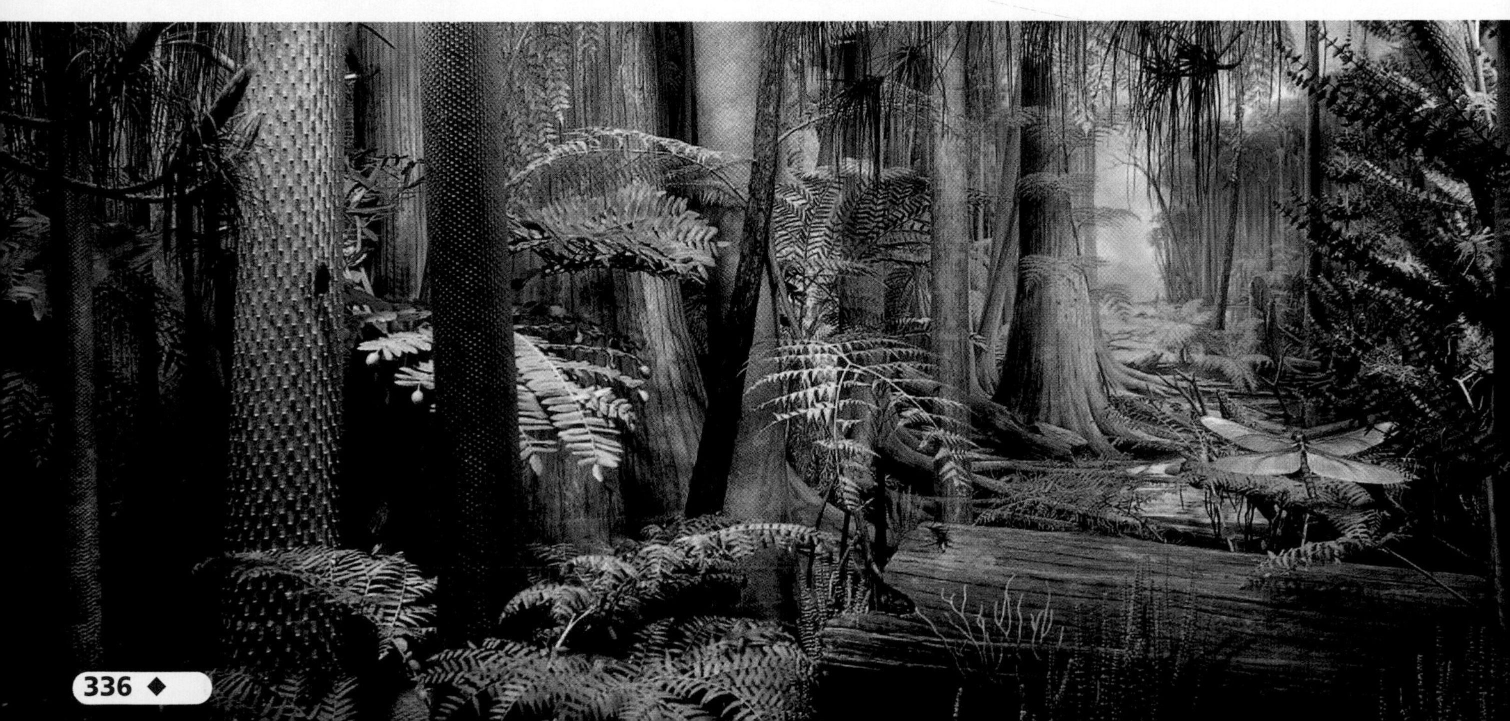

## Math Analyzing Data

### Mass Extinctions

The graph shows how the number of families of animals in Earth's oceans has changed.

1. **Reading Graphs** What variable is shown on the *x*-axis? On the *y*-axis of the graph?
2. **Interpreting Data** How long ago did the most recent mass extinction occur?
3. **Interpreting Data** Which mass extinction produced the greatest drop in the number of families of ocean animals?
4. **Relating Cause and Effect** In general, how did the number of families change between mass extinctions?

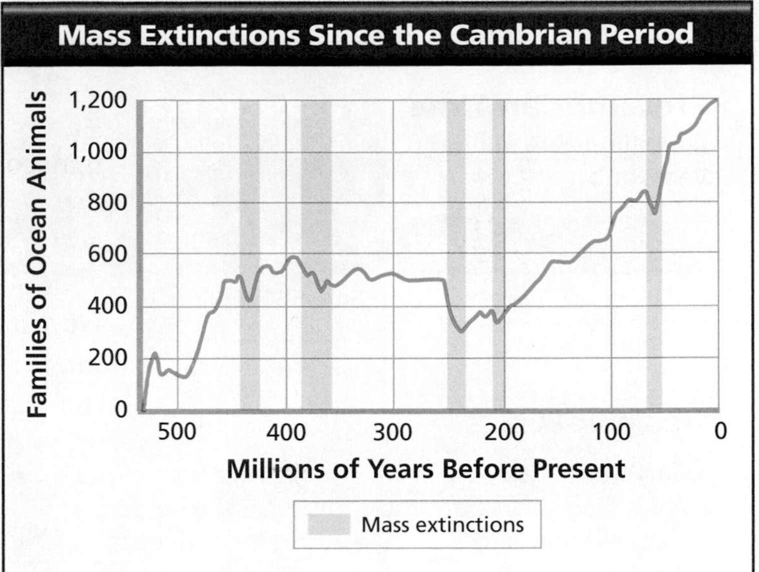


During the Carboniferous Period, winged insects evolved into many forms, including huge dragonflies and cockroaches. Giant ferns and cone-bearing plants and trees formed vast swampy forests called "coal forests." The remains of the coal forest plants formed thick deposits of sediment that changed into coal over millions of years.

**Mass Extinction Ends the Paleozoic** At the end of the Paleozoic Era, many kinds of organisms died out. This was a **mass extinction,** in which many types of living things became extinct at the same time. **The mass extinction at the end of the Paleozoic affected both plants and animals, on land and in the seas.** Scientists do not know what caused the mass extinction, but many kinds of organisms, such as trilobites, suddenly became extinct.

**The Supercontinent Pangaea** Scientists hypothesize that climate change resulting from continental drift may have caused the mass extinction at the end of the Paleozoic. **During the Permian Period, about 260 million years ago, Earth's continents moved together to form a great landmass, or supercontinent, called Pangaea** (pan JEE uh). The formation of Pangaea caused deserts to expand in the tropics. At the same time, sheets of ice covered land closer to the South Pole. Many organisms could not survive the new climate. After Pangaea formed, it broke apart again, as shown in Figure 22.

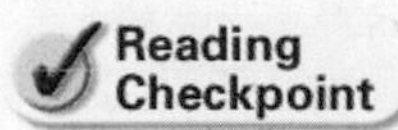

What was Pangaea?

**For:** Continental Drift activity
**Visit:** PHSchool.com
**Web Code:** cfp-1015

## Figure 22 Geologic History

| Period | Cambrian | Ordovician | Silurian |
|---|---|---|---|
| **Precambrian Time** 4.6 billion–544 million years ago | **Paleozoic Era** 544–245 million years ago | | |
| | 544–505 million years ago | 505–438 million years ago | 438–408 million years ago |
| **Geologic Events** • Earth forms about 4.6 billion years ago. • Oceans form and cover Earth about 4 billion years ago. • First sedimentary rocks form about 4 billion years ago. | • Shallow seas cover much of the land. • Ancient continents lie near or south of the equator. | • Warm, shallow seas cover much of Earth. • Ice cap covers what is now North Africa. | • Coral reefs develop. • Early continents collide with what is now North America, forming mountains. |
| **Development of Life** • Bacteria appear about 3.5 billion years ago. • Soft-bodied, multicellular organisms develop late in the Precambrian. • First mass extinction probably occurs near the end of the Precambrian. | • Great "explosion" of invertebrate life occurs in seas. • Invertebrates with shells appear, including trilobites and mollusks. | • Invertebrates dominate the oceans. • Early vertebrates—jawless fish—become common. | • Fish with jaws develop. • Land plants appear. • Insects and spiders appear. |

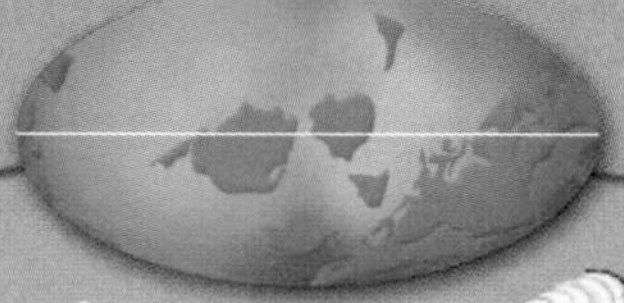

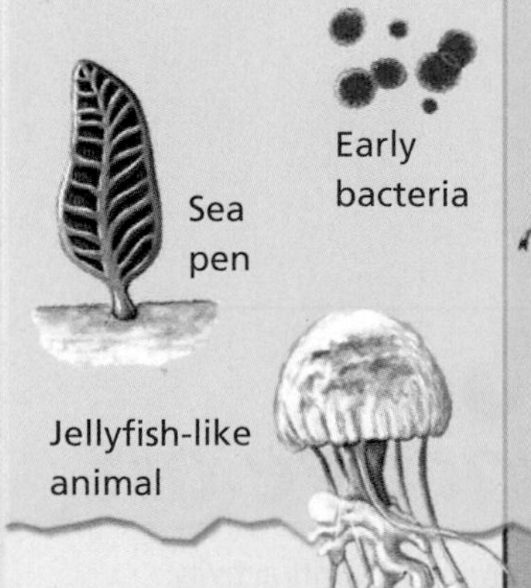

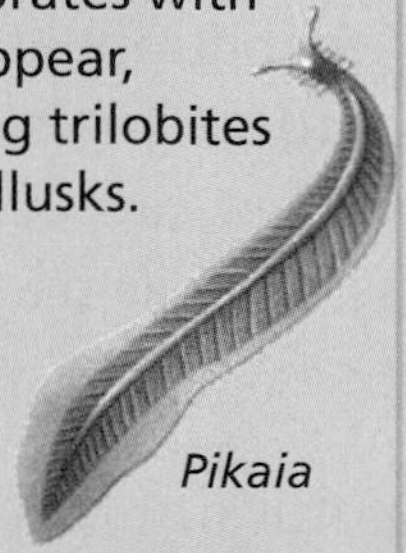

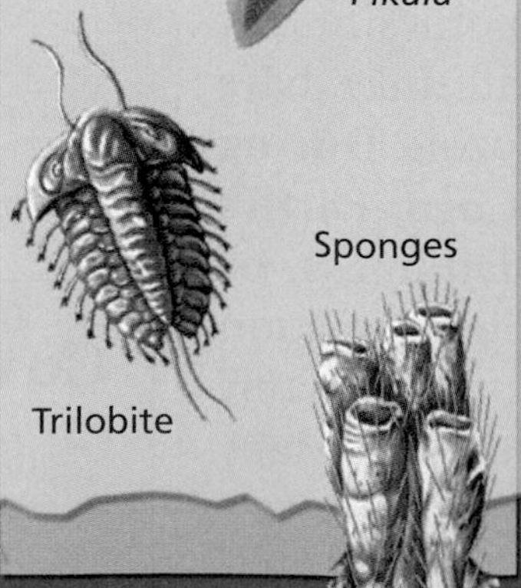

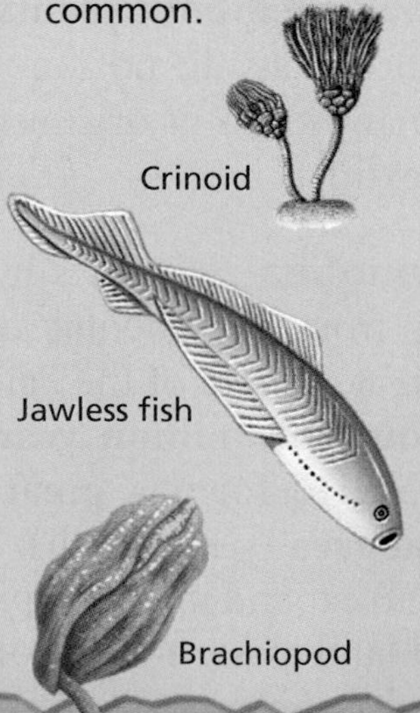

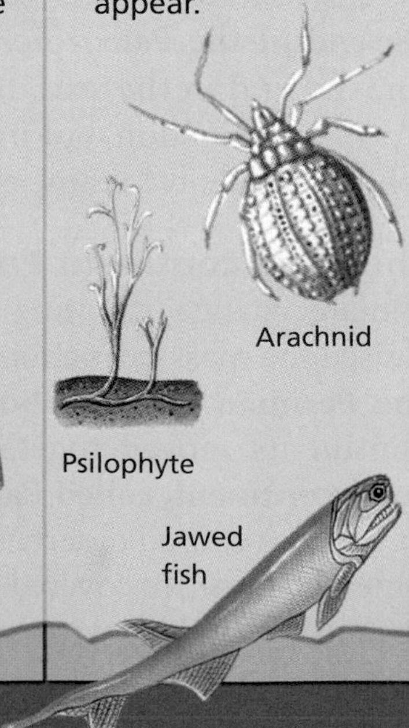

## Paleozoic Era

544–245 million years ago

| Devonian | Carboniferous 360–286 million years ago | | Permian |
|---|---|---|---|
| 408–360 million years ago | **Mississippian** 360–320 million years ago | **Pennsylvanian** 320–286 million years ago | 286–245 million years ago |

### Geologic Events

**Devonian**
- Seas rise and fall over what is now North America.

**Carboniferous**
- Appalachian Mountains begin to form.
- North America and Northern Europe lie in warm, tropical region.

**Permian**
- Deserts become larger in tropical regions.
- The supercontinent Pangaea forms as all continents join together.

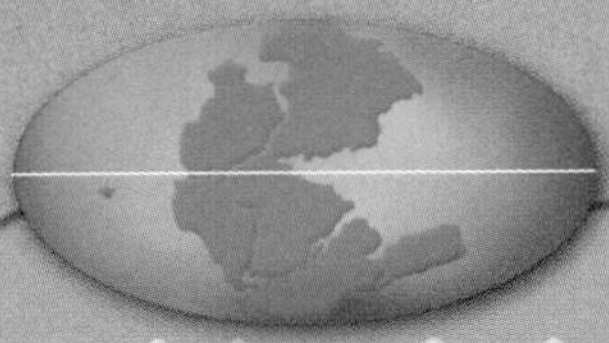

### Development of Life

**Devonian**
- Age of Fishes begins as sharks and fish with scales and bony skeletons become common.
- Trilobites and corals flourish in the oceans.
- Lungfish develop.
- First amphibians reach land.

Shark

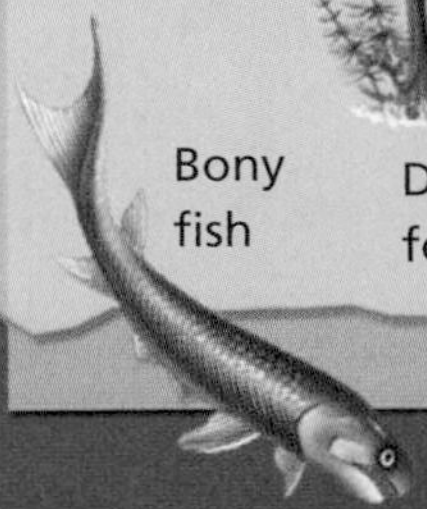

Bony fish

Devonian forest

**Carboniferous**
- Great swamp forests of huge, woody trees cover eastern North America and parts of Europe.
- First true reptiles appear.
- Winged insects appear.

Dragonfly

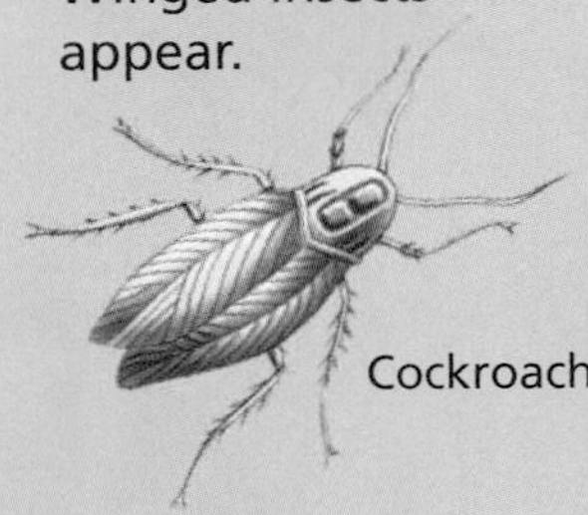

Cockroach

Coal forest

Amphibian

**Permian**
- Reptiles become dominant on land.
- Warm-blooded reptiles appear.
- Mass extinction of many marine invertebrates, including trilobites.

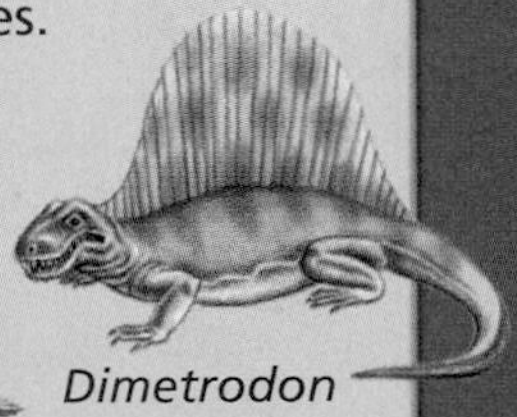

*Dimetrodon*

Conifer

*Dicynodon*

## Figure 22 Geologic History

### Mesozoic Era
245–66 million years ago

| Triassic | Jurassic |
|---|---|
| 245–208 million years ago | 208–144 million years ago |

#### Triassic

**Geologic Events**

- Pangaea holds together for much of the Triassic.
- Hot, dry conditions dominate the center of Pangaea.

**Development of Life**

- Age of Reptiles begins.
- First dinosaurs appear.
- First mammals, which evolve from warm-blooded reptiles, appear.
- First turtles and crocodiles appear.
- Conifers, palmlike trees, and ginkgo trees dominate forests.

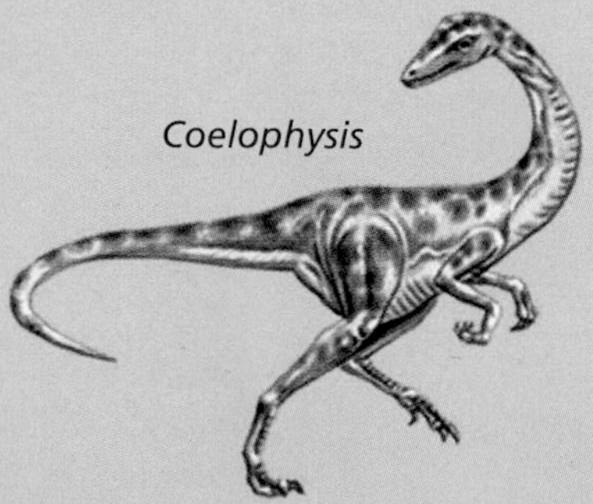

*Megazostrodon*

*Coelophysis*

Cycad

#### Jurassic

**Geologic Events**

- Pangaea breaks apart as North America separates from Africa and South America.

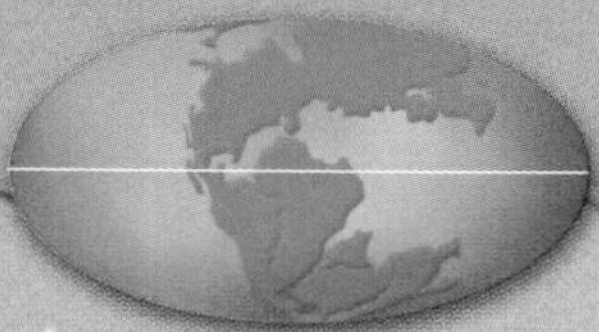

**Development of Life**

- Largest dinosaurs thrive, including *Stegosaurus*, *Diplodocus*, and *Apatosaurus.*
- First birds appear.
- First flying reptiles, pterosaurs, appear.

*Archaeopteryx*

*Morganucodon*

*Diplodocus*

## Mesozoic Era
245–66 million years ago

## Cenozoic Era
66 million years ago to present

| Cretaceous | Tertiary | Quaternary |
|---|---|---|
| 144–66 million years ago | 66–1.8 million years ago | 1.8 million years ago to the present |

### Geologic Events

**Cretaceous**

- Continents move toward their present-day positions, as South America splits from Africa.
- Widespread volcanic activity occurs.

**Tertiary**

- The Rocky Mountains and Himalayas form.
- Continents continue to move into present-day positions.
- Continental glacier covers Antarctica.

**Quaternary**

- Thick glaciers advance and retreat over much of North America and Europe, parts of South America and Asia, and all of Antarctica.

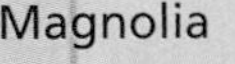

Magnolia

### Development of Life

**Cretaceous**

- First flowering plants appear.
- Dinosaurs, including *Tyrannosaurus rex,* dominate.
- First snakes appear.
- Mass extinction at end of period causes disappearance of many land and marine life forms, including dinosaurs.

**Tertiary**

- Flowering plants thrive.
- First grasses appear.
- Age of Mammals begins.
- Modern groups such as horses, elephants, bears, rodents, and primates appear.
- Ancestors of humans evolve.

**Quaternary**

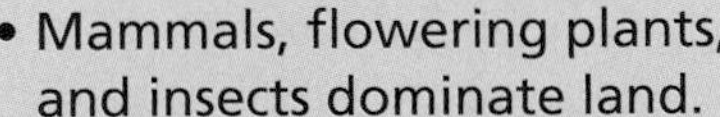

- Mammals, flowering plants, and insects dominate land.
- Modern humans evolve in Africa about 100,000 years ago.
- Giant mammals of North America and Eurasia become extinct when the Ice Age ends about 10,000 years ago.

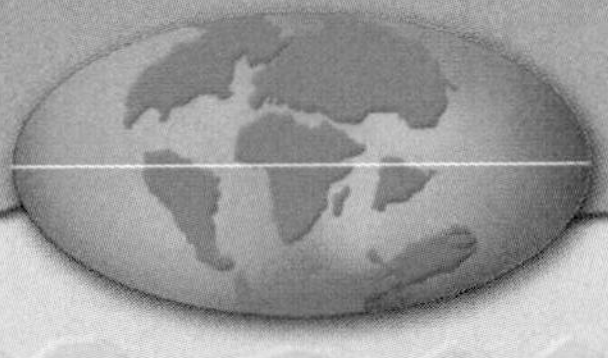

*Tyrannosaurus rex*

Creodonts

*Uintatherium*

*Plesiadapis*

*Hyracotherium*

*Megatherium*

*Homo sapiens*

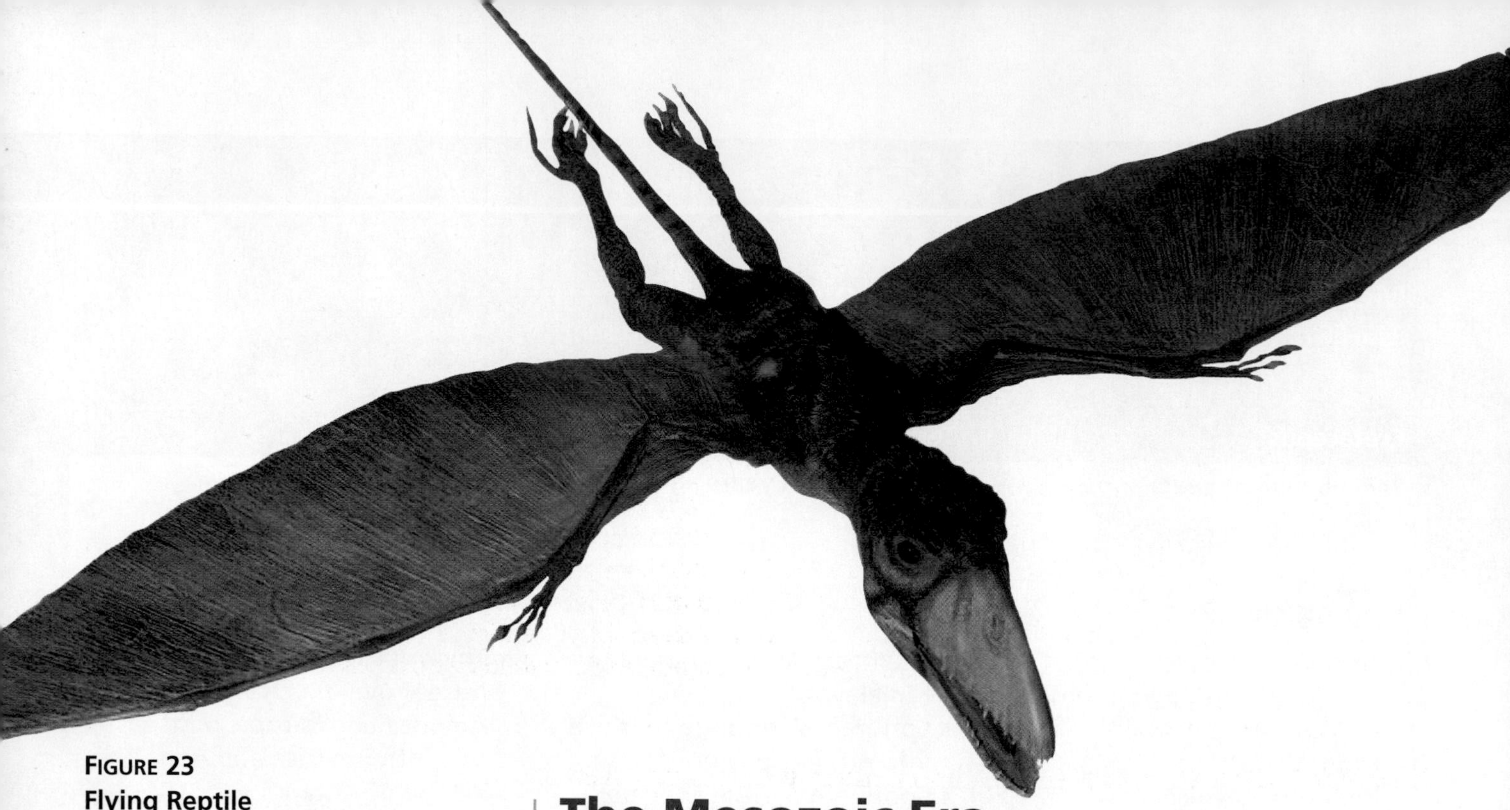

**FIGURE 23**
**Flying Reptile**
*Dimorphodon* was a flying reptile that lived during the Jurassic Period. Like dinosaurs, flying reptiles became extinct at the end of the Cretaceous period.
**Comparing and Contrasting** *How is* Dimorphodon *similar to the bird in Figure 24?*

## The Mesozoic Era

Millions of years flash by as your time machine travels. Watch out—there's a dinosaur! You're observing an era that you've read about in books and seen in movies.

**The Triassic Period** Some living things survived the Permian mass extinction. These organisms became the main forms of life early in the Triassic Period (try AS ik). Plants and animals that survived included fish, insects, reptiles, and cone-bearing plants called conifers. **Reptiles were so successful during the Mesozoic Era that this time is often called the Age of Reptiles.** About 225 million years ago, the first dinosaurs appeared. Mammals also first appeared during the Triassic Period. A **mammal** is a warm-blooded vertebrate that feeds its young milk. Mammals probably evolved from warm-blooded reptiles. The mammals of the Triassic Period were very small, about the size of a mouse or shrew. From these first small mammals, all mammals that live today evolved.

**The Jurassic Period** During the Jurassic Period (joo RAS ik), dinosaurs became the dominant animals on land. Scientists have identified several hundred different kinds of dinosaurs. Some were plant eaters, while others were meat eaters. Dinosaurs "ruled" Earth for about 150 million years, but different types lived at different times.

One of the first birds, called *Archaeopteryx*, appeared during the Jurassic Period. The name *Archaeopteryx* means "ancient wing thing." Many paleontologists now think that birds evolved from dinosaurs.

**FIGURE 24**
**Early Bird**
The artist of the illustration (left) has given *Archaeopteryx* colorful feathers. From a fossil (right), paleontologists can tell that *Archaeopteryx* was about 30 centimeters long, had feathers and teeth, and also had claws on its wings.

**The Cretaceous Period** Reptiles, including dinosaurs, were still the dominant vertebrates throughout the Cretaceous Period (krih TAY shus). Flying reptiles and birds competed for places in the sky. The hollow bones and feathers of birds made them better adapted to their environment than the flying reptiles, which became extinct during the Cretaceous Period. The Cretaceous Period also brought new forms of life. Flowering plants like the ones you see today evolved. Unlike the conifers, flowering plants produce seeds that are inside a fruit. The fruit helps the seeds survive.

**Another Mass Extinction** **At the close of the Cretaceous Period, about 65 million years ago, another mass extinction occurred. Scientists hypothesize that this mass extinction occurred when an object from space struck Earth.** This object was probably an asteroid. Asteroids are rocky masses that orbit the sun between Mars and Jupiter. Once in many millions of years, an asteroid may collide with Earth.

When the asteroid hit Earth, the impact threw huge amounts of dust and water vapor into the atmosphere. Many organisms on land and in the oceans died immediately. Dust and heavy clouds blocked sunlight around the world for years. Without sunlight, plants died, and plant-eating animals starved. This mass extinction wiped out over half of all plant and animal groups. No dinosaurs survived.

Not all scientists agree that an asteroid impact alone caused the mass extinction. Some scientists think that climate changes caused by increased volcanic activity were partly responsible.

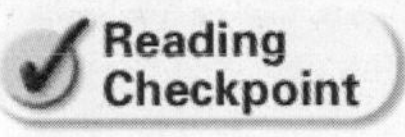


**What major groups of organisms developed during the Mesozoic Era?**

**FIGURE 25**
**The End of the Dinosaurs**
Many scientists hypothesize that during the Cretaceous an asteroid hit Earth near the present-day Yucatán Peninsula, in southeastern Mexico.

## Lab zone Try This Activity

### Life and Times

1. Place these events in their correct order: continental glaciers retreat; first fish appear; oldest fossils form; human ancestors appear; "explosion" of invertebrates occurs; dinosaurs become extinct; Pangaea forms.
2. Draw a timeline and graph these dates:
   - 3.5 billion years ago
   - 544 million years ago
   - 400 million years ago
   - 260 million years ago
   - 65 million years ago
   - 3.5 million years ago
   - 20,000 years ago

   Choose a scale so the oldest date fits on the paper.

**Interpreting Data** Match each event with the correct date on your timeline. How does the time since the dinosaurs became extinct compare with the time since the oldest fossil formed?

# The Cenozoic Era

Your voyage through time continues on through the Cenozoic Era—often called the Age of Mammals. During the Mesozoic Era, mammals had a hard time competing with dinosaurs for food and places to live. **The extinction of dinosaurs created an opportunity for mammals. During the Cenozoic Era, mammals evolved to live in many different environments—on land, in water, and even in the air.**

**The Tertiary Period** During the Tertiary Period, Earth's climates were generally warm and mild. In the oceans, marine mammals such as whales and dolphins evolved. On land, flowering plants, insects, and mammals flourished. When grasses evolved, they provided a food source for grazing mammals. These were the ancestors of today's cattle, deer, sheep, and other grass-eating mammals. Some mammals became very large, as did some birds.

**The Quaternary Period** The mammals that had evolved during the Tertiary Period eventually faced a changing environment. **Earth's climate cooled, causing a series of ice ages during the Quaternary Period.** Thick continental glaciers advanced and retreated over parts of Europe and North America. Then, about 20,000 years ago, Earth's climate began to warm. Over thousands of years, the continental glaciers melted, except in Greenland and Antarctica.

**FIGURE 26**
**Ice-Age Environment**
Large mammals roamed the ice-free parts of North America and Eurasia during the Ice Ages of the Quaternary Period.

In the oceans, algae, coral, mollusks, fish, and mammals thrived. Insects and birds shared the skies. On land, flowering plants and mammals such as bats, cats, dogs, cattle, and humans—just to name a few—became common.

The fossil record suggests that modern humans, or *Homo sapiens,* may have evolved as early as 100,000 years ago. By about 12,000 to 15,000 years ago, humans had migrated around the world to every continent except Antarctica.

Your time machine has now arrived back in the present. You and all organisms on Earth are living in the Quaternary Period of the Cenozoic Era. Is this the end of evolution and the changing of Earth's surface? No, these processes will continue as long as Earth exists. But you'll have to take your time machine into the future to see just what happens!

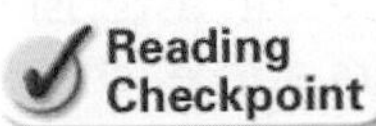

**How did Earth's climate change during the Quaternary Period?**

FIGURE 27
**Ice Age Art**
An early ancestor of modern humans painted these beautiful images of animals in a cave in France more than 15,000 years ago.

## Section 6 Assessment

**Target Reading Skill Previewing Visuals** Compare your questions and answers about Figure 22 with those of a partner.

### Reviewing Key Concepts

1. a. **Listing** What are the periods of the Paleozoic Era?
   b. **Describing** How did Earth's organisms change during the first period of the Paleozoic?
   c. **Relating Cause and Effect** What event do scientists think may have caused the mass extinction at the end of the Paleozoic?
2. a. **Reviewing** Which group of animals was dominant during the Mesozoic Era?
   b. **Inferring** How was their small size helpful to the mammals of the Mesozoic?
   c. **Developing Hypotheses** Many scientists think that the asteroid impact at the end of the Cretaceous prevented plant growth for many years. Although many dinosaurs were plant eaters, some were meat eaters. Develop a hypothesis to explain why no dinosaurs survived.
3. a. **Identifying** What term do scientists apply to the Cenozoic Era?
   b. **Inferring** What conditions allowed so many different kinds of mammals to evolve during the Cenozoic Era?

### Writing in Science

**Description** Suppose that you are going on a tour of Earth during one era of geologic time. Write a paragraph describing the organisms and environments that you see on the tour. Your tour should include at least one stop in each geologic period of the era you chose.

Lab zone **Skills Lab**

# As Time Goes By

## Problem

How can you make a model of geologic time?

## Skills

measuring, calculating, making models

## Materials

- worksheet with 2,000 asterisks
- one ream of paper

## Procedure

### PART 1 Table A

1. Copy Table A into your lab notebook. Figure how long ago these historic events happened and write the answers on your chart.
2. Obtain a worksheet with 2,000 asterisks printed on it. Each asterisk represents one year. The first asterisk at the top represents one year ago.
3. Starting from this asterisk, circle the asterisk that represents how many years ago each event in Table A occurred.
4. Label each circled asterisk to indicate the event.
5. Obtain a ream of copy paper. There are 500 sheets in a ream. If each sheet had 2,000 asterisks on it, there would be a total of 1 million asterisks. Therefore, each ream would represent 1 million years.

**Table A: Historic Events**

| Event | Date | Number of Years Ago |
|---|---|---|
| You are born. | | |
| One of your parents is born. | | |
| First space shuttle sent into space. | 1981 | |
| Neil Armstrong first walks on the moon. | 1969 | |
| World War I ends. | 1918 | |
| Civil War ends. | 1865 | |
| Declaration of Independence is signed. | 1776 | |
| Columbus crosses Atlantic Ocean. | 1492 | |
| Leif Ericson visits North America. | 1000 | |

| Table B: Geologic Events | | | |
|---|---|---|---|
| Event | Number of Years Ago | Reams or Sheets of Paper | Thickness of Paper |
| Last ice age ends. | 10,000 | | |
| Whales evolve. | 50 million | | |
| Pangaea begins to break up. | 225 million | | |
| First vertebrates develop. | 530 million | | |
| Multicellular organisms (algae) develop. | 1 billion | | |
| Single-celled organisms develop. | 3.5 billion | | |
| Oldest known rocks form. | 4.0 billion | | |
| Earth forms. | 4.6 billion | | |

### PART 2 Table B

6. Copy Table B into your lab notebook. Determine how much paper in reams or sheets would be needed to represent the events in geologic time found in Table B. (*Hint:* Recall that each ream represents 1 million years.)
7. Measure the thickness of a ream of paper. Use this thickness to calculate how thick a stack of paper would need to be to represent how long ago each geologic event occurred. (*Hint:* Use a calculator to multiply the thickness of the ream of paper by the number of reams.) Enter your results in Table B.

## Analyze and Conclude

1. **Measuring** Measure the height of your classroom. How many reams of paper would you need to reach the ceiling? How many years would the height of the ceiling represent? Which geologic events listed in Table B would fall on a ream of paper inside your classroom?
2. **Calculating** At this scale, how many classrooms would have to be stacked on top of each other to represent the age of Earth? The time when vertebrates appeared?
3. **Calculating** How many times higher would the thickness of the stack be for the age of Earth than for the breakup of Pangaea?
4. **Making Models** On your model, how could you distinguish one era or period from another? How could you show when particular organisms evolved and when they became extinct?
5. **Communicating** Is the scale of your model practical? What would be the advantages and disadvantages of a model that fit geologic time on a timeline 1 meter long?

## More to Explore

This model represents geologic time as a straight line. Can you think of other ways of representing geologic time graphically? Using colored pencils, draw your own version of the geologic time scale so that it fits on a single sheet of typing paper. (*Hint:* You could represent geologic time as a wheel, a ribbon, or a spiral.)

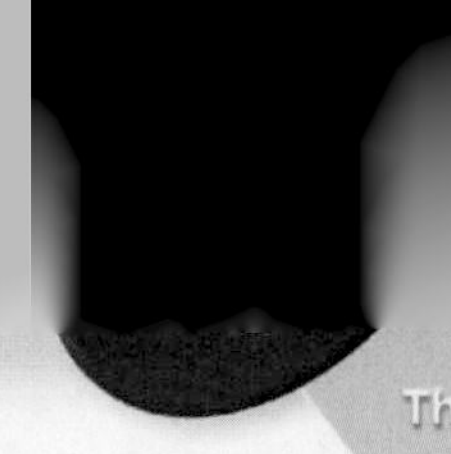

**The BIG Idea** **Earth's History** Evidence from rocks and fossils shows how Earth's geologic features and living things have changed over time.

## 1 Fossils

**Key Concepts**

- Most fossils form when living things die and are buried by sediments. The sediments slowly harden into rock and preserve the shapes of the organisms.
- Fossils found in rock include molds and casts, petrified fossils, carbon films, and trace fossils. Other fossils form when the remains of organisms are preserved in substances such as tar, amber, or ice.
- The fossil record provides evidence about the history of life and past environments on Earth. The fossil record also shows that different groups of organisms have changed over time.

**Key Terms**

fossil
sedimentary rock
mold
cast
petrified fossil
carbon film
trace fossil
paleontologist
scientific theory
evolution
extinct

## 2 The Relative Age of Rocks

**Key Concepts**

- According to the law of superposition, in horizontal sedimentary rock layers the oldest layer is at the bottom. Each higher layer is younger than the layers below it.
- To determine relative age, geologists also study extrusions and intrusions of igneous rock, faults, and gaps in the geologic record.
- Index fossils are useful because they tell the relative ages of the rock layers in which they occur.

**Key Terms**

relative age
absolute age
law of superposition
extrusion
intrusion
fault
unconformity
index fossil

## 3 Radioactive Dating

**Key Concepts**

- During radioactive decay, the atoms of one element break down to form atoms of another.
- Radioactive dating gives a rock's absolute age.

**Key Terms**

atom
element
radioactive decay
half-life

## 4 The Geologic Time Scale

**Key Concepts**

- Geologists use the geologic time scale to show the time span of Earth's history.
- After Precambrian Time, the basic units of the geologic time scale are eras and periods.

**Key Terms**

geologic time scale
era
period

## 5 Early Earth

**Key Concepts**

- Scientists hypothesize that Earth formed at the same time as the other planets and the sun, roughly 4.6 billion years ago.
- During early Precambrian Time, an atmosphere, oceans, and continents formed.
- Fossils of single-celled organisms have been dated to about 3.5 billion years ago.

**Key Terms**

comet
continental drift

## 6 Eras of Earth's History

**Key Concepts**

- At the beginning of the Paleozoic Era, many different kinds of organisms evolved.
- During the Permian Period, about 260 million years ago, the supercontinent Pangaea formed.

**Key Terms**

invertebrate
vertebrate
amphibian
reptile
mass extinction
mammal

# Review and Assessment

Go Online PHSchool.com
For: Self-Assessment
Visit: PHSchool.com
Web Code: cfa-2040

## Organizing Information

**Concept Mapping** Copy the concept map about fossils onto a piece of paper. Then complete it and add a title. (For more on concept maps, see the Skills Handbook.)

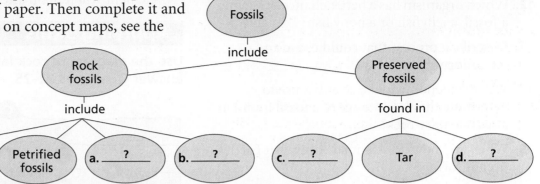

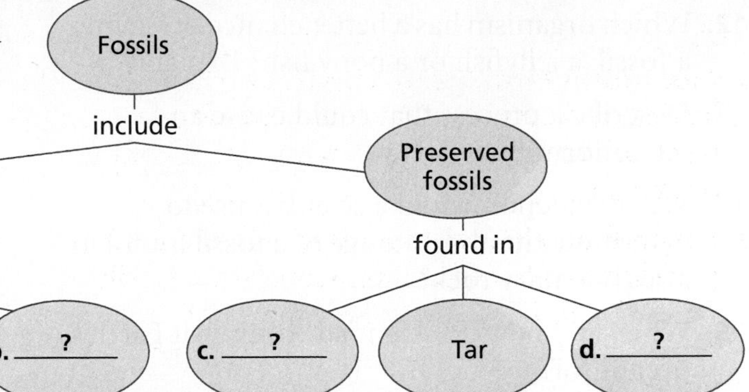


## Reviewing Key Terms

**Choose the letter of the best answer.**

1. A hollow area in sediment in the shape of all or part of an organism is called a
   **a.** mold. **b.** cast.
   **c.** trace fossil. **d.** carbon film.
2. A gap in the geologic record formed when sedimentary rocks cover an eroded surface is called a(n)
   **a.** intrusion. **b.** unconformity.
   **c.** fault. **d.** extrusion.
3. The time it takes for half of a radioactive element's atoms to decay is a(n)
   **a.** era. **b.** half-life.
   **c.** relative age. **d.** absolute age.
4. The geologic time scale is subdivided into
   **a.** relative ages.
   **b.** absolute ages.
   **c.** unconformities.
   **d.** eras and periods.
5. An animal that doesn't have a backbone is called a(n)
   **a.** vertebrate.
   **b.** mammal.
   **c.** invertebrate.
   **d.** amphibian.

**If the statement is true, write *true*. If it is false, change the underlined word or words to make the statement true.**

6. A dinosaur footprint in rock is an example of a <u>trace fossil</u>.
7. A <u>carbon film</u> is a fossil in which minerals have replaced all or part of an organism.
8. The <u>relative age</u> of something is the exact number of years since an event has occurred.
9. Earth's landmasses move slowly in a process called <u>continental drift</u>.
10. Scientists think dinosaurs became extinct as part of a(n) <u>intrusion</u> at the end of the Cretaceous Period.

## Writing in Science

**Field Guide** Write a field guide for visitors to the Grand Canyon. In your guide, explain how geologists have learned about Earth's past by studying the canyon walls and the fossils they contain.

*A Trip Through Geologic Time*
Video Preview
Video Field Trip
▶ Video Assessment

# Review and Assessment

## Checking Concepts

**11.** How does a petrified fossil form?

**12.** Which organism has a better chance of leaving a fossil: a jellyfish or a bony fish? Explain.

**13.** Describe a process that could cause an unconformity.

**14.** What evidence would a scientist use to determine the absolute age of a fossil found in a sedimentary rock?

**15.** When and how do scientists think that Earth's oceans formed?

**16.** How did Earth's environments change from the Tertiary Period to the Quarternary Period? Explain.

## Thinking Critically

**17. Applying Concepts** Paleontologists find a trilobite fossil in a rock layer at the top of a hill in South America. Then they find the same kind of fossil in a rock layer at the bottom of a cliff in Africa. What could the paleontologists conclude about the two rock layers?

**18. Problem Solving** Which of the elements in the table below would be better to use in dating a fossil from Precambrian time? Explain.

**Radioactive Elements**

| Element | Half-life (years) |
|---|---|
| Carbon-14 | 5,730 |
| Uranium-235 | 713 million |

**19. Relating Cause and Effect** When Pangaea formed, the climate changed and the land on Earth became drier. How was this climate change more favorable to reptiles than amphibians?

**20. Making Judgments** If you see a movie in which early humans fight giant dinosaurs, how would you judge the scientific accuracy of that movie? Give reasons for your judgment.

## Math Practice

**21. Percentage** What percentage of a radioactive element will remain after 9 half-lives?

## Applying Skills

**Use the diagram of rock layers below to answer Questions 22–25.**

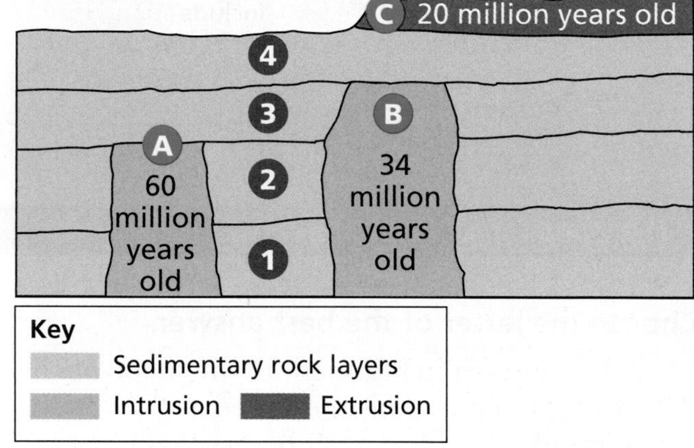


**22. Inferring** According to the Law of Superposition, which is the oldest layer of sedimentary rock? Which is the youngest? How do you know?

**23. Measuring** What method did a scientist use to determine the age of the intrusion and extrusion?

**24. Interpreting Data** What is the relative age of layer 3? (*Hint:* With what absolute ages can you compare it?)

**25. Interpreting Data** What is the relative age of layer 4?

## Lab zone Chapter Project

**Performance Assessment** You have completed your illustrations for the timeline and travel brochure. Now you are ready to present the story of the geologic time period you researched. Be sure to include the awesome sights people will see when they travel to this time period. Don't forget to warn them of any dangers that await them. In your journal, reflect on what you have learned about Earth's history.

# Standardized Test Prep

**Test-Taking Tip**

**Answering a Constructed-Response Question**

A constructed-response question asks you to compose an answer in your own words. Read the question carefully and note the type of information your response should contain. Your answer should address all the specific points asked for in the question. Before you begin writing, organize the information for your response.

***Sample Question***

Compare preserved remains and trace fossils. Give an example of each type of fossil.

***Answer***

Both preserved remains and trace fossils provide evidence of ancient life forms. However, with preserved remains, an organism has been fossilized with little or no change. An example of preserved remains would be an insect in amber. A trace fossil preserves evidence of an organism, not the organism itself. The footprint of a dinosaur would be an example of a trace fossil.

**Choose the letter of the best answer.**

**1.** A geologist finds identical index fossils in a rock layer in the Grand Canyon in Arizona and in a rock layer in northern Utah, more than 675 kilometers away. What inference can she make about the ages of the two rock layers?
- **A** the rock layer in the Grand Canyon is older
- **B** the rock layer in Utah is older
- **C** the two rock layers are about the same age
- **D** no inferences

**2.** What should you use so that the geologic time scale covering Earth's 4.6 billion year history can be drawn as a straight line on a poster board one meter high?
- **F** 1 cm = 1 million years
- **G** 1 cm = 10,000 years
- **H** 1 cm = 100,000 years
- **J** 1 cm = 50,000,000 years

*Use the diagram below and your knowledge of science to answer Question 3.*

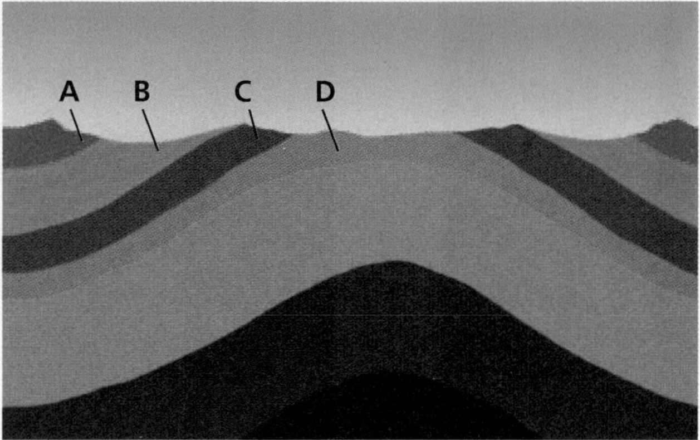


**3.** According to the law of superposition, the youngest layer of rock in this diagram is
- **A** Layer A
- **B** Layer B
- **C** Layer C
- **D** Layer D

**4.** What was used by geologists to define the beginnings and ends of the divisions of the geologic time scale?
- **F** radioactive dating
- **G** major changes in life forms
- **H** types of rocks present
- **J** volcanic events

**5.** A leaf falls into a shallow lake and is rapidly buried in the sediment that changes to rock over millions of years. Which type of fossil would be formed?
- **A** mold and cast
- **B** carbon film
- **C** trace fossil
- **D** amber

## Constructed Response

**6.** Describe two methods geologists use to determine the age of a rock. In your answer, be sure to mention igneous rock, sedimentary rock, the law of superposition, index fossils, radioactive decay, and half-life.

Chapter 11

# Energy Resources

The **BIG Idea**

Energy Resources and Technology

**What are the advantages and disadvantages of renewable and nonrenewable energy resources?**

## Chapter Preview

**1 Fossil Fuels**

***Discover*** What's in a Piece of Coal?

***Skills Activity*** Graphing

***Analyzing Data*** Fuels and Electricity

***At-Home Activity*** Heating Fuel Pros and Cons

**2 Renewable Sources of Energy**

***Discover*** Can You Capture Solar Energy?

***Try This*** Blowing in the Wind

***Technology Lab*** Design and Build a Solar Cooker

**3 Nuclear Energy**

***Discover*** Why Do They Fall?

***Skills Activity*** Calculating

***Active Art*** Nuclear Power Plant

***At-Home Activity*** Shoot the Nucleus

**4 Energy Conservation**

***Discover*** Which Bulb Is More Efficient?

***Tech & Design in History*** Energy-Efficient Products

***Consumer Lab*** Keeping Comfortable

***Technology and Society*** The Hybrid Car

Well-maintained electrical lines help ensure that electrical energy continues to flow. ▶

*Energy Resources*

▶ Video Preview
Video Field Trip
Video Assessment

Lab zone™ Chapter **Project**

## Energy Audit

How much energy does it take to keep your school running? In this chapter's project, you will work in a group to study energy use in your school.

**Your Goal** To report on one type of energy use in your school and make suggestions for saving energy

To complete this project, you must

- survey the types and amount of energy used in one area of your school
- identify ways to conserve energy in that area
- prepare a written report summarizing your observations and proposing your suggestions
- follow the safety guidelines in Appendix A

**Plan It!** Select an area of the school to study, such as a classroom, the cafeteria, or the school grounds. You could also consider the school's heating or cooling system or transportation to and from school. Then decide what type of data you will collect. When you begin your study, look for ways to reduce energy use.

Section 1

# Fossil Fuels

## Reading Preview

### Key Concepts

- How do fuels provide energy?
- What are the three major fossil fuels?
- Why are fossil fuels considered nonrenewable resources?

### Key Terms

- fuel • energy transformation
- combustion • fossil fuel
- hydrocarbon • petroleum
- refinery • petrochemical

### Target Reading Skill

**Building Vocabulary** Using a word in a sentence helps you think about how best to explain the word. After you read the section, reread the paragraphs that contain definitions of Key Terms. Use all the information you have learned to write a meaningful sentence using each Key Term.

## Lab zone Discover **Activity**

### What's in a Piece of Coal?

1. Observe a chunk of coal. Record your observations in as much detail as possible, including its color, texture, and shape.
2. Now use a hand lens to observe the coal more closely.
3. Examine your coal for fossils—imprints of plant or animal remains.

**Think It Over**

**Observing** What did you notice when you used the hand lens compared to your first observations? What do you think coal is made of?

How did you travel to school today? Whether you traveled in a car or a bus, walked, or rode your bike, you used some form of energy. The source of that energy was a fuel. A **fuel** is a substance that provides energy—such as heat, light, motion, or electricity—as the result of a chemical change.

## Energy Transformation and Fuels

Rub your hands together quickly for several seconds. Did they become warmer? When you moved your hands, they had mechanical energy, the energy of motion. The friction of your hands rubbing together converted the mechanical energy to thermal energy, which you felt as heat. A change from one form of energy to another is called an **energy transformation,** or an energy conversion.

Gasoline is a fossil fuel.

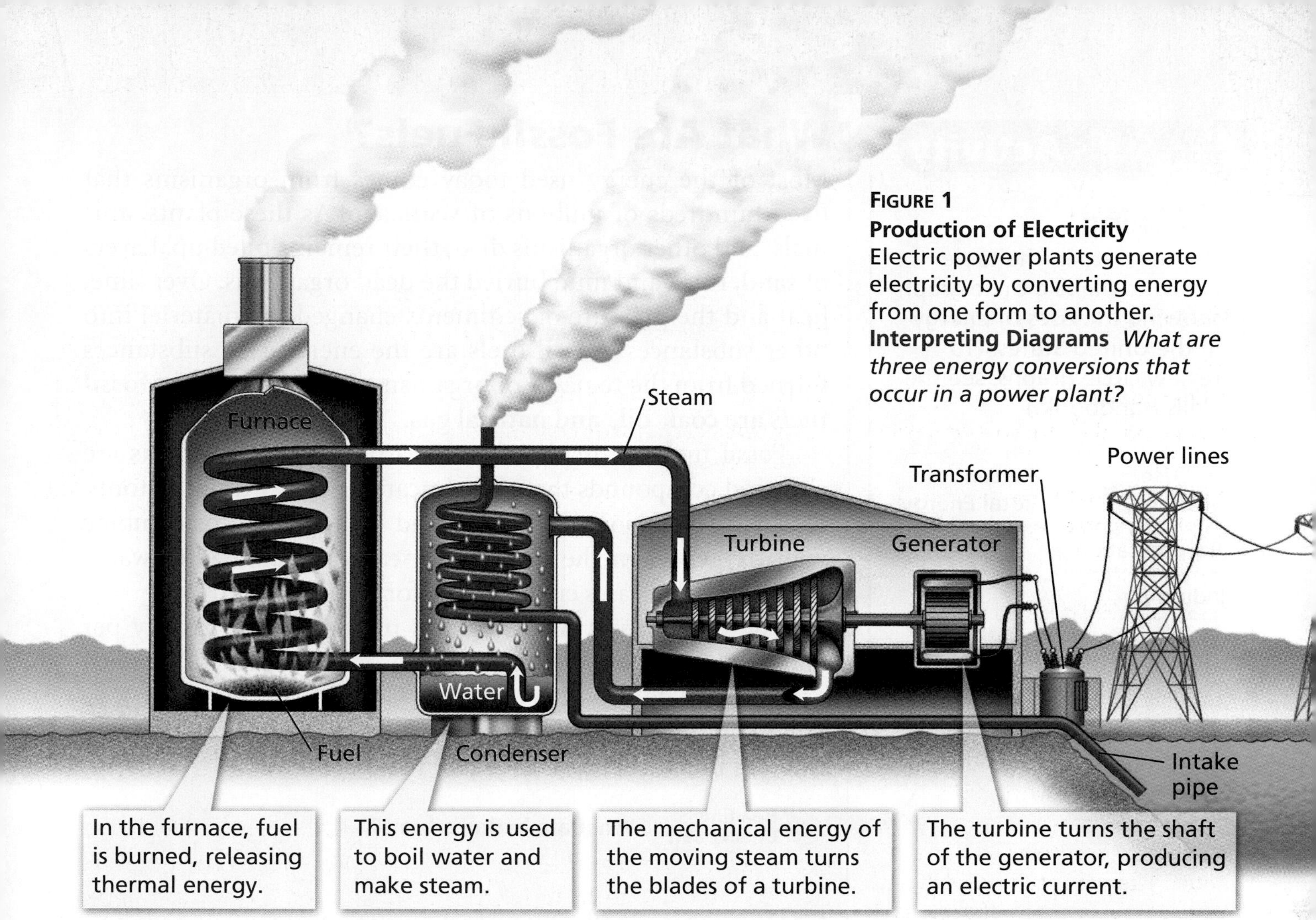

**FIGURE 1**
**Production of Electricity**
Electric power plants generate electricity by converting energy from one form to another.
**Interpreting Diagrams** *What are three energy conversions that occur in a power plant?*

Furnace
Steam
Water
Fuel
Condenser
Turbine
Generator
Transformer
Power lines
Intake pipe

In the furnace, fuel is burned, releasing thermal energy.

This energy is used to boil water and make steam.

The mechanical energy of the moving steam turns the blades of a turbine.

The turbine turns the shaft of the generator, producing an electric current.

**Combustion** Fuels contain stored chemical energy, which can be released by **combustion,** or burning. **When fuels are burned, the chemical energy that is released can be used to generate another form of energy, such as heat, light, motion, or electricity.** For example, when the gasoline in a car's engine is burned, it undergoes a chemical change. Some of the chemical energy stored in the gasoline is converted into thermal energy. This thermal energy is then converted to mechanical energy that moves the car.

**Production of Electricity** The chemical energy stored in fuels can be used to generate electricity. In an electric power plant, the thermal energy produced by burning fuel is used to boil water, making steam, as shown in Figure 1. The mechanical energy of the steam then turns a turbine. The turbine is connected to a generator, which consists of powerful magnets surrounded by coils of copper wire. As the magnets turn inside the wire coil, an electric current is produced. This current flows through power lines to homes and industries.

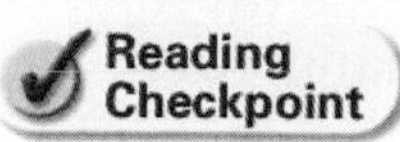

**What energy transformations occur in a car's engine?**

**For:** Links on fossil fuels
**Visit:** www.SciLinks.org
**Web Code:** scn-0551

## Lab zone Skills Activity

### Graphing

Use the data in the table below to make a circle graph showing the uses of energy in the United States. (To review circle graphs, see the Skills Handbook.)

| End Use of Energy | Percent of Total Energy |
|---|---|
| Transportation | 26.5 |
| Industry | 38.1 |
| Homes and businesses | 35.4 |

# What Are Fossil Fuels?

Most of the energy used today comes from organisms that lived hundreds of millions of years ago. As these plants, animals, and other organisms died, their remains piled up. Layers of sand, rock, and mud buried the dead organisms. Over time, heat and the pressure of sediments changed the material into other substances. **Fossil fuels** are the energy-rich substances formed from the remains of organisms. **The three major fossil fuels are coal, oil, and natural gas.**

Fossil fuels are made of hydrocarbons. **Hydrocarbons** are chemical compounds that contain carbon and hydrogen atoms. During combustion, the carbon and hydrogen atoms combine with oxygen from the air to form carbon dioxide and water. Combustion releases energy in the forms of heat and light.

The combustion of fossil fuels provides more energy per kilogram than does the combustion of other fuels. One kilogram of coal, for example, can provide twice as much energy as one kilogram of wood. Oil and natural gas can provide three times as much energy as an equal mass of wood.

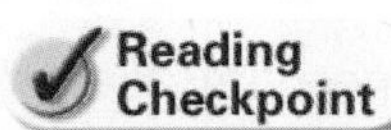

What are hydrocarbons?

**Coal** Coal is a solid fossil fuel formed from plant remains. Figure 2 shows the process by which coal forms. People have burned coal to produce heat for thousands of years. Wood was more convenient and cheaper than coal for most people until the Industrial Revolution of the 1800s, however. The huge energy needs of growing industries then made it worthwhile to find, mine, and transport coal. Today, coal makes up about 23 percent of the fuel used in the United States. Most of that coal fuels electrical power plants.

Before coal can be used to produce energy, it has to be mined, or removed from the ground. Miners use machines to chop the coal into chunks and lift it to the surface. Coal mining can be a dangerous job. Thousands of miners have been killed or injured in accidents in the mines. Many more suffer from lung diseases. Fortunately, modern safety procedures and better equipment have made coal mining safer.

Coal is the most plentiful fossil fuel in the United States. It is fairly easy to transport and provides a lot of energy when burned. But coal also has some disadvantages. Coal mining can increase erosion. Runoff from coal mines can cause water pollution. Burning most types of coal results in more air pollution than other fossil fuels. And coal mining can be dangerous.

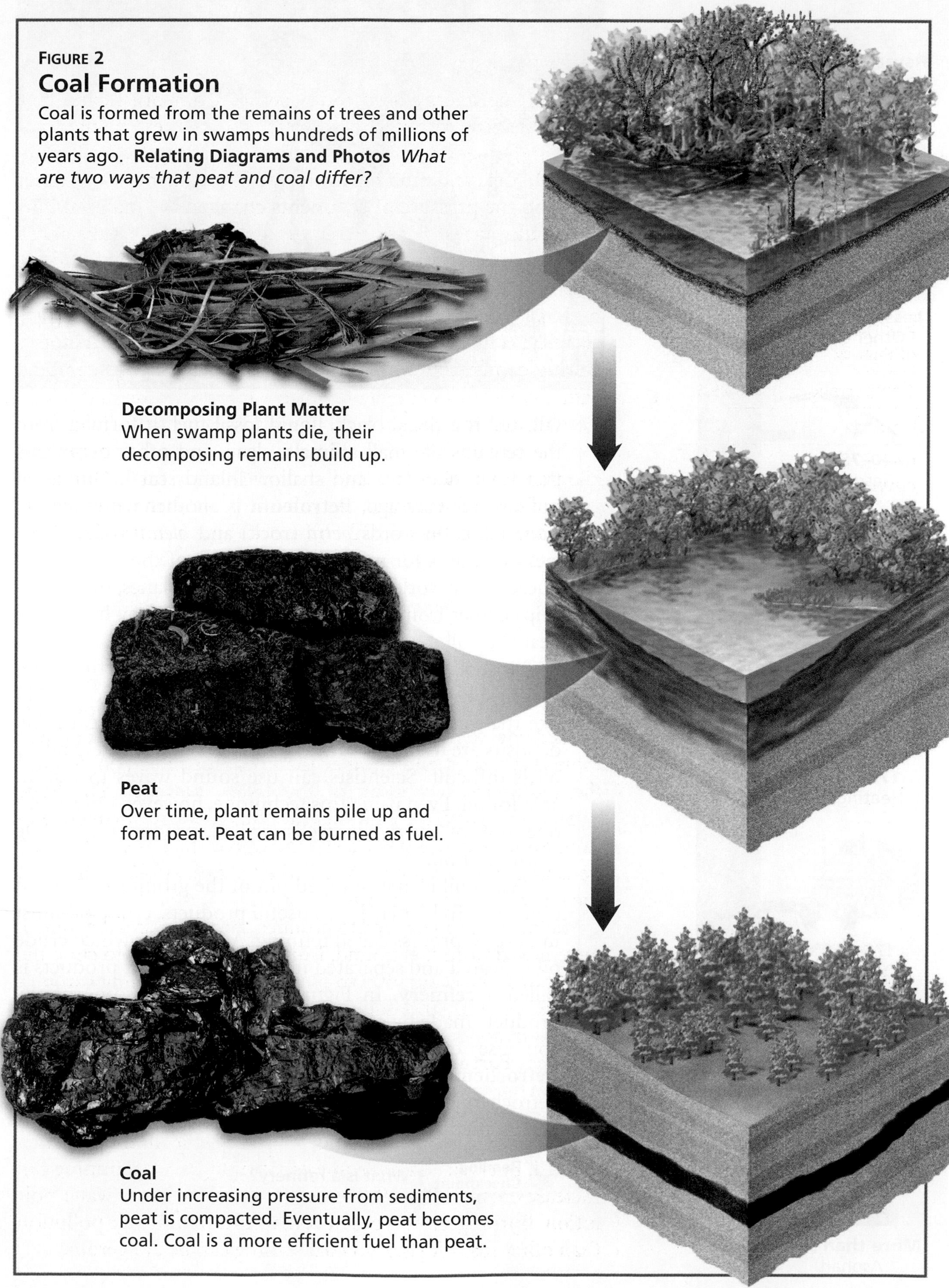

FIGURE 2
## Coal Formation

Coal is formed from the remains of trees and other plants that grew in swamps hundreds of millions of years ago. **Relating Diagrams and Photos** *What are two ways that peat and coal differ?*

**Decomposing Plant Matter**
When swamp plants die, their decomposing remains build up.

**Peat**
Over time, plant remains pile up and form peat. Peat can be burned as fuel.

**Coal**
Under increasing pressure from sediments, peat is compacted. Eventually, peat becomes coal. Coal is a more efficient fuel than peat.

FIGURE 3
**Oil Production**
Crude oil is first pumped out of the ground and then refined. In the refining process, crude oil is heated and separated to make different products.

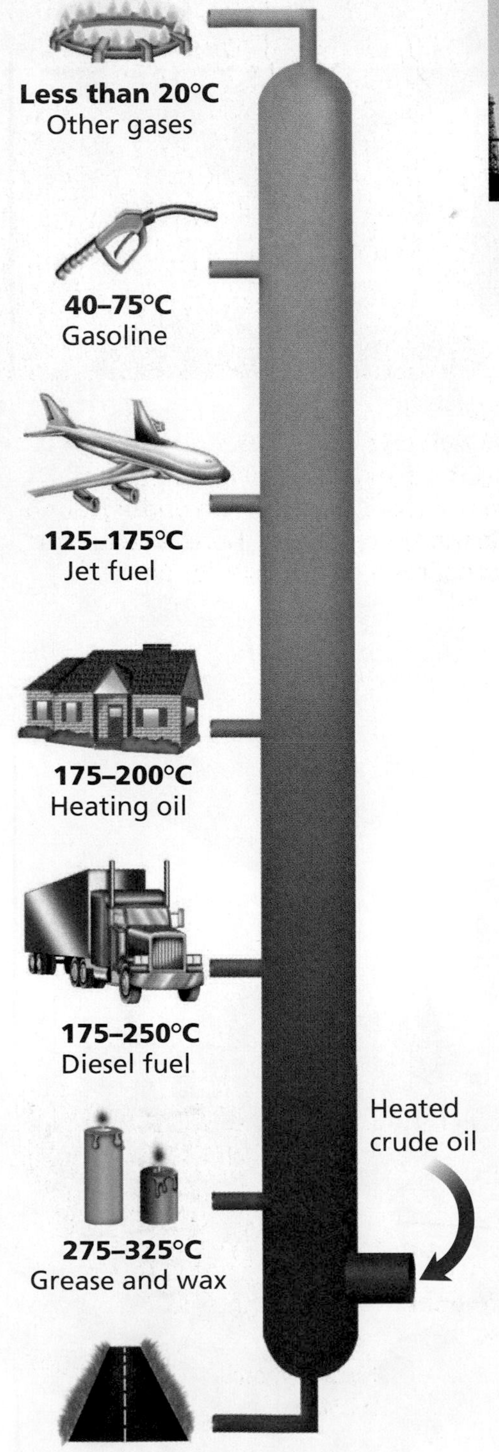

**Oil** Oil is a thick, black, liquid fossil fuel. It formed from the remains of small animals, algae, and other organisms that lived in oceans and shallow inland seas hundreds of millions of years ago. **Petroleum** is another name for oil, from the Latin words *petra* (rock) and *oleum* (oil). Petroleum accounts for more than one third of the energy produced in the world. Fuel for most cars, airplanes, trains, and ships comes from petroleum. In addition, many homes are heated by oil.

Most oil deposits are located underground in tiny holes in sandstone or limestone. The oil fills the holes somewhat like the way water fills the holes of a sponge. Because oil deposits are usually located deep below the surface, finding oil is difficult. Scientists can use sound waves to test an area for oil. Even using this technique, however, only about one out of every six wells drilled produces a usable amount of oil.

When oil is first pumped out of the ground, it is called crude oil. To be made into useful products, crude oil must undergo a process called refining. A factory in which crude oil is heated and separated into fuels and other products is called a **refinery.** In Figure 3, you can see some of the products made by refining crude oil. Many other products you use every day are also made from crude oil. **Petrochemicals** are compounds that are made from oil. Petrochemicals are used to make plastics, paints, medicines, and cosmetics.

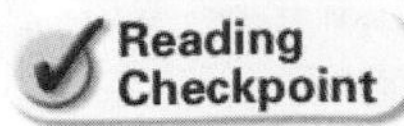

**What is a refinery?**

**Natural Gas** Natural gas is a mixture of methane and other gases. Natural gas forms from some of the same organisms as oil. Because it is less dense than oil, natural gas often rises above an oil deposit, forming a pocket of gas in the rock.

Pipelines transport natural gas from its source to the places where it is used. If all the gas pipelines in the United States were connected, they would reach to the moon and back—twice! Natural gas can also be compressed into a liquid and stored in tanks as fuel for trucks and buses.

Natural gas has several advantages. It produces large amounts of energy but lower levels of many air pollutants than coal or oil. It is also easy to transport once the network of pipelines is built. One disadvantage of natural gas is that it is highly flammable. A gas leak can cause a violent explosion and fire.

Gas companies help to prevent dangerous explosions from leaks. If you use natural gas in your home, you probably are familiar with the "gas" smell that alerts you whenever there is unburned gas in the air. You may be surprised to learn that natural gas actually has no odor at all. What causes the strong smell? Gas companies add a chemical with a distinct smell to the gas before it is piped to homes and businesses so that people can detect a gas leak.

FIGURE 4
**Natural Gas Pipelines**
More than 2,500,000 kilometers of natural gas pipelines run underground in the United States. Here, a technician prepares a new section of pipe.

## Math Analyzing Data

### Fuels and Electricity

The circle graph shows which energy sources are used to produce electricity in the United States.

1. **Reading Graphs** What does each wedge of the circle represent?
2. **Interpreting Data** Which energy source is used to generate most of the electricity in the United States?
3. **Drawing Conclusions** What percentage of the electricity production in the United States relies on fossil fuels?
4. **Predicting** How might the circle graph differ 50 years from now? Give reasons to support your prediction.

**United States Electricity Production by Energy Source**

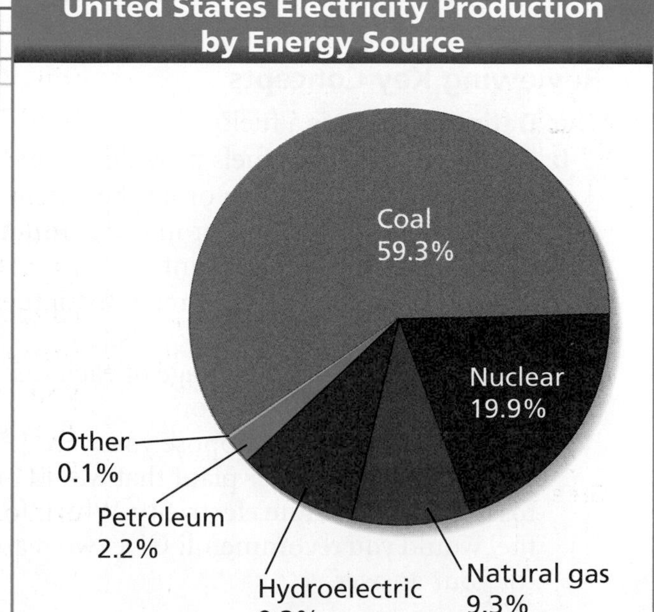

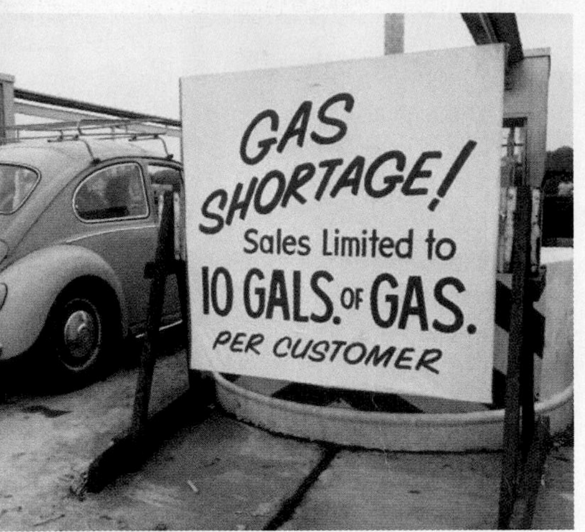


**FIGURE 5**
**Supply and Demand**
In the 1970s, a group of oil-exporting nations reduced their oil exports to the United States. Gasoline shortages resulted.

## Fuel Supply and Demand

The many advantages of using fossil fuels as an energy source have made them essential to modern life. **But since fossil fuels take hundreds of millions of years to form, they are considered nonrenewable resources.** For example, Earth's known oil reserves took 500 million years to form. One fourth of this oil has already been used. If fossil fuels continue to be used more rapidly than they are formed, the reserves will eventually be used up.

Many nations that consume large amounts of fossil fuels have very small reserves. They have to buy oil, natural gas, and coal from nations with large supplies. The United States, for example, uses about one third of all the oil produced in the world. But only 3 percent of the world's oil supply is located in this country. The difference must be purchased from countries with large oil supplies. The uneven distribution of fossil fuel reserves has often been a cause of political problems in the world.

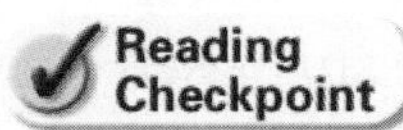


**Why are some nations dependent on others for fossil fuels?**

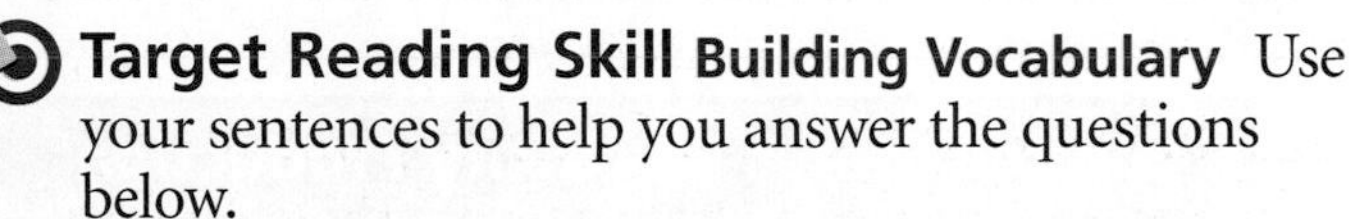


**Target Reading Skill Building Vocabulary** Use your sentences to help you answer the questions below.

### Reviewing Key Concepts

1. a. **Defining** What is a fuel?
   b. **Explaining** How do fuels provide energy?
   c. **Sequencing** Describe in order the energy transformations that occur in the production of electricity at a power plant.
2. a. **Listing** What are the three main fossil fuels?
   b. **Comparing and Contrasting** List an advantage and a disadvantage of each fossil fuel discussed in this section.
   c. **Making Judgments** Suppose you were designing a new power plant that would burn fossil fuel to generate electricity. Which fossil fuel would you recommend? Give two reasons for your answer.
3. a. **Reviewing** Why are fossil fuels considered nonrenewable resources?
   b. **Problem Solving** List three things you can do to reduce your dependence on fossil fuels.

**Lab zone At-Home Activity**

**Heating Fuel Pros and Cons** Talk to an adult family member to find out what type of fuel heats or cools your home. Then, with the family member, list some advantages and disadvantages of that type of fuel. Share what you learned with your classmates. What fuel source is used by the majority of students in your class?

Section 2

• Tech & Design •

# Renewable Sources of Energy

## Reading Preview

### Key Concepts

- What forms of energy does the sun provide?
- What are some renewable sources of energy?

### Key Terms

- solar energy
- hydroelectric power
- biomass fuel
- gasohol
- geothermal energy

### Target Reading Skill

**Previewing Visuals** Before you read, preview Figure 7. Then write two questions that you have about the diagram in a graphic organizer like the one below. As you read, answer your questions.

**Solar House**

| |
|---|
| Q. How does the house capture solar energy? |
| A. |
| Q. |

## Lab zone Discover Activity

### Can You Capture Solar Energy?

1. Pour 250 milliliters of water into each of two resealable, clear plastic bags.
2. Record the water temperature in each bag. Seal the bags.
3. Put one bag in a dark or shady place. Put the other bag in a place where it will receive direct sunlight.
4. Predict what the temperature of the water in each bag will be after 30 minutes.
5. Record the temperatures after 30 minutes.

**Think It Over**

**Developing Hypotheses** How did the water temperature in each bag change? What could account for these results?

You've just arrived at the campsite for your family vacation. The sun streaming through the trees warms your face. A breeze stirs, carrying with it the smell of a campfire. Maybe you'll start your day with a dip in the warm water of a nearby hot spring.

You might be surprised to learn that even in these woods, you are surrounded by energy resources. The sun warms the air, the wind blows, and heat from inside Earth warms the waters of the spring. These sources of energy are all renewable—they are constantly being supplied. Scientists are trying to find ways to put these renewable energy resources to work to meet people's energy needs.

Campers surrounded by renewable resources ▶

## Harnessing the Sun's Energy

The warmth you feel on a sunny day is **solar energy,** or energy from the sun. **The sun constantly gives off energy in the forms of light and heat.** Solar energy is the source, directly or indirectly, of most other renewable energy resources. In one day, Earth receives enough solar energy to meet the energy needs of the entire world for 40 years. Solar energy does not cause pollution, and it will not run out for billions of years.

So why hasn't solar energy replaced energy from fossil fuels? One reason is that solar energy is only available when the sun is shining. Another problem is that the energy Earth receives from the sun is very spread out. To obtain a useful amount of power, it is necessary to collect solar energy from a large area.

FIGURE 6
**Solar Collector**
This mirror collects energy from the sun and powers an electric plant in New South Wales, Australia. **Inferring** *Why is the Australian desert a practical location for a solar power plant?*

**Solar Power Plants** One way to capture the sun's energy involves using giant mirrors. In a solar power plant, rows of mirrors focus the sun's rays to heat a tank of water. The water boils, creating steam, which can then be used to generate electricity.

**Solar Cells** Solar energy can be converted directly into electricity in a solar cell. A solar cell has a negative and a positive terminal, like a battery. When light hits the cell, an electric current is produced. Solar cells power some calculators, lights, and other small devices. However, it would take more than 5,000 solar cells the size of your palm to produce enough electricity for a typical American home.

**Passive Solar Heating** Solar energy can be used to heat buildings with passive solar systems. A passive solar system converts sunlight into thermal energy, which is then distributed without using pumps or fans. Passive solar heating is what occurs in a parked car on a sunny day. Solar energy passes through the car's windows and heats the seats and other car parts. These parts transfer heat to the air, and the inside of the car warms. The same principle can be used to heat a home.

**Active Solar Heating** An active solar system captures the sun's energy, and then uses pumps and fans to distribute the heat. First, light strikes the dark metal surface of a solar collector. There, it is converted to thermal energy. Water is pumped through pipes in the solar collector to absorb the thermal energy. The heated water then flows to a storage tank. Finally, pumps and fans distribute the heat throughout the building.

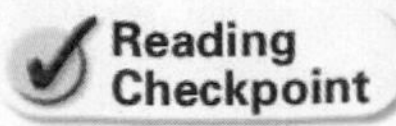

**How do solar cells work?**

FIGURE 7
## Solar House
A solar house uses passive and active heating systems to convert solar energy into heat and electricity.

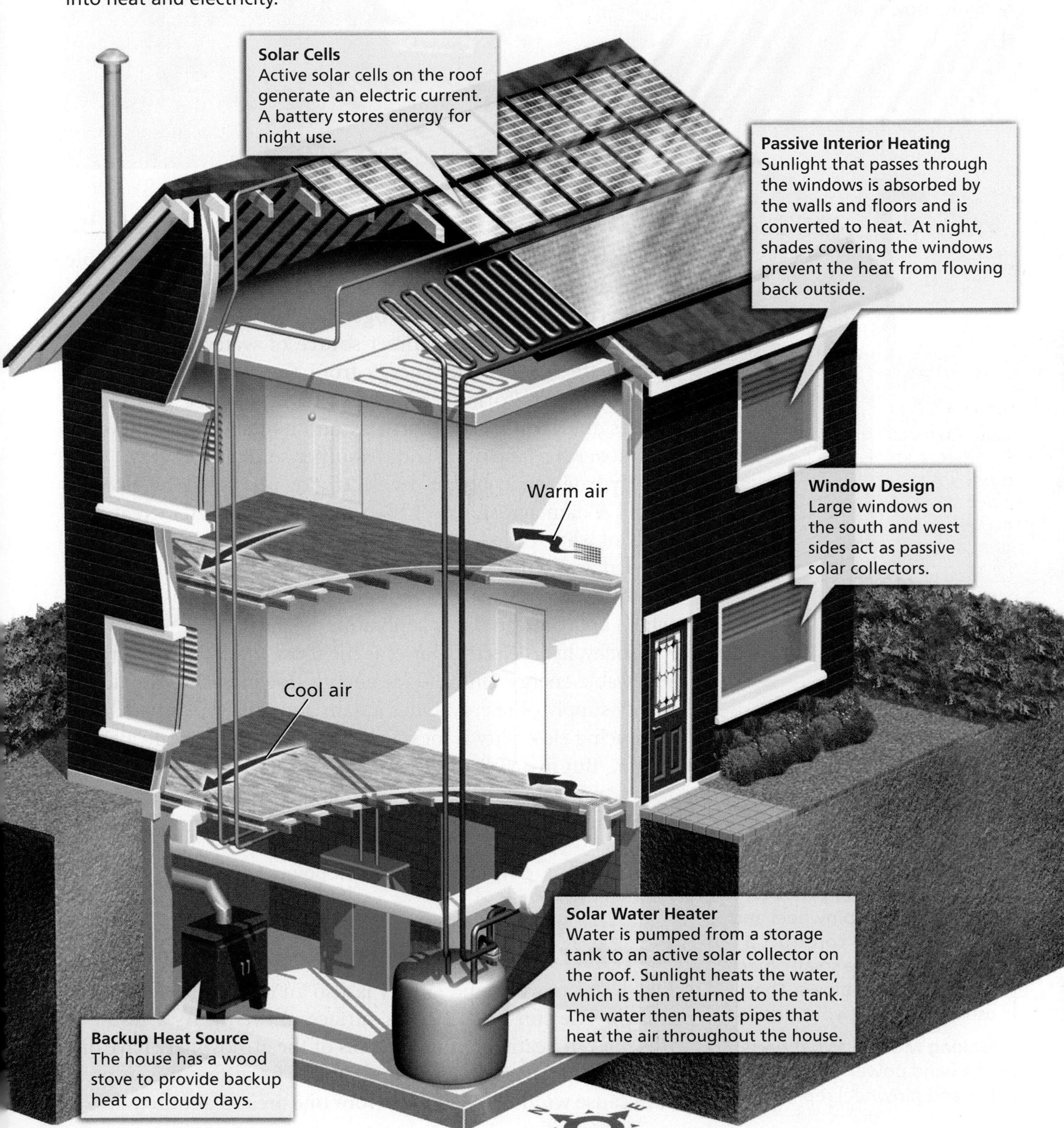

Solar Cells
Active solar cells on the roof generate an electric current. A battery stores energy for night use.
Passive Interior Heating
Sunlight that passes through the windows is absorbed by the walls and floors and is converted to heat. At night, shades covering the windows prevent the heat from flowing back outside.
Warm air
Window Design
Large windows on the south and west sides act as passive solar collectors.
Cool air
Solar Water Heater
Water is pumped from a storage tank to an active solar collector on the roof. Sunlight heats the water, which is then returned to the tank. The water then heats pipes that heat the air throughout the house.
Backup Heat Source
The house has a wood stove to provide backup heat on cloudy days.
N
E
S
W

FIGURE 8
**Water and Wind Power**
Both this dam in Arizona and this wind farm in California use renewable sources of energy to generate power.

## Hydroelectric Power

The sun is one source of renewable energy. **Other renewable sources of energy include water, the wind, biomass fuels, geothermal energy, and hydrogen.**

Solar energy is the indirect source of water power. Recall that in the water cycle, energy from the sun heats water on Earth's surface, forming water vapor. The water vapor condenses and falls back to Earth as rain and snow. As the water flows over the land, it provides another source of energy.

**Hydroelectric power** is electricity produced by flowing water. A dam across a river blocks the flow of water, creating a body of water called a reservoir. When a dam's control gates are opened, water flows through tunnels at the bottom of the dam. As the water moves through the tunnels, it turns turbines, which are connected to a generator.

Today, hydroelectric power is the most widely used source of renewable energy. Unlike solar energy, flowing water provides a steady supply of energy. Once a dam and power plant are built, producing electricity is inexpensive and does not create air pollution. But hydroelectric power has limitations. In the United States, most suitable rivers have already been dammed. And dams can have negative effects on the environment.

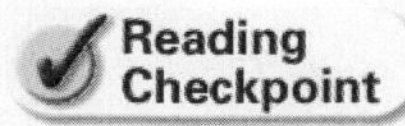

What is hydroelectric power?

### Lab zone Try This Activity

**Blowing in the Wind**

You can make a model that shows how wind can do the work necessary to produce energy. Using a pinwheel and other materials, construct a device that lifts a small object when the wind blows. Then use a fan to test your device.

**Making Models** What parts of a wind power plant do the fan and pinwheel represent?

## Capturing the Wind

Like water power, wind energy is also an indirect form of solar energy. The sun heats Earth's surface unevenly. As a result of this uneven heating, different areas of the atmosphere have different temperatures and air pressures. The differences in pressure cause winds as air moves from one area to another.

Wind can be used to turn a turbine and generate electricity. Wind farms consist of many windmills. Together, the windmills generate large amounts of power.

Wind is the fastest-growing energy source in the world. Wind energy does not cause pollution. In places where fuels are difficult to transport, wind energy is the major source of power.

But wind energy has drawbacks. Few places have winds that blow steadily enough to provide much energy. Wind energy generators are noisy and can be destroyed by very strong winds. Still, as fossil fuels become more scarce, wind energy will become more important.

**FIGURE 9**
**Biomass Fuels**
Biomass fuels are fuels that are made from living things.
**Comparing and Contrasting** *How are biomass fuels similar to energy sources such as wind and water? How are they different?*

## Biomass Fuels

Wood was probably the first fuel ever used for heat and light. Wood belongs to a group of fuels called **biomass fuels,** which are made from living things. Other biomass fuels include leaves, food wastes, and even manure. As fossil fuel supplies shrink, people are taking a closer look at biomass fuels. For example, when oil prices rose in the early 1970s, Hawaiian sugar cane farmers began burning sugar cane wastes to generate electricity. At one point, these wastes provided almost one fourth of the electricity used on the island of Kauai.

Aside from being burned as fuel, biomass materials can also be converted into other fuels. For example, corn, sugar cane, and other crops can be used to make alcohol. Adding the alcohol to gasoline forms a mixture called **gasohol.** Gasohol can be used as fuel for cars. Bacteria can produce methane gas when they decompose biomass materials in landfills. That methane can be used to heat buildings. And some crops, such as soybeans, can produce oil that can be used as fuel, which is called biodiesel fuel.

Biomass fuels are renewable resources. But it takes time for new trees to replace those that have been cut down. And producing alcohol and methane in large quantities is expensive. As a result, biomass fuels are not widely used today in the United States. But as fossil fuels become scarcer, biomass fuels may play a larger role in meeting energy needs.

▲ A woman uses a wood-fired oven in Nepal.

▲ This car runs on vegetable oil.

Reading Checkpoint **What is gasohol?**

For: Links on renewable energy
Visit: www.SciLinks.org
Web Code: scn-0552

## Tapping Earth's Energy

Below Earth's surface are pockets of very hot liquid rock called magma. In some places, magma is very close to the surface. The intense heat from Earth's interior that warms the magma is called **geothermal energy.**

In certain regions, such as Iceland and New Zealand, magma heats underground water to the boiling point. In these places, the hot water and steam can be valuable sources of energy. For example, in Reykjavík, Iceland, 90 percent of homes are heated by water warmed underground in this way. Geothermal energy can also be used to generate electricity, as shown in Figure 10.

Geothermal energy is an unlimited source of cheap energy. But it does have disadvantages. There are only a few places where magma comes close to Earth's surface. Elsewhere, very deep wells would be needed to tap this energy. Drilling deep wells is very expensive. Even so, geothermal energy is likely to play a part in meeting energy needs in the future.

**Reading Checkpoint** **How can geothermal energy be used to generate electricity?**

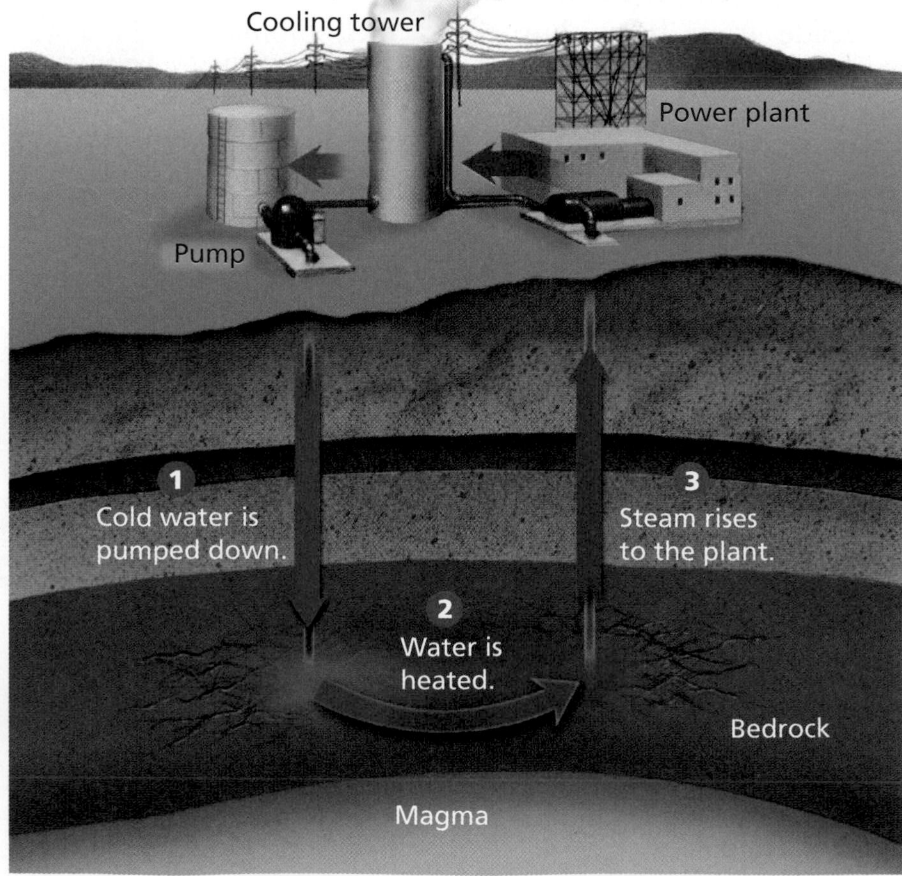


**FIGURE 10**
**Geothermal Energy**
A geothermal power plant uses heat from Earth's interior as an energy source. Cold water is piped deep into the ground, where it is heated by magma. The resulting steam can be used for heat or to generate electricity.
**Making Generalizations** *What is one advantage and one disadvantage of geothermal energy?*

## The Promise of Hydrogen Power

Now that you have read about so many energy sources, consider a fuel with this description: It burns cleanly. It creates no smog or acid rain. It exists on Earth in large supply.

This ideal-sounding fuel is real—it's hydrogen. Unfortunately, almost all the hydrogen on Earth is combined with oxygen in water. Pure hydrogen can be obtained by passing an electric current through water. But it takes more energy to obtain the hydrogen than is produced by burning it.

Still, scientists find hydrogen power promising. At present, hydroelectric plants decrease their activity when the demand for electricity is low. Instead, they could run at full capacity all the time, using the excess electricity to produce hydrogen. Similarly, solar power plants often generate more electricity than is needed during the day. This extra electricity could be used to produce hydrogen. Scientists are also searching for other ways to produce hydrogen cheaply from water.

Car manufacturers are now developing cars that run on hydrogen fuel cells. These would produce water as emissions. That water might then be used again as fuel. You can see that if scientists can find a way to produce hydrogen cheaply, it could someday be an important source of energy.

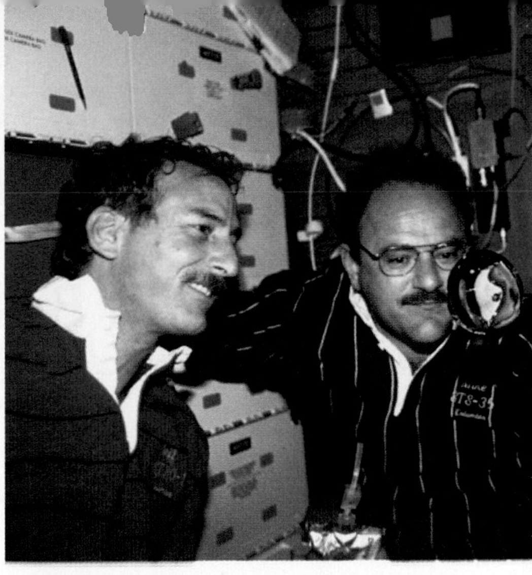

**FIGURE 11**
**Hydrogen Power**
The object fascinating these astronauts is a bubble of water—the harmless byproduct of the hydrogen fuel cells used on the space shuttle.

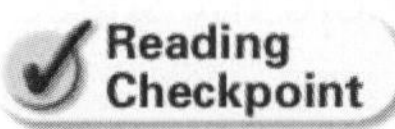

**Reading Checkpoint** **In what common substance is most hydrogen on Earth found?**

## Section 2 Assessment

**Target Reading Skill** **Previewing Visuals** Compare your questions and answers about Figure 7 with those of a partner.

### Reviewing Key Concepts

1. a. **Identifying** What two forms of energy does the sun supply?
   b. **Explaining** What are two reasons that solar energy has not replaced energy from fossil fuels?
   c. **Applying Concepts** A friend of yours argues that shopping malls should use solar energy to conserve fossil fuels. How would you respond?
2. a. **Listing** List five renewable energy sources other than solar energy.
   b. **Classifying** Which of the renewable energy sources that you listed are actually indirect forms of solar energy? Explain.
   c. **Predicting** Which source of renewable energy do you think is most likely to be used in your community in 50 years? Give reasons to support your answer.

### Writing in Science

**Advertisement** Write an advertisement for one of the renewable energy sources discussed in this section. Be sure to mention how its advantages make it superior to the other energy sources. Also mention how scientists might be able to overcome its disadvantages.

Lab zone

# Technology Lab

• Tech & Design •

## Design and Build a Solar Cooker

### Problem

What is the best shape for a solar cooker?

### Skills Focus

designing a solution, evaluating the design

### Materials

- scissors
- frozen vegetables
- 3 sheets of aluminum foil
- 3 sheets of oaktag paper
- wooden or plastic stirrers
- glue
- 3 thermometers
- tape
- clock or watch
- optional materials provided by your teacher

### Procedure  

**PART 1** **Research and Investigate**

1. Glue a sheet of aluminum foil, shiny side up, to each sheet of oaktag paper. Before the glue dries, gently smooth out any wrinkles in the foil.
2. Bend one sheet into a U shape. Leave another sheet flat. Bend another sheet into a shape of your own choosing.
3. Predict which shape will produce the largest temperature increase when placed in the sun. Write down your prediction and explain your reasons.
4. Place the aluminum sheets in direct sunlight. Use wood blocks or books to hold the sheets in position, if necessary.
5. Record the starting temperature on each thermometer.
6. Place the thermometer bulbs in the center of the aluminum shapes. After 15 minutes, record the final temperature on each thermometer.

## PART 2 Design and Build

7. Using what you learned in Part 1, design a solar cooker that can cook frozen vegetables. Your solar cooker should
   - be no larger than 50 cm on any side
   - cook the vegetables in less than 10 minutes
   - be made of materials approved by your teacher
8. Prepare a written description of your plan that includes a sketch of your cooker. Include a list of materials and an operational definition of a "well-cooked" vegetable. Obtain your teacher's approval for your design. Then build your solar cooker.

## PART 3 Evaluate and Redesign

9. Test your solar cooker by spearing some frozen vegetables on the stirrers. Time how long it takes to cook the vegetables. Make note of any problems with your solar cooker design.
10. Based on your test, decide how you could improve the design of your cooker. Then make any desired changes to your cooker and test how the improved cooker functions.

## Analyze and Conclude

1. **Identifying a Need** In what situations might it be important to have an efficient cooker that does not use fuel?
2. **Designing a Solution** How did you incorporate what you learned in Part 1 into your design in Part 2? For example, which shape did you use in your cooker design?
3. **Evaluating the Design** When you tested your solar cooker, what problems did you encounter?
4. **Redesigning** In what ways did you change your design for your second test? How did the redesign improve the performance of your cooker?
5. **Working With Design Constraints** Why might it be important for solar cookers to use inexpensive, readily available materials?
6. **Evaluating the Impact on Society** How can solar-powered devices help meet the world's future energy needs? What limitation do solar-powered devices have?

## Communicate

Design an advertisement for your solar cooker that will appear in a camping magazine. Make sure your ad describes the benefits of solar cookers in general, and of your design in particular.

# 3 Nuclear Energy

## Reading Preview

### Key Concepts

- What happens during a nuclear fission reaction?
- How does a nuclear power plant produce electricity?
- How does a nuclear fusion reaction occur?

### Key Terms

- nucleus • nuclear fission
- reactor vessel • fuel rod
- control rod • meltdown
- nuclear fusion

### Target Reading Skill

**Comparing and Contrasting**

As you read, compare fission and fusion reactions in a Venn diagram like the one below. Write the similarities in the space where the circles overlap and the differences on the left and right sides.

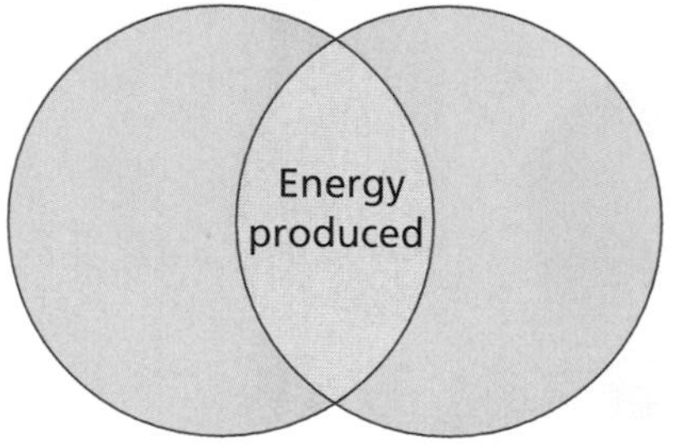


## Lab zone Discover Activity

### Why Do They Fall?

1. Line up 15 dominoes to form a triangle.
2. Knock over the first domino so that it falls against the second row of dominoes. Observe the results.
3. Set up the dominoes again, but then remove the dominoes in the third row from the lineup.
4. Knock over the first domino again. Observe what happens.

**Think It Over**

**Inferring** Suppose each domino produced a large amount of energy when it fell over. Why might it be helpful to remove the dominoes as you did in Step 3?

Wouldn't it be great if people could use the same method as the sun to produce energy? In a way, they can! The kind of reactions that power the sun involve the central cores of atoms. The central core of an atom that contains the protons and neutrons is called the **nucleus** (plural *nuclei*). Reactions that involve nuclei, called nuclear reactions, result in tremendous amounts of energy. Two types of nuclear reactions are fission and fusion.

## Nuclear Fission

Nuclear reactions convert matter into energy. As part of his theory of relativity, Albert Einstein developed a formula that described the relationship between energy and matter. You have probably seen this famous equation: $E = mc^2$. In the equation, the $E$ represents energy and the $m$ represents mass. The $c$, which represents the speed of light, is a very large number. This equation states that when matter is changed into energy, an enormous amount of energy is released.

▲ Albert Einstein 1879–1955

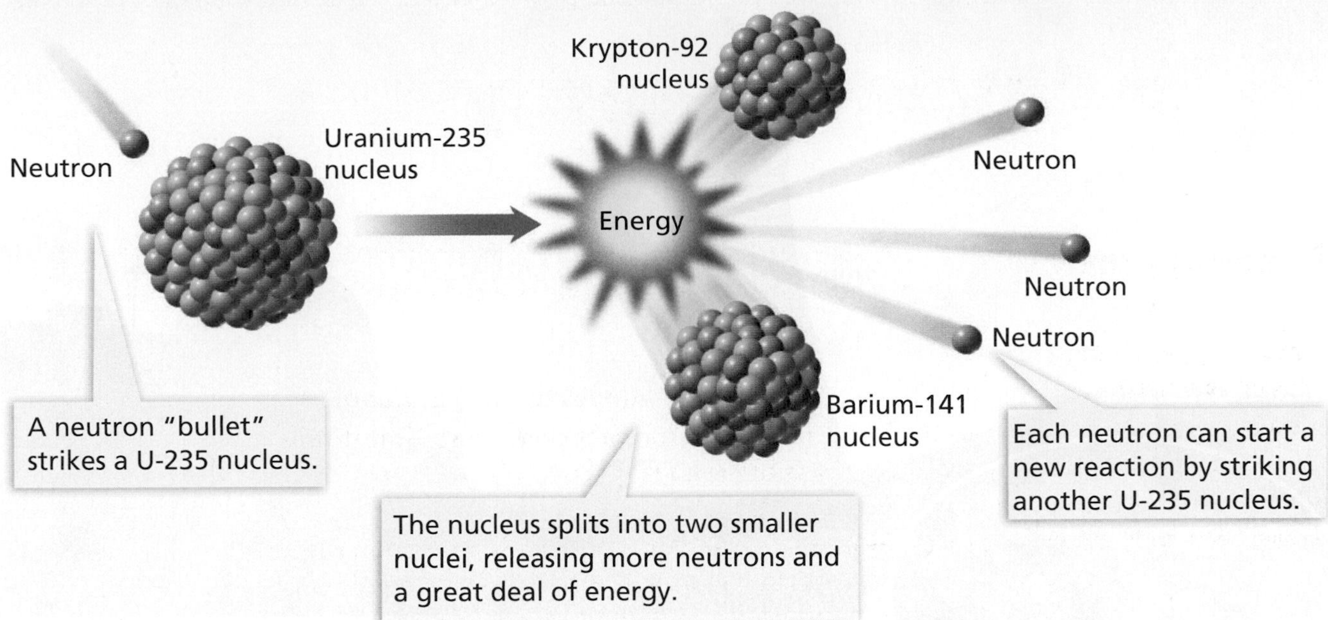
Neutron
Uranium-235 nucleus
Krypton-92 nucleus
Energy
Neutron
Neutron
Neutron
Barium-141 nucleus
A neutron "bullet" strikes a U-235 nucleus.
The nucleus splits into two smaller nuclei, releasing more neutrons and a great deal of energy.
Each neutron can start a new reaction by striking another U-235 nucleus.

**FIGURE 12**
**Nuclear Fission**
A great deal of energy is released in a nuclear fission reaction.
**Interpreting Diagrams** *How does a nuclear fission reaction begin?*

**Fission Reactions** **Nuclear fission** is the splitting of an atom's nucleus into two smaller nuclei. The fuel for the reaction is a large atom that has an unstable nucleus, such as uranium-235 (U-235). A neutron is shot at the U-235 atom at high speed. **When the neutron hits the U-235 nucleus, the nucleus splits apart into two smaller nuclei and two or more neutrons.** The total mass of all these particles is a bit less than the mass of the original nucleus. The small amount of mass that makes up the difference has been converted into energy—a lot of energy, as described by Einstein's equation.

Meanwhile, the fission reaction has produced three more neutrons. If any of these neutrons strikes another nucleus, the fission reaction is repeated. More neutrons and more energy are released. If there are enough nuclei nearby, the process repeats in a chain reaction, just like a row of dominoes falling. In a nuclear chain reaction, the amount of energy released increases rapidly with each step in the chain.

**Energy From Fission** What happens to all the energy released by these fission reactions? If a nuclear chain reaction is not controlled, the released energy causes a huge explosion. The explosion of an atomic bomb is an uncontrolled nuclear fission reaction. A few kilograms of matter explode with more force than several thousand tons of dynamite. However, if the chain reaction is controlled, the energy is released as heat, which can be used to generate electricity.

**Reading Checkpoint** **What happens if a nuclear chain reaction is not controlled?**

**Lab zone Skills Activity**

### Calculating

A pellet of U-235 produces as much energy as 615 liters of fuel oil. An average home uses 5,000 liters of oil a year. How many U-235 pellets would be needed to supply the same amount of energy?

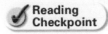

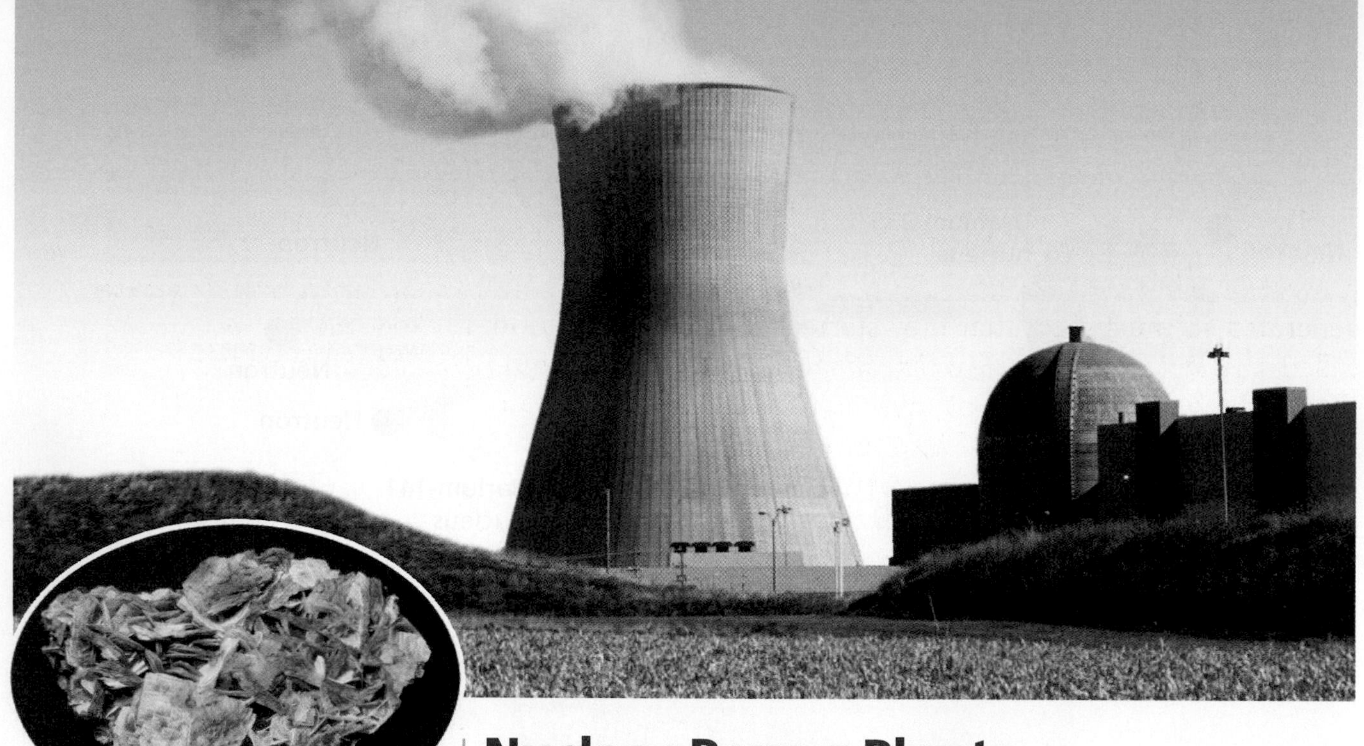

**FIGURE 13**
**Nuclear Power**
Nuclear power plants generate much of the world's electricity. The inset shows autunite, one of the ores of uranium. The uranium fuel for nuclear power plants is refined from uranium ores.

## Nuclear Power Plants

Controlled nuclear fission reactions take place inside nuclear power plants. Nuclear power plants generate much of the world's electricity—about 20 percent in the United States and more than 70 percent in France. **In a nuclear power plant, the heat released from fission reactions is used to change water into steam. The steam then turns the blades of a turbine to generate electricity.** Look at the diagram of a nuclear power plant in Figure 14. In addition to the generator, it has two main parts: the reactor vessel and the heat exchanger.

**Reactor Vessel** The **reactor vessel** is the part of the nuclear reactor where nuclear fission occurs. The reactor contains rods of U-235, called **fuel rods.** When several fuel rods are placed close together, a series of fission reactions occurs.

If the reactor vessel gets too hot, control rods are used to slow down the chain reactions. **Control rods,** made of the metal cadmium, are inserted between the fuel rods. The cadmium absorbs neutrons released during fission and slows the speed of the chain reactions. The cadmium control rods can then be removed to speed up the chain reactions again.

**Heat Exchanger** Heat is removed from the reactor vessel by water or another fluid that is pumped through the reactor. This fluid passes through a heat exchanger. There, the fluid boils water to produce steam, which runs the electrical generator. The steam is condensed again and pumped back to the heat exchanger.

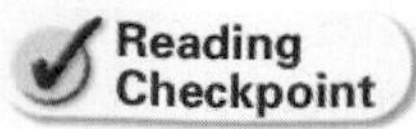

**What is the purpose of a control rod?**

**The Risks of Nuclear Power** At first, people thought that nuclear fission would provide an almost unlimited source of clean, safe energy. But accidents at nuclear power plants have led to safety concerns. In 1986, the reactor vessel in a nuclear power plant in Chernobyl, Ukraine, overheated. The fuel rods generated so much heat that they started to melt, a condition called a **meltdown.** The excess heat caused a series of explosions, which injured or killed dozens of people. In addition, radioactive materials escaped into the environment.

Accidents can be avoided by careful planning and improved safety features. A more difficult problem is the disposal of the radioactive wastes. Radioactive wastes remain dangerous for many thousands of years. Scientists must find a way to store these wastes safely for a long period of time.

Go Online
*active art*

**For:** Nuclear Power Plant activity
**Visit:** PHSchool.com
**Web Code:** cep-5053

FIGURE 14
**Nuclear Power Plant**
Nuclear fission provides the energy to generate electricity in a nuclear power plant. **Interpreting Diagrams** *In what part of the power plant does nuclear fission occur?*

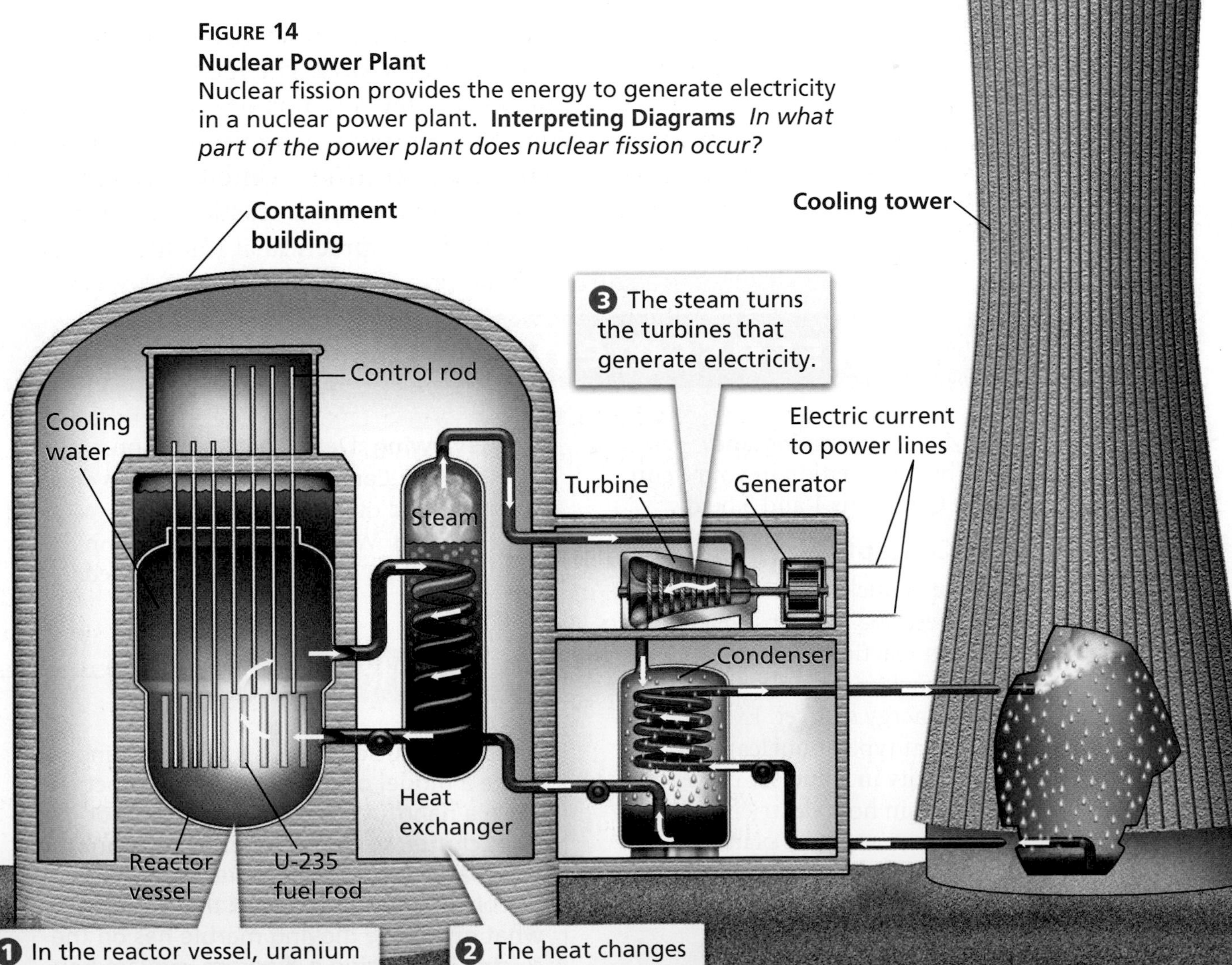
Containment building
Cooling tower
Control rod
Cooling water
Steam
Turbine
Generator
Electric current to power lines
Condenser
Heat exchanger
Reactor vessel
U-235 fuel rod
3 The steam turns the turbines that generate electricity.
1 In the reactor vessel, uranium fuel undergoes nuclear fission, producing heat.
2 The heat changes water into steam in the heat exchanger.

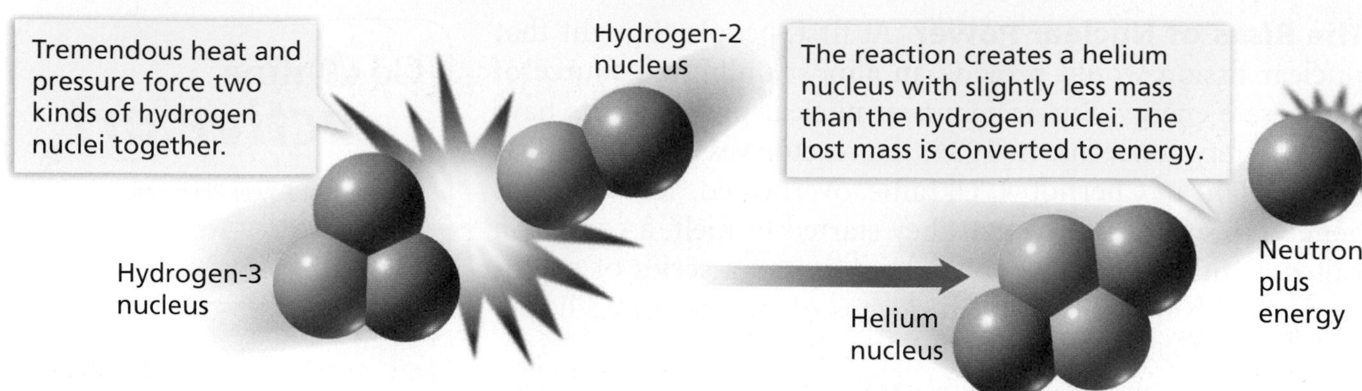
Tremendous heat and pressure force two kinds of hydrogen nuclei together.
Hydrogen-2 nucleus
The reaction creates a helium nucleus with slightly less mass than the hydrogen nuclei. The lost mass is converted to energy.
Hydrogen-3 nucleus
Helium nucleus
Neutron plus energy

**FIGURE 15**
**Nuclear Fusion**
In nuclear fusion, two hydrogen nuclei are forced together, forming a helium nucleus, a neutron, and energy.
**Interpreting Diagrams** *What is released during a fusion reaction?*

## The Quest to Control Fusion

**Nuclear fusion** is the combining of two atomic nuclei to produce a single larger nucleus. **In nuclear fusion, two hydrogen nuclei combine to create a helium nucleus, which has slightly less mass than the two hydrogen nuclei. The lost mass is converted to energy.**

Nuclear fusion could produce much more energy per unit of atomic mass than nuclear fission. The fuel for a fusion reactor is readily available—water contains one kind of hydrogen needed for fusion. Nuclear fusion should also produce less radioactive waste than nuclear fission. Unfortunately, the pressure and temperature required for a reaction make the construction of a fusion reactor impractical at this time.

## Section 3 Assessment

**Target Reading Skill Comparing and Contrasting** Use the information in your Venn diagram to answer Questions 1 and 3 below.

### Reviewing Key Concepts

1. a. **Defining** What is nuclear fission?
   b. **Sequencing** Describe the steps that occur in a nuclear fission reaction.
   c. **Classifying** Is nuclear fission a renewable or nonrenewable energy source? Explain.
2. a. **Identifying** What type of nuclear reaction produces electricity in a nuclear power plant?
   b. **Explaining** Explain how electricity is produced in a nuclear power plant.
   c. **Predicting** What might happen in a nuclear power plant if too many control rods were removed?
3. a. **Reviewing** Define nuclear fusion.
   b. **Relating Cause and Effect** How is energy produced during a nuclear fusion reaction?
   c. **Inferring** What is preventing fusion energy from filling our current energy needs?

### Lab zone At-Home **Activity**

**Shoot the Nucleus** With a family member, make a model of a nuclear fission reaction. Place a handful of marbles on the floor in a tight cluster, so that they touch one another. Step back about a half meter from the marbles. Shoot a marble at the cluster. Note what effect the moving marble has on the cluster. Then using a diagram, explain how this event models a nuclear fission reaction.

Section 4

# Energy Conservation

## Reading Preview

### Key Concept

- What are two ways to preserve our current energy sources?

### Key Terms

- efficiency
- insulation
- energy conservation

### Target Reading Skill

**Using Prior Knowledge** Before you read, write what you know about energy efficiency and conservation in a graphic organizer like the one below. As you read, write what you learn.

| What You Know |
|---|
| 1. I turn off lights to conserve energy.<br>2. |

| What You Learned |
|---|
| 1.<br>2. |

## Lab zone Discover **Activity**

### Which Bulb Is More Efficient?

1. Record the light output (listed in lumens) from the packages of a 60-watt incandescent light bulb and a 15-watt compact fluorescent bulb.
2. Place the fluorescent bulb in a lamp socket. **CAUTION:** *Make sure the lamp is unplugged.*
3. Plug in the lamp and turn it on. Hold the end of a thermometer about 8 centimeters from the bulb.
4. Record the temperature after five minutes.
5. Turn off and unplug the lamp. When the bulb is cool, remove it. Repeat Steps 2, 3, and 4 with the incandescent light bulb.

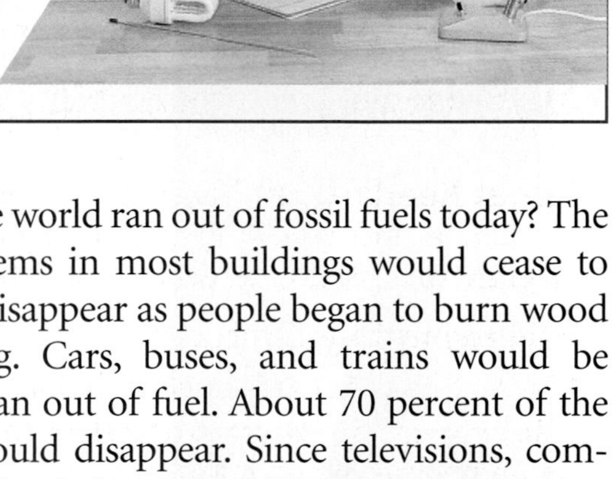

**Think It Over**

**Inferring** The 60-watt bulb uses four times as much energy as the 15-watt bulb. Does it also provide four times as much light output? If not, how can you account for the difference?

What would happen if the world ran out of fossil fuels today? The heating and cooling systems in most buildings would cease to function. Forests would disappear as people began to burn wood for heating and cooking. Cars, buses, and trains would be stranded wherever they ran out of fuel. About 70 percent of the world's electric power would disappear. Since televisions, computers, and telephones depend on electricity, communication would be greatly reduced. Lights, microwave ovens, and most other home appliances would no longer work.

Although fossil fuels won't run out immediately, they also won't last forever. Most people think that it makes sense to use fuels more wisely now to avoid fuel shortages in the future. **One way to preserve our current energy resources is to increase the efficiency of our energy use. Another way is to conserve energy whenever possible.**

## Energy Efficiency

One way to make energy resources last longer is to use fuels more efficiently. **Efficiency** is the percentage of energy that is actually used to perform work. The rest of the energy is "lost" to the surroundings, usually as heat. People have developed many ways to increase energy efficiency.

**Heating and Cooling** One method of increasing the efficiency of heating and cooling systems is insulation. **Insulation** is a layer of material that traps air to help block the transfer of heat between the air inside and outside a building. You have probably seen insulation made of fiberglass, which looks like pink cotton candy. A layer of fiberglass 15 centimeters thick insulates a room as well as a brick wall 2 meters thick!

Trapped air can act as insulation in windows, too. Many windows consist of two panes of glass with space between them. The air between the panes of glass acts as insulation.

## • Tech & Design in History •

### Energy-Efficient Products

Scientists and engineers have developed many technologies that improve energy efficiency and reduce energy use.

**1932 Fiberglass Insulation**
Long strands of glass fibers trap air and keep buildings from losing heat. Less fuel is used for heating.

**1936 Fluorescent Lighting**
Fluorescent bulbs were introduced to the public at the hundredth anniversary celebration of the United States Patent Office. Because these bulbs use less energy than incandescent bulbs, most offices and schools use fluorescent lights today.

**1958 Solar Cells**
More than 150 years ago, scientists discovered that silicon can convert light into electricity. The first useful application of solar cells was to power the radio on a satellite. Now solar cells are even used on experimental cars like the one above.

1930 1940 1950 1960

**Lighting** Much of the electricity used for home lighting is wasted. For example, less than 10 percent of the electricity that an incandescent light bulb uses is converted into light. The rest is given off as heat. In contrast, compact fluorescent bulbs use about one fourth as much energy to provide the same amount of light.

**Transportation** Engineers have improved the energy efficiency of cars by designing better engines and tires. Another way to save energy is to reduce the number of cars on the road. In many communities, public transit systems provide an alternative to driving. Other cities encourage carpooling. Many cities now set aside lanes for cars containing two or more people.

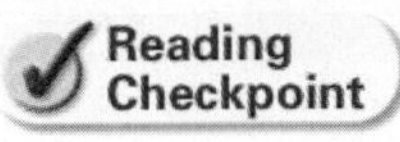


**What are two examples of insulation?**

## Writing in Science

**Research and Write** Design an advertisement for one of the energy-saving inventions described in this timeline. The advertisement may be a print, radio, or television ad. Be sure that your advertisement clearly explains the benefits of the invention.

**1967**
**Microwave Ovens**
The first countertop microwave oven for the home was introduced. Microwaves cook food by heating the water the food contains. Unlike a conventional oven, a microwave oven heats only the food. And preheating is unnecessary, saving even more energy.

**1981 High-Efficiency Window Coatings**
Materials that reflect sunlight were first used to coat windows in the early 1980s. This coating reduces the air conditioning needed to keep the inside of the building cool.

**1997 Hydrogen-Powered Vehicles**
Hydrogen fuel cells produce no polluting emissions. In 1997, two major automakers unveiled experimental hydrogen-powered cars. The first mass-produced hydrogen-powered cars are expected around 2010.

1970 | 1980 | 1990 | 2000

**FIGURE 16**
**Energy Conservation**
There are many ways you can conserve energy.

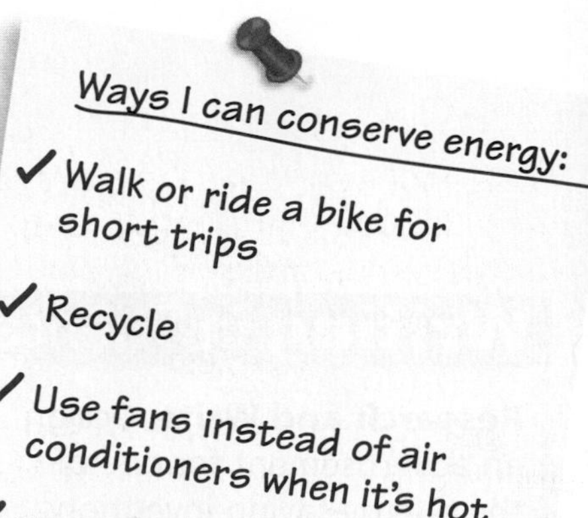

Ways I can conserve energy:
✓ Walk or ride a bike for short trips
✓ Recycle
✓ Use fans instead of air conditioners when it's hot
✓ Turn off the lights and television when leaving a room

## Energy Conservation

Another approach to making energy resources last longer is conservation. **Energy conservation** means reducing energy use.

You can reduce your personal energy use by changing your behavior in some simple ways. For example, if you walk to the store instead of getting a ride, you are conserving the gasoline it would take to drive to the store. You can also follow some of the suggestions in Figure 16.

While these suggestions seem like small things, multiplied by millions of people they add up to a lot of energy saved for the future.

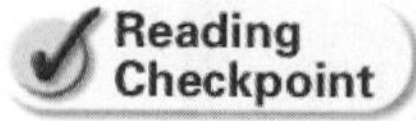

**What are two ways you can reduce your personal energy use?**

## Section 4 Assessment

**Target Reading Skill Using Prior Knowledge** Review your graphic organizer and revise it based on what you just learned in the section.

### Reviewing Key Concepts

1. a. **Identifying** What are the two keys to preserving our current energy resources?
   b. **Applying Concepts** How does insulating buildings help to preserve energy resources? How does carpooling preserve resources?
   c. **Predicting** One office building contains only incandescent lights. The building next door contains only fluorescent lights. Predict which building has higher energy bills. Explain your answer.

### Writing in Science

**Energy Savings Brochure**
Conduct an energy audit of your home. Look for places where energy is being lost, such as cracks around doors. Also look for ways to reduce energy use, such as running the dishwasher only when it is full. Then create a short, illustrated brochure of energy-saving suggestions. Keep the brochure where everyone can see it.

Lab zone **Consumer Lab**

# Keeping Comfortable

## Problem
How well do different materials prevent heat transfer?

## Skills Focus
measuring, controlling variables

## Materials 
- watch or clock
- beakers
- ice water
- hot water
- thermometers or temperature probes
- containers and lids made of paper, glass, plastic, plastic foam, and metal

## Procedure  
1. Use a pencil to poke a hole in the lid of a paper cup. Fill the cup halfway with cold water.

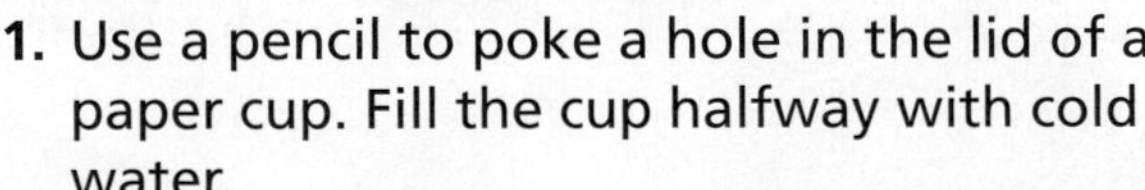

2. Put the lid on the cup. Insert a thermometer into the water through the hole. (If you are using a temperature probe, see your teacher for instructions.) When the temperature stops dropping, place the cup in a beaker. Add hot water to the beaker until the water level is about 1 cm below the lid.
3. Record the water temperature once every minute until it has increased by 5°C. Use the time it takes for the temperature to increase 5°C as a measure of the effectiveness of the paper cup in preventing heat transfer.
4. Choose three other containers and their matching lids to test. Design an experiment to compare how well those materials prevent heat transfer. You can use a similar procedure to the one you used in Steps 1–3.

## Analyze and Conclude
1. **Measuring** In Step 2, what was the starting temperature of the cold water? How long did it take for the temperature to increase by 5°C? In which direction did the heat flow? Explain.
2. **Making Models** If the materials in Steps 1–3 represented your home in very hot weather, which material would represent the rooms in your home? The outdoor weather? The building walls?
3. **Controlling Variables** In the experiment you conducted in Step 4, what were the manipulated and responding variables? What variables were kept constant?
4. **Drawing Conclusions** Which material was most effective at preventing the transfer of heat? Which was the least effective? Explain how your data support your conclusion.
5. **Communicating** Write a paragraph explaining why the results of your experiment could be useful to people building energy-efficient structures.

## Design an Experiment
Design an experiment to compare how well the materials you tested would work if the hot water were inside the cup and the cold water were outside. *Obtain your teacher's permission before carrying out your investigation.*

**For:** Data sharing
**Visit:** PHSchool.com
**Web Code:** ced-5054

# Technology and Society

• Tech & Design •

## The Hybrid Car

How do you get from here to there? Like most people, you probably rely on cars or buses. Engines that burn fossil fuels power most of these vehicles. To conserve fossil fuels, as well as to reduce air pollution, some car companies have begun to produce hybrid vehicles.

### How Are Hybrid Cars Different?

The power source for most cars is a gasoline engine that powers the transmission. Unlike conventional cars, hybrid cars can use both a gasoline engine and an electric motor to turn the transmission. The generated power can be used by the transmission to turn the wheels. Or power can be converted into electricity for later use by the electric motor. Any extra electricity is stored in the car's battery. The gasoline engine in a hybrid car is smaller, more efficient, and less polluting than the engine in a conventional car.

**Gasoline Engine** The engine burns fuel to provide energy to the car.

**Electric Motor and Generator** In this model, the electric motor draws energy from the car's battery to help the car speed up. As the car slows down, the generator produces electricity to recharge the car's battery.

**Transmission** This device transmits power from the engine to the axle that turns the wheels.

**Start** The car uses power from its battery to start the gasoline engine.

**Accelerate** When the car accelerates, the electric motor and the gasoline engine work together to power the car.

**Brake** When the car brakes, the motor acts like a generator and stores electrical energy in the battery.

## Are Hybrid Cars the Way to Go?

Hybrid cars consume less gas per mile and emit fewer pollutants than cars that run on gasoline alone. In spite of the benefits, there are some drawbacks to hybrid cars. In general, hybrid cars have less power for climbing steep hills and less acceleration than cars with larger engines. In addition, the large batteries could be an environmental hazard if they end up in a landfill. Drivers must make trade-offs in buying any car.

**Mileage per Tank of Gas**

Miles Traveled per Tank of Gas (13.2 gallons)

700
600
500
400
300
200
100
0

Conventional Hybrid

Type of Car

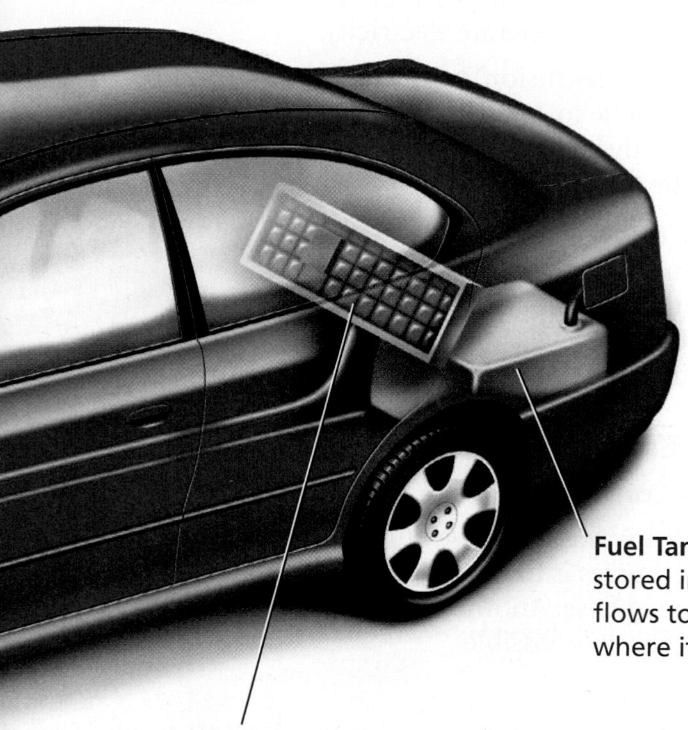

**Fuel Tank** Gasoline stored in the fuel tank flows to the engine where it's burned.

**Battery** The car's electric motor uses energy stored in the battery.

**Stop**
When the car stops or idles, the gasoline engine stops. It restarts when the driver steps on the gas pedal.

## Weigh the Impact

**1. Identify the Need**
Why are some car companies developing hybrid cars?

**2. Research**
Research hybrid cars currently on the market. Use your findings to list the advantages and disadvantages of hybrid-car technology.

**3. Write**
Should your family's next car be a conventional or hybrid model? Use the information here and your research findings to write several paragraphs supporting your opinion.

**For:** More on hybrid cars
**Visit:** PHSchool.com
**Web Code:** ceh-5050

# Chapter 11 Study Guide

**The BIG Idea** **Energy Resources and Technology** Renewable and nonrenewable energy resources differ in cost and availability. These resources also differ in the environmental effects of producing and using them.

## 1 Fossil Fuels

### Key Concepts

- When fuels are burned, the chemical energy that is released can be used to generate another form of energy, such as heat, light, motion, or electricity.
- The three major fossil fuels are coal, oil, and natural gas.
- Since fossil fuels take hundreds of millions of years to form, they are considered nonrenewable resources.

### Key Terms

fuel
energy transformation
combustion
fossil fuel
hydrocarbon
petroleum
refinery
petrochemical

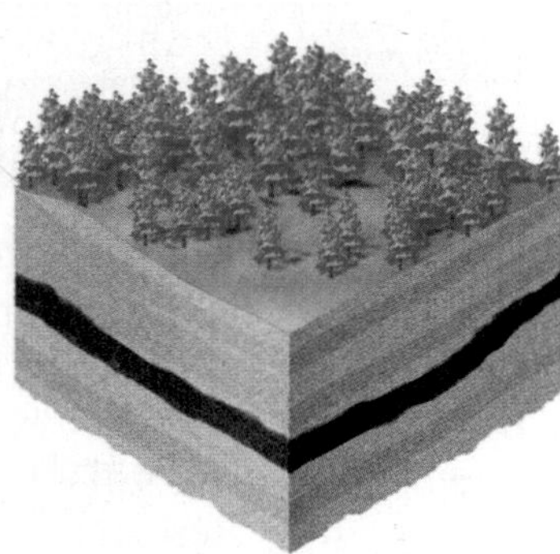

## 2 Renewable Sources of Energy

### Key Concepts

- The sun constantly gives off energy in the forms of light and heat.
- In addition to solar energy, renewable sources of energy include water, the wind, biomass fuels, geothermal energy, and hydrogen.

### Key Terms

solar energy
hydroelectric power
biomass fuel
gasohol
geothermal energy

## 3 Nuclear Energy

### Key Concepts

- During nuclear fission, when a neutron hits a U-235 nucleus, the nucleus splits apart into two smaller nuclei and two or more neutrons.
- In a nuclear power plant, the heat released from fission reactions is used to change water into steam. The steam then turns the blades of a turbine to generate electricity.
- In nuclear fusion, two hydrogen nuclei combine to create a helium nucleus, which has slightly less mass than the two hydrogen nuclei. The lost mass is converted to energy.

### Key Terms

nucleus
nuclear fission
reactor vessel
fuel rod
control rod
meltdown
nuclear fusion

## 4 Energy Conservation

### Key Concept

- One way to preserve our current energy resources is to increase the efficiency of our energy use. Another way is to conserve energy whenever possible.

### Key Terms

efficiency
insulation
energy conservation

# Review and Assessment

Go Online
PHSchool.com
For: Self-Assessment
Visit: PHSchool.com
Web Code: cea-5050

## Organizing Information

**Comparing and Contrasting** Copy the graphic organizer about sources of energy onto a separate sheet of paper. Then complete it and add a title. (For more on Comparing and Contrasting, see the Skills Handbook.)

| Energy Type | Advantage | Disadvantage |
|---|---|---|
| Coal | Easy to transport | a. ___?___ |
| Oil | b. ___?___ | Nonrenewable |
| Solar | c. ___?___ | d. ___?___ |
| Wind | e. ___?___ | f. ___?___ |
| Hydroelectric | No pollution | g. ___?___ |
| Geothermal | h. ___?___ | i. ___?___ |
| Nuclear | j. ___?___ | Radioactive waste |

## Reviewing Key Terms

**Choose the letter of the best answer.**

1. Which of the following is *not* a fossil fuel?
   **a.** coal
   **b.** wood
   **c.** oil
   **d.** natural gas
2. Wind and water energy are both indirect forms of
   **a.** nuclear energy.
   **b.** electrical energy.
   **c.** solar energy.
   **d.** geothermal energy.
3. Which of the following is *not* a biomass fuel?
   **a.** methane
   **b.** gasohol
   **c.** hydrogen
   **d.** sugar cane wastes
4. The particle used to start a nuclear fission reaction is a(n)
   **a.** neutron.
   **b.** electron.
   **c.** proton.
   **d.** atom.
5. A part of a nuclear power plant that undergoes a fission reaction is called a
   **a.** turbine.
   **b.** control rod.
   **c.** heat exchanger.
   **d.** fuel rod.

**If the statement is true, write *true.* If it is false, change the underlined word or words to make the statement true.**

6. The process of burning a fuel for energy is called <u>combustion</u>.
7. Most of the energy used today comes from <u>fossil fuels</u>.
8. Products made from petroleum are called <u>hydrocarbons</u>.
9. Geothermal energy is an example of a <u>nonrenewable</u> energy source.
10. <u>Insulation</u> means reducing energy use.

## Writing in Science

**Letter** In a letter to a friend, predict how solar energy will change your life over the next 20 years. Include specific details in your description.

*Energy Resources*
Video Preview
Video Field Trip
▶ Video Assessment

# Review and Assessment

## Checking Concepts

**11.** Describe how coal forms.

**12.** What is natural gas? How is natural gas transported to where it is needed?

**13.** Describe three features of a solar home. (Your answer may include passive and active solar systems.)

**14.** Explain why solar energy is the indirect source of hydroelectric power.

**15.** Explain how wind can be used to generate electricity.

**16.** How is a nuclear fission reaction controlled in a nuclear reactor?

**17.** Define energy efficiency. Give three examples of inventions that increase energy efficiency.

## Thinking Critically

**18. Comparing and Contrasting** Discuss how the three major fossil fuels are alike and how they are different.

**19. Predicting** Do you think you will ever live in a solar house? Support your prediction with details about the climate in your area.

**20. Classifying** State whether each of the following energy sources is renewable or nonrenewable: coal, solar power, natural gas, hydrogen. Give a reason for each answer.

**21. Making Judgments** Write a short paragraph explaining why you agree or disagree with the following statement: "The United States should build more nuclear power plants to prepare for the future shortage of fossil fuels."

**22. Relating Cause and Effect** In the nuclear reaction shown below, a neutron is about to strike a U-235 nucleus. What will happen next?

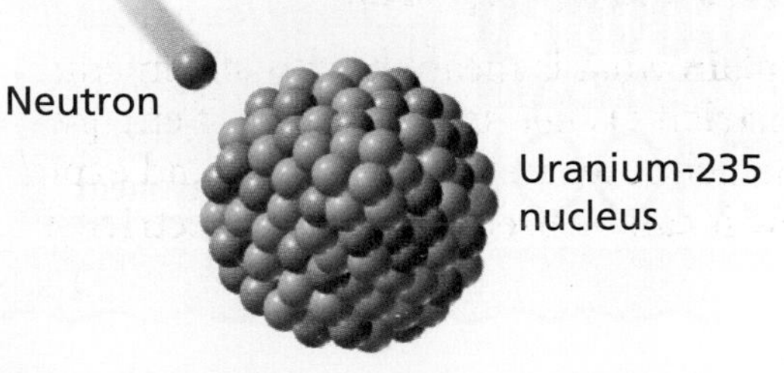


## Applying Skills

**Use the information in the table to answer Questions 23–27.**

*The table below shows the world's energy production in 1973 and today.*

| Energy Source | Units Produced 1973 | Units Produced Today |
|---|---|---|
| Oil | 2,861 | 3,574 |
| Natural gas | 1,226 | 2,586 |
| Coal | 2,238 | 3,833 |
| Nuclear | 203 | 2,592 |
| Hydroelectric | 1,300 | 2,705 |
| Total | 7,828 | 15,290 |

**23. Interpreting Data** How did the total energy production change from 1973 to today?

**24. Calculating** What percentage of the total world energy production did nuclear power provide in 1973? What percentage does it provide today?

**25. Classifying** Classify the different energy sources according to whether they are renewable or nonrenewable.

**26. Inferring** How has the importance of hydroelectric power changed from 1973 to the present?

**27. Predicting** How do you think the world's energy production will change over the next 40 years? Explain.

## Lab zone Chapter Project

**Performance Assessment** Share your energy-audit report with another group. The group should review the report for clarity, organization, and detail. Make revisions based on feedback from the other group. As a class, discuss each group's findings. Then prepare a class proposal with the best suggestions for conserving energy in your school.

# Standardized Test Prep

### Test-Taking Tip

**Eliminating Incorrect Answers**

When answering a multiple-choice question, you can often eliminate some answer choices because they are clearly incorrect. By doing this, you increase your odds of selecting the correct answer.

***Sample Question***

Geothermal energy is not a widely used source of energy because

**A** dams can have negative effects on the environment.
**B** methane gas is produced as a waste product.
**C** it is difficult to store.
**D** magma only comes close to Earth's surface in a few locations.

***Answer***

The correct answer is **D**. You can eliminate **A** because dams are used to produce hydroelectric power. You can also eliminate **B** because methane gas is produced when bacteria decompose biomass materials. Of the two remaining choices, **D** is correct because geothermal energy uses magma from Earth's interior as an energy source.

**Choose the letter of the best answer.**

**1.** The interior of your car heats up on a sunny day because of
**A** passive solar heating.
**B** solar cells.
**C** active solar heating.
**D** indirect solar heating.

**2.** The main function of a dam in producing electricity is to
**F** form a reservoir for recreation.
**G** prevent flooding after a heavy rain.
**H** provide a source of fast-moving water.
**J** provide a source of wind.

*Use the graph to answer Questions 3–4.*

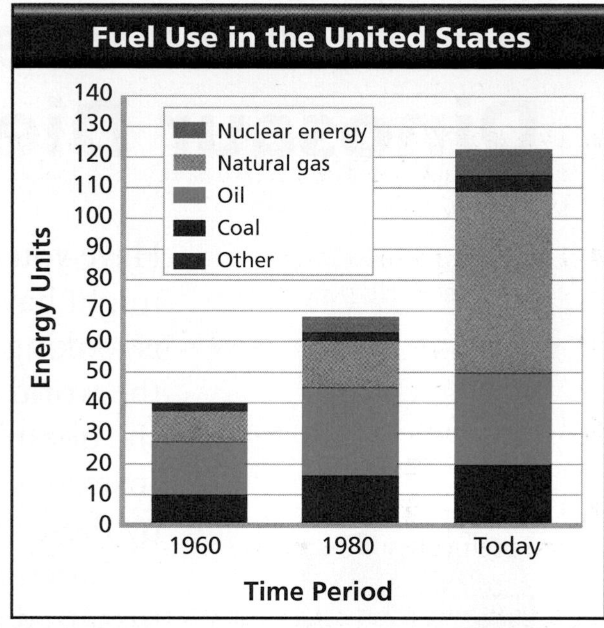


**3.** According to the graph, most of the fuel sources used in the United States today are
**A** renewable fuels. **B** nuclear fuels.
**C** fossil fuels. **D** solar energy.

**4.** Which statement about fuel use in the United States is best supported by the graph?
**F** Natural gas has become the most widely used fuel source.
**G** Nuclear energy is not used today.
**H** Coal is becoming the main source of fuel.
**J** The amount of oil being used today has greatly decreased since 1980.

**5.** Which of the following is the first step in producing electricity in a nuclear reactor?
**A** Steam turns the blades of a turbine.
**B** Water boils to produce steam.
**C** U-235 atoms are split by nuclear fission.
**D** Heat is released.

### Constructed Response

**6.** Explain what is meant by this statement: Electricity is *not* itself a source of energy. Then choose one energy source and explain how it can be used to produce electricity.

Careers in **Science**

# Fossils Reveal Dinosaur Diet

◀ *Tyrannosaurus rex*

Have you ever wondered what a *Tyrannosaurus rex* might have eaten for lunch? Paleontologist Karen Chin is looking for the answers to this question. She explores the world of ancient animals, including dinosaurs. But she doesn't do her research by digging up fossil bones. Instead, she relies on another kind of clue left behind by these fascinating animals.

Karen is a world-famous expert on coprolites—fossilized animal droppings. Because coprolites contain the undigested remains of food that has passed through an animal's digestive tract, they may provide clues about an animal's diet.

Studying coprolites may sound odd. But research can reveal important information about an animal and its environment. In fact, Karen has made some exciting discoveries about dinosaurs as a result of her research. And she's earned a nickname—The Queen of Coprolites.

## Career Path

**Dr. Karen Chin** has a master's degree in biology from Montana State University. She earned a Ph.D. in geology from the University of California at Santa Barbara. Currently, Karen is an Assistant Professor of Geology at the University of Colorado at Boulder. She is also a curator of paleontology at the University of Colorado Museum of Natural History, where she helps oversee the museum's fossil collection.

Using a slicing machine, Karen cuts thin sections of fossils to examine.

# *Talking With* Dr. Karen Chin

## How did you become interested in fossils?

As a child, I was interested in animals and plants. But I wasn't interested in studying extinct animals, so I never thought about becoming a paleontologist. As a young adult, I worked for many summers as a National Park naturalist. I enjoyed talking with the public about nature and science.

When I entered graduate school at Montana State University, I wanted to learn about museums, so I took a part-time job at the Museum of the Rockies. I did all sorts of things there, including helping to glue together fossil dinosaur bones and writing text for fossil exhibits. I became fascinated by the mystery of how we can learn about the prehistoric world by using clues from fossils. It was during this time that I got interested in coprolites.

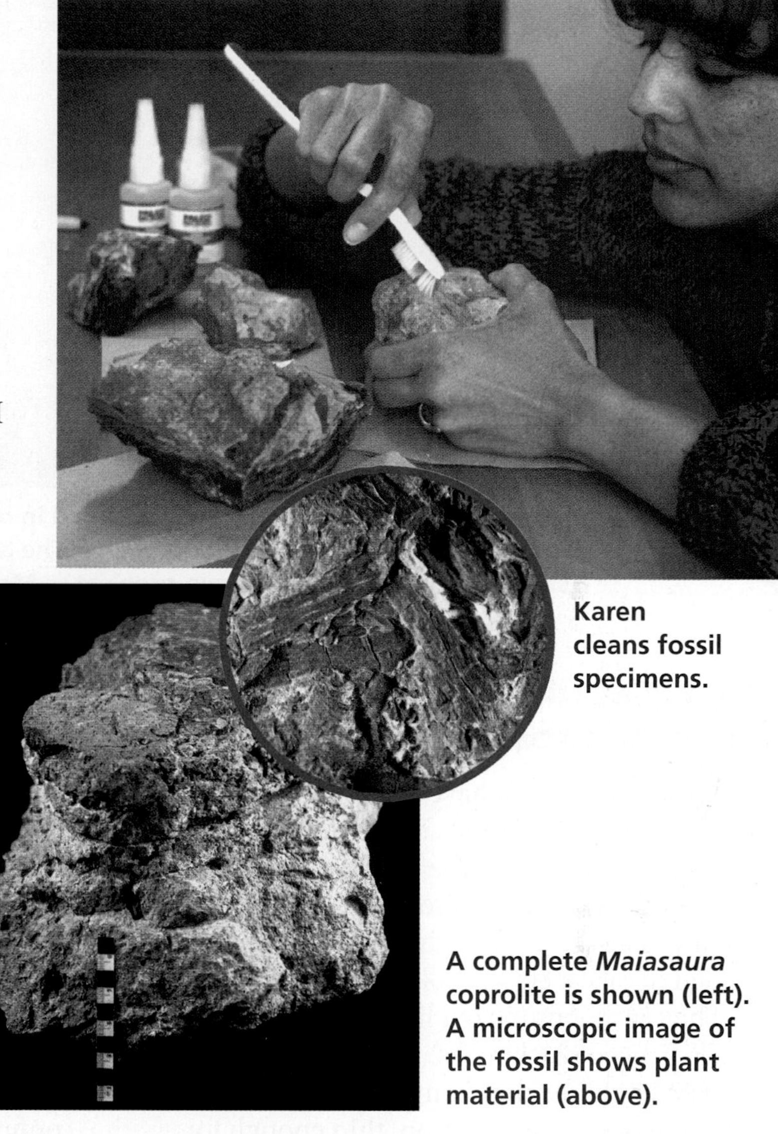

Karen cleans fossil specimens.

A complete *Maiasaura* coprolite is shown (left). A microscopic image of the fossil shows plant material (above).

## How do you identify coprolites?

When a team of paleontologists finds the fossilized bones of dinosaurs or other animals, they sometimes come across coprolites in the same area. Not all coprolites look alike. But they do have some characteristics in common. Coprolites from smaller animals often have a shape that reminds you of dog droppings. But the shapes of coprolites from giant animals like *Tyrannosaurus rex* are not always easy to recognize. In some cases, the coprolites contain clues in the form of chopped-up remains of things an animal ate. I often have to do a lot of investigating to figure out whether a fossil is a coprolite or not.

## What do these fossils tell you?

They can give us a good idea of a dinosaur's diet and digestion. I've seen many different types of food remains, including fish scales, broken bits of dinosaur bone, shells, and fragments of wood and other plant material. Those food remains also tell us what kinds of organisms lived together in the same environment in the ancient past. The coprolites found in Montana are an example of what specimens can reveal.

**Two Medicine Formation (above), located in northwestern Montana, is an important dinosaur site. The artwork (left) shows duck-billed dinosaurs in prehistoric Montana.**

## What did you find in the fossils?

Many dinosaur fossils have been found at the Two Medicine Formation site in Montana. Dr. Jack Horner, one of the paleontologists who discovered these fossils, also found some specimens he thought might be coprolites. I decided to take a closer look at them.

The specimens looked like nothing more than broken, jagged black rocks. But when I looked closely, I could see they contained plant material. I prepared a very thin section, thin enough for light to shine through, so I could examine it under the microscope. It showed that the rock was filled with chopped-up wood. That material was wood from coniferous trees.

These coprolites were probably produced by duck-billed dinosaurs that lived about 75 million years ago. This particular dinosaur, called *Maiasaura*, was very large, about 7 meters long and about one or two metric tons.

## What else did you learn?

I also noticed burrows in these coprolites. The burrows reminded me of dung beetles. Dung beetles are insects that feed on droppings. Some species of dung beetles create distinctive burrows as they feed. I asked a beetle expert to take a look. He confirmed that the burrows were the type made by dung beetles.

Now we had some new pieces of information. First of all, the presence of the dung beetles confirmed that these fossils were coprolites. Also, the coprolites showed that dung beetles and dinosaurs lived together in prehistoric Montana—something we didn't know before. Other coprolites at the site indicate the presence of snails. So we can infer that duck-billed dinosaurs, coniferous trees, dung beetles, and snails lived in close association.

**This large coprolite is thought to be from *Tyrannosaurus rex.* It is being weighed.**

## What fossils did you examine in Canada?

Another paleontologist sent me a possible coprolite collected near where a *T. rex* skeleton was dug up in Saskatchewan, Canada. These giant dinosaur species lived about 65 million years ago. They grew to 14 meters long and weighed as much as 5 metric tons.

I did some chemical tests on the specimen. My results showed that it was a coprolite and that it was produced by a meat-eating animal. The specimen contained many bone fragments. By looking at the cell structure of the bone fragments, I was able to tell that they probably belonged to a young plant-eating dinosaur.

This coprolite specimen was found in the same rock layers as several species of meat-eating dinosaurs. All the dinosaurs were fairly small. The only large one was *T. rex*. Because of the large size of the Saskatchewan coprolite, we inferred that it was probably produced by *T. rex*.

## What did you conclude?

This coprolite showed us that it is possible to find coprolites from large meat-eating dinosaurs. It gives us an idea of what to look for when we are searching for fossils. This coprolite provides physical evidence that *T. rex* ate other dinosaurs.

## What is your most surprising finding?

I identified a very large tyrannosaur coprolite, though not from *T. rex*. It contains not only bone fragments, but also impressions of muscle tissue. It was surprising to find the fossilized remains of undigested meat in a coprolite. This discovery shows that it is possible for droppings to become fossilized much more quickly than we thought.

## Why are these findings important?

It's exciting to use a different kind of fossil evidence to find out how these ancient animals lived and what their environments were like.

Karen looks at a very thin slice of coprolite under her microscope.

### Writing in Science

**Career Link** Karen Chin uses the clues she finds in coprolites to figure out what ancient animals ate and what their environment was like. Make a list of what you'd like to know about animals and plants that lived in prehistoric times. In a paragraph describe ways that studying fossils could help you learn the answers to your questions.

**Go Online** PHSchool.com

**For:** More on this career
**Visit:** PHSchool.com
**Web Code:** cfb-2000

Chapter

# 12 Fresh Water

The BIG Idea

Earth's Resources

**Where is fresh water found and how is it used?**

## Chapter Preview

**1 Water on Earth**

***Discover*** Where Does the Water Come From?

***Active Art*** The Water Cycle

***Skills Activity*** Calculating

**2 Surface Water**

***Discover*** What's in Pond Water?

***Try This*** A Natural Filter

**3 Water Underground**

***Discover*** Where Does the Water Go?

***Try This*** An Artesian Well

***Design Your Own Lab*** Soil Testing

**4 Using Freshwater Resources**

***Discover*** Can You Find a Balance?

***Analyzing Data*** Household Water Use

***At-Home Activity*** Monitoring Water Use

**5 Water to Drink**

***Discover*** How Can Water Be Cleaned?

***Math Skills*** Calculating a Concentration

***Consumer Lab*** Testing Water

These waterfalls in the Pacific Northwest ▶ show the abundance of water on Earth.

*Earth: The Water Planet*

▶ Video Preview
Video Field Trip
Video Assessment

Lab zone™ Chapter **Project**

## A Precious Resource

You need water to cook, to clean, to shower—and, most important, to survive. Water is a precious resource. But when people use water, it can become polluted. In this chapter project, you'll explore how to clean up water pollution.

**Your Goal** To design and build a water treatment system that will clean one liter of dirty water

Your treatment system should

- consist of at least two treatment steps
- be made from materials that have been approved by your teacher
- recover as much clean water as possible
- be assembled following the safety guidelines in Appendix A

**Plan It!** Your teacher will give you a sample of dirty water. Carefully observe your sample and record your observations. Preview the chapter to learn about water pollution and water treatment systems. Then choose materials for your model. After your teacher approves your design, build your model and conduct several trials to see how well it works. **CAUTION:** *Do not taste or drink the water samples before or after treatment.*

Section 1

# Water on Earth

## Reading Preview

### Key Concepts

- How does Earth's water move through the water cycle?
- Where are fresh water and salt water found on Earth?

### Key Terms

- water cycle
- precipitation
- groundwater

### Target Reading Skill

**Identifying Main Ideas** As you read the Distribution of Earth's Water section, write the main idea in a graphic organizer like the one below. Then write four supporting details that further explain the main idea.

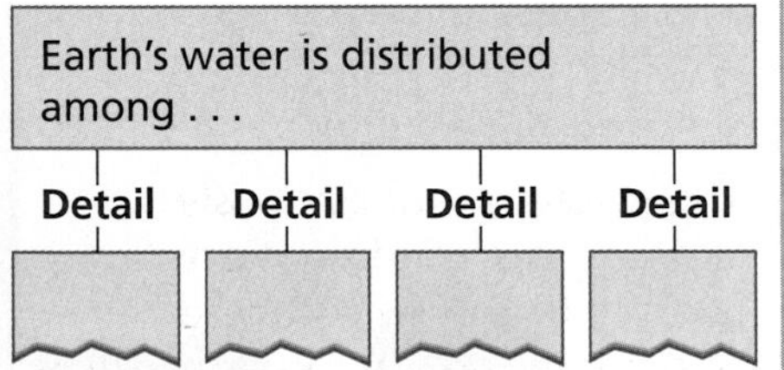


## Lab zone Discover Activity

### Where Does the Water Come From?

1. Fill a glass with ice cubes and water, taking care not to spill any water. Set the glass aside for 5 minutes.
2. Observe the outside of the glass. Pick up the glass and examine the surface it was sitting on.

**Think It Over**

**Inferring** Where did the water on the outside of the glass come from? How do you think it got there?

In a galaxy called the Milky Way, nine planets orbit a star known simply as the sun. Some of the planets have spectacular rings. Others have volcanoes that are larger than continents, or storms that last for centuries. But only one of the planets, Earth, has a surface covered mainly by water. In fact, oceans cover about 70 percent of our planet's surface. That's why Earth is often called the "water planet."

Earth differs from the other planets in another important way. It is the only place known thus far where you, your classmates, your pets, your plants, and every other living thing can survive. Life on Earth could not exist without water.

## The Water Cycle

Earth's water is naturally recycled through the water cycle. The **water cycle** is the continuous process by which water moves from Earth's surface to the atmosphere and back. **In the water cycle, water moves from bodies of water, land, and living things on Earth's surface to the atmosphere and back to Earth's surface.** As shown in Figure 1, the water cycle has three major steps—evaporation, condensation, and precipitation. The cycle itself has no beginning or end. But it is driven by an energy source—the sun.

◀ Earth, the "water planet"

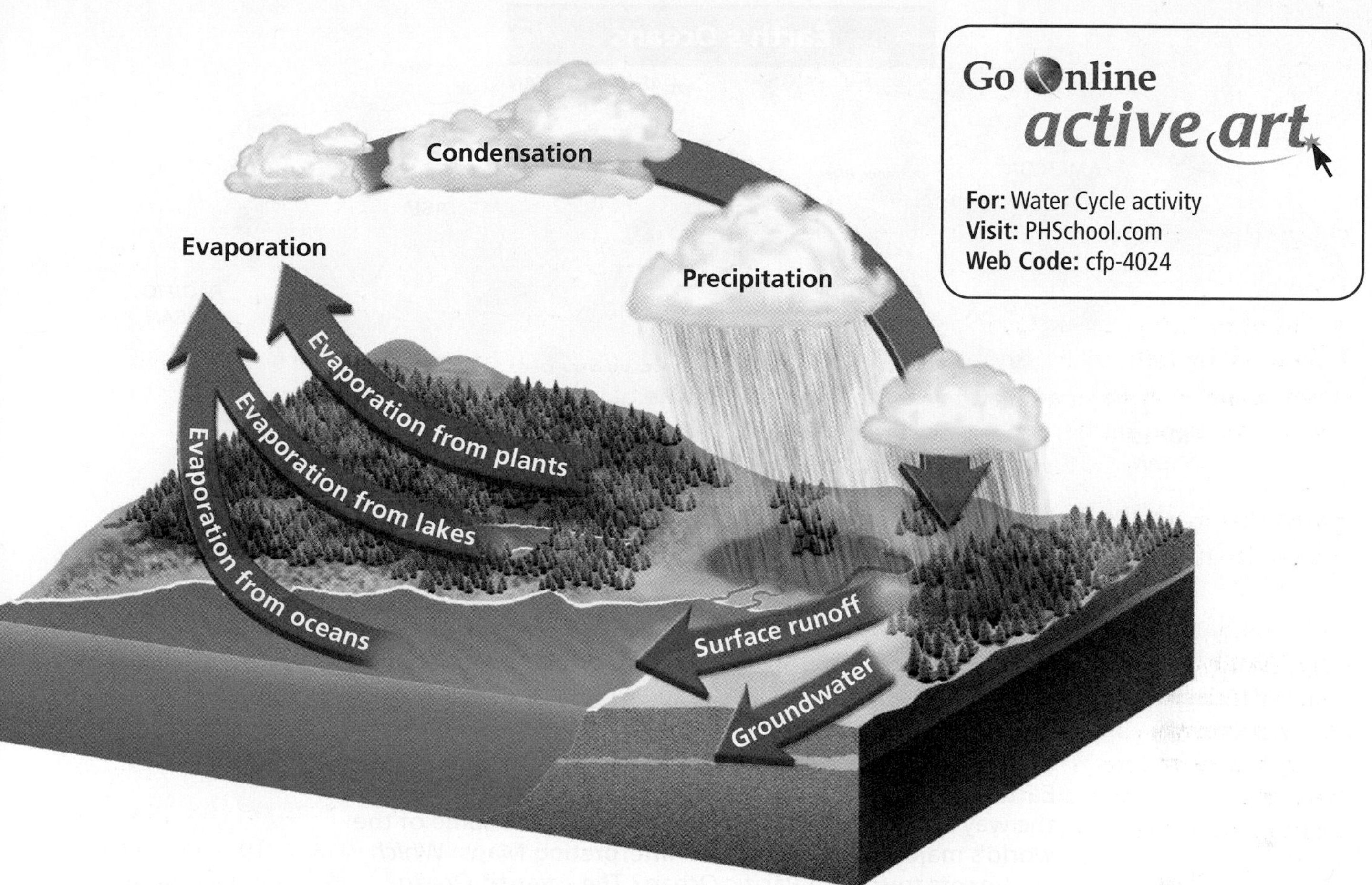


Go Online
active art
For: Water Cycle activity
Visit: PHSchool.com
Web Code: cfp-4024

FIGURE 1
## The Water Cycle
Water moves continuously through a cycle, from Earth's surface to the atmosphere and back. The sun's energy drives this process.
**Interpreting Diagrams** *In which step of the water cycle does water return to Earth's surface?*

**Water Evaporates** In the process of evaporation, liquid water changes to a gas called water vapor. Water is constantly evaporating from the surfaces of lakes and oceans and even from the soil. Plants play a role, too, in this step of the water cycle. Plants draw in water from the soil through their roots and release it through their leaves as water vapor.

**Condensation Forms Clouds** What happens after water evaporates? Warm air carries the water vapor upward. At higher altitudes, air tends to become much colder. Cold air cannot hold as much water vapor as warm air can. As a result, some of the water vapor cools and condenses into liquid water. Condensed droplets of water clump together around tiny dust particles in the air, forming clouds.

**Precipitation** As more water vapor condenses, the drops of water in the cloud grow larger. Eventually, the heavy drops fall back to Earth as **precipitation**—rain, snow, sleet, or hail. Most precipitation falls back into the ocean or lakes. The precipitation that falls on land may soak into the soil and become groundwater. Or the precipitation may run off the land, eventually flowing back into the ocean.

## Earth's Oceans

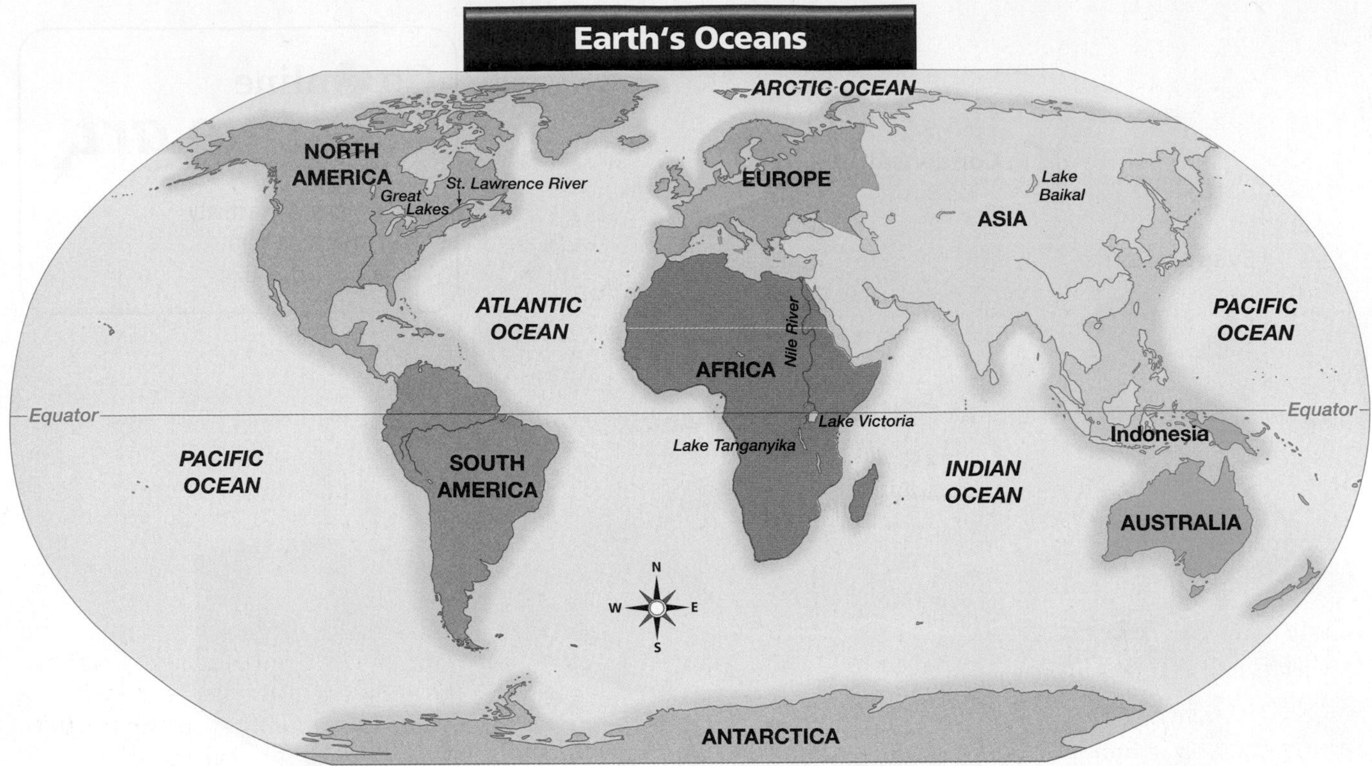


**FIGURE 2**
Earth's oceans are all connected, enabling a ship to sail all the way around the world. This map also shows some of the world's major rivers and lakes. **Interpreting Maps** *Which continents touch the Pacific Ocean? The Atlantic Ocean?*

## Distribution of Earth's Water

**Most of Earth's water—roughly 97 percent—is salt water found in oceans. Only 3 percent is fresh water.** Of that 3 percent, about three quarters is frozen in huge masses of ice near the North and South poles. Almost a quarter of the fresh water is underground. A tiny fraction of Earth's fresh water occurs in lakes and rivers. An even tinier fraction is in the atmosphere, most of it in the form of water vapor.

**Oceans** A vast, salty ocean covers an area greater than all the land on Earth combined. Pacific, Atlantic, Indian, and Arctic are the names used for the different parts of the ocean. But the waters are really all interconnected, making up one big ocean.

**Ice** Most of Earth's fresh water is locked in thick sheets of ice that cover Antarctica, near the South Pole, and Greenland, near the North Pole. Huge icebergs, floating chunks of ice made of fresh water, often break off the ice sheets. The icebergs slowly melt as they float toward warmer waters.

**What are icebergs?**

**Lab zone Skills Activity**

### Calculating

Your teacher has set up an aquarium filled with 20 liters of water to model all the water on Earth. How much water would you need to remove from the aquarium to model Earth's fresh water? (*Hint*: Refer to the graph in Figure 3.)

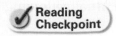

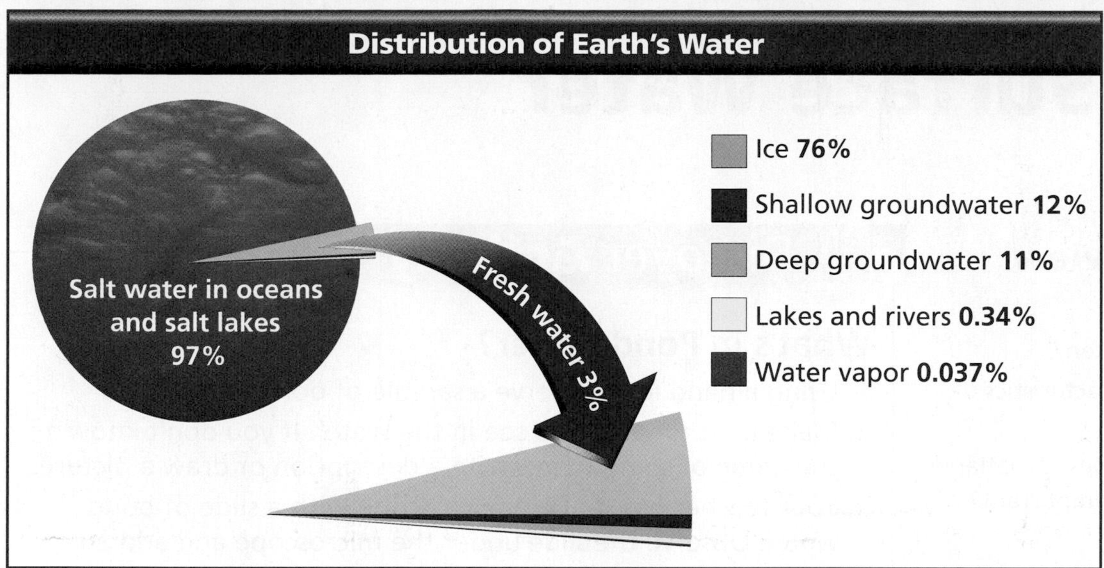


**FIGURE 3**
Most of Earth's water is salt water. Only 3 percent is fresh water. Of that fresh water, only a tiny fraction is available for human use. (Percentages have been rounded off.)

**Rivers and Lakes** Relatively little of Earth's fresh water is found in rivers and lakes. But rivers and lakes are important sources of fresh water for the people who live near them. North America's five Great Lakes contain nearly 20 percent of all the water in the world's freshwater lakes.

**Groundwater** Water that fills the cracks and spaces in underground soil and rock layers is called **groundwater.** When it rains or snows, some water soaks into the ground. This water trickles down through spaces between particles of soil and rock. Eventually the water reaches a layer of rock that it cannot move through. Far more fresh water is located underground than in all of Earth's rivers and lakes.

## Section 1 Assessment

**Target Reading Skill Identifying Main Ideas** Use your graphic organizer to help you answer Question 2 below.

### Reviewing Key Concepts

1. a. **Identifying** What three major steps make up the water cycle?
   b. **Explaining** How does water enter Earth's atmosphere? Explain your answer.
   c. **Relating Cause and Effect** Would cutting down trees affect the amount of evaporation in an area? Explain.
2. a. **Listing** What are Earth's four main sources of water?
   b. **Classifying** Which of the four main water sources contain salt water? Which contain fresh water?
   c. **Making Judgments** Which freshwater source is most important to people? Use facts to defend your answer.

### Writing in Science

**Moving Through the Water Cycle** Starting with a puddle on a sunny day, write a paragraph describing how water might move through the water cycle and eventually fall back as rain.

Section 2

# Surface Water

## Reading Preview

### Key Concepts

- What is a river system?
- What are the characteristics of ponds and lakes?
- What are three types of wetlands and why are they important?

### Key Terms

- tributary • watershed
- divide • habitat • reservoir
- wetland

### Target Reading Skill

**Outlining** As you read, make an outline of this section. Use the red headings for the main ideas and the blue headings for the supporting ideas.

**Surface Water**

I. River systems
  A. Tributaries
  B.
  C.
II. Ponds
  A.

## Lab zone Discover Activity

### What's in Pond Water?

1. Using a hand lens, observe a sample of pond water.
2. Make a list of what you see in the water. If you don't know the name of something, write a description or draw a picture.
3. Your teacher has set up a microscope with a slide of pond water. Observe the slide under the microscope and add any new items to your list. Wash your hands when you are done.

**Think It Over**

**Classifying** Use one of these systems to divide the items on your list into two groups: moving/still, living/nonliving, or microscopic/visible without a microscope. What does your classification system tell you about pond water?

Imagine that you are a raindrop falling from the clouds to Earth's surface. Down, down, you go and then, splash! You land in the tumbling waters of a fast-moving stream. You are in one of Earth's freshwater sources. Fresh water on Earth may be moving, as in streams and rivers, or still, as in ponds and lakes.

## River Systems

Rivers often begin in the mountains, where the runoff from melting snow forms small streams. As you followed one small stream downhill, you would notice that the stream reached another stream and joined it. These streams would flow into a small river. Eventually this path would lead you to a large river such as the Rio Grande, shown in Figure 4. The Rio Grande—the "Big River"—begins as trickles of melting snow high in the Rocky Mountains of Colorado.

◄ Kayaker in river rapids

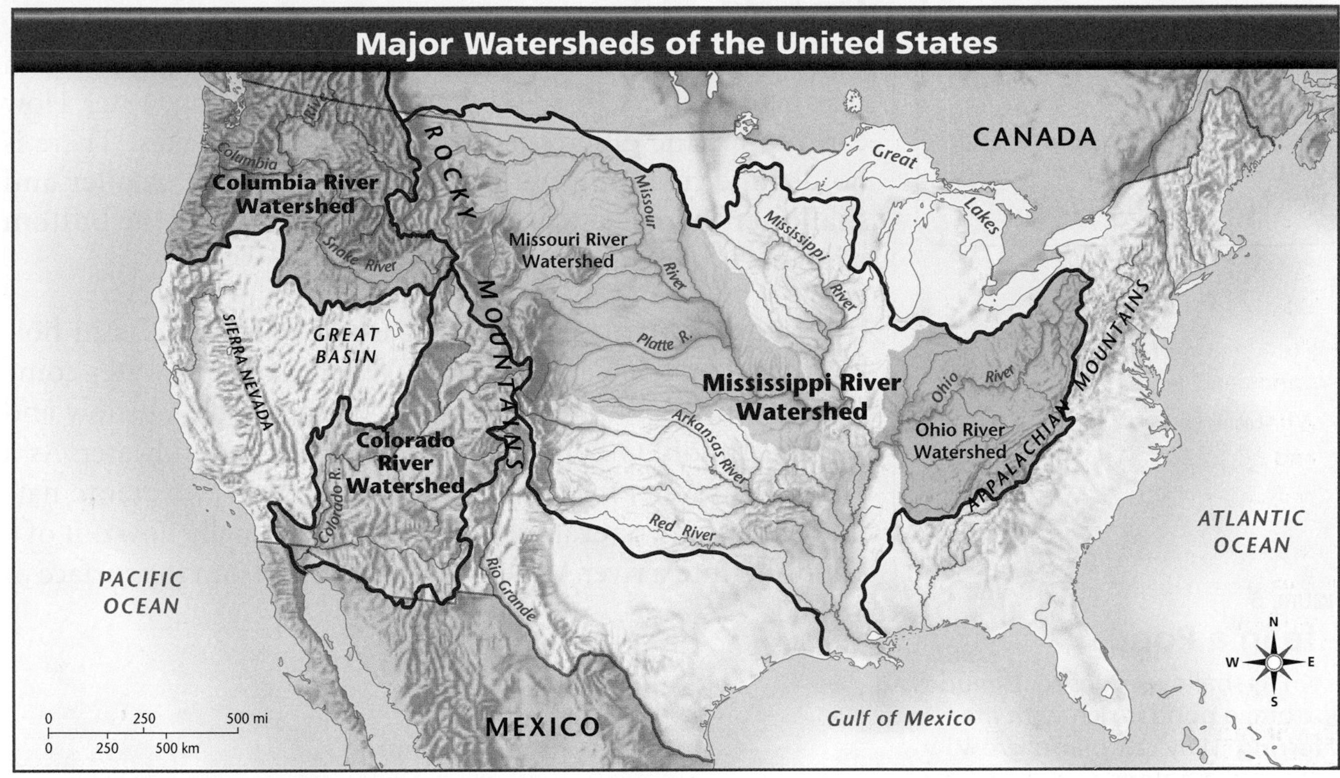


**FIGURE 4**
**Major Watersheds**
This map shows watersheds of several large rivers in the continental United States. Each river's watershed consists of the region drained by the river and all its tributaries. **Interpreting Maps** *What large rivers are tributaries of the Mississippi River?*

**Tributaries** The streams and smaller rivers that feed into a main river are called **tributaries.** Tributaries flow downward toward the main river, pulled by the force of gravity. **A river and all its tributaries together make up a river system.**

**Watersheds** Just as all the water in a bathtub flows toward the drain, all the water in a river system drains into a main river. The land area that supplies water to a river system is called a **watershed.** Watersheds are sometimes known as drainage basins.

As you can see in Figure 4, the Missouri and Ohio rivers are quite large. Yet they flow into the Mississippi River. So large rivers may be tributaries of still larger rivers. When rivers join another river system, the areas they drain become part of the largest river's watershed. You can identify a river's watershed on a map by drawing an imaginary line around the region drained by all its tributaries.

**Divides** What keeps watersheds separate? One watershed is separated from another by a ridge of land called a **divide.** Streams on each side of the divide flow in different directions. The Continental Divide, the longest divide in North America, follows the line of the Rocky Mountains.

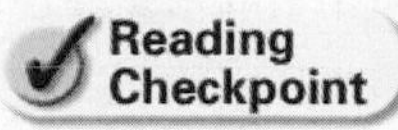

**What is a divide?**

For: More on surface water
Visit: PHSchool.com
Web Code: cfd-3013

## Ponds

Ponds are bodies of fresh water. Unlike the moving water in streams and rivers, ponds contain still, or standing, water. How can you tell the difference between ponds and lakes? There is no definite rule. **In general, however, ponds are smaller and shallower than lakes. Sunlight usually reaches to the bottom of all parts of a pond.**

**How Ponds Form** Ponds form when water collects in hollows and low-lying areas of land. Where does the water come from? Some ponds are supplied by rainfall, melting snow and ice, and runoff. Others are fed by rivers or groundwater. As a pond gains water from these sources, it also loses water to natural processes. For example, water may eventually flow out of a pond and into a river. Water also evaporates from the surface of a pond.

FIGURE 5
**Life in a Pond**
From its shallow edges to its muddy bottom, a pond is rich with life.
**Inferring** *Why can plants grow throughout a pond?*

Some of the most important pond dwellers are the smallest. Microscopic algae are the pond's basic food producers.

The roots of water lilies cling to the pond bottom, while their leaves float on the surface. Sponges live under the leaves. Dragonflies pause on top to rest.

A slender-bodied pickerel waits among the duckweed to grab a meal of insects at the water's edge.

**Exploring a Pond** If you've ever waded in a pond, you know that the muddy bottom is often covered with weeds. Because the water is shallow enough for sunlight to reach the bottom, plants grow throughout a pond. A quiet pond is actually a thriving habitat, supporting a wide diversity of living things, as shown in Figure 5. An organism's **habitat** is the place where it lives and obtains all the things it needs to survive.

Not all ponds exist year-round. Some ponds appear only in spring, when runoff from rain and melting snow collects in low areas. The ponds dry up by midsummer as the shallow water evaporates.

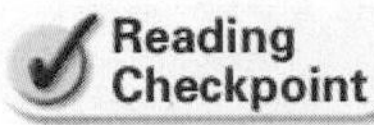

**What is a habitat?**

The shore is edged with grasses and trees that require a lot of water, such as willows and maples. These plants provide shelter and nesting places for red-winged blackbirds and other birds.

Frogs lay eggs in the shallow water near shore. They hatch in the water as tadpoles and move to the land as adults.

Sunfish and perch live in both the weedy shallows and the deeper waters of the pond.

Snails find food on the soft bottom of the pond.

Crayfish lie buried in the mud, waiting for bits of food to drift down.

**FIGURE 6**
**Lake Michigan**
Lake Michigan is a freshwater lake that looks large enough to be mistaken for the ocean.

## Lakes

Suppose you are shown a picture of waves breaking against large sand dunes. The water stretches as far as the eye can see. You might guess that this huge body of water is the ocean. But it could actually be a lake! You could be viewing a photo of dunes in Indiana, on the shore of Lake Michigan.

**Characteristics of Lakes** Most lakes are not as large as Lake Michigan. **But lakes are generally deeper and bigger than ponds. In addition, sunlight does not reach the bottom in a deep lake, as it does in a pond.** As a result, no plants and relatively few other organisms can live in a lake's chilly, dark depths. A lake bottom may consist of sand, pebble, or rock, whereas the bottom of a pond is usually covered with mud and algae.

**How Lakes Form** Lakes can form in several ways. Some lakes may form through the same processes that form ponds. Other lakes, especially larger ones, are the result of powerful forces that shape Earth's surface.

Some natural lakes, such as the Great Lakes, formed in depressions created by ice sheets that melted at the end of the Ice Age. Other lakes were created by movements of Earth's crust. Such movements formed the deep valleys in central Africa that lie below Lake Tanganyika and Lake Victoria. Still other lakes are the result of volcanoes. An erupting volcano can cause a flow of lava or mud that blocks a river and forms a lake. Some lakes form in the empty craters of volcanoes.

People can also create a lake by building a dam across a river. The lake may be used for supplying drinking water, for irrigating fields, and for recreation. A lake that stores water for human use is called a **reservoir.**

## Wetlands

A **wetland** is a land area that is covered with water during part or all of the year. Wetlands help control floods and provide habitats for many species. They form where water is trapped in low areas or where groundwater seeps to the surface. Some wetlands fill up during spring rains, but dry up during summer.

**Types of Wetlands** **The three common types of freshwater wetlands are marshes, swamps, and bogs.** Marshes are usually grassy areas covered by shallow water or a stream. They teem with cattails and other tall, grasslike plants. Swamps look more like flooded forests, with trees and shrubs sprouting from the water. Many swamps are located in warm, humid climates, where trees grow quickly. Bogs are more common in cooler northern areas. They often form in depressions left by melting ice sheets thousands of years ago. The water in bogs tends to be acidic, and mosses thrive in these conditions.

Wetlands along coasts usually contain both fresh and salt water. Coastal wetlands include salt marshes and mangrove forests. Salt marshes are found along both coasts of the United States. Tall, strong grasses grow in the rich, muddy bottoms of salt marshes. Mangrove forests are found along the southeastern coast of the United States. In these forests, the mangrove trees are short and have thick, tangled roots.

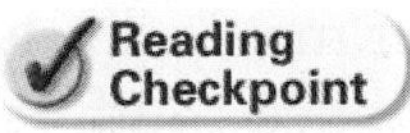

What is a salt marsh?

### Lab zone Try This **Activity**

#### A Natural Filter

1. In one end of a loaf pan, build a sloping hill of damp soil.
2. Add water to the other end of the pan to form a lake.
3. Use a watering can to sprinkle rain onto the hill. Observe what happens to the hill and the lake.

4. Empty the water out of the pan and rebuild the hill.
5. Now push a sponge into the soil across the bottom of the hill to model a wetland.
6. Repeat Steps 2 and 3.

**Observing** Based on your observations, describe how wetlands filter water.

FIGURE 7
**Freshwater Wetlands**
Swamps and bogs are two kinds of wetlands.

**Swamp** Curtains of Spanish moss hang from cypress trees in this Louisiana swamp.

**Bog** Mosses thrive in the acidic water in this bog in Montana.

**FIGURE 8**
**Florida Everglades**
A rich variety of living things, including this great egret, make their homes in Everglades National Park. **Interpreting Maps** *Describe the flow of fresh water through the Everglades. Where does it begin? Where does it reach salt water?*

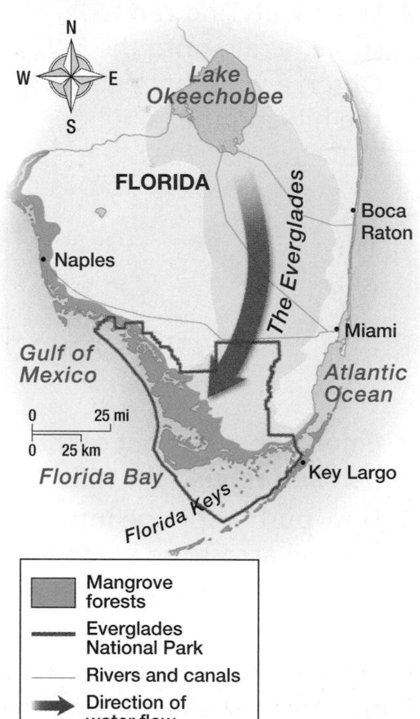

**The Everglades: A Wetland** If you were to walk down a path in Everglades National Park, you would feel the ground squish under your feet. Water is the key to the Everglades, a vast marsh in south Florida. A shallow stream of water moves slowly over the gently sloping land from Lake Okeechobee south to Florida Bay. Tall, sharp-edged blades of sawgrass grow in the water. The thick growth of sawgrass gave this region its Native American name, *Pa-hay-okee*, which means "river of grass."

The Everglades are home to many kinds of wildlife—alligators, fishes, snakes, and wading birds. The Everglades also provide habitats for many rare or endangered species, such as the Florida panther and the manatee.

Human activities near the Everglades threaten the region's water and wildlife. For example, farming has introduced harmful chemicals into the water. Water that once flowed into the Everglades from Lake Okeechobee has been diverted for farming and household use. New organisms brought into the area accidentally or for pest control compete with organisms that occur naturally in the Everglades.

Scientists have been trying for many years to develop a plan to preserve the Everglades and save its endangered wildlife. One plan involves building a system of pipes and canals to refill some drained areas with fresh water.

**For:** Links on wetlands
**Visit:** www.SciLinks.org
**Web Code:** scn-0814

**Importance of Wetlands** If you've ever enjoyed cranberry sauce or wild rice, you've eaten plants that grow in wetlands. Water in a wetland is shallow, and plant and animal materials add natural fertilizers to the water and soil. **Because of their sheltered waters and rich supply of nutrients, wetlands provide habitats for many living things.**

Wetlands are also important to people. Scientific studies show that wetlands help with pollution control and flood control. For example, as water moves slowly through a wetland, some waste materials settle out. Other wastes may be absorbed by plants. **In these ways, wetlands act as natural water filters. They also help control floods by absorbing extra runoff from heavy rains.** Wetlands are like giant sponges, storing rainwater until it gradually drains or evaporates. When wetlands are destroyed, the floodwaters are not absorbed. Instead, the water runs off the land quickly, worsening flood problems. Because of these important functions of wetlands, governments have passed laws to protect them.

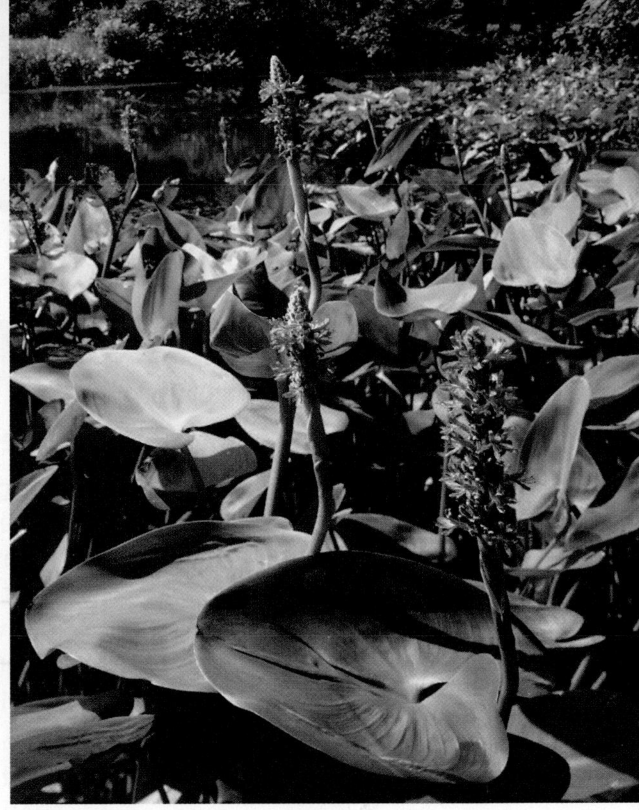

**FIGURE 9**
**Natural Filters**
Some wetland plants, such as the pickerel weed shown here, filter pollutants from water.

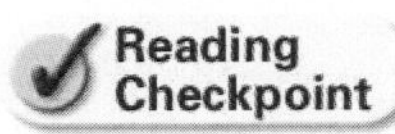

**What prompted wetlands protection laws?**

## Section 2 Assessment

**Target Reading Skill Outlining** Use the information in your outline to help you answer the questions below.

### Reviewing Key Concepts

1. a. **Identifying** What bodies of water make up a river system?
   b. **Summarizing** How is a watershed related to a river system?
   c. **Applying Concepts** How could you determine the boundaries of a river system by studying a map of the United States?
2. a. **Reviewing** How are lakes different from ponds?
   b. **Explaining** Explain how ponds and lakes form.
   c. **Comparing and Contrasting** What is the major difference between a reservoir and most other types of lakes?
3. a. **Defining** What is a wetland?
   b. **Classifying** What are the three major types of freshwater wetlands?
   c. **Comparing and Contrasting** How are the three major types of freshwater wetlands similar? How are they different?

**Lab zone** At-Home **Activity**

**Runoff** Show a family member how water runs off different materials. Pour some water in the grass and watch what happens. Then pour some water on the sidewalk or driveway. What happened to the water in each case? How does this relate to the role of wetlands in controlling floods?

Section 3

# Water Underground

## Reading Preview

### Key Concepts

- How does water move through underground layers of soil and rock?
- How do people obtain water from an aquifer?

### Key Terms

- permeable
- impermeable
- saturated zone
- water table
- unsaturated zone
- spring
- aquifer
- artesian well
- geyser

### Target Reading Skill

**Previewing Visuals** Before you read, preview Figure 12. Then write one question that you have about the diagram in a graphic organizer like the one below. As you read, answer your question.

**Springs and Wells**

| Q. What is an artesian well? |
|---|
| A. |
| Q. |

## Lab zone Discover Activity

### Where Does the Water Go?

1. Add pebbles to a jar to form a layer about 5 centimeters deep. Cover the pebbles with a layer of dry sand about 3 centimeters thick. Pour the sand in slowly to avoid moving the pebbles. These materials represent underground soil layers.
2. Sprinkle water onto the sand to simulate rainfall.
3. Looking through the side of the jar, observe the path of the water as it soaks through the layers. Wash your hands when you are finished with this activity.

**Think It Over**

**Observing** Describe what happened when the water reached the bottom of the jar.

When you were a little child, did you ever dig a hole in the ground hoping to find a buried treasure? You probably never found a trunk full of gold. But there was a certain kind of treasure hidden underground. If you had dug past the tangled grass roots and small stones, the bottom of your hole would have filled with water. You would have "struck groundwater"! In the days before public water systems, water underground was truly a hidden treasure. Today, many people still rely on the water underground to meet their water needs.

## How Water Moves Underground

Where does this underground water come from? Like the water in rivers, lakes, and glaciers, it comes from precipitation. Recall that precipitation can evaporate, run off the surface, or soak into the ground. If water soaks into the ground, it trickles downward, following the pull of gravity.

If you pour water into a glass full of pebbles, the water trickles down around the pebbles until it reaches the bottom of the glass. Then the water begins to fill up the spaces between the pebbles. **In the same way, water underground trickles down between particles of soil and through cracks and spaces in layers of rock.**

**Effects of Different Materials** Different types of rock and soil have different-sized spaces, or pores, between their particles, as shown in Figure 10. The size of the pores determines how easily water moves through rock and soil. If the pores are connected, this too affects water movement. Because they have large and connected pores, materials such as sand and gravel allow water to pass through, or permeate. They are thus known as **permeable** (PUR mee uh bul) materials.

As water soaks down through permeable rock and soil, it eventually reaches layers of material that it cannot pass through. These materials have few or no pores or cracks. Two examples are clay and granite. Clay and granite are **impermeable,** meaning that water cannot pass through easily.

**Water Zones** Once water reaches an impermeable layer, it is trapped. It can't soak any deeper. Instead, the water begins to fill up the spaces above the impermeable material. The area of permeable rock or soil that is totally filled, or saturated, with water is called the **saturated zone.** The top of the saturated zone is the **water table.** If you know the depth of the water table in your area, you can tell how deep you must dig to reach groundwater.

Soil and rock layers above the water table contain some moisture, too. But here the pores contain air as well as water. They are not saturated. Therefore, the layer of rocks and soil above the water table is called the **unsaturated zone.**

**Give an example of a permeable material.**

**For:** Links on water underground
**Visit:** www.SciLinks.org
**Web Code:** scn-0815

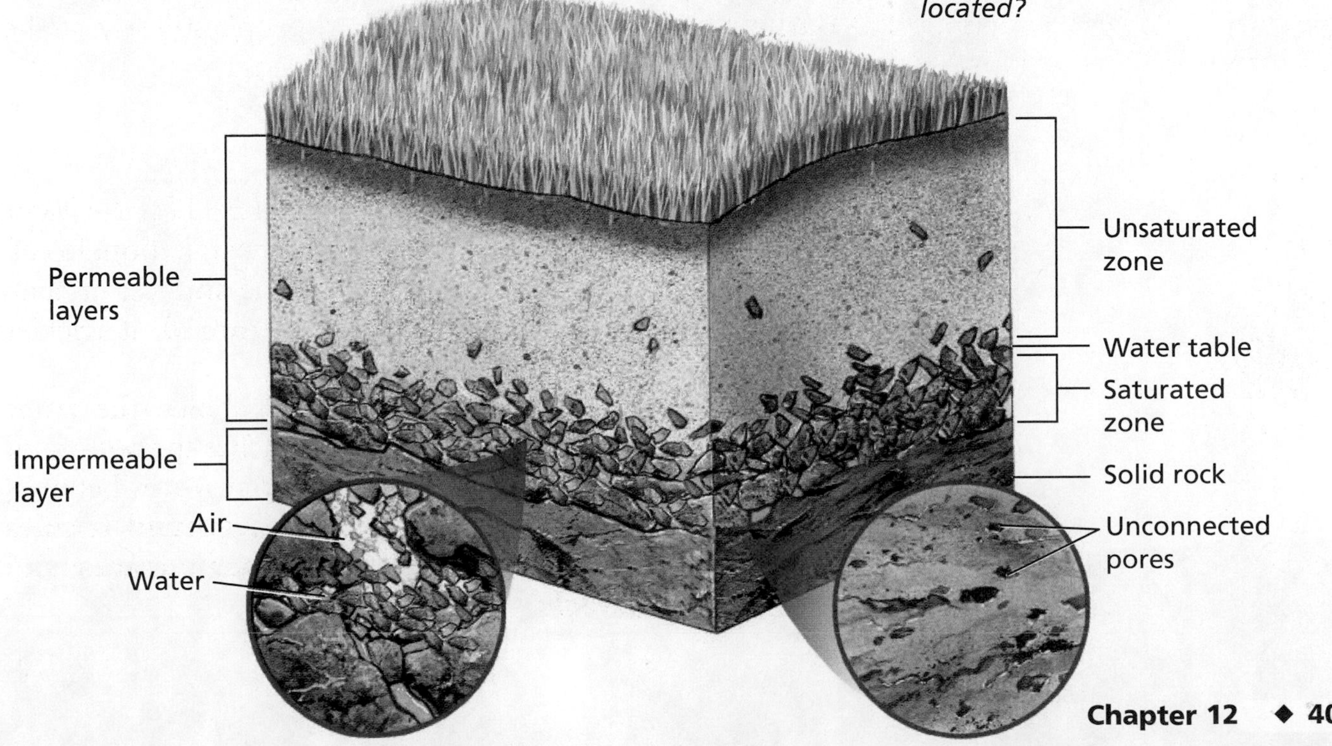


**FIGURE 10**
**Groundwater Formation**
Differences in the materials that form layers underground determine where groundwater forms. Water can move through certain layers but not others.
**Interpreting Diagrams** *What is the saturated zone? Where is it located?*

## Bringing Up Groundwater

Suppose you live far from a city, town, or body of fresh water. How could you reach groundwater to use it for your daily needs? You may be in luck: the water table in your area might be only a few meters underground. In fact, in some places the water table actually meets the surface. **Springs** can form as groundwater bubbles or flows out of cracks in the rock. A short distance away, the water table may be deep underground.

**Aquifers** Any underground layer of rock or sediment that holds water is called an **aquifer.** Aquifers can range in size from a small underground patch of permeable material to an area the size of several states. The huge Ogallala aquifer lies beneath the plains of the Midwest, from South Dakota to Texas. Millions of people obtain drinking water from this aquifer. The aquifer also provides water for crops and livestock.

Do you picture groundwater as a large, still pool beneath Earth's surface? In fact, the water is moving, seeping through layers of rock. The rate of movement depends largely on the slope of the aquifer and the permeability of the rocks. Groundwater in some aquifers moves only a few centimeters a day. At that rate, the water moves about 10 meters a year. Groundwater may travel hundreds of kilometers and stay in an aquifer for thousands of years before coming to the surface again.

**FIGURE 11**
**Ogallala Aquifer**
The Ogallala aquifer is a main source of water for farming, ranching, and human consumption in eight states.

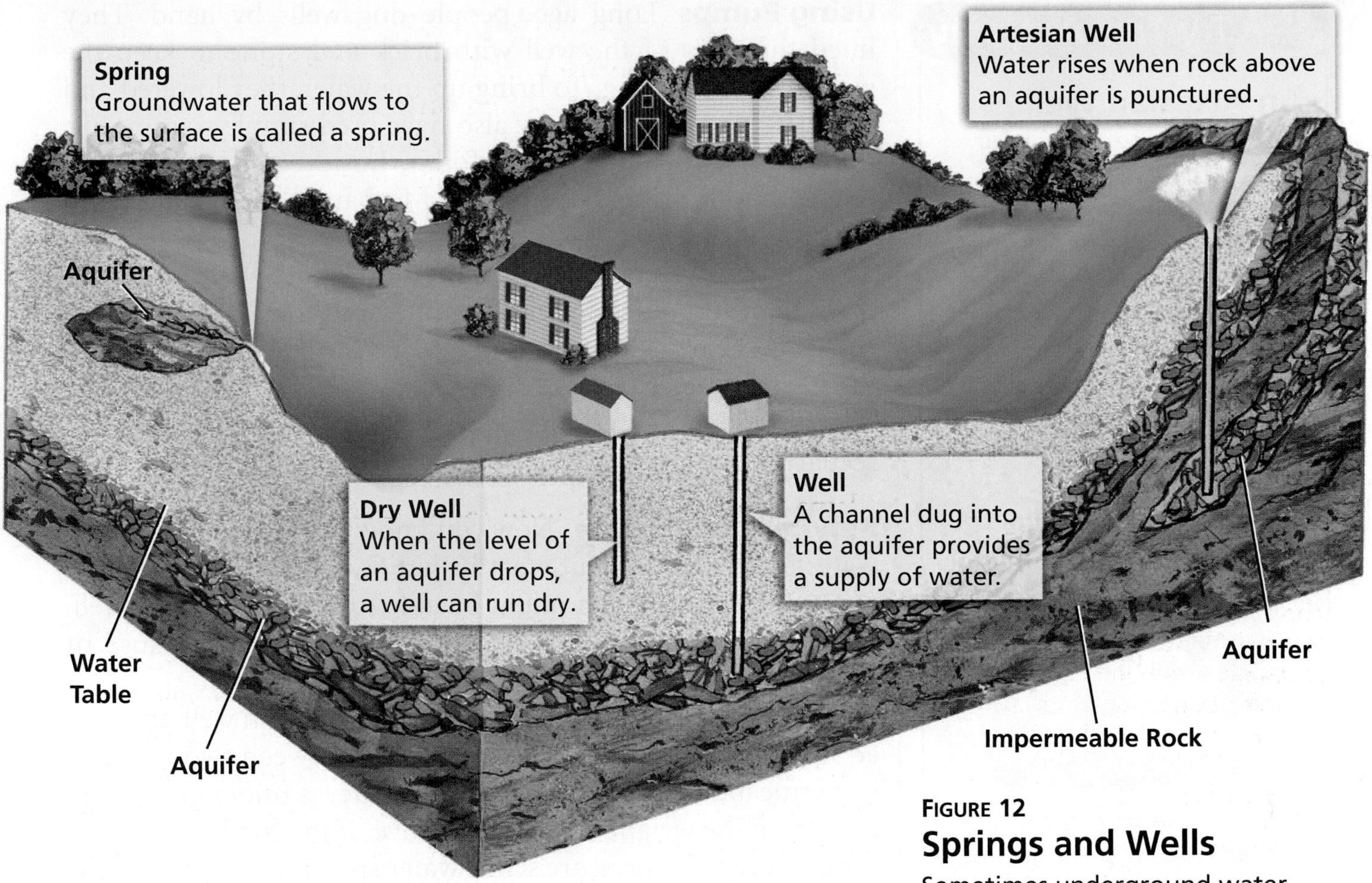

**Spring**
Groundwater that flows to the surface is called a spring.

**Artesian Well**
Water rises when rock above an aquifer is punctured.

**Aquifer**

**Dry Well**
When the level of an aquifer drops, a well can run dry.

**Well**
A channel dug into the aquifer provides a supply of water.

**Water Table**

**Aquifer**

**Aquifer**

**Impermeable Rock**

FIGURE 12
## Springs and Wells
Sometimes underground water comes to the surface naturally. Other times, people use energy to obtain groundwater.
**Comparing and Contrasting** *How do the ordinary well and the dry well differ?*

**Wells** The depth of a water table can vary greatly over a small area. Its level may vary as well. Generally, the level of a water table follows the shape of underground rock layers, as shown in Figure 12. But it can rise during heavy rains or snow melts, and then fall in times of dry weather. So what do you do if the depth and level of the water table in your area is far underground? How can you bring the water to the surface?

Since ancient times, people have brought groundwater to the surface for drinking and other everyday uses. **People can obtain groundwater from an aquifer by drilling a well below the water table.** Locate the well near the center of Figure 12. Because the bottom of the well is in a saturated zone, the well contains water. Notice the level of the bottom of the dry well in the diagram. Because this well does not reach below the water table, water cannot be obtained from it.

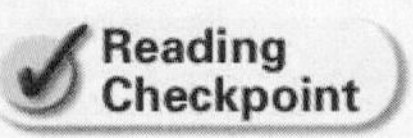

**Why might a water table rise? Why might a water table fall?**

## Lab zone Try This Activity

### An Artesian Well

For this activity, cover your desk with newspaper.

1. Cover the bottom of a loaf pan with clay. Pile the clay higher at one end. Cover the clay with about 4 cm of moist sand.
2. Cover the sand with a thin sheet of clay. Seal the edges of the clay tightly against the pan.
3. Push a funnel into the high end so the bottom of the funnel is in the sand.

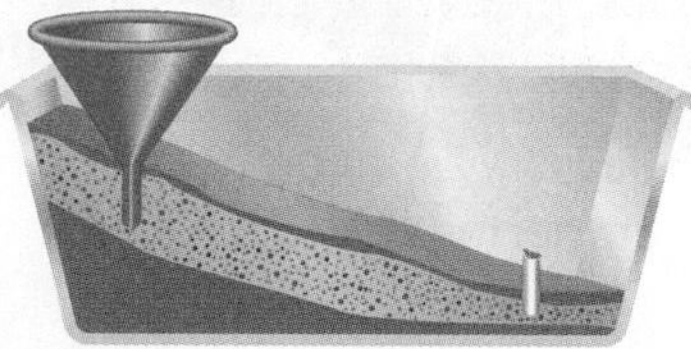

4. Insert a short piece of plastic straw through the clay and into the sand layer at the low end. Remove the straw, discard it, and then insert a new piece of straw into the same hole.
5. Slowly pour water into the funnel. Do not let the water overflow.
6. Observe the level of water in the straw.

**Making Models** How is your model like a real artesian well? How is it different?

**Using Pumps** Long ago, people dug wells by hand. They lined the sides of the well with brick and stone to keep the walls from collapsing. To bring up the water, they lowered and raised a bucket. People may also have used simple pumps, like the one shown in Figure 13. Today, however, most wells are dug with well-drilling equipment. Mechanical pumps bring up the groundwater.

Pumping water out of an aquifer lowers the water level near the well. If too much water is pumped out too fast, a well may run dry. The owners of the well will have to dig deeper to reach the lowered water table, or wait for rainfall to refill the aquifer. New water that enters the aquifer from the surface is called recharge.

**Relying on Pressure** Now you know how to bring groundwater to the surface. But what if that doesn't work? You might not be out of luck. You might be able to drill an artesian well. In an **artesian well** (ahr TEEZH un), water rises because of pressure within an aquifer.

Look back at Figure 13 and locate the artesian well. In some aquifers, groundwater becomes trapped between two layers of impermeable rock or sediment. This water is under great pressure from the weight of the rock above. If the top layer of rock is punctured, the pressure sends water spurting up through the hole. No pump is necessary—in an artesian well, pressure does the job.

FIGURE 13
**Working for Water** Here a resident of Bangladesh uses a hand pump to bring groundwater to the surface.
**Interpreting Photographs** *What is one disadvantage of a hand pump?*

**Springs and Geysers** Sometimes, groundwater comes to the surface through natural processes. Recall that places where groundwater bubbles or flows out of cracks in the rock are called springs. Most springs contain water at normal temperatures. Others, like those in Figure 14, contain water that is warmed by the hot rocks deep below the surface. The heated water bubbles to the surface in hot springs.

In some areas, you might see a fountain of boiling hot water and white steam burst into the air. This is a **geyser** (GY zur), a type of hot spring from which the water periodically erupts. The word *geyser* comes from an Icelandic word, *geysir*, which means "gusher."

A geyser forms when very hot water that has been circulating deep underground begins to rise through narrow passages in the rock. Heated gases and bubbles of steam are forced up these passages by the pressure of the hot water boiling below. Just as pressure builds up in a partly blocked water pipe, the pressure within these narrow openings in the rock increases. Finally, the gases, steam, and hot water erupt high into the air.

**FIGURE 14**
**A Hot Spring**
A Japanese macaque takes advantage of the warm water that rises to the surface of a hot spring in Nagano, Japan.

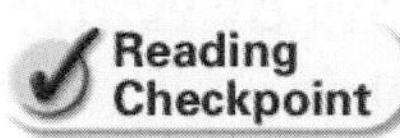


**How do geysers form?**

## Section 3 Assessment

**Target Reading Skill Previewing Visuals** Refer to your questions and answers about Figure 12 to help you answer Question 2 below.

### Reviewing Key Concepts

1. a. **Reviewing** How does water move underground?
   b. **Explaining** Explain the two factors that determine how easily water can move through underground materials.
   c. **Comparing and Contrasting** How are the saturated zone and the unsaturated zone similar? How are they different?
2. a. **Describing** How can people obtain water from an aquifer?
   b. **Interpreting Diagrams** Using Figure 12 as a guide, explain why is it important to know the depth of an aquifer before drilling a well.
   c. **Problem Solving** During the winter, you draw your water from a well on your property. Every summer, the well dries up. What might be the reason for the change?

### Writing in Science

**Formal Letter** Water use in your town has risen in recent years due to population growth. Your town obtains its water from a nearby aquifer. You are concerned that the water level of the aquifer may be going down. Write a letter to local government officials explaining your concerns. Describe the effect of heavy water use on the aquifer and suggest measures that can be taken to avoid a water shortage.

Lab zone **Design Your Own Lab**

# Soil Testing

## Problem

How fast does water move through sand, clay, and pebbles?

## Skills Focus

observing, developing hypotheses, designing experiments

## Suggested Materials

- hand lens
- 100 mL of sand
- stopwatch
- 3 rubber bands
- 3 100-mL beakers
- 300 mL of water
- 100 mL of pebbles
- 100 mL of powdered potter's clay
- 3 squares of cheesecloth
- 3 large funnels or cut-off plastic bottle tops

## Procedure   

### PART 1 Observing the Flow of Water Through Sand

1. Copy the data table in your notebook.
2. Use a hand lens to observe the sand sample closely. Record your observations in your data table.
3. Place a piece of cheesecloth over the bottom of one funnel or bottle top and secure it with a rubber band.
4. Place the sand in the funnel. Be sure that there is about 5 cm of space above the sand in the funnel.
5. Place the funnel on top of a beaker.

| Data Table | | |
|---|---|---|
| Material | Observations | Time for Water to Stop Dripping |
| Sand | | |
| Clay | | |
| Pebbles | | |
| | | |

6. Slowly pour 100 mL of water into the funnel. Do not let the water overflow the funnel.
7. Start the stopwatch when the water begins to flow or drip out of the funnel.
8. Stop the stopwatch when the water stops dripping out of the funnel or after 5 minutes. Record the time to the nearest second in your data table.

### PART 2 Comparing the Flow of Water Through Different Soil Samples

9. Use a hand lens to observe each of the two other material samples closely. Record your observations in the data table.
10. Using the procedures you followed in Part 1, design an experiment to compare the flow of water through sand, clay, and pebbles. Be sure to write a hypothesis and to control all necessary variables.
11. Submit your experimental plan to your teacher. After making any necessary changes, carry out your experiment. Record your observations in your data table.
12. When you are finished with this activity, dispose of the materials according to your teacher's instructions. Wash your hands thoroughly with soap.

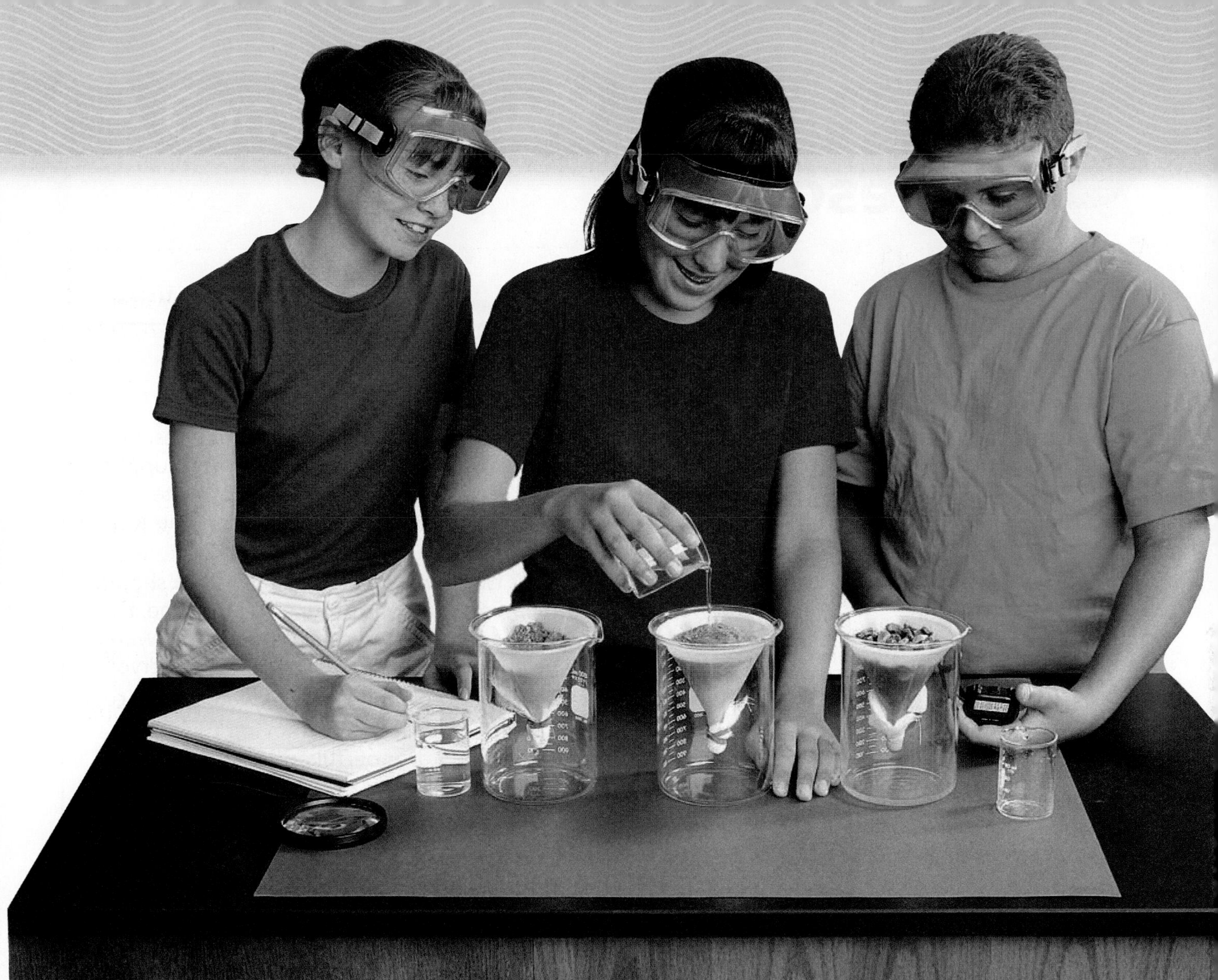

## Analyze and Conclude

1. **Observing** In Part 1, how did the sand look under the hand lens? How long did it take the water to flow through the sand?
2. **Developing Hypotheses** What hypothesis did you test in Part 2? On what did you base your hypothesis?
3. **Designing Experiments** What was the manipulated variable in Part 2? What was the responding variable?
4. **Drawing Conclusions** Through which material did water move the fastest? The slowest? What can you conclude about the permeability of the three materials?
5. **Predicting** Based on the results of this lab, would you expect to get more water from a well dug in sand, pebbles, or clay? Explain.
6. **Communicating** You and your neighbor are discussing your gardens. You're explaining that it's important for a gardener to know the permeability of different soils. Write your conversation in dialogue form. Use quotation marks for each speaker.

## More to Explore

Of the soil samples you tested, which do you think most resembles the soil on the grounds at your school? Explain your reasoning. How might you test your hypothesis?

Section 4

# Using Freshwater Resources

## Reading Preview

### Key Concepts

- How do people use water?
- What are some ways to conserve available fresh water?
- How do scientists classify sources of water pollution?

### Key Terms

- irrigation
- conservation
- water pollution
- pollutant
- point source
- nonpoint source

### Target Reading Skill

**Using Prior Knowledge** Before you read, write what you know about water conservation in a graphic organizer like the one below. As you read, write what you learn.

| What You Know |
|---|
| 1. I can conserve water by taking shorter showers. |
| 2. |

| What You Learned |
|---|
| 1. |
| 2. |

## Lab zone Discover Activity

### Can You Find a Balance?

1. Fill a large measuring cup with water to represent a reservoir. Record the level of the water. One partner, the water supplier, should have a plastic dropper and a small bowl of water. The other partner, the water user, should have a spoon and an empty bowl.
2. Start a stopwatch. For two minutes, the water supplier should add water to the measuring cup one dropperful at a time. Each time the water supplier adds a dropperful of water, the water user should remove one spoonful of water from the reservoir.
3. At the end of two minutes, record the level of water in the cup.
4. Now increase the rate of water use by removing two spoonfuls of water for every dropperful added.
5. After two minutes, record the level of water in the cup.

**Think It Over**

**Predicting** What changes will you need to make so that the water level in the reservoir stays constant?

If you have ever gone fishing, you know that it can be exciting. You cast your fishing line out over the smooth, dark blue water. As you gently reel in the line, suddenly you feel a slight pull that quickly grows to a strong tug. You've caught a fish!

Good fishing depends on a supply of clean, fresh water in rivers and lakes. Yet there are many other uses of fresh water. Some of these uses can reduce the overall water supply or make the water unsuitable for fishing.

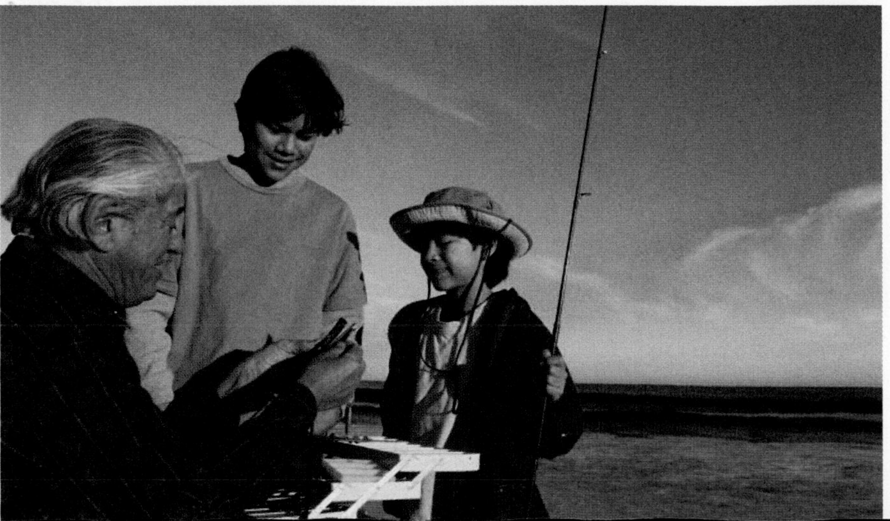

This family is enjoying a freshwater resource—fish. ▶

## How People Use Water

Think about the ways that people use water in your community. As you walk around your neighborhood on a hot summer afternoon, you might see young children running through a sprinkler. Nearby, someone is watering plants or washing a car. Across the United States, thousands of different uses consume more than 1,280 billion liters of water every day.

**People use water for household purposes, industry, transportation, agriculture, and recreation.** As cities grow, so too does the water needed for household uses. Industries also need water to cool machinery and produce materials such as paper. Meanwhile, farmers need a large amount to water their fields. Cities, industries, and farms compete for water rights—the legal right to take water from a particular source.

In some parts of the United States, such as the Southwest, water is scarce. As you know, water is constantly recycled in the water cycle. However, sometimes water is used faster than it can be replaced by precipitation. A water shortage occurs when there is too little water or too great a demand in an area—or both. A water shortage may occur because of natural processes or because of rapidly growing human water needs.

### Math Analyzing Data

#### Household Water Use

A family conducted a survey of their current water use. Their average daily use is shown in the bar graph. Study the graph and answer the following questions.

1. **Reading Graphs** What variable is shown on the horizontal axis? What variable is shown on the vertical axis?
2. **Interpreting Data** Where does this family use the greatest amount of water?
3. **Calculating** The family uses an average of about 800 liters of water per day. What percentage of the water is used for laundry?
4. **Inferring** Do you think the family's water use would vary during the year? Explain.

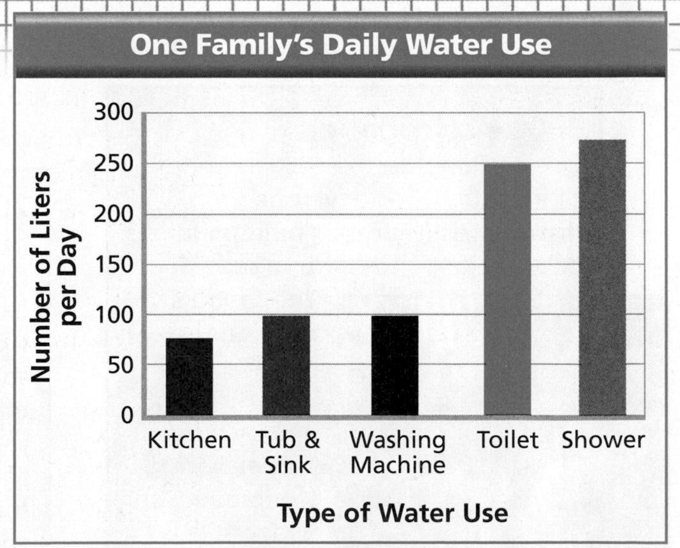


5. **Predicting** Suggest three ways that this family might be able to save a significant amount of water each day.

**In the Home** Take a minute to list all of the ways you used water this morning. You probably washed your face, brushed your teeth, and flushed the toilet. Perhaps you drank a glass of water or used water to make oatmeal. These are some common uses of water in the home.

**Industry and Transportation** Think about the objects in your backpack—books, pens, folders. Even though water is not part of these things, it plays a role in making them. Industries use water in other ways, too. For example, power plants and steel mills both need huge volumes of water to cool hot machinery. Water that is used for cooling can often be recycled.

Since ancient times, water has been used to transport people and goods. If you look at a map of the United States, you will notice that many large cities are located on the coasts. Ocean travel led to the growth of these port cities. In early America, rivers also served as natural highways.

## • Tech & Design in History •

### Water and Agriculture

Plants require a steady supply of water to grow. How have farmers throughout history provided their crops with water? This timeline shows some methods developed in different parts of the world.

**3000 B.C. Irrigation**
One of the oldest known methods of irrigation was developed for growing rice. Farmers built paddies, or artificial ponds with raised edges. The farmers flooded the paddies with water from a nearby stream. This ancient technique is still widely used throughout Southeast Asia.

**2000 B.C. Shadufs**
Egyptian farmers invented a device to raise water from the Nile River. The shaduf acted as a lever to make lifting a bucket of water easier. The farmers then emptied the water into a network of canals to irrigate their fields. The shaduf is still in use in Egypt, India, and other countries.

**700 B.C. Canals and Aqueducts**
Sennacherib, king of the ancient nation Assyria, surrounded the capital city of Nineveh with fruit trees and exotic plants. To help irrigate the gardens, he built a canal and an aqueduct to transport water from the nearby hills.

3000 B.C. | 2000 B.C. | 1000 B.C.

**Agriculture** Has your family ever had a garden? If so, you know that growing fruits and vegetables requires water. On a large farm, a constant supply of fresh water is essential. However, some areas don't receive enough regular rainfall for agriculture. In such places, farmland must be irrigated. **Irrigation** is the process of supplying water to areas of land to make them suitable for growing crops. In the United States, more water is used for irrigation than for any other single purpose.

**Recreation** Do you like to swim in a neighborhood pool? Catch fish from a rowboat in the middle of a lake? Walk along a beach collecting seashells? Or maybe just sit on the edge of a dock and dangle your feet in the water? Then you know some ways that water is used for recreation. And if you brave the winter cold to ski or skate, you are enjoying water in its frozen form.

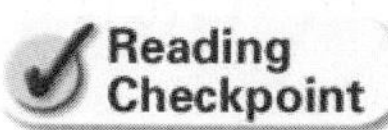

**List a household use, an industrial use, and an agricultural use of water.**

## Writing in Science

**Research and Write** Find out more about one of these agricultural techniques. Imagine that you are a farmer seeing the method in action for the first time. Write a letter to a friend describing the new technique. What problem will it solve? How will it improve your farming?

**A.D. 1200 *Chinampas***
To grow crops in swampy areas, the Aztecs built raised plots of farmland called *chinampas.* A grid of canals kept the crops wet and allowed the farmers to navigate boats between the *chinampas.*

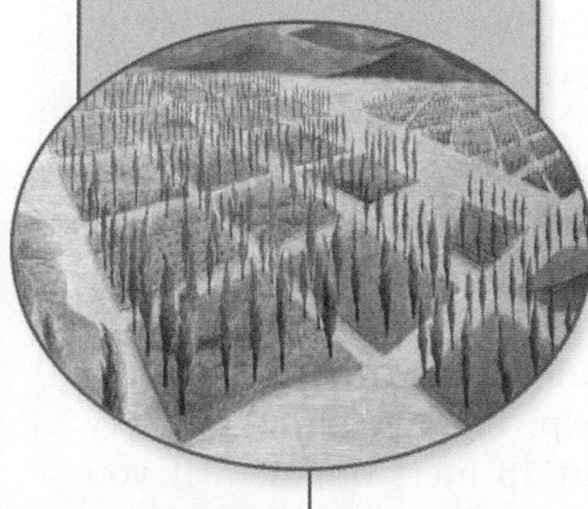

**A.D. 1870**
**Wind-Powered Pumps**
When homesteaders arrived on the dry Great Plains of the central United States, they had to rely on groundwater for irrigation. Windmills provided the energy to pump the groundwater to the surface. The farmers dug ditches to transport the water to their fields.

**Today Drip Irrigation**
Irrigation is the key to survival in desert regions. Today, methods such as drip irrigation ensure that very little water is wasted when crops are watered. Holes in the pipe allow water to drip directly onto the soil around the roots of each plant.

A.D. 1 A.D. 1000 A.D. 2000

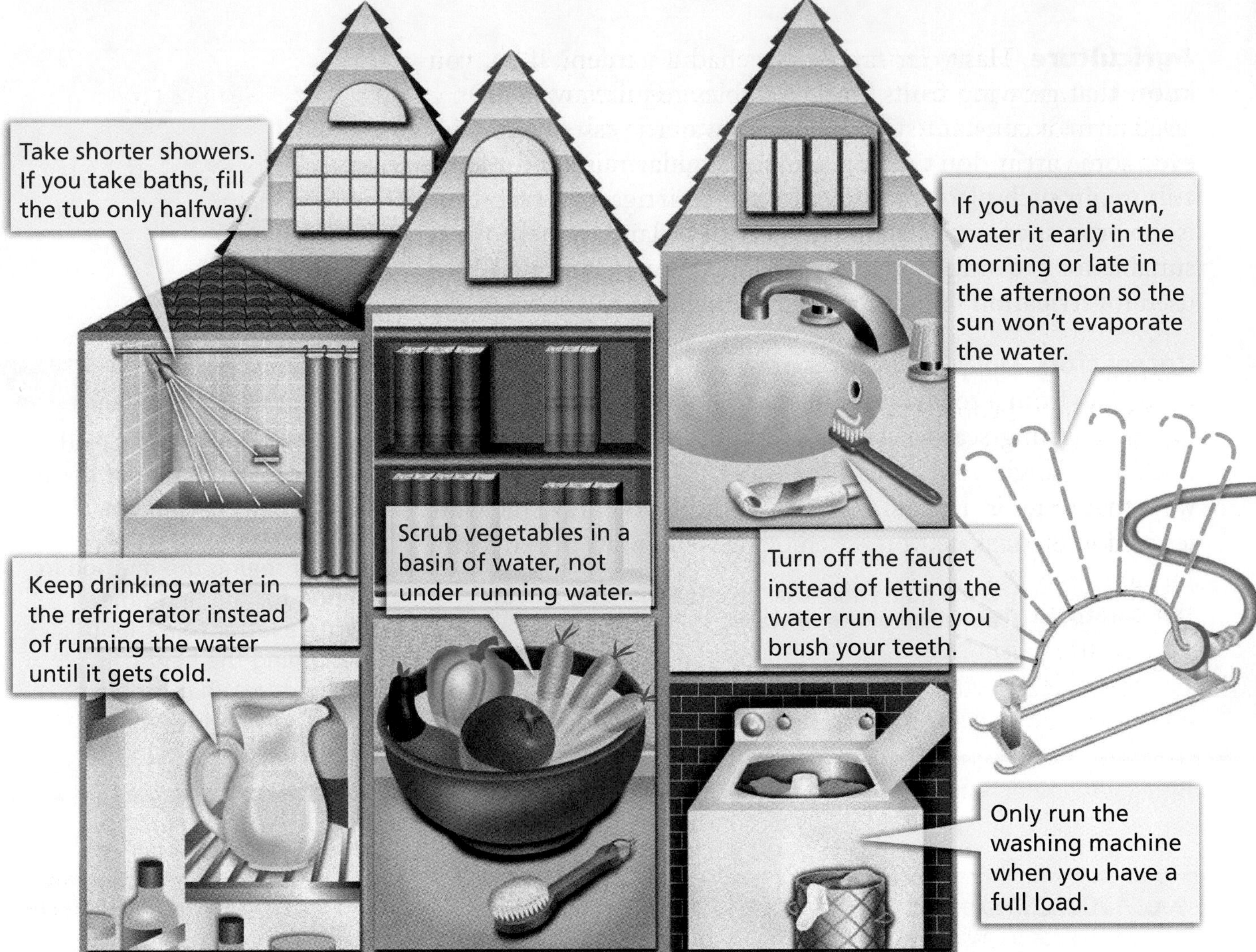

Take shorter showers. If you take baths, fill the tub only halfway.
If you have a lawn, water it early in the morning or late in the afternoon so the sun won't evaporate the water.
Scrub vegetables in a basin of water, not under running water.
Keep drinking water in the refrigerator instead of running the water until it gets cold.
Turn off the faucet instead of letting the water run while you brush your teeth.
Only run the washing machine when you have a full load.

FIGURE 15
**Conserving Water at Home**
There are many simple ways to conserve water at home.
**Developing Hypotheses** *Which of these ideas do you think would save the most water per day in your home? How could you test your hypothesis?*

## Conserving Water

During a water shortage, people often try to avoid wasting water. **Conservation** is the practice of using less of a resource so that it will not be used up. **Reducing water use, recycling water, and reusing water are three ways to conserve water.**

**In the Home** Most people in the United States have access to as much clean, safe water as they want. As a result, they often use more water than they need without thinking much about it. But as Figure 15 shows, there are some simple things you can do to help conserve water around your home.

Can these suggestions really help? Figure it out. For every minute you shower, you use about 18 liters of water. If you shower for 10 minutes, that's about 180 liters. But if you showered for 5 minutes, you would use only 90 liters. And if each student in a class of 25 showered for 5 minutes instead of 10, they would save a total of 2,250 liters of water!

**In Industry** Many industries have made changes in their manufacturing processes to use less water. For example, in the 1950s it took about 227,000 liters of water to make 1,000 kilograms of writing paper. By the 1980s, paper mills needed only half that much water to make the same amount of paper.

New water-saving techniques help industries save money in water costs and meet the requirements of environmental laws. These techniques conserve water while also reducing the amount of wastewater that plants release. For example, some factories that use water to cool machinery now build cooling pools on their property. The heated water cools off in the pools and then can be used again.

**In Agriculture** Agriculture accounts for the highest consumption of water in the United States. In the last few decades, farmers have found new ways to use less water. When water flows into fields in open ditches, much of it is lost through evaporation. Using pipes to carry water reduces the water loss.

Sprinkler irrigation and drip irrigation both use pipes to conserve water. Sprinkler irrigation sprays water onto crops from overhead pipes. Drip irrigation distributes water through pipes with tiny holes that lie close to the ground. Water drips onto the soil near the plants' roots so that very little is wasted.

**Reading Checkpoint** **How do sprinkler irrigation and drip irrigation differ?**

**For:** More on water conservation
**Visit:** PHSchool.com
**Web Code:** cfd-3021

FIGURE 16
**Conserving Water on Farms**
One way that farmers can conserve water is to use sprinkler irrigation systems to water their crops.
**Relating Cause and Effect** *How does sprinkler irrigation conserve water?*

FIGURE 17

## Pollution Solutions

People can prevent or clean up pollution in many ways. **Interpreting Diagrams** *What are two ways of reducing water pollution on farms?*

**Roads**
Using sand instead of salt on roadways reduces the amount of pollution in the winter.

**Factories**
Factories cool water and reuse it instead of dumping hot water into a river.

**Farms**
Farmers collect runoff from pastures and barnyards to use for irrigation. They also plant coarse grasses to filter pollutants before they reach rivers and ponds.

**Homes**
In rural areas, people place septic tanks away from freshwater sources and maintain their tanks to avoid leaking pollutants.

**Cities**
In the city, sewage treatment plants clean wastewater. Hazardous waste collection days discourage people from dumping pollutants such as motor oil down their drains.

**Wetlands**
Natural and artificial wetlands filter out pollutants from the runoff produced by mines.

## What Is Pollution?

**Water pollution** is the addition of any substance that has a negative effect on water or the living things that depend on the water. The substances that cause water pollution are called **pollutants.**

**Scientists classify sources of pollution, in part, by how they enter a body of water.** For example, suppose you notice a pipe gushing brightly colored water into a river. The pipe is a **point source,** a specific source of pollution that can be identified. In contrast, a widely spread source of pollution that can't be tied to a specific point of origin is called a **nonpoint source.** Examples of nonpoint sources include runoff from farm fields, streets, or construction sites.

There are many ways in which industries, farms, and homes can reduce water pollution. Figure 17 shows some of these techniques.

At home, you can help to reduce water pollution. Dispose of toxic substances properly. For example, never pour paint or motor oil down the drain. Instead, take these pollutants to sites that collect hazardous waste.

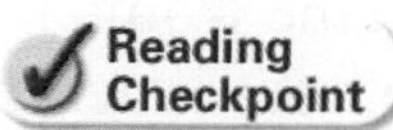
Reading Checkpoint: What are pollutants?

**FIGURE 18**
**Preventing Water Pollution**
One way you can help prevent water pollution is to educate others about its causes. This student has stenciled a storm drain to remind people of its connection to a nearby river.

## Section 4 Assessment

**Target Reading Skill Using Prior Knowledge** Revise your graphic organizer based on what you learned.

### Reviewing Key Concepts

1. a. **Listing** Name five ways that people use water.
   b. **Describing** How is water used in agriculture?
   c. **Predicting** What might happen to the supply of water for agriculture in a region with a rapidly growing city?
2. a. **Identifying** What are three ways to conserve water?
   b. **Describing** Describe the techniques that industries can use to conserve water.
   c. **Making Judgments** To conserve water, should communities limit how often people can water their lawns or wash their cars? Why or why not?
3. a. **Defining** What is a point source of pollution? What is a nonpoint source?
   b. **Classifying** In winter, some communities spread salt on the roads to melt ice. Runoff containing salt can flow into nearby streams or lakes. Is this an example of point source or nonpoint source pollution? Explain.

### Lab zone At-Home Activity

**Monitoring Water Use** To show family members one way of conserving water, brush your teeth twice. The first time, allow the water to run into the sink with a stopper in the drain. When you're finished brushing, mark the water level with a piece of tape. Drain the sink, then replace the stopper and brush again. This time, use the water only when you need to. Point out the difference in the amount of water used.

Section 5 • Tech & Design •

# Water to Drink

## Reading Preview

### Key Concepts

- What factors affect water quality?
- Why is drinking water often treated before people drink it?

### Key Terms

- water quality • concentration
- pH • hardness • coliform
- filtration • coagulation

### Target Reading Skill

**Sequencing** As you read, make a flowchart that shows the steps of drinking-water treatment. Put the steps of the process in separate boxes in the flowchart in the order in which they occur.

**Drinking-Water Treatment**

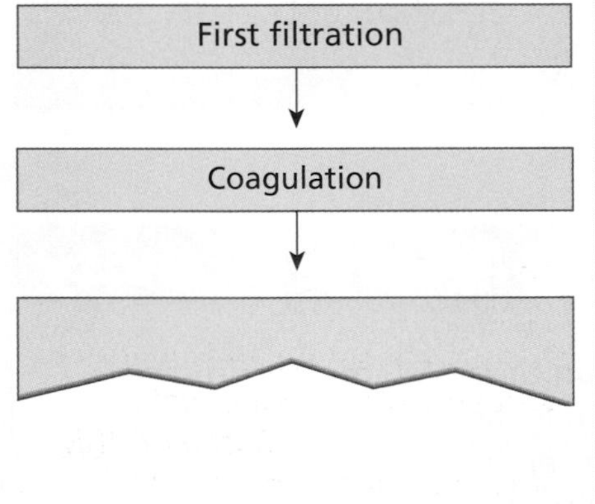


## Lab zone Discover Activity

### How Can Water Be Cleaned?

1. Cover an empty jar with a paper towel. Tuck the paper towel slightly into the mouth of the jar.
2. Fill a second jar with water. Add a handful of materials to the water, such as sand, soil, and leaves.
3. While holding the paper towel in place, slowly pour about half of the water onto the paper towel so that it enters the empty jar. Observe what happens as the water flows through the paper towel.

**Think It Over**

**Comparing and Contrasting** Describe the appearance of the water in the two jars. How could your observations help you in designing a process for treating drinking water?

Where does the water in your kitchen faucet come from? Its source may be a lake or reservoir, or it may come from water in underground rock layers. Most people in the United States get their drinking water from one of these sources.

Your drinking water comes from either a public or private water supply. In a public water supply, a community collects, treats, and distributes water to residents. In rural areas, private wells often supply water for individual families.

## Water Quality

Because water comes from different sources, it varies in quality. Would you drink water that was rust-colored or had a funny smell? Color and odor are factors that affect water quality.

**Standards of Quality** **Water quality** is a measurement of the substances in water besides water molecules. **Certain substances, such as iron, can affect the taste or color of water but are harmless unless present at very high levels. Other substances, such as certain chemicals and microorganisms, can be harmful to your health.**

In the United States, the Environmental Protection Agency (EPA) is responsible for developing water-quality standards. These standards, shown in Figure 19, set concentration limits for certain substances. A **concentration** is the amount of one substance in a certain volume of another substance.

**Acidity** The pH level of water also affects its quality. The **pH** of water is a measurement of how acidic or basic the water is, on a scale of 0 to 14. Pure water has a pH of 7—it is neutral, meaning it is neither an acid nor a base. The higher the pH, the more basic the water. The lower the pH, the more acidic the water. Acidic water can cause problems by dissolving lead or other metals from the pipes it passes through.

**Hardness** The combined level of two minerals—calcium and magnesium—in a sample of water is referred to as the **hardness** of that sample. Hard water contains high levels of calcium and magnesium. The minerals come from rocks, such as limestone, that water flows through underground.

The main drawback of hard water is that it does not form suds well when mixed with soap or detergent. The minerals in hard water can also form deposits that can clog pipes and machinery. Soft water, on the other hand, contains lower levels of calcium and magnesium. Soft water leaves fewer deposits and forms better soapsuds than hard water.

**Disease-Causing Organisms** The presence of disease-causing organisms affects water quality. Such organisms can be detected by a coliform count, which measures the number of *Escherichia coli* bacteria. **Coliform** bacteria are found in human and animal wastes. Their presence in water shows that it contains waste material. A high coliform count shows that the water may also contain other disease-causing organisms.

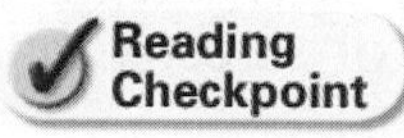


**What two minerals affect a water sample's hardness?**

**Math Skills**

### Calculating a Concentration

Concentrations are often measured in parts per million (ppm). What does this unit mean? If you own one compact disc by your favorite band, and the disc sells one million copies, your disc is one of the one million sold, or one part per million. When a concentration is written in this form, you can rewrite it as a fraction. To do this, put the number of parts on top, and the "whole" on the bottom.

$$1 \text{ part per million} = \frac{1}{1{,}000{,}000}$$

**Practice Problem** The concentration of iron in a water sample is 500 parts per million. Write this concentration as a fraction.

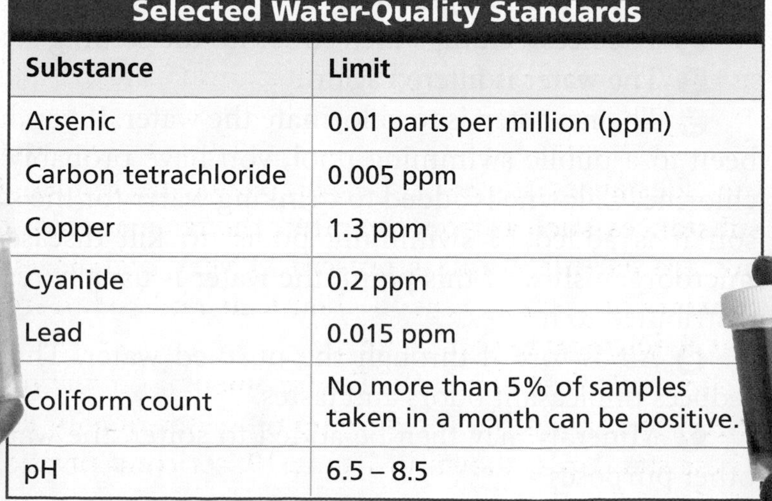

**Selected Water-Quality Standards**

| Substance | Limit |
|---|---|
| Arsenic | 0.01 parts per million (ppm) |
| Carbon tetrachloride | 0.005 ppm |
| Copper | 1.3 ppm |
| Cyanide | 0.2 ppm |
| Lead | 0.015 ppm |
| Coliform count | No more than 5% of samples taken in a month can be positive. |
| pH | 6.5 – 8.5 |

FIGURE 19
The EPA has set water-quality standards for drinking water. **Interpreting Data** *Based on this table, is a concentration of 0.09 ppm of arsenic in drinking water acceptable? Is a concentration of 0.05 ppm of cyanide acceptable?*

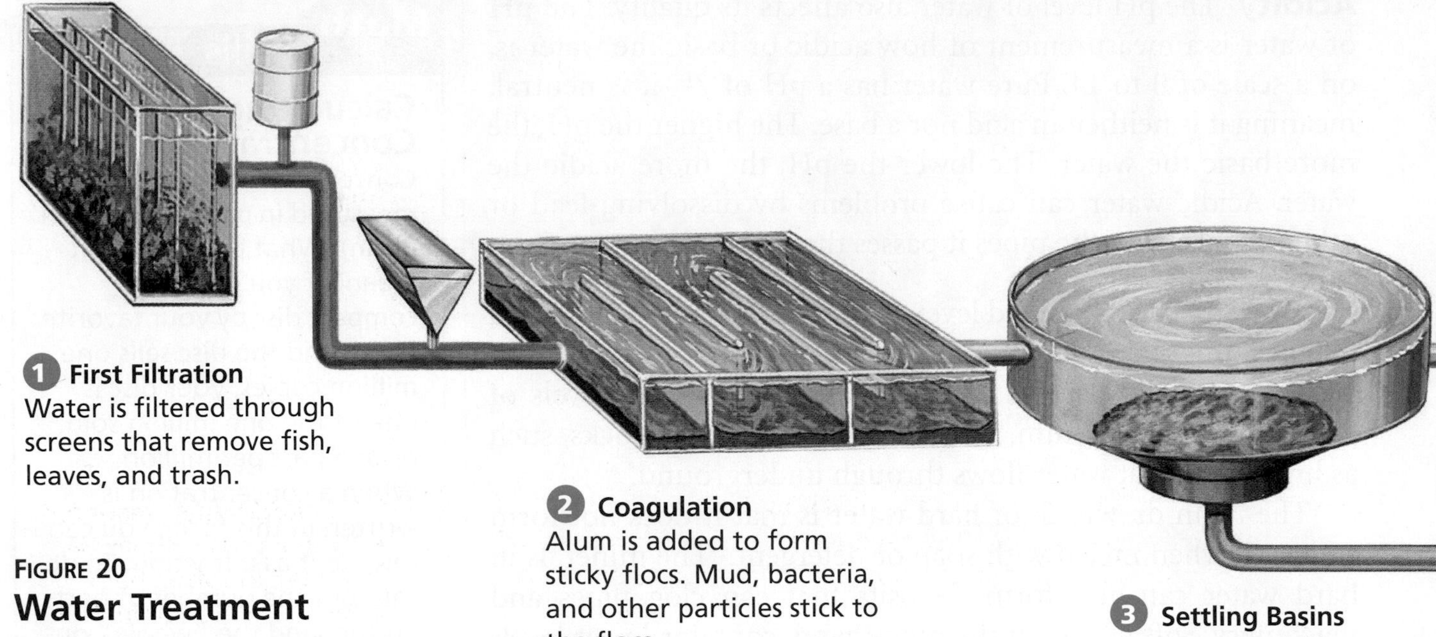

**1 First Filtration**
Water is filtered through screens that remove fish, leaves, and trash.

**2 Coagulation**
Alum is added to form sticky flocs. Mud, bacteria, and other particles stick to the flocs.

**3 Settling Basins**
The water and flocs then sink into settling basins.

**FIGURE 20**
**Water Treatment**
A typical drinking-water treatment process includes several steps that remove unwanted substances from water.
**Interpreting Diagrams** *What occurs during aeration?*

## Treating Drinking Water

How can you be sure that the quality of your drinking water is good? **Water from both public and private supplies often needs some treatment to ensure that it is clean and safe to drink.** Follow the steps in water treatment in Figure 20.

1 Treating water from a lake or river usually begins with filtration to remove trash, leaves, and other large objects. **Filtration** is the process of passing water through a series of screens that allows the water through, but not larger solid particles.

2 After filtration, a chemical is added to cause sticky globs, called flocs, to form. Other particles stick to the flocs, a process known as **coagulation.**

3 The heavy clumps then sink into the settling basins.

4 The water is filtered again.

5 The next step is to chlorinate the water. If you have ever been to a public swimming pool, you have probably smelled chlorine. Chlorine is added to drinking water for the same reason it is added to swimming pools: to kill disease-causing microorganisms. At this point, the water is usually ready to be distributed to homes.

6 Air is forced through the purified water. This process reduces unpleasant odors and tastes.

7 Minerals may then be added to soften the water or for other purposes.

**For:** More on water treatment
**Visit:** PHSchool.com
**Web Code:** cfd-3022

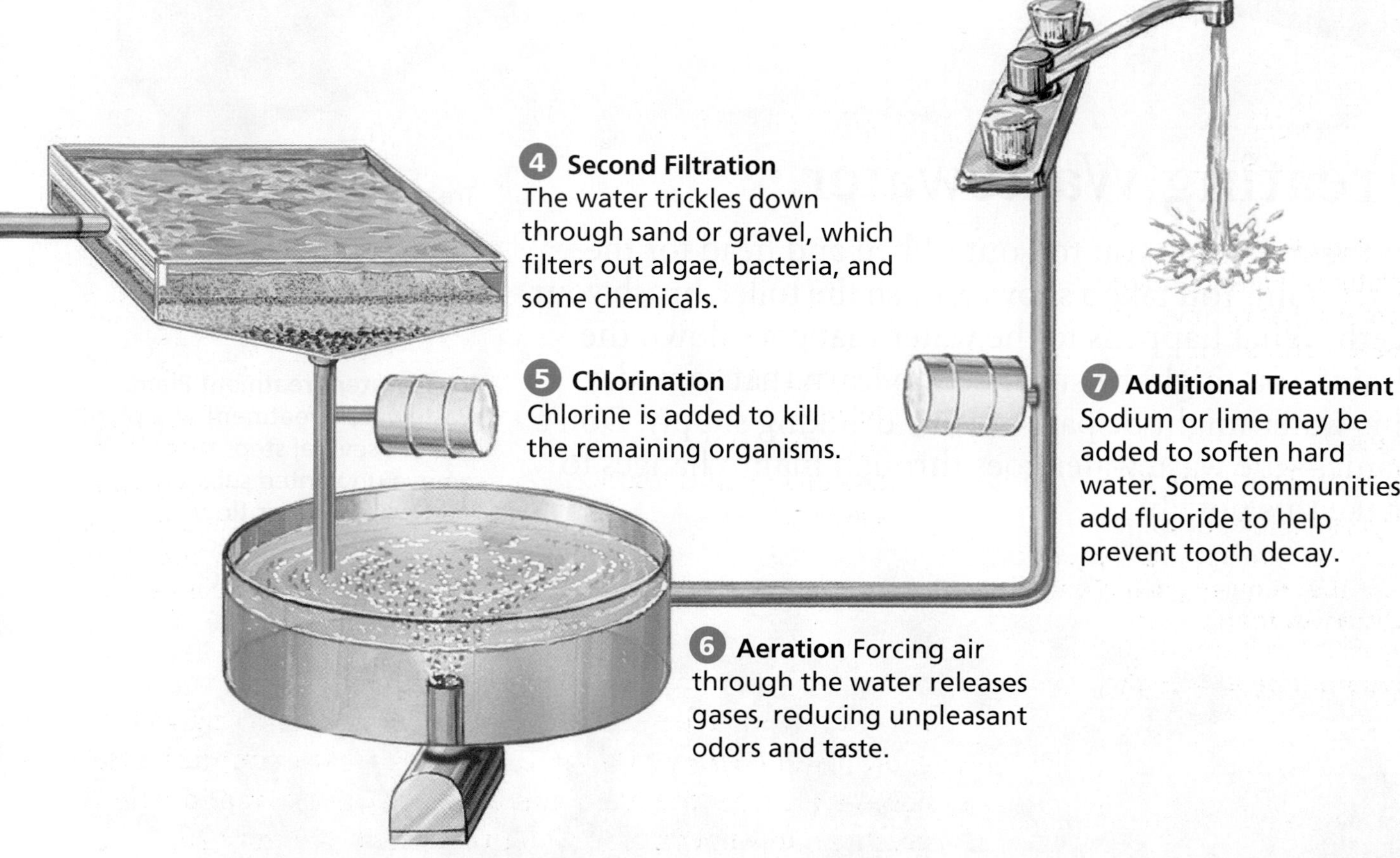

4 Second Filtration
The water trickles down through sand or gravel, which filters out algae, bacteria, and some chemicals.
5 Chlorination
Chlorine is added to kill the remaining organisms.
6 Aeration Forcing air through the water releases gases, reducing unpleasant odors and taste.
7 Additional Treatment
Sodium or lime may be added to soften hard water. Some communities add fluoride to help prevent tooth decay.

## Section 5 Assessment

**Target Reading Skill Sequencing** Refer to your flowchart about drinking-water treatment as you answer Question 2 below.

### Reviewing Key Concepts

1. a. **Listing** Name the factors that affect water quality.
   b. **Comparing and Contrasting** How does hard water differ from soft water?
   c. **Inferring** Dissolved lead has been found in your drinking supply. What can you infer about the acidity of your water? Explain.
2. a. **Reviewing** Explain why drinking water is treated.
   b. **Explaining** What is the purpose of coagulation in water treatment?
   c. **Interpreting Diagrams** Refer to Figure 20. Explain the steps in water treatment that remove and kill bacteria and other organisms in the water.

**Math Practice**

3. **Calculating a Concentration** Review the EPA selected water-quality standards in Figure 19. Note that the concentrations of the first five substances are limited to certain amounts, given in parts per million (ppm). Write the concentration of each substance as a fraction.

# Technology and Society

• Tech & Design •

## Treating Wastewater

In the morning, you roll out of bed and head for the bathroom. You take a shower, flush the toilet, brush your teeth. What happens to the water that goes down the drain? You might be surprised to learn that someday this water might be part of your drinking supply. Don't panic—the wastewater goes through many changes to make this possible.

Treated sludge can be used for fertilizer.

**Wastewater Treatment Plant**
Wastewater treatment at a plant includes several steps that remove unwanted substances from water. Water flows through the plant, becoming cleaner after each stage.

**1 Preliminary Treatment**
First, wastewater flows through screens to catch large particles such as food and bits of trash.

**2 Primary Treatment**
The flow of the water slows as it enters settling tanks. Gravity causes particles to settle to the bottom of the tanks, forming sludge.

**3 Secondary Treatment**
Next, the wastewater is filtered through a bed of gravel. The gravel is covered with colonies of bacteria. These bacteria break down the wastes left in the sewage.

## Public Treatment Systems

Most communities rely on public treatment systems to clean their wastewater. Different communities often use slightly different processes. A typical wastewater treatment process, like the one shown here, involves several steps. Once treatment is complete, the water is returned to the environment. The clean water may be released back into lakes, rivers, or oceans, or pumped back into the ground. There the water rejoins the water cycle.

## How Clean Is Clean?

Until recently, wastewater was often dumped into open gutters and allowed to run directly into rivers and oceans. This practice spread disease. Cleaning wastewater before it is returned to the environment is healthier for everyone. However, treating wastewater does have some tradeoffs. By law, costly chemical tests are performed regularly to verify the water's cleanliness. Updating old systems or increasing system capacities for growing populations is expensive also. Small amounts of unwanted substances may remain in the water after treatment. The long-term effects of these substances are not known.

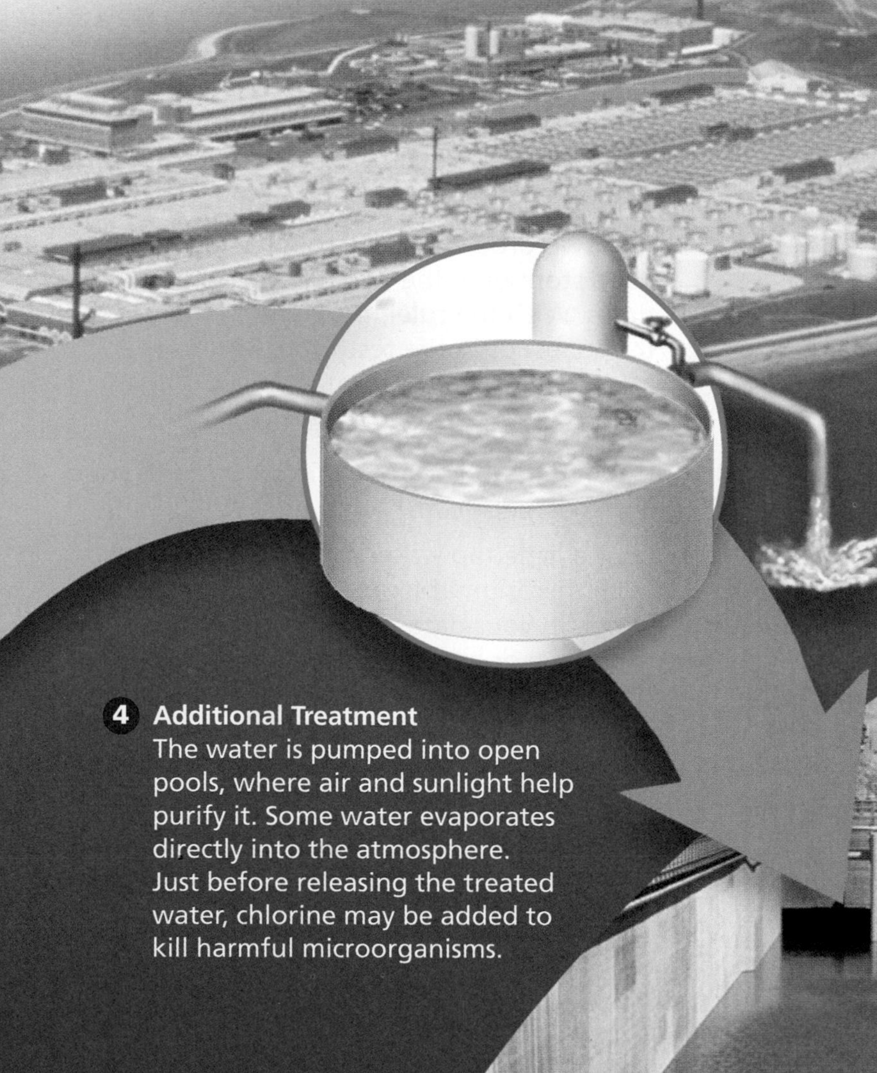

**4 Additional Treatment**
The water is pumped into open pools, where air and sunlight help purify it. Some water evaporates directly into the atmosphere. Just before releasing the treated water, chlorine may be added to kill harmful microorganisms.

## Weigh the Impact

**1. Identify the Need**
Why is wastewater treated?

**2. Research**
Use the Internet to research wastewater treatment. What new technologies are being developed? Choose one of these technologies and make a list of its advantages and disadvantages.

**3. Write**
Your community is considering upgrading its wastewater treatment plant. Some residents believe the plan can reduce water pollution. Others are concerned about the cost. State your views in a letter to the newspaper. Back up your opinions with facts from your research.

Go Online
PHSchool.com
**For:** More on wastewater treatment
**Visit:** PHSchool.com
**Web Code:** cfh-3020

Lab zone **Consumer Lab**

For: Data sharing
Visit: PHSchool.com
Web Code: cfd-3023

# Testing Water

## Problem

How do distilled water, spring water, and mineral water differ from tap water?

## Skills Focus

observing, inferring, drawing conclusions

## Materials

- hot plate
- liquid soap
- ruler
- wax pencil
- tap water, 200 mL
- distilled water, 200 mL
- spring water, 200 mL
- mineral water, 200 mL
- 4 250-mL beakers
- 4 test tubes and stoppers
- 4 pieces of pH paper
- test tube rack
- 25-mL graduated cylinder
- pH indicator chart
- 4 paper cups per person

## Procedure

1. Copy the data table into your notebook.
2. Label the beakers A, B, C, and D. Pour 100 mL of tap water into beaker A. Pour 100 mL of the other water samples into the correct beaker (refer to the data table).
3. Heat each water sample on a hot plate until about 20 mL remains. Do not allow the water to boil completely away. **CAUTION:** *Do not touch the hot plate or beakers with your bare hands.*
4. After the water samples have cooled, look for solids that make the water cloudy. Rank the samples from 1 to 4, where 1 has the fewest visible solids and 4 has the most visible solids. Record your rankings in the data table.
5. Label the test tubes A, B, C, and D. Pour 10 mL of each water sample from the source bottle into the correct test tube.
6. Dip a piece of pH paper into test tube A to measure its acidity. Match the color of the pH paper to a number on the pH indicator chart. Record the pH (0–14) in your data table.
7. Repeat Step 6 for the other samples.
8. Add two drops of liquid soap to test tube A. Put a stopper in the test tube and shake it 30 times. With the ruler, measure the height of the soapsuds in the test tube. Record the measurement in your data table.
9. Repeat Step 8 for the other samples.
10. Label the four cups A, B, C, and D. Write your name on each cup.
11. Pour a little tap water into cup A directly from the original source bottle. Taste the tap water. In your data table, describe the taste using one or more of these words: *salty, flat, bitter, metallic, refreshing, tasteless.* **CAUTION:** *Do not conduct the taste test in a lab room. Use a clean cup for each sample and discard it after use.*
12. Repeat Step 11 with the other samples.

**Data Table**

| Water Sample | Visible Solids (1–4) | pH (0–14) | Soapsud Height (cm) | Taste |
|---|---|---|---|---|
| A – Tap Water | | | | |
| B – Distilled Water | | | | |
| C – Spring Water | | | | |
| D – Mineral Water | | | | |

## Analyze and Conclude

1. **Observing** Review your data table. Compare each of the bottled water samples to the tap water sample. What similarities and differences did you detect?
2. **Inferring** Rank the samples from the one with the fewest soapsuds to the one with the most. Compare this ranking to the one for visible solids. What pattern do you see? What do both of these tests have to do with the hardness of water?
3. **Posing Questions** What other information about the water samples might you need before deciding which one to drink regularly? Explain.
4. **Drawing Conclusions** Based on your results, which sample would you most want to use for (a) drinking, (b) boiling in a teakettle, and (c) washing laundry? Which sample would you least want to use for each purpose? Explain.
5. **Communicating** Create a brochure to educate consumers about water quality. Include information about acidity, hardness, and other factors that can affect the appearance, taste, and safety of drinking water.

## More to Explore

Conduct a survey to find out what percentage of people buy bottled mineral water, distilled water, and spring water. Why do they buy each type of water, and how do they use it in their homes?

**The BIG Idea** **Earth's Resources** Surface fresh water is found in river systems, lakes, and ponds. Fresh water is also found underground. People use water for drinking and washing, industry, agriculture, transportation, recreation, and generating electrical power.

## 1 Water on Earth

### Key Concepts

- In the water cycle, water moves from bodies of water, land, and living things on Earth's surface to the atmosphere and back to Earth's surface.
- Most of Earth's water is salt water found in oceans. Only 3 percent is fresh water.

### Key Terms

water cycle
precipitation
groundwater

## 2 Surface Water

### Key Concepts

- A river and all its tributaries together make up a river system.
- In general, ponds are smaller and shallower than lakes. Sunlight usually reaches to the bottom of all parts of a pond.
- Lakes are generally bigger and deeper than ponds. Sunlight does not reach the bottom in a deep lake, as it does in a pond.
- The three common types of freshwater wetlands are marshes, swamps, and bogs.
- Wetlands provide habitats for many living things. Wetlands also act as natural water filters and help to control floods.

### Key Terms

tributary
watershed
divide
habitat
reservoir
wetland

## 3 Water Underground

### Key Concepts

- Water trickles down between particles of soil and through cracks and spaces in rock layers.
- People can obtain groundwater from an aquifer by drilling a well below the water table.

### Key Terms

permeable
impermeable
saturated zone
water table
unsaturated zone
spring
aquifer
artesian well
geyser

## 4 Using Freshwater Resources

### Key Concepts

- People use water for household purposes, industry, transportation, agriculture, and recreation.
- Reducing water use, recycling water, and reusing water are three ways to conserve water.
- Scientists classify sources of water pollution by how they enter a body of water.

### Key Terms

irrigation
conservation
water pollution
pollutant
point source
nonpoint source

## 5 Water to Drink

### Key Concepts

- Certain substances can affect the taste or color of water but are usually harmless. Other substances can be harmful to your health.
- Water often needs some treatment to ensure that it is clean and safe to drink.

### Key Terms

water quality
concentration
pH
hardness
coliform
filtration
coagulation

# Review and Assessment

For: Self-Assessment
Visit: PHSchool.com
Web Code: cja-3120

## Organizing Information

**Sequencing** Copy and complete the cycle diagram to show how water moves throughout the water cycle. (For more on Sequencing, see the Skills Handbook.)

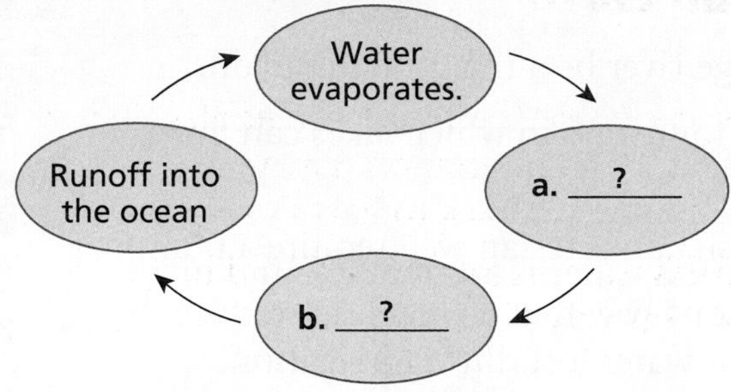


## Reviewing Key Terms

**Choose the letter of the best answer.**

1. More than 97 percent of Earth's total water supply is found in
   a. ice sheets.
   b. the atmosphere.
   c. the oceans.
   d. groundwater.
2. The land area that supplies water to a river system is called a
   a. divide.
   b. watershed.
   c. wetland.
   d. tributary.
3. Wetlands help control floods by absorbing
   a. silt and mud.
   b. extra runoff.
   c. nutrients.
   d. waste materials.
4. The water table is the top of the
   a. saturated zone.
   b. unsaturated zone.
   c. aquifer.
   d. artesian well.
5. Chlorine is added during water treatment in order to
   a. make particles form flocs.
   b. kill disease-causing organisms.
   c. improve the taste of the water.
   d. remove objects such as fish and trash.

**If the statement is true, write *true*. If it is false, change the underlined word or words to make the statement true.**

6. One watershed is separated from another by a <u>divide.</u>
7. An <u>aquifer</u> is an area of land covered with a shallow layer of water during some or all of the year.
8. Water moves easily through <u>permeable</u> materials.
9. <u>Conservation</u> is the practice of using less of a resource so that it will not be used up.
10. The <u>pH</u> of water is a measurement of the amount of calcium and magnesium it contains.

## Writing in Science

**Brochure** Write a brochure describing the Florida Everglades. Be sure to include information about why so many organisms live here and why people need to protect the Everglades.

*Earth: The Water Planet*
Video Preview
Video Field Trip
▶ Video Assessment

# Review and Assessment

## Checking Concepts

11. Why is so little of Earth's water available for human use?
12. Can a large river be a tributary? Explain.
13. Describe four ways in which lakes can form naturally.
14. Why doesn't an artesian well require a pump?
15. Describe one way that farmers can reduce the amount of water lost during irrigation.

## Thinking Critically

16. **Relating Cause and Effect** The water cycle begins as water evaporates from the surface of bodies of water. What is the energy source for this process? Explain.
17. **Applying Concepts** An engineer drilling a well finds water when the drill reaches 25 meters below the surface. What zone has the drill reached, what zone lies above it, and what do scientists call the level where the two zones meet? Explain.
18. **Inferring** Why are cities and towns often located along coasts or rivers?

**Drinking Water Sample Test Results**

| | |
|---|---|
| Lead | 0.2 parts per million |
| Copper | 0.006 parts per million |
| pH | 5.0 |
| Coliform count | 5 out of 5 samples positive |

19. **Inferring** A family tested their well to check the water quality. The test results are shown in the table above. Based on the data, is the well water safe to drink? Explain. (*Hint:* Compare these data with the data in Figure 19).
20. **Comparing and Contrasting** How would the variety of organisms in the center of a pond be different from those you would find in deep water at the center of a lake?

## Math Practice

21. **Calculating a Concentration** Look at the concentrations of lead and copper shown in the data table on this page. Write the concentrations in fraction form.

## Applying Skills

**Use the diagram of underground layers to answer Questions 22–25.**

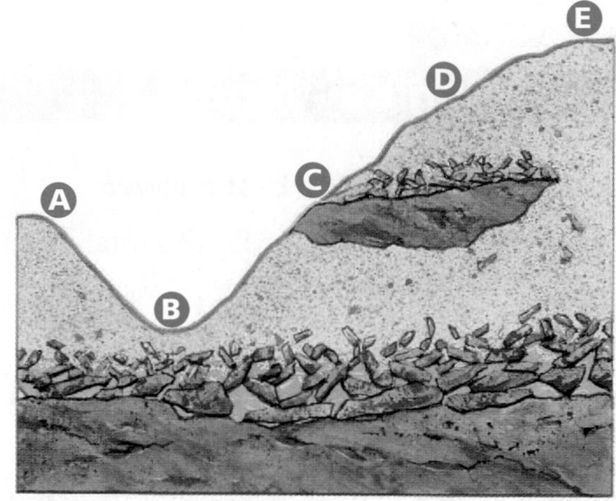


22. **Drawing Conclusions** Would point D or point E be a better location to dig a well? Explain your reasoning.
23. **Inferring** At which location could you obtain groundwater without having to use a pump? What is this location called?
24. **Interpreting Data** At which point is the water table closest to the surface?
25. **Predicting** Draw a simple diagram showing how this area might look during a very rainy season.

## Lab zone Chapter **Project**

**Performance Assessment** It's time to put your treatment system to the test! Use your system to clean up the dirty water sample. Measure the volume of water recovered by your system. Share your results with your classmates. How do your results compare with theirs?

# Standardized Test Prep

**Test-Taking Tip**

**Reading All the Answer Choices**

Always read *every* answer choice in a multiple-choice question before selecting the answer you think is correct. If you stop reading as soon as you find an answer that seems correct, you may not notice that "all of the above" is given as one of the answer choices.

***Sample Question***

Where on Earth is fresh water found?

**A** icebergs
**B** rivers and lakes
**C** groundwater
**D** all of the above

***Answer***

The correct answer is **D,** all of the above. Fresh water is found in icebergs, rivers and lakes, and groundwater.

**Choose the letter of the best answer.**

**1.** Why don't plants normally grow on the bottoms of deep lakes?
**A** The water is too salty.
**B** The water is too cold.
**C** Photosynthesis does not occur in water.
**D** There is not enough sunlight for photosynthesis to occur.

**2.** Which of the following is an example of a point source of water pollution?
**F** runoff of pesticides from wheat fields
**G** salt spread on parking lots to melt ice
**H** chemicals flowing from a factory into a stream
**J** fertilizer from corn fields that runs off into streams

**3.** For a science project you must build a model of an aquifer. What material would be the best to use for the layer that will hold water?
**A** an impermeable material, such as clay
**B** an impermeable material, such as granite
**C** a permeable material, such as gravel
**D** a material that does not have pores

*Use the diagram below and your knowledge of science to answer Questions 4–5.*

**4.** Which of the following is a process that occurs in the water cycle?
**F** evaporation
**G** precipitation
**H** condensation
**J** all of the above

**5.** What is the energy source that drives the continuous process shown in the diagram?
**A** the sun
**B** the ocean
**C** gravity
**D** the tides

## Constructed Response

**6.** Explain what a wetland is and why wetlands are important. Describe one threat to wetlands and the actions being taken to protect wetlands from this threat.

# Chapter 13 Ocean Motions

## The BIG Idea
Transfer of Energy

**What are the causes of waves, currents, and tides?**

### Chapter Preview

**1 Wave Action**
- ***Discover*** How Do Waves Change a Beach?
- ***Active Art*** Water Motion
- ***Try This*** Wave Motion
- ***Skills Activity*** Making Models
- ***At-Home Activity*** Wave Model

**2 Tides**
- ***Discover*** When Is High Tide?
- ***Analyzing Data*** Plotting Tides

**3 Ocean Water Chemistry**
- ***Discover*** Will the Eggs Sink or Float?
- ***Math Skills*** Calculating Density
- ***Technology Lab*** Investigating Changes in Density

**4 Currents and Climate**
- ***Discover*** Which Is More Dense?
- ***Skills Activity*** Drawing Conclusions
- ***At-Home Activity*** Modeling the Coriolis Effect
- ***Skills Lab*** Modeling Ocean Currents

**Powerful waves have created odd-looking landforms at Cape Kiwanda in Oregon.** ▶

*Ocean Motions*

▶ Video Preview
Video Field Trip
Video Assessment

Lab zone™ Chapter **Project**

## Design and Build an Erosion-Proof Beach

Waves, tides, and currents move Earth's waters in different ways. These movements change the land. In this project, you will build a model of a shoreline with a lighthouse and use the model to demonstrate how some ocean motions can affect the land along the coast.

**Your Goal** To design and build a model ocean beach and test methods for preventing shoreline erosion

To complete this project, you must

- build a model beach and use it to demonstrate the effects of wave erosion
- test methods of protecting the lighthouse from damage
- follow the safety guidelines outlined in Appendix A

**Plan It!** Begin now by previewing the chapter. Find out how engineers protect structures from beach erosion. Begin to design your model ocean beach. Consider what materials you will use for your shoreline and lighthouse. Then develop a plan for protecting your lighthouse.

Section 1

# Wave Action

## Reading Preview

### Key Concepts

- How does a wave form?
- How do waves change near the shore?
- How do waves affect shorelines and beaches?

### Key Terms

- wave • wavelength
- frequency • wave height
- tsunami • longshore drift
- rip current • groin

### Target Reading Skill

**Using Prior Knowledge** Before you read, look at the section headings and visuals to see what this section is about. Then write what you know about waves in a graphic organizer like the one below. As you read, continue to write in what you learn.

| What You Know |
|---|
| 1. There are waves in the ocean.<br>2. |

| What You Learned |
|---|
| 1.<br>2. |

## Lab zone Discover Activity

### How Do Waves Change a Beach?

1. In one end of an aluminum pan, build a "beach" of sand and pebbles. Put a book under that end of the pan to raise it about 5 centimeters.
2. Pour water slowly into the other end of the pan until it covers the edge of the sand, just as water touches the edge of a beach.
3. Place a wooden tongue depressor in the water. Move it back and forth gently in a regular rhythm to make waves in the pan. Continue for about 2 minutes.
4. Once the water has stopped moving, observe what has happened to the beach. Wash your hands after completing this activity.

**Think It Over**

**Observing** How has the motion of the water changed the edge of the beach?

Hundreds of years ago, kings and queens ruled the islands of Hawaii. If you could travel back in time, you could watch the royal family engaging in the islands' favorite sport. It wasn't baseball or tennis or polo. Instead, the ancient rulers paddled into the ocean on heavy wooden boards to catch the perfect wave. They were "wave-sliding," a sport we know today as surfing.

If you've ever seen a surfer like the one in Figure 1, you know that they make this difficult sport look almost easy. But even experienced surfers can seldom predict when the next good wave will roll into shore. As you will read in this section, many different forces influence the size, shape, and timing of waves.

## What Is a Wave?

When you watch a surfer's wave crash onto a beach, you are seeing the last step in the development of a wave. A **wave** is the movement of energy through a body of water. Wave development usually begins with wind. Without the energy of wind, the surface of the ocean would be as smooth as a mirror. **Most waves form when winds blowing across the water's surface transmit their energy to the water.**

**Wave Size** Waves start in the open ocean. The size of a wave depends on the strength of the wind and on the length of time it blows. A gentle breeze creates small ripples on the surface of the water. Stronger winds create larger waves.

The size of a wave also depends on the distance over which the wind blows. Winds blowing across longer distances build up bigger waves. Winds blowing across the Pacific Ocean can create bigger waves than winds blowing across the narrower Atlantic Ocean.

**Wave Energy** Although waves may appear to carry water toward shore, the water does not actually move forward in deep water. If it did, ocean water would eventually pile up on the coasts of every continent! The energy of the wave moves toward shore, but the water itself remains in place. You can test this by floating a cork in a bowl of water. Use a spoon to make a wave in the bowl. As the wave passes, the cork lurches forward a little; then it bobs backward. It ends up in almost the same spot where it started.

**FIGURE 1**
**Wave Energy**
A surfer cruises along a cresting wave. The wave's energy moves, but the water mostly stays in one place. **Applying Concepts** *In which direction is the energy of this wave moving?*

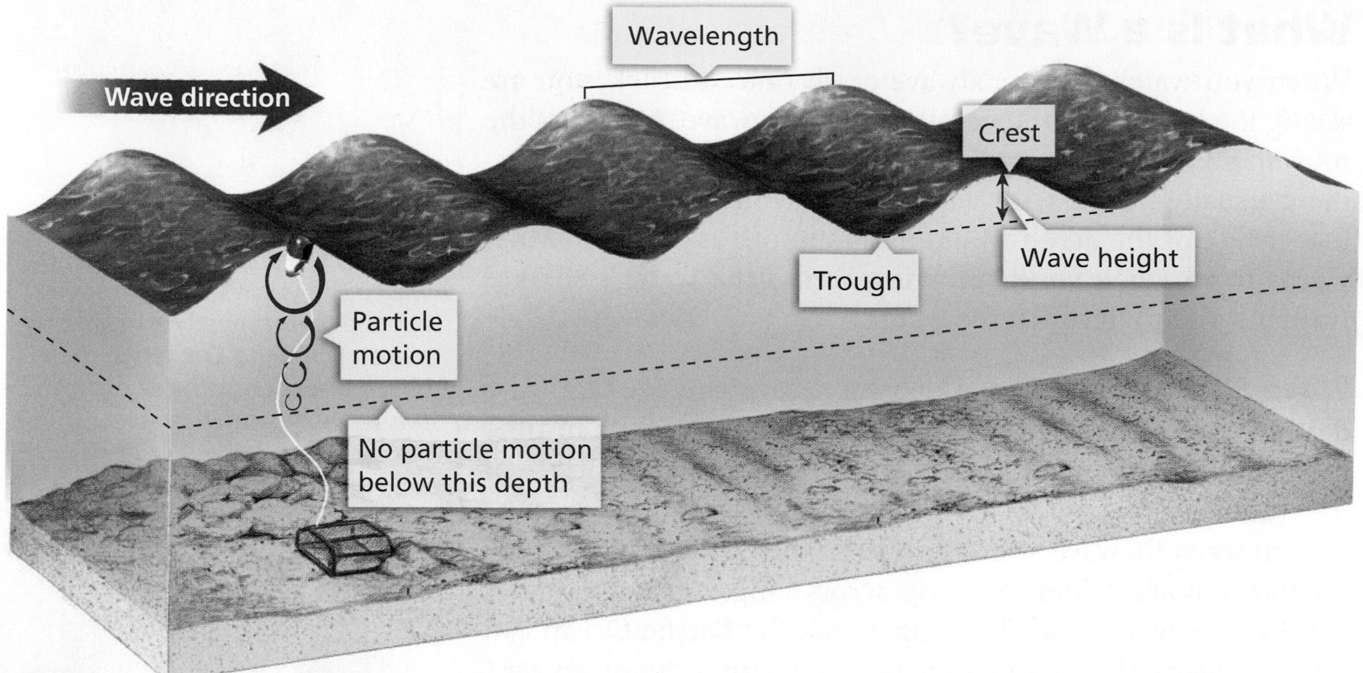


**FIGURE 2**
**Water Motion**
As a wave passes, water particles move in a circular motion. The buoy on the surface swings down into the trough of one wave, then back up to the crest of the next. Below the surface, water particles move in smaller circles. At a depth equal to about one half the wavelength, water particles are not affected by the surface wave.

For: Water Motion activity
Visit: PHSchool.com
Web Code: cfp-3031

**Water Motion** Figure 2 shows what happens to the water as a wave travels along. As the wave passes, water particles move in a circular path. They swing forward and down with the energy of the wave, then back up to their original position.

Notice that the deeper water particles move in smaller circles than those near the surface. The wind affects the water at the surface more than it affects the deep water. Below a certain depth, the water does not move at all as the wave passes. If you were inside a submarine in deep water, you would not be able to tell whether the water above you was rough or calm.

**Other Wave Characteristics** Scientists have a vocabulary of terms to describe the characteristics of waves. The name for the highest part of a wave is the crest. The horizontal distance between crests is the **wavelength.** Long, rolling waves with lots of space between crests have long wavelengths. Short, choppy waves have shorter wavelengths. Waves are also measured by their **frequency,** the number of waves that pass a point in a certain amount of time.

The lowest part of a wave is the trough. The vertical distance from the crest to the trough is the **wave height.** The energy and strength of a wave depend mainly on its wave height. In the open ocean, most waves are between 2 and 5 meters high. During storms, waves can grow much higher and more powerful.

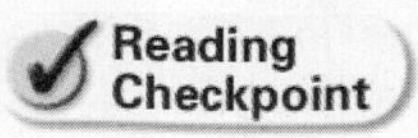


**Which have longer wavelengths—waves that are close together or waves that are far apart?**

## How Waves Change Near Shore

Have you ever seen an area of ocean water swell, resulting in a wave? Waves begin this way out in the ocean, but as they approach the shore, they change.

**Breakers** The white-capped waves that crash onto shore are often called "breakers." In deep water, these waves usually travel as long, low waves called swells. As the waves approach the shore, the water becomes shallower. Follow the waves in Figure 3 as they enter the shallow water. The bottoms of the waves begin to touch the sloping ocean floor. Friction between the ocean floor and the water causes the waves to slow down. As the speed of the waves decreases, their shapes change. **Near shore, wave height increases and wavelength decreases.** When the wave reaches a certain height, the crest of the wave topples. The wave breaks onto the shore, forming surf.

As the wave breaks, it continues to move forward. At first the breaker surges up the beach. But gravity soon slows it down, eventually stopping it. The water that had rushed up the beach then flows back out to sea. Have you ever stood at the water's edge and felt the pull of the water rushing back out to the ocean? This pull, often called an undertow, carries shells, seaweed, and sand away from the beach. A strong undertow can be dangerous to swimmers.

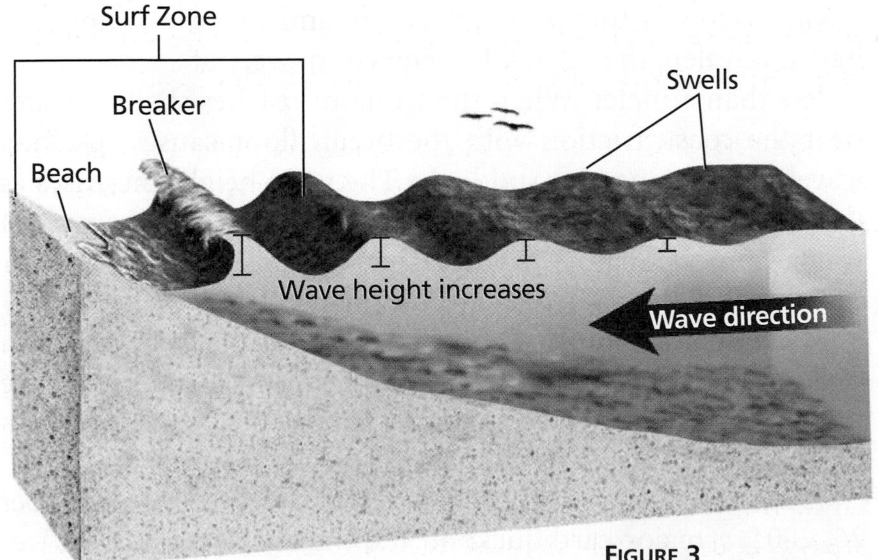


**FIGURE 3**
**How Breakers Change Near Shore**
Friction with the ocean floor causes waves to slow down in the shallow water near shore. The wave height increases until the waves break, forming surf.
**Comparing and Contrasting** *How do swells and breakers differ?*

**Lab zone Try This Activity**

### Wave Motion

This activity shows how waves that form at the surface affect deeper water.

1. Fill an aquarium about three-quarters full of water.
2. Tie enough metal washers to a cork so that the cork floats about 3 cm from the bottom of the tank.

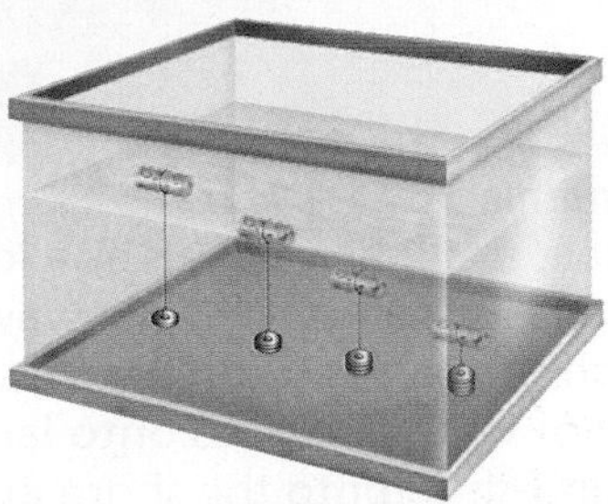

3. Repeat Step 2 with more corks so that they float 9 cm from the bottom, 15 cm from the bottom, and so on, until the last cork floats on the surface.
4. Make small, steady waves in the tank by moving your hand up and down in the water. Note what happens to each cork.
5. Repeat Step 4, increasing the height of the waves by moving your hand faster.

**Observing** How does increasing the wave height affect the motion of each cork?

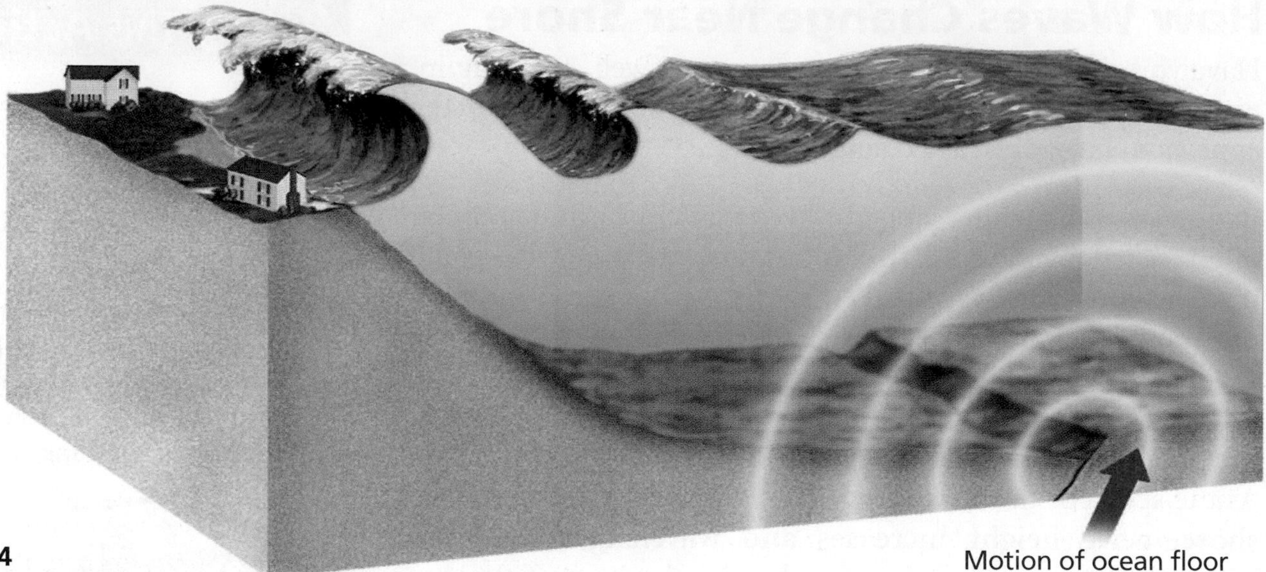


**FIGURE 4**
**Tsunamis**
At sea, a tsunami travels as a long, low wave. Near shore, the wave height increases suddenly. The wall of water smashes onto land, tossing ships onto the shore and destroying buildings.

**Tsunamis** So far you have been reading about waves that are caused by the wind. Another kind of wave, shown in Figure 4, forms far below the ocean surface. This type of wave, called a **tsunami,** is usually caused by an earthquake beneath the ocean floor. The abrupt movement of the ocean floor sends pulses of energy through the water above it. When tsunamis reach the coast, they can be as devastating as an earthquake on land, smashing buildings and bridges.

Despite the tremendous amount of energy a tsunami carries, people on a ship at sea may not even realize a tsunami is passing. How is this possible? A tsunami in deep water may have a wavelength of 200 kilometers or more, but a wave height of less than a meter. When the tsunami reaches shallow water near the coast, friction with the ocean floor causes the long wavelength to decrease suddenly. The wave height increases as the water "piles up." The tsunami becomes a towering wall of water. Some tsunamis have reached heights of 20 meters or more—taller than a five-story building!

Tsunamis are most common in the Pacific Ocean, often striking Alaska, Hawaii, and Japan. In response, nations in the Pacific have developed a warning system, which can alert them to an approaching tsunami.

But not all tsunamis occur in the Pacific Ocean. On December 26, 2004, a major earthquake in the Indian Ocean caused tremendous tsunamis that hit 11 nations. Tragically, these tsunamis took the lives of more than 230,000 people. Several nations are now developing a tsunami warning system for the Indian Ocean.

Discovery Channel School

*Ocean Motions*

Video Preview
▶ Video Field Trip
Video Assessment

## How Waves Affect the Shore

What happens on shore as waves pound the beach? Figure 5 shows some of their effects. Because wave direction at sea is determined by the wind, waves usually roll toward shore at an angle. But as they touch bottom, the shallower water slows the shoreward side of the wave first. The rows of waves gradually turn and become more nearly parallel to the shore.

**Longshore Drift** **As waves come into shore, water washes up the beach at an angle, carrying sand grains. The water and sand then run straight back down the beach.** This movement of sand along the beach is called **longshore drift.** As the waves slow down, they deposit the sand they are carrying on the shallow, underwater slope in a long ridge called a sandbar.

**Rip Currents** As a sandbar grows, it can trap the water flowing along the shore. In some places, water breaks through the sandbar and begins to flow back down the sloping ocean bottom. This process creates a **rip current,** a rush of water that flows rapidly back to sea through a narrow opening. Rip currents can carry a swimmer out into deep water. Because rip currents are narrow, a strong swimmer can usually escape by swimming across the current, parallel to the beach.

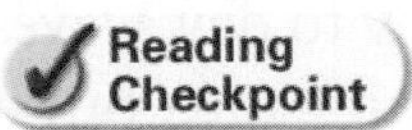


**In what direction does a rip current pull a swimmer?**

### Lab zone Skills Activity

**Making Models**

Half fill an aluminum pan with water. The pan represents the ocean floor. Make the "ocean floor" slope by placing a book or other object under one long end of the pan. Add enough sand in the middle of the pan to create a sandbar. Then pour water from a beaker onto the sand to model a rip current. Use the model to explain why rip currents can be dangerous to swimmers.



**FIGURE 5**
**Longshore Drift**
Waves approach the shore at an angle. This results in a gradual movement of sand along the beach. **Interpreting Diagrams** *In which direction is longshore drift moving the sand along this beach?*

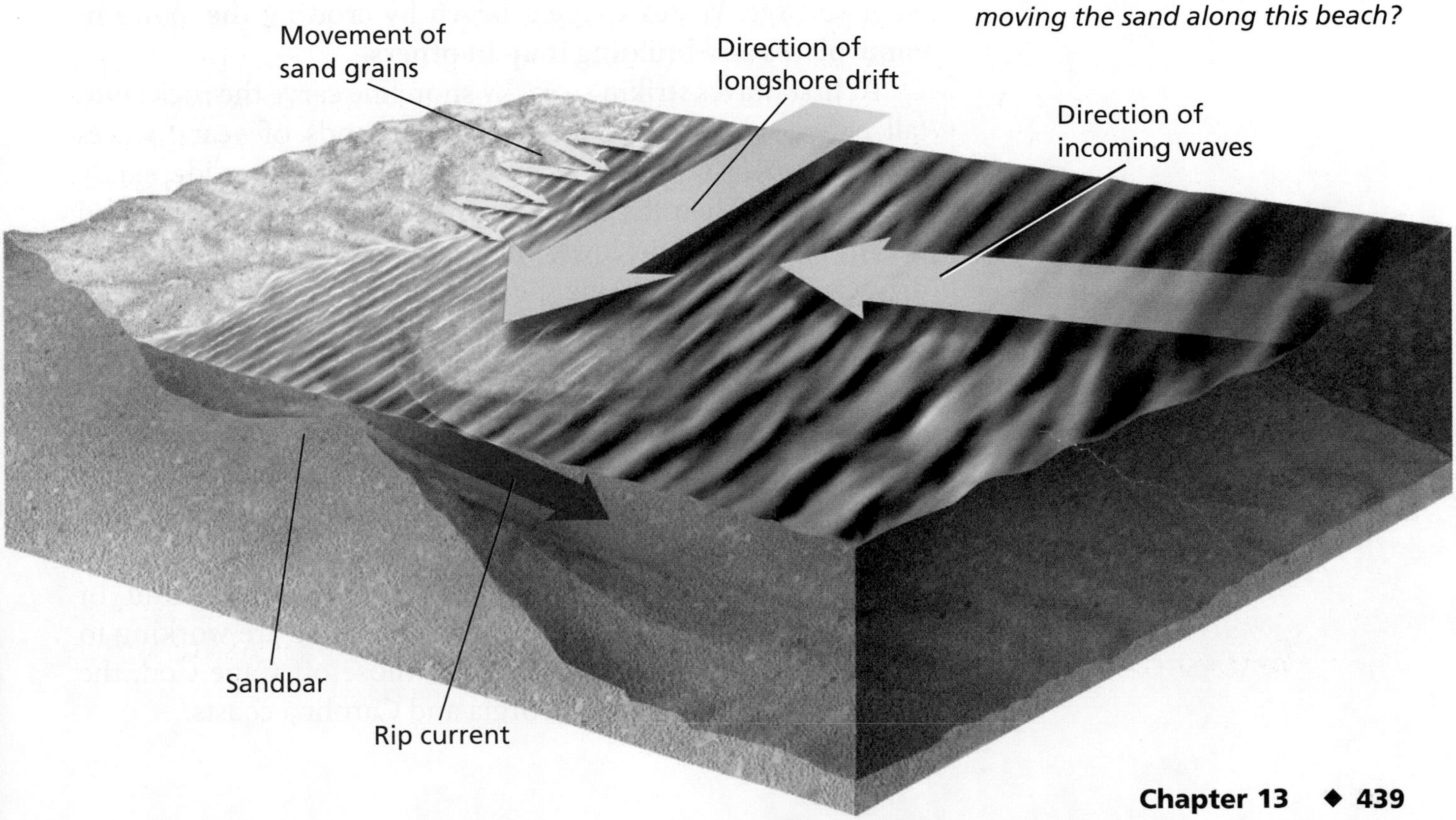

FIGURE 6
**A Barrier Beach**
Barrier beaches are sand deposits that form parallel to a shore. Sand dunes are hills of wind-blown sand that help protect the beach.
**Interpreting Photographs** *How does a barrier beach protect the mainland from erosion by waves?*

## Waves and Beach Erosion

The boundary between land and ocean is always changing shape. If you walk on the same beach every day, you might not notice that it is changing. From day to day, waves remove sand and bring new sand at about the same rate. But if you visit a beach just once each year, you might be startled by what you see. **Waves shape a beach by eroding the shore in some places and building it up in others.**

At first, waves striking a rocky shoreline carve the rocks into tall cliffs and arches. Over many thousands of years, waves break the rocks into pebbles and grains of sand. A wide, sandy beach forms. Then the waves begin to eat away at the exposed beach. The shoreline slowly moves farther inland. Longshore drift carries the sand along the coast and deposits it elsewhere. This process of breaking up rock and carrying it away is known as erosion.

**Barrier Beaches** A natural landform that protects shorelines from wave action occurs along low-lying beaches. Long sand deposits called barrier beaches form parallel to the shore. Such beaches are separated from the mainland by a shallow lagoon. Waves break against the barrier beach instead of against the land inside. For this reason, people are working to preserve natural barrier beaches like those off Cape Cod, the New Jersey shore, and the Georgia and Carolina coasts.

**FIGURE 7**
**Groins**
Sand piles up against a series of groins people have built along the New Jersey coast. Building groins to stop longshore drift is one way to reduce beach erosion.

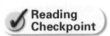

**Sand Dunes** Other natural landforms also help protect beaches and reduce erosion, although they can't completely stop the movement of sand. Sand dunes, which are hills of windblown sand, can make a beach more stable and protect the shore from erosion. The strong roots of dune plants, such as beach grass and sea oats, hold the sand in place. These plants help to slow erosion caused by wind and water. But the dunes and plants can be destroyed by cars, bicycles, or even by many people walking over them. Without plants to hold the sand in place, dunes can be easily washed away by wave action.

**Groins** Many people like to live near the ocean. But over time, erosion can wear away the beach. This threatens the homes and other buildings near the beach. To avoid losing their property, people look for ways to reduce the effect of erosion.

One method of reducing erosion along a stretch of beach is to build a wall of rocks or concrete, called a **groin,** outward from the beach. Sand carried by the water piles up against the groins instead of moving along the shore. Figure 7 shows how groins interrupt the movement of water. However, groins increase the amount of erosion farther down the beach.

**Name two natural landforms that help reduce beach erosion.**

## Section 1 Assessment

**Target Reading Skill Using Prior Knowledge** Review your graphic organizer and revise it based on what you just learned in the section.

### Reviewing Key Concepts

1. a. **Reviewing** How do waves form?
   b. **Explaining** Explain how both a wave's energy and the water in a wave move.
   c. **Applying Concepts** Why does an ocean buoy bob up and down as a wave passes by?
2. a. **Defining** What is the wavelength of a wave? What is wave height?
   b. **Describing** How do wavelength and wave height change as a wave enters shallow water?
   c. **Developing Hypotheses** Using what you know about the wavelength and wave height of tsunamis, propose an explanation of why tsunamis can cause so much damage when they reach the shore.
3. a. **Explaining** What is longshore drift, and how does it affect a shoreline?
   b. **Relating Cause and Effect** Explain how building a groin affects longshore drift. What happens to the beach on each side of the groin?

### Lab zone At-Home Activity

**Wave Model** With a family member, make a construction paper model of a wave. Your model should show the wave from the time it develops in the ocean to the time it breaks on the shore. Be sure to label the features of the wave, including crests, troughs, wavelengths, wave heights, swells, and breakers.

Section 2

Integrating Space Science

# Tides

## Reading Preview

### Key Concepts

- What causes tides?
- What affects the heights of tides?
- How are tides a source of energy?

### Key Terms

- tides • spring tide • neap tide

### Target Reading Skill

**Previewing Visuals** Before you read, preview Figure 11. Then write two questions that you have about the diagram in a graphic organizer like the one below. As you read, answer your questions.

**Spring and Neap Tides**

| Q. When do spring tides occur? |
|---|
| A. |
| Q. |

## Lab zone Discover Activity

### When Is High Tide?

Twice a day, the ocean rises and falls on Earth's coasts. These changes in water level are called tides. The map shows the times of the two high tides in two cities on a specific day.

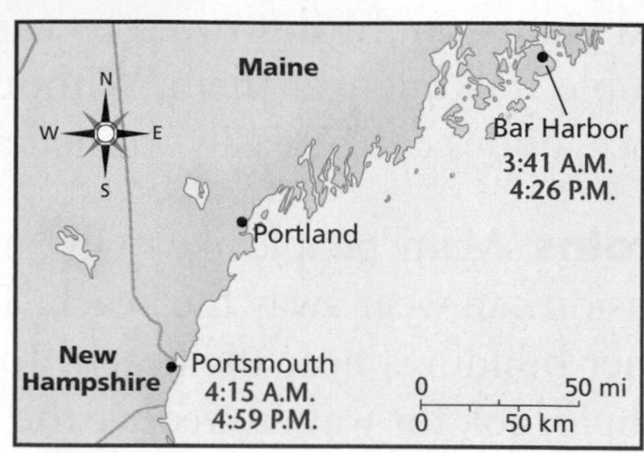


1. Calculate the length of time between the two high tides for each city. Remember to consider both hours and minutes.
2. Compare the times of the high tides in Bar Harbor and in Portsmouth. Do you see a pattern?

**Think It Over**

**Predicting** Based on the times of the high tides in Bar Harbor and Portsmouth, predict when the high tides will occur in Portland.

You're standing on a riverbank in the town of Saint John, New Brunswick, in Canada. In the distance there's a roaring sound. Suddenly a wall of water twice your height thunders past. The surge of water rushes up the river channel so fast that it almost looks as if the river is flowing backward!

This thundering wall of water is an everyday event at Saint John. The town is located where the Saint John River enters the Bay of Fundy, an arm of the Atlantic Ocean. The Bay of Fundy is famous for its dramatic daily tides. When the tide comes in, fishing boats float on the water near the piers. But once the tide goes out, the boats are stranded on the muddy harbor bottom!

**FIGURE 8**
**Differences in Tides**
The Bay of Fundy in Canada is noted for the great differences between its high and low tides. Near the mouth of the bay, boats float at high tide (left). At low tide, the boats are grounded (right).

## What Causes Tides?

The daily rise and fall of Earth's waters on its coastlines are called **tides.** As the tide comes in, the level of the water on the beach rises gradually. When the water reaches its highest point, it is high tide. Then the tide goes out, flowing back toward the sea. When the water reaches its lowest point, it is low tide. Unlike the surface waves you read about earlier, tides happen regularly no matter how the wind blows. Tides occur in all bodies of water, but they are most noticeable in the ocean and large lakes.

**Gravity and Tides** **Tides are caused by the interaction of Earth, the moon, and the sun.** How can distant objects like the moon and sun influence water on Earth? The answer is gravity. Gravity is the force exerted by an object that pulls other objects toward it. Gravity keeps you and everything around you on Earth's surface. As the distance between objects increases, however, gravity's pull grows weaker.

Figure 9 shows the effect of the moon's gravity on the water on Earth's surface. The moon pulls on the water on the side of Earth closest to it more strongly than it pulls on the center of the Earth. This pull creates a bulge of water, called a tidal bulge, on the side of Earth facing the moon. The water farthest from the moon is pulled toward the moon less strongly than are other parts of Earth. The water farthest from the moon is "left behind," forming a second bulge.

In the places where there are tidal bulges, high tide is occurring along the coastlines. In the places between the bulges, low tide is occurring. Earth's rotation through the tidal bulges causes most coastlines to experience two high tides and two low tides every 25 hours.

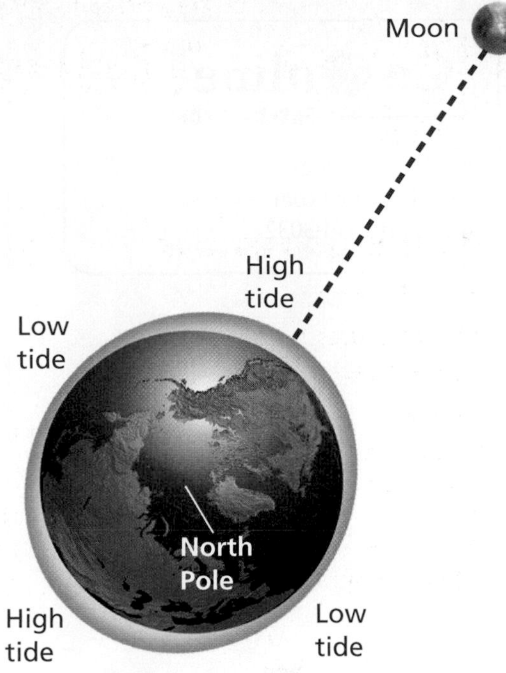


**FIGURE 9**
**How the Moon Causes Tides**
The pull of the moon's gravity on Earth's water causes tidal bulges to form on the side closest to the moon and the side farthest from the moon. **Inferring** *Why is the water level high on the side of Earth farthest from the moon?*

**What force causes tides to occur on Earth's surface?**

For: More on tides
Visit: PHSchool.com
Web Code: cfd-3032

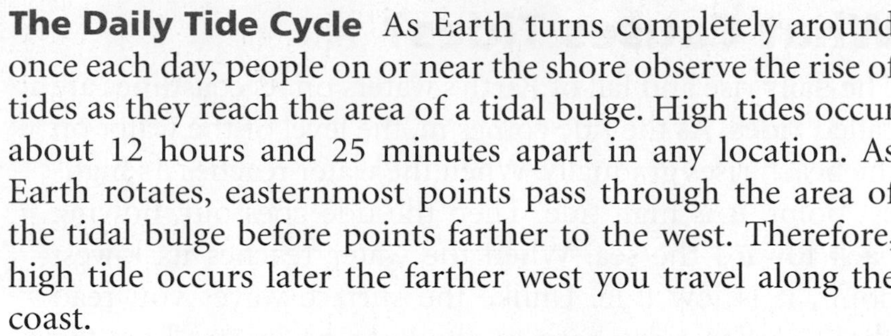

**The Daily Tide Cycle** As Earth turns completely around once each day, people on or near the shore observe the rise of tides as they reach the area of a tidal bulge. High tides occur about 12 hours and 25 minutes apart in any location. As Earth rotates, easternmost points pass through the area of the tidal bulge before points farther to the west. Therefore, high tide occurs later the farther west you travel along the coast.

In some places, the two high tides and two low tides are easy to observe each day. But in other places, the difference between high tide and low tide is less dramatic. One set of tides may even be so minimal that there appears to be only one high tide and one low tide per day.

Several factors affect the height of a tide in any particular location. For example, certain landforms can interrupt the water's movements. A basin at the mouth of a river can also increase the difference between high and low tide. The speed and depth of moving water increases as it flows into a narrower channel. That is what causes the dramatic tides in the mouth of the Saint John River you read about earlier.

FIGURE 10
**Sea Turtles and Spring Tides**
Some animals are very dependent on tide cycles. Sea turtles can only come to shore to lay their eggs during certain spring tides.

**The Monthly Tide Cycle** Even though the sun is about 150 million kilometers from Earth, it is so massive that its gravity affects the tides. The sun pulls the water on Earth's surface toward it. In Figure 11, you can follow the positions of Earth, the moon, and the sun at different times during a month. **Changes in the positions of Earth, the moon, and the sun affect the heights of the tides during a month.**

Twice a month, at the new moon and the full moon, the sun and moon are lined up. Their combined gravitational pull produces the greatest difference between the heights of high and low tide, called a **spring tide.** These tides get their name from an Old English word, *springen*, which means "to jump."

At the first and third quarters of the moon, the sun and moon pull at right angles to each other. This arrangement produces a **neap tide,** a tide with the least difference between low and high tide. During a neap tide, the sun's gravity pulls some of the water away from the tidal bulge facing the moon. This acts to "even out" the water level over Earth's surface, decreasing the difference between high and low tides.

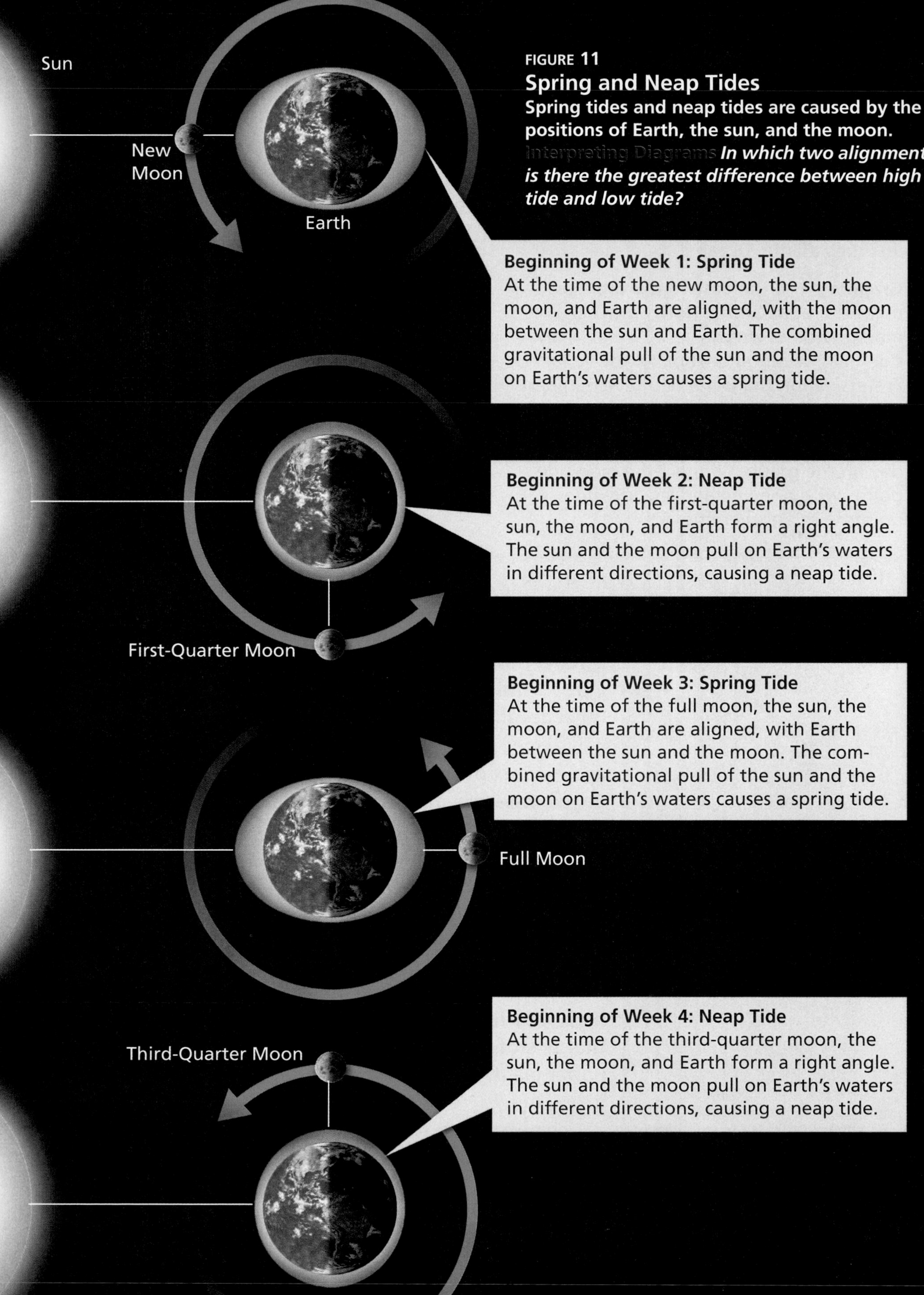

Sun
New Moon
Earth
First-Quarter Moon
Full Moon
Third-Quarter Moon
**Beginning of Week 1: Spring Tide**
At the time of the new moon, the sun, the moon, and Earth are aligned, with the moon between the sun and Earth. The combined gravitational pull of the sun and the moon on Earth's waters causes a spring tide.
**Beginning of Week 2: Neap Tide**
At the time of the first-quarter moon, the sun, the moon, and Earth form a right angle. The sun and the moon pull on Earth's waters in different directions, causing a neap tide.
**Beginning of Week 3: Spring Tide**
At the time of the full moon, the sun, the moon, and Earth are aligned, with Earth between the sun and the moon. The combined gravitational pull of the sun and the moon on Earth's waters causes a spring tide.
**Beginning of Week 4: Neap Tide**
At the time of the third-quarter moon, the sun, the moon, and Earth form a right angle. The sun and the moon pull on Earth's waters in different directions, causing a neap tide.


FIGURE 11
**Spring and Neap Tides**
**Spring tides and neap tides are caused by the positions of Earth, the sun, and the moon.** Interpreting Diagrams ***In which two alignments is there the greatest difference between high tide and low tide?***

## Math Analyzing Data

### Plotting Tides

This table lists the highest high tides and the lowest low tides for one week at the mouth of the Savannah River, where it meets the Atlantic Ocean in Georgia.

| Tide Table | | |
|---|---|---|
| Day | Highest High Tide (m) | Lowest Low Tide (m) |
| 1 | 1.9 | 0.2 |
| 2 | 2.1 | 0.1 |
| 3 | 2.3 | 0.0 |
| 4 | 2.4 | –0.2 |
| 5 | 2.5 | –0.2 |
| 6 | 2.6 | –0.3 |
| 7 | 1.9 | 0.3 |

1. **Graphing** Use the data in the table to make a graph. On the horizontal axis, mark the days. On the vertical axis, mark tide heights ranging from 3.0 to –1.0 meters. (*Hint:* Mark the negative numbers below the horizontal axis.)
2. **Graphing** Plot the tide heights for each day on the graph. Connect the high tide points with one line and the low tide points with another line.
3. **Interpreting Data** How do the high and low tides change during the week?
4. **Inferring** What type of tide might be occurring on Day 6? Explain.

**Tide Tables** Despite the complex factors affecting tides, scientists can predict tides quite accurately for many locations. They combine knowledge of the movements of the moon and Earth with information about the shape of the coastline and other local conditions. If you live near the coast, your local newspaper probably publishes a tide table. Knowing the times and heights of tides is important to sailors, marine scientists, people who fish, and coastal residents.

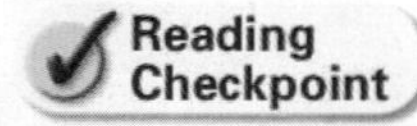


**What two types of information help scientists predict the times of tides?**

## Energy From Tides

Look at Figure 12. Can you almost hear the roar of the rushing water? **The movement of huge amounts of water between high and low tide is a source of potential energy—energy that is stored and can be used.** Engineers have designed tidal power plants that capture some of this energy as the tide moves in and out.

The first large-scale tidal power plant was built in 1967 on the Rance River in northwestern France. As high tide swirls up the river, the plant's gates open so that the water flows into a basin. As the tide retreats, the gates shut to trap the water. Gravity pulls the water back to sea through tunnels. The energy of the water moving through the tunnels powers generators that produce electricity, just as in a hydroelectric dam on a river.

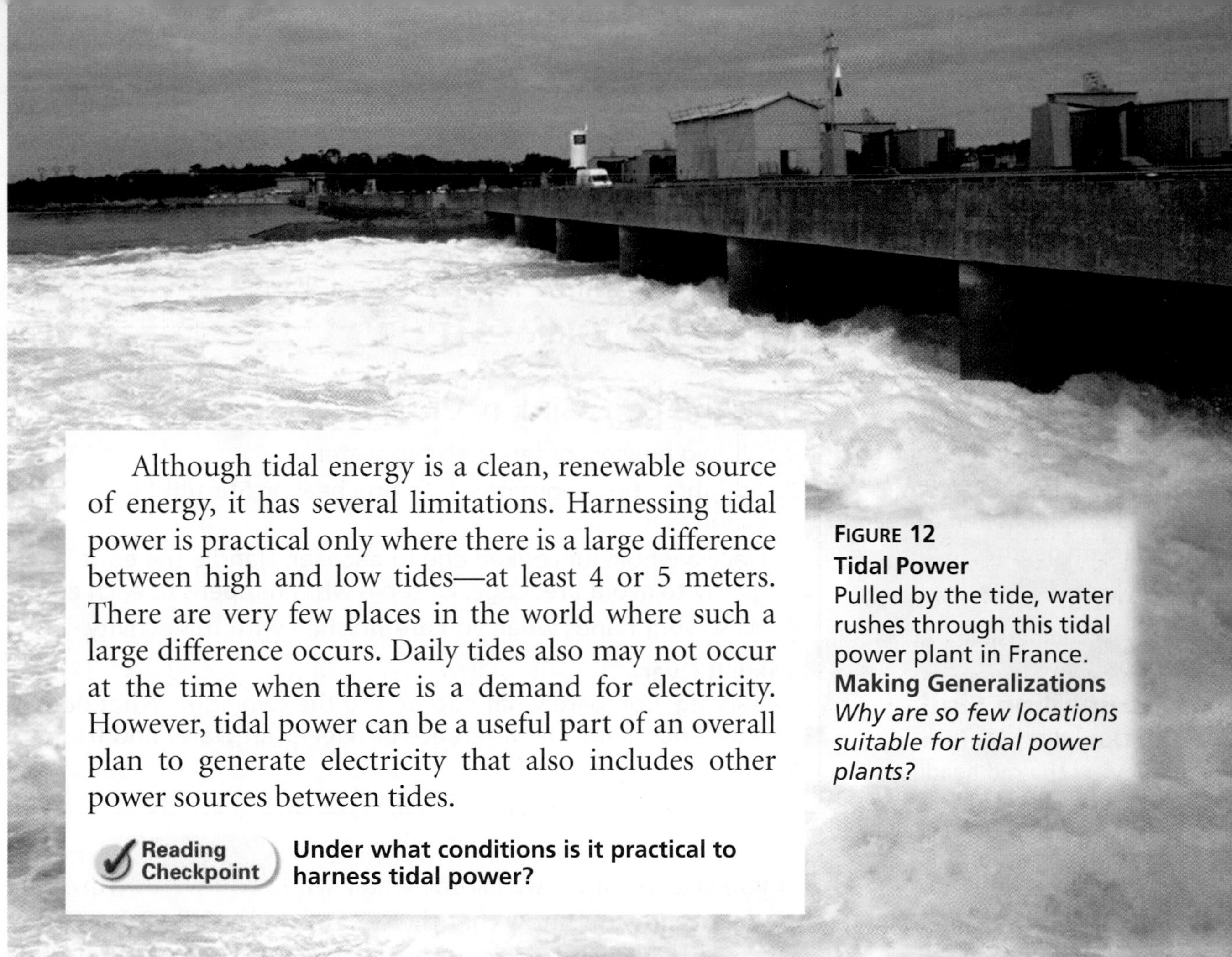

Although tidal energy is a clean, renewable source of energy, it has several limitations. Harnessing tidal power is practical only where there is a large difference between high and low tides—at least 4 or 5 meters. There are very few places in the world where such a large difference occurs. Daily tides also may not occur at the time when there is a demand for electricity. However, tidal power can be a useful part of an overall plan to generate electricity that also includes other power sources between tides.

**Reading Checkpoint** **Under what conditions is it practical to harness tidal power?**

**FIGURE 12**
**Tidal Power**
Pulled by the tide, water rushes through this tidal power plant in France.
**Making Generalizations** *Why are so few locations suitable for tidal power plants?*

## Section 2 Assessment

**Target Reading Skill Previewing Visuals** Refer to your questions and answers about Figure 11 to help you answer Question 2 below.

### Reviewing Key Concepts

1. a. **Defining** What is a tide? What causes tides?
   b. **Explaining** Explain why the moon causes a tidal bulge to form on the side of Earth closest to it.
   c. **Inferring** The sun is much bigger than the moon. Why doesn't the sun affect tides more than the moon does?
2. a. **Reviewing** Why do the heights of tides change during the course of a month?
   b. **Describing** Describe the positions of the sun, moon, and Earth during a spring tide and during a neap tide.
   c. **Applying Concepts** Imagine that you are the captain of a fishing boat. Why would it be helpful to consult a monthly tide table?
3. a. **Reviewing** How can tides be used to generate electricity?
   b. **Predicting** Do you think that tidal power will ever be a major source of energy worldwide? Why or why not?

### Writing in Science

**Firsthand Account** Imagine that you are fishing on a pier on the Bay of Fundy in Canada. It was high tide when you began fishing. Now it is low tide. Write a firsthand account describing the changes that you observed as the tide went out. Use clear, descriptive language in your writing.

Section 3

# Ocean Water Chemistry

## Reading Preview

### Key Concepts

- How salty is ocean water?
- How do the temperature and gas content of ocean water vary?
- How do conditions in the ocean change with depth?

### Key Terms

- salinity
- submersible

### Target Reading Skill

**Asking Questions** Before you read, preview the red headings. In a graphic organizer like the one below, ask a *how* or *what* question for each heading. As you read, answer your questions.

**Ocean Water Chemistry**

| Question | Answer |
|---|---|
| How salty is the ocean? | One kilogram of ocean water has . . . |
| | |

## Lab zone Discover Activity

### Will the Eggs Sink or Float?

1. Fill two beakers or jars with tap water.
2. Add three teaspoons of salt to one beaker. Stir until it dissolves.
3. Place a whole, uncooked egg in each jar. Handle the eggs gently to avoid breakage. Observe what happens to each egg.
4. Wash your hands when you are finished with this activity.

**Think It Over**

**Observing** Compare what happens to the two eggs. What does this tell you about the difference between salt water and fresh water?

If you've ever swallowed some water while you were swimming in the ocean, you know that the ocean is salty. Why? According to an old Swedish legend, it's all because of a magic mill. This mill could grind out anything its owner wanted, such as herring, porridge, or even gold. A greedy sea captain once stole the mill and took it away on his ship, but without finding out how to use it. He asked the mill to grind some salt but then could not stop it. The mill ground more and more salt, until the captain's ship sank from its weight. According to the tale, the mill is still at the bottom of the sea, grinding out salt!

Salt storage area ▼

## The Salty Ocean

Probably no one ever took this legend seriously, even when it was first told. The scientific explanation for the ocean's saltiness begins with the early stages of Earth's history, when the ocean covered much of the surface of the planet. Undersea volcanoes erupted, spewing chemicals into the water. Gradually, the lava from these volcanic eruptions built up areas of land. Rain fell on the bare land, washing more chemicals from the rocks into the ocean. Over time, these dissolved substances built up to the levels present in the ocean today.

**Salinity** Just how salty is the ocean? If you boiled a kilogram of ocean water in a pot until all the water was gone, there would be about 35 grams of salts left in the pot. **On average, one kilogram of ocean water contains about 35 grams of salts—that is, 35 parts per thousand.** The total amount of dissolved salts in a sample of water is the **salinity** of that sample.

The substance you know as table salt—sodium chloride—is the salt present in the greatest amount in ocean water. When sodium chloride dissolves in water, it separates into sodium and chloride particles called ions. Other salts, such as magnesium chloride, form ions in water in the same way. Together, chloride and sodium make up almost 86 percent of the ions dissolved in ocean water. Ocean water also contains smaller amounts of about a dozen other ions, including magnesium and calcium, and other substances that organisms need, such as nitrogen and phosphorus.

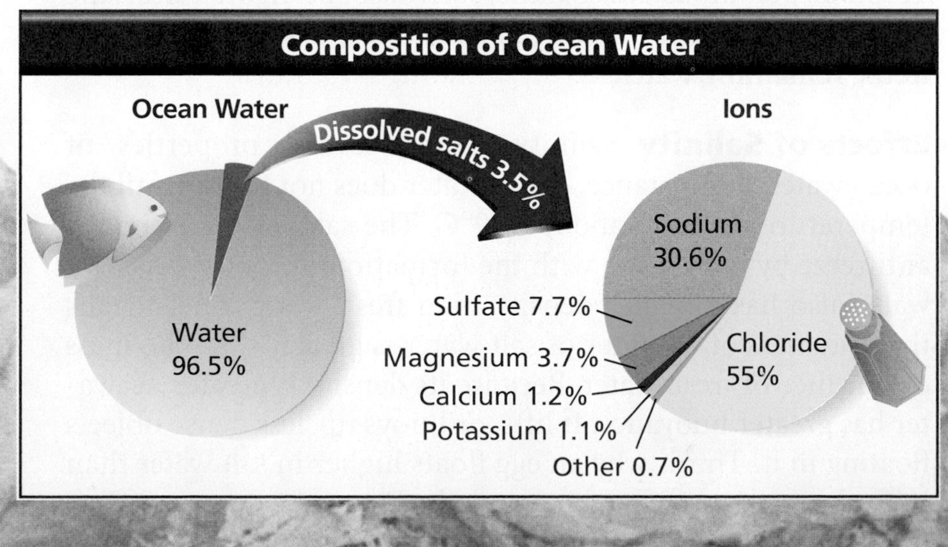


**FIGURE 13**
**Composition of Ocean Water**
Ocean water contains many different dissolved salts. When salts dissolve, they separate into particles called ions.
**Reading Graphs** *Which ion is most common in ocean water?*

**FIGURE 14**
**Salinity and Density**
These people are relaxing with the paper while floating in the water! The Dead Sea between Israel and Jordan is so salty that people float easily on its surface.
**Relating Cause and Effect** *How is the area's hot, dry climate related to the Dead Sea's high salinity?*

**Variations in Salinity** In most parts of the ocean, the salinity is between 34 and 37 parts per thousand. But near the ocean's surface, rain, snow, and melting ice add fresh water, lowering the salinity. Salinity is also lower near the mouths of large rivers such as the Amazon or Mississippi. These rivers empty great amounts of fresh water into the ocean. Evaporation, on the other hand, increases salinity, since the salt is left behind as the water evaporates. For example, in the Red Sea, where the climate is hot and dry, the salinity can be as high as 41 parts per thousand. Salinity can also be higher near the poles. As the surface water freezes into ice, the salt is left behind in the remaining water.

**Effects of Salinity** Salinity affects several properties of ocean water. For instance, ocean water does not freeze until the temperature drops to about –1.9°C. The salt acts as a kind of antifreeze by interfering with the formation of ice crystals. Salt water also has a higher density than fresh water. That means that the mass of one liter of salt water is greater than the mass of one liter of fresh water. Because its density is greater, seawater has greater buoyancy. It lifts, or buoys up, less dense objects floating in it. This is why an egg floats higher in salt water than in fresh water, and why the people in Figure 14 float so effortlessly in the Dead Sea.

**Why does salt water have greater buoyancy than fresh water?**

**Math Skills**

## Calculating Density

To calculate the density of a substance, divide the mass of the substance by its volume.

$$\text{Density} = \frac{\text{Mass}}{\text{Volume}}$$

For example, 1 liter (L) of ocean water has a mass of 1.03 kilograms (kg). Therefore,

$$\text{Density} = \frac{1.03 \text{ kg}}{1.00 \text{ L}}$$

$$\text{Density} = 1.03 \text{ kg/L}$$

**Practice Problems** A 5-liter sample of one type of crude oil has a mass of 4.10 kg. What is its density? If this oil spilled on the ocean's surface, would it sink or float? Explain your answer in terms of density.

## Other Ocean Properties

In New England, the news reports on New Year's Day often feature the shivering members of a "Polar Bear Club" taking a dip in the icy Atlantic Ocean. Yet on the same day, people enjoy the warm waters of a Puerto Rico beach. **Like temperatures on land, temperatures at the surface of the ocean vary with location and the seasons. Gases in ocean water vary as well.**

**Temperature of Ocean Water** Why do surface temperatures of the ocean vary from place to place? The broad surface of the ocean absorbs energy from the sun. Near the equator, surface ocean temperatures often reach 25°C, about room temperature. The temperature drops as you travel away from the equator.

Because warm water is less dense than cold water, warm water forms only a thin layer on the ocean surface. Generally, the deeper you descend into the ocean, the colder and denser the water becomes. When water temperature is lower, the water molecules stay closer together than at higher temperatures. So, a sample of cold water has more water molecules than a sample of warm water of the same volume. The sample of cold water is denser.

**Gases in Ocean Water** Just as land organisms use gases found in air, ocean organisms use gases found in ocean water. Two gases that ocean organisms use are carbon dioxide and oxygen.

Carbon dioxide is about 60 times as plentiful in the oceans as in the air. Algae need carbon dioxide for photosynthesis. Animals such as corals also use carbon dioxide, which provides the carbon to build their hard skeletons.

Unlike carbon dioxide, oxygen is scarcer in seawater than in air. Oxygen is most plentiful in seawater near the surface. Oxygen in seawater comes from the air and from algae in the ocean, as a product of photosynthesis. The amount of oxygen in seawater is affected by the water temperature. The cold waters in the polar regions contain more oxygen than warm, tropical waters. But there is still enough oxygen in tropical seas to support a variety of organisms.

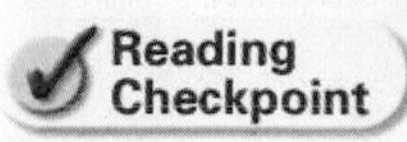


**What are two sources of oxygen in ocean water?**

**FIGURE 15**
**Organisms and Ocean Temperatures**
From the warmest tropical waters to the coldest Antarctic sea, you can find organisms that are adapted to extreme ocean temperatures.

▲ This longfin anthias fish swimming near Hawaii lives in one of the warmest parts of the Pacific Ocean.

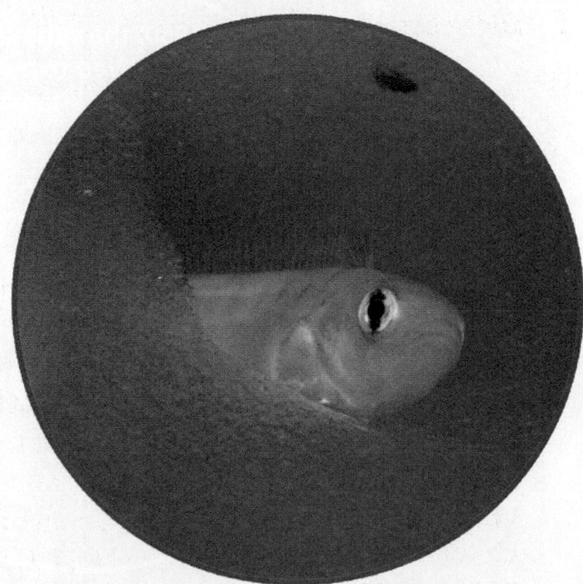

▲ This rockcod is swimming through a hole in an iceberg in near-freezing ocean water.

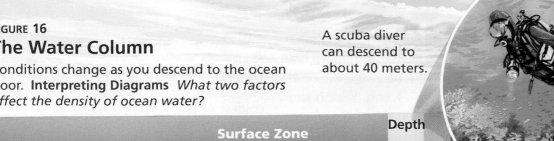

**FIGURE 16**

## The Water Column

Conditions change as you descend to the ocean floor. **Interpreting Diagrams** *What two factors affect the density of ocean water?*

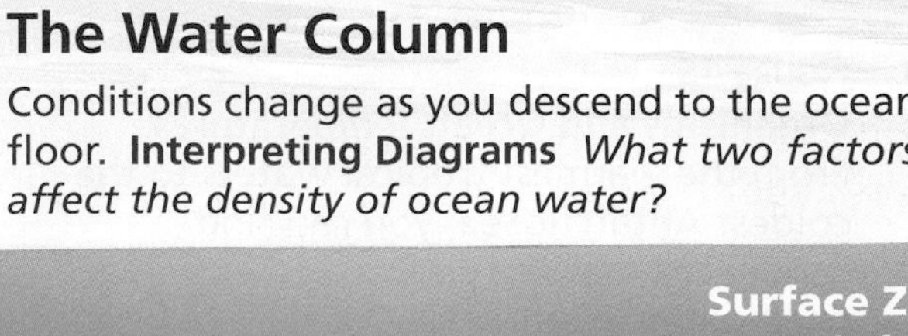

A scuba diver can descend to about 40 meters.

Depth

**Surface Zone**
Extends from the surface to about 200 meters. Average temperature worldwide is 17.5°C.

**Transition Zone**
Extends from bottom of the surface zone to about 1 kilometer. Temperature rapidly drops to 4°C.

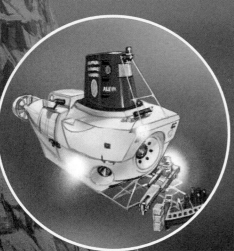

**Deep Zone**
Extends from about 1 kilometer to ocean floor. Average temperature is 3.5°C.

The submersible *Alvin* can descend to about 4 kilometers.

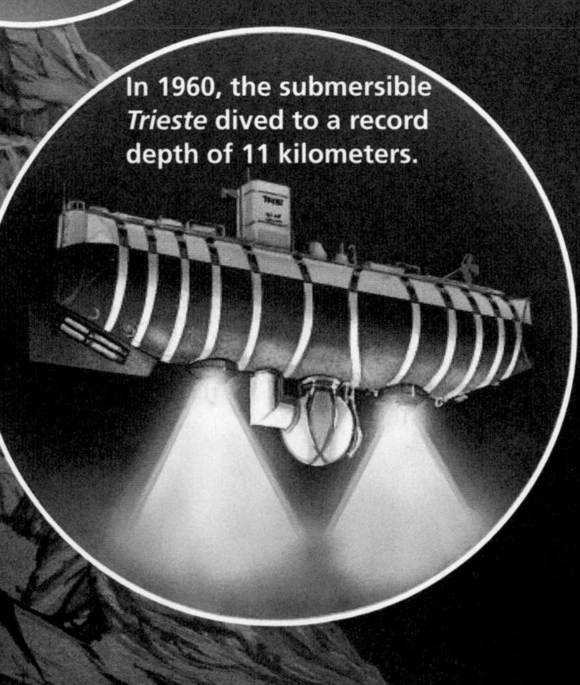

In 1960, the submersible *Trieste* dived to a record depth of 11 kilometers.

3.8 km Average ocean depth

**Color and Light**
Sunlight penetrates the surface of the ocean. It appears first yellowish, then blue-green, as the water absorbs the red light. No light reaches below about 200 meters.

**Temperature**
Near the surface, temperature is affected by the weather above. In the transition zone, the temperature drops rapidly. In the deep zone, the water is always extremely cold.

**Salinity**
Rainfall decreases salinity near the surface, while evaporation increases salinity in warm, dry areas. Below the surface zone, salinity remains fairly constant throughout the water column.

**Density**
The density of seawater depends on temperature and salinity. The ocean is generally least dense in the surface zone, where it is warmest. However, higher salinity also increases density. The most dense water is found in the cold deep zone.

**Pressure**
Pressure increases at the rate of 10 times the air pressure at sea level per 100 meters of depth.

## Changes With Depth

If you could descend from the ocean's surface to the ocean floor, you would pass through a vertical section of the ocean referred to as the water column. Figure 16 on the previous page shows some of the dramatic changes you would observe.

For: Links on ocean water chemistry
Visit: www.SciLinks.org
Web Code: scn-0833

**Decreasing Temperature** **As you descend through the ocean, the water temperature decreases.** There are three temperature zones in the water column. The surface zone is the warmest. It typically extends from the surface to between 100 and 500 meters. The transition zone extends from the bottom of the surface zone to about 1 kilometer. Temperatures drop very quickly as you descend through the transition zone, to about 4°C. Below the transition zone is the deep zone. Average temperatures there are 3.5°C in most of the ocean.

**Increasing Pressure** Water pressure is the force exerted by the weight of water. **Pressure increases continuously with depth in the ocean.** Because of the high pressure in the deep ocean, divers can descend safely only to about 40 meters. To observe the deep ocean, scientists must use a **submersible,** an underwater vehicle built of materials that resist pressure.

**What is a submersible?**

## Section 3 Assessment

**Target Reading Skill** **Asking Questions** Use the questions you wrote about the headings to help you answer the questions below.

### Reviewing Key Concepts

1. a. **Defining** What is salinity? What is the average salinity of ocean water?
   b. **Describing** Describe one factor that increases the salinity of seawater and one factor that decreases its salinity.
   c. **Inferring** Would you expect the seawater just below the floating ice in the Arctic Ocean to be higher or lower in salinity than the water in the deepest part of the ocean? Explain.
2. a. **Identifying** Where would you find the warmest ocean temperatures on Earth?
   b. **Comparing and Contrasting** How do carbon dioxide and oxygen levels in the oceans compare to those in the air?
   c. **Relating Cause and Effect** How does the temperature of ocean water affect oxygen levels in the water?
3. a. **Reviewing** How do temperature and pressure change as you descend in the ocean?
   b. **Predicting** Where in the water column would you expect to find the following conditions: the highest pressure readings; the densest waters; the warmest temperatures?

### Math Practice

4. **Calculating Density** Calculate the density of the following 1-L samples of ocean water. Sample A has a mass of 1.01 kg; Sample B has a mass of 1.06 kg. Which sample would likely have the higher salinity? Explain.

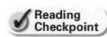

Lab zone **Technology Lab**
• Tech & Design •

# Investigating Changes in Density

## Problem

Can you design and build an instrument that can detect differences in density?

## Skills Focus

building a prototype, designing a solution, troubleshooting

## Materials

• thumbtacks • 250-mL graduated cylinder
• unsharpened pencil with eraser • metric ruler
• fine-point permanent marker • thermometer
• ice • balance • water • spoon • salt
• additional materials provided by your teacher

## Procedure  

### PART 1 Research and Investigate

1. One way to measure the density of a liquid is with a tool called a hydrometer. You can make a simple hydrometer using an unsharpened wooden pencil.
2. Starting at the unsharpened end of a pencil, use a permanent marker to make marks every 2 mm along the side of the pencil. Make longer marks for every whole centimeter. Continue until you have marked off 5 cm.
3. Label each of the long marks, starting at the unsharpened end of the pencil.
4. Insert 3 thumbtacks as weights into the eraser end of the pencil. **CAUTION:** *Be careful not to cut yourself on the sharp points of the thumbtacks.*
5. Fill the graduated cylinder with 250 mL of water at room temperature. Place the pencil in the water, eraser end down.
6. Add or remove thumbtacks and adjust their placement until the pencil floats upright, with about 2 cm sticking up above the surface of the water.
7. In your notebook, record the temperature of the water. Next to that number, record the reading on the pencil hydrometer at the surface of the water.
8. Fill the graduated cylinder with cold water. Place the pencil hydrometer into the water, eraser end down. Then repeat Step 7.

### PART 2 Design and Build

9. Using what you learned in Part 1, design and build a hydrometer that can detect density differences among different samples of water. Your hydrometer should
   • be able to measure density differences between hot water and cold water
   • be able to measure density differences between salt water and fresh water
   • be constructed of materials approved by your teacher

10. Sketch your design in your notebook and make a list of the materials you will need. Write a plan for how you will construct your hydrometer. After you have received your teacher's approval for your design, build your hydrometer.

## PART 3 Evaluate and Redesign

11. Test your hydrometer by using it to measure the density of water at different temperatures. Then test samples of water that have different salinities. Create a data table in which to record your results.

| Data Table | | |
|---|---|---|
| Temperature (°C) | Salinity $\left(\frac{\text{g salt}}{\text{L water}}\right)$ | Hydrometer Reading |
| | | |
| | | |
| | | |
| | | |

12. Based on your tests, decide how you could improve the design of your hydrometer. For example, how could you change your design so your hydrometer is able to detect smaller differences in density? Obtain your teacher's approval, then make the necessary changes, and test how your redesigned hydrometer functions.

## Analyze and Conclude

1. **Inferring** Explain why cold water is more dense than hot water. Explain why salt water is more dense than fresh water.
2. **Building a Prototype** How well did the pencil hydrometer you built in Part 1 work? What problems did you encounter with the hydrometer?

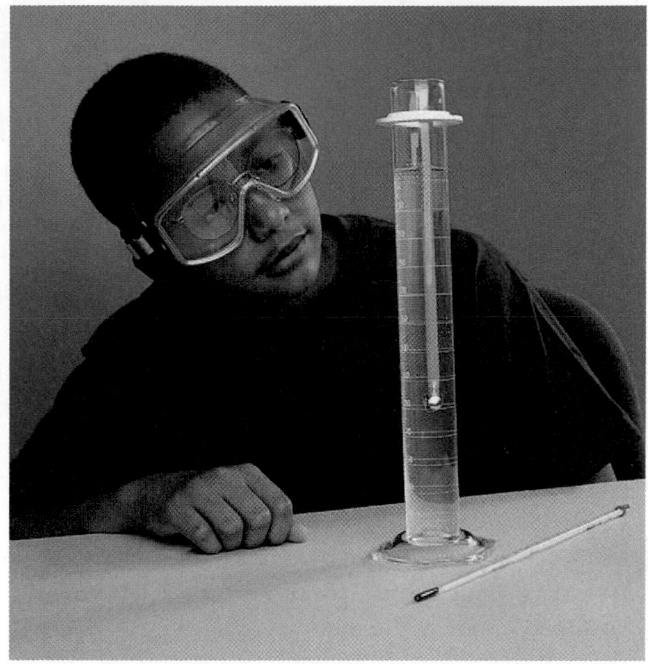

3. **Designing a Solution** How did you incorporate what you learned in Part 1 into your hydrometer design in Part 2? For example, how did your hydrometer address the problems you encountered in Part 1?
4. **Troubleshooting** In Part 3, how well did your hydrometer perform when you measured water samples of different densities? How did you redesign your hydrometer to improve its function?
5. **Evaluating the Design** What limitations did factors such as buoyancy, materials, time, costs, or other factors place on the design and function of your hydrometer? Describe how you adapted your design to work within these limitations.

## Communicate

Create an informative poster that describes how your hydrometer works. Include illustrations of your hydrometer and any important background information on density.

# 4 Currents and Climate

## Reading Preview

### Key Concepts

- What causes surface currents and how do they affect climate?
- What causes deep currents and what effects do they have?
- How does upwelling affect the distribution of nutrients in the ocean?

### Key Terms

- current
- Coriolis effect
- climate
- El Niño
- upwelling

### Target Reading Skill

**Relating Cause and Effect** As you read, identify the main factors that cause surface and deep currents in the oceans. Write the information in graphic organizers like the one below.

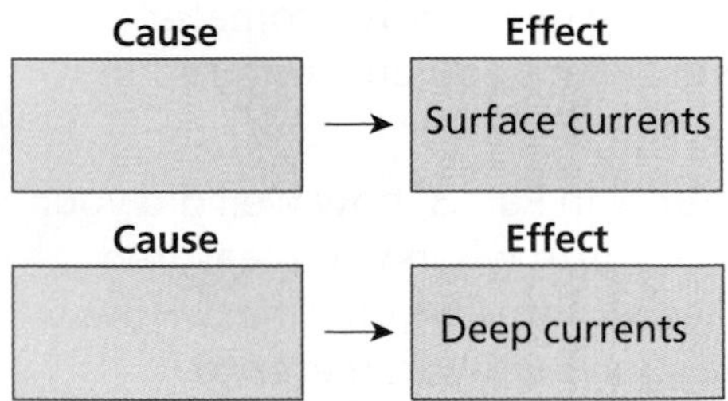


## Lab zone Discover **Activity**

### Which Is More Dense?

1. Fill a plastic container three-quarters full with warm water. Wait for the water to stop moving.
2. Add several drops of food coloring to a cup of ice water and stir.
3. Gently dribble colored water down the inside of the container. Observe.

**Think It Over**

**Inferring** Describe what happened to the cold water. Which is more dense, warm water or cold water? Explain.

One spring day, people strolling along a beach in Washington State saw an amazing sight. Hundreds of sneakers of all colors and sizes were washing ashore from the Pacific Ocean! This "sneaker spill" was eventually traced to a cargo ship accident. Containers of sneakers had fallen overboard and now the sneakers were washing ashore.

But the most amazing part of the story is this—scientists could predict where the sneakers would wash up next. And just as the scientists had predicted, sneakers washed up in Oregon, and then thousands of kilometers away in Hawaii!

How did the scientists know that the sneakers would float all the way to Hawaii? The answer lies in a type of ocean movement known as a current. A **current** is a large stream of moving water that flows through the oceans. Unlike waves, currents carry water from one place to another. Some currents move water at the surface of the ocean, while other currents move water deep in the ocean.

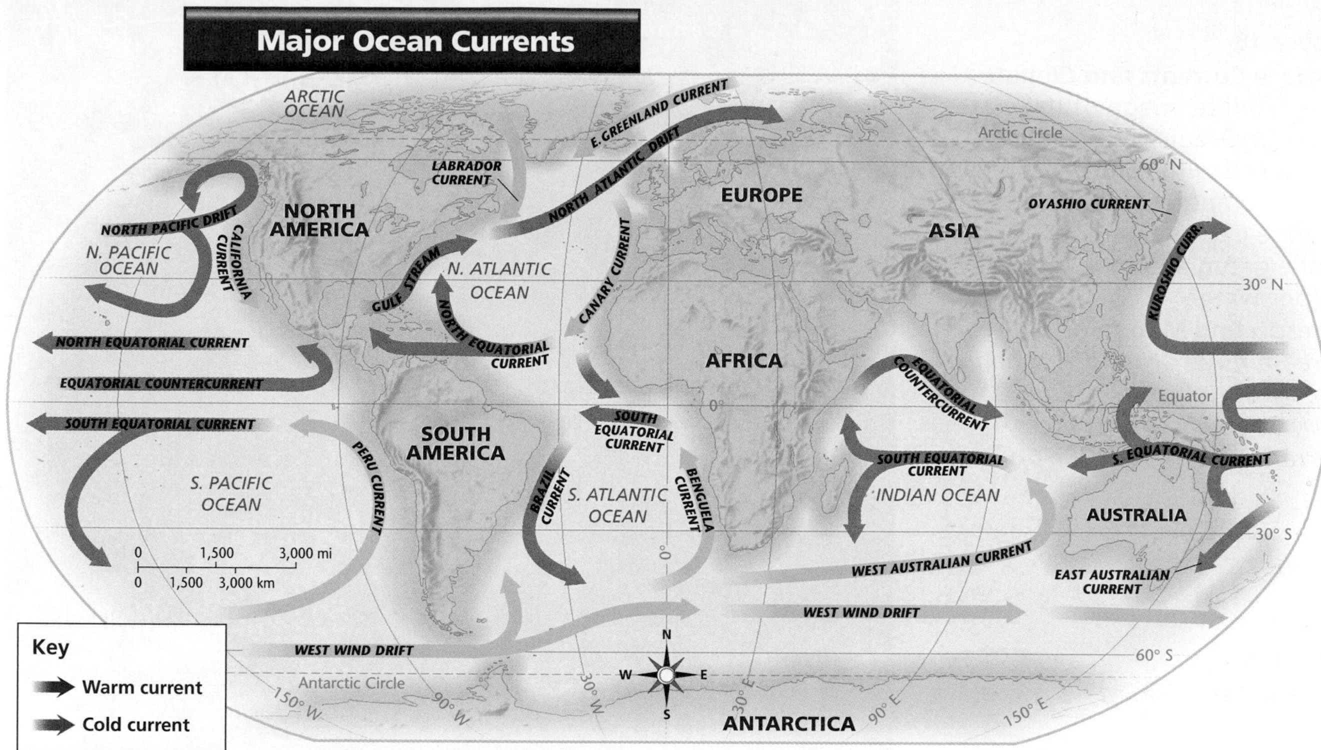


FIGURE 17
Large surface currents generally move in circular patterns in Earth's oceans. **Interpreting Maps** *Name four currents that flow along the coasts of North America. State whether each current is warm or cold.*

## Surface Currents

Figure 17 shows the major surface currents in Earth's oceans. **Surface currents, which affect water to a depth of several hundred meters, are driven mainly by winds.** Following Earth's major wind patterns, surface currents move in circular patterns in the five major oceans. Most of the currents flow east or west, and then double back to complete the circle.

**Coriolis Effect** Why do the currents move in these circular patterns? If Earth were standing still, winds and currents would flow in straight lines between the poles and the equator. But as Earth rotates, the paths of the winds and currents curve. This effect of Earth's rotation on the direction of winds and currents is called the **Coriolis effect** (kawr ee OH lis). In the Northern Hemisphere, the Coriolis effect causes the currents to curve to the right. In the Southern Hemisphere, the Coriolis effect causes the currents to curve to the left.

The largest and most powerful surface current in the North Atlantic Ocean, the Gulf Stream, is caused by strong winds from the west. It is more than 30 kilometers wide and 300 meters deep, and carries a volume of water 100 times greater than the Mississippi River. The Gulf Stream carries warm water from the Gulf of Mexico to the Caribbean Sea, then northward along the coast of the United States. Near Cape Hatteras, North Carolina, it curves eastward across the Atlantic, as a result of the Coriolis effect.

**For:** Links on ocean currents
**Visit:** www.SciLinks.org
**Web Code:** scn-0834

**FIGURE 18**
**Surface Currents and Climate**
This satellite image of the Atlantic Ocean has been enhanced with colors that show water temperature. Red and orange indicate warmer water, while green and blue indicate colder water.
**Interpreting Maps** *The Gulf Stream flows around Florida in the lower left of the map. Is the Gulf Stream warm or cold current?*

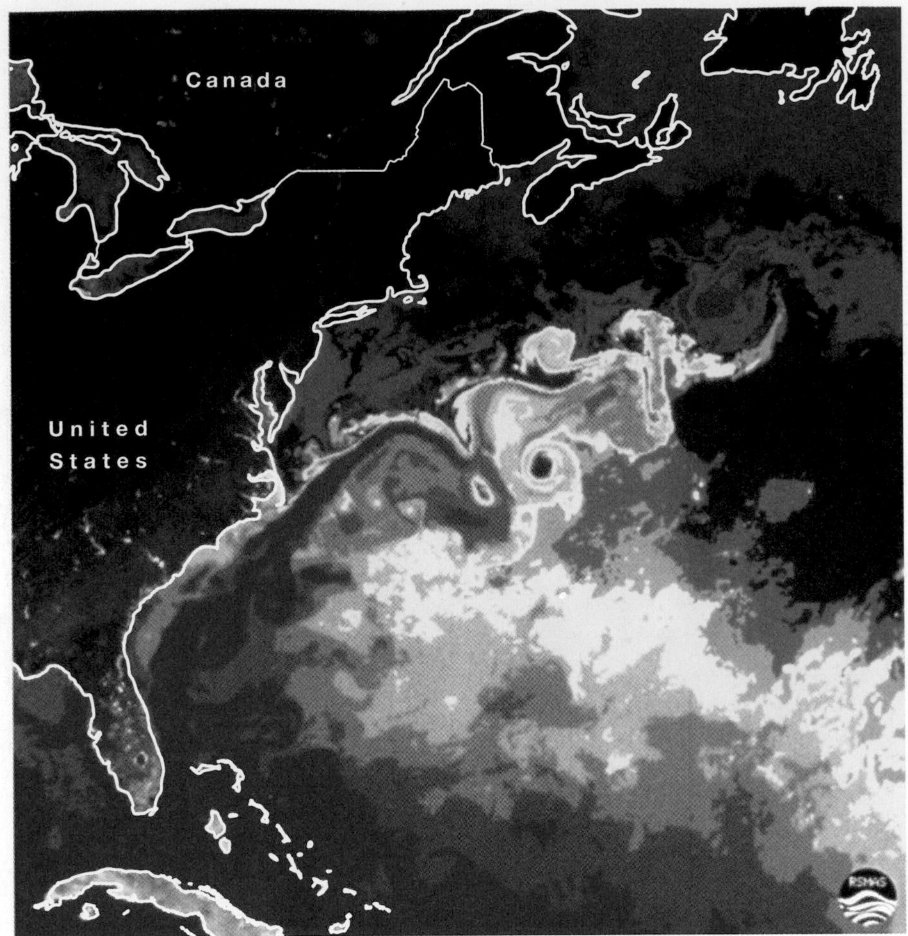


**Effects on Climate** The Gulf Stream and another warm current, the North Atlantic Drift, are very important to people in the city of Trondheim, Norway. Trondheim is located along Norway's western coast. Although it is very close to the Arctic Circle, winters there are fairly mild. Snow melts soon after it falls. And fortunately for the fishing boats, the local harbors are free of ice most of the winter. The two warm currents bring this area of Norway a mild climate. **Climate** is the pattern of temperature and precipitation typical of an area over a long period of time.

Currents affect climate by moving cold and warm water around the globe. In general, currents carry warm water from the tropics toward the poles and bring cold water back toward the equator. **A surface current warms or cools the air above it, influencing the climate of the land near the coast.**

Winds pick up moisture as they blow across warm-water currents. For example, the warm Kuroshio Current brings mild, rainy weather to the southern islands of Japan. In contrast, cold-water currents cool the air above them. Since cold air holds less moisture than warm air, these currents tend to bring cool, dry weather to the land areas in their path.

**Lab zone Skills Activity**

### Drawing Conclusions

Locate the Benguela Current in Figure 17 on the previous page. Near the southern tip of Africa, the winds blow from west to east. Using what you have learned about surface currents and climate, what can you conclude about the impact of this current on the climate of the south-western coast of Africa?

**El Niño** When changes in wind patterns and currents occur, they can have a major impact on the oceans and neighboring land. One example of such changes is **El Niño,** an abnormal climate event that occurs every two to seven years in the Pacific Ocean. El Niño begins when an unusual pattern of winds forms over the western Pacific. This causes a vast sheet of warm water to move eastward toward the South American coast. El Niño conditions can last for one to two years before the usual winds and currents return.

El Niño can have disastrous consequences. It causes shifts in weather patterns around the world, bringing unusual and often severe conditions to different areas. For example, a major El Niño occurred between 1997 and 1998 and caused an especially warm winter in the northeastern United States. However, it was also responsible for heavy rains, flooding, and mudslides in California, as well as a string of deadly tornadoes in Florida.

Although scientists do not fully understand the conditions that cause El Niño, they have been able to predict its occurrence using computer models of world climate. Knowing when El Niño will occur can reduce its impact. Scientists and public officials can plan emergency procedures and make changes to protect people and wildlife.

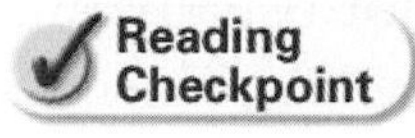


**Why is it helpful to be able to predict when El Niño will occur?**

**FIGURE 19**
**El Niño's Impact**
El Niño can cause severe weather all around the world.

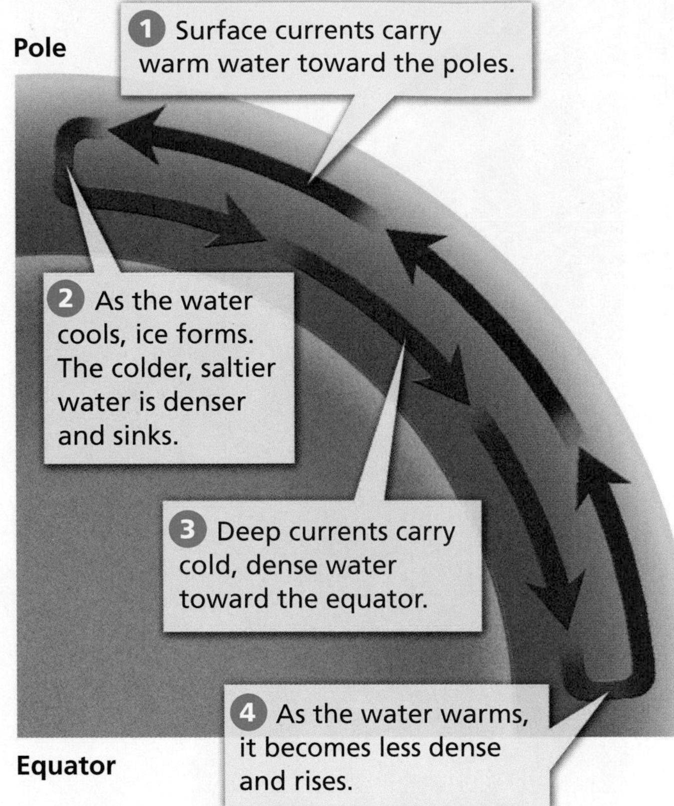

Pole
1 Surface currents carry warm water toward the poles.
2 As the water cools, ice forms. The colder, saltier water is denser and sinks.
3 Deep currents carry cold, dense water toward the equator.
4 As the water warms, it becomes less dense and rises.
Equator

**FIGURE 20**
**Deep Currents**
Deep currents are caused by differences in the density of ocean water.

## Deep Currents

Deep below the ocean surface, another type of current causes chilly waters to creep slowly across the ocean floor. **These deep currents are caused by differences in the density of ocean water.**

As you read earlier, the density of water depends on its temperature and its salinity. When a warm surface current moves from the equator toward one of the poles, it gradually cools. As ice forms near the poles, the salinity of the water increases from the salt left behind during freezing. As its temperature decreases and its salinity increases, the water becomes denser and sinks. Then, the cold water flows back along the ocean floor as a deep current. Deep currents are affected by the Coriolis effect, which causes them to curve.

**Deep currents move and mix water around the world. They carry cold water from the poles toward the equator.** Deep currents flow slowly. They may take as long as 1,000 years to flow from the pole to the equator and back again!

## Upwelling

In most parts of the ocean, surface waters do not usually mix with deep ocean waters. However, mixing sometimes occurs when winds cause upwelling. **Upwelling** is the movement of cold water upward from the deep ocean. As winds blow away the warm surface water, cold water rises to replace it.

**Upwelling brings up tiny ocean organisms, minerals, and other nutrients from the deeper layers of the water. Without this motion, the surface waters of the open ocean would be very scarce in nutrients.** Because nutrients are plentiful, zones of upwelling are usually home to huge schools of fish.

One major area of upwelling lies in the Pacific Ocean off the west coast of South America. Many people depend on this rich fishing area for food and jobs. The arrival of El Niño prevents upwelling from occurring. Without the nutrients brought by upwelling, fish die or go elsewhere to find food, reducing the fishing catch that season and hurting people's livelihoods.

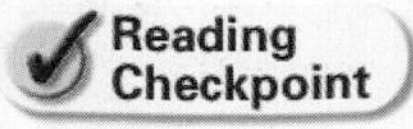

**What is upwelling?**

**FIGURE 21**
**Upwelling**
As cold water rises from the deep ocean, it brings a new supply of nutrients to the surface. The nutrients feed enormous schools of fish such as these anchovies.
**Relating Cause and Effect** *What causes cold water to rise during upwelling?*

## Section 4 Assessment

**Target Reading Skill Relating Cause and Effect** Refer to your graphic organizer about the causes of ocean currents to answer Questions 1 and 2 below.

### Reviewing Key Concepts

1. a. **Defining** What is a current?
   b. **Describing** What causes surface currents to occur? How do surface currents affect the climate of coastal areas?
   c. **Predicting** What type of climate might a coastal area have if nearby currents are cold?
2. a. **Explaining** Explain how deep currents form and move in the ocean.
   b. **Comparing and Contrasting** Compare the causes and effects of deep currents and surface currents.
3. a. **Reviewing** What causes upwelling?
   b. **Explaining** Why are huge schools of fish usually found in zones of upwelling?
   c. **Applying Concepts** Why would the ability to predict the occurrence of El Niño be important for the fishing industry on the western coast of South America?

### Lab zone At-Home Activity

**Modeling the Coriolis Effect** With the help of a family member, use chalk and a globe to model the Coriolis effect. Have your family member slowly rotate the globe in an easterly direction. As the globe rotates, draw a line from the North Pole to the equator. Use your knowledge of the Coriolis effect to explain why the line is curved.

Lab zone **Skills Lab**

# Modeling Ocean Currents

## Problem

How can you model the movement of ocean water caused by surface currents?

## Skills Focus

making models, observing, inferring

## Materials

- rectangular baking tray
- chalk
- modeling clay, 3 sticks
- ruler
- permanent marker
- hole puncher
- newspaper
- construction paper, blue and red
- jointed drinking straws, one per student
- light-reflecting rheoscopic fluid, 400 mL (or water and food coloring)

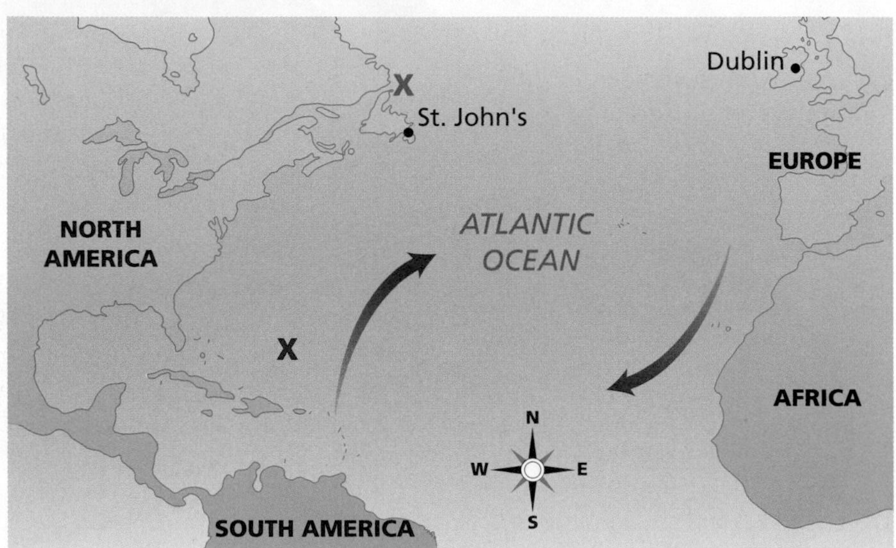


## Procedure

1. Cover your work area with newspaper. Place the baking tray on top of the newspaper.
2. Using the map as a guide, draw a chalk outline of the eastern coast of North and South America on the left side of the tray. Draw the outline of the west coast of Europe and Africa on the right side of the tray.
3. Use modeling clay to create the continents, roughly following the chalk outlines you have drawn. Build the continents to a depth of about 3 cm. Press the clay tightly to the pan to form a watertight seal.
4. Fill the ocean area of your model with rheoscopic fluid (or water and food coloring) to a depth of 1 cm.
5. Place 10 blue paper punches in the ocean area marked with a blue X on the map. Place 10 red paper punches in the area marked with a red X.
6. Select a drinking straw and bend it at the joint. Write your initials on the short end of the straw with the marker.
7. With a partner, simulate the pattern of winds that blow in this region of the world. One partner should position his or her straw across the westernmost bulge of Africa and blow toward the west (see arrow on map). The other partner should position his or her straw across the northern end of South America and blow toward the northeast (see arrow on map). Make sure that the straws are bent and that the short ends are parallel to the ocean surface. Both partners should begin blowing gently through the straws at the same time. Try to blow as continuously as possible for one to two minutes.
8. Observe the motion of the fluid and paper punches over the surface of the ocean. Notice what happens when the fluid and punches flow around landmasses.

## Analyze and Conclude

1. **Making Models** Draw a map that shows the pattern of ocean currents that was produced in your model. Use red arrows to show the flow of warm water moving north from the equator. Use blue arrows to show the flow of cold water away from the polar regions.
2. **Classifying** Use Figure 17 to add names to the currents you drew on your map. Which currents are warm-water currents? Which are cold-water currents?
3. **Observing** Based on what you observed with your model, describe the relationship between winds and surface currents in the ocean.
4. **Inferring** Dublin, Ireland, is located at the same latitude as St. John's in Newfoundland, Canada. However, when it's 8°C in Dublin in January, it's usually below 0°C in St. John's. Use your knowledge of ocean currents to explain why the climate in Dublin is different from the climate in St. John's.
5. **Communicating** Suppose you wanted to sail to Europe from the East Coast of the United States. Write a dialogue you might have with a crew member in which you discuss two natural factors that could help speed up the trip.

## Design an Experiment

Design an investigation in which you simulate an upwelling off the coast of Africa. (*Hint:* You may use a model similar to the one used in this investigation.) *Obtain your teacher's permission before carrying out your investigation.*

**The BIG Idea**

**Transfer of Energy** Most waves are caused by winds. Surface currents are driven by winds, and deep currents are caused by differences in water density. Tides are caused by the gravitational pull of the moon and sun.

## 1 Wave Action

### Key Concepts

- Most waves form when winds blowing across the water's surface transmit energy to the water.
- Near shore, wave height increases and wavelength decreases.
- As waves come ashore, water washes up the beach at an angle, carrying sand grains. The water and sand then run straight back down the beach. Waves erode the shore in some places and build it up in others.

### Key Terms

• wave • wavelength • frequency
• wave height • tsunami • longshore drift
• rip current • groin

## 2 Tides

### Key Concepts

- Tides are caused by the interaction of Earth, the moon, and the sun.
- Changes in the positions of Earth, the moon, and the sun affect the heights of the tides during a month.
- The movement of huge amounts of water between high and low tides is a source of potential energy.

### Key Terms

• tides • spring tide • neap tide

## 3 Ocean Water Chemistry

### Key Concepts

- On average, one kilogram of ocean water contains about 35 grams of salts.
- Like temperatures on land, temperatures at the surface of the ocean vary with location and the seasons. Gases in ocean water vary as well.
- As you descend through the ocean, the water temperature decreases. Pressure increases continuously with depth in the ocean.

### Key Terms

• salinity • submersible

## 4 Currents and Climate

### Key Concepts

- Surface currents are driven mainly by winds. A surface current warms or cools the air above it, influencing the climate of the land near the coast.
- Deep currents are caused by differences in the density of ocean water. Deep currents move and mix water around the world. They carry cold water from the poles toward the equator.
- Upwelling brings up tiny ocean organisms, minerals, and other nutrients from the deeper layers of the water.

### Key Terms

• current • Coriolis effect • climate
• El Niño • upwelling

# Review and Assessment

For: Self-Assessment
Visit: PHSchool.com
Web Code: cfa-3030

## Organizing Information

**Sequencing** Copy the flowchart about the movement of a wave onto a separate sheet of paper. Then complete it by putting the following three steps in the correct sequence: wave travels as low swell; wave breaks on shore; wavelength decreases and wave height increases. (For more on Sequencing, see the Skills Handbook.)

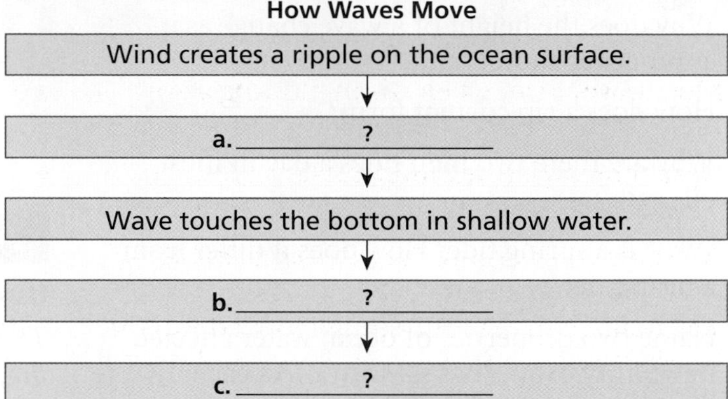

How Waves Move
Wind creates a ripple on the ocean surface.
a. ?
Wave touches the bottom in shallow water.
b. ?
c. ?

## Reviewing Key Terms

**Choose the letter of the best answer.**

1. Rolling waves with a large horizontal distance between crests have a long
   - **a.** wave height.
   - **b.** wavelength.
   - **c.** frequency.
   - **d.** trough.
2. Groins are built to reduce the effect of
   - **a.** tsunamis.
   - **b.** longshore drift.
   - **c.** rip currents.
   - **d.** deep currents.
3. At the full moon, the combined gravitational pulls of the sun and moon produce the biggest difference between low and high tide, called a
   - **a.** surface current.
   - **b.** neap tide.
   - **c.** spring tide.
   - **d.** rip current.
4. Ocean water is more dense than fresh water at the same temperature because of
   - **a.** pressure.
   - **b.** the Coriolis effect.
   - **c.** upwelling.
   - **d.** salinity.
5. Winds and currents move in curved paths because of
   - **a.** the Coriolis effect.
   - **b.** longshore drift.
   - **c.** wave height.
   - **d.** tides.
6. Cold and warm ocean water is carried around the world by
   - **a.** spring tides.
   - **b.** neap tides.
   - **c.** currents.
   - **d.** tsunamis.

## Writing in Science

**Essay** Suppose you were planning to take part in an around-the-world sailing race. Write a short essay about the knowledge of currents that you will need to prepare for the race.

# Review and Assessment

## Checking Concepts

7. What factors influence the size of a wave?
8. Why does the height of a wave change as it approaches shore?
9. How does a rip current form?
10. Why are there two high tides a day in most places?
11. What is a spring tide? How does it differ from a neap tide?
12. Name two properties of ocean water affected by salinity. How does salinity affect each?
13. What is the Coriolis effect? How does it influence ocean currents?
14. How do warm-water currents influence climate?
15. What is El Niño? What are some of its effects?
16. Describe the cause and effects of upwelling.

## Thinking Critically

17. **Predicting** How will the duck's location change as the wave moves? Explain your answer.

18. **Applying Concepts** Would you expect the salinity of the ocean to be high or low in a rainy region near the mouth of a river? Why?
19. **Comparing and Contrasting** In what ways is the ocean at 1,000 meters deep different from the ocean at the surface in the same location?
20. **Relating Cause and Effect** How does the movement of ocean currents explain the fact that much of western Europe has a mild, wet climate?
21. **Classifying** Classify the following movements of ocean water by stating whether or not each is caused by winds: waves, tides, surface currents, deep currents, upwelling.

## Math Practice

22. **Calculating Density** Two 1-liter samples of water were taken from the ocean. Both have the same salinity. Sample A has a mass of 1.02 kg. Sample B has a mass of 1.05 kg. Which sample was taken during the colder weather? Explain your answer.

## Applying Skills

**Use the data to answer Questions 23–25.**

*The temperature readings in the table were obtained in the Atlantic Ocean near Bermuda.*

**Ocean Temperatures**

| Depth (m) | Temp. (°C) | Depth (m) | Temp. (°C) |
|---|---|---|---|
| 0 | 19 | 1,000 | 9 |
| 200 | 18 | 1,200 | 5 |
| 400 | 18 | 1,400 | 5 |
| 600 | 16 | 1,600 | 4 |
| 800 | 12 | 1,800 | 4 |

23. **Graphing** Construct a line graph using the data in the table. Plot depth readings on the horizontal axis and temperature readings on the vertical axis.
24. **Drawing Conclusions** Use your graph to identify the temperature range in the transition zone.
25. **Predicting** Predict how the ocean temperature at depths of 0 meters and at 1,400 meters would change with the seasons in this location. Explain your reasoning.

## Lab zone Chapter Project

**Performance Assessment** Using your model, present your method of shoreline protection to the class. Show your classmates how the method you chose protects the lighthouse from ocean waves and the beach erosion that can result.

# Standardized Test Prep

### Test-Taking Tip

**Interpreting Diagrams**

When answering questions about a diagram, examine the diagram carefully, including all the labels. For example, the labels on the diagram below identify the shoreline, a series of groins, and the longshore drift. The arrow labeled *Longshore Drift* shows the direction of the drift. The diagram also has an arrow indicating which way is north on the diagram. Study the diagram and answer the sample question below it.

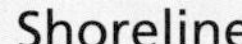


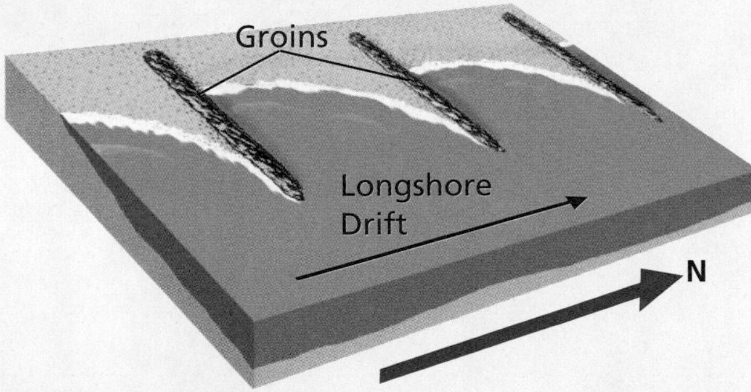


***Sample Question***

Where will sand pile up against the groins shown in the diagram?

**A** on the north side of the groins
**B** on the west side of the groins
**C** on the south side of the groins
**D** No sand will pile up against the groins.

***Answer***

The correct answer is **C.** By looking at the direction of the longshore drift and the north arrow, you can see that sand has begun to pile up on the south side of the groins.

**Choose the letter of the best answer.**

**1.** A scientist plans to test the effect temperature has on the density of ocean water. What will the manipulated variable be in her experiment?

**A** density
**B** salinity
**C** temperature
**D** water depth

**2.** In which of the following areas would the salinity of the ocean water be the highest?

**F** in a hot, dry area
**G** near a rainy coastal area close to the equator
**H** at the mouth of a large river
**J** in cold, deep water, near the ocean bottom

**3.** A major warm ocean surface current flows along a coastal area. What type of climate would you most likely find in the area influenced by the current?

**A** extremely hot and dry
**B** cool and dry
**C** extremely cool and wet
**D** mild and wet

*Use the wave diagram below and your knowledge of science to answer Questions 4–5.*

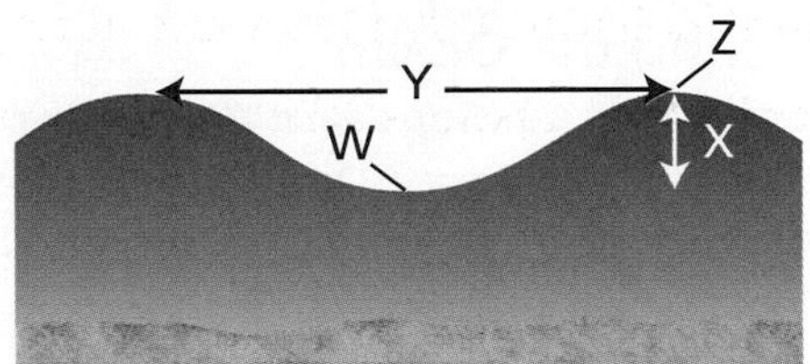


**4.** What is the wave feature labeled **W** in the diagram?

**F** wave crest
**G** wave trough
**H** wavelength
**J** wave height

**5.** What is the wave feature labeled **Y** in the diagram?

**A** wave crest
**B** wave trough
**C** wavelength
**D** wave height

### Constructed Response

**6.** Some people refer to a tsunami as a tidal wave. Explain why this is incorrect. In your answer, describe what a tsunami is and how it forms.

Chapter

# 14 Ocean Zones

## The BIG Idea

Ocean Structure and Environments

**How do scientists divide the ocean and ocean floor into zones?**

### Chapter Preview

**1 Exploring the Ocean**

***Discover*** What Can You Learn Without Seeing?
***Tech & Design in History*** Ocean Exploration
***At-Home Activity*** Mapping the Ocean
***Skills Lab*** The Shape of the Ocean Floor

**2 Ocean Habitats**

***Discover*** How Complex Are Ocean Feeding Relationships?
***Active Art*** Ocean Food Web
***Try This*** Hold On!
***Skills Activity*** Inferring

**3 Resources From the Ocean**

***Discover*** Is It From the Ocean?
***Try This*** Seaweed Candy
***Analyzing Data*** Ocean Oil Pollution
***At-Home Activity*** Modeling Ocean Pollution
***Skills Lab*** Cleaning Up an Oil Spill
***Science and Society*** Who Owns the Ocean's Minerals?

Sea stars and green sea anemones color this tide pool. ▶

Ocean Zones

▶ Video Preview
Video Field Trip
Video Assessment

Lab zone™ Chapter **Project**

## At Home in the Sea

Marine organisms are able to thrive in all ocean habitats, from sandy tropical beaches to the cold depths of the ocean floor. In this project, you will create a model of one ocean habitat.

**Your Goal** To build a three-dimensional model of a marine habitat and include some of the organisms that live there

To complete the project successfully, you will need to

- include the significant physical features of the habitat
- create a life-size model of one organism that lives in the habitat
- write an explanation of how the organism is adapted to its habitat
- follow the safety guidelines in Appendix A

**Plan It!** Begin now by previewing the visuals in the chapter to identify different ocean habitats. With your group, discuss which habitat you would like to learn more about. Make a list of questions you have about the habitat. Choose the materials you will need to build your model, then sketch your design. After your teacher approves your plan, begin to build the model and plan your written report.

Section 1

# Exploring the Ocean

## Reading Preview

### Key Concepts

- For what reasons have people studied the ocean?
- What are the main sections of the ocean floor?
- What are the different ocean zones?

### Key Terms

- sonar • continental shelf
- continental slope
- abyssal plain
- mid-ocean ridge • trench
- intertidal zone • neritic zone
- open-ocean zone

### Target Reading Skill

**Building Vocabulary**

A definition states the meaning of a word or phrase by telling about its most important feature or function. After you read the section, reread the paragraphs that contain definitions of Key Terms. Use all the information you have learned to write a definition of each Key Term in your own words.

## Lab zone Discover Activity

### What Can You Learn Without Seeing?

1. Your teacher will provide your group with ten plastic drinking straws and a covered box containing a mystery object. The top of the box has several holes punched in it. Using the straws as probes, try to determine the size, shape, and location of the object inside the box.
2. Based on the information you gathered, describe your object. What can you say about its length, shape, and position? Write down your hypothesis about the identity of the object.
3. Remove the box top to reveal the object.

**Think It Over**

**Inferring** Explain how you used the method of indirect observation to learn about the object.

Imagine going on a voyage around the world that will last three and a half years. Your assignment: to investigate everything about the sea. Your vessel: a ship powered by sails and a steam engine. On board there are thermometers for measuring the temperature of ocean water and cable for lowering dredges beneath the surface. With the dredges, you scrape sand, muck, and rock from the ocean floor. You drag nets behind the ship to collect ocean organisms.

The crew of a British ship, HMS *Challenger*, began such a voyage in 1872. By the end of the journey, scientists on the ship had gathered enough data to fill 50 volumes and had collected more than 4,000 new organisms! The scientists learned about ocean-water chemistry, currents, ocean life, and the shape of the ocean floor. The voyage of the *Challenger* was so successful that it became the model for many later ocean expeditions.

◀ **HMS *Challenger***

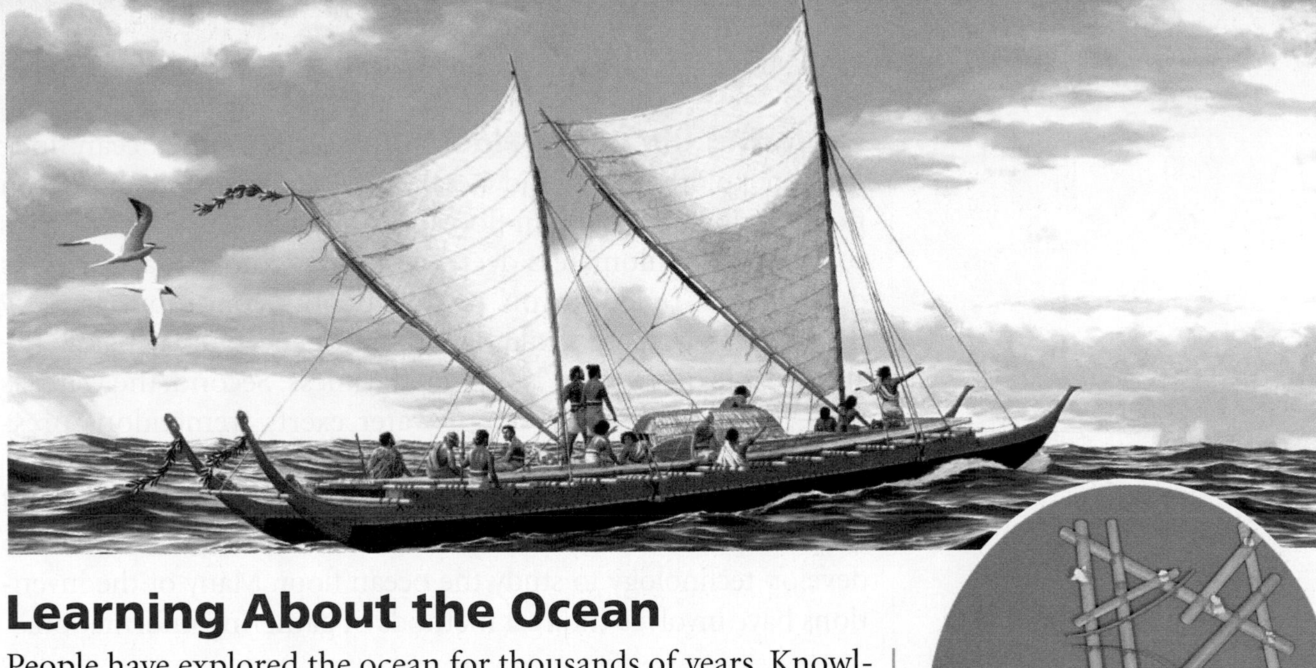

## Learning About the Ocean

People have explored the ocean for thousands of years. Knowledge of the ocean has always been important to the people living along its coasts. **People have studied the ocean since ancient times, because the ocean provides food and serves as a route for trade and travel. Modern scientists have studied the characteristics of the ocean's waters and the ocean floor.**

**Trading Routes** The Phoenicians, who lived along the Mediterranean Sea, were one of the earliest cultures to explore the oceans. By about 1200 B.C., they had established sea routes for trade with other nations around the Mediterranean. After the Phoenicians, people of many European, African, and Asian cultures sailed along the coasts to trade with distant lands.

In the Pacific Ocean around 2,000 years ago, the Polynesians left the safety of their islands and boldly sailed into the open ocean. Their knowledge of winds and currents enabled the Polynesians to settle the widely scattered islands of Hawaii, Tahiti, and New Zealand. To navigate the ocean, they used devices such as the one shown in Figure 1.

**FIGURE 1**
**Polynesian Explorers**
Around 2,000 years ago, Polynesians explored the Pacific Ocean in boats such as the one above. They used stick charts (above right) to navigate.
**Inferring** *Why is careful navigation important to explorers?*

**Scientific Discoveries** As modern science developed and trade increased, ocean exploration changed. Nations needed accurate maps of the oceans and lands bordering them. Governments also wanted their countries to be known for new scientific discoveries. For example, in the late 1700s, the British government hired Captain James Cook to lead three voyages of exploration. Cook's crew included scientists who studied the stars and those who collected new species of plants and animals.

Within a century of Cook's voyages, almost all of Earth's coastlines had been mapped. Scientists then turned to the study of the ocean's waters. The *Challenger* expedition marked the beginning of the modern science of oceanography.

**Exploring the Ocean Floor** Until recently, the ocean floor was unexplored. Why did it take so long to reach the ocean floor? Studying the ocean floor is difficult because the ocean is so deep—3.8 kilometers deep on average, more than twice as deep as the Grand Canyon. At such depths, conditions are very harsh. First, because sunlight does not penetrate far below the surface, the deep ocean is in total darkness. Second, the water is very cold. Finally, deep ocean water exerts tremendous pressure due to the mass of water pushing down from above.

Humans cannot survive the darkness, cold temperatures, and extreme pressure of the deep ocean. So scientists have had to develop technology to study the ocean floor. Many of the inventions have involved indirect methods of gathering information.

## • Tech & Design in History •

### Ocean Exploration

The timeline includes several inventions that have helped scientists overcome the challenges of studying the oceans.

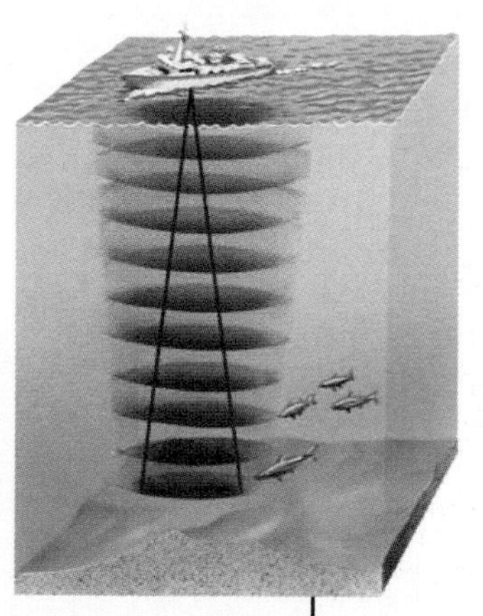

**1925 Sonar**
Scientists aboard the German ship *Meteor* used sonar to map the ocean floor. They used a device called an echo sounder to produce pulses of sound. The ship's crew then timed the return of the echoes.

**1943 SCUBA**
Jacques Cousteau and Emile Gagnan invented SCUBA, which stands for "**s**elf **c**ontained **u**nderwater **b**reathing **a**pparatus." A tank containing compressed air is strapped to the diver's back and connected by a tube to a mouthpiece. SCUBA enables divers to explore to a depth of 40 meters.

**1960 Submersibles**
Explorers traveled to the bottom of Challenger Deep, 11 kilometers below the ocean surface, protected by the thick metal hull of the submersible *Trieste*.

1920 1940 1960

One of the simplest methods, used by the *Challenger*'s crew, was to lower a weight on a long line into the water until the weight touched the bottom. The length of line that got wet was approximately equal to the water's depth. However, this method was slow and often inaccurate.

A major advance in ocean-floor mapping was **sonar,** which stands for **so**und **na**vigation and **r**anging. Sonar is a system that uses sound waves to calculate the distance to an object. The sonar equipment on a ship sends out pulses of sound that bounce off the ocean floor. The equipment then measures how quickly the sound waves return to the ship. Sound waves return quickly if the ocean floor is close. Sound waves take longer to return if the ocean floor is farther away.

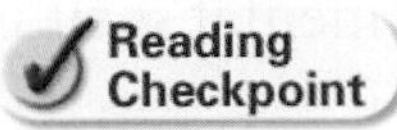


**What conditions exist in the depths of the ocean?**

## Writing in Science

**Research and Write** Each of the inventions shown in this timeline helped solve a challenge of ocean exploration. Find out more about one of these inventions. Write a short newspaper article telling the story of its development. Include details about the people who invented it and how it added to people's knowledge of the oceans.

**1978 Satellites**

*Seasat A* was the first satellite in Earth's orbit to study the oceans. Since satellites make millions of observations a day, they can provide data on rapidly changing ocean conditions. Such data include temperatures, algae growth patterns, and even the movement of large schools of fish.

**1986 Remote Underwater Manipulator**

The Remote Underwater Manipulator, or RUM III, is about the size of a small car. It is controlled by a computer aboard a ship at the surface. The RUM III can collect samples, take photographs, and map the ocean floor—all without a crew.

**2003 Deep Flight Aviator**

The Deep Flight Aviator, a new type of submersible, is launched in San Francisco Bay. Deep Flight Aviators maneuver faster and much more easily than other submersibles. Passengers can see much more, too.

1980 2000 2020

## The Ocean Floor

You might be surprised to find that the ocean floor is not a flat, sandy plain. If you could take a submarine voyage along the ocean floor, what would you see? **If you could travel along the ocean floor, you would see the continental shelf, the continental slope, the abyssal plain, and the mid-ocean ridge.** Trace your journey in Figure 2.

**Shallow Water** As you leave the harbor, your submarine first passes over a section of the ocean floor called the **continental shelf.** This gently sloping, shallow area of the ocean floor extends outward from the edge of a continent. At a depth of about 130 meters, the slope of the ocean floor gets steeper. This incline beyond the edge of the continental shelf is called the **continental slope.**

**Open Ocean** As you follow the ocean floor, it slopes gradually toward the deep ocean. Soon, you encounter mountains tall enough to break the ocean's surface, forming islands. Other mountains, called seamounts, are completely underwater.

FIGURE 2

### The Ocean Floor

The floor of the ocean has mountains, slopes, and other features. To show the major features of the ocean floor, thousands of kilometers have been "squeezed" into one illustration.

**Interpreting Diagrams** *Which is steeper, the continental slope or the continental shelf?*

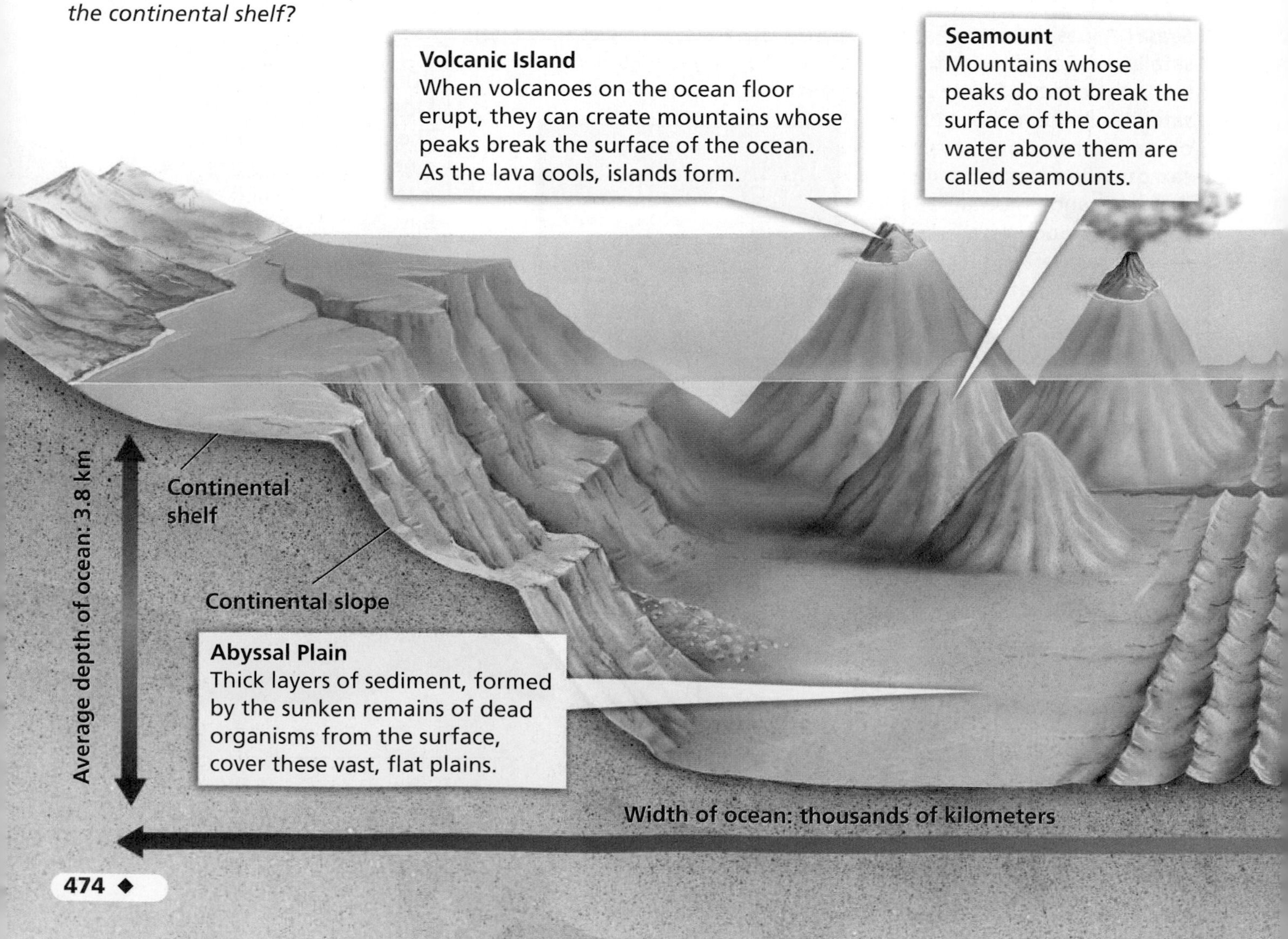

**Volcanic Island**
When volcanoes on the ocean floor erupt, they can create mountains whose peaks break the surface of the ocean. As the lava cools, islands form.
**Seamount**
Mountains whose peaks do not break the surface of the ocean water above them are called seamounts.
Continental shelf
Continental slope
Average depth of ocean: 3.8 km
**Abyssal Plain**
Thick layers of sediment, formed by the sunken remains of dead organisms from the surface, cover these vast, flat plains.
Width of ocean: thousands of kilometers

Next you cross a broad area covered with thick layers of mud and silt. This smooth, nearly flat region of the ocean floor is called the **abyssal plain** (uh BIHS ul). After gliding over the abyssal plain for many kilometers, you see a mountain range ahead. The **mid-ocean ridge** is made up of a range of mountains that winds through the oceans, much as the line of stitches winds around a baseball.

**Deepest Depths** You cross the ocean floor from the mid-ocean ridge toward the abyssal plain. Soon your submarine's lights reveal a dark gash in the ocean floor ahead of you. As you pass over it, you look down into a canyon in the ocean floor called a **trench.** The trench is so deep you cannot see the bottom.

Then your submarine slowly climbs the continental slope. You cross the continental shelf on this side of the ocean and maneuver the submarine into harbor.

Discovery Channel School

*Ocean Zones*

Video Preview
▶ Video Field Trip
Video Assessment

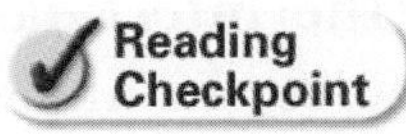


**Which ocean-floor feature makes up the deepest parts of the ocean?**

**Continental Slope**
A steady incline marks the continental slope. Continental slopes in the Pacific Ocean are steeper than those in the Atlantic Ocean. *Note: Because the vertical scale is exaggerated, the continental slope in this illustration appears steeper than it really is.*

**Continental Shelf**
This gradually sloping area borders each continent. Its width varies from just a few kilometers to as much as 1,300 kilometers.

**Mid-Ocean Ridge**
The mid-ocean ridge consists of many peaks along both sides of a central valley. This chain of undersea mountains runs all around the world.

**Trenches**
These canyons include Earth's deepest points. The Mariana Trench in the Pacific is 11 kilometers deep.

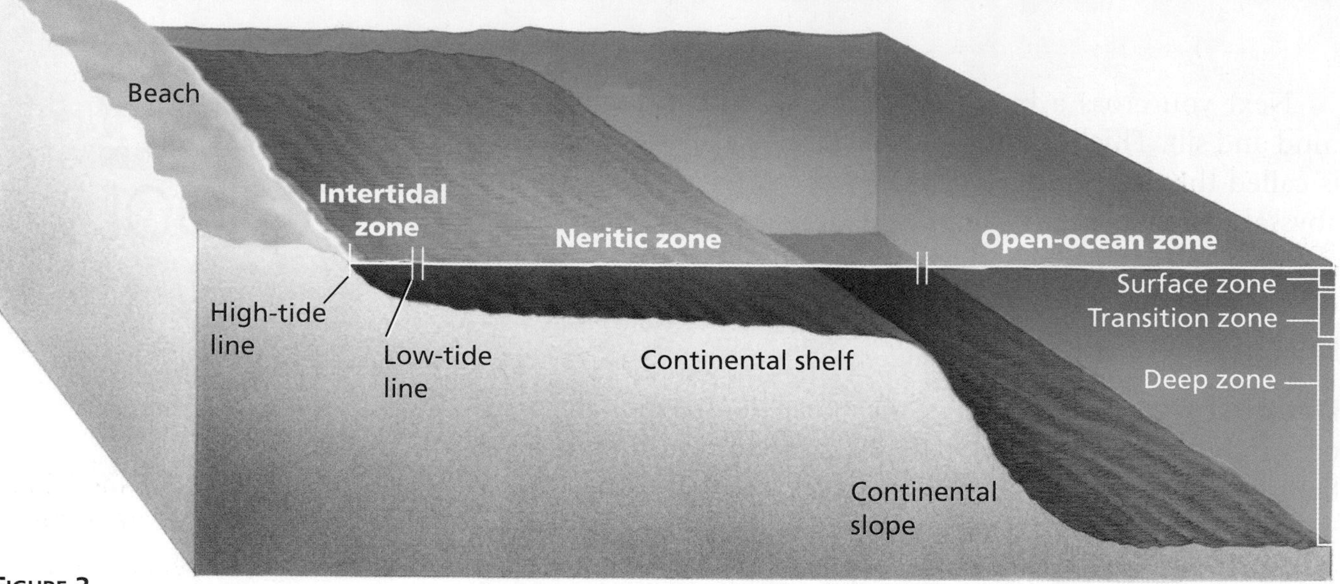


**FIGURE 3**
**Ocean Zones**
The three ocean zones are the intertidal zone, the neritic zone, and the open-ocean zone.
**Classifying** *Into what three zones is the open-ocean zone divided?*

## Ocean Zones

Just as the ocean floor can be divided into sections, the ocean can be divided into zones. **Ocean zones include the intertidal zone, the neritic zone, and the open-ocean zone.** At the highest high-tide line, the **intertidal zone** begins. The intertidal zone stretches out to the point exposed by the lowest low tide. The **neritic zone** extends from the low-tide line out to the edge of the continental shelf. Beyond the edge of the continental shelf lies the **open-ocean zone.** This zone includes the deepest, darkest part of the ocean. The physical conditions of each ocean zone help determine which organisms can live in that zone.

## Section 1 Assessment

**Target Reading Skill Building Vocabulary** Use your definitions to help answer the questions below.

### Reviewing Key Concepts

1. a. **Reviewing** Why have people in ancient and modern times explored the oceans?
   b. **Explaining** Why did the ocean floor remain unexplored until recently?
   c. **Summarizing** What is sonar? How did it finally enable scientists to map the ocean floor?
2. a. **Listing** List four sections of the ocean floor.
   b. **Interpreting Diagrams** Refer to Figure 2. Describe the characteristics of each of the four sections of the ocean floor that you listed above.
   c. **Sequencing** Put the following in order from steepest to least steep: continental slope, continental shelf, trench, abyssal plain.
3. a. **Identifying** Identify the three ocean zones.
   b. **Sequencing** Put the ocean zones in order from the shallowest to the deepest.

### Lab zone At-Home Activity

**Mapping the Ocean** Choose a room in your house and make a "room-floor" map. The ceiling is the ocean surface and the floor is the ocean bottom. Choose a straight path across the room. At regular intervals take a depth reading from the ceiling to the floor or to the top of any furniture in that spot. Plot the depths on a graph. Then challenge others to identify the room by looking at the graph.

Lab zone **Skills Lab**

# The Shape of the Ocean Floor

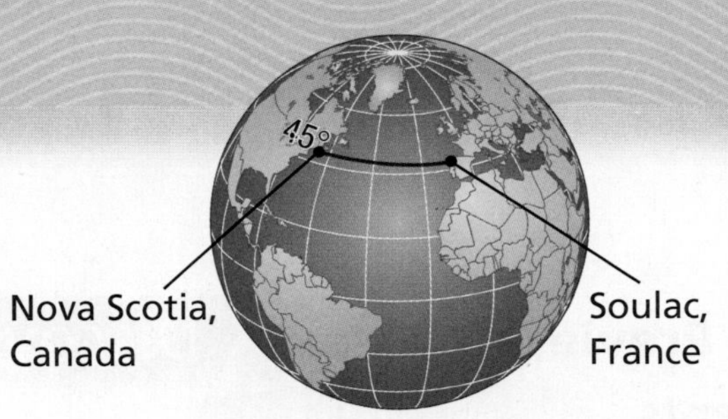


## Problem

Imagine you are an oceanographer traveling across the Atlantic along the 45° N latitude line marked on the map. You are gathering data on the depth of the ocean between Nova Scotia, Canada, and Soulac, France. How can you use data to determine the shape of the ocean floor?

## Skills Focus

graphing, predicting, inferring

## Materials

- pencil
- graph paper

## Procedure

1. Draw the axes of a graph. Label the horizontal axis *Longitude*. Mark from 65° W to 0° from left to right. Label the vertical axis *Ocean Depth*. Mark 0 meters at the top of the vertical axis to represent sea level. Mark −5,000 meters at the bottom to represent the depth of 5,000 meters below sea level. Mark depths at equal intervals along the vertical axis.
2. Examine the data in the table. The numbers in the Longitude column give the ship's location at 19 points in the Atlantic Ocean. Location 1 is Nova Scotia, and Location 19 is Soulac. The numbers in the Ocean Depth column give the depth measurements recorded at each location. Plot each measurement on your graph. Remember that the depths are represented on your graph as numbers below 0, or sea level.
3. Connect the points you have plotted with a line to create a profile of the ocean floor.

## Analyze and Conclude

1. **Graphing** On your graph, identify and label the continental shelf and continental slope.
2. **Predicting** Label the abyssal plain on your graph. How would you expect the ocean floor to look there?
3. **Graphing** Label the mid-ocean ridge on your graph. Describe the process occurring there.
4. **Inferring** What might the feature at 10° W be? Explain.
5. **Communicating** Imagine you are traveling along the ocean floor from Nova Scotia, Canada, to Soulac, France. Describe the features you would see along your journey.

## More to Explore

Use the depth measurements in the table to calculate the average depth of the Atlantic Ocean between Nova Scotia and France.

**Ocean Depth Sonar Data**

| Longitude | Ocean Depth (m) | Longitude | Ocean Depth (m) |
|---|---|---|---|
| 1. 64° W | 0 | 11. 28° W | 1,756 |
| 2. 60° W | 91 | 12. 27° W | 2,195 |
| 3. 55° W | 132 | 13. 25° W | 3,146 |
| 4. 50° W | 73 | 14. 20° W | 4,244 |
| 5. 48° W | 3,512 | 15. 15° W | 4,610 |
| 6. 45° W | 4,024 | 16. 10° W | 4,976 |
| 7. 40° W | 3,805 | 17. 05° W | 4,317 |
| 8. 35° W | 4,171 | 18. 04° W | 146 |
| 9. 33° W | 3,439 | 19. 01° W | 0 |
| 10. 30° W | 3,073 | | |

Section 2

Integrating Life Science

# Ocean Habitats

## Reading Preview

### Key Concepts

- How are marine organisms classified?
- What conditions must organisms in intertidal zones tolerate?
- What are the conditions in the neritic zone?
- What are the conditions in the open ocean?

### Key Terms

- plankton
- nekton
- benthos
- food web
- estuary
- atoll
- bioluminescence
- hydrothermal vent

### Target Reading Skill

**Using Prior Knowledge** Before you read, write what you know about conditions that might determine where ocean organisms live. Use a graphic organizer like the one below. As you read, write what you learn.

| What You Know |
|---|
| 1. Many organisms need sunlight.<br>2. |

| What You Learned |
|---|
| 1.<br>2. |

## Lab zone Discover Activity

### How Complex Are Ocean Feeding Relationships?

1. Form a circle of five students. Each student will represent one of the following marine organisms: algae, shrimp, fish, sea otter, and whale. Each student should write the name of his or her organism on a card.
2. Discuss the possible feeding relationships among the five organisms. What might your organism eat? What might eat the organism you represent?
3. Use string to connect your card to the cards of the organisms that may have feeding relationships with your organism.

**Think It Over**

**Inferring** Based on your results in Step 3, are the feeding relationships among ocean organisms simple or complex? Explain your answer.

As you walk along the beach on a sunny July day, your feet sink in the soft, wet sand. You stop to pick up some interesting shells that have washed up on the shore. A few gulls screech and swoop overhead. Otherwise, all is calm. The ocean stretches as far as the eye can see. Waves crash against the shore. But you see no sign of life on the shore.

Look closer. Right beneath your feet you can see evidence of living things. Tiny, round holes are signs of clams burrowing into the sand. If you wade into the water, you may be able to spot a sand crab feeding in the surf. And far out to sea, a school of dolphins swims by. Their bodies form graceful arcs as they dive in and out of the water. An ocean may seem lifeless, but many different organisms inhabit this vast, watery environment.

## Life in the Ocean

On land, most organisms live on or near the surface. The ocean, on the other hand, is inhabited by organisms at every depth. **Scientists classify marine organisms according to where they live and how they move.** Figure 4 shows the three categories of ocean organisms—plankton, nekton, and benthos.

**Plankton** **Plankton** are tiny algae and animals that float in the water and are carried by waves and currents. Algae plankton include geometrically shaped diatoms. Animal plankton include microscopic crustaceans, such as copepods, and some tiny young fish.

**Nekton** **Nekton** are free-swimming animals that can move throughout the water column. Squid, most fishes, and marine mammals such as whales and seals are nekton.

**Benthos** **Benthos** are organisms that inhabit the ocean floor. Some benthos, like crabs, sea stars, octopus, and lobsters, move from place to place. Others, like sponges and sea anemones, stay in one location.

**Reading Checkpoint** **Are sharks plankton, nekton, or benthos? Why?**

FIGURE 4
**Marine Organisms**
Marine organisms can be classified as plankton, nekton, or benthos.

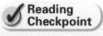

Polar bear
Arctic tern
Sea duck
Loons
Ringed seal
Arctic cod
Algae plankton
Animal plankton
Silversides
Beluga whale
Benthos

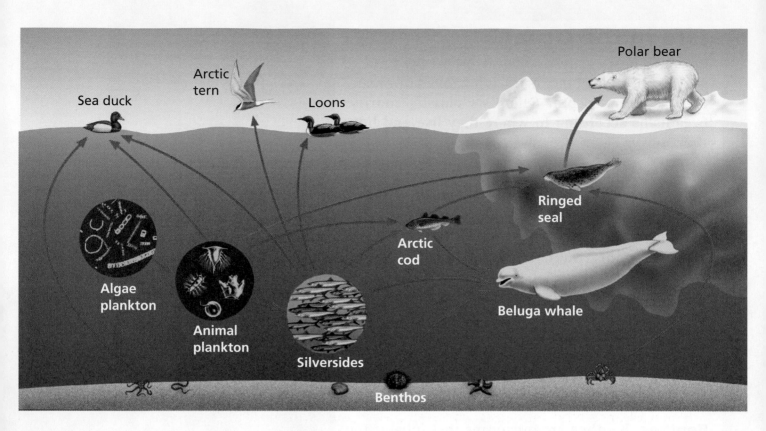

**FIGURE 5**
## An Ocean Food Web
This ocean food web includes typical organisms found in the Arctic Ocean. The arrows indicate what each organism eats.
**Interpreting Diagrams** *Which organisms feed directly on the Arctic cod? Which organisms depend indirectly on the cod?*

**For:** Ocean Food Web activity
**Visit:** PHSchool.com
**Web Code:** cfp-3042

**Relationships Among Organisms** Plankton, nekton, and benthos are all found in most marine habitats. Many plankton and benthos are algae. Like plants, algae use sunlight to produce their own food through photosynthesis. Photosynthetic plankton are called producers. Other plankton and benthos, as well as all nekton, eat either algae or other organisms. They are called consumers. Finally, some organisms, including many benthos, break down wastes and the remains of other organisms. They are called decomposers.

**Ocean Food Webs** All of the feeding relationships that exist in a habitat make up a **food web.** A typical ocean food web is shown in Figure 5. Each organism in this Arctic food web depends either directly or indirectly on the algae plankton. Throughout the ocean, plankton are a source of food for other organisms of all sizes. If you think of sharks as sharp-toothed, meat-eating hunters, you might be surprised to learn that the biggest sharks of all feed directly on tiny plankton! Many whales, including Earth's largest animal—the blue whale—also feed only on plankton.

**Which organisms in an ocean food web are the producers?**

## The Intertidal Zone

Intertidal zone

A wide variety of organisms, or living things, live in the different habitats of the intertidal zone. Estuaries, sandy shores, and rocky shores are three major habitats in the intertidal zone. The conditions in each of the habitats in the intertidal zone determine the types of organisms that can live there.

**Organisms that live in intertidal zones must be able to tolerate changes in both the salinity and temperature of the water, as well as periods of being underwater and periods exposed to the air. Some also experience pounding waves.** They must avoid drying out, hide from predators, and find food in this harsh setting.

**Estuaries** Many important environments along the ocean's edge are estuaries. **Estuaries** are coastal inlets or bays where fresh water from rivers mixes with salty ocean water. Water that is partly salty and partly fresh is brackish. Estuaries serve as valuable nurseries for fish and shellfish. They also serve as valuable feeding and resting areas for birds and land animals.

Estuaries are found on coasts wherever a river meets the ocean. The Chesapeake Bay is a huge estuary on the mid-Atlantic coast. It is a rich source of oysters, clams, and blue crabs. It is also a valuable feeding and resting stop for migrating birds. Monterey Bay on the California coast is another important estuary. It contains the Monterey Bay National Marine Sanctuary, one of the nation's largest research facilities and sanctuaries for ocean animals.

**Mangrove Forests** Coastal wetlands are found in and around estuaries. Along the coasts of the United States, most wetlands are either mangrove forests or salt marshes.

Mangroves are short, twisted trees that grow in brackish water. Mangrove forests are found in southern Florida and along the Gulf of Mexico. The mangroves' arching roots, shown in Figure 6, anchor the trees to the land. The roots create a protected nursery, rich in nutrients, for many young animals. Mangroves can also absorb the force of winds and waves, protecting the coastline during storms.

FIGURE 6
**A Mangrove Forest**
Arching prop roots anchor these mangrove trees firmly in the soft, sandy soil.
**Relating Cause and Effect** *How do mangrove forests protect the coastline?*

## Lab zone Try This Activity

### Hold On!

In this activity, you will model one way that an animal that lives in the intertidal zone might cling to a rock.

1. Your teacher will give you a ping-pong ball, a rock, and some other materials. The ping-pong ball represents the animal.
2. Attach the ping-pong ball to the rock.
3. Place the rock in a sink or deep pan. Run water over the rock. Observe how well your animal stays in place on the rock.

**Making Models** How well did your animal cling to the rock? In what ways did your model best represent a real intertidal-zone animal? In what ways did it most poorly represent one?

**Salt Marshes** A salt marsh oozes with smelly mud. The mud is made up of sediments, animal and plant matter, and nutrients carried into the marsh by fresh water and tides. Salt marshes are common along the east coast from Massachusetts to Florida.

Cordgrass is the most common plant in the marsh. Unlike most plants, cordgrass can survive in salt water. Some cordgrass is eaten by animals. The rest is decomposed by bacteria and fungi. The decomposed material supplies nutrients to marsh organisms.

Tidal channels run through the cordgrass. Waves break up as they enter the channels, so that organisms in the marsh are protected from the surf. Within the marsh, fish, crabs, shrimp, and oysters hatch and feed before entering the harsher ocean environment offshore. At low tide, crabs search for food in the rich mud. Birds such as herons and stilts prey on the crabs and other benthos exposed by the low tide.

**Sandy Shores** Sandy shores are also part of the intertidal zone. There are sandy shores on all the ocean coasts of the United States. It often looks like there is nothing on a sandy shore but sand and water. But that is because most of the animals live underground.

Like other organisms of the intertidal zone, the organisms on a sandy shore must tolerate changing water levels and temperatures. On a sandy shore, organisms must also deal with crashing waves and a sandy surface that is always moving. Burrowing underground protects animals such as clams, sand dollars, and sand crabs from the ever-changing conditions at the edge of the ocean.

**Rocky Shores** Imagine that your home has no walls or roof. Twice a day, a huge storm passes through, bringing a drenching downpour and winds so strong you can hardly keep your balance. At other times, the sun beats down, and you feel like you're baking. This is what life is like for organisms that live on rocky shores.

FIGURE 7
### A Rocky Shore
The constantly changing water level along a rocky shore in the intertidal zone creates different habitats.
**Comparing and Contrasting** *How are conditions different for organisms near the top of the rocks compared to organisms at the bottom?*

A rocky shore is another type of habitat in the intertidal zone. Rocky shores are found along much of both coasts of the United States. Figure 7 shows some of the colorful organisms that typically live along the California coast.

The highest rocks, above the highest high-tide line, make up the spray zone. The spray zone is never completely covered with water, but it gets wet as the waves break against the rocks. A stripe of black algae indicates the highest high-tide line.

The rocks below this level are covered with barnacles. Barnacles can close up their hard shells. This action traps a drop of water inside to carry the barnacles through the dry period until the next high tide. The rocks are also home to flat animals called limpets. Limpets have a large, muscular foot that allows them to hold tightly to the rocks. They release drops of mucus around the edges of their shells. The mucus forms a tight seal.

**Tide Pools** When the tide retreats from a rocky shore, some water remains in depressions among the rocks. These puddles are called tide pools. As the water in a tide pool is warmed by the sun, the water begins to evaporate. The remaining water becomes saltier. If it rains, however, the salinity quickly decreases. Organisms in the tide pool must be able to withstand these changes in temperature and salinity.

Tide-pool organisms must also withstand the force of waves. Sea stars cling to the rocks with rows of tiny suction cups. If the bottom is sandy, a spiny sea urchin can use its spines to dig a hole. The sea urchin then buries itself in the hole during heavy surf.

Under shady rock ledges, sponges and sea anemones wait for the incoming tide to bring a fresh supply of plankton and other food particles. Most sea anemones look delicate. But some sea anemones can survive out of water for more than two weeks. To do this, the anemone pulls its tentacles inside and folds up into a round blob.

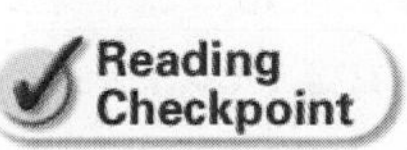


**What are three habitats of the intertidal zone?**

**For:** More on the intertidal zone
**Visit:** PHSchool.com
**Web Code:** cfd-3043

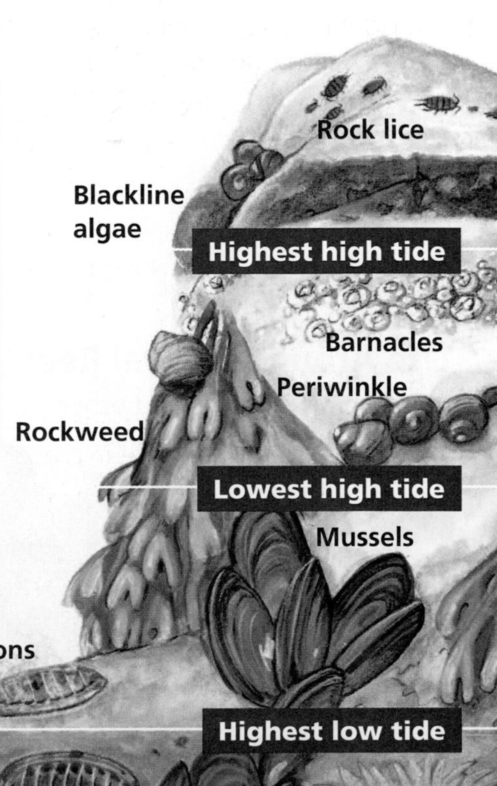

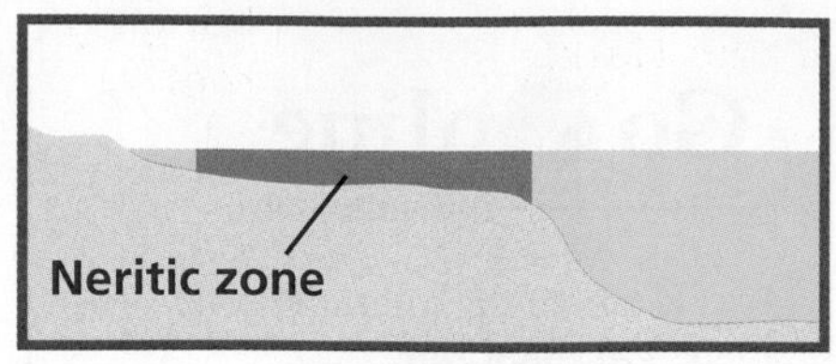

For: Links on coral reefs
Visit: www.SciLinks.org
Web Code: scn-0844

## Conditions in the Neritic Zone

Recall that the neritic zone extends from the low-tide line out to the edge of the continental shelf. A wide variety of organisms are found in the neritic zone, more than in any other ocean zone. Most of the world's major fishing grounds are found in this zone.

The neritic zone is home to so many living things because it is located over the continental shelf. **The shallow water over the continental shelf receives sunlight and a steady supply of nutrients washed from the land into the ocean. The light and nutrients enable large plantlike algae to grow.** These algae serve as a food source and shelter for other organisms.

In many parts of the neritic zone, upwelling brings additional nutrients to the surface. These nutrients support large numbers of plankton, which form the base of ocean food webs. Schools of fish such as sardines and herrings feed on the plankton. Important fisheries in upwelling areas include Monterey Canyon off California and Georges Bank off New England.

## Coral Reefs

A coral reef is another type of diverse habitat found in the neritic zone. A coral reef is made of living things and their remains. Coral reefs are created by colonies of tiny coral animals, each of which is not much larger than a pencil eraser. Each coral animal produces a hard structure that surrounds its body. After the coral dies, the empty structure remains. New coral animals attach to it and grow. Over many years, a reef is built.

FIGURE 8
**Life Around a Coral Reef**
Many animals, algae, and other organisms live in the diverse habitats of a coral reef.

Green moray eel ▼

▼ Coral animals

FIGURE 9

## How an Atoll Forms

An atoll develops in stages, beginning with a fringing reef that surrounds a volcanic island. **Relating Cause and Effect** *For an atoll to form, what must happen to the volcanic island?*

1 A fringing reef closely surrounds an island.

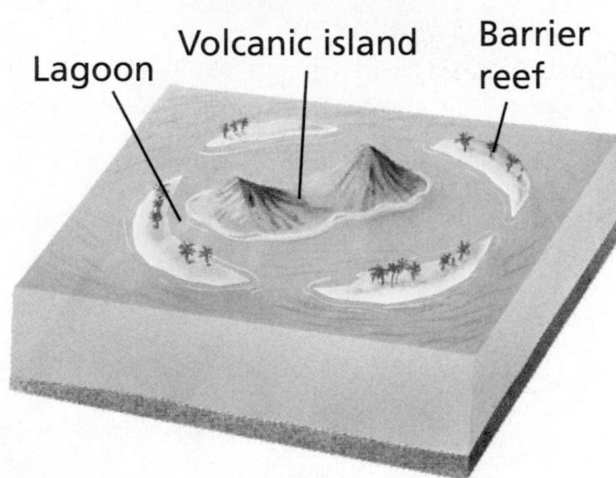


2 As the island sinks, a lagoon forms inside the barrier reef.

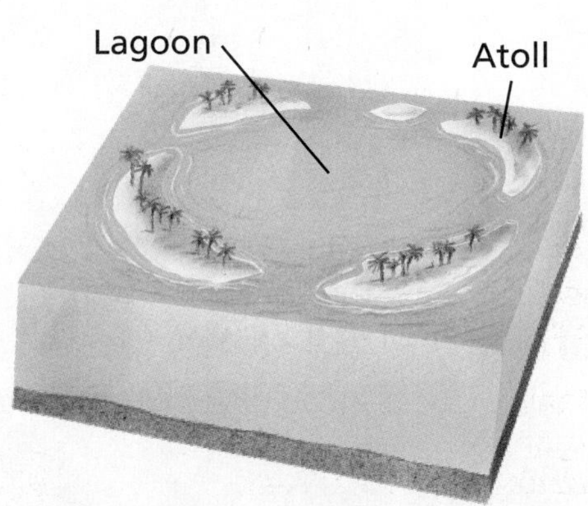


3 Finally, the island sinks, leaving a ring-shaped atoll.

**Environment of Coral Reefs** Microscopic algae live in the bodies of the coral animals and provide food for the corals. The algae need warm temperatures and sunlight. **Therefore, coral reefs can form only in shallow, tropical ocean waters.** The reefs grow above continental shelves or around volcanic islands, where the water is shallow.

**Ring-Shaped Reefs** In areas where the seafloor is sinking, a reef may develop over time into an atoll. An **atoll** is a ring-shaped reef surrounding a shallow lagoon. Figure 9 shows the development of an atoll. It begins as a fringing reef that closely surrounds the edges of the island. As the sea floor sinks, the island sinks with it, and the reef continues to grow upward. Water separates the top of the barrier reef from the island. The island continues to sink until it is entirely underwater, forming the atoll.

**Life Around a Reef** Coral can form a variety of shapes. These shapes are suggested by the names of coral species—elkhorn, brain, plate, star. Many animals live in and around a coral reef. Coral-reef animals include octopuses, spiny lobsters, shrimp, and fishes in all colors and sizes. Parrotfish scrape coral off the reef to eat. The parrotfish grind up the broken coral inside their bodies, producing the fine, soft sand commonly found around the reef.

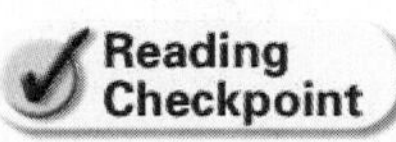


**What is an atoll?**

Clown fish ▼

**FIGURE 10**
**A Kelp Forest**
Kelp are large, heavy algae that grow in parts of the neritic zone. They require cold water and a rocky ocean floor in order to grow well. **Observing** *Why might this group of kelp be called a forest?*

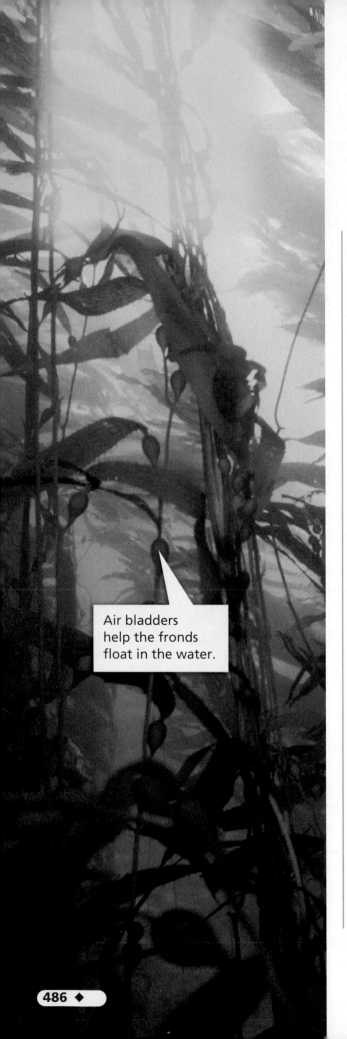

Air bladders help the fronds float in the water.

## Kelp Forests

Below the water's surface, stalks of giant kelp gently sway back and forth. Sunlight filters through the water, producing a greenish light. If you could examine one of the kelp strands close up, you would notice small bulbs at the base of each frond. These bulbs keep the heavy kelp fronds upright in the water.

**Environment of Kelp Forests** Conditions that favor kelp forests exist along the Pacific coast from Alaska to Mexico. **Kelp forests grow in cold neritic waters where the ocean has a rocky floor.** Kelp are large, heavy algae, and they require a solid, rocky bottom to anchor their stalks. A bundle of rootlike strands called a holdfast attaches the algae to the rocks. A stalk of giant kelp can grow to 30 meters in length. The air bladders keep the heavy kelp stalk upright in the water.

**Providing a Habitat** The kelp use the sunlight and dissolved gases in the neritic zone to produce their own food. The kelp also provide a habitat for many other organisms. The curtains of kelp hide young gray whales from predators while their mothers are feeding. Sea slugs and snails live amid the tangle of the holdfasts.

Sea otters play a particularly important role in a kelp forest. In addition to eating abalone, sea otters feed on sea urchins, which eat the kelp. In areas where sea otters have disappeared, armies of sea urchins have devoured the kelp. The once-thriving forest has become a barren rocky zone.

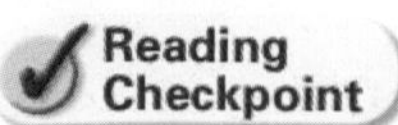

**What keeps kelp upright in water?**

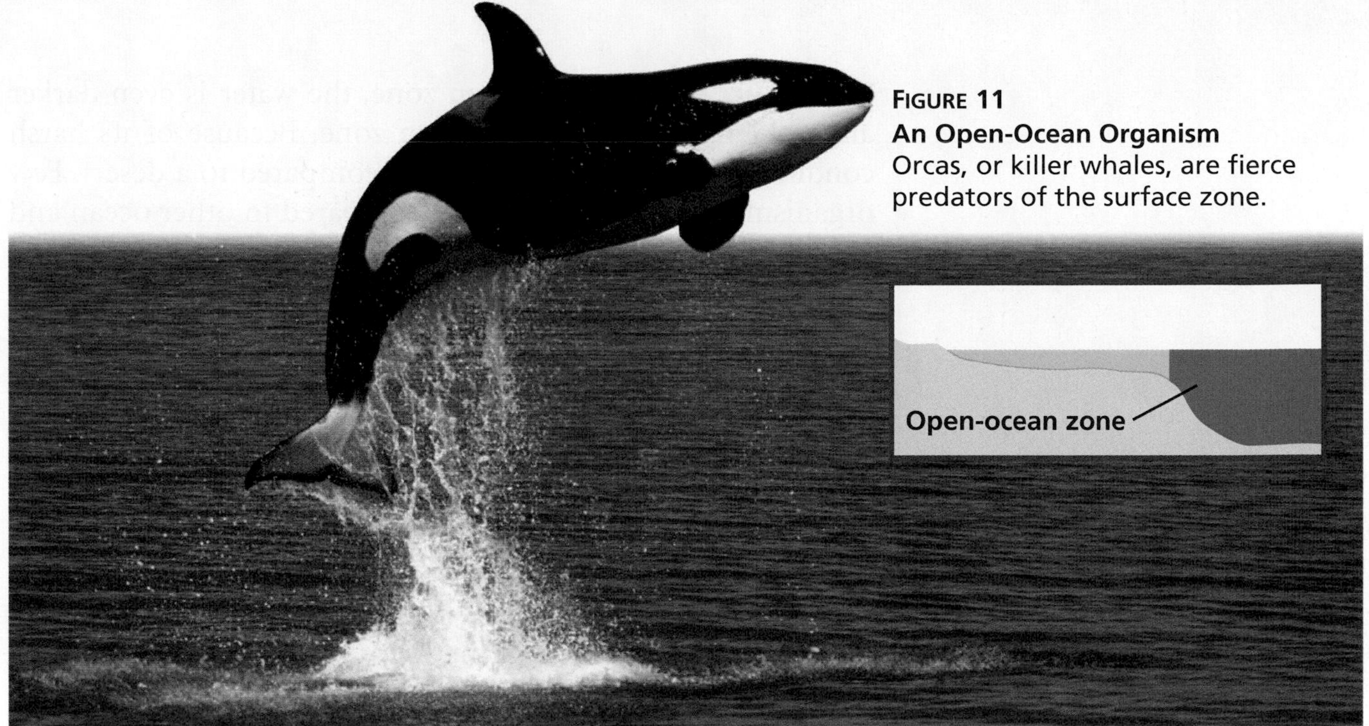


**FIGURE 11**
**An Open-Ocean Organism**
Orcas, or killer whales, are fierce predators of the surface zone.

## Conditions in the Open Ocean

The open ocean begins where the neritic zone ends, at the edge of the continental shelf. **The open ocean differs from the neritic zone in two important ways. First, only a small part of the open ocean receives sunlight. Second, the water has fewer nutrients.** As a result, the open ocean supports fewer organisms.

Diving into the open ocean is like walking down a long staircase that has a light only at the top. Sunlight penetrates only a short distance into the water. If the water is cloudy, sunlight does not reach as far. In clear tropical waters, however, sunlight may reach as deep as a few hundred meters.

Recall that the neritic zone receives a constant supply of nutrients from shore. In contrast, dissolved nutrients are less abundant in the open ocean.

**The Surface Zone** Recall that the water column in the open ocean can be divided into three zones. The surface zone extends as far as sunlight reaches below the surface. The surface zone is the only part of the open ocean that receives enough sunlight to support the growth of algae. These microscopic algae are the base of open-ocean food webs. Animal plankton that feed on the algae include shrimplike krill, as well as the young of crabs, mollusks, and fishes.

**The Transition Zone** The transition zone extends from the bottom of the surface zone to a depth of about 1 kilometer. The water here is darker and colder than in the surface zone.

**Lab zone Skills Activity**

### Inferring

To keep from sinking, many plankton rely on the friction between their bodies and the surrounding water. More friction is needed to stay afloat in warm water than in denser cold water. One of the copepods below is found in tropical ocean waters, while the other is found near the poles. Which do you think is which? Explain your reasoning. (*Hint:* More streamlined shapes create less friction with their surroundings.)

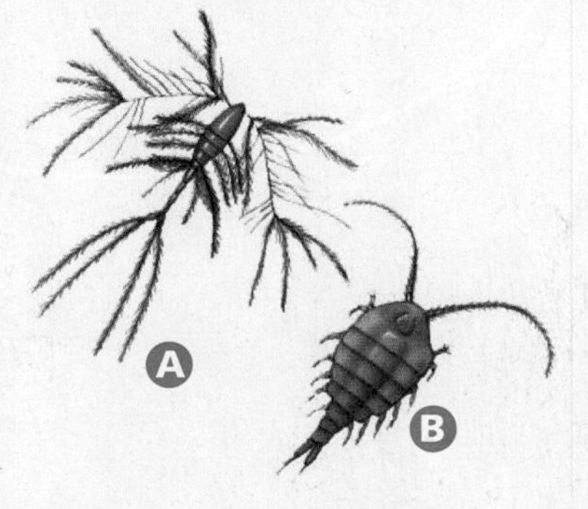

**The Deep Zone** In the deep zone, the water is even darker and colder than in the transition zone. Because of its harsh conditions, the deep ocean is often compared to a desert. Few organisms live in the deep zone, compared to other ocean and land environments. But unlike a desert, which bakes under the bright sun, the deep ocean is cold, dark, and wet.

Finding food in the darkness is a challenge. Many deep-sea fishes produce their own light. The production of light by living things is called **bioluminescence.** Chemical reactions in the cells of organisms produce bioluminescence.

In some cases, light is produced by bioluminescent bacteria that live on the bodies of fishes. In other cases, the chemical reactions take place in the bodies of the fishes, as they do in fireflies on land. For example, tiny light-producing structures are scattered over the surfaces of some fishes. Other fishes, such as the anglerfish, have light-producing organs. The anglerfish has a light organ on its head. The anglerfish lurks in the shadows below the pool of light created by its light organ. Shrimp and fishes that are attracted to the light become prey of the anglerfish.

The food supply in most of the deep ocean is much more limited than in shallower water. Therefore, animals in this zone must be good hunters to survive. The gaping mouths of many deep-sea fishes are filled with fanglike teeth. Rows of sharp teeth stick out at angles, ensuring that any animal it bites cannot escape.

**FIGURE 12**
**Organisms of the Deep Zone**
The angler fish (below) and the deep sea octopus (right) are animals that flourish in the cold and dark of the deep zone.

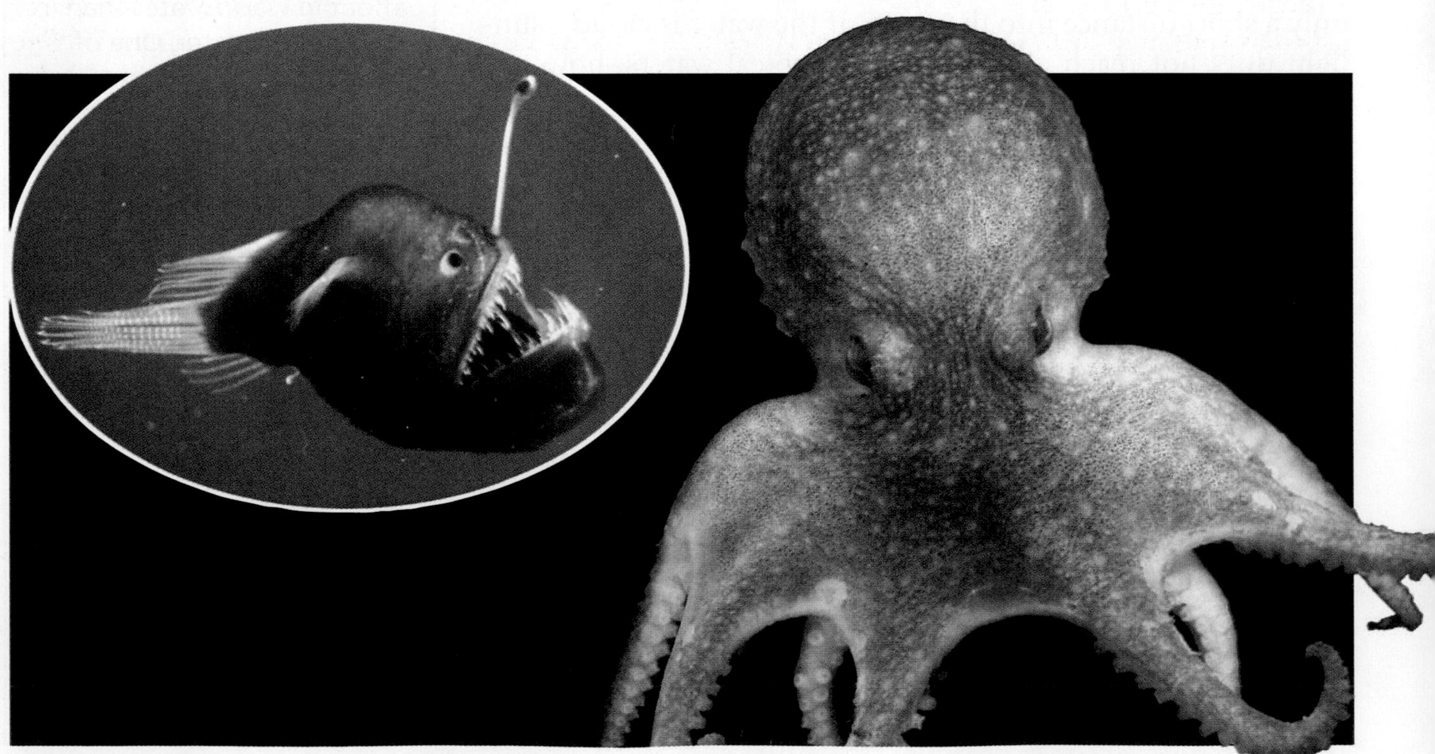

**Hydrothermal Vents** In most parts of the deep zone, food is very scarce. As a result, organisms there tend to be small and slow. However, there is one kind of deep-zone environment—a hydrothermal vent—that supports organisms of an unusual number, variety, and size. At a **hydrothermal vent,** hot water rises out of cracks in the ocean floor and is heated by the underlying magma.

The heated water coming from a vent carries gases and minerals from Earth's interior. Bacteria feed directly on these chemical nutrients. Like the algae in the surface zone that use sunlight to produce food, these bacteria use chemical nutrients to produce food.

These bacteria form the base of the food web at a hydrothermal vent. Other organisms, such as giant clams, feed on the bacteria. Red-tipped tube worms are supplied with food by bacteria living within their tissues. Meanwhile, scuttling crabs feed on the remains of the other inhabitants of their unusual habitat.

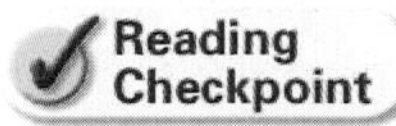

**What is a hydrothermal vent?**

FIGURE 13
**A Hydrothermal Vent**
Giant tube worms and crabs cluster around a hydrothermal vent on the ocean floor.

## Section 2 Assessment

**Target Reading Skill Using Prior Knowledge** Review your graphic organizer and revise it based on what you just learned in the section.

### Reviewing Key Concepts

1. a. **Identifying** Identify the three categories of ocean organisms and describe their characteristics.
   b. **Classifying** Sea cucumbers are small animals that crawl along the ocean floor. To which category of ocean organisms do they belong? Explain.
2. a. **Describing** What are conditions like in the intertidal zone?
   b. **Applying Concepts** How does the behavior of a sea anemone help it survive in the intertidal zone?
3. a. **Describing** Describe the physical conditions in the neritic zone.
   b. **Relating Cause and Effect** Explain how neritic-zone conditions support the growth of plankton.
   c. **Making Generalizations** Why are food webs in the neritic zone especially complex? (*Hint:* What is the role of plankton in food webs?)
4. a. **Reviewing** How do conditions in the open ocean and the neritic zone differ?
   b. **Summarizing** Summarize the conditions that exist around hydrothermal vents.
   c. **Applying Concepts** Are the organisms around a hydrothermal vent typical of deep-zone organisms? Explain.

### Writing in Science

**Editorial** You are a scientist studying a coral reef located near a tropical island. A forest on the island has been cut down. As a result, soil erosion is increasing. Write an editorial for the local newspaper explaining how this could affect the coral reef.

Section 3

# Resources From the Ocean

## Reading Preview

### Key Concepts

- How do people use living resources from the ocean?
- What are some nonliving ocean resources?
- What are the sources of ocean pollution?

### Key Terms

- aquaculture
- nodule

### Target Reading Skill

**Identifying Main Ideas** As you read the Nonliving Resources section, write the main idea—the biggest or most important idea—in a graphic organizer like the one below. Then write three supporting details that give examples of the main idea.

Main Idea

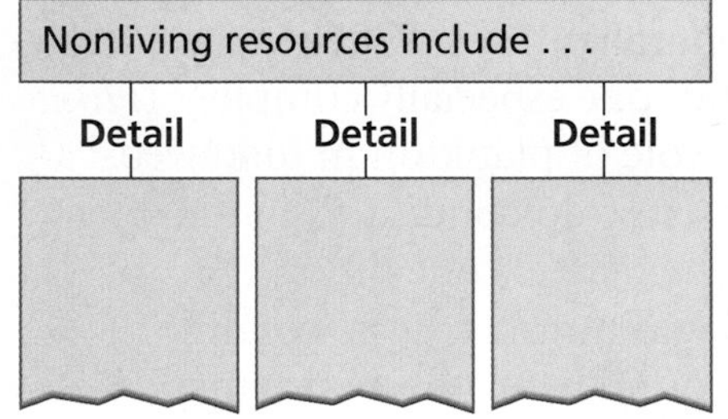


## Lab zone Discover Activity

### Is It From the Ocean?

1. Your teacher will give you some labels from common household products. Read the ingredient information on each label.
2. Divide the products into two piles—those you think include substances that come from the ocean and those that do not.

**Think It Over**

**Classifying** For each product you classified as coming from the ocean, name the ocean resource that is used to produce it. In which ocean zone is it found?

When European explorers began sailing to North America, they were astounded by the huge number of codfish off its eastern coast. Sailors reported that this area was so "swarming with fish that they could be taken not only with a net but in baskets let down and weighted with a stone." Others reported sailing through schools of cod so thick they slowed the boats down!

This cod fishery stretched from Newfoundland to a hook of land appropriately named Cape Cod. For more than 400 years, the seemingly endless supply of "King Cod" supported a thriving fishing industry. But starting in the early 1900s, it became clear that the cod population was decreasing. With the price of cod rising, there was more competition to catch fewer fish. In 1992, the Canadian government closed the fishery.

A cod catch ▶

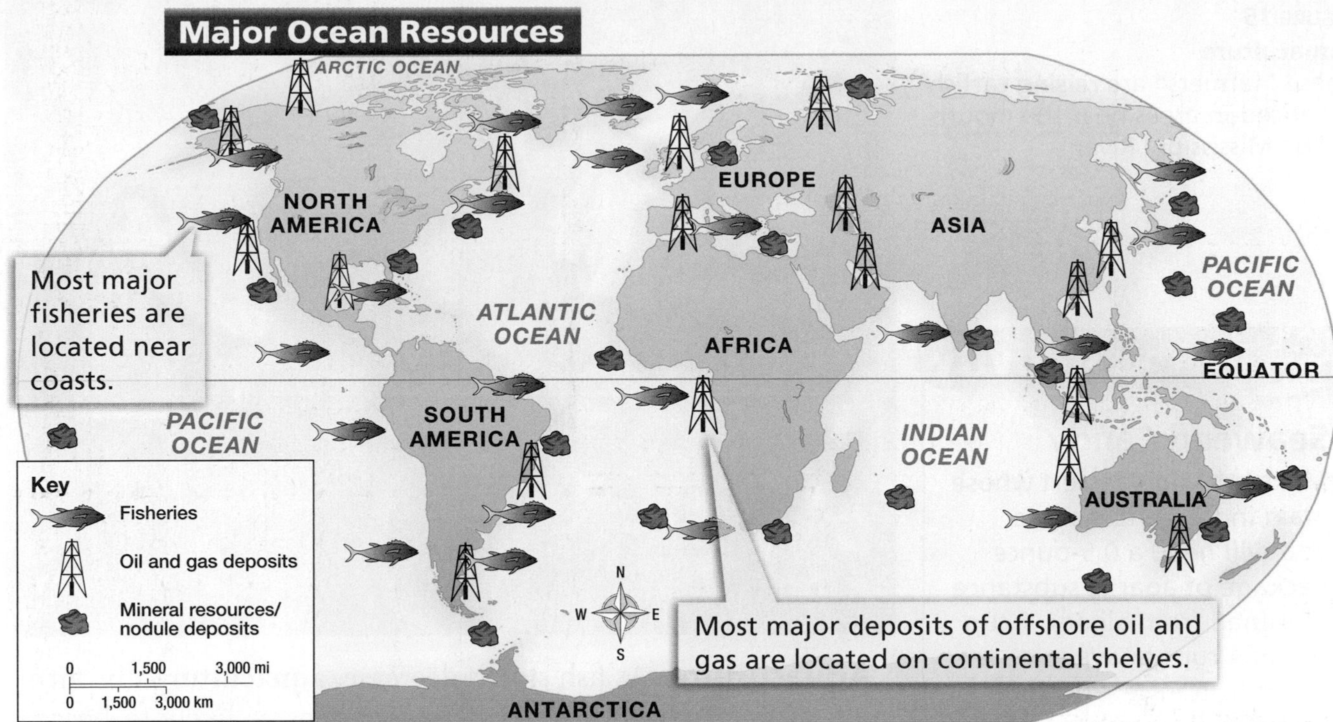


**FIGURE 14**
**Resources From the Ocean**
All over the world, the oceans are an important source of food, oil and gas, and minerals.
**Interpreting Maps** *Where are Africa's major fisheries located?*

## Living Resources

Cod are just one example of a living resource from the ocean. How many other kinds of seafood have you tasted: tuna, shrimp, flounder, lobster, clams, squid, oysters, seaweed, or mussels? **People depend heavily on fishes and other ocean organisms for food. Ocean organisms also provide materials that are used in products such as detergents and paints.**

**Harvesting Fish** Many kinds of fishes are caught to be eaten. Anchovies, pollock, mackerel, herring, and tuna make up most of the worldwide catch. Locate the world's major fisheries in Figure 14. You can see that they are all located close to coasts. Nearly all fishes caught are harvested from coastal waters or areas of upwelling. These waters contain nutrients and plankton on which the fish feed.

If used wisely, fisheries naturally renew themselves each year. New fish are born, replacing those that are caught, but only as long as the fishery is not overfished. Overfishing causes the supply of fish to decrease.

Better technology has enabled people to catch large numbers of fish very quickly. Sometimes the fish can be caught faster than they can reproduce. When fish reproduction decreases, there are fewer and fewer fish each season. Eventually, the fish in the fishery may become very scarce. This is what happened in the cod fishery you read about earlier.

**For:** Links on ocean resources
**Visit:** www.SciLinks.org
**Web Code:** scn-0845

**FIGURE 15**
**Aquaculture**
These "farmers" are raising catfish in fenced-in areas near the mouth of the Mississippi River.

**Lab zone** Try This **Activity**

## Seaweed Candy

Make an Asian dessert whose main ingredient is algae. You will need a 0.5-ounce package of agar (a substance obtained from algae), 1 cup sugar, 4 cups guava juice or other fruit juice, and food coloring. Remember to prepare food only in a nonscience classroom and to get permission before using a stove.

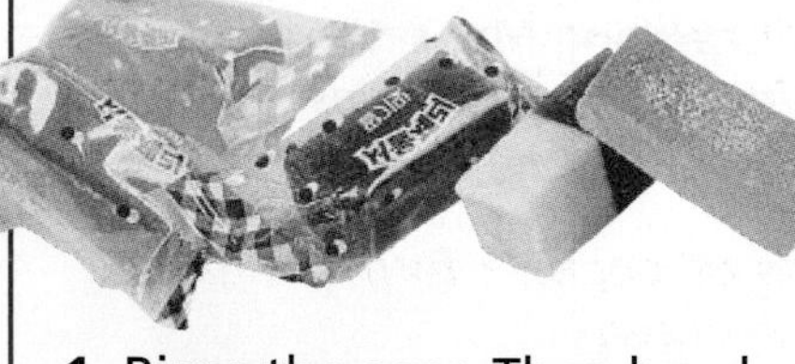

1. Rinse the agar. Then break the agar into cubes and place them in a saucepan.
2. Add the sugar and juice to the pan. Bring the mixture to a boil. Turn down the heat and cook, stirring until the agar dissolves.
3. Remove the pan from the heat and stir in a few drops of food coloring. Pour the mixture into a shallow pan. Let it cool.
4. Refrigerate the candy until it is firm. Cut it into blocks and serve.

**Inferring** What purpose does the agar serve in this recipe?

**Aquaculture** As fish stocks decrease, **aquaculture,** the farming of saltwater and freshwater organisms, is likely to become more common. Aquaculture has been practiced in some Asian countries for centuries.

Aquaculture involves creating an environment for the organisms. To help the organisms thrive, nutrient levels, water temperature, light, and other factors must be controlled. Oysters, abalone, and shrimp have successfully been farmed in artificial saltwater ponds and protected bays. Even landlocked regions can produce seafood using aquaculture. For example, salmon are now being raised in Nebraska fields that once were cattle ranches.

Aquaculture can have drawbacks, of course. For example, many shrimp farms require the clearing of mangrove forests. The United Nations has estimated that shrimp farming has destroyed 25 percent of the world's mangrove forests. But about 25 percent of the world's shrimp are raised on shrimp farms. So the shrimp farming debate will continue.

**Other Ocean Products** People harvest ocean organisms for many purposes besides food. Algae is an ingredient in many household products. Its gelatin-like texture makes it an ideal base for detergents, shampoos, cosmetics, paints, and even ice cream! Sediments containing the hard pieces of diatoms are used for abrasives and polishes. Many researchers believe that other marine organisms may be important sources of chemicals for medicines in the future.

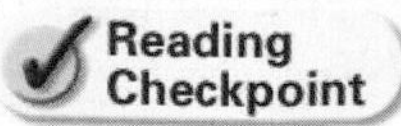

**What is aquaculture?**

## Nonliving Resources

In addition to living organisms, the ocean contains valuable nonliving resources. **Some nonliving ocean resources include water, fuels, and minerals.**

**Water** You have read how fresh water can be extracted from ocean water using desalination. Desalination provides fresh water for many dry areas and islands.

**Fuels** The remains of dead marine organisms are the source of another nonliving resource. The remains sink to the bottom of the ocean, where they are buried by sediments. As more sediments accumulate, the buried remains decompose. Over hundreds of thousands of years, the heat and pressure from the overlying layers gradually transform the organisms' remains into oil and natural gas.

As you know, many organisms live in the part of the ocean above the continental shelf. The thick sediments on the continental shelves bury the remains of living things. As a result, the richest deposits of oil and gas are often located on the continental shelves.

Oil rigs like the one in Figure 16 drill the rocky ocean floor as much as 300 meters below the surface. Imagine trying to dig a hole in the concrete bottom of a swimming pool, while standing on a raft floating on the surface of the water. You can see why drilling the ocean floor is very difficult! Ocean drilling is made even harder by strong currents, winds, and violent storms.

FIGURE 16
**An Oil Rig**
Lit up like a city at night, this Norwegian oil-drilling platform rises above the icy waters of the North Sea. Hundreds of people may live and work on an oil rig.
**Relating Cause and Effect** *How did oil deposits form beneath the ocean?*

**Minerals** Minerals are solid substances that are obtained from the ground and the water. When fresh water is removed from ocean water, the salts that are left behind are a valuable mineral resource. More than half of the world's supply of magnesium, a strong, light metal, is obtained from seawater in this way.

The ocean floor is another source of mineral resources. From the sediments covering the continental shelves, gravel and sand are mined for use in building construction. In some areas of the world, diamonds and gold are mined from sand deposits. Metals such as manganese also accumulate on the ocean floor. The metals concentrate around pieces of shell, forming black lumps called **nodules** (NAHJ oolz). Nodules sometimes occur in waters as deep as 5,000 meters. Therefore, recovering the nodules is a difficult process. The technology to gather them is still being developed.

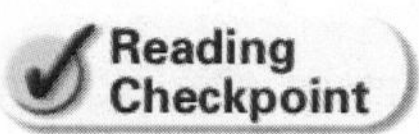


**What minerals are obtained from the oceans?**

## Ocean Pollution

The ocean is a self-cleaning system that can absorb some wastes without permanent damage. But dumping large amounts of wastes into the ocean threatens many marine organisms. Most ocean pollution comes from the land. **Although some ocean pollution is the result of natural occurrences, most pollution is related to human activities.**

### Math Analyzing Data

### Ocean Oil Pollution

The bar graph shows the main sources of oil pollution in the ocean. The source *Natural Seeps* refers to the natural process by which oil leaks out of oil deposits in the oceans. Study the graph, and then answer the following questions.

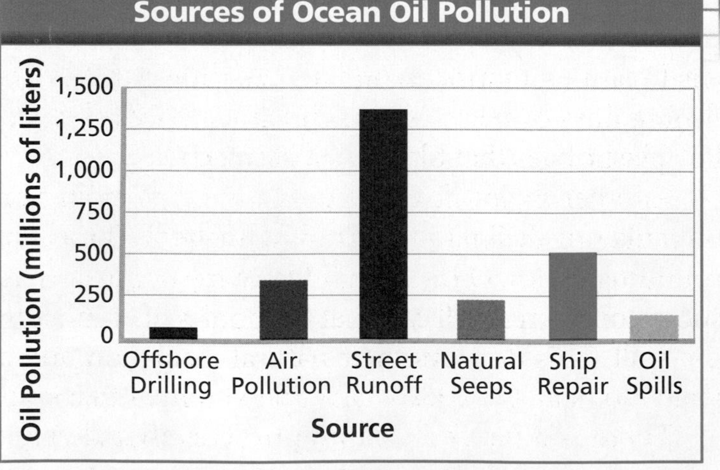


1. **Reading Graphs** How many sources of ocean oil pollution are shown on the graph?
2. **Interpreting Data** Which source causes the most oil pollution? The least?
3. **Classifying** Classify each source of oil pollution as either a natural cause or one that is caused by human actions.
4. **Problem Solving** Which source or sources of ocean oil pollution could you personally reduce? What actions could you take to reduce the sources?

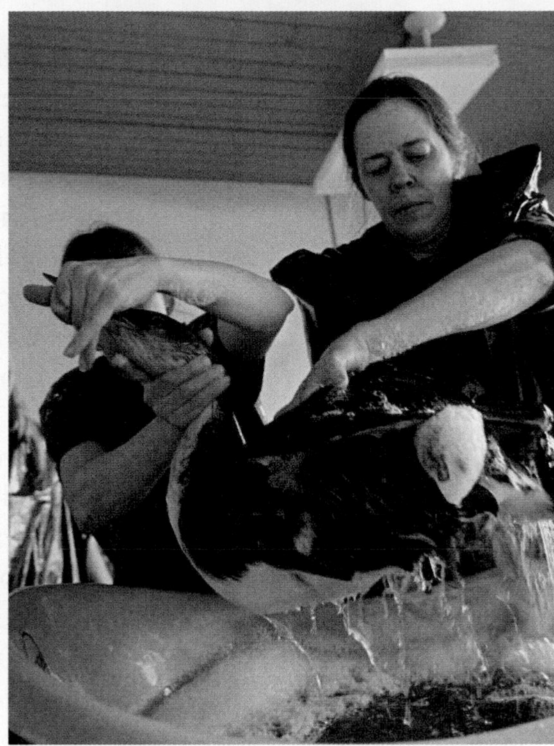

**FIGURE 17**
**Cleaning Up Oil**
This cleanup worker is using absorbent mops to remove oil from the sand (left). On the right, two workers try to clean oil from a bird's beak and feathers.
**Inferring** *What might have caused this oil pollution?*

**Natural Occurrences** Some pollution is the result of weather. For example, heavy rains wash fresh water into estuaries and out into the water offshore. This surge of fresh water pollutes the ocean by lowering its salinity. A sudden change in salinity may kill ocean animals that are unable to adjust to it.

**Human Activities** Sewage, chemicals, and trash dumped into coastal waters all come from human sources. Substances that run off fields and roads often end up in the ocean. These substances can harm ocean organisms directly. The pollutants can also build up in the organisms' bodies and poison other animals, including people, that feed on them. Trash can cause serious problems, too. Air-breathing marine mammals can drown if they get tangled in fishing lines or nets. Other animals are harmed when they swallow plastic bags that block their stomachs.

Another major threat to ocean life is oil pollution. When an oil tanker or drilling platform is damaged, oil leaks into the surrounding ocean. Oil is harmful to many organisms. As Figure 17 shows, oil from a spill can coat the bodies of animals that live near the spill. This destroys their natural insulation and affects their ability to float. Oil is also harmful to animals that swallow it.

There is a natural cleaning process that slowly takes place after oil spills. Certain bacteria that live in the ocean feed on the oil and multiply. It takes many years, but these bacteria can eventually clean an oil-covered beach. Of course, oil can cause much damage to an area in that time, so people often help to clean up large spills.

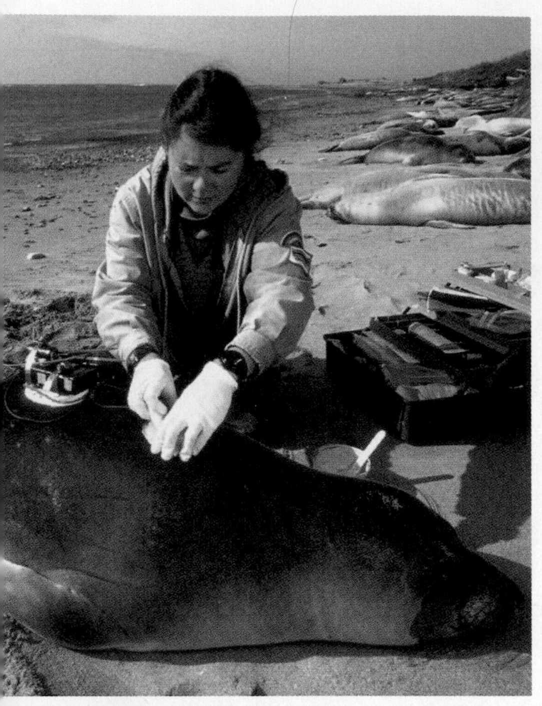

FIGURE 18
**A Marine Refuge**
This scientist is tagging an elephant seal in a marine refuge in California. Scientists will then be able to monitor the seal's travels.

**Protecting Earth's Oceans** Who owns the ocean and its resources? Who has the responsibility of protecting them? These are questions that nations have been struggling to answer for hundreds of years. Because the world ocean is a continuous body of water that has no boundaries, it is difficult to determine who, if anyone, should control portions of it. Nations must cooperate to manage and protect the oceans.

The United Nations has established different boundaries in the oceans. According to one treaty, a nation now controls the first 22 kilometers out from its coasts. The nation also controls the resources in the waters or on the continental shelf within 370 kilometers of shore. This treaty leaves approximately half of the ocean's surface waters as "high seas," owned by no nation. Ownership of the ocean floor beneath the high seas is still under debate.

Other international efforts have resulted in cooperation aimed at reducing ocean pollution. Examples include the establishment of marine refuges and regulations for building safer oil tankers.

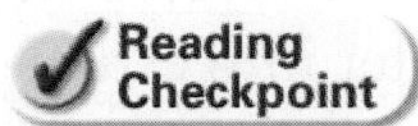


**Why is it difficult to determine who controls ocean resources?**

## Section 3 Assessment

**Target Reading Skill Identifying Main Ideas** Use your graphic organizer about Nonliving Resources to help you answer Question 2 below.

### Reviewing Key Concepts

1. a. **Reviewing** What are two ways in which people use ocean organisms?
   b. **Summarizing** What is aquaculture? What problem does it help address?
2. a. **Listing** List three nonliving ocean resources.
   b. **Describing** How is oil obtained from the ocean floor?
   c. **Inferring** Oil deposits are found beneath dry land as well the ocean. From which location—ocean or dry land—is it more difficult to obtain oil? Explain your answer.
3. a. **Reviewing** Identify one natural occurrence and three human activities that can pollute the oceans.
   b. **Explaining** Explain why one nation by itself cannot control ocean pollution.
   c. **Making Judgments** Should mineral resources on the ocean floor belong to whomever finds them, or to the closest nation? Consider each position and write a short paragraph stating your opinion.

### Lab zone At-Home Activity

**Modeling Ocean Pollution** Have a family member hook one end of a rubber band around his or her wrist. Stretch the rubber band across the back of the hand and hook the free end over three fingers as shown. Now ask the person to try to remove the rubber band without using the other hand. Explain that this shows how difficult it is for seals or dolphins to free themselves from a plastic beverage ring or piece of net. Can you propose any ways to reduce this threat to marine mammals?

Lab zone **Skills Lab**

# Cleaning Up an Oil Spill

## Problem

How can an oil spill be cleaned up?

## Skills Focus

making models, observing

## Materials

- water
- feather
- marking pen
- shallow pan
- paper towels
- paper cup
- cotton balls
- vegetable oil
- plastic dropper
- wooden sticks
- graduated cylinder, 100-mL

## Procedure    

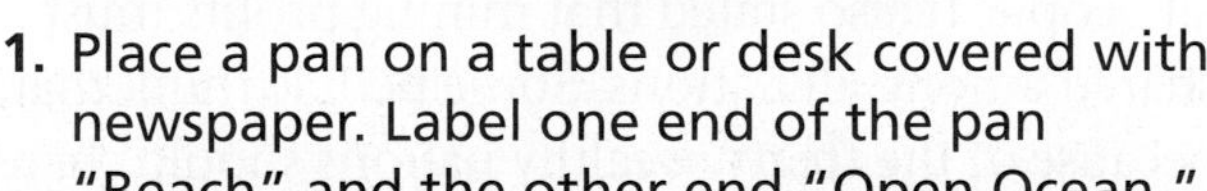

1. Place a pan on a table or desk covered with newspaper. Label one end of the pan "Beach" and the other end "Open Ocean."
2. Pour water into the pan to a depth of 2 cm.
3. Gently pour 20 mL of vegetable oil into the center of the pan. Record your observations.
4. Dip a feather and your finger into the oil. Observe how each is affected by the oil.
5. Try to wipe oil off the feather and your finger using cotton balls or paper towels. Record whether any oil is left on the feather or your skin.
6. Now try to clean up the spill. First, using the wooden sticks, try to keep the oil from reaching the "beach." Next, gently blow across the surface of the water from the "open ocean" side to simulate wind and waves. Then use the cotton balls, paper towels, and dropper to recover as much of the oil as possible. Record your observations with each step.
7. When you are finished, dispose of the oil and used items in the paper cup. Wash your hands.

## Analyze and Conclude

1. **Observing** How successful were you in cleaning up the oil? Did the water end up as clean as it was at the start?
2. **Making Models** How well were you able to keep the oil from reaching the beach? How does this activity model the problems that actual cleanup workers encounter?
3. **Inferring** Describe what happened when you cleaned the feather and your finger. What might happen to fish, birds, and other animals if they were coated with oil as a result of an oil spill?
4. **Predicting** Predict how storms with strong winds and waves would affect the cleanup of an oil spill.
5. **Communicating** Look at the used cleanup materials in the paper cup. What additional problems does this suggest for cleanup crews? Write instructions for procedures that cleanup crews might follow to deal with these problems.

## More to Explore

One way to reduce the threat of oil spills is to transport less oil across the oceans. To make that possible, people would need to use less oil in their daily lives. Use reference materials or the Internet to find tips on oil conservation. Then list at least three ways to reduce the amount of oil you and your family use.

Science and
**Society**

# Who Owns the Ocean's Minerals?

Rich mineral deposits lie on and just beneath the ocean floor. Coastal nations have the right to mine deposits near their shores. Today, they are mining minerals from the continental shelf. But mineral deposits on the ocean floor beyond are open for all nations. Who owns these valuable underwater minerals?

## The Issues

### Who Can Afford to Mine?

Mining the ocean floor will cost a huge amount of money. New technologies must be developed to obtain mineral deposits from the ocean floor. Only wealthy industrial nations will be able to afford the costs. Industrial nations that have spent money on mining think that they should keep the profits. But developing nations that lack money and technology and landlocked nations disagree.

### What Rights Do Nations Have?

By 2003, 157 nations had signed the Law of the Sea treaty. Among other things, this treaty stated that ocean mineral deposits are the common property of all people. It also stated that mining profits must be shared among all nations. Some people think that, because of the treaty, wealthy nations should share their technology and any profits they get from mining the ocean floor.

### Ocean-Floor Mining

Mining on the continental shelf is relatively easy. New technologies will be needed to mine the deep ocean beyond.

**Continental Shelf**
Diamonds are found near the shores of southwest Africa.

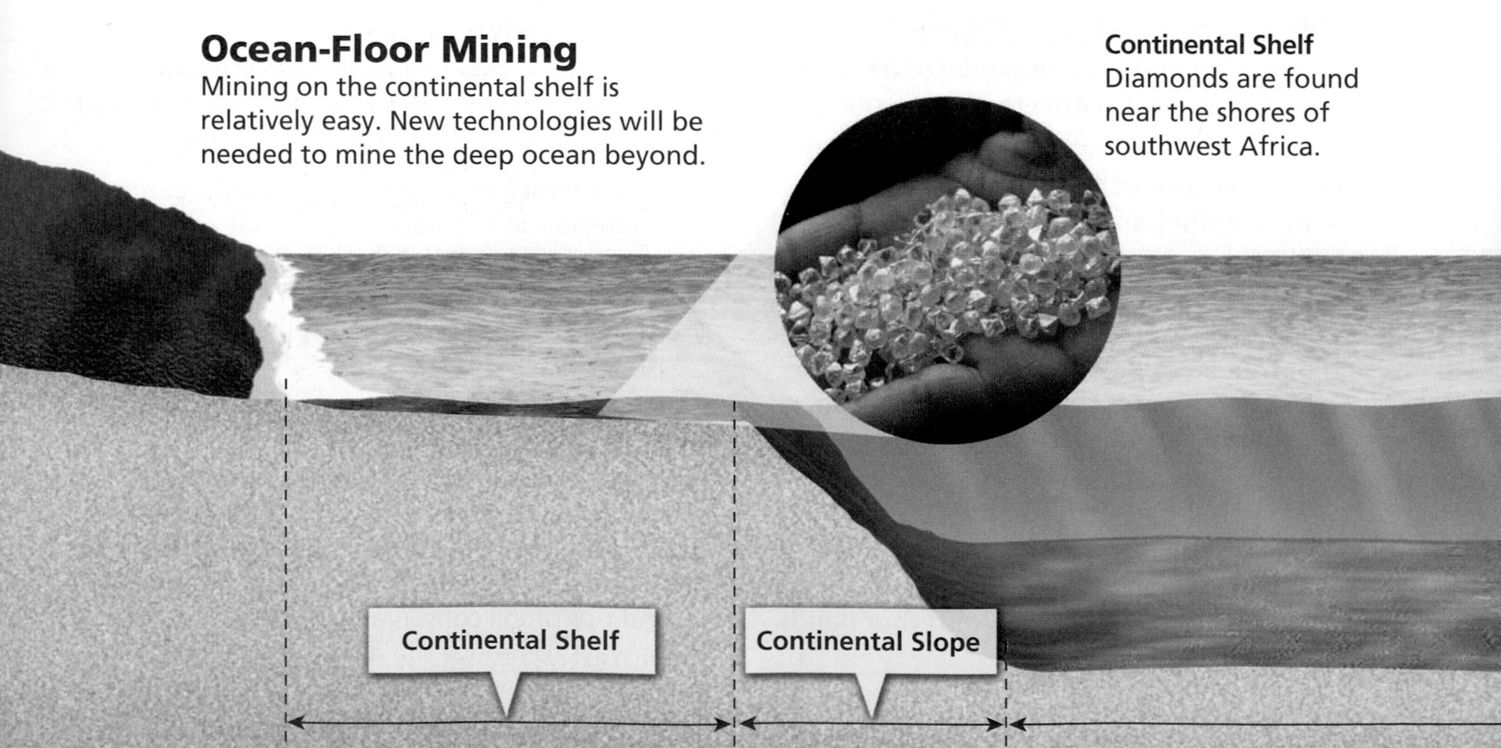

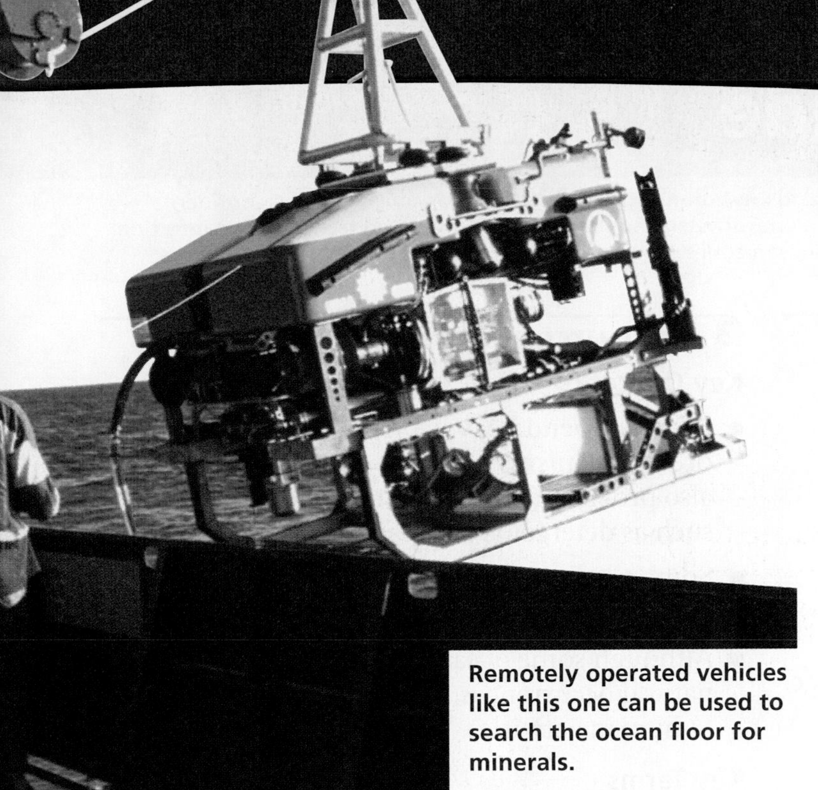

Remotely operated vehicles like this one can be used to search the ocean floor for minerals.

## How Can the Wealth Be Shared?

What can nations do to prevent conflict over mining the ocean floor? They might arrange a compromise. Perhaps wealthy nations should contribute part of their profits to help developing or landlocked nations. Developing nations could pool their money for ocean-floor mining. Whatever nations decide, some regulations for ocean-floor mining are necessary. In the future, these resources will be important to everyone.

## What Would You Do?

**1. Identify the Problem**
Summarize the controversy about ocean mineral rights.

**2. Analyze the Options**
Research this topic at the library or on the Internet. Then compare the concerns of wealthy nations with those of developing nations. How could you reassure developing nations that they will not be left out?

**3. Find a Solution**
Look at a map of the world. Who should share the mineral profits from the Pacific Ocean? From the Atlantic Ocean? Write one or two paragraphs stating your opinion. Support your ideas with facts.

**For:** More on who owns the ocean's minerals
**Visit:** PHSchool.com
**Web Code:** cfh-1040

**Abyssal Plain**
Minerals called manganese nodules form on the deep ocean floor. The metals cobalt, iron, nickel, and copper are also found here.

**Mid-Ocean Ridge**
Rich mineral deposits form from hot water solutions near mid-ocean ridges. Mining for gold, silver, copper, and other minerals might be possible here.

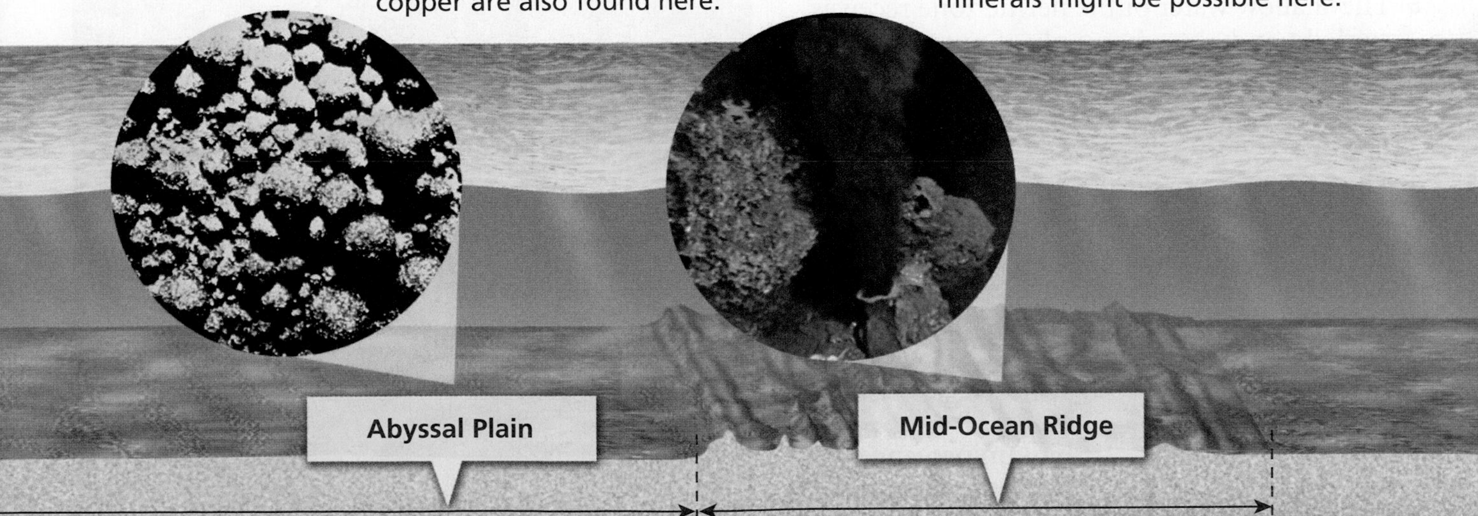

# Chapter 14 Study Guide

**The BIG Idea**

**Ocean Structure and Environments** The ocean floor consists of the continental shelf, continental slope, abyssal plain, mid-ocean ridges, and trenches. The intertidal, neritic, and open-ocean zones provide habitats for communities of living things.

## 1 Exploring the Ocean

### Key Concepts

- People have studied the ocean since ancient times, because the ocean provides food and serves as a route for trade and travel. Modern scientists have studied the characteristics of the ocean's waters and the ocean floor.
- If you could travel along the ocean floor, you would see the continental shelf, the continental slope, the abyssal plain, and the mid-ocean ridge.
- Ocean zones include the intertidal zone, the neritic zone, and the open-ocean zone.

### Key Terms

sonar
continental shelf
continental slope
abyssal plain
mid-ocean ridge
trench
intertidal zone
neritic zone
open-ocean zone

## 2 Ocean Habitats

### Key Concepts

- Scientists classify marine organisms according to where they live and how they move.
- Organisms that live in the intertidal zones must be able to tolerate changes in both the salinity and temperature of the water, as well as periods of being underwater and periods of being exposed to the air.
- The shallow water of the neritic zone receives sunlight and a steady supply of nutrients from the land. Coral reefs can form only in shallow, tropical ocean water. Kelp forests grow in cold neritic waters.
- The open ocean differs from the neritic zone in two important ways. First, only a small part of the open ocean receives sunlight. Second, the water has fewer nutrients.

### Key Terms

plankton
nekton
benthos
food web
estuary
atoll
bioluminescence
hydrothermal vent

## 3 Resources From the Ocean

### Key Concepts

- People depend heavily on fishes and other ocean organisms for food. Ocean organisms also provide materials that are used in products such as detergents and paints.
- Some nonliving ocean resources include water, fuels, and minerals.
- Although some ocean pollution is the result of natural occurrences, most pollution is related to human activities.

### Key Terms

aquaculture
nodule

# Review and Assessment

For: Self-Assessment
Visit: PHSchool.com
Web Code: cja-3140

## Organizing Information

**Comparing and Contrasting** Copy the table about ocean habitats onto a separate sheet of paper. Then complete it and add a title. (For more on Comparing and Contrasting, see the Skills Handbook.)

| Habitat | Zone | Conditions | Organisms |
|---|---|---|---|
| Tide pool | Intertidal | a. ___?___ | b. ___?___ |
| Coral reef | c. ___?___ | d. ___?___ | Coral, fishes, shrimp, eels |
| Surface zone | Open ocean | e. ___?___ | f. ___?___ |
| Hydrothermal vent | g. ___?___ | High pressure, dark, warm | h. ___?___ |

## Reviewing Key Terms

**Choose the letter of the best answer.**

1. A smooth, nearly flat region of the ocean floor is called a(n)
   **a.** trench.
   **b.** mid-ocean ridge.
   **c.** abyssal plain.
   **d.** seamount.
2. Free-swimming animals that can move throughout the water column are called
   **a.** plankton.
   **b.** benthos.
   **c.** coral.
   **d.** nekton.
3. An area where rivers flow into the ocean and fresh water and salt water mix is a(n)
   **a.** tide pool.
   **b.** hydrothermal vent.
   **c.** estuary.
   **d.** kelp forest.
4. Hydrothermal vents are located
   **a.** in coral reefs.
   **b.** in the intertidal zone.
   **c.** in kelp forests.
   **d.** in the deep zone.
5. Nodules consist of
   **a.** metals.
   **b.** algae.
   **c.** sediments.
   **d.** chemical nutrients.

**If the statement is true, write *true*. If it is false, change the underlined word or words to make the statement true.**

6. The steep edge of the continental shelf is called the <u>abyssal plain</u>.
7. The area between the high- and low-tide lines is the <u>neritic zone.</u>
8. An <u>estuary</u> is a coastal inlet or bay where fresh water mixes with salt water.
9. Many deep-sea fishes use their <u>bioluminescence</u> to attract prey.
10. <u>Aquaculture</u> is the farming of saltwater and freshwater organisms.

## Writing in Science

**Firsthand Account** Suppose you were going to travel to the deepest part of the ocean floor in a submersible. Write about your journey, describing each feature of the ocean floor that you see along the way.

# Review and Assessment

## Checking Concepts

**11.** Why do scientists use indirect methods to study the ocean floor?

**12.** What is a seamount?

**13.** Describe a typical ocean food web.

**14.** Describe three physical factors that organisms in the intertidal zone must overcome.

**15.** Explain why estuaries are especially vulnerable to pollution.

**16.** What is an atoll? How is it formed?

**17.** Explain why scientists were surprised to discover the variety of organisms living around hydrothermal vents.

## Thinking Critically

**18. Drawing Conclusions** Mauna Kea projects about 4,200 meters above sea level. Its base is on the floor of the Pacific Ocean, about 6,000 meters below sea level. Mt. Everest rises 8,850 meters from base to summit. Its base is located on land. Which mountain is taller: Mauna Kea or Mt. Everest?

**19. Classifying** Classify the organisms in each photo below as plankton, nekton, or benthos.

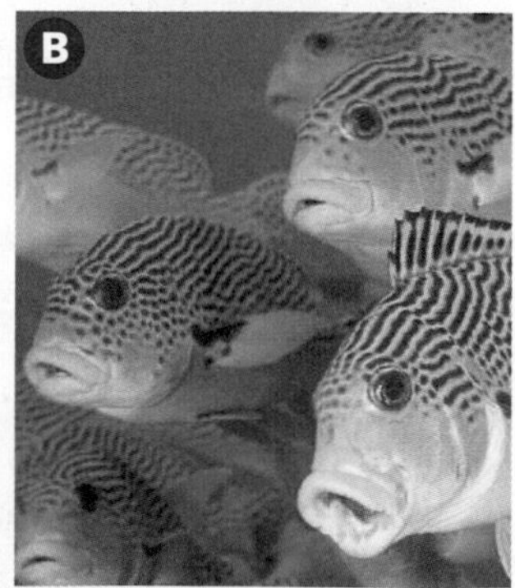


**20. Making Generalizations** Explain why many of the world's fisheries are located in the neritic zone.

**21. Relating Cause and Effect** How might fertilizers used on farmland result in ocean pollution near shore?

## Applying Skills

**Use the diagram of a portion of the ocean floor to answer Questions 22–25.**

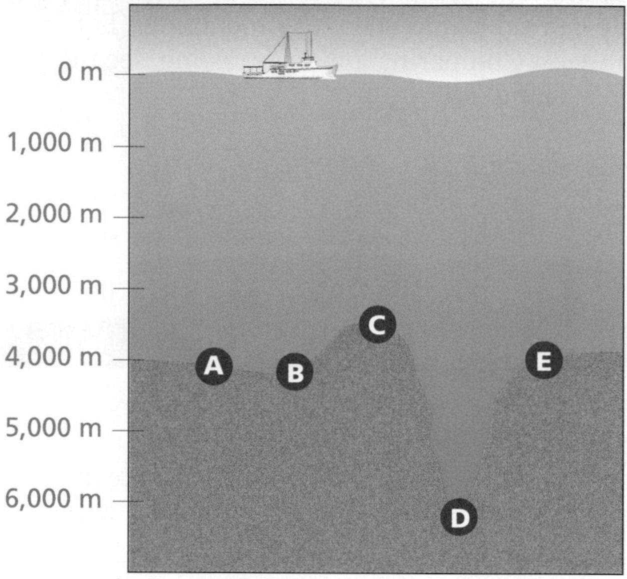


**22. Interpreting Diagrams** What is the approximate depth of the ocean floor at point A? At point C?

**23. Inferring** What might the feature between locations A and B be?

**24. Describing** What would you expect the physical conditions at point D to be like?

**25. Interpreting Diagrams** What is the approximate depth of the feature at point D? What might this feature be?

## Lab zone Chapter Project

**Performance Assessment** Prepare a guided tour of your marine environment. First, rehearse the tour with your group. As you rehearse, check to see that your marine environment is complete. Make any final changes now. Then take your classmates through your tour.

# Standardized Test Prep

**Test-Taking Tip**

**Choosing Among Similar Answers**

Sometimes two or more answer choices appear similar or closely related. You must read the question and all the answer choices carefully in order to select the correct answer.

***Sample Question***

What is the shallow, gently sloping area of the ocean floor that extends outward from the shoreline?

**A** the abyssal plain
**B** the continental shelf
**C** the continental slope
**D** the mid-ocean ridge

***Answer***

The correct answer is B. If you read the answer choices quickly, choices B and C might appear similar. However, the continental slope, answer choice C, does not extend from the shoreline, it is not a shallow area, and it has a steeper slope than the continental shelf.

**Choose the letter of the best answer.**

**1.** In which category of ocean organisms do sharks, tuna, killer whales, and squid belong?
**A** plankton
**B** nekton
**C** benthos
**D** none of the above

**2.** Use your knowledge of ocean zones to infer which adaptation would be most important for organisms in the intertidal zone.
**F** the ability to use bioluminescence
**G** the ability to withstand high pressures
**H** the ability to use chemical nutrients in the water
**J** the ability to withstand periods underwater and periods exposed to the air

*Use the diagram below and your knowledge of science to answer Questions 3–4.*

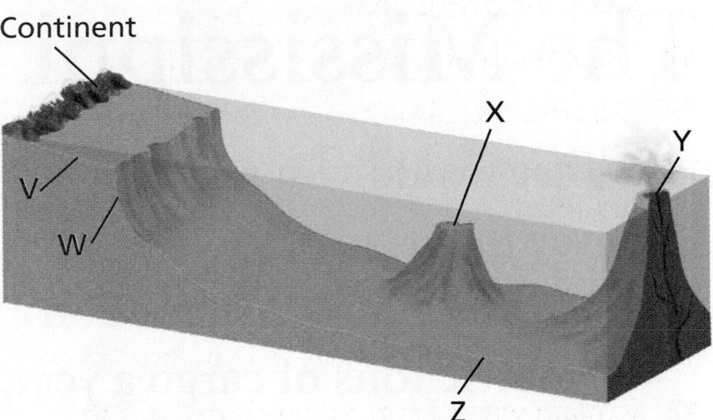


**3.** What is the feature labeled X on the diagram above?
**A** seamount
**B** abyssal plain
**C** mid-ocean ridge
**D** continental slope

**4.** In which part of the diagram would the greatest variety of organisms be found?
**F** part V
**G** part W
**H** part X
**J** part Z

**5.** If you were constructing a model of an estuary, which of the following elements would be the most important?
**A** the depth of water to which sunlight can penetrate
**B** the water temperature
**C** the mix of fresh water and salt water
**D** the presence of hydrothermal vents

**Constructed Response**

**6.** The coral reef ecosystem has a higher diversity of organisms than any other ecosystem. Explain the conditions necessary for coral reefs to form. Include in your explanation the relationship between coral and algae. Predict whether a coral reef would be likely to form near the mouth of a major river. Explain why or why not.

Interdisciplinary **Exploration**

# The Mississippi

## What would you name a river that—

- carries about 420 million metric tons of cargo a year,
- drains 31 states and 2 Canadian provinces,
- flows at about 18,100 cubic meters of water per second?

Native Americans called the river *misi sipi*, an Algonquin name meaning "big water," or "father of waters."

You might have traveled on a river or lake that feeds into the mighty Mississippi but never realized it. The map below shows the watershed of this great river. From the west, the Missouri River—the "Big Muddy"—carries soft silt eroded from the Great Plains. The Missouri joins the Mississippi near St. Louis, turning the river's clear water to muddy brown. From the east, the Ohio River flows in from the rocky Appalachian plateau, nearly doubling the volume of water in the river. In all, the huge Mississippi watershed drains about 40 percent of the United States.

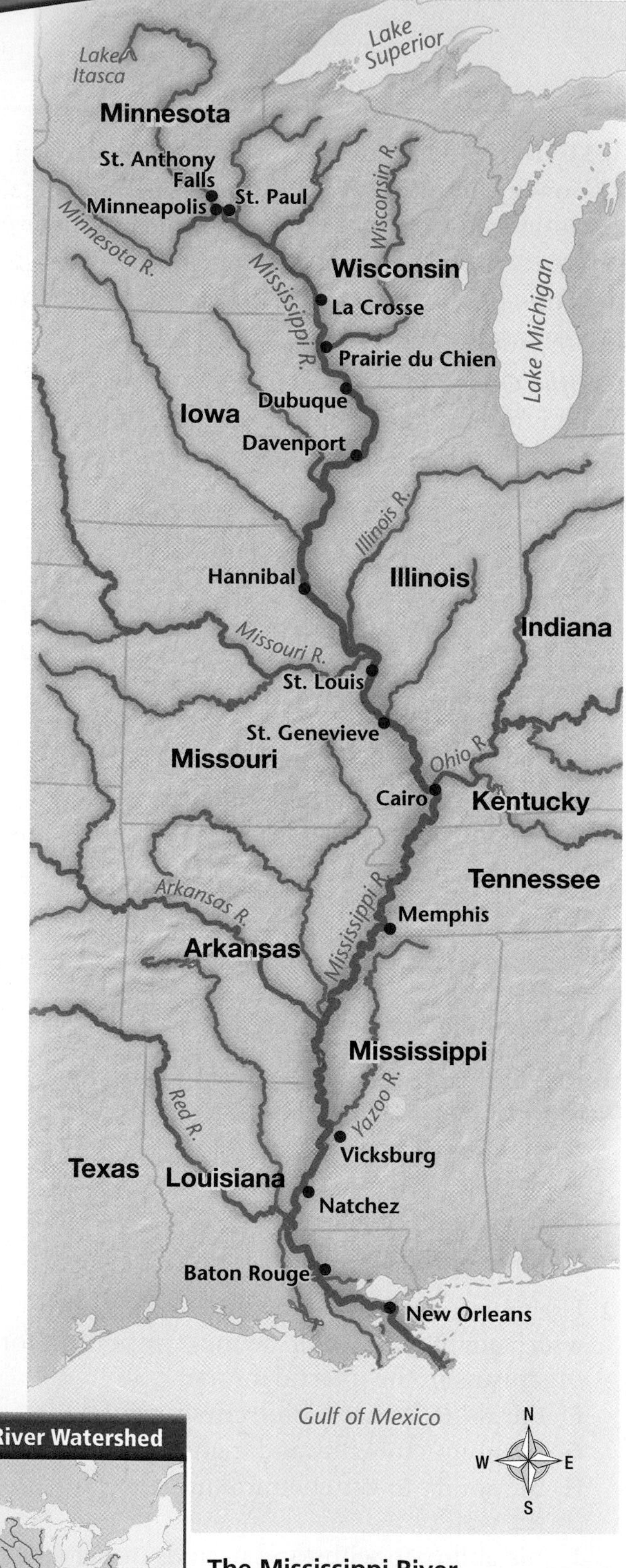


**The Mississippi River Watershed**

**The Mississippi River**
The Mississippi starts at Lake Itasca and flows through 10 states to the Gulf of Mexico. The river is a drainage point for hundreds of tributaries in the Mississippi watershed.

## A National Trade Route

Since Native Americans settled in villages along the Mississippi around 1,200 years ago, the river has served as a water highway for trade and travel.

In the late 1600s, French explorers, fur traders, and soldiers arrived in the Mississippi Valley. They chose strategic sites for forts and fur-trading posts —Prairie du Chien, St. Louis, and St. Genevieve. At first, traders used canoes, rafts, and flatboats to carry goods downstream. But traveling up the river was difficult. Crews had to use long poles to push narrow keelboats upstream against the current.

In 1811, the arrival of *The New Orleans,* the first steamboat on the Mississippi River, changed the river forever. Within 40 years, there were hundreds more steamboats and many new river towns. On the upper Mississippi, the city of Minneapolis grew up around flour mills near St. Anthony Falls. Farther downstream, Memphis became a center for transporting cotton. Later, it was a stopping point for showboats and musicians. New Orleans quickly became a world port. It received cotton, tobacco, and sugar cane from southern plantations and exported corn, wheat, and indigo to Europe. Imported luxury items, such as soap, coffee, shoes, and textiles, traveled upstream from the port of New Orleans. Up and down the river townspeople eagerly waited for the cry, "Steamboat comin'!"

**Flatboats**
Flatboat crews rode the river currents, steering with long oars.

**New Orleans**
The city has been a major trading port since its founding in 1718.

**The Mississippi River in Minnesota**

### Social Studies Activity

Research a city on the Mississippi River. Imagine that you are an early settler there. Write a letter to convince relatives to move to your city. Before writing, research the city's history by finding the answers to these questions:

- Who founded the city? When was it founded? Why did settlers move there? Where did they come from?
- What part did the Mississippi River play in the city's founding?
- What other physical features were important to the city?
- Where did the city's name come from?
- What products were grown, bought, or sold there?

## Taming the River

Navigating the sandbars, shallow water, and rocky rapids on the upper Mississippi River was treacherous in the 1800s. To make traveling easier, engineers in the early 1900s built a "water staircase," a series of 29 locks and dams between Minneapolis, Minnesota, and Alton, Illinois, above St. Louis.

A lock is an enclosed basin, with gates at each end. Locks allow engineers to raise or lower the water level in a certain area of the river. Between the locks on the upper Mississippi, the river forms wide pools of quiet water, maintaining a channel deep enough for large boats. Use the diagrams to trace how a boat "locks through" as it travels upstream.

### 1 The lock gate opens.

Your boat moves in and you tie up to the wall.

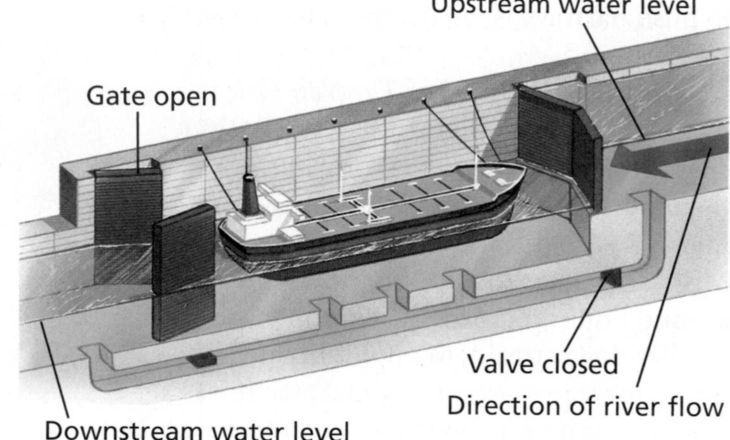


### 2 The gate closes, and water pours in.

As water fills the lock—like a bathtub filling—it lifts the boat a meter or more. When the water in the lock is even with the water level upstream, the gates at the upstream end open. You untie your boat and move out into the river.

If you were going downstream, you would "lock through" in reverse. The water would empty out of the lock, lowering the water level to match the level downstream.

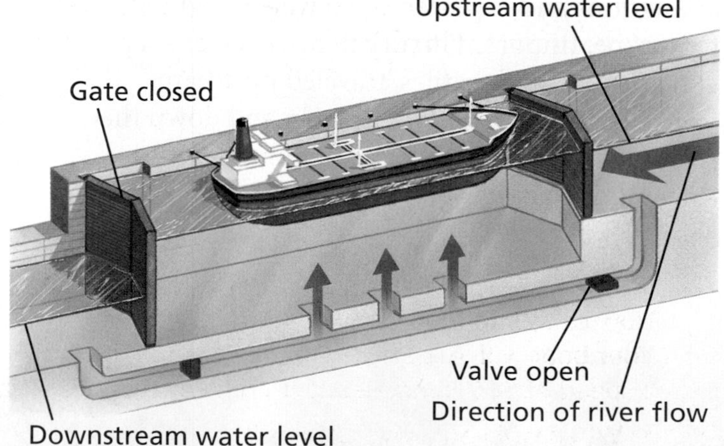


## Science Activity

Use a cardboard milk container to build a working model of a lock. Set up your lock following the illustration. Then demonstrate how your lock works, using a cork or pen cap as your ship and sailing it through the lock.

Cut-out side view

## All Aboard

The whistle blows. The gleaming white steamboat pulls away from the dock just below Fort Snelling, Minnesota. You head downstream toward New Orleans. As you watch the paddlewheel splashing in the water, you think of the old-time steamboats that traveled the Mississippi River in the 1800s.

Today you are cruising at a speed of 11.3 kilometers per hour. You want to stay awake until you enter Lock 3 at Red Wing, Minnesota. It's 4:30 P.M. on Monday now. You know that it's about 78.8 kilometers to Red Wing. It should take about 7 hours to reach the lock. So you'll be there at 11:30 P.M. and through the lock by midnight.

As your boat travels along the river, it will follow the schedule you see below. You will arrive in Mark Twain's hometown of Hannibal, Missouri, on Friday.

Look at the Upper Mississippi River schedule to answer the questions below. Distances are given from Fort Snelling.

- What is your average speed between Dubuque and Hannibal? Use the following equation:

$$\text{Speed} = \frac{\text{Distance}}{\text{Time}}$$

  Round to the nearest tenth.
- How long will you spend in Prairie du Chien?
- About how long does it take to travel from Prairie du Chien to Dubuque?

**Upper Mississippi Riverboat Schedule** May–Sept.

| Port | Arrival Time | Departure Time | Distance From Fort Snelling |
|---|---|---|---|
| Fort Snelling, MN | | 4:30 P.M. Mon. | 0 km |
| Lock 3, Red Wing, MN | 11:30 P.M. Mon. | 12:00 midnight | 78.8 km |
| Prairie du Chien, WI | 11:00 P.M. Tues. | 10:30 A.M. Wed. | 337.8 km |
| Dubuque, IA | 6:30 P.M. Wed. | 7:00 P.M. Wed. | 426.3 km |
| Hannibal, MO | 1:00 A.M. Fri. | ______ | 863.9 km |

### Math Activity

Now complete the riverboat schedule for the Lower Mississippi. Your boat will leave Hannibal at 6 P.M. Friday and will travel at a speed of 14.7 kilometers per hour for the rest of the journey.

- When will you arrive at Lock 26?
- You spend 34 minutes in the lock. When will you depart from Lock 26? Your boat travels on. When will it arrive in St. Louis?
- The boat will spend 4 hours in St. Louis and head to Cape Girardeau, arriving at 6:30 A.M. Sunday. How far is it from St. Louis to Cape Girardeau?

**Lower Mississippi Riverboat Schedule** May–Sept.

| Port | Arrival Time | Departure Time | Distance From Fort Snelling |
|---|---|---|---|
| Hannibal, MO | | 6 P.M. Fri. | 863.9 km |
| Lock 26, Alton, IL | a. ? | b. ? | 1,033.0 km |
| St. Louis, MO | c. ? | d. ? | 1,070.7 km |
| Cape Girardeau, MO | 6:30 A.M. Sun. | ______ | e. ? |

## Mark Three! Mark Twain!

To steer a boat on the Mississippi, early riverboat pilots had to memorize landmarks at every bend and curve of the river, going both upstream and down. They had to know where the channel was deep enough for the boat, where the current was strong, and where there were sandbars or sunken logs.

When Samuel Clemens was growing up in the small river town of Hannibal, Missouri, his ambition was to become a Mississippi River steamboat pilot. He was a pilot for a while. Later he became one of America's most famous writers, using the pen name Mark Twain. In the passage at right from his book *Life on the Mississippi*, Twain describes a lesson he learned from an experienced pilot, Mr. Bixby.

"My boy," [Bixby said] "you've got to know the shape of the river perfectly. It is all there is left to steer by on a very dark night. Everything else is blotted out and gone. But mind you, it hasn't the same shape in the night that it has in the daytime."

"How on earth am I ever going to learn it, then?"

"How do you follow a hall at home in the dark? Because you know the shape of it. You can't see it."

"Do you mean to say that I've got to know all the million trifling variations of shape in the banks of this interminable [endless] river as well as I know the shape of the front hall at home?"

"On my honor, you've got to know them better than any man ever did know the shapes of the halls in his own house."

"I wish I was dead!"

"Now I don't want to discourage you, but— . . . . You see, this has got to be learned; there isn't any getting around it. . . .

**What's in a Name?**
Mark Twain's name comes from a term that steamboat crews used to measure the depth of river water. *Twain* means "two." Dropping a weighted line, they would call out the depth:
"Mark twain!"—2 fathoms deep;
"Mark three!"—3 fathoms deep.
(Note: One fathom equals 1.8 meters.)

**Sunrise over the Mississippi River in Iowa**

"The river is a very different shape on a pitch-dark night from what it is on a starlight night. All shores seem to be straight lines, then, and mighty dim ones, too; and you'd run them for straight lines, only you know better. Then there's your gray mist. You take a night when there's one of these grisly, drizzly gray mists, and then there isn't any particular shape to a shore. A gray mist would tangle the head of the oldest man that ever lived. Well, then, different kinds of moonlight change the shape of the river in different ways. You see—"

"Oh, don't say any more, please! Have I got to learn the shape of the river according to all these five hundred thousand different ways? If I tried to carry all that cargo in my head, it would make me stoop-shouldered."

"No! You only learn the shape of the river; and you learn it with such absolute certainty that you can always steer by the shape that's in your head, and never mind the one that's before your eyes."

## Language Arts Activity

Read the excerpt, focusing on what the dialogue tells you about the characters of Mark Twain and Mr. Bixby.

- What lesson does Mark Twain learn?
- How does Mr. Bixby feel about the Mississippi River?

How can you tell?

Now, use dialogue to write an ending to this riverboat excerpt. Before you begin writing, think carefully about the characters, setting, and your conclusion.

## Tie It Together

### Celebrate the River

Plan a class fair featuring cities on the Mississippi River today, such as St. Louis (above). Set up a booth for each city and create a travel brochure to persuade people to visit.

Choose a city to represent. Then, research the city to find information on

- interesting attractions and events— zoos, museums, parks, sports events, and music festivals.
- influences of different groups on food, customs, music, and architecture.
- physical features around the city.
- famous people—writers, political figures, entertainers—who lived there.
- historic places to visit—monuments, houses, battlefields, and statues.
- illustrations and pictures of special attractions.
- maps of walking tours and historic areas.
- native plants and animals in the area.

Before starting your brochure, decide which attractions to highlight. Then set up your booth, display your brochure, and celebrate life on the Mississippi today.

Chapter 15

# The Atmosphere

## The BIG Idea

Structure of Earth's Atmosphere

**How do air pressure and temperature vary in the atmosphere?**

### Chapter Preview



**Bubbles are pockets of air surrounded by a thin film of liquid.** ▶

*The Atmosphere*

▶ Video Preview
Video Field Trip
Video Assessment

Lab zone™ Chapter **Project**

## Watching the Weather

The weather is always changing. If you pay close attention to weather patterns, you can learn to predict whether a storm is brewing or fair weather will continue. In this project, you will observe weather conditions without using instruments. Then you will look for hints about tomorrow's weather in the weather conditions today.

**Your Goal** Your project must

- include a plan for observing and describing a variety of weather conditions over a period of two to three weeks
- show your observations in a daily weather log
- display your findings about weather conditions

**Plan It!** Begin by discussing what weather conditions you can observe. Decide how, when, and where you will make your observations. Organize a notebook to record them. Think of ways to make comparisons from day to day. Then begin your observations. Look for patterns in your data. At the end of the chapter, you will display your weather observations to the class.

Section 1

# The Air Around You

## Reading Preview

### Key Concepts

- What is the composition of Earth's atmosphere?
- How is the atmosphere important to living things?

### Key Terms

- weather
- atmosphere
- ozone
- water vapor

### Target Reading Skill

**Using Prior Knowledge** Before you read, look at the section headings and visuals to see what this section is about. Then write what you know about the atmosphere in a graphic organizer like the one below. As you read, write what you learn.

| What You Know |
|---|
| 1. The atmosphere contains oxygen.<br>2. |

| What You Learned |
|---|
| 1.<br>2. |

## Lab zone Discover Activity

### How Long Will the Candle Burn?

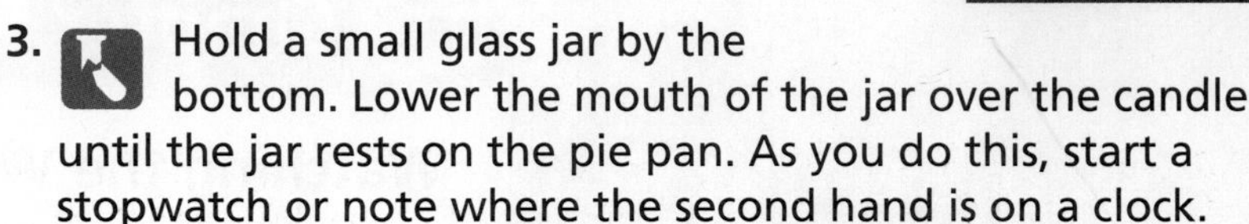

1. Put on your goggles.
2. Stick a small piece of modeling clay onto an aluminum pie pan. Push a short candle into the clay. Carefully light the candle.
3. Hold a small glass jar by the bottom. Lower the mouth of the jar over the candle until the jar rests on the pie pan. As you do this, start a stopwatch or note where the second hand is on a clock.
4. Watch the candle carefully. How long does the flame burn?
5. Wearing an oven mitt, remove the jar. Relight the candle and then repeat Steps 3 and 4 with a larger jar.

**Think It Over**

**Inferring** How would you explain any differences between your results in Steps 4 and 5?

The sky is full of thick, dark clouds. In the distance you see a bright flash. Thirty seconds later, you hear a crack of thunder. You begin to run and reach your home just as the downpour begins. That was close! From your window you look out to watch the storm.

Does the weather where you live change often, or is it fairly constant from day to day? **Weather** is the condition of Earth's atmosphere at a particular time and place. But what is the atmosphere? Earth's **atmosphere** (AT muh sfeer) is the envelope of gases that surrounds the planet. To understand the relative size of the atmosphere, imagine that Earth is the size of an apple. If you breathe on the apple, a thin film of water droplets will form on its surface. Earth's atmosphere is like that water on the apple—a thin layer of gases on Earth's surface.

◀ **From space, Earth's atmosphere appears as a thin layer near the horizon.**

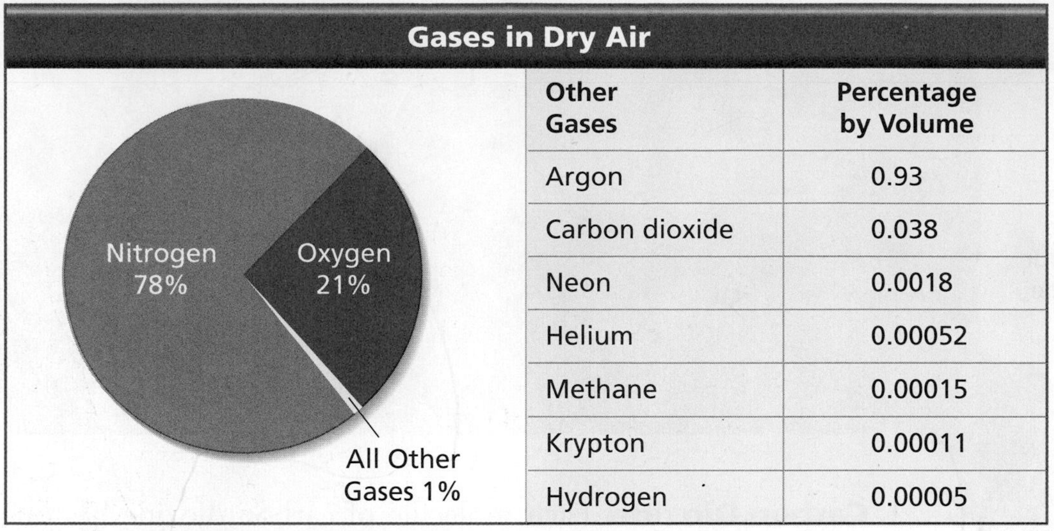


| Other Gases | Percentage by Volume |
|---|---|
| Argon | 0.93 |
| Carbon dioxide | 0.038 |
| Neon | 0.0018 |
| Helium | 0.00052 |
| Methane | 0.00015 |
| Krypton | 0.00011 |
| Hydrogen | 0.00005 |

**FIGURE 1**
Dry air in the lower atmosphere generally has about the same composition of gases.
**Interpreting Data** *What two gases make up most of the air?*

## Composition of the Atmosphere

The atmosphere is made up of a mixture of atoms and molecules of different kinds. An atom is the smallest unit of a chemical element that can exist by itself. Molecules are made up of two or more atoms. **Earth's atmosphere is made up of nitrogen, oxygen, carbon dioxide, water vapor, and many other gases, as well as particles of liquids and solids.**

**Nitrogen** As you can see in Figure 1, nitrogen is the most abundant gas in the atmosphere. It makes up a little more than three fourths of the air we breathe. Each nitrogen molecule consists of two nitrogen atoms.

**Oxygen** Even though oxygen is the second most abundant gas in the atmosphere, it makes up less than one fourth of the volume. Plants and animals take oxygen directly from the air and use it to release energy from their food.

Oxygen is also involved in many other important processes. Any fuel you can think of, from the gasoline in a car to the candles on a birthday cake, uses oxygen as it burns. Without oxygen, a fire will go out. Burning uses oxygen rapidly. During other processes, oxygen is used slowly. For example, steel in cars and other objects reacts slowly with oxygen to form iron oxide, or rust.

Most oxygen molecules have two oxygen atoms. **Ozone** is a form of oxygen that has three oxygen atoms in each molecule instead of the usual two. Have you ever noticed a pungent smell in the air after a thunderstorm? This is the odor of ozone, which forms when lightning interacts with oxygen in the air.

**Reading Checkpoint** What is ozone?

**FIGURE 2**
**Burning Uses Oxygen**
Oxygen is necessary in order for the wood to burn.

**FIGURE 3**
**Water Vapor in the Air**
There is very little water vapor in the air over the desert where this lizard lives. In the tropical rain forest (right), where the frog lives, as much as four percent of the air may be water vapor.

**Carbon Dioxide** Each molecule of carbon dioxide has one atom of carbon and two atoms of oxygen. Carbon dioxide is essential to life. Plants must have carbon dioxide to produce food. When the cells of plants and animals break down food to produce energy, they give off carbon dioxide as a waste product.

When fuels such as coal and gasoline are burned, they release carbon dioxide. Burning these fuels increases the amount of carbon dioxide in the atmosphere.

**Other Gases** Oxygen and nitrogen together make up 99 percent of dry air. Argon and carbon dioxide make up most of the other one percent. The remaining gases are called trace gases because only small amounts of them are present.

**Water Vapor** So far, we have discussed the composition of dry air. In reality, air is not dry because it contains water vapor. **Water vapor** is water in the form of a gas. Water vapor is invisible. It is not the same thing as steam, which is made up of tiny droplets of liquid water. Each water molecule contains two atoms of hydrogen and one atom of oxygen.

The amount of water vapor in the air varies greatly from place to place and from time to time. Water vapor plays an important role in Earth's weather. Clouds form when water vapor condenses out of the air to form tiny droplets of liquid water or crystals of ice. If these droplets or crystals become heavy enough, they can fall as rain or snow.

**Particles** Pure air contains only gases. But pure air exists only in laboratories. In the real world, air also contains tiny solid and liquid particles of dust, smoke, salt, and other chemicals. You can see some of these particles in the air around you, but most of them are too small to see.

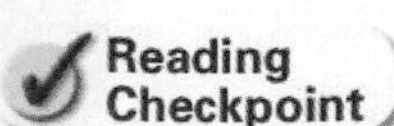


**What is water vapor?**

**Lab zone Try This Activity**

### Breathe In, Breathe Out

How can you detect carbon dioxide in the air you exhale?

1. Put on your goggles.
2. Fill a glass or beaker halfway with limewater.
3. Using a straw, slowly blow air through the limewater for about a minute. **CAUTION:** *Do not suck on the straw or drink the limewater.*
4. What happens to the limewater?

**Developing Hypotheses** What do you think would happen if you did the same experiment after jogging for 10 minutes? What would your results tell you about exercise and carbon dioxide?

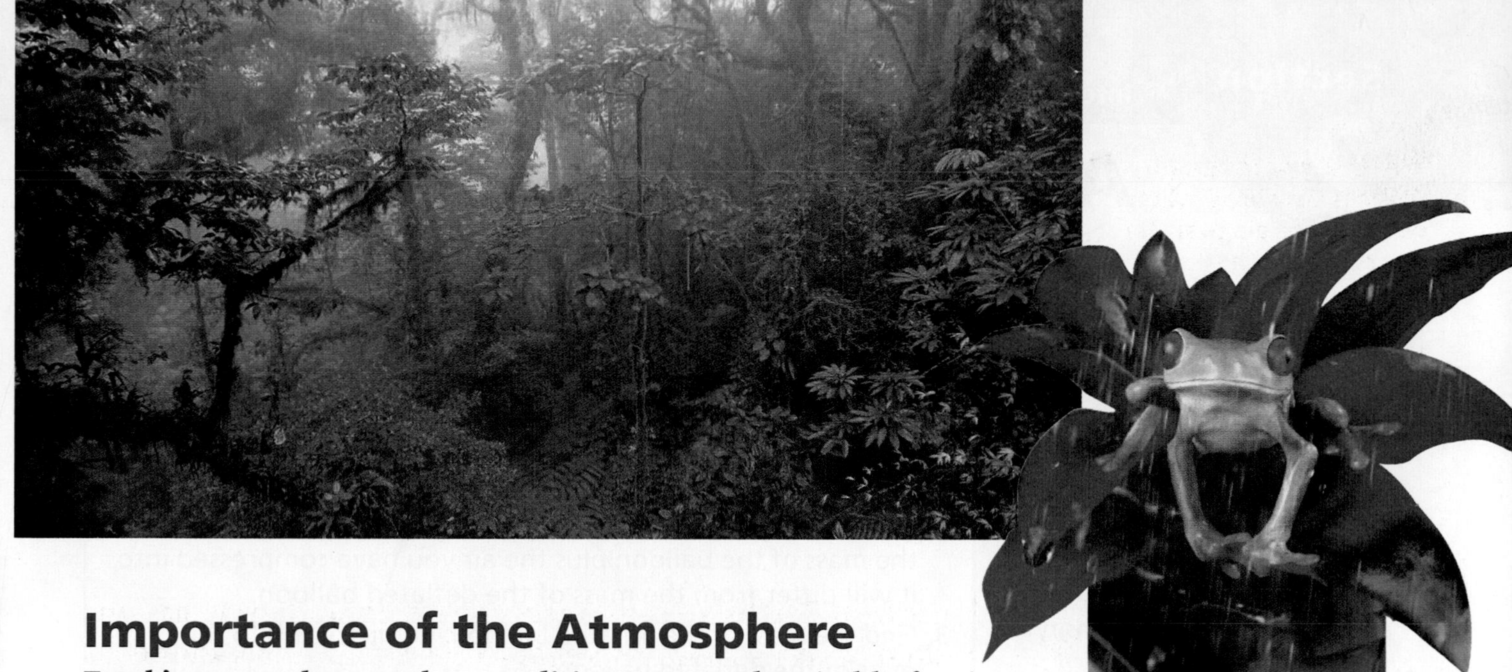

## Importance of the Atmosphere

**Earth's atmosphere makes conditions on Earth suitable for living things.** The atmosphere contains oxygen and other gases that you and other living things need to survive. In turn, living things affect the atmosphere. The atmosphere is constantly changing, with gases moving in and out of living things, the land, and the water.

Living things need warmth and liquid water. By trapping energy from the sun, the atmosphere keeps most of Earth's surface warm enough for water to exist as a liquid. In addition, Earth's atmosphere protects living things from dangerous radiation from the sun. The atmosphere also prevents Earth's surface from being hit by most meteoroids, or rocks from outer space.

For: Links on atmosphere
Visit: www.SciLinks.org
Web Code: scn-0911

## Section 1 Assessment

**Target Reading Skill Using Prior Knowledge** Review your graphic organizer and revise it based on what you just learned in the section.

### Reviewing Key Concepts

1. a. **Defining** What is the atmosphere?
   b. **Listing** What are the four most common gases in dry air?
   c. **Explaining** Why are the amounts of gases in the atmosphere usually shown as percentages of dry air?
2. a. **Describing** What are three ways in which the atmosphere is important to life on Earth?
   b. **Predicting** How would the amount of carbon dioxide in the atmosphere change if there were no plants?
   c. **Developing Hypotheses** How would Earth be different without the atmosphere?

### Writing in Science

**Summary** Write a paragraph that summarizes in your own words how oxygen from the atmosphere is important. Include its importance to living things and in other processes.

Section 2

Integrating Physics

# Air Pressure

## Reading Preview

### Key Concepts

- What are some of the properties of air?
- What instruments are used to measure air pressure?
- How does increasing altitude affect air pressure and density?

### Key Terms

- density
- pressure
- air pressure
- barometer
- mercury barometer
- aneroid barometer
- altitude

### Target Reading Skill

**Identifying Main Ideas** As you read the Properties of Air section, write the main idea—the biggest or most important idea—in a graphic organizer like the one below. Then write two supporting details. The supporting details give examples of the main idea.

Main Idea

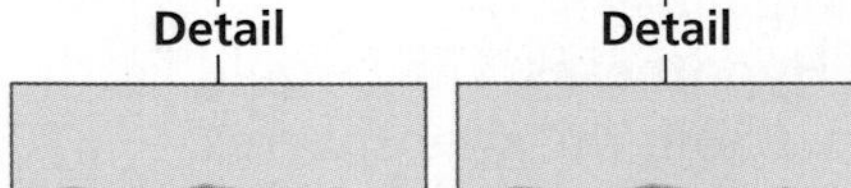
Because air has mass, it also . . .

Detail

Detail

## Lab zone Discover Activity

### Does Air Have Mass?

1. Use a balance to find the mass of a deflated balloon.
2. Blow up the balloon and tie the neck closed. Predict whether the mass of the balloon plus the air you have compressed into it will differ from the mass of the deflated balloon.
3. Find the mass of the inflated balloon. Compare this to the mass of the deflated balloon. Was your prediction correct?

**Think It Over**

**Drawing Conclusions** What can you conclude about whether air has mass? Explain your conclusion.

The air is cool and clear—just perfect for an overnight hiking trip. You've stuffed your backpack with your tent, sleeping bag, stove, and food. When you hoist your pack onto your back, its weight presses into your shoulders. That pack sure is heavy! By the end of the day, you'll be glad to take it off and get rid of all that weight.

But here's a surprise: Even when you take off your pack, your shoulders will still have pressure on them. The weight of the atmosphere itself is constantly pressing on your body.

**Like a heavy backpack pressing on your shoulders, the weight of the atmosphere causes air pressure.** ▶

## Properties of Air

It may seem to you that air has no mass. But in fact, air consists of atoms and molecules, which have mass. So air must have mass. **Because air has mass, it also has other properties, including density and pressure.**

**Density** The amount of mass in a given volume of air is its **density.** You can calculate the density of a substance by dividing its mass by its volume.

$$\text{Density} = \frac{\text{Mass}}{\text{Volume}}$$

If there are more molecules in a given volume, the density is greater. If there are fewer molecules, the density is less.

**Pressure** The force pushing on an area or surface is known as **pressure.** The weight of the atmosphere exerts a force on surfaces. **Air pressure** is the result of the weight of a column of air pushing down on an area. The column of air extends upward through the entire atmosphere, as shown in Figure 4.

The atmosphere is heavy. The weight of the column of air above your desk is about the same as the weight of a large schoolbus. So why doesn't air pressure crush your desk? The reason is that the molecules in air push in all directions—down, up, and sideways. The air pushing down on top of your desk is balanced by the air pushing up on the bottom of your desk.

Air pressure can change from day to day. A denser substance has more mass per unit volume than a less dense one. So denser air exerts more pressure than less dense air.

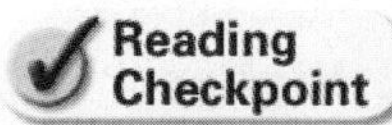


**How does the density of air affect air pressure?**

**FIGURE 4**
**Air Pressure**
There is a column of air above you all the time. The weight of the air in the atmosphere causes air pressure.

Lab zone Try This **Activity**

### Soda-Bottle Barometer

Here's how to build a device that shows changes in air pressure.

1. Fill a 2-liter soda bottle one-half full with water.
2. Lower a long straw into the bottle so that the end of the straw is in the water. Seal the mouth of the bottle around the straw with modeling clay.
3. Squeeze the sides of the bottle. What happens to the level of the water in the straw?
4. Let go of the sides of the bottle. Watch the level of the water in the straw.

**Inferring** Explain your results in terms of air pressure.

# Measuring Air Pressure

A **barometer** (buh RAHM uh tur) is an instrument that is used to measure air pressure. **Two common kinds of barometers are mercury barometers and aneroid barometers.**

**Mercury Barometers** Figure 5 shows the way a mercury barometer works. A **mercury barometer** consists of a glass tube open at the bottom end and partially filled with mercury. The space in the tube above the mercury is almost a vacuum—it contains very little air. The open end of the tube rests in a dish of mercury. The air pressure pushing down on the surface of the mercury in the dish is equal to the pressure exerted by the weight of the column of mercury in the tube. When the air pressure increases, it presses down more on the surface of the mercury. Greater air pressure forces the column of mercury higher. At sea level the mercury column is about 76 centimeters high, on average.

**Aneroid Barometers** If you have a barometer at home, it is probably an aneroid barometer. The word aneroid means "without liquid." An **aneroid barometer** (AN uh royd) has an airtight metal chamber, as shown in Figure 6. The metal chamber is sensitive to changes in air pressure. When air pressure increases, the thin walls of the chamber are pushed in. When the pressure drops, the walls bulge out. The chamber is connected to a dial by a series of springs and levers. As the shape of the chamber changes, the needle on the dial moves.

**For:** Measuring Air Pressure activity
**Visit:** PHSchool.com
**Web Code:** cfp-4012

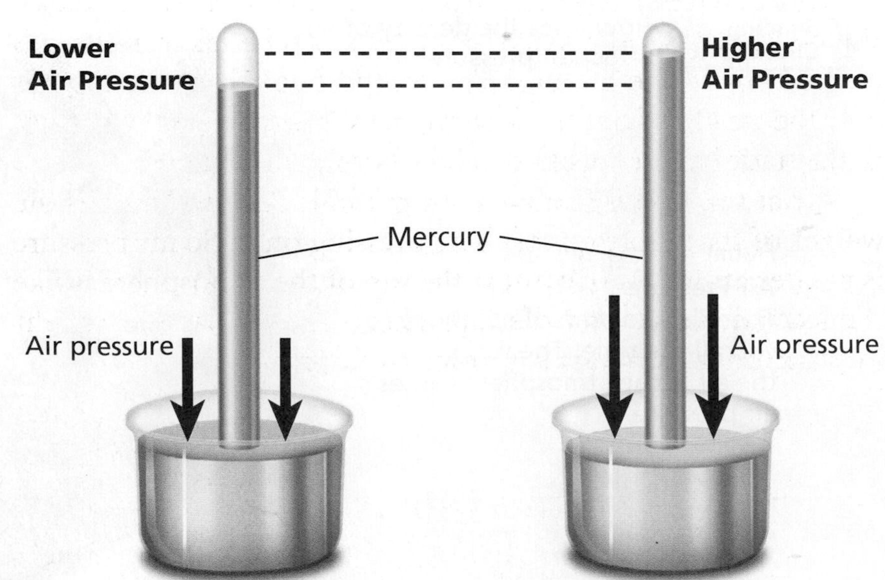


FIGURE 5
**Mercury Barometer**
Air pressure pushes down on the surface of the mercury in the dish, causing the mercury in the tube to rise. The air pressure is greater on the barometer on the right, so the mercury is higher in the tube.
**Predicting** *What happens to the level of mercury in the tube when the air pressure decreases?*

FIGURE 6
**Aneroid Barometer**
This diagram shows an aneroid barometer. Changes in air pressure cause the walls of the airtight metal chamber to flex in and out. The needle on the dial indicates the air pressure.

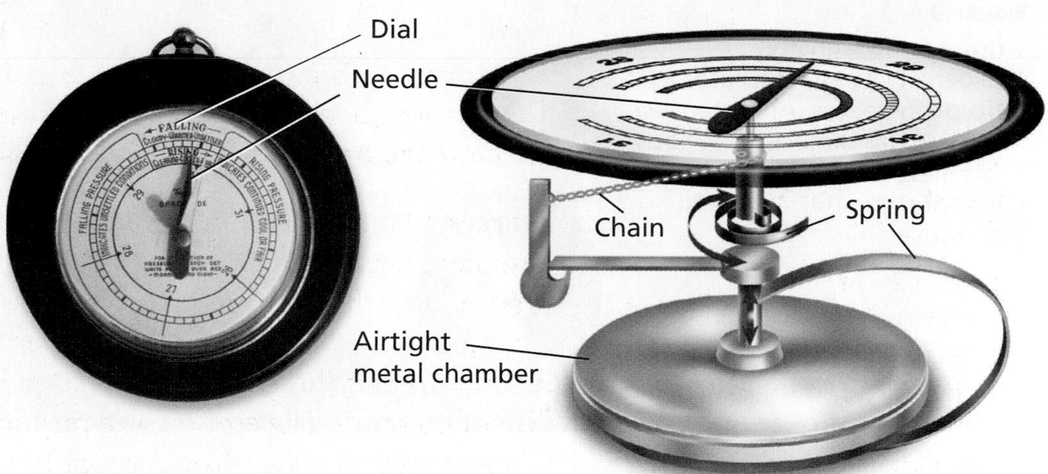


**Units of Air Pressure** Weather reports use several different units for air pressure. Most weather reports for the general public use inches of mercury. For example, if the column of mercury in a mercury barometer is 30 inches high, the air pressure is "30 inches of mercury" or just "30 inches."

National Weather Service maps indicate air pressure in millibars. One inch of mercury is approximately 33.87 millibars, so 30 inches of mercury is approximately equal to 1,016 millibars.

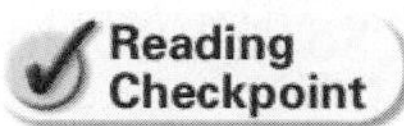

**What are two common units that are used to measure air pressure?**

## Altitude and the Properties of Air

At the top of a mountain, the air pressure is less than the air pressure at sea level. **Altitude,** or elevation, is the distance above sea level, the average level of the surface of the oceans. **Air pressure decreases as altitude increases. As air pressure decreases, so does density.**

**Altitude Affects Air Pressure** Imagine a stack of books. Which book has more weight on it, the second book from the top or the book at the bottom? The second book from the top has only the weight of one book on top of it. The book at the bottom of the stack has the weight of all the books pressing on it.

Air at sea level is like the bottom book. Sea-level air has the weight of the whole atmosphere pressing on it. So air pressure is greater at sea level. Air near the top of the atmosphere is like the second book from the top. There, the air has less weight pressing on it, and thus has lower air pressure.

FIGURE 7
**Air Pressure and Altitude**
Air pressure is greater at sea level and decreases as the altitude increases.

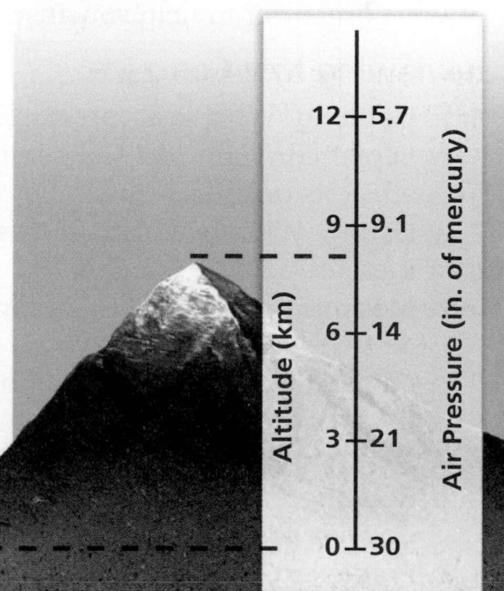

**FIGURE 8**
**Altitude and Density**
The density of air decreases as altitude increases. Air at sea level has more gas molecules in each cubic meter than air at the top of a mountain.

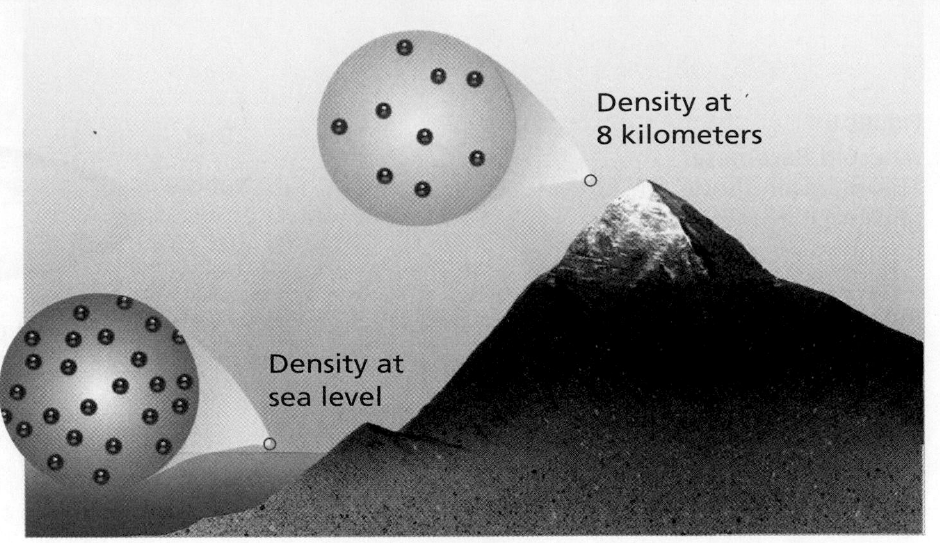

**Altitude Also Affects Density** As you go up through the atmosphere, the density of the air decreases. This means the gas molecules that make up the atmosphere are farther apart at high altitudes than they are at sea level. If you were near the top of a tall mountain and tried to run, you would quickly get out of breath. Why? The air contains 21 percent oxygen, whether you are at sea level or on top of a mountain. However, since the air is less dense at a high altitude, there are fewer oxygen molecules to breathe in each cubic meter of air than at sea level. So you would become short of breath quickly at high altitudes.

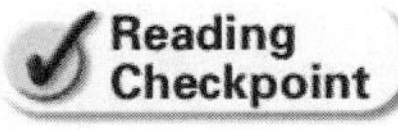

**Why is it hard to breathe at the top of a mountain?**

## Section 2 Assessment

**Target Reading Skill Identifying Main Ideas** Use your graphic organizer to help you answer Question 1 below.

### Reviewing Key Concepts

1. a. **Defining** What is air pressure?
   b. **Explaining** How does increasing the density of a gas affect its pressure?
2. a. **Listing** What two instruments are commonly used to measure air pressure?
   b. **Measuring** What units are commonly used to measure air pressure?
   c. **Calculating** How many millibars are equal to 27.23 inches of mercury?
3. a. **Defining** What is altitude?
   b. **Relating Cause and Effect** As altitude increases, how does air pressure change? How does density change?
   c. **Predicting** What changes in air pressure would you expect if you carried a barometer down a mine shaft?

### Lab zone At-Home Activity

**Model Air Pressure** Here's how you can show your family that air has pressure. Fill a glass with water. Place a piece of cardboard over the top of the glass. Hold the cardboard in place with one hand as you turn the glass upside down. **CAUTION:** *Be sure the cardboard does not bend.* Now remove your hand from the cardboard. What happens? Explain to your family that the cardboard doesn't fall because the air pressure pushing up on it is greater than the weight of the water pushing down.

Lab zone **Skills Lab**

# Working Under Pressure

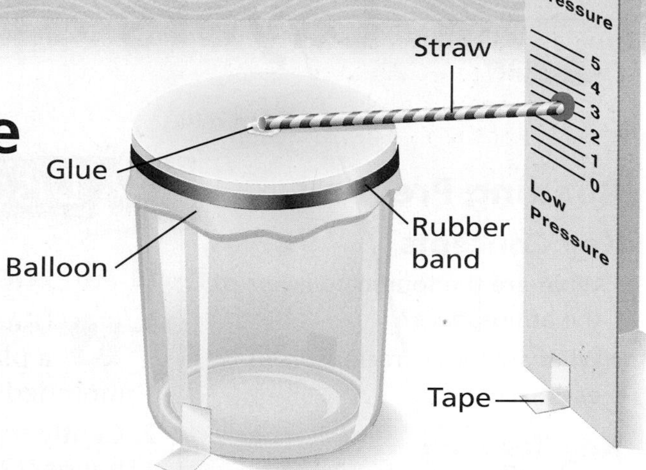


## Problem

How can a barometer detect changes in air pressure?

## Skills Focus

interpreting data, drawing conclusions

## Materials

- modeling clay • scissors • white glue
- tape • pencil • wide-mouthed glass jar
- metric ruler • cardboard strip, 10 cm × 25 cm
- rubber band • large rubber balloon
- drinking straw, 12–15 cm long

## Procedure  

1. Cut off the narrow opening of the balloon.
2. Fold the edges of the balloon outward. Carefully stretch the balloon over the open end of the glass jar. Use a rubber band to hold the balloon on the rim of the glass jar.
3. Place a small amount of glue on the center of the balloon top. Attach one end of the straw to the glue. Allow the other end to extend several centimeters beyond the edge of the glass jar. This is your pointer.
4. While the glue dries, fold the cardboard strip lengthwise and draw a scale along the edge with marks 0.5 cm apart. Write "High pressure" at the top of your scale and "Low pressure" at the bottom.
5. After the glue dries, add a pea-sized piece of modeling clay to the end of the pointer. Place your barometer and its scale in a location that is as free from temperature changes as possible. Note that the pointer of the straw must just reach the cardboard strip, as shown in the diagram.
6. Tape both the scale and the barometer to a surface so they do not move during your experiment.
7. Make a data table like the one below in your notebook. Record the date and time. Note the level of the straw on the cardboard strip.

| Data Table | | |
|---|---|---|
| Date and Time | Air Pressure | Weather Conditions |
| | | |
| | | |

8. Check the barometer twice a day. Record your observations in your data table.
9. Record the weather conditions for at least three days.

## Analyze and Conclude

1. **Interpreting Data** What change in atmospheric conditions must occur to cause the free end of the straw to rise? What change must occur for it to fall?
2. **Drawing Conclusions** Based on your observations, what kind of weather is usually associated with high air pressure? With low air pressure?
3. **Communicating** Write a paragraph in which you discuss what effect, if any, a large temperature change might have on the accuracy of your barometer.

## More to Explore

Compare your pressure readings with high and low pressure readings shown in newspaper weather maps for the same period. How do your readings compare with those in the newspaper?

# 3 Layers of the Atmosphere

## Reading Preview

### Key Concepts

- What are the four main layers of the atmosphere?
- What are the characteristics of each layer?

### Key Terms

- troposphere
- stratosphere
- mesosphere
- thermosphere
- ionosphere
- exosphere

### Target Reading Skill

**Previewing Visuals** Before you read this section, preview Figure 9. Then write at least two questions that you have about the diagram in a graphic organizer like the one below. As you read, answer your questions.

**Layers of the Atmosphere**

| Q. Where is the ozone layer? |
|---|
| A. |
| Q. |

## Lab zone Discover Activity

### Is Air There?

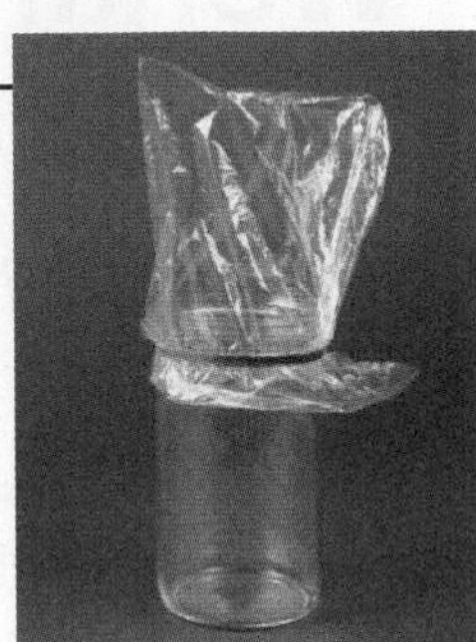

1. Use a heavy rubber band to tightly secure a plastic bag over the top of a wide-mouthed jar.
2. Gently try to push the bag into the jar. What happens? Is the air pressure higher inside or outside the bag?
3. Remove the rubber band and line the inside of the jar with the plastic bag. Use the rubber band to tightly secure the edges of the bag over the rim of the jar.
4. Gently try to pull the bag out of the jar with your fingertips. What happens? Is the air pressure higher inside or outside the bag?

**Think It Over**

**Predicting** Explain your observations in terms of air pressure. How do you think differences in air pressure would affect a balloon as it traveled up through the atmosphere?

Imagine taking a trip upward into the atmosphere in a hot-air balloon. You begin on a warm beach near the ocean, at an altitude of 0 kilometers above sea level.

You hear a roar as the balloon's pilot turns up the burner to heat the air in the balloon. The balloon begins to rise, and Earth's surface gets farther and farther away. As the balloon rises to an altitude of 3 kilometers, you realize that the air is getting colder. As you continue to rise, the air gets colder still. At 6 kilometers you begin to have trouble breathing. The air is becoming less dense. It's time to go back down.

What if you could have continued your balloon ride up through the atmosphere? As you rose higher, the air pressure and temperature would change dramatically.

**Scientists divide Earth's atmosphere into four main layers classified according to changes in temperature. These layers are the troposphere, the stratosphere, the mesosphere, and the thermosphere.** The four main layers of the atmosphere are shown in Figure 9. Read on to learn more about each of these layers.

▲ Hot-air balloon

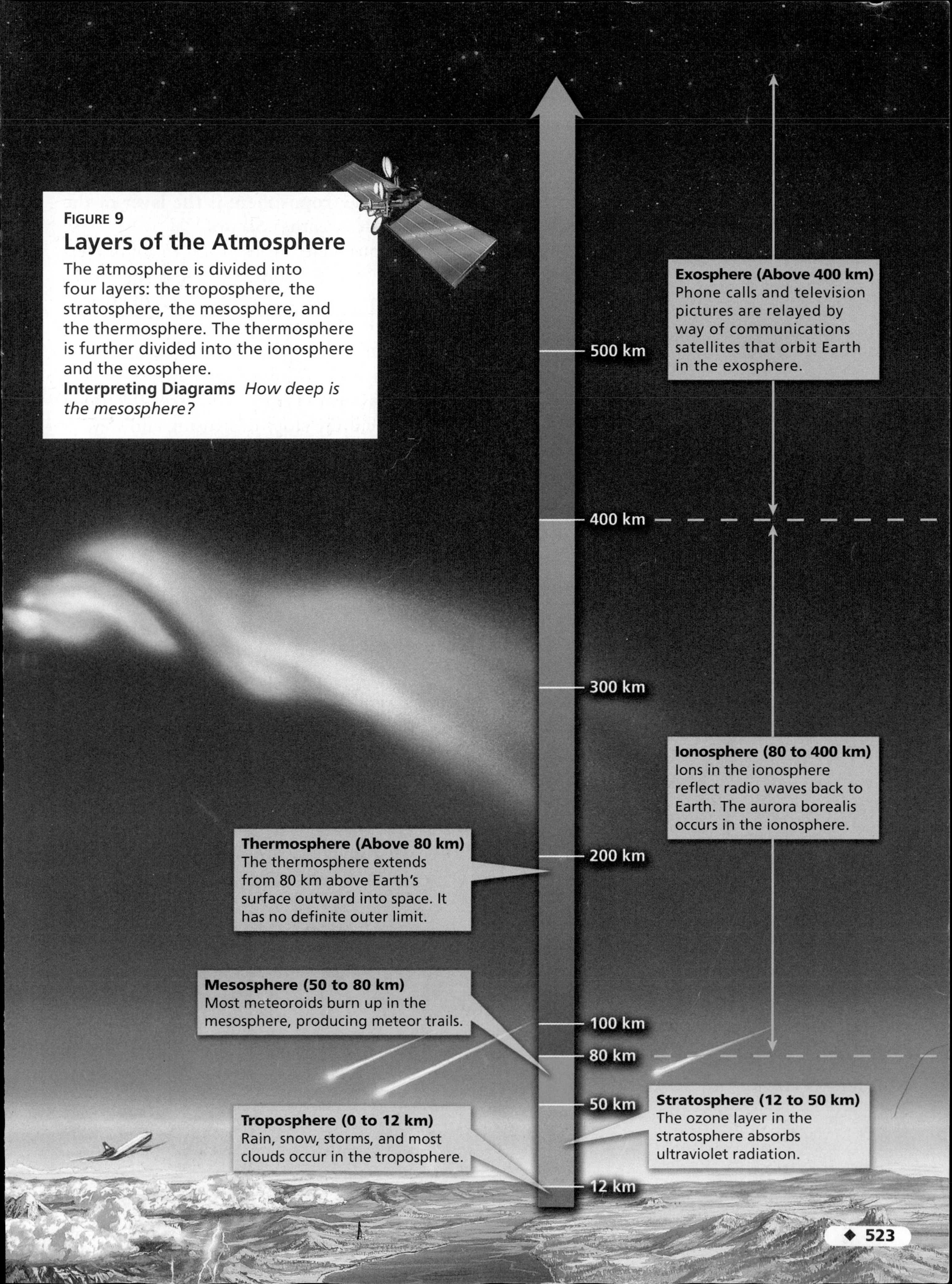

FIGURE 9

## Layers of the Atmosphere

The atmosphere is divided into four layers: the troposphere, the stratosphere, the mesosphere, and the thermosphere. The thermosphere is further divided into the ionosphere and the exosphere.

**Interpreting Diagrams** *How deep is the mesosphere?*

**Exosphere (Above 400 km)**
Phone calls and television pictures are relayed by way of communications satellites that orbit Earth in the exosphere.

**Ionosphere (80 to 400 km)**
Ions in the ionosphere reflect radio waves back to Earth. The aurora borealis occurs in the ionosphere.

**Thermosphere (Above 80 km)**
The thermosphere extends from 80 km above Earth's surface outward into space. It has no definite outer limit.

**Mesosphere (50 to 80 km)**
Most meteoroids burn up in the mesosphere, producing meteor trails.

**Stratosphere (12 to 50 km)**
The ozone layer in the stratosphere absorbs ultraviolet radiation.

**Troposphere (0 to 12 km)**
Rain, snow, storms, and most clouds occur in the troposphere.

500 km
400 km
300 km
200 km
100 km
80 km
50 km
12 km

For: More on the ozone layer
Visit: PHSchool.com
Web Code: cfd-4013

## The Troposphere

You live in the inner, or lowest, layer of Earth's atmosphere, the **troposphere** (TROH puh sfeer). *Tropo-* means "turning" or "changing." Conditions in the troposphere are more variable than in the other layers. **The troposphere is the layer of the atmosphere in which Earth's weather occurs.**

The depth of the troposphere varies from 16 kilometers above the equator to less than 9 kilometers above the North and South poles. Although it is the shallowest layer, the troposphere contains almost all of the mass of the atmosphere.

As altitude increases in the troposphere, the temperature decreases. On average, for every 1-kilometer increase in altitude, the air gets about 6.5 Celsius degrees cooler. At the top of the troposphere, the temperature stops decreasing and stays at about –60°C. Water here forms thin, feathery clouds of ice.

## • Tech & Design in History •

### Explorers of the Atmosphere

The atmosphere has been explored from the ground and from space.

**1643**
**Torricelli Invents the Barometer**
Italian physicist and mathematician Evangelista Torricelli improved existing scientific instruments and invented some new ones. In 1643 he invented the mercury barometer.

**1746**
**Franklin Experiments With Electricity**
American statesman and inventor Benjamin Franklin experimented with electricity in the atmosphere. To demonstrate that lightning is a form of electricity, Franklin flew a kite in a thunderstorm. However, Franklin did not hold the kite string in his hand, as this historical print shows.

**1804 Gay-Lussac Studies the Upper Troposphere**
French chemist Joseph-Louis Gay-Lussac ascended to a height of about 7 kilometers in a hydrogen balloon to study the upper troposphere. Gay-Lussac studied pressure, temperature, and humidity.

1600 1700 1800

## The Stratosphere

The **stratosphere** extends from the top of the troposphere to about 50 kilometers above Earth's surface. *Strato-* means "layer" or "spread out." **The stratosphere is the second layer of the atmosphere and contains the ozone layer.**

The lower stratosphere is cold, about –60°C. Surprisingly, the upper stratosphere is warmer than the lower stratosphere. Why is this? The middle portion of the stratosphere contains a layer of air where there is much more ozone than in the rest of the atmosphere. (Recall that ozone is the three-atom form of oxygen.) When the ozone absorbs energy from the sun, the energy is converted into heat, warming the air. The ozone layer is also important because it protects Earth's living things from dangerous ultraviolet radiation from the sun.

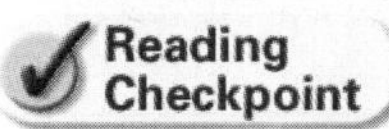


**Why is the upper stratosphere warmer than the lower stratosphere?**

**Writing in Science**

**Research and Write** Imagine you were one of the first people to travel into the atmosphere in a balloon. What would you need to take? Find out what the early explorers took with them in their balloons. Write at least two paragraphs about what you would take and why.

**1931 Piccard Explores the Stratosphere**
Swiss-Belgian physicist Auguste Piccard made the first ascent into the stratosphere. He reached a height of about 16 kilometers in an airtight cabin attached to a huge hydrogen balloon. Piccard is shown here with the cabin.

**1960 First Weather Satellite Launched**
*TIROS-1*, the first weather satellite equipped with a camera to send data back to Earth, was put into orbit by the United States. As later weather satellites circled Earth, they observed cloud cover and recorded temperatures and air pressures in the atmosphere.

**1999 *Terra* Satellite Launched**
The *Terra* satellite is equipped to study Earth's surface, atmosphere, and oceans from orbit. The data it gathers are used to help understand changes in Earth's climate.

1900 2000 2100

## Math Analyzing Data

### Changing Temperatures

The graph shows how temperatures in the atmosphere change with altitude. Use it to answer the questions below.

1. **Reading Graphs** What two variables are being graphed? In what unit is each measured?
2. **Reading Graphs** What is the temperature at the bottom of the stratosphere?
3. **Interpreting Data** Which layer of the atmosphere has the lowest temperature?
4. **Making Generalizations** Describe how temperature changes as altitude increases in the troposphere.

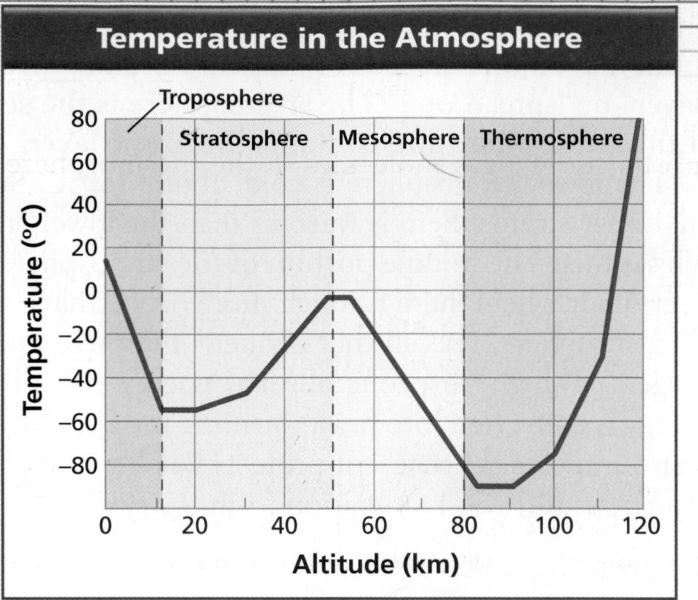


# The Mesosphere

Above the stratosphere, a drop in temperature marks the beginning of the next layer, the **mesosphere.** *Meso-* means "middle," so the mesosphere is the middle layer of the atmosphere. The mesosphere begins 50 kilometers above Earth's surface and ends at an altitude of 80 kilometers. In the outer mesosphere, temperatures approach –90°C.

**The mesosphere is the layer of the atmosphere that protects Earth's surface from being hit by most meteoroids.** Meteoroids are chunks of stone and metal from space. What you see as a shooting star, or meteor, is the trail of hot, glowing gases the meteoroid leaves behind in the mesosphere.

# The Thermosphere

Near the top of the atmosphere, the air is very thin. At 80 kilometers above Earth's surface, the air is only about 0.001 percent as dense as the air at sea level. It's as though you took a cubic meter of air at sea level and expanded it into 100,000 cubic meters at the top of the mesosphere. **The outermost layer of Earth's atmosphere is the thermosphere.** The **thermosphere** extends from 80 kilometers above Earth's surface outward into space. It has no definite outer limit, but blends gradually with outer space.

The *thermo-* in thermosphere means "heat." Even though the air in the thermosphere is thin, it is very hot, up to 1,800°C. This is because sunlight strikes the thermosphere first. Nitrogen and oxygen molecules convert this energy into heat.

Despite the high temperature, you would not feel warm in the thermosphere. An ordinary thermometer would show a temperature well below 0°C. Why is that? Temperature is the average amount of energy of motion of each molecule of a substance. The gas molecules in the thermosphere move very rapidly, so the temperature is very high. However, the molecules are spaced far apart in the thin air. There are not enough of them to collide with a thermometer and warm it very much.

FIGURE 10
**Aurora Borealis**
The aurora borealis, seen from Fairbanks, Alaska, creates a spectacular display in the night sky.

The thermosphere is divided into two layers. The lower layer, called the **ionosphere** (eye AHN uh sfeer), begins about 80 kilometers above the surface and extends to about 400 kilometers. Energy from the sun causes gas molecules in the ionosphere to become electrically charged particles called ions. Radio waves bounce off ions in the ionosphere back to Earth's surface. Brilliant light displays, such as those shown in Figure 10, also occur in the ionosphere. In the Northern Hemisphere, these displays are called the Northern Lights, or the aurora borealis. Auroras are caused by particles from the sun that enter the ionosphere near the poles. These particles strike atoms in the ionosphere, causing them to glow.

*Exo-* means "outer," so the **exosphere** is the outer portion of the thermosphere. The exosphere extends from about 400 kilometers outward for thousands of kilometers.

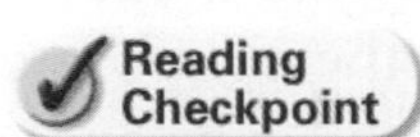


**What is the ionosphere?**

## Section 3 Assessment

**Target Reading Skill Previewing Visuals** Refer to your graphic organizer about Figure 9 to help you answer the following questions.

### Reviewing Key Concepts

1. a. **Listing** List the four main layers of the atmosphere, beginning with the layer closest to Earth's surface.
   b. **Classifying** What properties are used to distinguish the layers of the atmosphere?
   c. **Interpreting Diagrams** According to Figure 9, in which layer of the atmosphere do communications satellites orbit?
2. a. **Identifying** Give at least one important characteristic of each of the four main layers of Earth's atmosphere.
   b. **Comparing and Contrasting** How does temperature change as height increases in the troposphere? Compare this to how temperature changes with height in the stratosphere.
   c. **Applying Concepts** Why would you not feel warm in the thermosphere, even though temperatures can be up to 1,800°C?

### Writing in Science

**Cause and Effect Paragraph** How do you think Earth's surface might be different if it had no atmosphere? Write a paragraph explaining your ideas.

Section 4

Integrating Environmental Science

# Air Quality

## Reading Preview

### Key Concepts

- What are the major sources of air pollution?
- What causes smog and acid rain?
- What can be done to improve air quality?

### Key Terms

- pollutants
- photochemical smog
- acid rain

### Target Reading Skill

**Outlining** As you read, make an outline about air quality that you can use for review. Use the red headings for the main topics and the blue headings for the subtopics.

| Air Quality |
|---|
| I. Sources of air pollution |
| A. Natural sources |
| B. |
| C. |
| II. Smog and acid rain |
| A. |

## Lab zone Discover Activity

### What's on the Jar?

1. Put on your goggles.
2. Put a small piece of modeling clay on a piece of aluminum foil. Push a candle into the clay. Light the candle.
3. Wearing an oven mitt, hold a glass jar by the rim so that the bottom of the jar is just above the flame.

**Think It Over**

**Observing** What do you see on the jar? Where did it come from?

As you are reading this page, you are breathing without even thinking about it. Breathing brings air into your lungs, where the oxygen you need is taken into your body. But not everything in the air is healthful. You may also breathe in tiny particles or even a small amount of harmful gases.

If you live in a large city, you may have noticed a brown haze in the air. Even if you live far from a city, the air around you may contain pollutants. **Pollutants** are harmful substances in the air, water, or soil. Air that contains harmful particles and gases is said to be polluted.

Air pollution can affect the health of humans and other living things. Figure 12 identifies the effects of some pollutants.

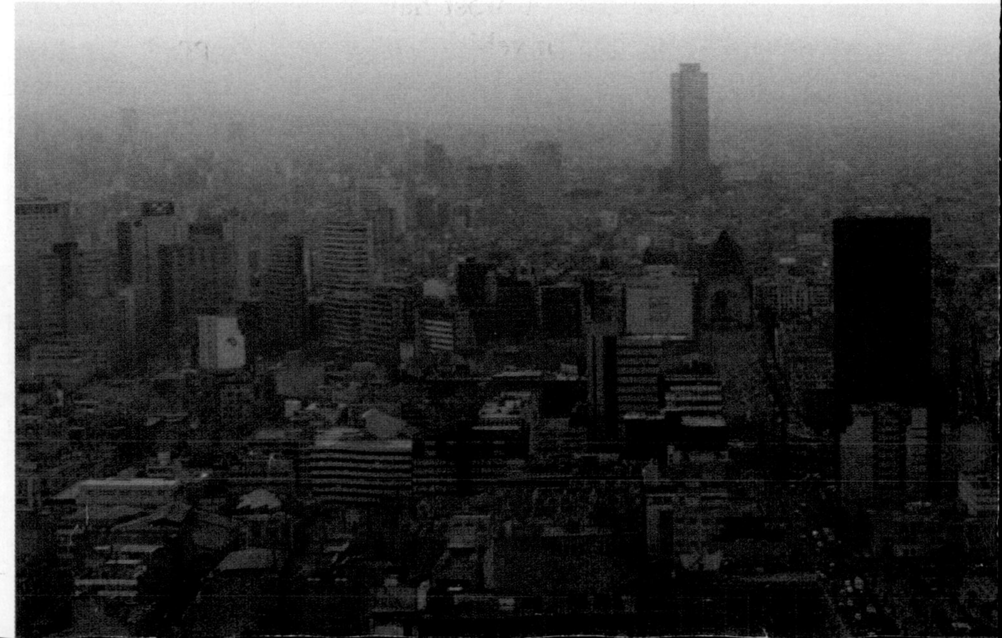

FIGURE 11
**Air Pollution**
Air pollution in large cities, such as Mexico City, can cause serious health problems.

| Effects of Air Pollution on Human Health | | |
|---|---|---|
| **Pollutant** | **Source** | **Health Effect** |
| Carbon monoxide | Burning of fossil fuels | Reduced ability of blood to deliver oxygen to cells |
| Nitrogen dioxide | Burning of fossil fuels | Breathing problems, lung damage |
| Ozone | Chemical reaction of certain carbon compounds | Breathing problems, asthma, eye irritation |
| Particles of dust, smoke, or soot | Burning of wood and fossil fuels, volcanic eruptions | Respiratory illnesses, nose and throat irritation |
| Sulfur dioxide | Burning of fossil fuels, volcanic eruptions | Breathing problems, lung damage |

**FIGURE 12**
Air pollution can cause many different problems. The table shows the health effects of air pollution. Pollen also can cause difficulties for people with allergies.

## Sources of Pollution

**Some air pollution occurs naturally. But many types of air pollution are the result of human activities.**

**Natural Sources** Many natural processes add particles to the atmosphere. Forest fires, soil erosion, and dust storms release a great deal of smoke and dust into the air. The wind carries particles of molds and pollen. Erupting volcanoes spew out clouds of dust and ash along with poisonous gases.

**Human Activities** Human activities, such as farming and construction, can send soil and dust into the air. But most air pollution is the result of burning fossil fuels, such as coal, oil, gasoline, and diesel fuel. Almost half of this pollution comes from cars and other motor vehicles. Factories and power plants that burn coal and oil also release pollution.

When fossil fuels burn, they release both particles and gases. When people burn wood or coal, particles of soot enter the air. Soot gives smoke its dark color. All fossil fuels contain hydrocarbons, compounds made of hydrogen and carbon. As fossil fuels burn, some hydrocarbons do not burn completely and escape into the air. Burning fossil fuels produces a variety of pollutants, including carbon monoxide, nitrogen oxides, and sulfur oxides.

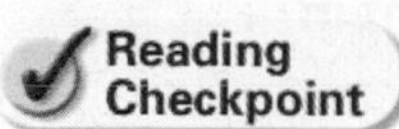


**What are some air pollutants produced by burning fossil fuels?**

**For:** More on air pollution
**Visit:** PHSchool.com
**Web Code:** cfd-4014

## Smog and Acid Rain

High levels of air pollution decrease the quality of the air. **The burning of fossil fuels can cause smog and acid rain.**

**London-Type Smog** One hundred years ago, the city of London, England, was dark and dirty. Factories burned coal, and most houses were heated by coal. The air was full of soot. In 1905, the term *smog* was created by combining the words *smoke* and *fog* to describe this type of air pollution. Typically, London-type smog forms when particles in coal smoke combine with water droplets in humid air. Today, people in London burn much less coal. As a result, the air in London now is much cleaner than it was 100 years ago.

**Photochemical Smog** Fortunately, London-type smog is no longer common in the United States. Instead, many cities today have another type of smog. The brown haze that develops in sunny cities is called **photochemical smog** (foh toh KEM ih kul). The *photo-* in photochemical means "light." Photochemical smog is formed by the action of sunlight on pollutants such as hydrocarbons and nitrogen oxides. These chemicals react to form a brownish mixture of ozone and other pollutants.

Recall that ozone in the stratosphere blocks ultraviolet radiation, thus protecting living things on Earth. But in the troposphere, ozone is a pollutant that can irritate the eyes, throat, and lungs. It can also harm plants and other living things and damage many materials.

FIGURE 13
**Results of Acid Rain**
This scientist is studying trees damaged by acid rain. Needle-leafed trees such as pines and spruce are especially sensitive to acid rain. Acid rain may make tree needles turn brown or fall off.

**Acid Rain** Another result of air pollution is acid rain. Rain is naturally slightly acidic, but rain that contains more acid than normal is known as **acid rain.**

How does acid rain form? The burning of coal that contains a lot of sulfur produces sulfur oxides, substances composed of oxygen and sulfur. Acid rain forms when nitrogen oxides and sulfur oxides combine with water in the air to form nitric acid and sulfuric acid. Rain, sleet, snow, fog, and even dry particles carry these two acids to trees and lakes.

Acid rain is sometimes strong enough to damage the surfaces of buildings and statues. It also harms lakes and ponds. Acid rain can make water so acidic that plants, amphibians, fish, and insects can no longer survive in it.

**What is the main pollutant in photochemical smog?**

## Improving Air Quality

**In the United States, the federal and state governments have passed a number of laws and regulations to reduce air pollution.** The Environmental Protection Agency (EPA) monitors air pollutants in the United States. Air quality in this country has generally improved over the past 30 years. The amounts of most major air pollutants have decreased. Many newer cars cause less pollution than older models. Recently built power plants are less polluting than power plants that have been in operation for many years.

However, there are now more cars on the road and more power plants burning fossil fuels than in the past. Unfortunately, the air in many American cities is still polluted. Voluntary measures, such as greater use of public transportation in place of driving, could reduce the total amount of air pollution produced. Many people think that stricter regulations are needed to control air pollution. Others argue that reducing air pollution can be very expensive and that the benefits of stricter regulations may not be worth the costs.

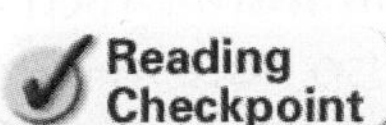

**Explain one way that air quality could be improved.**

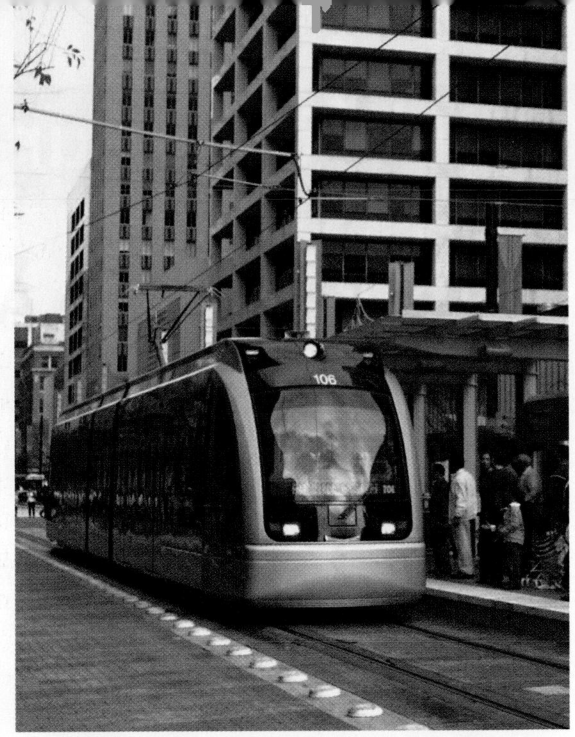


**FIGURE 14**
**Public Transportation**
Public transportation, like the light rail system above, can reduce air pollution.

## Section 4 Assessment

### Target Reading Skill

**Outlining** Use the information in your outline about air quality to help you answer the questions below.

### Reviewing Key Concepts

1. a. **Defining** What is a pollutant?
   b. **Identifying** Name three natural processes and three human activities that cause air pollution.
   c. **Summarizing** What is the major source of air pollution today?
2. a. **Identifying** What human activity is responsible for the formation of smog and acid rain?
   b. **Explaining** What kinds of harm does photochemical smog cause?
   c. **Inferring** Do you think that photochemical smog levels are higher during the winter or during the summer? Explain.
3. a. **Identifying** What government agency monitors air quality?
   b. **Summarizing** How and why has the air quality changed in the United States over the last 30 years?

### Lab zone At-Home Activity

**Dust in the Air** It's easy to see particles in the air. Gather your family members in a dark room. Open a window shade or blind slightly, or turn on a flashlight. Can they see tiny particles suspended in the beam of light? Discuss where the particles came from. What might be some natural sources? What might be some human sources?

Lab zone **Design Your Own Lab**

# How Clean Is the Air?

## Problem

How do weather and location affect the number of particles in the air?

## Skills Focus

measuring, interpreting data

## Materials

- rubber band
- coffee filters
- thermometer
- low-power microscope
- vacuum cleaner with intake hose (1 per class)

## Procedure 

### PART 1 Particles and Weather

1. Predict what factors will affect the number of particles you collect. How might different weather conditions affect your results?
2. In your notebook, make a data table like the one on the next page.
3. Place a coffee filter over the nozzle of the vacuum cleaner hose. Fasten the coffee filter securely to the hose with a rubber band. Make sure the air passes through the coffee filter as it enters the vacuum cleaner.
4. You will take air samples in the same outdoor location for five days. If necessary, you can run the vacuum cleaner cord out of a classroom window. **CAUTION:** *Do not use the vacuum cleaner outdoors on wet or rainy days.* If it is wet or rainy, collect the sample on the next clear day.
5. Hold the vacuum nozzle at least one meter above the ground each time you use the vacuum. Turn on the vacuum. Run the vacuum for 30 minutes.
6. While the vacuum is running, observe the weather conditions. Measure the outdoor temperature. Estimate the amount of precipitation, if any, since the previous observation. Note the direction from which the wind, if any, is blowing. Also note whether the wind is strong, light, or calm. Record your observations.
7. Shut off the vacuum. Remove the coffee filter from the nozzle. Label the filter with the place, time, and date. Draw a circle on the filter to show the area that was over the vacuum nozzle.
8. Place the coffee filter on the stage of a microscope (40 power). Be sure that the part of the filter that was over the vacuum nozzle is directly under the microscope lens. Without moving the coffee filter, count all the particles you see. Record the number in your data table.
9. Repeat Steps 3–8 each clear day.

### PART 2 Particles and Locations

10. Based on what you learned in Part 1, write a hypothesis for how the number of particles you collect can vary between two locations. The locations you choose should differ in some factor that might influence particle numbers.

| Data Table | | | | | |
|---|---|---|---|---|---|
| Date and Time | Temperature | Amount of Precipitation | Wind Direction | Wind Speed | Number of Particles |
| | | | | | |
| | | | | | |
| | | | | | |

11. Design an experiment to test your hypothesis. As you design your plan, consider the following:
    - What factors might affect the number of particles collected?
    - Which locations will you choose?
    - What procedure will you follow?
    - How will you control the variables in your experiment?
    - How will you record your new data?
12. Obtain your teacher's approval before carrying out your experiment. Be sure to record all your observations.

## Analyze and Conclude

1. **Measuring** In Part 1, was there a day of the week when you collected more particles?
2. **Interpreting Data** What factors changed during the week that could have caused changes in the particle count recorded in Part 1?
3. **Inferring** Did the weather have any effect on your day-to-day results? If so, which weather factor do you think was most important?
4. **Interpreting Data** Did your experiment in Part 2 prove or disprove your hypothesis?
5. **Controlling Variables** In your experiment in Part 2, which variables did you control? What was the manipulated variable? The responding variable?
6. **Classifying** Make a list of some possible sources of the particles you collected. Are these sources natural, or did the particles come from manufactured products?
7. **Designing Experiments** How could you improve your method to obtain more particles out of the air?
8. **Communicating** Identify areas in or around your school where there may be high levels of dust and other airborne particles. Write a brochure that suggests what people should do to protect themselves in these areas. Include suggestions for improvements that might lower the levels of particles in the identified areas.

## More to Explore

Do you think time of day will affect the number of particles you collect? Develop a hypothesis and a plan for testing it. Could you work with other classes to get data at different times of the day? Before carrying out your plan, get your teacher's approval.

Go Online PHSchool.com

**For:** Data sharing
**Visit:** PHSchool.com
**Web Code:** cfd-4010

Science and
**Society**

# Cars and Clean Air

New technology and strict laws have brought cleaner air to many American cities. But in some places the air is still polluted. Cars and trucks cause about half the air pollution in cities. And there are more motor vehicles on the road every year!

Worldwide, there are nearly 600 million cars. More cars will mean more traffic jams and more air pollution. What can people do to reduce air pollution by cars?

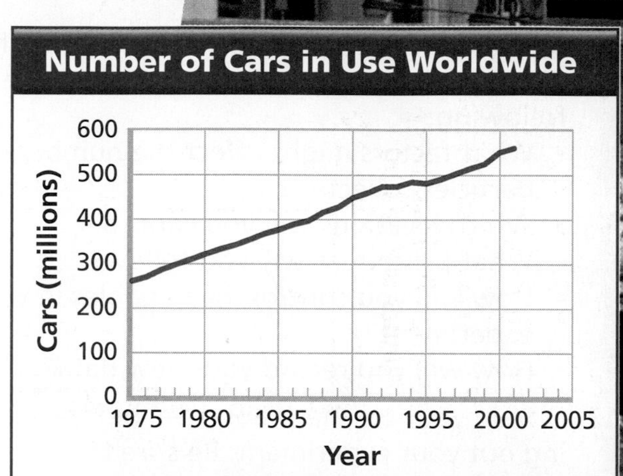


## The Issues

### Can Cars Be Made to Pollute Less?

From 1975 until 1987, the fuel economy of new cars and light trucks improved significantly. However, since 1987, the average fuel economy of such vehicles has gotten slightly worse. Why? People are driving larger vehicles, such as trucks, vans, and SUVs. These vehicles have more power, but get fewer miles per gallon of gasoline. As a result, the total amount of pollution from motor vehicles has been increasing in recent years.

New technologies offer the promise of improved fuel economy in the future. Hybrid vehicles use a combination of gasoline and electricity to obtain much improved gas mileage. A few vehicles use fuels such as hydrogen or natural gas in place of gasoline. Vehicles using such fuels produce little pollution.

Battery-powered electric cars produce no air pollution. But the electricity to charge the batteries comes from power plants that may burn oil or coal. So electric cars produce some pollution indirectly.

**A futuristic hybrid car** ▼

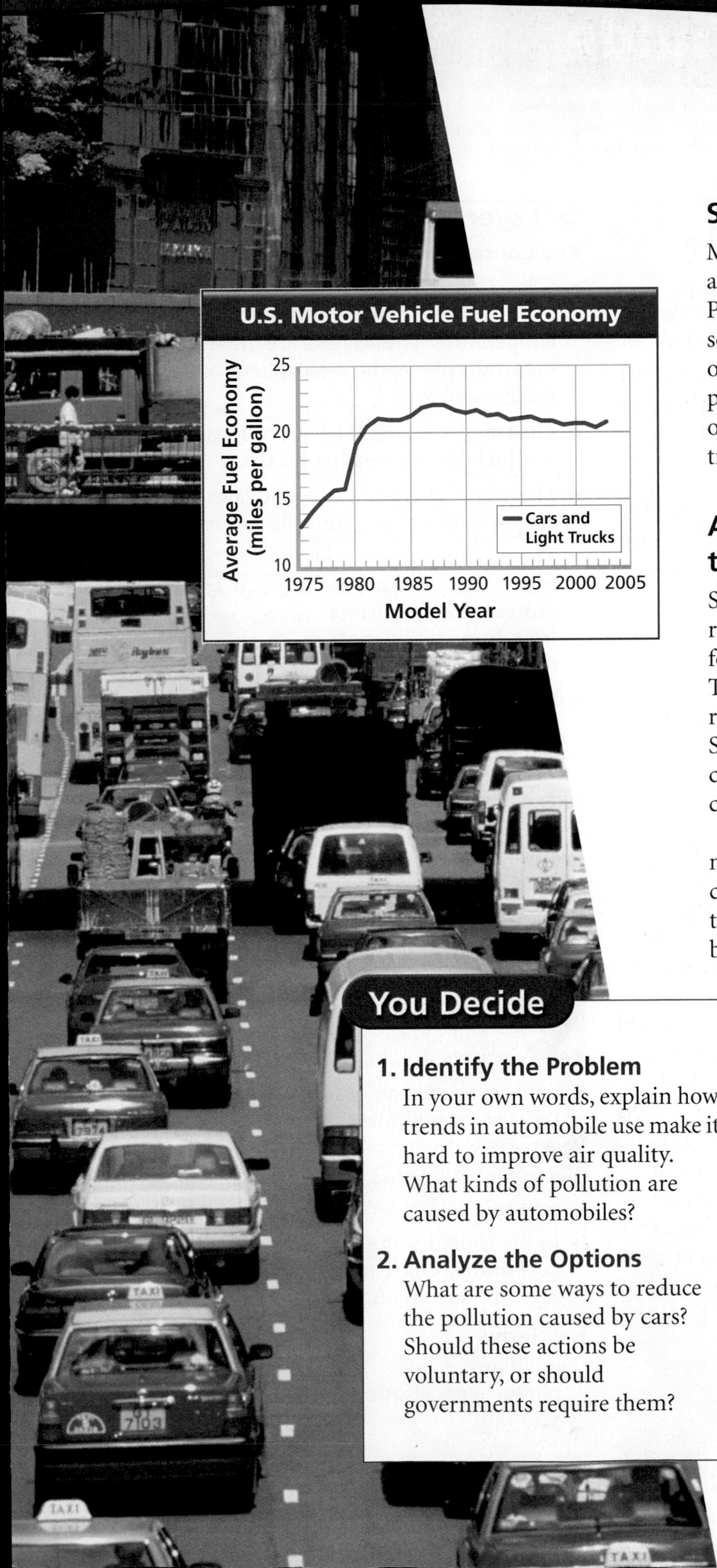

**U.S. Motor Vehicle Fuel Economy**

Average Fuel Economy (miles per gallon)

25
20
15
10

1975 1980 1985 1990 1995 2000 2005

Model Year

Cars and Light Trucks

## Should People Drive Less?

Many car trips are shorter than a mile—an easy distance for most people to walk. People might also consider riding a bicycle sometimes instead of driving. Many cars on the road are occupied by just one person. People might consider riding with others in car pools or taking buses or trains instead of driving.

## Are Stricter Standards or Taxes the Answer?

Some state governments have led efforts to reduce pollution. The state of California, for example, has strict anti-pollution laws. These laws set standards for gradually reducing pollutants released by cars. Stricter pollution laws might make new cars more expensive and old cars more costly to maintain.

Another approach is to make driving more expensive so that people use their cars less. That might mean higher gasoline taxes or fees for using the highways at busy times.

## You Decide

### 1. Identify the Problem

In your own words, explain how trends in automobile use make it hard to improve air quality. What kinds of pollution are caused by automobiles?

### 2. Analyze the Options

What are some ways to reduce the pollution caused by cars? Should these actions be voluntary, or should governments require them?

### 3. Find a Solution

How would you encourage people to try to reduce the pollution from cars? Create a visual essay from newspaper and magazine clippings. Write captions to explain your solution.

**For:** More on cars and clean air
**Visit:** PHSchool.com
**Web Code:** cfh-4010

# Chapter 15 Study Guide

**The BIG Idea**

**Structure of Earth's Atmosphere** Air pressure and temperature vary with altitude, location, and time. Changes in temperature with altitude result in distinct atmospheric layers: the troposphere, stratosphere, mesosphere, and exosphere.

## 1 The Air Around You

### Key Concepts

- Earth's atmosphere is made up of nitrogen, oxygen, carbon dioxide, water vapor, and many other gases, as well as particles of liquids and solids.
- Earth's atmosphere makes conditions on Earth suitable for living things.

### Key Terms

weather
atmosphere
ozone
water vapor

## 2 Air Pressure

### Key Concepts

- Because air has mass, it also has other properties, including density and pressure.
- Two common kinds of barometers are mercury barometers and aneroid barometers.
- Air pressure decreases as altitude increases. As air pressure decreases, so does density.

### Key Terms

density
pressure
air pressure
barometer
mercury barometer
aneroid barometer
altitude

## 3 Layers of the Atmosphere

### Key Concept

- Scientists divide Earth's atmosphere into four main layers classified according to changes in temperature. These layers are the troposphere, the stratosphere, the mesosphere, and the thermosphere.
- The troposphere is the layer of the atmosphere in which Earth's weather occurs.
- The stratosphere is the second layer of the atmosphere and contains the ozone layer.
- The mesosphere is the layer of the atmosphere that protects Earth's surface from being hit by most meteoroids.
- The outermost layer of Earth's atmosphere is the thermosphere.

### Key Terms

troposphere
stratosphere
mesosphere
thermosphere
ionosphere
exosphere

## 4 Air Quality

### Key Concepts

- Some air pollution occurs naturally. But many types of air pollution are the result of human activities.
- The burning of fossil fuels can cause smog and acid rain.
- In the United States, the federal and state governments have passed a number of laws and regulations to reduce air pollution.

### Key Terms

pollutant
photochemical smog
acid rain

# Review and Assessment

For: Self-Assessment
Visit: PHSchool.com
Web Code: cfa-4010

## Organizing Information

**Concept Mapping** Copy the concept map about air pressure onto a separate sheet of paper. Then complete it and add a title. (For more on concept mapping, see the Skills Handbook.)

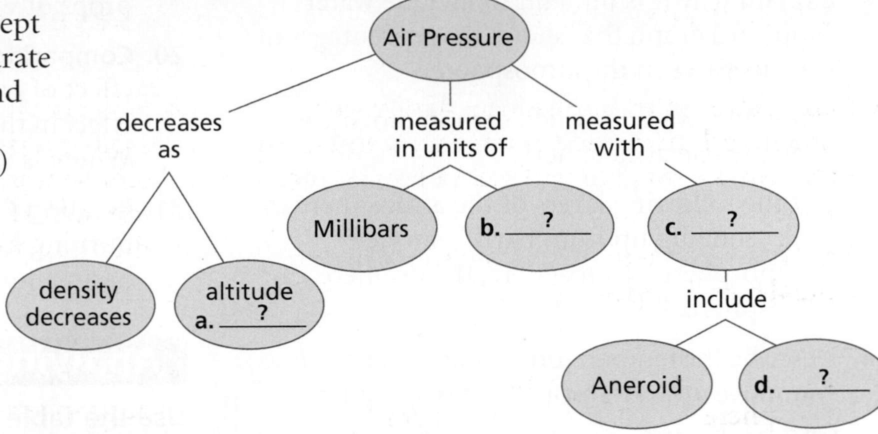


## Reviewing Key Terms

**Choose the letter of the best answer.**

1. The most abundant gas in the atmosphere is
   - **a.** ozone.
   - **b.** water vapor.
   - **c.** oxygen.
   - **d.** nitrogen.
2. Air pressure is typically measured with a
   - **a.** thermometer.
   - **b.** satellite.
   - **c.** barometer.
   - **d.** hot-air balloon.
3. The layers of the atmosphere are classified according to changes in
   - **a.** altitude.
   - **b.** temperature.
   - **c.** air pressure.
   - **d.** pollutants.
4. The layer of the atmosphere that reflects radio waves is called the
   - **a.** mesosphere.
   - **b.** troposphere.
   - **c.** ionosphere.
   - **d.** stratosphere.
5. Most air pollution is caused by
   - **a.** ozone.
   - **b.** acid rain.
   - **c.** photochemical smog.
   - **d.** the burning of fossil fuels.

**If the statement is true, write *true*. If it is false, change the underlined word or words to make the statement true.**

6. <u>Weather</u> is the condition of Earth's atmosphere at a particular time and place.
7. The force pushing on an area or surface is known as <u>density</u>.
8. Earth's weather occurs in the <u>thermosphere</u>.
9. The ozone layer is found in the <u>exosphere</u>.
10. When sulfur and nitrogen oxides mix with water in the air, they form <u>photochemical smog</u>.

## Writing in Science

**Descriptive Paragraph** Suppose you are on a hot air balloon flight to the upper levels of the troposphere. Describe how the properties of the atmosphere, such as air pressure and amount of oxygen, would change during your trip.

*The Atmosphere*

Video Preview
Video Field Trip
▶ Video Assessment

# Review and Assessment

## Checking Concepts

11. Explain why it is difficult to include water vapor in a graph that shows the percentages of various gases in the atmosphere.
12. Name two ways in which carbon dioxide is added to the atmosphere.
13. List the following layers of the atmosphere in order, moving up from Earth's surface: thermosphere, stratosphere, troposphere, mesosphere.
14. Describe the temperature changes that occur as you move upward through the troposphere.
15. What is the difference between photochemical smog and London-type smog?
16. How does acid rain form and what kinds of problems can it cause?

## Thinking Critically

17. **Applying Concepts** Why can an aneroid barometer be used to indicate changes in elevation as well as air pressure?
18. **Reading Graphs** According to the graph below, what is the air pressure at an altitude of 4 km? In general, how does air pressure change with altitude?

**Air Pressure and Altitude**

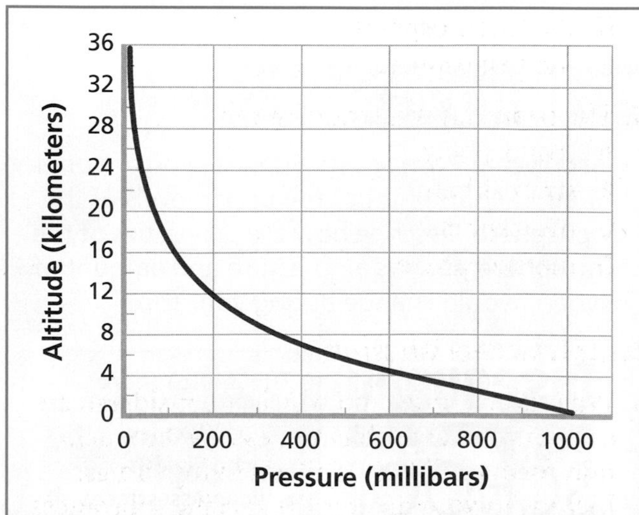


19. **Inferring** Why are clouds at the top of the troposphere made of ice crystals rather than drops of water?
20. **Comparing and Contrasting** Compare the effect of ozone in the troposphere with its effect in the stratosphere. Where is it harmful? Where is it helpful?
21. **Relating Cause and Effect** How could burning high-sulfur coal in a power plant harm a forest hundreds of kilometers away?

## Applying Skills

**Use the table below to answer the questions that follow.**

*The table shows the temperature at various altitudes above Omaha, Nebraska on a January day.*

| Altitude (kilometers) | 0 | 1.6 | 3.2 | 4.8 | 6.4 | 7.2 |
|---|---|---|---|---|---|---|
| Temperature (°C) | 0 | −4 | −9 | −21 | −32 | −40 |

22. **Graphing** Make a line graph of the data in the table. Put temperature on the horizontal axis and altitude on the vertical axis. Label your graph.
23. **Reading Graphs** At about what height above the ground was the temperature −15°C?
24. **Reading Graphs** What was the approximate temperature 2.4 kilometers over Omaha?
25. **Calculating** Suppose an airplane was about 6.8 kilometers above Omaha on this day. What was the approximate temperature at 6.8 kilometers? How much colder was the temperature at 6.8 kilometers above the ground than at ground level?

## Lab zone Chapter Project

**Performance Assessment** For your class presentation, prepare a display of your weather observations. Include drawings, graphs, and tables that summarize the weather you observed. Practice presenting your project to your group.

# Standardized Test Prep

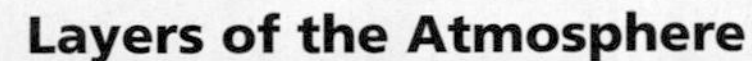

### Test-Taking Tip

**Reading All the Answer Choices**

When you answer a multiple-choice question, always read *every* answer choice before selecting an answer. One choice may be more complete than another choice, which may be only partially correct. Also "all of the above" may be a possible answer. If you stop reading as soon as you find an answer that seems correct, you won't notice that "all of the above" is an option.

***Sample Question***

The troposphere is the layer of the atmosphere

- **A** in which Earth's weather occurs.
- **B** that is closest to Earth's surface.
- **C** that contains most of the mass of the atmosphere.
- **D** all of the above

***Answer***

If you know that Earth's weather occurs in the troposphere, you might be tempted to stop reading and select choice **A.** However, choices **B** and **C** are also true. Therefore, the most complete answer is **D**, all of the above.

**Choose the letter of the best answer.**

**1.** What two gases make up approximately 99% of Earth's atmosphere?

- **A** nitrogen and carbon dioxide
- **B** oxygen and carbon dioxide
- **C** nitrogen and hydrogen
- **D** nitrogen and oxygen

**2.** In the troposphere, as altitude increases

- **F** air pressure decreases.
- **G** temperature decreases.
- **H** air density decreases.
- **J** all of the above

**Layers of the Atmosphere**

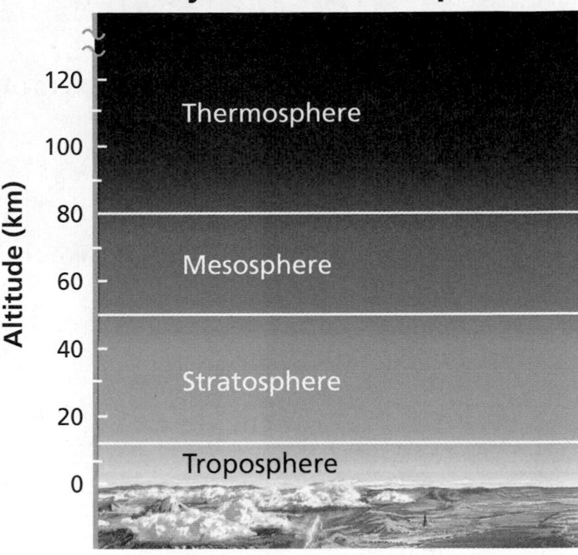


*Use the the diagram above and your knowledge of science to answer Questions 3 and 4.*

**3.** Use the diagram to estimate the depth of the stratosphere.

- **A** about 50 kilometers
- **B** about 40 kilometers
- **C** about 30 kilometers
- **D** about 20 kilometers

**4.** According to the diagram, where is a meteoroid when it is 75 kilometers above Earth's surface?

- **F** the mesosphere
- **G** the stratosphere
- **H** the thermosphere
- **J** the troposphere

**5.** The ozone layer is found in the

- **A** troposphere.
- **B** stratosphere.
- **C** mesosphere.
- **D** thermosphere.

### Constructed Response

**6.** What is acid rain, and why is it considered an environmental problem? Describe how acid rain forms and how it affects living things. Include in your answer the specific substances that combine to form acid rain.

# Chapter 16 Weather Factors

## The BIG Idea
Transfer of Energy

**What factors interact to produce changes in weather?**

### Chapter Preview

**1 Energy in Earth's Atmosphere**
- ***Discover*** Does a Plastic Bag Trap Heat?
- ***At-Home Activity*** Heating Your Home
- ***Skills Lab*** Heating Earth's Surface

**2 Heat Transfer**
- ***Discover*** What Happens When Air Is Heated?
- ***Math Skills*** Converting Units
- ***Try This*** Temperature and Height

**3 Winds**
- ***Discover*** Does the Wind Turn?
- ***Try This*** Build a Wind Vane
- ***Active Art*** Global Winds
- ***Technology Lab*** Measuring the Wind

**4 Water in the Atmosphere**
- ***Discover*** How Does Fog Form?
- ***Active Art*** The Water Cycle
- ***Analyzing Data*** Determining Relative Humidity
- ***At-Home Activity*** Water in the Air

**5 Precipitation**
- ***Discover*** How Can You Make Hail?
- ***Skills Activity*** Calculating

Rain is an important factor in helping these black-eyed Susans grow. ▶

**Weather Factors**

- ▶ Video Preview
- Video Field Trip
- Video Assessment

## Lab zone™ Chapter Project

### Design and Build Your Own Weather Station

In this chapter, you will learn about a variety of weather factors—such as air pressure, precipitation, and wind speed. As you learn about these factors, you will build your own weather station. Your weather station will include simple instruments that you will use to monitor the weather.

**Your Goal** To design and build a weather station to monitor at least three weather factors and to look for patterns that can be used to predict the next day's weather

You must

- design and build instruments for your weather station
- use your instruments to collect and record data in a daily log
- display your data in a set of graphs
- use your data to try to predict the weather
- follow the safety guidelines in Appendix A

**Plan It!** Begin your project by deciding where your weather station will be located. Plan which instruments you will build and how you will make your measurements. Prepare a log to record your daily observations. Finally, graph the data and look for any patterns that you can use to predict the next day's weather.

Section 1

# Energy in Earth's Atmosphere

## Reading Preview

### Key Concepts

- In what forms does energy from the sun travel to Earth?
- What happens to the sun's energy when it reaches Earth?

### Key Terms

- electromagnetic waves
- radiation
- infrared radiation
- ultraviolet radiation
- scattering
- greenhouse effect

### Target Reading Skill

**Sequencing** As you read, make a flowchart that shows how the sun's energy reaches Earth's surface. Put each step of the process in a separate box in the order in which it occurs.

**How Earth's Atmosphere Gets Energy**

Sun gives off energy.

↓

Energy travels to Earth as electromagnetic radiation.

↓

[ ]

## Lab zone Discover Activity

### Does a Plastic Bag Trap Heat?

1. Record the initial temperatures on two thermometers. (You should get the same readings.)
2. Place one of the thermometers in a plastic bag. Put a small piece of paper in the bag so that it shades the bulb of the thermometer. Seal the bag.
3. Place both thermometers on a sunny window ledge or near a light bulb. Cover the bulb of the second thermometer with a small piece of paper. Predict what you think will happen.
4. Wait five minutes. Then record the temperatures on the two thermometers.

**Think It Over**

**Measuring** Were the two temperatures the same? How could you explain any difference?

In the deserts of Arizona, summer nights can be chilly. In the morning, the sun is low in the sky and the air is cool. As the sun rises, the temperature increases. By noon it is quite hot. As you will learn in this chapter, heat is a major factor in the weather. The movement of heat in the atmosphere causes temperatures to change, winds to blow, and rain to fall.

## Energy From the Sun

Where does this heat come from? Nearly all the energy in Earth's atmosphere comes from the sun. This energy travels to Earth as **electromagnetic waves,** a form of energy that can move through the vacuum of space. Electromagnetic waves are classified according to wavelength, or distance between waves. **Radiation** is the direct transfer of energy by electromagnetic waves.

What kinds of energy do we receive from the sun? Is all of the energy the same? **Most of the energy from the sun travels to Earth in the form of visible light and infrared radiation. A small amount arrives as ultraviolet radiation.**

As the sun rises, energy in the form of electromagnetic waves reaches Earth's surface.

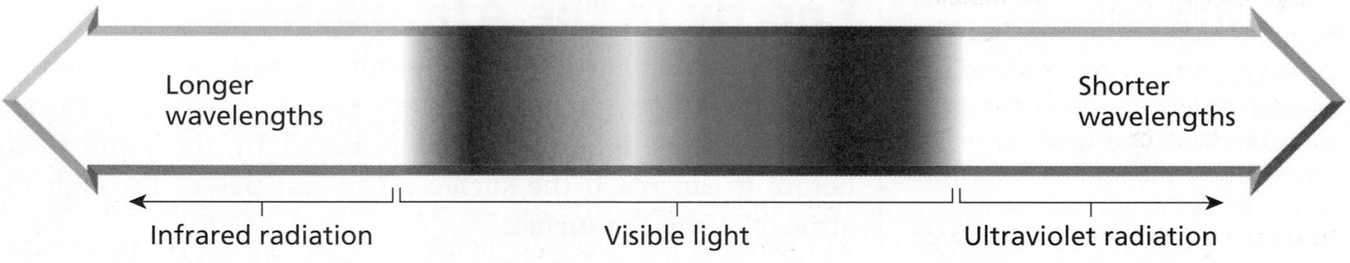


**FIGURE 1**
**Radiation From the Sun**
Energy from the sun travels to Earth as infrared radiation, visible light, and ultraviolet radiation.
**Interpreting Diagrams** *What type of radiation has wavelengths that are shorter than visible light?*

**Visible Light** Visible light includes all of the colors that you see in a rainbow: red, orange, yellow, green, blue, and violet. The different colors are the result of different wavelengths. Red and orange light have the longest wavelengths, while blue and violet light have the shortest wavelengths, as shown in Figure 1.

**Non-Visible Radiation** One form of electromagnetic energy, **infrared radiation,** has wavelengths that are longer than red light. Infrared radiation is not visible, but can be felt as heat. The sun also gives off **ultraviolet radiation,** which is an invisible form of energy with wavelengths that are shorter than violet light. Ultraviolet radiation can cause sunburns. This radiation can also cause skin cancer and eye damage.

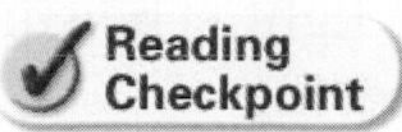

**Which color of visible light has the longest wavelengths?**

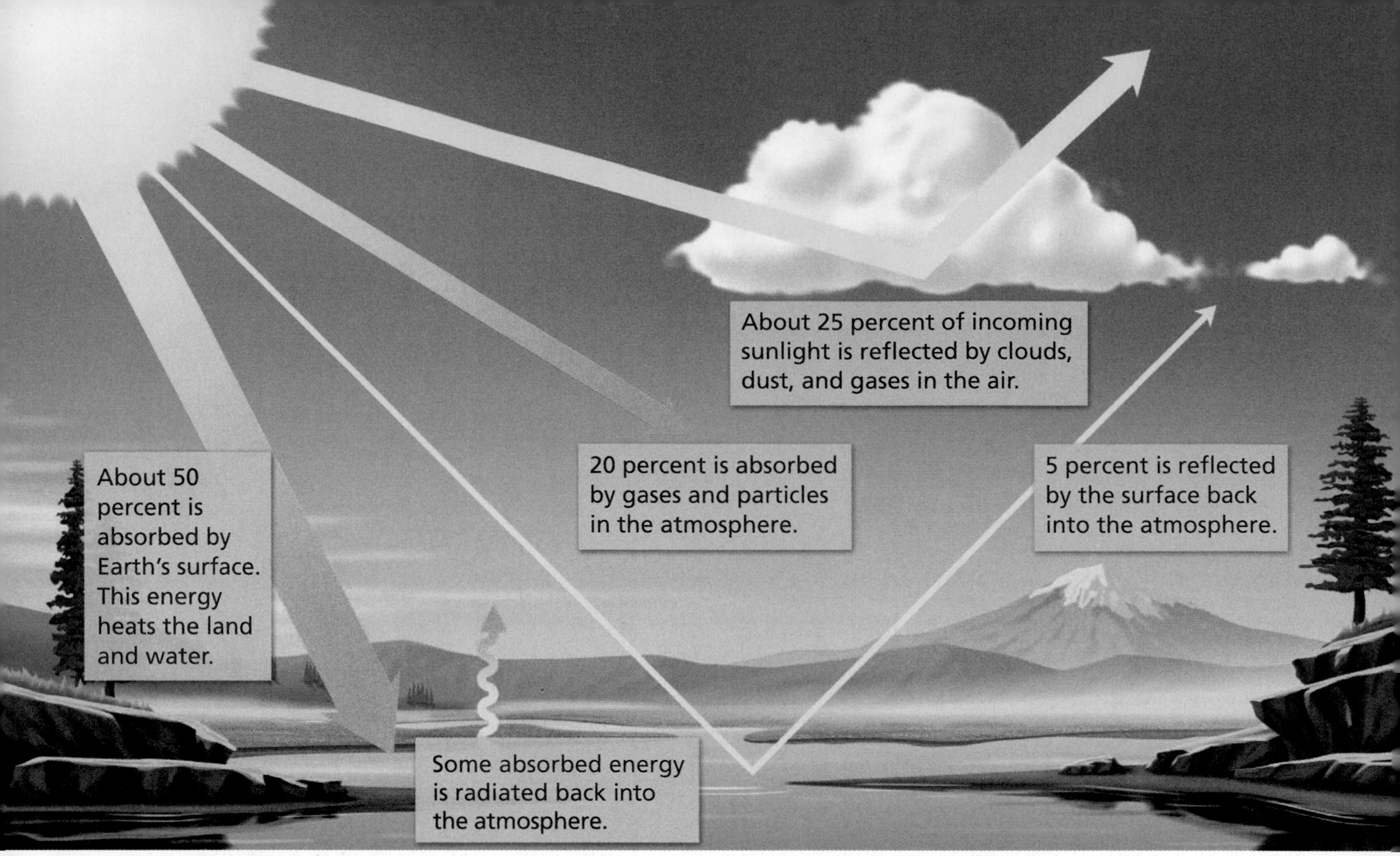

About 25 percent of incoming sunlight is reflected by clouds, dust, and gases in the air.

About 50 percent is absorbed by Earth's surface. This energy heats the land and water.

20 percent is absorbed by gases and particles in the atmosphere.

5 percent is reflected by the surface back into the atmosphere.

Some absorbed energy is radiated back into the atmosphere.

**FIGURE 2**
**Energy in the Atmosphere**
The sun's energy interacts with Earth's atmosphere and surface in several ways. About half is either reflected back into space or absorbed by the atmosphere. The rest reaches Earth's surface.

## Energy in the Atmosphere

Before reaching Earth's surface, sunlight must pass through the atmosphere. The path of the sun's rays is shown in Figure 2. **Some sunlight is absorbed or reflected by the atmosphere before it can reach the surface. The rest passes through the atmosphere to the surface.**

Part of the sun's energy is absorbed by the atmosphere. The ozone layer in the stratosphere absorbs most of the ultraviolet radiation. Water vapor and carbon dioxide absorb some infrared radiation. Clouds, dust, and other gases also absorb energy.

Some sunlight is reflected. Clouds act like mirrors, reflecting sunlight back into space. Dust particles and gases in the atmosphere reflect light in all directions, a process called **scattering.** When you look at the sky, the light you see has been scattered by gas molecules in the atmosphere. Gas molecules scatter short wavelengths of visible light (blue and violet) more than long wavelengths (red and orange). Scattered light therefore looks bluer than ordinary sunlight. This is why the daytime sky looks blue.

When the sun is rising or setting, its light passes through a greater thickness of the atmosphere than when the sun is higher in the sky. More light from the blue end of the spectrum is removed by scattering before it reaches your eyes. The remaining light contains mostly red and orange light. The sun looks red, and clouds around it become very colorful.

**For:** Links on energy in Earth's atmosphere
**Visit:** www.SciLinks.org
**Web Code:** scn-0921

## Energy at Earth's Surface

Some of the sun's energy reaches Earth's surface and is reflected back into the atmosphere. About half of the sun's energy, however, is absorbed by the land and water and changed into heat.

**When Earth's surface is heated, it radiates most of the energy back into the atmosphere as infrared radiation.** As shown in Figure 3, much of this infrared radiation cannot travel all the way through the atmosphere back into space. Instead, it is absorbed by water vapor, carbon dioxide, methane, and other gases in the air. The energy from the absorbed radiation heats the gases in the air. These gases form a "blanket" around Earth that holds heat in the atmosphere. The process by which gases hold heat in the air is called the **greenhouse effect.**

The greenhouse effect is a natural process that keeps Earth's atmosphere at a temperature that is comfortable for most living things. Over time, the amount of energy absorbed by the atmosphere and Earth's surface is in balance with the amount of energy radiated into space. In this way, Earth's average temperatures remain fairly constant. However, as you will learn later, emissions from human activities may be altering this process.

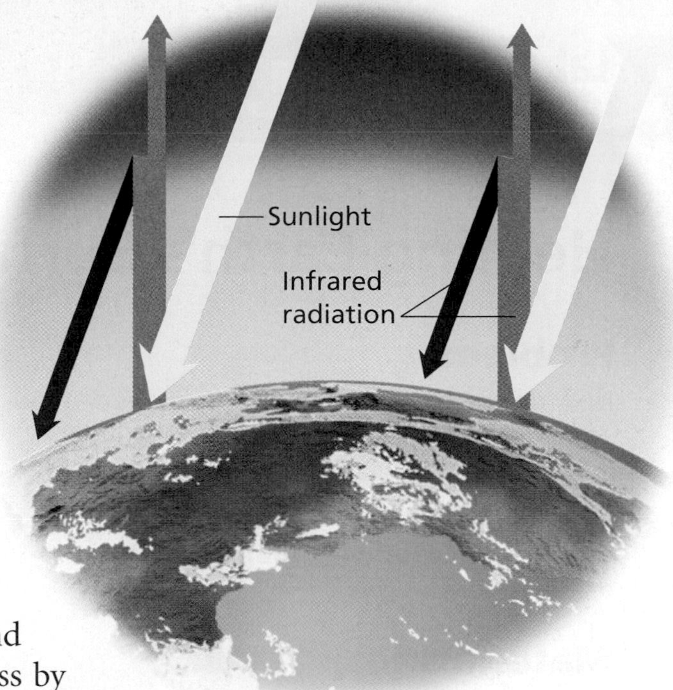


**FIGURE 3**
**Greenhouse Effect**
Sunlight travels through the atmosphere to Earth's surface. Earth's surface then gives off infrared radiation. Much of this energy is held by the atmosphere, warming it.

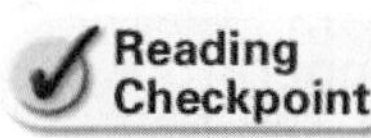


**What is the greenhouse effect?**

## Section 1 Assessment

### Target Reading Skill

**Sequencing** Refer to your flowchart about how the sun's energy reaches Earth's surface as you answer Question 2.

### Reviewing Key Concepts

1. a. **Listing** List three forms of radiation from the sun.
   b. **Comparing and Contrasting** Which form of radiation from the sun has the longest wavelength? The shortest wavelength?
2. a. **Summarizing** What happens to most of the sunlight that reaches Earth?
   b. **Interpreting Diagrams** What percentage of incoming sunlight is reflected by clouds, dust, and gases in the atmosphere?
   c. **Applying Concepts** Why are sunsets red?
3. a. **Describing** What happens to the energy from the sun that is absorbed by Earth's surface?
   b. **Predicting** How might conditions on Earth be different without the greenhouse effect?

### Lab zone At-Home **Activity**

**Heating Your Home** With an adult family member, explore the role radiation from the sun plays in heating your home. Does it make some rooms warmer in the morning? Are other rooms warmer in the afternoon? How does opening and closing curtains or blinds affect the temperature of a room? Explain your observations to your family.

Lab zone **Skills Lab**

# Heating Earth's Surface

## Problem

How do the heating and cooling rates of sand and water compare?

## Skills Focus

developing hypotheses, graphing, drawing conclusions

## Materials 

- 2 thermometers or temperature probes
- 2 beakers, 400-mL
- sand, 300 mL
- water, 300 mL
- lamp with 150-W bulb
- metric ruler
- clock or stopwatch
- string
- graph paper
- ring stand and two ring clamps

## Procedure   

1. Which do you think will heat up faster—sand or water? Record your hypothesis. Then follow these steps to test your hypothesis.
2. Copy the data table into your notebook. Add enough rows to record data for 15 minutes.
3. Fill one beaker with 300 mL of dry sand.
4. Fill the second beaker with 300 mL of water at room temperature.
5. Arrange the beakers side by side beneath the ring stand.
6. Place one thermometer in each beaker. If you are using a temperature probe, see your teacher for instructions.
7. Suspend the thermometers from the ring stand with string. This will hold the thermometers in place so they do not fall.
8. Adjust the height of the clamp so that the bulb of each thermometer is covered by about 0.5 cm of sand or water in a beaker.
9. Position the lamp so that it is about 20 cm above the sand and water. There should be no more than 8 cm between the beakers. **CAUTION:** *Be careful not to splash water onto the hot light bulb.*
10. Record the temperature of the sand and water in your data table.
11. Turn on the lamp. Read the temperature of the sand and water every minute for 15 minutes. Record the temperatures in the *Temperature With Light On* column in the data table.
12. Which material do you think will cool off more quickly? Record your hypothesis. Again, give reasons why you think your hypothesis is correct.
13. Turn the light off. Read the temperature of the sand and water every minute for another 15 minutes. Record the temperatures in the *Temperature With Light Off* column (16–30 minutes).

**Data Table**

| Temperature With Light On (°C) | | | Temperature With Light Off (°C) | | |
|---|---|---|---|---|---|
| Time (min) | Sand | Water | Time (min) | Sand | Water |
| Start | | | 16 | | |
| 1 | | | 17 | | |
| 2 | | | 18 | | |
| 3 | | | 19 | | |
| 4 | | | 20 | | |
| 5 | | | 21 | | |
| | | | | | |

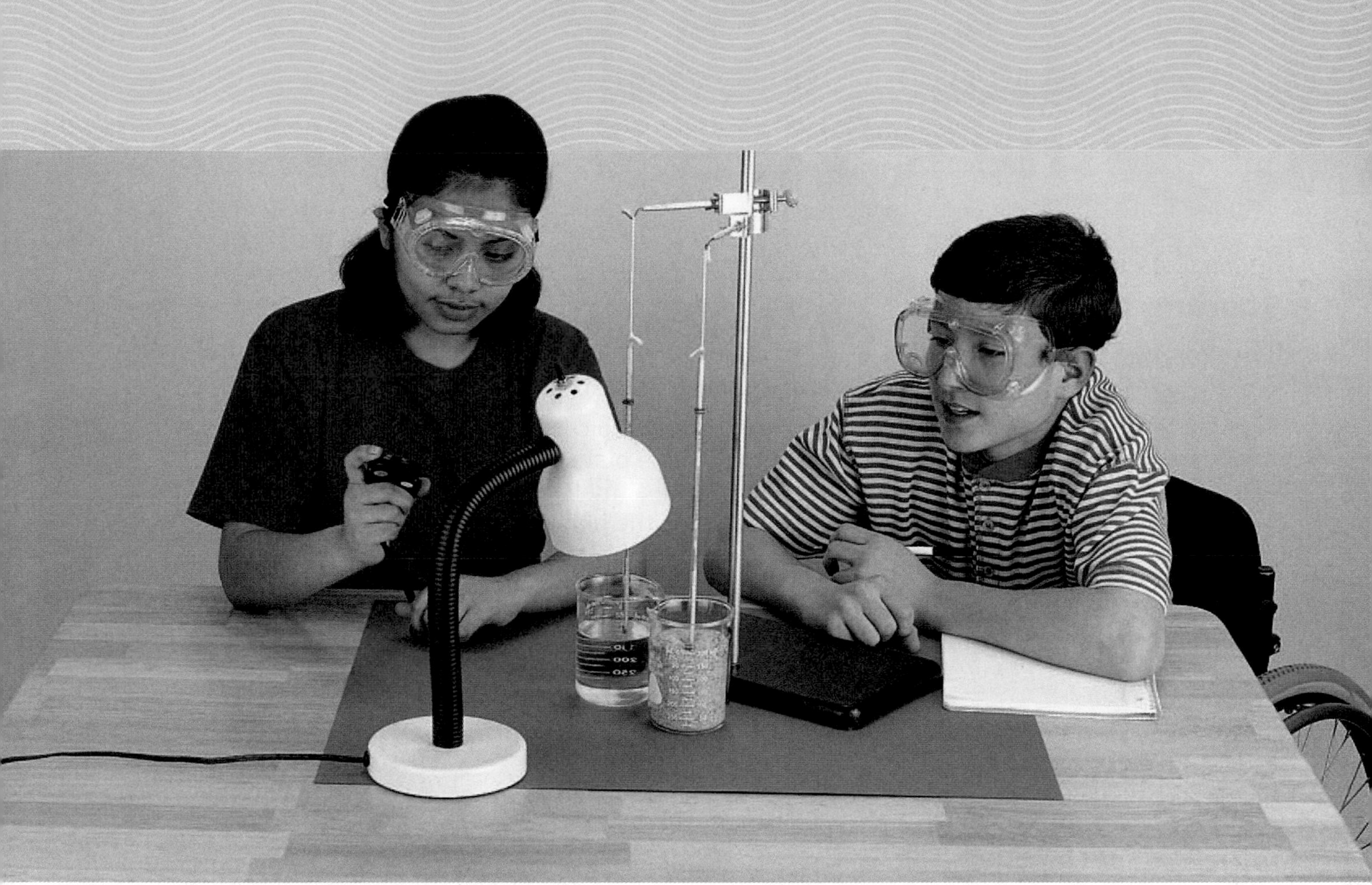

## Analyze and Conclude

1. **Graphing** Draw two line graphs to show the data for the temperature change in sand and water over time. Label the horizontal axis from 0 to 30 minutes and the vertical axis in degrees Celsius. Draw both graphs on the same piece of graph paper. Use a dashed line to show the temperature change in water and a solid line to show the temperature change in sand.
2. **Calculating** Calculate the total change in temperature for each material.
3. **Interpreting Data** Based on your data, which material had the greater increase in temperature?
4. **Drawing Conclusions** What can you conclude about which material absorbed heat faster? How do your results compare with your hypothesis?
5. **Interpreting Data** Review your data again. In 15 minutes, which material cooled faster?
6. **Drawing Conclusions** How do these results compare to your second hypothesis?
7. **Developing Hypotheses** Based on your results, which do you think will heat up more quickly on a sunny day: the water in a lake or the sand surrounding it? After dark, which will cool off more quickly?
8. **Communicating** If your results did not support either of your hypotheses, why do you think the results differed from what you expected? Write a paragraph in which you discuss the results and how they compared to your hypotheses.

## Design an Experiment

Do you think all solid materials heat up as fast as sand? For example, consider gravel, crushed stone, or different types of soil. Write a hypothesis about their heating rates as an "If ... then...." statement. With the approval and supervision of your teacher, develop a procedure to test your hypothesis. Was your hypothesis correct?

# Heat Transfer

## Reading Preview

### Key Concepts

- How is temperature measured?
- In what three ways is heat transferred?
- How is heat transferred in the troposphere?

### Key Terms

- temperature
- thermal energy
- thermometer
- heat
- conduction
- convection
- convection currents

### Target Reading Skill

**Outlining** As you read, make an outline about how heat is transferred. Use the red headings for the main topics and the blue headings for the subtopics.

**Heat Transfer**

I. Thermal energy and temperature
  A. Measuring temperature
  B.
II. How heat is transferred
  A.

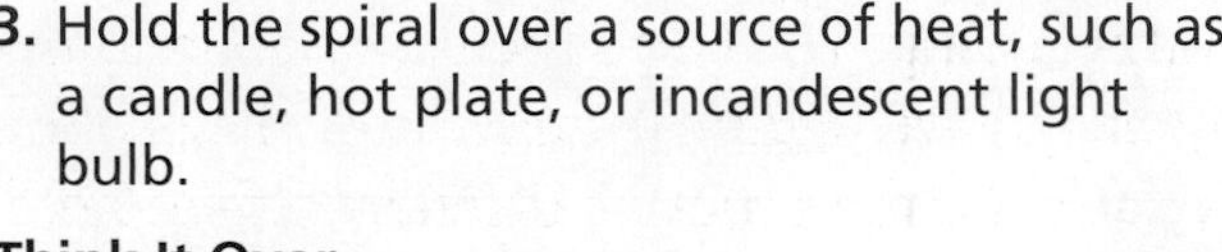


### What Happens When Air Is Heated?

1. Use heavy scissors to cut the flat part out of an aluminum pie plate. Use the tip of the scissors to poke a small hole in the middle of the flat part of the plate.
2. Cut the part into a spiral shape, as shown in the photo. Tie a 30-centimeter piece of thread to the middle of the spiral.
3. Hold the spiral over a source of heat, such as a candle, hot plate, or incandescent light bulb.

**Think It Over**

**Inferring** What happened to the spiral? Why do you think this happened?

You pour a cup of steaming tea from a teapot. Your teacup is warm to the touch. Somehow, heat was transferred from one object (the cup) to another (your hand) that it was touching. This is an example of conduction, one of three ways that heat can be transferred. As you'll learn in this section, heat transfer in the troposphere plays an important role in influencing Earth's weather.

**It takes only a small amount of energy to heat up a cup of tea.** ▶

**FIGURE 4**
**Movement of Molecules** The iced tea is cold, so its molecules move slowly. The herbal tea is hot, so its molecules move faster than the molecules in the iced tea.
**Inferring** *Which liquid has a higher temperature?*

## Thermal Energy and Temperature

The tea in the cup and in the teapot are at the same temperature but have a different amount of total energy. To understand this, you need to know that all substances are made up of tiny particles that are constantly moving. The faster the particles are moving, the more energy they have. Figure 4 shows how the motion of the particles is related to the amount of energy they hold. **Temperature** is the *average* amount of energy of motion of each particle of a substance. That is, temperature is a measure of how hot or cold a substance is. In contrast, the *total* energy of motion in the particles of a substance is called **thermal energy.** The hot tea in the teapot has more thermal energy than the hot tea in the cup because it has more particles.

**Measuring Temperature** Temperature is one of the most important factors affecting the weather. **Air temperature is usually measured with a thermometer.** A **thermometer** is a thin glass tube with a bulb on one end that contains a liquid, usually mercury or colored alcohol.

Thermometers work because liquids expand when they are heated and contract when they are cooled. When the air temperature increases, the temperature of the liquid in the bulb also increases. This causes the liquid to expand and rise up the column.

**Temperature Scales** Temperature is measured in units called degrees. Two temperature scales are commonly used: the Celsius scale and the Fahrenheit scale. Scientists use the Celsius scale. On the Celsius scale, the freezing point of pure water is 0°C (read "zero degrees Celsius"). The boiling point of pure water at sea level is 100°C. Weather reports in the United States use the Fahrenheit scale. On the Fahrenheit scale, the freezing point of water is 32°F and the boiling point is 212°F.

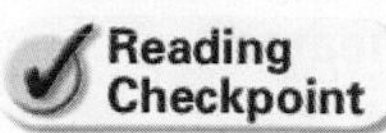


**Which temperature scale do scientists use?**

### Converting Units

Temperatures in weather reports use the Fahrenheit scale, but scientists use the Celsius scale. Temperature readings can be converted from the Fahrenheit scale to the Celsius scale using the following equation:

$$°C = \frac{5}{9}(°F - 32)$$

If the temperature is 68°F, what is the temperature in degrees Celsius?

$$°C = \frac{5}{9}(68 - 32)$$

$$°C = 20°C$$

**Practice Problem** Use the equation to convert the following temperatures from Fahrenheit to Celsius: 35.0°F, 60.0°F, and 72.0°F.

For: Links on heat transfer
Visit: www.SciLinks.org
Web Code: scn-0922

Lab zone **Try This Activity**

### Temperature and Height

How much difference is there between air temperatures near the ground and higher up? Give reasons for your prediction.

1. Take all of your measurements outside at a location that is sunny all day.
2. Early in the morning, measure the air temperature 1 cm and 1.25 m above the ground. Record the time and temperature for each height. Repeat your measurements late in the afternoon.
3. Repeat Step 2 for two more days.
4. Graph your data for each height with temperature on the vertical axis and time of day on the horizontal axis. Use the same graph paper and same scale for each graph. Label each graph.

**Interpreting Data** At which height did the temperature vary the most? How can you explain the difference?

## How Heat Is Transferred

**Heat** is the transfer of thermal energy from a hotter object to a cooler one. **Heat is transferred in three ways: radiation, conduction, and convection.**

**Radiation** Have you ever felt the warmth of the sun's rays on your face? You were feeling energy coming directly from the sun as radiation. Recall that radiation is the direct transfer of energy by electromagnetic waves. Most of the heat you feel from the sun travels to you as infrared radiation. You cannot see infrared radiation, but you can feel it as heat.

**Conduction** Have you ever walked barefoot on hot sand? Your feet felt hot because heat moved directly from the sand into your feet. The direct transfer of heat from one substance to another substance that it is touching is called **conduction.** When a fast-moving sand molecule bumps into a slower-moving molecule, the faster molecule transfers some of its energy.

The closer together the atoms or molecules in a substance are, the more effectively they can conduct heat. Conduction works well in some solids, such as metals, but not as well in liquids and gases. Air and water do not conduct heat very well.

**Convection** In fluids (liquids and gases), particles can move easily from one place to another. As the particles move, their energy goes along with them. The transfer of heat by the movement of a fluid is called **convection.**

**Heating the Troposphere** **Radiation, conduction, and convection work together to heat the troposphere.** During the day, the sun's radiation heats Earth's surface. The land becomes warmer than the air. Air near Earth's surface is warmed by both radiation and conduction. However, heat is not easily transferred from one air particle to another by conduction. Only the first few meters of the troposphere are heated by conduction. Thus, the air close to the ground is usually warmer than the air a few meters up.

Within the troposphere, heat is transferred mostly by convection. When the air near the ground is heated, its particles move more rapidly. As a result, they bump into each other and move farther apart. The air becomes less dense. Cooler, denser air sinks toward the surface, forcing the warmer air to rise. The upward movement of warm air and the downward movement of cool air form **convection currents.** Convection currents move heat throughout the troposphere.

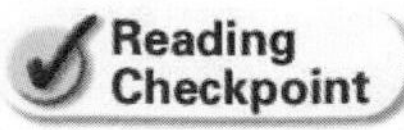

**How is the air near Earth's surface heated?**

**FIGURE 5**
**Heat Transfer**
All three types of heat transfer—radiation, conduction, and convection—help to warm the troposphere.

## Section 2 Assessment

**Target Reading Skill Outlining** Use the information in your outline about heat transfer to help you answer the questions below.

### Reviewing Key Concepts

1. **a. Defining** What is temperature?
   **b. Identifying** What instrument is used to measure air temperature?
   **c. Comparing and Contrasting** A pail of water is the same temperature as a lake. Compare the amount of thermal energy of the water in the lake and the water in the pail.
2. **a. Naming** Name three ways that heat can be transferred.
   **b. Describing** How do the three types of heat transfer work together to heat the troposphere?
   **c. Identifying** What is the major way that heat is transferred in the troposphere?
   **d. Applying Concepts** Explain how a hawk or eagle can sometimes soar upward without flapping its wings.

**Math Practice**

3. **Converting Units** Use the equation from the Math Skills Activity to convert the following temperatures from Fahrenheit to Celsius: 52°F, 86°F, 77°F, and 97°F.

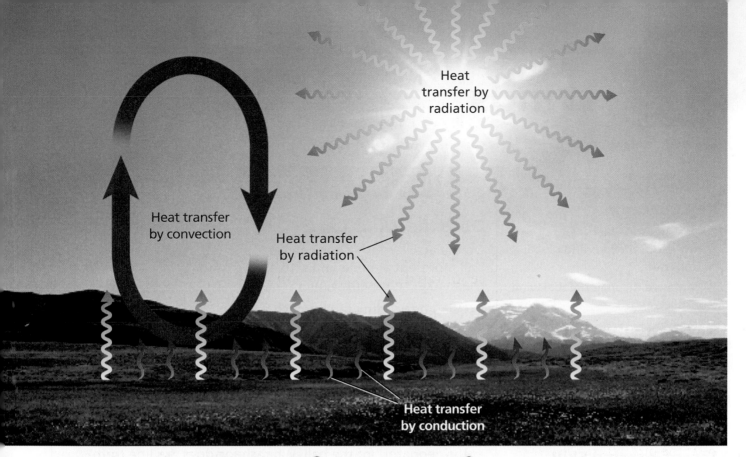

Section 3

# Winds

## Reading Preview

### Key Concepts

- What causes winds?
- How do local winds and global winds differ?
- Where are the major global wind belts located?

### Key Terms

- wind
- anemometer
- wind-chill factor
- local winds
- sea breeze
- land breeze
- global winds
- Coriolis effect
- latitude
- jet stream

### Target Reading Skill

**Relating Cause and Effect** As you read, identify how the unequal heating of the atmosphere causes the air to move. Write the information in a graphic organizer like the one below.

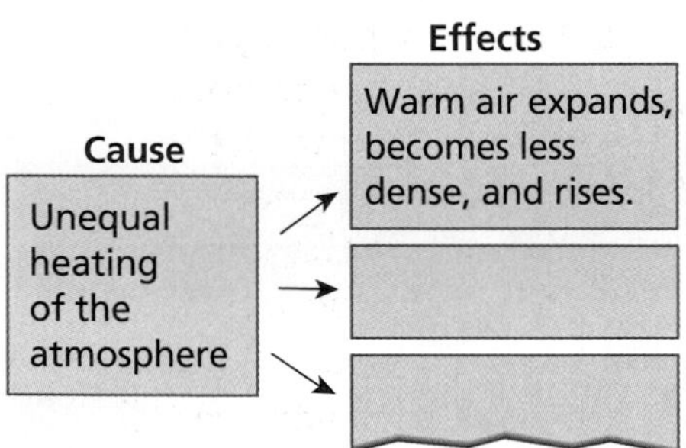
Effects
Cause
Unequal heating of the atmosphere
Warm air expands, becomes less dense, and rises.

A kite festival in Cape Town, South Africa ▶

## Lab zone Discover Activity

### Does the Wind Turn?

Do this activity with a partner. Let the ball represent a model of Earth and the marker represent wind.

1. Using heavy-duty tape, attach a pencil to a large smooth ball so that you can spin the ball from the top without touching it.
2. One partner should hold the pencil. Slowly turn the ball counterclockwise when seen from above.
3. While the ball is turning, the second partner should use a marker to try to draw a straight line from the "North Pole" to the "equator" of the ball. What shape does the line form?

**Think It Over**

**Making Models** If cold air were moving south from Canada into the continental United States, how would its movement be affected by Earth's rotation?

Have you ever flown a kite? Start by unwinding a few meters of string with the kite downwind from you. Have a friend hold the kite high overhead. Then, as your friend releases the kite, run directly into the wind. If you're lucky, the kite will start to rise. Once the kite is stable, you can unwind your string to let the wind lift the kite high into the sky. But what exactly is the wind that lifts the kite, and what causes it to blow?

## What Is Wind?

Because air is a fluid, it can move easily from place to place. Differences in air pressure cause the air to move. A **wind** is the horizontal movement of air from an area of high pressure to an area of lower pressure. **Winds are caused by differences in air pressure.**

Most differences in air pressure are caused by the unequal heating of the atmosphere. Convection currents form when an area of Earth's surface is heated by the sun's rays. Air over the heated surface expands and becomes less dense. As the air becomes less dense, its air pressure decreases. If a nearby area is not heated as much, the air above the less-heated area will be cooler and denser. The cool, dense air with a higher pressure flows underneath the warm, less dense air. This forces the warm air to rise.

**Measuring Wind** Winds are described by their direction and speed. Wind direction is determined with a wind vane. The wind swings the wind vane so that one end points into the wind. The name of a wind tells you where the wind is coming from. For example, a south wind blows from the south toward the north. A north wind blows to the south.

Wind speed can be measured with an **anemometer** (an uh MAHM uh tur). An anemometer has three or four cups mounted at the ends of spokes that spin on an axle. The force of the wind against the cups turns the axle. A meter on the axle shows the wind speed.

**Wind-Chill Factor** On a warm day, a cool breeze can be refreshing. But during the winter, the same breeze can make you feel uncomfortably cold. The wind blowing over your skin removes body heat. The stronger the wind, the colder you feel. The increased cooling a wind can cause is called the **wind-chill factor.** Thus a weather report may say, "The temperature outside is 20 degrees Fahrenheit. But with a wind speed of 30 miles per hour, the wind-chill factor makes it feel like 1 degree above zero."

**Lab zone Try This Activity**

### Build a Wind Vane

1. Use scissors to cut out a pointer and a slightly larger tail fin from construction paper.
2. Make a slit 1 cm deep in each end of a soda straw.
3. Slide the pointer and tail fin into place on the straw, securing them with small pieces of tape.

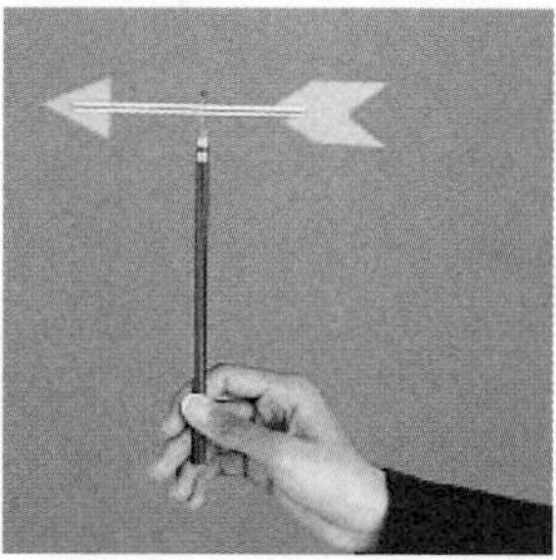

4. Hold the straw on your finger to find the point at which it balances.
5. Carefully push a pin through the balance point and into the eraser of a pencil. Make sure the wind vane can spin freely.

**Observing** How can you use your wind vane to tell the direction of the wind?

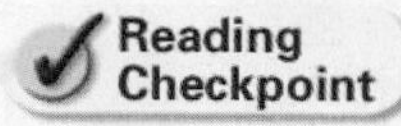


**Toward what direction does a west wind blow?**

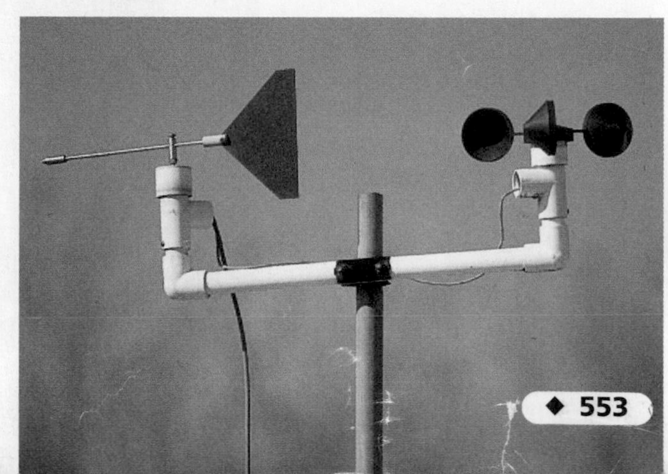

FIGURE 6
**Wind Direction and Speed**
The wind vane on the left points in the direction the wind is blowing from. The anemometer on the right measures wind speed. The cups catch the wind, turning faster when the wind blows faster.

## Local Winds

Have you ever noticed a breeze at the beach on a hot summer day? Even if there is no wind inland, there may be a cool breeze blowing in from the water. This breeze is an example of a local wind. **Local winds** are winds that blow over short distances. **Local winds are caused by the unequal heating of Earth's surface within a small area.** Local winds form only when large-scale winds are weak.

**Sea Breeze** Unequal heating often occurs along the shore of a large body of water. It takes more energy to warm up a body of water than it does to warm up an equal area of land. As the sun heats Earth's surface during the day, the land warms up faster than the water. As a result, the air over the land becomes warmer than the air over the water. The warm air expands and rises, creating a low-pressure area. Cool air blows inland from over the water and moves underneath the warm air, causing a sea breeze. A **sea breeze** or a lake breeze is a local wind that blows from an ocean or lake. Figure 7 shows a sea breeze.

**Land Breeze** At night, the process is reversed. Land cools more quickly than water, so the air over the land becomes cooler than the air over the water. As the warmer air over the water expands and rises, cooler air from the land moves beneath it. The flow of air from land to a body of water is called a **land breeze.**

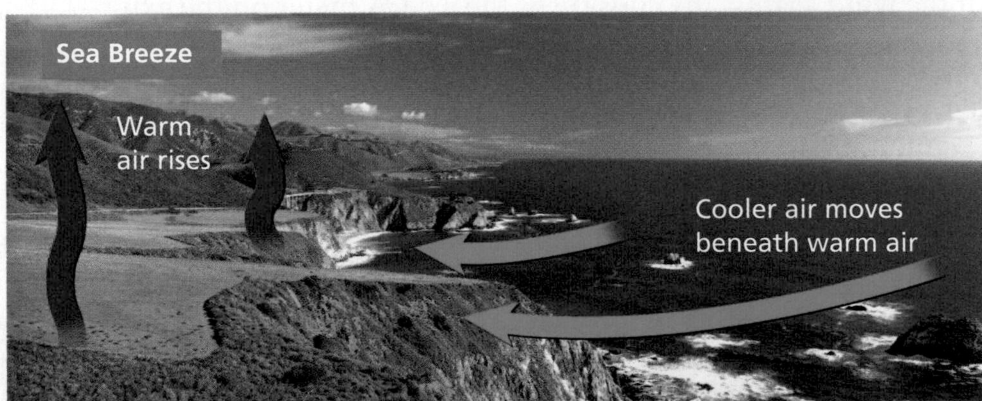


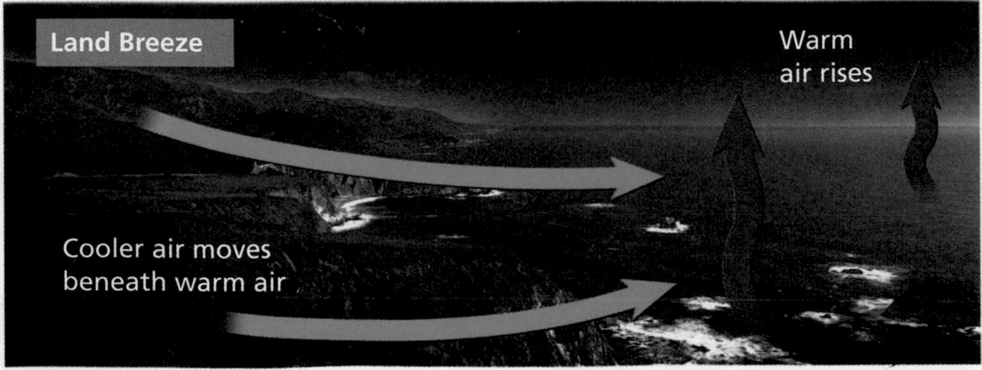


**FIGURE 7**
**Local Winds**
During the day, cool air moves from the sea to the land, creating a sea breeze. At night, cooler air moves from the land to the sea.
**Forming Operational Definitions** *What type of breeze occurs at night?*

## Global Winds

**Global winds** are winds that blow steadily from specific directions over long distances. **Like local winds, global winds are created by the unequal heating of Earth's surface. But unlike local winds, global winds occur over a large area.** Recall how the sun's radiation strikes Earth. In the middle of the day near the equator, the sun is almost directly overhead. The direct rays from the sun heat Earth's surface intensely. Near the poles, the sun's rays strike Earth's surface at a lower angle. The sun's energy is spread out over a larger area, so it heats the surface less. As a result, temperatures near the poles are much lower than they are near the equator.

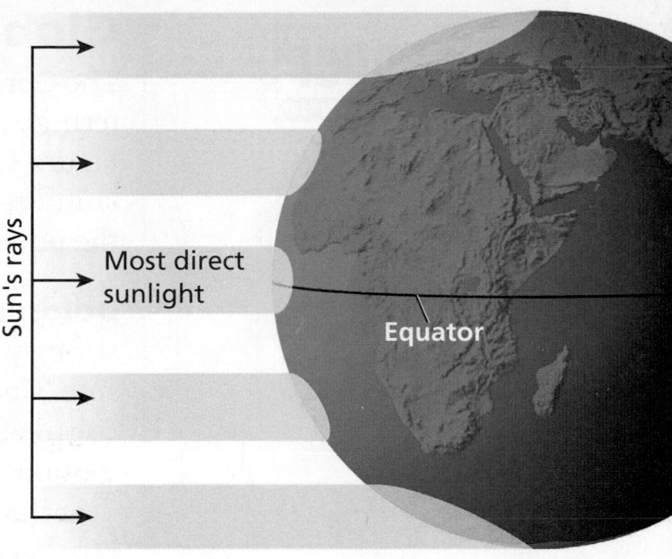


FIGURE 8
**Angle of Sun's Rays**
Near the equator, energy from the sun strikes Earth almost directly. Near the poles, the same amount of energy is spread out over a larger area.

**Global Convection Currents** How do global winds develop? Temperature differences between the equator and the poles produce giant convection currents in the atmosphere. Warm air rises at the equator, and cold air sinks at the poles. Therefore air pressure tends to be lower near the equator and greater near the poles. This difference in pressure causes winds at Earth's surface to blow from the poles toward the equator. Higher in the atmosphere, however, air flows away from the equator toward the poles. Those air movements produce global winds.

**The Coriolis Effect** If Earth did not rotate, global winds would blow in a straight line from the poles toward the equator. Because Earth is rotating, however, global winds do not follow a straight path. As the winds blow, Earth rotates from west to east underneath them, making it seem as if the winds have curved. The way Earth's rotation makes winds curve is called the **Coriolis effect** (kawr ee OH lis).

Because of the Coriolis effect, global winds in the Northern Hemisphere gradually turn toward the right. As Figure 9 shows, a wind blowing toward the south gradually turns toward the southwest. In the Southern Hemisphere, winds curve toward the left.

**Which way do winds turn in the Southern Hemisphere?**

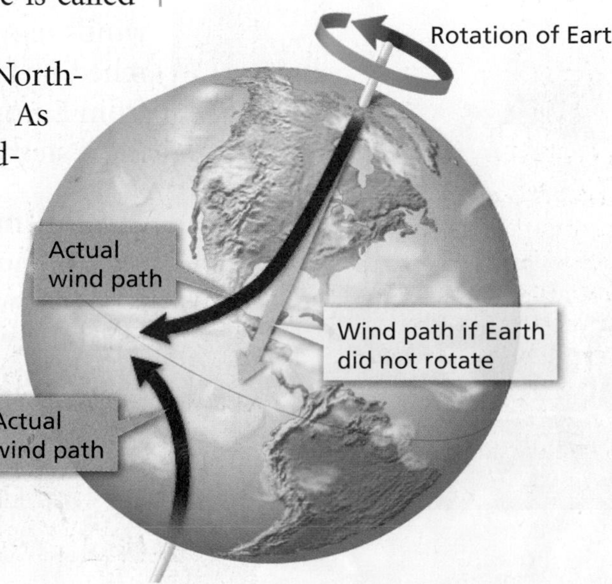


FIGURE 9
**Coriolis Effect**
As Earth rotates, the Coriolis effect turns winds in the Northern Hemisphere toward the right.

## Global Wind Belts

The Coriolis effect and other factors combine to produce a pattern of calm areas and wind belts around Earth, as shown in Figure 11. The calm areas include the doldrums and the horse latitudes. **The major global wind belts are the trade winds, the polar easterlies, and the prevailing westerlies.**

**Doldrums** Near the equator, the sun heats the surface strongly. Warm air rises steadily, creating an area of low pressure. Cool air moves into the area, but is warmed rapidly and rises before it moves very far. There is very little horizontal motion, so the winds near the equator are very weak. Regions near the equator with little or no wind are called the doldrums.

**Horse Latitudes** Warm air that rises at the equator divides and flows both north and south. **Latitude** is distance from the equator, measured in degrees. At about 30° north and south latitudes, the air stops moving toward the poles and sinks. In each of these regions, another belt of calm air forms. Hundreds of years ago, sailors becalmed in these waters ran out of food and water for their horses and had to throw the horses overboard. Because of this, the latitudes 30° north and south of the equator came to be called the horse latitudes.

**Trade Winds** When the cold air over the horse latitudes sinks, it produces a region of high pressure. This high pressure causes surface winds to blow both toward the equator and away from it. The winds that blow toward the equator are turned west by the Coriolis effect. As a result, winds in the Northern Hemisphere between 30° north latitude and the equator generally blow from the northeast. In the Southern Hemisphere between 30° south latitude and the equator, the winds blow from the southeast. For hundreds of years, sailors relied on these winds to move ships carrying valuable cargoes from Europe to the West Indies and South America. As a result, these steady easterly winds are called the trade winds.

**Prevailing Westerlies** In the mid-latitudes, between 30° and 60° north and south, winds that blow toward the poles are turned toward the east by the Coriolis effect. Because they blow from the west to the east, they are called prevailing westerlies. The prevailing westerlies blow generally from the southwest in north latitudes and from the northwest in south latitudes. The prevailing westerlies play an important part in the weather of the United States.

**FIGURE 10**
**Ocean Sailing**
Sailing ships relied on global winds to speed their journeys to various ports around the world.
**Applying Concepts** *How much effect do you think the prevailing winds have on shipping today?*

FIGURE 11
## Global Winds
A series of wind belts circles Earth. Between the wind belts are calm areas where air is rising or falling. **Interpreting Diagrams** *Which global wind belt would a sailor choose to sail from eastern Canada to Europe?*

**Go Online** *active art*
**For:** Global Winds activity
**Visit:** PHSchool.com
**Web Code:** cfp-4023

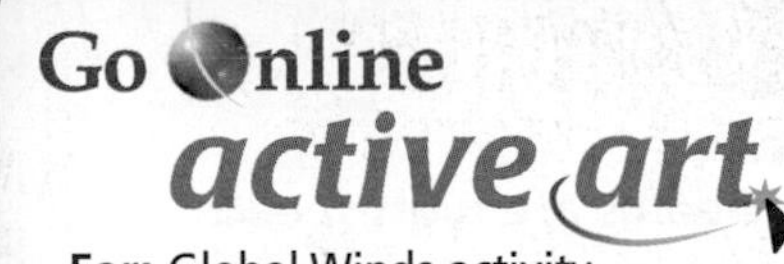

90°N
Polar Easterlies
60°N
Prevailing Westerlies blow away from the horse latitudes.
Prevailing Westerlies
Horse Latitudes are calm areas of falling air.
Horse Latitudes
30°N
Trade Winds
Doldrums are a calm area where warm air rises.
Equator 0°
Doldrums
Trade Winds
Trade Winds blow from the horse latitudes toward the equator.
Horse Latitudes
30°S
Prevailing Westerlies
60°S
Polar Easterlies blow cold air away from the poles.
90°S
N
W
E
S

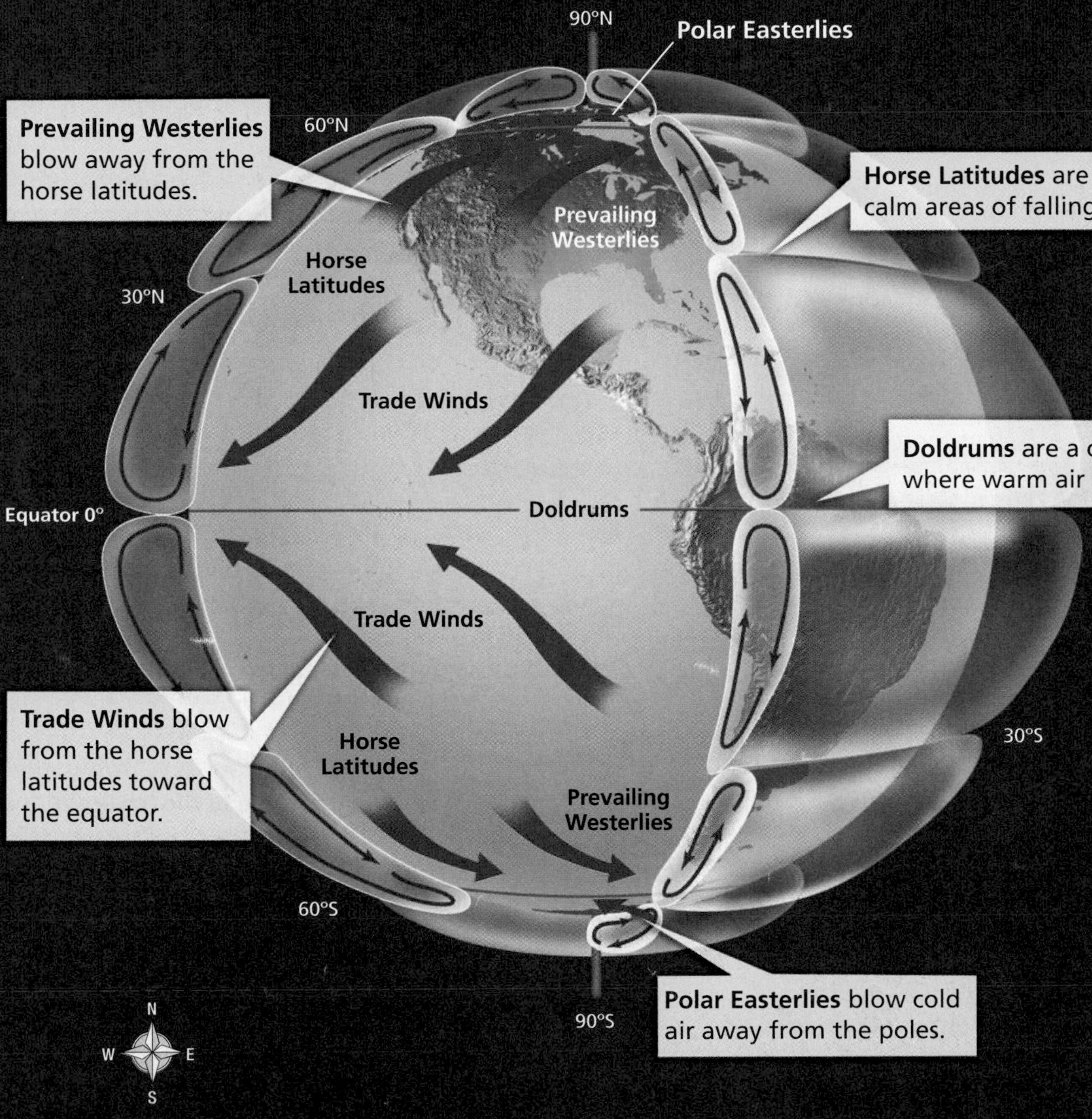

**FIGURE 12**
**Jet Streams**
The jet streams are high-speed bands of winds occurring at the top of the troposphere. By traveling east in a jet stream, pilots can save time and fuel.

**Polar Easterlies** Cold air near the poles sinks and flows back toward lower latitudes. The Coriolis effect shifts these polar winds to the west, producing the polar easterlies. The polar easterlies meet the prevailing westerlies at about 60° north and 60° south latitudes, along a region called the polar front. The mixing of warm and cold air along the polar front has a major effect on weather in the United States.

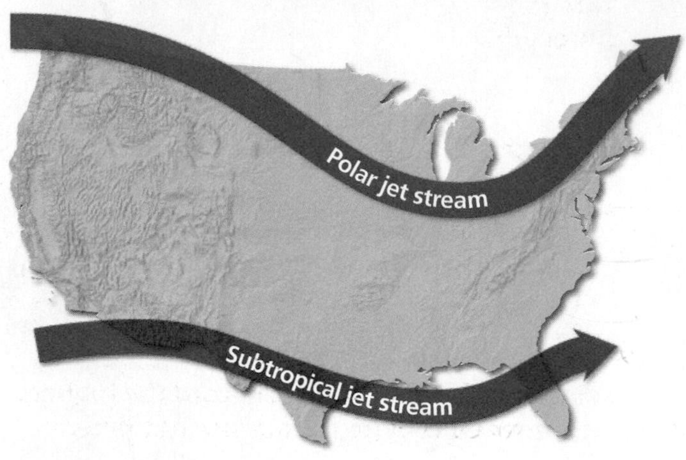


**Jet Streams** About 10 kilometers above Earth's surface are bands of high-speed winds called **jet streams.** These winds are hundreds of kilometers wide but only a few kilometers deep. Jet streams generally blow from west to east at speeds of 200 to 400 kilometers per hour, as shown in Figure 12. As jet streams travel around Earth, they wander north and south along a wavy path.

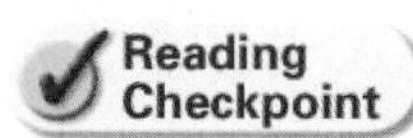

**What are the jet streams?**

## Section 3 Assessment

### Target Reading Skill

**Relating Cause and Effect** Refer to your graphic organizer about the effects of unequal heating to help you answer Question 1 below.

### Reviewing Key Concepts

1. a. **Defining** What is wind?
   b. **Relating Cause and Effect** How is wind related to air temperature and air pressure?
   c. **Applying Concepts** It's fairly warm but windy outside. Use the concept of wind-chill factor to explain why it may be a good idea to wear a jacket.
2. a. **Defining** What are local winds?
   b. **Summarizing** What causes local winds?
   c. **Comparing and Contrasting** Compare the conditions that cause a sea breeze with those that cause a land breeze.
3. a. **Identifying** Name the three major global wind belts.
   b. **Describing** Briefly describe the three major global wind belts and where they are located.
   c. **Interpreting Diagrams** Use Figure 9 and Figure 11 to describe how the Coriolis effect influences the direction of the trade winds in the Northern Hemisphere. Does it have the same effect in the Southern Hemisphere? Explain.

### Writing in Science

**Explanation** Imagine that you are a hot-air balloonist. You want to fly your balloon across the continental United States. To achieve the fastest time, would it make more sense to fly east-to-west or west-to-east? Explain how the prevailing winds influenced your decision.

Lab zone **Technology Lab**

• Tech & Design •

# Measuring the Wind

## Problem

Can you design and build an anemometer to measure the wind?

## Design Skills

evaluating the design, redesigning

## Materials

- pen
- round toothpick
- masking tape
- 2 wooden coffee stirrers
- meter stick
- corrugated cardboard sheet, 15 cm × 20 cm
- wind vane

## Procedure

1. Begin by making a simple anemometer that uses wooden coffee stirrers to indicate wind speed. On a piece of cardboard, draw a curved scale like the one shown in the diagram. Mark it in equal intervals from 0 to 10.
2. Carefully use the pen to make a small hole where the toothpick will go. Insert the toothpick through the hole.
3. Tape the wooden coffee stirrers to the toothpick as shown in the diagram, one on each side of the cardboard.
4. Copy the data table into your notebook.

| Data Table | | |
|---|---|---|
| Location | Wind Direction | Wind Speed |
| | | |
| | | |
| | | |

5. Take your anemometer outside the school. Stand about 2–3 m away from the building and away from any corners or large plants.
6. Use the wind vane to find out what direction the wind is coming from. Hold your anemometer so that the card is straight, vertical, and parallel to the wind direction.

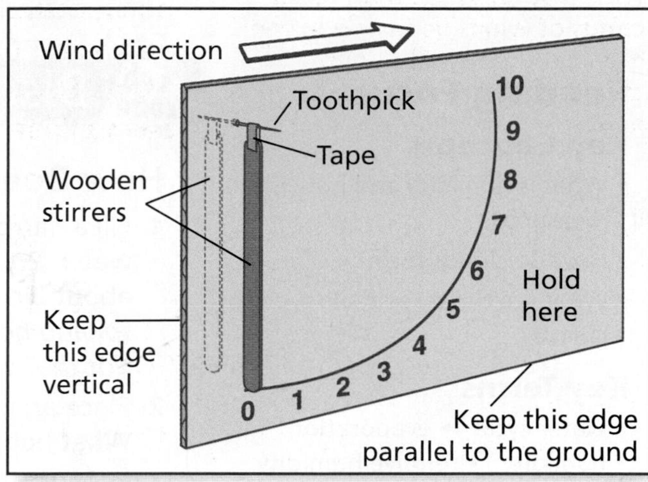


7. Observe the wooden stirrer on your anemometer for one minute. Record the highest wind speed that occurs during that time.
8. Repeat your measurements on all the other sides of the building. Record your data.

## Analyze and Conclude

1. **Interpreting Data** Was the wind stronger on one side of the school than on the other sides? Explain your observations.
2. **Applying Concepts** Based on your data, which side of the building provides the best location for a door?
3. **Evaluating the Design** Do you think your anemometer accurately measured all of the winds you encountered? How could you improve its accuracy?
4. **Redesigning** What was the hardest part of using your anemometer? How could you change your design to make it more useful at very low or at very high wind speeds? Explain.
5. **Working With Design Constraints** How did having to use the materials provided by your teacher affect your anemometer? How would your design have changed if you could have used any materials you wanted to?

## Communicate

Write a brochure describing the benefits of your anemometer. Make sure your brochure explains how the anemometer works and its potential uses.

# Section 4 Water in the Atmosphere

## Reading Focus

### Key Concepts

- What is humidity and how is it measured?
- How do clouds form?
- What are the three main types of clouds?

### Key Terms

- water cycle
- evaporation
- humidity
- relative humidity
- psychrometer
- condensation
- dew point
- cirrus
- cumulus
- stratus

### Target Reading Skill

**Asking Questions** Before you read, preview the red headings. In a graphic organizer like the one below, ask *what* or *how* questions for each heading. As you read, write answers to your questions.

**The Water Cycle**

| Question | Answer |
|---|---|
| How does the water cycle work? | During the water cycle . . . |
| | |

## Lab zone Discover Activity

### How Does Fog Form?

1. Fill a narrow-necked plastic bottle with hot tap water. Pour out most of the water, leaving about 3 cm at the bottom. **CAUTION:** *Avoid spilling hot water. Do not use water that is so hot that you cannot safely hold the bottle.*
2. Place an ice cube on the mouth of the bottle. What happens?
3. Repeat Steps 1 and 2 using cold water instead of hot water. What happens?

**Think It Over**

**Developing Hypotheses** How can you explain your observations? Why is there a difference between what happens with the hot water and what happens with the cold water?

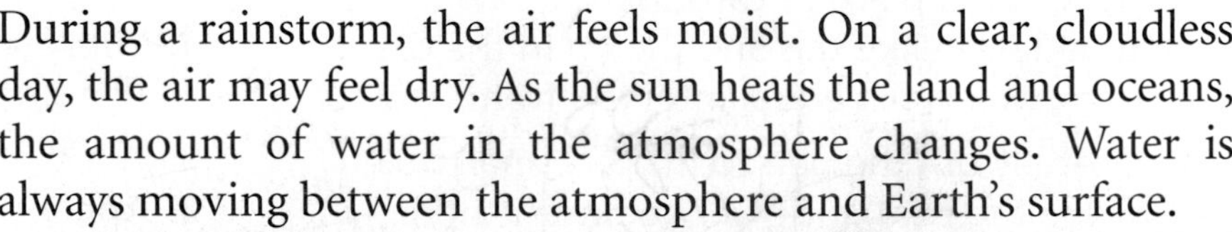

During a rainstorm, the air feels moist. On a clear, cloudless day, the air may feel dry. As the sun heats the land and oceans, the amount of water in the atmosphere changes. Water is always moving between the atmosphere and Earth's surface.

The movement of water between the atmosphere and Earth's surface is called the **water cycle.** As you can see in Figure 13, water vapor enters the air by evaporation from the oceans and other bodies of water. **Evaporation** is the process by which water molecules in liquid water escape into the air as water vapor. Water vapor is also added to the air by living things. Water enters the roots of plants, rises to the leaves, and is released as water vapor.

As part of the water cycle, some of the water vapor in the atmosphere condenses to form clouds. Rain and snow fall from the clouds toward the surface. The water then runs off the surface or moves through the ground, back into the lakes, streams, and eventually the oceans.

## Humidity

How is the quantity of water vapor in the atmosphere measured? **Humidity** is a measure of the amount of water vapor in the air. Air's ability to hold water vapor depends on its temperature. Warm air can hold more water vapor than cool air.

**Relative Humidity** Weather reports usually refer to the water vapor in the air as relative humidity. **Relative humidity** is the percentage of water vapor that is actually in the air compared to the maximum amount of water vapor the air can hold at a particular temperature. For example, at 10°C, 1 cubic meter of air can hold at most 8 grams of water vapor. If there actually were 8 grams of water vapor in the air, then the relative humidity of the air would be 100 percent. Air with a relative humidity of 100 percent is said to be saturated. If the air had 4 grams of water vapor, the relative humidity would be half, or 50 percent.

FIGURE 13
**Water Cycle**
In the water cycle, water moves from oceans, lakes, rivers, and plants into the atmosphere and then falls back to Earth.

For: Water Cycle activity
Visit: PHSchool.com
Web Code: cfp-4024

Condensation

Precipitation

Evaporation from plants

Evaporation from oceans, lakes, and streams

Surface runoff

**FIGURE 14**
**Sling Psychrometer**
A sling psychrometer is used to measure relative humidity.

**Measuring Relative Humidity** **Relative humidity can be measured with an instrument called a psychrometer.** A **psychrometer** (sy KRAHM uh tur) has two thermometers, a wet-bulb thermometer and a dry-bulb thermometer, as shown in Figure 14. The bulb of the wet-bulb thermometer has a cloth covering that is moistened with water. When the psychrometer is "slung," or spun by its handle, air blows over both thermometers. Because the wet-bulb thermometer is cooled by evaporation, its reading drops below that of the dry-bulb thermometer.

If the relative humidity is high, the water on the wet bulb evaporates slowly, and the wet-bulb temperature does not change much. If the relative humidity is low, the water on the wet bulb evaporates rapidly, and the wet-bulb temperature drops. The relative humidity can be found by comparing the temperatures of the wet-bulb and dry-bulb thermometers.

**What instrument measures relative humidity?**

## Math Analyzing Data

### Determining Relative Humidity

Relative humidity is affected by temperature. Use the data table to answer the questions below. First, find the dry-bulb temperature in the left column of the table. Then find the difference between the wet- and dry-bulb temperatures across the top of the table. The number in the table where these two readings intersect indicates the relative humidity in percent.

**Relative Humidity**

| Dry-Bulb Reading (°C) | Difference Between Wet- and Dry-Bulb Readings (°C) | | | | |
|---|---|---|---|---|---|
| | 1 | 2 | 3 | 4 | 5 |
| 10 | 88 | 76 | 65 | 54 | 43 |
| 12 | 88 | 78 | 67 | 57 | 48 |
| 14 | 89 | 79 | 69 | 60 | 50 |
| 16 | 90 | 80 | 71 | 62 | 54 |
| 18 | 91 | 81 | 72 | 64 | 56 |
| 20 | 91 | 82 | 74 | 66 | 58 |
| 22 | 92 | 83 | 75 | 68 | 60 |

1. **Interpreting Data** At noon, the readings on a sling psychrometer are 18°C for the dry-bulb thermometer and 14°C for the wet-bulb thermometer. What is the relative humidity?
2. **Interpreting Data** At 5 P.M., the psychrometer is used again. The reading on the dry-bulb thermometer is 12°C, and the reading on the wet-bulb thermometer is 11°C. Determine the new relative humidity.
3. **Interpreting Data** How did the temperature change between noon and 5 P.M.?
4. **Interpreting Data** How did relative humidity change during the course of the day?
5. **Drawing Conclusions** How was the relative humidity affected by air temperature? Explain your answer.

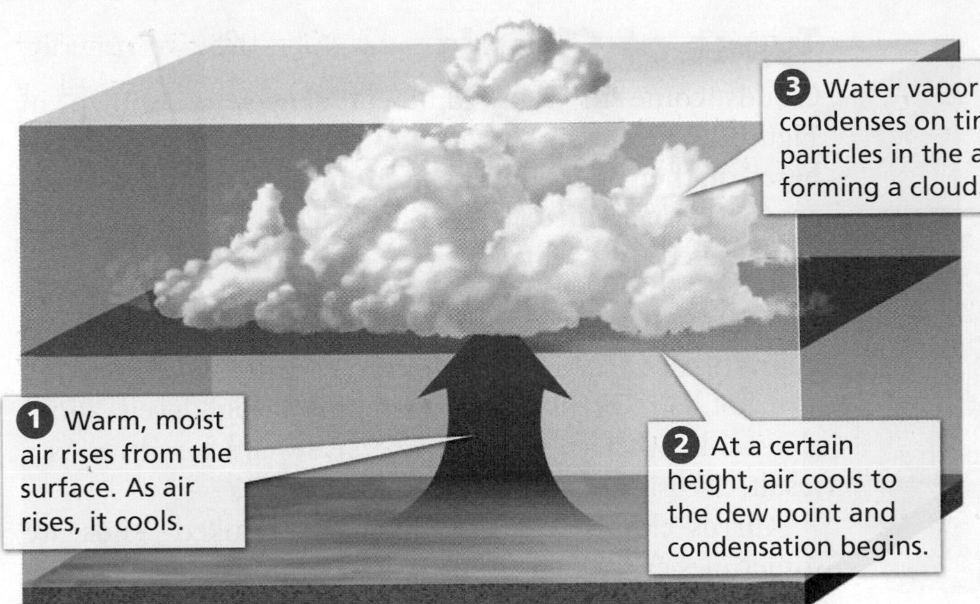
3 Water vapor condenses on tiny particles in the air, forming a cloud.
1 Warm, moist air rises from the surface. As air rises, it cools.
2 At a certain height, air cools to the dew point and condensation begins.

**FIGURE 15**
**Cloud Formation**
Clouds form when warm, moist air rises and cools. Water vapor condenses onto tiny particles in the air.

## How Clouds Form

When you look at a cloud, you are seeing millions of tiny water droplets or ice crystals. **Clouds form when water vapor in the air condenses to form liquid water or ice crystals.** Molecules of water vapor in the air become liquid water in the process of **condensation.** How does water in the atmosphere condense? Two conditions are required for condensation: cooling of the air and the presence of particles in the air.

**The Role of Cooling** As you have learned, cold air holds less water vapor than warm air. As air cools, the amount of water vapor it can hold decreases. The water vapor condenses into tiny droplets of water or ice crystals.

The temperature at which condensation begins is called the **dew point.** If the dew point is above freezing, the water vapor forms water droplets. If the dew point is below freezing, the water vapor may change directly into ice crystals.

**The Role of Particles** But something else besides a change in temperature is needed for cloud formation. For water vapor to condense, tiny particles must be present so the water has a surface on which to condense. In cloud formation, most of these particles are salt crystals, dust from soil, and smoke. Water vapor also condenses onto solid surfaces, such as blades of grass or window panes. Liquid water that condenses from the air onto a cooler surface is called dew. Ice that has been deposited on a surface that is below freezing is called frost.

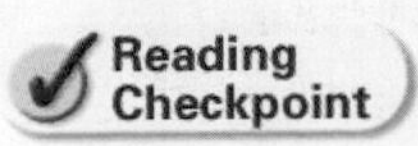
Reading Checkpoint

**What two factors are required for condensation to occur?**

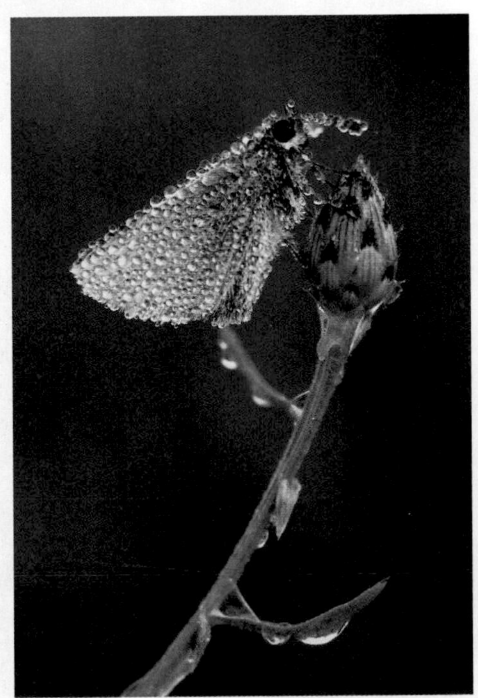

**FIGURE 16**
**Condensation**
Water vapor condensed on this insect to form dew. **Predicting** *What would happen if the surface were below freezing?*

Cirrus clouds

Cumulus clouds

Stratus clouds

## Types of Clouds

Clouds come in many different shapes, as shown in Figure 17. **Scientists classify clouds into three main types based on their shape: cirrus, cumulus, and stratus. Clouds are further classified by their altitude.** Each type of cloud is associated with a different type of weather.

**Cirrus Clouds** Wispy, feathery clouds are known as **cirrus** (SEER us) clouds. *Cirrus* comes from a word meaning a curl of hair. Cirrus clouds form only at high levels, above about 6 kilometers, where temperatures are very low. As a result, cirrus clouds are made of ice crystals.

Cirrus clouds that have feathery "hooked" ends are sometimes called mare's tails. Cirrocumulus clouds, which look like rows of cotton balls, often indicate that a storm is on its way. The rows of cirrocumulus clouds look like the scales of a fish. For this reason, the term "mackerel sky" is used to describe a sky full of cirrocumulus clouds.

**Cumulus Clouds** Clouds that look like fluffy, rounded piles of cotton are called **cumulus** (KYOO myuh lus) clouds. The word *cumulus* means "heap" or "mass" in Latin. Cumulus clouds form less than 2 kilometers above the ground, but they may grow in size and height until they extend upward as much as 18 kilometers. Cumulus clouds that are not very tall usually indicate fair weather. These clouds, which are common on sunny days, are called "fair weather cumulus." Towering clouds with flat tops, called cumulonimbus clouds, often produce thunderstorms. The suffix *-nimbus* means "rain."

**Stratus Clouds** Clouds that form in flat layers are called **stratus** (STRAT us) clouds. Recall that *strato* means "spread out." Stratus clouds usually cover all or most of the sky and are a uniform dull, gray color. As stratus clouds thicken, they may produce drizzle, rain, or snow. They are then called nimbostratus clouds.

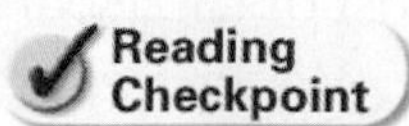

**What are stratus clouds?**

FIGURE 17
## Clouds

The three main types of clouds are cirrus, cumulus, and stratus. A cloud's name contains clues about its height and structure. **Interpreting Diagrams** *What type of cloud is found at the highest altitudes?*

**FIGURE 18**
**Fog Around the Golden Gate Bridge**
The cold ocean water of San Francisco Bay is often covered by fog in the early morning.
**Predicting** *What will happen as the sun rises and warms the air?*

**Altocumulus and Altostratus** Part of a cloud's name may be based on its height. The names of clouds that form between 2 and 6 kilometers above Earth's surface have the prefix *alto-*, which means "high." The two main types of these clouds are altocumulus and altostratus. These are "middle-level" clouds that are higher than regular cumulus and stratus clouds, but lower than cirrus and other "high" clouds.

**Fog** Clouds that form at or near the ground are called fog. Fog often forms when the ground cools at night after a warm, humid day. The ground cools the air just above the ground to the air's dew point. The next day the heat of the morning sun "burns" the fog off as its water droplets evaporate. Fog is more common in areas near bodies of water or low-lying marshy areas. In mountainous areas, fog can form as warm, moist air moves up the mountain slopes and cools.

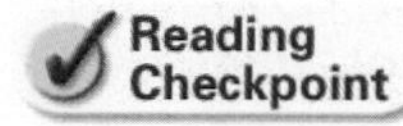

**What is fog?**

## Section 4 Assessment

### Target Reading Skill

**Asking Questions** Use the answers to the questions you wrote about the headings to help answer the questions below.

### Reviewing Key Concepts

1. a. **Reviewing** What is humidity?
   b. **Comparing and Contrasting** How are humidity and relative humidity different?
   c. **Calculating** Suppose a sample of air can at most hold 10 grams of water vapor. If the sample actually has 2 grams of water vapor, what is its relative humidity?
2. a. **Identifying** What process is involved in cloud formation?
   b. **Summarizing** What two conditions are needed for clouds to form?
   c. **Inferring** When are clouds formed by ice crystals instead of drops of liquid water?
3. a. **Listing** What are the three main types of clouds?
   b. **Describing** Briefly describe each of the three main types of clouds.
   c. **Classifying** Classify each of the following cloud types as low-level, medium-level, or high-level: altocumulus, altostratus, cirrostratus, cirrus, cumulus, fog, nimbostratus, and stratus.

### Lab zone At-Home Activity

**Water in the Air** Fill a large glass half full with cold water. Show your family members what happens as you add ice cubes to the water. Explain to your family that the water that appears on the outside of the glass comes from water vapor in the atmosphere. Also explain why the water on the outside of the glass only appears after you add ice to the water in the glass.

Section 5

# Precipitation

## Reading Focus

### Key Concepts

- What are the common types of precipitation?
- How is precipitation measured?

### Key Terms

- precipitation
- drought
- cloud seeding
- rain gauge

### Target Reading Skill

**Using Prior Knowledge** Before you read, write what you know about precipitation in a graphic organizer like the one below. As you read, write what you learn.

| What You Know |
|---|
| 1. Precipitation can be rain or snow.<br>2. |

| What You Learned |
|---|
| 1.<br>2. |

## Lab zone Discover Activity

### How Can You Make Hail?

1. Put on your goggles.
2. Put 15 g of salt into a beaker. Add 50 mL of water. Stir the solution until most of the salt is dissolved.
3. Put 15 mL of cold water in a clean test tube.
4. Place the test tube in the beaker.
5. Fill the beaker almost to the top with crushed ice. Stir the ice mixture every minute for six minutes.
6. Remove the test tube from the beaker and drop an ice chip into the test tube. What happens?

**Think It Over**

**Inferring** Based on your observation, what conditions are necessary for hail to form?

In Arica, Chile, the average rainfall is less than 1 millimeter per year. But in Hawaii, the average rainfall on Mount Waialeale is about 12 meters per year. As you can see, rainfall varies greatly around the world.

Water evaporates from every water surface on Earth and from living things. This water eventually returns to the surface as precipitation. **Precipitation** (pree sip uh TAY shun) is any form of water that falls from clouds and reaches Earth's surface.

Not all clouds produce precipitation. For precipitation to occur, cloud droplets or ice crystals must grow heavy enough to fall through the air. One way that cloud droplets grow is by colliding and combining with other droplets. As the droplets grow larger, they move faster and collect more small droplets. Finally, the droplets become heavy enough to fall out of the cloud as raindrops.

Typical Droplet Size (Diameter)

Cloud droplet (0.02 mm)

Mist droplet (0.005–0.05 mm)

Drizzle droplet (0.05–0.5 mm)

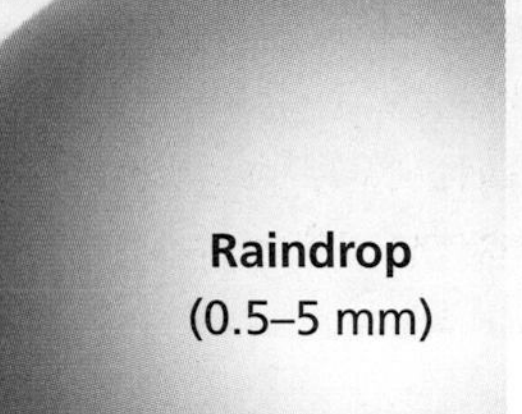

Raindrop (0.5–5 mm)

**FIGURE 19**
**Water Droplets**
Droplets come in many sizes. Believe it or not, a raindrop has about one million times as much water in it as a cloud droplet.

For: Links on precipitation
Visit: www.SciLinks.org
Web Code: scn-0925

## Types of Precipitation

In warm parts of the world, precipitation is almost always in the form of rain. In colder regions, precipitation may fall as snow or ice. **Common types of precipitation include rain, sleet, freezing rain, snow, and hail.**

**Rain** The most common kind of precipitation is rain. Drops of water are called rain if they are at least 0.5 millimeter in diameter. Precipitation made up of smaller drops of water is called drizzle. Precipitation of even smaller drops is called mist. Drizzle and mist usually fall from stratus clouds.

**Sleet** Sometimes raindrops fall through a layer of air that is below 0°C, the freezing point of water. As they fall, the raindrops freeze into solid particles of ice. Ice particles smaller than 5 millimeters in diameter are called sleet.

**Freezing Rain** Sometimes raindrops falling through cold air near the ground do not freeze in the air. Instead, they freeze when they touch a cold surface. This kind of precipitation is called freezing rain. In an ice storm, a smooth, thick layer of ice builds up on every surface. The weight of the ice may break tree branches and cause them to fall onto power lines, causing power failures. Freezing rain and sleet can make sidewalks and roads slippery and dangerous.

**What is sleet?**

FIGURE 20
**Rain and Freezing Rain**
Rain is the most common form of precipitation. Freezing rain coats objects with a layer of ice.
**Relating Cause and Effect** *What conditions are necessary for freezing rain to occur?*

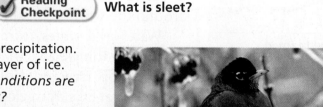

**Snow** Often water vapor in a cloud is converted directly into ice crystals called snowflakes. Snowflakes have an endless number of different shapes and patterns, all with six sides or branches. Snowflakes often join together into larger clumps of snow in which the six-sided crystals are hard to see.

**FIGURE 21**
**Snowflake**
Snowflakes are tiny ice crystals. They all have six sides or branches.

**Hail** Round pellets of ice larger than 5 millimeters in diameter are called hailstones. Hail forms only inside cumulonimbus clouds during thunderstorms. A hailstone starts as an ice pellet inside a cold region of a cloud. Strong updrafts carry the hailstone up through the cold region many times. Each time the hailstone goes through the cold region, a new layer of ice forms around it. Eventually the hailstone becomes heavy enough to fall to the ground. If you cut a hailstone in half, you often see shells of ice, like the layers of an onion, as shown in Figure 22. Because hailstones can grow quite large before finally falling to the ground, hail can cause tremendous damage to crops, buildings, and vehicles.

**FIGURE 22**
**How Hail Forms**
Hailstones start as small pellets of ice in cumulonimbus clouds. They grow larger as they are repeatedly tossed up and down, until they become so heavy that they fall to the ground.

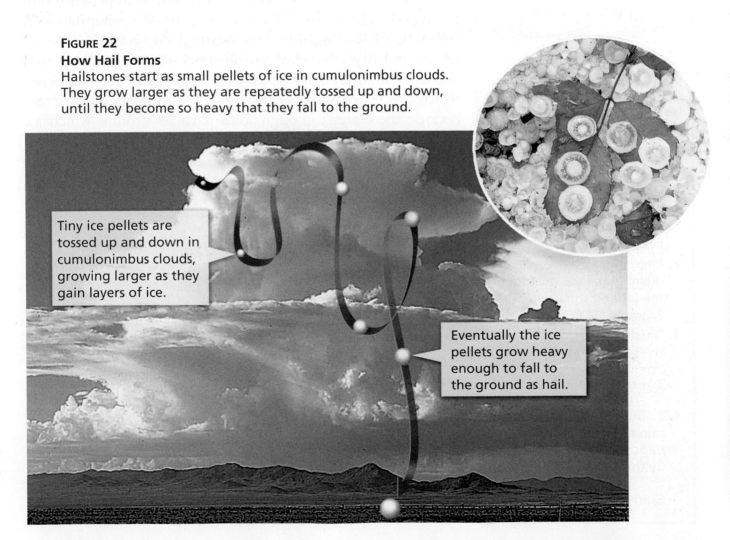

Tiny ice pellets are tossed up and down in cumulonimbus clouds, growing larger as they gain layers of ice.

Eventually the ice pellets grow heavy enough to fall to the ground as hail.

**FIGURE 23**
**Cloud Seeding**
Small planes are used to sprinkle chemicals into clouds to try to produce rain.

**Modifying Precipitation** Sometimes a region goes through a period of weather that is much drier than usual. Long periods of unusually low precipitation are called **droughts.** Droughts can cause great hardship.

Since the 1940s, scientists have been trying to produce rain during droughts. One method used to modify precipitation is called **cloud seeding.** In cloud seeding, tiny crystals of silver iodide and dry ice (solid carbon dioxide) are sprinkled into clouds from airplanes. Many clouds contain droplets of water which are supercooled below 0°C. The droplets don't freeze because there aren't enough solid particles around which ice crystals can form. Water vapor can condense on the particles of silver iodide, forming rain or snow. Dry ice cools the droplets even further, so that they will freeze without particles being present. However, to date cloud seeding has not been very effective in producing precipitation.

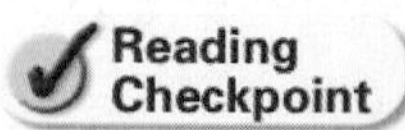

**What is a drought?**

**Lab zone Skills Activity**

### Calculating

Make a rain gauge by putting a funnel into a narrow, straight-sided glass jar. Here's how to calculate how much more rain your funnel collects than the jar alone.

1. First measure the diameter of the top of the funnel and square it.
   Example: $4 \times 4 = 16$
2. Then measure the diameter of the bottom of the jar and square it.
   Example: $2 \times 2 = 4$
3. Divide the first square by the second square.
   Example: $\frac{16}{4} = 4$
4. To find the actual depth of rain that fell, divide the depth of water in the jar by the ratio from Step 3.
   Example: $\frac{8 \text{ cm}}{4} = 2 \text{ cm}$

## Measuring Precipitation

There are various ways to measure the amount of rain or snow. **Scientists measure precipitation with various instruments, including rain gauges and measuring sticks.**

**Snowfall Measurement** Snowfall is usually measured in two ways; using a simple measuring stick or by melting collected snow and measuring the depth of water it produces. On average, 10 centimeters of snow contains about the same amount of water as 1 centimeter of rain. However, light, fluffy snow contains far less water than heavy, wet snow.

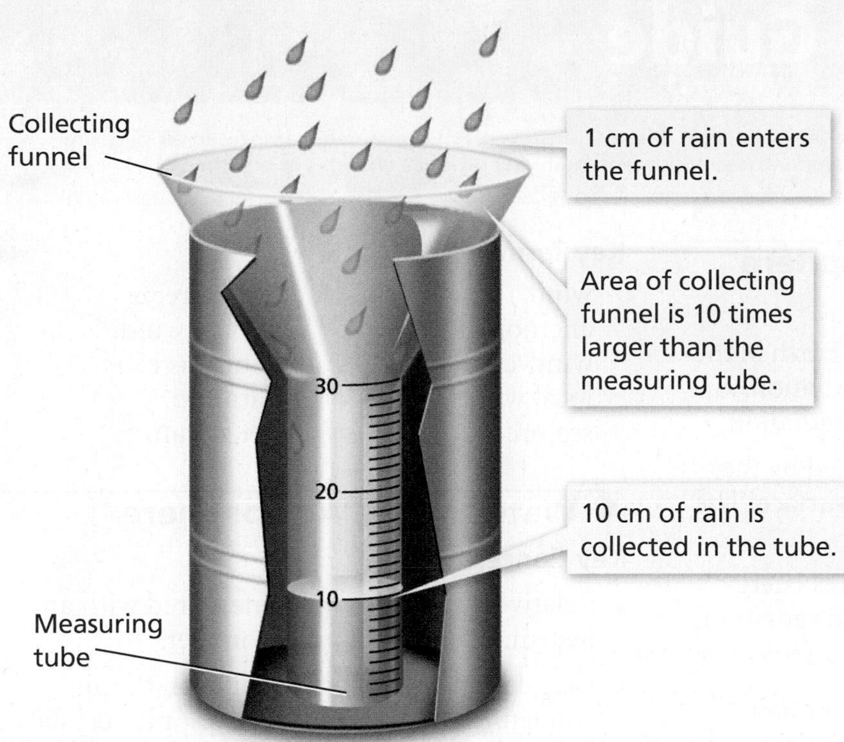

Collecting funnel
1 cm of rain enters the funnel.
Area of collecting funnel is 10 times larger than the measuring tube.
30
20
10 cm of rain is collected in the tube.
10
Measuring tube

**FIGURE 24**
**Rain Gauge**
A rain gauge measures the depth of rain that falls.
**Observing** *How much rain was collected in the measuring tube of this rain gauge?*

**Rain Measurements** An open-ended can or tube that collects rainfall is called a **rain gauge.** The amount of rainfall is measured by dipping a ruler into the water or by reading a marked scale. To increase the accuracy of the measurement, the top of a rain gauge may have a funnel that collects ten times as much rain as the tube alone, as shown in Figure 24. The funnel collects a greater depth of water that is easier to measure. To get the actual depth of rain, it is necessary to divide by ten. The narrow opening of the tube helps to minimize evaporation.

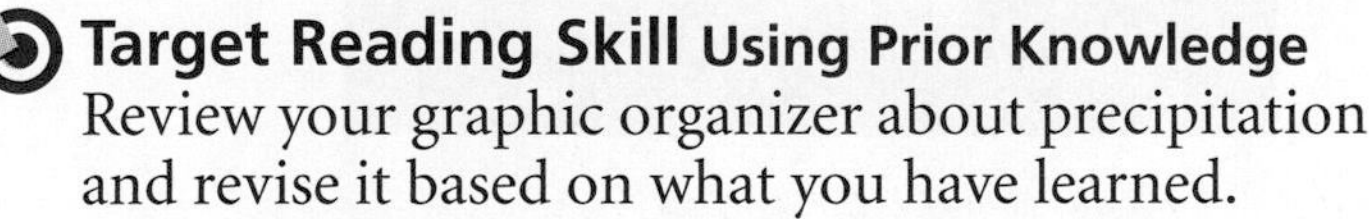

## Section 5 Assessment

**Target Reading Skill Using Prior Knowledge** Review your graphic organizer about precipitation and revise it based on what you have learned.

### Reviewing Key Concepts

1. a. **Listing** Name the five common types of precipitation.
   b. **Comparing and Contrasting** Compare and contrast freezing rain and sleet.
   c. **Classifying** A thunderstorm produces precipitation in the form of ice particles that are about 6 millimeters in diameter. What type of precipitation would this be?
   d. **Relating Cause and Effect** How do hailstones become so large in cumulonimbus clouds?
2. a. **Identifying** How can a rain gauge be used to measure precipitation?
   b. **Explaining** How does the funnel in a rain gauge increase the accuracy of the measurement?

### Writing in Science

**Firsthand Account** Think about the most exciting experience you have had with precipitation. Write a paragraph about that event. Make sure you describe the precipitation itself as well as the effect it had on you.

**The BIG Idea** **Transfer of Energy** Energy transfers resulting from differences in air pressure, air temperature, winds, and humidity produce changes in weather.

## 1 Energy in Earth's Atmosphere

### Key Concepts

- Most energy from the sun travels to Earth in the form of visible light and infrared radiation. A small amount arrives as ultraviolet radiation.
- Some sunlight is absorbed or reflected by the atmosphere before it can reach the surface. The rest passes through to the surface.
- When the surface is heated, it radiates energy back into the atmosphere as infrared radiation.

### Key Terms

electromagnetic waves
radiation
infrared radiation
ultraviolet radiation
scattering
greenhouse effect

## 2 Heat Transfer

### Key Concepts

- Air temperature is usually measured with a thermometer.
- Heat is transferred in three ways: radiation, conduction, and convection.
- Radiation, conduction, and convection work together to heat the troposphere.

### Key Terms

temperature
thermal energy
thermometer
heat
conduction
convection
convection currents

## 3 Winds

### Key Concepts

- Winds are caused by differences in air pressure.
- Local winds are caused by the unequal heating of Earth's surface within a small area.
- Like local winds, global winds are created by the unequal heating of Earth's surface. Unlike local winds, global winds occur over large areas.
- The major global wind belts are the trade winds, the polar easterlies, and the prevailing westerlies.

### Key Terms

wind
anemometer
wind-chill factor
local winds
sea breeze
land breeze
global winds
Coriolis effect
latitude
jet stream

## 4 Water in the Atmosphere

### Key Concepts

- Relative humidity can be measured with an instrument called a psychrometer.
- Clouds form when water vapor in the air condenses to form liquid water or ice crystals.
- Scientists classify clouds into three main types based on their shape: cirrus, cumulus, and stratus. Clouds are also classified by altitude.

### Key Terms

water cycle
evaporation
humidity
relative humidity
psychrometer
condensation
dew point
cirrus
cumulus
stratus

## 5 Precipitation

### Key Concepts

- Common types of precipitation include rain, sleet, freezing rain, snow, and hail.
- Scientists measure precipitation with various instruments, including rain gauges and measuring sticks.

### Key Terms

precipitation
drought
cloud seeding
rain gauge

# Review and Assessment

Go Online
PHSchool.com
For: Self-Assessment
Visit: PHSchool.com
Web Code: cfa-4020

## Organizing Information

**Concept Mapping** Copy the concept map about Earth's winds onto a separate sheet of paper. Then complete it and add a title. (For more on Concept Mapping, see the Skills Handbook).

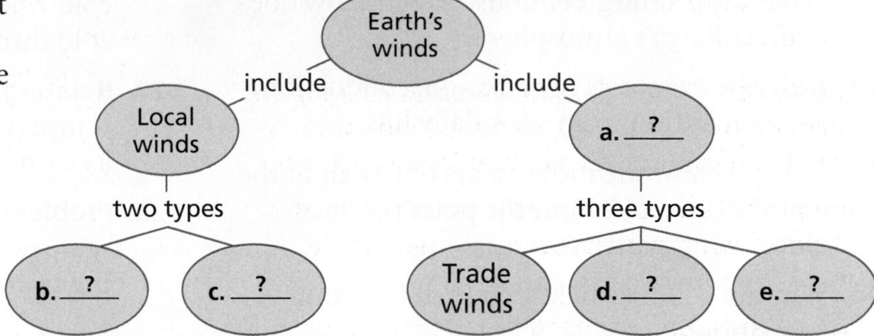


## Reviewing Key Terms

**Choose the letter of the best answer.**

1. Energy from the sun travels to Earth's surface by
   **a.** radiation.
   **b.** convection.
   **c.** evaporation.
   **d.** conduction.
2. Rising warm air transports thermal energy by
   **a.** conduction.
   **b.** convection.
   **c.** radiation.
   **d.** condensation.
3. Bands of high-altitude, high-speed winds are called
   **a.** jet streams.
   **b.** sea breezes.
   **c.** land breezes.
   **d.** local winds.
4. A type of cloud that forms in flat layers and often covers much of the sky is
   **a.** cirrus.
   **b.** cumulus.
   **c.** fog.
   **d.** stratus.
5. Rain, sleet, and hail are all forms of
   **a.** evaporation.
   **b.** condensation.
   **c.** precipitation.
   **d.** convection.

**If the statement is true, write *true*. If it is false, change the underlined word or words to make the statement true.**

6. Infrared radiation and <u>ultraviolet radiation</u> make up most of the energy Earth receives from the sun.
7. The transfer of heat by the movement of a fluid is called <u>conduction.</u>
8. Winds that blow steadily from specific directions for long distances are called <u>sea breezes.</u>
9. <u>Cirrus</u> clouds are made mostly of ice crystals.
10. Rainfall is measured by a(n) <u>anemometer.</u>

## Writing in Science

**Descriptive Paragraph** Suppose you are preparing for an around-the-world sailing trip. Select a route. Then write a description of the types of winds you would expect to find along different parts of your route.

## Checking Concepts

**11.** What causes the greenhouse effect? How does it affect Earth's atmosphere?

**12.** Describe examples of radiation, conduction, and convection from your daily life.

**13.** Describe how the movements of hot air at the equator and cold air at the poles produce global wind patterns.

**14.** Why are solid particles required for cloud formation?

**15.** Why do clouds usually form high in the air instead of near Earth's surface?

**16.** Describe sleet, hail, and snow in terms of how each one forms.

## Math Practice

**17. Converting Units** Suppose the outside temperature is 60°F. What is the temperature in degrees Celsius?

**18. Converting Units** What is 30°C in degrees Fahrenheit?

## Thinking Critically

**19. Inferring** Venus has an atmosphere that is mostly carbon dioxide. How do you think the greenhouse effect has altered Venus?

**20. Interpreting Diagrams** Describe the journey of a small particle of water through the water cycle, using the terms in the diagram below.

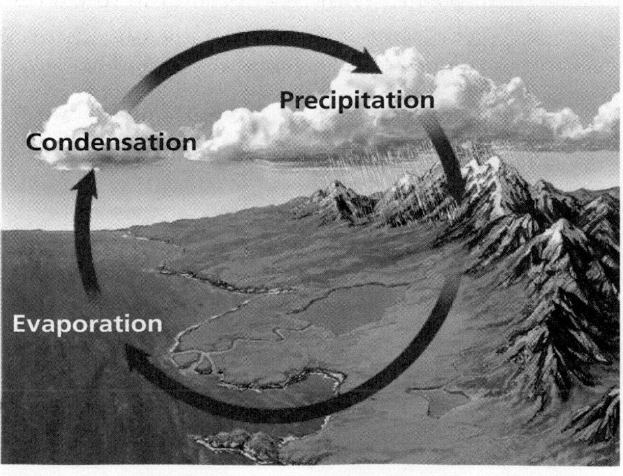


**21. Applying Concepts** What type of heat transfer is responsible for making you feel cold when you are swimming in a pool that is cold throughout?

**22. Relating Cause and Effect** What circumstances could cause a nighttime land breeze in a city near the ocean?

**23. Problem Solving** A psychrometer gives the same reading on both thermometers. What is the relative humidity?

## Applying Skills

**Use the table to answer questions 24–26.**

**Average Monthly Rainfall**

| Month | Rainfall | Month | Rainfall |
|---|---|---|---|
| January | 1 cm | July | 49 cm |
| February | 1 cm | August | 57 cm |
| March | 1 cm | September | 40 cm |
| April | 2 cm | October | 20 cm |
| May | 25 cm | November | 4 cm |
| June | 52 cm | December | 1 cm |

**24. Graphing** Use the information in the table to draw a bar graph that shows the rainfall for each month at this location.

**25. Calculating** What is the total amount of rainfall each year at this location?

**26. Classifying** Which months of the year would you classify as "dry"? Which months would you classify as "wet"?

## Lab zone Chapter Project

**Performance Assessment** Decide how to present the findings from your weather station to the class. For example, you could put your graphs and predictions on a poster or use a computer to make a slide show. Make sure your graphs are neatly drawn and easy to understand.

# Standardized Test Prep

### Test-Taking Tip

**Using Formulas**

Some test questions require you to use a formula. Read the question carefully and recall information or equations that might help you answer the question. For example, in the question below, to convert temperature readings in degrees Fahrenheit (°F) to degrees Celsius (°C) you need to use the following formula:

$$°C = \frac{5}{9}(°F - 32)$$

To solve for a quantity in a formula, substitute known values, including units, for the variables. Be sure to include units in your final answer.

***Sample Question***

The temperature at noon in Denver, Colorado, was 68° F. What was the temperature in degrees Celsius?

**A** 55°C
**B** 41°C
**C** 20°C
**D** 64.8°C

***Answer***

You are given that the temperature is 68° F. Substitute this value in the formula for °F.

$$°C = \frac{5}{9}(68-32)$$

$$= \frac{5}{9}(36)$$

$$= 20°C$$

The correct answer is **C.**

**Choose the letter of the best answer.**

**1.** When the temperature equals the dew point, the relative humidity is

**A** zero.
**B** about 10 percent.
**C** about 50 percent.
**D** 100 percent.

**2.** What equipment would you need to design an experiment to determine the relative humidity of the air?

**F** a rain gauge and a thermometer
**G** an anemometer or a thermometer
**H** a psychrometer or two thermometers
**J** an anemometer and a rain gauge

**3.** What is the temperature in degrees Celsius when a room thermometer reads 77°F?

**A** 25°C
**B** 32°C
**C** 45°C
**D** 77°C

*The table below shows the actual air temperature when the wind speed is zero. Use the table and your knowledge of science to answer Questions 4 and 5.*

**Wind-Chill Temperature Index**

| Wind Speed | Equivalent Air Temperature (°C) | | | |
|---|---|---|---|---|
| 0 km/h | 5° | 0° | −5° | −10° |
| 10 km/h | 2.7° | −3.3° | −9.3° | −15.3° |
| 15 km/h | 1.7° | −4.4° | −10.6° | −16.7° |
| 20 km/h | 1.1° | −5.2° | −11.6° | −17.9° |

**4.** On a windy winter's day, the actual air temperature is −5°C and the wind speed is 15 kilometers per hour. What would the wind-chill factor make the temperature feel like to a person outdoors?

**F** 1.7°C
**G** −5°C
**H** −10.6°C
**J** −16.7°C

**5.** Use trends shown in the data table to predict how cold the air temperature would feel if the actual temperature was 0°C, and the wind speed was 25 km/h.

**A** about 0°C
**B** about −6°C
**C** about −15°C
**D** about −5°C

### Constructed Response

**6.** Describe the process by which a cloud forms. What two conditions are necessary for this process to occur? How does this process compare to the process by which dew or frost is formed?

# Chapter 17 Weather Patterns

## The BIG Idea
### Weather Systems

**How do air masses produce changes in weather?**

### Chapter Preview

*Weather Patterns*

▶ Video Preview
Video Field Trip
Video Assessment

Lab zone™ Chapter **Project**

## The Weather Tomorrow

When the sky turns dark and threatening, it's not hard to predict the weather. A storm is likely on its way. But wouldn't you rather know about an approaching storm before it arrives? In this project you will get a chance to make your own weather forecasts and compare them to the forecasts of professionals. Good luck!

**Your Goal** To predict the weather for your own community and two other locations in the United States

To complete the project you must

- compare weather maps for several days at a time
- look for patterns in the weather
- draw maps to show your weather predictions

**Plan It!** Begin by previewing the chapter to learn about weather maps and symbols. Start a project folder to store daily national weather maps and a description of the symbols used on the maps. Choose two locations that are at least 1,000 kilometers away from your town and from each other. As you collect weather maps, look for patterns in day-to-day weather changes. Then predict the next day's weather and compare your predictions to professional forecasts and to the actual weather.

Section 1

# Air Masses and Fronts

## Reading Preview

### Key Concepts

- What are the major types of air masses in North America, and how do they move?
- What are the main types of fronts?
- What type of weather is associated with cyclones and anticyclones?

### Key Terms

- air mass
- tropical
- polar
- maritime
- continental
- front
- occluded
- cyclone
- anticyclone

### Target Reading Skill

**Comparing and Contrasting** As you read, compare and contrast the four types of fronts by completing a table like the one below.

Types of Fronts

| Front | How Forms | Type of Weather |
|---|---|---|
| Cold front | A cold air mass overtakes a warm air mass. | |
| Warm front | | |
| Occluded front | | |

## Lab zone Discover Activity

### How Do Fluids of Different Densities Behave?

1. Put on your apron. Place a cardboard divider across the middle of a plastic shoe box.
2. Add a few drops of red food coloring to a liter of warm water. Pour the red liquid, which represents low-density warm air, into the shoe box on one side of the divider.
3. Add about 100 mL of table salt and a few drops of blue food coloring to a liter of cold water. Pour the blue liquid, which represents high-density cold air, into the shoe box on the other side of the divider.
4. What do you think will happen if you remove the divider?
5. Now quickly remove the divider. Watch carefully from the side. What happens?

**Think It Over**

**Developing Hypotheses** Based on this activity, write a hypothesis stating what would happen if a mass of cold air ran into a mass of warm air.

Listen to the evening news in the winter and you may hear a weather forecast like this: "A huge mass of Arctic air is moving our way, bringing freezing temperatures." Today's weather can be influenced by air from thousands of kilometers away—perhaps from Canada or the Pacific Ocean. A huge body of air that has similar temperature, humidity, and air pressure at any given height is called an **air mass.** A single air mass may spread over millions of square kilometers and be up to 10 kilometers deep.

FIGURE 1
**Major Snowstorm**
In winter, humid air masses bring heavy snowstorms to areas like New York City.

## Types of Air Masses

Scientists classify air masses according to two characteristics: temperature and humidity. **Four major types of air masses influence the weather in North America: maritime tropical, continental tropical, maritime polar, and continental polar.**

The characteristics of an air mass depend on the temperatures and moisture content of the region over which the air mass forms. Remember that temperature affects air pressure. Cold, dense air has a higher pressure, while warm, less dense air has a lower pressure. **Tropical,** or warm, air masses form in the tropics and have low air pressure. **Polar,** or cold, air masses form north of 50° north latitude and south of 50° south latitude. Polar air masses have high air pressure.

Whether an air mass is humid or dry depends on whether it forms over water or land. **Maritime** air masses form over oceans. Water evaporates from the oceans, so the air can become very humid. **Continental** air masses form over land. Continental air masses have less exposure to large amounts of moisture from bodies of water. Therefore, continental air masses are drier than maritime air masses.

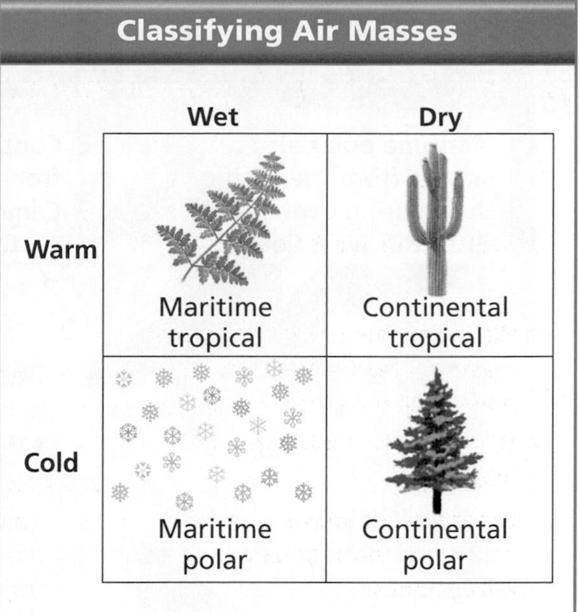


**FIGURE 2**
Air masses can be classified according to their temperature and humidity. **Identifying** *What type of air mass consists of warm, moist air?*

**Maritime Tropical** Warm, humid air masses form over tropical oceans. Maritime tropical air masses that form over the Gulf of Mexico and the Atlantic Ocean move first into the southeastern United States. These air masses then move north and northeast, where they influence weather in the central and eastern United States. In the west, maritime tropical air masses form over the Pacific Ocean. They mainly affect the weather on the West Coast. As they cross the coastal mountain ranges, the Pacific air masses lose moisture.

In summer, maritime tropical air masses usually bring hot, humid weather. Many summer showers and thunderstorms in the eastern United States develop in air masses that have formed over the Gulf of Mexico. In winter, a humid air mass can bring heavy rain or snow.

**North American Air Masses**

**Maritime polar air masses** from the Pacific Ocean bring cool, humid air to the West Coast.

**Continental polar air masses** from central and northern Canada bring cold air to the central and eastern United States.

**Maritime polar air masses** from the Atlantic Ocean are often pushed out to sea by westerly winds.

Pacific Ocean

Atlantic Ocean

Gulf of Mexico

**Maritime tropical air masses** from the Pacific Ocean bring warm, humid air to California and the West Coast.

**Continental tropical air masses** from the South bring hot, dry air to the southern plains.

**Maritime tropical air masses** from the Gulf of Mexico bring warm, humid air to the eastern United States.

FIGURE 3
Air masses can be warm or cold, and humid or dry. As an air mass moves into an area, the weather changes.

**Maritime Polar** Cool, humid air masses form over the icy cold North Pacific and North Atlantic oceans. Maritime polar air masses affect the West Coast more than the East Coast. Even in summer, these masses of cool, humid air often bring fog, rain, and cool temperatures to the West Coast.

**Continental Tropical** Hot, dry air masses form mostly in summer over dry areas of the Southwest and northern Mexico. Continental tropical air masses cover a smaller area than other air masses. They occasionally move northeast, bringing hot, dry weather to the southern Great Plains.

**Continental Polar** Large continental polar air masses form over central and northern Canada and Alaska, as shown in Figure 3. Air masses that form near the Arctic Circle can bring bitterly cold weather with very low humidity. In winter, continental polar air masses bring clear, cold, dry air to much of North America. In summer, the air mass is milder. Storms may occur when continental polar air masses move south and collide with maritime tropical air masses moving north.

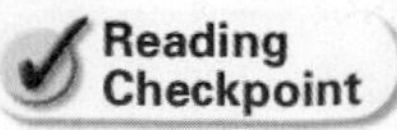

**Where do continental polar air masses come from?**

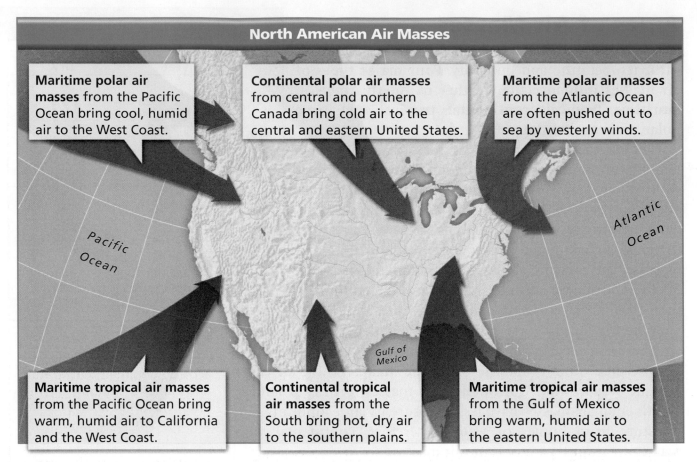

## How Air Masses Move

When an air mass moves into an area and interacts with other air masses, it causes the weather to change. **In the continental United States, air masses are commonly moved by the prevailing westerlies and jet streams.**

**Prevailing Westerlies** The prevailing westerlies, the major wind belts over the continental United States, generally push air masses from west to east. For example, maritime polar air masses from the Pacific Ocean are blown onto the West Coast, bringing low clouds and showers.

**Jet Streams** Embedded within the prevailing westerlies are jet streams. Recall that jet streams are bands of high-speed winds about 10 kilometers above Earth's surface. As jet streams blow from west to east, air masses are carried along their tracks.

**Fronts** As huge masses of air move across the land and the oceans, they collide with each other. But the air masses do not easily mix. Think about a bottle of oil and water. The less dense oil floats on top of the denser water. Something similar happens when two air masses with a different temperature and humidity collide. The air masses do not easily mix. The boundary where the air masses meet becomes a **front.** Storms and changeable weather often develop along fronts, as shown in Figure 4.

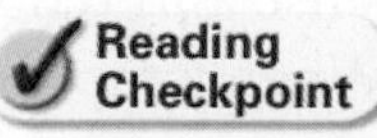


**In what direction does the jet stream move storms?**

### Lab zone Skills Activity

#### Calculating

When planes fly from west to east, they fly with the jet stream, and therefore can fly faster. When traveling from east to west, planes fly against the jet stream, and travel slower. To calculate the rate at which the planes fly, divide the distance traveled by the time it takes.

$$\text{Rate} = \frac{\text{Distance}}{\text{Time}}$$

If a plane flies from Denver, Colorado, to New York City, a distance of about 2,618 kilometers, it takes about 3 hours and 30 minutes. The return flight takes about 4 hours. Calculate the rates of air travel, in km/h, in each direction. How much extra speed does the jet stream add to the west-to-east flight?

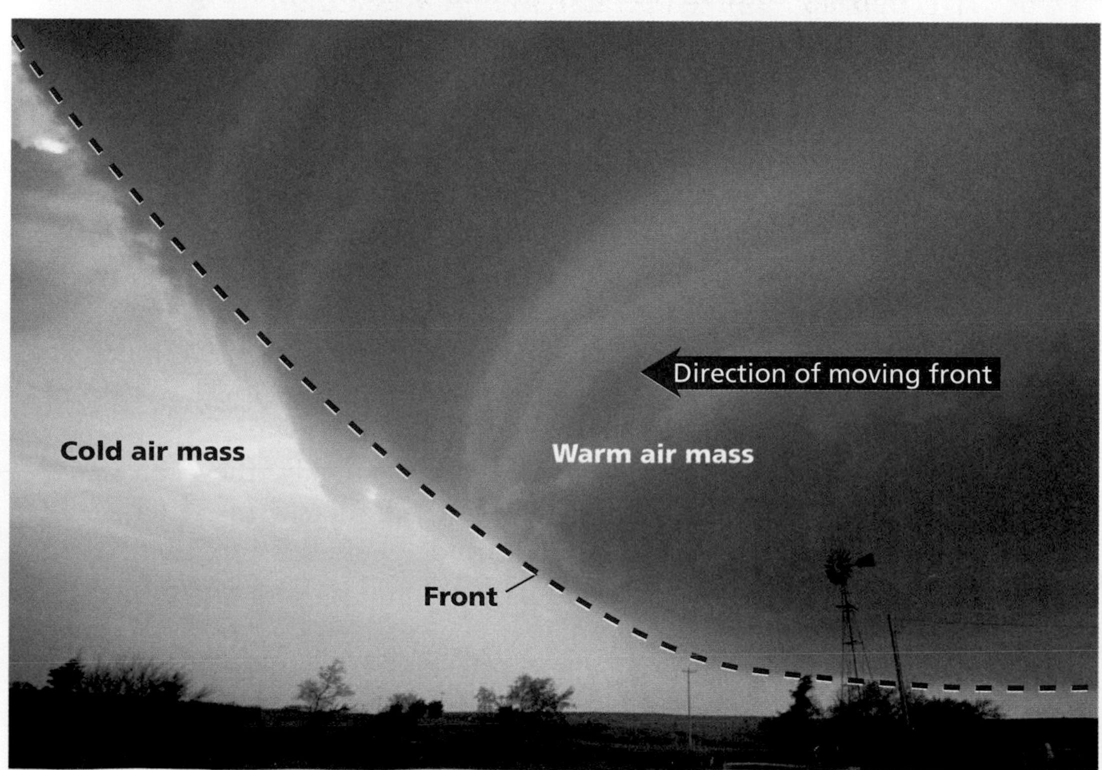


FIGURE 4
**How a Front Forms**
The boundary where unlike air masses meet is called a front. A front may be 15 to 600 kilometers wide and extend high into the troposphere.

FIGURE 5
## Types of Fronts
There are four types of fronts: cold fronts, warm fronts, stationery fronts, and occluded fronts.
**Interpreting Diagrams** *What kind of weather occurs at a warm front?*

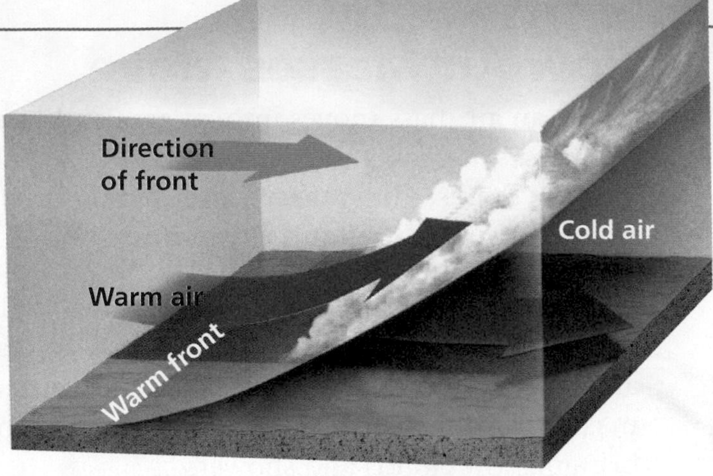


▲ **Warm Front**
A warm air mass overtakes a slow-moving cold air mass.

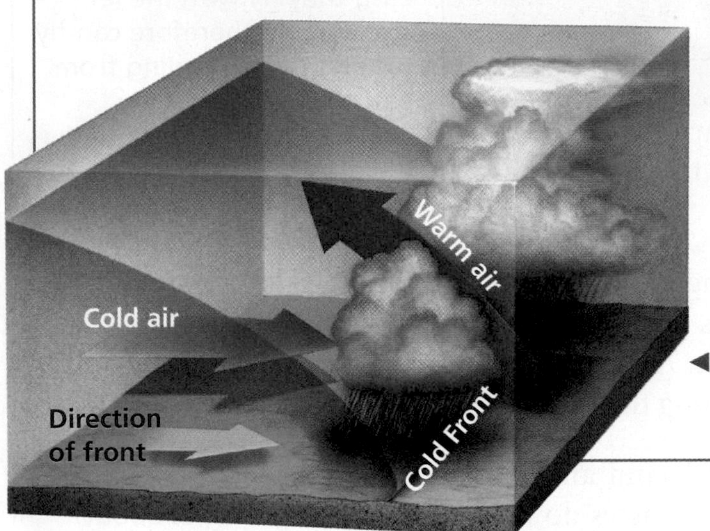


◀ **Cold Front**
A fast-moving cold air mass overtakes a warm air mass.

## Types of Fronts

**Colliding air masses can form four types of fronts: cold fronts, warm fronts, stationary fronts, and occluded fronts.** The kind of front that develops depends on the characteristics of the air masses and how they are moving.

**Cold Fronts** As you have learned, cold air is dense and tends to sink. Warm air is less dense and tends to rise. When a rapidly moving cold air mass runs into a slowly moving warm air mass, the denser cold air slides under the lighter warm air. The warm air is pushed upward along the leading edge of the colder air, as shown in Figure 5. A cold front forms.

As the warm air rises, it expands and cools. Remember that warm air can hold more water vapor than cool air. The rising air soon reaches the dew point, the temperature at which the water vapor in the air condenses into droplets of liquid water or forms tiny ice crystals. Clouds form. If there is a lot of water vapor in the warm air, heavy rain or snow may fall. If the warm air mass contains only a little water vapor, then the cold front may be accompanied by only cloudy skies.

Since cold fronts tend to move quickly, they can cause abrupt weather changes, including thunderstorms. After a cold front passes through an area, colder, drier air moves in, often bringing clear skies, a shift in wind, and lower temperatures.

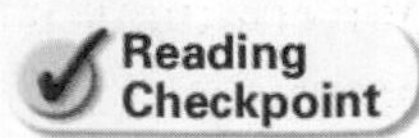
**Reading Checkpoint** **What type of weather do cold fronts bring?**

**Lab zone Skills Activity**

### Classifying
At home, watch the weather forecast on television. Make a note of each time the weather reporter mentions a front. Classify the fronts mentioned or shown as cold, warm, stationary, or occluded. What type of weather is predicted to occur when the front arrives? Note the specific weather conditions, such as temperature and air pressure, associated with the front. Is each type of front always associated with the same type of weather?

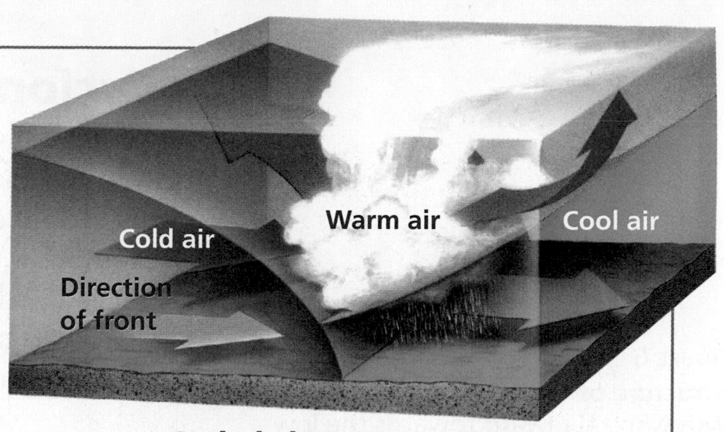


▲ **Occluded Front**
A warm air mass is caught between two cooler air masses.

▼ **Stationary Front**
Cold and warm air masses meet, but neither can move the other.

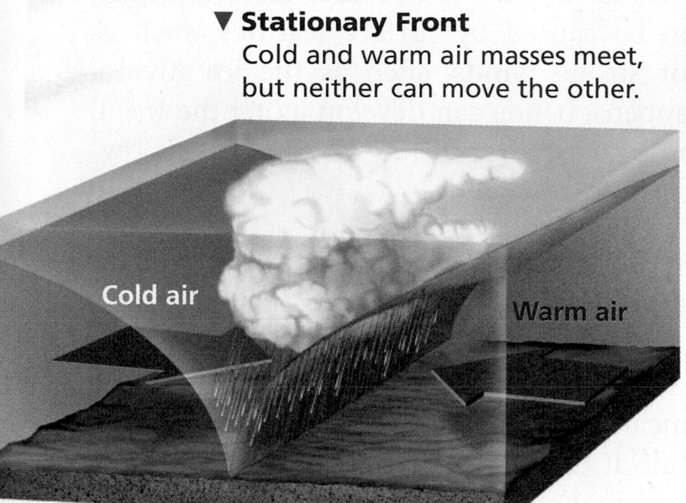


**Go Online active art**
**For:** Weather Fronts activity
**Visit:** PHSchool.com
**Web Code:** cfp-4031

**Warm Fronts** Clouds and precipitation also accompany warm fronts. At a warm front, a fast-moving warm air mass overtakes a slowly moving cold air mass. Because cold air is denser than warm air, the warm air moves over the cold air. If the warm air is humid, light rain or snow falls along the front. If the warm air is dry, scattered clouds form. Because warm fronts move slowly, the weather may be rainy or cloudy for several days. After a warm front passes through an area, the weather is likely to be warm and humid.

**Stationary Fronts** Sometimes cold and warm air masses meet, but neither one can move the other. The two air masses face each other in a "standoff." In this case, the front is called a stationary front. Where the warm and cool air meet, water vapor in the warm air condenses into rain, snow, fog, or clouds. If a stationary front remains stalled over an area, it may bring many days of clouds and precipitation.

**Occluded Fronts** The most complex weather situation occurs at an occluded front, where a warm air mass is caught between two cooler air masses. The denser cool air masses move underneath the less dense warm air mass and push the warm air upward. The two cooler air masses meet in the middle and may mix. The temperature near the ground becomes cooler. The warm air mass is cut off, or **occluded,** from the ground. As the warm air cools and its water vapor condenses, the weather may turn cloudy and rain or snow may fall.

## Cyclones and Anticyclones

As air masses collide to form fronts, the boundary between the fronts sometimes becomes distorted. This distortion can be caused by surface features, such as mountains, or strong winds, such as the jet stream. When this happens, bends can develop along the front. The air begins to swirl. The swirling air can cause a low-pressure center to form.

**FIGURE 6**
**Structure of Cyclones and Anticyclones**
Winds spiral inward towards the low-pressure center of a cyclone. Winds spiral outward from the high-pressure center of an anticyclone.
**Interpreting Diagrams** *Do cyclone winds spin clockwise or counter-clockwise in the Northern Hemisphere?*

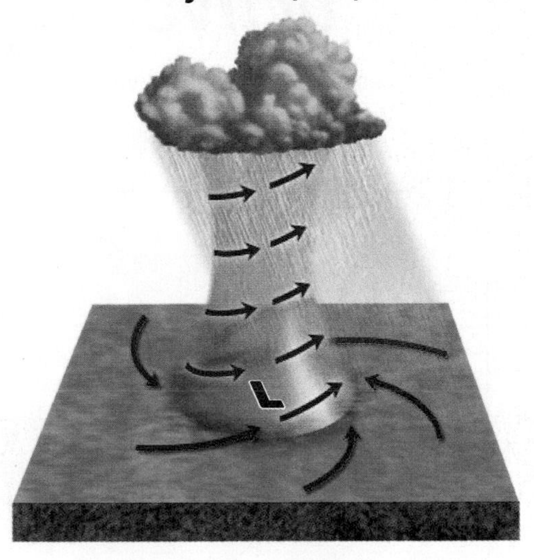


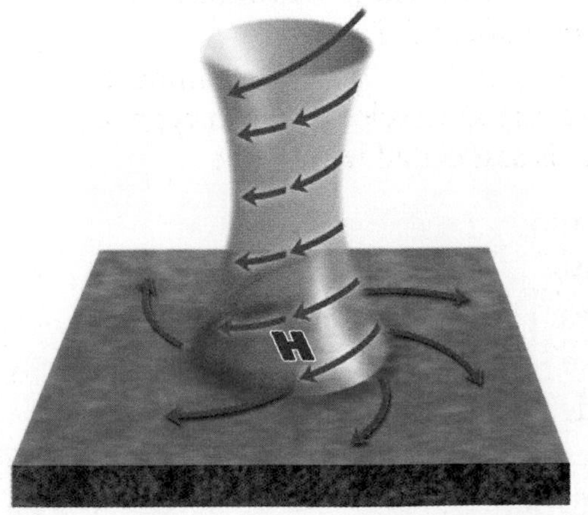


**Cyclones** If you look at a weather map, you will see areas marked with an *L*. The L stands for "low," and indicates an area of relatively low air pressure. A swirling center of low air pressure is called a **cyclone,** from a Greek word meaning "wheel."

As warm air at the center of a cyclone rises, the air pressure decreases. Cooler air blows toward this low-pressure area from nearby areas where the air pressure is higher. As shown in Figure 6, winds spiral inward toward the center of the system. Recall that, in the Northern Hemisphere, the Coriolis effect deflects winds to the right. Because of this deflection, winds in a cyclone spin counterclockwise in the Northern Hemisphere when viewed from above.

Cyclones play a large part in the weather of the United States. As air rises in a cyclone, the air cools, forming clouds and precipitation. **Cyclones and decreasing air pressure are associated with clouds, wind, and precipitation.**

**Anticyclones** As its name suggests, an anticyclone is the opposite of a cyclone. **Anticyclones** are high-pressure centers of dry air. Anticyclones are usually called "highs"—*H* on a weather map. Winds spiral outward from the center of an anticyclone, moving toward areas of lower pressure. Because of the Coriolis effect, winds in an anticyclone spin clockwise in the Northern Hemisphere. Because air moves out from the center of the anticyclone, cool air moves downward from higher in the troposphere. As the cool air falls, it warms up, so its relative humidity drops. **The descending air in an anticyclone generally causes dry, clear weather.**

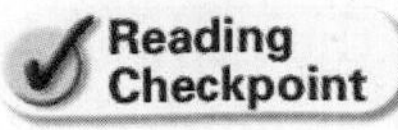

What is an anticyclone?

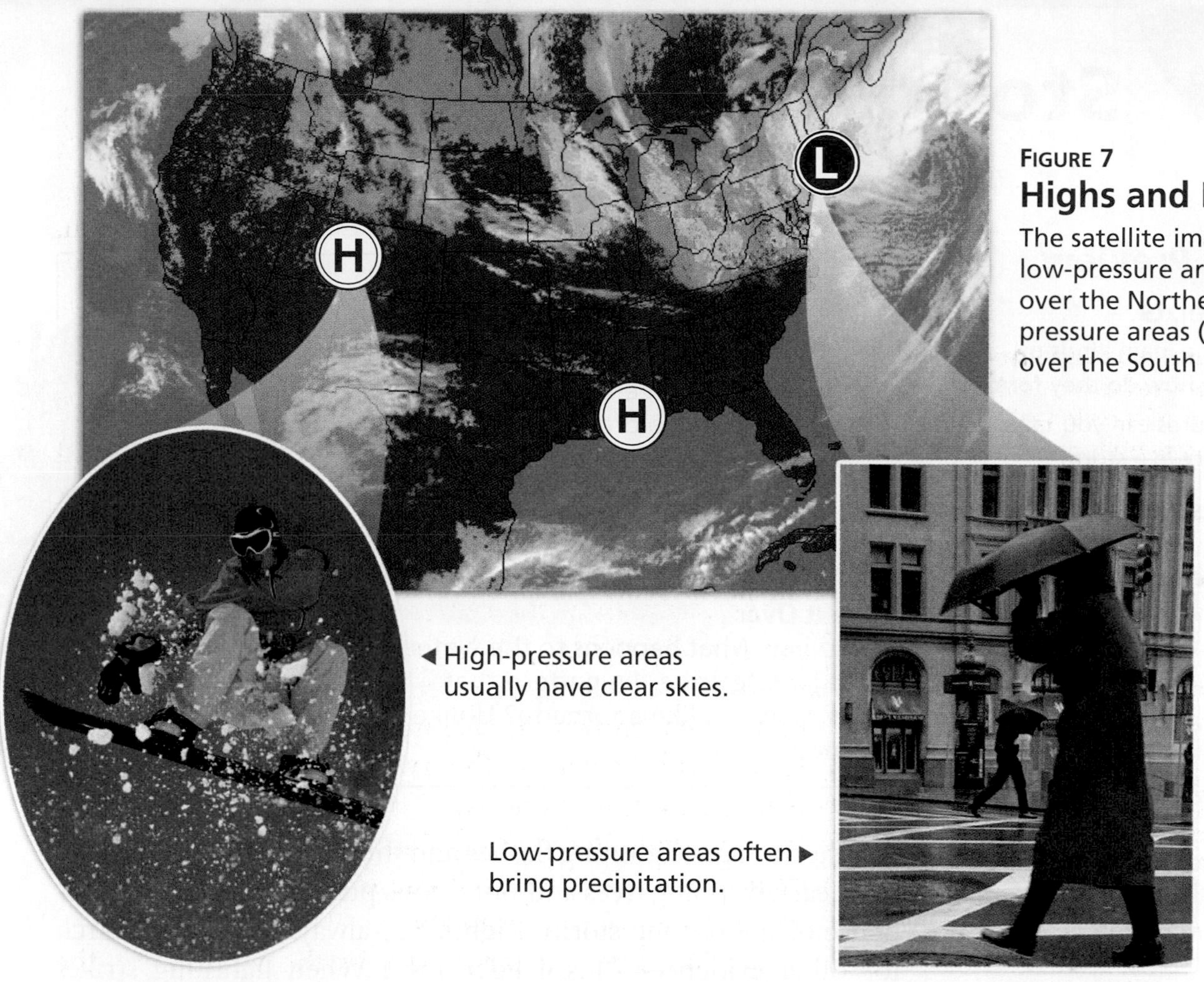


FIGURE 7
## Highs and Lows
The satellite image shows a low-pressure area (cyclone) over the Northeast and high-pressure areas (anticyclones) over the South and West.

◀ High-pressure areas usually have clear skies.

Low-pressure areas often ▶ bring precipitation.

# Section 1 Assessment

**Target Reading Skill Comparing and Contrasting** Use the information in your table about fronts to help you answer Question 2 below.

### Reviewing Key Concepts

1. a. **Reviewing** What two characteristics are used to classify air masses?
   b. **Classifying** Classify the four major types of air masses according to whether they are dry or humid.
   c. **Applying Concepts** What type of air mass would form over the northern Atlantic Ocean?
2. a. **Defining** What is a front?
   b. **Describing** Name the four types of fronts and describe the type of weather each brings.
   c. **Classifying** What type of front would most likely be responsible for several days of rain and clouds?
3. a. **Identifying** What is a cyclone?
   b. **Relating Cause and Effect** How does air move in an anticyclone? How does this movement affect the weather?
   c. **Comparing and Contrasting** Compare cyclones and anticyclones. What type of weather is associated with each?

## Writing in Science

**News Report** Suppose you are a television weather reporter covering a severe thunderstorm. Write a brief report to explain to viewers the conditions that caused the thunderstorm.

# 2 Storms

## Reading Preview

### Key Concepts

- What are the main kinds of storms, and how do they form?
- What measures can you take to ensure safety in a storm?

### Key Terms

- storm
- thunderstorm
- lightning
- tornado
- hurricane
- storm surge
- evacuate

### Target Reading Skill

**Sequencing** As you read, make a flowchart like the one below that shows how a hurricane forms. Write each step of the process in the flowchart in a separate box in the order in which it occurs.

**Hurricane Formation**

Begins as a low-pressure area over warm water, or a tropical disturbance.

↓

Warm, humid air rises and begins to spiral.

↓

## Lab zone Discover Activity

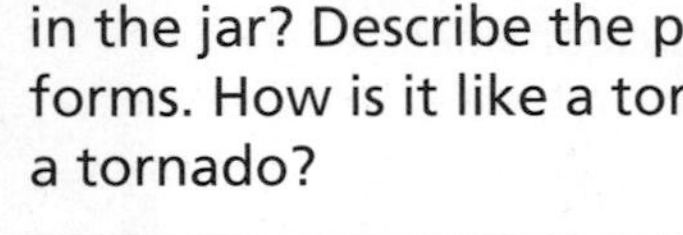

### Can You Make a Tornado?

1. Fill a large jar three-quarters full with water. Add a drop of liquid dish detergent and a penny or a marble.
2. Put the lid on the jar tightly. Now move the jar in a circle until the water inside begins to spin.

**Think It Over**

**Observing** What happens to the water in the jar? Describe the pattern that forms. How is it like a tornado? Unlike a tornado?

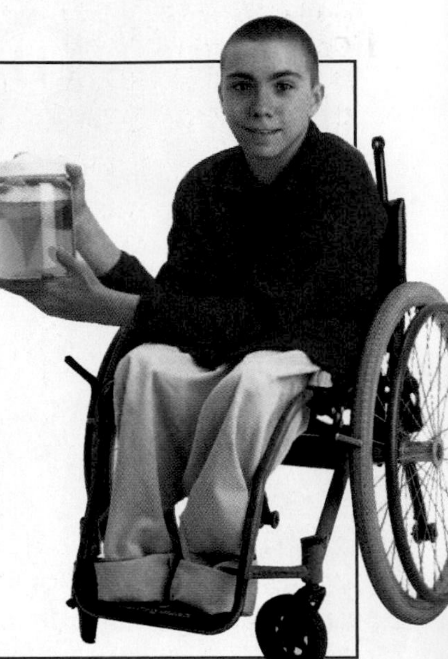

As a storm rages, lightning flashes and thunder rumbles. After the sky clears, dripping trees and numerous puddles are the only evidence of the passing storm. Right? Not always. Scientists search for other evidence—"fossil lightning"! When lightning strikes sand or sandy soil, the sand grains are fused together to form a fulgurite. The shape of the fulgurite reflects the path of the lightning bolt that formed it, as shown in Figure 8. These structures clearly show the tremendous power of storms.

A **storm** is a violent disturbance in the atmosphere. Storms involve sudden changes in air pressure, which in turn cause rapid air movements. Conditions that bring one kind of storm often cause other kinds of storms in the same area. For example, the conditions that cause thunderstorms can also cause tornadoes. There are several types of severe storms.

FIGURE 8
**Fulgurites**
A fulgurite forms when lightning strikes sand or sandy soil. The temperature of the lightning is so high that it melts the sand and forms a tube.

**FIGURE 9**
**Thunderstorm Formation**
A thunderstorm forms when warm, humid air rises rapidly within a cumulonimbus cloud.
**Applying Concepts** *Why do cumulonimbus clouds often form along cold fronts?*

## Thunderstorms

Do you find thunderstorms frightening? Exciting? As you watch the brilliant flashes of lightning and listen to long rolls of thunder, you may wonder what caused them.

**How Thunderstorms Form** A **thunderstorm** is a small storm often accompanied by heavy precipitation and frequent thunder and lightning. **Thunderstorms form in large cumulonimbus clouds, also known as thunderheads.** Most cumulonimbus clouds form on hot, humid afternoons. They also form when warm air is forced upward along a cold front. In both cases, the warm, humid air rises rapidly. The air cools, forming dense thunderheads. Heavy rain falls, sometimes along with hail. Within the thunderhead are strong upward and downward winds—updrafts and downdrafts—as shown in Figure 9. Many thunderstorms form in the spring and summer in southern states or on the Western Plains.

**Lightning and Thunder** During a thunderstorm, areas of positive and negative electrical charges build up in the storm clouds. **Lightning** is a sudden spark, or electrical discharge, as these charges jump between parts of a cloud, between nearby clouds, or between a cloud and the ground. Lightning is similar to the shocks you sometimes feel when you touch a metal object on a very dry day, but on a much larger scale.

What causes thunder? A lightning bolt can heat the air near it to as much as 30,000°C, much hotter than the sun's surface. The rapidly heated air expands suddenly and explosively. Thunder is the sound of the explosion. Because light travels much faster than sound, you see lightning before you hear thunder.

**Lab zone** Try This **Activity**

### Lightning Distances

Because light travels faster than sound, you see a lightning flash before you hear the clap of thunder. Here's how to calculate your distance from a thunderstorm. **CAUTION:** *Only do this activity inside a building.*

1. Count the number of seconds between the moment when you see the lightning and when you hear the thunder.
2. Divide the number of seconds you counted by three to get the approximate distance in kilometers. Example:

$$\frac{15 \text{ s}}{3 \text{ s/km}} = 5 \text{ km}$$

**Calculating** Wait for another lightning flash and calculate the distance again. How can you tell whether a thunderstorm is moving toward you or away from you?

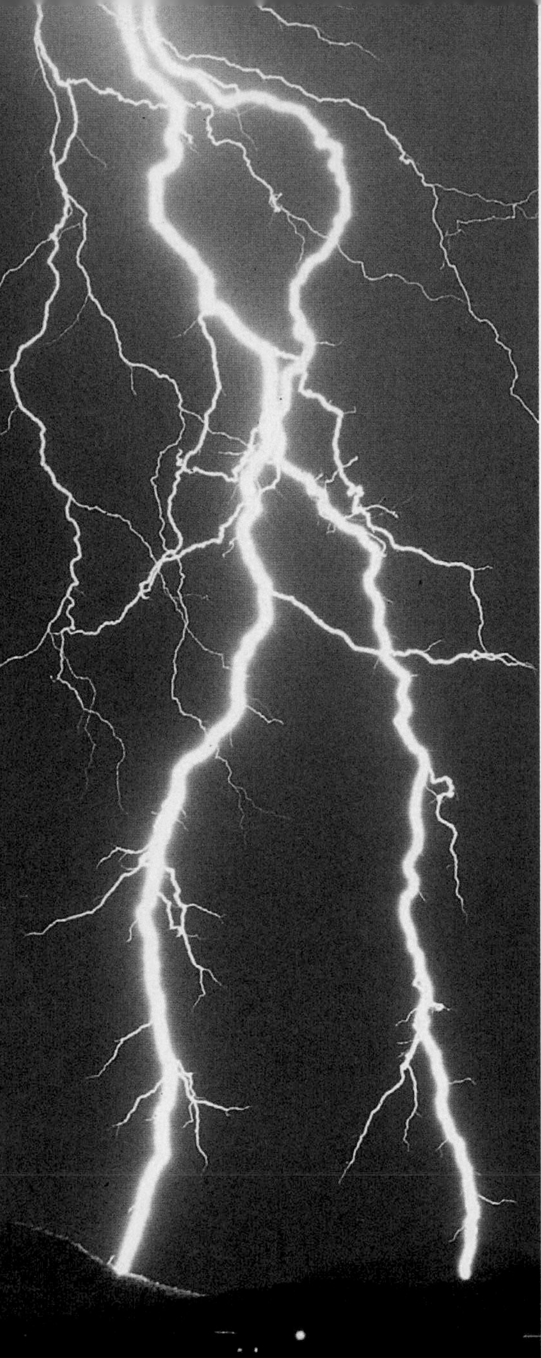

**FIGURE 10**
**Lightning Striking Earth**
Lightning occurs when electricity jumps within clouds, between clouds, or between clouds and the ground. Lightning can cause fires or serious injuries.

For: More on thunder and lightning
Visit: PHSchool.com
Web Code: cfd-4032

**Thunderstorm Damage** Thunderstorms can cause severe damage. The heavy rains associated with thunderstorms can flood low-lying areas. Lightning can also cause damage. When lightning strikes the ground, the hot, expanding air can shatter tree trunks or start forest fires. When lightning strikes people or animals, it acts like a powerful electric shock. Lightning can cause unconsciousness, serious burns, or even heart failure.

**Floods** A major danger during severe thunderstorms is flooding. Floods occur when so much water pours into a stream or river that its banks overflow, covering the surrounding land. In urban areas, floods can occur when the ground is already saturated by heavy rains. The water can't soak into the water-logged ground or the many areas covered with buildings, roads, and parking lots. A flash flood is a sudden, violent flood that occurs shortly after a storm.

**Thunderstorm Safety** The safest place to be during a thunderstorm is indoors. If you are inside a house, avoid touching telephones, electrical appliances, or plumbing fixtures, all of which can conduct electricity. It is usually safe to stay in a car with a hard top during a thunderstorm. The electricity will move along the metal skin of the car and jump to the ground. However, do not touch any metal inside the car. **During thunderstorms, avoid places where lightning may strike. Also avoid objects that can conduct electricity, such as metal objects and bodies of water.**

How can you remain safe if you are caught outside during a thunderstorm? It is dangerous to seek shelter under a tree, because lightning may strike the tree and you. Instead, find a low area away from trees, fences, and poles. Crouch with your head down. If you are swimming or in a boat, get to shore and find shelter away from the water.

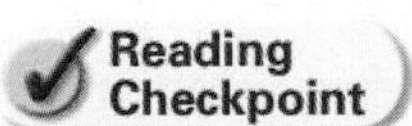
**How can lightning be dangerous?**

## Tornadoes

A tornado is one of the most frightening and destructive types of storms. A **tornado** is a rapidly whirling, funnel-shaped cloud that reaches down from a storm cloud to touch Earth's surface. If a tornado occurs over a lake or ocean, the storm is known as a waterspout. Tornadoes are usually brief, but can be deadly. They may touch the ground for 15 minutes or less and be only a few hundred meters across. But wind speeds in the most intense tornadoes may approach 500 kilometers per hour.

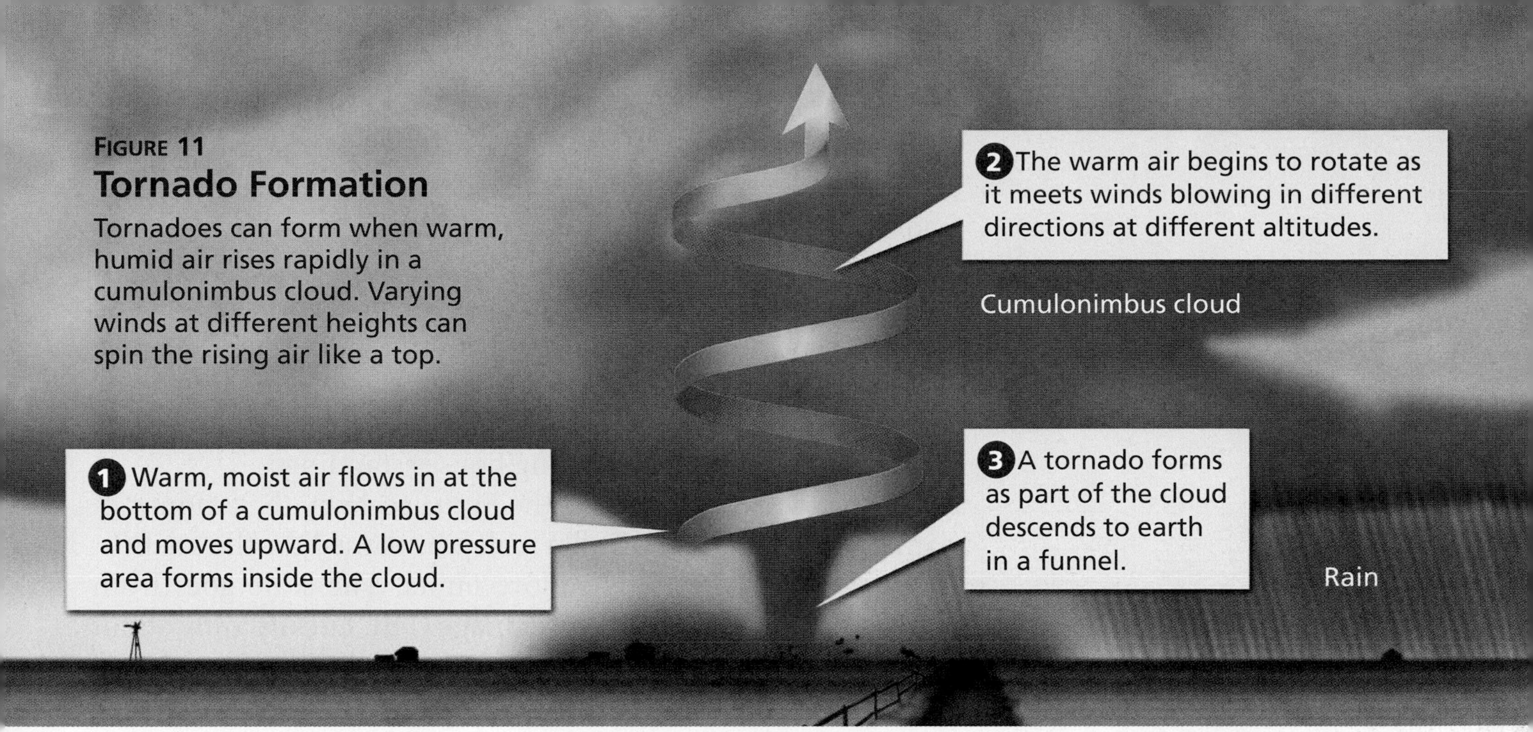

FIGURE 11
## Tornado Formation

Tornadoes can form when warm, humid air rises rapidly in a cumulonimbus cloud. Varying winds at different heights can spin the rising air like a top.

1 Warm, moist air flows in at the bottom of a cumulonimbus cloud and moves upward. A low pressure area forms inside the cloud.

2 The warm air begins to rotate as it meets winds blowing in different directions at different altitudes.

Cumulonimbus cloud

3 A tornado forms as part of the cloud descends to earth in a funnel.

Rain

**How Tornadoes Form** Tornadoes can form in any situation that produces severe weather. **Tornadoes most commonly develop in thick cumulonimbus clouds—the same clouds that bring thunderstorms.** Tornadoes are most likely to occur when thunderstorms are likely—in spring and early summer, often late in the afternoon when the ground is warm. The Great Plains often have the kind of weather pattern that is likely to create tornadoes: A warm, humid air mass moves north from the Gulf of Mexico into the lower Great Plains. A cold, dry air mass moves south from Canada. When the air masses meet, the cold air moves under the warm air, forcing it to rise. A squall line of thunderstorms is likely to form, with storms traveling from southwest to northeast. A single squall line can produce ten or more tornadoes.

**Tornado Alley** Tornadoes occur more often in the United States than in any other country. About 800 tornadoes occur in the United States every year. Weather patterns on the Great Plains result in a "tornado alley," as shown in Figure 12. However, tornadoes can and do occur in nearly every part of the United States.

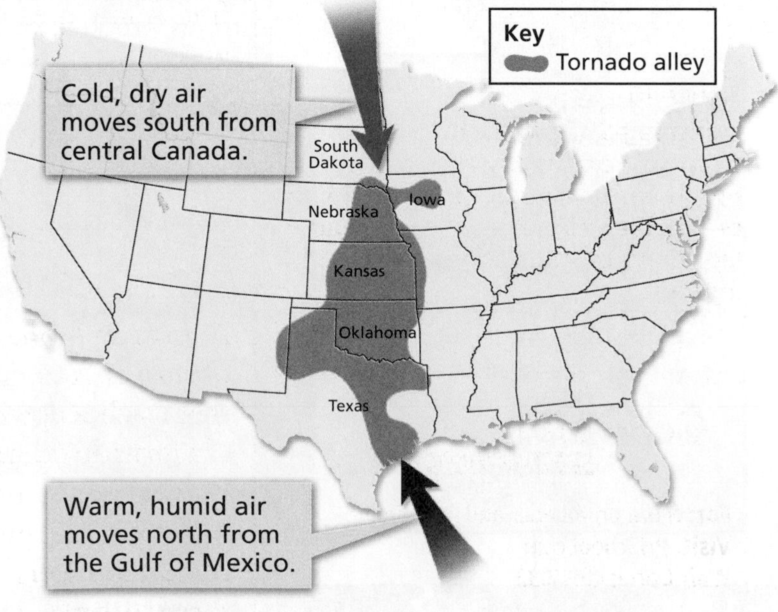
Key
Tornado alley
Cold, dry air moves south from central Canada.
South Dakota
Nebraska
Iowa
Kansas
Oklahoma
Texas
Warm, humid air moves north from the Gulf of Mexico.

FIGURE 12
**Tornado Alley**
Tornadoes in the U.S. are most likely to occur in a region known as Tornado Alley. **Interpreting Maps** *Name five states that Tornado Alley crosses.*

**Tornado Damage** Tornado damage comes from both strong winds and flying debris. The low pressure inside the tornado sucks dust and other objects into the funnel. Tornadoes can move large objects—sheds, trailers, cars—and scatter debris many miles away. One tornado tore off a motel sign in Broken Bow, Oklahoma, and dropped it 30 miles away in Arkansas! One of the reasons that tornadoes are so frightening is that they are unpredictable. A tornado can level houses on one street but leave neighboring houses standing.

Tornadoes are ranked on the Fujita scale by the amount of damage they cause. The Fujita scale was named for the scientist who devised it, Dr. T. Theodore Fujita. The scale goes from light damage (F0) to extreme damage (F5). Luckily, only about one percent of tornadoes are ranked as F4 or F5.

## Science and **History**

### Weather That Changed History

Unanticipated storms have caused incredible damage, killed large numbers of people, and even changed the course of history.

**1281 Japan**
In an attempt to conquer Japan, Kublai Khan, the Mongol emperor of China, sent a fleet of ships carrying a huge army. A hurricane from the Pacific brought high winds and towering waves that sank the ships. The Japanese named the storm *kamikaze*, meaning "divine wind."

**1588 England**
King Philip II of Spain sent the Spanish Armada, a fleet of 130 ships, to invade England. Strong winds in the English Channel trapped the Armada near shore. Some Spanish ships escaped, but storms wrecked most of them.

**1620 Massachusetts**
English Pilgrims set sail for the Americas in the *Mayflower*. They had planned to land near the mouth of the Hudson River, but turned back north because of rough seas and storms. When the Pilgrims landed farther north, they decided to stay and so established Plymouth Colony.

1200 1600 1700

**Tornado Safety** What should you do if a tornado is predicted in your area? A "tornado watch" is an announcement that tornadoes are possible in your area. Watch for approaching thunderstorms. A "tornado warning" is an announcement that a tornado has been seen in the sky or on weather radar. If you hear a tornado warning, move to a safe area as soon as you can. Do not wait until you actually see the tornado.

**The safest place to be during a tornado is in a storm shelter or the basement of a well-built building.** If the building you are in does not have a basement, move to the middle of the ground floor. Stay away from windows and doors to avoid flying debris. Lie on the floor under a sturdy piece of furniture, such as a large table. If you are outdoors, lie flat in a ditch.

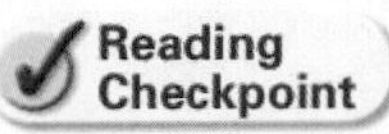


**What is a tornado warning?**

## Writing in Science

**Research and Write**
Many of these events happened before forecasters had the equipment to predict weather scientifically. Research one of the events in the timeline. Write a paragraph describing the event and how history might have been different if the people involved had had accurate weather predictions.

**1837 North Carolina**
The steamship *Home* sank during a hurricane off Ocracoke, North Carolina. In one of the worst storm-caused disasters at sea, 90 people died. In response, the U.S. Congress passed a law requiring sea-going ships to carry a life preserver for every passenger.

**1870 Great Lakes**
Learning that more than 1,900 boats had sunk in storms on the Great Lakes in 1869, Congress set up a national weather service, the Army Signal Corps. In 1891 the job of issuing weather warnings and forecasts went to a new agency, the U.S. Weather Bureau.

**1900 and 1915 Texas**
When a hurricane struck the port city of Galveston in 1900, it killed at least 8,000 people and destroyed much of the city. As a result, a seawall 5 meters high and 16 kilometers long was built. When another hurricane struck in 1915, the seawall greatly reduced the amount of damage.

1800 1900 2000

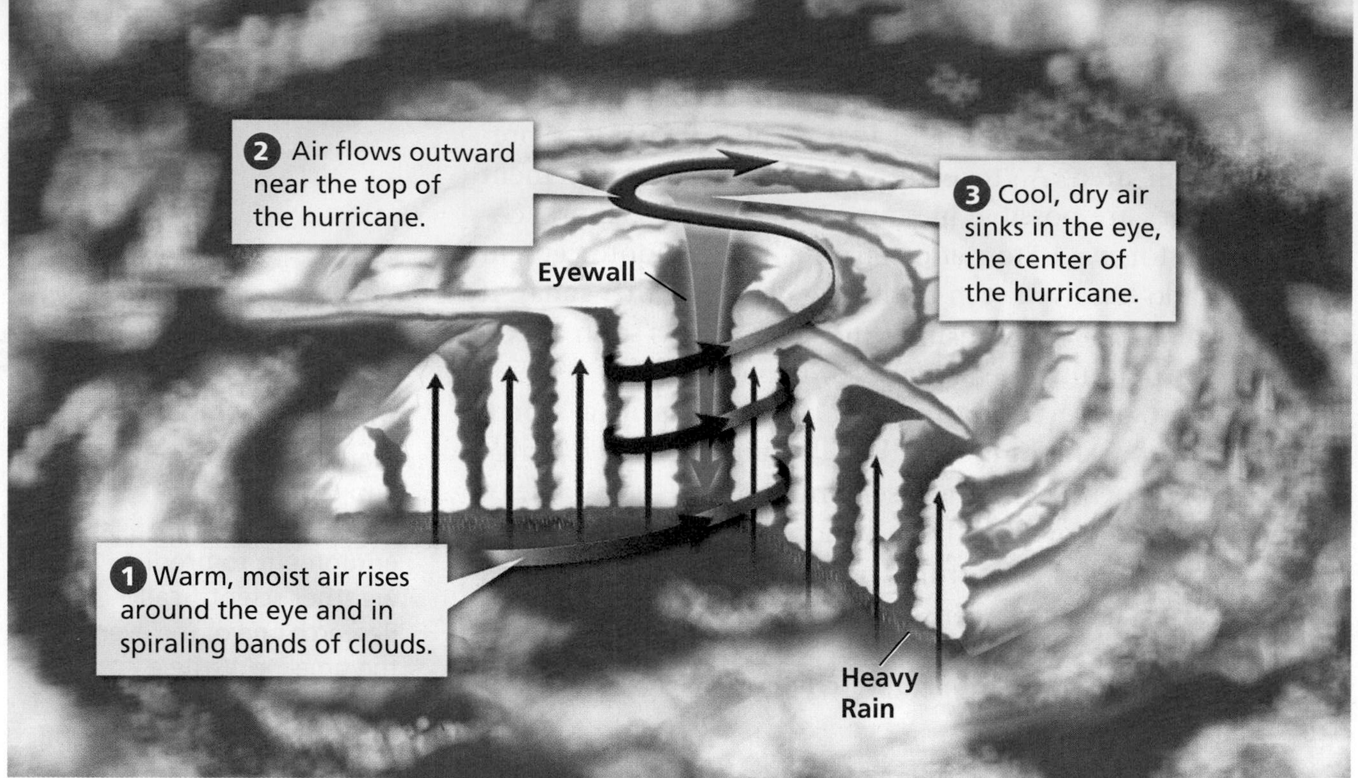

2 Air flows outward near the top of the hurricane.
3 Cool, dry air sinks in the eye, the center of the hurricane.
Eyewall
1 Warm, moist air rises around the eye and in spiraling bands of clouds.
Heavy Rain

FIGURE 13
**Structure of a Hurricane**
In a hurricane, air moves rapidly around a low-pressure area called the eye.

## Hurricanes

A **hurricane** is a tropical cyclone that has winds of 119 kilometers per hour or higher. A typical hurricane is about 600 kilometers across. Hurricanes form in the Atlantic, Pacific, and Indian oceans. In the western Pacific Ocean, hurricanes are called typhoons.

**How Hurricanes Form** A typical hurricane that strikes the United States forms in the Atlantic Ocean north of the equator in August, September, or October. **A hurricane begins over warm ocean water as a low-pressure area, or tropical disturbance.** If the tropical disturbance grows in size and strength, it becomes a tropical storm, which may then become a hurricane.

A hurricane draws its energy from the warm, humid air at the ocean's surface. As this air rises and forms clouds, more air is drawn into the system. Inside the storm are bands of very high winds and heavy rains. Winds spiral inward toward the area of lowest pressure at the center. The lower the air pressure at the center of a storm, the faster the winds blow toward the center. Hurricane winds may be as strong as 320 kilometers per hour.

Look at Figure 13. Hurricane winds are strongest in a narrow band around the center of the storm. At the center is a ring of clouds, called the eyewall, that enclose a quiet "eye." The wind gets stronger as the eye approaches. When the eye arrives, the weather changes suddenly. The air grows calm and the sky may clear. After the eye passes, the storm resumes, but the wind blows from the opposite direction.

**How Hurricanes Move** Hurricanes last longer than other storms, usually a week or more. During that period, they can travel quite a distance. Hurricanes that form in the Atlantic Ocean are steered by easterly trade winds toward the Caribbean islands and the southeastern United States. After a hurricane passes over land, it no longer has warm, moist air to draw energy from. The hurricane gradually loses strength, although heavy rainfall may continue for several days.

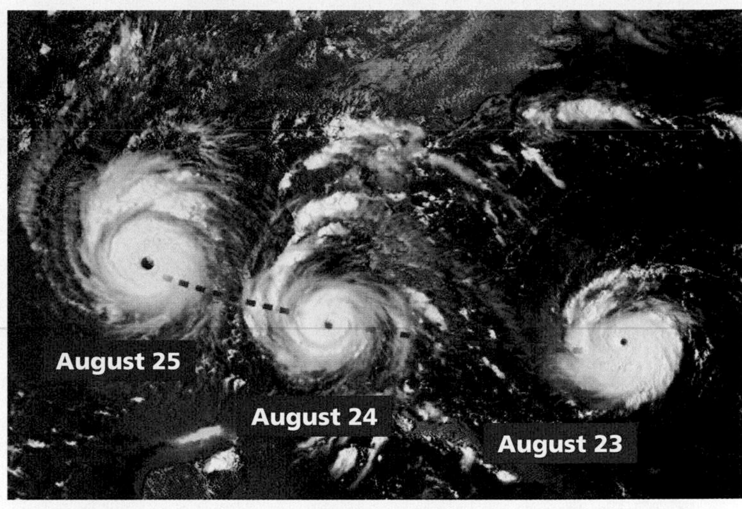


**FIGURE 14**
**Hurricane Andrew**
The path of Hurricane Andrew over three consecutive days can be seen in this photo montage.

**Hurricane Damage** When a hurricane comes ashore, it brings high waves and severe flooding as well as wind damage. The low pressure and high winds of the hurricane over the ocean raise the level of the water up to 6 meters above normal sea level. The result is a **storm surge,** a "dome" of water that sweeps across the coast where the hurricane lands. Storm surges can cause great damage, washing away beaches, destroying buildings along the coast, and eroding the coastlines.

**Hurricane Safety** Until the 1950s, a fast-moving hurricane could strike with little warning. People now receive information well in advance of an approaching hurricane.

A "hurricane watch" indicates that hurricane conditions are possible in an area within the next 36 hours. You should be prepared to **evacuate** (ee VAK yoo ayt), or move away temporarily. A "hurricane warning" means that hurricane conditions are expected within 24 hours. **If you hear a hurricane warning and are told to evacuate, leave the area immediately.**

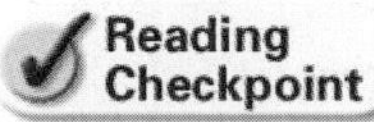


What is a storm surge?

**FIGURE 15**
**Hurricane Katrina**
Hurricane Katrina caused tremendous damage to New Orleans and the Gulf Coast in 2005. Here, a rescue crew in Bay St. Louis, Mississippi, assists a family that was trapped atop their car by rising flood waters.

## Winter Storms

In the winter in the northern United States, a large amount of precipitation falls as snow. **All year round, most precipitation begins in clouds as snow. If the air is colder than 0°C all the way to the ground, the precipitation falls as snow.** Heavy snowfalls can block roads, trapping people in their homes and making it hard for emergency vehicles to move. Extreme cold can damage crops and cause water pipes to freeze and burst.

**FIGURE 16**
**Lake-Effect Snow**
As cold dry air moves across the warmer water, it becomes more humid as water vapor evaporates from the lake surface. When the air reaches land and cools, lake-effect snow falls.
**Interpreting Maps** *Which two cities on the map receive large amounts of lake-effect snow?*

**Lake-Effect Snow** Two of the snowiest cities in the United States are Buffalo and Rochester in upstate New York. On average, nearly three meters of snow falls on each of these cities every winter. Why do Buffalo and Rochester get so much snow?

Study Figure 16. Notice that Buffalo is located east of Lake Erie, and Rochester is located south of Lake Ontario. In the fall and winter, the land near these lakes cools much more rapidly than the water in the lakes. Although the water in these lakes is cold, it is still much warmer than the surrounding land and air.

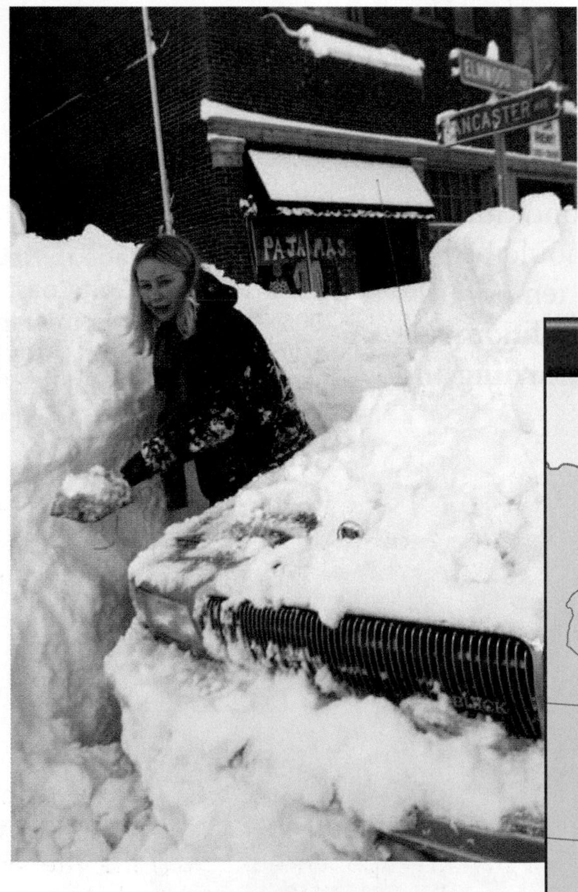


When a cold, dry air mass from central Canada moves southeast across one of the Great Lakes, it picks up water vapor and heat from the lake. As soon as the air mass reaches the other side of the lake, the air rises and cools again. The water vapor condenses and falls as snow, usually within 40 kilometers of the lake.

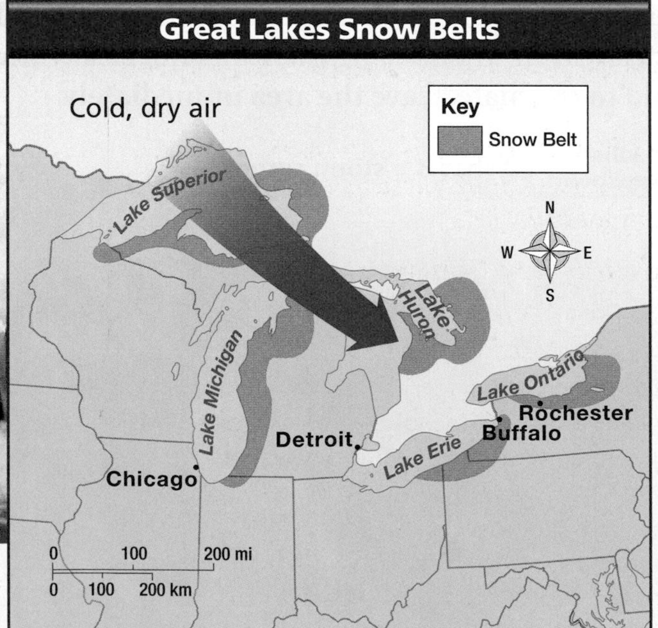

**FIGURE 17**
**Winter Storm Damage**
Major winter storms can cause a great deal of damage. Here, utility workers in Maine remove a pole snapped by a fierce winter storm.

**Snowstorm Safety** Imagine being caught in a snowstorm when the wind suddenly picks up. High winds can blow falling snow sideways or pick up snow from the ground and suspend it in the air. This situation can be extremely dangerous because the blowing snow limits your vision and makes it easy to get lost. Also, strong winds cool a person's body rapidly. **If you are caught in a snowstorm, try to find shelter from the wind.** Cover exposed parts of your body and try to stay dry. If you are in a car, the driver should keep the engine running only if the exhaust pipe is clear of snow.

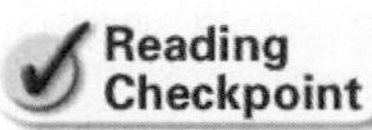
**Reading Checkpoint** How can snowstorms be dangerous?

## Section 2 Assessment

**Target Reading Skill Sequencing** Refer to your flowchart about hurricane formation as you answer Question 3.

### Reviewing Key Concepts

1. a. **Defining** What is a thunderstorm?
   b. **Listing** List two dangers associated with thunderstorms.
   c. **Describing** What safety precautions should you follow during a thunderstorm?
2. a. **Identifying** What weather conditions are most likely to produce tornadoes?
   b. **Developing Hypotheses** Why do tornadoes occur most often in the area known as "tornado alley"?
3. a. **Defining** What is a hurricane?
   b. **Relating Cause and Effect** How do hurricanes form?
4. a. **Explaining** What is lake-effect snow?
   b. **Inferring** Why doesn't lake-effect snow fall to the north or west of the Great Lakes?
   c. **Describing** What should you do if you are caught in a snowstorm?

### Lab zone At-Home Activity

**Storm Eyewitness** Interview a family member or other adult about a dramatic storm that he or she has experienced. Before the interview, make a list of questions you would like to ask. For example, when and where did the storm occur? Write up your interview in a question-and-answer format, beginning with a short introduction.

Lab zone **Skills Lab**

# Tracking a Hurricane

## Problem

How can you predict when and where a hurricane will come ashore?

## Skills Focus

interpreting data, predicting, drawing conclusions

## Materials

- ruler
- red, blue, green, and brown pencils
- tracing paper

## Procedure

1. Look at the plotted path of the hurricane on the map. Each dot represents the location of the eye of the hurricane at six-hour intervals. The last dot shows where the hurricane was located at noon on August 30.
2. Predict the path you think the hurricane will take. Place tracing paper over the map below. Using a red pencil, place an *X* on your tracing paper where you think the hurricane will first reach land. Next to your *X*, write the date and time you think the hurricane will come ashore.
3. Hurricane warnings are issued for an area that is likely to experience a hurricane within 24 hours. On your tracing paper, shade in red the area for which you would issue a hurricane warning.
4. Using the following data table, plot the next five positions for the storm using a blue pencil. Use your ruler to connect the dots to show the hurricane's path.

**Data Table**

| Date and Time | Latitude | Longitude |
|---|---|---|
| August 30, 6:00 P.M. | 28.3° N | 86.8° W |
| August 31, midnight | 28.4° N | 86.0° W |
| August 31, 6:00 A.M. | 28.6° N | 85.3° W |
| August 31, noon | 28.8° N | 84.4° W |
| August 31, 6:00 P.M. | 28.8° N | 84.0° W |

5. Based on the new data, decide if you need to change your prediction of where and when the hurricane will come ashore. Mark your new predictions in blue pencil on your tracing paper.
6. During September 1, you obtain four more positions. (Plot these points only after you have completed Step 5.) Based on these new data, use the green pencil to indicate when and where you now think the hurricane will come ashore.

**Data Table**

| Date and Time | Latitude | Longitude |
|---|---|---|
| September 1, midnight | 28.8° N | 83.8° W |
| September 1, 6:00 A.M. | 28.6° N | 83.9° W |
| September 1, noon | 28.6° N | 84.2° W |
| September 1, 6:00 P.M. | 28.9° N | 84.8° W |

7. The next day, September 2, you plot four more positions using a brown pencil. (Plot these points only after you have completed Step 6.)

**Data Table**

| Date and Time | Latitude | Longitude |
|---|---|---|
| September 2, midnight | 29.4° N | 85.9° W |
| September 2, 6:00 A.M. | 29.7° N | 87.3° W |
| September 2, noon | 30.2° N | 88.8° W |
| September 2, 6:00 P.M. | 31.0° N | 90.4° W |

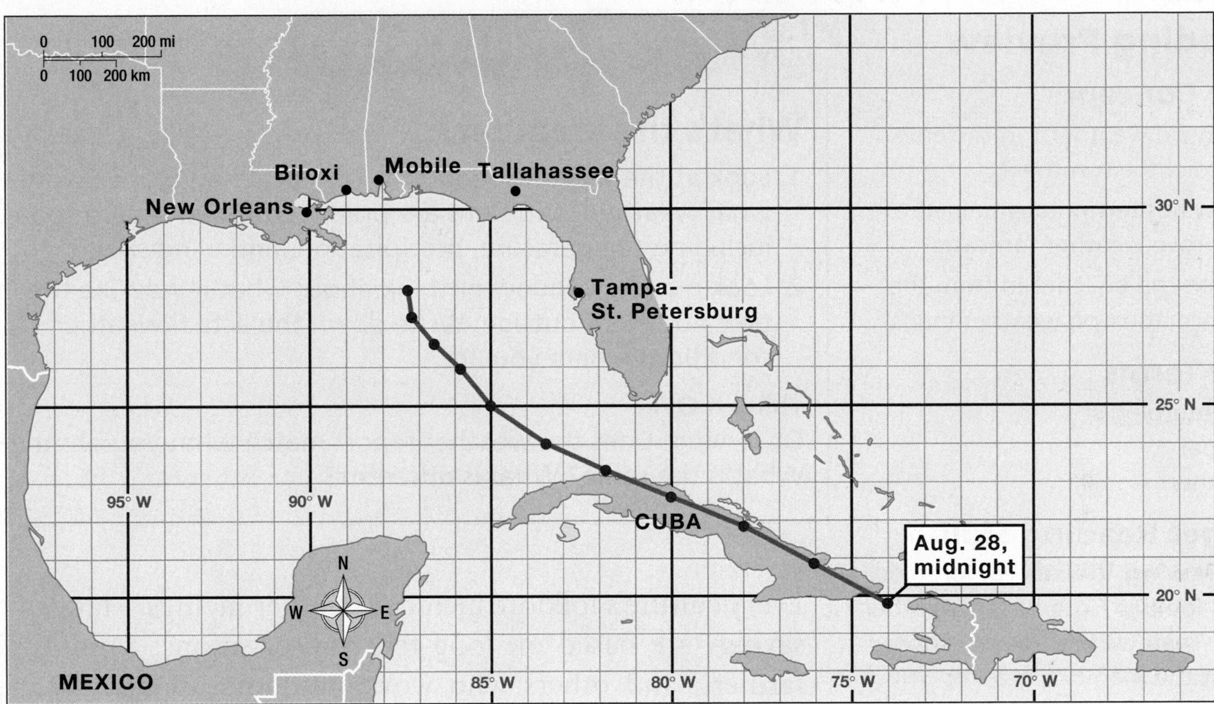


## Analyze and Conclude

1. **Interpreting Data** Describe in detail the complete path of the hurricane you tracked. Include where it came ashore and identify any cities that were in the vicinity.
2. **Predicting** How did your predictions in Steps 2, 5, and 6 compare to what actually happened?
3. **Interpreting Data** What was unusual about your hurricane's path?
4. **Inferring** How do you think hurricanes with a path like this one affect the issuing of hurricane warnings?
5. **Drawing Conclusions** Why do you have to be so careful when issuing warnings? What problems might be caused if you issued an unnecessary hurricane warning? What might happen if a hurricane warning were issued too late?
6. **Communicating** In this activity you only had data for the hurricane's position. If you were tracking a hurricane and issuing warnings, what other types of information would help you make decisions about the hurricane's path? Write a paragraph describing the additional information you would need.

## More to Explore

With your teacher's help, search the Internet for more hurricane tracking data. Map the data and try to predict where the hurricane will come ashore.

Section 3

• Tech & Design •

# Predicting the Weather

## Reading Preview

### Key Concepts

- How do weather forecasters predict the weather?
- How has technology helped to improve weather forecasts?
- What can be learned from the information on weather maps?

### Key Terms

- meteorologist
- isobar
- isotherm

### Target Reading Skill

**Previewing Visuals** Before you read, look at Figure 21, a weather map. Then write three questions about the map in a graphic organizer like the one below. As you read, answer your questions.

**Weather Map**

| |
|---|
| **Q.** What type of front is located west of Oklahoma City? |
| **A.** |
| **Q.** |

## Lab zone Discover Activity

### What's the Weather?

1. Look at the weather report in your local newspaper. Note what weather conditions are predicted for your area today, including temperature, precipitation, and wind speed.
2. Look out the window or think about what it was like the last time you were outside. Write down the actual weather conditions where you are.

**Think It Over**

**Observing** Does the weather report match what you observe? What is the same? What is different?

Every culture's folklore includes weather sayings. Many of these sayings are based on long-term observations. Sailors, pilots, farmers, and others who work outdoors are usually careful observers of clouds, winds, and other signs of changes in the weather. Two examples are shown below.

Why do these two weather sayings agree that a red morning sky means bad weather? Recall that in the United States storms usually move from west to east. Clouds in the west may indicate an advancing low-pressure area, bringing stormy weather. If there are high clouds in the west in the morning, the rising sun in the east turns these clouds red. The reverse is true at sunset. As the sun sets in the west, it turns clouds in the east red. Clouds in the east may indicate that a storm is moving away to the east. A red sky is one kind of observation that helps people to predict the weather.

**FIGURE 18**
**Red Sky**
The red sky shown in this sunrise may indicate an approaching storm.

Evening red and morning gray
Will send the traveler on his way;
Evening gray and morning red
Will bring down rain upon his head.

Red sky in the morning,
sailors take warning;
Red sky at night,
sailor's delight.

**FIGURE 19**
**Meteorologist at Work**
Professional meteorologists use computers to help track and forecast the weather. **Inferring** *Why might a meteorologist need to refer to more than one computer screen?*

## Weather Forecasting

The first step in forecasting is to collect data, either from simple, direct observations or through the use of instruments. For example, if a barometer shows that the air pressure is falling, you can expect a change in the weather. Falling air pressure usually indicates an approaching low-pressure area, possibly bringing rain or snow.

**Making Simple Observations** You can read weather signs in the clouds, too. Cumulus clouds often form on warm afternoons when warm air rises. If you see these clouds growing larger and taller, you can expect them to become cumulonimbus clouds, which may produce a thunderstorm. If you can see thin cirrus clouds high in the sky, a warm front may be approaching.

Even careful weather observers often turn to professional meteorologists for weather information. **Meteorologists** (mee tee uh RAHL uh jists) are scientists who study the causes of weather and try to predict it.

**Interpreting Complex Data** Meteorologists are able to interpret information from a variety of sources, including local weather observers, instruments carried by balloons, satellites, and weather stations around the world. **Meteorologists use maps, charts, and computers to analyze weather data and to prepare weather forecasts.** They often use radar to track areas of rain or snow and to locate severe storms such as tornadoes. Forecasters can also follow the path of a storm system.

Where do weather reporters get their information? Most weather information comes from the National Weather Service. The National Weather Service uses balloons, satellites, radar, and surface instruments to gather weather data.

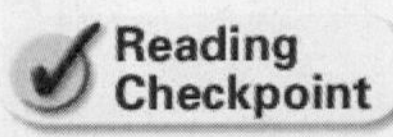

**What is a meteorologist?**

## Weather Technology

Techniques for predicting weather have changed dramatically in recent years. Short-range forecasts—forecasts for up to five days—are now fairly reliable. Meteorologists can also make somewhat accurate long-range predictions. **Technological improvements in gathering weather data and using computers have improved the accuracy of weather forecasts.**

**Weather Balloons** Weather balloons carry instruments high into the troposphere and lower stratosphere. Remember that these are the two lowest layers of the atmosphere. The instruments measure temperature, air pressure, and humidity.

**Weather Satellites** The first weather satellite, *TIROS-1*, was launched in 1960. Satellites orbit Earth in the exosphere, the uppermost layer of the atmosphere. Cameras on weather satellites in the exosphere can make images of Earth's surface, clouds, storms, and snow cover. These images are then transmitted to meteorologists on Earth, who interpret the information. New technologies, such as NASA's *Terra* satellite, shown in Figure 20, provide large amounts of data to meteorologists. Modern satellites collect data on temperature, humidity, solar radiation, wind speed and wind direction, and provide images of clouds and storm systems.

**FIGURE 20**
**Satellite Technology**
The large satellite image shows an intense cyclone over Ireland and Great Britain. The *Terra* satellite (right) collects data on weather and environmental conditions.

**Automated Weather Stations** Data are also gathered from surface locations for temperature, air pressure, relative humidity, rainfall, and wind speed and direction. The National Weather Service has established a network of over 1,700 surface weather observation sites.

**Computer Forecasts** Computers are widely used to help forecast weather. Instruments can now gather large amounts of data, including temperature, humidity, air pressure, wind speed and direction, and other factors. Computers process such information quickly to help forecasters make predictions. To make a forecast, the computer starts with weather conditions reported from various weather stations over a large area. The computer then works through thousands of calculations using equations from weather models. These data are used to make forecasts for 12 hours, 24 hours, 36 hours, and so on. Each forecast builds on the previous forecast. When new weather data come in, the computer forecasts are revised.

**Reading Checkpoint** How are computers used to produce weather forecasts?

**For:** More on weather maps
**Visit:** PHSchool.com
**Web Code:** cfd-4033

**Math** Analyzing Data

## Computer Weather Forecasting

Scientists use computers to develop different models of how a front may move. These predictions are then used to make weather forecasts. As more data become available, some models are found to be incorrect, while others are found to closely fit the predicted conditions. The upper graph shows predicted air pressure from two models. The lower graph shows actual data for air pressure.

1. **Reading Graphs** What two variables are being graphed?
2. **Interpreting Data** How is air pressure predicted to change according to each model in the top graph?
3. **Inferring** Which computer model most closely matches the actual air pressure data?
4. **Predicting** What weather would you forecast for Monday and Tuesday? Explain. (*Hint:* Remember that falling air pressure usually means an approaching low-pressure area and possible precipitation.)

**Weather Forecasting Data**

FIGURE 21

## Reading Weather Map Symbols

The figure below shows what various weather symbols mean. At right, the weather map shows data collected from many weather stations.

| Wind Speed (mph) | Symbol |
|---|---|
| 1 – 2 | |
| 3 – 8 | |
| 9 – 14 | |
| 15 – 20 | |
| 21 – 25 | |
| 26 – 31 | |
| 32 – 37 | |
| 38 – 43 | |
| 44 – 49 | |
| 50 – 54 | |
| 55 – 60 | |
| 61 – 66 | |
| 67 – 71 | |
| 72 – 77 | |

**Weather Map Symbol**

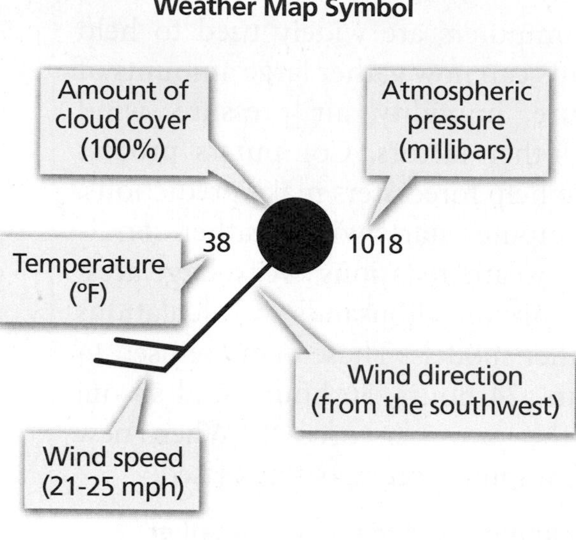


| Cloud Cover (%) | Symbol |
|---|---|
| 0 | |
| 10 | |
| 20–30 | |
| 40 | |
| 50 | |
| 60 | |
| 70–80 | |
| 90 | |
| 100 | |

**Lab zone Skills Activity**

### Interpreting Data

Use Figure 21 to help you answer questions about this weather station data.

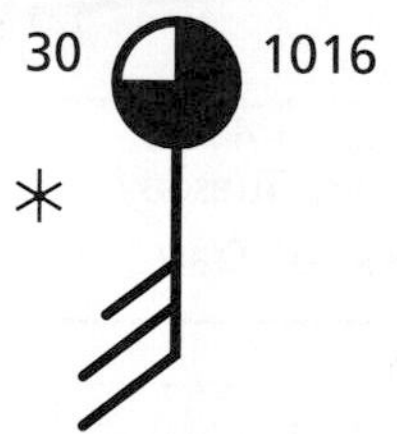


1. What is the temperature at this station?
2. What is the wind speed?
3. Which way is the wind blowing?
4. What is the air pressure?
5. What percent of the sky is covered by clouds?
6. What type of precipitation, if any, is falling?

## Reading Weather Maps

A weather map is a "snapshot" of conditions at a particular time over a large area. There are many types of weather maps. Weather forecasters often present maps generated by computers from surface data, radar, or satellite information.

**Weather Service Maps** Data from many local weather stations all over the country are assembled into weather maps at the National Weather Service. The data collected by a typical station is summarized in Figure 21 above. The simplified weather map on the next page includes most of the weather station data shown in the key.

On some weather maps, you see curved lines. These lines connect places where certain conditions—temperature or air pressure—are the same. **Isobars** are lines joining places on the map that have the same air pressure. (*Iso* means "equal" and *bar* means "pressure.") The numbers on the isobars are the pressure readings. Air pressure readings may be given in inches of mercury or in millibars or both. The isobars in Figure 21 are shown in both millbars and inches of mercury.

**Isotherms** are lines joining places that have the same temperature. The isotherm may be labeled with the temperature in degrees Fahrenheit, degrees Celsius, or both.

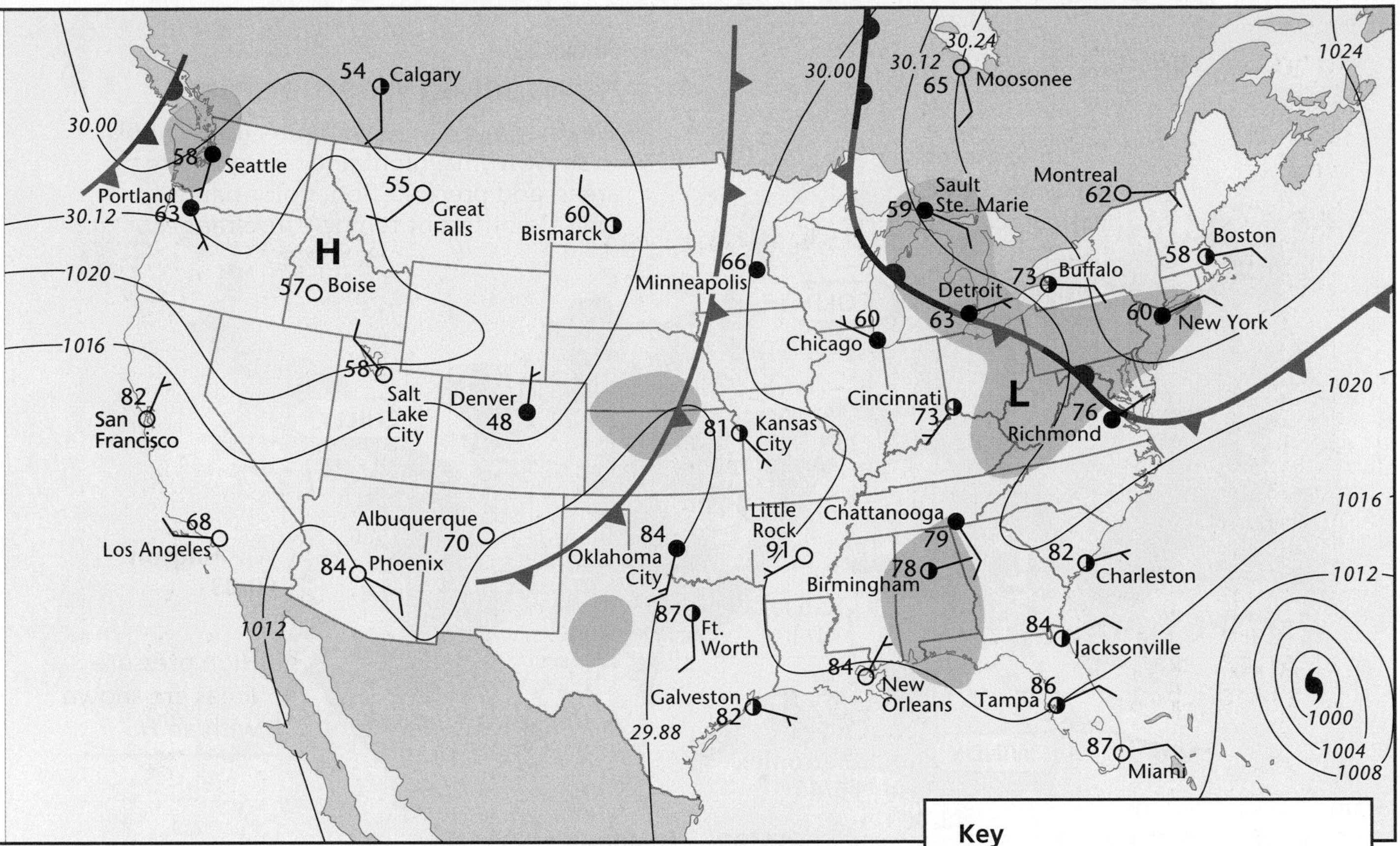

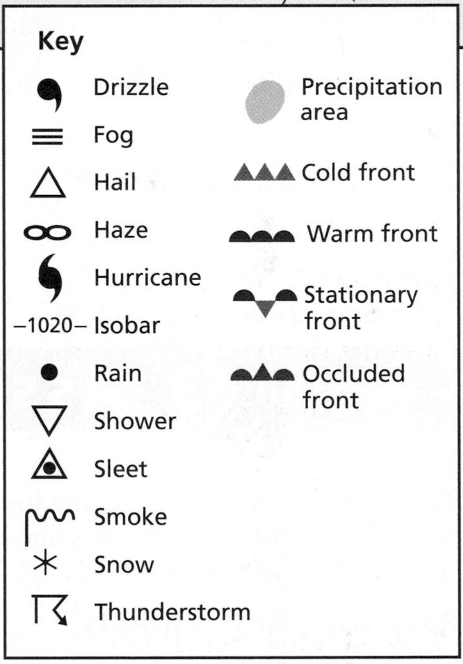

Key

- Drizzle
- Fog
- Hail
- Haze
- Hurricane
- –1020– Isobar
- Rain
- Shower
- Sleet
- Smoke
- Snow
- Thunderstorm
- Precipitation area
- Cold front
- Warm front
- Stationary front
- Occluded front

**Newspaper Weather Maps** Maps in newspapers are simplified versions of maps produced by the National Weather Service. Figure 22 on the next page shows a typical newspaper weather map. From what you have learned in this chapter, you can probably interpret most of the symbols on this map. **Standard symbols on weather maps show fronts, areas of high and low pressure, types of precipitation, and temperatures.** Note that the high and low temperatures are given in degrees Fahrenheit instead of Celsius.

**Limits of Weather Forecasts** As computers have grown more powerful, and new satellites and radar technologies have been developed, scientists have been able to make better forecasts. But even with extremely fast computers, it is unlikely that forecasters will ever be able to predict the weather a month in advance with great accuracy. This has to do with the so-called "butterfly effect." The atmosphere works in such a way that a small change in the weather today can mean a larger change in the weather a week later! The name refers to a scientist's suggestion that even the flapping of a butterfly's wings causes a tiny disturbance in the atmosphere. This tiny event might cause a larger disturbance that could—eventually—grow into a large storm.

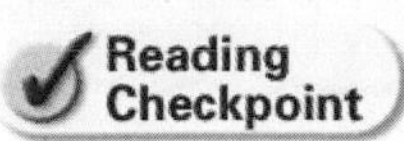


**What is the "butterfly effect"?**

FIGURE 22
## Newspaper Weather Map
Weather maps in newspapers use symbols to show fronts, high- and low-pressure areas, and precipitation. Color bands indicate different temperature ranges.

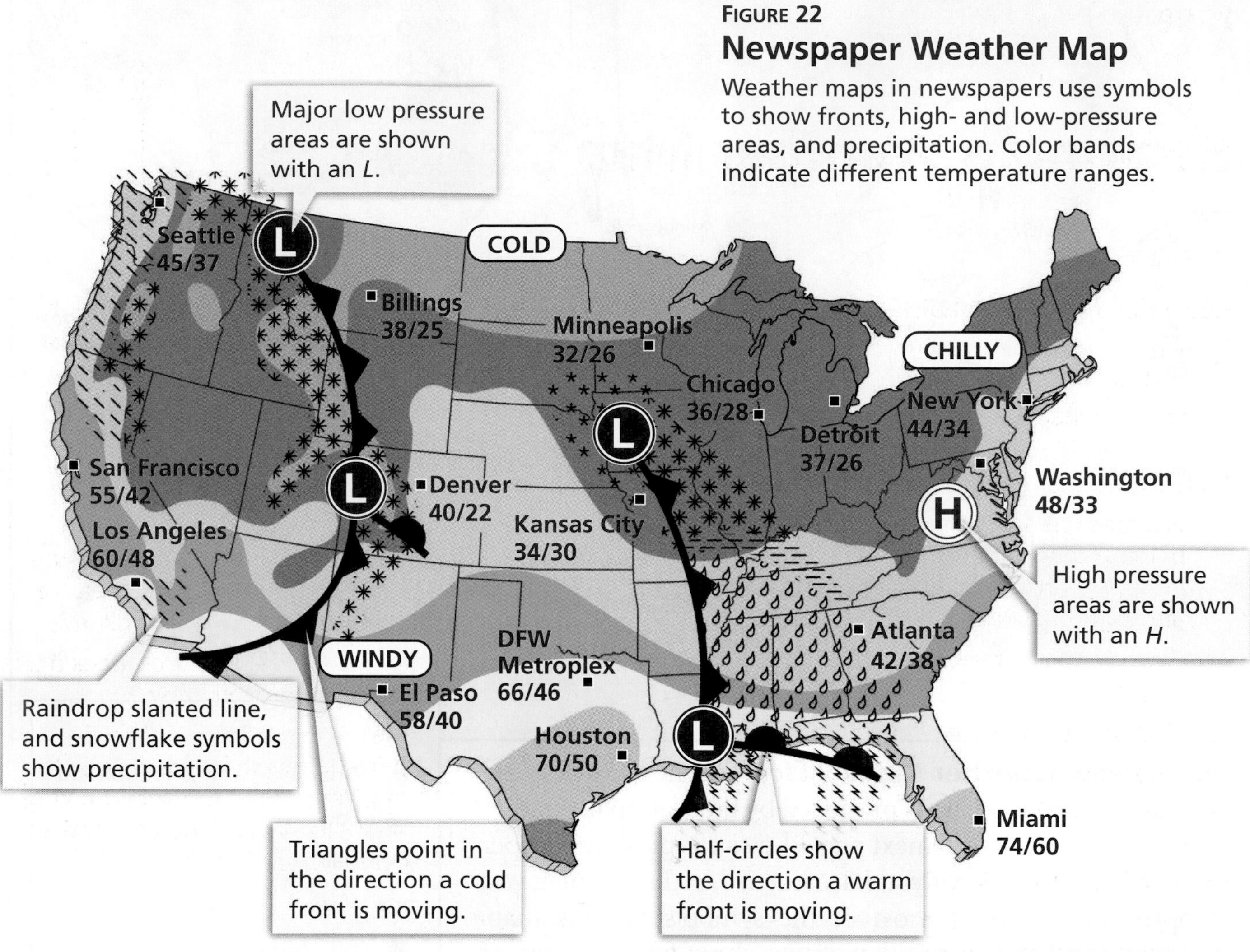


# Section 3 Assessment

**Target Reading Skill Previewing Visuals** Refer to your questions and answers about weather maps to help you answer Question 3 below.

### Reviewing Key Concepts

1. a. **Describing** What is a meteorologist?
   b. **Explaining** What tools do meteorologists rely on to forecast the weather?
2. a. **Listing** List three technologies used to gather weather data.
   b. **Summarizing** Describe the types of weather data gathered by satellites.
   c. **Drawing Conclusions** How does the large amount of weather data gathered by various modern technologies affect the accuracy of weather forecasts?
3. a. **Identifying** What is the symbol for a cold front on a weather map?
   b. **Explaining** How is wind direction indicated on a weather map?
   c. **Interpreting Diagrams** According to Figure 22, what is the weather like in Chicago? How might this change in a few hours?

## Writing in Science

**Weather Report** Find a current weather map from a newspaper. Use the map to write a brief weather report for your region. Include a description of the various weather symbols used on the map.

Lab zone **Skills Lab**

# Reading a Weather Map

## Problem

How does a weather map communicate data?

## Skills Focus

interpreting maps, observing, drawing conclusions

## Procedure

1. Examine the symbols on the weather map below. For more information about the symbols used on the map, refer to Figure 21 and Figure 22 earlier in this section.
2. Observe the different colors on the weather map below.
3. Find the symbols for snow and rain.
4. Locate the warm fronts and cold fronts.
5. Locate the symbols for high and low pressure.

## Analyze and Conclude

1. **Interpreting Maps** What color represents the highest temperatures? What color represents the lowest temperatures?
2. **Interpreting Maps** Which city has the highest temperature? Which city has the lowest temperature?
3. **Interpreting Maps** Where on the map is it raining? Where on the map is it snowing?
4. **Interpreting Maps** How many different kinds of fronts are shown on the map?
5. **Observing** How many areas of low pressure are shown on the map? How many areas of high pressure are shown on the map?
6. **Drawing Conclusions** What season does this map represent? How do you know?
7. **Communicating** The triangles and semicircles on the front lines show which way the front is moving. What type of front is moving toward Minneapolis? What kind of weather do you think it will bring?

## More to Explore

Compare this weather map to one shown on a television news report. Which symbols on these maps are similar? Which symbols are different?

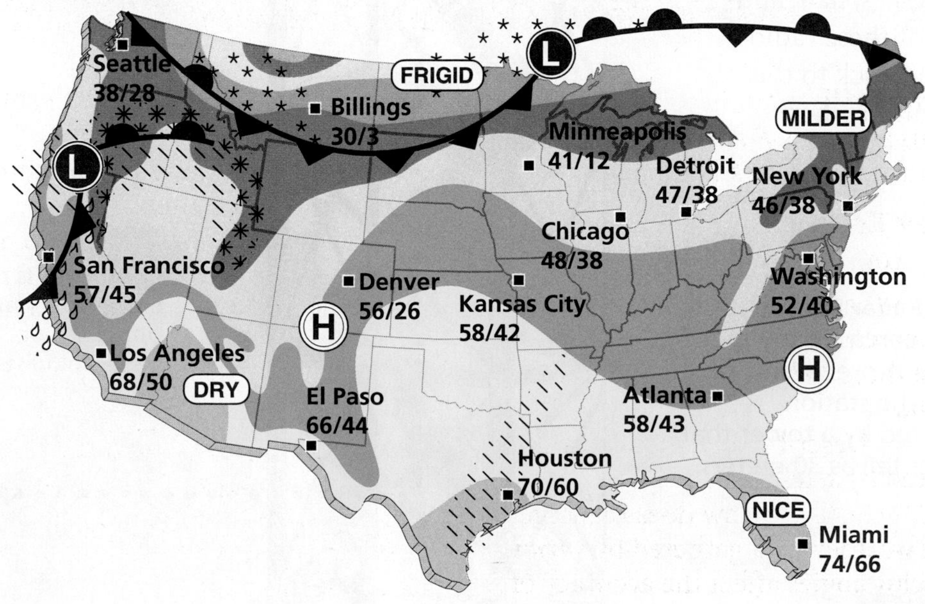

Technology and **Society** • Tech & Design •

# Doppler Radar

"Let's look at our Doppler radar screen," says a TV meteorologist pointing to a weather map with moving color blotches. The colors represent different locations and intensities of precipitation. "The purple area here shows a severe storm moving rapidly into our area." Doppler radar helps meteorologists make more accurate weather forecasts by tracking the speed and direction of precipitation.

## What Is Doppler Radar?

Doppler radar gets its name from the "Doppler effect," which describes the changes that occur in radio waves as they bounce off a moving object. Nearly 150 Doppler radar stations throughout the United States continuously send out radio waves. These waves bounce off particles in the air, such as raindrops, snowflakes, hail, and even dust. Some of these radio waves are reflected back to the Doppler radar station where computers process the data.

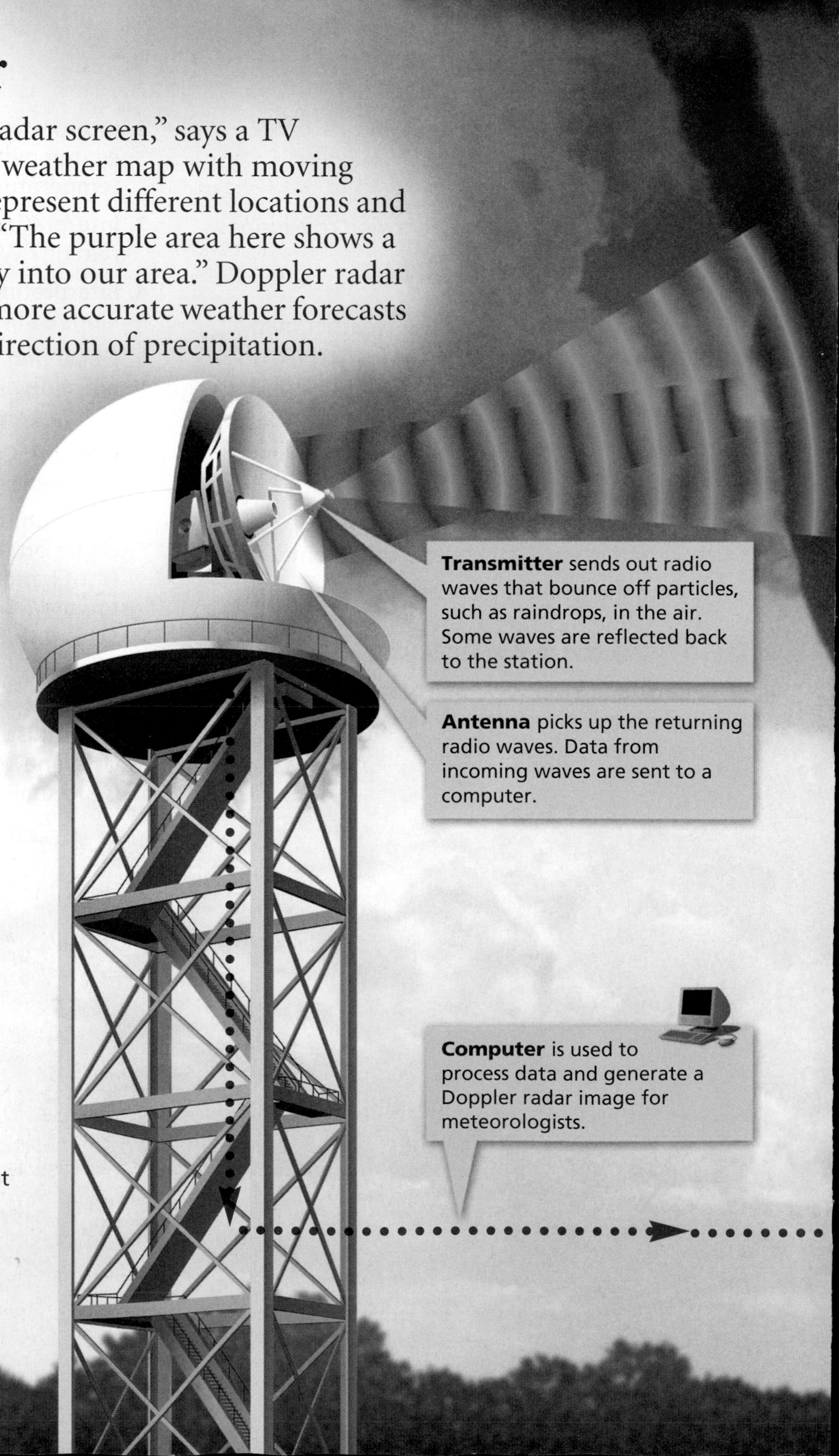

**Transmitter** sends out radio waves that bounce off particles, such as raindrops, in the air. Some waves are reflected back to the station.

**Antenna** picks up the returning radio waves. Data from incoming waves are sent to a computer.

**Doppler Radar Station**
Rotating continuously inside the protective housing, the station is supported by a tower that may be as tall as 30 meters.

**Computer** is used to process data and generate a Doppler radar image for meteorologists.

## How Effective Is Doppler Radar?

Before Doppler radar, it was hard to track fast-moving storms such as tornadoes. Tornado warnings were issued an average of just five minutes in advance. Today, Doppler radar can give people several extra minutes to prepare. People also use Doppler images to make decisions about everyday activities.

But the technology does have limitations. Doppler radar doesn't "see" everything. Sometimes mountains or buildings block the radio waves. In addition, Doppler radar doesn't always pick up light precipitation such as drizzle. Meteorologists must review the completeness of the data and decide how it might affect the forecast.

## Weigh the Impact

**1. Identify the Need**
How is Doppler radar an important technology in weather forecasting?

**2. Research**
Using the Internet, research Doppler radar reports for your city. Examine a Doppler image and explain each element on the map, including the different colors and the direction of motion.

**3. Write**
As a TV meteorologist, write the script for a local weather forecast. Describe areas with precipitation, the amount of precipitation, and the direction of weather systems. Use your research and notes.

**For:** More on Doppler radar
**Visit:** PHSchool.com
**Web Code:** cfh-4030

**Tornado**
Doppler radar can detect the air movements in thunderstorms that may lead to tornadoes. A tornado is a rapidly spinning, funnel-shaped cloud formed of condensed water particles.

**Doppler Radar Screens**

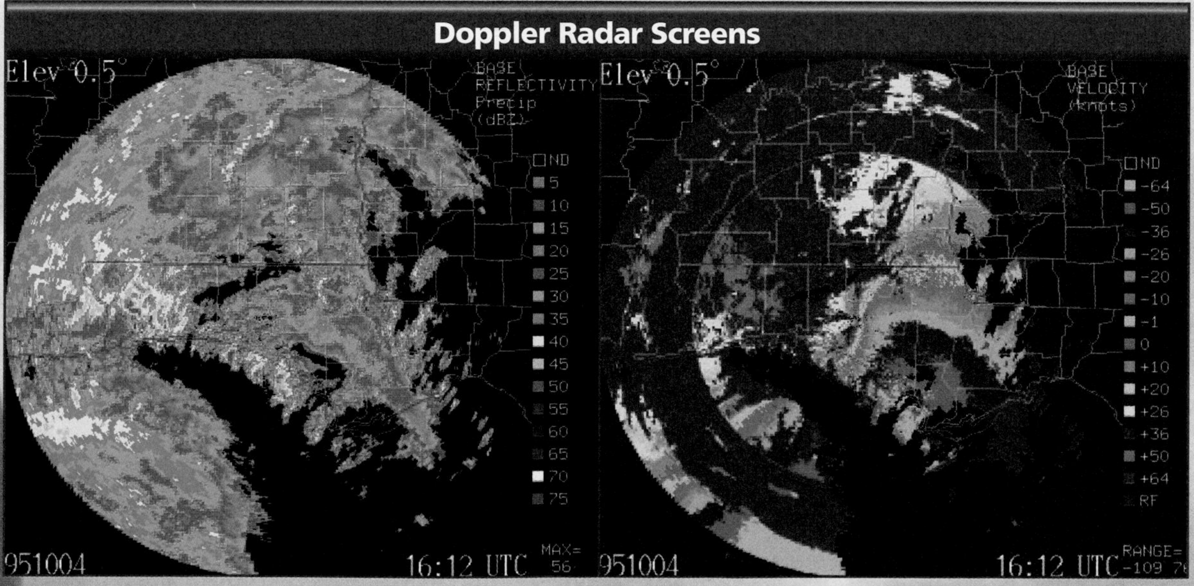


The amount of precipitation is shown above by using different colors.

The different colors above show the speed and direction of precipitation.

# Chapter 17 Study Guide

**The BIG Idea** **Weather Systems** When air masses collide, they form fronts. Storms and rapid changes in weather often develop along fronts.

## 1 Air Masses and Fronts

### Key Concepts

- Four major types of air masses influence the weather in North America: maritime tropical, continental tropical, maritime polar, and continental polar.
- In the continental United States, air masses are commonly moved by the prevailing westerlies and jet streams.
- Colliding air masses can form four types of fronts: cold fronts, warm fronts, stationary fronts, and occluded fronts.
- Cyclones and decreasing air pressure are associated with clouds, wind, and precipitation.
- The descending air in an anticyclone generally causes dry, clear weather.

### Key Terms

• air mass • tropical • polar • maritime
• continental • front • occluded • cyclone
• anticyclone

## 2 Storms

### Key Concepts

- Thunderstorms form in large cumulonimbus clouds, also known as thunderheads.
- During thunderstorms, avoid places where lightning may strike. Also avoid objects that can conduct electricity, such as metal objects and bodies of water.
- Tornadoes most commonly develop in thick cumulonimbus clouds—the same clouds that bring thunderstorms.
- The safest place to be during a tornado is in a storm shelter or the basement of a well-built building.
- A hurricane begins over warm ocean water as a low-pressure area, or tropical disturbance.
- If you hear a hurricane warning and are told to evacuate, leave the area immediately.
- All year round, most precipitation begins in clouds as snow.
- If you are caught in a snowstorm, try to find shelter from the wind.

### Key Terms

• storm • thunderstorm • lightning
• tornado • hurricane • storm surge
• evacuate

## 3 Predicting the Weather

### Key Concepts

- Meteorologists use maps, charts, and computers to analyze weather data and to prepare weather forecasts.
- Technological improvements in gathering weather data and using computers have improved the accuracy of weather forecasts.
- Standard symbols on weather maps show fronts, areas of high and low pressure, types of precipitation, and temperatures.

### Key Terms

meteorologist
isobar
isotherm

# Review and Assessment

For: Self-Assessment
Visit: PHSchool.com
Web Code: cfa-4030

## Organizing Information

**Comparing and Contrasting** Copy the table, which compares and contrasts thunderstorms, tornadoes, and hurricanes, onto a separate sheet of paper. Then complete it and add a title. (For more on Comparing and Contrasting, see the Skills Handbook.)

| Type of Storm | Where Forms | Typical Time of Year | Safety Rules |
|---|---|---|---|
| Thunderstorm | Within large cumulonimbus clouds | a. ___?___ | b. ___?___ |
| Tornado | c. ___?___ | Spring, early summer | d. ___?___ |
| Hurricane | e. ___?___ | f. ___?___ | Evacuate or move inside a well-built building |

## Reviewing Key Terms

**Choose the letter of the best answer.**

1. An air mass that forms over an ocean is called
   a. tropical.
   b. continental.
   c. maritime.
   d. polar.
2. Cool, clear weather usually follows a
   a. warm front.
   b. cold front.
   c. stationary front.
   d. occluded front.
3. A rotating funnel-shaped cloud with high winds that extends from a storm cloud to Earth's surface is a
   a. storm surge.
   b. thunderstorm.
   c. hurricane.
   d. tornado.
4. Very large tropical cyclones with high winds are called
   a. hurricanes.
   b. tornadoes.
   c. air masses.
   d. anticyclones.
5. Lines joining places that have the same temperature are
   a. isobars.
   b. isotherms.
   c. fronts.
   d. occluded.

**If the statement is true, write *true*. If it is false, change the underlined word or words to make the statement true.**

6. Summers in the Southwest are hot and dry because of <u>maritime tropical</u> air masses.
7. A <u>cyclone</u> is a high-pressure center of dry air.
8. Cumulonimbus clouds may produce both thunderstorms and <u>hurricanes.</u>
9. <u>Lightning</u> is a sudden spark or electrical discharge, as electrical charges jump between parts of a cloud, between nearby clouds, or between a cloud and the ground.
10. On a weather map, <u>isotherms</u> join places on the map with the same air pressure.

## Writing in Science

**Descriptive Paragraph** Imagine that you are a hurricane hunter—a scientist who flies into a hurricane to collect data. Describe what it would feel like as you flew through the hurricane's eyewall into its eye.

*Weather Patterns*
Video Preview
Video Field Trip
▶ Video Assessment

# Review and Assessment

## Checking Concepts

11. Describe how wind patterns affect the movement of air masses in North America.
12. How does a cold front form?
13. What safety precautions should you take if a tornado is predicted in your area? If a hurricane is predicted?
14. What happens to a hurricane when it moves onto land? Why?
15. Explain how lake-effect snow forms.
16. What are some of the sources of information that meteorologists use to predict the weather?

## Thinking Critically

17. **Relating Cause and Effect** How do differences in air density influence the movement of air along cold and warm fronts?
18. **Making Generalizations** What type of weather is most likely to form at the front shown below?

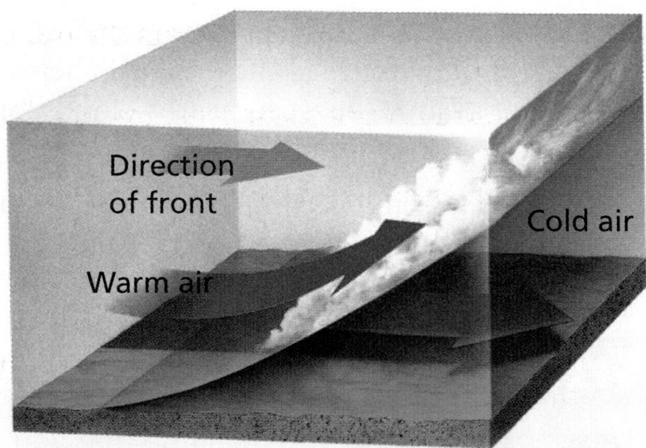


19. **Comparing and Contrasting** Compare thunderstorms and tornadoes. How are they similar? How are they different?
20. **Predicting** If you observe that air pressure is decreasing, what kind of weather do you think is coming?
21. **Applying Concepts** Would you expect hurricanes to form over the oceans off the northeast or northwest coasts of the United States? Explain.
22. **Making Judgments** What do you think is the most important thing people should do to reduce the dangers of storms?
23. **Applying Concepts** Why can't meteorologists accurately forecast the weather a month in advance?

## Applying Skills

**Use the map to answer Questions 24–27.**

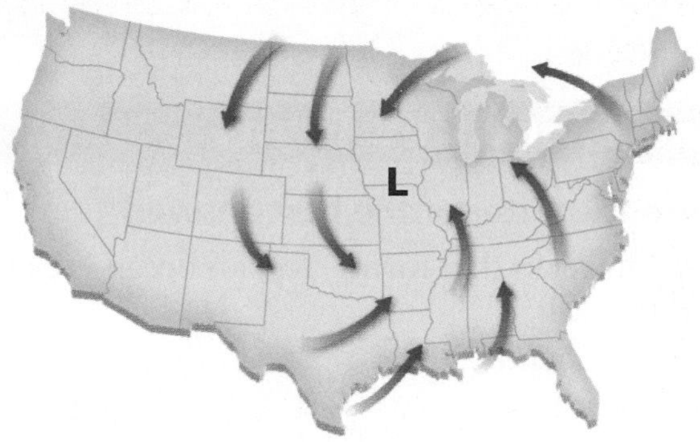


24. **Interpreting Maps** Does the map show a cyclone or an anticyclone? How can you tell?
25. **Interpreting Data** What do the arrows show about the movement of the winds in this pressure center? What else indicates wind direction?
26. **Making Models** Using this diagram as an example, draw a similar diagram to illustrate a high-pressure area. Remember to indicate wind direction in your diagram.
27. **Posing Questions** If you saw a pressure center like the one shown above on a weather map, what could you predict about the weather? What questions would you need to ask in order to make a better prediction?

## Lab zone Chapter **Project**

**Performance Assessment** Present your weather maps and weather forecasts to the class. Discuss how accurate your weather predictions were. Explain why inaccuracies may have occurred in your forecasts.

# Standardized Test Prep

**Test-Taking Tip**

**Interpreting Graphs**

A bar graph is used to compare quantities of different things. Each bar represents a quantity or amount of something. When answering a question with a bar graph, keep the following tips in mind. Read the title of the graph; the title should help you identify what information is shown on the graph. Then carefully examine the labels for the axes to determine what variables are plotted.

***Sample Question***

Use the graph at the right to determine how many tornadoes occurred in January.

**A** 30
**B** 25
**C** 5
**D** 15

***Answer***

First, find **J** for January on the *x*-axis. Then check the length of the bar and determine on the *y*-axis how many tornadoes occurred. The answer is **C**—five tornadoes occurred in January.

**Choose the letter of the best answer.**

**1.** How are air masses classified?
**A** by temperature and pressure
**B** by pressure and humidity
**C** by temperature and density
**D** by temperature and humidity

**2.** A rapidly moving cold air mass meets a slowly moving warm air mass and forms a front. What will most likely occur at this front?
**F** The two air masses will mix together.
**G** The warm air will slide under the cold air. The cold air will rise and get warmer.
**H** Cold air will slide under the warm air. Warm air will rise and cool. Clouds will form.
**J** The less dense warm air will sink and cool. Clouds will form.

*Use the graph below and your knowledge of science to answer Questions 3–4.*

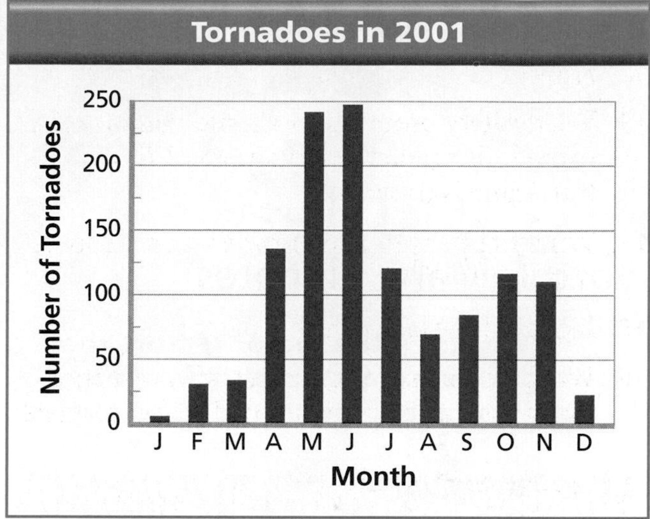


**3.** According to the graph, which two months in 2001 had the most tornadoes?
**A** April and May
**B** May and July
**C** May and June
**D** June and July

**4.** Which statement best summarizes the trend shown in the graph?
**F** Tornadoes always occur most frequently in May and June.
**G** Tornadoes occur when the weather is warmest.
**H** In 2001, tornadoes were most frequent in April, May, and June.
**J** Tornadoes are generally most frequent in the winter.

## Constructed Response

**5.** Sound travels at a speed of about 330 m/s. How could you use this information to determine how far away lightning bolts are from you during a thunderstorm? Use an example to show how you would calculate the distance.

# Chapter 18
# Climate and Climate Change

## The BIG Idea
Earth's Many Climates

**What are the major factors that influence a region's climate?**

### Chapter Preview

❶ **What Causes Climate?**
***Discover*** How Does Latitude Affect Climate?
***Skills Activity*** Inferring
***Math Skills*** Percentage
***Active Art*** The Seasons
***Skills Lab*** Sunny Rays and Angles

❷ **Climate Regions**
***Discover*** How Do Climates Differ?
***Try This*** Modeling a Climate
***Skills Activity*** Classifying
***At-Home Activity*** What's Your Climate?
***Consumer Lab*** Cool Climate Graphs

❸ **Long-Term Changes in Climate**
***Discover*** What Story Can Tree Rings Tell?
***Analyzing Data*** Ice Ages and Temperature
***Active Art*** Continental Drift

❹ **Global Changes in the Atmosphere**
***Discover*** What Is the Greenhouse Effect?
***Try This Activity*** It's Your Skin!
***At-Home Activity*** Sun Protection

These emperor penguins thrive in Antarctica's polar climate. ▶

*Climate and Climate Change*

▶ Video Preview
Video Field Trip
Video Assessment

## Lab zone™ Chapter Project

### Investigating Microclimates

A microclimate is a small area with its own climate. As you work through this chapter, you will investigate microclimates in your community.

**Your Goal** To compare weather conditions from at least three microclimates

To complete your project, you must

- hypothesize how the microclimates in three areas differ from each other
- collect data from your locations at the same time each day
- relate each microclimate to the plants and animals found there

**Plan It!** Begin by brainstorming a list of nearby places that may have different microclimates. How are the places different? Keep in mind weather factors such as temperature, precipitation, humidity, wind direction, and wind speed. Consider areas that are grassy, sandy, sunny, or shaded. You will need to measure daily weather conditions and record them in a logbook. Collect the instruments you need before you begin your investigation. Once you have collected all the data, construct your graphs and look for patterns. Then plan your presentation.

Section 1

# What Causes Climate?

## Reading Preview

### Key Concepts

- What factors influence temperature?
- What factors influence precipitation?
- What causes the seasons?

### Key Terms

- climate
- microclimate
- tropical zone
- polar zone
- temperate zone
- marine climate
- continental climate
- windward
- leeward
- monsoon

### Target Reading Skill

**Building Vocabulary** After you read the section, reread the paragraphs that contain definitions of Key Terms. Use all the information you have learned to write a meaningful sentence using each Key Term.

## Lab zone Discover **Activity**

### How Does Latitude Affect Climate?

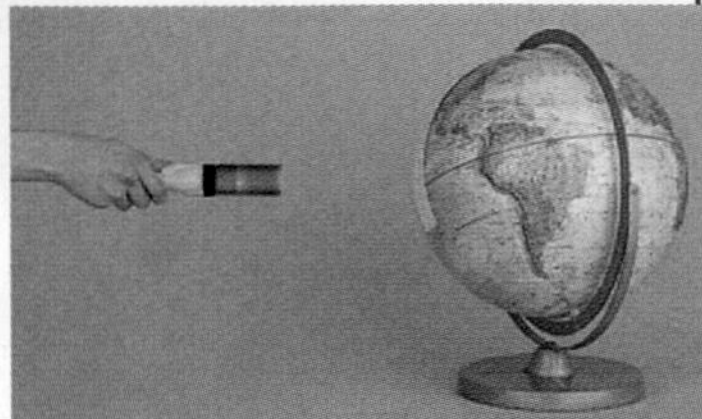

1. On a globe, tape a strip of paper from the equator to the North Pole. Divide the tape into three equal parts. Label the top section *poles,* the bottom section *equator,* and the middle section *mid-latitudes.*
2. Tape the end of an empty toilet paper roll to the end of a flashlight. Hold the flashlight about 30 cm from the equator. Turn on the flashlight to represent the sun. On the paper strip, have a partner draw the area the light shines on.
3. Move the flashlight up slightly to aim at the "mid-latitudes." Keep the flashlight horizontal and at the same distance from the globe. Again, draw the lighted area.
4. Repeat Step 3, but this time aim the light at the "poles."

**Think It Over**

**Observing** How does the size of the illuminated area change? Do you think the sun's rays heat Earth's surface evenly?

The weather in an area changes every day. At a given location, the weather may be cloudy and rainy one day and clear and sunny the next. **Climate,** on the other hand, refers to the average, year-after-year conditions of temperature, precipitation, winds, and clouds in an area. For example, California's Mojave Desert, shown below, has a hot, dry climate.

Scientists use two main factors—precipitation and temperature—to describe the climate of a region. A climate region is a large area that has similar climate conditions throughout. For example, the climate in the southwestern United States is dry, with hot summers.

The factors that affect large climate regions also affect smaller areas. Have you ever noticed that it is cooler and more humid in a grove of trees than in an open field? A small area with climate conditions that differ from those around it may have its own **microclimate.**

An oasis in the Mojave Desert ▼

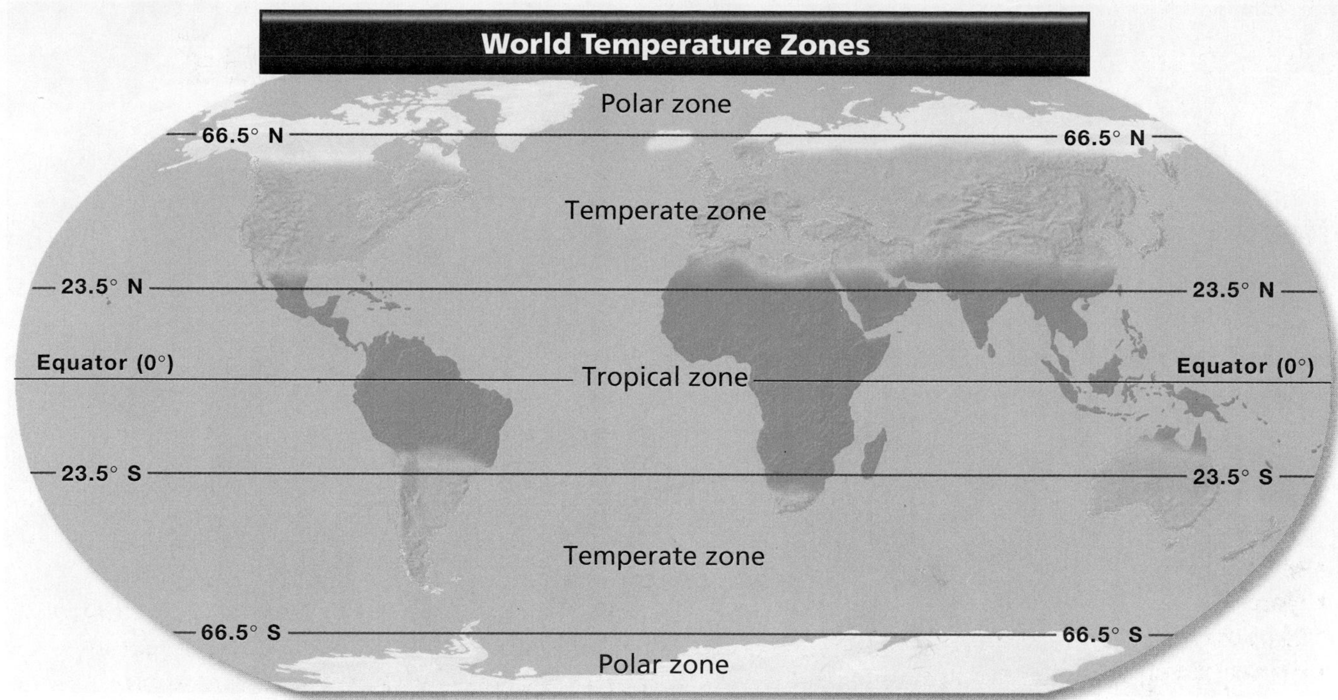


**FIGURE 1**
The tropical zone has the warmest climates. Cold climates occur in the polar zone. In between lies the temperate zone, where climates vary from warm to cool.
**Interpreting Maps** *In which temperature zone is most of the United States located?*

## Factors Affecting Temperature

Why are some places warm and others cold? **The main factors that influence temperature are latitude, altitude, distance from large bodies of water, and ocean currents.**

**Latitude** In general, climates of locations near the equator are warmer than climates of areas far from the equator. The reason is that the sun's rays hit Earth's surface most directly at the equator. At the poles, the same amount of solar radiation is spread over a larger area, and therefore brings less warmth.

Recall that latitude is the distance from the equator, measured in degrees. Based on latitude, Earth's surface can be divided into the three temperature zones shown in Figure 1. The **tropical zone** is the area near the equator, between about 23.5° north latitude and 23.5° south latitude. The tropical zone receives direct or nearly direct sunlight all year round, making climates there warm.

In contrast, the sun's rays always strike at a lower angle near the North and South poles. As a result, the areas near both poles have cold climates. These **polar zones** extend from about 66.5° to 90° north and 66.5° to 90° south latitudes.

Between the tropical zones and the polar zones are the **temperate zones.** In summer, the sun's rays strike the temperate zones more directly. In winter, the sun's rays strike at a lower angle. As a result, the weather in the temperate zones ranges from warm or hot in summer to cool or cold in winter.

**FIGURE 2**
**Effect of Altitude**
Mount Kilimanjaro, in Tanzania, is near the equator.
**Relating Cause and Effect** *What factor is responsible for the difference between the climate at the mountaintop and the climate at the base?*

**Altitude** The peak of Mount Kilimanjaro towers high above the plains of East Africa. Kilimanjaro is covered in snow all year round, as shown in Figure 2. Yet it is located near the equator, at 3° south latitude. Why is Mount Kilimanjaro so cold?

In the case of high mountains, altitude is a more important climate factor than latitude. In the troposphere, temperature decreases about 6.5 Celsius degrees for every 1-kilometer increase in altitude. As a result, highland areas everywhere have cool climates, no matter what their latitude. At nearly 6 kilometers, the air at the top of Kilimanjaro is about 39 Celsius degrees colder than the air at sea level at the same latitude.

**Distance From Large Bodies of Water** Oceans or large lakes can also affect temperatures. Oceans greatly moderate, or make less extreme, the temperatures of nearby land. Water heats up more slowly than land. It also cools down more slowly. Therefore, winds off the ocean often prevent extremes of hot and cold in coastal regions. Much of the west coasts of North America, South America, and Europe have mild **marine climates,** with relatively mild winters and cool summers.

The centers of North America and Asia are too far inland to be warmed or cooled by the ocean. Most of Canada and of Russia, as well as the central United States, have continental climates. **Continental climates** have more extreme temperatures than marine climates. Winters are cold, while summers are warm or hot.

**Ocean Currents** Marine climates are influenced by ocean currents, streams of water within the oceans that move in regular patterns. Some warm ocean currents move from the tropics towards the poles. This affects climate as the warm ocean water warms the air above it. The warmed air then moves over nearby land. In the same way, cold currents bring cold water from the polar zones toward the equator. A cold current brings cool air.

As you read about the following currents, trace their paths on the map in Figure 3. The best-known warm-water current is the Gulf Stream. The Gulf Stream begins in the Gulf of Mexico, then flows north along the east coast of the United States. When it crosses the North Atlantic, it becomes the North Atlantic Drift. This warm current brings mild, humid air to Ireland and southern England. As a result, these areas have a mild, wet climate despite their relatively high latitude.

In contrast, the cool California Current flows southward down the West Coast of the United States. The California Current makes climates along the West Coast cooler than you would expect at those latitudes.

**Reading Checkpoint** **What effect do oceans have on the temperatures of nearby land areas?**

**Lab zone Skills Activity**

### Inferring

Look at the currents in the South Pacific, South Atlantic, and Indian oceans. What pattern can you observe? Now compare currents in the South Atlantic to those in the North Atlantic. What might be responsible for differences in the current patterns?

**FIGURE 3**
On this map, warm currents are shown in red and cold currents in blue. **Interpreting Maps** *What type of current occurs around Antarctica?*

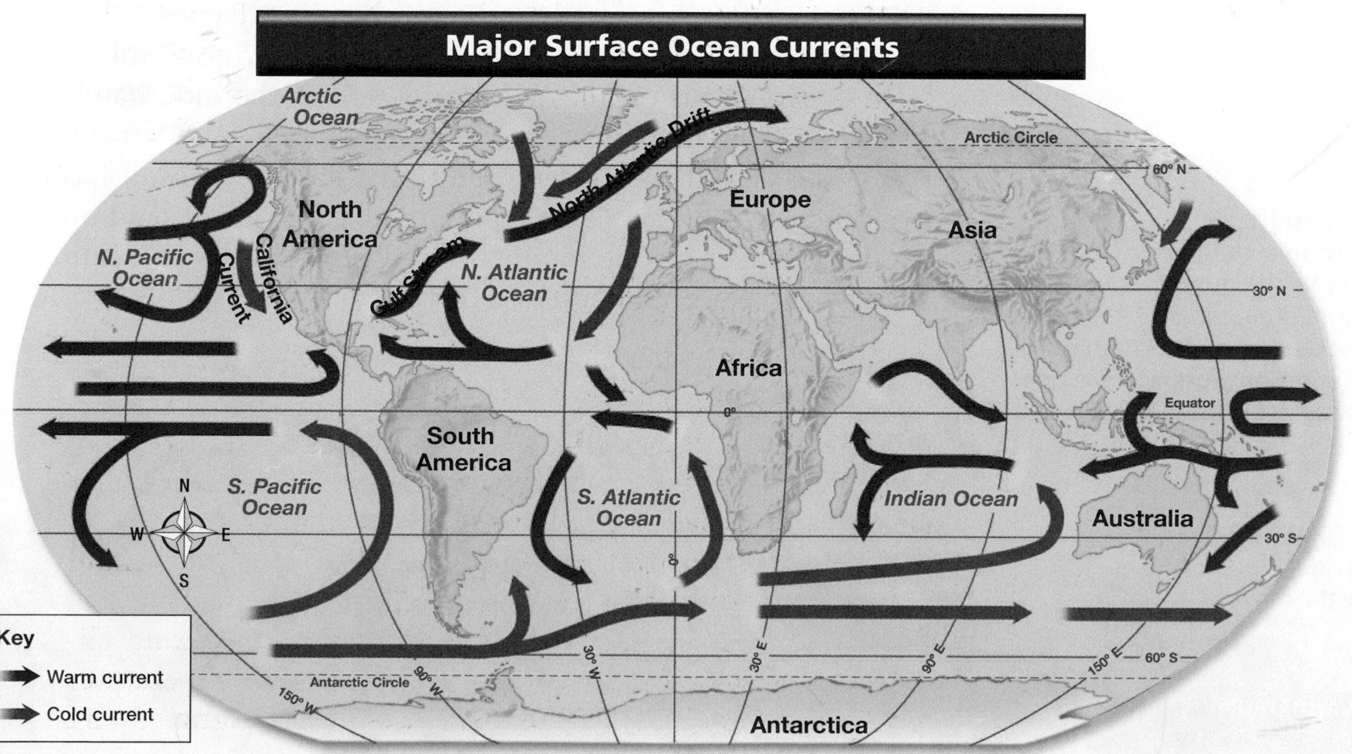

## Factors Affecting Precipitation

The air masses that pass over an area may bring rain or snow. The amount of precipitation varies from year to year. But over time, total precipitation tends toward a yearly average. What determines the amount of precipitation an area receives? **The main factors that affect precipitation are prevailing winds, the presence of mountains, and seasonal winds.**

**Prevailing Winds** As you know, weather patterns depend on the movement of huge air masses. Air masses are moved from place to place by prevailing winds, the directional winds that usually blow in a region. Air masses can be warm or cool, dry or humid. The amount of water vapor in the air mass influences how much rain or snow will fall.

The amount of water vapor in prevailing winds also depends on where the winds come from. Winds that blow inland from oceans or large lakes carry more water vapor than winds that blow from over land. For example, winter winds generally blow from west to east across the Great Lakes. The winds pick up moisture that evaporates from the lakes. As a result, areas that are downwind can receive large amounts of snow.

**Mountain Ranges** A mountain range in the path of prevailing winds can also influence where precipitation falls. When humid winds blow from the ocean toward coastal mountains, they are forced to rise, as shown in Figure 4. The rising air cools and its water vapor condenses, forming clouds. Rain or snow falls on the **windward** side of the mountains, the side the wind hits.

By the time the air has moved over the mountains, it has lost much of its water vapor, so it is cool and dry. The land on the **leeward** side of the mountains—downwind—is in a rain shadow. Little precipitation falls there.

**FIGURE 4**
**Rain Shadow**
A mountain range can form a barrier to the movement of humid air. Humid air cools as it is blown up the side of a mountain range.
**Applying Concepts** *Where does the heaviest rainfall occur?*

Warm, moist air blows in from the ocean and is pushed up by the mountains.
Warm, moist air
As the air rises, it cools and water vapor condenses. Moisture in the air is released as precipitation.

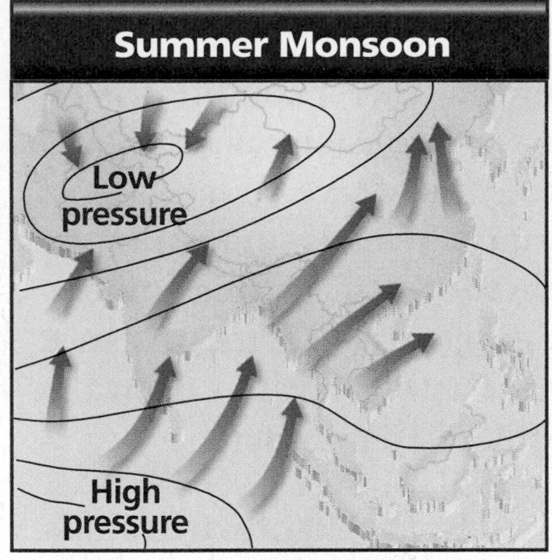

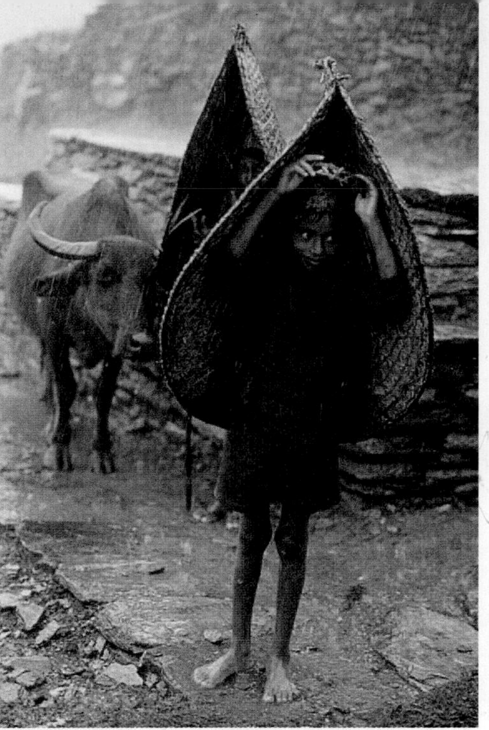

**FIGURE 5**
**Monsoons**
In a summer monsoon, wind blows from the ocean to the land. In the winter, the monsoon reverses and blows from the land to the ocean. Summer monsoons in Nepal cause heavy rain (above).

**Seasonal Winds** A seasonal change in wind patterns can affect precipitation. These seasonal winds are similar to land and sea breezes, but occur over a wider area. Sea and land breezes over a large region that change direction with the seasons are called **monsoons.** What produces a monsoon? In the summer in South and Southeast Asia, the land gradually gets warmer than the ocean. A "sea breeze" blows steadily inland from the ocean all summer, even at night. The air blowing from the ocean during this season is very warm and humid. As the humid air rises over the land, the air cools. This causes water vapor to condense into clouds, producing heavy rains.

Thailand and parts of India receive much of their rain from the summer monsoons. These rains supply the water needed by rice and other crops. Monsoon winds also bring rain to coastal areas in West Africa and northeastern South America.

Regions affected by monsoon winds receive very little rain in winter. In the winter, the land cools and becomes colder than the ocean. A "land breeze" blows steadily from the land to the ocean. These winds carry little moisture.

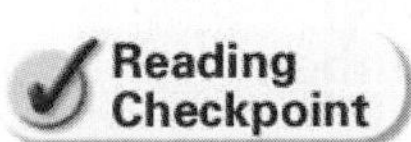


**Why does precipitation fall mainly on the windward sides of mountains?**

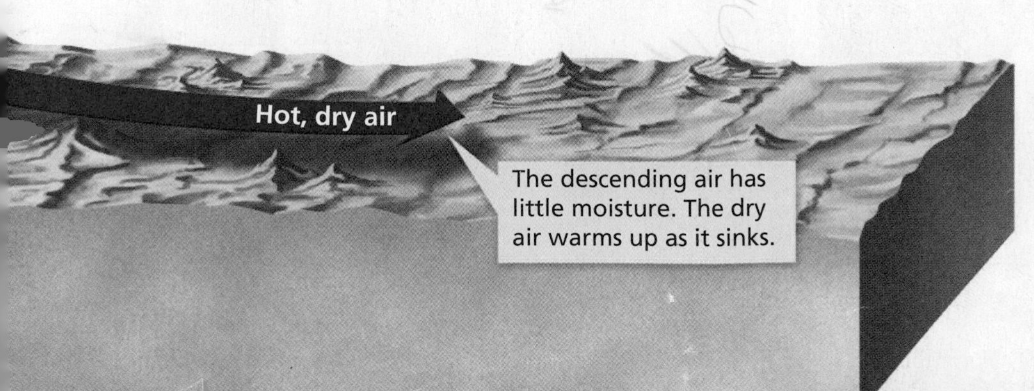

Hot, dry air
The descending air has little moisture. The dry air warms up as it sinks.

## Math Skills

**Percentage** Light from the sun strikes Earth's surface at different angles. An angle is made up of two lines that meet at a point. Angles are measured in degrees. A full circle has 360 degrees.

When the sun is directly overhead near the equator, it is at an angle of 90° to Earth's surface. A 90° angle is called a right angle. What percentage of a circle is it?

$$\frac{90 \text{ degrees}}{360 \text{ degrees}} = \frac{d\%}{100\%}$$

$$90 \times 100 = 360 \times d$$

$$\frac{90 \times 100}{360} = d = 25$$

A 90° angle is 25 percent of a full circle.

**Practice Problem** Earth's axis is tilted at an angle of 23.5°. About what percentage of a right angle is this?

# The Seasons

Although you can describe the average weather conditions of a climate region, these conditions are not constant all year long. Instead, most places outside the tropics have four seasons: winter, spring, summer, and autumn. When it is summer in the Northern Hemisphere it is winter in the Southern Hemisphere. So the seasons are not a result of changes in the distance between Earth and the sun. In fact, Earth is farthest from the sun during the summer in the Northern Hemisphere.

**Tilted Axis** **The seasons are caused by the tilt of Earth's axis as Earth travels around the sun.** The axis is an imaginary line through Earth's center that passes through both poles. Earth rotates, or turns, around this axis once each day. Earth's axis is not straight up and down, but is tilted at an angle of 23.5°. As Earth travels around the sun, its axis always points in the same direction. So the north end of the axis is pointed away from the sun for one part of the year and toward the sun for another part of the year.

**Effect of the Tilted Axis** Look at Figure 7. Which way is the north end of Earth's axis tilted in June? Notice that the Northern Hemisphere receives more direct rays from the sun. Also, in June the days in the Northern Hemisphere are longer than the nights. The combination of more direct rays and longer days makes Earth's surface warmer in the Northern Hemisphere than at any other time of the year. It is summer in the Northern Hemisphere. At the same time, the Southern Hemisphere is experiencing winter.

In December, on the other hand, the north end of Earth's axis is tilted away from the sun. It is winter in the Northern Hemisphere and summer in the Southern Hemisphere.

**In June, what season is it in the Southern Hemisphere?**

**FIGURE 6**
**Summer and Winter**
There can be a striking difference between summer and winter in the same location. **Inferring** *During which season does the area shown receive more solar energy?*

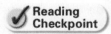

**FIGURE 7**
**The Seasons**
**The seasons are a result of Earth's tilted axis. The seasons change as the amount of energy each hemisphere receives from the sun changes.**

Go Online
active art
**For:** The Seasons activity
**Visit:** PHSchool.com
**Web Code:** cfp-5012

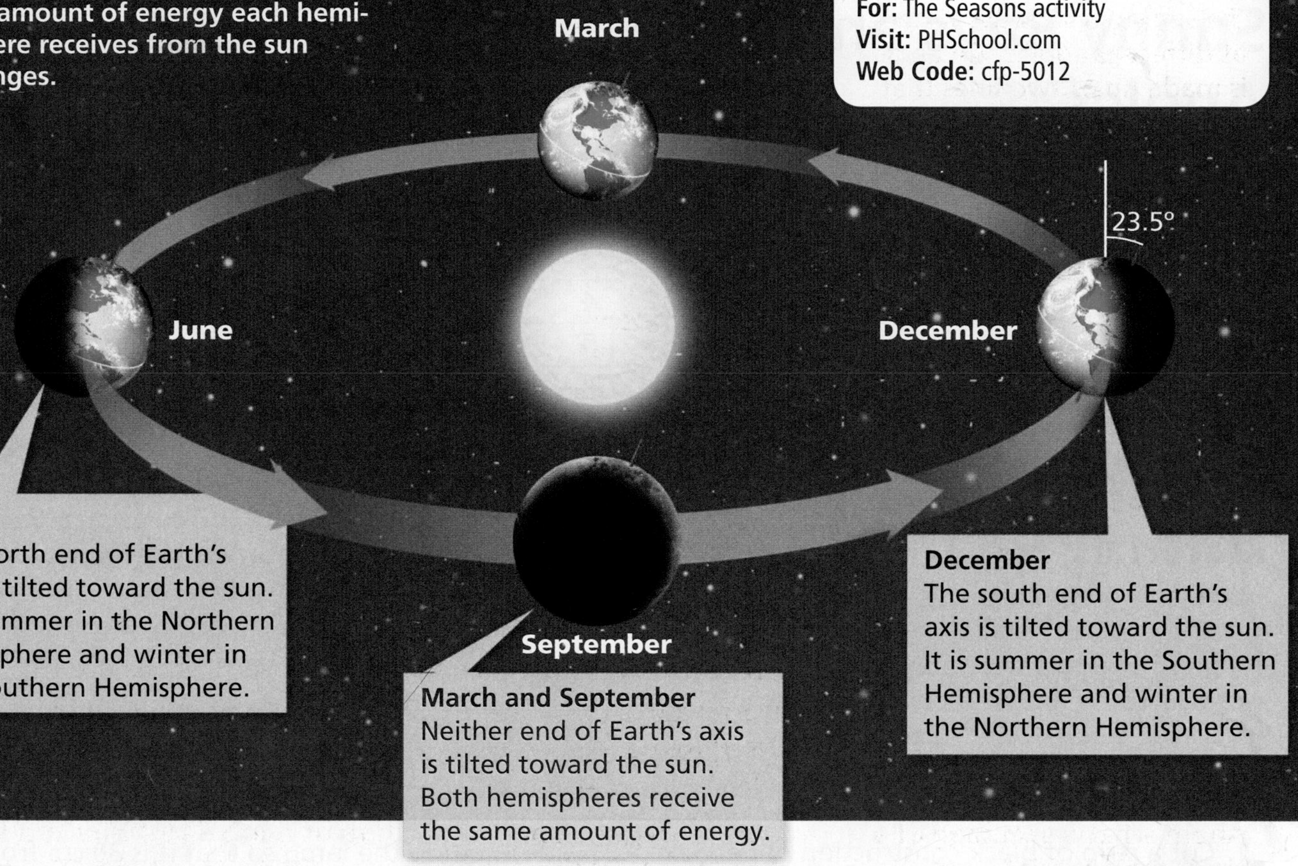

March

June

December

23.5°

September

**June**
The north end of Earth's axis is tilted toward the sun. It is summer in the Northern Hemisphere and winter in the Southern Hemisphere.

**March and September**
Neither end of Earth's axis is tilted toward the sun. Both hemispheres receive the same amount of energy.

**December**
The south end of Earth's axis is tilted toward the sun. It is summer in the Southern Hemisphere and winter in the Northern Hemisphere.

## Section 1 Assessment

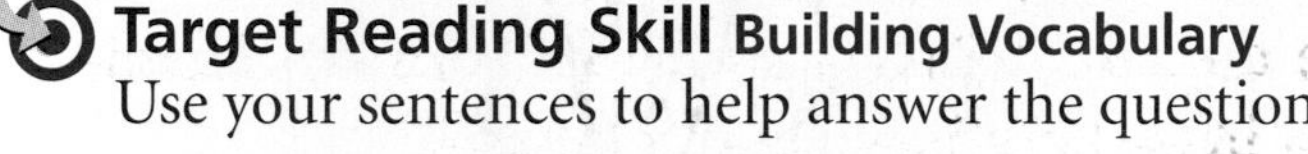

**Target Reading Skill Building Vocabulary** Use your sentences to help answer the questions.

### Reviewing Key Concepts

1. a. **Identifying** Name four factors that affect temperature.
   b. **Describing** How does temperature vary in Earth's temperature zones?
   c. **Comparing and Contrasting** Two locations are at the same latitude in the temperate zone. One is in the middle of a continent. The other is on a coast affected by a warm ocean current. How will their climates differ?
2. a. **Listing** List three factors that affect precipitation.
   b. **Summarizing** How do prevailing winds affect the amount of precipitation an area receives?
   c. **Relating Cause and Effect** How does a mountain range in the path of prevailing winds affect precipitation on either side of the mountains?
3. a. **Reviewing** What causes the seasons?
   b. **Describing** Describe how the seasons are related to Earth's orbit around the sun.
   c. **Developing Hypotheses** How might Earth's climates be different if Earth were not tilted on its axis?

**Math Practice**

4. **Percentage** At noon at a particular location, the sun makes an angle of 66.5° with Earth's surface. What percentage of a full circle is this?

Lab zone **Skills Lab**

# Sunny Rays and Angles

## Problem

How does the angle of a light source affect the rate at which the temperature of a surface changes?

## Skills Focus

controlling variables, graphing, interpreting data, making models

## Materials 

- books • graph paper • pencil
- watch or clock • ruler • clear tape
- 3 thermometers or temperature probes
- protractor • 100-W incandescent lamp
- scissors • black construction paper

## Procedure  

1. Cut a strip of black construction paper 5 cm by 10 cm. Fold the paper in half and tape two sides to form a pocket.
2. Repeat Step 1 to make two more pockets.

| Data Table | | | |
|---|---|---|---|
| Time (min.) | Temperature (°C) | | |
| | 0° Angle | 45° Angle | 90° Angle |
| Start | | | |
| 1 | | | |
| 2 | | | |
| 3 | | | |
| 4 | | | |
| 5 | | | |

3. Place the bulb of a thermometer inside each pocket. If you're using a temperature probe, see your teacher for instructions.
4. Place the pockets with thermometers close together, as shown in the photo. Place one thermometer in a vertical position (90° angle), one at a 45° angle, and the third one in a horizontal position (0° angle). Use a protractor to measure the angles. Support the thermometers with books.
5. Position the lamp so that it is 30 cm from each of the thermometer bulbs. Make sure the lamp will not move during the activity.
6. Copy a data table like the one above into your notebook.

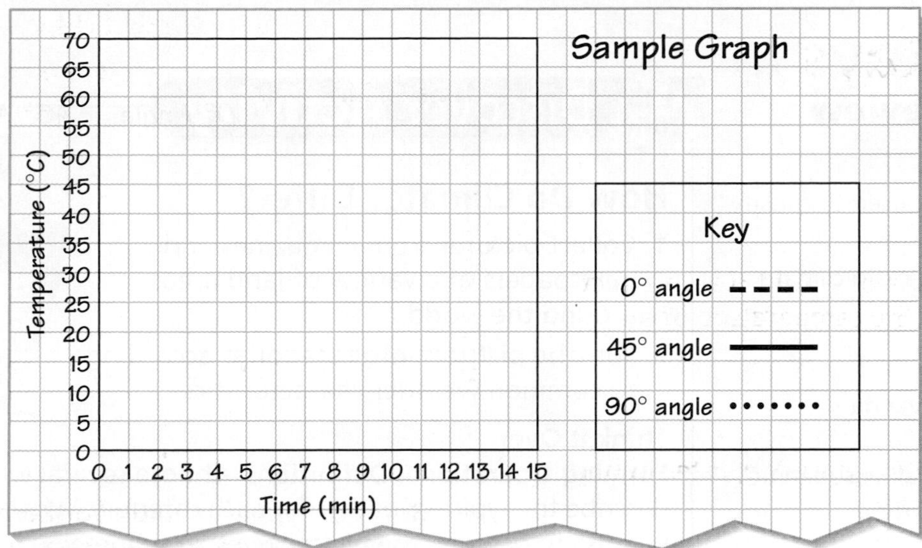


7. In your data table, record the temperature on all three thermometers. (All three temperatures should be the same.)
8. Switch on the lamp. In your data table, record the temperature on each thermometer every minute for 15 minutes. **CAUTION:** *Be careful not to touch the hot lampshade.*
9. After 15 minutes, switch off the lamp.

## Analyze and Conclude

1. **Controlling Variables** In this experiment, what was the manipulated variable? What was the responding variable?
2. **Graphing** Graph your data. Label the horizontal axis and vertical axis of your graph as shown on the sample graph. Use solid, dashed, and dotted lines to show the results from each thermometer, as shown in the key.
3. **Interpreting Data** Based on your data, at which angle did the temperature increase the most?
4. **Interpreting Data** At which angle did the temperature increase the least?
5. **Making Models** What part of Earth's surface does each thermometer represent?
6. **Drawing Conclusions** Why is air at the North Pole still very cold in the summer even though the Northern Hemisphere is tilted toward the sun?
7. **Communicating** Write a paragraph explaining what variables were held constant in this experiment.

## Design an Experiment

Design an experiment to find out how the results of the investigation would change if the lamp were placed farther from the thermometers. Then, design another experiment to find out what happened if the lamp were placed closer to the thermometers.

# 2 Climate Regions

## Reading Preview

### Key Concepts

- What factors are used to classify climates?
- What are the six main climate regions?

### Key Terms

- rain forest • savanna
- desert • steppe
- humid subtropical • subarctic
- tundra • permafrost

### Target Reading Skill

**Comparing and Contrasting**

As you read, compare and contrast the six main climate regions by completing a table like the one below.

**Climate Regions**

| Climate Region | Precipitation | Temperature |
|---|---|---|
| Tropical Rainy | Heavy precipitation | |
| Dry | | |
| Temper-ate Marine | | |

## Lab zone Discover Activity

### How Do Climates Differ?

1. Collect pictures from magazines and newspapers of a variety of land areas around the world.
2. Sort the pictures into categories according to common weather characteristics.

**Think It Over**

**Forming Operational Definitions** Choose several words that describe the typical weather for each category. What words would you use to describe the typical weather where you live?

Suppose you lived for an entire year near the equator. It would be very different from where you live now. The daily weather, the amount of sunlight, and the pattern of seasons would all be new to you. You would be in another climate region.

**Scientists classify climates according to two major factors: temperature and precipitation.** They use a system developed around 1900 by Wladimir Köppen (KEP un). Besides temperature and precipitation, Köppen also looked at the distinct vegetation in different areas. This system identifies broad climate regions, each of which has smaller subdivisions.

**There are six main climate regions: tropical rainy, dry, temperate marine, temperate continental, polar, and highlands.** These climate regions are shown in Figure 10.

Maps can show boundaries between the climate regions. In the real world, of course, no clear boundaries mark where one climate region ends and another begins. Each region blends gradually into the next.

## Tropical Rainy Climates

**The tropics have two types of rainy climates: tropical wet and tropical wet-and-dry.** Tropical wet climates are found in low-lying lands near the equator.

**Tropical Wet** In areas that have a tropical wet climate, many days are rainy, often with afternoon thunderstorms. These thunderstorms are triggered by midday heating. Another source of precipitation is prevailing winds. In many areas with a tropical wet climate, the trade winds bring moisture from the oceans. With year-round heat and heavy rainfall, vegetation grows lush and green. Dense rain forests grow in these rainy tropical climates. **Rain forests** are forests in which large amounts of rain fall year-round. Tropical rain forests are important because it is thought that at least half of the world's species of land plants and animals are found there.

In the United States, only the windward sides of the Hawaiian islands have a tropical wet climate. Rainfall is very heavy—over 10 meters per year on the windward side of the Hawaiian island of Kauai. The rain forests of Hawaii have a large variety of plants, including ferns, orchids, and many types of vines and trees.

FIGURE 8
**Tropical Rain Forests**
Lush tropical rain forests grow in the tropical wet climate.

**Tropical Wet-and-Dry** Areas that have tropical wet-and-dry climates receive slightly less rain than tropical climates and have distinct dry and rainy seasons. Instead of rain forests, there are tropical grasslands called **savannas.** Scattered clumps of trees that can survive the dry season dot the coarse grasses. Only a small part of the United States—the southern tip of Florida—has a tropical wet-and-dry climate. The graphs in Figure 9 show how temperature and precipitation vary in Makindu, Kenya, in East Africa.

**Reading Checkpoint** **What parts of the United States have tropical rainy climates?**

FIGURE 9
**Climate Graphs**
A graph of average temperature (left) can be combined with a graph of average precipitation (middle) to form a climate graph. These graphs show data for a tropical wet-and-dry region.

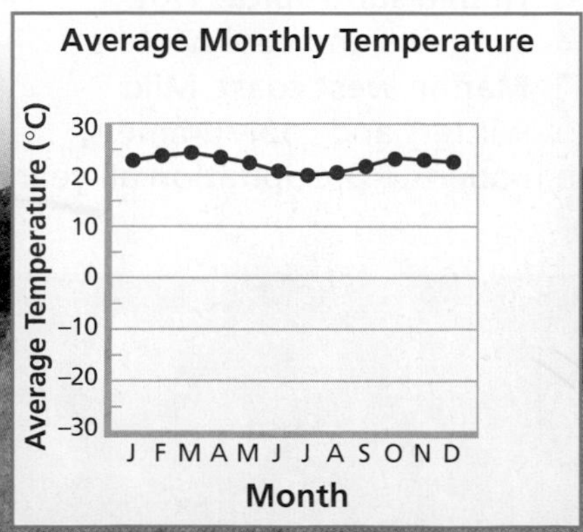


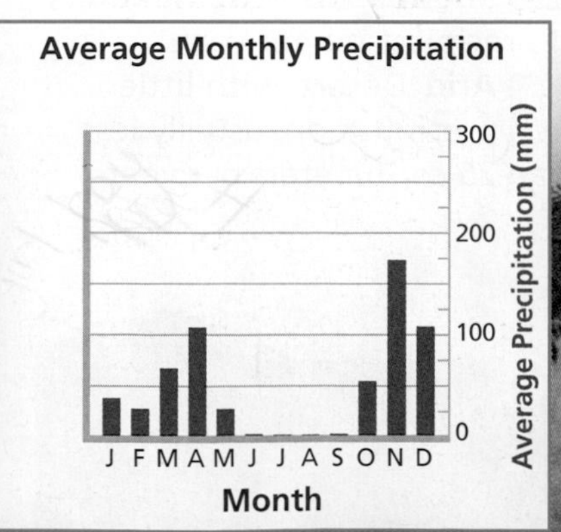


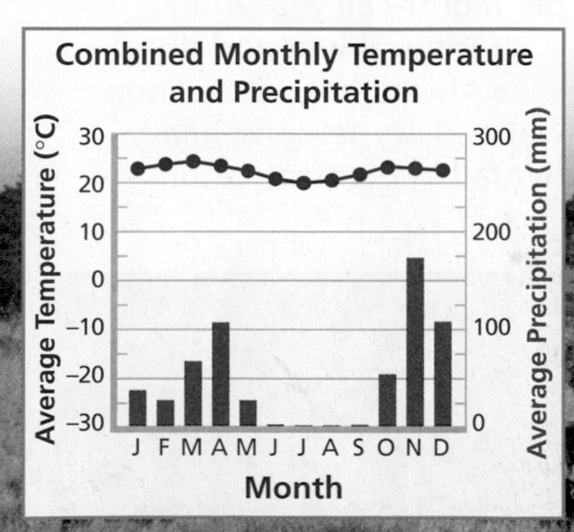

FIGURE 10
## Climate Regions

Climate regions are classified according to a combination of temperature and precipitation. Climates in highland regions change rapidly as altitude changes.

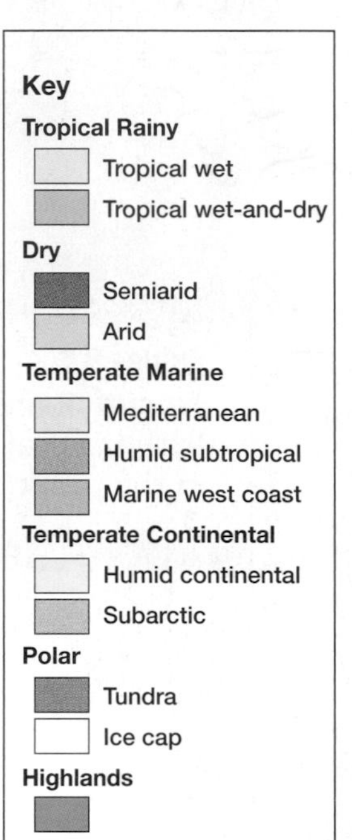


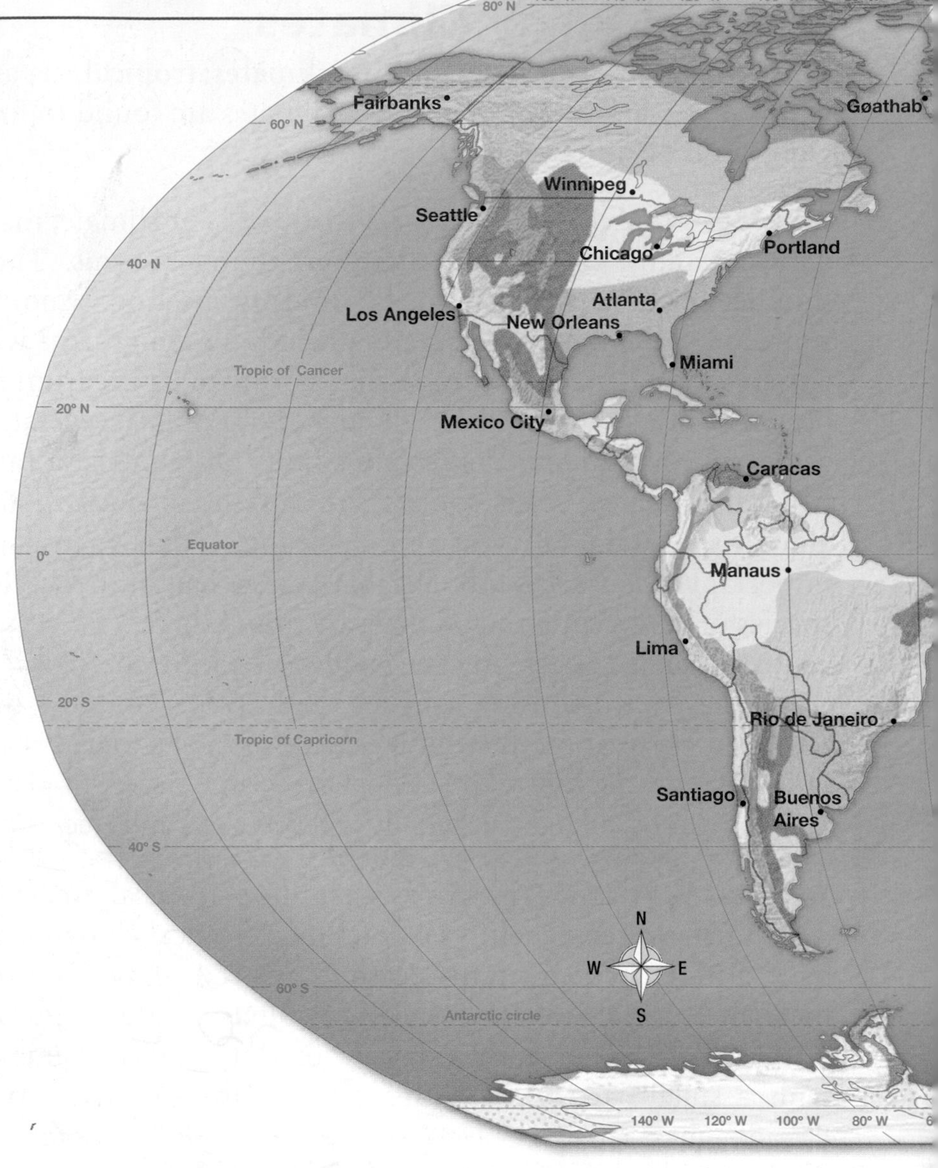


**Tropical Rainy**
Temperature always 18°C or above

**Tropical wet** Always hot and humid, with heavy rainfall (at least 6 centimeters per month) all year round

**Tropical wet-and-dry** Always hot; alternating wet and dry seasons; heavy rainfall in the wet season

**Dry**
Occurs wherever potential evaporation is greater than precipitation; may be hot or cold

**Semiarid** Dry but receives about 25 to 50 centimeters of precipitation per year

**Arid** Desert, with little precipitation, usually less than 25 centimeters per year

**Temperate Marine**
Averages 10°C or above in warmest month, between –3°C and 18°C in the coldest month

**Mediterranean** Warm, dry summers and rainy winters

**Humid subtropical** Hot summers and cool winters

**Marine west coast** Mild winters and cool summers, with moderate precipitation all year

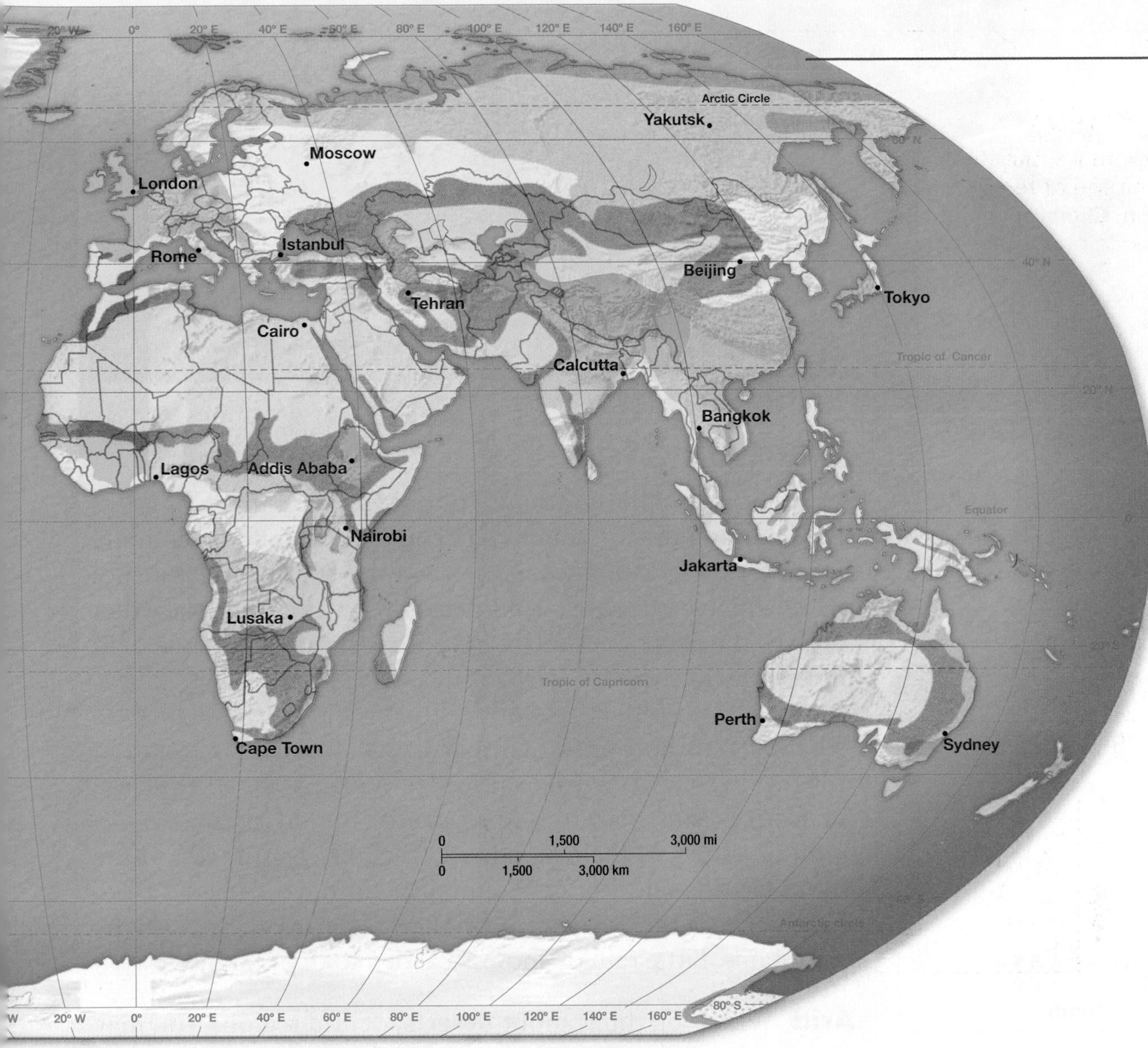

Arctic Circle
Yakutsk
Moscow
London
Istanbul
Rome
Beijing
Tokyo
Tehran
Cairo
Tropic of Cancer
Calcutta
Bangkok
Lagos
Addis Ababa
Equator
Nairobi
Jakarta
Lusaka
Tropic of Capricorn
Perth
Sydney
Cape Town
0 1,500 3,000 mi
0 1,500 3,000 km
Antarctic circle

20° W 0° 20° E 40° E 60° E 80° E 100° E 120° E 140° E 160° E

**Temperate Continental**
Average temperature 10°C or above in the warmest month, –3°C or below in the coldest month

**Humid continental** Hot, humid summers and cold winters, with moderate precipitation year round

**Subarctic** Short, cool summers and long, cold winters; light precipitation, mainly in summer

**Polar**
Average temperature below 10°C in the warmest month

**Tundra** Always cold with a short, cool summer—warmest temperature about 10°C

**Ice cap** Always cold, average temperature at or below 0°C

**Highlands**
Generally cooler and wetter than nearby lowlands; temperature decreasing with altitude

**FIGURE 11**
**Arid Climate**
Deserts of the southwestern United States are home to the western patchnose snake.
**Interpreting Graphs** *Which month has the highest average temperature?*

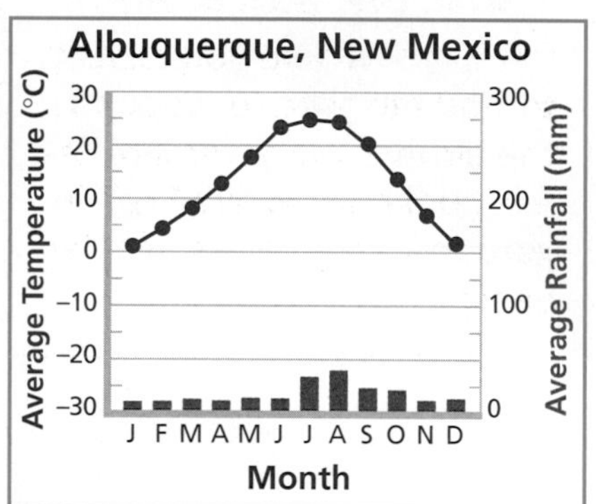


## Dry Climates

A climate is "dry" if the amount of precipitation that falls is less than the amount of water that could potentially evaporate. Because water evaporates more slowly in cool weather, a cool place with low rainfall may not be as dry as a warmer place that receives the same amount of rain. **Dry climates include arid and semiarid climates.**

Look at the map of world climate regions in Figure 10. What part of the United States is dry? Why is precipitation in this region so low? As you can see, dry regions often lie inland, far from oceans that are the source of humid air masses. In addition, much of the region lies in the rain shadow east of the Sierra Nevada and Rocky Mountains. Humid air masses from the Pacific Ocean lose much of their water as they cross the mountains. Little rain or snow is carried to dry regions.

**Arid** When you think about **deserts,** or arid regions, you may picture blazing heat and drifting sand dunes. Some deserts are hot and sandy, but others are cold or rocky. On average, arid regions, or deserts, get less than 25 centimeters of rain a year. Some years may bring no rain at all. Only specialized plants such as cactus and yucca can survive the desert's dryness and extremes of hot and cold. In the United States there are arid climates in portions of California, the Great Basin, and the Southwest.

**Semiarid** Locate the semiarid regions in Figure 10. As you can see, large semiarid areas are usually located on the edges of deserts. These semiarid areas are called steppes. A **steppe** is dry but gets enough rainfall for short grasses and low bushes to grow. For this reason, a steppe may also be called a prairie or grassland. The Great Plains are the steppe region of the United States.

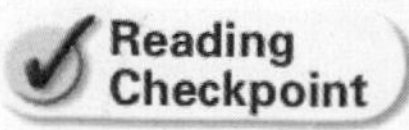

**What is a desert?**

## Temperate Marine Climates

Look once again at Figure 10. Along the coasts of continents in the temperate zones, you will find the third main climate region, temperate marine. **There are three kinds of temperate marine climates: marine west coast, humid subtropical, and Mediterranean.** Because of the moderating influence of oceans, all three are humid and have mild winters.

**Marine West Coast** The coolest temperate marine climates are found on the west coasts of continents north of 40° north latitude and south of 40° south latitude. Humid ocean air brings mild, rainy winters. Summer precipitation can vary considerably.

In North America, the marine west coast climate extends from northern California to southern Alaska. In the northwestern United States, humid air from the Pacific Ocean hits the western slopes of the Coastal Ranges. The air rises up the slopes of the mountains, and it cools. As the air cools, large amounts of rain or snow fall on the western slopes. The eastern slopes lie in the rain shadow of the mountains and receive little precipitation.

Because of the heavy precipitation, thick forests of tall trees grow in this region, including coniferous, or cone-bearing, trees such as Sitka spruce, Douglas fir, redwoods, and Western red cedar, as shown in Figure 12. One of the main industries of this region is harvesting and processing wood for lumber, paper, and furniture.

**Lab zone Try This Activity**

### Modeling a Climate

Here's how you can create humidity.

1. Put the same amount of water in each of two small plastic bowls.
2. Place a sheet of transparent plastic wrap over each bowl. Secure each sheet with a rubber band.
3. Place one bowl on a warm, sunny windowsill or near a radiator. Put the other bowl in a cool location.
4. Wait a day and then look at the two bowls. What do you see on the plastic wrap over each bowl?

**Inferring** Would you expect to find more water vapor in the air in a warm climate or in a cool one? Why? Explain your results in terms of solar energy.

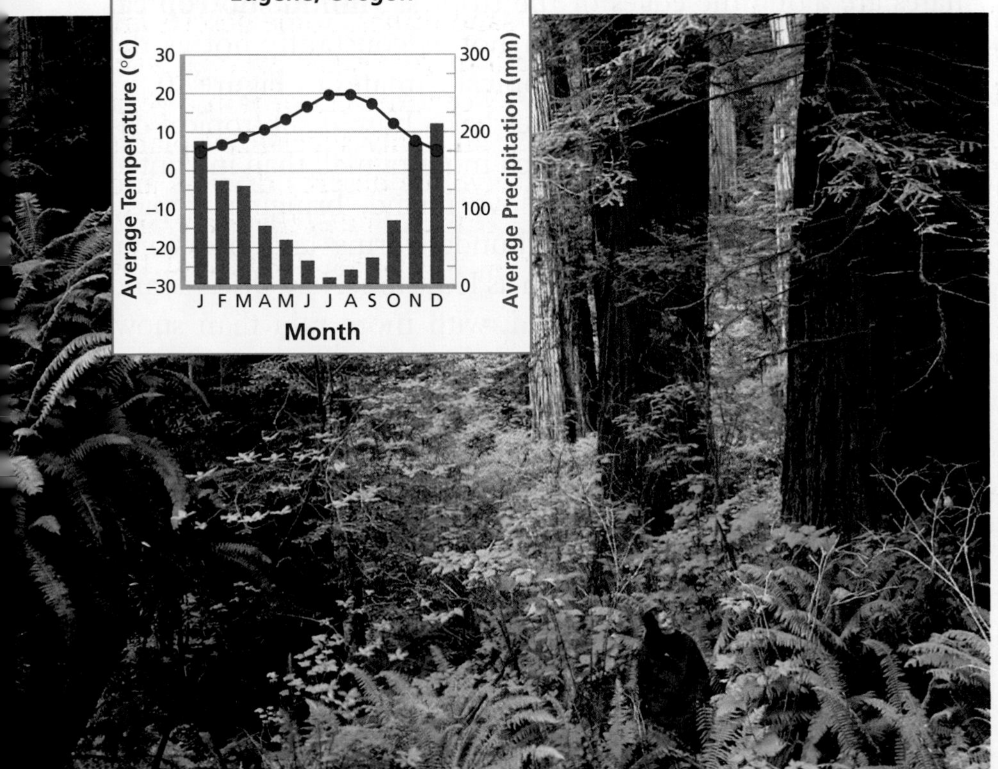


FIGURE 12
**Marine West Coast Climate**
Redwoods, Douglas firs, and Sitka spruce dominate the lush forests found in marine west coast climates.

**FIGURE 13**
**Mediterranean Climate**
Santa Barbara, on the coast of southern California, has a Mediterranean climate. Mild temperatures throughout the year make the area ideal for growing olives and citrus fruits.
**Interpreting Graphs** *How much precipitation does Santa Barbara receive in July? In January?*

**Mediterranean** A coastal climate that is drier and warmer than west coast marine is known as Mediterranean. Most areas with this climate are found around the Mediterranean Sea. In the United States, the southern coast of California has a Mediterranean climate. This climate is mild, with two seasons. In winter, marine air masses bring cool, rainy weather. Summers are somewhat warmer, with little rain.

Mediterranean climates have two main vegetation types. One is made up of dense shrubs and small trees, called chaparral (chap uh RAL). The other vegetation type includes grasses with a few large trees.

Agriculture is important to the economy of California's Mediterranean climate region. Using irrigation, farmers grow many different crops, including rice, many vegetables, fruits, and nuts.

**Humid Subtropical** The warmest temperate marine climates are along the edges of the tropics. **Humid subtropical** climates are wet and warm, but not as constantly hot as the tropics. Locate the humid subtropical climates in Figure 10.

The southeastern United States has a humid subtropical climate. Summers are hot, with much more rainfall than in winter. Maritime tropical air masses move inland, bringing tropical weather conditions, including thunderstorms and occasional hurricanes, to southern cities such as Houston, New Orleans, and Atlanta. Winters are cool to mild, with more rain than snow. However, polar air masses moving in from the north can bring freezing temperatures and frosts.

Mixed forests of oak, ash, hickory, and pines grow in the humid subtropical region of the United States. Important crops in this region include oranges, peaches, peanuts, sugar cane, and rice.

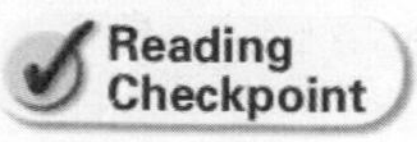
**Reading Checkpoint** **What region of the United States has a humid subtropical climate?**

**Lab zone Skills Activity**

## Classifying

The table shows some climate data for three cities.

| | City A | City B | City C |
|---|---|---|---|
| Average Jan. Temp. (°C) | 12.8 | 18.9 | –5.6 |
| Average July Temp. (°C) | 21.1 | 27.2 | 20 |
| Annual Precipitation (cm) | 33 | 152 | 109 |

Describe the climate you would expect each city to have. Identify the cities of Miami, Florida; Los Angeles, California; and Portland, Maine. Use Figure 10 to help identify each city's climate.

**FIGURE 14**
**Subarctic Climate**
Subarctic climates have cool summers and cold winters. The world's largest subarctic regions are in Russia, Canada, and Alaska. This emperor goose is breeding in the subarctic climate region in Alaska.

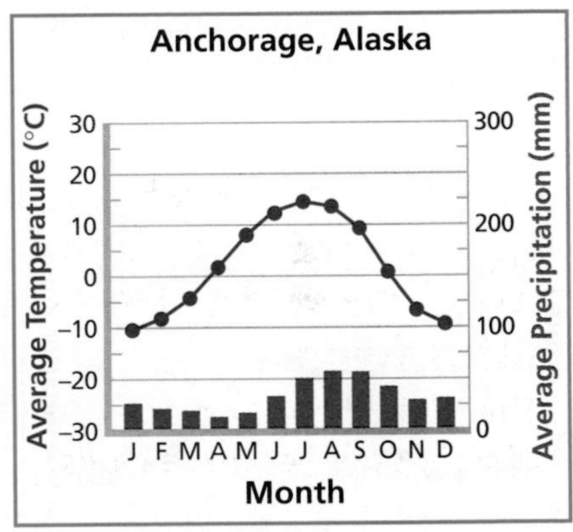


## Temperate Continental Climates

Temperate continental climates are not influenced very much by oceans, so they commonly have extremes of temperature. **Temperate continental climates are only found on continents in the Northern Hemisphere, and include humid continental and subarctic.** The parts of continents in the Southern Hemisphere south of 40° south latitude are not far enough from oceans for dry continental air masses to form.

**Humid Continental** Shifting tropical and polar air masses bring constantly changing weather to humid continental climates. In winter, continental polar air masses move south, bringing bitterly cold weather. In summer, tropical air masses move north, bringing heat and high humidity. Humid continental climates receive moderate amounts of rain in the summer. Smaller amounts of rain or snow fall in winter.

What parts of the United States have a humid continental climate? The eastern part of the region—the Northeast—has a range of forest types, from mixed forests in the south to coniferous forests in the north. Much of the western part of this region—the Midwest—was once tall grasslands, but is now farmland.

**Subarctic** The **subarctic** climates lie north of the humid continental climates. Summers in the subarctic are short and cool. Winters are long and bitterly cold.

In North America, coniferous trees such as spruce and fir make up a huge northern forest that stretches from Alaska to eastern Canada. Wood products from this forest are an important part of the economy. Many large mammals, including bears and moose, live in the forest. Birds of many species breed in the subarctic.

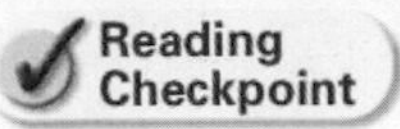


**Which area of the United States has a subarctic climate?**

**For:** Links on climates of the world
**Visit:** www.SciLinks.org
**Web Code:** scn-0942

## Polar Climates

**The polar climate is the coldest climate region, and includes the ice cap and tundra climates.** Ice cap and tundra climates are found only in the far north and south, near the North and South poles. Most polar climates are relatively dry, because the cold air holds little moisture.

**Ice Cap** As Figure 10 shows, ice cap climates are found mainly on Greenland and in Antarctica. With average temperatures always at or below freezing, the land in ice cap climate regions is covered with ice and snow. Intense cold makes the air dry. Lichens and a few low plants may grow on the rocks.

**Tundra** The **tundra** climate region stretches across northern Alaska, Canada, and Russia. Short, cool summers follow bitterly cold winters. Because of the cold, some layers of the tundra soil are always frozen. This permanently frozen tundra soil is called **permafrost.** Because of the permafrost, water cannot drain away, so the soil is wet and boggy in summer.

It is too cold on the tundra for trees to grow. Despite the harsh climate, during the short summers the tundra is filled with life. Mosquitoes and other insects hatch in the ponds and marshes above the frozen permafrost. Mosses, grasses, lichens, wildflowers, and shrubs grow quickly during the short summers. In North America, herds of caribou eat the vegetation and are in turn preyed upon by wolves. Some birds, such as the white-tailed ptarmigan, live on the tundra year-round. Others, such as the arctic tern and many waterfowl, spend only their summer breeding seasons there.

**What type of vegetation is found on the tundra?**

**FIGURE 15**
**Tundra Climate**
The Nenet people are reindeer herders on the tundra of northern Russia. These reindeer are grazing on some short shrubs typical of tundra plants.

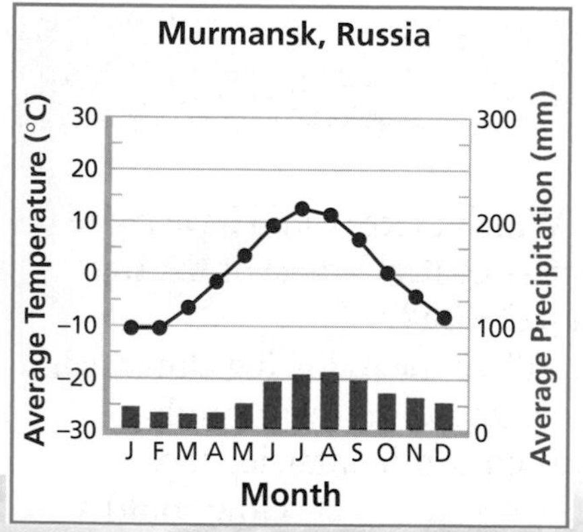

## Highlands

Why are highlands a distinct climate region? **Temperature falls as altitude increases, so highland regions are colder than the regions that surround them.** Increasing altitude produces climate changes similar to the climate changes you would expect with increasing latitude. Precipitation also increases as air masses carrying moisture pass over highland areas.

The climate on the lower slopes of a mountain range is like that of the surrounding countryside. The Rocky Mountain foothills, for instance, share the semi-arid climate of the Great Plains. But as you go higher up into the mountains, temperatures become lower and precipitation increases. Climbing 1,000 meters up in elevation is like traveling 1,200 kilometers toward the poles. The climate higher in the mountains is like that of the subarctic: cool with coniferous trees.

Above a certain elevation—the tree line—temperatures are too low for trees to grow. The climate above the tree line is like that of the tundra. Only low plants, mosses, and lichens can grow there.

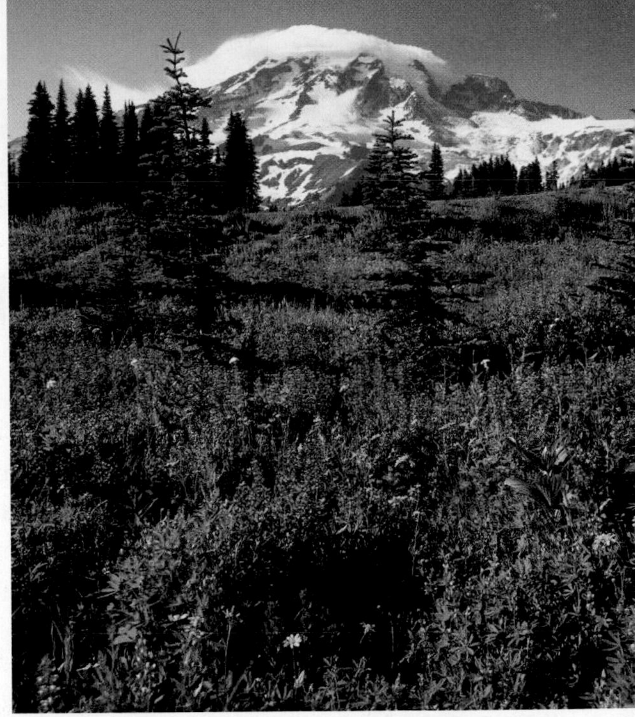

**FIGURE 16**
**Highland Climate**
Highland climates are generally cooler than surrounding regions. The Mount Rainier area in Washington State has short summers and long, severe winters.
**Classifying** *What climate zone does the mountaintop resemble?*

## Section 2 Assessment

**Target Reading Skill Comparing and Contrasting** Use the information in your table about climate regions to help you answer Question 1.

### Reviewing Key Concepts

1. a. **Listing** What two major factors are used to classify climates?
   b. **Reviewing** What other factor did Köppen use in classifying climates?
2. a. **Identifying** What are the six main climate regions?
   b. **Comparing and Contrasting** How is a tropical wet climate similar to a tropical wet-and-dry climate? How are they different?
   c. **Inferring** In what climate region would you find plains covered with short grasses and small bushes? Explain.
   d. **Relating Cause and Effect** Why do marine west coast climates have abundant precipitation?
   e. **Predicting** Which place would have more severe winters—central Russia or the west coast of France? Why?
   f. **Sequencing** Place the following climates in order from coldest to warmest: tundra, subarctic, humid continental, ice cap.
   g. **Relating Cause and Effect** How could a forest grow on a mountain that is surrounded by a desert?

### Lab zone At-Home Activity

**What's Your Climate?** Describe to your family the characteristics of the climate region in which you live. What plants and animals live in your climate region? What characteristics do these plants and animals have that make them well-adapted to the region?

Lab zone **Consumer Lab**

# Cool Climate Graphs

## Problem

Based on climate data, what is the best time of year to visit various cities to enjoy particular recreational activities?

## Skills Focus

graphing, interpreting data

## Materials

- calculator
- ruler
- 3 pieces of graph paper
- black, blue, red, and green pencils
- climate map on pages 626–627
- U.S. map with city names and latitude lines

## Procedure

1. Work in groups of three. Each person should graph the data for a different city, A, B, or C.
2. On graph paper, use a black pencil to label the axes as on the climate graph below. Title your climate graph City A, City B, or City C.
3. Use your green pencil to make a bar graph of the monthly average amount of precipitation. Place a star below the name of each month that has more than a trace of snow.
4. Use a red pencil to plot the average monthly maximum temperature. Make a dot for the temperature in the middle of each space for the month. When you have plotted data for all 12 months, connect the points into a smooth curved line.
5. Use a blue pencil to plot the average monthly minimum temperature for your city. Use the same procedure as in Step 4.
6. Calculate the total average annual precipitation for this city and include it in your observations. Do this by adding the average precipitation for each month.

## Analyze and Conclude

Use all three climate graphs, plus the graph for Washington, D.C., to answer these questions.

1. **Interpreting Data** Which of the four cities has the least change in average temperatures during the year?
2. **Interpreting Maps** Use the map on pages 626–627 to help find the climate region in which each city is located.

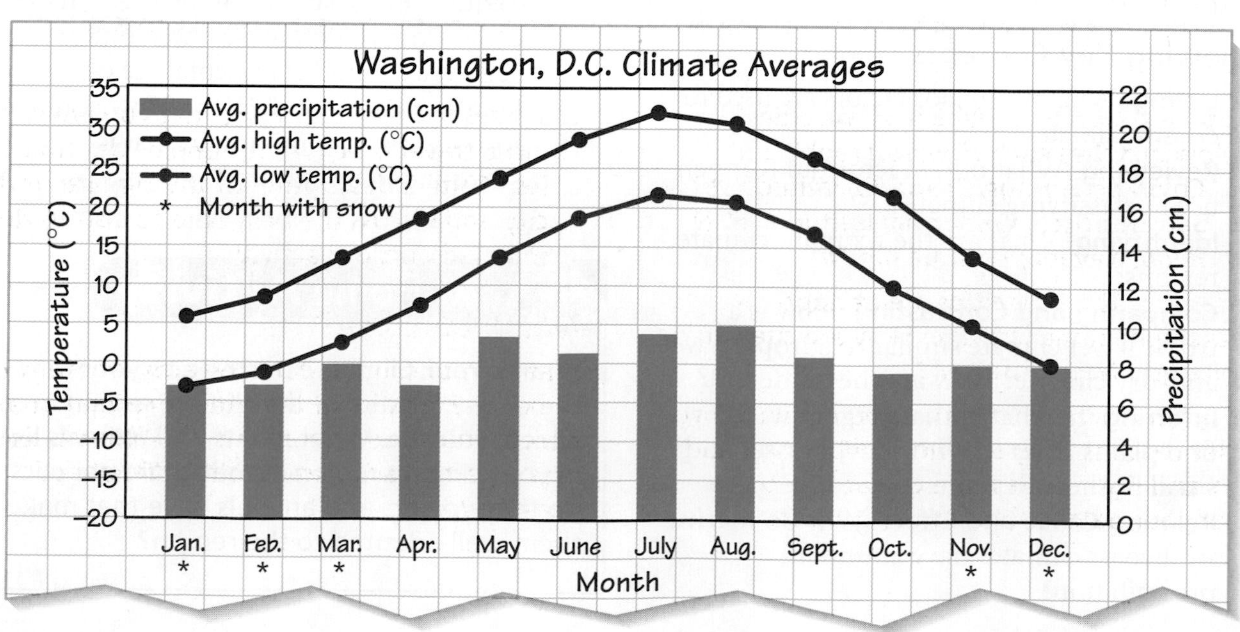

| Climate Data | | | | | | | | | | | | |
|---|---|---|---|---|---|---|---|---|---|---|---|---|
| **Washington, D.C.** | **Jan.** | **Feb.** | **Mar.** | **April** | **May** | **June** | **July** | **Aug.** | **Sept.** | **Oct.** | **Nov.** | **Dec.** |
| Average High Temp. (°C) | 6 | 8 | 14 | 19 | 24 | 29 | 32 | 31 | 27 | 21 | 14 | 8 |
| Average Low Temp. (°C) | –3 | –2 | 3 | 8 | 14 | 19 | 22 | 21 | 17 | 10 | 5 | 0 |
| Average Precipitation (cm) | 6.9 | 6.9 | 8.1 | 6.9 | 9.4 | 8.6 | 9.7 | 9.9 | 8.4 | 7.6 | 7.9 | 7.9 |
| Months With Snow | * | * | * | trace | — | — | — | — | — | trace | * | * |
| **City A** | **Jan.** | **Feb.** | **Mar.** | **April** | **May** | **June** | **July** | **Aug.** | **Sept.** | **Oct.** | **Nov.** | **Dec.** |
| Average High Temp. (°C) | 13 | 16 | 16 | 17 | 17 | 18 | 18 | 19 | 21 | 21 | 17 | 13 |
| Average Low Temp. (°C) | 8 | 9 | 9 | 10 | 11 | 12 | 12 | 13 | 13 | 13 | 11 | 8 |
| Average Precipitation (cm) | 10.4 | 7.6 | 7.9 | 3.3 | 0.8 | 0.5 | 0.3 | 0.3 | 0.8 | 3.3 | 8.1 | 7.9 |
| Months With Snow | trace | trace | trace | — | — | — | — | — | — | — | — | trace |
| **City B** | **Jan.** | **Feb.** | **Mar.** | **April** | **May** | **June** | **July** | **Aug.** | **Sept.** | **Oct.** | **Nov.** | **Dec.** |
| Average High Temp. (°C) | 5 | 7 | 10 | 16 | 21 | 26 | 29 | 27 | 23 | 18 | 11 | 6 |
| Average Low Temp. (°C) | –9 | –7 | –4 | 1 | 6 | 11 | 14 | 13 | 8 | 2 | –4 | –8 |
| Average Precipitation (cm) | 0.8 | 1.0 | 2.3 | 3.0 | 5.6 | 5.8 | 7.4 | 7.6 | 3.3 | 2.0 | 1.3 | 1.3 |
| Months With Snow | * | * | * | * | * | — | — | — | trace | * | * | * |
| **City C** | **Jan.** | **Feb.** | **Mar.** | **April** | **May** | **June** | **July** | **Aug.** | **Sept.** | **Oct.** | **Nov.** | **Dec.** |
| Average High Temp. (°C) | 7 | 11 | 13 | 18 | 23 | 28 | 33 | 32 | 27 | 21 | 12 | 8 |
| Average Low Temp. (°C) | –6 | –4 | –2 | 1 | 4 | 8 | 11 | 10 | 5 | 1 | –3 | –7 |
| Average Precipitation (cm) | 2.5 | 2.3 | 1.8 | 1.3 | 1.8 | 1 | 0.8 | 0.5 | 0.8 | 1 | 2 | 2.5 |
| Months With Snow | * | * | * | * | * | trace | — | — | trace | trace | * | * |

3. **Applying Concepts** Which of the cities below matches each climate graph?
   Colorado Springs, Colorado; latitude 39° N
   San Francisco, California; latitude 38° N
   Reno, Nevada; latitude 40° N
4. **Inferring** The four cities are at approximately the same latitude. Why are their climate graphs so different?
5. **Graphing** What factors do you need to consider when setting up and numbering the left and right *y*-axes of a climate graph so that your data will fit on the graph?
6. **Communicating** Imagine that you are writing a travel brochure for one of the four cities. Write a description of the climate of the city and discuss the best time to visit to do a selected outdoor activity.

## More to Explore

What type of climate does the area where you live have? Find out what outdoor recreational opportunities your community has. How is each activity particularly suited to the climate of your area?

Section 3

# Long-Term Changes in Climate

## Reading Preview

### Key Concepts

- What principle do scientists follow in studying ancient climates?
- What changes occur on Earth's surface during an ice age?
- What factors can cause climate change?

### Key Terms

- ice age
- sunspot

### Target Reading Skill

**Identifying Supporting Evidence** As you read, identify the evidence that is used to show that climates change. Write the evidence in a graphic organizer like the one below.

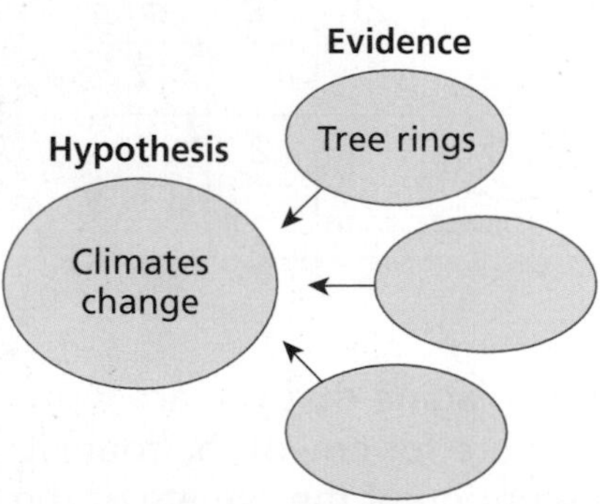


## Lab zone Discover Activity

### What Story Can Tree Rings Tell?

1. Look at the photo of tree rings in Figure 18. Tree rings are the layers of new wood that form each year as a tree grows.
2. Look closely at the tree rings. Note whether they are all the same thickness.
3. What weather conditions might cause a tree to form thicker or thinner tree rings?

**Think It Over**

**Inferring** How could you use tree rings to tell you about weather in the past?

One of the greatest Native American cultures in the American Southwest was the Ancestral Pueblos. These farming people built great pueblos, or "apartment houses," of stone and sun-baked clay, with hundreds of rooms, as shown in Figure 17. By about the year 1000, the Ancestral Pueblos were flourishing. Evidence from tree rings indicates that several periods of intense drought then occurred. These droughts may have contributed to a breakdown in their society. By the late 1200s, they had abandoned the pueblos and moved to other areas.

Although weather varies from day to day, climates usually change more slowly. But climates do change, both in small areas and throughout the world. Although climate change is usually slow, its consequences are great.

**FIGURE 17**
**Ancient Pueblo Dwellings**
The Ancestral Pueblos lived in these buildings, now in Mesa Verde National Park in southwestern Colorado, about 1,000 years ago.

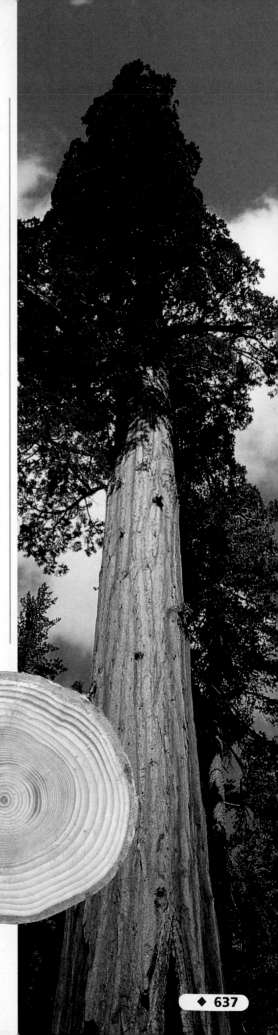

## Studying Climate Change

Climate changes have affected many regions in addition to the Southwest. For example, Greenland today is mostly covered by an ice cap. But 80 million years ago, Greenland had a warm, moist climate. Fossils of magnolias and palm trees found in Greenland provide evidence for this climate change. Today magnolia and palm trees grow only in warm, moist climates. Scientists assume that the ancestors of these trees required similar conditions. **In studying ancient climates, scientists follow an important principle: If plants or animals today need certain conditions to live, then similar plants and animals in the past also required those conditions.**

**Pollen** One source of information about ancient climates is pollen records. Each type of plant has a particular type of pollen. The bottoms of some lakes are covered with thick layers of mud and plant material, including pollen that fell to the bottom of the lake over thousands of years. Scientists can drill down into these layers and bring up cores to examine. By looking at the pollen present in each layer, scientists can tell what types of plants lived in the area. From pollen data, scientists can infer that an ancient climate was similar to the climate where the same plants grow today.

**Tree Rings** Tree rings can also be used to learn about ancient climates. Every summer, a tree grows a new layer of wood just under its bark. These layers form rings, as shown in Figure 18. In cool climates, the amount the tree grows—the thickness of a ring—depends on the length of the warm growing season. In dry climates, the thickness of each ring depends on the amount of rainfall. Scientists study the pattern of thick or thin tree rings. From these data they can see whether previous years were warm or cool, wet or dry.

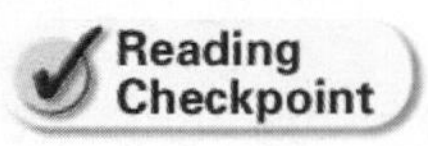


**What are two ways scientists study ancient climates?**

FIGURE 18
**Evidence of Climate Change**
The width of tree rings provides information on temperature and rainfall. A thin ring indicates that the year was cool or dry. A thick ring indicates that the year was warm or wet. **Inferring** *Which tree rings would provide information about climate close to the time that the tree was cut down?*

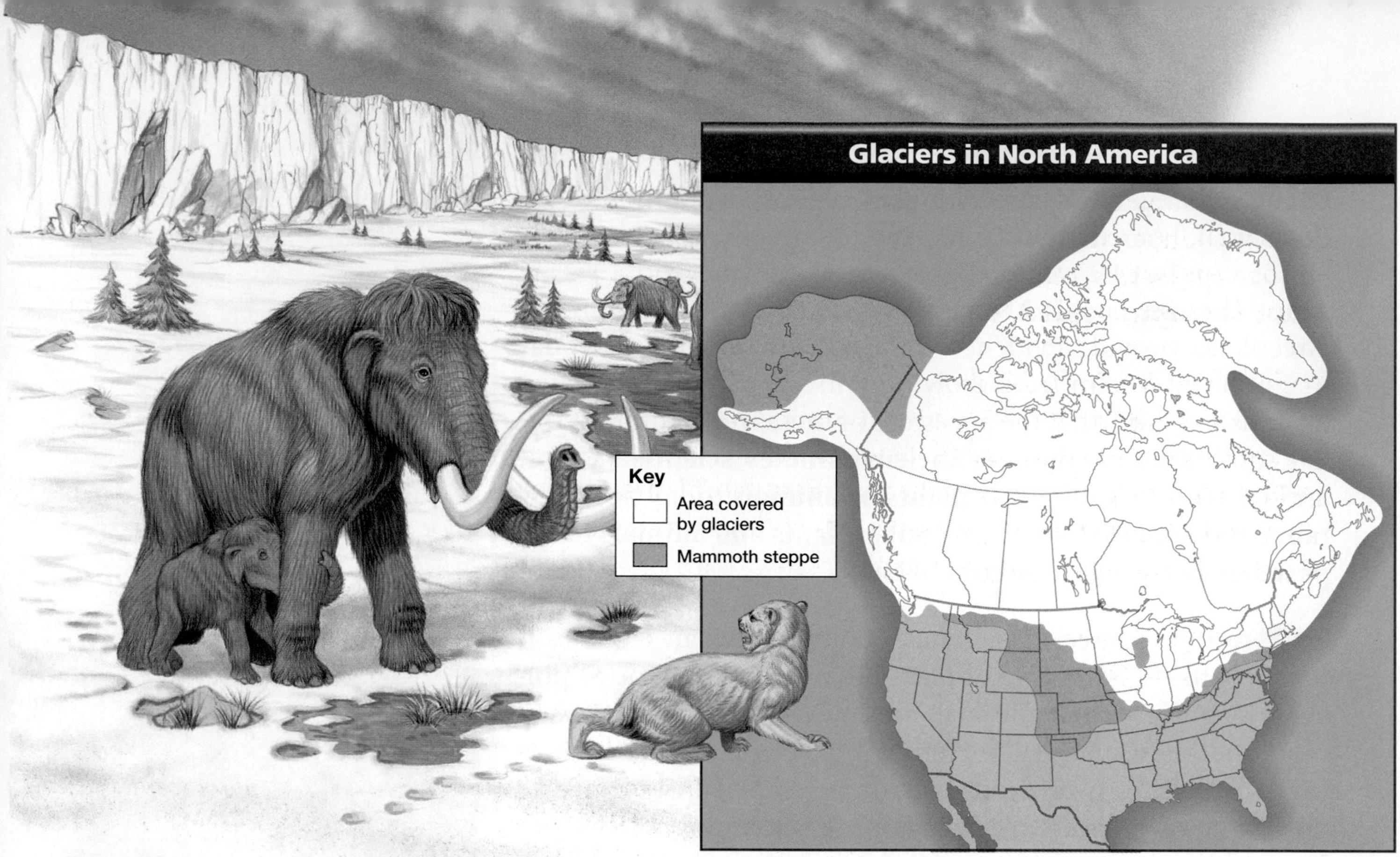

Glaciers in North America

Key
Area covered by glaciers
Mammoth steppe

**FIGURE 19**
**The Last Ice Age**
The map shows the parts of North America that were covered by glaciers 18,000 years ago. On the steppe near the glaciers lived many mammals that are now extinct, including woolly mammoths.

## Ice Ages

Throughout Earth's history, climates have gradually changed. Over millions of years, warm periods have alternated with cold periods known as **ice ages,** or glacial episodes. **During each ice age, huge sheets of ice called glaciers covered large parts of Earth's surface.**

Glaciers transform the landscape by carving giant grooves in solid rock, depositing enormous piles of sediment, and moving huge boulders hundreds of kilometers. From this evidence and from fossils, scientists have concluded that in the past two million years there have been many major ice ages. Each one lasted 100,000 years or longer. Long, warmer periods occurred between the ice ages. Some scientists think that we are now in a warm period between ice ages.

The last ice age ended only about 10,500 years ago. Ice sheets covered much of northern Europe and North America, reaching as far south as present-day Iowa and Nebraska, as shown in Figure 19. In some places, the ice was more than 3 kilometers thick. So much water was frozen in the ice sheets that the average sea level was much lower than it is today. When the ice sheets melted, the rising oceans flooded coastal areas. Inland, the Great Lakes formed.

**Why were the oceans lower during the ice ages than they are now?**

## Causes of Climate Change

Why do climates change? **Possible explanations for major climate changes include variations in the position of Earth relative to the sun, changes in the sun's energy output, major volcanic eruptions, and the movement of the continents.**

**Earth's Position** As Earth revolves around the sun, the time of year when Earth is closest to the sun shifts from January to July and back again over a period of about 23,000 years. The angle at which Earth's axis tilts and the shape of Earth's orbit around the sun also change slightly over long periods of time. The combined effects of these changes may be the main cause of ice ages.

**Solar Energy** Short-term changes in climate have been linked to changes in the number of **sunspots**—dark, cooler regions on the surface of the sun. Sunspots increase and decrease in fairly regular 11-year cycles. Satellite measurements have shown that the amount of energy the sun produces increases slightly when there are more sunspots. This may cause Earth's temperature to warm.

**Volcanic Activity** Major volcanic eruptions release huge quantities of gases and ash into the atmosphere. These materials can stay in the upper atmosphere for months or years. Scientists think that the gases and ash filter out some of the incoming solar radiation, and may lower temperatures.

### Math Analyzing Data

#### Ice Ages and Temperature

The graph shows the estimated average worldwide temperature over the last 350,000 years. During this time, cold glacial periods (blue) alternated with warmer interglacial periods (pink).

1. **Reading Graphs** What does the *x*-axis of the graph represent? What does the *y*-axis represent?
2. **Interpreting Data** What pattern do you see in these data? How would you explain this pattern?
3. **Predicting** Based on the pattern over the last 350,000 years, predict how global temperature will change in the future.

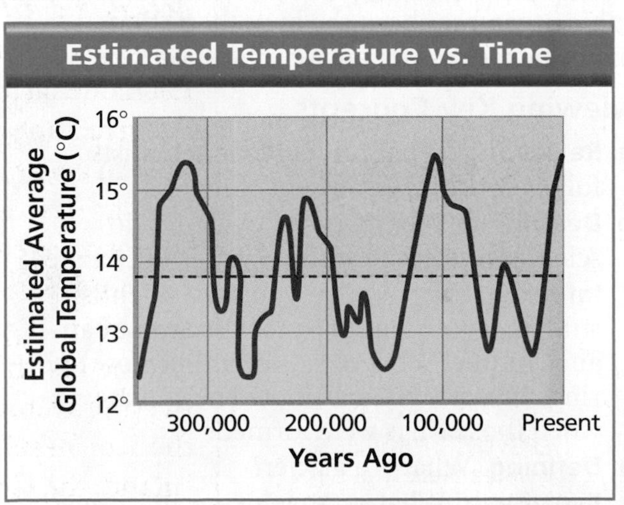

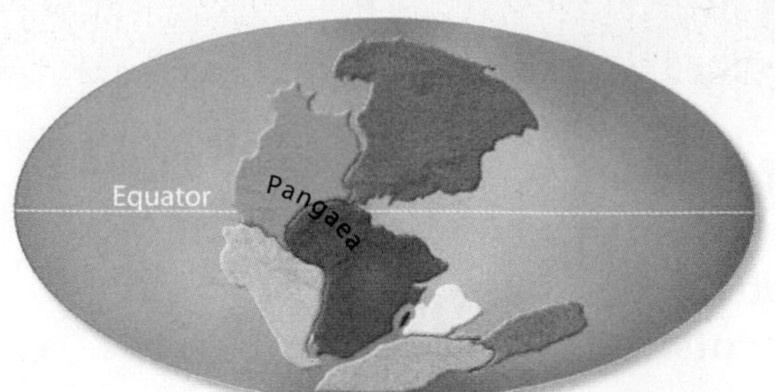


**225 Million Years Ago**

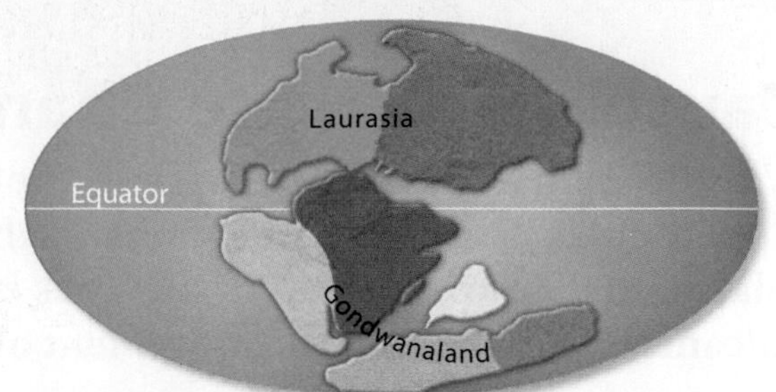


**180–200 Million Years Ago**

**FIGURE 20**
**Moving Continents**
The continents have moved over millions of years.
**Interpreting Maps** *Which present-day continents broke away from Gondwanaland? Which broke away from Laurasia?*

**For:** Continental Drift activity
**Visit:** PHSchool.com
**Web Code:** cfp-1015

**Movement of Continents** The continents have not always been located where they are now. About 225 million years ago, most of the land on Earth was part of a single continent called Pangaea (pan JEE uh), as Figure 20 shows. At that time, most continents were far from their present positions. Continents that are now in the polar zones were once near the equator. This movement explains how tropical plants such as magnolias and palm trees could once have grown in Greenland.

The movements of continents over time changed the locations of land and sea. These changes affected the global patterns of winds and ocean currents, which in turn slowly changed climates. And as the continents continue to move, climates will continue to change.

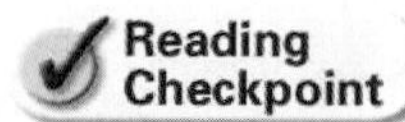 **Reading Checkpoint** What was Pangaea?

## Section 3 Assessment

### Target Reading Skill

**Identifying Supporting Evidence** Refer to your graphic organizer about the hypothesis that climate changes as you answer Question 1 below.

### Reviewing Key Concepts

1. a. **Reviewing** What principle do scientists follow in studying ancient climates?
   b. **Describing** What types of evidence do scientists gather to study changes in climate?
   c. **Inferring** Suppose that you are a scientist studying tree rings in a cross-section of an ancient tree. What could several narrow tree rings in a row tell you about the climate when those rings were formed?
2. a. **Defining** What is a glacier?
   b. **Explaining** What occurs during an ice age?
   c. **Comparing and Contrasting** Compare the climate today with it during an ice age.
3. a. **Listing** What are four factors that could be responsible for changing Earth's climate?
   b. **Summarizing** Select one of the four factors that could cause climate change and summarize how it may cause the climate to change.

### Writing in Science

**Procedure for Data Collection** Suppose that you are a scientist who wants to use pollen data from a lake bed to learn about ancient climates. Write the steps for the procedure that you would follow to collect and analyze your data.

Section 4

Integrating Environmental Science

# Global Changes in the Atmosphere

## Reading Preview

### Key Concepts

- What events can cause short-term climate changes?
- How might human activities be affecting the temperature of Earth's atmosphere?
- How have human activities affected the ozone layer?

### Key Terms

- El Niño
- La Niña
- global warming
- greenhouse gas
- chlorofluorocarbon

### Target Reading Skill

**Asking Questions** Before you read, preview the red headings. Ask a *what* or *how* question for each heading, for example, "How does short-term climate change occur?" As you read, write the answers to your questions.

## Lab zone Discover Activity

### What Is the Greenhouse Effect?

1. Cut two pieces of black construction paper to fit the bottoms of two shoe boxes.
2. Place a thermometer in each box. Record the temperatures on the thermometers. Cover one box with plastic wrap.
3. Place the boxes together where sunlight or a light bulb can shine on them equally. Make sure the thermometers are shaded by the sides of the boxes.
4. Wait 15 minutes and read the thermometers again. Record the temperatures.

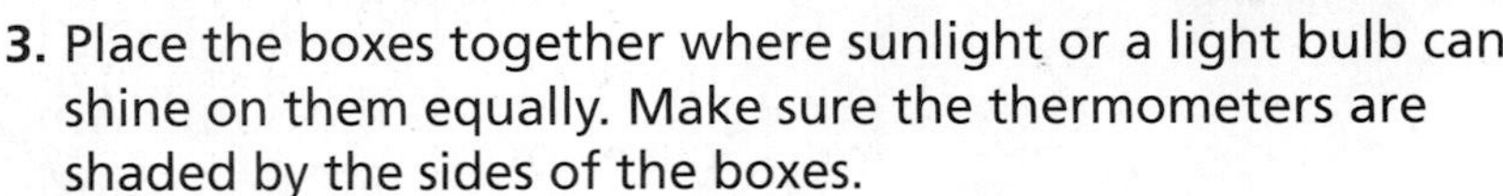

**Think It Over**

**Inferring** How can you explain any temperature difference between the two boxes?

If you live in one area for several years, you get to know the area's climate. But in some years, the weather is so unusual that you might think the climate has changed. That's what happened in several different parts of the world during 1997–1998. Droughts occurred in parts of Africa, Asia, and Australia. Heavy rains struck parts of South America. In the United States, very heavy rains swept across California and the South.

What produced these global changes? During the droughts and floods of 1998, parts of the Pacific Ocean were much warmer than usual. Even the ocean's winds and currents changed. Scientists have evidence that these changes in the Pacific Ocean led to wild weather in other parts of the world.

◄ In 1998, mudslides from heavy rains caused severe damage in California.

▲ In **normal years**, water in the eastern Pacific is kept relatively cool by currents along the coast of North and South America.

▲ When **El Niño** occurs, warm surface water from the western Pacific moves east toward the coast of South America.

▲ **La Niña** occurs when surface waters in the eastern Pacific Ocean are colder than normal.

FIGURE 21
**El Niño and La Niña**
In these satellite images, warmer water is red and white. Cooler water is blue and purple.

## Short-Term Climate Change

Changes in ocean currents and winds can greatly affect climate. **El Niño and La Niña are short-term changes in the tropical Pacific Ocean caused by changes in ocean surface currents and prevailing winds.** El Niño and La Niña both influence weather patterns all over the world.

**El Niño** The warm-water event known as **El Niño** begins when an unusual pattern of winds forms over the western Pacific. This causes a vast sheet of warm water to move eastward toward the South American coast, as shown in Figure 21. El Niño causes the surface of the ocean in the eastern Pacific to be unusually warm. El Niño typically occurs every two to seven years.

The arrival of El Niño's warm surface water disrupts the cold ocean currents along the western coast of South America and changes weather patterns there. El Niño also affects weather patterns around the world, often bringing severe conditions such as heavy rains or droughts. El Niño conditions can last for one to two years before normal winds and currents return.

**La Niña** When surface waters in the eastern Pacific are colder than normal, a climate event known as **La Niña** occurs. A La Niña event is the opposite of an El Niño event. La Niña events typically bring colder than normal winters and greater precipitation to the Pacific Northwest and the north central United States. Another major effect of La Niña is greater hurricane activity in the western Atlantic.

**How often does El Niño typically occur?**

## Global Warming

Most changes in world climates are caused by natural factors. But recently scientists have observed climate changes that could be the result of human activities. For example, over the last 120 years, the average temperature of the troposphere has risen by about 0.7 Celsius degree. This gradual increase in the temperature of Earth's atmosphere is called **global warming.**

**The Greenhouse Hypothesis** Recall that gases in Earth's atmosphere hold in heat from the sun, keeping the atmosphere at a comfortable temperature for living things. The process by which gases in Earth's atmosphere trap this energy is called the greenhouse effect. Look at the greenhouse in Figure 22. Notice that sunlight does not heat the air in the greenhouse directly. Instead, sunlight first heats the soil, benches, and pots. Then infrared radiation from these surfaces heats the air in the greenhouse. The greenhouse effect in Earth's atmosphere is similar in some ways.

Gases in the atmosphere that trap energy are called **greenhouse gases.** Carbon dioxide, water vapor, and methane are some of the greenhouse gases. **Many scientists have hypothesized that human activities that add greenhouse gases to the atmosphere may be warming Earth's atmosphere.**

**FIGURE 22**
**Greenhouse Effect**
Sunlight enters a greenhouse and is absorbed. The interior of the greenhouse radiates back energy in the form of infrared radiation, or heat. Much of the heat is trapped and held inside the greenhouse, warming it.
**Applying Concepts** *What gases in Earth's atmosphere can trap heat like a greenhouse?*

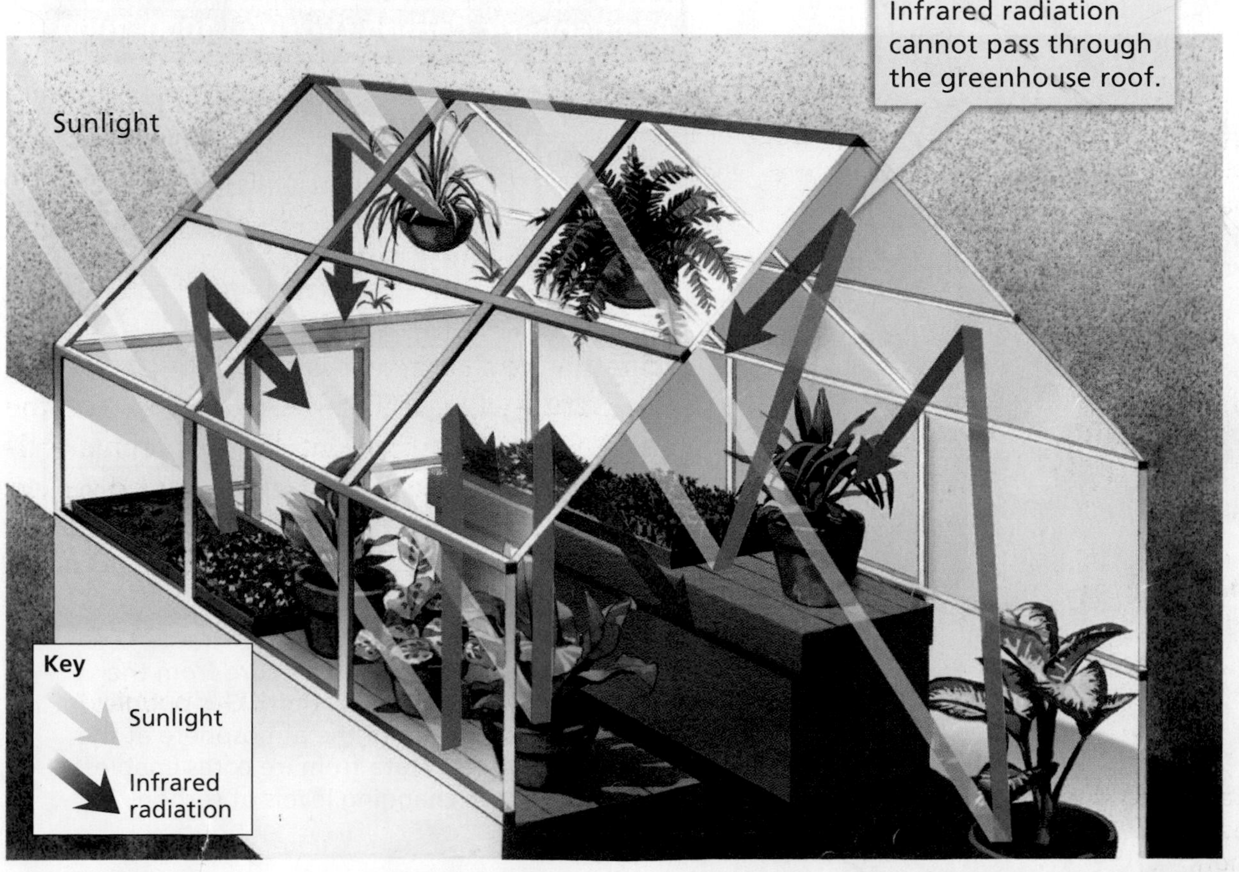
Infrared radiation cannot pass through the greenhouse roof.
Sunlight
Key
Sunlight
Infrared radiation

**Changing Levels of Carbon Dioxide** Scientists think that an increase in carbon dioxide is a major factor in global warming. Until the late 1800s, the level of carbon dioxide in the atmosphere remained about the same. How did scientists determine this? They measured the amount of carbon dioxide in air bubbles trapped in Antarctic ice. They obtained these samples of ancient air from ice cores, as shown in Figure 23. The glacier that covers Antarctica formed over millions of years. Gas bubbles in the ice cores provide samples of air from the time the ice formed.

Is global warming caused by human activities, or does it have a natural cause? Scientists have done a great deal of research to try to answer this question.

Since the late 1800s, the level of carbon dioxide in the atmosphere has increased steadily, as shown in Figure 23. Most scientists think that this change is a result of increased human activities. For example, the burning of wood, coal, oil, and natural gas adds carbon dioxide to the air. During the last 100 years, these activities have increased greatly in many different countries. Some scientists predict that the level of carbon dioxide could double by the year 2100. If that happens, then global temperature could rise by several Celsius degrees.

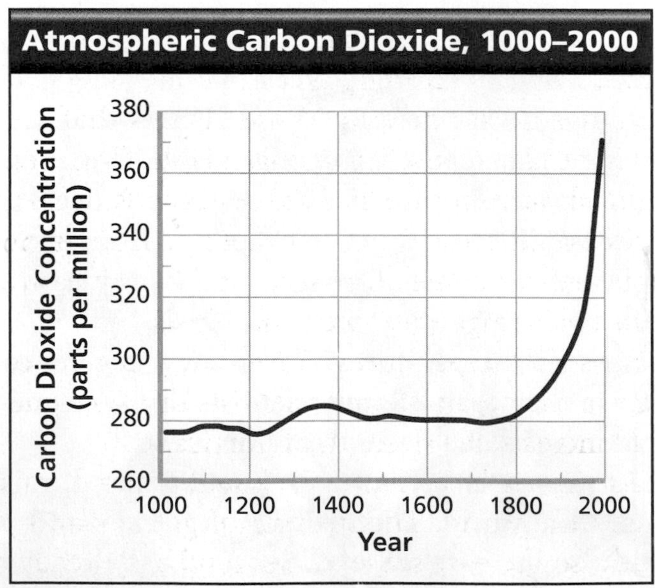


FIGURE 23
**Carbon Dioxide Levels**
These scientists are taking an ice core from the glacier that covers Antarctica (left). Gas bubbles in the ice provide samples of the atmosphere at the time the ice formed. Data from ice cores enables scientists to graph changing levels of carbon dioxide (above).

**FIGURE 24**
**Melting Glaciers**
The photos show the Burroughs glacier in Alaska. The photo on the left was taken in 1960. The photo on the right was taken in1990, and shows the large amount of melting that has taken place.

**Climate Variation Hypothesis** Not all scientists agree about the causes of global warming. Some scientists think that the 0.7 Celsius degree rise in global temperatures over the past 120 years may be due in part to natural variations in climate.

Satellite measurements have shown that the amount of energy the sun produces increases and decreases from year to year. Even such small changes in solar energy could be causing periods of warmer and cooler climates. Climate change could be a result of changes in both carbon dioxide levels and the amount of solar energy.

**Possible Effects** Global warming could have some positive effects. Farmers in some areas that are now cool could plant two crops a year instead of one. Places that are too cold for farming today could become farmland. However, many effects of global warming are likely to be less positive. Higher temperatures would cause water to evaporate from exposed soil, such as plowed farmland. Dry soil blows away easily. Thus, some fertile fields might become "dust bowls."

A rise in temperatures of even a few degrees could warm up water in the oceans. Some scientists think warmer ocean water could increase the strength of hurricanes.

As the water warmed, it would expand, raising sea level around the world. The melting of glaciers and polar ice caps could also increase sea level. Sea level has already risen by 10 to 20 centimeters over the last 100 years, and could rise another 25 to 80 centimeters by the year 2100. Even such a small rise in sea level would flood low-lying coastal areas.

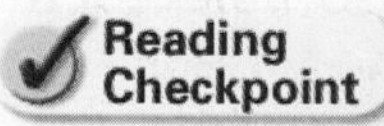

**What are three possible effects of global warming?**

**For:** More on the greenhouse effect
**Visit:** PHSchool.com
**Web Code:** cfd-4044

## Lab zone Try This Activity

### It's Your Skin!

Compare how well sunscreens block out ultraviolet rays.

1. Close the blinds or curtains in the room. Place one square of sun-sensitive paper inside each of three plastic sandwich bags.
2. Place three drops of one sunscreen on the outside of one bag. Spread the sunscreen as evenly as possible. Label this bag with the SPF number of the sunscreen.
3. On another bag, repeat Step 2 using a sunscreen with a different SPF. Wash your hands after spreading the sunscreen. Leave the third bag untreated as a control.
4. Place the bags outside in direct sunlight. Bring them back inside after 3 minutes or after one of the squares turns completely white.

**Drawing Conclusions** Did both of the sunscreens block ultraviolet radiation? Was one better than the other? Explain.

## Ozone Depletion

Another global change in the atmosphere involves the ozone layer. Ozone in the stratosphere filters out much of the harmful ultraviolet radiation from the sun, as shown in Figure 25.

In the 1970s, scientists noticed that the ozone layer over Antarctica was growing thinner each spring. A large area of reduced ozone, or ozone hole, was being created. In 2000, the ozone hole reached a record size of more than 28.5 million $km^2$—almost the size of Africa. By 2004, the maximum size of the ozone hole decreased to about 20 million $km^2$. What created the ozone hole? **Chemicals produced by humans have been damaging the ozone layer.**

**Chlorofluorocarbons** A major cause of ozone depletion is a group of compounds called **chlorofluorocarbons,** or CFCs. CFCs were used in air conditioners and refrigerators, as cleaners for electronic parts, and in aerosol sprays, such as deodorants.

Most chemical compounds released into the air eventually break down. CFCs, however, can last for decades and rise all the way to the stratosphere. In the stratosphere, ultraviolet radiation breaks down the CFC molecules into atoms, including chlorine. The chlorine atoms then break ozone down into oxygen atoms.

**Results of Ozone Depletion** Because ozone blocks ultraviolet radiation, a decrease in ozone means an increase in the amount of ultraviolet radiation that reaches Earth's surface. Ultraviolet radiation can cause eye damage and several kinds of skin cancer.

In the late 1970s, the United States and many other countries banned most uses of CFCs in aerosol sprays. In 1990, many nations agreed to phase out the production and use of CFCs. Because ozone depletion affects the whole world, such agreements must be international to be effective. Worldwide production of the chemicals has greatly decreased. In the United States, at the current rate it will take until 2010 to completely eliminate the use of CFCs. The size of the ozone hole is expected to gradually shrink over time as these agreements take effect.

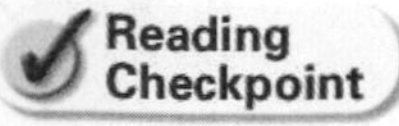

What are CFCs?

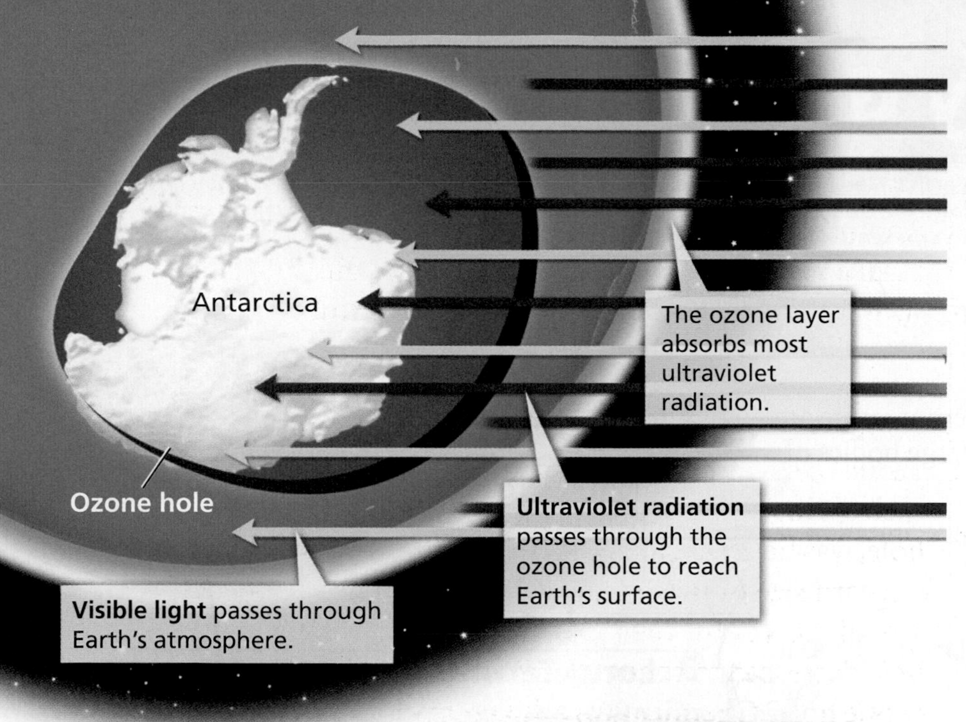
Antarctica
Ozone hole
The ozone layer absorbs most ultraviolet radiation.
Ultraviolet radiation passes through the ozone hole to reach Earth's surface.
Visible light passes through Earth's atmosphere.

FIGURE 25
### The Ozone Hole
The ozone layer blocks much of the ultraviolet radiation (purple) coming from the sun. Visible light (yellow) can pass through the ozone layer. The satellite images below show the concentration of ozone over the South Pole for three years. The dark area shows where the ozone layer is thinnest. **Observing** *How has the size of the ozone layer changed over time?*

1979

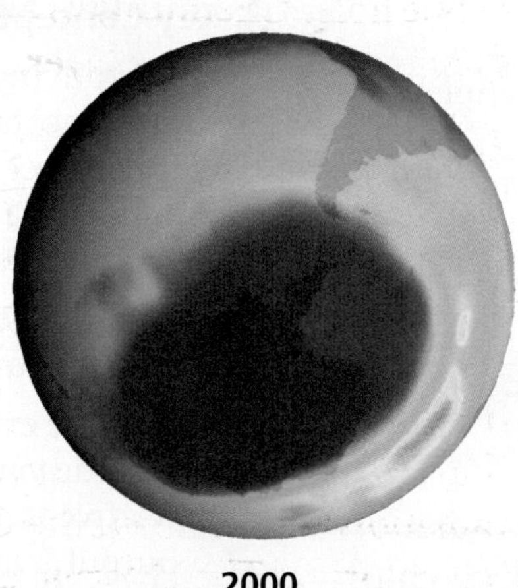
2000

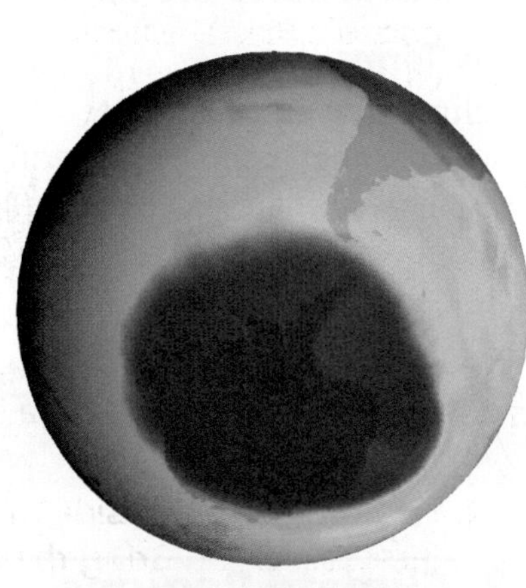
2003

## Section 4 Assessment

### Target Reading Skill
**Asking Questions** Use the answers to your *what* and *how* questions to help you answer the questions below.

### Reviewing Key Concepts
1. a. **Listing** What are two events that can cause short-term climate change?
   b. **Describing** Describe the changes that occur in the Pacific Ocean and the atmosphere above it during El Niño.
   c. **Relating Cause and Effect** What effects does El Niño have on weather and climate?
2. a. **Defining** What is global warming?
   b. **Relating Cause and Effect** How do scientists think that increased carbon dioxide levels contributed to global warming?
3. a. **Reviewing** What effect have human activities had on the ozone layer?
   b. **Summarizing** Summarize the cause of ozone depletion and the steps taken to reverse it.

### Lab zone At-Home Activity
**Sun Protection** Visit a drugstore with your family. Compare the SPF (sun protection factor) of the various sunscreens for sale. Explain why it is important to protect your skin from ultraviolet radiation. Ask your family members to determine the best value for the money in terms of SPF rating and price.

# Chapter 18 Study Guide

**The BIG Idea**

**Earth's Many Climates** The major factors that influence a region's climate are latitude, distance from large bodies of water, ocean currents, prevailing winds, the presence of mountains, and seasonal winds.

## 1 What Causes Climate?

### Key Concepts

- The main factors that influence temperature are latitude, altitude, distance from large bodies of water, and ocean currents.
- The main factors that influence precipitation are prevailing winds, the presence of mountains, and seasonal winds.
- The seasons are caused by the tilt of Earth's axis as Earth travels around the sun.

### Key Terms

- climate • microclimate • tropical zone
- polar zone • temperate zone
- marine climate • continental climate
- windward • leeward • monsoon

## 2 Climate Regions

### Key Concepts

- Scientists classify climates according to two major factors: temperature and precipitation.
- There are six main climate regions: tropical rainy, dry, temperate marine, temperate continental, polar, and highlands.
- The tropics have two types of rainy climates: tropical wet and tropical wet-and-dry.
- Dry climates can be arid and semiarid climates.
- There are three kinds of temperate marine climates: marine west coast, humid subtropical, and Mediterranean.
- Temperate continental climates are only found on continents in the Northern Hemisphere, and include humid continental and subarctic.
- The polar climate is the coldest climate region, and includes the ice cap and tundra climates.
- Temperature falls as altitude increases, so highland regions are colder than regions that surround them.

### Key Terms

rain forest
savanna
desert
steppe
humid subtropical
subarctic
tundra
permafrost

## 3 Long-Term Changes in Climate

### Key Concepts

- In studying ancient climates, scientists follow an important principle: If plants or animals today need certain conditions to live, then similar plants and animals in the past also required those conditions.
- During each ice age, huge sheets of ice called glaciers covered large parts of Earth's surface.
- Possible explanations for major climate changes include variations in the position of Earth relative to the sun, changes in the sun's energy output, major volcanic eruptions, and the movement of continents.

### Key Terms

ice age
sunspot

## 4 Global Changes in the Atmosphere

### Key Concepts

- El Niño and La Niña are short-term changes in the tropical Pacific Ocean caused by changes in ocean surface currents and prevailing winds.
- Human activities that add greenhouse gases to the atmosphere may be warming Earth's atmosphere.
- Chemicals produced by humans have been damaging the ozone layer.

### Key Terms

- El Niño • La Niña • global warming
- greenhouse gas • chlorofluorocarbon

# Review and Assessment

Go Online
PHSchool.com
For: Self-Assessment
Visit: PHSchool.com
Web Code: cfa-4040

## Organizing Information

**Concept Mapping** Copy the graphic organizer about climate onto a separate sheet of paper. Then complete it and add a title. (For more on Concept Mapping, see the Skills Handbook.)

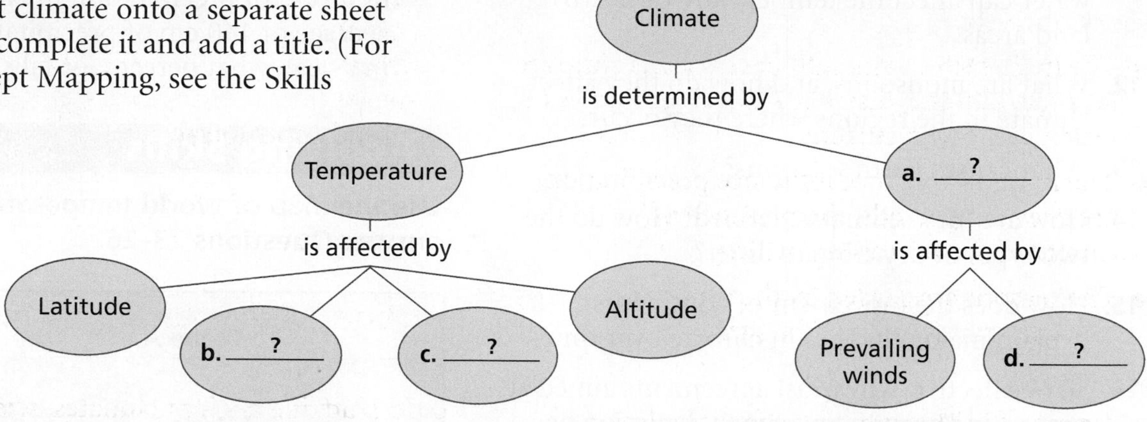


## Reviewing Key Terms

**Choose the letter of the best answer.**

1. The average conditions of temperature, precipitation, wind, and clouds in an area over a period of years make up its
   a. weather. b. latitude.
   c. climate. d. season.
2. Temperatures range from warm or hot in summer to cool or cold in winter in
   a. polar zones.
   b. tropical zone.
   c. tundra climates.
   d. temperate zones.
3. A wet, warm climate zone on the edge of the tropics is
   a. humid subtropical.
   b. tundra.
   c. subarctic.
   d. continental climate.
4. A tropical grassland with scattered clumps of trees is a
   a. steppe. b. desert.
   c. savanna. d. rain forest.
5. The main cause of ozone depletion is
   a. global warming.
   b. chlorofluorocarbons.
   c. greenhouse gases.
   d. sunspots.

**If the statement is true, write *true*. If it is false, change the underlined word or words to make the statement true.**

6. The climate conditions that exist in a small area are its <u>microclimate</u>.
7. Rain or snow usually falls on the <u>leeward</u> side of a mountain range.
8. Permanently frozen soil is called <u>tundra</u>.
9. During <u>ice ages</u> large parts of Earth's surface are covered by glaciers.
10. Carbon dioxide is a <u>chlorofluorocarbon</u> that traps energy in the atmosphere.

## Writing in Science

**Expedition Plan** Suppose that you are preparing to take a trip back in time to the last ice age. Write a list of the equipment you will need to bring with you and describe what the climate will be like.

*Climate and Climate Change*
Video Preview
Video Field Trip
▶ Video Assessment

# Review and Assessment

## Checking Concepts

**11.** Explain how distance from large bodies of water can affect the temperature of nearby land areas.

**12.** What are monsoons, and how do they affect climate in the regions where they occur?

**13.** What causes Earth's seasons?

**14.** How are "dry" climates defined? How do the two types of dry climate differ?

**15.** How does the movement of continents explain major changes in climate over time?

**16.** To be effective, why must agreements aimed at preventing or reducing ozone depletion be international?

## Thinking Critically

**17. Relating Cause and Effect** Describe three ways in which water influences climate.

**18. Relating Cause and Effect** Why do parts of the United States have a semiarid climate while neighboring areas have a humid continental climate?

**19. Reading Graphs** Which month shown on the graph has the warmest average temperature? Which month is the wettest? What type of climate is indicated by the graph?

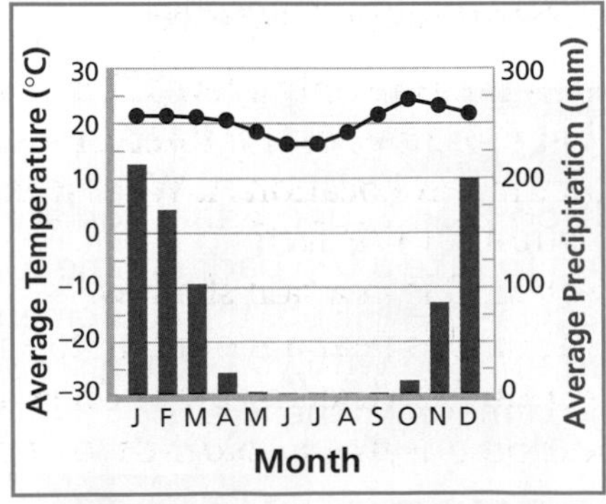


**20. Inferring** How is Earth's climate affected by major volcanic eruptions?

**21. Comparing and Contrasting** How is global warming different from earlier changes in Earth's climate?

## Math Practice

**22. Percentage** Suppose a city receives an average of 35 cm of precipitation in November. If an average of 140 cm of precipitation falls there in a year, what percentage falls in November?

## Applying Skills

**Use the map of world temperature zones to answer Questions 23–26.**

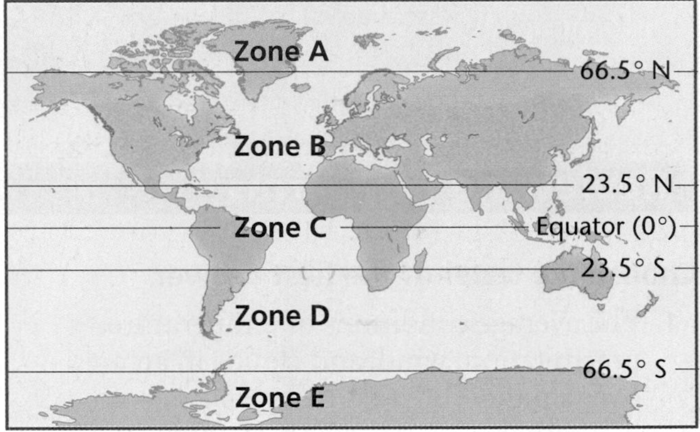


**23. Interpreting Maps** Name each of the five zones shown on the map.

**24. Measuring** What is the name of the temperature zone that includes the equator? How many degrees of latitude does this zone cover?

**25. Interpreting Data** Which of the five zones shown on the map has the greatest amount of land area suitable for people to live?

**26. Drawing Conclusions** Which zone has the highest average temperatures all year round? Explain why.

## Lab zone Chapter Project

**Performance Assessment** Now share your project with your class. In your presentation, describe the patterns you found in your graphs. Then explain what you think causes different microclimates. After your presentation, think about how you could have improved your investigation.

# Standardized Test Prep

**Test-Taking Tip**

**Eliminating Incorrect Answers**

When answering a multiple-choice question, you can often eliminate one or more of the answer choices because they are clearly incorrect. By doing this you increase your odds of selecting the correct answer.

***Sample Question***

Which climate is warm, wet, and located on the edges of the tropics?

**A** humid subtropical  **B** humid continental
**C** semiarid  **D** subarctic

***Answer***

You can eliminate **C** and **D** right away. Semiarid climates are dry, not wet, and subarctic climates are not located on the edges of the tropics. You have narrowed the choices to **A** or **B.** The correct answer is **A**—humid subtropical.

**Choose the letter of the best answer.**

**1.** Predict what type of climate would be the most likely in an area located in the interior of a large continent, on the east side of a major mountain range. Winds in the area commonly blow from west to east.
**A** dry  **B** polar
**C** temperate marine  **D** tropical rainy

**2.** What two major factors are usually used to classify climates?
**F** precipitation and altitude
**G** temperature and air pressure
**H** temperature and precipitation
**J** air pressure and humidity

**3.** What is the major result at Earth's surface of ozone depletion in the stratosphere?
**A** an increase in the amount of ultraviolet radiation reaching the surface
**B** a decrease in the amount of ultraviolet radiation reaching the surface
**C** an increase in global temperatures
**D** a decrease in global temperatures

*The graphs below show average monthly precipitation for two locations in Arizona. Use the information and your knowledge of science to answer Questions 4–5.*

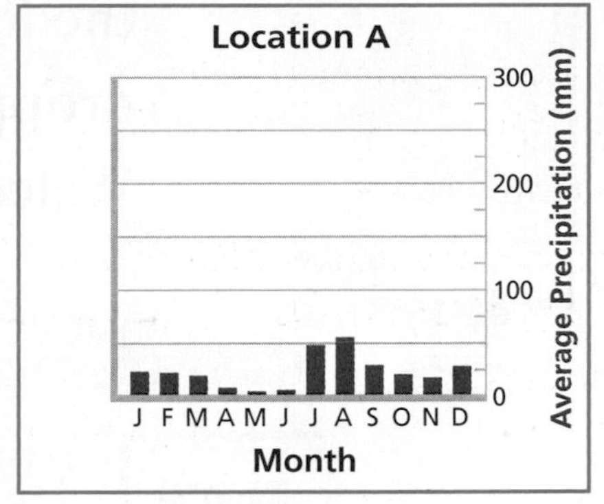


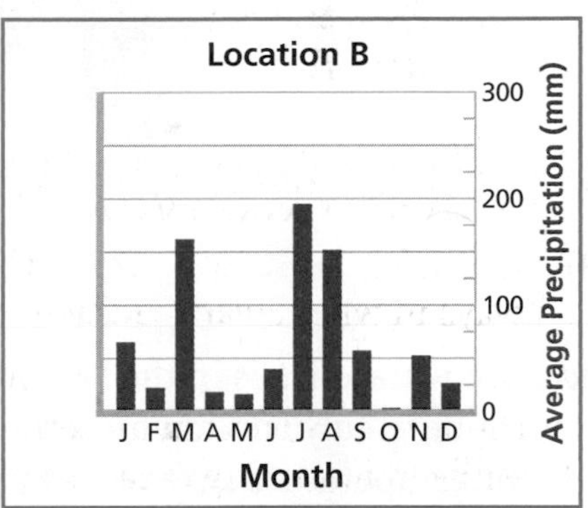


**4.** During which months do these locations receive the most precipitation?
**F** January through March
**G** April through June
**H** July through September
**J** October through December

**5.** Although they are only a few kilometers apart, Location B receives nearly three times as much precipitation as Location A. What is the best explanation for this fact?
**A** Location B is in a rain shadow.
**B** Location B is near a mountain top.
**C** Location A is dried by prevailing winds.
**D** Location A is much colder than Location B.

## Constructed Response

**6.** Ice ages have occurred at several times during Earth's history. What is an ice age, and how does an ice age affect the land surface and the oceans?

Interdisciplinary **Exploration**

# Antarctica

## On July 21, 1983, the temperature at the Russian research station Vostok dropped to a world record low of −89°C. Welcome to Antarctica!

**Amundsen-Scott Station**
This is one of the United States stations at the South Pole.

Because Antarctica is in the Southern Hemisphere, July is midwinter there. But the temperature isn't very warm in summer, either. The average summer temperature at Vostok is −33°C. Antarctica's climate is unusual in other ways. It's the windiest continent as well as the coldest. Even though Antarctica is covered with snow and ice, it's also the driest continent—a snowy desert. Less than five centimeters of precipitation falls in the interior in a year. Antarctic blizzards are terrifying, but they don't bring much new snow. They just blow drifts from one place to another.

Many countries have set up research stations in Antarctica to study climate, temperature, and the atmosphere. Scientists in Antarctica also research wildlife and geology.

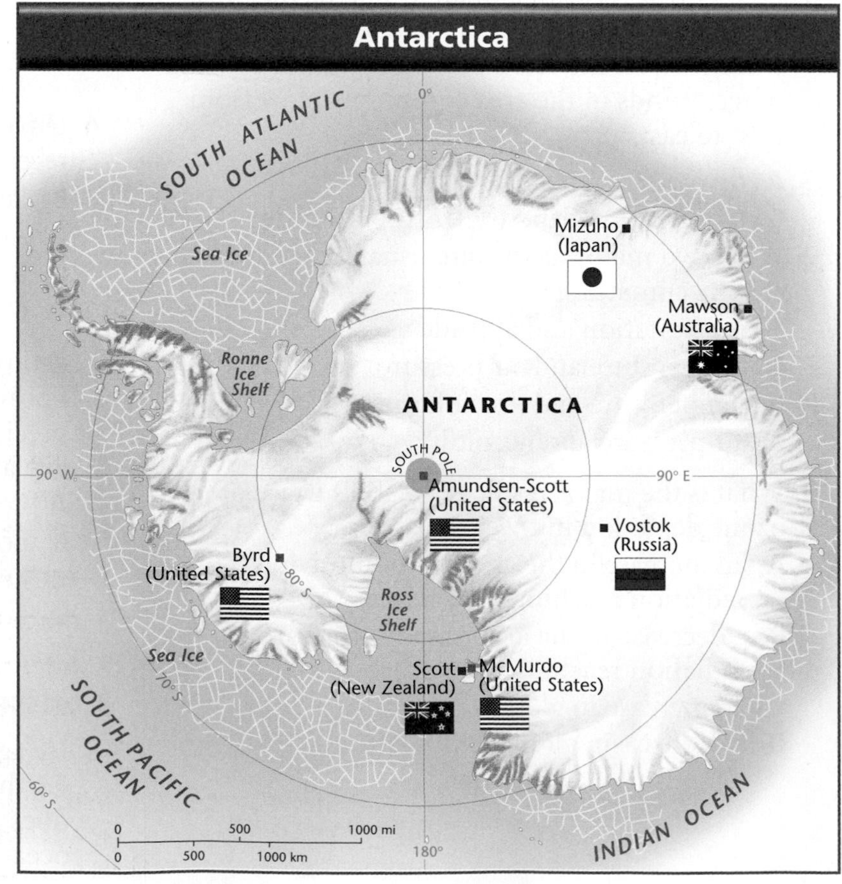


**Antarctica**
The map shows major research stations established in Antarctica by countries around the world.

# Race to the South Pole

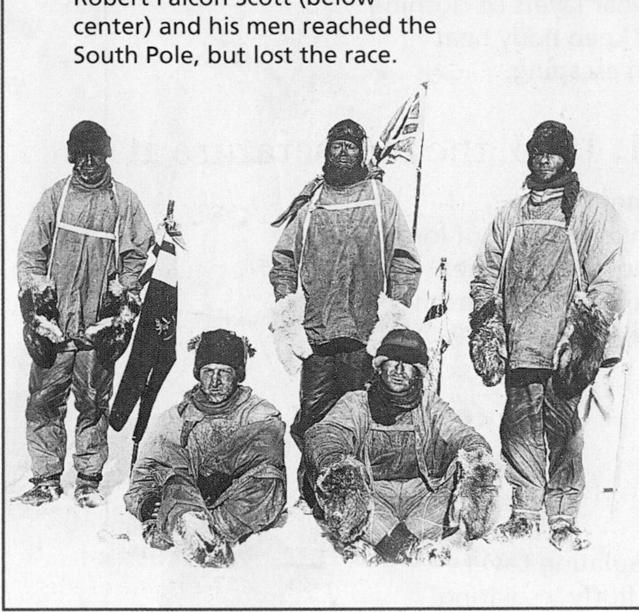

**1912**
Robert Falcon Scott (below center) and his men reached the South Pole, but lost the race.

Would you brave the darkness and cold of Antarctica? In the early 1900s, several famous explorers began a "race to the pole." Their attempts to reach the South Pole produced stories of heroism—and tragedy.

In October 1911, the British explorer Robert Scott traveled to the South Pole. He started overland with dog teams, motorized sleds, and ponies. He and four other explorers reached the South Pole in January 1912—only to find that a Norwegian expedition led by Roald Amundsen had beaten them there by a month! Scott's team had lost the race!

Soon after, Scott and his crew started back. But all of them died in a blizzard. Searchers later found their tent, Scott's diary, and photographs. Scott's team had been only 18 kilometers from a supply camp.

In 1914, Sir Ernest Shackleton was the hero of an incredible Antarctic survival story. On the way to the South Pole, ice trapped and crushed his ship. He and his men escaped to an island. Shackleton and a few others sailed in a small whaleboat to find help. Amazingly, everyone was rescued.

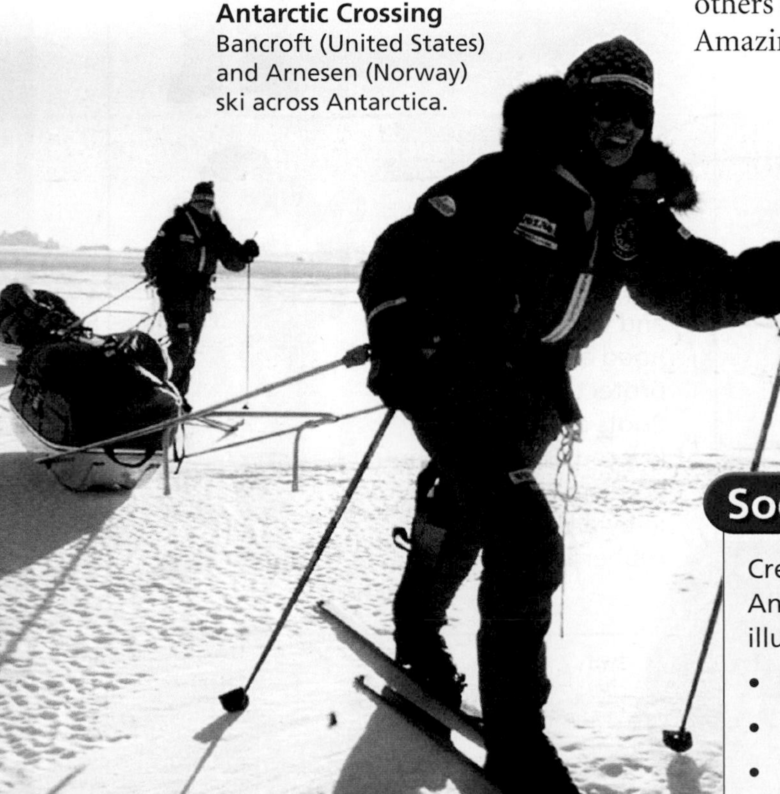

**Antarctic Crossing**
Bancroft (United States) and Arnesen (Norway) ski across Antarctica.

Other expeditions followed. In 1929, American explorer Richard E. Byrd led the first flight over the South Pole. More recently, in 2001, Ann Bancroft and Liv Arnesen became the first women to cross Antarctica.

## Social Studies Activity

Create a timeline of important events in Antarctica. Find photos or draw sketches to illustrate the events. Include the following events:

- early expeditions
- "race to the pole" in the early 1900s
- International Geophysical Year
- Antarctic Treaty
- new research stations

Why did it take courage and endurance to try to reach the South Pole in the early 1900s?

Science

# Continent of Extremes

Why is Antarctica so cold? Its high latitude and months of darkness are important reasons. In addition, the broad expanses of white snow and icy glaciers reflect back sunlight before much heat is absorbed.

As on every continent, climates vary from place to place. Warmer parts of Antarctica are at lower elevations, at lower latitudes, or near the coast. Coastal areas are warmer because the nearby ocean moderates temperatures. These areas also have bare land, which absorbs heat.

Summer weather patterns in Antarctica are different from winter patterns. The short summer warm-up starts in October. The warmest temperatures are from mid-December to mid-January. Then temperatures drop suddenly. So by mid-March, the beginning of winter, the temperature has fallen to winter levels. Over the next six months Antarctica remains very cold—and dark.

## Science Activity

Staying warm is essential for life in the Antarctic. Set up an experiment to test how well different materials keep heat from escaping. Use socks made of nylon, silk, cotton, and wool. You will need a jar for each material plus one jar as a control.

- Fill jars with equal amounts of very hot water. The water in each jar should be the same temperature.
- Record the temperature of each jar and screw each cap on.
- Place each jar, except the control, inside a sock. Refrigerate all the jars for 30 minutes.
- Remove the jars and record the water temperature of each.

Which jar cooled fastest? Which materials retained the heat best?

## Cold-Weather Clothing

The secret to staying warm is to wear layers of clothing that keep body heat from escaping.

**Inner Layer**
An inner layer of long underwear carries moisture away from the skin.

**Insulating Layer**
A fluffy insulating layer, such as fleece or down, traps pockets of air that are warmed by body heat.

**Outer Layer**
The outer shell layer protects against wind and water. An insulated hood and a face mask protect against wind. Boots and gloves are layered, too. Fleece in boots may be sealed in by a waterproof rubber layer.

**Protective Gear**
Goggles, or sunglasses worn by this man in Antarctica, reduce the glare of sunlight and protect eyes from freezing.

## Sky Watch

It's March 21—the beginning of winter—and you're watching the sun set very, very slowly. It takes 30 hours—more than a day—for the sun to disappear below the horizon. Once it's gone, you won't see sunshine again until September! April and early May aren't completely dark, but there is hardly enough light to cast a shadow. Then it's dark for two months. In August, light begins again. The sky brightens quickly until the polar sunrise.

The tilt of Earth on its axis affects the hours of daylight and darkness from season to season. At the poles, midsummer brings the "midnight sun," which circles around the sky but does not set. Midwinter brings almost total darkness.

Anvers Island in Antarctica

### Math Activity

The table (right) shows hours of daylight on the 15th of each month. It shows readings at two different Antarctic locations—the Amundsen-Scott station and Japan's Mizuho station.

Use the table to make a graph that shows hours of daylight for the Mizuho station and the Amundsen-Scott station.

- On the horizontal axis of the graph, list the months.
- On the vertical axis, mark off spaces for 0 to 24 hours.
- Choose a different color marker for each latitude. Above the month for each location, place a colored dot at the correct hour mark. Connect the dots to show changes in daylight at each place during a year.
- How are the changes in darkness and daylight in Antarctica like those you see at home? How are they different?

**Hours of Daylight in Antarctica***

| Month | Mizuho Station 70° S | Amundsen-Scott Station 90° S |
|---|---|---|
| January | 24 | 24 |
| February | 18 | 24 |
| March | 14 | 24 |
| April | 9 | 0 |
| May | 3 | 0 |
| June | 0 | 0 |
| July | 0 | 0 |
| August | 7 | 0 |
| September | 11 | 0 |
| October | 16 | 24 |
| November | 22 | 24 |
| December | 24 | 24 |

*Sunrise to sunset, rounded to nearest hour

## Alone in Antarctica

Admiral Richard Byrd worked in the Antarctic for nearly 30 years after his flight over the South Pole. He led several expeditions and set up research stations at Little America. Byrd's book *Alone* is based on the journal he kept while spending the winter of 1934 alone at a weather station outpost. During his four-and-a-half-month stay, Byrd nearly gave up mentally and physically. He endured, however, and kept up his weather research until help arrived in August.

In this memoir of his days in early April, 1934, Byrd describes some of the problems of working in the intense cold.

**Admiral Byrd**
In his small shack at Little America, Byrd tries to keep warm.

At times I felt as if I were the last survivor of an Ice Age, striving to hold on with the flimsy tools bequeathed by an easy-going, temperate world. Cold does queer things. At 50° Fahrenheit below zero a flashlight dies out in your hand. At −55° Fahrenheit kerosene will freeze, and the flame will dry up on the wick.

At −60° Fahrenheit rubber turns brittle. One day, I remember, the antenna wire snapped in my hands when I tried to bend it to make a new connection. Below −60° Fahrenheit cold will find the last microscopic touch of oil in an instrument and stop it dead. If there is the slightest breeze, you can hear your breath freeze as it floats away, making a sound like that of Chinese firecrackers. . . . And if you work too hard and breathe too deeply, your lungs will sometimes feel as if they were on fire.

Cold—even April's relatively moderate cold—gave me plenty to think about. . . . Two cases of tomato juice shattered their bottles. Whenever I brought canned food inside the shack I had to let it stand all day near the stove to thaw. . . . Frost was forever collecting on the electrical contact points of the wind vane and wind cups. Some days I climbed the twelve-foot anemometer pole two and three times to clean them. It was a bitter job, especially on blustery nights. With my legs twined around the slender pole, my arms flung over the cleats, and my free hands trying to scrape the contact point clean with a knife and at the same time hold a flashlight to see, I qualified for the world's coldest flagpole sitter. I seldom came down from that pole without a frozen finger, toe, nose, or cheek.

The shack was always freezingly cold in the morning. I slept with the door open [for ventilation]. When I arose the inside temperature (depending upon the surface weather) might be anywhere from 10° to 40° Fahrenheit below zero. Frost coated the sleeping bag where my breath had condensed during the night; my socks and boots, when I picked them up, were so stiff with frozen sweat that I first had to work them between my hands. A pair of silk gloves hung from a nail over the bunk, where I could grab them the first thing. Yet, even with their protection, my fingers would sting and burn from the touch of the lamp and stove as I lighted them.

## Language Arts Activity

From this passage, what can you conclude about Byrd's attitude toward his research? Although you've probably never traveled to Antarctica, you may have had an outdoor adventure—at summer camp or even in a city park. Use descriptive writing to recapture that experience. Remember to include concrete, sensory details like those in Byrd's journal. If you prefer, write about an imaginary event or adventure in the outdoors.

Port Lockroy in Antarctica

## Tie It Together

### Plan a Cool Expedition

You're on your way to Antarctica! Good planning is the key to a successful expedition. Work in small groups to plan your expedition. When your group has finished planning, meet with your class to present your program.

Consider these questions and issues in making your plan:

- What research will you do—weather, wildlife, geology, or another topic?
- Where will you work? Will you work near the coast? Will you join an existing research station?
- Will you travel? Plot your travel course and location on a map of Antarctica.
- How long do you plan to stay?
- What equipment will you take—climbing gear to cross glaciers, boats and kayaks, tents for camping?
- What clothing will you need? Check the illustration of protective clothing.
- What supplies will you take? Plan the kinds and amounts of food that you will take.

**Cold-Weather Clothing**
How are these young people staying warm?

Chapter 19

# Earth, Moon, and Sun

## The BIG Idea

Motion and Forces

**What effects are caused by the motion of Earth and the moon?**

### Chapter Preview

1. **Earth in Space**
   - ***Discover*** What Causes Day and Night?
   - ***Try This*** Sun Shadows
   - ***Active Art*** The Seasons
2. **Gravity and Motion**
   - ***Discover*** Can You Remove the Bottom Penny?
   - ***Analyzing Data*** Gravity Versus Distance
3. **Phases, Eclipses, and Tides**
   - ***Discover*** How Does the Moon Move?
   - ***Active Art*** Phases of the Moon
   - ***Active Art*** Lunar Eclipses
   - ***Skills Activity*** Making Models
   - ***Skills Lab*** A "Moonth" of Phases
4. **Earth's Moon**
   - ***Discover*** Why Do Craters Look Different From Each Other?
5. **Traveling Into Space**
   - ***Discover*** What Force Moves a Balloon?
   - ***Try This*** Be a Rocket Scientist
   - ***Active Art*** Multistage Rocket
   - ***Skills Activity*** Calculating
   - ***Technology Lab*** Design and Build a Water Rocket

This time-lapse photo shows an eclipse of the moon as it rises over the Golden Gate Bridge in San Francisco.

*Earth, Moon, and Sun*
▶ Video Preview
Video Field Trip
Video Assessment

Lab zone™ Chapter **Project**

## Track the Moon

How does the moon move across the sky? How does its appearance change over the course of a month? In this project, you will observe how the position and apparent shape of the moon change over time.

**Your Goal** To observe the shape of the moon and its position in the sky every day for one month

To complete this project, you must

- observe the compass direction in which you see the moon, its phase, and its height above the horizon
- use your observations to explain the phases of the moon
- develop rules you can use to predict when and where you might see the moon each day

**Plan It!** Begin by preparing an observation log. You will record the date and time of each observation, the direction and height of the moon, a sketch of its shape, and notes about cloud cover and other conditions. Observe the moon every clear night, looking for patterns. Make a map of your observation site on which you will plot the direction of the moon. You can measure the moon's height in degrees above the horizon by making a fist and holding it at arm's length. One fist above the horizon is 10°, two fists are 20°, and so on. On at least one day, compare your observations of the moon an hour or two apart.

# Section 1 Earth in Space

## Reading Preview

### Key Concepts

- How does Earth move in space?
- What causes the cycle of seasons on Earth?

### Key Terms

- astronomy
- axis
- rotation
- revolution
- orbit
- solstice
- equinox

### Target Reading Skill

**Using Prior Knowledge** Your prior knowledge is what you already know before you read about a topic. Before you read, write what you know about seasons on Earth in a graphic organizer like the one below. As you read, write in what you learn.

| What You Know |
|---|
| 1. The sun's rays heat Earth.<br>2. |

| What You Learned |
|---|
| 1.<br>2. |

## Lab zone Discover Activity

### What Causes Day and Night?

1. Place a lamp with a bare bulb on a table to represent the sun. Put a globe at the end of the table about 1 meter away to represent Earth.
2. Turn the lamp on and darken the room. Which parts of the globe have light shining on them? Which parts are in shadow?

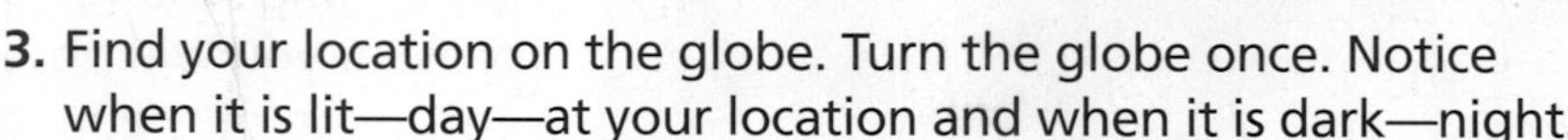

3. Find your location on the globe. Turn the globe once. Notice when it is lit—day—at your location and when it is dark—night.

**Think It Over**

**Making Models** What does one complete turn of the globe represent? In this model, how many seconds represent one day? How could you use the globe and bulb to represent a year?

Each year, ancient Egyptian farmers eagerly awaited the flood of the Nile River. For thousands of years, their planting was ruled by it. As soon as the Nile's floodwaters withdrew, the farmers had to be ready to plow and plant their fields along the river. Therefore, the Egyptians wanted to predict when the flood would occur. Around 3000 B.C., people noticed that the bright star Sirius first became visible in the early morning sky every year shortly before the flood began. The Egyptians used this knowledge to predict each year's flood. The ancient Egyptians were among the first people to study the stars. The study of the moon, stars, and other objects in space is called **astronomy.**

**FIGURE 1**
**Ancient Egyptian Farmers**
Egyptian farmers watched the sky in order to be prepared to plow and plant their fields.

## How Earth Moves

Ancient astronomers studied the movements of the sun and the moon as they appeared to travel across the sky. It seemed to them as though Earth was standing still and the sun and moon were moving. Actually, the sun and moon seem to move across the sky each day because Earth is rotating on its axis. Earth also moves around the sun. **Earth moves through space in two major ways: rotation and revolution.**

**Rotation** The imaginary line that passes through Earth's center and the North and South poles is Earth's **axis.** The spinning of Earth on its axis is called **rotation.**

Earth's rotation causes day and night. As Earth rotates eastward, the sun appears to move westward across the sky. It is day on the side of Earth facing the sun. As Earth continues to turn to the east, the sun appears to set in the west. Sunlight can't reach the side of Earth facing away from the sun, so it is night there. It takes Earth about 24 hours to rotate once. As you know, each 24-hour cycle of day and night is called a day.

**Revolution** In addition to rotating on its axis, Earth travels around the sun. **Revolution** is the movement of one object around another. One complete revolution of Earth around the sun is called a year. Earth follows a path, or **orbit,** as it revolves around the sun. Earth's orbit is not quite circular. It is a slightly elongated circle, or ellipse.

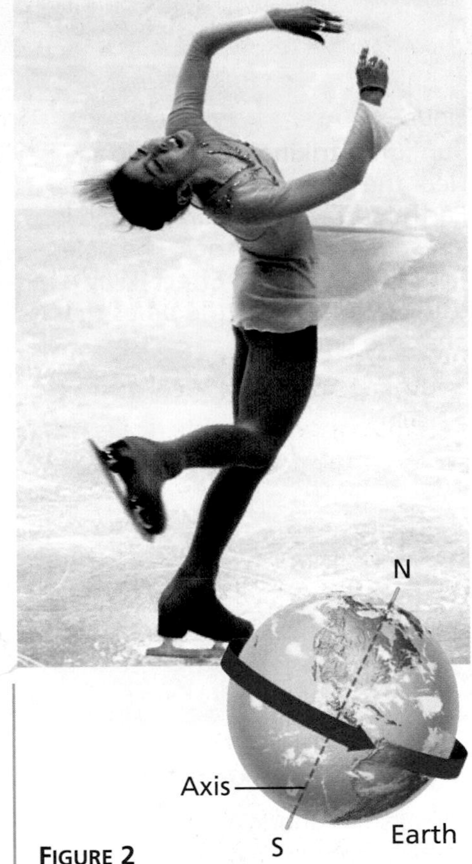


**FIGURE 2**
**Rotation**
The rotation of Earth on its axis is similar to the movement of the figure skater as she spins.

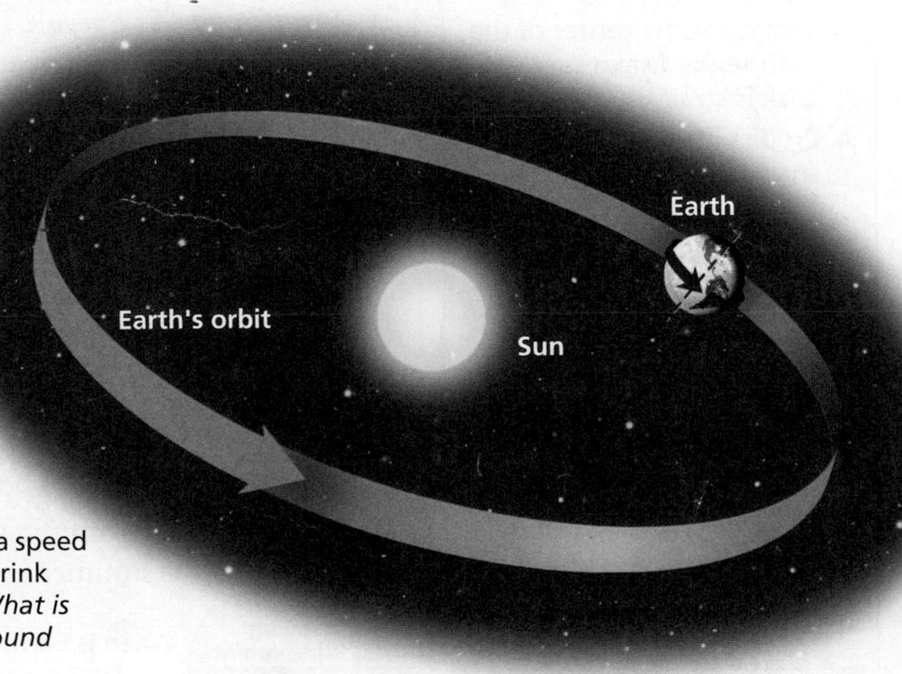


**FIGURE 3**
**Revolution**
Earth revolves around the sun just as a speed skater travels around the center of a rink during a race. **Applying Concepts** *What is one complete revolution of Earth around the sun called?*

**FIGURE 4**
**Sunlight Striking Earth's Surface**
Near the equator, sunlight strikes Earth's surface more directly and is less spread out than near the poles.
**Relating Cause and Effect** *Why is it usually colder near the poles than near the equator?*

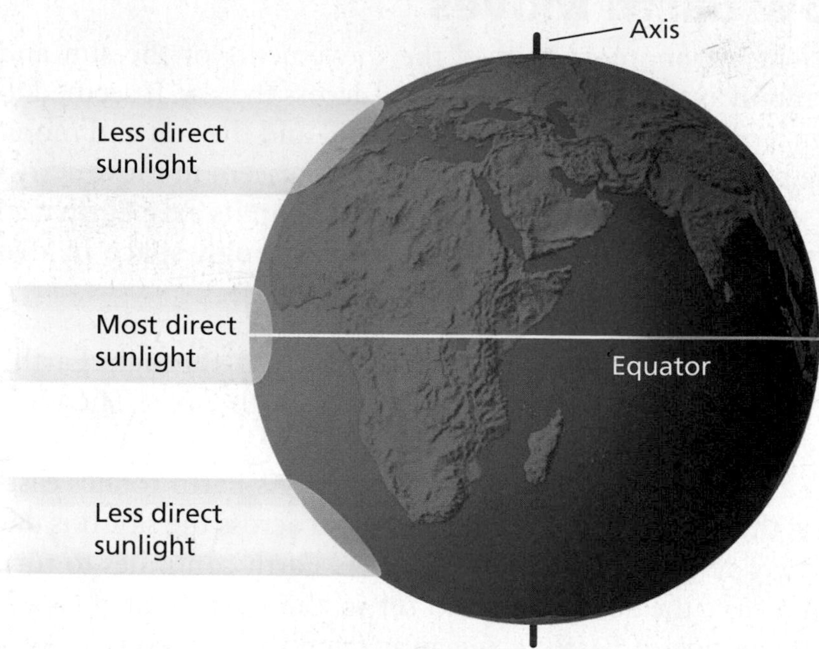


**Lab zone Try This Activity**

### Sun Shadows

The sun's shadow changes predictably through the day.

1. On a sunny day, stand outside in the sun and use a compass to find north.
2. Have your partner place a craft stick about one meter to the north of where you are standing. Repeat for east, south, and west.
3. Insert a meter stick in the ground at the center of the craft sticks. Make sure the stick is straight up.
4. Predict how the sun's shadow will move throughout the day.
5. Record the direction and length of the sun's shadow at noon and at regular intervals during the day.

**Predicting** How did the actual movement of the sun's shadow compare with your prediction? How do you think the direction and length of the sun's shadow at these same times would change over the next six months?

## The Seasons on Earth

Most places outside the tropics and polar regions have four distinct seasons: winter, spring, summer, and autumn. But there are great differences in temperature from place to place. For instance, it is generally warmer near the equator than near the poles. Why is this so?

**How Sunlight Hits Earth** Figure 4 shows how sunlight strikes Earth's surface. Notice that sunlight hits Earth's surface most directly near the equator. Near the poles, sunlight arrives at a steep angle. As a result, it is spread out over a greater area. That is why it is warmer near the equator than near the poles.

**Earth's Tilted Axis** If Earth's axis were straight up and down relative to its orbit, temperatures would remain fairly constant year-round. There would be no seasons. **Earth has seasons because its axis is tilted as it revolves around the sun.**

Notice in Figure 5 that Earth's axis is always tilted at an angle of 23.5° from the vertical. As Earth revolves around the sun, the north end of its axis is tilted away from the sun for part of the year and toward the sun for part of the year.

Summer and winter are caused by Earth's tilt as it revolves around the sun. The change in seasons is not caused by changes in Earth's distance from the sun. In fact, Earth is farthest from the sun when it is summer in the Northern Hemisphere.

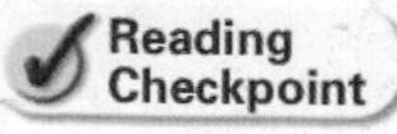

**When is Earth farthest from the sun?**

FIGURE 5

## The Seasons

**The yearly cycle of the seasons is caused by the tilt of Earth's axis as it revolves around the sun.**



**June Solstice**
The north end of Earth's axis is tilted toward the sun. It is summer in the Northern Hemisphere and winter in the Southern Hemisphere.



**March and September Equinoxes**
Neither end of Earth's axis is tilted toward the sun. Both hemispheres receive the same amount of energy.

**December Solstice**
The south end of Earth's axis is tilted toward the sun. It is summer in the Southern Hemisphere and winter in the Northern Hemisphere.

The height of the sun above the horizon varies with the season.
**Interpreting Graphics** *When is the sun at its maximum height in the Northern Hemisphere?*

**June Solstice**

**March and September Equinoxes**

**December Solstice**

FIGURE 6
**Solstices and Equinoxes**

Summer in the Southern Hemisphere (left) occurs at the same time as winter in the Northern Hemisphere (right). Similarly, when it is spring in the Southern Hemisphere, it is fall in the Northern Hemisphere.
**Interpreting Photographs** *In which direction was Earth's axis pointing at the time that each of the photographs was taken?*

**Earth in June** In June, the north end of Earth's axis is tilted toward the sun. In the Northern Hemisphere, the noon sun is high in the sky and there are more hours of daylight than darkness. The combination of direct rays and more hours of sunlight heats the surface more in June than at any other time of the year. It is summer in the Northern Hemisphere.

At the same time south of the equator, the sun's energy is spread over a larger area. The sun is low in the sky and days are shorter than nights. The combination of less direct rays and fewer hours of sunlight heats Earth's surface less than at any other time of the year. It is winter in the Southern Hemisphere.

**Earth in December** In December, people in the Southern Hemisphere receive the most direct sunlight, so it is summer there. At the same time, the sun's rays in the Northern Hemisphere are more slanted and there are fewer hours of daylight. So it is winter in the Northern Hemisphere.

**Solstices** The sun reaches its greatest distance north or south of the equator twice each year. Each of these days, when the sun is farthest north or south of the equator, is known as a **solstice** (SOHL stis). The day when the sun is farthest north of the equator is the summer solstice in the Northern Hemisphere. It is also the winter solstice in the Southern Hemisphere. This solstice occurs around June 21 each year. It is the longest day of the year in the Northern Hemisphere and the shortest day of the year in the Southern Hemisphere.

Similarly, around December 21, the sun is farthest south of the equator. This is the winter solstice in the Northern Hemisphere and the summer solstice in the Southern Hemisphere.

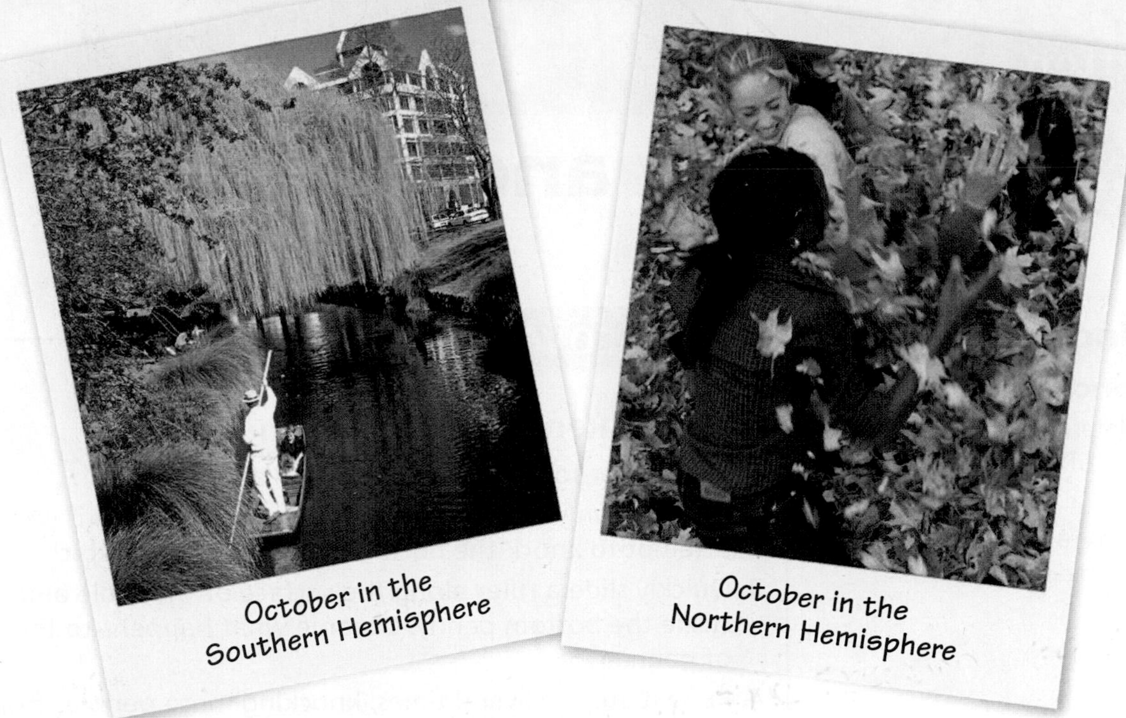
October in the Southern Hemisphere

October in the Northern Hemisphere

**Equinoxes** Halfway between the solstices, neither hemisphere is tilted toward or away from the sun. This occurs twice a year, when the noon sun is directly overhead at the equator. Each of these days is known as an **equinox,** which means "equal night." During an equinox, day and night are each about 12 hours long everywhere on Earth. The vernal (spring) equinox occurs around March 21 and marks the beginning of spring in the Northern Hemisphere. The autumnal equinox occurs around September 22. It marks the beginning of fall in the Northern Hemisphere.

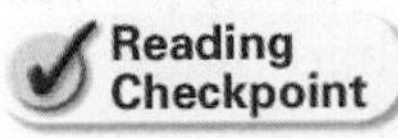

**What is an equinox?**

## Section 1 Assessment

**Target Reading Skill Using Prior Knowledge** Review your graphic organizer and revise it based on what you just learned in this section. Use it to help answer Question 2.

### Reviewing Key Concepts

1. a. **Identifying** What are the two major motions of Earth as it travels through space?
   b. **Explaining** Which motion causes day and night?
2. a. **Relating Cause and Effect** What causes the seasons?
   b. **Comparing and Contrasting** What are solstices and equinoxes? How are they related to the seasons?
   c. **Predicting** How would the seasons be different if Earth were not tilted on its axis?

### Writing in Science

**Descriptive Paragraph** What seasons occur where you live? Write a detailed paragraph describing the changes that take place each season in your region. Explain how seasonal changes in temperature and hours of daylight relate to changes in Earth's position as it moves around the sun.

# 2 Gravity and Motion

## Reading Preview

### Key Concepts

- What determines the strength of the force of gravity between two objects?
- What two factors combine to keep the moon and Earth in orbit?

### Key Terms

- force
- gravity
- law of universal gravitation
- mass
- weight
- inertia
- Newton's first law of motion

### Target Reading Skill

**Asking Questions** Before you read, preview the red headings. In a graphic organizer like the one below, ask a question for each heading. As you read, write answers to your questions.

Gravity

| Question | Answer |
|---|---|
| What is gravity? | Gravity is . . . |
| | |

## Lab zone Discover Activity

### Can You Remove the Bottom Penny?

1. Place 25 or so pennies in a stack on a table.
2. Write down your prediction of what will happen if you attempt to knock the bottom penny out of the stack.
3. Quickly slide a ruler along the surface of the table and strike the bottom penny. Observe what happens to the stack of pennies.
4. Repeat Step 3 several times, knocking more pennies from the bottom of the stack.

**Think It Over**

**Developing Hypotheses** Explain what happened to the stack of pennies as the bottom penny was knocked out of the stack.

Earth revolves around the sun in a nearly circular orbit. The moon orbits Earth in the same way. But what keeps Earth and the moon in orbit? Why don't they just fly off into space?

The first person to answer these questions was the English scientist Isaac Newton. Late in his life, Newton told a story of how watching an apple fall from a tree in 1666 had made him think about the moon's orbit. Newton realized that there must be a force acting between Earth and the moon that kept the moon in orbit. A **force** is a push or a pull. Most everyday forces require objects to be in contact. Newton realized that the force that holds the moon in orbit is different in that it acts over long distances between objects that are not in contact.

## Gravity

Newton hypothesized that the force that pulls an apple to the ground also pulls the moon toward Earth, keeping it in orbit. This force, called **gravity,** attracts all objects toward each other. In Newton's day, most scientists thought that forces on Earth were different from those elsewhere in the universe. Although Newton did not discover gravity, he was the first person to realize that gravity occurs everywhere. Newton's **law of universal gravitation** states that every object in the universe attracts every other object.

The force of gravity is measured in units called newtons, named after Isaac Newton. **The strength of the force of gravity between two objects depends on two factors: the masses of the objects and the distance between them.**

**Gravity, Mass, and Weight** According to the law of universal gravitation, all of the objects around you, including Earth and even this book, are pulling on you, just as you are pulling on them. Why don't you notice a pull between you and the book? Because the strength of gravity depends in part on the masses of each of the objects. **Mass** is the amount of matter in an object.

Because Earth is so massive, it exerts a much greater force on you than this book does. Similarly, Earth exerts a gravitational force on the moon, large enough to keep the moon in orbit. The moon also exerts a gravitational force on Earth, as you will learn later in this chapter when you study the tides.

The force of gravity on an object is known as its **weight**. Unlike mass, which doesn't change, an object's weight can change depending on its location. For example, on the moon you would weigh about one sixth of your weight on Earth. This is because the moon is much less massive than Earth, so the pull of the moon's gravity on you would be far less than that of Earth's gravity.

**Gravity and Distance** The strength of gravity is affected by the distance between two objects as well as their masses. The force of gravity decreases rapidly as distance increases. For example, if the distance between two objects were doubled, the force of gravity between them would decrease to one fourth of its original value.

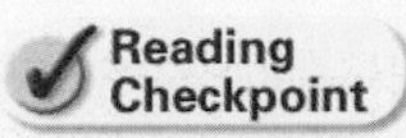

What is an object's weight?

FIGURE 7
**Gravity, Mass, and Distance**
The strength of the force of gravity between two objects depends on their masses and the distance between them.
**Inferring** *How would the force of gravity change if the distance between the objects decreased?*

m m
Gravity attracts all objects toward one another.

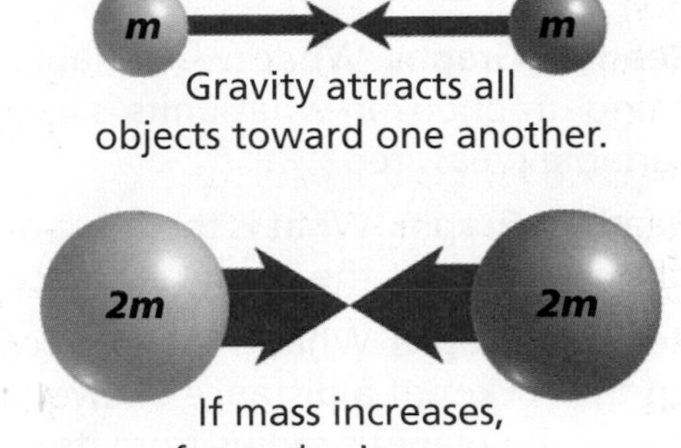


If mass increases, force also increases.

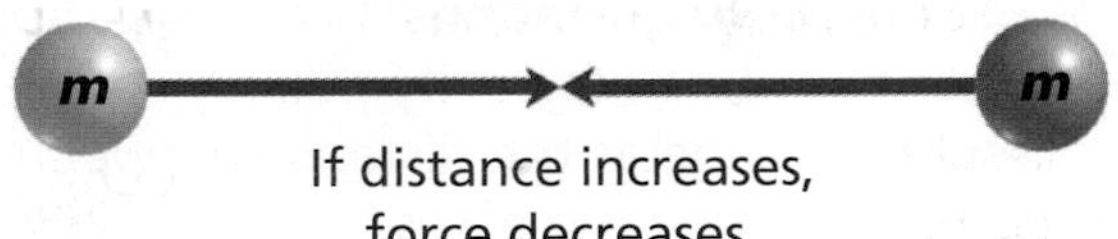


If distance increases, force decreases.

FIGURE 8
**Earth Over the Moon**
The force of gravity holds Earth and the moon together.

## Math Analyzing Data

### Gravity Versus Distance

As a rocket leaves a planet's surface, the force of gravity between the rocket and the planet changes. Use the graph at the right to answer the questions below.

1. **Reading Graphs** What two variables are being graphed? In what units is each variable measured?
2. **Reading Graphs** What is the force of gravity on the rocket at the planet's surface?
3. **Reading Graphs** What is the force of gravity on the rocket at a distance of two units (twice the planet's radius from its center)?
4. **Making Generalizations** In general, how does the force of gravity pulling on the rocket change as the distance between it and the planet increases?

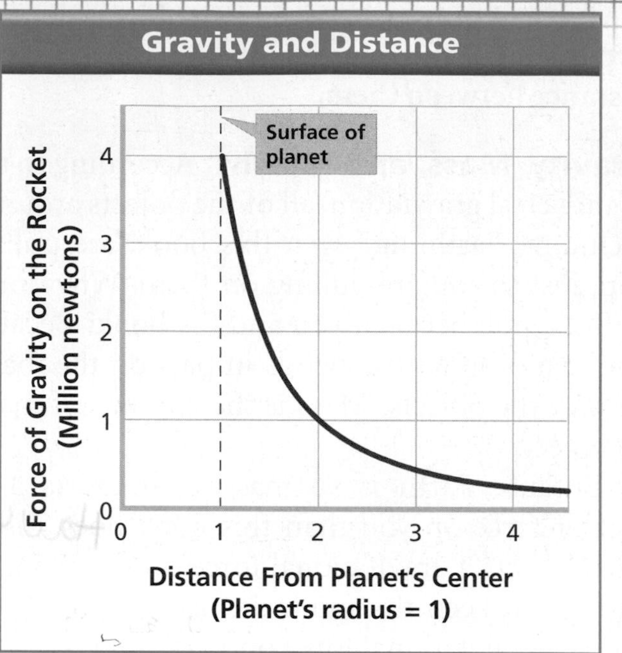


## Inertia and Orbital Motion

If the sun and Earth are constantly pulling on one another because of gravity, why doesn't Earth fall into the sun? Similarly, why doesn't the moon crash into Earth? The fact that such collisions have not occurred shows that there must be another factor at work. That factor is called inertia.

**Inertia** The tendency of an object to resist a change in motion is **inertia.** You feel the effects of inertia every day. When you are riding in a car and it stops suddenly, you keep moving forward. If you didn't have a seat belt on, your inertia could cause you to bump into the car's windshield or the seat in front of you. The more mass an object has, the greater its inertia. An object with greater inertia is more difficult to start or stop.

Isaac Newton stated his ideas about inertia as a scientific law. **Newton's first law of motion** says that an object at rest will stay at rest and an object in motion will stay in motion with a constant speed and direction unless acted on by a force.

**What is inertia?**

**For:** Links on gravity
**Visit:** www.SciLinks.org
**Web Code:** scn-0612

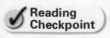

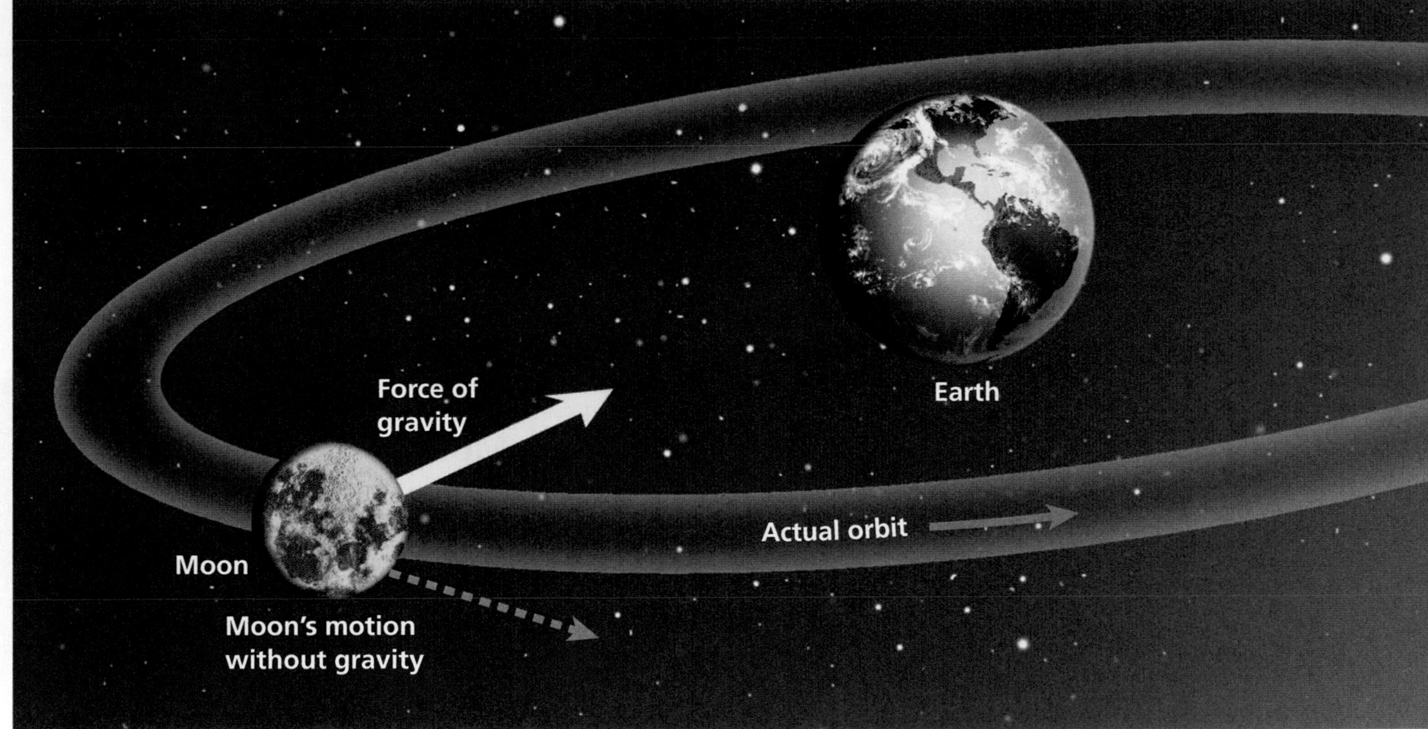


**FIGURE 9**
**Gravity and Inertia**
A combination of gravity and inertia keeps the moon in orbit around Earth. If there were no gravity, inertia would cause the moon to travel in a straight line.
**Interpreting Diagrams** *What would happen to the moon if it were not moving in orbit?*

**Orbital Motion** Why do Earth and the moon remain in their orbits? **Newton concluded that two factors—inertia and gravity—combine to keep Earth in orbit around the sun and the moon in orbit around Earth.**

As shown in Figure 9, Earth's gravity keeps pulling the moon toward it, preventing the moon from moving in a straight line. At the same time, the moon keeps moving ahead because of its inertia. If not for Earth's gravity, inertia would cause the moon to move off through space in a straight line. In the same way, Earth revolves around the sun because the sun's gravity pulls on it while Earth's inertia keeps it moving ahead.

## Section 2 Assessment

**Target Reading Skill Asking Questions** Use your graphic organizer about the headings to help answer the questions below.

### Reviewing Key Concepts

1. a. **Summarizing** What is the law of universal gravitation?
   b. **Reviewing** What two factors determine the force of gravity between two objects?
   c. **Predicting** Suppose the moon were closer to Earth. How would the force of gravity between Earth and the moon be different?
2. a. **Identifying** What two factors act together to keep Earth in orbit around the sun?
   b. **Applying Concepts** Why doesn't Earth simply fall into the sun?
   c. **Predicting** How would Earth move if the sun (including its gravity) suddenly disappeared? Explain your answer.

### Writing in Science

**Cause and Effect Paragraph** Suppose you took a trip to the moon. Write a paragraph describing how and why your weight would change. Would your mass change too?

Section 3

# Phases, Eclipses, and Tides

## Reading Preview

### Key Concepts

- What causes the phases of the moon?
- What are solar and lunar eclipses?
- What causes the tides?

### Key Terms

- phases
- eclipse
- solar eclipse
- umbra
- penumbra
- lunar eclipse
- tide
- spring tide
- neap tide

### Target Reading Skill

**Previewing Visuals** Preview Figure 11. Then write two questions about the diagram of the phases of the moon in a graphic organizer like the one below. As you read, answer your questions.

**Phases of the Moon**

| |
|---|
| Q. Why does the moon have phases? |
| A. |
| Q. |

## Lab zone Discover Activity

### How Does the Moon Move?

1. Place a quarter flat on your desk to represent Earth. Put a penny flat on your desk to represent the moon.
2. One side of the moon always faces Earth. Move the moon through one revolution around Earth, keeping Lincoln's face always looking at Earth. How many times did the penny make one complete rotation?

**Think It Over**

**Inferring** From the point of view of someone on Earth, does the moon seem to rotate? Explain your answer.

When you look up at the moon, you may see what looks like a face. Some people call this "the man in the moon." What you are really seeing is a pattern of light-colored and dark-colored areas on the moon's surface that just happens to look like a face. Oddly, this pattern never seems to move. That is, the same side of the moon, the "near side," always faces Earth. The "far side" of the moon always faces away from Earth. The reason has to do with how the moon moves in space.

## Motions of the Moon

Like Earth, the moon moves through space in two ways. The moon revolves around Earth and also rotates on its own axis.

As the moon revolves around Earth, the relative positions of the moon, Earth, and sun change. **The changing relative positions of the moon, Earth, and sun cause the phases of the moon, eclipses, and tides.**

The moon rotates once on its axis in the same amount of time as it revolves around Earth. Thus, a "day" and a "year" on the moon are the same length. For this reason, the same side of the moon always faces Earth. The length of the moon's day is somewhat shorter than the 29.5 days between consecutive full moons. This is because as Earth revolves around the sun, the moon revolves around Earth.

The same side of the moon always faces Earth.

**FIGURE 10**
**The Moon in Motion**
The moon rotates on its axis and revolves around Earth in the same amount of time. As a result, the near side of the moon (shown with a flag) always faces Earth.
**Interpreting Diagrams** *Would Earth ever appear to set below the horizon for someone standing next to the flag on the moon? Explain.*

## Phases of the Moon

On a clear night when the moon is full, the bright moonlight can keep you awake. But the moon does not produce the light you see. Instead, it reflects light from the sun. Imagine taking a flashlight into a dark room. If you were to shine the flashlight on a chair, you would see the chair because the light from your flashlight would bounce, or reflect, off the chair. In the same way that the chair wouldn't shine by itself, the moon doesn't give off light by itself. You can see the moon because it reflects the light of the sun.

When you see the moon in the sky, sometimes it appears round. Other times you see only a thin sliver, or crescent. The different shapes of the moon you see from Earth are called **phases.** The moon goes through its whole set of phases each time it makes a complete revolution around Earth.

Phases are caused by changes in the relative positions of the moon, Earth, and the sun. Because the sun lights the moon, half the moon is almost always in sunlight. However, since the moon revolves around Earth, you see the moon from different angles. The half of the moon that faces Earth is not always the half that is sunlit. **The phase of the moon you see depends on how much of the sunlit side of the moon faces Earth.**

## The Moon Seen From Earth

**1 New Moon** The sunlit side faces away from Earth.

**2 Waxing Crescent** The portion of the moon you can see is waxing, or growing, into a crescent shape.

**3 First Quarter** You can see half of the sunlit side of the moon.

**4 Waxing Gibbous** The moon continues to wax. The visible shape of the moon is called gibbous.

FIGURE 11
## Phases of the Moon

The photos at the top of the page show how the phases of the moon appear when you look up at the moon from Earth's surface. The circular diagram at the right shows how the Earth and moon would appear to an observer in space as the moon revolves around Earth.
**Interpreting Diagrams** *During what phases are the moon, Earth, and sun aligned in a straight line?*

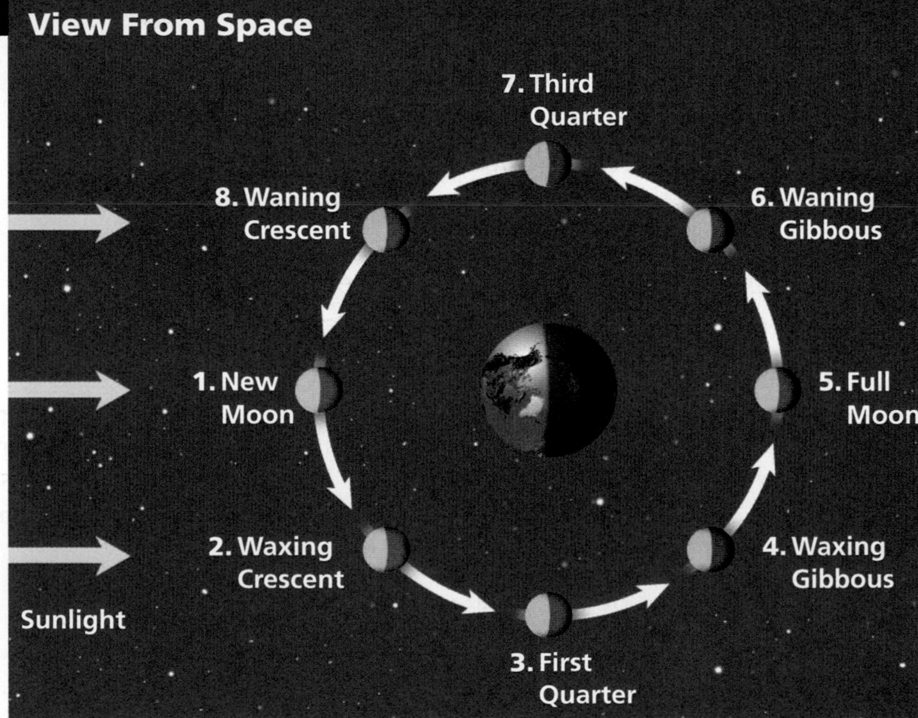

**For:** Moon Phases and Eclipses activity
**Visit:** PHSchool.com
**Web Code:** cfp-5013

**5 Full Moon**
The entire sunlit side faces Earth.

**6 Waning Gibbous**
The portion of the moon you can see wanes, or shrinks.

**7 Third Quarter**
You can see half of the moon's lighted side.

**8 Waning Crescent**
You see a crescent once again.

To understand the phases of the moon, study Figure 11. During the new moon, the side of the moon facing Earth is not lit because the sun is behind the moon. As the moon revolves around Earth, you see more and more of the lighted side of the moon every day, until the side of the moon you see is fully lit. As the moon continues in its orbit, you see less and less of the lighted side. About 29.5 days after the last new moon, the cycle is complete, and a new moon occurs again.

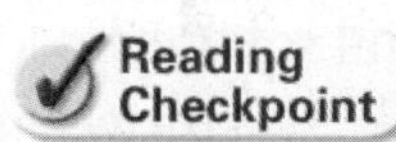

**What is a new moon?**

## Eclipses

As Figure 12 shows, the moon's orbit around Earth is slightly tilted with respect to Earth's orbit around the sun. As a result, in most months the moon revolves around Earth without moving into Earth's shadow or the moon's shadow hitting Earth.

**When the moon's shadow hits Earth or Earth's shadow hits the moon, an eclipse occurs.** When an object in space comes between the sun and a third object, it casts a shadow on that object, causing an **eclipse** (ih KLIPS) to take place. There are two types of eclipses: solar eclipses and lunar eclipses. (The words *solar* and *lunar* come from the Latin words for "sun" and "moon.")

**FIGURE 12**
**The Moon's Orbit**
The moon's orbit is tilted about 5 degrees relative to Earth's orbit around the sun.

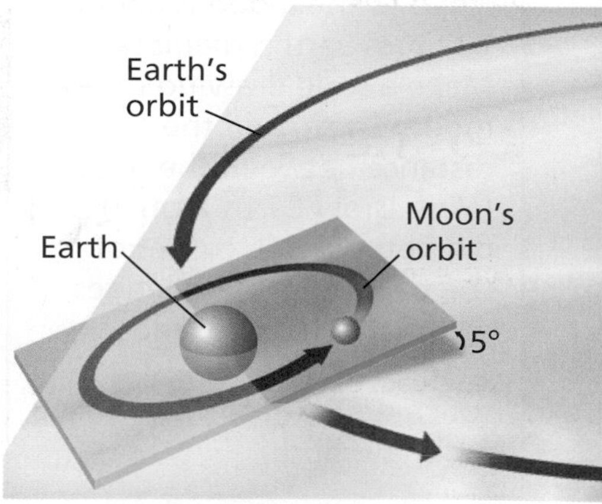

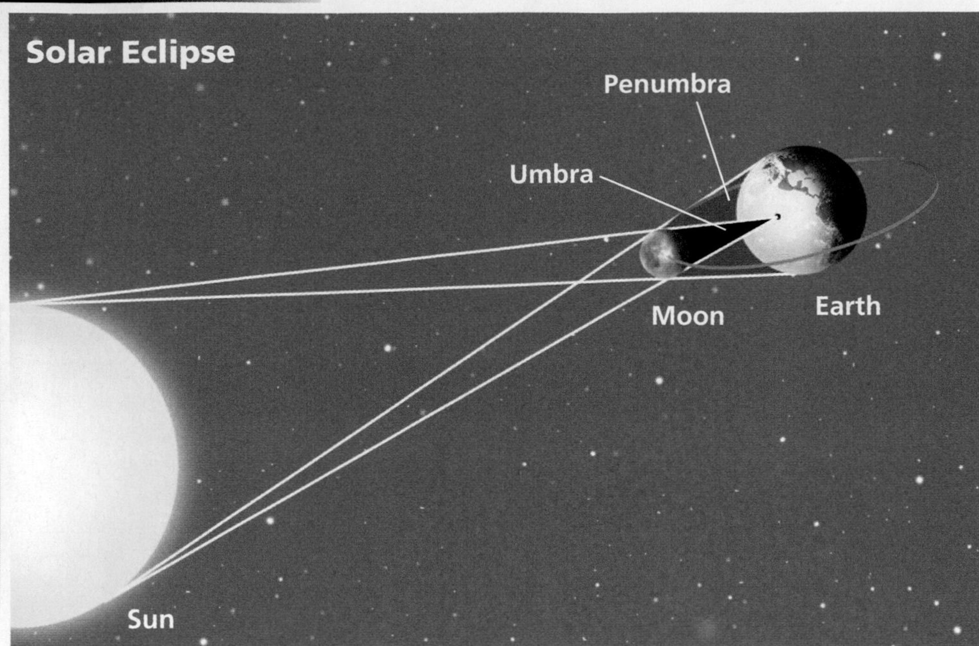


**FIGURE 13**
The outer layer of the sun's atmosphere, the solar corona, is visible surrounding the dark disk of the moon during a solar eclipse. During a solar eclipse, the moon blocks light from the sun, preventing sunlight from reaching parts of Earth's surface.

**When Do Solar Eclipses Occur?** During a new moon, the moon lies between Earth and the sun. But most months, as you have seen, the moon travels a little above or below the sun in the sky. **A solar eclipse occurs when the moon passes directly between Earth and the sun, blocking sunlight from Earth.** The moon's shadow then hits Earth, as shown in Figure 13. So a **solar eclipse** occurs when a new moon blocks your view of the sun.

**Total Solar Eclipses** The very darkest part of the moon's shadow, the **umbra** (UM bruh), is cone-shaped. From any point in the umbra, light from the sun is completely blocked by the moon. The moon's umbra happens to be long enough so that the point of the cone can just reach a small part of Earth's surface. Only the people within the umbra experience a total solar eclipse. During the short period of a total solar eclipse, the sky grows as dark as night, even in the middle of a clear day. The air gets cool and the sky becomes an eerie color. You can see the stars and the solar corona, which is the faint outer atmosphere of the sun.

**Partial Solar Eclipses** In Figure 13, you can see that the moon casts another part of its shadow that is less dark than the umbra. This larger part of the shadow is called the **penumbra** (peh NUM bruh). In the penumbra, part of the sun is visible from Earth. During a solar eclipse, people in the penumbra see only a partial eclipse. Since an extremely bright part of the sun still remains visible, it is not safe to look directly at the sun during a partial solar eclipse (just as you wouldn't look directly at the sun during a normal day).

**Lab zone Skills Activity**

### Making Models

Here is how you can draw a scale model of a solar eclipse. The moon's diameter is about one fourth Earth's diameter. The distance from Earth to the moon is about 30 times Earth's diameter. Make a scale drawing of the moon, Earth, and the distance between them. (*Hint:* Draw Earth 1 cm in diameter in one corner of the paper.) From the edges of the moon, draw and shade in a triangle just touching Earth to show the moon's umbra.

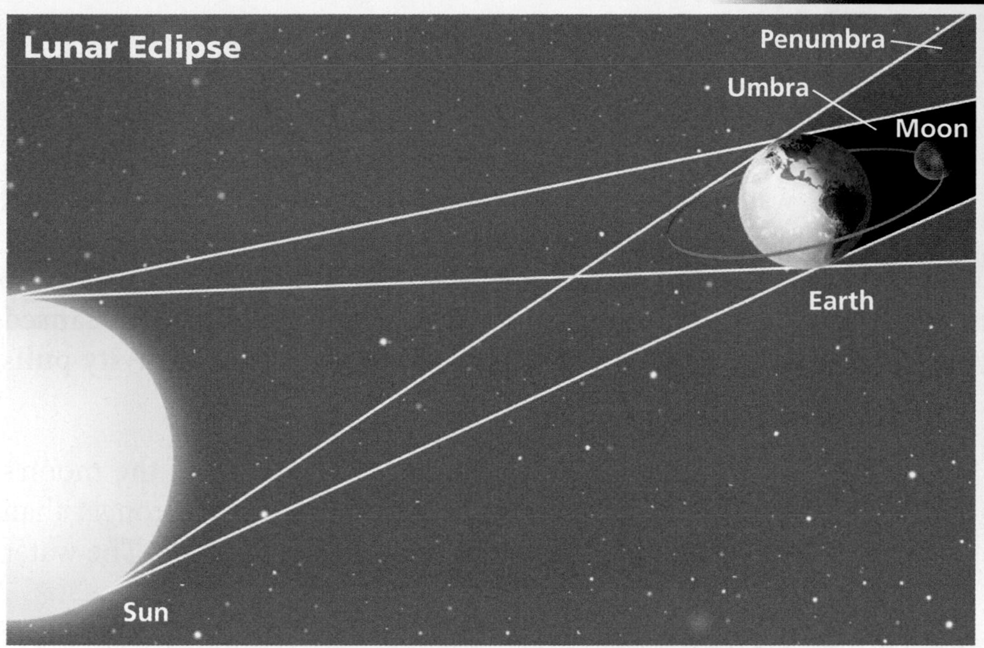

**When Do Lunar Eclipses Occur?** During most months, the moon moves near Earth's shadow but not quite into it. A **lunar eclipse** occurs at a full moon when Earth is directly between the moon and the sun. You can see a lunar eclipse in Figure 14. **During a lunar eclipse, Earth blocks sunlight from reaching the moon.** The moon is then in Earth's shadow and looks dim from Earth. Lunar eclipses occur only when there is a full moon because the moon is closest to Earth's shadow at that time.

**Total Lunar Eclipses** Like the moon's shadow in a solar eclipse, Earth's shadow has an umbra and a penumbra. When the moon is in Earth's umbra, you see a total lunar eclipse. You can see the edge of Earth's shadow on the moon before and after a total lunar eclipse.

Unlike a total solar eclipse, a total lunar eclipse can be seen anywhere on Earth that the moon is visible. So you are more likely to see a total lunar eclipse than a total solar eclipse.

**Partial Lunar Eclipses** For most lunar eclipses, Earth, the moon, and the sun are not quite in line, and only a partial lunar eclipse results. A partial lunar eclipse occurs when the moon passes partly into the umbra of Earth's shadow. The edge of the umbra appears blurry, and you can watch it pass across the moon for two or three hours.

**During which phase of the moon can lunar eclipses occur?**

**FIGURE 14**
During a lunar eclipse, Earth blocks sunlight from reaching the moon's surface. The photo of the moon above was taken during a total lunar eclipse. The moon's reddish tint occurs because Earth's atmosphere bends some sunlight toward the moon.
**Interpreting Diagrams** *What is the difference between the umbra and the penumbra?*

**For:** Moon Phases and Eclipses activity
**Visit:** PHSchool.com
**Web Code:** cfp-5013

High Tide

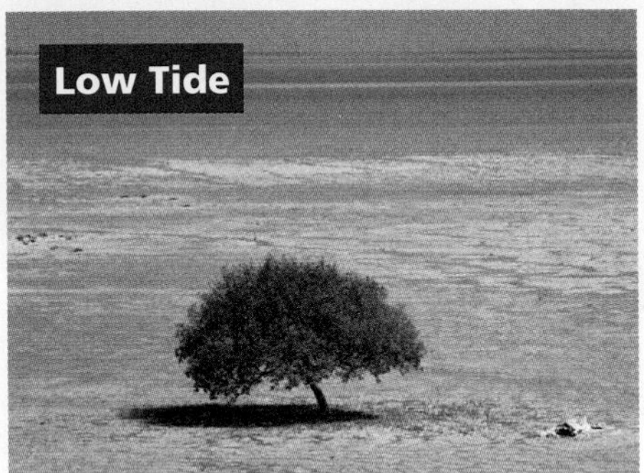
Low Tide

**FIGURE 15**
**High and Low Tides**
In some locations, such as along this beach in Australia, there can be dramatic differences between the height of high and low tides.

## Tides

Have you ever built a sand castle on an ocean beach? Was it washed away by rising water? This is an example of **tides,** the rise and fall of ocean water that occurs every 12.5 hours or so. The water rises for about six hours, then falls for about six hours, in a regular cycle.

The force of gravity pulls the moon and Earth (including the water on Earth's surface) toward each other. **Tides are caused mainly by differences in how much the moon's gravity pulls on different parts of Earth.**

**The Tide Cycle** Look at Figure 16. The force of the moon's gravity at point A, which is closer to the moon, is stronger than the force of the moon's gravity on Earth as a whole. The water flows toward point A, and a high tide forms.

The force of the moon's gravity at point C, which is on the far side of Earth from the moon, is weaker than the force of the moon's gravity on Earth as a whole. Earth is pulled toward the moon more strongly than the water at point C, so the water is "left behind." Water flows toward point C, and a high tide occurs there too. Between points A and C, water flows away from points B and D, causing low tides.

At any one time there are two places with high tides and two places with low tides on Earth. As Earth rotates, one high tide stays on the side of Earth facing the moon. The second high tide stays on the opposite side of Earth. Each location on Earth sweeps through those two high tides and two low tides every 25 hours or so.

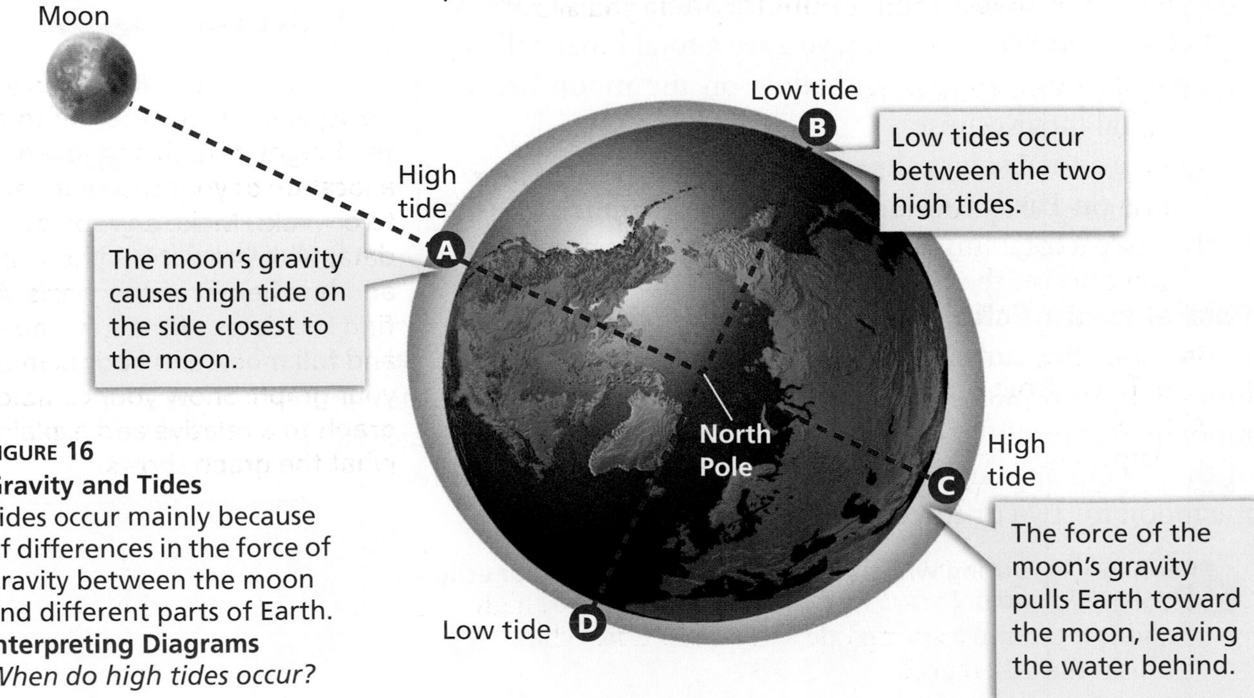
Moon
Low tide
B
Low tides occur between the two high tides.
High tide
A
The moon's gravity causes high tide on the side closest to the moon.
North Pole
High tide
C
The force of the moon's gravity pulls Earth toward the moon, leaving the water behind.
Low tide
D

**FIGURE 16**
**Gravity and Tides**
Tides occur mainly because of differences in the force of gravity between the moon and different parts of Earth.
**Interpreting Diagrams**
*When do high tides occur?*

**Spring Tides** The sun's gravity also pulls on Earth's waters. As shown in the top diagram of Figure 17, the sun, moon, and Earth are nearly in a line during a new moon. The gravity of the sun and the moon pull in the same direction. Their combined forces produce a tide with the greatest difference between consecutive low and high tides, called a **spring tide.**

At full moon, the moon and the sun are on opposite sides of Earth. Since there are high tides on both sides of Earth, a spring tide is also produced. It doesn't matter in which order the sun, Earth, and moon line up. Spring tides occur twice a month, at new moon and at full moon.

**Neap Tides** During the moon's first-quarter and third-quarter phases, the line between Earth and the sun is at right angles to the line between Earth and the moon. The sun's pull is at right angles to the moon's pull. This arrangement produces a **neap tide,** a tide with the least difference between consecutive low and high tides. Neap tides occur twice a month.

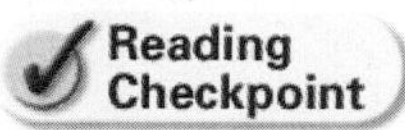

**What is a neap tide?**

**FIGURE 17**
**Spring and Neap Tides**
When Earth, the sun, and the moon are in a straight line (top), a spring tide occurs. When the moon is at a right angle to the sun (bottom), a neap tide occurs.

**Spring Tide**

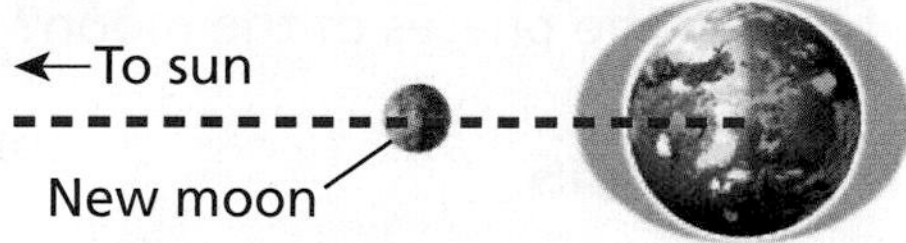


**Neap Tide**

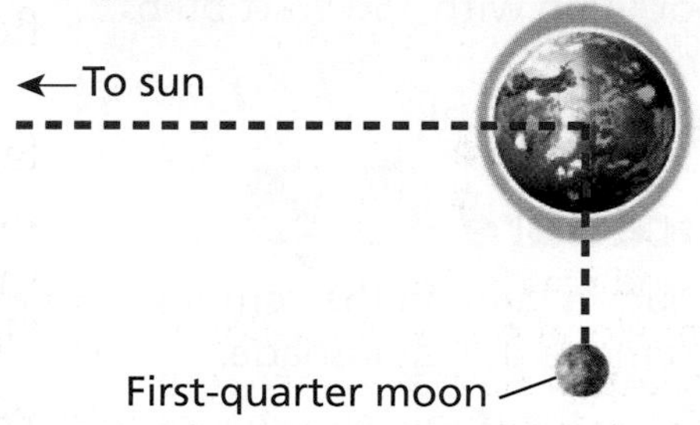


## Section 3 Assessment

**Target Reading Skill Previewing Visuals** Refer to your questions and answers about Figure 11 to help you answer Question 1 below.

### Reviewing Key Concepts

1. a. **Explaining** What causes the moon to shine?
   b. **Relating Cause and Effect** Why does the moon appear to change shape during the course of a month?
   c. **Interpreting Diagrams** Use Figure 11 to explain why you can't see the moon at the time of a new moon.
2. a. **Explaining** What is an eclipse?
   b. **Comparing and Contrasting** How is a solar eclipse different from a lunar eclipse?
   c. **Relating Cause and Effect** Why isn't there a solar eclipse and a lunar eclipse each month?
3. a. **Summarizing** What causes the tides?
   b. **Explaining** Explain why most coastal regions have two high tides and two low tides each day.
   c. **Comparing and Contrasting** Compare the size of high and low tides in a spring tide and a neap tide. What causes the difference?

**Lab zone At-Home Activity**

**Tracking the Tides** Use a daily newspaper or the Internet to track the height of high and low tides at a location of your choice for at least two weeks. Make a graph of your data, with the date as the *x*-axis and tide height as the *y*-axis. Also find the dates of the new moon and full moon and add them to your graph. Show your completed graph to a relative and explain what the graph shows.

Lab zone **Skills Lab**

# A "Moonth" of Phases

## Problem

What causes the phases of the moon?

## Skills Focus

making models, observing, drawing conclusions

## Materials

- floor lamp with 150-watt bulb
- pencils
- plastic foam balls

## Procedure  

1. Place a lamp in the center of the room. Remove the lampshade.
2. Close the doors and shades to darken the room, and switch on the lamp.
3. Carefully stick the point of a pencil into the plastic foam ball so that the pencil can be used as a "handle."
4. Draw 8 circles on a sheet of paper. Number them 1–8.
5. Have your partner hold the plastic foam ball at arm's length in front and slightly above his or her head so that the ball is between him or her and the lamp. **CAUTION:** *Do not look directly at the bulb.*
6. The ball should be about 1 to 1.5 m away from the lamp. Adjust the distance between the ball and the lamp so that the light shines brightly on the ball.
7. Stand directly behind your partner and observe what part of the ball facing you is lit by the lamp. If light is visible on the ball, draw the shape of the lighted part of the ball in the first circle.
8. Have your partner turn 45° to the left while keeping the ball in front and at arm's length.
9. Repeat Step 7. Be sure you are standing directly behind your partner.
10. Repeat Steps 8 and 9 six more times until your partner is facing the lamp again. See the photograph for the 8 positions.
11. Change places and repeat Steps 4–10.

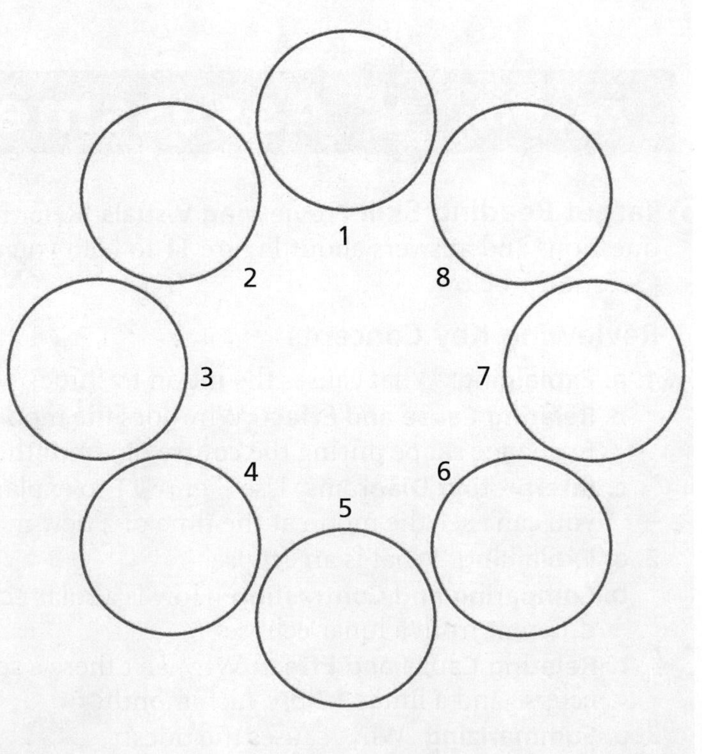

## Analyze and Conclude

1. **Making Models** In your model, what represents Earth? The sun? The moon?
2. **Observing** Refer back to your 8 circles. How much of the lighted part of the ball did you see when facing the lamp?
3. **Classifying** Label your drawings with the names of the phases of the moon. Which drawing represents a full moon? A new moon? Which represents a waxing crescent? A waning crescent?
4. **Observing** How much of the lighted part of the ball did you see after each turn?
5. **Drawing Conclusions** Whether you could see it or not, how much of the ball's surface was always lit by the lamp? Was the darkness of the new moon caused by an eclipse? Explain your answer.
6. **Communicating** Write a brief analysis of this lab. How well did making a model help you understand the phases of the moon? What are some disadvantages of using models? What is another way to make a model to represent the various phases of the moon?

## More to Explore

Design a model to show a lunar eclipse and a solar eclipse. What objects would you use for Earth, the sun, and the moon? Use the model to demonstrate why there isn't an eclipse every full moon and new moon.

# Earth's Moon

## Reading Preview

### Key Concepts

- What features are found on the moon's surface?
- What are some characteristics of the moon?
- How did the moon form?

### Key Terms

- telescope
- maria
- craters
- meteoroids

### Target Reading Skill

**Identifying Main Ideas** As you read "The Moon's Surface," write the main idea—the biggest or most important idea—in a graphic organizer like the one below. Then write three supporting details that further explain the main idea.

**Main Idea**

The moon's surface has a variety of features, such as . . .

**Detail** **Detail** **Detail**

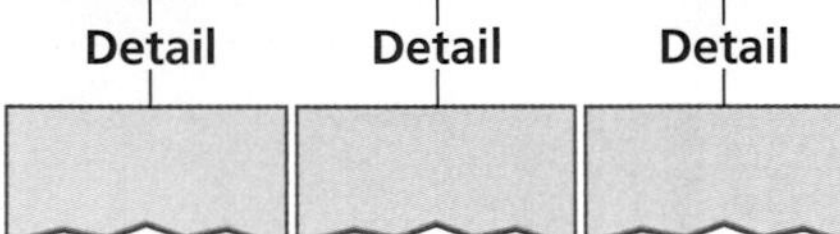

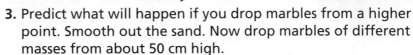

## Lab zone Discover Activity

### Why Do Craters Look Different From Each Other?

The moon's surface has pits in it, called craters.

1. Put on your goggles. Fill a large plastic basin to a depth of 2 cm with sand.
2. Drop marbles of different masses from about 20 cm high. Take the marbles out and view the craters they created.
3. Predict what will happen if you drop marbles from a higher point. Smooth out the sand. Now drop marbles of different masses from about 50 cm high.
4. Take the marbles out and view the craters they left.

**Think It Over**

**Developing Hypotheses** In which step do you think the marbles were moving faster when they hit the sand? If objects hitting the moon caused craters, how did the speeds of the objects affect the sizes of the craters? How did the masses of the objects affect the sizes of the craters?

For thousands of years, people could see shapes on the surface of the moon, but didn't know what caused them. The ancient Greeks thought that the moon was perfectly smooth. It was not until about 400 years ago that scientists could study the moon more closely.

In 1609, the Italian scientist Galileo Galilei heard about a **telescope,** a device built to observe distant objects by making them appear closer. Galileo soon made his own telescope by putting two lenses in a wooden tube. The lenses focused the light coming through the tube, making distant objects seem closer. When Galileo pointed his telescope at the moon, he was able to see much more detail than anyone had ever seen before. What Galileo saw astounded him. Instead of the perfect sphere imagined by the Greeks, he saw that the moon has an irregular surface with a variety of remarkable features.

Galileo used a telescope to help make this drawing of the moon.

The dark, flat areas on the moon's surface are called maria.

The light-colored features that cover much of the moon's surface are highlands.

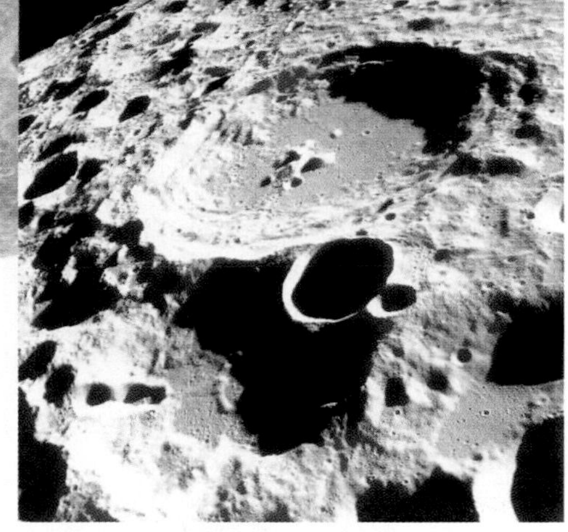

**FIGURE 18**
**The Moon's Surface**
The moon's surface is covered by craters, maria, and highlands. Craters on the moon formed from the impact of meteoroids. Most large craters are named after famous scientists or philosophers.
**Observing** *What are the light regions in the top photograph called?*

## The Moon's Surface

Recent photos of the moon show much more detail than Galileo could see with his telescope. **Features on the moon's surface include maria, craters, and highlands.**

**Maria** The moon's surface has dark, flat areas, which Galileo called **maria** (MAH ree uh), the Latin word for "seas." Galileo incorrectly thought that the maria were oceans. The maria are actually hardened rock formed from huge lava flows that occurred between 3 and 4 billion years ago.

**Craters** Galileo saw that the moon's surface is marked by large round pits called **craters.** Some craters are hundreds of kilometers across. For a long time, many scientists mistakenly thought that these craters had been made by volcanoes. Scientists now know that these craters were caused by the impacts of **meteoroids,** chunks of rock or dust from space.

The maria have few craters compared to surrounding areas. This means that most of the moon's craters formed from impacts early in its history, before the maria formed. On Earth, such ancient craters have disappeared. They were worn away over time by water, wind, and other forces. But since the moon has no liquid water or atmosphere, its surface has changed little for billions of years.

**Highlands** Galileo correctly inferred that some of the light-colored features he saw on the moon's surface were highlands, or mountains. The peaks of the lunar highlands and the rims of the craters cast dark shadows, which Galileo could see. The rugged lunar highlands cover much of the moon's surface.

What are maria?

**For:** Links on Earth's moon
**Visit:** www.SciLinks.org
**Web Code:** scn-0614

## Characteristics of the Moon

Would you want to take a vacation on the moon? At an average distance of about 384,000 kilometers (about 30 times Earth's diameter), the moon is Earth's closest neighbor in space. Despite its proximity, the moon is very different from Earth. **The moon is dry and airless. Compared to Earth, the moon is small and has large variations in its surface temperature.** If you visited the moon, you would need to wear a bulky space suit to provide air to breathe, protect against sunburn, and to keep you at a comfortable temperature.

**FIGURE 19**
**The Moon's Size**
The diameter of the moon is a little less than the distance across the contiguous United States.
**Calculating** *What is the ratio of the moon's diameter to the distance between Earth and the moon?*

**Size and Density** The moon is 3,476 kilometers in diameter, a little less than the distance across the United States. This is about one-fourth Earth's diameter. However, the moon has only one-eightieth as much mass as Earth. Though Earth has a very dense core, its outer layers are less dense. The moon's average density is similar to the density of Earth's outer layers.

**Temperature and Atmosphere** On the moon's surface, temperatures range from a torrid 130°C in direct sunlight to a frigid –180°C at night. Temperatures on the moon vary so much because it has no atmosphere. The moon's surface gravity is so weak that gases can easily escape into space.

**Water** The moon has no liquid water. However, there is evidence that there may be large patches of ice near the moon's poles. Some areas are shielded from sunlight by crater walls. Temperatures in these regions are so low that ice there would remain frozen. If a colony were built on the moon in the future, any such water would be very valuable. It would be very expensive to transport large amounts of water to the moon from Earth.

**Reading Checkpoint** **Where on the moon is there evidence of the existence of ice?**

**FIGURE 20**
**The Moon's Surface**
This photo of a large boulder field and hills on the moon's surface was taken by one of the crew members of *Apollo 17.*

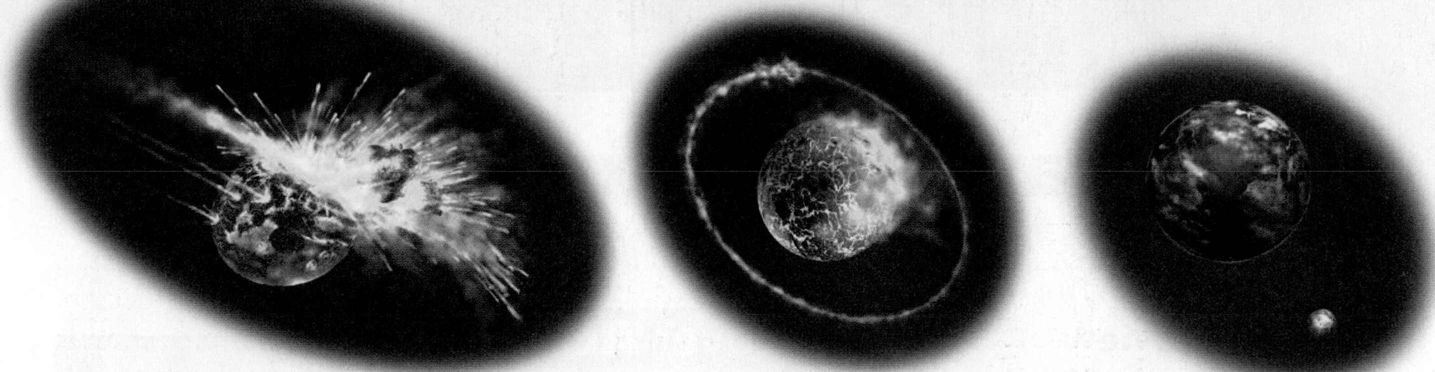

## The Origin of the Moon

People have long wondered how the moon formed. Scientists have suggested many possible theories. For example, was the moon formed elsewhere in the solar system and captured by Earth's gravity as it came near? Was the moon formed near Earth at the same time that Earth formed? Scientists have found reasons to reject these ideas.

The theory of the moon's origin that seems to best fit the evidence is called the collision-ring theory. It is illustrated in Figure 21. About 4.5 billion years ago, when Earth was very young, the solar system was full of rocky debris. Some of this debris was the size of small planets. **Scientists theorize that a planet-sized object collided with Earth to form the moon.** Material from the object and Earth's outer layers was ejected into orbit around Earth, where it formed a ring. Gravity caused this material to combine to form the moon.

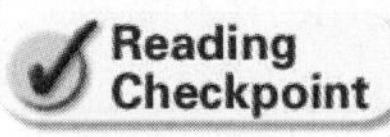


**What theory best explains the moon's origin?**

**FIGURE 21**
**Formation of the Moon**
According to the collision-ring theory, the moon formed early in Earth's history when a planet-sized object struck Earth. The resulting debris formed the moon.

## Section 4 Assessment

**Target Reading Skill Identifying Main Ideas** Use your graphic organizer to help you answer Question 1 below.

### Reviewing Key Concepts

1. a. **Identifying** Name three major features of the moon's surface.
   b. **Explaining** How did the moon's craters form?
   c. **Relating Cause and Effect** Why is the moon's surface much more heavily cratered than Earth's surface?
2. a. **Describing** Describe the range of temperatures on the moon.
   b. **Comparing and Contrasting** Compare Earth and the moon in terms of size and surface gravity.
   c. **Relating Cause and Effect** What is the relationship between the moon's surface gravity, lack of an atmosphere, and temperature range?
3. a. **Describing** What was the solar system like when the moon formed?
   b. **Sequencing** Explain the various stages in the formation of the moon.

### Lab zone At-Home Activity

**Moonwatching** With an adult, observe the moon a few days after the first-quarter phase. Make a sketch of the features you see. Label the maria, craters, and highlands.

Section 5

# Traveling Into Space

## Reading Preview

### Key Concepts

- How does a rocket work?
- What is the main advantage of a multistage rocket?
- What was the space race, and what were the major events in the human exploration of the moon?
- What are the roles of space shuttles, space stations, and space probes?

### Key Terms

- rocket • thrust
- velocity • orbital velocity
- escape velocity • satellite
- space shuttle • space station
- space probe • rover

### Target Reading Skill

**Building Vocabulary** Carefully read the definition of each key term. Also read the neighboring sentences. Then write a definition of each key term in your own words.

## Lab zone Discover Activity

### What Force Moves a Balloon?

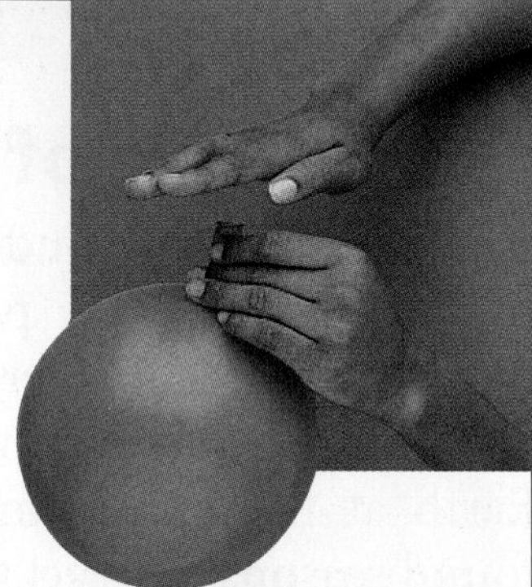

1. Put on your goggles. Blow up a balloon and hold its neck closed with your fingers.
2. Point the far end of the balloon in a direction where there are no people. Put your free hand behind the balloon's neck, so you will be able to feel the force of the air from the balloon on your hand. Let go of the balloon. Observe what happens.
3. Repeat Steps 1 and 2 without your free hand behind the neck of the balloon.

**Think It Over**

**Inferring** What happened when you let go of the balloon? Which direction did the balloon move in comparison to the direction the air moved out of the balloon? What force do you think caused the balloon to move in that direction? Did the position of your free hand affect the balloon's movement?

You have probably seen a colorful fireworks display on the Fourth of July. As the fireworks moved skyward, you may have noticed a fiery gas rushing out of the tail end. Fireworks are actually rockets. A **rocket** is a device that expels gas in one direction to move in the opposite direction. The first rockets were made in China in the 1100s. These early rockets were very simple—they were arrows coated with a flammable powder that were lighted and shot with bows. By about 1200, the Chinese were using gunpowder inside their rockets.

Modern rockets were first developed in the early 1900s. The Russian physicist Konstantin Tsiolkovsky first described how rockets work and proposed designs for advanced rockets. The American physicist Robert Goddard went a step further and built rockets to test his designs.

Rocket design made major advances during World War II. The Germans used a rocket called the V2 to destroy both military and civilian targets. The designer of the V2, Wernher von Braun, came to the United States after the war. Von Braun later designed rockets used in the United States space program.

## How Do Rockets Work?

A rocket works in much the same way as a balloon that is propelled through the air by releasing gas. In most rockets, fuel is burned to make hot gas. The gas pushes outward in every direction, but it can leave the rocket only through openings at the back. The movement of gas out of these openings moves the rocket forward. **A rocket moves forward when gases shooting out the back of the rocket push it in the opposite direction.**

**Action and Reaction Forces** The movement of a rocket demonstrates a basic law of physics: For every force, or action, there is an equal and opposite force, or reaction. The force of the air moving out of a balloon is an action force. An equal force—the reaction force—pushes the balloon forward.

The reaction force that propels a rocket forward is called **thrust.** The amount of thrust depends on several factors, including the mass and speed of the gases propelled out of the rocket. The greater the thrust, the greater a rocket's velocity. **Velocity** is speed in a given direction.

**Orbital and Escape Velocity** In order to lift off the ground, a rocket must have more upward thrust than the downward force of gravity. Once a rocket is off the ground, it must reach a certain velocity in order to go into orbit. **Orbital velocity** is the velocity a rocket must achieve to establish an orbit around Earth. If the rocket moves slower than orbital velocity, Earth's gravity will cause it to fall back to the surface. If the rocket has a velocity of 40,200 km/h or more, it can escape Earth's gravity and fly off into space. **Escape velocity** is the velocity a rocket must reach to fly beyond a planet's gravitational pull.

### Lab zone Try This **Activity**

### Be a Rocket Scientist

You can build a rocket.

1. Use a plastic or paper cup as the rocket body. Cut out a paper nose cone. Tape it to the bottom of the cup.
2. Obtain an empty film canister with a lid that snaps on inside the canister. Go outside to do Steps 3–5.
3. Fill the canister about one-quarter full with water.
4. Put on your goggles. Now add half of a fizzing antacid tablet to the film canister and quickly snap on the lid.
5. Place the canister on the ground with the lid down. Place your rocket over the canister and stand back.

**Observing** What action happened inside the film canister? What was the reaction of the rocket?

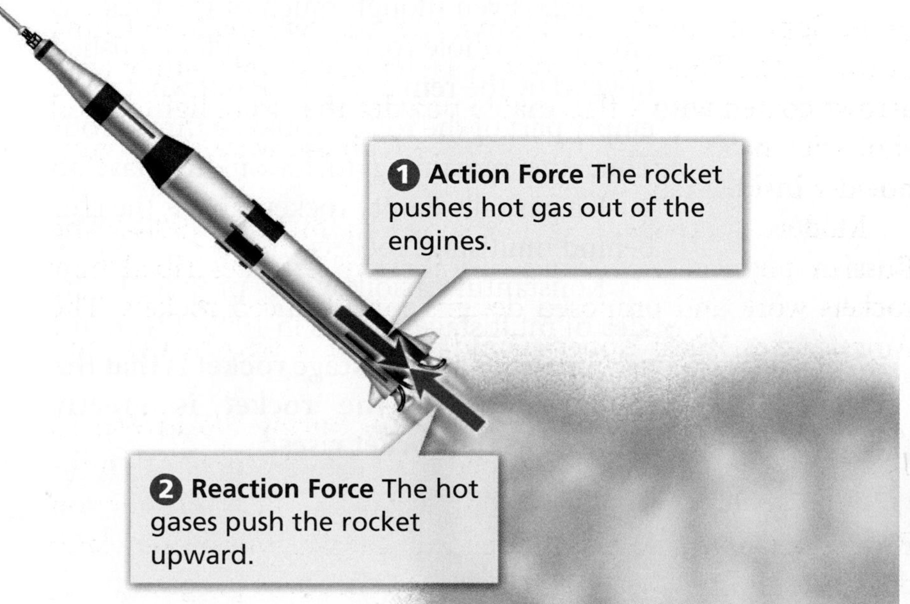

1 **Action Force** The rocket pushes hot gas out of the engines.
2 **Reaction Force** The hot gases push the rocket upward.


FIGURE 22
**Rocket Action and Reaction**
The force of gas propelled out of the back of a rocket (action) produces an opposing force (reaction) that propels the rocket forward.
**Interpreting Diagrams** *How can a rocket rise from the ground into space?*

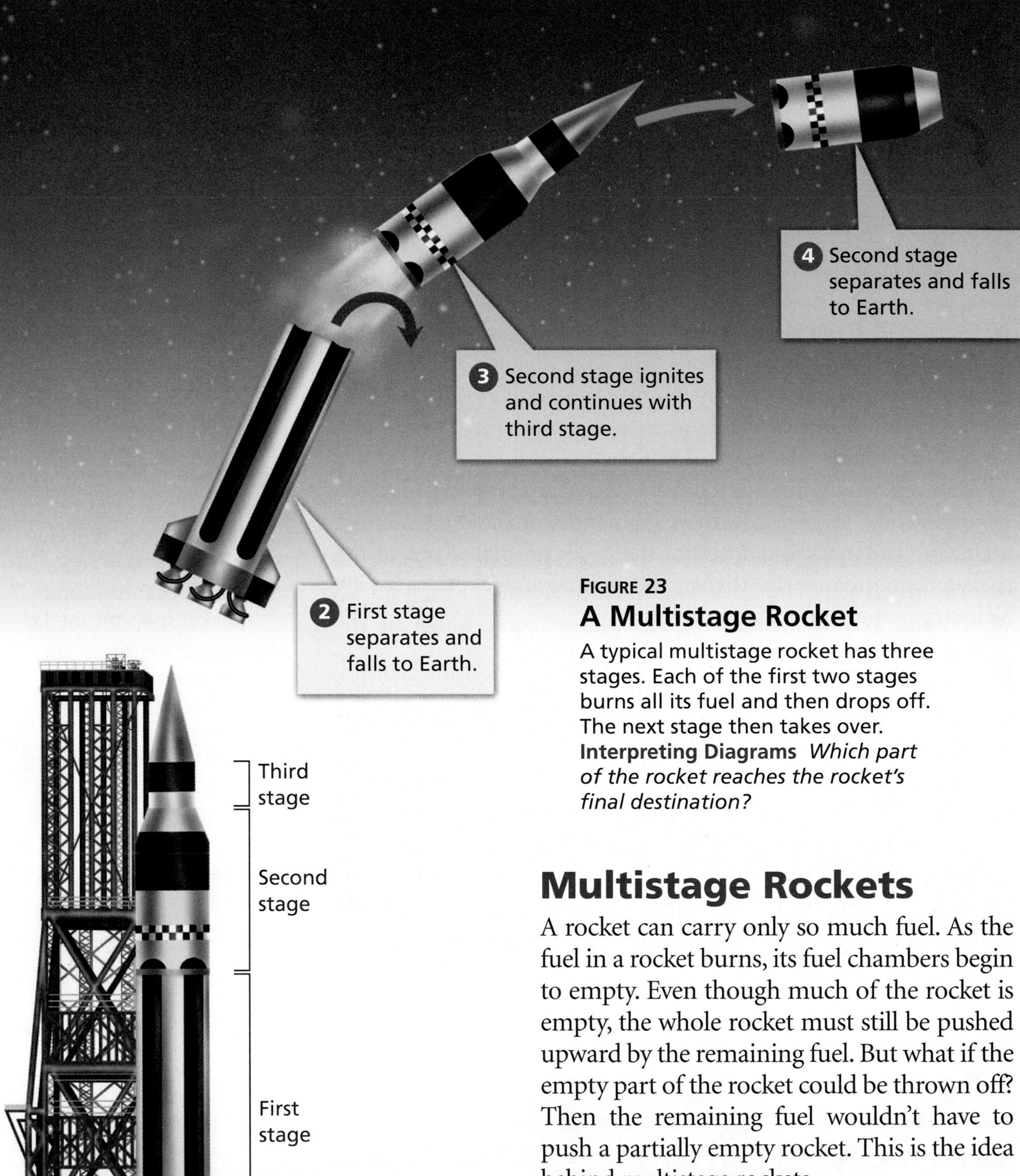
4 Second stage separates and falls to Earth.
3 Second stage ignites and continues with third stage.
2 First stage separates and falls to Earth.
Third stage
Second stage
First stage
1 Heavy first stage provides thrust for launch.

FIGURE 23
### A Multistage Rocket
A typical multistage rocket has three stages. Each of the first two stages burns all its fuel and then drops off. The next stage then takes over.
**Interpreting Diagrams** *Which part of the rocket reaches the rocket's final destination?*

## Multistage Rockets

A rocket can carry only so much fuel. As the fuel in a rocket burns, its fuel chambers begin to empty. Even though much of the rocket is empty, the whole rocket must still be pushed upward by the remaining fuel. But what if the empty part of the rocket could be thrown off? Then the remaining fuel wouldn't have to push a partially empty rocket. This is the idea behind multistage rockets.

Konstantin Tsiolkovsky proposed the idea of multistage rockets in 1903. **The main advantage of a multistage rocket is that the total weight of the rocket is greatly reduced as the rocket rises.**

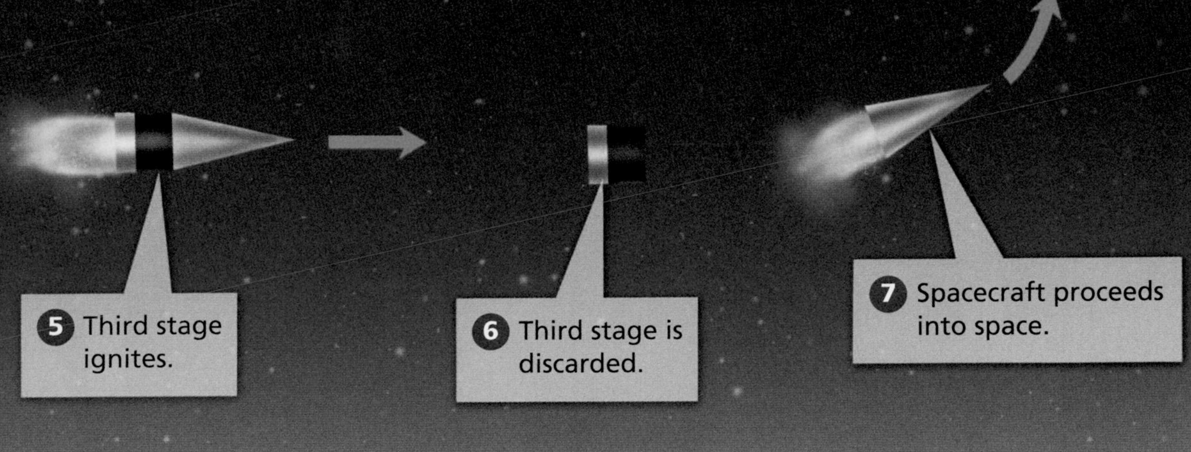

For: Multistage Rocket activity
Visit: PHSchool.com
Web Code: cfp-5021

In a multistage rocket, smaller rockets, or stages, are placed one on top of the other and then fired in succession. Figure 23 shows how a multistage rocket works. As each stage of the rocket uses up its fuel, the empty fuel container falls away. The next stage then ignites and continues powering the rocket toward its destination. At the end, there is just a single stage left, the very top of the rocket.

In the 1960s, the development of powerful multistage rockets such as the *Saturn V* made it possible to send spacecraft to the moon and the solar system beyond. The mighty *Saturn V* rocket stood 111 meters tall—higher than the length of a football field. It was by far the most powerful rocket ever built. Today, multistage rockets are used to launch a wide variety of satellites and space probes.

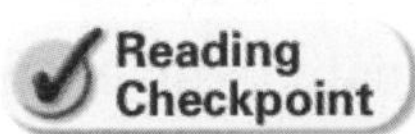

**What is a multistage rocket?**

## The Race for Space

In the 1950s, the United States and the Soviet Union began to compete in the exploration of space. At that time, the Soviet Union was the greatest rival to the United States in politics and military power. The tensions between the two countries were so high that they were said to be in a "cold war." These tensions increased in 1957 when the Soviets launched a satellite, *Sputnik I,* into orbit. The United States responded by speeding up its own space program. **The rivalry between the United States and the Soviet Union over the exploration of space was known as the "space race."**

**FIGURE 24**
**John Glenn**
*Friendship 7* lifted off from Cape Canaveral, Florida, in February 1962. It carried astronaut John Glenn, the first American to orbit Earth. The closeup photo shows Glenn climbing into the *Friendship 7* space capsule.
**Observing** *Where on the rocket was the space capsule located?*

**The First Artificial Satellites** A **satellite** is an object that revolves around another object in space. The moon is a natural satellite of Earth. A spacecraft orbiting Earth is an artificial satellite. *Sputnik I* was the first artificial satellite. This success by the Soviets caused great alarm in the United States.

The United States responded in early 1958 by launching its own satellite, *Explorer 1,* into orbit. Over the next few years, both the United States and the Soviet Union placed many more satellites into orbit around Earth.

Later in 1958, the United States established a government agency in charge of its space program, called the National Aeronautics and Space Administration (NASA). NASA brought together the talents of many scientists and engineers who worked together to solve the many difficult technical problems of space flight.

**Humans in Space** In 1961 the space race heated up even more when the Soviets launched the first human into space. Yuri Gagarin flew one orbit around Earth aboard *Vostok 1*. Less than a month later, astronaut Alan Shepard became the first American in space. His tiny spacecraft, called *Freedom 7,* was part of the U.S. Mercury space program. Other Soviet cosmonauts and American astronauts soon followed into space.

The first American to orbit Earth was John Glenn, who was launched into space in 1962 aboard *Friendship 7*. The spacecraft he traveled in was called a space capsule because it was like a small cap on the end of the rocket. The tiny capsule orbited Earth three times before returning to the surface.

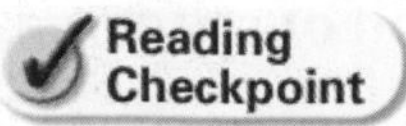

**Who was the first American in space?**

## Missions to the Moon

"I believe that this nation should commit itself to achieving the goal, before the decade is out, of landing a man on the moon and returning him safely to Earth." With these words from a May 1961 speech, President John F. Kennedy launched an enormous program of space exploration and scientific research. **The American effort to land astronauts on the moon was named the Apollo program.**

**Exploring the Moon** Between 1964 and 1972, the United States and the Soviet Union sent many unpiloted spacecraft to explore the moon. When a U.S. spacecraft called *Surveyor* landed on the moon, it didn't sink into the surface. This proved that the moon had a solid surface. Next, scientists searched for a suitable place to land humans on the moon.

**The Moon Landings** In July 1969, three American astronauts circled the moon aboard *Apollo 11*. Once in orbit, Neil Armstrong and Buzz Aldrin entered a tiny spacecraft called *Eagle*. On July 20, the *Eagle* descended toward a flat area on the moon's surface called the Sea of Tranquility. When Armstrong radioed that the *Eagle* had landed, cheers rang out at the NASA Space Center in Houston. A few hours later, Armstrong and Aldrin left the *Eagle* to explore the moon. When Armstrong first set foot on the surface, he said, "That's one small step for man, one giant leap for mankind." Armstrong meant to say, "That's one small step for *a* man," meaning himself, but in his excitement he never said the "a."

**Lab zone Skills Activity**

### Calculating

If you went to the moon, your weight would be about one sixth of your weight on Earth. Recall that in SI, weight is measured in newtons (1 lb ≈ 4.5 N). To find the approximate weight of an object on the moon, divide its weight on Earth by six.

An astronaut weighs 667 N on Earth. She wears a spacesuit and equipment that weigh 636 N on Earth. What is the astronaut's total weight on the moon?

FIGURE 25
*Apollo 11*
On July 20, 1969, *Apollo 11* astronaut Neil Armstrong became the first person to walk on the moon. He took this photograph of Buzz Aldrin. The inset photo shows Armstrong's footprint on the lunar soil.

## Exploring Space Today

After the great success of the moon landings, the question for space exploration was, "What comes next?" Scientists and public officials decided to build space shuttles and space stations where astronauts can live and work. They also sent space probes to explore the rest of the solar system.

**Space Shuttles** Before 1983, spacecraft could be used only once. In contrast, a space shuttle is like an airplane—it can fly, land, and then fly again. A **space shuttle** is a spacecraft that can carry a crew into space, return to Earth, and then be reused for the same purpose. A shuttle includes large rockets that launch it into orbit and then fall away. At the end of a mission, a shuttle returns to Earth by landing like an airplane. **NASA has used space shuttles to perform many important tasks. These include taking satellites into orbit, repairing damaged satellites, and carrying astronauts and equipment to and from space stations.**

**Space Stations** A **space station** is a large artificial satellite on which people can live and work for long periods. **A space station provides a place where long-term observations and experiments can be carried out in space.** In the 1970s and 1980s, both the United States and the Soviet Union placed space stations in orbit.

In the 1980s, the United States and 15 other countries began planning the construction of the International Space Station. The first module, or section, of the station was placed into orbit in 1998. Since then, many other modules have been added. On board, astronauts and scientists from many countries are carrying out experiments in various fields of science.

**FIGURE 26**
**International Space Station**
This is an artist's view of how the International Space Station will look when completed. It will be longer than a football field, and the living space will be about as large as the inside of the largest passenger jet.

**Space Probes** People have not yet traveled farther than the moon. Yet, scientists have gathered great amounts of information about other parts of the solar system. This data was collected by space probes. A **space probe** is a spacecraft that carries scientific instruments that can collect data, but has no human crew. **Space probes gather data about distant parts of the solar system where humans cannot easily travel.**

Each space probe is designed for a specific mission. Some probes are designed to land on a certain planet. Other probes are designed to fly by and collect data about more than one planet. Thus, each probe is unique. Still, probes have some features in common. Each probe has a power system to produce electricity, a communication system to send and receive signals, and scientific instruments to collect data or perform experiments.

The scientific instruments that a probe contains depend on the probe's mission. Some probes are equipped to photograph and analyze the atmosphere of a planet. Other probes are equipped to land on a planet and analyze the materials on its surface. Some probes have small robots called **rovers** that move around on the surface. A rover typically has instruments that collect and analyze soil and rock samples.

**FIGURE 27**
*Cassini*
The space probe *Cassini* is exploring Saturn's moons. It launched a smaller probe, *Huygens*, to explore Titan, Saturn's largest moon.

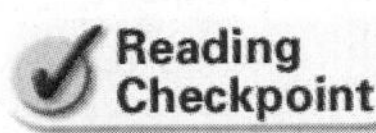


**What is a rover?**

## Section 5 Assessment

**Target Reading Skill Building Vocabulary** Use your definitions to help answer the questions below.

### Reviewing Key Concepts

1. a. **Explaining** What is a rocket?
   b. **Explaining** How do rockets create thrust?
   c. **Interpreting Diagrams** Use Figure 22 to explain how a rocket moves forward.
2. a. **Describing** Describe how a multistage rocket works.
   b. **Comparing and Contrasting** What is the main advantage of a multistage rocket compared to a single-stage rocket?
3. a. **Summarizing** What was the "space race"?
   b. **Sequencing** Place these events in the correct sequence: first humans on the moon, *Sputnik I,* first American in space, John Glenn orbits Earth, NASA formed, Yuri Gagarin orbits Earth.
4. a. **Describing** What is the space shuttle? What is its main advantage?
   b. **Defining** What is a space station? A space probe?
   c. **Comparing and Contrasting** What are the roles of space shuttles, space stations, and probes in the space program?

### Lab zone At-Home Activity

**Landmarks in Space Flight** Interview someone who remembers the early space programs. Prepare your questions in advance, such as: What did you think when you heard that *Sputnik* was in orbit? How did you feel when the first Americans went into space? Did you watch any of the space flights on TV? You may want to record your interview and then write it out later.

Lab zone

# Technology Lab

• Tech & Design •

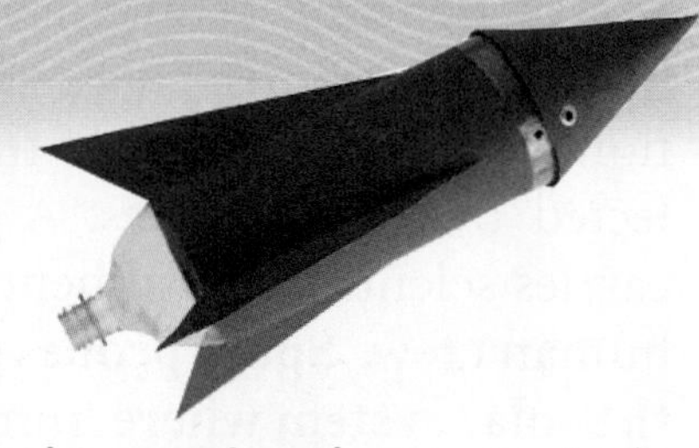

# Design and Build a Water Rocket

## Problem

Can you design and build a rocket propelled by water and compressed air?

## Design Skills

observing, evaluating the design, redesigning

## Materials

- large round balloon • tap water
- graduated cylinder • modeling clay
- 50 paper clips in a plastic bag
- empty 2-liter soda bottle • poster board
- scissors • hot glue gun or tape
- bucket, 5 gallon • stopwatch
- rocket launcher and tire pump (one per class)

## Procedure   

### PART 1 Research and Investigate

1. Copy the data table onto a separate sheet of paper.

| Data Table | |
|---|---|
| Volume of Water (mL) | Motion of Balloon |
| No water | |
| | |
| | |
| | |

2. In an outdoor area approved by your teacher, blow up a large round balloon. Hold the balloon so the opening is pointing down. Release the balloon and observe what occurs. ***CAUTION:*** *If you are allergic to latex, do not handle the balloon.*
3. Measure 50 mL of water with a graduated cylinder. Pour the water into the balloon. Blow it up to about the same size as the balloon in Step 2. Hold the opening down and release the balloon. Observe what happens.
4. Repeat Step 3 twice, varying the amount of water each time. Record your observations in the data table.

### PART 2 Design and Build

5. You and a partner will design and build a water rocket using the materials provided or approved by your teacher. Your rocket must
   - be made from an empty 2-liter soda bottle
   - have fins and a removable nosecone
   - carry a load of 50 paper clips
   - use air only or a mixture of air and water as a propulsion system
   - be launched on the class rocket launcher
   - remain in the air for at least 5 seconds
6. Begin by thinking about how your rocket will work and how you would like it to look. Sketch your design and make a list of materials that you will need.
7. Rockets often have a set of fins to stabilize them in flight. Consider the best shape for fins, and decide how many fins your rocket needs. Use poster board to make your fins.
8. Decide how to safely and securely carry a load of 50 paper clips in your rocket.
9. Based on what you learned in Part 1, decide how much, if any, water to pour into your rocket.
10. After you obtain your teacher's approval, build your rocket.

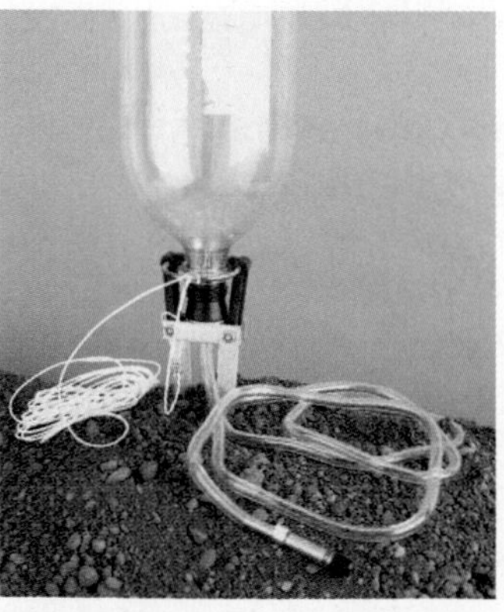

◀ Rocket launcher

## PART 3 Evaluate and Redesign

11. Test your rocket by launching it on the rocket launcher provided by your teacher. **CAUTION:** *Make sure that the rocket is launched vertically in a safe, open area that is at least 30 m across. All observers should wear goggles and stay at least 8–10 m away from the rocket launcher. The rocket should be pumped to a pressure of no more than 50 pounds per square inch.*
12. Use a stopwatch to determine your rocket's flight time (how long it stays in the air).
13. Record in a data table the results of your own launch and your classmates' launches.
14. Compare your design and results with those of your classmates.

## Analyze and Conclude

1. **Observing** What did you observe about the motion of the balloon as more and more water was added?
2. **Drawing Conclusions** What purpose did adding water to the balloon serve?
3. **Designing a Solution** How did your results in Part 1 affect your decision about how much water, if any, to add to your rocket?
4. **Evaluating the Design** Did your rocket meet all the criteria listed in Step 5? Explain.
5. **Evaluating the Design** How did your rocket design compare to the rockets built by your classmates? Which rocket had the greatest flight time? What design features resulted in the most successful launches?
6. **Redesigning** Based on your launch results and your response to Question 5, explain how you could improve your rocket. How do you think these changes would help your rocket's performance?
7. **Evaluating the Impact on Society** Explain how an understanding of rocket propulsion has made space travel possible.

## Communicate

Write a paragraph that describes how you designed and built your rocket. Explain how it worked. Include a labeled sketch of your design.

**For:** Data sharing
**Visit:** PHSchool.com
**Web Code:** cfd-5021

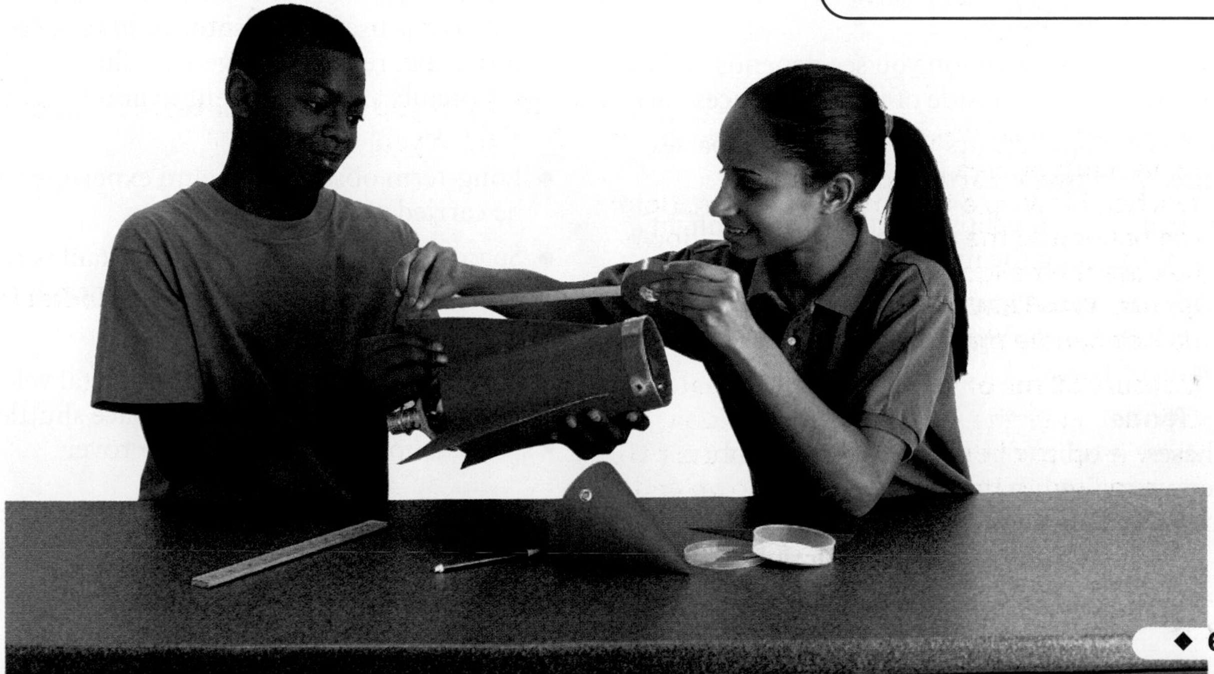

# Chapter 19 Study Guide

**The BIG Idea** **Motion and Forces** The motions of Earth and the moon and their position relative to the sun result in day and night, the seasons, phases of the moon, eclipses, and tides.

## 1 Earth in Space

### Key Concepts

- Earth moves through space in two major ways: rotation and revolution.
- Earth has seasons because its axis is tilted as it revolves around the sun.

### Key Terms

• astronomy • axis • rotation • revolution
• orbit • solstice • equinox

## 2 Gravity and Motion

### Key Concepts

- The strength of the force of gravity between two objects depends on two factors: the masses of the objects and the distance between them.
- Inertia and gravity combine to keep Earth and the moon in their orbits.

### Key Terms

• force • gravity • law of universal gravitation
• mass • weight • inertia
• Newton's first law of motion

## 3 Phases, Eclipses, and Tides

### Key Concepts

- The changing relative positions of the moon, Earth, and sun cause the phases of the moon, eclipses, and tides.
- The phase of the moon you see depends on how much of the sunlit side of the moon faces Earth.
- A solar eclipse occurs when the moon passes directly between Earth and the sun.
- During a lunar eclipse, Earth blocks sunlight from reaching the moon.
- Tides are caused mainly by differences in how much the moon's gravity pulls on different parts of Earth.

### Key Terms

• phases • eclipse • solar eclipse • umbra
• penumbra • lunar eclipse • tide
• spring tide • neap tide

## 4 Earth's Moon

### Key Concepts

- Features on the moon's surface include maria, craters, and highlands.
- The moon is dry and airless. Compared to Earth, the moon is small and has large variations in its surface temperature.
- Scientists theorize that a planet-sized object collided with Earth to form the moon.

### Key Terms

• telescope • maria • craters
• meteoroids

## 5 Traveling Into Space

### Key Concepts

- A rocket moves forward when gases shooting out the back of the rocket push it in the opposite direction.
- In a multistage rocket, the total weight of the rocket is greatly reduced as the rocket rises.
- The rivalry between the United States and the Soviet Union over the exploration of space was known as the "space race."
- The American effort to land astronauts on the moon was named the Apollo program.
- NASA has used space shuttles to take satellites into orbit, repair damaged satellites, and carry astronauts and equipment to and from space stations.
- Long-term observations and experiments can be carried out in space stations.
- Space probes gather data about distant parts of the solar system where humans cannot easily travel.

### Key Terms

• rocket • thrust • velocity • orbital velocity
• escape velocity • satellite • space shuttle
• space station • space probe • rover

# Review and Assessment

**Go Online** PHSchool.com
**For:** Self-Assessment
**Visit:** PHSchool.com
**Web Code:** cja-5190

## Organizing Information

**Comparing and Contrasting** Copy the graphic organizer onto a separate sheet of paper. Then complete it and add a title. (For more on Comparing and Contrasting, see the Skills Handbook.)

| Astronaut | Year | Spacecraft | Accomplishment |
|---|---|---|---|
| Yuri Gagarin | 1961 | a. ___?___ | First human in space |
| Alan Shepard | b. ___?___ | *Freedom 7* | c. ___?___ |
| d. ___?___ | 1962 | *Friendship 7* | e. ___?___ |
| Neil Armstrong | f. ___?___ | g. ___?___ | First human to walk on the moon |

## Reviewing Key Terms

**Choose the letter of the best answer.**

1. The movement of Earth around the sun once a year is called Earth's
   **a.** inertia. **b.** rotation.
   **c.** revolution. **d.** axis.
2. The tendency of an object to resist a change in motion is called
   **a.** gravity.
   **b.** inertia.
   **c.** force.
   **d.** the law of universal gravitation.
3. When Earth's shadow falls on the moon, the shadow causes a
   **a.** new moon.
   **b.** solar eclipse.
   **c.** full moon.
   **d.** lunar eclipse.
4. The craters on the moon were caused by
   **a.** tides.
   **b.** volcanoes.
   **c.** meteoroids.
   **d.** maria.
5. A device that expels gas in one direction to move in the opposite direction is a
   **a.** rocket. **b.** space probe.
   **c.** space station. **d.** rover.

**If the statement is true, write *true*. If it is false, change the underlined word or words to make the statement true.**

6. Earth's spinning on its axis is called <u>rotation</u>.
7. The force that attracts all objects toward each other is called <u>inertia</u>.
8. The tilt of Earth's axis as Earth revolves around the sun causes <u>eclipses</u>.
9. The greatest difference between low and high tides occurs during a <u>neap</u> tide.
10. A large artificial satellite on which people can live for long periods is a <u>space station</u>.

## Writing in Science

**News Report** Imagine that you are a reporter asked to write a story about the origin of the moon. Write an article explaining how the moon formed.

*Earth, Moon, and Sun*
Video Preview
Video Field Trip
▶ Video Assessment

# Review and Assessment

## Checking Concepts

**11.** Explain how the length of the day and year are related to Earth's movement through space.

**12.** Suppose you moved two objects farther apart. How would this affect the force of gravity between those objects?

**13.** Explain Newton's first law of motion in your own words.

**14.** Why does the moon have phases?

**15.** Why do more people see a total lunar eclipse than a total solar eclipse?

**16.** Why is there a high tide on the side of Earth closest to the moon? On the side of Earth farthest from the moon?

**17.** Does the diagram below show a spring tide or a neap tide? How do you know?

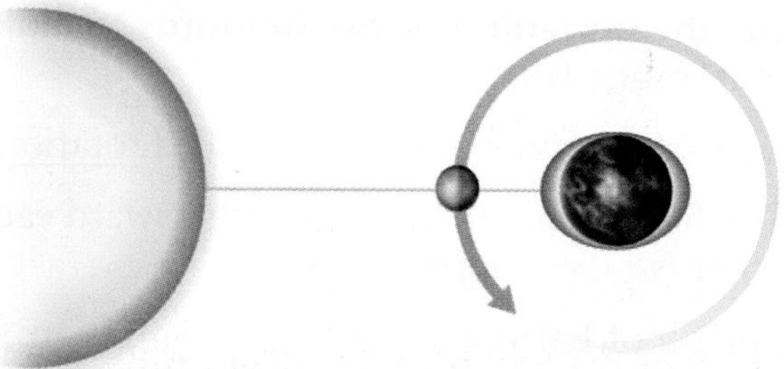

**18.** How did the invention of the telescope contribute to our knowledge of the moon's surface?

**19.** Why do temperatures vary so much on the moon?

**20.** Explain how scientists think the moon originated.

## Thinking Critically

**21. Inferring** Mars's axis is tilted at about the same angle as Earth's axis. Do you think Mars has seasons? Explain your answer.

**22. Comparing and Contrasting** How are mass and weight different?

**23. Calculating** Suppose a person weighs 450 newtons (about 100 pounds) on Earth. How much would she weigh on the moon?

**24. Posing Questions** Suppose you were assigned to design a spacesuit for astronauts to wear on the moon. What characteristics of the moon would be important to consider in your design?

**25. Making Judgments** Do you think that the benefits of the Apollo program outweighed the program's costs? Explain.

## Applying Skills

**Use the illustration below to answer Questions 26–28.**

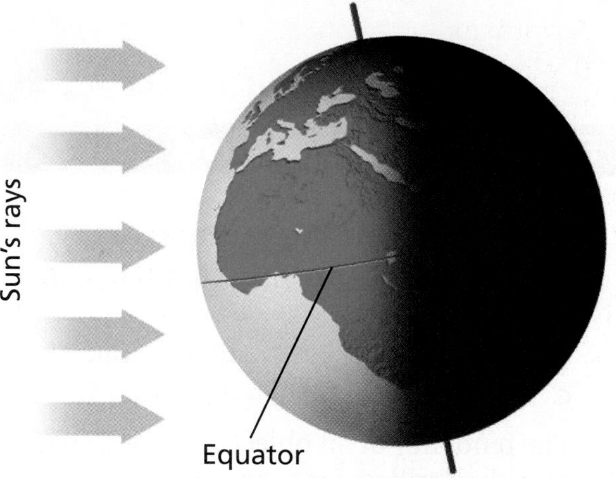


**26. Interpreting Diagrams** On which hemisphere are the sun's rays falling most directly?

**27. Inferring** In the Northern Hemisphere, is it the summer solstice, winter solstice, or one of the equinoxes? How do you know?

**28. Predicting** Six months after this illustration, Earth will have revolved halfway around the sun. Draw a diagram that shows which end of Earth's axis will be tilted toward the sun.

## Lab zone Chapter Project

**Performance Assessment** Present your observation log, map, and drawings of the moon. Some ways to graph your data include time of moonrise for each date; how often you saw the moon in each direction; or how often you saw the moon at a specific time. Display your graphs. Discuss any patterns that you discovered.

# Standardized Test Prep

**Test-Taking Tip**

**Interpreting a Diagram**

When answering questions about diagrams, examine the diagram carefully, including labels. For example, the numbers on the diagram shown above Question 5 indicate the locations of the moon in its orbit around Earth. Study the diagram and answer the sample question below.

***Sample Question***

When the moon is in location 3, a person standing on Earth at night would see

A a full moon.
B a crescent moon.
C a quarter moon.
D a new moon.

***Answer***

The correct answer is **A.** The diagram shows that when the moon is at location 3, Earth is between the moon and the sun. Therefore, the sun lights the entire side of the moon facing Earth.

**Choose the letter of the best answer.**

**1.** You observe a thin crescent moon in the western sky during the early evening. About two weeks later, a full moon is visible in the eastern sky during the early evening. Which conclusion is best supported by these observations?

A The moon revolves around Earth.
B The moon rotates on its axis.
C Earth revolves around the sun.
D Earth's axis is tilted relative to the moon.

**2.** Only one side of the moon is visible from Earth because

F the moon does not rotate on its axis.
G the moon does not revolve around Earth.
H the moon rotates faster than it revolves.
J the moon revolves once and rotates once in the same period of time.

**3.** What type of eclipse occurs when Earth's umbra covers the moon?

A a partial solar eclipse
B a total solar eclipse
C a partial lunar eclipse
D a total lunar eclipse

**4.** What force must a rocket overcome to be launched into space?

F thrust
G gravity
H orbital velocity
J escape velocity

*The diagram below shows the relative positions of the sun, moon, and Earth. The numbers indicate specific locations of the moon in its orbit. Use the diagram to answer Questions 5 and 6.*

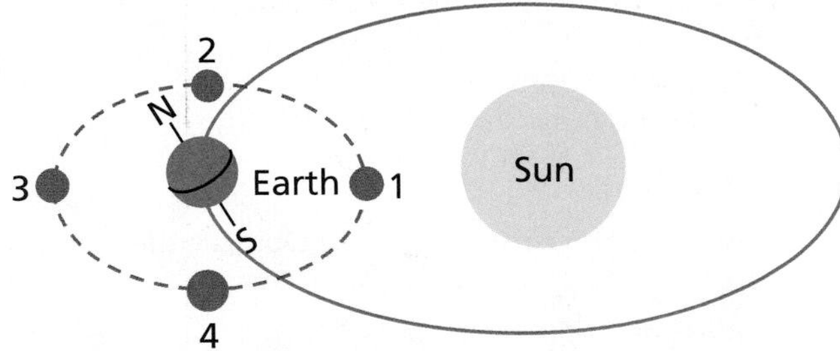


**5.** Which of the following can occur when the moon is at location 1?

A only a lunar eclipse
B only a solar eclipse
C both a solar and a lunar eclipse
D neither a solar nor a lunar eclipse

**6.** When the moon is at location 2, at most coastal locations there would be

F only one high tide each day.
G only one low tide each day.
H two high tides and two low tides each day, with the most difference between high and low tide.
J two high tides and two low tides each day, with the least difference between high and low tide.

**Constructed Response**

**7.** The sun rises on the east coast of the United States before it rises on the west coast of the United States. Explain why this happens.

# Chapter 20 The Solar System

The BIG Idea
Structure of the Solar System

**What types of objects are found in the solar system?**

**Chapter Preview**



This illustration shows the planets in orbit around the sun. ▶

The Solar System

▶ Video Preview
Video Field Trip
Video Assessment

Lab zone™ Chapter **Project**

## Build a Model of the Solar System

The solar system is a vast region containing the sun, planets, and many other objects. To help you understand the huge distances involved, you will design three different scale models of the solar system.

**Your Goal** To design scale models of the solar system

To complete this project, you will

- design a model to show the planets' distances from the sun
- design a model to show the planets' sizes compared to the sun
- test different scales to see if you can use the same scale for both size and distance in one model

**Plan It!** Begin by previewing the planet tables in this chapter. With a group of classmates, brainstorm how to build your models. Then design two models—one to show distances and one to show diameters. Next, design a third model that uses the same scale for both size and distance. Try several different scales to find which works best. Prepare a data table to record your calculations.

Section 1

# Observing the Solar System

## Reading Preview

### Key Concepts

- What are the geocentric and heliocentric systems?
- How did Copernicus, Galileo, and Kepler contribute to our knowledge of the solar system?
- What objects make up the solar system?

### Key Terms

- geocentric
- heliocentric
- ellipse

### Target Reading Skill

**Previewing Visuals** Preview Figure 2 and Figure 3. Then write two questions that you have about the diagrams in a graphic organizer. As you read, answer your questions.

**Models of the Universe**

| Q. What is a geocentric model? |
|---|
| A. |
| Q. |

## Lab zone Discover Activity

### What Is at the Center?

1. Stand about 2 meters from a partner who is holding a flashlight. Have your partner shine the flashlight in your direction. Tell your partner not to move the flashlight.
2. Continue facing your partner, but move sideways in a circle, staying about 2 meters away from your partner.
3. Record your observations about your ability to see the light.
4. Repeat the activity, but this time remain stationary and continually face one direction. Have your partner continue to hold the flashlight toward you and move sideways around you, remaining about 2 meters from you.
5. Record your observations about your ability to see the light.

**Think It Over**

**Drawing Conclusions** Compare your two sets of observations. If you represent Earth and your partner represents the sun, is it possible, just from your observations, to tell whether Earth or the sun is in the center of the solar system?

Have you ever gazed up at the sky on a starry night? If you watch for several hours, the stars seem to move across the sky. The sky seems to be rotating right over your head. In fact, from the Northern Hemisphere, the sky appears to rotate completely around the North Star once every 24 hours.

Now think about what you see every day. During the day, the sun appears to move across the sky. From here on Earth, it seems as if Earth is stationary and that the sun, moon, and stars are moving around Earth. But is the sky really moving above you? Centuries ago, before there were space shuttles or even telescopes, there was no easy way to find out.

**FIGURE 1**
**Star Trails**
This photo was made by exposing the camera film for several hours. Each star appears as part of a circle, and all the stars seem to revolve around the North Star.

## Earth at the Center

When the ancient Greeks watched the stars move across the sky, they noticed that the patterns of the stars didn't change. Although the stars seemed to move, they stayed in the same position relative to one another. These patterns of stars, called constellations, kept the same shapes from night to night and from year to year.

**Greek Observations** As the Greeks observed the sky, they noticed something surprising. Several points of light seemed to wander slowly among the stars. The Greeks called these objects *planets,* from the Greek word meaning "wanderers." The Greeks made careful observations of the motions of the planets that they could see. You know these planets by the names the ancient Romans later gave them: Mercury, Venus, Mars, Jupiter, and Saturn.

Most early Greek astronomers believed the universe to be perfect, with Earth at the center. The Greeks thought that Earth is inside a rotating dome they called the celestial sphere. Since *geo* is the Greek word for "Earth," an Earth-centered model is known as a **geocentric** (jee oh SEN trik) system. **In a geocentric system, Earth is at the center of the revolving planets and stars.**

**Ptolemy's Model** About A.D. 140, the Greek astronomer Ptolemy (TAHL uh mee) further developed the geocentric model. Like the earlier Greeks, Ptolemy thought that Earth is at the center of a system of planets and stars. In Ptolemy's model, however, the planets move on small circles that move on bigger circles.

Even though Ptolemy's geocentric model was incorrect, it explained the motions observed in the sky fairly accurately. As a result, the geocentric model of the universe was widely accepted for nearly 1,500 years after Ptolemy.

**Reading Checkpoint** What is a geocentric system?

**FIGURE 2**
**Geocentric System**
In a geocentric system, the planets and stars are thought to revolve around a stationary Earth. In the 1500s, an astronomy book published the illustration of Ptolemy's geocentric system shown below.
**Interpreting Diagrams** *Where is Earth located in each illustration?*

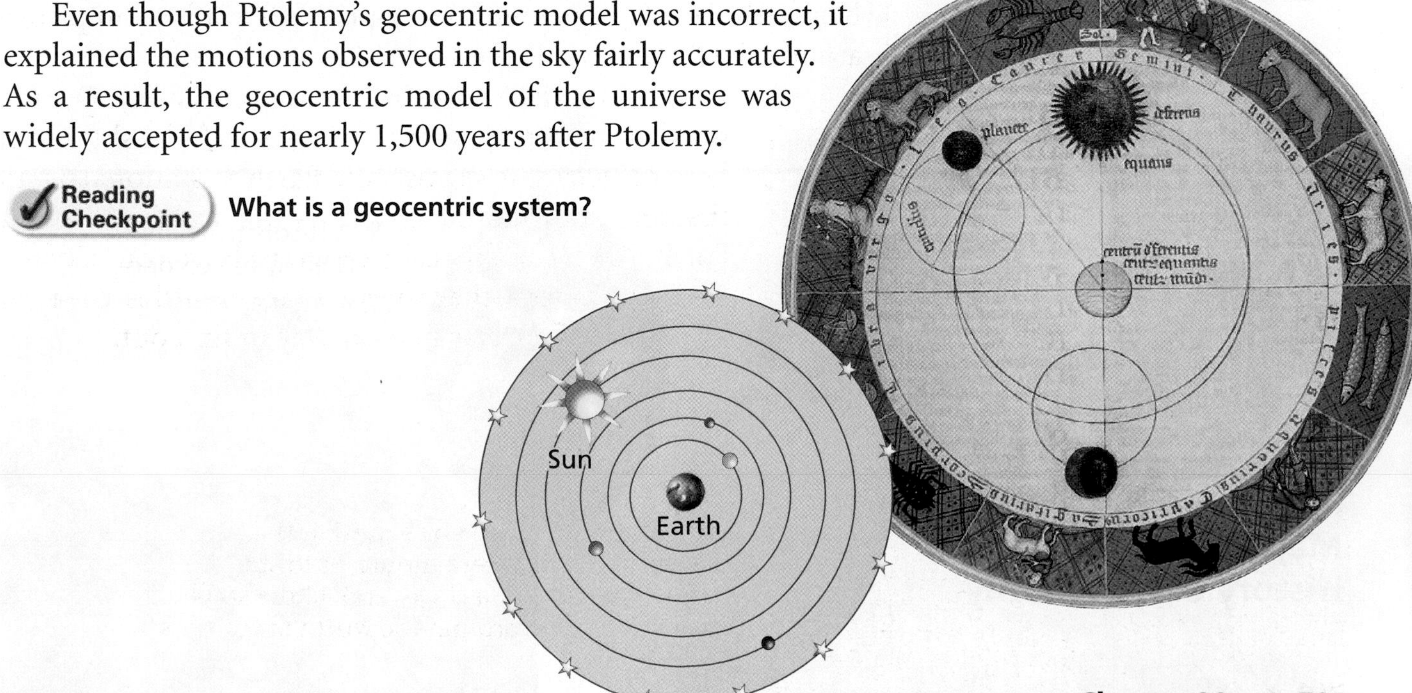

## Sun at the Center

Not everybody believed in the geocentric system. An ancient Greek scientist developed another explanation for the motion of the planets. This sun-centered model is called a **heliocentric** (hee lee oh SEN trik) system. *Helios* is Greek for "sun." **In a heliocentric system, Earth and the other planets revolve around the sun.** This model was not well received in ancient times, however, because people could not accept that Earth is not at the center of the universe.

FIGURE 3
**Heliocentric System**
In a heliocentric system, Earth and the other planets revolve around the sun. The illustration by Andreas Cellarius (top) was made in the 1660s.
**Interpreting Diagrams** *In a heliocentric model, what revolves around Earth?*

**The Copernican Revolution** In 1543, the Polish astronomer Nicolaus Copernicus further developed the heliocentric model. **Copernicus was able to work out the arrangement of the known planets and how they move around the sun.** Copernicus's theory would eventually revolutionize the science of astronomy. But at first, many people were unwilling to accept his theory. They needed more evidence to be convinced.

In the 1500s and early 1600s, most people still believed in the geocentric model. However, evidence collected by the Italian scientist Galileo Galilei gradually convinced others that the heliocentric model was correct.

**Galileo's Evidence** **Galileo used the newly invented telescope to make discoveries that supported the heliocentric model.** For example, in 1610, Galileo used a telescope to discover four moons revolving around Jupiter. The motion of these moons proved that not everything in the sky revolves around Earth.

**Nicolaus Copernicus**
**1473–1543**

▼ A reconstruction of Galileo's telescope

**Galileo Galilei**
**1564–1642**

FIGURE 4
**Major Figures in the History of Astronomy**

Galileo's observations of Venus also supported the heliocentric system. Galileo knew that Venus is always seen near the sun. He discovered that Venus goes through a series of phases similar to those of Earth's moon. But Venus would not have a full set of phases if it circled around Earth. Therefore, Galileo reasoned, the geocentric model must be incorrect.

**Tycho Brahe's Observations** Copernicus correctly placed the sun at the center of the planets. But he incorrectly assumed that the planets travel in orbits that are perfect circles. Copernicus had based his ideas on observations made by the ancient Greeks.

In the late 1500s, the Danish astronomer Tycho Brahe (TEE koh BRAH uh) and his assistants made much more accurate observations. For more than 20 years, they carefully observed and recorded the positions of the planets. Surprisingly, these observations were made without using a telescope. Telescopes had not yet been invented!

**Kepler's Calculations** Tycho Brahe died in 1601. His assistant, Johannes Kepler, went to work analyzing the observations. Kepler began by trying to figure out the shape of Mars's orbit. At first, he assumed that the orbit was circular. But his calculations did not fit the observations. Kepler eventually found that Mars's orbit was a slightly flattened circle, or ellipse. An **ellipse** is an oval shape, which may be elongated or nearly circular.

After years of detailed calculations, Kepler reached a remarkable conclusion about the motion of the planets. **Kepler found that the orbit of each planet is an ellipse.** Kepler had used the evidence gathered by Tycho Brahe to disprove the long-held belief that the planets move in perfect circles.

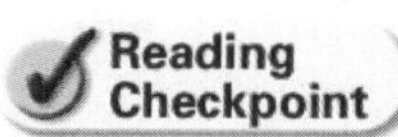


**What is an ellipse?**

Lab zone **Try This Activity**

## A Loopy Ellipse

You can draw an ellipse.

1. Carefully stick two pushpins about 10 cm apart through a sheet of white paper on top of corrugated cardboard. One pushpin represents the sun.
2. Tie the ends of a 30-cm piece of string together. Place the string around the pushpins.
3. Keeping the string tight, move a pencil around inside the string.
4. Now place the pushpins 5 cm apart. Repeat Step 3.

**Predicting** How does changing the distance between the pushpins affect the ellipse's shape? What shape would you draw if you used only one pushpin? Is the "sun" at the center of the ellipse?

**Tycho Brahe**
**1546–1601**

◀ Brahe's observatory on an island between Denmark and Sweden

**Johannes Kepler**
**1571–1630**

**FIGURE 5**
**The Sun and Planets**
This illustration shows the average distances of the planets from the sun. The solar system also includes smaller objects, such as Pluto. These distances are drawn to scale, but the sizes of the planets are not drawn to the same scale.
**Observing** *Which planet is closest to the sun?*

## Modern Discoveries

Today, people talk about the "solar system" rather than the "Earth system." This shows that people accept the idea that Earth and the other planets revolve around the sun.

Since Galileo's time, our knowledge of the solar system has increased dramatically. Galileo knew the same planets that the ancient Greeks had known—Mercury, Venus, Earth, Mars, Jupiter, and Saturn. Since Galileo's time, astronomers have discovered two more planets—Uranus and Neptune, as well as Pluto, which is no longer considered to be a planet. Astronomers have also identified many other objects in the solar system, such as comets and asteroids. **Today we know that the solar system consists of the sun, the planets and their moons, and several kinds of smaller objects that revolve around the sun.**

**Math** Analyzing Data

### Planet Speed Versus Distance

Johannes Kepler discovered a relationship between the speed of a planet and its distance from the sun. Use the graph to help discover what Kepler learned.

1. **Reading Graphs** According to the graph, what is Earth's average speed?
2. **Interpreting Data** Which is closer to the sun, Mercury or Mars? Which moves faster?
3. **Drawing Conclusions** What is the general relationship between a planet's speed and its average distance from the sun?
4. **Predicting** The planet Uranus is about 2,900 million km from the sun. Predict whether its speed is greater or less than Jupiter's speed. Explain your answer.

**Speed of Planets**

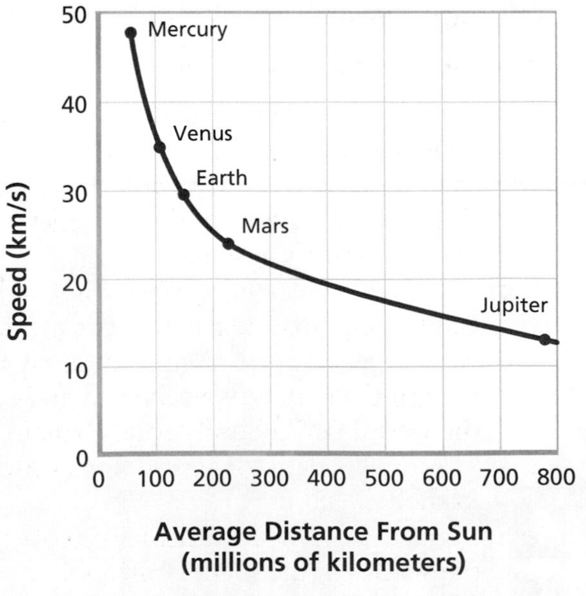

Uranus
2,873,000,000 km

Neptune
4,495,000,000 km

Pluto
5,870,000,000 km

Galileo used a telescope to observe the solar system from Earth's surface. Astronomers today still use telescopes located on Earth, but they have also placed telescopes in space to gain a better view of the universe beyond Earth. Scientists have also sent astronauts to the moon and launched numerous space probes to explore the far reaches of the solar system. Our understanding of the solar system continues to grow every day. Who knows what new discoveries will be made in your lifetime!

**Which six planets were known to the ancient Greeks?**

**For:** Solar System activity
**Visit:** PHSchool.com
**Web Code:** cfp-5031

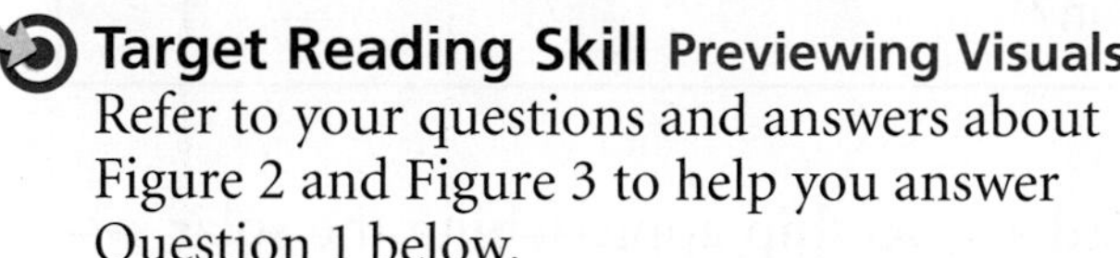

## Section 1 Assessment

**Target Reading Skill Previewing Visuals** Refer to your questions and answers about Figure 2 and Figure 3 to help you answer Question 1 below.

### Reviewing Key Concepts

1. a. **Explaining** What are the geocentric and heliocentric systems?
   b. **Comparing and Contrasting** How was Copernicus's model of the universe different from Ptolemy's model?
   c. **Drawing Conclusions** What discoveries by Galileo support the heliocentric model?
   d. **Applying Concepts** People often say the sun rises in the east, crosses the sky, and sets in the west. Is this literally true? Explain.
2. a. **Interpreting Data** How did Kepler use Tycho Brahe's data?
   b. **Describing** What did Kepler discover about the shapes of the planets' orbits?
   c. **Inferring** How did Tycho Brahe and Kepler employ the scientific method?
3. a. **Describing** What objects make up the solar system?
   b. **Listing** What are the planets, in order of increasing distance from the sun?
   c. **Interpreting Diagrams** Use Figure 5 to find the planet with the closest orbit to Earth.

### Writing in Science

**Dialogue** Write an imaginary conversation between Ptolemy and Galileo about the merits of the geocentric and heliocentric systems. Which system would each scientist favor? What evidence could each offer to support his view? Do you think that one scientist could convince the other to change his mind? Use quotation marks around the comments of each scientist.

Section 2

# The Sun

## Reading Preview

### Key Concepts

- What are the three layers of the sun's interior?
- What are the three layers of the sun's atmosphere?
- What features form on or above the sun's surface?

### Key Terms

- core
- nuclear fusion
- radiation zone
- convection zone
- photosphere
- chromosphere
- corona
- solar wind
- sunspot
- prominence
- solar flare

### Target Reading Skill

**Outlining** As you read, make an outline about the sun that you can use for review. Use the red headings for main topics and the blue headings for subtopics.

| The Sun |
|---|
| I. The sun's interior |
| A. The core |
| B. |
| C. |
| II. The sun's atmosphere |
| A. The photosphere |

## Lab zone Discover Activity

### How Can You Safely Observe the Sun?

1. Clamp a pair of binoculars to a ring stand as shown in the photo.
2. Cut a hole in a 20-cm by 28-cm sheet of thin cardboard so that it will fit over the binoculars, as shown in the photo. The cardboard should cover one lens, but allow light through the other lens. Tape the cardboard on securely.
3. Use the binoculars to project an image of the sun onto a sheet of white paper. The cardboard will shade the white paper. Change the focus and move the paper back and forth until you get a sharp image. **CAUTION:** *Never look directly at the sun. You will hurt your eyes if you do. Do not look up through the binoculars.*

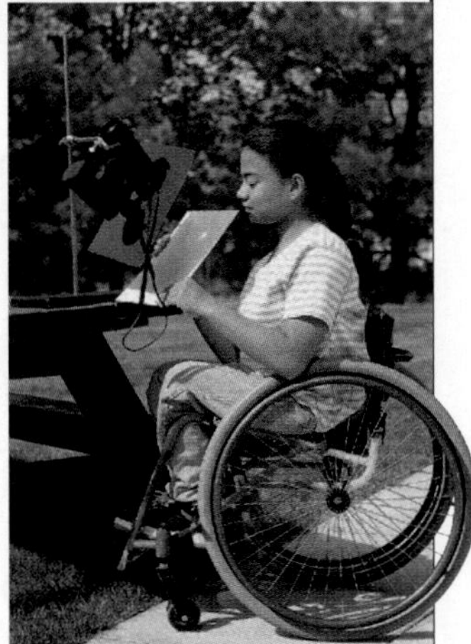

**Think It Over**

**Observing** Draw what you see on the paper. What do you see on the surface of the sun?

Suppose you are aboard a spaceship approaching the solar system from afar. Your first impression of the solar system might be that it consists of a single star with a few tiny objects orbiting around it. Your first impression wouldn't be that far off. In fact, the sun accounts for 99.8 percent of the solar system's total mass. As a result of its huge mass, the sun exerts a powerful gravitational force throughout the solar system. Although this force decreases rapidly with distance, it is strong enough to hold all the planets and other distant objects in orbit.

**FIGURE 6**
**Active Sun**
The sun is a huge, hot ball of glowing gas.

## The Sun's Interior

Unlike Earth, the sun does not have a solid surface. Rather, the sun is a ball of glowing gas through and through. About three fourths of the sun's mass is hydrogen and one fourth is helium. There are also small amounts of other elements. Like Earth, the sun has an interior and an atmosphere. **The sun's interior consists of the core, the radiation zone, and the convection zone.**

**The Core** The sun produces an enormous amount of energy in its **core,** or central region. This energy is not produced by burning fuel. Rather, the sun's energy comes from nuclear fusion. In the process of **nuclear fusion,** hydrogen atoms join together to form helium. Nuclear fusion occurs only under conditions of extremely high temperature and pressure. The temperature inside the sun's core reaches about 15 million degrees Celsius, high enough for nuclear fusion to take place.

The total mass of the helium produced by nuclear fusion is slightly less than the total mass of the hydrogen that goes into it. What happens to this mass? It is changed into energy. This energy slowly moves outward from the core, eventually escaping into space.

**The Radiation Zone** The energy produced in the sun's core moves outward through the middle layer of the sun's interior, the radiation zone. The **radiation zone** is a region of very tightly packed gas where energy is transferred mainly in the form of electromagnetic radiation. Because the radiation zone is so dense, energy can take more than 100,000 years to move through it.

**The Convection Zone** The **convection zone** is the outermost layer of the sun's interior. Hot gases rise from the bottom of the convection zone and gradually cool as they approach the top. Cooler gases sink, forming loops of gas that move energy toward the sun's surface.

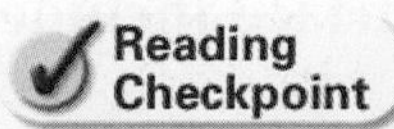


**What is nuclear fusion?**

**For:** More on the sun
**Visit:** PHSchool.com
**Web Code:** cfd-5032

FIGURE 7
**The Sun's Corona**
During a total solar eclipse, you can see light from the corona, the outer layer of the sun's atmosphere around the dark disk of the moon.

## The Sun's Atmosphere

**The sun's atmosphere includes the photosphere, the chromosphere, and the corona.** Each layer has unique properties.

**The Photosphere** The inner layer of the sun's atmosphere is called the **photosphere** (FOH tuh sfeer). The Greek word *photos* means "light," so *photosphere* means the sphere that gives off visible light. The sun does not have a solid surface, but the gases of the photosphere are thick enough to be visible. When you look at an image of the sun, you are looking at the photosphere. It is considered to be the sun's surface layer.

**The Chromosphere** During a total solar eclipse, the moon blocks light from the photosphere. The photosphere no longer produces the glare that keeps you from seeing the sun's faint, outer layers. At the start and end of a total eclipse, a reddish glow is visible just around the photosphere. This glow comes from the middle layer of the sun's atmosphere, the **chromosphere** (KROH muh sfeer). The Greek word *chroma* means "color," so the chromosphere is the "color sphere."

**The Corona** During a total solar eclipse an even fainter layer of the sun becomes visible, as you can see in Figure 7. This outer layer, which looks like a white halo around the sun, is called the **corona,** which means "crown" in Latin. The corona extends into space for millions of kilometers. It gradually thins into streams of electrically charged particles called the **solar wind.**

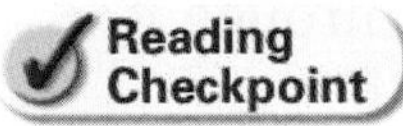

**During what event could you see the sun's corona?**

**Lab zone Try This Activity**

### Viewing Sunspots

You can observe changes in the number of sunspots.

1. Make a data table to record the number of sunspots you see each day.
2. Decide on a time to study sunspots each day.
3. View the sun's image in the way described in the Discover activity in this section. **CAUTION:** *Never look directly at the sun. You will hurt your eyes if you do.*
4. Make and record your observations.

**Interpreting Data** How much did the number of sunspots change from day to day?

## Features on the Sun

For hundreds of years, scientists have used telescopes to study the sun. They have spotted a variety of features on the sun's surface. **Features on or just above the sun's surface include sunspots, prominences, and solar flares.**

**Sunspots** Early observers noticed dark spots on the sun's surface. These became known as sunspots. Sunspots look small. But in fact, they can be larger than Earth. **Sunspots** are areas of gas on the sun's surface that are cooler than the gases around them. Cooler gases don't give off as much light as hotter gases, which is why sunspots look darker than the rest of the photosphere. Sunspots seem to move across the sun's surface, showing that the sun rotates on its axis, just as Earth does. The number of sunspots on the sun varies over a period of about 11 years.

## FIGURE 8
## The Layers of the Sun

The sun has an interior and an atmosphere, each of which consists of several layers. The diameter of the sun (not including the chromosphere and the corona) is about 1.4 million kilometers. **Interpreting Diagrams** *Name the layers of the sun's interior, beginning at its center.*

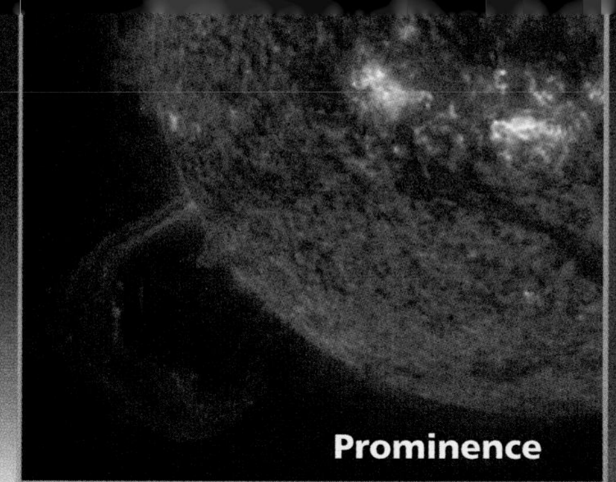
Prominence

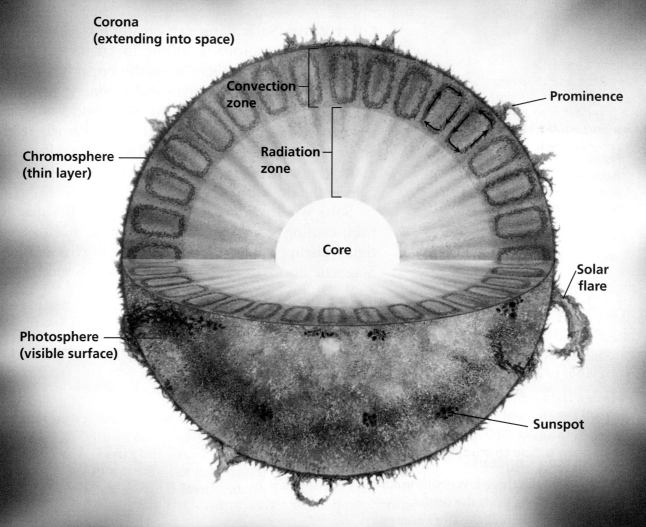

Corona (extending into space)

Convection zone

Prominence

Radiation zone

Chromosphere (thin layer)

Core

Solar flare

Photosphere (visible surface)

Sunspot

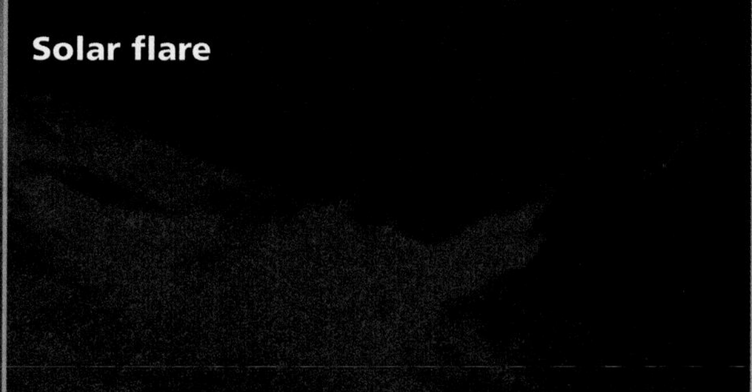
Solar flare

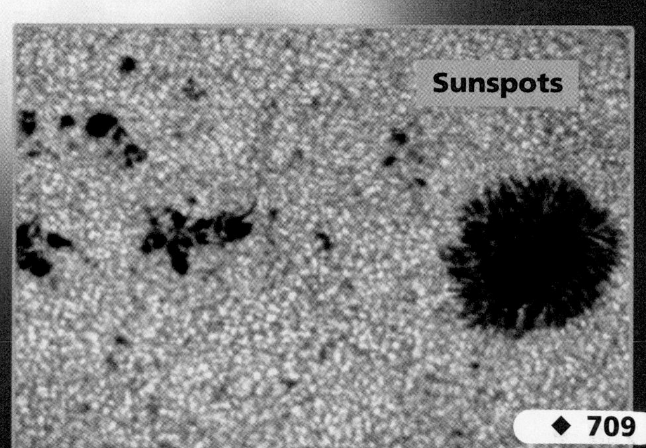
Sunspots

**FIGURE 9**
**Auroras**
Auroras such as this can occur near Earth's poles when particles of the solar wind strike gas molecules in Earth's upper atmosphere.

**Prominences** Sunspots usually occur in groups. Huge, reddish loops of gas called **prominences** often link different parts of sunspot regions. When a group of sunspots is near the edge of the sun as seen from Earth, these loops can be seen extending over the edge of the sun.

**Solar Flares** Sometimes the loops in sunspot regions suddenly connect, releasing large amounts of magnetic energy. The energy heats gas on the sun to millions of degrees Celsius, causing the gas to erupt into space. These eruptions are called **solar flares.**

**Solar Wind** Solar flares can greatly increase the solar wind from the corona, resulting in an increase in the number of particles reaching Earth's upper atmosphere. Normally, Earth's atmosphere and magnetic field block these particles. However, near the North and South poles, the particles can enter Earth's atmosphere, where they create powerful electric currents that cause gas molecules in the atmosphere to glow. The result is rippling sheets of light in the sky called auroras.

Solar wind particles can also affect Earth's magnetic field, causing magnetic storms. Magnetic storms sometimes disrupt radio, telephone, and television signals. Magnetic storms can also cause electrical power problems.

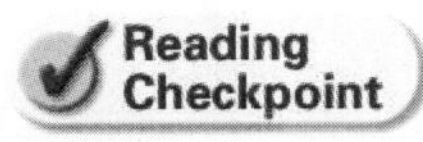

**What is a prominence?**

## Section 2 Assessment

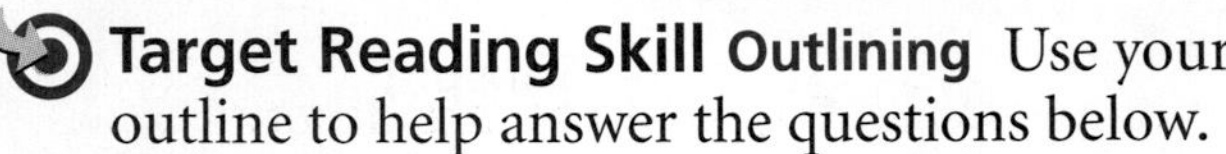

**Target Reading Skill Outlining** Use your outline to help answer the questions below.

### Reviewing Key Concepts

1. a. **Listing** List the three layers of the sun's interior, starting from the center.
   b. **Explaining** Where is the sun's energy produced?
   c. **Comparing and Contrasting** Compare how energy moves through the radiation zone and the convection zone.
2. a. **Listing** What three layers make up the sun's atmosphere?
   b. **Identifying** Which of the sun's layers produces its visible light?
   c. **Relating Cause and Effect** Why is it usually impossible to see the sun's corona from Earth?
3. a. **Describing** Describe three features found on or just above the sun's surface.
   b. **Relating Cause and Effect** Why do sunspots look darker than the rest of the sun's photosphere?

### Lab zone At-Home **Activity**

**Sun Symbols** As the source of heat and light, the sun is an important symbol in many cultures. With family members, look around your home and neighborhood for illustrations of the sun on signs, flags, clothing, and in artwork. Which parts of the sun's atmosphere do the illustrations show?

Lab zone **Skills Lab**

# Stormy Sunspots

## Problem
How are magnetic storms on Earth related to sunspot activity?

## Skills Focus
graphing, interpreting data

## Materials
- graph paper
- ruler

## Procedure
1. Use the data in the table of Annual Sunspot Numbers to make a line graph of sunspot activity between 1972 and 2002.
2. On the graph, label the *x*-axis "Year." Use a scale with 2-year intervals, from 1972 to 2002.
3. Label the *y*-axis "Sunspot Number." Use a scale of 0 through 160 in intervals of 10.
4. Graph a point for the Sunspot Number for each year.
5. Complete your graph by drawing lines to connect the points.

**Annual Sunspot Numbers**

| Year | Sunspot Number | Year | Sunspot Number |
|---|---|---|---|
| 1972 | 68.9 | 1988 | 100.2 |
| 1974 | 34.5 | 1990 | 142.6 |
| 1976 | 12.6 | 1992 | 94.3 |
| 1978 | 92.5 | 1994 | 29.9 |
| 1980 | 154.6 | 1996 | 8.6 |
| 1982 | 115.9 | 1998 | 64.3 |
| 1984 | 45.9 | 2000 | 119.6 |
| 1986 | 13.4 | 2002 | 104.0 |

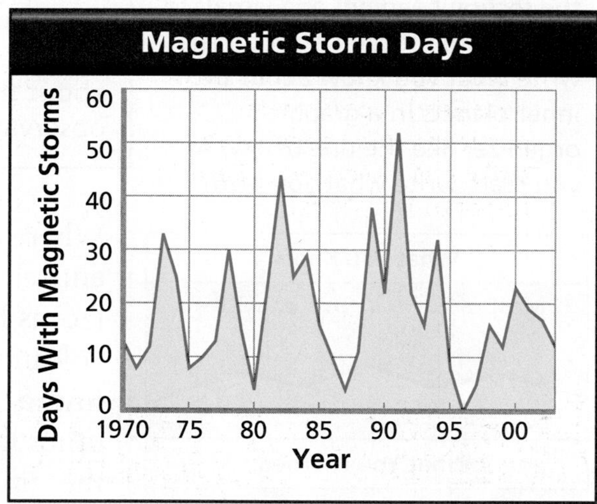


## Analyze and Conclude
1. **Graphing** Based on your graph, which years had the highest Sunspot Number? The lowest Sunspot Number?
2. **Interpreting Data** How often does the cycle of maximum and minimum activity repeat?
3. **Interpreting Data** When was the most recent maximum sunspot activity? The most recent minimum sunspot activity?
4. **Inferring** Compare your sunspot graph with the magnetic storms graph. What relationship can you infer between periods of high sunspot activity and magnetic storms? Explain.
5. **Communicating** Suppose you are an engineer working for an electric power company. Write a brief summary of your analysis of sunspot data. Explain the relationship between sunspot number and electrical disturbances on Earth.

## More to Explore
Using the pattern of sunspot activity you found, predict the number of peaks you would expect in the next 30 years. Around which years would you expect the peaks to occur?

Section 3

# The Inner Planets

## Reading Preview

### Key Concepts

- What characteristics do the inner planets have in common?
- What are the main characteristics that distinguish each of the inner planets?

### Key Terms

- terrestrial planets
- greenhouse effect

### Target Reading Skill

**Using Prior Knowledge** Look at the section headings and visuals to see what this section is about. Then write what you know about the inner planets in a graphic organizer like the one below. As you read, write what you learn.

| What You Know |
|---|
| 1. Most of Earth is covered with water.<br>2. |

| What You Learned |
|---|
| 1.<br>2. |

## Lab zone Discover Activity

### How Does Mars Look From Earth?

1. Work in pairs. On a sheet of paper, draw a circle 20 cm across to represent Mars. Draw about 100 small lines, each about 1 cm long, at random places inside the circle.
2. Have your partner look at your drawing of Mars from the other side of the room. Your partner should draw what he or she sees.
3. Compare your original drawing with what your partner drew. Then look at your own drawing from across the room.

**Think It Over**

**Observing** Did your partner draw any connecting lines that were not actually on your drawing? What can you conclude about the accuracy of descriptions of other planets based on observations from Earth?

Where could you find a planet whose atmosphere has almost entirely leaked away into space? How about a planet whose surface is hot enough to melt lead? And how about a planet with volcanoes higher than any on Earth? Finally, where could you find a planet with oceans of water brimming with fish and other life? These are descriptions of the four planets closest to the sun, known as the inner planets.

Earth and the three other inner planets—Mercury, Venus, and Mars—are more similar to each other than they are to the five outer planets. **The four inner planets are small and dense and have rocky surfaces.** The inner planets are often called the **terrestrial planets,** from the Latin word *terra,* which means "Earth." Figure 10 summarizes data about the inner planets.

## Earth

As you can see in Figure 11, Earth has three main layers—a crust, a mantle, and a core. The crust includes the solid, rocky surface. Under the crust is the mantle, a layer of hot molten rock. When volcanoes erupt, this hot material rises to the surface. Earth has a dense core made of mainly iron and nickel. The outer core is liquid, but the inner core is solid.

**The Inner Planets**

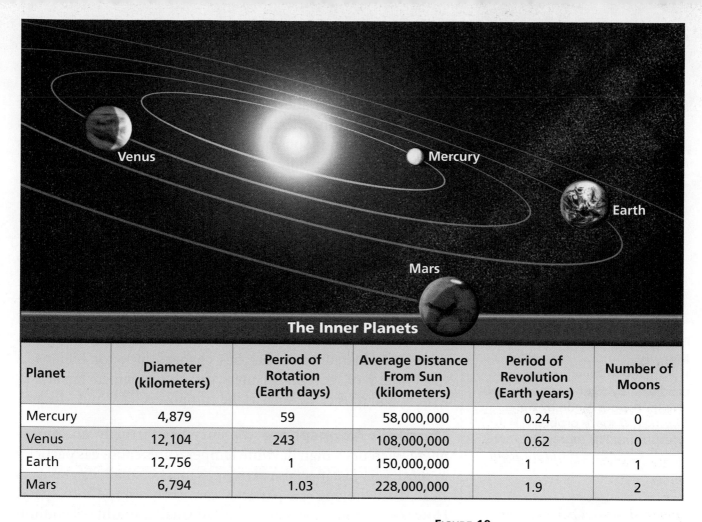

| Planet | Diameter (kilometers) | Period of Rotation (Earth days) | Average Distance From Sun (kilometers) | Period of Revolution (Earth years) | Number of Moons |
|---|---|---|---|---|---|
| Mercury | 4,879 | 59 | 58,000,000 | 0.24 | 0 |
| Venus | 12,104 | 243 | 108,000,000 | 0.62 | 0 |
| Earth | 12,756 | 1 | 150,000,000 | 1 | 1 |
| Mars | 6,794 | 1.03 | 228,000,000 | 1.9 | 2 |

**FIGURE 10**
The inner planets take up only a small part of the solar system. Note that sizes and distances are not drawn to scale.

**Water** **Earth is unique in our solar system in having liquid water at its surface.** In fact, most of Earth's surface, about 70 percent, is covered with water. Perhaps our planet should be called "Water" instead of "Earth"! Earth has a suitable temperature range for water to exist as a liquid, gas, or solid. Water is also important in shaping Earth's surface, wearing it down and changing its appearance over time.

**Atmosphere** Earth has enough gravity to hold on to most gases. These gases make up Earth's atmosphere, which extends more than 100 kilometers above its surface. Other planets in the solar system have atmospheres too, but only Earth has an atmosphere that is rich in oxygen. The oxygen you need to live makes up about 20 percent of Earth's atmosphere. Nearly all the rest is nitrogen, with small amounts of other gases such as argon and carbon dioxide. The atmosphere also includes varying amounts of water in the form of a gas. Water in a gaseous form is called water vapor.

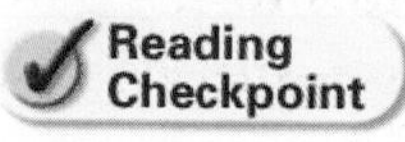

**What two gases make up most of Earth's atmosphere?**

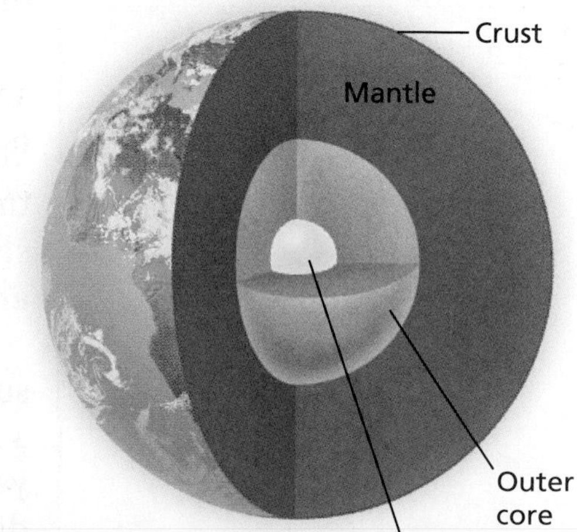


**FIGURE 11**
**Earth's Layers**
Earth has a solid, rocky surface.
**Interpreting Diagrams** *What are Earth's three main layers?*

**FIGURE 12**
**Mercury**
This image of Mercury was produced by combining a series of smaller images made by the *Mariner 10* space probe.
**Interpreting Photographs** *How is Mercury's surface different from Earth's?*

Size of Mercury compared to Earth

## Mercury

**Mercury is the smallest terrestrial planet and the planet closest to the sun.** Mercury is not much larger than Earth's moon and has no moons of its own. The interior of Mercury is probably made up mainly of the dense metal iron.

**Exploring Mercury** Because Mercury is so close to the sun, it is hard to see from Earth. Much of what astronomers know about Mercury's surface came from a single probe, *Mariner 10.* It flew by Mercury three times in 1974 and 1975. Two new missions to Mercury are planned. The first of these, called *MESSENGER,* is scheduled to go into orbit around Mercury in 2009.

*Mariner 10*'s photographs show that Mercury has many flat plains and craters on its surface. The large number of craters shows that Mercury's surface has changed little for billions of years. Many of Mercury's craters have been named for artists, writers, and musicians, such as the composers Bach and Mozart.

**Mercury's Atmosphere** Mercury has virtually no atmosphere. Mercury's high daytime temperatures cause gas particles to move very fast. Because Mercury's mass is small, its gravity is weak. Fast-moving gas particles can easily escape into space. However, astronomers have detected small amounts of sodium and other gases around Mercury.

Mercury is a planet of extremes, with a greater temperature range than any other planet in the solar system. It is so close to the sun that during the day, the side facing the sun reaches temperatures of 430°C. Because Mercury has almost no atmosphere, at night its heat escapes into space. Then its temperature drops below −170°C.

## Venus

Venus is so similar in size and mass to Earth that it is sometimes called "Earth's twin." **Venus's density and internal structure are similar to Earth's. But, in other ways, Venus and Earth are very different.**

Venus takes about 7.5 Earth months to revolve around the sun. It takes about 8 months for Venus to rotate once on its axis. Thus, Venus rotates so slowly that its day is longer than its year! Oddly, Venus rotates from east to west, the opposite direction from most other planets and moons. Astronomers hypothesize that a large object struck Venus long ago, causing the planet to change its direction of rotation.

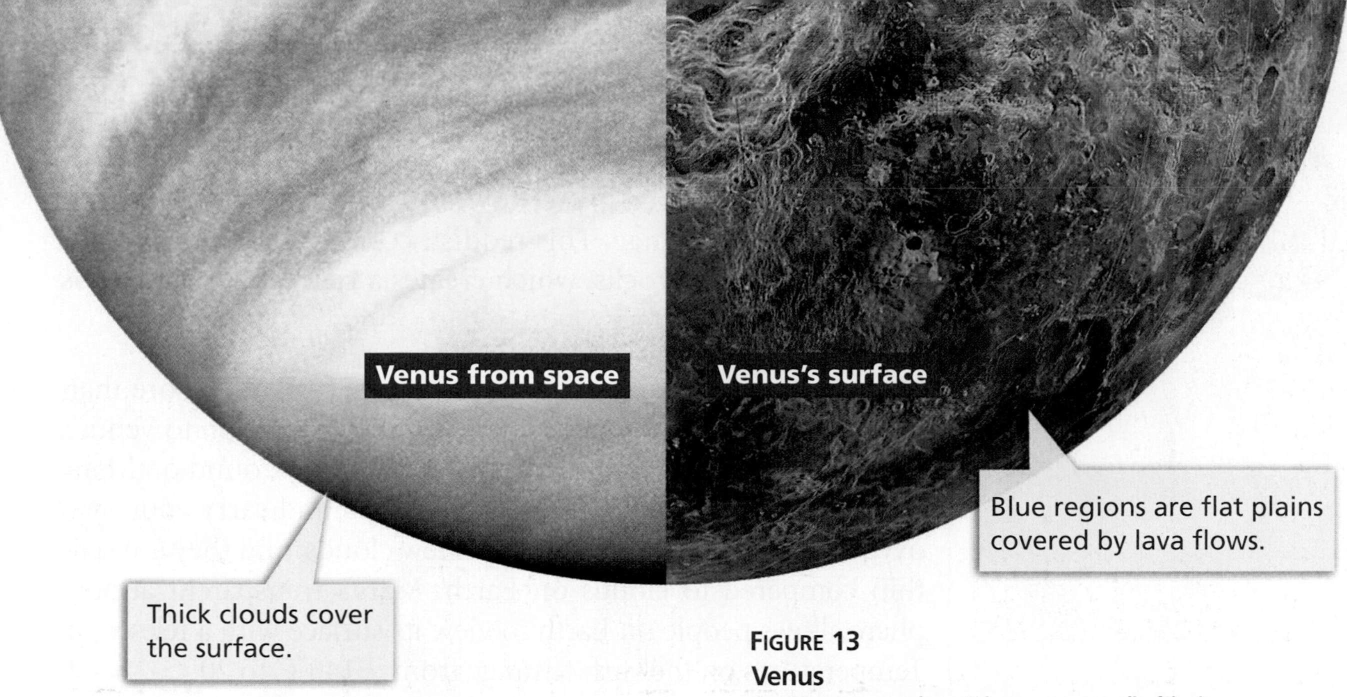

Venus from space
Venus's surface
Blue regions are flat plains covered by lava flows.
Thick clouds cover the surface.

**FIGURE 13**
**Venus**
An image made with a camera (left) shows Venus's thick atmosphere. A radar image (right) penetrates Venus's clouds to reveal the surface. Both images are false color.

**Venus's Atmosphere** Venus's atmosphere is so thick that it is always cloudy there. From Earth or space, astronomers can see only a smooth cloud cover over Venus. The clouds are made mostly of droplets of sulfuric acid.

If you could stand on Venus's surface, you would quickly be crushed by the weight of its atmosphere. The pressure of Venus's atmosphere is 90 times greater than the pressure of Earth's atmosphere. You couldn't breathe on Venus because its atmosphere is mostly carbon dioxide.

Because Venus is closer to the sun than Earth is, it receives more solar energy than Earth does. Much of this radiation is reflected by Venus's atmosphere. However, some radiation reaches the surface and is later given off as heat. The carbon dioxide in Venus's atmosphere traps heat so well that Venus has the hottest surface of any planet. At 460°C, its average surface temperature is hot enough to melt lead. This trapping of heat by the atmosphere is called the **greenhouse effect.**

Size of Venus compared to Earth

**Exploring Venus** Many space probes have visited Venus. The first probe to land on the surface and send back data, *Venera 7*, landed in 1970. The *Magellan* probe reached Venus in 1990, carrying radar instruments. Radar works through clouds, so *Magellan* was able to map nearly the entire surface. The *Magellan* data confirmed that Venus is covered with rock. Venus's surface has many volcanoes and broad plains formed by lava flows.

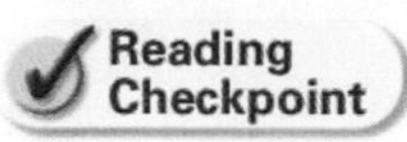


**How is Venus's surface temperature affected by the greenhouse effect?**

**For:** Links on the planets
**Visit:** www.SciLinks.org
**Web Code:** scn-0633

Size of Mars compared to Earth

## Mars

Mars is called the "red planet." When you see it in the sky, it has a slightly reddish tinge. This reddish color is due to the breakdown of iron-rich rocks, which creates a rusty dust that covers much of Mars's surface.

**Mars's Atmosphere** The atmosphere of Mars is more than 95 percent carbon dioxide. It is similar in composition to Venus's atmosphere, but much thinner. You could walk around on Mars, but you would have to wear an airtight suit and carry your own oxygen, like a scuba diver. Mars has few clouds, and they are very thin compared to clouds on Earth. Mars's transparent atmosphere allows people on Earth to view its surface with a telescope. Temperatures on the surface range from $-140^{\circ}C$ to $20^{\circ}C$.

**Water on Mars** Images of Mars taken from space show a variety of features that look as if they were made by ancient streams, lakes, or floods. There are huge canyons and features that look like the remains of ancient coastlines. **Scientists think that a large amount of liquid water flowed on Mars's surface in the distant past.** Scientists infer that Mars must have been much warmer and had a thicker atmosphere at that time.

At present, liquid water cannot exist for long on Mars's surface. Mars's atmosphere is so thin that any liquid water would quickly turn into a gas. So where is Mars's water now? Some of it is located in the planet's two polar ice caps, which contain frozen water and carbon dioxide. A small amount also exists as water vapor in Mars's atmosphere. Some water vapor has probably escaped into space. But scientists think that a large amount of water may still be frozen underground.

**FIGURE 14**
**Mars**
Because of its thin atmosphere and its distance from the sun, Mars is quite cold. Mars has ice caps at both poles. **Inferring** *Why is it easy to see Mars's surface from space?*



**Seasons on Mars** Because Mars has a tilted axis, it has seasons just as Earth does. During the Martian winter, an ice cap grows larger as a layer of frozen carbon dioxide covers it. Because the northern and southern hemispheres have opposite seasons, one ice cap grows while the other one shrinks.

As the seasons change on the dusty surface of Mars, windstorms arise and blow the dust around. Since the dust is blown off some regions, these regions look darker.

**FIGURE 15**
**Mars's Surface**
The surface of Mars is rugged and rocky.

**Exploring Mars** Many space probes have visited Mars. The first ones seemed to show that Mars is barren and covered with craters like the moon. Recently, two new probes landed on Mars's surface. NASA's *Spirit* and *Opportunity* rovers explored opposite sides of the planet. They examined a variety of rocks and soil samples. At both locations, the rovers found strong evidence that liquid water was once present.

Some regions of Mars have giant volcanoes. Astronomers see signs that lava flowed from the volcanoes in the past, but the volcanoes are no longer active. *Olympus Mons* on Mars is the largest volcano in the solar system.

*The Solar System*

Video Preview
▶ Video Field Trip
Video Assessment

**What is the largest volcano in the solar system?**

## Section 3 Assessment

### Target Reading Skill

**Using Prior Knowledge** Review your graphic organizer and revise it based on what you just learned in the section.

### Reviewing Key Concepts

1. a. **Listing** List the four inner planets in order of size, from smallest to largest.
   b. **Comparing and Contrasting** How are the four inner planets similar to one another?
2. a. **Describing** Describe an important characteristic of each inner planet.
   b. **Comparing and Contrasting** Compare the atmospheres of the four inner planets.
   c. **Relating Cause and Effect** Venus is much farther from the sun than Mercury is. Yet average temperatures on Venus's surface are much higher than those on Mercury. Explain why.

### Writing in Science

**Travel Brochure** Select one of the inner planets other than Earth. Design a travel brochure for your selected planet, including basic facts and descriptions of places of interest. Also include a few sketches or photos to go along with your text.

Science and **Society**

# Space Exploration—Is It Worth the Cost?

Imagine that your spacecraft has just landed on the moon or on Mars. You've spent years planning for this moment. Canyons, craters, plains, and distant mountains stretch out before you. Perhaps a group of scientists has already begun construction of a permanent outpost. You check your spacesuit and prepare to step out onto the rocky surface.

Is such a trip likely? Would it be worthwhile? How much is space flight really worth to human society? Scientists and public officials have already started to debate such questions. Space exploration can help us learn more about the universe. But exploration can be risky and expensive. Sending people into space costs billions of dollars and risks the lives of astronauts. How can we balance the costs and benefits of space exploration?

▼ **Moon Landing**
A rocket is preparing to dock with a lander on the moon's surface in this imaginative artwork.

## The Issues

### Should Humans Travel Into Space?

Many Americans think that Neil Armstrong's walk on the moon in 1969 was one of the great moments in history. Learning how to keep people alive in space has led to improvements in everyday life. Safer equipment for firefighters, easier ways to package frozen food, and effective heart monitors have all come from space program research.

### What Are the Alternatives?

Space exploration can involve a project to establish a colony on the moon or Mars. It also can involve a more limited use of scientific instruments near Earth, such as the Hubble Space Telescope. Instead of sending people, we could send space probes like *Cassini* to other planets.

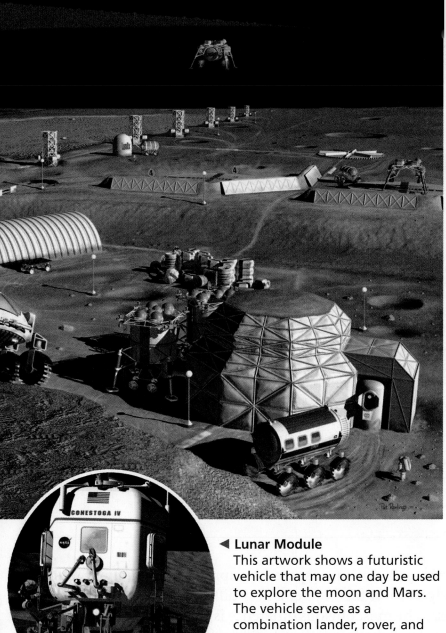

◀ **Lunar Outpost**
A mining operation on the moon is shown in this imaginative artwork. Such a facility may someday harvest oxygen from the moon's soil.

◀ **Lunar Module**
This artwork shows a futuristic vehicle that may one day be used to explore the moon and Mars. The vehicle serves as a combination lander, rover, and habitat for astronauts.

## Is Human Space Exploration Worth the Cost?

Scientists who favor human travel into space say that only people can collect certain kinds of information. They argue that the technologies developed for human space exploration will have many applications on Earth. But no one knows if research in space really provides information more quickly than research that can be done on Earth. Many critics of human space exploration think that other needs are more important. One United States senator said, "Every time you put money into the space station, there is a dime that won't be available for our children's education or for medical research."

## You Decide

1. **Identify the Problem**
In your own words, list the various costs and benefits of space exploration.

2. **Analyze the Options**
Make a chart of three different approaches to space exploration: sending humans to the moon or another planet, doing only Earth-based research, and one other option. What are the benefits and drawbacks of each of these approaches?

3. **Find a Solution**
Imagine that you are a member of Congress who has to vote on a new budget. There is a fixed amount of money to spend, so you have to decide which needs are most important. Make a list of your top ten priorities. Explain your decisions.

**For:** More on space exploration
**Visit:** PHSchool.com
**Web Code:** cfh-5030

Section 4

# The Outer Planets

## Reading Preview

### Key Concepts

- What characteristics do the gas giants have in common?
- What characteristics distinguish each of the outer planets?

### Key Terms

- gas giant
- ring

### Target Reading Skill

**Identifying Main Ideas** As you read the *Gas Giants and Pluto* section, write the main idea—the biggest or most important idea—in a graphic organizer like the one below. Then write three supporting details that further explain the main idea.

**Main Idea**

The four gas giants are similar in . . .

Detail | Detail | Detail

## Lab zone Discover Activity

### How Big Are the Planets?

The table shows the diameters of the outer planets compared to Earth. For example, Jupiter's diameter is about 11 times Earth's diameter.

| Planet | Diameter (Earth = 1) |
|---|---|
| Earth | 1.0 |
| Jupiter | 11.2 |
| Saturn | 9.4 |
| Uranus | 4.0 |
| Neptune | 3.9 |

1. Measure the diameter of a quarter in millimeters. Trace the quarter to represent Earth.
2. If Earth were the size of a quarter, calculate how large Jupiter would be. Now draw a circle to represent Jupiter.
3. Repeat Step 2 for each of the other planets in the table.

**Think It Over**

**Classifying** List the outer planets in order from largest to smallest. What is the largest outer planet?

Imagine you are in a spaceship approaching Jupiter. You'll quickly discover that Jupiter is very different from the terrestrial planets. The most obvious difference is Jupiter's great size. Jupiter is so large that more than 1,300 Earths could fit within it!

As your spaceship enters Jupiter's atmosphere, you encounter thick, colorful bands of clouds. Next, you sink into a denser and denser mixture of hydrogen and helium gas. Eventually, if the enormous pressure of the atmosphere does not crush your ship, you'll reach an incredibly deep "ocean" of liquid hydrogen and helium. But where exactly is Jupiter's surface? Surprisingly, there isn't a solid surface. Like the other giant planets, Jupiter has no real surface, just a solid core buried deep within the planet.

◀ **An illustration of the space probe *Galileo* approaching the cloud-covered atmosphere of Jupiter.**

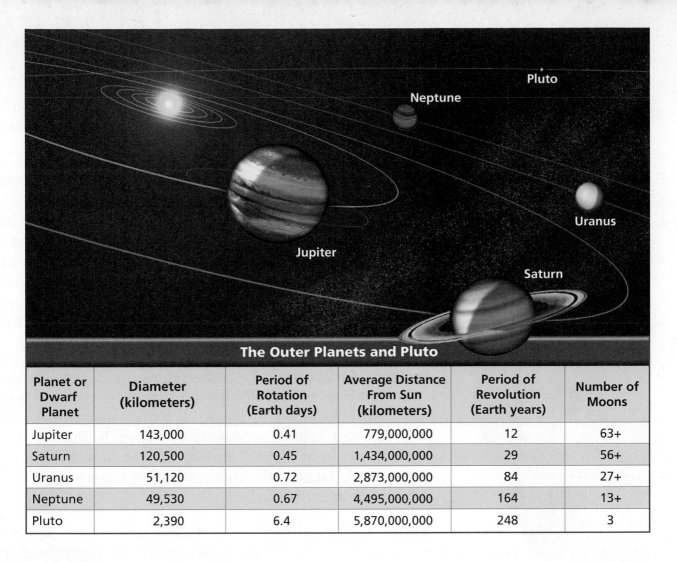

**The Outer Planets and Pluto**

| Planet or Dwarf Planet | Diameter (kilometers) | Period of Rotation (Earth days) | Average Distance From Sun (kilometers) | Period of Revolution (Earth years) | Number of Moons |
|---|---|---|---|---|---|
| Jupiter | 143,000 | 0.41 | 779,000,000 | 12 | 63+ |
| Saturn | 120,500 | 0.45 | 1,434,000,000 | 29 | 56+ |
| Uranus | 51,120 | 0.72 | 2,873,000,000 | 84 | 27+ |
| Neptune | 49,530 | 0.67 | 4,495,000,000 | 164 | 13+ |
| Pluto | 2,390 | 6.4 | 5,870,000,000 | 248 | 3 |

**FIGURE 16**
The outer planets are much farther apart than the inner planets. Pluto is now considered to be a dwarf planet. Note that planet sizes and distances are not drawn to scale. **Observing** *Which outer planet has the most moons?*

## Gas Giants and Pluto

Jupiter and the other planets farthest from the sun are called the outer planets. **The four outer planets—Jupiter, Saturn, Uranus, and Neptune—are much larger and more massive than Earth, and they do not have solid surfaces.** Because these four planets are all so large, they are often called the **gas giants.** Figure 16 provides information about these planets. It also includes Pluto, which is now classified as a dwarf planet.

Like the sun, the gas giants are composed mainly of hydrogen and helium. Because they are so massive, the gas giants exert a much stronger gravitational force than the terrestrial planets. Gravity keeps the giant planets' gases from escaping, so they have thick atmospheres. Despite the name "gas giant," much of the hydrogen and helium is actually in liquid form because of the enormous pressure inside the planets. The outer layers of the gas giants are extremely cold because of their great distance from the sun. Temperatures increase greatly within the planets.

All the gas giants have many moons. In addition, each of the gas giants is surrounded by a set of rings. A **ring** is a thin disk of small particles of ice and rock.

**For:** More on the planets
**Visit:** PHSchool.com
**Web Code:** ced-5034

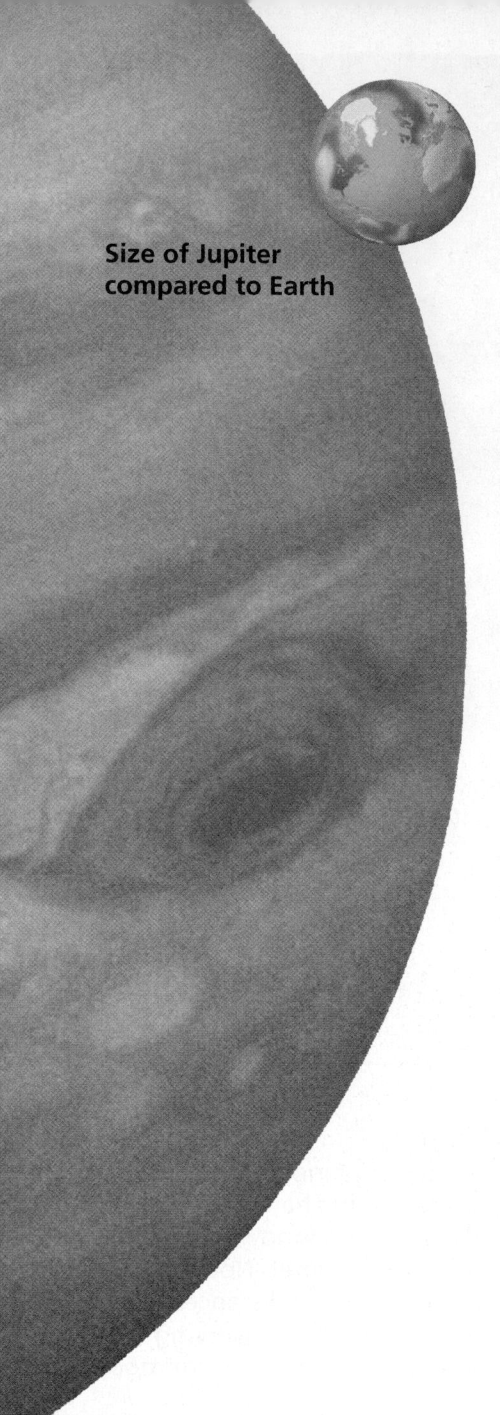


## Jupiter

**Jupiter is the largest and most massive planet.** Jupiter's enormous mass dwarfs the other planets. In fact, its mass is about $2\frac{1}{2}$ times that of all the other planets combined!

**Jupiter's Atmosphere** Like all of the gas giants, Jupiter has a thick atmosphere made up mainly of hydrogen and helium. An especially interesting feature of Jupiter's atmosphere is its Great Red Spot, a storm that is larger than Earth! The storm's swirling winds blow hundreds of kilometers per hour, similar to a hurricane. But hurricanes on Earth weaken quickly as they pass over land. On Jupiter, there is no land to weaken the huge storm. The Great Red Spot, which was first observed in the mid-1600s, shows no signs of going away soon.

**Jupiter's Structure** Astronomers think that Jupiter, like the other giant planets, probably has a dense core of rock and iron at its center. As shown in Figure 17, a thick mantle of liquid hydrogen and helium surrounds this core. Because of the crushing weight of Jupiter's atmosphere, the pressure at Jupiter's core is estimated to be about 30 million times greater than the pressure at Earth's surface.

**Jupiter's Moons** Recall that Galileo discovered Jupiter's four largest moons. These moons, which are highlighted in Figure 18, are named Io (EYE oh), Europa, Ganymede, and Callisto. All four are larger than Earth's own moon. However, they are very different from one another. Since Galileo's time, astronomers have discovered dozens of additional moons orbiting Jupiter. Many of these are small moons that have been found in the last few years thanks to improved technology.

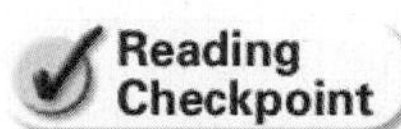

**What is Jupiter's atmosphere composed of?**

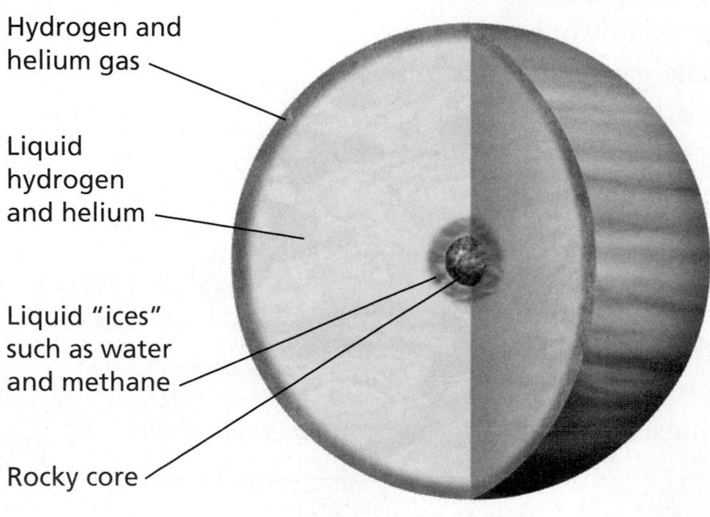


FIGURE 17
**Jupiter's Structure**
Jupiter is composed mainly of the elements hydrogen and helium. Although Jupiter is often called a "gas giant," much of it is actually liquid.
**Comparing and Contrasting** *How does the structure of Jupiter differ from that of a terrestrial planet?*

FIGURE 18
## Jupiter's Moons
The astronomer Galileo discovered Jupiter's four largest moons. These images are not shown to scale. **Interpreting Photographs** *Which is the largest of Jupiter's moons?*

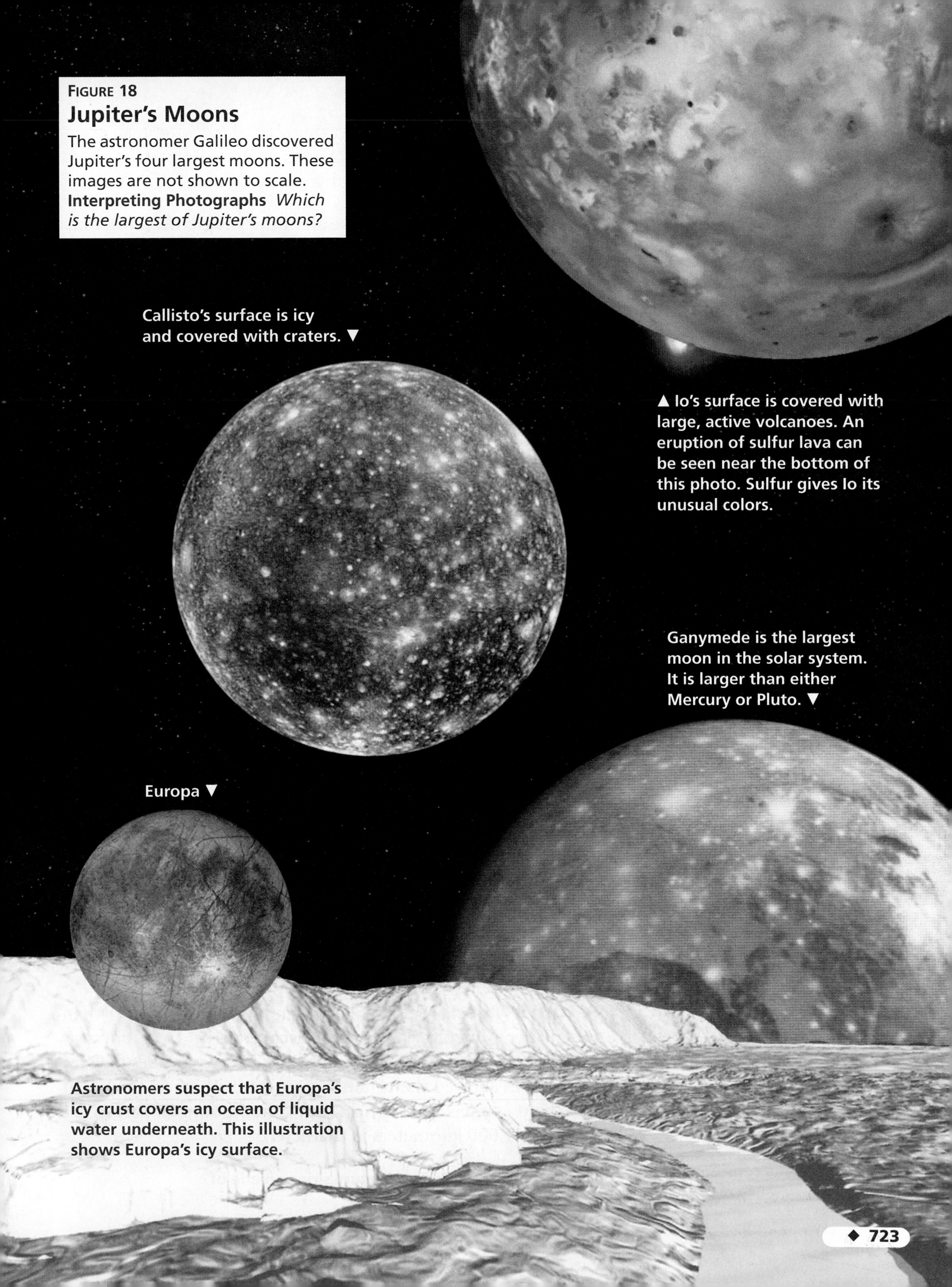

Callisto's surface is icy and covered with craters. ▼

▲ Io's surface is covered with large, active volcanoes. An eruption of sulfur lava can be seen near the bottom of this photo. Sulfur gives Io its unusual colors.

Ganymede is the largest moon in the solar system. It is larger than either Mercury or Pluto. ▼

Europa ▼

Astronomers suspect that Europa's icy crust covers an ocean of liquid water underneath. This illustration shows Europa's icy surface.

**FIGURE 19**
**Exploring Saturn**
The *Cassini* probe is exploring Saturn and its moons.
**Observing** *Why might it be hard to see Saturn's rings when their edges are facing Earth?*

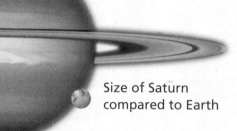

Size of Saturn compared to Earth

## Saturn

The second-largest planet in the solar system is Saturn. The *Voyager* probes showed that Saturn, like Jupiter, has a thick atmosphere made up mainly of hydrogen and helium. Saturn's atmosphere also contains clouds and storms, but they are less dramatic than those on Jupiter. Saturn is the only planet whose average density is less than that of water.

**Saturn's Rings** When Galileo first looked at Saturn with a telescope, he could see something sticking out on the sides. But he didn't know what it was. A few decades later, an astronomer using a better telescope discovered that Saturn had rings around it. These rings are made of chunks of ice and rock, each traveling in its own orbit around Saturn.

**Saturn has the most spectacular rings of any planet.** From Earth, it looks as though Saturn has only a few rings and that they are divided from each other by narrow, dark regions. The *Voyager* spacecraft discovered that each of these obvious rings is divided into many thinner rings. Saturn's rings are broad and thin, like a compact disc.

**Saturn's Moons** Saturn's largest moon, Titan, is larger than the planet Mercury. Titan was discovered in 1665 but was known only as a point of light until the *Voyager* probes flew by. The probes showed that Titan has an atmosphere so thick that little light can pass through it. Four other moons of Saturn are each over 1,000 kilometers in diameter.

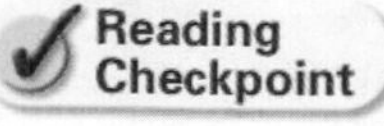

**Reading Checkpoint** **What are Saturn's rings made of?**

**Lab zone Skills Activity**

### Making Models

1. Use a plastic foam sphere 8 cm in diameter to represent Saturn.
2. Use an overhead transparency to represent Saturn's rings. Cut a circle 18 cm in diameter out of the transparency. Cut a hole 9 cm in diameter out of the center of the circle.
3. Stick five toothpicks into Saturn, spaced equally around its equator. Put the transparency on the toothpicks and tape it to them. Sprinkle baking soda on the transparency.
4. Use a peppercorn to represent Titan. Place the peppercorn 72 cm away from Saturn on the same plane as the rings.
5. What do the particles of baking soda represent?

Size of Uranus compared to Earth

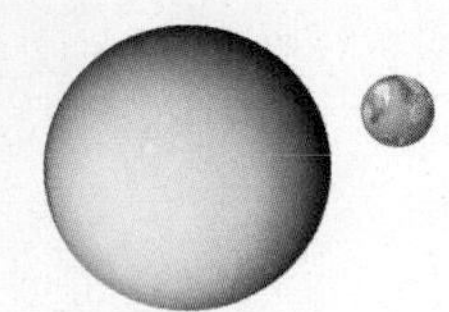

## Uranus

Although the gas giant Uranus (YOOR uh nus) is about four times the diameter of Earth, it is still much smaller than Jupiter and Saturn. Uranus is twice as far from the sun as Saturn, so it is much colder. Uranus looks blue-green because of traces of methane in its atmosphere. Like the other gas giants, Uranus is surrounded by a group of thin, flat rings, although they are much darker than Saturn's rings.

**Discovery of Uranus** In 1781, Uranus became the first new planet discovered since ancient times. Astronomer William Herschel, in England, found a fuzzy object in the sky that did not look like a star. At first he thought it might be a comet, but it soon proved to be a planet beyond Saturn. The discovery made Herschel famous and started an era of active solar system study.

**Exploring Uranus** About 200 years after Herschel's discovery, *Voyager 2* arrived at Uranus and sent back close-up views of that planet. Images from *Voyager 2* show only a few clouds on Uranus's surface. But even these few clouds allowed astronomers to calculate that Uranus rotates in about 17 hours.

**Uranus's axis of rotation is tilted at an angle of about 90 degrees from the vertical.** Viewed from Earth, Uranus is rotating from top to bottom instead of from side to side, the way most of the other planets do. Uranus's rings and moons rotate around this tilted axis. Astronomers think that billions of years ago Uranus was hit by an object that knocked it on its side.

**Uranus's Moons** Photographs from *Voyager 2* show that Uranus's five largest moons have icy, cratered surfaces. The craters show that rocks from space have hit the moons. Uranus's moons also have lava flows on their surfaces, suggesting that material has erupted from inside each moon. *Voyager 2* images revealed 10 moons that had never been seen before. Recently, astronomers discovered several more moons, for a total of at least 27.

**FIGURE 20**
**Uranus**
The false color image of Uranus below was taken by the Hubble Space Telescope. Unlike most other planets, Uranus rotates from top to bottom rather than side to side.
**Inferring** *How must Uranus's seasons be unusual?*

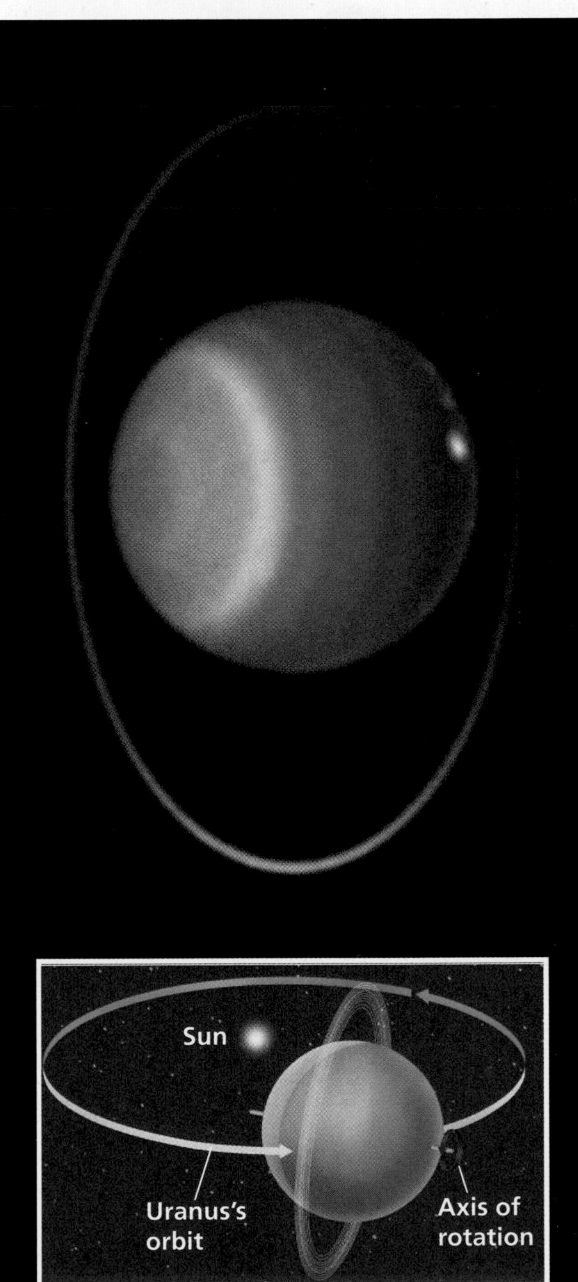


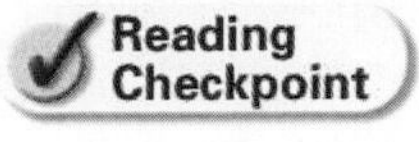

**Who discovered Uranus?**

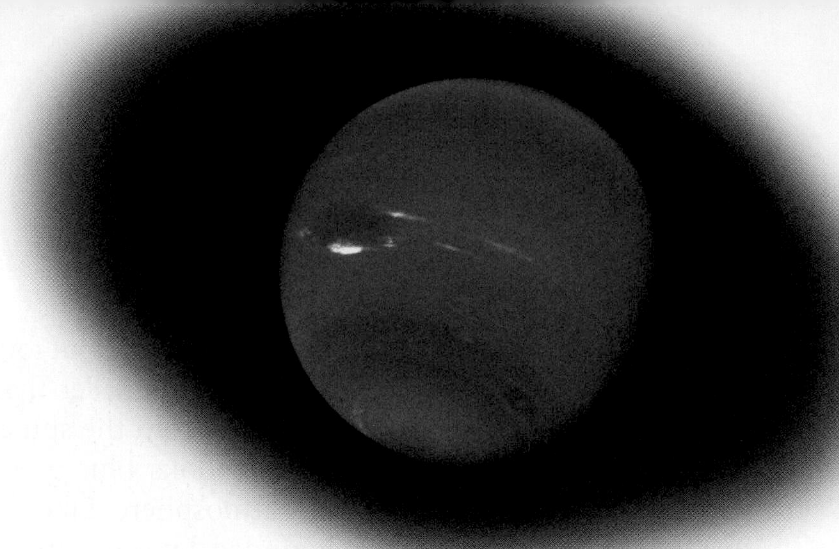

**FIGURE 21**
**Neptune**
The Great Dark Spot was a giant storm in Neptune's atmosphere. White clouds, probably made of methane ice crystals, can also be seen in the photo.

Size of Neptune compared to Earth

## Math Skills

### Circumference

To calculate the circumference of a circle, use this formula:

$$C = 2\pi r$$

In the formula, $\pi \approx 3.14$, and $r$ is the circle's radius, which is the distance from the center of the circle to its edge. The same formula can be used to calculate the circumference of planets, which are nearly spherical.

Neptune's radius at its equator is about 24,800 km. Calculate its circumference.

$$C = 2\pi r$$
$$= 2.00 \times 3.14 \times 24{,}800 \text{ km}$$
$$= 156{,}000 \text{ km}$$

**Practice Problem** Saturn's radius is 60,250 km. What is its circumference?

## Neptune

Neptune is even farther from the sun than Uranus. In some ways, Uranus and Neptune look like twins. They are similar in size and color. **Neptune is a cold, blue planet. Its atmosphere contains visible clouds.** Scientists think that Neptune, shown in Figure 21, is slowly shrinking, causing its interior to heat up. As this energy rises toward Neptune's surface, it produces clouds and storms in the planet's atmosphere.

**Discovery of Neptune** Neptune was discovered as a result of a mathematical prediction. Astronomers noted that Uranus was not quite following the orbit predicted for it. They hypothesized that the gravity of an unseen planet was affecting Uranus's orbit. By 1846, mathematicians in England and France had calculated the orbit of this unseen planet. Shortly thereafter, an observer saw an unknown object in the predicted area of the sky. It was the new planet, now called Neptune.

**Exploring Neptune** In 1989, *Voyager 2* flew by Neptune and photographed a Great Dark Spot about the size of Earth. Like the Great Red Spot on Jupiter, the Great Dark Spot was probably a giant storm. But the storm didn't last long. Images taken five years later showed that the Great Dark Spot was gone. Other, smaller spots and regions of clouds on Neptune also seem to come and go.

**Neptune's Moons** Astronomers have discovered at least 13 moons orbiting Neptune. The largest moon is Triton, which has a thin atmosphere. The *Voyager* images show that the region near Triton's south pole is covered by nitrogen ice.

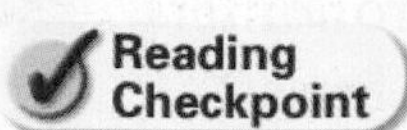


**Before they could see Neptune, what evidence led scientists to conclude that it existed?**

Size of Pluto compared to Earth

**FIGURE 22**
**Pluto and Charon**
The illustration above shows Pluto (lower right) and its moon Charon. Charon is more than half the size of Pluto.

## Pluto

Pluto is very different from the gas giants. **Pluto has a solid surface and is much smaller and denser than the outer planets.** In fact, Pluto is smaller than Earth's moon.

Pluto has three known moons. The largest of these, Charon, is more than half of Pluto's size.

**Pluto's Orbit** Pluto is so far from the sun that it revolves around the sun only once every 248 Earth years. Pluto's orbit is very elliptical, bringing it closer to the sun than Neptune on part of its orbit.

**Dwarf Planets** Until recently, Pluto was considered to be the ninth planet in our solar system. Pluto was always thought to be something of an oddball because of its small size and unusual orbit. Then, in recent years, astronomers discovered many icy objects beyond Neptune's orbit. Some of these were fairly similar to Pluto in size and makeup. Following the discovery of a body that is even larger and farther from the sun than Pluto, astronomers decided to create a new class of objects called "dwarf planets." A dwarf planet, like a planet, is round and orbits the sun. But unlike a planet, a dwarf planet has not cleared out the neighborhood around its orbit. Astronomers classified Pluto and two other bodies as dwarf planets.

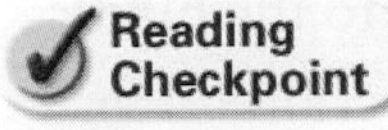


How is Pluto now classified?

## Section 4 Assessment

**Target Reading Skill Identifying Main Ideas** Use your graphic organizer about the structure of the gas giants to help you answer Question 1 below.

### Reviewing Key Concepts

1. a. **Describing** How are the gas giants similar to one another?
   b. **Explaining** Why do all of the gas giants have thick atmospheres?
   c. **Listing** List the outer planets in order of size, from smallest to largest.
   d. **Comparing and Contrasting** Compare the structure of a typical terrestrial planet with that of a gas giant.
2. a. **Describing** Describe an important characteristic of each outer planet that helps to distinguish it from the other outer planets.
   b. **Comparing and Contrasting** How is Pluto different from the gas giants?
   c. **Classifying** Why did astronomers reclassify Pluto as a dwarf planet?

**Math Practice**

3. **Circumference** Jupiter's radius is about 71,490 km. What is its circumference?

Lab zone

# Design Your Own Lab

## Speeding Around the Sun

### Problem

How does a planet's distance from the sun affect its period of revolution?

### Skills Focus

making models, developing hypotheses, designing experiments

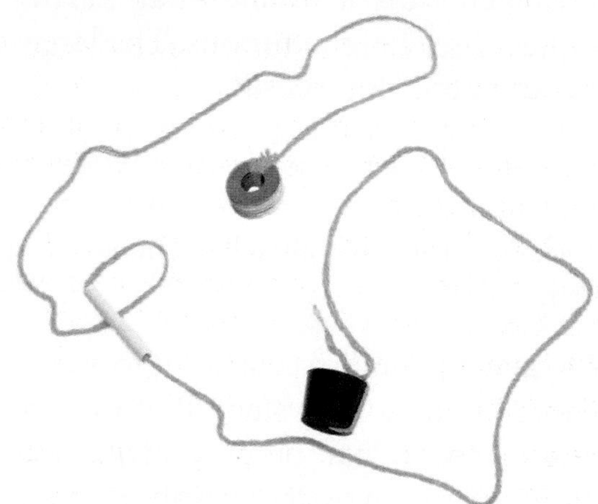

### Materials

- string, 1.5 m
- plastic tube, 6 cm
- meter stick
- weight or several washers
- one-hole rubber stopper
- stopwatch or watch with second hand

### Procedure  

#### PART 1 Modeling Planetary Revolution

1. Copy the data table onto a sheet of paper.

| Data Table | | | | |
|---|---|---|---|---|
| Distance (cm) | Period of Revolution | | | |
| | Trial 1 | Trial 2 | Trial 3 | Average |
| 20 | | | | |
| 40 | | | | |
| 60 | | | | |

2. Make a model of a planet orbiting the sun by threading the string through the rubber stopper hole. Tie the end of the string to the main part of the string. Pull tightly to make sure that the knot will not become untied.
3. Thread the other end of the string through the plastic tube and tie a weight to that end. Have your teacher check both knots.
4. Pull the string so the stopper is 20 cm away from the plastic tube. Hold the plastic tube in your hand above your head. Keeping the length of string constant, swing the rubber stopper in a circle above your head just fast enough to keep the stopper moving. The circle represents a planet's orbit, and the length of string from the rubber stopper to the plastic tube represents the distance from the sun. **CAUTION:** *Stand away from other students. Make sure the swinging stopper will not hit students or objects. Do not let go of the string.*
5. Have your lab partner time how long it takes for the rubber stopper to make ten complete revolutions. Determine the period for one revolution by dividing the measured time by ten. Record the time in the data table.
6. Repeat Step 5 two more times. Be sure to record each trial in a data table. After the third trial, calculate and record the average period of revolution.

## PART 2 Designing an Experiment

7. Write your hypothesis for how a planet's period of revolution would be affected by changing its distance from the sun.
8. Design an experiment that will enable you to test your hypothesis. Write the steps you plan to follow to carry out your experiment. As you design your experiment, consider the following factors:
   - What different distances will you test?
   - What variables are involved in your experiment and how will you control them?
   - How many trials will you run for each distance?
9. Have your teacher review your step-by-step plan. After your teacher approves your plan, carry out your experiment.

## Analyze and Conclude

1. **Making Models** In your experiment, what represents the planet and what represents the sun?
2. **Making Models** What force does the pull on the string represent?
3. **Interpreting Data** What happened to the period of revolution when you changed the distance in Part 2? Did your experiment prove or disprove your hypothesis?
4. **Drawing Conclusions** Which planets take less time to revolve around the sun—those closer to the sun or those farther away? Use the model to support your answer.
5. **Designing Experiments** As you were designing your experiment, which variable was the most difficult to control? How did you design your procedure to control that variable?
6. **Communicating** Write a brief summary of your experiment for a science magazine. Describe your hypothesis, procedure, and results in one or two paragraphs.

## More to Explore

Develop a hypothesis for how a planet's mass might affect its period of revolution. Then, using a stopper with a different mass, modify the activity to test your hypothesis. Before you swing your stopper, have your teacher check your knots.

# 5 Comets, Asteroids, and Meteors

## Reading Preview

### Key Concepts

- What are the characteristics of comets?
- Where are most asteroids found?
- What are meteoroids and how do they form?

### Key Terms

- comet • coma • nucleus
- Kuiper belt • Oort cloud
- asteroid • asteroid belt
- meteoroid • meteor
- meteorite

### Target Reading Skill

**Comparing and Contrasting**
As you read, compare and contrast comets, asteroids, and meteoroids by completing a table like the one below.

**Comets, Asteroids, and Meteoroids**

| Feature | Comets | Asteroids |
|---|---|---|
| Origin | Kuiper belt and Oort cloud | |
| Size | | |
| Composition | | |

## Lab zone Discover Activity

### Which Way Do Comet Tails Point?

1. Form a small ball out of modeling clay to represent a comet.
2. Using a pencil point, push three 10-cm lengths of string into the ball. The strings represent the comet's tail. Stick the ball onto the pencil point, as shown.
3. Hold the ball about 1 m in front of a fan. The air from the fan represents the solar wind. Move the ball toward the fan, away from the fan, and from side to side. **CAUTION:** *Keep your fingers away from the fan blades.*

**Think It Over**
**Inferring** How does moving the ball affect the direction in which the strings point? What determines which way the tail of a comet points?

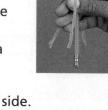

Imagine watching a cosmic collision! That's exactly what happened in July 1994. The year before, Eugene and Carolyn Shoemaker and David Levy discovered a comet that had previously broken into pieces near Jupiter. When their orbit passed near Jupiter again, the fragments crashed into Jupiter. On Earth, many people were fascinated to view images of the huge explosions—some were as large as Earth!

As this example shows, the sun, planets, and moons aren't the only objects in the solar system. There are also many smaller objects moving through the solar system. These objects are classified as comets, asteroids, or meteoroids.

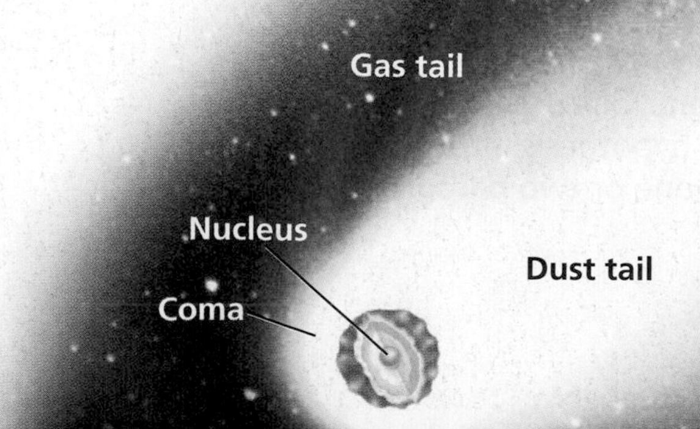


**FIGURE 23**
**Structure of a Comet**
The main parts of a comet are the nucleus, the coma, and the tail. The nucleus is deep within the coma. Most comets have two tails—a bluish gas tail and a white dust tail.

## Comets

One of the most glorious things you can see in the night sky is a comet. But what exactly is a comet? You can think of a **comet** as a "dirty snowball" about the size of a mountain. **Comets are loose collections of ice, dust, and small rocky particles whose orbits are usually very long, narrow ellipses.**

**For:** Links on comets, asteroids, and meteors
**Visit:** www.SciLinks.org
**Web Code:** scn-0635

**A Comet's Head** When a comet gets close enough to the sun, the energy in the sunlight turns the ice into gas, releasing gas and dust. Clouds of gas and dust form a fuzzy outer layer called a **coma.** Figure 23 shows the coma and the **nucleus,** the solid inner core of a comet. The brightest part of a comet, the comet's head, is made up of the nucleus and coma.

**A Comet's Tail** As a comet approaches the sun and heats up, some of its gas and dust stream outward, forming a tail. The name *comet* means "long-haired star" in Greek. Most comets have two tails—a gas tail and a dust tail. Both tails usually point away from the sun, as shown in Figure 24.

A comet's tail can be more than 100 million kilometers long and stretch across most of the sky. The material is stretched out very thinly, however, so there is little mass in a comet's tail.

**Origin of Comets** Most comets are found in one of two distant regions of the solar system: the Kuiper belt and the Oort cloud. The **Kuiper belt** is a doughnut-shaped region that extends from beyond Neptune's orbit to about 100 times Earth's distance from the sun. The **Oort cloud** is a spherical region of comets that surrounds the solar system out to more than 1,000 times the distance between Pluto and the sun.

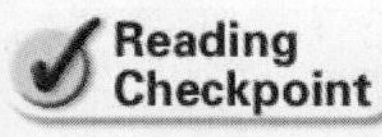


**What is the Oort cloud?**

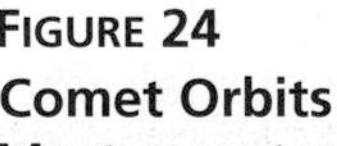

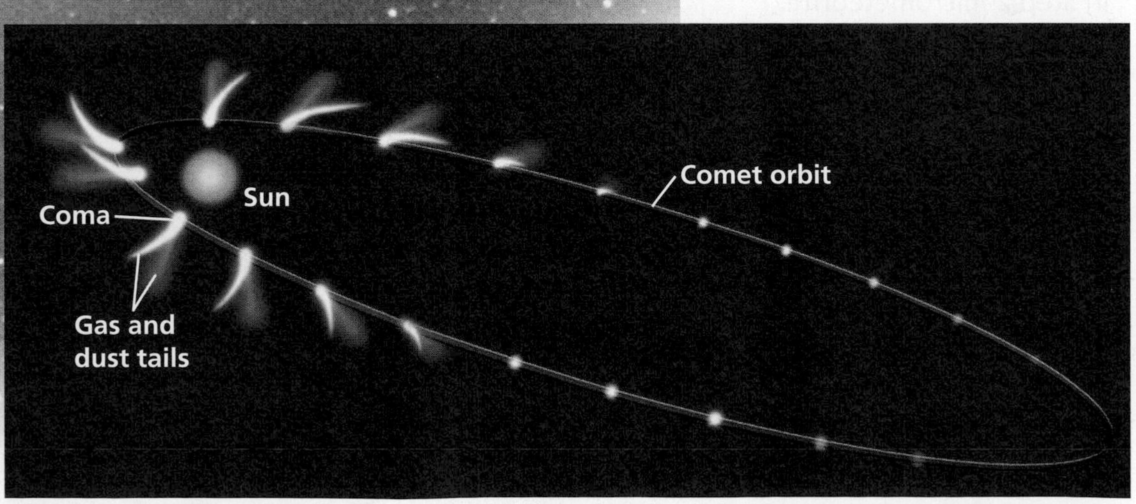


**FIGURE 24**
**Comet Orbits**
Most comets revolve around the sun in very long, narrow orbits. Gas and dust tails form as the comet approaches the sun. **Observing** *What shape is a comet's orbit?*

## Lab zone Try This Activity

### Micrometeorites

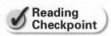

An estimated 300 tons of material from space fall on Earth each day. Much of this is micrometeorites, tiny, dust-sized meteorites.

1. To gather magnetic micrometeorites, tie a string to a small, round magnet and place the magnet in a plastic freezer bag. Lower the magnet close to the ground as you walk along sidewalk cracks, drain spouts, or a parking lot.
2. To gather nonmagnetic and magnetic micrometeorites, cover one side of a few microscope slides with petroleum jelly. Leave the slides outside for several days in a place where they won't be disturbed.
3. Use a microscope to examine the materials you have gathered. Any small round spheres you see are micrometeorites.

**Estimating** Which technique allows you to gather a more complete sample of micrometeorites? Were all the particles that were gathered in Step 2 micrometeorites? How could you use the method described in Step 2 to estimate the total number of micrometeorites that land on Earth each day?

# Asteroids

Between 1801 and 1807, astronomers discovered four small objects between the orbits of Mars and Jupiter. They named the objects Ceres, Pallas, Juno, and Vesta. Over the next 80 years, astronomers found 300 more. These rocky objects, called **asteroids,** are too small and too numerous to be considered full-fledged planets. **Most asteroids revolve around the sun between the orbits of Mars and Jupiter.** This region of the solar system, shown in Figure 25, is called the **asteroid belt.**

Astronomers have discovered more than 100,000 asteroids, and they are constantly finding more. Most asteroids are small—less than a kilometer in diameter. Only Ceres, Pallas, Vesta, and Hygiea are more than 300 kilometers across. The largest asteroid, Ceres, was recently classified as a dwarf planet. At one time, scientists thought that asteroids were the remains of a shattered planet. However, the combined mass of all the asteroids is too small to support this idea. Scientists now hypothesize that the asteroids are leftover pieces of the early solar system that never came together to form a planet.

Some asteroids have very elliptical orbits that bring them closer to the sun than Earth's orbit. Someday, one of these asteroids could hit Earth. One or more large asteroids did hit Earth about 65 million years ago, filling the atmosphere with dust and smoke and blocking out sunlight around the world. Scientists hypothesize that many species of organisms, including the dinosaurs, became extinct as a result.

**Reading Checkpoint** **Name the four largest asteroids.**

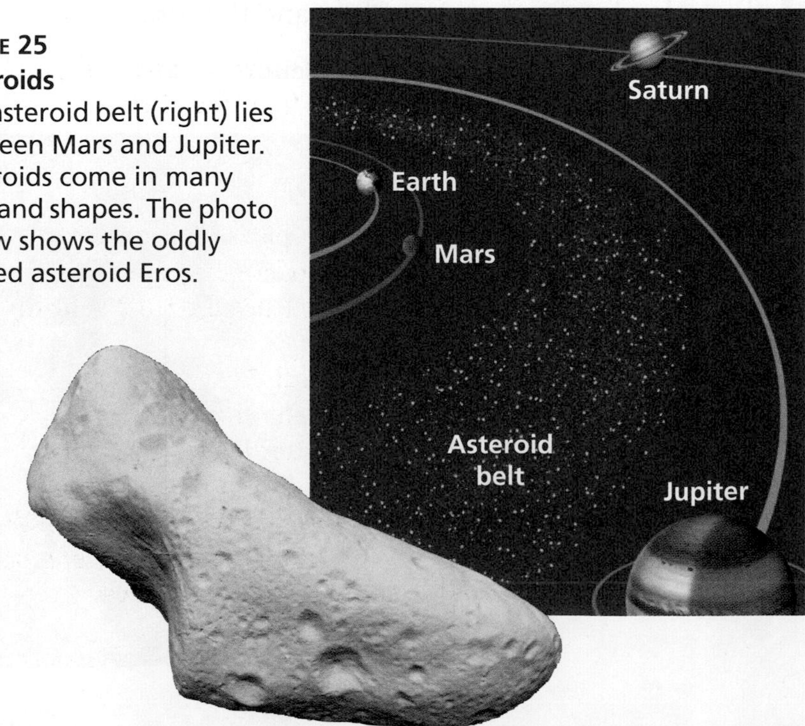


**FIGURE 25**
**Asteroids**
The asteroid belt (right) lies between Mars and Jupiter. Asteroids come in many sizes and shapes. The photo below shows the oddly shaped asteroid Eros.

## Meteors

It's a perfect night for stargazing—dark and clear. Suddenly, a streak of light flashes across the sky. For an hour or so, you see a streak at least once a minute. You are watching a meteor shower. Meteor showers happen regularly, several times a year.

Even when there is no meteor shower, you often can see meteors if you are far from city lights and the sky is not cloudy. On average, a meteor streaks overhead every 10 minutes.

A **meteoroid** is a chunk of rock or dust in space. **Meteoroids come from comets or asteroids.** Some meteoroids form when asteroids collide in space. Others form when a comet breaks up and creates a cloud of dust that continues to move through the solar system. When Earth passes through one of these dust clouds, bits of dust enter Earth's atmosphere.

When a meteoroid enters Earth's atmosphere, friction with the air creates heat and produces a streak of light in the sky—a **meteor.** If the meteoroid is large enough, it may not burn up completely. Meteoroids that pass through the atmosphere and hit Earth's surface are called **meteorites.** The craters on the moon were formed by meteoroids.

**FIGURE 26 Meteors**
Meteoroids make streaks of light called meteors as they burn up in the atmosphere.

## Section 5 Assessment

**Target Reading Skill Comparing and Contrasting** Use the information in your table about comets, asteroids, and meteoroids to help you answer the questions below.

### Reviewing Key Concepts

1. a. **Defining** What is a comet?
   b. **Listing** What are the different parts of a comet?
   c. **Relating Cause and Effect** How does a comet's appearance change as it approaches the sun? Why do these changes occur?
2. a. **Describing** What is an asteroid?
   b. **Explaining** Where are most asteroids found?
   c. **Summarizing** How did the asteroids form?
3. a. **Describing** What is a meteoroid?
   b. **Explaining** What are the main sources of meteoroids?
   c. **Comparing and Contrasting** What are the differences between meteoroids, meteors, and meteorites?

### Lab zone At-Home Activity

**Observing Meteors** Meteor showers occur regularly on specific dates. (The Perseid meteor shower, for example, occurs around August 12 each year.) Look in the newspaper, on the Internet, or in an almanac for information about the next meteor shower. With adult family members, go outside on that night and look for meteors. Explain to your family what causes the display.

Section 6

Integrating Life Science

# Is There Life Beyond Earth?

## Reading Preview

### Key Concepts

- What conditions do living things need to exist on Earth?
- Why do scientists think Mars and Europa are good places to look for signs of life?

### Key Term

- extraterrestrial life

### Target Reading Skill

**Asking Questions** Before you read, preview the red headings. In a graphic organizer like the one below, ask a question for each heading. As you read, write the answers to your questions.

**Is There Life Beyond Earth?**

| Question | Answer |
|---|---|
| What are the "Goldilocks" conditions? | The "Goldilocks" conditions are . . . |
| | |

## Lab zone Discover Activity

### Is Yeast Alive or Not?

1. Open a package of yeast and pour it into a bowl.
2. Look at the yeast carefully. Make a list of your observations.
3. Fill the bowl about halfway with warm water (about 20°C). Add a spoonful of sugar. Stir the mixture with the spoon. Wait 5 minutes.
4. Now look at the yeast again and make a list of your observations.

**Think It Over**

**Forming Operational Definitions** Which of your observations suggest that yeast is not alive? Which observations suggest that yeast is alive? How can you tell if something is alive?

Most of Antarctica is covered with snow and ice. You would not expect to see rocks lying on top of the whiteness. But surprisingly, people have found rocks lying on Antarctica's ice. When scientists examined the rocks, they found that many were meteorites. A few of these meteorites came from Mars. Astronomers think that meteoroids hitting the surface of Mars blasted chunks of rock into space. Some of these rocks eventually entered Earth's atmosphere and landed on its surface.

In 1996, a team of scientists announced that a meteorite from Mars found in Antarctica has tiny shapes that look like fossils—the remains of ancient life preserved in rock—though much smaller. Most scientists doubt that the shapes really are fossils. But if they are, it would be a sign that microscopic lifeforms similar to bacteria once existed on Mars. Life other than that on Earth would be called **extraterrestrial life.**

**FIGURE 27**
**Meteorites in Antarctica**
Dr. Ursula Marvin (lying down) studies meteorites like this one in Antarctica.

## Life on Earth

Sometimes it can be hard to tell whether something is alive or not. But all living things on Earth have several characteristics in common. Living things are made up of one or more cells. Living things take in energy and use it to grow and develop. They reproduce, producing new living things of the same type. Living things also give off waste.

**The "Goldilocks" Conditions** No one knows whether life exists anywhere other than Earth. Scientists often talk about the conditions needed by "life as we know it." **Earth has liquid water and a suitable temperature range and atmosphere for living things to survive.** Scientists sometimes call these favorable conditions the "Goldilocks" conditions. That is, the temperature is not too hot and not too cold. It is just right. If Earth were much hotter, water would always be a gas—water vapor. If Earth were much colder, water would always be solid ice.

Are these the conditions necessary for life? Or are they just the conditions that Earth's living things happen to need? Scientists have only one example to study: life on Earth. Unless scientists find evidence of life somewhere else, there is no way to answer these questions for certain.

FIGURE 28
**Hot Spring**
Bacteria that thrive in near-boiling water help to produce the striking colors of Grand Prismatic Spring in Wyoming. **Inferring** *How does studying unusual organisms on Earth help scientists predict what extraterrestrial life might be like?*

**Extreme Conditions** Recently, scientists have discovered living things in places where it was once believed that life could not exist. Giant tubeworms have been found under the extremely high pressures at the bottom of the ocean. Single-celled organisms have been found in the near-boiling temperatures of hot springs. Tiny life-forms have been discovered deep inside solid rock. Scientists have even found animals that do not require the energy of sunlight, but instead get their energy from chemicals.

These astounding discoveries show that the range of conditions in which life can exist is much greater than scientists once thought. Could there be life-forms in the solar system that do not need the "Goldilocks" conditions?

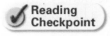

**Reading Checkpoint** What are some characteristics of all living things?

**Lab zone Skills Activity**

**Communicating** You are writing a letter to a friend who lives on another planet. Your friend has never been to Earth and has no idea what the planet is like. Explain in your letter why the conditions on Earth make it an ideal place for living things.

For: Links on extraterrestrial life
Visit: www.SciLinks.org
Web Code: scn-0636

## Life Elsewhere in the Solar System?

Recall that Mars is the planet most similar to Earth. That makes Mars the most obvious place to look for living things.

**Life on Mars?** Spacecraft have found regions on the surface of Mars that look like streambeds with crisscrossing paths of water. Shapes like those shown in Figure 29 were almost certainly formed by flowing water. **Since life as we know it requires water, scientists hypothesize that Mars may have once had the conditions needed for life to exist.**

In 1976 twin *Viking* spacecraft reached Mars. Each of the *Viking* landers carried a small laboratory meant to search for life forms. These laboratories tested Mars's air and soil for signs of life. None of these tests showed evidence of life.

More recently, the *Spirit* and *Opportunity* rovers found rocks and other surface features on Mars that were certainly formed by liquid water. However, the rovers were not equipped to search for past or present life.

Interest in life on Mars was increased by a report in 1996 about a meteorite from Mars that may contain fossils. The scientists' report started a huge debate. What were the tube-shaped things in the meteorite? Some scientists have suggested that the tiny shapes found in the meteorite are too small to be the remains of life forms. The shapes may have come from natural processes on Mars.

The most effective way to answer these questions is to send more probes to Mars. Future Mars missions should be able to bring samples of rocks and soil back to Earth for detailed analysis. Scientists may not yet have evidence of life on Mars, but hope is growing that we can soon learn the truth.

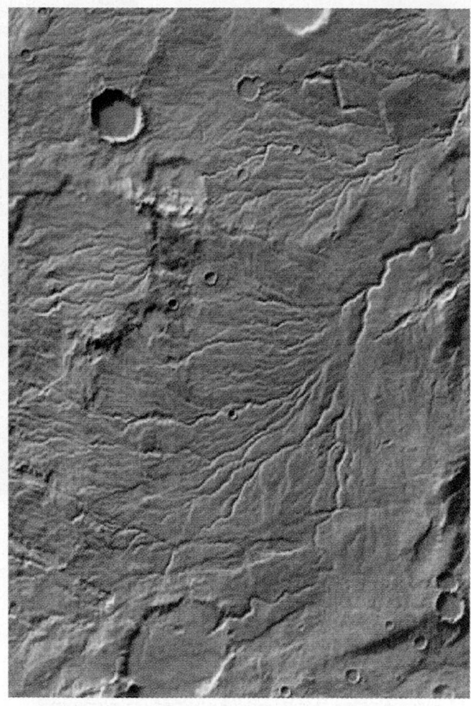

**FIGURE 29**
**Liquid Water on Mars**
The river-like patterns on the surface of Mars indicate that liquid water once flowed there.
**Applying Concepts** *Why does this evidence make it more likely that there may once have been life on Mars?*

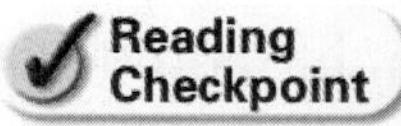


**What did the *Spirit* and *Opportunity* rovers discover on Mars?**

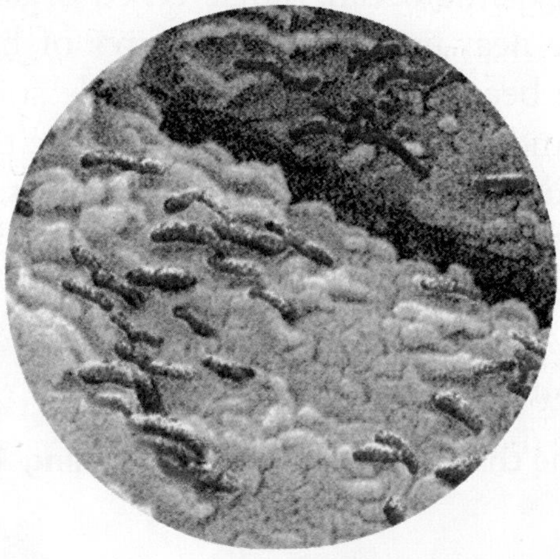

**FIGURE 30**
**Martian Fossils?**
This false-color electron microscope image shows tiny fossil-like shapes found in a meteorite from Mars. These structures are less than one-hundredth the width of a human hair.

**Life on Europa?** Many scientists think that Europa, one of Jupiter's moons, may have the conditions necessary for life to develop. Europa has a smooth, icy crust with giant cracks. Close-up views from the *Galileo* space probe show that Europa's ice has broken up and re-formed, resulting in large, twisted blocks of ice. Similar patterns occur in the ice crust over Earth's Arctic Ocean. Scientists hypothesize that there is a liquid ocean under Europa's ice. The water in the ocean could be kept liquid by heat from inside Europa. **If there is liquid water on Europa, there might also be life.**

How could scientists study conditions under Europa's ice sheet? Perhaps a future space probe might be able to use radar to "see" through Europa's icy crust. After that, robotic probes could be sent to drill through the ice to search for life in the water below.

**FIGURE 31**
**Exploring Europa**
Scientists have discussed sending a robotic probe to search for life in the ocean below Europa's icy crust.

## Section 6 Assessment

**Target Reading Skills** **Asking Questions** Use the answers to the questions you wrote about the section headings to help answer the questions.

### Reviewing Key Concepts

1. a. **Relating Cause and Effect** What conditions does life on Earth need to survive?
   b. **Summarizing** Why is Earth said to have the "Goldilocks" conditions?
   c. **Applying Concepts** Do you think there could be life as we know it on Neptune? Explain. (*Hint*: Review Section 4.)
2. a. **Explaining** Why do astronomers think there could be life on Europa?
   b. **Identifying** Scientists think that in the past Mars may have had the conditions needed for life to exist. What are these conditions? Do they still exist?
   c. **Making Generalizations** What characteristic do Mars and Europa share with Earth that makes them candidates to support extraterrestrial life?

### Lab zone At-Home Activity

**Making a Message** Imagine that scientists have found intelligent extraterrestrial life. With family members, make up a message to send to the extraterrestrials. Remember that they will not understand English, so you should use only symbols and drawings in your message.

# Chapter 20 Study Guide

**The BIG Idea** **Structure of the Solar System** The solar system includes the sun, the planets and their moons, and smaller objects such as comets, asteroids, and meteoroids.

## 1 Observing the Solar System

### Key Concepts

- In a geocentric system, Earth is perceived to be at the center of the revolving planets and stars. In a heliocentric system, Earth and the other planets revolve around the sun.
- Galileo's discoveries supported the heliocentric model. Kepler found that the orbit of each planet is an ellipse.
- The solar system consists of the sun, the planets and their moons, and a series of smaller objects that revolve around the sun.

### Key Terms

• geocentric • heliocentric • ellipse

## 2 The Sun

### Key Concepts

- The sun's interior consists of the core, radiation zone, and convection zone. The sun's atmosphere consists of the photosphere, chromosphere, and corona.
- Features on or just above the sun's surface include sunspots, prominences, and solar flares.

### Key Terms

• core • nuclear fusion • radiation zone
• convection zone • photosphere
• chromosphere • corona • solar wind
• sunspot • prominence • solar flare

## 3 The Inner Planets

### Key Concepts

- The four inner planets are small and dense and have rocky surfaces. Earth is unique in our solar system in having liquid water at its surface.
- Mercury is the smallest terrestrial planet.
- Venus's internal structure is similar to Earth's.
- Scientists think that a large amount of liquid water flowed on Mars's surface in the distant past.

### Key Terms

• terrestrial planets • greenhouse effect

## 4 The Outer Planets

### Key Concepts

- Jupiter, Saturn, Uranus, and Neptune are much larger and more massive than Earth.
- Jupiter is the largest and most massive planet in the solar system. Saturn has the most spectacular rings of any planet.
- Uranus's axis of rotation is tilted at an angle of about 90 degrees from the vertical.
- Neptune is a cold, blue planet. Its atmosphere contains visible clouds.
- Pluto has a solid surface and is much smaller and denser than the outer planets.

### Key Terms

• gas giant • ring

## 5 Comets, Asteroids, and Meteors

### Key Concepts

- Comets are loose collections of ice, dust, and small rocky particles whose orbits are usually very long, narrow ellipses.
- Most asteroids revolve around the sun between the orbits of Mars and Jupiter.
- Meteoroids come from comets or asteroids.

### Key Terms

• comet • coma • nucleus • Kuiper belt
• Oort cloud • asteroid • asteroid belt
• meteoroid • meteor • meteorite

## 6 Is There Life Beyond Earth?

### Key Concepts

- Earth has liquid water and a suitable temperature range and atmosphere for life.
- Scientists hypothesize that Mars may have once had the conditions for life to exist.
- If there is liquid water on Europa, there might also be life.

### Key Term

• extraterrestrial life

# Review and Assessment

For: Self-Assessment
Visit: PHSchool.com
Web Code: cja-5200

## Organizing Information

**Comparing and Contrasting** Fill in the graphic organizer to compare and contrast the geocentric system and the heliocentric system. (For more on Comparing and Contrasting, see the Skills Handbook.)

| Feature | Geocentric System | Heliocentric System |
|---|---|---|
| Object at center | Earth | a. ___?___ |
| Objects that move around center | Planets and sun | b. ___?___ |
| Proposed by | c. ___?___ | Copernicus |
| Supporters | Ptolemy | d. ___?___ |

## Reviewing Key Terms

**Choose the letter of the best answer.**

1. Copernicus thought that the solar system was
   a. an ellipse.
   b. a constellation.
   c. geocentric.
   d. heliocentric.
2. The part of the sun where nuclear fusion occurs is the
   a. photosphere.
   b. core.
   c. chromosphere.
   d. corona.
3. Pluto is a(n)
   a. inner planet.
   b. terrestrial planet.
   c. dwarf planet.
   d. gas giant.
4. The region between Mars and Jupiter where many rocky objects are found is the
   a. asteroid belt.
   b. Oort cloud.
   c. convection zone.
   d. Kuiper belt.
5. A meteoroid that reaches Earth's surface is called a(n)
   a. comet.
   b. meteorite.
   c. meteor.
   d. asteroid.

**If the statement is true, write *true*. If it is false, change the underlined word or words to make the statement true.**

6. The shape of the orbit of each planet is a(n) ellipse.
7. Prominences are regions of cooler gases on the sun.
8. The trapping of heat by a planet's atmosphere is called nuclear fusion.
9. All the terrestrial planets are surrounded by rings.
10. The solid inner core of a comet is its coma.

## Writing in Science

**News Report** Imagine you are on a mission to explore the solar system. Write a brief news report telling the story of your trip from Earth to another terrestrial planet and to a gas giant. Include a description of each planet.

*The Solar System*
Video Preview
Video Field Trip
▶ Video Assessment

# Review and Assessment

## Checking Concepts

11. Describe the contributions Tycho Brahe and Johannes Kepler made to modern astronomy.
12. What is the solar wind?
13. Why does Mercury have very little atmosphere?
14. Why can astronomers see the surface of Mars clearly but not the surface of Venus?
15. What evidence do astronomers have that water once flowed on Mars?

## Math Practice

16. **Circumference** Mars has a radius of 3,397 km at its equator. Find its circumference.
17. **Circumference** Jupiter has a circumference of about 449,000 km at its equator. Calculate its radius.

## Thinking Critically

18. **Applying Concepts** Explain why Venus is hotter than it would be if it had no atmosphere.
19. **Predicting** Do you think astronomers have found all of the moons of the outer planets? Explain.
20. **Comparing and Contrasting** Compare and contrast comets, asteroids, and meteoroids.
21. **Classifying** Look at the diagram below. Do you think it represents the structure of a terrestrial planet or a gas giant? Explain.

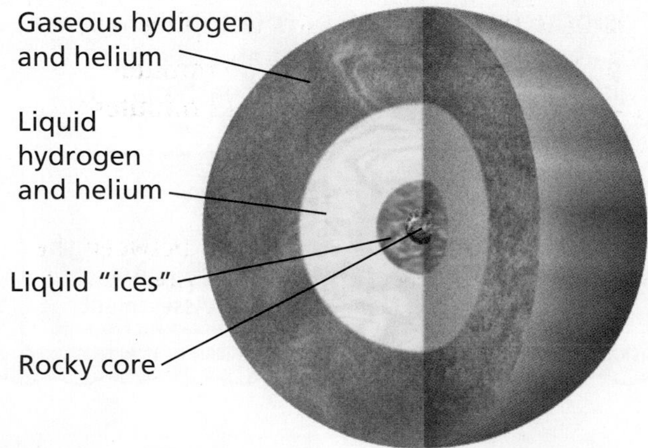


22. **Making Generalizations** Why would the discovery of liquid water on another planet be important?

## Applying Skills

**Use the diagram of an imaginary, newly discovered planetary system around Star X to answer Questions 23–25.**

*The periods of revolution of planets A, B, and C are 75 Earth days, 200 Earth days, and 300 Earth days.*

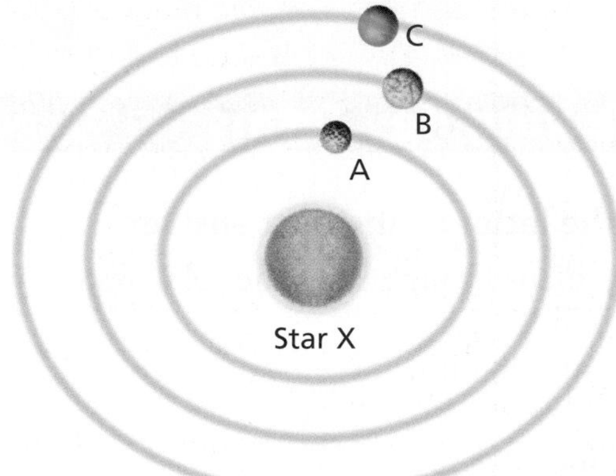


23. **Interpreting Data** Which planet in this new planetary system revolves around Star X in the shortest amount of time?
24. **Making Models** In 150 days, how far will each planet have revolved around Star X? Copy the diagram and sketch the positions of the three planets to find out. How far will each planet have revolved around Star X in 400 days? Sketch their positions.
25. **Drawing Conclusions** Can Planet C ever be closer to Planet A than to Planet B? Study your drawings to figure this out.

## Lab zone Chapter Project

**Performance Assessment** Present your scale models of the solar system. Display your data tables showing how you did the calculations and how you checked them for accuracy.

# Standardized Test Prep

### Test-Taking Tip

**Interpreting a Data Table**

When answering a question that is related to a data table, read the headings of the columns and rows to see how the data is organized. Think about the relationship between the columns and rows. For example, the table shown before Question 3 gives data about period of rotation, period of revolution, and average distance from the sun (column headings) for five planets (row headings). Do not spend much time trying to examine all the data, because you may not need total understanding to answer the questions.

***Sample Question***

Which of the following conclusions about planets is supported by information in the table?

**A** As distance from the sun increases, period of rotation increases.
**B** As distance from the sun increases, period of revolution increases.
**C** As distance from the sun increases, period of revolution decreases.
**D** There is no relationship between distance from the sun and period of revolution.

***Answer***

The correct answer is **B**. The table shows that planets' periods of revolution increase the farther they are from the sun. There is no relationship between a planet's distance from the sun and its period of rotation.

**Choose the letter of the best answer.**

**1.** What characteristic do all of the inner planets share?
**A** They are larger and more massive than the sun.
**B** They have thick atmospheres of hydrogen and helium.
**C** They have rocky surfaces.
**D** They each have many moons.

**2.** Mercury has a daytime temperature of about 430°C and a nighttime temperature below –170°C. What is the best explanation?
**F** Mercury has a greenhouse effect.
**G** Global warming is occurring on Mercury.
**H** Mercury is the closest planet to the sun.
**J** Mercury has no real atmosphere.

*The table below shows data for five planets in our solar system. Use the table and your knowledge of science to answer Questions 3–5.*

| **Planet** | **Period of Rotation** (Earth days) | **Period of Revolution** (Earth years) | **Average Distance From the Sun** (million km) |
|---|---|---|---|
| Mars | 1.03 | 1.9 | 228 |
| Jupiter | 0.41 | 12 | 779 |
| Saturn | 0.45 | 29 | 1,434 |
| Uranus | 0.72 | 84 | 2,873 |
| Neptune | 0.67 | 164 | 4,495 |

**3.** Which of these planets' orbits is farthest from Earth's orbit?
**A** Mars
**B** Jupiter
**C** Uranus
**D** Neptune

**4.** Which planet has a "day" that is most similar in length to a day on Earth?
**F** Mars
**G** Jupiter
**H** Uranus
**J** Neptune

**5.** Light takes about 8 minutes and 20 seconds to travel from the sun to Earth, 150 million kilometers away. About how long does it take light to travel from the sun to Jupiter?
**A** 10 minutes
**B** 25 minutes
**C** 43 minutes
**D** 112 minutes

### Constructed Response

**6.** Describe three major differences between the terrestrial planets and the gas giants.

Chapter 21

# Stars, Galaxies, and the Universe

## The BIG Idea

### Structure of the Universe

**How do astronomers learn about the structure of the universe?**

### Chapter Preview

1. **Telescopes**
   - ***Discover*** How Does Distance Affect an Image?
   - ***Try This*** Locating Radio Waves
   - ***Technology Lab*** Design and Build a Telescope
2. **Characteristics of Stars**
   - ***Discover*** How Does Your Thumb Move?
   - ***Skills Activity*** Inferring
   - ***Try This*** Star Bright
   - ***At-Home Activity*** Observing Orion
   - ***Skills Lab*** How Far Is That Star?
3. **Lives of Stars**
   - ***Discover*** What Determines How Long Stars Live?
   - ***Skills Activity*** Predicting
   - ***Active Art*** The Lives of Stars
4. **Star Systems and Galaxies**
   - ***Discover*** Why Does the Milky Way Look Hazy?
   - ***Try This*** A Spiral Galaxy
   - ***Math Skills*** Scientific Notation
5. **The Expanding Universe**
   - ***Discover*** How Does the Universe Expand?
   - ***Analyzing Data*** Speeding Galaxies
   - ***At-Home Activity*** Stargazing

**The dark Horsehead Nebula is visible against red-glowing hydrogen gas.** ▶

Stars, Galaxies, and the Universe
▶ Video Preview
Video Field Trip
Video Assessment

Lab zone™ Chapter **Project**

## Star Stories

Many years ago, people created stories to explain the patterns of stars they saw in the sky. In your project, you'll learn how the names of these constellations reflect the cultures of the people who named them.

**Your Goal** To complete the project you will

- learn the star patterns of at least three constellations
- research the myths that gave one constellation its name
- create your own star myth

**Plan It!** Begin by making a list of constellations that you have heard about. Then use the star charts in the appendix to locate constellations in the night sky. Make a sketch of the constellations that you locate. Choose one constellation, and research the myths that gave it its name. Draw a new picture for the star pattern in your constellation, and choose a name for it. Finally, write a story about your constellation. At the end of the chapter, you will present your constellation and a story that explains its name.

Section 1 • Tech & Design •

# Telescopes

## Reading Preview

### Key Concepts

- What are the regions of the electromagnetic spectrum?
- What are telescopes and how do they work?
- Where are most large telescopes located?

### Key Terms

- telescope
- electromagnetic radiation
- visible light
- wavelength
- spectrum
- optical telescope
- refracting telescope
- convex lens
- reflecting telescope
- radio telescope
- observatory

### Target Reading Skill

**Building Vocabulary** Carefully read the definition of each key term. Also read the neighboring sentences. Then write a definition of each key term in your own words.

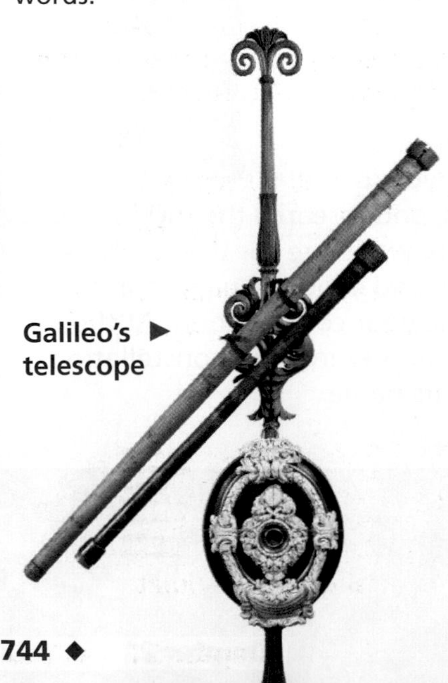

Galileo's ▶ telescope

## Lab zone Discover Activity

### How Does Distance Affect an Image?

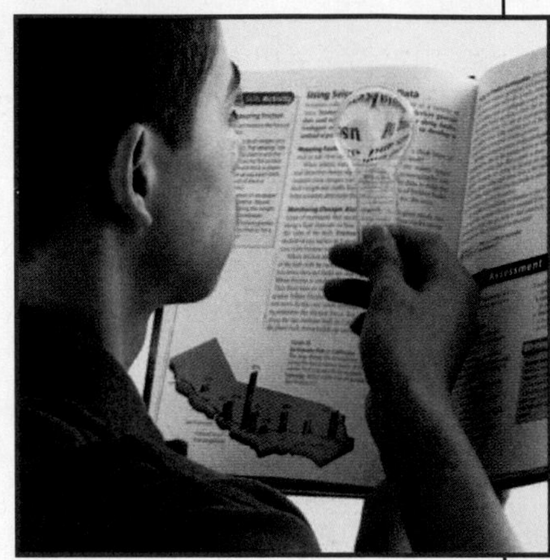

1. Hold a plastic hand lens about 7 cm away from your eye and about 5 cm away from a printed letter on a page. Move the lens slowly back and forth until the letter is in clear focus.
2. Keep the letter about 5 cm from the lens as you move your eye back to about 20 cm from the lens. Then, keeping the distance between your eye and the lens constant, slowly move the object away from the lens.

**Think It Over**

**Observing** What did the letter look like through the lens in Step 1 compared with how it looked without the lens? How did the image change in Step 2?

Ancient peoples often gazed up in wonder at the many points of light in the night sky. But they could see few details with their eyes alone. It was not until the invention of the telescope in 1608 that people could observe objects in the sky more closely. Recall that a **telescope** is a device that makes distant objects appear to be closer. The telescope revolutionized astronomy. Scientists now had a tool that allowed them to see many objects in space for the first time.

Although Galileo was not the first to use a telescope, he soon made it famous as he turned his homemade instrument to the sky. With his telescope, Galileo saw things that no one had even dreamed of. He was the first to see sunspots, Saturn's rings, and the four large moons of Jupiter. Galileo could see fine details, such as mountains on the moon, which cannot be seen clearly by the unaided eye.

Since Galileo's time, astronomers have built ever larger and more powerful telescopes. These telescopes have opened up a whole universe of wonders that would have amazed even Galileo.

## Electromagnetic Radiation

To understand how telescopes work, it's useful to understand the nature of electromagnetic radiation. Light is a form of **electromagnetic radiation** (ih lek troh mag NET ik), or energy that can travel through space in the form of waves. You can see stars when the light that they produce reaches your eyes.

For: Links on telescopes
Visit: www.SciLinks.org
Web Code: scn-0641

**Forms of Radiation** Scientists call the light you can see **visible light.** Visible light is just one of many types of electromagnetic radiation. Many objects give off radiation that you can't see. For example, in addition to their reddish light, the glowing coils of an electric heater give off infrared radiation, which you feel as heat. Radio transmitters produce radio waves that carry signals to radios and televisions. Objects in space give off all types of electromagnetic radiation.

**The Electromagnetic Spectrum** As shown in Figure 1, the distance between the crest of one wave and the crest of the next wave is called **wavelength.** Visible light has very short wavelengths, less than one millionth of a meter. Some electromagnetic waves have even shorter wavelengths. Other waves have much longer wavelengths, even several meters long.

If you shine white light through a prism, the light spreads out to make a range of different colors with different wavelengths, called a **spectrum.** The spectrum of visible light is made of the colors red, orange, yellow, green, blue, and violet. **The electromagnetic spectrum includes the entire range of radio waves, infrared radiation, visible light, ultraviolet radiation, X-rays, and gamma rays.**

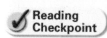

**Reading Checkpoint** **What are two kinds of electromagnetic waves that you might experience every day?**

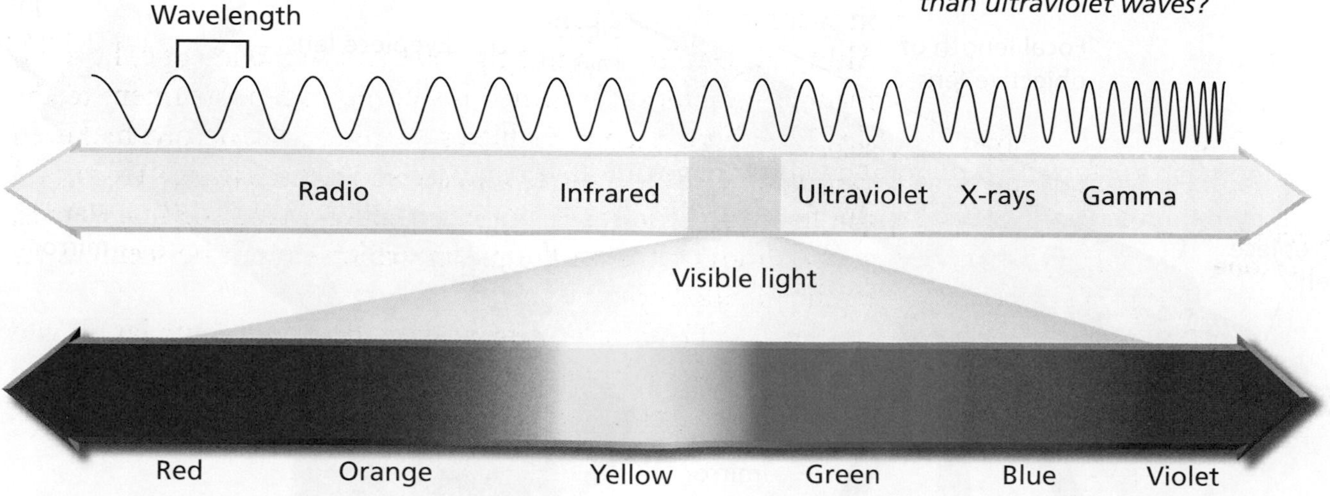


**FIGURE 1**
**The Electromagnetic Spectrum** The electromagnetic spectrum ranges from long-wavelength radio waves through short-wavelength gamma rays.
**Interpreting Diagrams** *Are infrared waves longer or shorter than ultraviolet waves?*

## Types of Telescopes

On a clear night, your eyes can see at most a few thousand stars. But with a telescope, you can see many millions. Why? The light from stars spreads out as it moves through space, and your eyes are too small to gather much light.

**Telescopes are instruments that collect and focus light and other forms of electromagnetic radiation.** Telescopes make distant objects appear larger and brighter. A telescope that uses lenses or mirrors to collect and focus visible light is called an **optical telescope.** The two major types of optical telescope are refracting telescopes and reflecting telescopes.

Modern astronomy is based on the detection of many forms of electromagnetic radiation besides visible light. Non-optical telescopes collect and focus different types of electromagnetic radiation, just as optical telescopes collect visible light.

**Refracting Telescopes** A **refracting telescope** uses convex lenses to gather and focus light. A **convex lens** is a piece of transparent glass, curved so that the middle is thicker than the edges.

Figure 2 shows a simple refracting telescope. This telescope has two convex lenses, one at each end of a long tube. Light enters the telescope through the large objective lens at the top. The objective lens focuses the light at a certain distance from the lens. This distance is the focal length of the lens. The larger the objective lens, the more light the telescope can collect. This makes it easier for astronomers to see faint objects.

The smaller lens at the lower end of a refracting telescope is the eyepiece lens. The eyepiece lens magnifies the image produced by the objective lens.

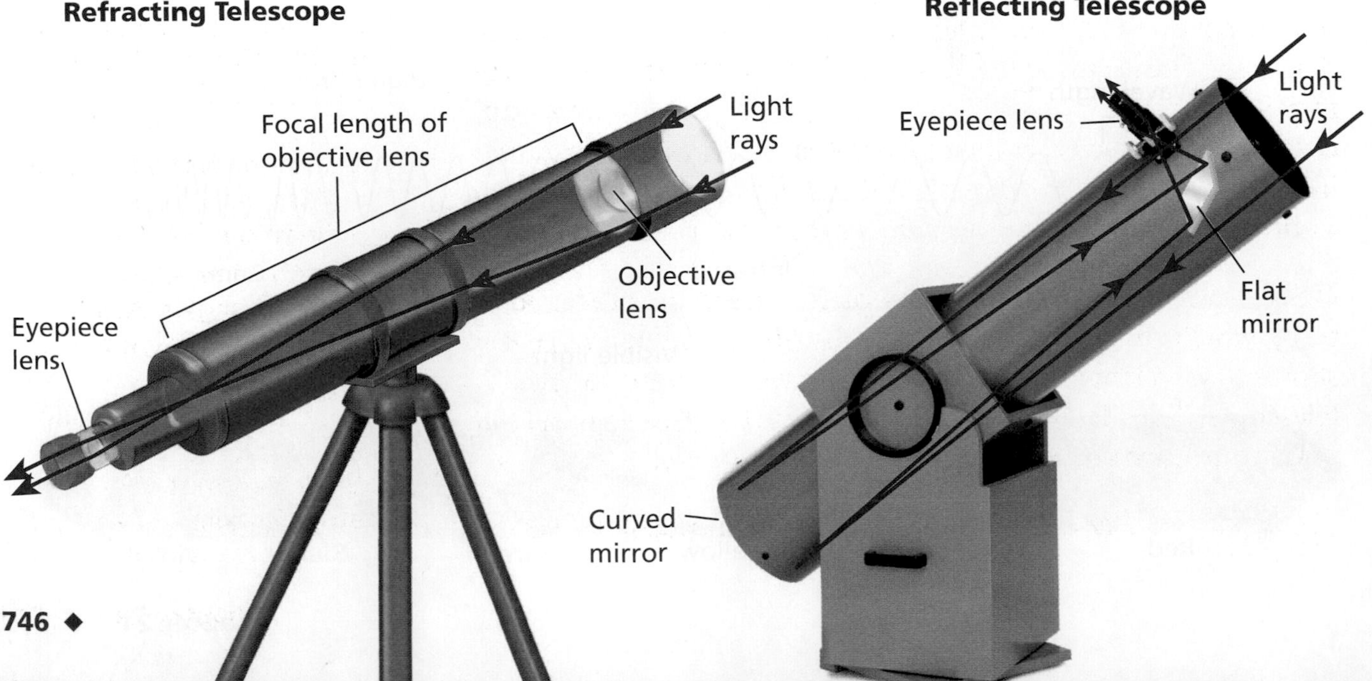


FIGURE 2
**Refracting and Reflecting Telescopes**
A refracting telescope uses convex lenses to focus light. A reflecting telescope has a curved mirror in place of an objective lens.

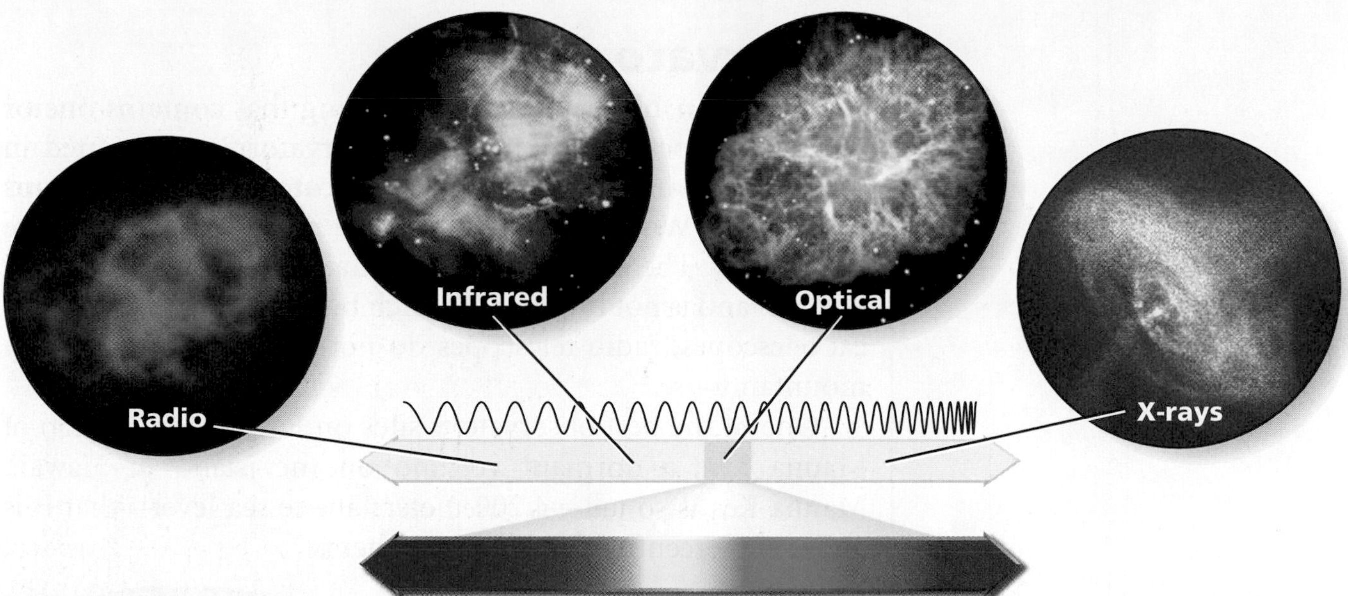


FIGURE 3
**Four Views of the Crab Nebula**
Different types of telescopes collect electromagnetic radiation at different wavelengths. Astronomers are able to learn a great deal about the Crab Nebula by examining these different images. The images are shown at different scales.

**Reflecting Telescopes** In 1668, Isaac Newton built the first reflecting telescope. A **reflecting telescope** uses a curved mirror to collect and focus light. Like the objective lens in a refracting telescope, the curved mirror in a reflecting telescope focuses a large amount of light onto a small area. The larger the mirror, the more light the telescope can collect. The largest optical telescopes today are all reflecting telescopes.

**Radio Telescopes** Devices used to detect radio waves from objects in space are called **radio telescopes.** Most radio telescopes have curved, reflecting surfaces—up to 305 meters in diameter. These surfaces focus radio waves the way the mirror in a reflecting telescope focuses light waves. The surfaces concentrate the faint radio waves from space onto small antennas like those on radios. As with optical telescopes, the larger a radio telescope is, the more radio waves it can collect.

**Other Telescopes** Some telescopes detect infrared radiation, which has longer wavelengths than visible light but shorter wavelengths than radio waves. There are also telescopes that detect the shortest wavelengths—ultraviolet radiation, X-rays, and gamma rays.

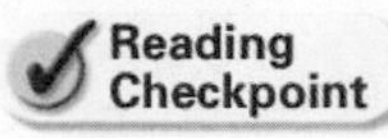

**Who built the first reflecting telescope?**

Lab zone **Try This Activity**

## Locating Radio Waves

You can use an umbrella to focus radio waves.

1. Line the inside of an open umbrella with aluminum foil.
2. Turn on a small radio and tune it to a station.
3. Move the radio up and down along the umbrella handle. Find the position where the station is clearest. Radio waves reflecting off the foil focus at this point. Tape the radio to the handle.
4. Hold the umbrella at different angles. At which angle is the station the clearest?

**Inferring** In which direction do you think the radio station's transmitter is located? Explain.

## Observatories

In general, an **observatory** is a building that contains one or more telescopes. However, some observatories are located in space. **Many large observatories are located on mountaintops or in space.** Why? Earth's atmosphere makes objects in space look blurry. The sky on some mountaintops is clearer than at sea level and is not brightened much by city lights. Unlike optical telescopes, radio telescopes do not need to be located on mountaintops.

One of the best observatory sites on Earth is on the top of Mauna Kea, a dormant volcano on the island of Hawaii. Mauna Kea is so tall—4,200 meters above sea level—that it is above 40 percent of Earth's atmosphere.

## • Tech & Design in History •

### Development of Modern Telescopes

During the last century, astronomers have built larger telescopes, which can collect more visible light and other types of radiation. Today's astronomers use tools that could not have been imagined 100 years ago.

**1897 Yerkes Telescope**

The 1-meter-diameter telescope at Yerkes Observatory in Wisconsin is the largest refracting telescope ever built. Because its main lens is so large, the Yerkes telescope can collect more light than any other refracting telescope.

**1931 Beginning of Radio Astronomy**

Karl Jansky, an American engineer, was trying to find the source of static that was interfering with radio communications. Using a large antenna, he discovered that the static was radio waves given off by objects in space. Jansky's accidental discovery led to the beginning of radio astronomy.

**1963 Arecibo Radio Telescope**

This radio telescope in Puerto Rico was built in a natural bowl in the ground. It is 305 meters in diameter, the largest radio telescope in existence.

1900 | 1940 | 1960

**Advanced Telescopes** Today, many large optical telescopes are equipped with systems that significantly improve the quality of their images. Optical telescopes on Earth equipped with such systems are able to produce images of small regions of the sky that rival those of optical telescopes based in space.

Some new telescopes are equipped with computer systems that correct images for problems such as telescope movement and changes in air temperature or mirror shape. Other advanced telescopes use lasers to monitor conditions in the atmosphere. The shape of the telescope's mirror is automatically adjusted thousands of times each second in response to changes in the atmosphere.

## Writing in Science

**Research and Write**
Research one of these telescopes or another large telescope. Create a publicity brochure in which you describe the telescopes features, when and where it was built, and what types of research it is used for.

### 1980 Very Large Array

The Very Large Array is a set of 27 radio telescopes in New Mexico. The telescopes can be moved close together or far apart. The telescopes are linked, so they can be used as if they were one giant radio telescope 25 kilometers in diameter.

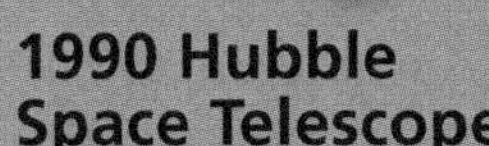

### 1990 Hubble Space Telescope

The Hubble Space Telescope views objects in space from high above the atmosphere. As a result, it can produce extremely sharp images.

### 2003 Spitzer Space Telescope

The Spitzer Space Telescope is a powerful 0.85-meter diameter telescope that surveys the sky in the infrared range of the spectrum.

1980 2000 2020

**FIGURE 4**
**Repairing Hubble**
Astronauts have repaired and upgraded the Hubble Space Telescope on several occasions.

**Telescopes in Space** X-rays, gamma rays, and most ultraviolet radiation are blocked by Earth's atmosphere. To detect these wavelengths, astronomers have placed telescopes in space. Some space telescopes are designed to detect visible light or infrared radiation, since Earth's atmosphere interferes with the transmission of these forms of radiation.

The Hubble Space Telescope is a reflecting telescope with a mirror 2.4 meters in diameter. Because the Hubble telescope orbits Earth above the atmosphere, it can produce very detailed images in visible light. It also collects ultraviolet and infrared radiation. The spectacular Hubble telescope images have changed how astronomers view the universe.

The hottest objects in space give off X-rays. The Chandra X-ray Observatory produces images in the X-ray portion of the spectrum. Chandra's X-ray images are much more detailed than those of earlier X-ray telescopes.

The most recent addition to NASA's lineup of telescopes in space is the Spitzer Space Telescope. Launched in 2003, the Spitzer telescope produces images in the infrared portion of the spectrum.

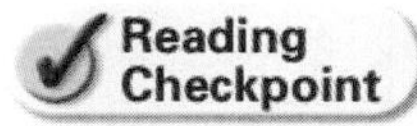


**What is an observatory?**

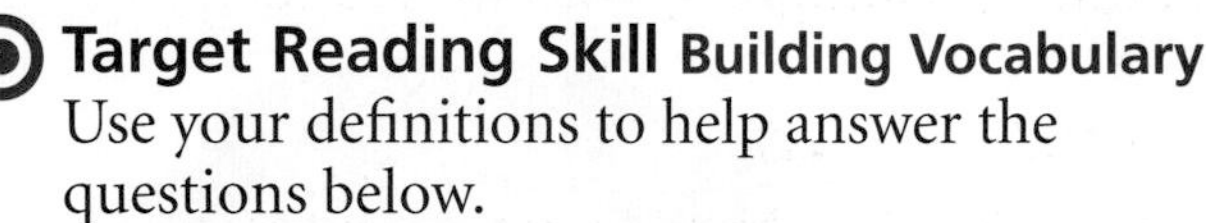

## Section 1 Assessment

**Target Reading Skill Building Vocabulary** Use your definitions to help answer the questions below.

### Reviewing Key Concepts

1. a. **Sequencing** List the main types of electromagnetic waves, from longest wavelength to shortest.
   b. **Applying Concepts** Why are images from the Hubble Space Telescope clearer than images from telescopes on Earth?
2. a. **Identifying** What are the two major types of optical telescope?
   b. **Explaining** How does a refracting telescope work?
   c. **Comparing and Contrasting** Use Figure 2 to explain the major differences between reflecting and refracting telescopes.
3. a. **Summarizing** How does the atmosphere affect electromagnetic radiation?
   b. **Explaining** Why are many large optical telescopes located on mountaintops?
   c. **Applying Concepts** Would it make sense to place an X-ray or gamma ray telescope on a mountaintop? Explain why or why not.

### Writing in Science

**Writing Instructions** Write a short explanation of how to build a reflecting telescope for a booklet to be included in a model telescope kit. Be sure to describe the shape and position of each of the lenses or mirrors. You may include drawings.

Lab zone

# Technology Lab

• Tech & Design •

## Design and Build a Telescope



### Problem

Can you design and build a telescope?

### Skills Focus

evaluating the design, redesigning

### Materials

- 2 paper towel tubes of slightly different diameters
- several plastic objective lenses
- several plastic eyepiece lenses
- meter stick
- foam holder for eyepiece
- transparent tape

### Procedure

1. Fit one of the paper towel tubes inside the other. Make sure you can move the tubes but that they will not slide on their own.
2. Place the large objective lens flat against the end of the outer tube. Tape the lens in place.
3. Insert the small eyepiece lens into the opening in the foam holder.
4. Place the foam eyepiece lens holder into the inner tube at the end of the telescope opposite to the objective lens.
5. Tape a meter stick to the wall. Look through the eyepiece at the meter stick from 5 m away. Slide the tubes in and out to focus your telescope so that you can clearly read the numbers on the meter stick. Draw your telescope. On the drawing, mark the tube position that allows you to read the numbers most clearly.
6. Use your telescope to look at other objects at different distances, both in your classroom and through the window. For each object you view, draw your telescope, marking the tube position at which you see the object most clearly. **CAUTION:** *Do not look at the sun. You will damage your eyes.*
7. Design and build a better telescope. Your new telescope should make objects appear larger than your first model from the same observing distance. It should have markings on the inner tube to enable you to pre-focus the telescope for a given observing distance.
8. Draw a design for your new telescope. List the materials you'll need. Obtain your teacher's approval. Then build your new model.

### Analyze and Conclude

1. **Inferring** Why do you need two tubes?
2. **Observing** If you focus on a nearby object and then focus on something farther away, do you have to move the tubes together or apart?
3. **Evaluating the Design** How could you improve on the design of your new telescope? What effects would different lenses or tubes have on its performance?
4. **Redesigning** Describe the most important factors in redesigning your telescope.

### Communicate

Write a product brochure for your new telescope. Be sure to describe in detail why your new telescope is better than the first telescope.

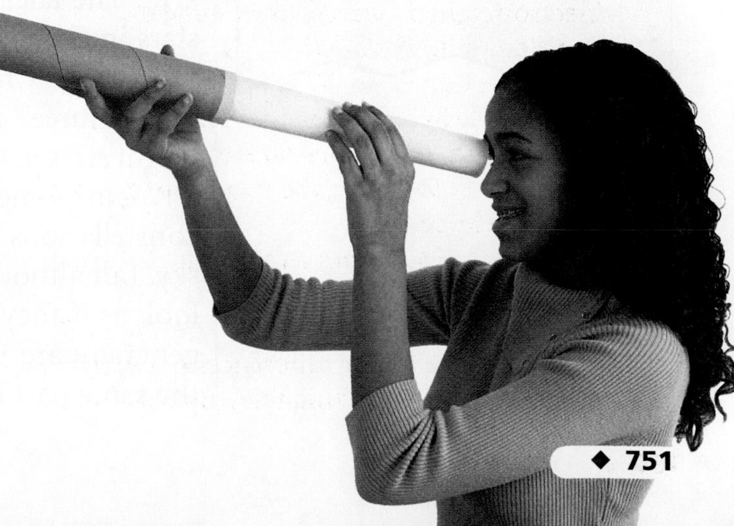

Section 2

# Characteristics of Stars

## Reading Preview

### Key Concepts

- How are stars classified?
- How do astronomers measure distances to the stars?
- What is an H-R diagram and how do astronomers use it?

### Key Terms

- constellation
- spectrograph
- apparent brightness
- absolute brightness
- light-year
- parallax
- Hertzsprung-Russell diagram
- main sequence

### Target Reading Skill

**Using Prior Knowledge** Before you read, write what you know about the characteristics of stars in a graphic organizer like the one below. As you read, write what you learn.

| What You Know |
|---|
| 1. Stars are bright and hot.<br>2. |

| What You Learned |
|---|
| 1.<br>2. |

## Lab zone Discover Activity

### How Does Your Thumb Move?

1. Stand facing a wall, at least an arm's length away. Stretch your arm out with your thumb up and your fingers curled.
2. Close your right eye and look at your thumb with your left eye. Line your thumb up with something on the wall.
3. Now close your left eye and open your right eye. How does your thumb appear to move along the wall?
4. Bring your thumb closer to your eye, about half the distance as before. Repeat Steps 2 and 3.

**Think It Over**

**Observing** How does your thumb appear to move in Step 4 compared to Step 3? How are these observations related to how far away your thumb is at each step? How could you use this method to estimate distances?

When ancient observers around the world looked up at the night sky, they imagined that groups of stars formed pictures of people or animals. Today, we call these imaginary patterns of stars **constellations.**

Different cultures gave different names to the constellations. For example, a large constellation in the winter sky is named Orion, the Hunter, after a Greek myth. In this constellation, Orion is seen with a sword in his belt and an upraised arm. The ancient Sumerians thought that the stars in Orion formed the outline of a sheep. In ancient China, this group of stars was called "three," probably because of the three bright stars in Orion's belt.

Astronomers use the patterns of the constellations to locate objects in the night sky. But although the stars in a constellation look as if they are close to one another, they generally are not. They just happen to lie in the same part of the sky as seen from Earth.

**Illustration of Orion ▼**

## Classifying Stars

Like the sun, all stars are huge spheres of glowing gas. They are made up mostly of hydrogen, and they produce energy through the process of nuclear fusion. This energy makes stars shine brightly. Astronomers classify stars according to their physical characteristics. **Characteristics used to classify stars include color, temperature, size, composition, and brightness.**

For: More on types of stars
Visit: PHSchool.com
Web Code: cfd-5042

**Color and Temperature** If you look at the night sky, you can see slight differences in the colors of the stars. For example, Betelgeuse (BAY tul jooz), the bright star in Orion's shoulder, looks reddish. Rigel, the star in Orion's heel, is blue-white.

Like hot objects on Earth, a star's color reveals its surface temperature. If you watch a toaster heat up, you can see the wires glow red-hot. The wires inside a light bulb are even hotter and glow white. Similarly, the coolest stars—with a surface temperature of about 3,200 degrees Celsius—appear reddish in the sky. With a surface temperature of about 5,500 degrees Celsius, the sun appears yellow. The hottest stars in the sky, with surface temperatures of over 20,000 degrees Celsius, appear bluish.

**Size** When you look at stars in the sky, they all appear to be points of light of the same size. Many stars are actually about the size of the sun, which is a medium-sized star. However, some stars are much larger than the sun. Very large stars are called giant stars or supergiant stars. If the supergiant star Betelgeuse were located where our sun is, it would be large enough to fill the solar system as far out as Jupiter.

Most stars are much smaller than the sun. White dwarf stars are about the size of Earth. Neutron stars are even smaller, only about 20 kilometers in diameter.

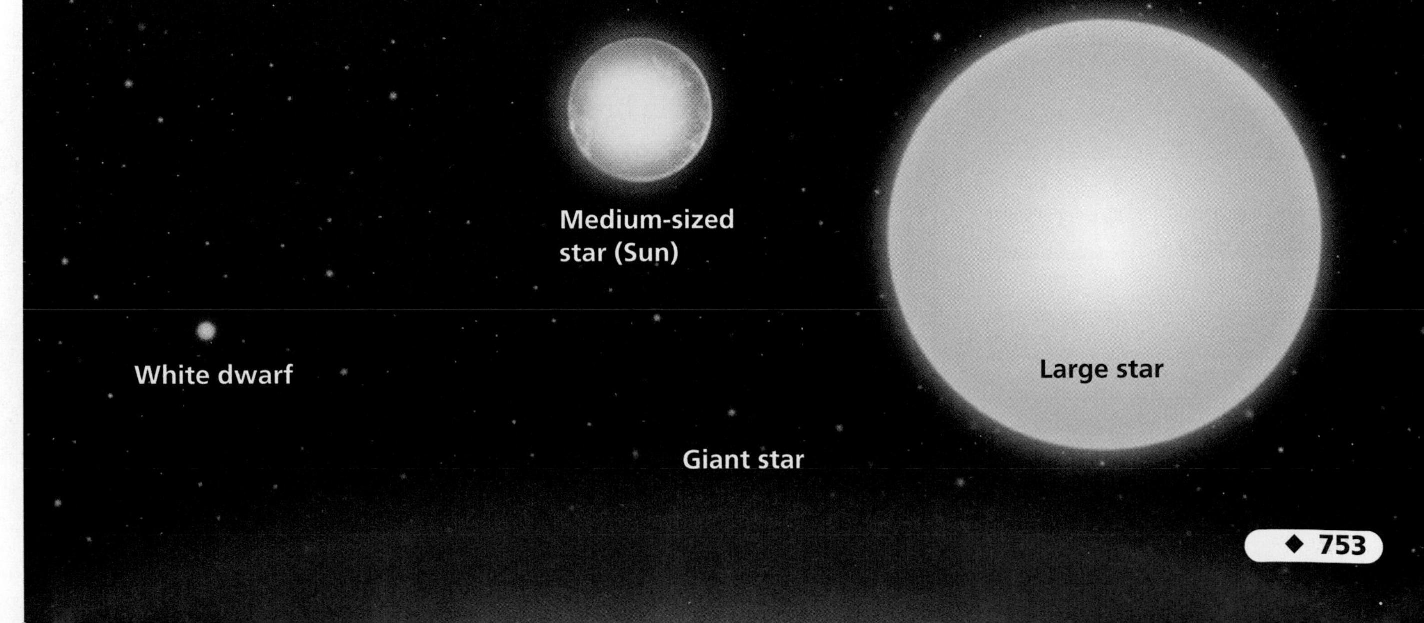


**FIGURE 5**
**Star Size**
Stars vary greatly in size. Giant stars are typically 10 to 100 times larger than the sun and more than 1,000 times the size of a white dwarf. **Calculating** *Betelgeuse has a diameter of 420 million kilometers. How many times larger is this than the sun, which has a diameter of 1.4 million kilometers?*

**FIGURE 6**
**Spectrums of Four Stars**
Astronomers can use line spectrums to identify the chemical elements in a star. Each element produces a characteristic pattern of spectral lines.

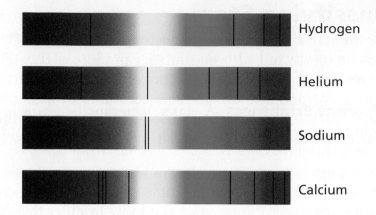

**Chemical Composition** Stars vary in their chemical composition. The chemical composition of most stars is about 73 percent hydrogen, 25 percent helium, and 2 percent other elements by mass. This is similar to the composition of the sun.

Astronomers use spectrographs to determine the elements found in stars. A **spectrograph** (SPEK truh graf) is a device that breaks light into colors and produces an image of the resulting spectrum. Most large telescopes have spectrographs.

The gases in a star's atmosphere absorb some wavelengths of light produced within the star. When the star's light is seen through a spectrograph, each absorbed wavelength is shown as a dark line on a spectrum. Each chemical element absorbs light at particular wavelengths. Just as each person has a unique set of fingerprints, each element has a unique set of lines for a given temperature. Figure 6 shows the spectral lines of four elements. By comparing a star's spectrum with the spectrums of known elements, astronomers can infer how much of each element is found in the star.

**What is a spectrograph?**

**Lab zone Skills Activity**

### Inferring

The lines on the spectrums below are from three different stars. Each of these star spectrums is made up of an overlap of spectrums from the individual elements shown in Figure 6. In star A, which elements have the strongest lines? Which are the strongest in star B? In star C?

## Brightness of Stars

Stars also differ in brightness, the amount of light they give off. **The brightness of a star depends upon both its size and temperature.** Recall that the photosphere is the layer of a star that gives off light. Betelgeuse is fairly cool, so a square meter of its photosphere doesn't give off much light. But Betelgeuse is very large, so it shines brightly.

Rigel, on the other hand, is very hot, so each square meter of Rigel's photosphere gives off a lot of light. Even though it is smaller than Betelgeuse, Rigel shines more brightly.

How bright a star looks from Earth depends on both its distance from Earth and how bright the star truly is. Because of these two factors, the brightness of a star can be described in two ways: apparent brightness and absolute brightness.

**Apparent Brightness** A star's **apparent brightness** is its brightness as seen from Earth. Astronomers can measure apparent brightness fairly easily using electronic devices. However, astronomers can't tell how much light a star gives off just from the star's apparent brightness. Just as a flashlight looks brighter the closer it is to you, a star looks brighter the closer it is to Earth. For example, the sun looks very bright. This does not mean that the sun gives off more light than all other stars. The sun looks so bright simply because it is so close. In reality, the sun is a star of only average brightness.

**Absolute Brightness** A star's **absolute brightness** is the brightness the star would have if it were at a standard distance from Earth. Finding a star's absolute brightness is more complex than finding its apparent brightness. An astronomer must first find out both the star's apparent brightness and its distance from Earth. The astronomer can then calculate the star's absolute brightness.

Astronomers have found that the absolute brightness of stars can vary tremendously. The brightest stars are more than a billion times brighter than the dimmest stars!

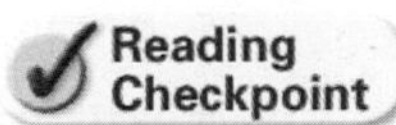

**What is a star's absolute brightness?**

**Lab zone Try This Activity**

### Star Bright

You can compare absolute and apparent brightness.

1. Dim the lights. Put two equally bright flashlights next to each other on a table. Turn them on.
2. Look at the flashlights from the other side of the room. Think of the flashlights as two stars. Then compare them in terms of absolute and apparent brightness.
3. Move one of the flashlights closer to you and repeat Step 2.
4. Replace one of the flashlights with a brighter one. Repeat Steps 1 and 2 with the unequally bright flashlights.

**Making Models** How could you place the flashlights in Step 4 so that they have the same apparent brightness? Try it.

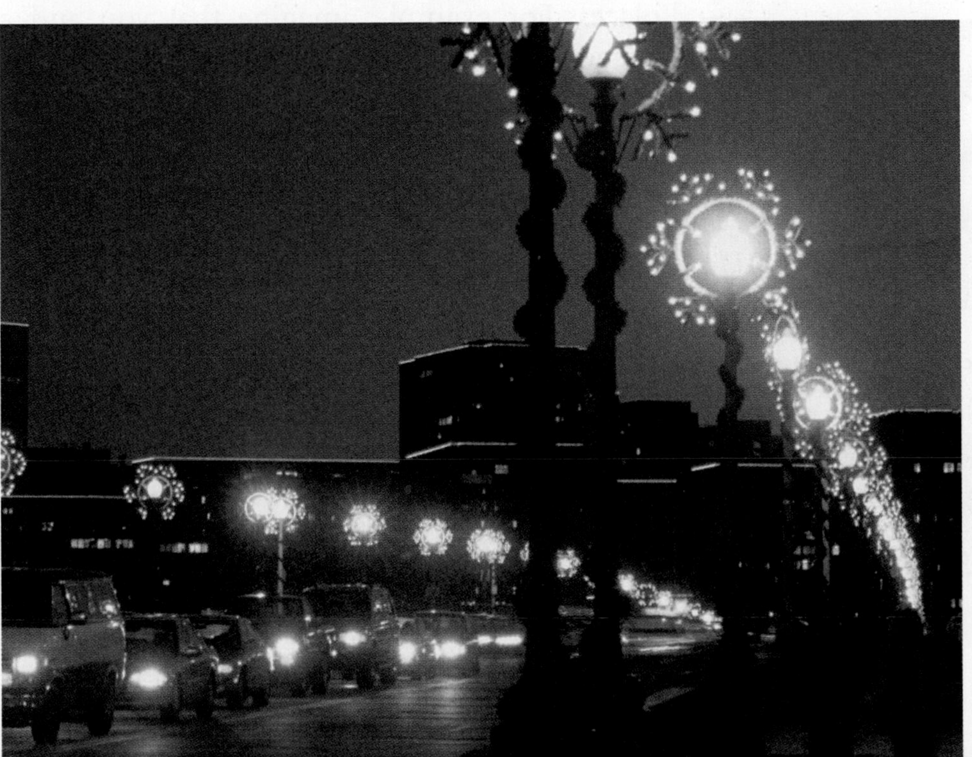

FIGURE 7
**Absolute Brightness**
The streetlights in this photo all give off about the same amount of light, and so have about the same absolute brightness.
**Applying Concepts** *Why do the closer streetlights appear brighter than the more distant lights?*

## Measuring Distances to Stars

Imagine that you could travel to the stars at the speed of light. To travel from Earth to the sun would take about 8 minutes, not very much time for such a long trip. The next nearest star, Proxima Centauri, is much farther away. A trip to Proxima Centauri at the speed of light would take 4.2 years!

**The Light-Year** Distances on Earth's surface are often measured in kilometers. However, distances to the stars are so large that kilometers are not very practical units. **Astronomers use a unit called the light-year to measure distances between the stars.** In space, light travels at a speed of about 300,000 kilometers per second. A **light-year** is the distance that light travels in one year, about 9.5 million million kilometers.

Note that the light-year is a unit of distance, not time. To help you understand this, consider an everyday example. If you bicycle at 10 kilometers per hour, it would take you 1 hour to go to a mall 10 kilometers away. You could say that the mall is "1 bicycle-hour" away.

**Parallax** Standing on Earth looking up at the sky, it may seem as if there is no way to tell how far away the stars are. However, astronomers have found ways to measure those distances. **Astronomers often use parallax to measure distances to nearby stars.**

**Parallax** is the apparent change in position of an object when you look at it from different places. For example, imagine that you and a friend have gone to a movie. A woman with a large hat sits down in front of you, as shown in Figure 8. Because you and your friend are sitting in different places, the woman's hat blocks different parts of the screen. If you are sitting on her left, the woman's hat appears to be in front of the large dinosaur. But to your friend on the right, she appears to be in front of the bird.

Have the woman and her hat moved? No. But because you changed your position, she appears to have moved. This apparent movement when you look from two different directions is parallax.

**FIGURE 8**
**Parallax at the Movies**
You and your friend are sitting behind a woman with a large hat. **Applying Concepts** *Why is your view of the screen different from your friend's view?*

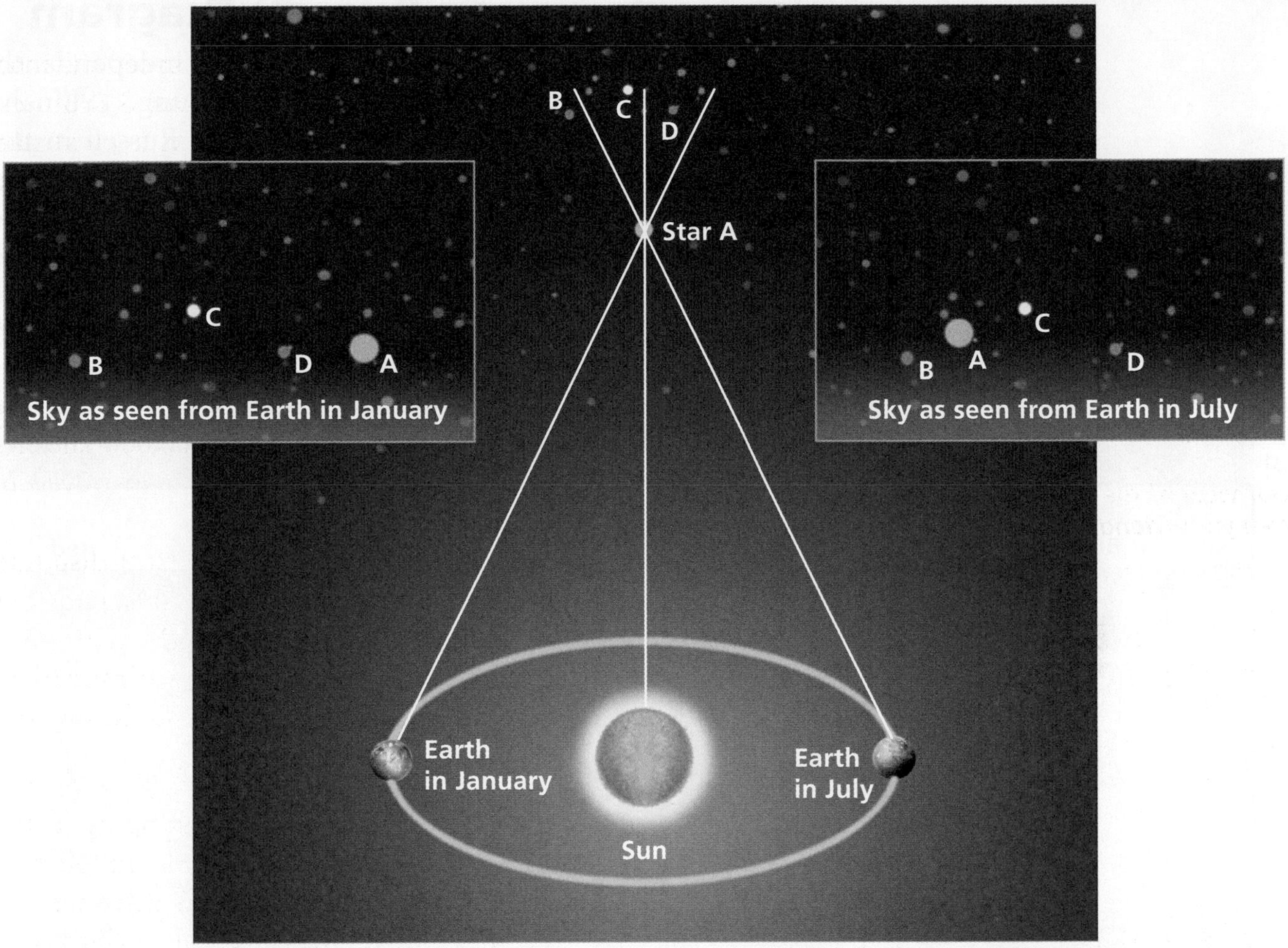

**Parallax in Astronomy** Astronomers are able to measure the parallax of nearby stars to determine their distances. As shown in Figure 9, astronomers look at a nearby star when Earth is on one side of the sun. Then they look at the same star again six months later, when Earth is on the opposite side of the sun. Astronomers measure how much the nearby star appears to move against a background of stars that are much farther away. They can then use this measurement to calculate the distance to the nearby star. The less the nearby star appears to move, the farther away it is.

Astronomers can use parallax to measure distances up to a few hundred light-years from Earth. The parallax of any star that is farther away is too small to measure accurately.

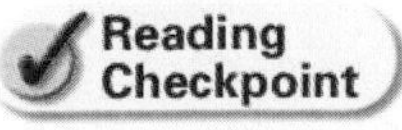

**How is parallax useful in astronomy?**

FIGURE 9
**Parallax of Stars**
The apparent movement of a star when seen from a different position is called parallax. Astronomers use parallax to calculate the distance to nearby stars. Note that the diagram is not to scale.
**Interpreting Diagrams** *Why do nearby stars appear to change position between January and July?*

## The Hertzsprung-Russell Diagram

About 100 years ago, two scientists working independently made the same discovery. Both Ejnar Hertzsprung (EYE nahr HURT sprung) in Denmark and Henry Norris Russell in the United States made graphs to find out if the temperature and the absolute brightness of stars are related. They plotted the surface temperatures of stars on the *x*-axis and their absolute brightness on the *y*-axis. The points formed a pattern. The graph they made is still used by astronomers today. It is called the **Hertzsprung-Russell diagram,** or H-R diagram.

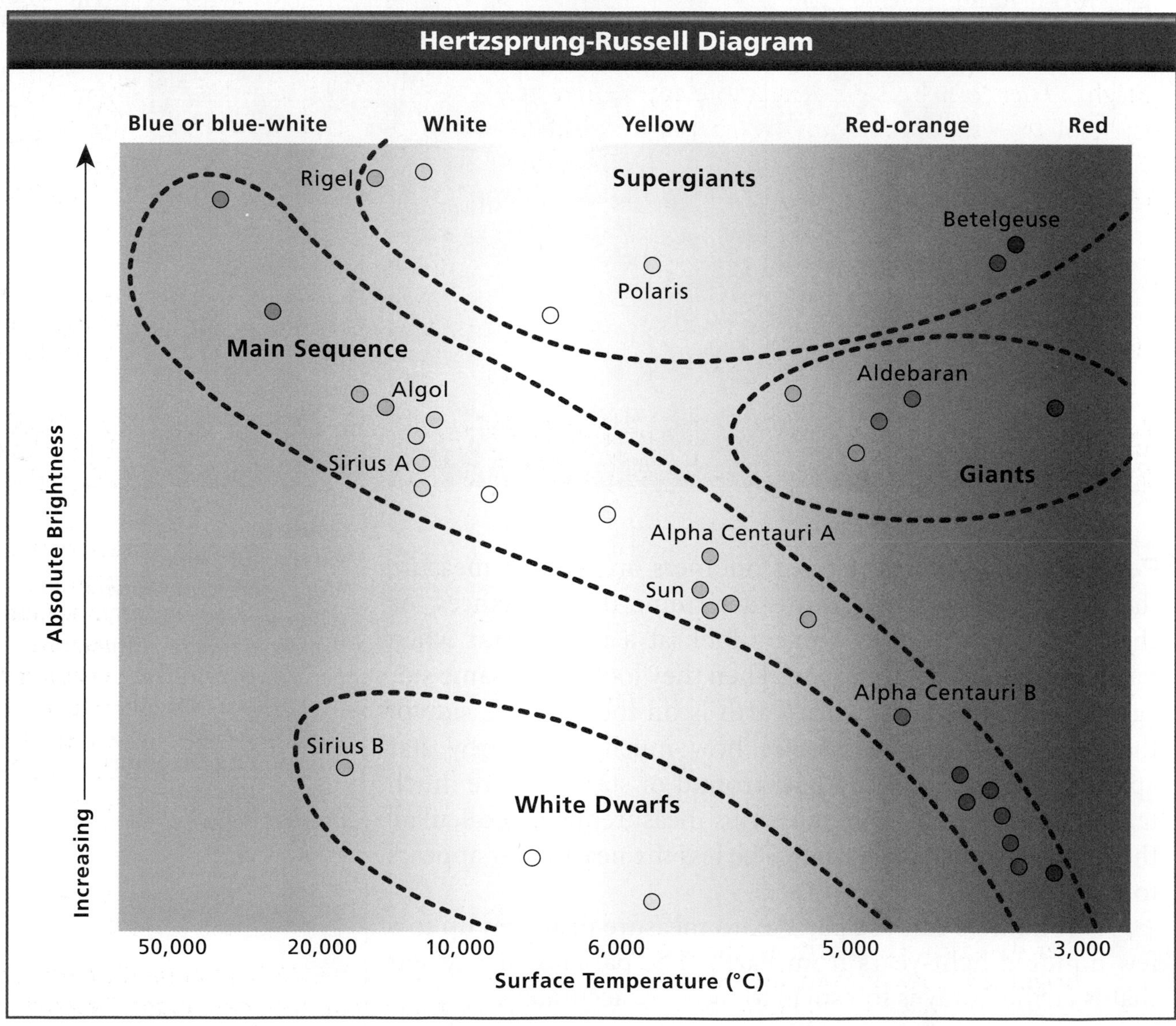


**FIGURE 10**
The Hertzsprung-Russell diagram shows the relationship between the surface temperature and absolute brightness of stars.
**Interpreting Diagrams** *Which star has a hotter surface: Rigel or Aldebaran?*

**Astronomers use H-R diagrams to classify stars and to understand how stars change over time.** As you can see in Figure 10, most of the stars in the H-R diagram form a diagonal area called the **main sequence.** More than 90 percent of all stars, including the sun, are main-sequence stars. Within the main sequence, surface temperature increases as absolute brightness increases. Thus, hot bluish stars are located at the left of an H-R diagram and cooler reddish stars are located at the right of the diagram.

The brightest stars are located near the top of an H-R diagram, while the dimmest stars are located at the bottom. Giant and supergiant stars are very bright. They can be found near the top center and right of the diagram. White dwarfs are hot, but not very bright, so they appear at the bottom left or bottom center of the diagram.

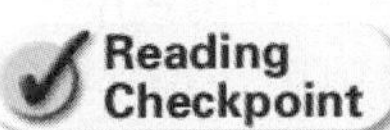

What is the main sequence?

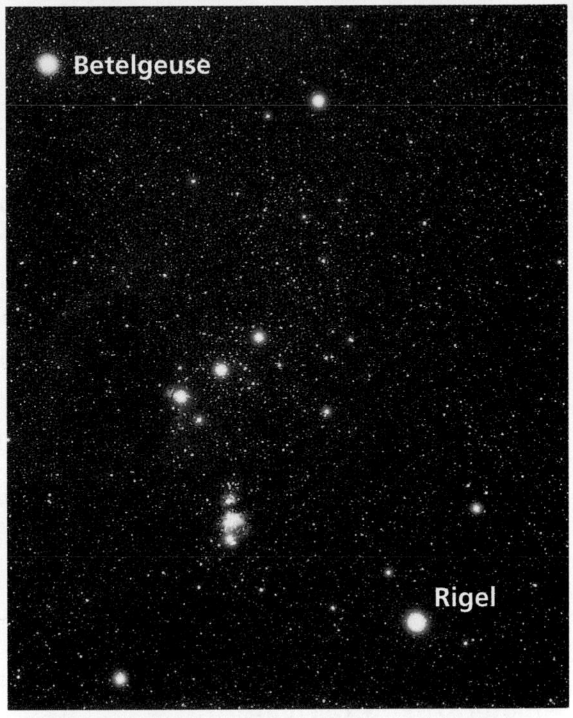


**FIGURE 11**
**Orion**
Orion includes the red supergiant Betelgeuse, the blue supergiant Rigel, and many other main-sequence and giant stars.

## Section 2 Assessment

**Target Reading Skill Using Prior Knowledge** Review your graphic organizer and revise it based on what you just learned in the section.

### Reviewing Key Concepts

1. a. **Listing** Name three characteristics used to classify stars.
   b. **Comparing and Contrasting** What is the difference between apparent brightness and absolute brightness?
   c. **Applying Concepts** Stars A and B have about the same apparent brightness, but Star A is about twice as far from Earth as Star B. Which star has the greater absolute brightness? Explain your answer.
2. a. **Measuring** What is a light-year?
   b. **Defining** What is parallax?
   c. **Predicting** Vega is 25.3 light-years from Earth and Arcturus is 36.7 light-years away. Which star would have a greater parallax? Explain.
3. a. **Summarizing** What two characteristics of stars are shown in an H-R diagram?
   b. **Identifying** Identify two ways in which astronomers can use an H-R diagram.
   c. **Classifying** The star Procyon B has a surface temperature of 6,600° Celsius and an absolute brightness that is much less than the sun's. What type of star is Procyon B? (*Hint:* Refer to the H-R diagram.)

**Lab zone At-Home Activity**

**Observing Orion** With adult family members, go outside on a clear, dark night. Determine which way is south. Using the star charts in the appendix, look for the constellation Orion, which is visible in the evening during winter and spring. Find the stars Betelgeuse and Rigel in Orion and explain to your family why they are different colors.

Lab zone **Skills Lab**

# How Far Is That Star?

## Problem

How can parallax be used to determine distances?

## Skills Focus

inferring, calculating, predicting

## Materials

- masking tape
- paper clips
- pen
- black and red pencils
- metric ruler
- paper
- meter stick
- calculator
- lamp without a shade, with 100-watt light bulb
- copier paper box (without the lid)
- flat rectangular table, about 1 m wide

## Procedure 

### PART 1 Telescope Model

1. Place the lamp on a table in the middle of the classroom.
2. Carefully use the tip of the pen to make a small hole in the middle of one end of the box. The box represents a telescope.
3. At the front of the classroom, place the box on a flat table so the hole points toward the lamp. Line the left side of the box up with the left edge of the table.
4. Put a small piece of tape on the table below the hole. Use the pen to make a mark on the tape directly below the hole. The mark represents the position of the telescope when Earth is on one side of its orbit.

### PART 2 Star 1

5. Label a sheet of paper Star 1 and place it inside the box as shown in the drawing. Hold the paper in place with two paper clips. The paper represents the film in a telescope.
6. Darken the room. Turn on the light to represent the star.
7. With the red pencil, mark the paper where you see a dot of light. Label this dot A. Dot A represents the image of the star on the film.
8. Move the box so the right edge of the box lines up with the right edge of the table. Repeat Step 4. The mark on the tape represents the position of the telescope six months later, when Earth is on the other side of its orbit.

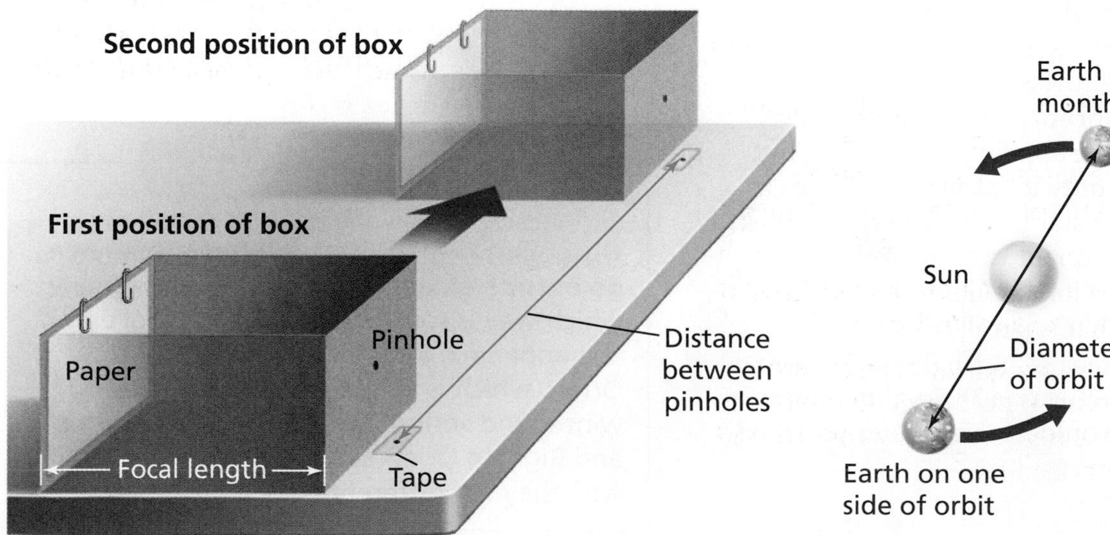

| Data Table | | | | | | |
|---|---|---|---|---|---|---|
| Star | Parallax Shift (mm) | Focal Length (mm) | Diameter of Orbit (mm) | Calculated Distance to Star (mm) | Calculated Distance to Star (m) | Actual Distance to Star (m) |
| | | | | | | |
| | | | | | | |

9. Repeat Step 7, using a black pencil to mark the second dot B. Dot B represents the image of the star as seen 6 months later from the other side of Earth's orbit.
10. Remove the paper. Before you continue, copy the data table into your notebook.
11. Measure and record the distance in millimeters between dots A and B. This distance represents the parallax shift for Star 1.
12. Measure and record the distance from the hole in the box to the lamp. This distance represents the actual distance to the star.
13. Measure and record the distance from the hole (lens) to the back of the box in millimeters. This distance represents the focal length of your telescope.
14. Measure and record the distance in millimeters between the marks on the two pieces of masking tape. This distance represents the diameter of Earth's orbit.

### PART 3 Stars 2 and 3

15. Move the lamp away from the table—about half the distance to the back of the room. The bulb now represents Star 2. Predict what you think will happen to the light images on your paper.
16. Repeat Steps 6–12 with a new sheet of paper to find the parallax shift for Star 2.
17. Move the lamp to the back of the classroom. The bulb now represents Star 3. Repeat Steps 6–12 with a new sheet of paper to find the parallax shift for Star 3.

## Analyze and Conclude

1. **Inferring** What caused the apparent change in position of the dots of light for each star? Explain.
2. **Calculating** Use the following formula to calculate the distance from the telescope to Star 1.

$$\text{Distance} = \frac{\text{Diameter} \times \text{Focal length}}{\text{Parallax shift}}$$

3. **Calculating** Divide your result from Question 2 by 1,000 to get the distance to the light bulb in meters.
4. **Calculating** Repeat Questions 2 and 3 for Stars 2 and 3.
5. **Predicting** Was your prediction in Step 15 correct? Why or why not?
6. **Interpreting Data** How did your calculation for Star 3 compare with the actual distance? What could you do to improve your results?
7. **Communicating** Write a paragraph that explains how parallax shift varies with distance. Relate each star's parallax shift to its distance from Earth.

## Design an Experiment

What would happen if you kept moving the lamp away from the box? Is there a distance at which you can no longer find the distance to the star? Design an experiment to find out.

Section

# 3 Lives of Stars

## Reading Preview

### Key Concepts

- How does a star form?
- What determines how long a star will exist?
- What happens to a star when it runs out of fuel?

### Key Terms

- nebula
- protostar
- white dwarf
- supernova
- neutron star
- pulsar
- black hole

### Target Reading Skill

**Sequencing** As you read, make a flowchart like the one below that shows the stages in the life of a star like the sun. Write each step of the process in a separate box in the flowchart in the order that it occurs.

**Life Cycle of a Sun-like Star**

Protostar forms from a nebula.
↓
A star is born as fusion begins.
↓
[ ]

## Lab zone Discover Activity

### What Determines How Long Stars Live?

1. This graph shows how the mass of a star is related to its lifetime—how long the star lives before it runs out of fuel.
2. How long does a star with 0.75 times the mass of the sun live? How long does a star with 3 times the mass of the sun live?

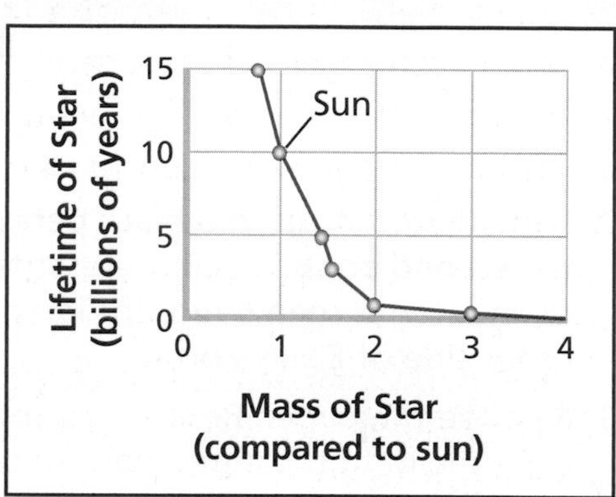


**Think It Over**

**Drawing Conclusions** Describe the general relationship between a star's mass and its lifetime.

Imagine that you want to study how people age. You wish you could watch a few people for 50 years, but your project is due next week! You have to study a lot of people for a short time, and classify the people into different age groups. You may come up with groups like *babies, young adults,* and *elderly people.* You don't have time to see a single person go through all these stages, but you know the stages exist.

Astronomers have a similar problem in trying to understand how stars age. They can't watch a single star for billions of years. Instead, they study many stars and other objects in space. Over time, astronomers have figured out that these objects represent different stages in the lives of stars.

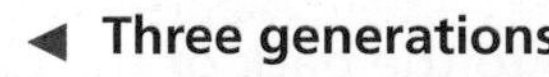
◀ Three generations

## The Lives of Stars

Stars do not last forever. Each star is born, goes through its life cycle, and eventually dies. (Of course, stars are not really alive. The words *born, live,* and *die* are just helpful comparisons.)

**A Star Is Born** All stars begin their lives as parts of nebulas. A **nebula** is a large cloud of gas and dust spread out in an immense volume. A star, on the other hand, is made up of a large amount of gas in a relatively small volume.

In the densest part of a nebula, gravity pulls gas and dust together. A contracting cloud of gas and dust with enough mass to form a star is called a **protostar.** *Proto* means "earliest" in Greek, so a protostar is the earliest stage of a star's life.

**A star is born when the contracting gas and dust from a nebula become so dense and hot that nuclear fusion starts.** Recall that nuclear fusion is the process by which atoms combine to form heavier atoms. In the sun, for example, hydrogen atoms combine to form helium. During nuclear fusion, enormous amounts of energy are released. Nuclear fusion has not yet begun in a protostar.

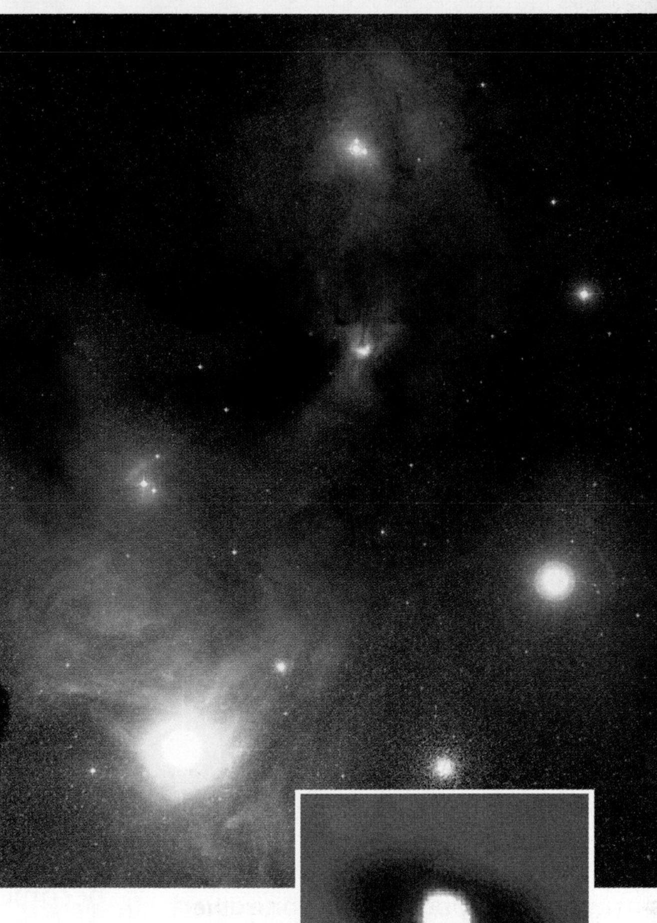

**FIGURE 12**
**Young Stars**
New stars are forming in the nebula on top. The bottom photo shows a protostar in the Orion Nebula. **Applying Concepts** *How do some of the gas and dust in a nebula become a protostar?*

**Lifetimes of Stars** **How long a star lives depends on its mass.** You might think that stars with more mass would last longer than stars with less mass. But the reverse is true. You can think of stars as being like cars. A small car has a small gas tank, but it also has a small engine that burns gas slowly. A large car has a larger gas tank, but it also has a larger engine that burns gas rapidly. So the small car can travel farther on a tank of gas than the larger car. Small-mass stars use up their fuel more slowly than large-mass stars, so they have much longer lives.

Generally, stars that have less mass than the sun use their fuel slowly, and can live for up to 200 billion years. Medium-mass stars like the sun live for about 10 billion years. Astronomers think the sun is about 4.6 billion years old, so it is almost halfway through its lifetime.

Stars that have more mass than the sun have shorter lifetimes. A star that is 15 times as massive as the sun may live only about ten million years. That may seem like a long time, but it is only one tenth of one percent of the lifetime of the sun.

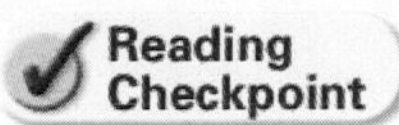


**How long will a star that is the mass of the sun live?**

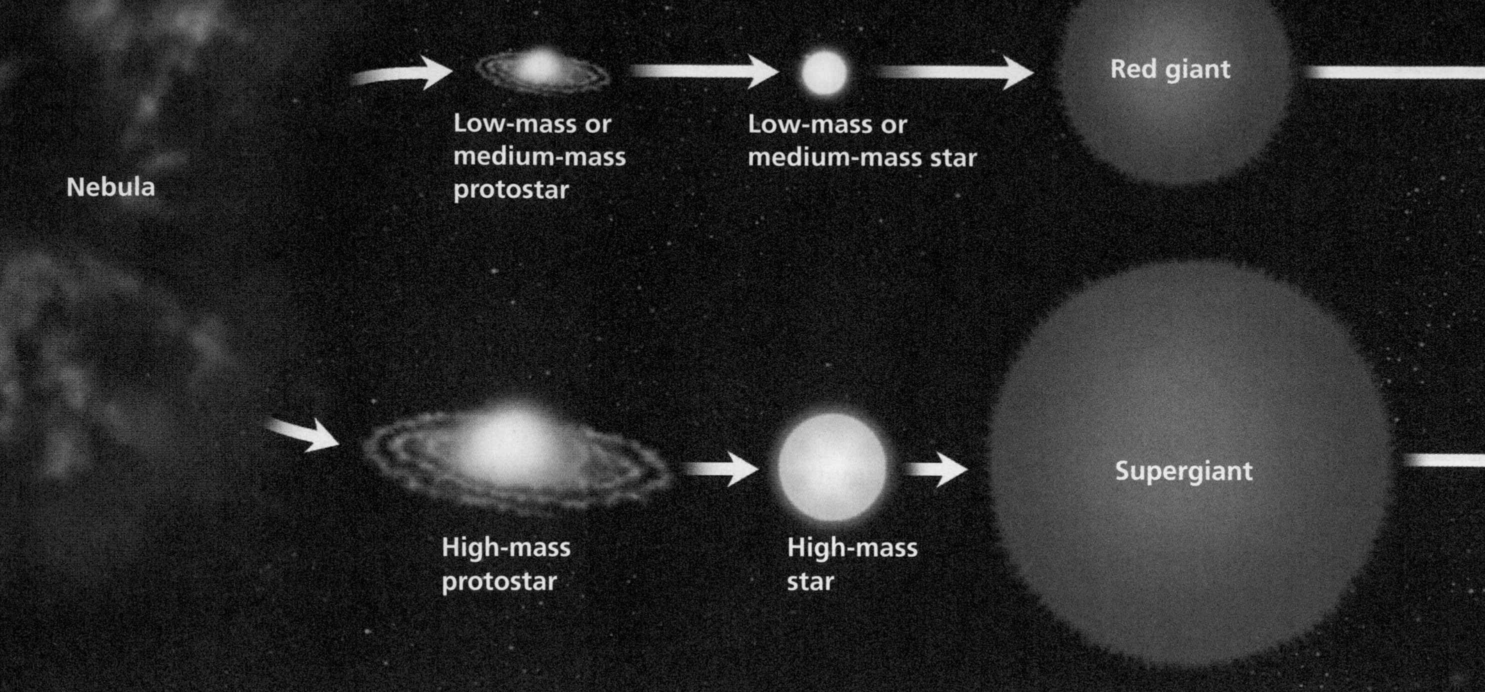


FIGURE 13
**The Lives of Stars**
A star's life history depends on its mass. A low-mass main-sequence star uses up its fuel slowly and eventually becomes a white dwarf. A high-mass star uses up its fuel quickly. After its supergiant stage, it will explode as a supernova, producing a neutron star or a black hole.
**Interpreting Diagrams** *What type of star produces a planetary nebula?*

## Deaths of Stars

When a star begins to run out of fuel, its core shrinks and its outer portion expands. Depending on its mass, the star becomes either a red giant or a supergiant. All main-sequence stars eventually become red giants or supergiants. As shown in Figure 13, red giants and supergiants evolve in very different ways. **After a star runs out of fuel, it becomes a white dwarf, a neutron star, or a black hole.**

**White Dwarfs** Low-mass stars and medium-mass stars like the sun take billions of years to use up their nuclear fuel. As they start to run out of fuel, their outer layers expand, and they become red giants. Eventually, the outer parts grow larger still and drift out into space, forming a glowing cloud of gas called a planetary nebula. The blue-white core of the star that is left behind cools and becomes a **white dwarf.**

White dwarfs are only about the size of Earth, but they have about as much mass as the sun. Since a white dwarf has the same mass as the sun but only one millionth the volume, it is one million times as dense as the sun. A spoonful of material from a white dwarf has as much mass as a large truck. White dwarfs have no fuel, but they glow faintly from leftover energy. After billions of years, a white dwarf eventually stops glowing. Then it is called a black dwarf.

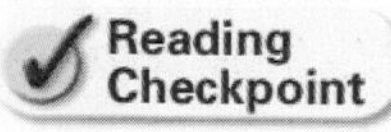

What is a white dwarf?

**Lab zone Skills Activity**

### Predicting

Find Algol, Sirius B, and Polaris in Figure 10, the H-R diagram. What type of star is each of these now? Predict what the next stage in each star's life will be.

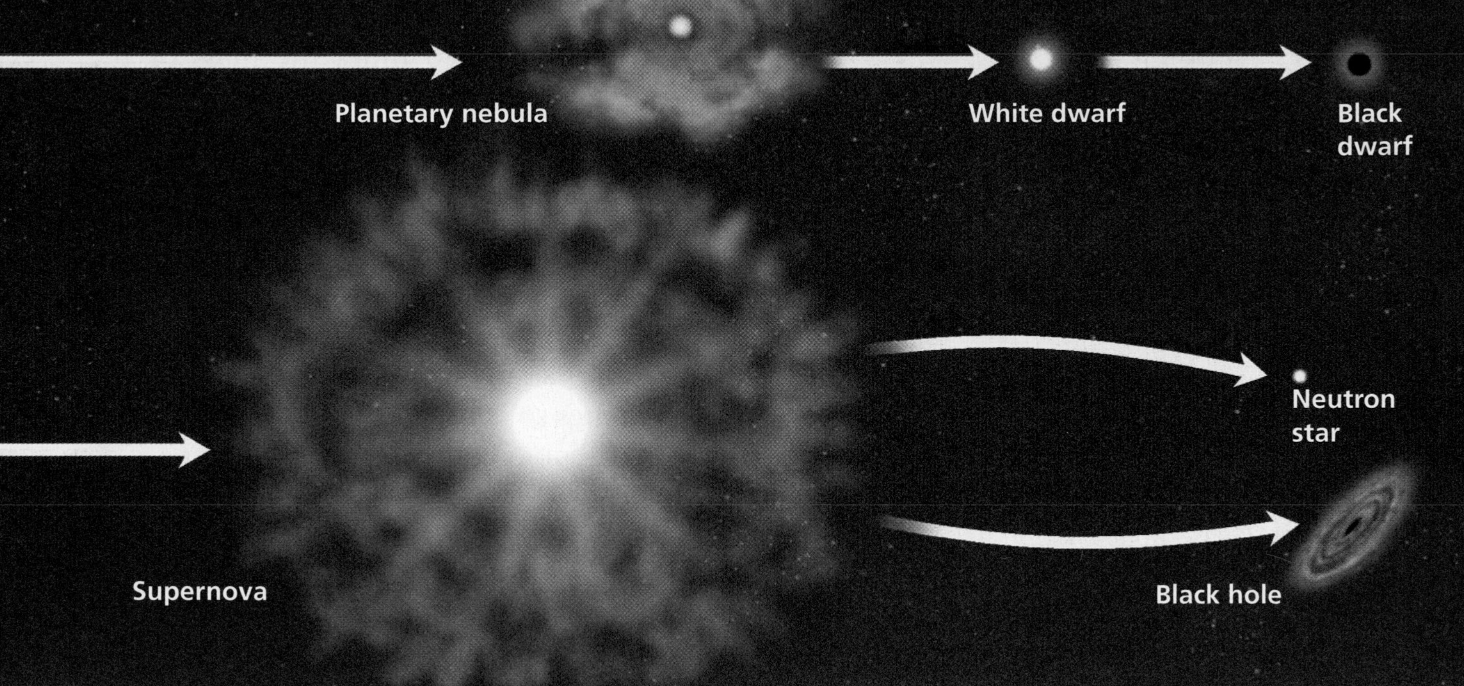


**Supernovas** The life cycle of a high-mass star is quite different from the life cycle of a low-mass or medium-mass star. High-mass stars quickly evolve into brilliant supergiants. When a supergiant runs out of fuel, it can explode suddenly. Within hours, the star blazes millions of times brighter. The explosion is called a **supernova.** After a supernova, some of the material from the star expands into space. This material may become part of a nebula. This nebula can then contract to form a new, partly recycled star. Astronomers think the sun began as a nebula that contained material from a supernova.

**For:** The Lives of Stars activity
**Visit:** PHSchool.com
**Web Code:** cfp-5043

**Neutron Stars** After a supergiant explodes, some of the material from the star is left behind. This material may form a neutron star. **Neutron stars** are the remains of high-mass stars. They are even smaller and denser than white dwarfs. A neutron star may contain as much as three times the mass of the sun but be only about 25 kilometers in diameter, the size of a city.

In 1967, Jocelyn Bell, a British astronomy student, detected an object in space that appeared to give off regular pulses of radio waves. Some astronomers hypothesized that the pulses might be a signal from an extraterrestrial civilization. At first, astronomers even named the source LGM, for the "Little Green Men" in early science-fiction stories. Soon, however, astronomers concluded that the source of the radio waves was really a rapidly spinning neutron star. Spinning neutron stars are called **pulsars,** short for pulsating radio sources. Some pulsars spin hundreds of times per second!

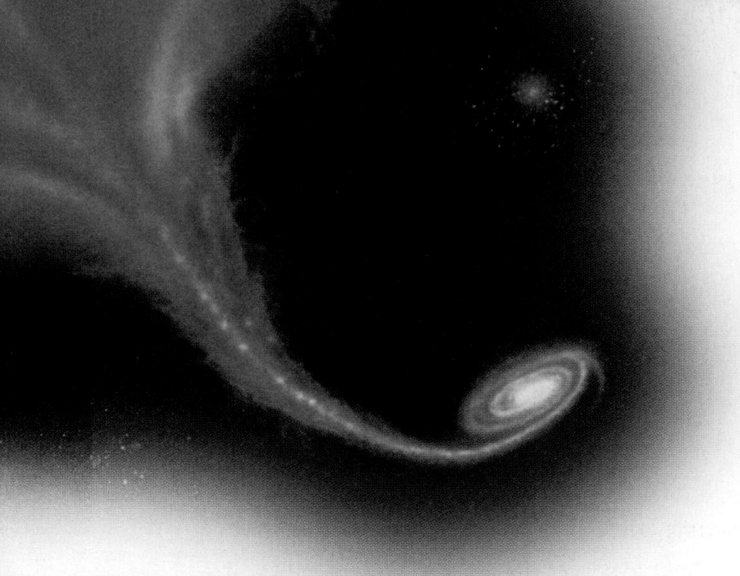

**Black Holes** The most massive stars—those having more than 40 times the mass of the sun—may become black holes when they die. A **black hole** is an object with gravity so strong that nothing, not even light, can escape. After a very massive star dies in a supernova explosion, more than five times the mass of the sun may be left. The gravity of this mass is so strong that the gas is pulled inward, packing the gas into a smaller and smaller space. The gas becomes so densely packed that its intense gravity will not allow even light to escape. The remains of the star have become a black hole.

**FIGURE 14**
**Black Holes**
The remains of the most massive stars collapse into black holes. This artist's impression shows a black hole pulling matter from a companion star. The material glows as it is pulled into the black hole. **Applying Concepts** *If it is impossible to detect a black hole directly, how do astronomers find them?*

No light, radio waves, or any other form of radiation can ever get out of a black hole, so it is not possible to detect a black hole directly. But astronomers can detect black holes indirectly. For example, gas near a black hole is pulled so strongly that it revolves faster and faster around the black hole. Friction heats the gas up. Astronomers can detect X-rays coming from the hot gas and infer that a black hole is present. Similarly, if another star is near a black hole, astronomers can calculate the mass of the black hole from the effect of its gravity on the star. Scientists have detected dozens of star-size black holes with the Chandra X-ray Observatory. They have also detected huge black holes that are millions or billions of times the sun's mass.

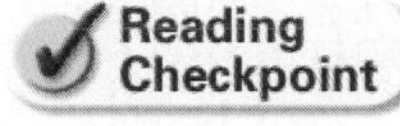

**What is a black hole?**

## Section 3 Assessment

**Target Reading Skill Sequencing** Refer to your flowchart as you answer the questions.

### Reviewing Key Concepts

1. a. **Defining** What is a nebula?
   b. **Explaining** How does a star form from a nebula?
   c. **Comparing and Contrasting** How is a protostar different from a star?
2. a. **Identifying** What factor determines how long a star lives?
   b. **Applying Concepts** A star is twice as massive as the sun. Will its lifespan be longer, shorter, or the same as that of the sun?
3. a. **Comparing and Contrasting** What is a white dwarf? How is it different from a neutron star?
   b. **Relating Cause and Effect** Why do some stars become white dwarfs and others become neutron stars or black holes?
   c. **Predicting** What will happen to the sun when it runs out of fuel? Explain.

### Writing in Science

**Descriptive Paragraph** Write a description of one of the stages in the life of a star, such as a nebula, red giant, supernova, or white dwarf. Include information on how it formed and what will happen next in the star's evolution.

Section 4

# Star Systems and Galaxies

## Reading Preview

### Key Concepts

- What is a star system?
- What are the major types of galaxies?
- How do astronomers describe the scale of the universe?

### Key Terms

- binary star
- eclipsing binary
- open cluster
- globular cluster
- galaxy
- spiral galaxy
- elliptical galaxy
- irregular galaxy
- quasar
- universe
- scientific notation

### Target Reading Skill

**Building Vocabulary** Carefully read the definition of each key term. Also read the neighboring sentences. Then write a definition of each key term in your own words.

## Lab zone Discover Activity

### Why Does the Milky Way Look Hazy?

1. Using a pencil, carefully poke at least 20 holes close together in a sheet of white paper.
2. Tape the paper to a chalkboard or dark-colored wall.
3. Go to the other side of the room and look at the paper. From the far side of the room, what do the dots look like? Can you see individual dots?

**Think It Over**

**Making Models** How is looking at the paper from the far side of the room like trying to see many very distant stars that are close together? How does your model compare to the photograph of the Milky Way below?

On a clear, dark night in the country, you can see a hazy band of light stretched across the sky. This band of stars is called the Milky Way. It looks as if the Milky Way is very far away. Actually, though, Earth is inside the Milky Way! The Milky Way looks milky or hazy from Earth because the stars are too close together for your eyes to see them individually. The dark blotches in the Milky Way are clouds of dust that block light from stars behind them.

The Milky Way

## Star Systems and Clusters

Our solar system has only one star, the sun. But this is not the most common situation for stars. **Most stars are members of groups of two or more stars, called star systems.** If you were on a planet in one of these star systems, at times you might see two or more suns in the sky! At other times, one or more of these suns would be below the horizon.

**Multiple Star Systems** Star systems that have two stars are called double stars or **binary stars.** (The prefix *bi* means "two.") Those with three stars are called triple stars. The nearby star Proxima Centauri may be part of a triple star system. The other two stars in the system, Alpha Centauri A and Alpha Centauri B, form a double star. Scientists are not sure whether Proxima Centauri is really part of the system or is just passing close to the other two stars temporarily.

Often one star in a binary star is much brighter and more massive than the other. Astronomers can sometimes detect a binary star even if only one of the stars can be seen from Earth. Astronomers can often tell that there is a dim star in a binary system by observing the effects of its gravity. As the dim companion star revolves around a bright star, the dim star's gravity causes the bright star to wobble back and forth. Imagine watching a pair of dancers who are twirling each other around. Even if one dancer were invisible, you could tell that the invisible dancer was there from watching the motion of the visible dancer.

**FIGURE 15**
**Invisible Partners**
If you saw someone dancing but couldn't see a partner, you could infer that the partner was there by watching the dancer you could see. Astronomers use a similar method to detect faint stars in star systems.

**Eclipsing Binaries** A wobble is not the only clue that a star has a dim companion. A dim star in a binary star may pass in front of a brighter star and eclipse it. From Earth, the binary star would suddenly look much dimmer. A system in which one star periodically blocks the light from another is called an **eclipsing binary.** As Figure 16 shows, the star Algol is actually an eclipsing binary star system.

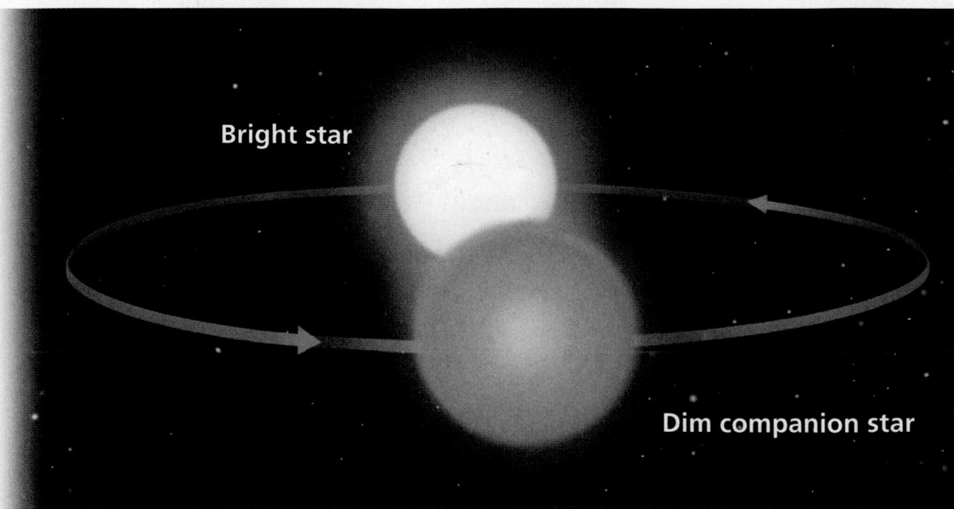


**FIGURE 16**
**Eclipsing Binary**
Algol is an eclipsing binary star system consisting of a bright star and a dim companion. Each time the dimmer star passes in front of the brighter one, Algol appears less bright.
**Interpreting Diagrams** *When does Algol appear brighter?*

**Planets Around Other Stars** In 1995, astronomers first discovered a planet revolving around another ordinary star. They used a method similar to the one used in studying binary stars. The astronomers observed that a star was moving slightly toward and away from us. They knew that the invisible object causing the movement didn't have enough mass to be a star. They inferred that it must be a planet.

Since then, astronomers have discovered more than 100 planets around other stars, and new ones are being discovered all of the time. Most of these new planets are very large, with at least half of the mass of Jupiter. A small planet would be hard to detect because it would have little gravitational effect on the star it orbited.

Could there be life on planets in other solar systems? Some scientists think it is possible. A few astronomers are using radio telescopes to search for signals that could not have come from natural sources. Such a signal might be evidence that an extraterrestrial civilization was sending out radio waves.

**Star Clusters** Many stars belong to larger groupings called star clusters. All of the stars in a particular cluster formed from the same nebula at about the same time and are about the same distance from Earth.

There are two major types of star clusters: open clusters and globular clusters. **Open clusters** have a loose, disorganized appearance and contain no more than a few thousand stars. They often contain many bright supergiants and much gas and dust. In contrast, **globular clusters** are large groupings of older stars. Globular clusters are round and densely packed with stars—some may contain more than a million stars.

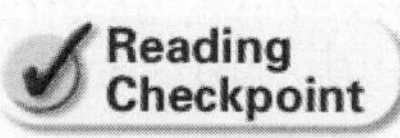


**What is a globular cluster?**

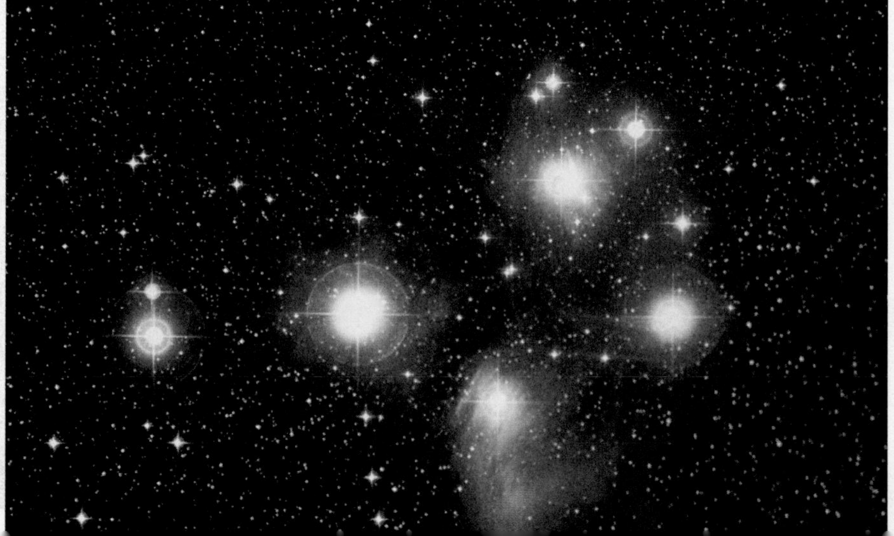

**FIGURE 17**
**Star Clusters**
The stars in a globular cluster (above) are all about the same age and the same distance from Earth. The Pleiades (left), also called the *Seven Sisters*, is an open cluster.

**FIGURE 18**
**Types of Galaxies**
There are three major types of galaxies: spiral, elliptical, and irregular.

## Galaxies

A **galaxy** is a huge group of single stars, star systems, star clusters, dust, and gas bound together by gravity. There are billions of galaxies in the universe. The largest galaxies have more than a trillion stars. **Astronomers classify most galaxies into the following types: spiral, elliptical, and irregular.** Figure 18 shows examples of these three.

**Spiral Galaxies** Some galaxies appear to have a bulge in the middle and arms that spiral outward, like pinwheels. Such galaxies are called **spiral galaxies.** The spiral arms contain many bright, young stars as well as gas and dust. Most new stars in spiral galaxies form in these spiral arms. Relatively few new stars are forming in the central bulge. Some spiral galaxies, called barred-spiral galaxies, have a huge bar-shaped region of stars and gas that passes through their center.

**Elliptical Galaxies** Not all galaxies have spiral arms. **Elliptical galaxies** look like round or flattened balls. These galaxies contain billions of stars but have little gas and dust between the stars. Because there is little gas or dust, stars are no longer forming. Most elliptical galaxies contain only old stars.

**Irregular Galaxies** Some galaxies do not have regular shapes. These are known as **irregular galaxies.** Irregular galaxies are typically smaller than other types of galaxies. They generally have many bright, young stars and lots of gas and dust to form new stars.

**Quasars** In the 1960s, astronomers discovered objects that are very bright, but also very far away. Many of these objects are 10 billion light-years or more away, making them among the most distant objects in the universe. These distant, enormously bright objects looked almost like stars. Since *quasi* means "something like" in Latin, these objects were given the name quasi-stellar objects, or **quasars.**

What could be so bright at such a great distance from Earth? Astronomers have concluded that quasars are active young galaxies with giant black holes at their centers. Each of these black holes has a mass a billion times or more as great as that of the sun. As enormous amounts of gas revolve around the black hole, the gas heats up and shines brightly.

For: Links on galaxies
Visit: www.SciLinks.org
Web Code: scn-0644

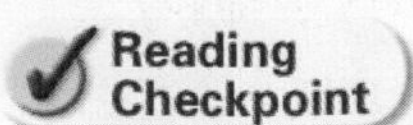


**What is a quasar?**

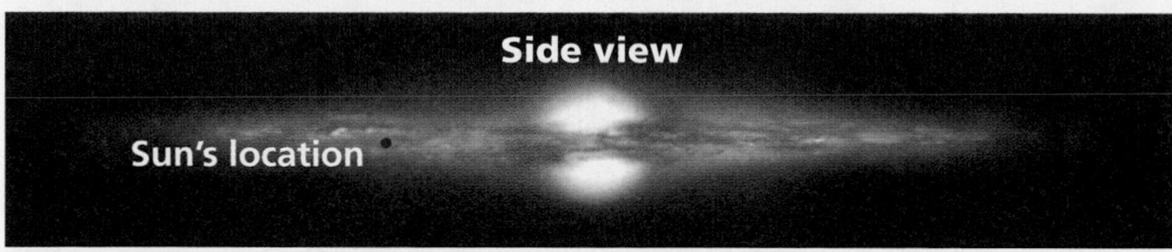


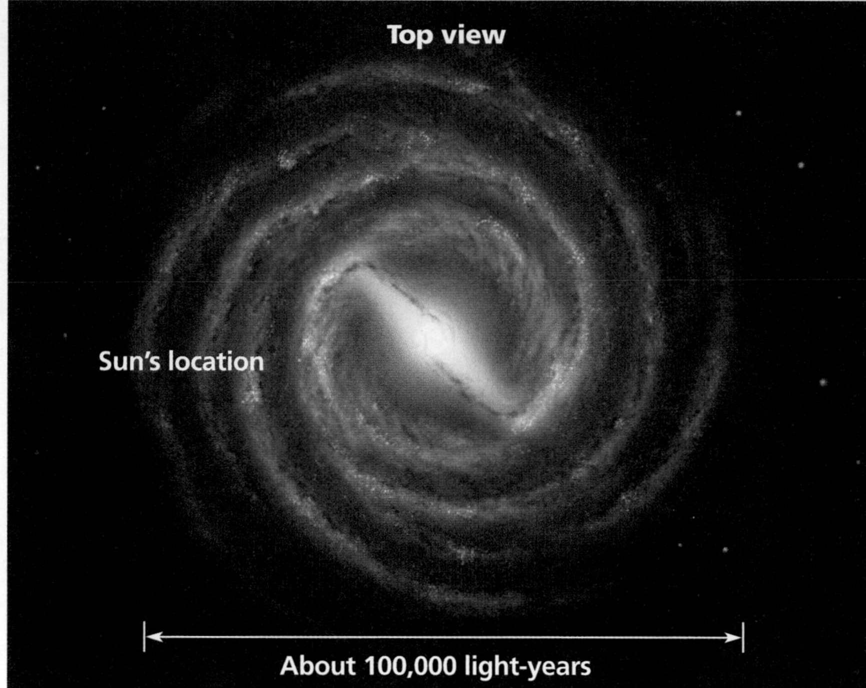


**FIGURE 19**
**Structure of the Milky Way**
From the side, the Milky Way appears to be a narrow disk with a bulge in the middle. The galaxy's spiral structure is visible only from above or below the galaxy.
**Interpreting Diagrams** *Where in the galaxy is the sun located?*

## The Milky Way

**Our solar system is located in a spiral galaxy called the Milky Way.** As Figure 19 shows, the shape of the Milky Way varies depending on your vantage point. From the side, the Milky Way would look like a narrow disk with a large bulge in the middle. But from the top or bottom, the Milky Way would have a spiral, pinwheel shape. You can't see the spiral shape of the Milky Way from Earth because our solar system is inside the galaxy in one of the spiral arms.

The Milky Way is usually thought of as a standard spiral galaxy. However, recent evidence suggests that the Milky Way is a barred-spiral galaxy instead.

When you see the Milky Way at night during the summer, you are looking toward the center of our galaxy. The center of the galaxy is about 25,000 light-years away, but it is hidden from view by large clouds of dust and gas. However, astronomers can study the center using X-rays, infrared radiation, and radio waves.

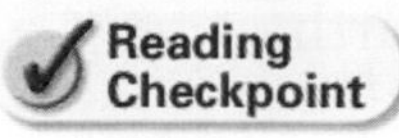

**How far away is the center of the galaxy?**

**Lab zone Try This Activity**

### A Spiral Galaxy

You can make a model of our galaxy.

1. Using pipe cleaners, make a pinwheel with two spirals.
2. View the spirals along the surface of the table. Sketch what you see.
3. Next, view the spirals from above the table and sketch them.

**Observing** The sun is inside a flat spiral galaxy. From Earth's position on the flat surface, is it possible to get a good view of stars in the spiral arms? Why or why not?

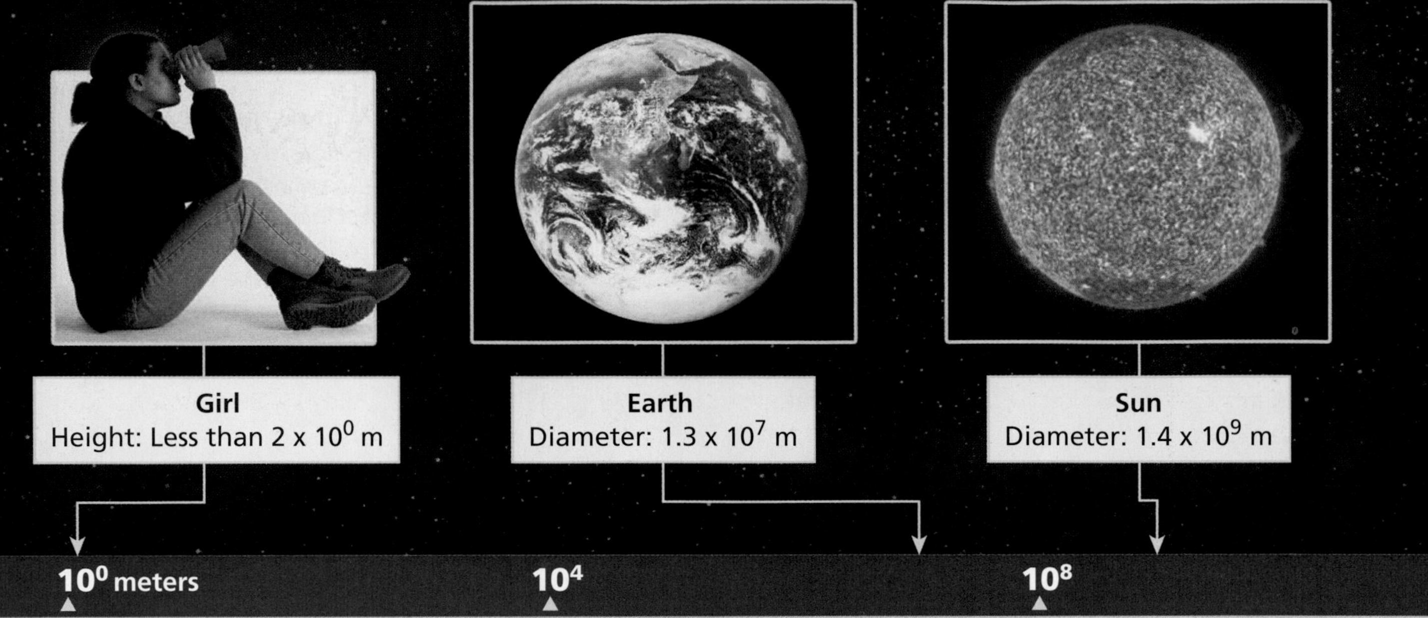


## The Scale of the Universe

Astronomers define the **universe** as all of space and everything in it. The universe is enormous, almost beyond imagination. Astronomers study objects as close as the moon and as far away as quasars. They study incredibly large objects, such as galaxies that are millions of light-years across. They also study the behavior of tiny particles, such as the atoms within stars. **Since the numbers astronomers use are often very large or very small, they frequently use scientific notation to describe sizes and distances in the universe.**

**Scientific Notation** **Scientific notation** uses powers of ten to write very large or very small numbers in shorter form. Each number is written as the product of a number between 1 and 10 and a power of 10. For example: 1,200 is written as $1.2 \times 10^3$. One light-year is about 9,500,000,000,000,000 meters. Since there are 15 digits after the first digit, in scientific notation this number is written as $9.5 \times 10^{15}$ meters.

**The Immensity of Space** The structures in the universe vary greatly in scale. To understand the scale of these structures, imagine that you are going on a journey through the universe. Refer to Figure 20 as you take your imaginary trip. Start at the left with something familiar—a girl looking through binoculars. She is about 1.5 meters tall. Now shift to the right and change the scale by 10,000,000 or $10^7$. You're now close to the diameter of Earth, $1.28 \times 10^7$ meters. As you move from left to right across Figure 20, the scale increases. The diameter of the sun is about 100 times that of Earth.

**Math Skills**

### Scientific Notation

The bright star Deneb is about 3,230 light-years from Earth. To express this number in scientific notation, first insert a decimal point in the original number so that you have a number between one and ten. In this case, the number is 3.23.

To determine the power of 10, count the number of places that the decimal point moved. Here the decimal point moved three places.

3,230 light-years =
$3.23 \times 10^3$ light-years

**Practice Problem** The sun takes about 220,000,000 years to revolve once around the center of the galaxy. Express this length of time in scientific notation.

Beyond the solar system, the sizes of observable objects become much larger. For example, within our galaxy, the beautiful Cat's Eye Nebula is about $3 \times 10^{16}$ meters across.

Beyond our galaxy are billions of other galaxies, many of which contain billions of stars. For example, the nearby spiral galaxy Andromeda is about $2 \times 10^{21}$ meters across. The Milky Way is part of a cluster of 50 or so galaxies called the Local Group. The Local Group is part of the Virgo Supercluster, which contains hundreds of galaxies. The size of the observable universe is about $10^{10}$ light years, or $10^{26}$ meters.

**FIGURE 20**
**Scientific Notation**
Scientists often use scientific notation to help describe the vast sizes and distances in space.
**Calculating** *About how many times larger is the Cat's Eye Nebula than Earth?*

## Section 4 Assessment

**Target Reading Skill Building Vocabulary** Use your definitions to help answer the questions.

### Reviewing Key Concepts

1. a. **Defining** What is a binary star?
   b. **Classifying** Are all binary stars part of star systems? Explain.
   c. **Applying Concepts** Some binary stars are called eclipsing binaries. Explain why this term is appropriate. (*Hint:* Think about Algol as you write your answer.)
2. a. **Listing** Name the main types of galaxies.
   b. **Classifying** What type of galaxy is the Milky Way?
   c. **Classifying** Suppose astronomers discover a galaxy that contains only old stars. What type of galaxy is it likely to be?
3. a. **Reviewing** What is scientific notation?
   b. **Explaining** How is scientific notation useful to astronomers?
   c. **Calculating** How large is the Cat's Eye Nebula in light-years? (*Hint:* Refer to Figure 20.)

**Math Practice**

4. **Scientific Notation** The star Betelgeuse has a diameter of 940,000,000 km. Betelgeuse is 427 light-years from Earth. Write each of these figures in scientific notation.

Section 5

# The Expanding Universe

## Reading Preview

### Key Concepts

- What is the big bang theory?
- How did the solar system form?
- What do astronomers predict about the future of the universe?

### Key Terms

- big bang
- Hubble's law
- cosmic background radiation
- solar nebula
- planetesimal
- dark matter
- dark energy

### Target Reading Skill

**Identifying Supporting Evidence** As you read, identify the evidence that supports the big bang theory. Write the evidence in a graphic organizer like the one below.

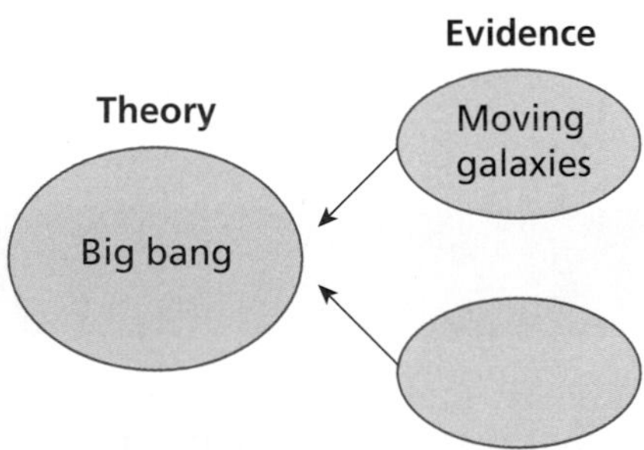


## Lab zone Discover Activity

### How Does the Universe Expand?

1. Use a marker to put 10 dots on an empty balloon. The dots represent galaxies.
2. Blow up the balloon. What happens to the distances between galaxies that are close together? Galaxies that are far apart?

**Think It Over**

**Inferring** If the universe is expanding, do galaxies that are close together move apart faster or slower than galaxies that are far apart? Explain.

The Andromeda Galaxy is the most distant object that the human eye can see. Light from this galaxy has traveled for about 3 million years before reaching Earth. When that light finally reaches your eye, you are seeing how the galaxy looked 3 million years ago. It is as though you are looking back in time.

Astronomers have photographed galaxies that are billions of light-years away. Light from these galaxies traveled for billions of years before it reached Earth. From these observations, astronomers are able to infer the age of the universe.

## How the Universe Formed

Astronomers theorize that the universe began billions of years ago. At that time, the part of the universe we can now see was no larger than the period at the end of this sentence. This tiny universe was incredibly hot and dense. The universe then exploded in what astronomers call the **big bang.**

◀ **Nearly every visible object in this image is a distant galaxy.**

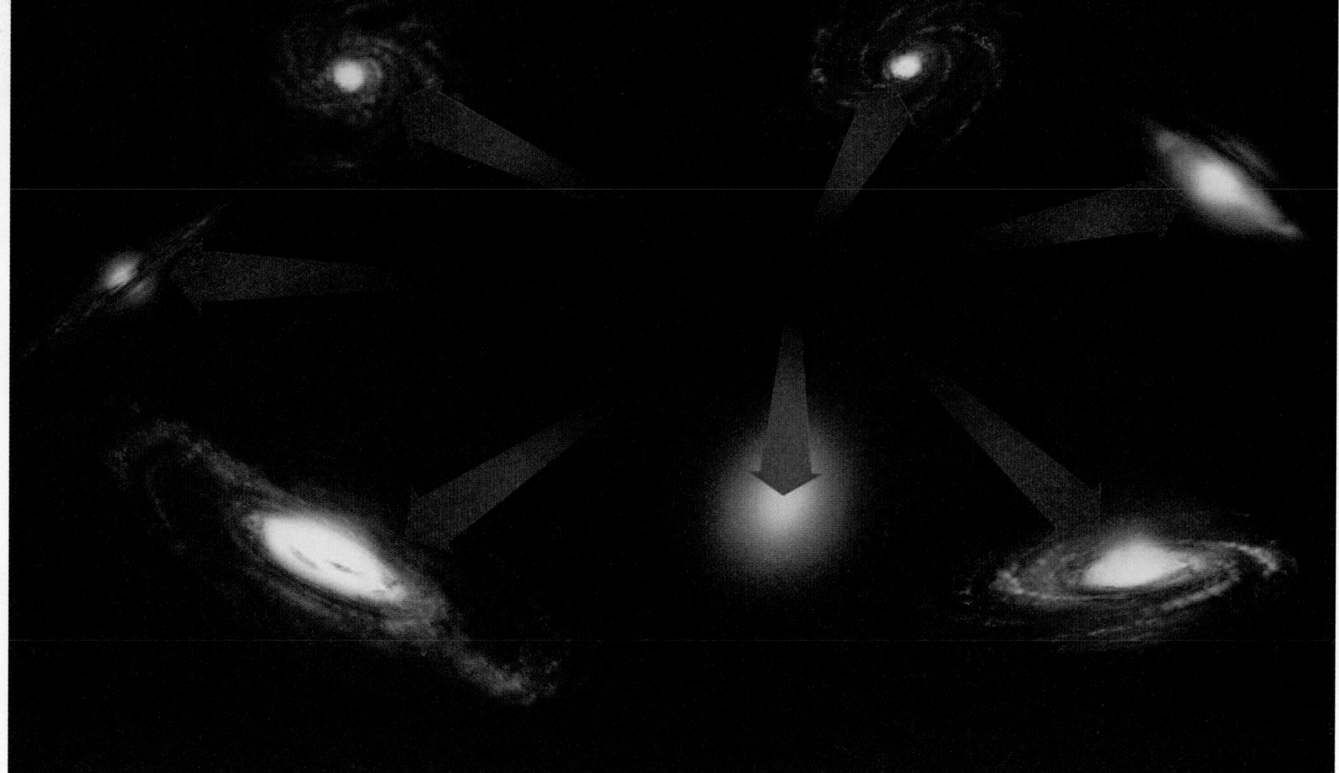

**FIGURE 21**
**Retreating Galaxies**
All of the distant galaxies astronomers have observed are moving rapidly away from our galaxy and from each other.

**According to the big bang theory, the universe formed in an instant, billions of years ago, in an enormous explosion.** Since the big bang, the size of the universe has been increasing rapidly. The universe is billions of times larger now than it was early in its history.

As the universe expanded, it gradually cooled. After a few hundred thousand years, atoms formed. About 200 million years after the big bang, the first stars and galaxies formed.

If the big bang theory is accurate, what evidence might you expect to find in today's universe? You might expect that the matter that had been hurled apart by the big bang would still be moving apart. You might also expect to find evidence of energy left over from the explosion.

**Moving Galaxies** An American astronomer, Edwin Hubble, discovered important evidence that later helped astronomers to develop the big bang theory. In the 1920s, Hubble studied the spectrums of many galaxies at various distances from Earth. By examining a galaxy's spectrum, Hubble could tell how fast the galaxy is moving and whether it is moving toward our galaxy or away from it.

Hubble discovered that, with the exception of a few nearby galaxies, all galaxies are moving away from us and from each other. Hubble found that there is a relationship between the distance to a galaxy and its speed. **Hubble's law** states that the farther away a galaxy is, the faster it is moving away from us. Hubble's law strongly supports the big bang theory.

## Math Analyzing Data

### Speeding Galaxies

Use the graph to answer the questions below about moving clusters of galaxies.

1. **Reading Graphs** How far away is the Bootes cluster? How fast is it moving?
2. **Reading Graphs** Which galaxy is moving away the fastest? Which galaxy is closest to Earth?
3. **Drawing Conclusions** How are the distance and speed of a galaxy related?
4. **Predicting** Predict the speed of a galaxy that is 5 billion light-years from Earth.

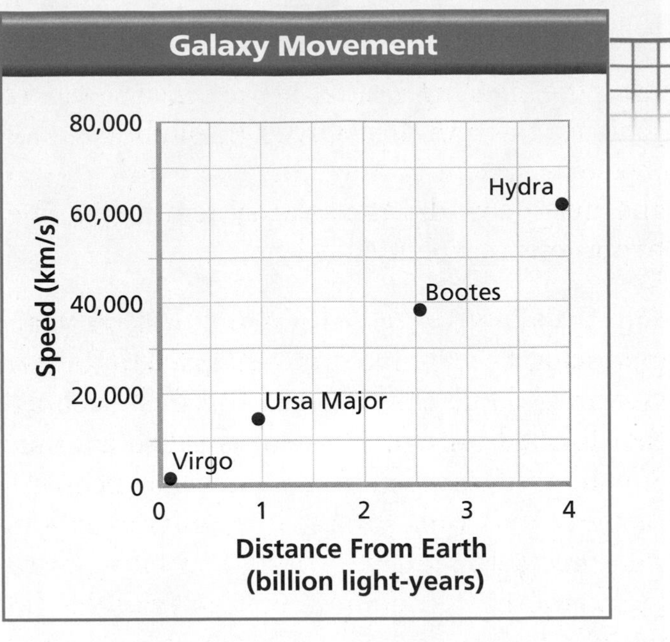


FIGURE 22
**Rising Dough**
The galaxies in the universe are like the raisins in rising bread dough. **Making Models** *How does rising raisin bread dough resemble the expanding universe?*

To understand how the galaxies are moving, think of raisin bread dough that is rising. If you could shrink yourself to sit on a raisin, you would see all the other raisins moving away from you. The farther a raisin was from you, the faster it would move away, because there would be more bread dough to expand between you and the raisin. No matter which raisin you sat on, all the other raisins would seem to be moving away from you. You could tell that the bread dough was expanding by watching the other raisins.

The universe is like the bread dough. Like the raisins in the dough, the galaxies in the universe are moving away from each other. In the universe, it is space that is expanding, like the dough between the raisins.

**Cosmic Background Radiation** In 1965, two American physicists, Arno Penzias and Robert Wilson, accidentally detected faint radiation on their radio telescope. This mysterious glow was coming from all directions in space. Scientists later concluded that this glow, now called **cosmic background radiation,** is the leftover thermal energy from the big bang. This energy was distributed in every direction as the universe expanded.

**Age of the Universe** Since astronomers can measure approximately how fast the universe is expanding now, they can infer how long it has been expanding. Based on careful measurements of how fast distant galaxies are moving away from us and the cosmic background radiation, astronomers estimate that the universe is about 13.7 billion years old.

# Formation of the Solar System

After the big bang, matter in the universe separated into galaxies. Gas and dust spread throughout space. Where the solar system is now, there was only cold, dark gas and dust. How did the solar system form? The leading hypothesis is explained below.

**The Solar Nebula** **About five billion years ago, a giant cloud of gas and dust collapsed to form our solar system.** A large cloud of gas and dust such as the one that formed our solar system is called a **solar nebula.** Slowly, gravity began to pull the solar nebula together. As the solar nebula shrank, it spun faster and faster. The solar nebula flattened, forming a rotating disk. Gravity pulled most of the gas into the center of the disk, where the gas eventually became hot and dense enough for nuclear fusion to begin. The sun was born.

**Planetesimals** In the outer parts of the disk, gas and dust formed small asteroid-like and comet-like bodies called **planetesimals.** These formed the building blocks of the planets. Planetesimals collided and grew larger by sticking together, eventually combining to form the planets.

**The Inner Planets** When the solar system formed, temperatures were very high. It was so hot close to the sun that most water and other ice-forming materials simply vaporized. Most gases escaped the gravity of the planets that were forming in this region. As a result, the inner planets, Mercury, Venus, Earth, and Mars, are relatively small and rocky.

**The Outer Planets** In contrast, farther from the sun it was much cooler. As the planets in this region grew, their gravity increased and they were able to capture much of the hydrogen and helium gas in the surrounding space. As a result, the planets Jupiter, Saturn, Uranus, and Neptune became very large. Most comets formed near Jupiter and Saturn. They were later flung out to the outer solar system. Beyond the gas giants, a huge disk of ice and other substances formed. Pluto also formed in this region.

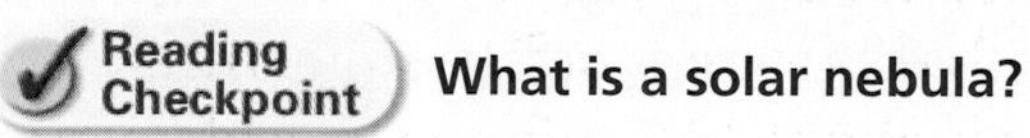

**What is a solar nebula?**

A cloud of gas and dust formed a spinning disk.

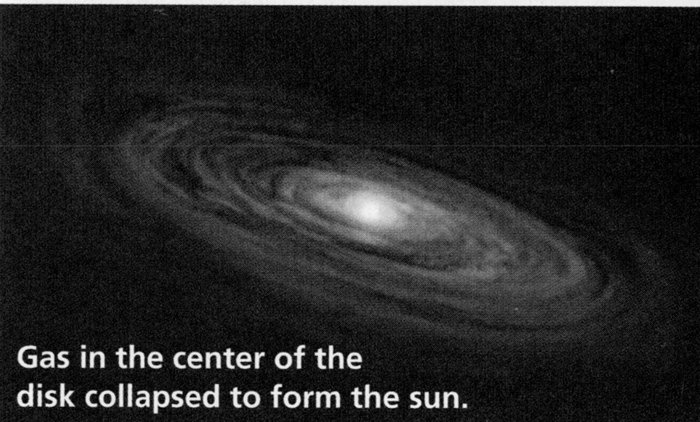
Gas in the center of the disk collapsed to form the sun.

The remaining gas and dust formed the planets.

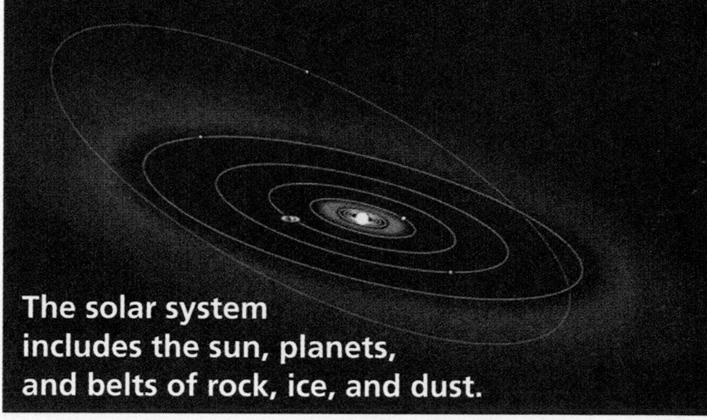
The solar system includes the sun, planets, and belts of rock, ice, and dust.

FIGURE 23
**How the Solar System Formed**
The solar system formed from a collapsing cloud of gas and dust.

**For:** Links on the expanding universe
**Visit:** www.SciLinks.org
**Web Code:** scn-0645

## The Future of the Universe

What will happen to the universe in the future? One possibility is that the universe will continue to expand, as it is doing now. All of the stars will eventually run out of fuel and burn out, and the universe will be cold and dark. Another possibility is that the force of gravity will begin to pull the galaxies back together. The result would be a reverse big bang, or "big crunch." All of the matter in the universe would be crushed into an enormous black hole.

Which of these possibilities is more likely? Recent discoveries have produced a surprising new view of the universe that is still not well understood. **New observations lead many astronomers to conclude that the universe will likely expand forever.**

**Dark Matter** Until fairly recently, astronomers assumed that the universe consisted solely of the matter they could observe directly. But this idea was disproved by the American astronomer Vera Rubin. Rubin made detailed observations of the rotation of spiral galaxies. She discovered that the matter that astronomers can see, such as stars and nebulas, makes up as little as ten percent of the mass in galaxies. The remaining mass exists in the form of dark matter.

**Dark matter** is matter that does not give off electromagnetic radiation. Dark matter cannot be seen directly. However, its presence can be inferred by observing the effect of its gravity on visible objects, such as stars, or on light.

Astronomers still don't know much about dark matter—what it is made of or all of the places where it is found. But astronomers estimate that about 23 percent of the universe's mass is made of dark matter.

**An Accelerating Expansion** In the late 1990s, astronomers observed that the expansion of the universe appears to be accelerating. That is, galaxies seem to be moving apart at a faster rate now than in the past. This observation was puzzling, as no known force could account for it. Astronomers infer that a mysterious new force, which they call **dark energy,** is causing the expansion of the universe to accelerate. Current estimates indicate that most of the universe is made of dark energy and dark matter.

Astronomy is one of the oldest sciences, but there are still many discoveries to be made and puzzles to be solved about this universe of ours!

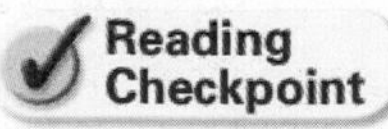


**What is the effect of dark energy?**

**FIGURE 24**
**Vera Rubin**
Astronomer Vera Rubin's observations proved the existence of dark matter.

**FIGURE 25**
**Dark Matter**
Astronomers measured the effect of gravity on light to produce this computer image of how dark matter (in blue) is distributed across a cluster of galaxies.

## Section 5 Assessment

**Target Reading Skill Identifying Supporting Evidence** Refer to your graphic organizer about the big bang theory as you answer Question 1 below.

### Reviewing Key Concepts

1. a. **Defining** What was the big bang?
   b. **Summarizing** When did the big bang occur?
   c. **Describing** Describe two pieces of evidence that support the big bang theory.
2. a. **Summarizing** How old is the solar system?
   b. **Relating Cause and Effect** What force caused the solar system to form?
   c. **Sequencing** Place the following events in the proper order: planets form; planetesimals form; solar nebula shrinks; nuclear fusion begins in the sun.
3. a. **Defining** What is dark matter?
   b. **Explaining** How do scientists know that dark matter exists?
   c. **Predicting** What evidence has led scientists to predict that the universe will continue to expand forever?

### Lab zone At-Home Activity

**Stargazing** Plan an evening of stargazing with adult family members. Choose a dark, clear night. Use binoculars if available and the star charts in the appendix to locate the Milky Way and some interesting stars that you have learned about. Explain to your family what you know about the Milky Way and each constellation that you observe.

# Chapter 21 Study Guide

**The BIG Idea**

**Structure of the Universe** Astronomers learn about the structure of the universe and how it has changed over time by studying stars, galaxies, and other objects in space.

## 1 Telescopes

### Key Concepts

- The electromagnetic spectrum includes radio waves, infrared radiation, visible light, ultraviolet radiation, X-rays, and gamma rays.
- Telescopes are instruments that collect and focus electromagnetic radiation.
- Many large observatories are located on mountaintops or in space.

### Key Terms

- telescope
- visible light
- wavelength
- spectrum
- optical telescope
- electromagnetic radiation
- refracting telescope
- convex lens
- reflecting telescope
- radio telescope
- observatory

## 2 Characteristics of Stars

### Key Concepts

- Characteristics used to classify stars include color, temperature, size, composition, and brightness.
- The brightness of a star depends upon both its size and temperature.
- Astronomers use a unit called the light-year to measure distances between the stars.
- Astronomers often use parallax to measure distances to nearby stars.
- Astronomers use H-R diagrams to classify stars and to understand how stars change over time.

### Key Terms

- constellation • spectrograph
- apparent brightness • absolute brightness
- light-year • parallax
- Hertzsprung-Russell diagram
- main sequence

## 3 Lives of Stars

### Key Concepts

- A star is born when nuclear fusion starts.
- How long a star lives depends on its mass.
- After a star runs out of fuel, it becomes a white dwarf, a neutron star, or a black hole.

### Key Terms

- nebula • protostar • white dwarf
- supernova • neutron star • pulsar
- black hole

## 4 Star Systems and Galaxies

### Key Concepts

- Most stars are members of groups of two or more stars called star systems.
- Astronomers classify most galaxies into the following types: spiral, elliptical, and irregular.
- Our solar system is located in a spiral galaxy called the Milky Way.
- Astronomers often use scientific notation to describe sizes and distances in the universe.

### Key Terms

- binary star • eclipsing binary • open cluster
- globular cluster • galaxy • spiral galaxy
- elliptical galaxy • irregular galaxy
- quasar • universe • scientific notation

## 5 The Expanding Universe

### Key Concepts

- According to the big bang theory, the universe formed in an instant, billions of years ago, in an enormous explosion.
- About five billion years ago, a giant cloud of gas and dust collapsed to form our solar system.
- New observations lead astronomers to conclude that the universe will likely expand forever.

### Key Terms

- big bang • Hubble's law
- cosmic background radiation • solar nebula
- planetesimal • dark matter • dark energy

# Review and Assessment

For: Self-Assessment
Visit: PHSchool.com
Web Code: cfa-5040

## Organizing Information

**Concept Mapping** Copy the concept map about telescopes onto a separate sheet of paper. Then complete it and add a title. (For more on Concept Mapping, see the Skills Handbook.)

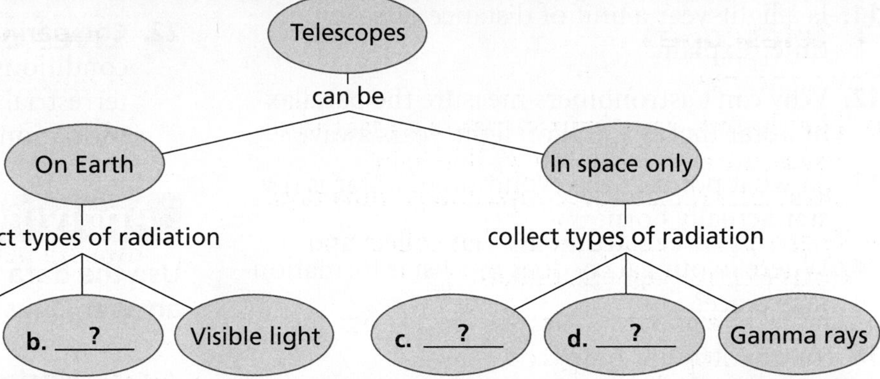


## Reviewing Key Terms

**Choose the letter of the best answer.**

1. Visible light is a form of
   a. spectrum.
   b. electromagnetic radiation.
   c. wavelength.
   d. cosmic background radiation.
2. An H-R diagram is a graph of stars' temperature and
   a. apparent brightness.
   b. main sequence.
   c. absolute brightness.
   d. parallax.
3. A low-mass main sequence star will eventually evolve into a
   a. white dwarf. b. protostar.
   c. black hole. d. nebula.
4. A star system in which one star blocks the light from another is called a(n)
   a. open cluster.
   b. quasar.
   c. binary star.
   d. eclipsing binary.
5. Astronomers theorize that the universe began in an enormous explosion called the
   a. solar nebula.
   b. supernova.
   c. big bang.
   d. big crunch.

**If the statement is true, write *true*. If it is false, change the underlined word or words to make the statement true.**

6. A <u>reflecting telescope</u> uses convex lenses to gather and focus light.
7. Astronomers use <u>spectrographs</u> to determine the chemical composition of stars.
8. Pulsars are a kind of <u>neutron star</u>.
9. A galaxy shaped like a ball and containing only older stars is most likely a <u>spiral galaxy</u>.
10. <u>Globular clusters</u> are small asteroid-like bodies that formed the building blocks of the planets.

## Writing in Science

**News Article** Imagine that you are a journalist covering current research in astronomy, including stars and black holes. Write an article explaining what black holes are, how they form, and how they can be detected.

*Stars, Galaxies, and the Universe*
Video Preview
Video Field Trip
▶ Video Assessment

# Review and Assessment

## Checking Concepts

**11.** Is a light-year a unit of distance or a unit of time? Explain.

**12.** Why can't astronomers measure the parallax of a star that is a million light-years away?

**13.** At what point in the evolution of a star is the star actually born?

**14.** Where in our galaxy does most star formation take place?

**15.** What is Hubble's law?

**16.** How can astronomers detect dark matter if they cannot observe it directly?

## Math Practice

**17. Calculating** The bright star Spica is 262 light-years from our solar system. How many kilometers is this?

**18. Scientific Notation** The star Antares is approximately 604 light-years from Earth. Write this distance in scientific notation.

## Thinking Critically

**19. Inferring** What advantage might there be to locating a telescope, such as the one shown below, on the moon?

**20. Applying Concepts** Describe a real-world situation involving absolute and apparent brightness. (*Hint:* Think about riding in a car at night.)

**21. Relating Cause and Effect** How does a star's mass affect its lifetime?

**22. Comparing and Contrasting** Compare the conditions that led to the formation of the terrestrial planets with those that led to the formation of the gas giants.

## Applying Skills

**Use the data in the H-R diagram below to answer Questions 23–26.**

**Hertzsprung-Russell Diagram**

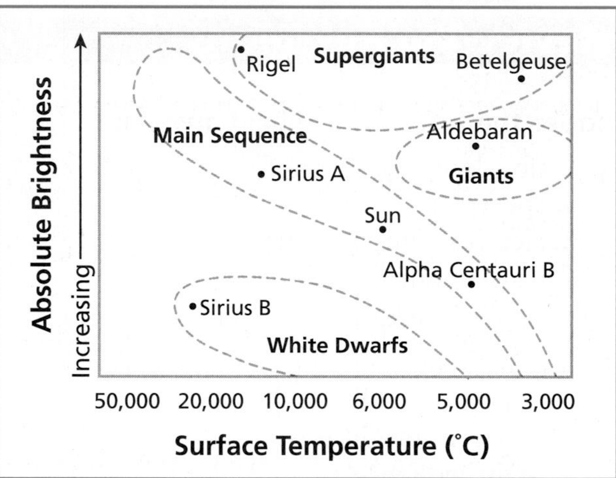


**23. Interpreting Diagrams** Which star has a greater absolute brightness, Aldebaran or Sirius B?

**24. Interpreting Diagrams** Which stars have higher surface temperatures than Sirius A?

**25. Applying Concepts** Which star is most likely to be red: Rigel, Sirius B, or Betelgeuse?

**26. Comparing and Contrasting** Compare Aldebaran and the sun in terms of size, temperature, and absolute brightness.

## Lab zone Chapter Project

**Performance Assessment** Check the final draft of your constellation story for correct spelling, grammar, punctuation, and usage. Then decide how you will present your story. For example, you could make a poster, read your story aloud, or perform it as a skit or a play.

# Standardized Test Prep

**Test-Taking Tip**
**Sequencing Events**
Some questions ask you to arrange a series of events in order. For example, you might be asked which event comes first or last, or which event comes before another event. Before looking at the answer choices, first try to recall the sequence of events in the entire process. If you have an idea of the sequence beforehand, you should find it easier to identify the correct answer.

***Sample Question***
Which of the following correctly describes the evolution of a sun-like star from young to old?
**A** white dwarf, red giant, main-sequence star, protostar
**B** red giant, main-sequence star, white dwarf, protostar
**C** protostar, main-sequence star, white dwarf, red giant
**D** protostar, main-sequence star, red giant, white dwarf

***Answer***
The correct answer is **D**. Choice **A** gives the correct order from old to young, rather than young to old. Choices **B** and **C** do not correctly sequence the life cycle of any star.

**Choose the letter of the best answer.**

**1.** The most common chemical element in most stars is
**A** oxygen.
**B** hydrogen.
**C** helium.
**D** nitrogen.

**2.** The main factor that affects the evolution of a star is its
**F** color.
**G** apparent brightness.
**H** mass.
**J** parallax.

**3.** The color of a star is related to its temperature. Which of the following color sequences correctly identifies the temperatures of stars in order from hottest to coldest?
**A** red, red-orange, yellow, white, blue
**B** yellow, white, blue, red, red-orange
**C** blue, yellow, red-orange, red, white
**D** blue, white, yellow, red-orange, red

*The table below gives an estimate of the distribution of stars in the Milky Way galaxy. Use the table and your knowledge of science to answer Questions 4 and 5.*

| Type of Star | Percentage of Total |
|---|---|
| Main sequence | 90.75% |
| Red Giant | 0.50% |
| Supergiant | $< 0.0001\%$ |
| White Dwarf | 8.75% |

**4.** According to the table, the most common type of stars in the Milky Way is
**F** main-sequence stars.
**G** red giants.
**H** supergiants.
**J** white dwarfs.

**5.** If there are a total of 400 billion stars in the Milky Way, about how many white dwarfs are there in the galaxy?
**A** 8.75 billion
**B** 35 billion
**C** 87.5 billion
**D** 3,500 billion

## Constructed Response

**6.** Describe the appearance of the Milky Way as you would see it both from Earth and from a point directly above or below the galaxy. Why does the galaxy look different from different vantage points?

# Think Like a Scientist

**Scientists have a particular way of looking at the world, or scientific habits of mind. Whenever you ask a question and explore possible answers, you use many of the same skills that scientists do. Some of these skills are described on this page.**

## Observing

When you use one or more of your five senses to gather information about the world, you are **observing.** Hearing a dog bark, counting twelve green seeds, and smelling smoke are all observations. To increase the power of their senses, scientists sometimes use microscopes, telescopes, or other instruments that help them make more detailed observations.

An observation must be an accurate report of what your senses detect. It is important to keep careful records of your observations in science class by writing or drawing in a notebook. The information collected through observations is called evidence, or data.

## Inferring

When you interpret an observation, you are **inferring,** or making an inference. For example, if you hear your dog barking, you may infer that someone is at your front door. To make this inference, you combine the evidence—the barking dog—and your experience or knowledge—you know that your dog barks when strangers approach—to reach a logical conclusion.

Notice that an inference is not a fact; it is only one of many possible interpretations for an observation. For example, your dog may be barking because it wants to go for a walk. An inference may turn out to be incorrect even if it is based on accurate observations and logical reasoning. The only way to find out if an inference is correct is to investigate further.

## Predicting

When you listen to the weather forecast, you hear many predictions about the next day's weather—what the temperature will be, whether it will rain, and how windy it will be. Weather forecasters use observations and knowledge of weather patterns to predict the weather. The skill of **predicting** involves making an inference about a future event based on current evidence or past experience.

Because a prediction is an inference, it may prove to be false. In science class, you can test some of your predictions by doing experiments. For example, suppose you predict that larger paper airplanes can fly farther than smaller airplanes. How could you test your prediction?

### Activity

**Use the photograph to answer the questions below.**

**Observing** Look closely at the photograph. List at least three observations.

**Inferring** Use your observations to make an inference about what has happened. What experience or knowledge did you use to make the inference?

**Predicting** Predict what will happen next. On what evidence or experience do you base your prediction?

## Classifying

Could you imagine searching for a book in the library if the books were shelved in no particular order? Your trip to the library would be an all-day event! Luckily, librarians group together books on similar topics or by the same author. Grouping together items that are alike in some way is called **classifying.** You can classify items in many ways: by size, by shape, by use, and by other important characteristics.

Like librarians, scientists use the skill of classifying to organize information and objects. When things are sorted into groups, the relationships among them become easier to understand.

**Activity**

**Classify the objects in the photograph into two groups based on any characteristic you choose. Then use another characteristic to classify the objects into three groups.**

## Making Models

Have you ever drawn a picture to help someone understand what you were saying? Such a drawing is one type of model. A model is a picture, diagram, computer image, or other representation of a complex object or process. **Making models** helps people understand things that they cannot observe directly.

Scientists often use models to represent things that are either very large or very small, such as the planets in the solar system, or the parts of a cell. Such models are physical models—drawings or three-dimensional structures that look like the real thing. Other models are mental models—mathematical equations or words that describe how something works.

**Activity**

**This student is using a model to demonstrate what causes day and night on Earth. What do the flashlight and the tennis ball in the model represent?**

## Communicating

Whenever you talk on the phone, write a report, or listen to your teacher at school, you are communicating. **Communicating** is the process of sharing ideas and information with other people. Communicating effectively requires many skills, including writing, reading, speaking, listening, and making models.

Scientists communicate to share results, information, and opinions. Scientists often communicate about their work in journals, over the telephone, in letters, and on the Internet. They also attend scientific meetings where they share their ideas with one another in person.

**Activity**

**On a sheet of paper, write out clear, detailed directions for tying your shoe. Then exchange directions with a partner. Follow your partner's directions exactly. How successful were you at tying your shoe? How could your partner have communicated more clearly?**

# Making Measurements

**By measuring, scientists can express their observations more precisely and communicate more information about what they observe.**

## Measuring in SI

The standard system of measurement used by scientists around the world is known as the International System of Units, which is abbreviated as SI (**Système International d'Unités,** in French). SI units are easy to use because they are based on powers of 10. Each unit is ten times larger than the next smallest unit and one tenth the size of the next largest unit. The table lists the prefixes used to name the most common SI units.

**Common SI Prefixes**

| Prefix | Symbol | Meaning |
|---|---|---|
| kilo- | k | 1,000 |
| hecto- | h | 100 |
| deka- | da | 10 |
| deci- | d | 0.1 (one tenth) |
| centi- | c | 0.01 (one hundredth) |
| milli- | m | 0.001 (one thousandth) |

**Length** To measure length, or the distance between two points, the unit of measure is the **meter (m).** The distance from the floor to a doorknob is approximately one meter. Long distances, such as the distance between two cities, are measured in kilometers (km). Small lengths are measured in centimeters (cm) or millimeters (mm). Scientists use metric rulers and meter sticks to measure length.

**Common Conversions**

| | | |
|---|---|---|
| 1 km | = | 1,000 m |
| 1 m | = | 100 cm |
| 1 m | = | 1,000 mm |
| 1 cm | = | 10 mm |

**Activity**

**The larger lines on the metric ruler in the picture show centimeter divisions, while the smaller, unnumbered lines show millimeter divisions. How many centimeters long is the shell? How many millimeters long is it?**

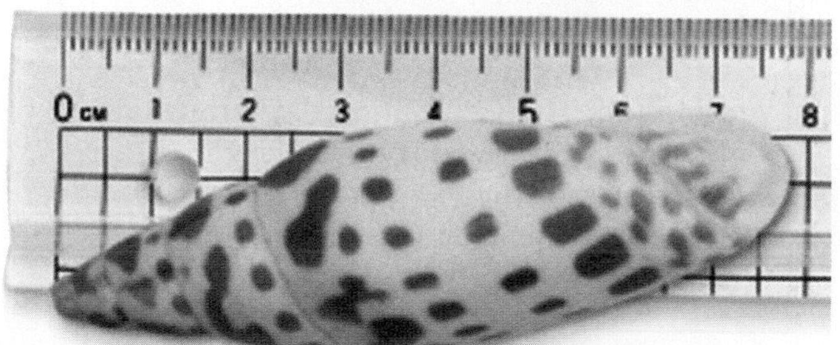


**Liquid Volume** To measure the volume of a liquid, or the amount of space it takes up, you will use a unit of measure known as the **liter (L).** One liter is the approximate volume of a medium-size carton of milk. Smaller volumes are measured in milliliters (mL). Scientists use graduated cylinders to measure liquid volume.

**Activity**

**The graduated cylinder in the picture is marked in milliliter divisions. Notice that the water in the cylinder has a curved surface. This curved surface is called the *meniscus*. To measure the volume, you must read the level at the lowest point of the meniscus. What is the volume of water in this graduated cylinder?**

**Common Conversion**

| | | |
|---|---|---|
| 1 L | = | 1,000 mL |

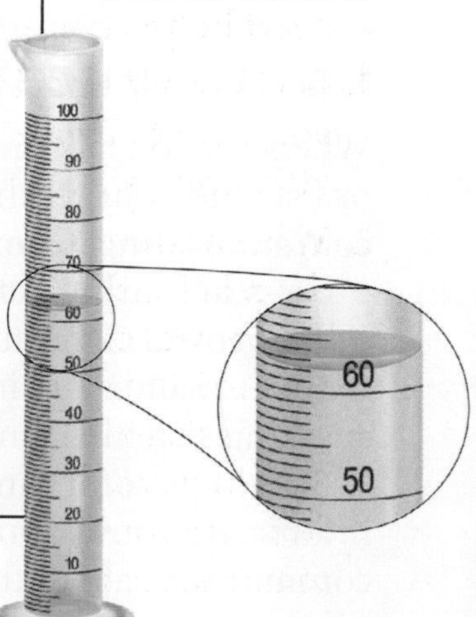

**Mass** To measure mass, or the amount of matter in an object, you will use a unit of measure known as the **gram (g).** One gram is approximately the mass of a paper clip. Larger masses are measured in kilograms (kg). Scientists use a balance to find the mass of an object.

| Common Conversion |
|---|
| 1 kg = 1,000 g |

**Activity**

**The mass of the potato in the picture is measured in kilograms. What is the mass of the potato? Suppose a recipe for potato salad called for one kilogram of potatoes. About how many potatoes would you need?**

**Temperature** To measure the temperature of a substance, you will use the **Celsius scale.** Temperature is measured in degrees Celsius (°C) using a Celsius thermometer. Water freezes at 0°C and boils at 100°C.

**Time** The unit scientists use to measure time is the **second (s).**

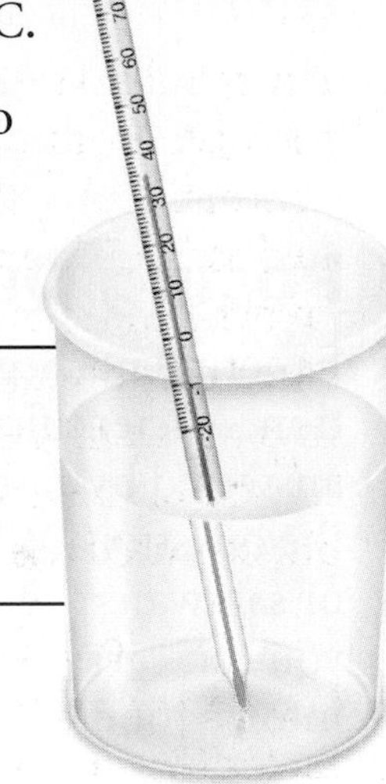

**Activity**

**What is the temperature of the liquid in degrees Celsius?**

## Converting SI Units

To use the SI system, you must know how to convert between units. Converting from one unit to another involves the skill of **calculating,** or using mathematical operations. Converting between SI units is similar to converting between dollars and dimes because both systems are based on powers of ten.

Suppose you want to convert a length of 80 centimeters to meters. Follow these steps to convert between units.

1. Begin by writing down the measurement you want to convert—in this example, 80 centimeters.
2. Write a conversion factor that represents the relationship between the two units you are converting. In this example, the relationship is 1 meter = 100 centimeters. Write this conversion factor as a fraction, making sure to place the units you are converting from (centimeters, in this example) in the denominator.
3. Multiply the measurement you want to convert by the fraction. When you do this, the units in the first measurement will cancel out with the units in the denominator. Your answer will be in the units you are converting to (meters, in this example).

### *Example*

80 centimeters = ■ meters

$$80 \text{ centimeters} \times \frac{1 \text{ meter}}{100 \text{ centimeters}} = \frac{80 \text{ meters}}{100}$$

$$= 0.8 \text{ meters}$$

**Activity**

**Convert between the following units.**

1. 600 millimeters = ■ meters
2. 0.35 liters = ■ milliliters
3. 1,050 grams = ■ kilograms

# Conducting a Scientific Investigation

**In some ways, scientists are like detectives, piecing together clues to learn about a process or event. One way that scientists gather clues is by carrying out experiments. An experiment tests an idea in a careful, orderly manner. Although experiments do not all follow the same steps in the same order, many follow a pattern similar to the one described here.**

## Posing Questions

Experiments begin by asking a scientific question. A scientific question is one that can be answered by gathering evidence. For example, the question "Which freezes faster—fresh water or salt water?" is a scientific question because you can carry out an investigation and gather information to answer the question.

## Developing a Hypothesis

The next step is to form a hypothesis. A **hypothesis** is a possible explanation for a set of observations or answer to a scientific question. In science, a hypothesis must be something that can be tested. A hypothesis can be worded as an *If . . . then . . .* statement. For example, a hypothesis might be *"If I add table salt to fresh water, then the water will freeze at a lower temperature."* A hypothesis worded this way serves as a rough outline of the experiment you should perform.

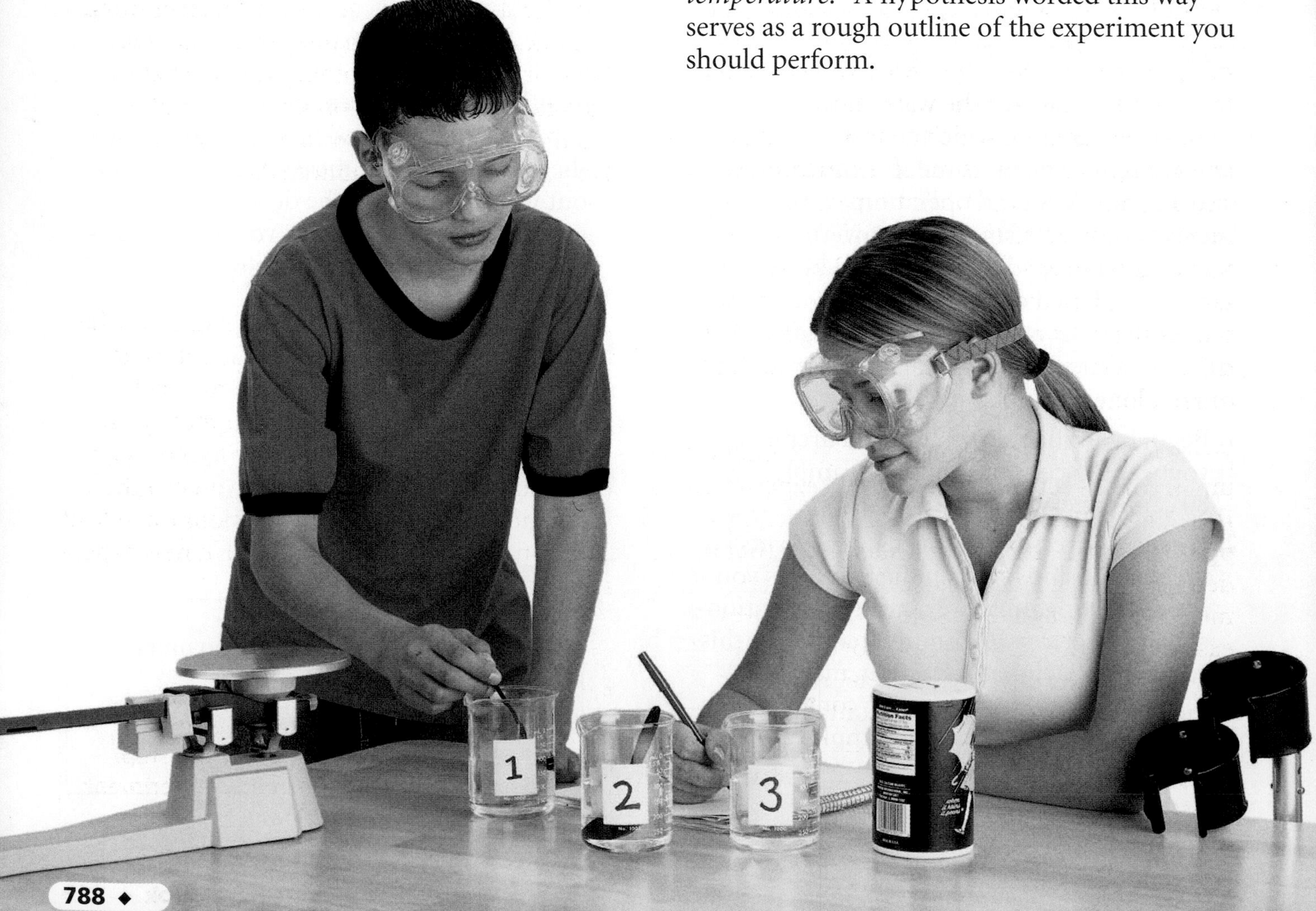

## Designing an Experiment

Next you need to plan a way to test your hypothesis. Your plan should be written out as a step-by-step procedure and should describe the observations or measurements you will make.

Two important steps involved in designing an experiment are controlling variables and forming operational definitions.

**Controlling Variables** In a well-designed experiment, you need to keep all variables the same except for one. A **variable** is any factor that can change in an experiment. The factor that you change is called the **manipulated variable.** In this experiment, the manipulated variable is the amount of table salt added to the water. Other factors, such as the amount of water or the starting temperature, are kept constant.

The factor that changes as a result of the manipulated variable is called the **responding variable.** The responding variable is what you measure or observe to obtain your results. In this experiment, the responding variable is the temperature at which the water freezes.

An experiment in which all factors except one are kept constant is called a **controlled experiment.** Most controlled experiments include a test called the control. In this experiment, Container 3 is the control. Because no salt is added to Container 3, you can compare the results from the other containers to it. Any difference in results must be due to the addition of salt alone.

**Forming Operational Definitions** Another important aspect of a well-designed experiment is having clear operational definitions. An **operational definition** is a statement that describes how a particular variable is to be measured or how a term is to be defined. For example, in this experiment, how will you determine if the water has frozen? You might decide to insert a stick in each container at the start of the experiment. Your operational definition of "frozen" would be the time at which the stick can no longer move.

| Experimental Procedure | |
|---|---|
| 1. | Fill 3 containers with 300 milliliters of cold |
| | tap water. |
| | |
| 2. | Add 10 grams of salt to Container 1; stir. |
| | Add 20 grams of salt to Container 2; stir. |
| | Add no salt to Container 3. |
| | |
| 3. | Place the 3 containers in a freezer. |
| | |
| 4. | Check the containers every 15 minutes. |
| | Record your observations. |
| | |

## Interpreting Data

The observations and measurements you make in an experiment are called **data.** At the end of an experiment, you need to analyze the data to look for any patterns or trends. Patterns often become clear if you organize your data in a data table or graph. Then think through what the data reveal. Do they support your hypothesis? Do they point out a flaw in your experiment? Do you need to collect more data?

## Drawing Conclusions

A **conclusion** is a statement that sums up what you have learned from an experiment. When you draw a conclusion, you need to decide whether the data you collected support your hypothesis or not. You may need to repeat an experiment several times before you can draw any conclusions from it. Conclusions often lead you to pose new questions and plan new experiments to answer them.

### Activity

**Is a ball's bounce affected by the height from which it is dropped? Using the steps just described, plan a controlled experiment to investigate this problem.**

# Technology Design Skills

**Engineers are people who use scientific and technological knowledge to solve practical problems. To design new products, engineers usually follow the process described here, even though they may not follow these steps in the exact order. As you read the steps, think about how you might apply them in technology labs.**

## Identify a Need

Before engineers begin designing a new product, they must first identify the need they are trying to meet. For example, suppose you are a member of a design team in a company that makes toys. Your team has identified a need: a toy boat that is inexpensive and easy to assemble.

## Research the Problem

Engineers often begin by gathering information that will help them with their new design. This research may include finding articles in books, magazines, or on the Internet. It may also include talking to other engineers who have solved similar problems. Engineers often perform experiments related to the product they want to design.

For your toy boat, you could look at toys that are similar to the one you want to design. You might do research on the Internet. You could also test some materials to see whether they will work well in a toy boat.

**Drawing for a boat design ▼**

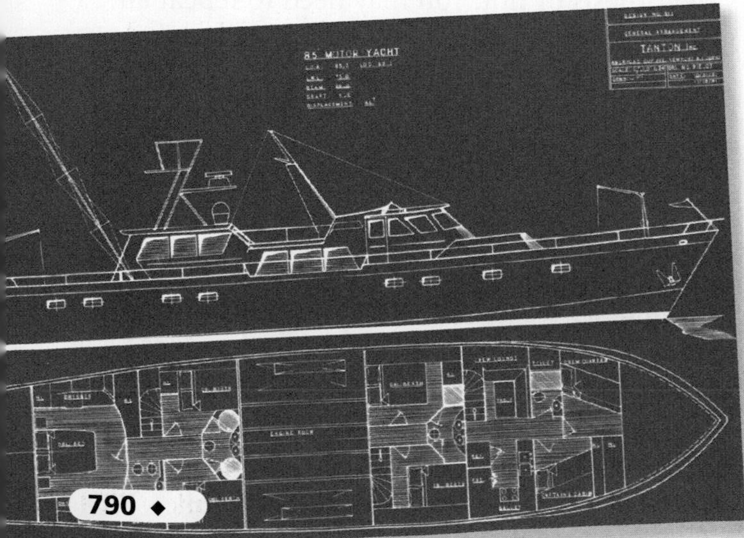


## Design a Solution

Research gives engineers information that helps them design a product. When engineers design new products, they usually work in teams.

**Generating Ideas** Often design teams hold brainstorming meetings in which any team member can contribute ideas. **Brainstorming** is a creative process in which one team member's suggestions often spark ideas in other group members. Brainstorming can lead to new approaches to solving a design problem.

**Evaluating Constraints** During brainstorming, a design team will often come up with several possible designs. The team must then evaluate each one.

As part of their evaluation, engineers consider constraints. **Constraints** are factors that limit or restrict a product design. Physical characteristics, such as the properties of materials used to make your toy boat, are constraints. Money and time are also constraints. If the materials in a product cost a lot, or if the product takes a long time to make, the design may be impractical.

**Making Trade-offs** Design teams usually need to make trade-offs. In a **trade-off,** engineers give up one benefit of a proposed design in order to obtain another. In designing your toy boat, you will have to make trade-offs. For example, suppose one material is sturdy but not fully waterproof. Another material is more waterproof, but breakable. You may decide to give up the benefit of sturdiness in order to obtain the benefit of waterproofing.

## Build and Evaluate a Prototype

Once the team has chosen a design plan, the engineers build a prototype of the product. A **prototype** is a working model used to test a design. Engineers evaluate the prototype to see whether it works well, is easy to operate, is safe to use, and holds up to repeated use.

Think of your toy boat. What would the prototype be like? Of what materials would it be made? How would you test it?

## Troubleshoot and Redesign

Few prototypes work perfectly, which is why they need to be tested. Once a design team has tested a prototype, the members analyze the results and identify any problems. The team then tries to **troubleshoot,** or fix the design problems. For example, if your toy boat leaks or wobbles, the boat should be redesigned to eliminate those problems.

## Communicate the Solution

A team needs to communicate the final design to the people who will manufacture and use the product. To do this, teams may use sketches, detailed drawings, computer simulations, and word descriptions.

### Activity

**You can use the technology design process to design and build a toy boat.**

**Research and Investigate**

1. Visit the library or go online to research toy boats.
2. Investigate how a toy boat can be powered, including wind, rubber bands, or baking soda and vinegar.
3. Brainstorm materials, shapes, and steering for your boat.

**Design and Build**

4. Based on your research, design a toy boat that
   - is made of readily available materials
   - is no larger than 15 cm long and 10 cm wide
   - includes a power system, a rudder, and an area for cargo
   - travels 2 meters in a straight line carrying a load of 20 pennies
5. Sketch your design and write a step-by-step plan for building your boat. After your teacher approves your plan, build your boat.

**Evaluate and Redesign**

6. Test your boat, evaluate the results, and troubleshoot any problems.
7. Based on your evaluation, redesign your toy boat so it performs better.

# Creating Data Tables and Graphs

**How can you make sense of the data in a science experiment? The first step is to organize the data to help you understand them. Data tables and graphs are helpful tools for organizing data.**

## Data Tables

You have gathered your materials and set up your experiment. But before you start, you need to plan a way to record what happens during the experiment. By creating a data table, you can record your observations and measurements in an orderly way.

Suppose, for example, that a scientist conducted an experiment to find out how many Calories people of different body masses burn while doing various activities. The data table shows the results.

Notice in this data table that the manipulated variable (body mass) is the heading of one column. The responding variable (for Experiment 1, the number of Calories burned while bicycling) is the heading of the next column. Additional columns were added for related experiments.

**Calories Burned in 30 Minutes**

| Body Mass | Experiment 1: Bicycling | Experiment 2: Playing Basketball | Experiment 3: Watching Television |
|---|---|---|---|
| 30 kg | 60 Calories | 120 Calories | 21 Calories |
| 40 kg | 77 Calories | 164 Calories | 27 Calories |
| 50 kg | 95 Calories | 206 Calories | 33 Calories |
| 60 kg | 114 Calories | 248 Calories | 38 Calories |

## Bar Graphs

To compare how many Calories a person burns doing various activities, you could create a bar graph. A bar graph is used to display data in a number of separate, or distinct, categories. In this example, bicycling, playing basketball, and watching television are the three categories.

To create a bar graph, follow these steps.

1. On graph paper, draw a horizontal, or *x*-, axis and a vertical, or *y*-, axis.
2. Write the names of the categories to be graphed along the horizontal axis. Include an overall label for the axis as well.
3. Label the vertical axis with the name of the responding variable. Include units of measurement. Then create a scale along the axis by marking off equally spaced numbers that cover the range of the data collected.
4. For each category, draw a solid bar using the scale on the vertical axis to determine the height. Make all the bars the same width.
5. Add a title that describes the graph.

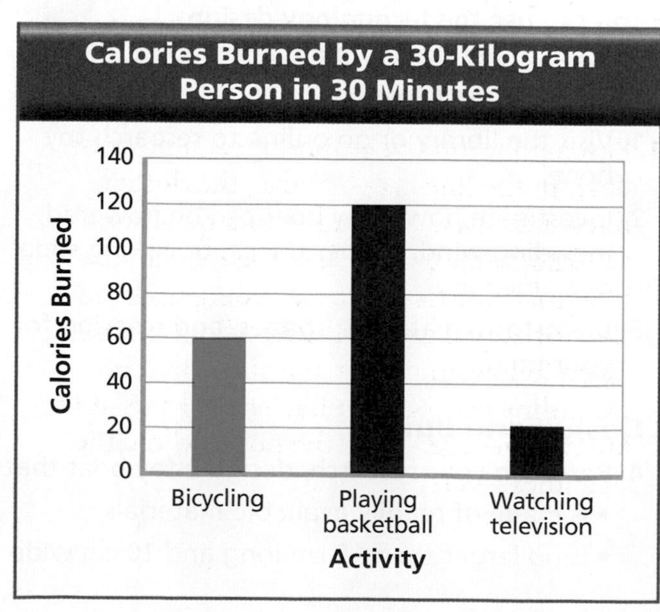

## Line Graphs

To see whether a relationship exists between body mass and the number of Calories burned while bicycling, you could create a line graph. A line graph is used to display data that show how one variable (the responding variable) changes in response to another variable (the manipulated variable). You can use a line graph when your manipulated variable is *continuous,* that is, when there are other points between the ones that you tested. In this example, body mass is a continuous variable because there are other body masses between 30 and 40 kilograms (for example, 31 kilograms). Time is another example of a continuous variable.

Line graphs are powerful tools because they allow you to estimate values for conditions that you did not test in the experiment. For example, you can use the line graph to estimate that a 35-kilogram person would burn 68 Calories while bicycling.

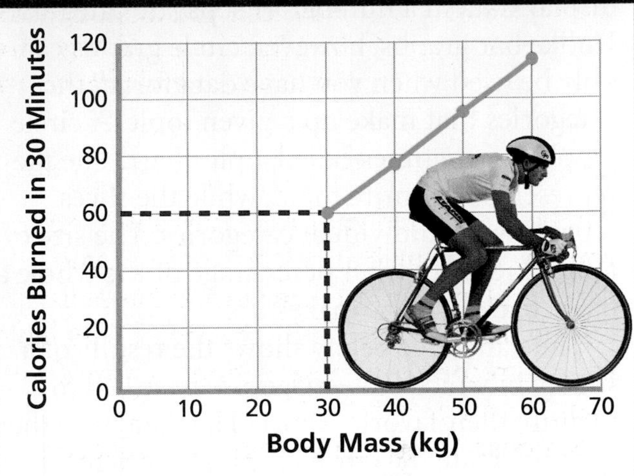


To create a line graph, follow these steps.

1. On graph paper, draw a horizontal, or *x*-, axis and a vertical, or *y*-, axis.
2. Label the horizontal axis with the name of the manipulated variable. Label the vertical axis with the name of the responding variable. Include units of measurement.
3. Create a scale on each axis by marking off equally spaced numbers that cover the range of the data collected.
4. Plot a point on the graph for each piece of data. In the line graph above, the dotted lines show how to plot the first data point (30 kilograms and 60 Calories). Follow an imaginary vertical line extending up from the horizontal axis at the 30-kilogram mark. Then follow an imaginary horizontal line extending across from the vertical axis at the 60-Calorie mark. Plot the point where the two lines intersect.
5. Connect the plotted points with a solid line. (In some cases, it may be more appropriate to draw a line that shows the general trend of the plotted points. In those cases, some of the points may fall above or below the line. Also, not all graphs are linear. It may be more appropriate to draw a curve to connect the points.)
6. Add a title that identifies the variables or relationship in the graph.

### Activity

**Create line graphs to display the data from Experiment 2 and Experiment 3 in the data table.**

### Activity

**You read in the newspaper that a total of 4 centimeters of rain fell in your area in June, 2.5 centimeters fell in July, and 1.5 centimeters fell in August. What type of graph would you use to display these data? Use graph paper to create the graph.**

# Circle Graphs

Like bar graphs, circle graphs can be used to display data in a number of separate categories. Unlike bar graphs, however, circle graphs can only be used when you have data for *all* the categories that make up a given topic. A circle graph is sometimes called a pie chart. The pie represents the entire topic, while the slices represent the individual categories. The size of a slice indicates what percentage of the whole a particular category makes up.

The data table below shows the results of a survey in which 24 teenagers were asked to identify their favorite sport. The data were then used to create the circle graph at the right.

| Favorite Sports | |
|---|---|
| Sport | Students |
| Soccer | 8 |
| Basketball | 6 |
| Bicycling | 6 |
| Swimming | 4 |

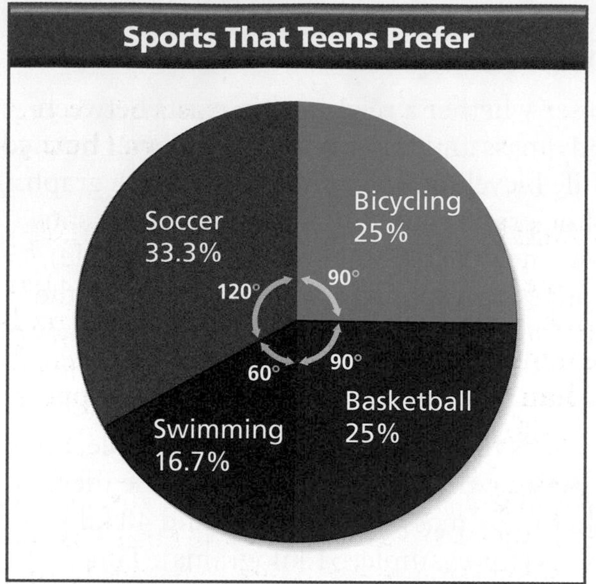


To create a circle graph, follow these steps.

1. Use a compass to draw a circle. Mark the center with a point. Then draw a line from the center point to the top of the circle.
2. Determine the size of each "slice" by setting up a proportion where $x$ equals the number of degrees in a slice. (*Note:* A circle contains 360 degrees.) For example, to find the number of degrees in the "soccer" slice, set up the following proportion:

$$\frac{\text{Students who prefer soccer}}{\text{Total number of students}} = \frac{x}{\text{Total number of degrees in a circle}}$$

$$\frac{8}{24} = \frac{x}{360}$$

Cross-multiply and solve for $x$.

$$24x = 8 \times 360$$
$$x = 120$$

The "soccer" slice should contain 120 degrees.

3. Use a protractor to measure the angle of the first slice, using the line you drew to the top of the circle as the 0° line. Draw a line from the center of the circle to the edge for the angle you measured.
4. Continue around the circle by measuring the size of each slice with the protractor. Start measuring from the edge of the previous slice so the wedges do not overlap. When you are done, the entire circle should be filled in.
5. Determine the percentage of the whole circle that each slice represents. To do this, divide the number of degrees in a slice by the total number of degrees in a circle (360), and multiply by 100%. For the "soccer" slice, you can find the percentage as follows:

$$\frac{120}{360} \times 100\% = 33.3\%$$

6. Use a different color for each slice. Label each slice with the category and with the percentage of the whole it represents.
7. Add a title to the circle graph.

## Activity

**In a class of 28 students, 12 students take the bus to school, 10 students walk, and 6 students ride their bicycles. Create a circle graph to display these data.**

# Math Review

**Scientists use math to organize, analyze, and present data. This appendix will help you review some basic math skills.**

## Mean, Median, and Mode

The **mean** is the average, or the sum of the data divided by the number of data items. The middle number in a set of ordered data is called the **median.** The **mode** is the number that appears most often in a set of data.

**Example**

A scientist counted the number of distinct songs sung by seven different male birds and collected the data shown below.

| Male Bird Songs | | | | | | | |
|---|---|---|---|---|---|---|---|
| Bird | A | B | C | D | E | F | G |
| Number of Songs | 36 | 29 | 40 | 35 | 28 | 36 | 27 |

To determine the mean number of songs, add the total number of songs and divide by the number of data items—in this case, the number of male birds.

$$\text{Mean} = \frac{231}{7} = 33 \text{ songs}$$

To find the median number of songs, arrange the data in numerical order and find the number in the middle of the series.

**27 28 29 35 36 36 40**

The number in the middle is 35, so the median number of songs is 35.

The mode is the value that appears most frequently. In the data, 36 appears twice, while each other item appears only once. Therefore, 36 songs is the mode.

**Practice**

Find out how many minutes it takes each student in your class to get to school. Then find the mean, median, and mode for the data.

## Probability

**Probability** is the chance that an event will occur. Probability can be expressed as a ratio, a fraction, or a percentage. For example, when you flip a coin, the probability that the coin will land heads up is 1 in 2, or $\frac{1}{2}$, or 50 percent.

The probability that an event will happen can be expressed in the following formula.

$$P(\text{event}) = \frac{\text{Number of times the event can occur}}{\text{Total number of possible events}}$$

**Example**

A paper bag contains 25 blue marbles, 5 green marbles, 5 orange marbles, and 15 yellow marbles. If you close your eyes and pick a marble from the bag, what is the probability that it will be yellow?

$$P(\text{yellow marbles}) = \frac{\text{15 yellow marbles}}{\text{50 marbles total}}$$

$$P = \frac{15}{50}, \text{ or } \frac{3}{10}, \text{ or } 30\%$$

**Practice**

Each side of a cube has a letter on it. Two sides have *A*, three sides have *B*, and one side has *C*. If you roll the cube, what is the probability that *A* will land on top?

## Area

The **area** of a surface is the number of square units that cover it. The front cover of your textbook has an area of about 600 $cm^2$.

**Area of a Rectangle and a Square** To find the area of a rectangle, multiply its length times its width. The formula for the area of a rectangle is

$$A = \ell \times w, \text{ or } A = \ell w$$

Since all four sides of a square have the same length, the area of a square is the length of one side multiplied by itself, or squared.

$$A = s \times s, \text{ or } A = s^2$$

**Example**

A scientist is studying the plants in a field that measures 75 m × 45 m. What is the area of the field?

$$A = \ell \times w$$

$$A = 75 \text{ m} \times 45 \text{ m}$$

$$A = 3{,}375 \text{ m}^2$$

**Area of a Circle** The formula for the area of a circle is

$$A = \pi \times r \times r, \text{ or } A = \pi r^2$$

The length of the radius is represented by $r$, and the value of $\pi$ is approximately $\frac{22}{7}$.

**Example**

Find the area of a circle with a radius of 14 cm.

$$A = \pi r^2$$

$$A = 14 \times 14 \times \frac{22}{7}$$

$$A = 616 \text{ cm}^2$$

**Practice**

Find the area of a circle that has a radius of 21 m.

## Circumference

The distance around a circle is called the circumference. The formula for finding the circumference of a circle is

$$C = 2 \times \pi \times r, \text{ or } C = 2\pi r$$

**Example**

The radius of a circle is 35 cm. What is its circumference?

$$C = 2\pi r$$

$$C = 2 \times 35 \times \frac{22}{7}$$

$$C = 220 \text{ cm}$$

**Practice**

What is the circumference of a circle with a radius of 28 m?

## Volume

The volume of an object is the number of cubic units it contains. The volume of a wastebasket, for example, might be about 26,000 $cm^3$.

**Volume of a Rectangular Object** To find the volume of a rectangular object, multiply the object's length times its width times its height.

$$V = \ell \times w \times h, \text{ or } V = \ell wh$$

**Example**

Find the volume of a box with length 24 cm, width 12 cm, and height 9 cm.

$$V = \ell wh$$

$$V = 24 \text{ cm} \times 12 \text{ cm} \times 9 \text{ cm}$$

$$V = 2{,}592 \text{ cm}^3$$

**Practice**

What is the volume of a rectangular object with length 17 cm, width 11 cm, and height 6 cm?

## Fractions

A **fraction** is a way to express a part of a whole. In the fraction $\frac{4}{7}$, 4 is the numerator and 7 is the denominator.

**Adding and Subtracting Fractions** To add or subtract two or more fractions that have a common denominator, first add or subtract the numerators. Then write the sum or difference over the common denominator.

To find the sum or difference of fractions with different denominators, first find the least common multiple of the denominators. This is known as the least common denominator. Then convert each fraction to equivalent fractions with the least common denominator. Add or subtract the numerators. Then write the sum or difference over the common denominator.

**Example**

$$\frac{5}{6} - \frac{3}{4} = \frac{10}{12} - \frac{9}{12} = \frac{10 - 9}{12} = \frac{1}{12}$$

**Multiplying Fractions** To multiply two fractions, first multiply the two numerators, then multiply the two denominators.

**Example**

$$\frac{5}{6} \times \frac{2}{3} = \frac{5 \times 2}{6 \times 3} = \frac{10}{18} = \frac{5}{9}$$

**Dividing Fractions** Dividing by a fraction is the same as multiplying by its reciprocal. Reciprocals are numbers whose numerators and denominators have been switched. To divide one fraction by another, first invert the fraction you are dividing by—in other words, turn it upside down. Then multiply the two fractions.

**Example**

$$\frac{2}{5} \div \frac{7}{8} = \frac{2}{5} \times \frac{8}{7} = \frac{2 \times 8}{5 \times 7} = \frac{16}{35}$$

**Practice**

Solve the following: $\frac{3}{7} \div \frac{4}{5}$.

## Decimals

Fractions whose denominators are 10, 100, or some other power of 10 are often expressed as decimals. For example, the fraction $\frac{9}{10}$ can be expressed as the decimal 0.9, and the fraction $\frac{7}{100}$ can be written as 0.07.

**Adding and Subtracting With Decimals** To add or subtract decimals, line up the decimal points before you carry out the operation.

**Example**

$$\begin{array}{r} 27.4 \\ +\ 6.19 \\ \hline 33.59 \end{array} \qquad \begin{array}{r} 278.635 \\ -\ 191.4 \\ \hline 87.235 \end{array}$$

**Multiplying With Decimals** When you multiply two numbers with decimals, the number of decimal places in the product is equal to the total number of decimal places in each number being multiplied.

**Example**

$$\begin{array}{rl} 46.2 & \text{(one decimal place)} \\ \times\ 2.37 & \text{(two decimal places)} \\ \hline 109.494 & \text{(three decimal places)} \end{array}$$

**Dividing With Decimals** To divide a decimal by a whole number, put the decimal point in the quotient above the decimal point in the dividend.

**Example**

$$15.5 \div 5$$

$$5\overline{)15.5} = 3.1$$

To divide a decimal by a decimal, you need to rewrite the divisor as a whole number. Do this by multiplying both the divisor and dividend by the same multiple of 10.

**Example**

$$1.68 \div 4.2 = 16.8 \div 42$$

$$42\overline{)16.8} = 0.4$$

**Practice**

Multiply 6.21 by 8.5.

## Ratio and Proportion

A **ratio** compares two numbers by division. For example, suppose a scientist counts 800 wolves and 1,200 moose on an island. The ratio of wolves to moose can be written as a fraction, $\frac{800}{1,200}$, which can be reduced to $\frac{2}{3}$. The same ratio can also be expressed as 2 to 3 or 2 : 3.

A **proportion** is a mathematical sentence saying that two ratios are equivalent. For example, a proportion could state that $\frac{800 \text{ wolves}}{1,200 \text{ moose}} = \frac{2 \text{ wolves}}{3 \text{ moose}}$. You can sometimes set up a proportion to determine or estimate an unknown quantity. For example, suppose a scientist counts 25 beetles in an area of 10 square meters. The scientist wants to estimate the number of beetles in 100 square meters.

**Example**

1. Express the relationship between beetles and area as a ratio: $\frac{25}{10}$, simplified to $\frac{5}{2}$.
2. Set up a proportion, with $x$ representing the number of beetles. The proportion can be stated as $\frac{5}{2} = \frac{x}{100}$.
3. Begin by cross-multiplying. In other words, multiply each fraction's numerator by the other fraction's denominator.

$$5 \times 100 = 2 \times x, \text{ or } 500 = 2x$$

4. To find the value of $x$, divide both sides by 2. The result is 250, or 250 beetles in 100 square meters.

**Practice**

Find the value of $x$ in the following proportion: $\frac{6}{7} = \frac{x}{49}$.

## Percentage

A **percentage** is a ratio that compares a number to 100. For example, there are 37 granite rocks in a collection that consists of 100 rocks. The ratio $\frac{37}{100}$ can be written as 37%. Granite rocks make up 37% of the rock collection.

You can calculate percentages of numbers other than 100 by setting up a proportion.

**Example**

Rain falls on 9 days out of 30 in June. What percentage of the days in June were rainy?

$$\frac{9 \text{ days}}{30 \text{ days}} = \frac{d\%}{100\%}$$

To find the value of $d$, begin by cross-multiplying, as for any proportion:

$$9 \times 100 = 30 \times d \qquad d = \frac{900}{30} \qquad d = 30$$

**Practice**

There are 300 marbles in a jar, and 42 of those marbles are blue. What percentage of the marbles are blue?

## Significant Figures

The **precision** of a measurement depends on the instrument you use to take the measurement. For example, if the smallest unit on the ruler is millimeters, then the most precise measurement you can make will be in millimeters.

The sum or difference of measurements can only be as precise as the least precise measurement being added or subtracted. Round your answer so that it has the same number of digits after the decimal as the least precise measurement. Round up if the last digit is 5 or more, and round down if the last digit is 4 or less.

**Example**

Subtract a temperature of 5.2°C from the temperature 75.46°C.

$$75.46 - 5.2 = 70.26$$

5.2 has the fewest digits after the decimal, so it is the least precise measurement. Since the last digit of the answer is 6, round up to 3. The most precise difference between the measurements is 70.3°C.

**Practice**

Add 26.4 m to 8.37 m. Round your answer according to the precision of the measurements.

**Significant figures** are the number of nonzero digits in a measurement. Zeroes between nonzero digits are also significant. For example, the measurements 12,500 L, 0.125 cm, and 2.05 kg all have three significant figures. When you multiply and divide measurements, the one with the fewest significant figures determines the number of significant figures in your answer.

**Example**

Multiply 110 g by 5.75 g.

$$110 \times 5.75 = 632.5$$

Because 110 has only two significant figures, round the answer to 630 g.

## Scientific Notation

A **factor** is a number that divides into another number with no remainder. In the example, the number 3 is used as a factor four times.

An **exponent** tells how many times a number is used as a factor. For example, $3 \times 3 \times 3 \times 3$ can be written as $3^4$. The exponent $^4$ indicates that the number 3 is used as a factor four times. Another way of expressing this is to say that 81 is equal to 3 to the fourth power.

**Example**

$$3^4 = 3 \times 3 \times 3 \times 3 = 81$$

**Scientific notation** uses exponents and powers of ten to write very large or very small numbers in shorter form. When you write a number in scientific notation, you write the number as two factors. The first factor is any number between 1 and 10. The second factor is a power of 10, such as $10^3$ or $10^6$.

**Example**

The average distance between the planet Mercury and the sun is 58,000,000 km. To write the first factor in scientific notation, insert a decimal point in the original number so that you have a number between 1 and 10. In the case of 58,000,000, the number is 5.8.

To determine the power of 10, count the number of places that the decimal point moved. In this case, it moved 7 places.

$$58{,}000{,}000 \text{ km} = 5.8 \times 10^7 \text{ km}$$

**Practice**

Express 6,590,000 in scientific notation.

# Reading Comprehension Skills

**Each section in your textbook introduces a Target Reading Skill. You will improve your reading comprehension by using the Target Reading Skills described below.**

## Using Prior Knowledge

Your prior knowledge is what you already know before you begin to read about a topic. Building on what you already know gives you a head start on learning new information. Before you begin a new assignment, think about what you know. You might look at the headings and the visuals to spark your memory. You can list what you know. Then, as you read, consider questions like these.

- How does what you learn relate to what you know?
- How did something you already know help you learn something new?
- Did your original ideas agree with what you have just learned?

## Asking Questions

Asking yourself questions is an excellent way to focus on and remember new information in your textbook. For example, you can turn the text headings into questions. Then your questions can guide you to identify the important information as you read. Look at these examples:

**Heading:** Using Seismographic Data

**Question:** How are seismographic data used?

**Heading:** Kinds of Faults

**Question:** What are the kinds of faults?

You do not have to limit your questions to text headings. Ask questions about anything that you need to clarify or that will help you understand the content. *What* and *how* are probably the most common question words, but you may also ask *why*, *who*, *when*, or *where* questions.

## Previewing Visuals

Visuals are photographs, graphs, tables, diagrams, and illustrations. Visuals contain important information. Before you read, look at visuals and their labels and captions. This preview will help you prepare for what you will be reading.

Often you will be asked what you want to learn about a visual. For example, after you look at the normal fault diagram below, you might ask: What is the movement along a normal fault? Questions about visuals give you a purpose for reading—to answer your questions.

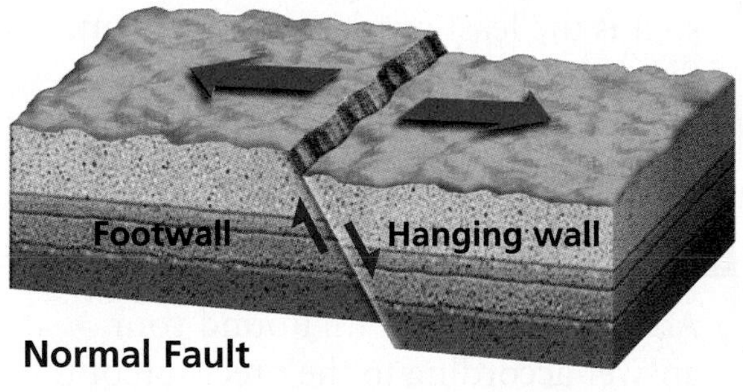


**Normal Fault**

## Outlining

An outline shows the relationship between main ideas and supporting ideas. An outline has a formal structure. You write the main ideas, called topics, next to Roman numerals. The supporting ideas, called subtopics, are written under the main ideas and labeled A, B, C, and so on. An outline looks like this:

**Technology and Society**

I. Technology through history
II. The impact of technology on society
   A.
   B.

## Identifying Main Ideas

When you are reading science material, it is important to try to understand the ideas and concepts that are in a passage. Each paragraph has a lot of information and detail. Good readers try to identify the most important—or biggest—idea in every paragraph or section. That's the main idea. The other information in the paragraph supports or further explains the main idea.

Sometimes main ideas are stated directly. In this book, some main ideas are identified for you as key concepts. These are printed in boldface type. However, you must identify other main ideas yourself. In order to do this, you must identify all the ideas within a paragraph or section. Then ask yourself which idea is big enough to include all the other ideas.

## Comparing and Contrasting

When you compare and contrast, you examine the similarities and differences between things. You can compare and contrast in a Venn diagram or in a table.

**Venn Diagram** A Venn diagram consists of two overlapping circles. In the space where the circles overlap, you write the characteristics that the two items have in common. In one of the circles outside the area of overlap, you write the differing features or characteristics of one of the items. In the other circle outside the area of overlap, you write the differing characteristics of the other item.

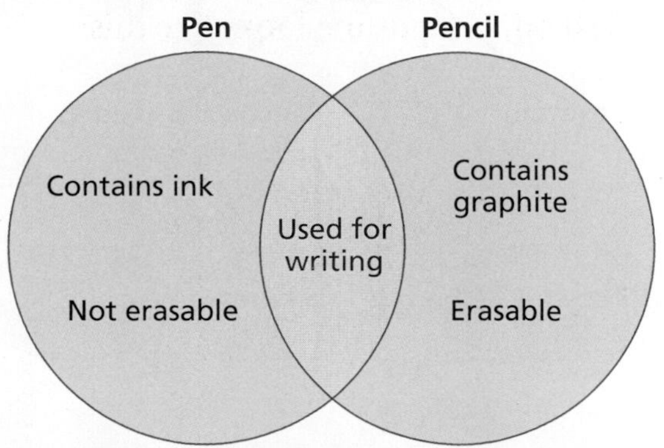


**Table** In a compare/contrast table, you list the characteristics or features to be compared across the top of the table. Then list the items to be compared in the left column. Complete the table by filling in information about each characteristic or feature.

| Blood Vessel | Function | Structure of Wall |
|---|---|---|
| Artery | Carries blood away from heart | |
| Capillary | | |
| Vein | | |

## Identifying Supporting Evidence

A hypothesis is a possible explanation for observations made by scientists or an answer to a scientific question. Scientists must carry out investigations and gather evidence that either supports or disproves the hypothesis.

Identifying the supporting evidence for a hypothesis or theory can help you understand the hypothesis or theory. Evidence consists of facts—information whose accuracy can be confirmed by testing or observation.

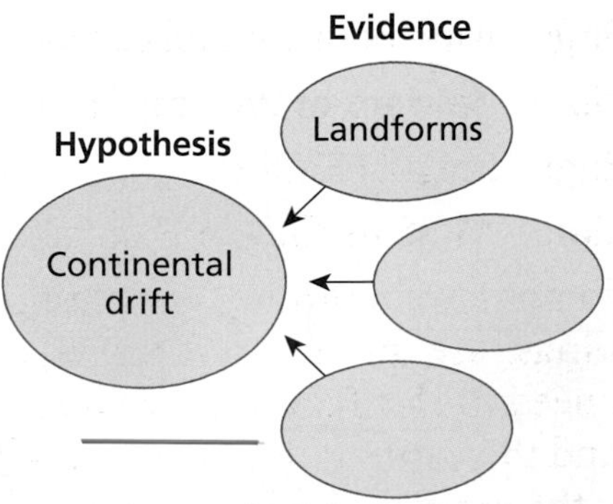

## Sequencing

A sequence is the order in which a series of events occurs. A flowchart or a cycle diagram can help you visualize a sequence.

**Flowchart** To make a flowchart, write a brief description of each step or event in a box. Place the boxes in order, with the first event at the top of the chart. Then draw an arrow to connect each step or event to the next.

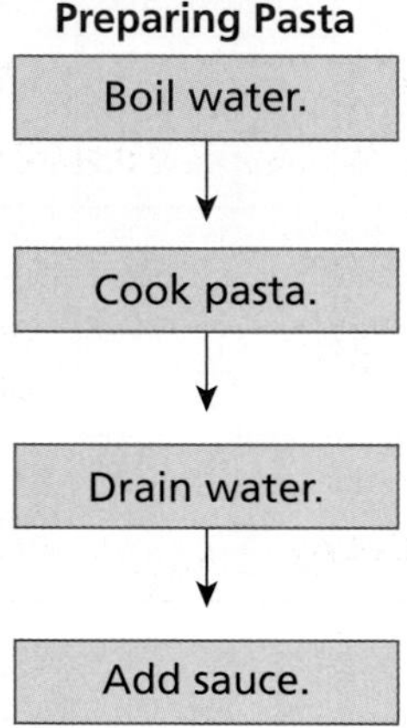


**Cycle Diagram** A cycle diagram shows a sequence that is continuous, or cyclical. A continuous sequence does not have an end because when the final event is over, the first event begins again. To create a cycle diagram, write the starting event in a box placed at the top of a page in the center. Then, moving in a clockwise direction, write each event in a box in its proper sequence. Draw arrows that connect each event to the one that occurs next.

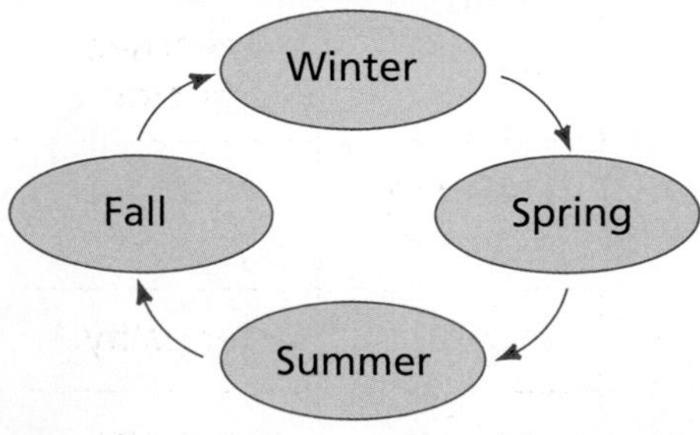


## Relating Cause and Effect

Science involves many cause-and-effect relationships. A cause makes something happen. An effect is what happens. When you recognize that one event causes another, you are relating cause and effect.

Words like *cause, because, effect, affect,* and *result* often signal a cause or an effect. Sometimes an effect can have more than one cause, or a cause can produce several effects.

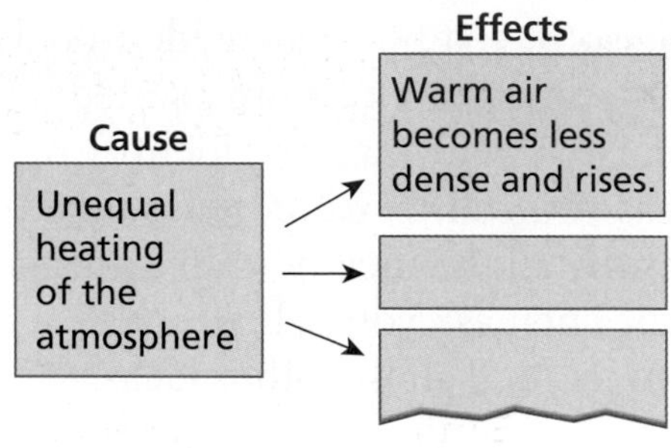


## Concept Mapping

Concept maps are useful tools for organizing information on any topic. A concept map begins with a main idea or core concept and shows how the idea can be subdivided into related subconcepts or smaller ideas.

You construct a concept map by placing concepts (usually nouns) in ovals and connecting them with linking words (usually verbs). The biggest concept or idea is placed in an oval at the top of the map. Related concepts are arranged in ovals below the big idea. The linking words connect the ovals.

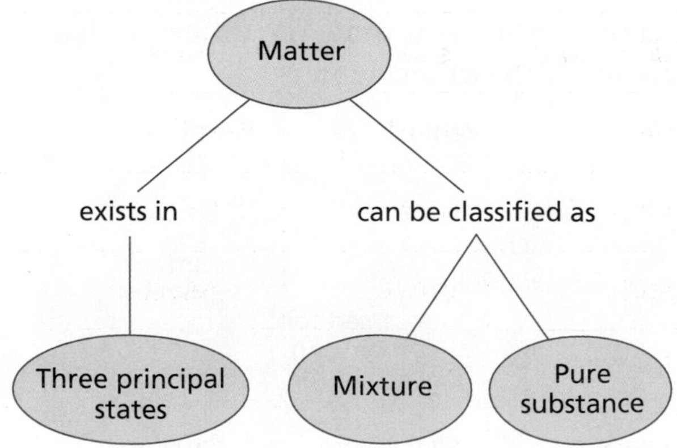

# Building Vocabulary

**Knowing the meaning of these prefixes, suffixes, and roots will help you understand the meaning of words you do not recognize.**

**Word Origins** Many science words come to English from other languages, such as Greek and Latin. By learning the meaning of a few common Greek and Latin roots, you can determine the meaning of unfamiliar science words.

| Greek and Latin Roots | | |
|---|---|---|
| **Greek Roots** | **Meaning** | **Example** |
| *ast-* | star | astronaut |
| *geo-* | Earth | geology |
| *metron-* | measure | kilometer |
| *opt-* | eye | optician |
| *photo-* | light | photograph |
| *scop-* | see | microscope |
| *therm-* | heat | thermostat |
| **Latin Roots** | **Meaning** | **Example** |
| *aqua-* | water | aquarium |
| *aud-* | hear | auditorium |
| *duc-, duct-* | lead | conduct |
| *flect-* | bend | reflect |
| *fract-, frag-* | break | fracture |
| *ject-* | throw | reject |
| *luc-* | light | lucid |
| *spec-* | see | inspect |

**Prefixes** A prefix is a word part that is added at the beginning of a root or base word to change its meaning.

**Suffixes** A suffix is a word part that is added at the end of a root word to change the meaning.

| Prefixes and Suffixes | | |
|---|---|---|
| **Prefix** | **Meaning** | **Example** |
| *com-, con-* | with | communicate, concert |
| *de-* | from; down | decay |
| *di-* | two | divide |
| *ex-, exo-* | out | exhaust |
| *in-, im-* | in, into; not | inject, impossible |
| *re-* | again; back | reflect, recall |
| *trans-* | across | transfer |
| **Suffix** | **Meaning** | **Example** |
| *-al* | relating to | natural |
| *-er, -or* | one who | teacher, doctor |
| *-ist* | one who practices | scientist |
| *-ity* | state of | equality |
| *-ology* | study of | biology |
| *-tion, -sion* | state or quality of | reaction, tension |

# Safety Symbols

**These symbols warn of possible dangers in the laboratory and remind you to work carefully.**

**Safety Goggles** Wear safety goggles to protect your eyes in any activity involving chemicals, flames or heating, or glassware.

**Lab Apron** Wear a laboratory apron to protect your skin and clothing from damage.

**Breakage** Handle breakable materials, such as glassware, with care. Do not touch broken glassware.

**Heat-Resistant Gloves** Use an oven mitt or other hand protection when handling hot materials such as hot plates or hot glassware.

**Plastic Gloves** Wear disposable plastic gloves when working with chemicals and harmful organisms. Keep your hands away from your face, and dispose of the gloves according to your teacher's instructions.

**Heating** Use a clamp or tongs to pick up hot glassware. Do not touch hot objects with your bare hands.

**Flames** Before you work with flames, tie back loose hair and clothing. Follow instructions from your teacher about lighting and extinguishing flames.

**No Flames** When using flammable materials, make sure there are no flames, sparks, or other exposed heat sources present.

**Corrosive Chemical** Avoid getting acid or other corrosive chemicals on your skin or clothing or in your eyes. Do not inhale the vapors. Wash your hands after the activity.

**Poison** Do not let any poisonous chemical come into contact with your skin, and do not inhale its vapors. Wash your hands when you are finished with the activity.

**Fumes** Work in a ventilated area when harmful vapors may be involved. Avoid inhaling vapors directly. Only test an odor when directed to do so by your teacher, and use a wafting motion to direct the vapor toward your nose.

**Sharp Object** Scissors, scalpels, knives, needles, pins, and tacks can cut your skin. Always direct a sharp edge or point away from yourself and others.

**Animal Safety** Treat live or preserved animals or animal parts with care to avoid harming the animals or yourself. Wash your hands when you are finished with the activity.

**Plant Safety** Handle plants only as directed by your teacher. If you are allergic to certain plants, tell your teacher; do not do an activity involving those plants. Avoid touching harmful plants such as poison ivy. Wash your hands when you are finished with the activity.

**Electric Shock** To avoid electric shock, never use electrical equipment around water, or when the equipment is wet or your hands are wet. Be sure cords are untangled and cannot trip anyone. Unplug equipment not in use.

**Physical Safety** When an experiment involves physical activity, avoid injuring yourself or others. Alert your teacher if there is any reason you should not participate.

**Disposal** Dispose of chemicals and other laboratory materials safely. Follow the instructions from your teacher.

**Hand Washing** Wash your hands thoroughly when finished with the activity. Use soap and warm water. Rinse well.

**General Safety Awareness** When this symbol appears, follow the instructions provided. When you are asked to develop your own procedure in a lab, have your teacher approve your plan before you go further.

# Science Safety Rules

## General Precautions

Follow all instructions. Never perform activities without the approval and supervision of your teacher. Do not engage in horseplay. Never eat or drink in the laboratory. Keep work areas clean and uncluttered.

## Dress Code

Wear safety goggles whenever you work with chemicals, glassware, heat sources such as burners, or any substance that might get into your eyes. If you wear contact lenses, notify your teacher.

Wear a lab apron or coat whenever you work with corrosive chemicals or substances that can stain. Wear disposable plastic gloves when working with organisms and harmful chemicals. Tie back long hair. Remove or tie back any article of clothing or jewelry that can hang down and touch chemicals, flames, or equipment. Roll up long sleeves. Never wear open shoes or sandals.

## First Aid

Report all accidents, injuries, or fires to your teacher, no matter how minor. Be aware of the location of the first-aid kit, emergency equipment such as the fire extinguisher and fire blanket, and the nearest telephone. Know whom to contact in an emergency.

## Heating and Fire Safety

Keep all combustible materials away from flames. When heating a substance in a test tube, make sure that the mouth of the tube is not pointed at you or anyone else. Never heat a liquid in a closed container. Use an oven mitt to pick up a container that has been heated.

## Using Chemicals Safely

Never put your face near the mouth of a container that holds chemicals. Never touch, taste, or smell a chemical unless your teacher tells you to.

Use only those chemicals needed in the activity. Keep all containers closed when chemicals are not being used. Pour all chemicals over the sink or a container, not over your work surface. Dispose of excess chemicals as instructed by your teacher.

Be extra careful when working with acids or bases. When mixing an acid and water, always pour the water into the container first and then add the acid to the water. Never pour water into an acid. Wash chemical spills and splashes immediately with plenty of water.

## Using Glassware Safely

If glassware is broken or chipped, notify your teacher immediately. Never handle broken or chipped glass with your bare hands.

Never force glass tubing or thermometers into a rubber stopper or rubber tubing. Have your teacher insert the glass tubing or thermometer if required for an activity.

## Using Sharp Instruments

Handle sharp instruments with extreme care. Never cut material toward you; cut away from you.

## Animal and Plant Safety

Never perform experiments that cause pain, discomfort, or harm to animals. Only handle animals if absolutely necessary. If you know that you are allergic to certain plants, molds, or animals, tell your teacher before doing an activity in which these are used. Wash your hands thoroughly after any activity involving animals, animal parts, plants, plant parts, or soil.

During field work, wear long pants, long sleeves, socks, and closed shoes. Avoid poisonous plants and fungi as well as plants with thorns.

## End-of-Experiment Rules

Unplug all electrical equipment. Clean up your work area. Dispose of waste materials as instructed by your teacher. Wash your hands after every experiment.

# Appendix B Common Minerals

| Group 1: Metallic Luster, Mostly Dark-Colored | | | | | | |
|---|---|---|---|---|---|---|
| Mineral/ Formula | Hardness | Density ($g/cm^3$) | Luster | Streak | Color | Other Properties/Remarks |
| **Pyrite** $FeS_2$ | 6–6.5 | 5.0 | Metallic | Greenish, brownish black | Light yellow | Called "fool's gold," but harder than gold and very |
| **Magnetite** $Fe_3O_4$ | 6 | 5.2 | Metallic | Black | Iron black | Very magnetic; important iron ore; some varieties known as "lodestone" |
| **Hematite** $Fe_2O_3$ | 5.5–6.5 | 4.9–5.3 | Metallic or earthy | Red or red brown | Reddish brown to black | Most important ore of iron; used as red pigment in paint |
| **Pyrrhotite** FeS | 4 | 4.6 | Metallic | Gray black | Brownish | Less hard than pyrite; slightly magnetic |
| **Sphalerite** ZnS | 3.5–4 | 3.9–4.1 | Resinous | Brown to light yellow | Brown to | Most important zinc ore |
| **Chalcopyrite** $CuFeS_2$ | 3.5–4 | 4.1–4.3 | Metallic | Greenish black | Golden yellow, often tarnished | Most important copper ore; softer than pyrite and more yellow |
| **Copper** Cu | 2.5–3 | 8.9 | Metallic | Copper red | Copper red to black | Used in making electrical wires, coins, pipes |
| **Gold** Au | 2.5–3 | 19.3 | Metallic | Yellow | Rich yellow | High density; does not tarnish; used in jewelry, coins, dental fillings |
| **Silver** Ag | 2.5–3 | 10.0–11. | Metallic | Silver to light gray | Silver white (tarnishes) | Used in jewelry, coins, electrical wire, photography |
| **Galena** PbS | 2.5 | 7.4–7.6 | Metallic | Lead gray | Lead gray | Main ore of lead; used in shields against radiation |
| **Graphite** C | 1–2 | 2.3 | Metallic to dull | Black | Black | Feels greasy; very soft; used as pencil "lead" and as a |
| **Group 2: Nonmetallic Luster, Mostly Dark-Colored** | | | | | | |
| **Corundum** $Al_2O_3$ | 9 | 3.9–4.1 | Brilliant to glassy | White | Usually brown | Very hard; used as an abrasive; transparent crystals used as "ruby" (red) and "sapphire" (blue) gems |
| **Garnet** $(Ca,Mg,Fe)_3(Al,Fe,Cr)_2(SiO_4)_3$ | 7–7.5 | 3.5–4.3 | Glassy to resinous | White, light brown | Red, brown, black, green | A group of minerals used in jewelry, as a birthstone, and as an abrasive |
| **Olivine** $(Mg,Fe)_2SiO_4$ | 6.5–7 | 3.3–3.4 | Glassy | White or gray | Olive green | Found in igneous rocks; sometimes used as a gem |
| **Augite** $Ca(Mg,Fe,Al)(Al,Si)_2O_6$ | 5–6 | 3.2–3.4 | Glassy | Greenish gray | Dark green to black | Found in igneous rocks |
| **Hornblende** $NaCa_2(Mg,Fe,Al)_5(Si,Al)_8O_{22}(OH)_2$ | 5–6 | 3.0–3.4 | Glassy, silky | White to gray | Dark green, brown, black | Found in igneous and metamorphic rocks |

| Group 2: Nonmetallic Luster, Mostly Dark-Colored | | | | | | |
|---|---|---|---|---|---|---|
| **Mineral/ Formula** | **Hardness** | **Density ($g/cm^3$)** | **Luster** | **Streak** | **Color** | **Other Properties/Remarks** |
| **Apatite** $Ca_5(PO_4)_3F$ | 5 | 3.1–3.2 | Glassy | White | Green, brown, red, blue | Sometimes used as a gem; source of the phosphorus needed by plants |
| **Azurite** $Cu_3(CO_3)_2(OH)_2$ | 3.5–4 | 3.8 | Glassy to dull | Pale blue | Intense blue | Ore of copper; used as a gem |
| **Biotite** $K(Mg,Fe)_3$ $AlSiO_{10}(OH)_2$ | 2.5–3 | 2.8–3.4 | Glassy or pearly | White to gray | Dark green, brown, or black | A type of mica; sometimes used as a lubricant |
| **Serpentine** $Mg_6Si_4O_{10}(OH)_8$ | 2–5 | 2.2–2.6 | Greasy, waxy, silky | White | Usually green | Once used in insulation but found to cause cancer; used in fireproofing; can be in the form of asbestos |
| **Bauxite** aluminum oxides | 1–3 | 2.0–2.5 | Dull to earthy | Colorless to gray | Brown, yellow, gray, white | Ore of aluminum, smells like clay when wet; a mixture, not strictly a mineral |
| **Group 3: Nonmetallic Luster, Mostly Light-Colored** | | | | | | |
| **Diamond** C | 10 | 3.5 | Brilliant | White | Colorless and varied | Hardest substance; used in jewelry, abrasives, cutting tools |
| **Topaz** $Al_2SiO_4(F,OH)_2$ | 8 | 3.5–3.6 | Glassy | White | Straw yellow, pink, bluish | Valuable gem |
| **Quartz** $SiO_2$ | 7 | 2.6 | Glassy, greasy | White | Colorless, white; any color when not pure | The second most abundant mineral; many varieties are gems (amethyst, jasper); used in making glass |
| **Feldspar** (K,Na,Ca) $(AlSi_3O_8)$ | 6 | 2.6 | Glassy | Colorless, white | Colorless, white; various colors | As a family, the most abundant of all minerals; the feldspars make up over 60 percent of Earth's crust |
| **Fluorite** $CaF_2$ | 4 | 3.0–3.3 | Glassy | Colorless | Purple, light green, yellow, bluish green | Some types are fluorescent (glow in ultraviolet light); used in making steel |
| **Calcite** $CaCO_3$ | 3 | 2.7 | Glassy | White to grayish | Colorless, white | Easily scratched; bubbles in dilute hydrochloric acid; frequently fluorescent |
| **Halite** NaCl | 2.5 | 2.1–2.6 | Glassy | White | Colorless | Perfect cubic crystals; has salty taste |
| **Gypsum** $CaSO_4 \cdot 2H_20$ | 2 | 2.3 | Glassy, pearly | White | Colorless, white | Very soft; used in plaster of Paris; form known as alabaster used for statues |
| **Sulfur** S | 2 | 2.0–2.1 | Resinous to greasy | White | Yellow to brown | Used in medicines, in production of sulfuric acid, and in vulcanizing rubber |
| **Talc** $Mg_3Si_4O_{10}(OH)_2$ | 1 | 2.7–2.8 | Pearly to greasy | White | Gray, white, greenish | Very soft; used in talcum powder; also called "soapstone" |

Use these star charts to locate bright stars and major constellations in the night sky at different times of year. Choose the appropriate star chart for the current season.

## Autumn Sky

This chart works best at the following dates and times: September 1 at 10:00 P.M., October 1 at 8:00 P.M., or November 1 at 6:00 P.M. Look for the constellations Ursa Minor (the Little Dipper) and Cassiopeia in the northern sky, and for the star Deneb, which is nearly overhead in autumn.

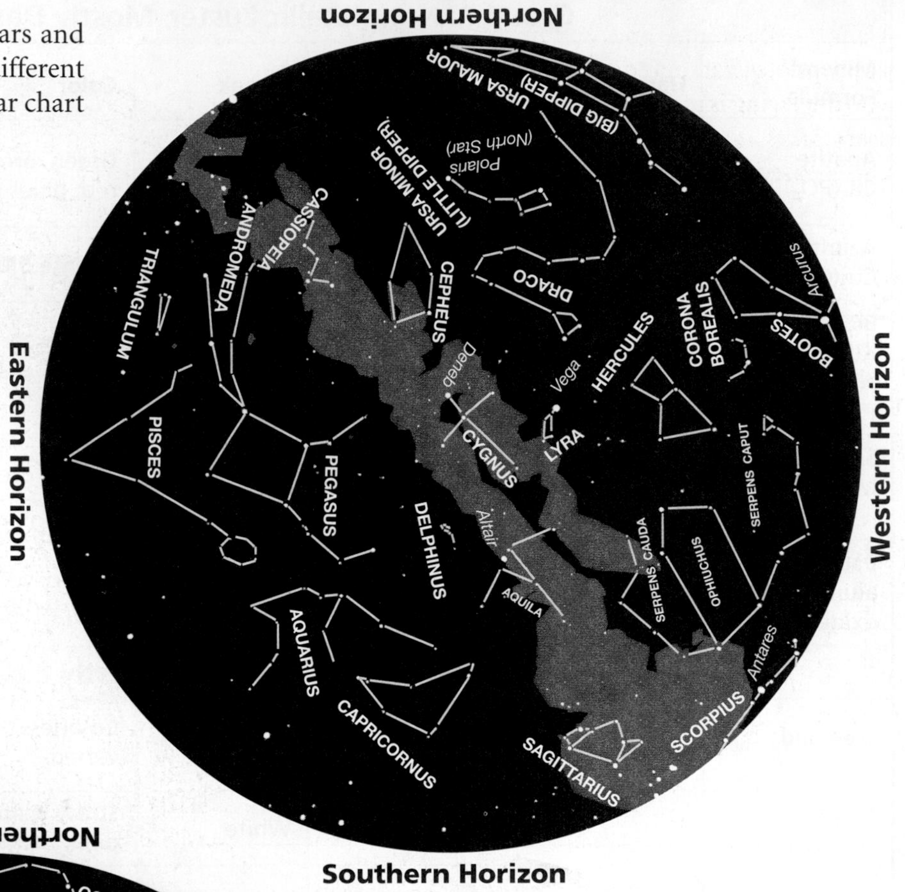


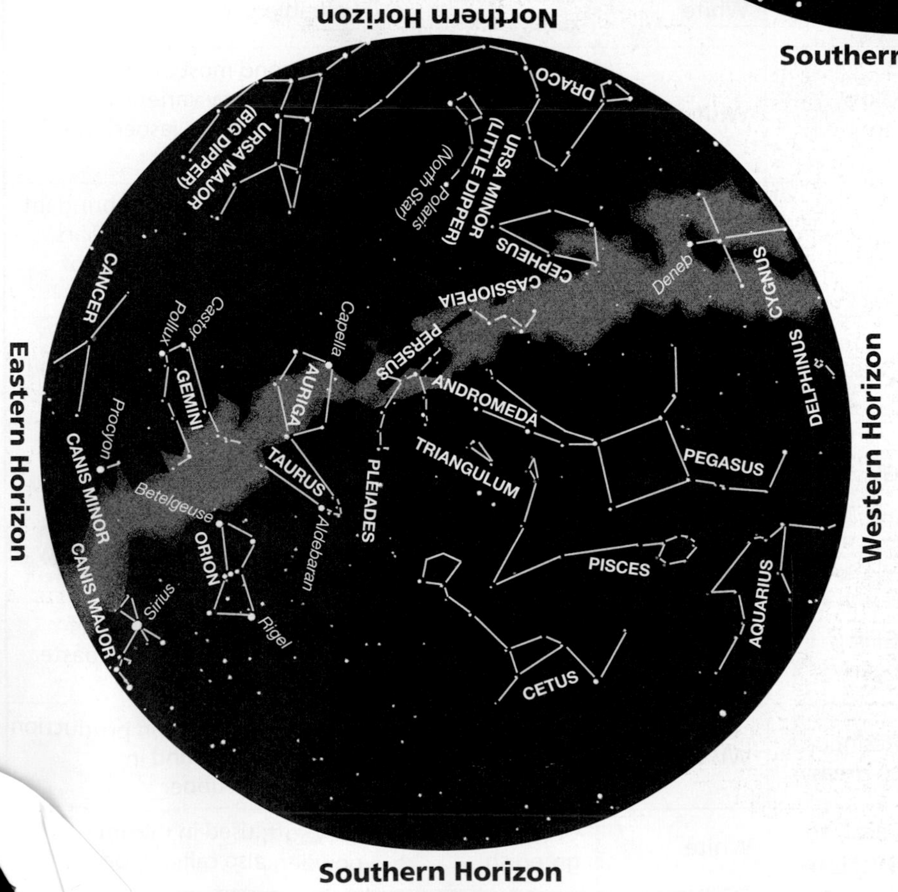


## Winter Sky

This chart works best at the following dates and times: December 1 at 10:00 P.M., January 1 at 8:00 P.M., or February 1 at 6:00 P.M. Look for the constellations Orion and Gemini, the bright star Sirius, and the Pleiades, a star cluster, in the winter sky.

Using a flashlight and a compass, hold the appropriate chart and turn it so that the direction you are facing is at the bottom of the chart. These star charts work best at 34° north latitude, but can be used at other central latitudes.

## Spring Sky

This chart works best at the following dates and times: March 1 at 10:00 P.M., March 15 at 9:00 P.M., or April 1 at 8:00 P.M. Look for the constellations Ursa Major (which contains the Big Dipper), Bootes, and Leo in the spring sky. The bright stars Arcturus and Spica can be seen in the east.

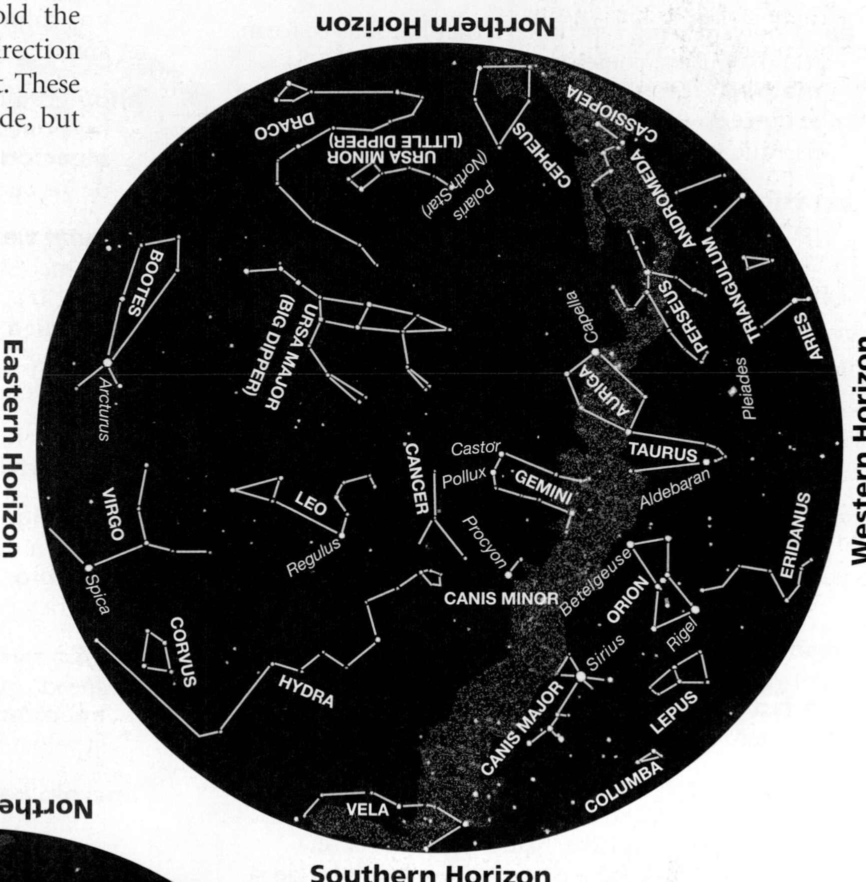

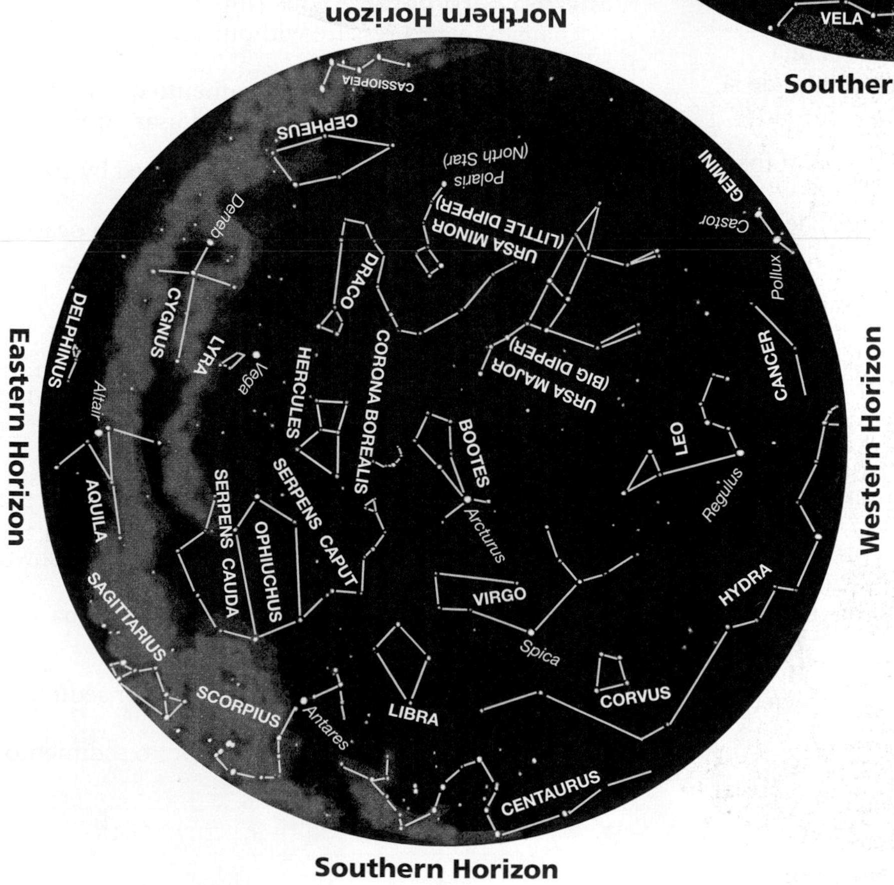

Northern Horizon

Eastern Horizon

Western Horizon

Southern Horizon

## Summer Sky

This chart works best at the following dates and times: May 15 at 11:00 P.M., June 1 at 10:00 P.M., or June 15 at 9:00 P.M. Look for the bright star Arcturus in the constellation Bootes overhead in early summer. Towards the east look for the bright stars Vega, Altair, and Deneb, which form a triangle.

# English and Spanish Glossary

## A

**aa** A slow-moving type of lava that hardens to form rough chunks; cooler than pahoehoe. (p. 208)
**malpaís** Tipo de lava de movimiento lento que al endurecerse forma aglutinaciones ásperas; es más fría que la lava cordada.

**abrasion** The grinding away of rock by other rock particles carried in water, ice, or wind. (pp. 241, 287)
**abrasión** Desgaste de la roca por otras partículas de roca llevadas por el agua, el viento o el hielo.

**absolute age** The age of a rock given as the number of years since the rock formed. (p. 317)
**edad absoluta** Edad de una roca basada en el número de años desde que se formó la roca.

**absolute brightness** The brightness of a star if it were at a standard distance from Earth. (p. 755)
**magnitud absoluta** Brillo que tendría una estrella si estuviera a una distancia estándar de la Tierra.

**abyssal plain** A smooth, nearly flat region of the deep ocean floor. (p. 475)
**llanura abisal** Región llana, casi plana, de la cuenca oceánica profunda.

**acid rain** Rain that contains more acid than normal. (p. 530)
**lluvia ácida** Lluvia que contiene más acidez de la normal.

**aftershock** An earthquake that occurs after a larger earthquake in the same area. (p. 188)
**réplica** Sismo que ocurre después de un terremoto mayor en la misma área.

**air mass** A huge body of air that has similar temperature, humidity, and air pressure throughout. (p. 578)
**masa de aire** Gran volumen de aire que tiene temperatura, humedad y presión similares en todos sus puntos.

**air pressure** The pressure caused by the weight of a column of air pushing down on an area. (p. 517)
**presión de aire** Presión causada por el peso de una columna de aire que empuja hacia abajo en un área.

**alloy** A solid mixture of two or more elements, at least one of which is a metal. (p. 85)
**aleación** Mezcla sólida de dos o más elementos, de los cuales por lo menos uno es un metal.

**alluvial fan** A wide, sloping deposit of sediment formed where a stream leaves a mountain range. (p. 277)
**abanico aluvial** Depósito ancho de sedimento en declive, que se forma donde un arroyo sale de una cordillera.

**altitude** Elevation above sea level. (p. 519)
**altitud** Elevación sobre el nivel del mar.

**amphibian** A vertebrate that lives part of its life on land and part of its life in water. (p. 336)
**anfibio** Vertebrado que vive parte de su vida en la tierra y parte en el agua.

**anemometer** An instrument used to measure wind speed. (p. 553)
**anemómetro** Instrumento que se usa para medir la velocidad del viento.

**aneroid barometer** An instrument that measures changes in air pressure without using a liquid. (p. 518)
**barómetro aneroide** Instrumento que mide los cambios en la presión del aire sin usar líquido.

**anticline** An upward fold in rock formed by compression of Earth's crust. (p. 166)
**anticlinal** Pliegue de la roca hacia arriba ocasionado por compresión de la corteza terrestre.

**anticyclone** A high-pressure center of dry air. (p. 584)
**anticiclón** Centro de aire seco de alta presión.

**apparent brightness** The brightness of a star as seen from Earth. (p. 755)
**magnitud aparente** Brillo de una estrella visto desde la Tierra.

**aquaculture** The farming of saltwater and freshwater organisms. (p. 492)
**acuicultura** Crianza de organismos de agua salada y dulce.

**aquifer** An underground layer of rock or sediment that holds water. (p. 406)
**acuífero** Capa subterránea de roca o sedimento que retiene agua.

**artesian well** A well in which water rises because of pressure within the aquifer. (p. 408)
**pozo artesiano** Pozo por el que el agua se eleva debido a la presión dentro del acuífero.

**asteroid** Rocky objects revolving around the sun that are too small and numerous to be considered planets. (p. 732)
**asteroides** Objetos rocosos que se mueven alrededor del Sol y que son demasiado pequeños y numerosos como para ser considerados planetas.

**asteroid belt** The region of the solar system between the orbits of Mars and Jupiter, where many asteroids are found. (p. 732)
**cinturón de asteroides** Región del sistema solar entre las órbitas de Marte y Júpiter, donde se encuentran muchos asteroides.

**asthenosphere** The soft layer of the mantle on which the lithosphere floats. (p. 129)
**astenosfera** Capa suave del manto en la que flota la litosfera.

**astronomer** A scientist who studies the universe beyond Earth. (p. 17)
**astrónomo** Científico que estudia el universo más allá de la Tierra.

**astronomy** The study of the moon, stars and other objects in space. (p. 660)
**astronomía** Estudio de la luna, las estrellas y otros objetos del espacio.

**atmosphere** The envelope of gases that surrounds Earth. (p. 512)
**atmósfera** Capa de gases que rodea la Tierra.

**atoll** A ring-shaped coral reef that surrounds a shallow lagoon. (p. 485)
**atolón** Arrecife de coral con forma de anillo que rodea a una laguna poco profunda.

**atom** The smallest particle of an element. (p. 324)
**átomo** Partícula más pequeña de un elemento.

**axis** An imaginary line that passes through Earth's center and the North and South poles, about which Earth rotates. (p. 661)
**eje** Línea imaginaria que pasa a través del centro de la Tierra, por los polos Norte y Sur, sobre el cual gira la Tierra.

N
Axis
S
Earth

## B

**barometer** An instrument used to measure changes in air pressure. (p. 518)
**barómetro** Instrumento que se usa para medir cambios en la presión del aire.

**basalt** A dark, dense, igneous rock with a fine texture, found in oceanic crust. (pp. 95, 128)
**basalto** Roca ígnea, oscura y densa, de textura fina, que se encuentra en la corteza oceánica.

**base-isolated building** A building mounted on bearings designed to absorb the energy of an earthquake. (p. 191)
**edificio de base aislada** Edificio montado sobre soportes diseñados para absorber la energía liberada por los terremotos.

**batholith** A mass of rock formed when a large body of magma cools inside the crust. (p. 222)
**batolito** Masa de roca formada cuando una gran masa de magma se enfría dentro de la corteza.

**beach** Wave-washed sediment along a coast. (p. 299)
**playa** Sedimento depositado por las olas a lo largo de una costa.

**bedrock** The solid layer of rock beneath the soil.
**lecho rocoso** Capa sólida de roca debajo del suelo. (p. 248)

**benthos** Organisms that live on the bottom of the ocean or other body of water. (p. 479)
**bentos** Organismos que viven en el fondo del océano u otro cuerpo de agua.

**big bang** The initial explosion that resulted in the formation and expansion of the universe. (p. 774)
**Big Bang** Explosión inicial que dio como resultado la formación y expansión del universo.

**binary star** A star system with two stars. (p. 768)
**estrella binaria** Sistema de estrellas con dos estrellas.

**bioluminescence** The production of light by living things. (p. 488)
**bioluminiscencia** Producción de luz por seres vivos.

**biomass fuel** Fuel made from living things. (p. 365)
**combustible de biomasa** Combustible formado a partir de seres vivos.

**black hole** An object whose gravity is so strong that nothing, not even light, can escape. (p. 766)
**agujero negro** Objeto cuya gravedad es tan fuerte que nada, ni siquiera la luz, puede escapar.

## C

**caldera** The large hole at the top of a volcano formed when the roof of a volcano's magma chamber collapses. (p. 220)
**caldera** Gran agujero en la parte superior de un volcán que se forma cuando la tapa de la cámara magmática del volcán se desploma.

**carbon film** A type of fossil consisting of an extremely thin coating of carbon on rock. (p. 312)
**película de carbono** Tipo de fósil que consiste en una capa de carbono extremadamente fina que recubre la roca.

**cast** A fossil that is a copy of an organism's shape, formed when minerals seep into a mold. (p. 311)
**vaciado** Fósil que es una copia de la forma de un organismo, formado cuando los minerales penetran en un molde.

**cementation** The process by which dissolved minerals crystallize and glue particles of sediment together into one mass. (p. 103)
**cementación** Proceso mediante el cual minerales disueltos se cristalizan y adhieren partículas de sedimento para formar una masa.

**chemical property** Any property of a substance that produces a change in the composition of matter. (p. 206)
**propiedad química** Cualquier propiedad de una substancia que produce cambios en la composición de la materia.

**chemical rock** Sedimentary rock that forms when minerals crystallize from a solution. (p. 105)
**roca química** Roca sedimentaria que se forma cuando los minerales en una solución se cristalizan.

**chemical weathering** The process that breaks down rock through chemical changes. (p. 242)
**desgaste químico** Proceso que erosiona la roca mediante cambios químicos.

**chlorofluorocarbons** Chlorine compounds that are the main cause of ozone depletion. (p. 646)
**clorofluorocarbonos** Compuestos de cloro que son la causa principal de la destrucción del ozono.

**chromosphere** The middle layer of the sun's atmosphere. (p. 708)
**cromosfera** Capa central en la atmósfera del Sol.

**cinder cone** A steep, cone-shaped hill or small mountain made of volcanic ash, cinders, and bombs piled up around a volcano's opening. (p. 218)
**cono de escoria** Colina o pequeña montaña escarpada en forma de cono que se forma cuando ceniza volcánica, escoria y bombas se acumulan alrededor de la boca de un volcán.

**cirrus** Wispy, feathery clouds made mostly of ice crystals that form at high levels. (p. 564)
**cirros** Nubes parecidas a plumas o pinceladas blancas formadas principalmente por cristales de hielo que se crean a grandes altitudes.

**clastic rock** Sedimentary rock that forms when rock fragments are squeezed together under high pressure. (p. 104)
**roca clástica** Roca sedimentaria que se forma cuando fragmentos de roca se unen bajo una gran presión.

**cleavage** A mineral's ability to split easily along flat surfaces. (p. 72)
**exfoliación** La facilidad con la que un mineral se divide en capas planas.

**climate** The average, year-after-year conditions of temperature, precipitation, winds, and clouds in an area. (pp. 458, 614)
**clima** Promedio, año a año, de las condiciones de temperatura, precipitación, viento y nubes en un área.

**cloud seeding** Process of producing rain during droughts by sprinkling silver iodide crystals and dry ice into clouds from airplanes. (p. 422)
**siembra de nubes** Proceso por el cual se produce lluvia durante las sequías al rociar desde aviones cristales de yoduro de plata y hielo seco en las nubes.

**coagulation** The process by which particles in a liquid clump together. (p. 422)
**coagulación** Proceso por el cual partículas presentes en un líquido forman cúmulos.

**coliform** A type of bacteria found in human and animal wastes. (p. 421)
**coliforme** Tipo de bacteria que se halla en los desperdicios humanos y animales.

**coma** The fuzzy outer layer of a comet. (p. 731)
**coma** Capa exterior y difusa de un cometa.

**combustion** The process of burning a fuel. (p. 355)
**combustión** Proceso en el que se quema un combustible.

**comet** A loose collection of ice, dust and small rocky particles, typically with a long, narrow orbit of the sun. (pp. 332, 731)
**cometa** Conjunto no compacto de hielo, polvo y partículas rocosas pequeñas, que normalmente tiene una órbita larga y estrecha del Sol.

**compaction** The process by which sediments are pressed together under their own weight. (p. 103)
**compactación** Proceso mediante el cual los sedimentos se unen por la presión de su propio peso.

**composite volcano** A tall, cone-shaped mountain in which layers of lava alternate with layers of ash and other volcanic materials. (p. 219)
**volcán compuesto** Montaña alta con forma de cono en la que las capas de lava se alternan con capas de ceniza y otros materiales volcánicos.

**compound** A substance in which two or more elements are chemically joined. (p. 205)
**compuesto** Sustancia en la que dos o más elementos están unidos químicamente.

**compression** Stress that squeezes rock until it folds or breaks. (p. 163)
**compresión** Esfuerzo que oprime una roca hasta que ésta se pliega o rompe.

**concentration** The amount of one substance in a certain volume of another substance. (p. 420)
**concentración** Cantidad de una sustancia que hay en cierto volumen de otra sustancia.

**condensation** The process by which molecules of water vapor in the air become liquid water. (p. 563)
**condensación** Proceso por el cual las moléculas de vapor de agua en el aire se convierten en agua líquida.

**conduction** The direct transfer of thermal energy from one substance to another substance that it is touching. (pp. 133, 550)
**conducción** Transferencia directa de energía térmica de una sustancia a otra que la toca.

**conservation** The practice of using less of a resource so that it will not be used up. (p. 416)
**conservación** Práctica de usar menos de un recurso para que no se agote.

**conservation plowing** Soil conservation method in which the dead stalks from the previous year's crop are left in the ground to hold the soil in place. (p. 259)
**arada de conservación** Método de conservación del suelo en el cual los tallos muertos de la cosecha del año anterior se dejan en la tierra para que sujeten el suelo en su lugar.

**constellation** An imaginary pattern of stars in the sky. (p. 752)
**constelación** Patrón imaginario de estrellas en el cielo.

**constructive force** A force that builds up mountains and landmasses on Earth's surface. (p. 15)
**fuerza constructiva** Fuerza que crea montañas y masas terrestres sobre la superficie de la Tierra.

**continental (air mass)** A dry air mass that forms over land. (p. 579)
**masa de aire continental** Masa de aire seco que se forma sobre la tierra.

**continental climate** The climate of the centers of continents, with cold winters and warm or hot summers. (p. 616)
**clima continental** Clima del centro de los continentes, con inviernos fríos y veranos templados o calurosos.

**continental drift** The hypothesis that the continents slowly move across Earth's surface.
**deriva continental** Hipótesis según la cual los continentes se desplazan lentamente en la superficie de la Tierra. (pp. 137, 332)

**continental glacier** A glacier that covers much of a continent or large island. (p. 292)
**glaciar continental** Glaciar que cubre gran parte de un continente o una isla grande.

**continental shelf** A gently sloping, shallow area of the ocean floor that extends outward from the edge of a continent. (p. 474)
**plataforma continental** Área poco profunda con pendiente suave del suelo oceánico que se extiende desde los márgenes de un continente.

**continental slope** A steep incline of the ocean floor leading down from the edge of the continental shelf. (p. 474)
**talud continental** Región del suelo oceánico con pendiente empinada que baja del borde de la plataforma continental.

**contour interval** The difference in elevation from one contour line to the next. (p. 55)
**intervalo entre curvas de nivel** Diferencia de elevación de una curva de nivel a otra.

**contour line** A line on a topographic map that connects points of equal elevation. (p. 55)
**curva de nivel** Línea en un mapa topográfico que conecta puntos de igual elevación.

**contour plowing** Plowing fields along the curves of a slope to prevent soil loss. (p. 259)
**arada en contorno** Arar los campos siguiendo las curvas de una pendiente para evitar que el suelo se suelte.

**control rod** A cadmium rod used in a nuclear reactor to absorb neutrons from fission reactions. (p. 372)
**varilla de control** Varilla de cadmio que se usa en un reactor nuclear para absorber los neutrones emitidos por las reacciones de la fisión.

**controlled experiment** An experiment in which only one variable is manipulated at a time. (p. 9)
**experimento controlado** Experimento en el cual sólo una variable es manipulada a la vez.

**convection** The transfer of thermal energy by the movement of a fluid. (pp. 134, 550)
**convección** Transferencia de energía térmica por el movimiento de un líquido.

**convection current** The movement of a fluid, caused by differences in temperature, that transfers heat from one part of the fluid to another. (pp. 134, 550)

**corriente de convección** Movimiento de un líquido ocasionado por diferencias en la temperatura, que transfiere calor de un punto del líquido a otro.

**convection zone** The outermost layer of the sun's interior. (p. 707)
**zona de convección** Capa más superficial del interior del Sol.

**convergent boundary** A plate boundary where two plates move toward each other. (p. 153)
**borde convergente** Borde de placa donde dos placas se deslizan una hacia la otra.

**convex lens** A piece of transparent glass curved so that the middle is thicker than the edges. (p. 746)
**lente convexa** Trozo de cristal transparente curvado de tal manera que el centro es más grueso que los extremos.

**coral reef** A structure of calcite skeletons built up by coral animals in warm, shallow ocean water.
**arrecife de coral** Estructura de esqueletos calcáreos formada por corales en aguas oceánicas templadas y poco profundas. (p. 108)

**core** The central region of the sun, where nuclear fusion takes place. (p. 707)
**úcleo** Región central del Sol, donde ocurre la ón nuclear.

**Coriolis effect** The effect of Earth's rotation on the direction of winds and currents. (pp. 457, 555)
**efecto de Coriolis** Efecto de la rotación terrestre sobre la dirección de los vientos y las corrientes.

**corona** The outer layer of the sun's atmosphere. (p. 708)
**corona** Capa externa de la atmósfera del Sol.

**cosmic background radiation** The electromagnetic radiation left over from the big bang. (p. 776)
**radiación cósmica de fondo** Radiación electromagnética que quedó del Big Bang.

**crater** A bowl-shaped area that forms around a volcano's central opening (p. 210); a large round pit caused by the impact of a meteoroid (p. 681).
**cráter** Área en forma de tazón que se forma alrededor de la entrada central de un volcán; gran cuenca redonda causada por el impacto de un meteoroide.

**crop rotation** The planting of different crops in a field each year to maintain the soil's fertility. (p. 259)
**rotación de cultivos** Plantación de cultivos diferentes en un campo cada año para mantener la fertilidad del suelo.

**crust** The layer of rock that forms Earth's outer surface. (p. 128)
**corteza** Capa de rocas que forma la superficie externa de la Tierra.

**crystal** A solid in which the atoms are arranged in a pattern that repeats again and again. (p. 67)
**cristal** Sólido en el que los átomos están dispuestos en un patrón que se repite una y otra vez.

**crystallization** The process by which atoms are arranged to form a material with a crystal structure. (p. 76)
**cristalización** Proceso mediante el cual los átomos se organizan para formar materiales con estructura cristalina.

**cumulus** Fluffy, white clouds, usually with flat bottoms, that look like rounded piles of cotton. (p. 564)
**cúmulos** Nubes blancas, que normalmente tienen la parte inferior plana, que parecen grandes masas de algodón esponjosas y redondas.

**current** A large stream of moving water that flows through the oceans. (p. 456)
**corriente** Un gran volumen de agua que fluye por los océanos.

**cyclone** A swirling center of low air pressure.
**ciclón** Centro de un remolino de aire de baja presión. (p. 584)

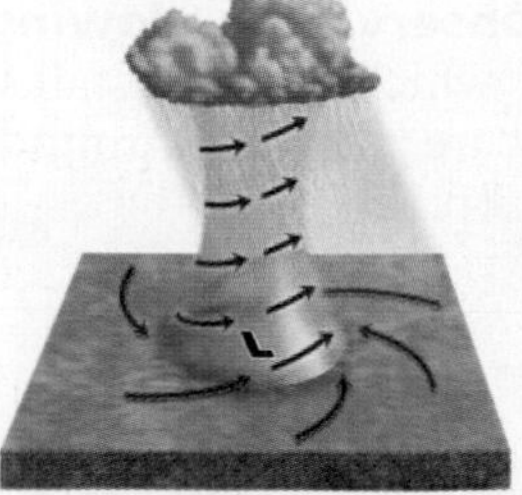

## D

**dark energy** A mysterious force that appears to be causing the expansion of the universe to accelerate. (p. 778)
**energía negra** Misteriosa fuerza que parece acelerar la expansión del universo.

**dark matter** Matter that does not give off electromagnetic radiation but appears to be quite abundant in the universe. (p. 778)
**materia negra** Materia que no despide radiación electromagnética, pero que es muy abundante en el universo.

**data** Facts, figures, and other evidence gathered through observations. (p. 10)
**dato** Hecho, cifra u otra evidencia reunida por medio de las observaciones.

**decomposer** Soil organism that breaks down the remains of organisms and digests them. (p. 253)
**descomponedor** Organismo del suelo que desintegra los restos de organismos y los digiere.

**deep-ocean trench** A deep valley along the ocean floor beneath which oceanic crust slowly sinks toward the mantle. (p. 146)
**fosa oceánica profunda** Valle profundo a lo largo del suelo oceánico debajo del cual la corteza oceánica se hunde lentamente hacia el manto.

**deflation** Wind erosion that removes surface materials. (p. 302)
**deflación** Erosión por viento que se lleva materiales superficiales.

**degree** A unit used to measure distances around a circle. One degree equals 1/360 of a full circle. (p. 41)
**grado** Unidad usada para medir distancias alrededor de un círculo. Un grado es igual a 1/360 de un círculo completo.

**delta** A landform made of sediment that is deposited where a river flows into an ocean or lake. (p. 277)
**delta** Accidente geográfico formado por sedimentos que se depositan en la desembocadura de un río a un océano o lago.

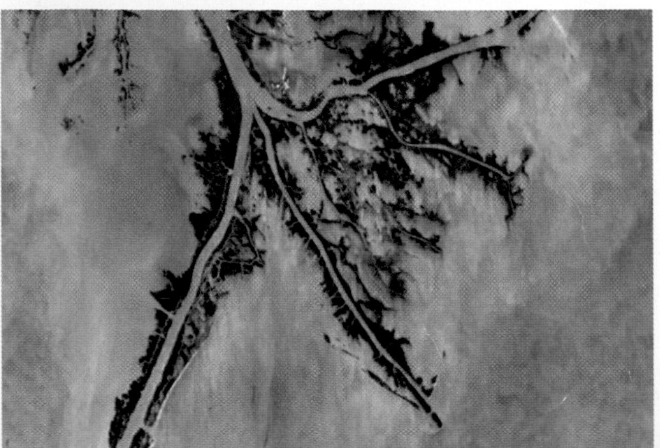

**density** The amount of mass of a substance in a given volume; mass per unit volume. (pp. 134, 517)
**densidad** Cantidad de masa en un espacio dado; masa por unidad de volumen.

**deposition** Process in which sediment is laid down in new locations. (pp. 103, 267)
**sedimentación** Proceso por el cual se asientan sedimentos en sitios nuevos.

**desert** An arid region that on average receives less than 25 centimeters of rain a year. (p. 628)
**desierto** Región árida que, como promedio, recibe menos de 25 centímetros de lluvia al año.

**destructive force** A force that slowly wears away mountains and other features on the surface of Earth. (p. 15)
**fuerza destructiva** Fuerza que desgasta lentamente las montañas y otros accidentes geográficos de la superficie de la Tierra.

**dew point** The temperature at which condensation begins. (p. 563)
**punto de rocío** Temperatura a la que comienza la condensación

**digitizing** Converting information to numbers for use by a computer. (p. 49)
**digitalizar** Convertir información a números para que pueda ser usada por una computadora.

**dike** A slab of volcanic rock formed when magma forces itself across rock layers. (p. 221)
**dique discordante** Placa de roca volcánica formada cuando el magma se abre paso a través de las capas de roca.

**divergent boundary** A plate boundary where two plates move away from each other. (p. 152)
**borde divergente** Borde de placa donde dos placas se separan.

**divide** A ridge of land that separates one watershed from another. (p. 397)
**divisoria de aguas** Elevación de terreno que separa una cuenca hidrográfica de otra.

**dormant** A volcano that is not currently active, but that may become active in the future. (p. 215)
**inactivo** Volcán que en la actualidad no está activo, pero que puede volver a ser activo en el futuro.

**drought** A long period of low precipitation. (p. 570)
**sequía** Largo período de poca precipitación.

**Dust Bowl** The area of the Great Plains where wind erosion caused soil loss during the 1930s. (p. 258)
**Cuenca del polvo** Área de las Grandes Llanuras donde la erosión por el viento causó la pérdida de suelo durante la década de 1930.

## E

**Earth science** The science that focuses on planet Earth and its place in the universe. (p. 14)
**ciencia de la Tierra** Ciencia que se centra en el planeta Tierra y en su lugar en el universo.

**earthquake** The shaking that results from the movement of rock beneath Earth's surface. (p. 169)
**terremoto** Temblor que resulta del movimiento de la roca debajo de la superficie de la Tierra.

**eclipse** The partial or total blocking of one object in space by another. (p. 673)
**eclipse** Bloqueo parcial o total de un objeto en el espacio por otro.

**eclipsing binary** A binary star system in which one star periodically blocks the light from another.
**eclipse binario** Sistema de estrella binaria en el que una estrella bloquea periódicamente la luz de la otra. (p. 768)

**efficiency** The percentage of energy that is used to perform work. (p. 376)
**eficiencia** Porcentaje de energía usada para realizar trabajo.

**El Niño** A climate event that occurs every two to seven years in the Pacific Ocean, during which winds shift and push warm water toward the coast of South America (pp. 459, 642)
**El Niño** Fenómeno climático que ocurre cada dos a siete años en el Océano Pacífico, durante el cual los vientos se desvían y empujan el agua templado hacia la costa de América del Sur.

**electromagnetic radiation** Energy that travels through space in the form of waves. (p. 745)
**radiación electromagnética** Energía que viaja a través del espacio en forma de ondas.

**electromagnetic wave** Waves that can transfer electric and magnetic energy through the vacuum of space. (p. 542)
**ondas electromagnéticas** Ondas que transfieren energía eléctrica y magnética a través del vacío.

**element** A substance in which all the atoms are the same that cannot be broken down into other substances. (pp. 205, 324)
**elemento** Substancia que no puede descomponerse en otras substancias en la cual todos los átomos son iguales.

**elevation** Height above sea level. (p. 35)
**elevación** Altura sobre el nivel del mar.

**ellipse** An oval shape, which may be elongated or nearly circular. (p. 703)
**elipse** Figura ovalada, alargada o casi circular.

**elliptical galaxy** A galaxy shaped like a round or flattened ball, generally ball, generally containing only old stars. (p. 770)
**galaxia elíptica** Galaxia con forma de pelota aplastada, que generalmente está formada sólo de estrellas viejas.

**energy** The ability to do work or cause change. (pp. 14, 286)
**energía** Capacidad para realizar trabajo o producir cambios.

**energy conservation** The practice of reducing energy use. (p. 378)
**conservación de la energía** Práctica de reducción del uso de energía.

**energy transformation** A change from one form of energy to another. (p. 354)
**transformación de la energía** Cambio de una forma de energía a otra.

**engineer** A person who is trained to use both technological and scientific knowledge to solve practical problems. (p. 21)
**ingeniero** Persona capacitada para usar conocimientos tecnológicos y científicos para resolver problemas prácticos.

**environmental scientist** A scientist who studies the effects of human activities on Earth's land, air, water, and living things and also tries to solve problems relating to the use of resources. (p. 17)
**científico ambientalista** Científico que estudia los efectos de las actividades humanas en el suelo, aire, agua y seres vivos de la Tierra, y que también trata de solucionar problemas relacionados con el uso de los recursos.

**epicenter** The point on Earth's surface directly above an earthquake's focus. (p. 169)
**epicentro** Punto en la superficie de la Tierra directamente sobre el foco de un terremoto.

**equator** An imaginary line that circles Earth halfway between the North and South poles. (p. 42)
**ecuador** Línea imaginaria que rodea la Tierra por el centro, entre los polos Norte y Sur.

**equinox** The two days of the year on which neither hemisphere is tilted toward or away from the sun. (p. 665)
**equinoccio** Los dos días del año en los que ningún hemisferio está inclinado hacia el Sol ni más lejos de él.

**era** One of the three long units of geologic time between the Precambrian and the present. (p. 329)
**era** Cada una de las tres unidades largas del tiempo geológico entre el Precámbrico y el presente.

**erosion** The process by which water, ice, wind, or gravity moves weathered rock or soil. (pp. 103, 239, 266)
**erosión** Proceso por el cual el agua, el hielo, el viento, o la gravedad desplazan rocas degastadas y suelo.

**escape velocity** The velocity a rocket must reach to fly beyond a planet's or moon's gravitational pull. (p. 685)
**velocidad de escape** Velocidad que debe alcanzar un objeto para salir del campo de gravedad de un planeta o luna.

**estuary** A coastal inlet or bay where fresh water from rivers mixes with salty ocean water. (p. 482)
**estuario** Ensenada o bahía costera donde el agua dulce de los ríos se mezcla con el agua salada del mar.

**evacuate** To move away from an area temporarily to avoid hurricane conditions. (p. 593)
**evacuar** Alejarse de un área temporalmente para evitar las condiciones de un huracán.

**evaporation** The process by which water molecules in liquid water escape into the air as water vapor. (p. 560)
**evaporación** Proceso por el cual las moléculas de agua líquida son liberadas al aire como vapor de agua.

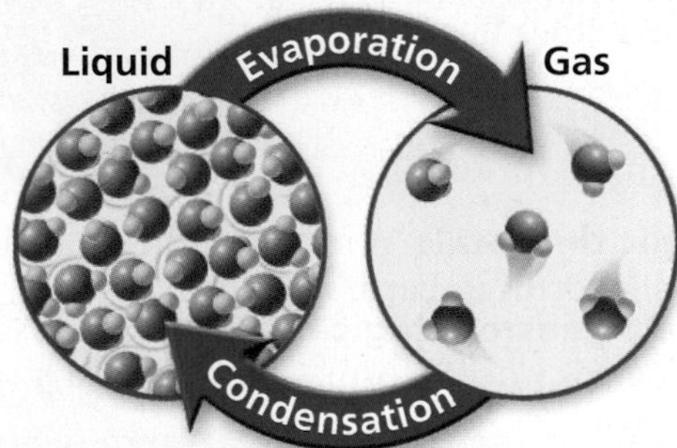


**evolution** The process by which all the different kinds of living things have changed over time. (p. 316)
**evolución** Proceso por el cual los diferentes tipos de seres vivos han cambiado con el tiempo.

**exosphere** The outer layer of the thermosphere.
**exosfera** Capa externa de la termosfera. (p. 527)

**extinct** A volcano that is no longer active and is unlikely to erupt again (p. 215); describes a type of organism that no longer exists anywhere on Earth. (p. 316)
**extinto** Volcán que ya no es activo y es poco probable que haga erupción otra vez; describe un tipo de organismo que ya no existe en la Tierra.

**extraterrestrial life** Life that exists other than that on Earth. (p. 734)
**vida extraterrestre** Vida que existe fuera de la Tierra.

**extrusion** An igneous rock layer formed when lava flows onto Earth's surface and hardens. (p. 319)
**extrusión** Capa de roca ígnea formada cuando la lava fluye  hacia la superficie de la Tierra y se endurece.

**extrusive rock** Igneous rock that forms from lava on Earth's surface. (p. 98)
**roca extrusiva** Roca ígnea que se forma de la lava en la superficie de la Tierra.

## F

**fault** A break or crack in Earth's lithosphere along which the rocks move. (pp. 152, 319)
**falla** Fisura o grieta en la litosfera de la Tierra a lo largo de la cual se mueven las rocas.

**fertility** A measure of how well soil supports plant growth. (p. 249)
**fertilidad** Medida de lo apropiado de un suelo para mantener el crecimiento de las plantas.

**filtration** The process of passing water through a series of screens that allow the water through, but not larger solid particles. (p. 422)
**filtración** Proceso en el que el agua pasa por una serie de mallas que impiden el paso de partículas sólidas grandes.

**flood plain** Wide valley through which a river flows. (p. 275)
**llanura de aluvión** Valle ancho por el cual fluye un río.

**focus** The point beneath Earth's surface where rock breaks under stress and causes an earthquake. (p. 169)
**foco** Punto debajo de la superficie de la Tierra en el que la roca se rompe a raíz del esfuerzo, y causa un terremoto.

**foliated** Term used to describe metamorphic rocks that have grains arranged in parallel layers or bands. (p. 111)
**esquistocidad** Término usado para describir las rocas metamórficas que tienen granos dispuestos en capas paralelas o bandas.

**food web** The feeding relationships in a habitat. (p. 480)
**red alimentaria** Relaciones de alimentación en un hábitat.

**footwall** The block of rock that forms the lower half of a fault. (p. 164)
**labio inferior** Bloque de roca que constituye la mitad inferior de una falla.

**force** A push or a pull exerted on an object. (p. 666)
**fuerza** Empuje o atracción ejercida sobre un objeto.

**fossil** A trace of an ancient organism that has been preserved in rock. (pp. 138, 310)
**fósil** Vestigio de un organismo de la antigüedad que se ha preservado en la roca u otra sustancia.

**fossil fuel** An energy-rich substance (such as coal, oil, or natural gas) formed from the remains of organisms. (p. 356)
**combustible fósil** Sustancia rica en energía (como carbón mineral, petróleo o gas natural) que se forma a partir de los restos de organismos.

**fracture** The way a mineral looks when it breaks apart in an irregular way. (p. 73)
**fractura** Apariencia de un mineral cuando se rompe irregularmente.

**frequency** The number of waves that pass a specific point in a given amount of time. (p. 436)
**frecuencia** Número de ondas u olas que pasan por un punto dado en cierto tiempo.

**friction** The force that opposes the motion of one surface as it moves across another surface. (pp. 182, 289)
**fricción** Fuerza que se opone al movimiento de una superficie a medida que se mueve a través de otra superficie.

**front** The boundary where unlike air masses meet but do not mix. (p. 581)
**frente** Límite en donde se encuentran masas de aire diferentes, pero no se mezclan.

**fuel** A substance that provides energy as the result of a chemical change. (p. 354)
**combustible** Sustancia que libera energía como resultado de un cambio químico.

**fuel rod** A uranium rod that undergoes fission in a nuclear reactor. (p. 372)
**varilla de combustible** Varilla de uranio que se somete a la fisión en un reactor nuclear.

## G

**galaxy** A huge group of single stars, star systems, star clusters, dust, and gas bound together by gravity. (p. 770)
**galaxia** Enorme grupo de estrellas individuales, sistemas de estrellas, cúmulos de estrellas, polvo y gas unidos por la gravedad.

**gas giant** The name often given to the first four outer planets: Jupiter, Saturn, Uranus, and Neptune. (p. 721)
**gigantes gaseosos** Nombre que normalmente se da a los cuatro primeros planetas exteriores: Júpiter, Saturno, Urano y Neptuno.

**gasohol** A mixture of gasoline and alcohol. (p. 365)
**gasohol** Mezcla de gasolina y alcohol.

**gemstone** A hard, colorful mineral that has a brilliant or glassy luster and is valued for its appearance. (p. 81)
**gema** Mineral duro y colorido, con lustre brillante o vidrioso.

**geocentric** A model of the universe in which Earth is at the center of the revolving planets and stars. (p. 701)
**geocéntrico** Modelo del universo en el que la Tierra es el centro de los planetas y estrellas que giran alrededor de ella.

**geode** A hollow rock inside which mineral crystals have formed.
**geoda** Roca hueca dentro de la que se forman cristales minerales. (p. 76)

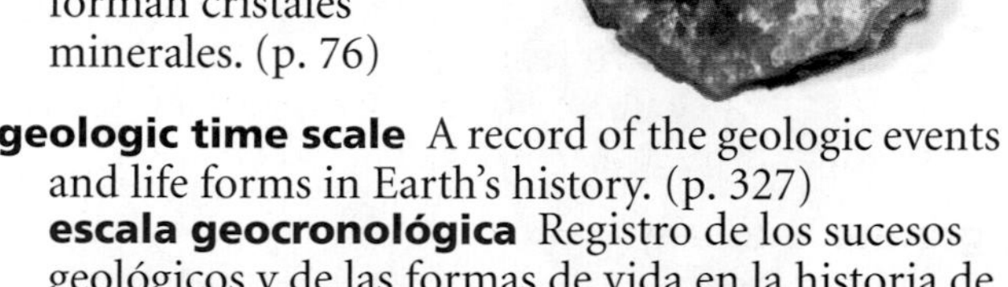

**geologic time scale** A record of the geologic events and life forms in Earth's history. (p. 327)
**escala geocronológica** Registro de los sucesos geológicos y de las formas de vida en la historia de la Tierra.

**geologist** A scientist who studies the forces that make and shape planet Earth. (p. 16)
**geólogo** Científico que estudia las fuerzas que crean y forman el planeta Tierra.

**geothermal activity** The heating of underground water by magma. (p. 222)
**actividad geotérmica** Calentamiento del agua subterránea por el magma.

**geothermal energy** Heat from Earth's interior.
**energía geotérmica** Calor del interior de la Tierra. (p. 366)

**geyser** A fountain of water and steam that builds up pressure underground and erupts at regular intervals. (pp. 223, 409)
**géiser** Fuente de agua y vapor que acumula presión subterránea y hace erupción a intervalos regulares.

**glacier** A large mass of moving ice and snow on land. (p. 292)
**glaciar** Gran masa de hielo y nieve que se mantiene en movimiento sobre la tierra.

**Global Positioning System** A method of finding latitude and longitude using a network of satellites. (p. 51)
**sistema de posicionamiento global** Método para hallar la latitud y longitud usando una red de satélites.

**global warming** A gradual increase in the temperature of Earth's atmosphere. (p. 643)
**calentamiento global** Aumento gradual en la temperatura promedio de la atmósfera terrestre.

**global winds** Winds that blow steadily from specific directions over long distances. (p. 555)
**vientos globales** Vientos que soplan constantemente desde direcciones específicas por largas distancias.

**globe** A sphere that represents Earth's entire surface.
**globo terráqueo** Esfera que representa toda la superficie de la Tierra. (p. 40)

**globular cluster** A large, round, densely-packed grouping of older stars. (p. 769)
**cúmulo globular** Conjunto grande y redondo de estrellas viejas densamente apretadas.

**grains** The particles of minerals or other rocks that give a rock its texture. (p. 96)
**granos** Partículas de minerales o de otras rocas que dan la textura a una roca.

**granite** A usually light-colored igneous rock that is found in continental crust. (pp. 95, 128)
**granito** Roca usualmente de color claro que se encuentra en la corteza continental.

**gravity** A force that moves rocks and other materials downhill; the force that pulls objects toward each other. (pp. 267, 666)
**gravedad** Fuerza que mueve rocas y otros materiales cuesta abajo; fuerza que atrae objectos entre sí.

**greenhouse effect** The process by which heat is trapped in the atmosphere by water vapor, carbon dioxide, methane, and other gases that form a "blanket" around Earth; the trapping of heat by a planet's atmosphere. (pp. 545, 715)
**efecto invernadero** Proceso por el cual el calor queda atrapado en la atmósfera por gases que forman una "manta" alrededor de la Tierra; acumulación de calor en la atmósfera de un planeta.

**greenhouse gases** Gases in the atmosphere, such as carbon dioxide, that trap solar energy. (p. 643)
**gases de invernadero** Gases de la atmósfera, como el dióxido de carbono, que atrapan la energía solar.

**groin** A wall made of rocks or concrete that is built outward from a beach to reduce erosion. (p. 441)
**escollera** Pared de piedra o concreto que se construye perpendicularmente a una playa para reducir la erosión.

**groundwater** Water that fills the cracks and spaces in underground soil and rock layers. (pp. 280, 395)
**aguas freáticas** Aguas que llenan las grietas y huecos de las capas subterráneas de tierra y roca.

**gully** A large channel in soil formed by erosion.
**barranco** Canal grande en el suelo, formado por la erosión. (p. 274)

## H

**habitat** The place where an organism lives and where it obtains all the things it needs to survive. (p. 399)
**hábitat** Lugar donde vive un organismo y donde obtiene todo lo que necesita para sobrevivir.

**half-life** The time it takes for half of the atoms of a radioactive element to decay. (p. 324)
**vida media** Tiempo que demoran en desintegrarse la mitad de los átomos de un elemento radiactivo.

**hanging wall** The block of rock that forms the upper half of a fault. (p. 164)
**labio superior** Bloque de roca que constituye la mitad superior de una falla.

**hardness** The level of the minerals calcium and magnesium in water. (p. 421)
**dureza** Cantidad de los minerales calcio y magnesio que contiene el agua.

**headland** A part of the shore that sticks out into the ocean. (p. 297)
**promontorio** Parte de la costa que se interna en el mar.

**heat** The transfer of thermal energy from one object to another because of a difference in temperature. (p. 550)
**calor** Transferencia de energía térmica de un objeto a otro debido a una diferencia de temperatura.

**heliocentric** A model of the solar system in which Earth and the other planets revolve around the sun. (p. 702)
**heliocéntrico** Modelo del sistema solar en el que la Tierra y otros planetas giran alrededor del Sol.

**hemisphere** One half of the sphere that makes up Earth's surface. (p. 42)
**hemisferio** La mitad de la esfera que forma la superficie de la Tierra.

**Hertzsprung-Russell diagram** A graph relating the surface temperatures and absolute brightnesses of stars. (p. 758)
**diagrama Hertzsprung-Russel** Gráfica que muestra la relación entre las temperaturas en la superficie de las estrellas y su magnitud absoluta.

**hot spot** An area where magma from deep within the mantle melts through the crust above it. (p. 203)
**punto caliente** Área por donde el magma de las profundidades del manto atraviesa la corteza.

**Hubble's law** The observation that the farther away a galaxy is, the faster it is moving away. (p. 775)
**ley de Hubble** Observación que enuncia que mientras más lejos de nosotros se encuentra una galaxia, más rápido se está alejando.

**humid subtropical** A wet and warm climate found on the edges of the tropics. (p. 630)
**subtropical húmedo** Clima húmedo y templado que se encuentra en los límites de los trópicos.

**humidity** The amount of water vapor in a given volume of air. (p. 561)
**humedad** Cantidad de vapor de agua en un volumen de aire definido.

**humus** Dark-colored organic material in soil. (p. 249)
**humus** Material orgánico de color oscuro en el suelo.

**hurricane** A tropical storm that has winds of about 119 kilometers per hour or higher. (p. 592)
**huracán** Tormenta tropical que tiene vientos de cerca de 119 kilómetros por hora o mayores.

**hydrocarbon** An energy-rich chemical compound that contains carbon and hydrogen atoms. (p. 356)
**hidrocarburo** Compuesto químico rico en energía que contiene átomos de carbono e hidrógeno.

**hydroelectric power** Electricity produced using the energy of flowing water. (p. 364)
**energía hidroeléctrica** Electricidad que se produce usando la energía de una corriente de agua.

**hydrothermal vent** An area where ocean water sinks through cracks in the ocean floor, is heated by the underlying magma, and rises again through the cracks. (p. 489)
**chimenea hidrotermal** Área en la que aguas oceánicas se cuelan por grietas del suelo oceánico, son calentadas por el magma subyacente y ascienden otra vez por las grietas.

**hypothesis** A possible explanation for a set of observations or answer to a scientific question; must be testable. (p. 8)
**hipótesis** Explicación posible para un conjunto de observaciones o respuesta a una pregunta científica; debe ser verificable.

## I

**ice age** Time in the past when continental glaciers covered large parts of Earth's surface.
**glaciación** Época del pasado en la que glaciares continentales cubrieron grandes extensiones de la superficie terrestre. (pp. 292, 638)

**ice wedging** Process that splits rock when water seeps into cracks, then freezes and expands. (p. 241)
**efecto cuña de hielo** Proceso que parte la roca cuando el agua penetra en las grietas, y luego se congela y expande.

**igneous rock** A type of rock that forms from the cooling of molten rock at or below the surface. (p. 97)
**roca ígnea** Tipo de roca que se forma cuando se enfrían las rocas fundidas en la superficie o debajo de la superficie.

**impermeable** A characteristic of materials, such as clay and granite, through which water does not easily pass. (p. 405)
**impermeable** Característica de los materiales, como la arcilla y el granito, que no dejan pasar fácilmente el agua.

**index contours** On a topographic map, a heavier contour line that is labeled with elevation of that contour line in round units. (p. 55)
**curva de nivel índice** En un mapa topográfico, una curva de nivel más gruesa que lleva rotulada la elevación de esa curva de nivel en unidades redondeadas.

**index fossil** Fossils of widely distributed organisms that lived during only one short period. (p. 320)
**fósil indicador** Fósiles de organismos ampliamente dispersos que vivieron durante un período corto.

**inertia** The tendency of an object to resist a change in motion. (p. 668)
**inercia** Tendencia de un objeto a resistir un cambio en su movimiento.

**inferring** The process of making an inference, an interpretation based on observations and prior knowledge. (p. 7)
**inferir** Proceso de realizar una inferencia; interpretación basada en observaciones y en el conocimiento previo.

**infrared radiation** Electromagnetic waves with wavelengths that are longer than visible light but shorter than microwaves. (p. 543)
**radiación infrarroja** Ondas electromagnéticas con longitudes de onda más largas que la luz visible, pero más cortas que las microondas.

**inner core** A dense sphere of solid iron and nickel at the center of Earth. (p. 130)
**núcleo interno** Densa esfera de hierro y níquel situada en el centro de la Tierra.

**inorganic** Not formed from living things or the remains of living things. (p. 67)
**inorgánico** Que no está formado de seres vivos o los restos de seres vivos.

**insulation** Material that blocks heat transfer between the air inside and outside a building. (p. 376)
**aislante** Material que impide la transferencia de calor entre el interior y el exterior de un edificio.

**intertidal zone** An area that stretches from the highest high-tide line on land out to the point on the continental shelf exposed by the lowest low tide. (p. 476)
**zona intermareal** Área que se extiende desde la línea más alta de pleamar en tierra hasta el punto de la plataforma continental expuesto por la bajamar más baja.

**intrusion** An igneous rock layer formed when magma hardens beneath Earth's surface. (p. 319)
**intrusión** Capa de roca ígnea formada cuando el magma se endurece bajo la superficie de la Tierra.

**intrusive rock** Igneous rock that forms when magma hardens beneath Earth's surface. (p. 99)
**roca intrusiva** Roca ígnea que se forma cuando el magma se endurece bajo la superficie de la Tierra.

**invertebrate** An animal without a backbone. (p. 335)
**invertebrado** Animal sin columna vertebral.

**ionosphere** The lower part of the thermosphere. (p. 527)
**ionosfera** Parte inferior de la termosfera.

**irregular galaxy** A galaxy that does not have a regular shape. (p. 770)
**galaxia irregular** Galaxia que no tiene una forma regular.

**irrigation** The process of supplying water to areas of land to make them suitable for growing crops. (p. 415)
**irrigación** Proceso mediante el cual se suministra agua a áreas de terreno para que pueda sembrarse en ellas.

**island arc** A string of islands formed by the volcanoes along a deep-ocean trench. (p. 202)
**arco de islas** Cadena de islas formadas por los volcanes que se encuentran a lo largo de una fosa oceánica profunda.

**isobar** A line on a weather map that joins places that have the same air pressure. (p. 602)
**isobara** Línea en un mapa del tiempo que une lugares que tienen la misma presión de aire.

**isotherm** A line on a weather map that joins places that have the same temperature. (p. 602)
**isoterma** Línea en un mapa del tiempo que une lugares que tienen la misma temperatura.

## J

**jet streams** Bands of high-speed winds about 10 kilometers above Earth's surface. (p. 558)
**corriente de chorro** Banda de vientos de alta velocidad a unos 10 kilómetros sobre la superficie de la Tierra.

## K

**karst topography** A region in which a layer of limestone close to the surface creates deep valleys, caverns and sinkholes. (p. 280)
**topografía kárstica** Región en la que una capa de piedra caliza cercana a la superficie forma valles profundos, grutas y dolinas.

**kettle** A small depression that forms when a chunk of ice is left in glacial till. (p. 294)
**marmita** Pequeña depresión que se forma cuando queda un trozo de hielo en la tillita.

**key** A list of the symbols used on a map. (p. 40)
**clave** Lista de símbolos usados en un mapa.

**kinetic energy** The energy an object has due to its motion. (p. 286)
**energía cinética** Energía que tiene un objeto por el hecho de estar en movimiento.

**Kuiper belt** A doughnut-shaped region that stretches from around Pluto's orbit to about 100 times Earth's distance from the sun. (p. 731)
**cinturón de Kuiper** Región en forma de disco que se extiende desde la órbita de Plutón hasta alrededor de 100 veces la distancia de la Tierra al Sol.

## L

**La Niña** A climate event in the eastern Pacific Ocean in which surface waters are colder than normal. (p. 642)
**La Niña** Fenómeno climático que ocurre en la parte este del océano Pacífico, en el cual las aguas superficiales están más frías que lo normal.

**land breeze** The flow of air from land to a body of water. (p. 554)
**brisa terrestre** Flujo de aire desde la tierra a una masa de agua.

**landform** A feature of topography formed by the processes that shape Earth's surface. (p. 35)
**accidente geográfico** Característica de la topografía creada por los procesos de formación de la superficie terrestre.

**landform region** A large area of land where the topography is similar. (p. 38)
**región con accidentes geográficos** Gran extensión de tierra con topografía similar.

**latitude** The distance in degrees north or south of the equator. (pp. 44, 556)
**latitud** Distancia en grados al norte o al sur del ecuador.

**lava** Liquid magma that reaches the surface; also, the rock formed when liquid lava hardens. (pp. 77, 200)
**lava** Magma líquida que sale a la superficie; también, la roca que se forma cuando la lava líquida se solidifica.

**lava flow** The area covered by lava as it pours out of a volcano's vent. (p. 210)
**colada de lava** Área cubierta de lava a medida que ésta sale por la boca del volcán.

**law of superposition** The geologic principle that states that in horizontal layers of sedimentary rock, each layer is older than the layer above it and younger than the layer below it. (p. 318)
**ley de la superposición** Principio geológico que enuncia que en las capas horizontales de la roca sedimentaria, cada capa es más vieja que la capa superior y más joven que la capa inferior.

**law of universal gravitation** The scientific law that states that every object in the universe attracts every other object. (p. 666)
**ley de la gravitación universal** Ley científica que establece que todos los objetos del universo se atraen entre ellos.

**leeward** The side of a mountain range that faces away from the oncoming wind. (p. 618)
**sotavento** Lado de una cadena montañosa que está resguardado del viento.

**lightning** A sudden spark, or energy discharge, caused when electrical charges jump between parts of a cloud, between nearby clouds, or between a cloud and the ground. (p. 587)
**rayo** Chispa repentina o descarga de energía causada por cargas eléctricas que saltan entre partes de una nube, entre nubes cercanas o entre una nube y la tierra.

**light-year** The distance that light travels in one year, about 9.5 million million kilometers. (p. 756)
**año luz** Distancia a la que viaja la luz en un año; alrededor de 9.5 millones de millones de kilómetros.

**liquefaction** The process by which an earthquake's violent movement suddenly turns loose soil into liquid mud. (p. 188)
**licuefacción** Proceso mediante el que las violentas sacudidas de un terremoto de pronto convierten la tierra suelta en lodo líquido.

**lithosphere** A rigid layer made up of the uppermost part of the mantle and the crust. (p. 129)
**litosfera** Capa rígida constituida por la parte superior del manto y la corteza.

**litter** The loose layer of dead plant leaves and stems on the surface of the soil. (p. 252)
**mantillo** Capa suelta de hojas y tallos de plantas muertas en la superficie del suelo.

**load** The amount of sediment that a river or stream carries. (p. 287)
**carga** La cantidad de sedimento que lleva un río o arroyo.

**loam** Rich, fertile soil that is made up of about equal parts of clay, sand, and silt. (p. 249)
**limo arcilloso arenoso** Suelo rico y fértil que está formado por partes casi iguales de arcilla, arena y limo.

**local winds** Winds that blow over short distances.
**vientos locales** Vientos que soplan por distancias cortas. (p. 554)

**loess** A wind-formed deposit made of fine particles of clay and silt. (p. 303)
**loes** Depósito de partículas finas de arcilla y limo arrastradas por el viento.

**longitude** The distance in degrees east or west of the prime meridian. (p. 44)
**longitud** Distancia en grados al este o al oeste del primer meridiano.

**longshore drift** The movement of water and sediment down a beach caused by waves coming in to shore at an angle. (pp. 299, 439)
**deriva litoral** Movimiento de agua y sedimentos paralelo a una playa debido a la llegada de olas inclinadas respecto a la costa.

**lunar eclipse** The blocking of sunlight to the moon that occurs when Earth is directly between the sun and the moon. (p. 675)
**eclipse lunar** Bloqueo de la luz solar sobre la Luna llena que ocurre cuando la Tierra se interpone entre el Sol y la Luna.

**luster** The way a mineral reflects light from its surface. (p. 69)
**brillo** La manera en la que un mineral refleja la luz en su superficie.

## M

**magma** The molten mixture of rock-forming substances, gases, and water from the mantle. (pp. 77, 200)
**magma** Mezcla fundida de las sustancias que forman las rocas, gases y agua, proveniente del manto.

**magma chamber** The pocket beneath a volcano where magma collects. (p. 210)
**cámara magmática** Bolsa debajo de un volcán en la que se acumula el magma.

**magnitude** The measurement of an earthquake's strength based on seismic waves and movement along faults. (p. 172)
**magnitud** Medida de la fuerza de un sismo basada en las ondas sísmicas y en el movimiento que ocurre a lo largo de las fallas.

**main sequence** A diagonal area on an H-R diagram that includes more than 90 percent of all stars. (p. 759)
**secuencia principal** Área diagonal en un diagrama de H-R que incluye más del 90 por ciento de todas las estrellas.

**mammal** A warm-blooded vertebrate that feeds its young milk. (p. 342)
**mamífero** Vertebrado de sangre caliente que alimenta con leche a su crías.

**manipulated variable** The one factor that a scientist changes during an experiment; also called independent variable. (p. 9)
**variable manipulada** Único factor que un científico cambia durante un experimento; también llamada variable independiente.

**mantle** The layer of hot, solid material between Earth's crust and core. (p. 129)
**manto** Capa de material caliente y sólido entre la corteza terrestre y el núcleo.

**map** A flat model of all or part of Earth's surface as seen from above. (p. 40)
**mapa** Modelo plano de toda la superficie de la Tierra o parte de ella tal y como se ve desde arriba.

**map projection** A framework of lines that helps to show landmasses on a flat surface. (p. 46)
**proyección cartográfica** Sistema de líneas que ayuda a mostrar volúmenes de tierra en una superficie plana.

**maria** Dark, flat areas on the moon's surface formed from huge ancient lava flows. (p. 681)
**maria** Áreas oscuras y llanas en la superficie de la Luna formadas por enormes flujos de lava antiguos.

**marine climate** The climate of some coastal regions, with relatively warm winters and cool summers. (p. 616)
**clima marino** Clima de algunas regiones costeras, con inviernos relativamente templados y veranos fríos.

**maritime (air mass)** A humid air mass that forms over oceans. (p. 579)
**masa de aire marítima** Masa de aire húmedo que se forma sobre los océanos.

**mass** The amount of matter in an object. (p. 667)
**masa** Cantidad de materia que hay en un objeto.

**mass extinction** When many types of living things become extinct at the same time. (p. 337)
**extinción en masa** Cuando muchos tipos de seres vivos se extinguen al mismo tiempo.

**mass movement** Any one of several processes by which gravity moves sediment downhill. (p. 267)
**movimiento de masas** Cualquiera de varios procesos por los cuales la gravedad desplaza sedimentos cuesta abajo.

**meander** A looplike bend in the course of a river. (p. 276)
**meandro** Curva muy pronunciada en el curso de un río.

**mechanical weathering** The type of weathering in which rock is physically broken into smaller pieces. (p. 240)
**desgaste mecánico** Tipo de desgaste en el cual una roca se rompe físicamente en trozos más pequeños.

**meltdown** A dangerous condition in which fuel rods inside a nuclear reactor melt. (p. 373)
**fusión (del núcleo de un reactor)** Condición peligrosa en la cual las varillas de combustible dentro del reactor nuclear se derriten.

**Mercalli scale** A scale that rates earthquakes according to their intensity and how much damage they cause at a particular place. (p. 172)
**escala de Mercalli** Escala con la que se miden los sismos basándose en la intensidad y el daño que ocasionan.

**mercury barometer** An instrument that measures changes in air pressure, consisting of a glass tube partially filled with mercury, with its open end resting in a dish of mercury. (p. 518)
**barómetro de mercurio** Instrumento que mide los cambios en la presión del aire; consiste de un tubo de vidrio parcialmente lleno de mercurio con su extremo abierto posado en un recipiente con mercurio.

**mesosphere** The layer of Earth's atmosphere immediately above the stratosphere. (p. 526)
**mesosfera** Capa de la atmósfera de la Tierra inmediatamente sobre la estratosfera.

**metamorphic rock** A type of rock that forms from an existing rock that is changed by heat, pressure, or chemical reactions. (p. 97)
**roca metamórfica** Tipo de roca que se forma cuando una roca es transformada por el calor, presión o reacciones químicas.

**meteor** A streak of light in the sky produced by the burning of a meteoroid in Earth's atmosphere. (p. 733)
**meteoro** Rayo de luz en el cielo producido por el incendio de un meteoroide en la atmósfera de la Tierra.

**meteorite** A meteoroid that passes through the atmosphere and hits Earth's surface. (p. 733)
**meteorito** Meteoroide que pasa por la atmósfera y golpea la superficie de la Tierra.

**meteoroid** A chunk of rock or dust in space. (pp. 681, 733)
**meteoroide** Pedazo de roca o polvo en el espacio.

**meteorologist** A scientist who studies the causes of weather and tries to predict it. (pp. 17, 599)
**meteorólogo** Científico que estudia las causas del tiempo e intentan predecirlo.

**microclimate** Climate conditions within a small area that differ from those in the surrounding area.
**microclima** Condiciones climáticas en una área pequeña que son diferentes del clima de las áreas de alrededor. (p. 614)

**mid-ocean ridge** An undersea mountain chain where new ocean floor is produced. (pp. 142, 475)
**dorsal oceánica** Cordillera montañosa submarina donde se produce nuevo suelo oceánico.

**mineral** A naturally occurring, inorganic solid that has a crystal structure and a definite chemical composition. (p. 66)
**mineral** Sólido inorgánico que ocurre en la naturaleza, de estructura cristalina y composición química definida.

**Mohs hardness scale** A scale ranking ten minerals from softest to hardest; used in testing the hardness of minerals. (p. 70)
**escala de dureza de Mohs** Escala en la que se clasifican diez minerales del más blando al más duro; se usa para probar la dureza de los minerales.

**mold** A fossil formed when an organism buried in sediment dissolves, leaving a hollow area. (p. 311)
**molde** Fósil que se forma cuando un organismo enterrado en sedimento se disuelve y deja un área hueca.

**moment magnitude scale** A scale that rates earthquakes by estimating the total energy released by an earthquake. (p. 173)
**escala de magnitud del momento** Escala con la que se miden los sismos estimando la cantidad total de energía liberada por un terremoto.

**monsoon** Sea or land breeze over a large region that changes direction with the seasons. (p. 619)
**monzón** Vientos marinos o terrestres que soplan sobre una extensa región y cambian de dirección según las estaciones.

**moraine** A ridge formed by the till deposited at the edge of a glacier. (p. 294)
**morrena** Montículo formado por la tillita depositada en el borde de un glaciar.

**mountain** A landform with high elevation and high relief. (p. 37)
**montaña** Accidente geográfico con una elevación alta y un relieve alto.

**mountain range** A series of mountains that have the same general shape and structure. (p. 37)
**cordillera** Serie de montañas que tienen la misma forma y estructura generales.

## N

**natural resource** Anything in the environment that humans use. (p. 257)
**recurso natural** Cualquier cosa de la naturaleza que usan los humanos.

**neap tide** A tide with the least difference between low and high tide that occurs when the sun and moon pull at right angles to each other at the first and third quarters of the moon. (pp. 444, 677)
**marea muerta** Marea con la mínima diferencia entre pleamar y bajamar; se presenta cuando el Sol y la Luna ejercen su atracción en direcciones que forman un ángulo recto, durante los cuartos creciente y menguante de la Luna.

**nebula** A large cloud of gas and dust in space, spread out in an immense volume. (p. 763)
**nebulosa** Gran nube de gas y polvo en el espacio, expandida en un volumen inmenso.

**nekton** Free-swimming animals that can move throughout the water column. (p. 479)
**necton** Animales que nadan libremente y pueden desplazarse por la columna de agua.

**neritic zone** The area of the ocean that extends from the low-tide line out to the edge of the continental shelf. (p. 476)
**zona nerítica** Área del océano que se extiende desde la línea de bajamar hasta el borde de la plataforma continental.

**neutron star** The small, dense remains of a high-mass star after a supernova. (p. 765)
**estrella de neutrones** Restos pequeños y densos de una estrella de gran masa después de una supernova.

**Newton's first law of motion** The scientific law that states that an object at rest will stay at rest and an object in motion will stay in motion with a constant speed and direction unless acted on by a force. (p. 668)
**primera ley de Newton del movimiento** Ley científica que establece que un objeto en reposo se mantendrá en reposo y un objeto en movimiento se mantendrá en movimiento con una velocidad y dirección constante a menos que se ejerza una fuerza sobre él.

**nodule** A lump on the ocean floor that forms when metals such as manganese build up around pieces of shell. (p. 494)
**nódulo** Protuberancia formada en el suelo oceánico cuando metales, como el manganeso, se depositan sobre pedazos de concha.

**nonpoint source** A widely spread source of pollution that is difficult to link to a specific point of origin. (p. 419)
**fuente dispersa** Fuente muy extendida de contaminación que es difícil vincular a un punto específico de origen.

**normal fault** A type of fault where the hanging wall slides downward; caused by tension in the crust. (p. 164)
**falla normal** Tipo de falla en la cual el labio superior se desliza hacia abajo como resultado de la tensión en la corteza.

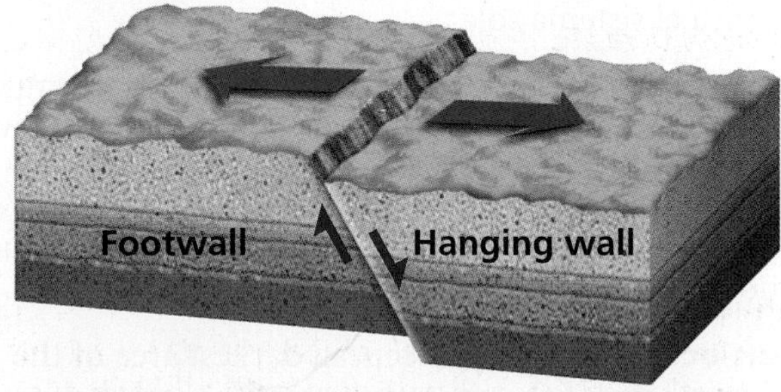


**nuclear fission** The splitting of an atom's nucleus into two smaller nuclei and neutrons. (p. 371)
**fisión nuclear** División del núcleo de un átomo en dos núcleos más pequeños y neutrones.

**nuclear fusion** The combining of two atomic nuclei to produce a single larger nucleus and much energy (p. 374); the process by which hydrogen atoms join together in the sun's core to form helium. (p. 707)
**fusión nuclear** Unión de dos núcleos atómicos para producir un núcleo único más grande y liberar energía; proceso por el cual los átomos de hidrógeno se unen en el núcleo del Sol para formar helio.

**nucleus** The central core of an atom that contains the protons and neutrons (p. 370); the solid inner core of a comet. (p. 731)
**núcleo** Parte central de un átomo, que contiene protones y neutrones; centro interno sólido de un cometa.

**observatory** A building that contains one or more telescopes. (p. 748)
**observatorio** Edificio que contiene uno o más telescopios.

**observing** The process of using one or more of your senses to gather information. (p. 7)
**observar** Proceso de usar uno o más de tus sentidos para reunir información.

**occluded** Cut off, as in a front where warm air mass is caught between two cooler air masses. (p. 583)
**ocluido** Aislado o cerrado, como cuando la masa de aire cálido queda atrapada entre dos masas de aire más frío.

**oceanographer** A scientist who studies Earth's oceans. (p. 16)
**oceanógrafo** Científico que estudia los océanos de la Tierra.

**Oort cloud** A spherical region of comets that surrounds the solar system. (p. 731)
**nube de Oort** Región esférica de cometas que rodea el sistema solar.

**open cluster** A star cluster that has a loose, disorganized appearance and contains no more than a few thousand stars. (p. 769)
**cúmulo abierto** Cúmulo de estrellas que tiene una apariencia no compacta y desorganizada, y que no contiene más de unos pocos miles de estrellas.

**open-ocean zone** The deepest, darkest area of the ocean beyond the edge of the continental shelf. (p. 476)
**zona de mar abierto** Zona más profunda y oscura del océano, más allá de la plataforma continental.

**optical telescope** A telescope that uses lenses or mirrors to collect and focus visible light. (p. 746)
**telescopio óptico** Telescopio que usa lentes o espejos para captar y enfocar la luz visible.

**orbit** The path of an object as it revolves around another object in space. (p. 661)
**órbita** Trayectoria de un objeto a medida que gira alrededor de otro en el espacio.

**orbital velocity** The velocity a rocket must achieve to establish an orbit around a body in space. (p. 685)
**velocidad orbital** Velocidad que un cohete debe alcanzar para establecer una órbita alrededor de un cuerpo en el espacio.

**ore** Rock that contains a metal or economically useful mineral. (p. 82)
**mena** Roca que contiene un metal o un mineral de importancia económica.

**organic rock** Sedimentary rock that forms from remains of organisms deposited in thick layers. (p. 104)
**roca orgánica** Roca sedimentaria que se forma cuando los restos de organismos se depositan en capas gruesas.

**outer core** A layer of molten iron and nickel that surrounds the inner core of Earth. (p. 130)
**núcleo externo** Capa de hierro y níquel fundidos que rodea el núcleo interno de la Tierra.

**oxbow lake** A meander cut off from a river. (p. 276)
**meandro abandonado** Meandro que ha quedado aislado de un río.

**oxidation** A chemical change in which a substance combines with oxygen, as when iron oxidizes, forming rust. (p. 243)
**oxidación** Cambio químico en el cual una sustancia se combina con el oxígeno, como cuando el hierro se oxida y se forma herrumbre.

**ozone** A form of oxygen that has three oxygen atoms in each molecule instead of the usual two. (p. 513)
**ozono** Forma de oxígeno que tiene tres átomos de oxígeno en cada molécula en vez de las dos normales.

**P wave** A type of seismic wave that compresses and expands the ground. (p. 171)
**onda P** Tipo de onda sísmica que comprime y expande el suelo.

**pahoehoe** A hot, fast-moving type of lava that hardens to form smooth, ropelike coils. (p. 208)
**pahoehoe** Tipo de lava caliente de movimiento muy veloz que al endurecerse forma espirales lisas en forma de cuerda.

**paleontologist** A scientist who studies fossils to learn about organisms that lived long ago. (p. 314)
**paleontólogo** Científico que estudia fósiles para aprender acerca de los organismos que vivieron hace mucho tiempo.

**Pangaea** The name of the single landmass that broke apart 200 million years ago and gave rise to today's continents. (p. 137)
**Pangea** Nombre de la masa terrestre única que se dividió hace 200 millones de años, dando origen a los continentes actuales.

**parallax** The apparent change in position of an object when seen from different places. (p. 756)
**paralaje** Cambio aparente en la posición de un objeto cuando es visto desde diferentes lugares.

**penumbra** The part of a shadow surrounding the darkest part. (p. 674)
**penumbra** Parte de una sombra que rodea la parte más oscura.

**period** One of the units of geologic time into which geologists divide eras. (p. 329)
**período** Una de las unidades del tiempo geológico dentro de las cuales los geólogos dividen las eras.

**permafrost** Permanently frozen soil found in the tundra climate region. (p. 632)
**permagélido** Suelo permanentemente helado que se encuentra en la región climática de la tundra.

**permeable** Characteristic of a material that is full of tiny, connected air spaces that water can seep through. (pp. 244, 405)
**permeable** Característica de un material que está lleno de diminutos espacios de aire conectados entre sí, por los que puede penetrar el agua.

**petrified fossil** A fossil in which minerals replace all or part of an organism. (p. 312)
**fósil petrificado** Fósil en el cual los minerales reemplazan todo el organismo o parte de él.

**petrochemical** A compound made from oil. (p. 358)
**petroquímico** Compuesto que se obtiene del petróleo.

**petroleum** Liquid fossil fuel; oil. (p. 358)
**petróleo** Combustible fósil líquido.

**pH** The measurement of how acidic or basic a substance is, on a scale of 0 (very acidic) to 14 (very basic). (p. 421)
**pH** Medida de qué tan ácida o básica es una sustancia, en una escala de 0 (muy ácida) a 14 (muy básica).

**phase** One of the different apparent shapes of the moon as seen from Earth. (p. 671)
**fase** Una de las diferentes formas aparentes de la Luna según se ve desde la Tierra.

**photochemical smog** A brownish haze that is a mixture of ozone and other chemicals, formed when pollutants react with each other in the presence of sunlight. (p. 530)
**neblina tóxica fotoquímica** Densa bruma parduscaque es una mezcla de ozono y otras sustancias químicas, que se forma cuando los contaminantes reaccionan entre ellos en presencia de luz solar.

**photosphere** The inner layer of the sun's atmosphere that gives off its visible light; the sun's surface. (p. 708)
**fotosfera** Capa más interna de la atmósfera del Sol que provoca la luz que vemos; superficie del Sol.

**physical property** Any characteristic of a substance that can be observed or measured without changing the composition of the substance. (p. 206)
**propiedad física** Cualquier característica de una sustancia que se puede observar o medir sin que cambie la composición de la misma.

**pipe** A long tube through which magma moves from the magma chamber to Earth's surface. (p. 210)
**chimenea** Largo tubo por el que el magma sube desde la cámara magmática hasta la superficie.

**pixels** The tiny dots in a satellite image. (p. 50)
**píxeles** Puntos diminutos en una imagen de satélite.

**plain** A landform made up of flat or gently rolling land with low relief. (p. 36)
**llanura** Accidente geográfico que consiste en un terreno plano o ligeramente ondulado con un relieve bajo.

**planetesimal** One of the small asteroid-like bodies that formed the building blocks of the planets. (p. 777)
**planetésimo** Uno de los cuerpos pequeños parecidos a asteroides que dieron origen a los planetas.

**plankton** Tiny algae and animals that float in water and are carried by waves and currents. (p. 479)
**plancton** Algas y animales diminutos que flotan en el agua a merced de las olas y las corrientes.

**plate** A section of the lithosphere that slowly moves over the asthenosphere, carrying pieces of continental and oceanic crust. (p. 150)
**placa** Sección de la litosfera que se desplaza lentamente sobre la astenosfera, llevando consigo trozos de la corteza continental y de la oceánica.

**plate tectonics** The theory that pieces of Earth's lithosphere are in constant motion, driven by convection currents in the mantle. (p. 151)
**tectónica de placas** Teoría según la cual las partes de la litosfera de la Tierra están en continuo movimiento, impulsadas por las corrientes de convección del manto.

**plateau** A landform that has high elevation and a more or less level surface. (pp. 37, 168)
**meseta** Accidente geográfico que tiene una elevación alta y cuya superficie está más o menos nivelada.

**plucking** The process by which a glacier picks up rocks as it flows over the land. (p. 293)
**arranque glaciar** Proceso por el cual un glaciar arranca rocas al fluir sobre la tierra.

**point source** A specific source of pollution that can be identified. (p. 419)
**fuente localizada** Fuente específica de contaminación que puede identificarse.

**polar (air mass)** A cold air mass that forms north of 50° north latitude or south of 50° south latitude and has high air pressure. (p. 579)
**masa de aire polar** Masa de aire frío que se forma al norte de los 50° de latitud norte o al sur de los 50° de latitud sur y que tiene presión alta.

**polar zone** The areas near both poles, from about 66.5° to 90° north and 66.5° to 90° south latitudes. (p. 615)
**zona polar** Áreas cercana a los polos, desde unos 66.5° a 90° de latitud norte y 66.5° a 90° de latitud sur.

**pollutant** A harmful substance in the air, water, or soil. (p. 528)
**contaminante** Sustancia dañina en el aire, agua o suelo.

**potential energy** Energy that is stored and available to be used later. (p. 286)
**energía potencial** Energía que se encuentra almacenada y puede utilizarse posteriormente.

**precipitation** Any form of water that falls from clouds and reaches Earth's surface. (pp. 393, 567)
**precipitación** Cualquier forma de agua que cae desde las nubes y llega a la superficie de la Tierra.

**predicting** The process of forecasting what will happen in the future based on past experience or evidence. (p. 7)
**predecir** Proceso de pronosticar lo que va a suceder en el futuro, basado en la experiencia pasada o en evidencia.

**pressure** The force exerted on a surface divided by the total area over which the force is exerted. (pp. 127, 517)
**presión** Fuerza ejercida sobre una superficie dividida por el área total sobre la cual se ejerce la fuerza.

**prime meridian** The line that makes a half circle from the North Pole to the South Pole and that passes through Greenwich, England. (p. 43)
**primer meridiano** Línea que forma medio círculo desde el Polo Norte al Polo Sur y que pasa por Greenwich, Inglaterra.

**prominence** A huge, reddish loop of gas that protrudes from the sun's surface, linking parts of sunspot regions. (p. 710)
**protuberancia solar** Enorme arco rojizo de gas que sobresale de la superfice del Sol, que une partes de las regiones de las manchas solares.

**protostar** A contracting cloud of gas and dust with enough mass to form a star. (p. 763)
**protoestrella** Nube de gas y polvo que se contrae, con suficiente masa como para formar una estrella.

**psychrometer** An instrument used to measure relative humidity, consisting of a wet-bulb thermometer and a dry-bulb thermometer. (p. 562)
**psicrómetro** Instrumento que se usa para medir la humedad relativa y que consiste de un termómetro de bulbo húmedo y de un termómetro de bulbo seco.

**pulsar** A rapidly spinning neutron star that produces radio waves. (p. 765)
**púlsar** Estrella de neutrones que gira rápidamente y produce ondas de radio.

**pyroclastic flow** The expulsion of ash, cinders, bombs, and gases during an explosive volcanic eruption. (p. 213)
**flujo piroclástico** Emisión de ceniza, escoria, bombas y gases durante una erupción volcánica explosiva.

## Q

**quasar** An enormously bright, distant galaxy with a giant black hole at its center. (p. 770)
**quásar** Galaxia extraordinariamente luminosa y distante con un agujero negro gigante en el centro.

## R

**radiation** The direct transfer of energy through space by electromagnetic waves. (pp. 133, 542)
**radiación** Transferencia directa de energía a través del espacio por ondas electromagnéticas.

**radiation zone** A region of very tightly packed gas in the sun's interior where energy is transferred mainly in the form of light. (p. 707)
**zona radiactiva** Región de gases estrechamente comprimidos en el interior del Sol en donde se transfiere la energía principalmente en forma de luz.

**radio telescope** A device used to detect radio waves from objects in space. (p. 747)
**radiotelescopio** Aparato usado para detectar ondas de radio de los objetos en el espacio.

**radioactive decay** The breakdown of a radioactive element, releasing particles and energy. (p. 324)
**desintegración radiactiva** Descomposición de un elemento radiactivo que libera partículas y energía.

**rain forest** A forest in the tropical wet climate zone in which large amounts of rain fall year-round.
**bosque tropical** Selva ubicada dentro de la zona de clima tropical húmedo en la cual caen grandes cantidades de lluvia todo el año. (p. 625)

**rain gauge** An instrument used to measure precipitation. (p. 571)
**pluviómetro** Instrumento que se usa para medir la precipitación.

**reactor vessel** The part of a nuclear reactor where nuclear fission occurs. (p. 372)
**cuba de reactor** Parte de un reactor nuclear donde ocurre la fisión nuclear.

**refinery** A factory in which crude oil is heated and separated into fuels and other products. (p. 358)
**refinería** Planta en la que el petróleo crudo se calienta y fracciona en combustibles y otros productos.

**reflecting telescope** A telescope that uses a curved mirror to collect and focus light. (p. 747)
**telescopio reflector** Telescopio que usa un espejo curvado para captar y enfocar la luz.

**refracting telescope** A telescope that uses convex lenses to gather and focus light. (p. 746)
**telescopio refractor** Telescopio que usa lentes convexas para captar y enfocar la luz.

**relative age** The age of a rock compared to the ages of rock layers. (p. 317)
**edad relativa** Edad de una roca comparada con la edad de las capas de roca.

**relative humidity** The percentage of water vapor in the air compared to the maximum amount of water vapor that air can contain at a particular temperature. (p. 561)
**humedad relativa** Porcentaje de vapor de agua en el aire comparado con la cantidad máxima de vapor de agua que puede contener el aire a una temperatura particular.

**relief** The difference in elevation between the highest and lowest parts of an area. (p. 35)
**relieve** Diferencia en la elevación entre las partes más altas y más bajas en un área.

**reptile** A vertebrate with scaly skin that lays eggs with tough, leathery shells. (p. 336)
**reptil** Vertebrado con piel de escamas que pone huevos de cascarón duro y correoso.

**reservoir** A lake that stores water for human use. (p. 400)
**embalse** Lago en el que se almacena agua para uso humano.

**responding variable** The factor that changes as a result of changes to the manipulated, or independent, variable in an experiment; also called dependent variable. (p. 9)
**variable respuesta** Factor que cambia como resultado de cambios a la variable manipulada, o independiente, en un experimento; también llamada variable dependiente.

**reverse fault** A type of fault where the hanging wall slides upward; caused by compression in the crust. (p. 165)
**falla inversa** Tipo de falla en la cual el labio superior se desliza hacia arriba como resultado de compresión en la corteza.

**revolution** The movement of an object around another object. (p. 661)
**revolución** Movimiento de un objeto alrededor de otro.

**Richter scale** A scale that rates an earthquake's magnitude based on the size of its seismic waves. (p. 172)
**escala de Richter** Escala con la que se mide la magnitud de un terremoto basándose en el tamaño de sus ondas sísmicas.

**rift valley** A deep valley that forms where two plates move apart. (p. 152)
**valle de fisura** Valle profundo que se forma cuando dos placas se separan.

**rill** A tiny groove in soil made by flowing water. (p. 274)
**arroyuelo** Pequeño surco en el suelo que deja el agua al fluir.

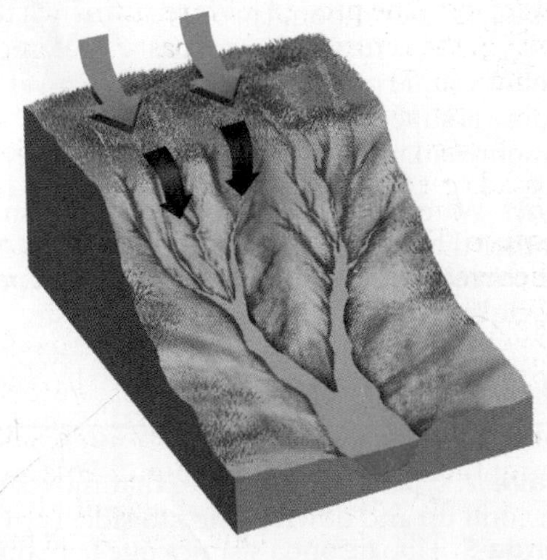

**ring** A thin disk of small ice and rock particles surrounding a planet. (p. 721)
**anillo** Disco fino de pequeñas partículas de hielo y roca que rodea un planeta.

**Ring of Fire** A major belt of volcanoes that rims the Pacific Ocean. (p. 201)
**Cinturón de Fuego** Gran cadena de volcanes que rodea el océano Pacífico.

**rip current** A rush of water that flows rapidly back to sea through a narrow opening in a sandbar. (p. 439)
**corriente de resaca** Torrente de agua que fluye con fuerza desde una playa hacia mar adentro por un canal estrecho en un banco de arena.

**rock cycle** A series of processes on the surface and inside Earth that slowly changes rocks from one kind to another. (p. 114)
**ciclo de las rocas** Serie de processos en la superficie y dentro de la Tierra que lentamente transforman las rocas de un tipo de roca a otro.

**rocket** A device that expels gas in one direction to move in the opposite direction. (p. 684)
**cohete** Aparato que expulsa gas en una dirección para moverse en la dirección opuesta.

**rock-forming minerals** The common minerals that make up most of the rocks of Earth's crust. (p. 95)
**minerales formadores de rocas** Los minerales comunes de los que están compuestas la mayoría de las rocas de la corteza de la Tierra.

**rotation** The spinning motion of a planet on its axis. (p. 661)
**rotación** Movimiento giratorio de un planeta sobre su eje.

**rover** A small robotic space probe that can move about the surface of a planet or moon. (p. 691)
**róver** Pequeña sonda espacial robótica que puede moverse sobre la superficie de un planeta o sobre la Luna.

**runoff** Water that flows over the ground surface rather than soaking into the ground. (p. 273)
**escorrentía** Agua que fluye sobre la superficie del suelo en lugar de ser absorbida por éste.

## S

**S wave** A type of seismic wave that moves the ground up and down or side to side. (p. 171)
**onda S** Tipo de onda sísmica que hace que el suelo se mueva de arriba abajo, o de lado a lado.

**salinity** The total amount of dissolved salts in a water sample. (p. 449)
**salinidad** Cantidad total de sales disueltas en una muestra de agua.

**sand dune** A deposit of wind-blown sand. (p. 301)
**duna de arena** Depósito de arena arrastrada por el viento.

**satellite** An object that revolves around another object in space. (p. 688)
**satélite** Objeto que gira alrededor de otro objeto en el espacio.

**satellite images** Pictures of the land surface based on computer data collected from satellites. (p. 50)
**imágenes satelitales** Fotografías de la superficie terrestre basadas en información computarizada reunida por satélites.

**saturated zone** A layer of permeable rock or soil in which the cracks and pores are totally filled with water. (p. 405)
**zona saturada** Capa de roca o suelo permeable cuyas grietas y poros están totalmente llenos de agua.

**savanna** A tropical grassland with scattered clumps of trees. (p. 625)
**sabana** Pradera tropical con grupos de árboles.

**scale** Used to compare distance on a map or globe to distance on Earth's surface. (p. 40)
**escala** Se usa para comparar la distancia en un mapa o globo terráqueo con la distancia en la superficie de la Tierra.

**scattering** Reflection of light in all directions. (p. 544)
**dispersión** Reflexión de la luz en todas las direcciones.

**science** A way of learning about the natural world through observations and logical reasoning; leads to a body of knowledge. (p. 6)
**ciencia** Método para aprender acerca del mundo natural a través de observaciones y del razonamiento lógico; conduce a un conjunto de conocimientos.

**scientific inquiry** The ongoing process of discovery in science; the diverse ways in which scientists study the natural world and propose explanations based on evidence they gather. (p. 8)
**investigación científica** Proceso continuo de descubrimiento en la ciencia; diversidad de métodos con los que los científicos estudian el mundo natural y proponen explicaciones del mismo basadas en la evidencia que reúnen.

**scientific law** A statement that describes what scientists expect to happen every time under a particular set of conditions. (p. 12)
**ley científica** Enunciado que describe lo que los científicos esperan que suceda cada vez que se da una serie de condiciones determinadas.

**scientific notation** A mathematical method of writing numbers using powers of ten. (p. 772)
**notación científica** Método matemático de escritura de números que usa la potencia de diez.

**scientific theory** A well-tested concept that explains a wide range of observations. (pp. 12, 150, 316)
**teoría científica** Concepto bien comprobado que explica un amplia gama de observaciones.

**sea breeze** The flow of cooler air from over an ocean or lake toward land. (p. 554)
**brisa marina** Flujo de aire más frío desde un océano o lago hacia la costa.

**sea-floor spreading** The process by which molten material adds new oceanic crust to the ocean floor. (p. 143)
**expansión del suelo oceánico** Proceso mediante el cual la materia fundida añade nueva corteza oceánica al suelo oceánico.

**sediment** Small, solid pieces of material that come from rocks or organisms; earth materials deposited by erosion. (pp. 102, 267)
**sedimento** Partículas sólidas de materiales que provienen de rocas u organismos; materiales terrestres depositados por la erosión.

**sedimentary rock** A type of rock that forms when particles from other rocks or the remains of plants and animals are pressed and cemented together. (pp. 97, 310)
**roca sedimentaria** Tipo de roca que se forma cuando las partículas de otras rocas o los restos de plantas y animales son presionados y cementados.

**seismic waves** Vibrations that travel through Earth carrying the energy released during an earthquake. (p. 126)
**ondas sísmicas** Vibraciones que se desplazan por la Tierra, llevando la energía liberada durante un terremoto.

**seismogram** The record of an earthquake's seismic waves produced by a seismograph. (p. 179)
**sismograma** Registro producido por un sismógrafo de las ondas sísimicas de un terremoto.

**seismograph** A device that records ground movements caused by seismic waves as they move through Earth. (p. 172)
**sismógrafo** Aparato con el que se registran los movimientos del suelo ocasionados por las ondas sísmicas a medida que éstas se desplazan por la Tierra.

**shearing** Stress that pushes masses of rock in opposite directions, in a sideways movement. (p. 163)
**cizallamiento** Esfuerzo que presiona masas de roca en sentidos opuestos.

**shield volcano** A wide, gently sloping mountain made of layers of lava and formed by quiet eruptions. (p. 218)
**volcán en escudo** Montaña ancha de pendientes suaves, compuesta por capas de lava y formada durante erupciones no violentas.

**silica** A material found in magma that is formed from the elements oxygen and silicon. (pp. 100, 207)
**sílice** Material presente en el magma, compuesto por los elementos oxígeno y silicio.

**sill** A slab of volcanic rock formed when magma squeezes between layers of rock. (p. 221)
**dique concordante** Placa de roca volcánica formada cuando el magma se mete entre las capas de roca.

**smelting** The process by which ore is melted to separate the useful metal from other elements. (p. 84)
**fundición** Proceso mediante el que una mena se funde para separar el mineral útil de otros elementos.

**sod** A thick mass of grass roots and soil. (p. 256)
**tepe** Masa gruesa de raíces de hierbas y suelo.

**soil** The loose, weathered material on Earth's surface in which plants can grow. (p. 248)
**suelo** Material suelto y desgastado sobre la superficie de la Tierra en donde crecen las plantas.

**soil conservation** The management of soil to prevent its destruction. (p. 259)
**conservación del suelo** Cuidado del suelo para prevenir su destrucción.

**soil horizon** The layer of soil that differs in color and texture from the layers above or below it. (p. 250)
**horizonte de suelo** Capa de suelo que se diferencia en color y textura de las capas que tiene encima o debajo.

**solar eclipse** The blocking of sunlight to Earth that occurs when the moon is directly between the sun and Earth. (p. 674)
**eclipse solar** Bloqueo de la luz solar en su camino a la Tierra que ocurre cuando la Luna se interpone entre el Sol y la Tierra.

**solar energy** Energy from the sun. (p. 362)
**energía solar** Energía del Sol.

**solar flare** An eruption of gas from the sun's surface that occurs when the loops in sunspot regions suddenly connect. (p. 710)
**fulguración solar** Erupción de gas desde la superficie del Sol que ocurre cuando los arcos en las regiones de las manchas solares se unen repentinamente.

**solar nebula** A large cloud of gas and dust such as the one that formed our solar system. (p. 777)
**nebulosa solar** Gran nube de gas y polvo como de la que formo nuestro sistema solar.

**solar wind** A stream of electrically charged particles that emanates from the sun's corona. (p. 708)
**viento solar** Flujo de partículas cargadas eléctricamente que emanan de la corona del Sol.

**solstice** The two days of the year on which the sun reaches its greatest distance north or south of the equator. (p. 664)
**solsticio** Los dos días del año en que el Sol está a mayor distancia hacia el norte o hacia el sur del ecuador.

**solution** A mixture in which one substance is dissolved in another. (p. 77)
**solución** Mezcla en la que una substancia se halla disuelta en otra.

**sonar** A device that determines the distance of an object under water by recording echoes of sound waves. (pp. 142, 473)
**sonar** Aparato con el cual se determina la distancia de un objeto sumergido en el agua mediante el registro del eco de las ondas sonoras.

**space probe** A spacecraft that has various scientific instruments that can collect data, including visual images, but has no human crew. (p. 691)
**sonda espacial** Nave espacial que tiene varios instrumentos científicos que pueden reunir datos, incluyendo imágenes, pero que no lleva tripulación.

**space shuttle** A spacecraft that can carry a crew into space, return to Earth, and then be reused for the same purpose. (p. 690)
**transbordador espacial** Nave espacial que puede llevar a una tripulación al espacio, volver a la Tierra, y luego volver a ser usada para el mismo propósito.

**space station** A large artificial satellite on which people can live and work for long periods. (p. 690)
**estación espacial** Enorme satélite artificial en el que la gente puede vivir y trabajar durante largos períodos.

**spectrograph** An instrument that separates light into colors and makes an image of the resulting spectrum. (p. 754)
**espectrógrafo** Instrumento que separa la luz en colores y crea una imagen del espectro resultante.

**spectrum** The range of wavelengths of electromagnetic waves. (p. 745)
**espectro** Gama de longitudes de ondas electromagnéticas.

**spiral galaxy** A galaxy with a bulge in the middle and arms that spiral outward in a pinwheel pattern. (p. 770)
**galaxia espiral** Galaxia con una protuberancia en el centro y brazos que giran en espiral hacia el exterior, como un remolino.

**spit** A beach formed by longshore drift that projects like a finger out into the water. (p. 300)
**banco de arena** Playa formada por la deriva litoral; que se interna como un dedo dentro del agua.

**spring** A place where groundwater flows to the surface. (p. 406)
**manantial** Lugar donde las aguas freáticas fluyen a la superficie.

**spring tide** A tide with the greatest difference between high and low tide that occurs when the sun and the moon are aligned with Earth at the new moon and the full moon. (pp. 444, 677)
**marea viva** Marea que presenta la mayor diferencia entre pleamar y bajamar; se presenta cuando el Sol y la Luna están alineados con la Tierra en la luna nueva y la luna llena.

**stalactite** A calcite deposit that hangs from the roof of a cave. (p. 280)
**estalactita** Depósito de calcita que cuelga del techo de una gruta.

**stalagmite** A cone-shaped calcite deposit that builds up from the floor of a cave. (p. 280)
**estalagmita** Depósito cónico de calcita que se forma en el piso de una gruta.

**steppe** A prairie or grassland found in the semiarid climate region. (p. 628)
**estepa** Pradera o pastizal que se encuentra en las regiones semiáridas.

**storm** A violent disturbance in the atmosphere. (p. 586)
**tormenta** Alteración violenta en la atmósfera.

**storm surge** A "dome" of water that sweeps across the coast where a hurricane lands. (p. 593)
**marejadas** "Cúpula" de agua que se desplaza a lo largo de la costa donde aterriza un huracán.

**stratosphere** The second-lowest layer of Earth's atmosphere. (p. 525)
**estratosfera** Segunda capa inferior de la atmósfera de la Tierra.

**stratus** Clouds that form in flat layers and often cover much of the sky. (p. 564)
**estratos** Nubes que forman capas planas y que a menudo cubren gran parte del cielo.

**streak** The color of a mineral's powder. (p. 69)
**raya** El color del polvo de un mineral.

**stream** A channel through which water is continually flowing downhill. (p. 274)
**arroyo** Canal por el cual fluye continuamente agua cuesta abajo.

**stress** A force that acts on rock to change its shape or volume. (p. 162)
**esfuerzo** Fuerza que al actuar sobre una roca cambia su forma o volumen.

**strike-slip fault** A type of fault where rocks on either side move past each other sideways with little up-or-down motion. (p. 165)
**falla transcurrente** Tipo de falla en la cual las rocas a ambos lados se deslizan horizontalmente en sentidos opuestos, con poco desplazamiento hacia arriba o abajo.

**subarctic** A climate zone that lies north of the humid continental climates, with short, cool summers and long, cold winters. (p. 631)
**subártico** Zona climática que se encuentra al norte de los climas continentales húmedos.

**subduction** The process by which oceanic crust sinks beneath a deep-ocean trench and back into the mantle at a convergent plate boundary. (p. 146)
**subducción** Proceso mediante el cual la corteza oceánica se hunde debajo de una fosa oceánica profunda y vuelve al manto por el borde de una placa convergente.

**submersible** An underwater vehicle built of strong materials to resist pressure. (p. 453)
**sumergible** Vehículo submarino de materiales fuertes para resistir la presión.

**subsoil** The layer of soil beneath the topsoil that contains mostly clay and other minerals. (p. 250)
**subsuelo** Capa del suelo bajo el suelo superior que contiene principalmente arcilla y otros minerales.

**sunspot** A dark area of gas on the sun's surface that is cooler than surrounding gases. (pp. 639, 708)
**mancha solar** Área oscura de gas en la superficie del Sol, que está más fría que los gases que la rodean.

**supernova** The brilliant explosion of a dying supergiant star. (p. 765)
**supernova** Explosión brillante de una estrella supergigante en extinción.

**surface wave** A type of seismic wave that forms when P waves and S waves reach Earth's surface. (p. 171)
**onda superficial** Tipo de onda sísmica que se forma cuando las ondas P y las ondas S llegan a la superficie de la Tierra.

**surveying** The process of gathering data for a map by using instruments and the principles of geometry to determine distance and elevations. (p. 49)
**agrimensura** Proceso de reunir información para un mapa usando instrumentos y los principios de geometría para determinar distancias y elevaciones.

**symbol** On a map, pictures used by mapmakers to stand for features on Earth's surface. (p. 40)
**símbolos** En un mapa, los dibujos que usan los cartógrafos para representar características de la superficie de la Tierra.

**syncline** A downward fold in rock formed by compression in Earth's crust. (p. 166)
**sinclinal** Pliegue de la roca hacia abajo ocasionado por la compresión de la corteza terrestre.

**system** A group of related parts that work together. (p. 15)
**sistema** Grupo de partes relacionadas que funcionan en conjunto.

## T

**technology** How people modify the world around them to meet their needs or to solve practical problems. (p. 20)
**tecnología** Cómo la gente modifica el mundo que la rodea para satisfacer sus necesidades o para solucionar problemas prácticos.

**telescope** A device built to observe distant objects by making them appear closer. (pp. 680, 744)
**telescopio** Aparato construido para observar objetos distantes que hace que aparezcan más cercanos.

**temperate zones** The areas between the tropical and the polar zones, from about 23.5° to 66.5° north and 23.5° to 66.5° south latitude. (p. 615)
**zonas templadas** Áreas entre las zonas tropicales y polares, que se encuentran entre 23.5° a 66.5° latitud norte y 23.5° a 66.5° latitud sur.

**temperature** A measure of how hot or cold an object is compared to a reference point. (p. 549)
**temperatura** Medida de lo caliente o frío que está un objeto comparado con un punto de referencia.

**tension** Stress that stretches rock so that it becomes thinner in the middle. (p. 163)
**tensión** Esfuerzo que estira una roca, haciéndola más delgada en el centro.

**terrestrial planets** The name often given to the four inner planets: Mercury, Venus, Earth, and Mars. (p. 712)
**planetas telúricos** Nombre dado normalmente a los cuatro planetas interiores: Mercurio, Venus, Tierra y Marte.

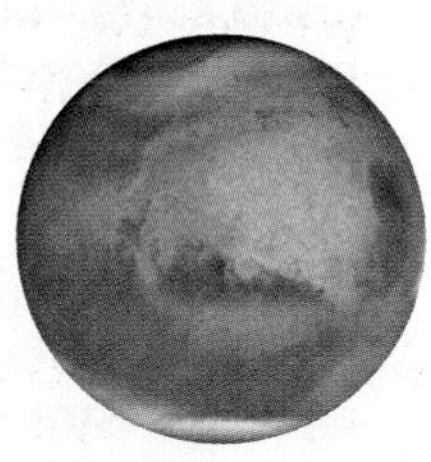

**texture** The look and feel of a rock's surface, determined by the size, shape, and pattern of a rock's grains. (p. 96)
**textura** Apariencia y sensación producida por la superficie de una roca, determinadas por el tamaño, forma y patrón de los granos de la roca.

**thermal energy** The total energy of motion in the particles of a substance. (p. 549)
**energía térmica** Energía de movimiento total en las partículas de una sustancia.

**thermometer** An instrument used to measure temperature, consisting of a thin glass tube with a bulb on one end that contains a liquid (usually mercury or alcohol). (p. 549)
**termómetro** Instrumento que se usa para medir la temperatura; consiste en un tubo de fino vidrio con un bulbo en un extremo que contiene un líquido (normalmente mercurio o alcohol).

**thermosphere** The outermost layer of Earth's atmosphere. (p. 526)
**termosfera** Capa exterior de la atmósfera de la Tierra.

**thrust** The reaction force that propels a rocket forward. (p. 685)
**empuje** Fuerza de reacción que propulsa un cohete hacia delante.

**thunderstorm** A small storm often accompanied by heavy precipitation and frequent thunder and lightning. (p. 587)
**tronada** Pequeña tormenta acompañada de fuerte precipitación y frecuentes rayos y truenos.

**tides** The daily rise and fall of Earth's waters on its coastlines. (pp. 443, 676)
**mareas** Ascenso y descenso diario de las aguas de la Tierra en las costas.

**till** The sediments deposited directly by a glacier. (p. 294)
**tillita** Sedimentos depositados directamente por un glaciar.

**topographic map** A map that shows the surface features of an area. (p. 55)
**mapa topográfico** Mapa que muestra los accidentes geográficos de la superficie terrestre de un área.

**topography** The shape of the land determined by elevation, relief, and landforms. (p. 34)
**topografía** Forma del terreno determinada por la elevación, el relieve y los accidentes geográficos.

**topsoil** Mixture of humus, clay, and other minerals that forms the crumbly, topmost layer of soil. (p. 250)
**suelo superior** Mezcla de humus, arcilla y otros minerales que forman la capa superior y suelta del suelo.

**tornado** A rapidly whirling, funnel-shaped cloud that reaches down from a storm cloud to touch Earth's surface. (p. 588)
**tornado** Nube con forma de embudo que gira rápidamente y que desciende hasta la superficie terrestre.

**trace fossil** A type of fossil that provides evidence of the activities of ancient organisms. (p. 312)
**vestigios fósiles** Tipo de fósil que da evidencia de las actividades de los organismos antiguos.

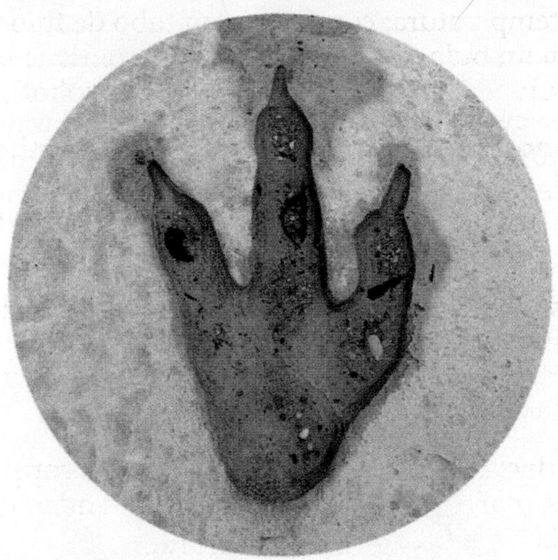

**transform boundary** A plate boundary where two plates move past each other in opposite directions. (p. 153)
**borde de transformación** Borde de placa donde dos placas se deslizan una respecto a la otra, pero en sentidos opuestos.

**trench** A deep, steep-sided canyon in the ocean floor. (p. 475)
**fosa** Cañón profundo, de lados empinados, en el suelo oceánico.

**tributary** A stream or smaller river that feeds into a main river. (pp. 274, 397)
**afluente** Arroyo o río más pequeño que desemboca en un río principal.

**tropical (air mass)** A warm air mass that forms in the tropics and has low air pressure. (p. 579)
**masa de aire tropical** Masa de aire templado que se forma en los trópicos y tiene presión baja.

**tropical zone** The area near the equator, between about 23.5° north latitude and 23.5° south latitude. (p. 615)
**zona tropical** Área cercana al ecuador, entre aproximadamente los 23.5° de latitud norte y los 23.5° de latitud sur.

**troposphere** The lowest layer of Earth's atmosphere. (p. 524)
**troposfera** Capa más inferior de la atmósfera de la Tierra.

**tsunami** A giant wave usually caused by an earthquake beneath the ocean floor. (pp. 189, 438)
**tsunami** Ola gigantesca, casi siempre causada por un sismo bajo el suelo oceánico.

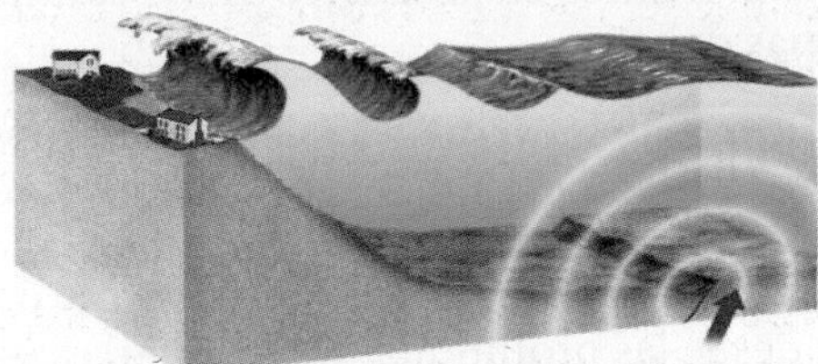

**tundra** A polar climate region, found across northern Alaska, Canada, and Russia, with short, cool summers and bitterly cold winters. (p. 632)
**tundra** Región climática polar que se encuentra en el norte de Alaska, Canadá y Rusia, que tiene veranos cortos y fríos, e inviernos extremadamente fríos.

**turbulence** A type of movement of water in which, rather than moving downstream, the water moves every which way. (p. 289)
**turbulencia** Tipo de movimiento del agua en el que, en vez de moverse corriente abajo, el agua se mueve en todas direcciones.

## U

**ultraviolet radiation** Electromagnetic waves with wavelengths that are shorter than visible light but longer than X-rays. (p. 543)
**radiación ultravioleta** Ondas electromagnéticas con longitudes de onda más cortas que la luz visible, pero más largas que los rayos X.

**umbra** The darkest part of a shadow. (p. 674)
**umbra** La parte más oscura de una sombra.

**unconformity** A place where an old, eroded rock surface is in contact with a newer rock layer. (p. 320)
**discordancia** Lugar donde una superficie rocosa erosionada y vieja está en contacto con una capa de rocas más nueva.

**uniformitarianism** The geologic principle that the same geologic processes that operate today operated in the past to change Earth's surface. (p. 239)
**uniformismo** Principio geológico que enuncia que los mismos procesos geológicos que cambian la superficie de la Tierra en la actualidad, ocurrían en el pasado.

**universe** All of space and everything in it. (p. 772)
**universo** Todo el espacio y todo lo que hay en él.

**unsaturated zone** A layer of rocks and soil above the water table in which the pores contain air as well as water. (p. 405)
**zona insaturada** Capa de rocas y suelo encima del nivel freático en la cual los poros contienen aire además de agua.

**upwelling** The movement of cold water upward from the deep ocean that is caused by wind. (p. 460)
**afloramiento** Movimiento ascendente de aguas frías desde las profundidades del mar, causado por los vientos.

## V

**valley glacier** A long, narrow glacier that forms when snow and ice build up in a mountain valley. (p. 292)
**glaciar de valle** Glaciar largo y angosto que se forma por acumulación de hielo y nieve en un valle de montaña.

**variable** A factor that can change in an experiment. (p. 9)
**variable** Factor que puede cambiar en un experimento.

**vein** A narrow deposit of a mineral that is sharply different from the surrounding rock. (p. 78)
**vena** Acumulación delgada de un mineral que es marcadamente distint de la roca que la rodea.

**velocity** Speed in a given direction. (p. 685)
**velocidad** Rapidez en una dirección dada.

**vent** The opening through which molten rock and gas leave a volcano. (p. 210)
**boca** Abertura a través de la que la roca en fusión y los gases salen de un volcán.

**vertebrate** An animal with a backbone. (p. 335)
**vertebrado** Animal con columna vertebral.

**viscosity** A liquid's resistance to flowing. (p. 206)
**viscosidad** Resistencia a fluir que presenta un líquido.

**visible light** Electromagnetic radiation that can be seen with the unaided eye. (p. 745)
**luz visible** Radiación electromagnética que se puede ver a simple vista.

**volcanic neck** A deposit of hardened magma in a volcano's pipe. (p. 221)
**cuello volcánico** Depósito de magma solidificada en la chimenea de un volcán.

**volcano** A weak spot in the crust where magma has come to the surface. (p. 200)
**volcán** Punto débil en la corteza por donde el magma escapa hacia la superficie.

## W

**water cycle** The continual movement of water among Earth's atmosphere, oceans, and land surface through evaporation, condensation, and precipitation. (pp. 392, 560)
**ciclo del agua** Movimiento continuo de agua entre la atmósfera, los océanos y la superficie de la Tierra mediante la evaporación, condensación y precipitación.

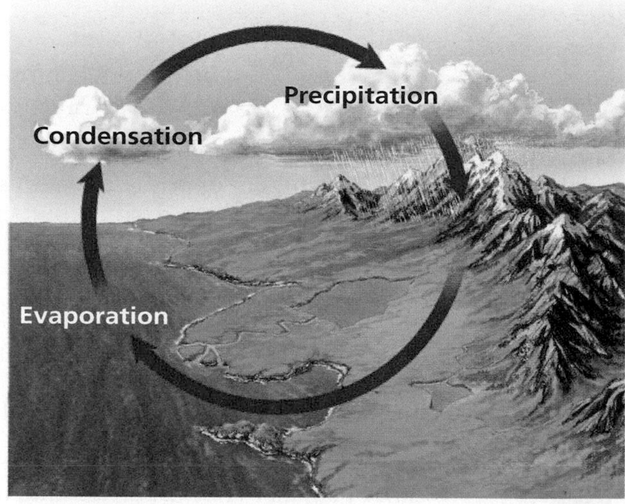


**water pollution** The addition of any substance that has a negative effect on water or the living things that depend on the water. (p. 419)
**contaminación del agua** Adición de cualquier sustancia que tiene un efecto negativo al agua o los seres viv

**water quality** The degree of purity of water, determined by measuring the substances in water besides water molecules. (p. 420)
**calidad del agua** Grado de pureza del agua, determinado por medición de las sustancias que el agua contiene además de sus propias moléculas.

**watershed** The land area that supplies water to a river system. (p. 397)
**cuenca hidrográfica** Área de terreno que suministra agua a un sistema fluvial.

**water table** The top of the saturated zone, or depth to the groundwater under Earth's surface. (p. 405)
**nivel freático** Límite superior de la zona saturada, o distancia hasta las aguas freáticas bajo la superficie terrestre.

**water vapor** Water in the form of a gas. (p. 514)
**vapor de agua** Agua en forma de gas.

**wave** The movement of energy through a body of water. (p. 435)
**ola** Movimiento de energía a través de un cuerpo de agua.

**wave height** The vertical distance from the crest of a wave to the trough. (p. 436)
**altura de una ola** Distancia vertical desde la cresta de una ola hasta el valle.

**wavelength** The horizontal distance between the crest of one wave and the crest of the next wave. (pp. 436, 745)
**longitud de onda** Distancia horizontal entre la cresta de una onda y la cresta de la siguiente onda.

**weather** The condition of Earth's atmosphere at a particular time and place. (p. 512)
**tiempo meteorológico** Condición de la atmósfera de la Tierra en un tiempo y lugar determinados.

**weathering** The chemical and physical processes that break down rock at Earth's surface. (p. 239)
**desgaste** Procesos químicos y físicos que rompen las rocas de la superficie de la Tierra.

**weight** The force of gravity on an object. (p. 667)
**peso** Fuerza de la gravedad que actúa sobre un objeto.

**wetland** A land area that is covered with a shallow layer of water during some or all of the year. (p. 401)
**humedal** Área de terreno cubierta por una capa superficial de agua durante una parte del año, o todo el tiempo.

**white dwarf** The blue-white hot core of a star that is left behind after its outer layers have expanded and drifted out into space. (p. 764)
**enana blanca** Núcleo caliente azul blanquecino de una estrella, que queda después de que sus capas externas se han expandido y dispersado por el espacio.

**wind** The horizontal movement of air from an area of high pressure to an area of lower pressure. (p. 553)
**viento** Movimiento horizontal de aire de un área de alta presión a un área de menor presión.

**wind-chill factor** A measure of cooling combining temperature and wind speed. (p. 553)
**factor de sensación térmica** Medida de enfriamiento que combina la temperatura y la velocidad del viento.

**windward** The side of a mountain range that faces the oncoming wind. (p. 618)
**barlovento** Lado de una cadena montañosa donde pega el viento de frente.

# Index

Page numbers for key terms are printed in **boldface** type.
Page numbers for illustrations, maps, and charts are printed in *italics*.

# Index

Page numbers for key terms are printed in **boldface** type.
Page numbers for illustrations, maps, and charts are printed in *italics*.

# Index

Page numbers for key terms are printed in **boldface** type.
Page numbers for illustrations, maps, and charts are printed in *italics*.

## G

# Index

Page numbers for key terms are printed in **boldface** type.
Page numbers for illustrations, maps, and charts are printed in *italics*.

# Index

Page numbers for key terms are printed in **boldface** type.
Page numbers for illustrations, maps, and charts are printed in *italics*.

# Index

Page numbers for key terms are printed in **boldface** type.
Page numbers for illustrations, maps, and charts are printed in *italics*.

# Index

Page numbers for key terms are printed in **boldface** type.
Page numbers for illustrations, maps, and charts are printed in *italics*.



## S

# Index

Page numbers for key terms are printed in **boldface** type.
Page numbers for illustrations, maps, and charts are printed in *italics*.

# Index

Page numbers for key terms are printed in **boldface** type.
Page numbers for illustrations, maps, and charts are printed in *italics*.

# Acknowledgments

**Grateful acknowledgment is made to the following for copyrighted material:**

Acknowledgment for pages 224–225: "Gelatin Volcanoes" by R. Fisk and D. Jackson from *Exploring Planets in the Classroom.* Copyright by Hawaii Space Grant Consortium, based on experiments done by R. Fisk and D. Jackson, U.S. Geological Survey.

Acknowledgment for page 233: "Rune of Riches" by Florence Converse from *Sung Under the Silver Umbrella.* Copyright © 1935 by the Macmillan Company. Reprinted with permission of the Association for Childhood Education International, 17904 Georgia Avenue, Suite 215, Olney, Maryland.

Acknowledgement for page 656: Excerpt from *Alone* by Richard E. Byrd. Copyright © 1938 by Richard E. Byrd, copyright © renewed 1966 by Marie A. Byrd. Reprinted by permission of Island Press.

Activity on page 685 is from *Exploring Planets in the Classroom* by Hawaii Space Grant Consortium. Based on a concept developed by Dale Olive.

Note: Every effort has been made to locate the copyright owner of material reproduced in this component. Omissions brought to our attention will be corrected in subsequent editions.

## Staff Credits

Scott Andrews, Jennifer Angel, Carolyn Belanger, Barbara A. Bertell, Peggy Bliss, James Brady, Anne M. Bray, Kerry Cashman, Jonathan Cheney, Joshua D. Clapper, Lisa J. Clark, Patricia M. Dambry, Frederick Fellows, Jonathan Fisher, Patti Fromkin, Paul Gagnon, Robert Graham, Kerri Hoar, Anne Jones, Kelly Kelliher, Toby Klang, Dotti Marshall, Constance J. McCarty, Carolyn McGuire, Ranida Touranont McKneally, Richard McMahon, Natania Mlawer, Dorothy Preston, Rashid Ross, Siri Schwartzman, Laurel Smith, Kara Stokes, Jennifer A. Teece, Amanda M. Watters, Merce Wilczek, Amy Winchester, Char Lyn Yeakley **Additional Credits** Louise Gachet, Terence Hegarty, Kevin Keane, Greg Lam, Marcy Rose

## Illustration

**Articulate Graphics:** 72, 73; **Morgan Cain & Associates:** 53, 97, 99, 103, 115, 126, 129r, 131r, 135, 143, 144, 158l, 163, 164, 165, 166, 179, 181, 197, 202, 218, 219, 221, 228l, 229, 249, 252, 253, 267, 268, 269, 290, 302, 324t, 326, 358, 371, 374, 379, 416, 460, 518, 519t, 521, 549, 557, 567, 619t, 713b, 721, 722b, 725b, 731, 732, 745, 751, 753, 754, 757, 758, 760, 764, 765, 768, 776; **David Corrente:** 503; **Warren Cutler:** 398, 399, 482, 483; **Dorling Kindersley:** 128, 129l; **John Edwards & Associates:** 287, 288, 293r, 311, 332, 333, 355, 366, 373, 424, 425, 436, 437, 438, 439, 443, 461, 476, 479, 520, 521, 582, 583, 621, 704, 705, 713t, 721, 771, 775, 777; **Forge FX:** 170, 171; **Chris Forsey:** 146, 152, 153, 205, 474, 475, 485; **Geosystems Global Corporation:** 35b, 38, 55, 397, 402, 491, 597, 603, 626, 627, 638r; **Dale Gustafson:** 192, 193; **Robert Hynes:** 78, 79, 88; **Kevin Jones Associates:** 36, 37, 57, 240, 241, 274, 293b, 298, 299, 303, 306, 314, 315, 357, 363, 380, 381, 393, 407, 418, 498, 499; **Jared D. Lee:** 756; **Martucci Design:** 228r, 602; **Steve McEntee:** 220, 543, 544, 545, 555t, 556, 565, 579, 584, 592, 606, 607, 618, 619b, 643; **Rich McMahon:** 338, 339, 340, 341, 571, 589t; **Rich McMahon with J/B Woolsey Associates:** 328; **Karen Minot:** 273; **Paul Mirocha:** 480; **Ortelius Design, Inc.:** 462, 615; **Matthew Pippin:** 84, 250, 278, 279, 294, 295, 405, 422, 423, 452, 517, 523; **Brucie Rosch:** 147; **Walter Stuart:** 638l; **J/B Woolsey Associates:** 167, 316, 318, 321, 322, 502; **XNR Productions:** 40, 41b, 45, 46, 47, 138, 139, 142, 151, 177, 187, 201, 222, 258, 280, 394, 457, 555b, 558, 580, 589b, 594, 617, 647; **Rose Zgodzinski:** 449. **All tables and graphs by Matt Mayerchak.**

## Photography

**Photo Research** Sue McDermott, John Judge, Paula Wehde, Kerri Hoar
**Cover image top,** Ron Watts/Corbis; **bottom,** ©John Cancalosi/Peter Arnold, Inc.

### Chapter 1

**Pages 4–5,** NASA; **5 inset,** Richard Haynes; **7,** Douglas Peebles/Corbis; **7 inset,** Ben Hankins/USGS; **8–9,** Jeff Hunter/Getty Images, Inc.; **9r,** The Granger Collection, NY; **11 all,** Richard Haynes; **12,** Carr Clifton Photography; **13,** Ken O'Donoghue; **14–15,** Corbis; **16l,** M.W.Franke/Peter Arnold, Inc.; **16r,** L. Gould/OSF/Animals Animals/Earth Scenes; **17l,** Bob Crandall/Stock Boston; **17m,** Frank Pederick/The Image Works; **17r,** D. Parker/Photo Researchers, Inc.; **18,** David Parker/Science Photo Library/Photo Researchers, Inc.; **19,** Richard Haynes; **20l,** Getty Images, Inc.; **20ml,** Corbis; **20m,** Casio, Inc.; **20mr,** Corbis; **20r,** Dorling Kindersley; **21, 22,** Richard Haynes; **23t,** Russ Lappa; **23b,** Tom Stewart/Corbis; **24, 25,** Richard Haynes; **26tl,** Getty Images, Inc.; **26ml,** Royalty-Free/Corbis; **26bl, 26tr, 26r,** Getty Images, Inc.; **26 br,** Richard Haynes.

### Chapter 2

**Pages 32–33,** Image courtesy of NASA Landsat Project Science Office and USGS EROS Data Center; **33,** Richard Haynes; **34,** National Museum of American History/Smithsonian Institution; **36,** Tom Bean; **37l,** David Muench; **37r,** Tom Bean; **39,** Russ Lappa; **41,** Jim Wark/Airphoto; **42l,** The Granger Collection, NY; **42m,** Bodleian Library, Oxford, U.K.; **42r,** Royal Geographical Society, London, UK/Bridgeman Art Library; **43l,** British Library, London/Bridgeman Art Library, London/Superstock, Inc.; **43m, 43r,** The Granger Collection, NY; **48,** Richard Haynes; **49t,** Russ Lappa; **49b,** Geographix; **50l,** Library of Congress; **50r,** USGS; **52–53,** Index Stock Imagery; **52t,** Copyright Boeing, all rights reserved; **52b,** Forest Johnson/Masterfile; **53, 54t,** Richard Haynes; **54b,** Mitch Wojnarowicz/The Image Works; **55,** Elliot Cohen/Janelco; **56,** U.S. Geological Survey; **58 ,** Robert Rathe/Stock Boston; **59,** Richard Haynes; **60,** British Library, London/Bridgeman Art Library, London/Superstock, Inc.; **62,** U.S. Geological Survey.

### Chapter 3

**Pages 64–65,** Kevin Downey; **65 inset, 66t,** Richard Haynes; **66–67b,** Anthony Bannister/Gallo Images/Corbis; **67t,** Tim Wright/Corbis; **67b,** DK Picture Library; **68tl,** Colin Keates/Dorling Kindersley Media Library; **68tm, 68tr,** Breck P. Kent; **68b,** AFP/Corbis; **69t,** Russ Lappa; **69m, 69mr,** Charles D. Winters/Photo Researchers, Inc.; **69bl,** Ken Lucas/Visuals Unlimited; **69bm,** Breck P. Kent; **69br,** Barry Runk/Grant Heilman Photography, Inc.; **70 all, 71l, 71ml,** Dorling Kindersley; **71m,** Charles D. Winters/Photo Researchers, Inc.; **71mr, 71r,** Dorling Kindersley; **72 all,** Breck P. Kent; **73tl,** Chip Clark; **73tr,** E.R. Degginger/Color Pic. Inc.; **73bl, 73bm,** Breck P. Kent; **73br,** Charles D. Winters/Photo Researchers, Inc.; **74tl, 74ml,** E.R. Degginger/Color Pic, Inc.; **74bl,** Breck P. Kent/Animals Animals/Earth Scenes; **74bm,** Colin Keates/Dorling Kindersley Media Library; **74br,** Ken Lucas/Visuals Unlimited; **76t,** Richard Haynes; **76b,** Breck P. Kent/Animals Animals/Earth Scenes; **77,** Kevin Downey; **78,** Jane Burton/Bruce Coleman, Inc.; **79t,** Ken Lucas/Visuals Unlimited; **79b,** Colin Keates/Dorling Kindersley Media Library; **80,** © 1986 The Field Museum/Ron Testa; **81,** Art Resource, NY; **82l,** C. M. Dixon; **82m,** Scala/Art Resource, NY; **82r,** C. M. Dixon; **83t,** The Granger Collection, NY; **83b,** Mark Mainz/Getty Images, Inc.; **85,** Bettmann/Corbis; **87t,** Getty Images, Inc.; **87b,** Richard Haynes; **88,** Russ Lappa; **90,** Breck P. Kent.

### Chapter 4

**Pages 92–93,** Corbis; **93 inset,** Richard Haynes; **94t, 94m,** Breck P. Kent; **94b,** Jonathan Blair/Corbis; **95tl,** E.R. Degginger/Color Pic, Inc.; **95tm,** Breck P. Kent; **95mr,** E.R. Degginger/Color Pic, Inc.; **95tr,** Barry Runk/Grant Heilman Photography, Inc.; **95ml,** Breck P. Kent; **95b,** David Reed/Corbis; **96tl,** E.R. Degginger/Color Pic, Inc.; **96tm, 96tr, 96ml, 96mr,** Breck P. Kent; **96bl,** Jeff Scovil; **96br,** Breck P. Kent; **98t,** Doug Martin/Photo Researchers, Inc.; **98b,** Barry Runk/Grant Heilman Photography, Inc.; **99 all,** Breck P. Kent; **100,** Jan Hinsch/SPL/Photo Researchers, Inc.; **101,** Michele & Tom Grimm/Getty Images, Inc.; **102,** Tom Lazar/Animals Animals/Earth Scenes; **104l,** Runk/Schoenberger/Grant Heilman Photography, Inc.; **104m,** Jeff Scovil; **104r,** North Museum/Franklin and Marshall College/Grant Heilman Photography, Inc.; **105tl,** Charles R. Belinky/Photo Researchers, Inc.; **105tm,** E.R. Degginger/Color Pic, Inc.; **105tr,** Breck Kent; **105b,** Mark Newman/Photo Researchers, Inc; **106,** Jeff Greenberg/Photo Agora; **107t,** Ted Clutter/Photo Researchers, Inc.; **107b,** Dave Fleetham/Tom Stack & Associates; **108t,** Stuart Westmorland/Corbis; **108b,** Jean-Marc Trucher/Stone/Getty Images, Inc.; **109,** Richard Thom/Visuals Unlimited; **111tl,** Barry Runk/Grant Heilman Photography, Inc.; **111tm,** Jeff Scovil; **111tr,** Breck P. Kent; **111bl,** Andrew J. Martinez/Photo Researchers, Inc.; **111bm,** Barry Runk/Grant Heilman Photography, Inc.; **111br,** Runk/Schoenberger/Grant Heilman Photography, Inc.; **112,** Catherine Karnow/Corbis; **113,** Richard Haynes; **114l, 114m,** Jeff Scovil; **114r,** Breck P. Kent; **115tl,** Francois Gohier/Photo Researchers, Inc.; **115tr,** David J. Wrobel/Visuals Unlimited; **115bl,** Breck P. Kent; **115br,** N.R. Rowan/Stock Boston; **116,** Corbis; **117 all,** Russ Lappa; **118,** Richard Haynes; **120tl,** Andrew J. Martinez/Photo Researchers, Inc.; **120tr,** Breck P. Kent; **120b,** E.R. Degginger/Color Pic, Inc.

### Chapter 5

**Pages 122–123,** Mats Wibelund; **123 inset,** Richard Haynes; **124-125b,** David Briscoe/AP/Wide World Photos; **125l,** Jeff Greenberg/PhotoEdit; **125r,** Michael Nichols/Magnum; **127,** Tracy Frankel/Getty Images, Inc.; **128,** Dorling Kindersley; **129,** Getty Images, Inc.; **131,** Runk/Schoenberger/Grant Heilman Photography, Inc.; **132, 133, 134,** Richard Haynes; **136,** Dorling Kindersley/Stephen Oliver; **139,** Ken Lucas/Visuals Unlimited; **140,** Bettmann/Corbis; **141,** Jeffrey L. Rotman/Corbis; **144–145b,** SIO Archives/UCSD; **148 all, 149 both,** Richard Haynes; **150, 155,** Russ Lappa.

# Periodic Table of Elements

**Key**

| | |
|---|---|
| C | Solid |
| Br | Liquid |
| H | Gas |
| Tc | Not found in nature |

| Period | 1 | 2 | 3 | 4 | 5 | 6 | 7 | 8 | 9 |
|---|---|---|---|---|---|---|---|---|---|
| 1 | 1<br>**H**<br>Hydrogen<br>1.0079 | | | | | | | | |
| 2 | 3<br>**Li**<br>Lithium<br>6.941 | 4<br>**Be**<br>Beryllium<br>9.0122 | | | | | | | |
| 3 | 11<br>**Na**<br>Sodium<br>22.990 | 12<br>**Mg**<br>Magnesium<br>24.305 | | | | | | | |
| 4 | 19<br>**K**<br>Potassium<br>39.098 | 20<br>**Ca**<br>Calcium<br>40.08 | 21<br>**Sc**<br>Scandium<br>44.956 | 22<br>**Ti**<br>Titanium<br>47.90 | 23<br>**V**<br>Vanadium<br>50.941 | 24<br>**Cr**<br>Chromium<br>51.996 | 25<br>**Mn**<br>Manganese<br>54.938 | 26<br>**Fe**<br>Iron<br>55.847 | 27<br>**Co**<br>Cobalt<br>58.933 |
| 5 | 37<br>**Rb**<br>Rubidium<br>85.468 | 38<br>**Sr**<br>Strontium<br>87.62 | 39<br>**Y**<br>Yttrium<br>88.906 | 40<br>**Zr**<br>Zirconium<br>91.22 | 41<br>**Nb**<br>Niobium<br>92.906 | 42<br>**Mo**<br>Molybdenum<br>95.94 | 43<br>**Tc**<br>Technetium<br>(98) | 44<br>**Ru**<br>Ruthenium<br>101.07 | 45<br>**Rh**<br>Rhodium<br>102.91 |
| 6 | 55<br>**Cs**<br>Cesium<br>132.91 | 56<br>**Ba**<br>Barium<br>137.33 | 71<br>**Lu**<br>Lutetium<br>174.97 | 72<br>**Hf**<br>Hafnium<br>178.49 | 73<br>**Ta**<br>Tantalum<br>180.95 | 74<br>**W**<br>Tungsten<br>183.85 | 75<br>**Re**<br>Rhenium<br>186.21 | 76<br>**Os**<br>Osmium<br>190.2 | 77<br>**Ir**<br>Iridium<br>192.22 |
| 7 | 87<br>**Fr**<br>Francium<br>(223) | 88<br>**Ra**<br>Radium<br>(226) | 103<br>**Lr**<br>Lawrencium<br>(262) | 104<br>**Rf**<br>Rutherfordium<br>(261) | 105<br>**Db**<br>Dubnium<br>(262) | 106<br>**Sg**<br>Seaborgium<br>(263) | 107<br>**Bh**<br>Bohrium<br>(264) | 108<br>**Hs**<br>Hassium<br>(265) | 109<br>**Mt**<br>Meitnerium<br>(268) |

**Lanthanides**

| | | | | | |
|---|---|---|---|---|---|
| 57<br>**La**<br>Lanthanum<br>138.91 | 58<br>**Ce**<br>Cerium<br>140.12 | 59<br>**Pr**<br>Praseodymium<br>140.91 | 60<br>**Nd**<br>Neodymium<br>144.24 | 61<br>**Pm**<br>Promethium<br>(145) | 62<br>**Sm**<br>Samarium<br>150.4 |

**Actinides**

| | | | | | |
|---|---|---|---|---|---|
| 89<br>**Ac**<br>Actinium<br>(227) | 90<br>**Th**<br>Thorium<br>232.04 | 91<br>**Pa**<br>Protactinium<br>231.04 | 92<br>**U**<br>Uranium<br>238.03 | 93<br>**Np**<br>Neptunium<br>(237) | 94<br>**Pu**<br>Plutonium<br>(244) |